THE ENLIGHTENMENT THAT FAILED

The Enlightenment that Failed

Ideas, Revolution, and Democratic Defeat, 1748–1830

JONATHAN I. ISRAEL

OXFORD
UNIVERSITY PRESS

OXFORD
UNIVERSITY PRESS

Great Clarendon Street, Oxford, OX2 6DP,
United Kingdom

Oxford University Press is a department of the University of Oxford.
It furthers the University's objective of excellence in research, scholarship,
and education by publishing worldwide. Oxford is a registered trade mark of
Oxford University Press in the UK and in certain other countries

First Edition published in 2019

Impression: 1

Published in the United States of America by Oxford University Press
198 Madison Avenue, New York, NY 10016, United States of America

British Library Cataloguing in Publication Data
Data available

Library of Congress Control Number: 2019941431

ISBN 978–0–19–873840–4

Printed and bound in Great Britain by
Clays Ltd, Elcograf S.p.A.

Contents

1

Introduction

Radical Enlightenment and "Modernity" (1650–1850)

1.1. BASIC ARGUMENT AND SCOPE

A quarter century after originally formulating my Radical Enlightenment thesis, this volume extends the project's core themes by reaching back before 1650, to consider the underground movements of the "Radical Renaissance" and "Radical Reformation" in relation to the Enlightenment, and forwards to encompass a range of relevant contexts thus far not covered or brought together, such as women's emancipation, black emancipation, race theory, the rise of the Spanish American republics, education reform, law reform, and the advent of economics and especially post-1789 revolutionary upheavals in the trans-Atlantic world and the early nineteenth century. The volume also addresses key objections raised in the escalating controversy surrounding the thesis.

In recent decades, an important response of the historiography to the growing need to reassess the overall Enlightenment phenomenon in both its unity and diversity, given the burgeoning wealth of detail research has made available and the growing need also to adopt a much wider geographical perspective than was once usual, has been to reorganize the topic primarily in terms of "plural enlightenments" and focus increasingly on particular national and religious contexts. The core argument presented in *Radical Enlightenment* (2001) and developed further in *Enlightenment Contested* (2006) and *Democratic Enlightenment* (2011) was that the Western Enlightenment as a whole resulted from a shared outpouring of basic new findings and ideas in philosophy, science and general scholarship, especially concepts of a liberating, tolerationist, secularizing kind, bringing in its wake, during the latter half of the eighteenth century, numerous wide-ranging practical improvements. Consequently, basing one's view of the Enlightenment on a "diverse family" typology, though understandable as a reaction to the historiographical problems, weakens our sense of the Enlightenment's unity, universal pretensions, and cosmopolitan flavor, as well as near global reach, *and* our sense of its continuing relevance to politics and society today.

Greater awareness of the unifying threads of the unfolding Enlightenment seems no less essential than increasing responsiveness to the Enlightenment's geographical range and diversity. The new criteria and findings of science combined with post-Cartesian philosophy to generate a vast panorama of fresh, innovative spheres of intellectual interest ranging from law reform to economics, ethnology, and what today are called the social sciences. This led, in turn, to an explosion of schemes and projects of amelioration aspiring to raise the level of human wellbeing by improving society's institutions, education, and basic organization. If this was a shared trans-Atlantic experience, while some of the welter of new ideas and reform projects were of a bold, far-reaching character, others were just adjustments to the prevailing status quo; whereas some were so transformative in implications and effects as to threaten the entire framework of society, religion, and politics, others could be easily absorbed within existing social conditions and structures of authority. Hence, what is chiefly required, arguably, is not a "family of enlightenments" typology but a carefully defined binary classification of ideas and reform projects into socially endorsing and socially oppositional blocs, differentiating those backed by state and church from those rejected. In this way we can more adequately profile the overall scenario and understand the international Enlightenment's shared internal tensions and conflicts. Projects intellectual and practical aiming at improvements inevitably divided into two basic kinds: schemes conserving the main components of the existing *ancien régime* framework, established religious authority, and social hierarchy based on aristocracy and monarchy especially, versus those challenging and potentially revolutionizing the existing foundations of society, culture, and education with wholly new forms of thought and practice.

As the latter category, that of the radical enlighteners, was generally considered a threat to society and religion, and both their writings and activities remained comprehensively banned until 1789, they tended to detach themselves to an extent from the rest of the Enlightenment, and society, forming clandestine networks of gatherings, organization, and book culture. Starting as a few minuscule groups, they evolved into a widely condemned underground intellectual "sect" adopting clandestine practices to camouflage, publicly screen, their challenging the beliefs, practices, and institutions of the then prevailing social and religious system. Growing from the 1660s down to the 1830s and 1840s, Radical Enlightenment little by little (though never completely) divested itself of its early clandestine practices but never its oppositional character. Some commentators assume the "Radical Enlightenment" category proposed encompasses all writers and thinkers rejecting the sway of theology and religious belief.[1] But that is not the case. Many essentially irreligious Enlightenment thinkers such as Voltaire, La Mettrie, Hume, Gibbon, and Goethe abjured the religious assumptions of the past privately, but not the social hierarchy, principle of monarchy, traditional moral norms (at least for most people), and outward religious

[1] See, for instance, Robertson, *The Enlightenment*, 6, 15–16, 136.

format—so that these too must be excluded from any meaningful radical category. Neither Moderate nor Radical Enlightenment can in fact be satisfactorily defined in terms of religious or irreligious Enlightenment. Unitarian, Arian, and other heterodox freethinking religious fringes existed, opposing church sway and conventionally-accepted Christian theology and inclined to embrace universal and equal rights, from whose ranks emerged several prominent "radical enlighteners" like the great Welshman Richard Price (1723–91).[2]

From the 1670s for over a century, the most common nomenclature applied to these underground Enlightenment radicals, albeit rather less so in England and America than continental Europe, was to label them *Spinosistes*, as they were known in France. As we shall see, there has been much dispute as to what significance, if any, should be attached to this nomenclature. But the important point for now is that although, throughout the period from 1670 down to the 1830s, "Radical Enlightenment" generally had some (mostly indirect and tenuous) connection with the actual philosophical and textual legacy of Spinoza, Spinoza had nothing to do with the existence of the radical tendency as such which stemmed directly from the deep divisions in the Dutch Republic between Orangists and anti-Orangists in the third quarter of the seventeenth century; it was never part of the argument to claim the Radical Enlightenment "originated in Spinoza" as hostile commentators regularly misrepresent the argument. Claiming the "Radical Enlightenment thesis" fails because it artificially imposes Spinoza's philosophy as a kind of "package logic" onto texts and thinkers when some of these, like Condorcet, rarely if ever mention Spinoza and showed no direct sign of his influence, is distorting the debate with inapplicable objections. Radical Enlightenment here remains what it was in the earlier volumes—refusal of religious guidance of society on philosophical grounds combined with universal principles rejecting aristocracy and monarchy in favour of representative, democratizing republicanism, nothing more nor less.

After the third volume of the series, *Democratic Enlightenment* (2011), appeared two specialized studies, *Revolutionary Ideas* (2014) on the French Revolution, and *The Expanding Blaze* (2017), on the American Revolution, requisite as preliminaries to this volume, especially to provide enough evidence and analysis of texts to substantiate overarching arguments relating to the revolutionary era and beyond on which, ultimately, the entire "Radical Enlightenment thesis" rests. The conclusions reached diverge from much of the previous historiography. Although the vast upheaval and turmoil of the French Revolution was chiefly due to the crown's financial breakdown and mass movements of protest, the democratic republican orientation, direction and legislation of 1789–93, these works argue, flowed principally from a vanguard of philosophical republicans who were actual or virtual republicans mixing in *philosophique* circles well before 1789, often among the coteries of Diderot, d'Holbach, and Helvétius.

[2] Israel, *Revolution of the Mind*, 30–1; Duthille, *Discours Radical*, 87–8, 94, 104–5.

Also, from 1789, a much noisier, more public rift manifested itself among enlighteners than had existed earlier. Many enlighteners recoiled from the new democratic and secularist credo, aligning defensively with monarchy, church, and aristocracy against the democratic republicans while others, in many countries, supported the Revolution in its more democratic mode, embracing "general will" in its non-Rousseauist format, universal and equal rights and egalitarian principles. Revolutionary turmoil, inevitably, sharply polarized and widely publicized enlighteners' splits, pushing them into two openly, soon violently opposed camps. While democratic republican secularizing groups plainly belonged to the Radical Enlightenment category, powerful factions of constitutional royalists commanded another main thrust within the Revolution, led by figures such as Mounier, Lally-Tollendal, Malouet, Maury, and Barnave, rejecting radical ideas and claiming the Revolution must compromise with monarchy, aristocracy, and established religion,[3] and are hence classified as heirs to the Moderate Enlightenment. Moderate enlighteners strove to steer between democratic Enlightenment and outright reaction, scorning the scorning of all enlightened change characterizing Counter-Enlightenment. Hence, post-1789 "moderate enlighteners", including the French *monarchiens*, Adams, Burke, Gibbon, and Ferguson, and, even more, the post-1806 Prussian court reformers, still believed further reform, secularization, and rationalization were needed (up to a point) and should be carried further whether on the basis of the "mixed government" British model derived from the Lockean "Revolution principles" of 1688 or that of "enlightened despotism," as under Napoleon's or Czar Alexander I's rule.

Revolutionary era moderate enlighteners hence opposed both the radicals on one side and encroaching Counter-Enlightenment on the other. The education reformer Johann Ludwig Ewald (1747–1822), writing in 1792, for example, urged Germany's princes fighting the democratic republican challenge not to retreat into mere repression and rejection but instead build on the Enlightenment of Frederick the Great (reigned: 1740–86) and Joseph II (reigned: 1780–90), restructure monarchy, and continue reforming their realms, but cautiously, always allied to ecclesiastical authority and Christianity.[4] Under the 1814–15 Restoration, after Napoleon's final defeat, radicals and moderates came under renewed pressure from reactionary Counter-Enlightenment, though frequently this had the opposite effect to that intended. In Ireland, Canada, and the United States as well as Britain, what made the "idealized, radical Enlightenment vision appear even more inspirational and heroic" to hardened political dissidents than it had before, as one scholar expressed it, was the "violent resistance it met from British authorities."[5] In Britain, this intensified climate of reactionary repression lasted four decades, from 1792 down to the Great Reform Bill of 1832.

Both basic categories of Enlightenment, then, moderate and radical, are deemed "revolutionary." The central role ascribed to both in the American, French, and other

[3] Ewald, *Über Revolutionen*, 244.
[4] Ewald, *Über Revolutionen*, 237–47.
[5] Cotlar, *Tom Paine's America*, 78.

revolutions makes this a fundamental point. Both Enlightenment streams sought to curb despotism, reduce religious policing, enhance individual freedom, expand freedom of the press and expression, and generally ameliorate society by spreading "enlightened" ideas and expanding education. For all this, the trans-Atlantic revolutions were indebted to the international Enlightenment as a whole. The core thesis regarding the French Revolution is that the two divergent streams during 1787–93 both contributed to the making of the Revolution but became competing revolutionary ideological blocs within it, a struggle continuing until the Montagnard coup of June 1793. This brought to the fore a third force, one rhetorically appealing to (but at the same time vigorously repressing) the *sans-culottes*, using a dramatically different, anti-intellectualist, and in some respects more Rousseauist, essentially populist authoritarian, Counter-Enlightenment ideology.

Fundamental to the "Radical Enlightenment" throughout was that its "democratizing republicanism" was always focused on "representative democracy": all Radical Enlightenment theorists from Spinoza to d'Holbach, Condorcet, Price, Volney, Destutt. and Bentham rejected pure "direct democracy," considering the common people of their time still too ignorant, superstitious, and prey to "priestcraft" to understand the issues, though they hoped, and some optimistically expected, this would change in the future. For "democracy", as they understood it, to work, the "common good," or "general will," contrary to Rousseau's teaching, must be represented by responsible, aware, and well-educated spokesmen and delegates. Radical Enlightenment hence invariably opted for "representative democracy" or, in its most sophisticated versions—as with Condorcet or the post-1810 Bentham—a complex balancing of representative and direct democracy backed by frequent re-election of representatives.[6] Pure "direct democracy," by contrast, the voice of the streets, Rousseau's dispensing with representation, radical thinkers down to 1848 invariably abjured as "unenlightened" and dangerous. Failing to see this, critics assuring readers the thesis collapses because key radical enlighteners like d'Holbach and Volney repudiated "direct democracy," as indeed they did, are confusing the issue.[7]

What is sometimes called Robespierre's "ultra-democratic project," direct popular sovereignty, was intrinsically alien to the Radical Enlightenment creed which remained relentless in stressing the ignorance of "the multitude," albeit "multitude" understood not in terms of class but in terms of ability or inability to understand the "reality of things." In Spinoza and d'Holbach this exacting standard by no means ruled out unprivileged, poor, and humble individuals who are perceptive and aware. But their "multitude" definitely did encompass most kings, princes, courtiers, aristocrats, professors, and clergymen who, radical enlighteners typically assumed, either fail to grasp

[6] Urbinati, "Condorcet's Democratic Theory," 56–7; Israel, *Radical Ideas*, 346–9.

[7] Israel, *Revolution of the Mind*, 62–4; Israel, *Democratic Enlightenment*, 644, 813–21, 948; Israel, *Radical Ideas*, 348, 357–8, 365; Peonidis, "Jeremy Bentham," 448; for examples of this confusion, see Chisick, "Of Radical and Moderate Enlightenment," 63; 66, 348; Kim, "Volney and the French Revolution," 236; see also Steenbakkers' review of Ducheyne's *Reassessing the Radical Enlightenment* in BMGN for 2018.

or deliberately obfuscate the reality of things. Radical Enlightenment was inherently and always entirely at odds with Rousseau's "sublime science of simple souls."[8]

Another key argument about the revolutionary era elaborated in *The Expanding Blaze* is that until the Montagnard coup of June 1793 there existed enough basic parallels between the American and French Revolutions, especially egalitarian concepts and "universal and equal rights," to persuade leading radical publicists of the era, like Franklin, Price, Paine, Jefferson, Barlow, Mirabeau, Brissot, Condorcet, Volney, Cooper, and Priestley, that the two revolutions' core principles were closely linked or, as Paine expressed it, "identical." Unlike former revolutions which he dismissed as just "a change of persons, or an alteration of local circumstances," the American and French revolutions, for Enlightenment radicals either side of the Atlantic, together constituted "a renovation of the natural order of things, a system of principles as universal as truth and the existence of man . . . "[9] American and French radicals, as democratic republicans, shared a common creed. When the revolutionary American Congress convened, in Philadelphia 1775–6, no privileged status of any kind was permitted or acknowledged, no social orders were separately represented, observed Condorcet, in 1788, before the onset of the French Revolution when, already firmly republican, he wished to justify excluding the French aristocracy from the future national legislature.[10] Shutting the clergy altogether out of America's state constitutions, concurred Cérutti, in 1788, was likewise a vital lesson for Europeans.[11] The American Revolution's role in inspiring the ideological framing and especially the universal and equal rights discourse and reformism of the French Revolution was indeed basic.[12]

Unsurprisingly, given its centrality, Radical Enlightenment is no new concept. Since the 1920s, first introduced as a pivotal idea by Leo Strauss, the term has infused the historiography for almost a century, even if most historians and general readers only became aware of its importance from the 1970s. My own work seeks to extend the meaning and scope of this century-old concept. Many eighteenth-century political figures often characterized in history books as "radicals" but whose intellectual assumptions and arguments focused less on universal principles applying to all men deriving from "natural right" or "natural rights", and more on longstanding constitutional traditions and precedents real or alleged particular to their own country, are excluded from the category as employed here. Such figures may have been "radical" in local contexts, but were not "enlighteners" promoting general radical principles internationally. Thus, many eighteenth-century British and American figures often referred to as "radicals" are excluded because in their pamphlets, speeches, and publicity they relied primarily on localized, particularist, constitutionalist arguments,

8 Neidleman, "Sublime Science," 823, 830, 833.
9 Paine, *Rights of Man*, 144.
10 Condorcet, *Sentimens d'un républicain* (1788), 18–21, 25.
11 Cérutti, *Mémoire pour le peuple* (1788), 22–3.
12 Gauchet, *Révolution des droits*, 48–54; Israel, *Expanding Blaze*, 252–74.

and played little part in international Enlightenment debates or drawing the connection between political radicalism and rejecting religious authority.

The main constituent claims, or sub-theses, underpinning the overall argument down to *Democratic Enlightenment* (2011), were the initiating role in the 1660s and 1670s of the *cercle spinoziste*, the earliest intellectual ferment combining rejection of religious authority with democratic republicanism; second, the amplifying role of Huguenot and other French intellectuals around 1700 in disseminating "Spinozistic" ideas projecting the now Europe-wide clash between the moderation of Lockean Enlightenment dualism and radical one-substance monism;[13] third, the mediating, intermediary role of the English "deists," especially Toland, Tindal and Collins; fourth, the war between opposing Enlightenment factions between 1756 and 1765 over whether or not the *Encyclopédie* was so subversive of monarchy as well as religion that it should be banned; fifth, the public rift with which Voltaire became intensely preoccupied in the last decade of his life, what he called the "guerre civile" [civil war] dividing the French enlighteners, with one wing assailing the alleged alliance of kings and priests, and Voltaire and his following insisting on focusing on "priests" alone. Especially the *cercle spinoziste* theme and second and third sub-theses diverge from Margaret Jacob's rival thesis that the "first stirrings" of the "radicals of the Enlightenment" subscribing to what she calls a "pantheistic conception of the universe" occurred in England "after the Revolution of 1688–9."[14]

Following on from the above points, this volume brings into the picture the extension of the basic rift into new areas, especially women's emancipation, race theory, and black emancipation, the "parallel" profiles of the French and American revolutions (until June 1793); *Robespierrisme* as a populist Counter-Enlightenment to which all veritable radical enlighteners were adamantly opposed; continuation of the basic Enlightenment rift after 1815 through the 1820s revolutions; and, lastly, the argument that a growing rift arose between socialism and Radical Enlightenment in the 1830s and 1840s, friction that among much else led to Karl Marx's conversion from a Radical Enlightenment outlook to his post-1844 economics-based socialism.

1.2. DEFINITIONS AND CATEGORIES

The incipient "Radical Enlightenment" of the 1660s and 1670s, the philosophically revolutionary phenomenon seeking to sweep all before it, commencing among the *cercle spinoziste* in Holland, emerged against a backcloth of a much older and wider

[13] On this general point, if nowhere else, one finds considerable overlap between Jacob's account and my own, Jacob, "Heavenly City," 52–3.

[14] Jacob, *Radical Enlightenment*, p. xiv; in her latest book, however, Jacob seems to have modified her position and become more willing to acknowledge the decisive role of pre-1688 clandestine philosophical literature and the pre-1688 Dutch context: see Jacob, *Secular Enlightenment*, 8, 64-9, 78–9, 91, 100–1, 103, 164–7, 180, 185, 189, 197–8.

dissident fringe. It stood out from a longstanding mix of Epicureans, sceptics, *libertins érudits*, anti-establishment eclectics, alienated types, and philosophical and political rebels, a milieu fertilized by texts scholars today label *clandestina*, that is clandestine manuscripts occasionally supplemented by anonymous and illicitly printed texts, promoting intellectual traditions and structures of thought condemned, banned, and severely repressed by state and church.[15] By contrast, the new tendency commencing in the 1660s and 1670s had a much tighter inner philosophical coherence and more dynamic conception of the relationship between forbidden thought and action. But assuredly it fed on the now long-established older clandestine milieu of furtive copying and discussion of forbidden subversive texts primarily in Latin and French, and clandestine networking. Diffusing slowly from the seventeenth century's third quarter onwards, Radical Enlightenment's illicit spread was aided by the older intellectual substratum of forbidden philosophy which had long nurtured a tenacious, carefully masked, underground social structure with its own hierarchies, practices, and contacts often built around "under the counter" booksellers and elusive printers. Simultaneously a social, cultural, and intellectual phenomenon, Radical Enlightenment forged a new, separate intellectual identity, fundamentally rewriting the relation between thought and action, while diffusing, organizing, and expanding amidst a complex, diverse milieu of rival clandestine philosophical agendas, a bewildering medley of Neo-Epicureanism, skepticism, Averroism, rebellious eclecticism, underground "deism," Iberian crypto-Judaism, Socinianism, radical fideism, a vast mix of underground theologico-philosophical currents long challenging established theological tenets.

Largely due to their concealed, marginal character, both the older, broader, more passive as well as variegated underground culture of the sixteenth and seventeenth centuries, and the more activist new phenomenon starting in the 1660s, based on hidden philosophical manuscripts and banned printed texts, unified only by a common tendency in one way or another to resist religion's sway, rarely attracted mainstream scholarly attention until recent decades. Latterly, though, the early modern clandestine philosophical literature has become a field of intensive study with many significant discoveries being brought to light by such outstanding scholars as Gianni Paganini, Miguel Benítez, Martin Mulsow, Silvia Berti, Winfried Schröder, and Antony McKenna.[16]

Since Radical Enlightenment arose out of, and early on was chiefly nourished by, a wider hidden substratum, a collection of underground social and intellectual hidden networks in several countries, diverse but always antagonistic to mainstream

[15] Paganini, *Filosofie clandestine*, 149–67; Paganini, "Enlightenment before the Enlightenment," 183–5.

[16] For the post-1660 clandestine philosophical literature in relation to the Radical Enlightenment's origins, see Israel, *Radical Enlightenment*, 684–703; Israel, "Radical Enlightenment: A Game-Changing Concept," 15–47; Israel, "'Lumières radicales" comme théorie générale," 387–436; Israel, "Democratic Republicanism and One-Substance Philosophy," 14–43; and the new two-volume expanded edition of Mulsow's *Moderne aus dem Untergrund* entitled *Radikale Frühaufklärung in Deutschland, 1680–1720* (2 vols., Göttingen, 2018) especially vol. 2, entitled *Clandestine Vernunft.*

religious, educational, and political culture, it has to be understood as inherently a social-cultural opposition movement as much as an intellectual phenomenon. Classifying the split between Radical and Moderate Enlightenment philosophically, in intellectual terms, as "reason" alone versus reason tempered by truths "above reason" and accessible only to theology, hence represents only one side of the coin, one side of the "Radical Enlightenment thesis," as it has evolved since the early 1990s. The intellectual aspect by itself hardly suffices for a proper appreciation of this revisionism; for it focuses equally on the social, cultural, and educational dimensions and repercussions of this escalating struggle, not least the post-1770 intensifying quarrel over whether all of society needed enlightening, as radical enlighteners insisted, or whether Enlightenment should (or unavoidably had to) be restricted just to society's elites, as moderates like Voltaire and Frederick the Great maintained. Since "moderates" had no wish to abolish existing social hierarchies and broadly endorsed the existing order, they perceived no pressing need for everyone, or indeed anyone beyond the elites, to become "enlightened." It was unnecessary and unrealistic, argued Voltaire and Prussia's celebrated "enlightened despot," to try to enlighten more than a small proportion of society. Enlightened despots like Frederick, Catherine, Joseph II of Austria, and indeed Napoleon, consequently assigned ecclesiastics and the churches an imposing slice of moral, legal, educational, social, and political power, responsibility and censorship and sanctioned the ecclesiastical grip over society—even if, as became obvious at elite level and at court, not with any great personal conviction.

Throughout the more than a century and a half of its existence, the radical tendency undeviatingly sought to exclude theology and organized religion from science, political theory, education, and philosophy. In this respect it proceeded quite differently from mainstream early Enlightenment, from figures like Locke, Newton, Le Clerc, and Leibniz aiming at reconciling science and religion by means of the "argument from design," Locke's "above reason," Leibniz's monads, and other pertinent dualistic devices. But here the Radical Enlightenment also strikingly contrasted with earlier clandestine philosophical currents: philosophically, it was the irreconcilable foe not just of the established order but also of skepticism, eclecticism, Socinianism, Neo-Epicureanism, crypto-Judaism, and radical fideism—all the strands of the earlier and wider underground dissident mix. Taking its cue from the mathematical logic of the post-Galilean Cartesian laws of science, the naturalistic philosophical underground proclaimed philosophical-scientific reason the exclusive criterion of truth, a unified and total system, the sole path to verifying "the truth" of things. Wholly usurping the previous role of theology, at least in its own estimation, this new creed, or "sect" as Bayle, Le Clerc, and Toland called it, became uniquely linked, as we shall see, to a revolutionary new concept of science as universally applicable, unchanging, unalterable general "natural laws" explaining the whole of reality which should hence also be the basis of men's understanding of society and politics. The clandestine radical tendency's proposed reforms it sought to anchor in the natural laws allegedly determining human behavior, morality, and thought while at the same time—again in contrast to Moderate Enlightenment—excluding all alternative or rival sources of truth verification and authority, all principles based on tradition, religion, common law, older philosophy, and the status quo.

While reconciling reason and faith following Locke, Newton, or Leibniz long remained hegemonic in the public sphere, privately or in small-group discussion, Locke's and Leibniz's reputedly cogent reconciling of "reason" and faith progressively eroded, leaving many among the intellectually sophisticated unconvinced, even among those most eager to compromise with religion and the political and social status quo. The latter therefore found themselves forced back on less philosophically confident solutions, and less compelling social arguments, of the kind resorted to by Montesquieu and Voltaire. The necessity of ecclesiastical guidance, if not for themselves, then, as they saw it, for society's unschooled lower orders, continued to be insisted on even by such notorious religious skeptics as Montesquieu, Voltaire, Hume, Gibbon, and Frederick the Great, but without offering much philosophical argument with which to ward off the radicals. This vulnerability ceaselessly aiding the radical wing's advance hence long remained a central factor from around 1660, even during the tendency's most inconspicuous and clandestine early phase.

From the late 1740s onwards, in France, constraints on the clandestine philosophical underground slowly loosened due to gradual easing and circumvention. New modes of surreptitious expression with frequent publishing of passages affirming the opposite of what was meant indicated with sly literary winks and nods, beside discreet appeals to police and administrative authorities to soften enforcement of prohibition of illicit books, became a cumulative shift in which Diderot played a pivotal part. Typically for this mid-eighteenth-century successor phase, subversive ideas, extracted from the founding texts, were increasingly surreptitiously propagated through innuendo and carefully guarded hints buried in more generally available published texts, like the *Encyclopédie* of Diderot and d'Alembert, making possible a much wider general impact than seemed attainable prior to the 1740s.[17]

Nevertheless, as the radical underground's writings diffused in a more direct, complete, and uninhibited fashion than earlier during the eighteenth century's middle decades, their more openly irreligious and anti-establishment writings still circulated only inconspicuously and in highly restricted quantities. Only from 1770, with the anonymous publication of the *Histoire philosophique des Deux Indes* (1770) and equally explosive, anonymous *Système de la nature* (1770), was a new stage reached when production and dissemination of Radical Enlightenment literature suddenly escalated to become a vastly larger, more formidable challenge to the existing order of things than in the past. This produced not just a much wider diffusion of Radical Enlightenment concepts in the 1770s and 1780s than had occurred earlier, but also a more open, general cultural drive by promoters of moderate Enlightenment, Religious

[17] Le Ru, *Subversives Lumières*, 7–20; Duflo, "Diderot et la fin," 26–9.

Enlightenment, and *anti-philosophes*, first in France, but soon conspicuously in Britain, Germany, and America too, to alert opinion and mobilize the public against what was now widely viewed as the overwhelming general menace of "la philosophie moderne"—the very antithesis of theology, authority, moderation, aristocratic primacy in the social hierarchy, monarchy, and faith.

Already, three years before the Revolution, Adrien Lamourette (1742–94), a key Catholic Enlightenment reformer seeking to reconcile theology and science using an element of skepticism, warned of the danger of a universal morally and socially destructive "révolution deplorable," stemming from clandestine philosophical premises. The threatened upheaval, he admonished in 1786, would cause the overthrow of religion and total negation of monarchy and aristocracy, leading to the remaking of all the laws on the principle of "equality": "le vrai dessein de la philosophie est de tout bouleverser [the true goal of the [modern] philosophy is to overthrow everything]."[18] But in proclaiming "modern philosophy" a contagion affecting all social strata, explained Lamourette, he meant to target only those behind the irreligious anonymous subversive texts, not "les systèmes modérés" of *philosophes* like Montesquieu, to him a stalwart defender of Christianity, or Rousseau, deemed by him far more respectful of religion and "virtue" than his former friends (Diderot and d'Holbach), the primary authors of the intellectual subversion he styled a malign force, dishonest, dogmatic, and overbearing, "as much an enemy of throne as of altar."[19]

Since radical enlighteners by definition repudiated theology and guidance by churchmen, most of society tended to characterize their pre-1770 underground, where they knew of it, as "atheistic." Radical enlighteners themselves, however, certainly before 1770, usually denied being "atheists," claiming to have a naturalistic anti-theological notion of "God." What their thought world did reject altogether was assuming that any prophets, spokesmen, or chosen individuals exist, or ever could exist, who stand closer to God than anyone else and are qualified to explain his ways and commands to everyone else. Theology and what they called "priestcraft," society's existing structure and established "morality," was not to them a system of law divinely delivered via any prophet, pope, or church, nor comprised practices intended or sanctioned by God or any supernatural events. While "atheism as a concept" was by no means unfamiliar to erudite academic debate during the late seventeenth and early eighteenth century but rather a topic inherent in the "mental furniture of the Christian learned world,"[20] arguing for the intellectual and moral superiority of "atheism," or non-religious philosophy, over Christian revelation and teaching, remained strictly forbidden, illegitimate in the eyes of governments, universities, and most contemporaries, and everywhere vigorously repressed, as was arguing

[18] Lamourette, *Pensées sur la philosophie*, 55–7, 83–5, 92; Israel, *Democratic Enlightenment*, 142, 148; Lehner, *Catholic Enlightenment*, 210–11.

[19] Lamourette, *Pensées sur la philosophie*, 83–4, 89, 113–15, 203; Sorkin, *Religious Enlightenment*, 276–9.

[20] Kors, *Naturalism and Unbelief*, 2.

human morality needs elevating by being stripped of its theological underpinning. Denying miracles and divine providence, insisting everything, without exception, including the origins of life and morality, is governed by mathematically precise natural laws without any knowing or benevolent divine intervention remained entirely illicit. Equally condemned was outright anti-Scripturalism, all Bible criticism maintaining divine revelation does not exist, that miracles are impossible, that there are no *supernaturalia*.

The pivotal role of anti-Scripturalism and one-substance doctrine in this broad international scenario, of itself assured Spinoza an exceptional status in Enlightenment history. Hobbes, La Peyrère, and one or two others undoubtedly preceded him in developing a powerful, sophisticated anti-Scripturalism, "but no-one smote the foundations of the Pentateuch more completely than Spinoza," insisted the eminent Zurich scholar Johann Heinrich Heidegger (1633–98), among the key Swiss theologians of the age, or did so with greater *audacia*.[21] Furthermore, Spinoza was the first anti-Scripturalist systematically to combine a rigorous new Bible criticism with a sophisticated metaphysics eliminating all *supernaturalia* and divine providence philosophically while viewing these components as "necessarily" linked to seeing the democratic republic as the best and most natural type of state. Hence, there is nothing surprising in Spinoza's unparalleled, posthumous presiding role in theorizing the early Radical Enlightenment or in the rapid forming, first in Holland in the 1670s, of a "Spinozist" sect, nor in his legacy remaining central to key debates subsequently. Samuel Clarke simply reflected the contemporary reality, in 1705, when ranking him as the early Enlightenment's number one challenger of theology's hegemony and calling "Spinoza, the most celebrated patron of atheism in our time (who thought that there is no difference of substances but the whole and every part of the material world is a necessarily existing being), and that there is no other God but the universe . . . "[22]

During the mid-eighteenth century, strict constraints as to how and in what manner philosophy and religion were presented everywhere remained in force and Spinoza still retained his earlier unique status among those challenging this overriding status quo. When Diderot embarked on his philosophical odyssey in the late 1740s, he was already steeped in the clandestine philosophical literature, but at that point possessed only a sketchy knowledge of Spinoza's philosophy.[23] Yet, in a key text of these years, the *Promenade du sceptique*, written in 1747 but not published until decades later, a clandestine text the Paris police searched for and came close to obliterating, Spinoza's system plays a central role. In this debate between a set of mutually disagreeing thinkers all rejecting revealed religion—a deist, sceptic, *spinoziste*, and representative of a crudely mechanistic, immoral atheism reminiscent of La Mettrie—it is the *spinoziste* who ends up presenting the most cogent, compelling,

[21] Heidegger, *Exercitationes Biblicae*, 304, 369, 385.

[22] Clarke, *A Demonstration*, 20.

[23] Goggi, "Spinoza contre Rousseau," 180–2.

and morally uplifting stance.[24] That *spinozisme* emerges from Diderot's clandestine conference, defeating deism, skepticism, and immoral atheism in this way, is deeply symbolic, heralding both Diderot's own allegiance and *spinozisme*'s, or perhaps better *le néo-spinozisme*'s or *neo-Spinozism*'s, emerging ascendancy during the eighteenth century's third quarter over French underground radical thought more generally. In the *Encyclopédie* volume XV, Diderot warns that his "Spinosistes modernes," holding as they do different views about biology, should not be confused with the "Spinosistes anciens" but also emphasizes that, aside from their views on living organisms, new *spinozistes* (among whom he placed himself) follow *l'ancien spinosisme* "in all its consequences."[25]

But here further qualification and clarification is needed given that many scholars oppose my core argument, a mass of critics here termed the "negative critique," while others, without endorsing every feature, react more positively. The controversy has become large and complex. Two recent volumes of essays presenting a balanced mix of both sides, one in English, Steffen Ducheyne's *Reassessing the Radical Enlightenment* (2017), the other in French, have helpfully set out the arguments *pro et contra* enabling readers to gain, with reasonable ease, an overview of the still escalating debate.[26] For the German context, the same applies to a third collection presenting both sides, Carl Niekerk (ed.), *The Radical Enlightenment in Germany*.[27] The "negative critique," probably still the larger phalanx,[28] frequently assumes what is being argued is that the Radical Enlightenment "originated in" as some put it, or evolved from Spinoza's philosophy, that the argument is "Spinoza-based." This is incorrect on

[24] Vernière, *Spinoza et la pensée française*, 568–70, 699; Venturi, *Jeunesse de Diderot*, 117–18; Quintili, *Pensée critique*, 150, 159; Paganini, *Filosofie clandestine*, 160–1; Benítez, *Foyer clandestin* i, 462–6; Blom, *Enlightening the World*, 42, 53; Israel, *Enlightenment Contested*, 818–21.

[25] Diderot, article "Spinosistes" in Diderot and d'Alembert, *Encyclopédie* XV. 474; Wolfe, "Determinism/Spinozism," 49; Métraux, "Über Denis Diderots physiologisch interpretierten Spinoza," 128–9; Villaverde, *Rousseau y el pensamiento*, 38, 44–5, 49.

[26] See Marta García-Alonso (ed.), *Les Lumières radicales et le politique* (Paris, 2017).

[27] Carl Niekerk (ed.), *The Radical Enlightenment in Germany* (Leiden, 2018).

[28] The main "negative" critiques of the Radical Enlightenment thesis thus far are those of Antoine Lilti, Anthony La Vopa, Johnson Kent Wright, Harvey Chisick, Ann Thomson, Ursula Goldenbaum, Samuel Moyn, Dale Van Kley, Annelien De Dijn, Paolo Casini, Carolina Armenteros, Francesco Benigno, Darryn McMahon, Eduardo Tortarolo, Theo Verbeeck, Vincenzo Ferrone, Helena Rosenblatt, Joanne Stalnaker, Lynn Hunt, Jose Peña, Keith Michael Baker, Margaret Jacob, Eric Schliesser, Jeremy Popkin, Dan Edelstein, David Bell, Minchul Kim, Andreas Pečar, and Damien Tricoire; among the foremost and most cited publications presenting their arguments are: Antoine Lilti, "Comment écrit-on l'histoire intellectuelle des Lumières? Spinozisme, radicalisme et philosophie," *Annales. Histoire, Sciences Sociales* (2009), 171–206; A. J. La Vopa, "A New Intellectual History? Jonathan Israel's Enlightenment," *Historical Journal* 52 (2009), 717–38; and Harvey Chisick, "Interpreting the Enlightenment," *The European Legacy*, (2008), 35–57; for four hostile interventions against the "Radical Enlightenment" approach to the French Revolution, see *H-France Forum*, vol. 9 issue 1 (Winter 2014), no. 5; for overviews of the whole debate, see Villaverde, "L'Abbé Raynal," 230–44, 248–51, and Borghero, *Interpretazioni, categorie*, 311–28, 505–7; the most extended critique in German is Andreas Pečar and Damien Tricoire, *Falsche Freunde: War die Auklärung wirklich die Geburtsstunde der Moderne?* (Frankfurt, 2015), originating in the 2012 debate on "Radical Enlightenment" at the Halle Center for Enlightenment Studies.

three counts.[29] First, "Radical Enlightenment" in this series means use of philosophy to reject religious authority linked to broadly democratizing republican schemes for reform so that certain groups and individuals not "Spinozists" in any specific sense could still belong to this category. These non-Spinozist elements included both radical Christian Socinians, Arians, and Unitarians like Jarig Jelles, Richard Price, and Joseph Priestley opposing theological mysteries they deemed incompatible with philosophical-scientific reason while espousing a democratic tendency, and also "deists" like Shaftesbury, meeting the criteria for inclusion under our rubric, who either expressly repudiated Spinoza on moral or some other grounds or, like Mandeville, Franklin, and also Jefferson (who called himself an "Epicurean"), stopped short of expressly renouncing a creator God separate from Nature.

Wrongly assuming that my argument holds that the radical tendency "originated" in Spinoza has led "negative critique" proponents to focus on one or another part of the tradition's complex transmission process, trying to show Spinoza played little or no direct role in a particular thinker's intellectual development. A notable instance is d'Holbach's indubitably substantial debt to Toland.[30] Several discussants point to the strong connection between Toland and d'Holbach, a tie evident not least from the contents of d'Holbach's personal library,[31] but then wrongly infer this means "Spinozism" did not shape d'Holbach's radicalism. Recent research on Toland, however, only reinforces claims that his Bible criticism and attack on priestcraft, and systematic subversion of Locke, rejection of Locke's dualism and "supra rationem," were steeped in Spinozism. Far from misplaced, concludes one scholar, "the extent of a general Spinozistic influence [on Toland] has been—if anything—under-determined and under-appreciated;" the same then applies to d'Holbach.[32] In any case, being a social as much as an intellectual underground Radical Enlightenment did and could not "originate" in the philosophy of any particular thinker. Obviously, if such a movement existed it was a social and cultural as much as intellectual movement drawing vitality, impetus, durability, and ultimately its broad meaning from the social, economic, and political tensions amidst which it flourished.[33]

Intellectually, the group, the *cercle spinoziste*, was a collaborative endeavour with significant contributions to what evolved into "Spinozism" being made by several others beside Spinoza himself—Franciscus van den Enden, Adriaen Koerbagh, Lodewijk Meyer, the Brothers De La Court, and others.[34] One of the few critics to fully appreciate this, Pierre-François Moreau, seeing Spinoza was by no means the first to combine abjuring religious authority with democratic republicanism, and that several of the circle were more explicitly republican, democratic, and hostile to religion, as well more libertarian in sexual matters, than Spinoza himself, inquired with

[29] Israel, "Radical Enlightenment: A Game-Changing Concept," 37–9.
[30] Jacob, *Radical Enlightenment*, 20, 154, 286; Borghero, *Interpretazioni, categorie*, 23–4, 113, 323.
[31] *Catalogue de livres de la Bibliothèque de feu M. le baron d'Holbach*, 24, 176.
[32] Leask, "Speaking for Spinoza?," 144.
[33] Israel, "Radical Enlightenment: A Game-Changing Concept," 36–40.
[34] Israel, *Radical Enlightenment*, 175–274.

an ironic flourish: "was Spinoza then a 'Spinozist'"?[35] The frequently-encountered eighteenth-century French label "spinoziste," Moreau suggested, casting doubt on whether Spinoza does actually evince a "revolutionary impulse," is a misnomer; he questioned whether the "Spinozist conception of the common good" does advance the cause of equality and a political and social revolution based on the "general will," stirring a lively dispute about the revolutionary potential of Spinoza's philosophy among Spinoza specialists. Nevertheless, all Spinoza scholars agree there are cogent grounds for viewing Spinoza as a deliberate political and religious subversive, so that even if one accepts the view of those arguing Spinoza opposed all violent revolutionary upheaval (which I do not), that would not of itself negate the claim that his stance entails opposition to religion's sway combined with opposition to kings and restricted oligarchies. We would still be left with a broad, enduring opposition movement exerting a major historical impact over a long period commencing with the efforts of a particular circle, shaped by a particular historical context, later becoming a growing force extending across Europe and eventually the entire Atlantic world, with one philosopher's contribution having a continuous, long-term presence in the tradition.

Radical Enlightenment, then, "originated" not in anyone's ideas, but rather in group intellectual responses to challenging historical realities, first in Holland, and later more generally in reaction to profound antagonisms within European and New World society and politics. The Radical Enlightenment thesis does not hold, therefore, that the late seventeenth and eighteenth century historical phenomenon contemporaries labeled "Spinozism" or the "sect of Spinozists" was necessarily tightly anchored in Spinoza's own texts as such. It is hard to dispute the findings of Paul Vernière's classic monograph, of 1954, that leading French radicals of the High Enlightenment era—Diderot, d'Holbach, Helvétius, and Condorcet—mostly had only a fleeting, superficial knowledge of Spinoza's texts and rarely cite him directly, albeit Diderot and d'Holbach were in the habit of echoing Spinoza more frequently than is usually realized.[36] Nor can one dispute that Spinoza's texts generally ceased to be as widely known and intensively studied as they had been after the first quarter of the eighteenth century (before reviving again strongly in Germany, in the 1780s).[37] In 1726, when reviewing Wollaston, Le Clerc observed that the "system of Spinoza" which earlier, as he himself had remarked, had gained a large following, having since the 1670s attracted many supporters,[38] was now no longer the chief vehicle of free-thinkers to the extent it had been, no longer "la grande mode des Libertins."[39] But it is wrong to infer from this that the continuing frequent use of labels "Spinosiste" and "Spinosisme" through the eighteenth century was therefore just a vague rhetorical

[35] Moreau, "Spinoza est-il spinoziste?," 292–3; on this point, see Villaverde, "L'Abbé Raynal," 235 and Henry, "L'Égalitarisme," 50.
[36] Goggi, *De l'*Encyclopédie *à l'éloquence républicaine*, 100–2, 174–83, 397–414.
[37] Vernière, *Spinoza et la pensée française*, 699–700.
[38] De Vet, "Spinoza en Spinozisme," 3.
[39] De Vet, Spinoza en Spinozisme," 3, 23.

ploy, a set of insignificant catch-all phrases essentially unconnected with Spinoza's system, a piece of frippery, as Yves Citton suggested, declaimed for purely rhetorical purposes by hundreds of writers with little grasp of the content of Spinoza's philosophy.[40]

Many scholars, including some eminent names, find the Postmodernist deconstruction techniques applied here by scholars like Antoine Lilti and Yves Citton compelling. Antonio Negri, convinced the thesis "Spinoza is the foundation of the radical Enlightenment" is wrong, compliments Lilti's "remarkable analysis" for demolishing it altogether.[41] Rather than a "theoretical corpus," Spinozism, contends Lilti, following Daniel Roche—and this constitutes Lilti's prime argument against the "Radical Enlightenment" thesis—is just "un scandale, la figure extreme de l'hétérotoxie," a term lacking content and irredeemably ambivalent in meaning and problematic.[42] The argument that different writers meant all manner of different things by "Spinozism," that the eighteenth-century cultural phenomenon *spinozisme* possessed no unity of content or cultural cohesion, that much of the talk of *spinozisme* was generated by detractors misunderstanding it or distorting it for polemical purposes, that eighteenth-century "Spinozism" is just a meaningless pool of ambivalence, is hugely applauded. Many scholars want Lilti's contention to be true; but it is not even remotely tenable. For it would mean that even though all over Europe, from around 1670, writers frequently identified Spinoza and "Spinozism" as the most audacious existing philosophical threat to religion, previous philosophy, and the moral order, nevertheless they did not mean anything concrete by this. Such an approach could not even begin to explain the systematic deployment of "Spinozism" in crucial passages of Leibniz, Le Clerc, Toland, Montesquieu, Diderot, and Voltaire (for whom it played a central role in the controversies of the last decade of his life); nor account for the concept's all too obtrusive coherence as institutionalized in the era's major encyclopedic compendia such as Bernard Picart's and Jean-Frédéric Bernard's *Céremonies et coûtumes religieuses*, Diderot's *Encyclopédie*, and Baumgarten's *Nachrichten*.

Not only did Clarke, Le Clerc, Montesquieu, Voltaire, Diderot, Kant, and many others become entangled in complex controversies about "spinozisme" obviously meaning something highly specific by this term, but all the Postmodernism in the world cannot make *spinozisme* as found in texts like Diderot's *Promenade* and the *Encyclopédie* compatible with revelation, miracles, divine providence, religious authority, deism, mysticism, fideism, eclecticism, moral relativism, Aristotelian substances, Platonic ideals, Prisca theologia (natural religion), Cartesian dualism, Lockean dualism based on *supra rationem*, double truth, fixity of species, Epicurean swerves, La Mettrie's materialism, or the durable and powerful thrust of skepticism. This does not mean there was absolutely no element of ambiguity or uncertainty; *spinozisme* was not always a precise philosophical-theological category. Some commentators, including Leibniz, claimed *spinozisme* was closely related to Stoicism, that

[40] Citton, "L'Invention du spinozisme," 310–12. [41] Negri, *Spinoza for our Time*, 16–17.

[42] Lilti, "Comment écrit-on l'histoire intellectuelle," 188–9, 192; Borghero, *Interpretazioni, categorie*, 506.

ancient Stoics were "presque spinozistes," while others demurred, aligning *Spinosistes* closer to Epicureanism. But the phenomenon invariably meant an unremitting naturalism, anti-Scripturalism, and rejection of all *supernaturalia* within a highly integrated philosophical "system," a rigorous atheism opposed to all theology and viewing organized religion as a prop to a wider apparatus of tyranny. If Spinoza's style, his "geometric method," appeared "terribly archaic" to Diderot and the "new Spinozists" of the 1750s, the latter, as Lilti himself concedes at one point, nevertheless intended "to follow [Spinoza] in the 'consequences' of his system." What matters far more than Spinoza's style of argumentation historically, is the tight interlinking of his system's main components—the attack on priestcraft, revelation, miracles, and preference for democracy as the most "natural form of government," is closely tied to the oneness of substance, God, and nature, his monism conceiving movement as inherent in matter, and a strictly social conception of morality and "good" and "bad," and, finally, to the question of how to reorganize life and politics, how thought relates to action, philosophy to improving individual life and humanity in general. To regard Diderot's, Montesquieu's, or Voltaire's repeated, clear usage of the term *spinozisme* as so elastic as to have little real meaning would be as reckless and absurd in an Enlightenment scholar as to suppose this with respect to Lessing, Goethe, Herder, Fichte, or Hegel. Rather than showing acumen, excessive preoccupation with "signification slippage" led the Postmodernist challenge to severe misconstruing of Spinoza's Enlightenment legacy and also of other elements of the story, including Bayle's legacy, which Lilti wrongly supposed one of skepticism instead of as anti-skeptical, anti-theological moral rationalism.[43]

Whether only a sketchy knowledge of Spinoza was revealed, as in Diderot's *Promenade*, or whether a given writer showed a profound, familiarity, *spinozisme*, wherever deployed in Enlightenment controversies, invariably entails an anti-Lockean and anti-Newtonian (and hence anti-Voltairean) comprehensive eradication of theism and theology in favour of a philosophy rooted in mathematically expressed universal laws of science.[44] Contrary to Roche, Lilti, Citton, Negri, and here also Borghero, "Spinozism" *was* broadly coherent and meaningful as a concept and tradition, albeit not infrequently detached from Spinoza's political and social thought so that, in practice, one could, like Boulainvilliers, La Mettrie, or Goethe, be a "Spinozist" in important respects, and in Boulainvilliers' case a key figure of the clandestine literature, without strictly being part of the Radical Enlightenment at all. Laurent Bove is very likely correct in arguing that Boulainvilliers' "spinozisme" was confined to his attack on religion, and not reflected in his political and social writing to the extent I earlier suggested; still, this does not obviate the main reason for including Boulainvilliers as a notable contributor to the rise of the Radical

[43] Lilti, "How Do We Write the Intellectual History?," cue 55; Israel, "L'Histoire intellectuelle," 209–10.
[44] Israel, "L'Histoire intellectuelle," 211–15.

Enlightenment given his pivotal role as an underground transmitter of Spinozist texts and concepts in France.[45]

The social reformist and political aspects of Spinoza were not as conspicuously or solidly embedded in the cultural phenomenon "spinozisme" in royalist France and princely Germany as the assault on religious authority. Yet, while possible, it was never easy, theoretically, to detach Spinoza's rigorous naturalism from its social and political consequences, as we discern not only in his own works and the *cercle spinoziste*, but also Toland and, from the late 1760s, Diderot, as he became politically more radical. For it follows directly from Spinoza's metaphysical stance that morality is a purely social tool invented by men to reconcile individual self-interest with the common interest; and from this that an entire new morality is required if we are to build a "happier" society based on worldly justice and equality and, from this, that the existing laws urgently needed reforming on many points, that numerous social abuses, as Diderot and his circle viewed them, such as penalizing homosexuality, prohibiting divorce, collecting tithes, and the social role of nunneries, needed eradicating. *Spinozisme*, like the *Encyclopédie* was hence always a social and political as much as philosophical *machine de guerre* geared to assault broader forms of "tyranny" than just oppression by religious authorities. "Spinozism" always implied that what Spinozists and Tolandists called "priestcraft" not only unjustly invades freedom of thought and conscience, persecutes dissenters, and distorts the academic agenda, but bolsters society's general oppressiveness by abetting political tyranny. What the specifically "democratizing" tendency consisted of, prior to the American Revolution, was not so much electoral practices tending toward universal suffrage as yet than the idea of elevating the autonomy of every individual on an equal basis and pursuing the "common good" or "general will" in the sense of promoting the well-being of society as a whole.

By 1775, and the outbreak of the American Revolution, the age of small hidden networks and clandestine manuscripts was definitely over, even if the Radical Enlightenment still remained in part a clandestine sphere, with d'Holbach, for example, carefully preserving his anonymity. Some illicitly published books, in French especially, were beginning to sell in large quantities, even if the trade remained illegal and even though, in Germany, demand for legally-sold French books tended to fall off after 1770.[46] Radical enlighteners had become an increasingly vocal and conspicuous (though often still anonymous) international fraternity, a now fast growing and relatively large, widely scattered intellectual elite predominantly formed by informal literary, academic, student, and professional enclaves, but now sporadically able to mobilize support well beyond those limits. Such fringes coalesced into a trans-Atlantic political and social movement present especially across France, Germany, Britain, Italy, Holland, Switzerland, Scandinavia, Ireland, and the United States.

[45] Israel, *Radical Enlightenment*, 566–74; Bove, "Boulainvilliers lecteur," 373–9.
[46] Freedman, *Books without Borders*, 81, 84, 239, 243–4, 267–8.

By 1786 the combined, integrated threat this posed to kings and religion was, as Lamourette contended, manifest.

By the 1770s, the battle between moderate (aristocratic-courtly) and Radical (democratizing republican) Enlightenment had hence completed its arduous historical transition from the world of clandestine manuscripts and anonymous illicit publications to unyielding and often ferocious open ideological warfare in newspapers, pamphlets, journals, lecture-halls, and courtrooms. By the 1790s, this was a battle equally intense, bitter, and formative in America *and* Europe.[47] One unavoidable consequence, massively evident everywhere Enlightenment thought counted, was that from the 1770s the Enlightenment itself became not just deeply, but now, as Lamourette also noted,[48] self-consciously and publicly divided in basic premises and general principles into bitterly warring factions, for and against democratizing republicanism linked to rejection, or alternatively acceptance, of ecclesiastical authority. In America, the main split within the Revolution was between a dominant "aristocratic" Federalist faction led by John Adams, Alexander Hamilton, Gouverneur Morris, John Jay, and their associates adopting "British mixed government" as their highest political ideal, and their chief ideological foes to the Left, the Jeffersonian so-called "true republicans" rejecting the British model and demanding elimination of "aristocracy" and wider suffrages, the two sides unrelenting in denouncing each other.

Little of this, the reader should note, had much to do with broad cultural shifts, cultural turns, or general "sociability," notions in recent decades much cherished by mainstream Enlightenment scholarship and decidedly part of the explanation why the revolutionary era's basic ideological and intellectual mechanics remain, much of the time, so obscured from view. While popular grievances and resentment generated the basic motive force behind the revolutionary developments of 1775–1848 so that in a primal sense revolutionary impetus did derive from society as a whole, including the disadvantaged and downtrodden, it is largely untrue that the complex revolutionary ideas that changed the world during those decades, the theories about how and why society must be transformed, what is good and bad for society, politics, and education, stemmed from mainstream culture's mostly vague and directionless generalized sociability or its discontents. Leadership and articulation of demands derived rather from small, besieged and highly restricted intellectual fringes. The prime shaping force generating and diffusing the new principles, political theories, democratic outcomes, rhetoric, terminology, and zeal to crush ecclesiastical authority, above all the revolutionary new principle of "universal and equal rights," did not arise from mainstream society, and had little direct derivation from public opinion as normally conceived. Rather, as we shall see, a very sharp opposition arose, as acute in Britain and America as France, the Low Countries, and Germany, between revolutionary ideas as a "universal and equal rights" programme and the conventional

[47] See Cotlar, *Tom Paine's America*, 4–60; Newman, "Paine, Jefferson and Revolutionary Radicalism," 71–94; Stewart, *Nature's God*, 133–363; Israel, *Revolutionary Ideas*, 30–52.

[48] Lamourette, *Pensées sur la philosophie*, 105–6, 203.

thinking of the populace at large. Democratic republican revolutionary ideals, equal rights, and attacking organized religion, derived not from general cultural shifts, or mainstream culture, but overwhelmingly from the still basically fringe sources and intellectual traditions of the Radical Enlightenment.

1.3. THE END OF THE ENLIGHTENMENT?

Although by longstanding convention historians place the end of the Enlightenment, viewed as an epoch, at 1789 or 1800, this poses something of a problem given that the objectives and concerns of many prominent early nineteenth-century intellectual and political figures were still broadly characteristic, indeed conscious continuations, of the late Enlightenment. Schemes of philosophically defined, non-religious political, legal, and social reform, not primarily focused on economic goals, proliferated. Bentham and the Benthamite Utilitarians in England, the French *Idéologues*, (the post-1815) Sismondi in Switzerland, the Spanish revolutionaries of 1820, the Von Humboldts in Germany, some Decembrists in Russia, Bolívar in Spanish America, and not least Napoleon and his brothers, and some of his subordinates, all exemplify this powerful post-1800 prolongation of bold Enlightenment projects reorganizing and rationalizing, at least purportedly, to ameliorate humanity. Hence, even if most historians prefer to adhere to convention and stop around 1800, there are undeniably grounds for postulating a resolutely reforming Enlightenment continuing at least until the 1830 revolutions. Within this perspective, "liberalism" as a distinctive label customarily applied by historians to the early nineteenth century becomes a somewhat superfluous term for the Enlightenment's late phase, a powerful continuing tendency operative at a time when "nationalism" and socialism, still relatively weak, were not yet major ideological rivals.

This does not mean all or most thinkers, publicists, and orators, active when these reform schemes were introduced, necessarily still belonged to the Enlightenment. If many middle-of-the-road conservatives and so-called "liberals" lacking enthusiasm for large-scale Enlightenment projects did still favour reform up to a point, there arose also a revivified and strengthened Counter-Enlightenment movement both Catholic and Protestant (and in eastern Europe, Jewish) resolutely and aggressively opposing Enlightenment core concepts and values on the basis of faith, political loyalism, and tradition. Around 1820, outright intellectual foes of the Enlightenment, "anti-philosophes" as their French representatives were called, abounded and received widespread political support in elaborating anti-Enlightenment ideologies amounting to far more than just obscurantist attitudes, fanaticism, and religious militancy, though enlighteners moderate and radical generally dismissed these figures as "fanatics."

Overtly Counter-Enlightenment revolt against "the Enlightenment," urging the populace to reject the supposedly arrogant and overconfident "enlightened" spirit of the age, remained a striking feature of the trans-Atlantic world certainly down to the 1820s. An exceptionally eloquent example is *Objections to the Spirit of the Century* (1823) by the poet Isaac da Costa (1798–1860). Son of an Amsterdam Sephardic merchant and a sister of the famous economist David Ricardo, after converting to Christianity, da Costa became a leading early nineteenth-century Dutch literary figure who vehemently protested against the "enlightened" spirit in his view still towering over Europe, especially its sweeping plans to supposedly improve society through education, law reform, vaccination, and alterations to economic life. He objected too to secularizing society by placing all churches together on the same subordinate level under state supervision, as the new ruler of the United Netherlands, William I (reigned: 1815–43), a former pawn of Napoleon, prided himself on doing.[49] Da Costa fervently resisted the Enlightenment's triumphant sense of advancing social and political progress on secular lines, what he saw as its upstart but illusory belief in the power of human reason, and especially its ignoring what to him was humanity's unalterably abject character, the innate shortcomings of human capacity viewed from what he considered the genuinely Christian perspective.

Da Costa did not portray the Enlightenment as a whole as irreligious and hostile to religion. Many enlighteners strove, he knew, to fuse Enlightenment strategies with traditional belief and defense of religious authority in the tradition of Locke, Le Clerc, Leibniz, Wolff, and Burke, or, if not reconcile, then at least, as with Voltaire, Hume, and Kant, compromise with organized religion for reasons of social and political expediency, conserving the existing order's religious frame for the sake of social stability. But even among sincere believers, following the path of moderation, it had always been the non-religious component of their plans for improvement that rendered their efforts integral to the Enlightenment. The category "Religious Enlightenment" only meaningfully applies to reformers who, while sincere believers or at least defenders of ecclesiastical authority (not at all the same thing), nevertheless aimed to reform Christendom, or in the case of Moses Mendelssohn, Judaism, by rejecting, or greatly toning down, confessional barriers, intolerance, and dogmatism. Religious Enlightenment qualified as Enlightenment specifically through advancing toleration and inter-confessional dialogue, by banishing religious conflict, and espousing strands of modern science, Newtonianism above all, suited to reconciling religion with science, and hence religion with philosophy.[50] Both "Religious Enlightenment" and such reconciling strategies remained typical features of the continuing Enlightenment of the 1820s.

In the eyes of counter-enlighteners, both wings of the Enlightenment, moderate and radical, remained in essence non-religious since the basic tools of Enlightenment compromise with religion, toleration and reasonable dialogue, resort to the "argument from design", in themselves seemed not to be religious undertakings. Rather,

[49] Da Costa, *Bezwaren*, 10, 13–15, 81, 84; Lok, "Vijanden van de Verlichting," 212; De Vet, "Verlichting en Christendom," 122.

[50] Sorkin, *Religious Enlightenment*, 5–6.

both reflect Enlightenment secularizing of the Christian conception of "redemption," leaving ample room for more ardent faith-based approaches comprehensively repudiating enlightened values and objectives. The torrent of anti-Christian texts authored by Voltaire, Diderot, Rousseau, Helvétius, and the rest, contended Da Costa, had yielded no genuine moral or social improvement; rather, the world had witnessed only regression into selfishness, licentiousness, and disorder. The revolutionary conceit that mankind could be dramatically refashioned on a vastly improved basis by recasting society's political, educational, and other institutions employing abstract ideas, philosophical principles, rather than embracing the God-given divine moral and social order, struck Da Costa as disastrous—as did Enlightenment stress on individual freedom which, from his faith-based perspective, meant immorality and "spiritual slavery." Enlighteners demanded tolerance, but enlightened *Tolerantismus* he pronounced bogus since reprehensible, vicious intolerance remained utterly alien to true Christian believers: it is found, instead, among non-believers as the French revolutionary Terror of 1793–4 proved for all to see. Were not Robespierre and Marat crueler, more oppressive violators of human freedom than Alva and the Inquisition? Christendom, led by religious leaders, monarchs, and teachers, must rise up and overcome every conception of the "modern" underpinned by "Enlightenment."[51]

Writers like De Maistre, Chateaubriand, De Lamennais, Bonald, and Da Costa demanded an uncompromising revival of religious faith and feeling (which, among much else, moved Da Costa to head a protest group resisting compulsory vaccination against smallpox and other endemic diseases).[52] As these all rightly saw, non-religious, non-traditional, philosophical-scientific preoccupation with schemes for sweeping change aimed at general improvement in politics, administration, health-care, education, moral attitudes, legal and penal systems, plans primarily non-economic in character but often including schemes to spread prosperity more evenly, remained the Western world's hegemonic cultural and political tendency during the nineteenth century's first quarter. Despite the noisily acclaimed 1814–15 Restoration following Napoleon's defeat, and its vow to reorder the world on the basis of faith, monarchy, and aristocracy, the truth was, all these counter-enlighteners complained, that religion continued to be systematically elbowed aside from education, healthcare, social institutions, and economic policy by leading publicists and intellectuals and some Western governments.

The justifications historiography offers for the old convention of selecting the French Revolution or Restoration of 1814–15 as the Enlightenment's conclusion are distinctly unsatisfactory. The Restoration was far less of a break with the Enlightenment than historians once assumed. Still less does it make sense to identify the Enlightenment's end with the events of 1789, claiming the Revolution demonstrated for all to see "how reason could fail," that social and political efforts inspired and

[51] Da Costa, *Bezwaren*, 24.

[52] De Vet, "Verlichting en Christendom," 120.

"conditioned by reason need not result in progress."[53] Even if that was the French Revolution's legacy (which is questionable), it was decidedly not the lesson those governing France or the rest of western Europe drew following Robespierre's overthrow. Rather, as counter-enlighteners complained, continuing confidence in the power of human reason, opposing the Holy Alliance's and Congress of Vienna's often ineffective efforts to spur political and religious reaction, belief in the power of "philosophy" to transform the world, barely receded at all.[54] The lesson guiding figures mostly drew from the Terror and unruliness of the *sans-culottes* was that reason and Enlightenment imperatives had abominably lapsed temporarily, betrayed by dishonest populist leaders like Marat, Robespierre, and Saint-Just whom all genuine enlighteners reviled as reprehensible deceivers of the people applying vile techniques of disinformation and lies, fraudulent opinion manipulators flattering popular ignorance.

The moral usually drawn from the experience of the Robespierre "tyranny" was not the Enlightenment's basic failure but, on the contrary, the need for redoubled effort to raise the common people's educational level and political awareness, improve attitudes and political culture on the basis of Enlightenment reason, and elevate the general level of society, to more effectively counter the irrationality of unreasoning populism and eradicate the manipulative mass politics that in the hands of Robespierre's Jacobinism proved so utterly destructive of Enlightenment values, ideals, and promise. It was exclusively *anti-philosophes* and prophets of Counter-Enlightenment who sought to pin Robespierre *to* the Enlightenment, all too plainly using the charge as a propaganda weapon for discrediting the Enlightenment in the public's minds.

One might agree up to a point and still object that whatever the basic post-1800 continuities, ending in 1789 or 1815 is so much the convention among practically all Enlightenment historians that terminating several decades later disturbs the entire shape of our received historiography of "modernity," especially the almost universally accepted practice of firmly separating the nineteenth century from the eighteenth, using the term "liberalism" as if it represented something fundamentally new. But there were no significant early nineteenth-century "liberal" projects that were not equally pre-1800 Enlightenment projects while the habit of using the term "liberal" to cover both anti-democratic "moderate" reformers, like Guizot in France, and those advocating universal male suffrage and other schemes that were democratic in orientation, serves only to blur vital distinctions. Certainly the great Enlightenment projects of the 1800–30 period were no mere emulation of past efforts. Some new elements appeared. But these are all best viewed either as applications of typically pre-1800 principles in new contexts, as with Bolivar's revolution in South America, or extensions of eighteenth-century concerns as with Bentham's schemes for

[53] O'Hara, *The Enlightenment*, 25, 27, 104–5, 113, 196; also Stalnaker, "How Does Enlightenment End?," 49–50; and Vermij, *Geest uit de fles*, 17–18.

[54] Da Costa, *Bezwaren*, 54, 84.

reorganizing representative government and the prison system, or Sismondi's proposals for spreading prosperity more evenly and ending slavery.

A prime instance of late Enlightenment universalism, concern with individual liberty, eschewing of theology and religious elements, and preoccupation with changing men's ideas, as the path to general improvement were the Prussian educational reform projects of Wilhelm von Humboldt (1767–1835). These aimed at ennobling humanity "by the very things which now, though beautiful in themselves, so often go to degrade it." Von Humboldt believed it possible to draw the mass of society, men and women equally, away from ignorance, superstition, religious fanaticism, low-level thinking, and soul-destroying drudgery, from crass entertainments and empty pastimes (as well as inflammatory, unreasoning politics), by means of far-reaching projects to re-educate everyone, peasants and artisans included, so as to understand enough about art, literature, and philosophy to ennoble them, and transform their ways of envisaging the world, work, leisure, and society. "The more a man accustoms himself to dwell in the region of higher thoughts and sensations, and the more refined and vigorous his moral and intellectual powers become, the more he longs to confine himself to such external objects only as furnish ampler scope and material for his internal development."[55] The process involved teaching how, aided by society's new schemes for public education, each individual's own inner striving for cultural elevation, or *Bildung*, could be what Von Humboldt optimistically deemed the vital path to greater happiness for all.

In Von Humboldt's vision, admittedly, one discerns a streak of "inwardness" revealing him to have been, besides one of the last great enlighteners, a bridging figure between Enlightenment and Romanticism. If one accepts Hegel's definition of Romanticism as "absolute inwardness," and agrees Rousseau was a founding figure of the Romantic movement,[56] there should be little difficulty in recognizing Romanticism as being in part a form of reaction, an abandonment, even a revulsion and protest, against the Enlightenment with its emphasis on "reason" and social projects. But though an anti-Enlightenment reaction, often an arm of Counter-Enlightenment, by exerting a strong impact on revolutionaries as well as counter-revolutionaries, Romanticism also acted as an intensifier serving to sharpen the rift between radical and moderate forms of Enlightenment as we see with the undeniable streak of Romanticism and nostalgia infusing the radical politics and social thought of figures like Shelley, Heine, Michelet, and Lamartine.

Meanwhile, in contrast to budding socialism and Romanticism, other widely proclaimed "new" elements historians customarily invoke as period markers supposedly fencing the nineteenth century off from the eighteenth, in particular nationalism, appear to have had much less bearing or significance in reality, at least before the 1830s and 1840s than has in the past been assigned to them. Nationalism did become a major factor eventually, but played remarkably little part in shaping reform schemes

[55] Von Humboldt, *Sphere and Duties*, 28. [56] Blanning, *Romantic Revolution*, 9.

during the Napoleonic era even in Spain and Germany where some claimed to detect evidence of a "national" awakening among the public. Nationalism did not count for much in the revolutions of the 1820s which in Spain, Portugal, Naples, Piedmont, and Latin America were chiefly about escaping repressive monarchical forms of government and antiquated systems of laws, press control, and ecclesiastical guidance rather than, as in Greece (tenuously), about national unification, strengthening national awareness, and nation-building.

This granted, one might infer that the Enlightenment "continued throughout the nineteenth century,"[57] but that would stretch the concept beyond all useful limits. From the 1830s (except among socialists), and then more decisively after the final outburst of democratic revolutions, those of 1848, a less reform-oriented, less ambitious if in many ways steadier, more quiescent and settled phase in the Western world commenced in which "nationalism," imperialism, racism, and general reaction against Enlightenment cosmopolitanism became, together with socialism, the guiding forces, the new predominant ideologies. The prolonged phase of social, political, and cultural stability following 1848 finally extinguished, west of Russia at least, the revolutionary ardour of past decades. A predominantly complacent, conservative aura presided over the successful monarchies of Victoria, Napoleon III, Prussia's king (after 1871 the Kaiser), and the new Italian royal house. After 1848 followed an age of relative social harmony lasting until 1914, already presaged earlier by the quietening, steadying constitutional outcome of several of the 1830 revolutions, like that in Belgium and in more repressive fashion Poland, and most strikingly by the 1832 limited constitutional reforms in Britain that long quelled the pre-1830 pressure for further, more far-reaching political reform in the world's then leading empire and economy.

Socialism, it is true, in many instances shared some features with the Enlightenment. But in general it was essentially a new tendency without real eighteenth-century roots or predecessors. Indeed, many socialists, Proudhon most notably, combined socialism with a decidedly anti-Enlightenment (and in his case also ferociously anti-Semitic) outlook. During the transition phase of the 1830s and 1840s, Europe's and America's socialists succeeded in refashioning and redirecting the Left intelligentsia's outlook fundamentally: the intellectual plans of the pre-1848 democratic radicals for social amelioration were discarded for something broadly different. Replacing late Enlightenment reformism with an alternative opposition culture, Europe's and America's socialists developed fresh and distinctive ideologies for general improvement based far more on economic and labour theory, and labour reorganization, than changing men's basic ideas, or overcoming credulity, "ignorance," and "superstition." The aspiration now was for improvement via labour reform and basic economic adjustments, whether revolutionary or gradualist, in place of the pre-1830 political, legal, and educational reform schemes of the late Enlightenment.

[57] Conrad, "Enlightenment," 1001.

Arguably the most basic continuity linking the first third of the nineteenth century with the Enlightenment past was the early nineteenth-century reformers, including the Russian Decembrists, finding themselves compelled by circumstance to divide between those willing to ally with organized religion in part, leaving primary education largely with the churches, and compromising with the principles of monarchy and aristocracy, like Napoleon and his brothers following Bonaparte's concordat with the Papacy, in 1801, and those basically rejecting compromise with the principles of crown, altar, and social hierarchy, like the post-1815 Bentham, Bolivar, Sismondi, the *Idéologues*, and some Decembrists. These latter were the radicals that counter-enlighteners rightly differentiated from the moderate enlighteners because they systematically opposed the sway of religion in every respect, along with the traditional social and political order based on hierarchy and aristocracy.[58] This leads us back once more to the fundamental rift between the long divergent moderate and radical Enlightenment blocs.

Nothing better exemplifies this volume's argument than the address Spanish America's greatest hero, Bolívar, delivered before the Venezuelan legislature, at Angostura, in February 1819. Bolívar has often presented problems for adherents of our existing historiographical categories. One scholar tried to set the record straight by linking Bolívar's passionate republicanism to the "classical republican" tradition sketched by Pocock and Skinner.[59] He rightly claimed Bolívar's complex, crucially important ideology had little to do with traditional Spanish American Creole patriotism: colonial-era white Creole resentment did indeed exalt the white elite and the Conquest, accepting the basic institutional framework of the Spanish *ancien régime* while complaining bitterly of the privileged position assigned to European Spaniards in Spanish America in preference to American-born "Spaniards." None of this held much interest for Bolívar who cared relatively little for the Spanish American past. Yet, despite his fondness for ancient Sparta, Bolívar's republicanism had little to do either, it turns out, with "classical republicanism," since he was serious about eliminating slavery and drawing the non-white population into a framework of democratic equality. As Bolívar saw it (others disputed his claims), his vision was emphatically a "democratic republicanism" formed by his favourite authors in social and political thought—the post-1815 Sismondi, Volney, Gorani, Helvétius, Filangieri, Bentham, and the Venezuelan Simon Rodríguez, none of whom were nationalists, liberals, or socialists, none of whom were classical republicans or moderates; all of whom were specifically and solidly "Radical Enlightenment" writers.

The ideological program Bolívar spelt out at Angostura had no meaningful relation to traditional Creole patriotism, "classical republicanism," liberalism, or nationalism. His goal, he explained, was to achieve in northern South America a "democratic republic." But he also explained, in classic Radical Enlightenment fashion, that this could not yet be a question of one man one vote since it was vital to exclude the

[58] Da Costa, *Bezwaren*, 54–5. [59] Brading, *Classical Republicanism*, 9, 11.

illiterate and completely ignorant from participation, and from voting, given that ability to read laws and newspapers, and overcome superstition and credulity, is the foundation of all proper political awareness and capacity for citizenship. The ignorant, superstitious, and credulous he declared, are and will always remain victims of oppression, deception, and manipulation. "The most perfect system of government is that which produces the greatest amount of happiness possible, the greatest level of social security and the highest level of political stability."[60] Therefore, for the time being, the majority must be excluded from voting while the republic undertook the burden of educating and enlightening its population. His approach was democratic in the sense that his desired outcome would produce the highest level of freedom, satisfaction, and equality for all, based on an exclusively secular and egalitarian definition of the "common good." He fully concurred with the goals of the first Venezuela constitution of 1811 in so far as this forbade all vestiges of monarchy, aristocracy, and privilege, and affirmed the universal and equal "rights of man" and liberty of work, thought, speech, and writing. Revolutionary in expressly rejecting the *ancien régime* in every respect, Bolívar pointedly cited Volney, a classic radical enlightener, to underline his fervent hope that the infinite errors and misfortunes of the Old World rendering most of its inhabitants wretched, miserable, and ignorant would prove to be lessons imparting wisdom and happiness to the New.[61]

1.4. THE CONCEPT "RADICAL ENLIGHTENMENT'

"Radical Enlightenment," in short, is the key to a great deal in historical studies, philosophy, political thought, Latin American studies, and the social sciences, an intellectual revolution profoundly affecting religion, morality, law, institutions, politics, healthcare, and education, as well as sexual attitudes and general culture while entailing also a sweepingly reformist and innately revolutionary new democratic approach to society and politics. By 1819 there were many Radical Enlightenment writers and orators and their global impact was vast. By Bolívar's time, Radical Enlightenment displayed a high degree of inner cohesion and consistency centering around the "universal and equal rights of man" understood as the "general will" not in Rousseau's but in Diderot's, d'Holbach's, and Volney's more lastingly important cosmopolitan sense as a body of universal truth, universally applicable. By contrast, from the outset, in the 1760s, Rousseau "rejected the notion of a universal bond obliging mankind," as it has been put, opening up a huge gulf between his then massively acclaimed thought and Radical Enlightenment.[62]

[60] Bolívar, *Discurso*, 25; Brading, *Classical Republicanism*, 15; Rojas, *Ideas educativas*, 44–5, 47.

[61] Bolívar, *Discurso*, 22.

[62] For a succinct summary of the difference between Diderot's (Radical Enlightenment) "general will" and Rousseau's "general will", see Shklar, "General Will," 276.

Counter-Enlightenment, meanwhile, did not deny the scale or grandiose hopes for improvement of the radical social projects of the post-1800 era; what it denied was that such radical schemes could in practice produce anything other than disorder, confusion, and setbacks. Philosophical champions of black emancipation on a republican basis planned not just to abolish slavery like some Christians, noted Da Costa, but "destroy the aristocracy of [white] skin colour"—they sought to end the oppression and *avilissement* of the blacks, by raising the blacks to the same level of freedom, education, and integration in society of the whites![63] In his view the only outcome of their ambitious schemes in the Caribbean (where dwelt several of his own relatives) had been devastation of colonies, slaughter of the white planters (as in Haiti), and bouts of cruel and bloody warfare.[64] Counter-Enlightenment preached submission to established authority, above all monarchy and ecclesiastics, along with total abandonment of such far-reaching schemes as Brissot and Condorcet had conjured up for black emancipation. Admittedly, Enlightenment moderates, like Burke, Guizot, and many others, acknowledged counter-enlighteners, also like them flatly rejected "universal and equal rights, black emancipation, women's emancipation, equality for Jews, eliminating religion's sway, and democratic republicanism, nearly as fervently sometimes as they did. But moderate enlighteners embraced *Tolerantismus*, schemes for constitutional and educational improvement, limiting monarchical power, depleting aristocracy, and spreading healthcare in ways corroding true Christian submission and the authentic mystique of aristocracy and monarchy. Da Costa fiercely denounced the widely acclaimed Spanish revolution of 1820–3 for its efforts to enthrone constitutionalism and elections, and dilute the sanctified majesty and authority of royalty and legitimacy as ordained by God.[65]

Radical Enlightenment defined as rejection of religious authority tied to democratic republicanism and universal and equal rights subsequently remained the chief agent of intellectual and political opposition to the existing order through the early nineteenth century, down to the 1848 revolutions. However, from the 1830s onwards it found itself increasingly challenged by a new and rival opposition movement, "socialism," which increasingly displaced the radical tendency. The two impulses, radical democratic ideas and socialism, already incipiently opposed earlier, noted Sismondi in 1819, became conscious, outright rivals during the 1830s and 1840s. Radical Enlightenment and socialism fully concurred that most men live in what d'Holbach called a "vale of tears," weighed down by tyrannical regimes and social systems, that the lot of the great majority is needlessly impoverished, oppressed, and wretched. The reason most men live in misery and in chains under debased and degrading conditions, both concurred further, is that the great majority are exploited, preyed on, taken advantage of, by cliques of privileged and wealthy persons. Radical enlighteners and socialists both believed dominant social elites deliberately deployed religion, conventional thinking, education, and ordinary public discourse, to dupe

[63] Brissot, *Mémoires* ii. 293.
[64] Da Costa, *Bezwaren*, 27–8.
[65] Da Costa, *Bezwaren*, 24, 58.

and mislead the people. It lies, the two movements further agreed, within humanity's power to create a much "happier" and more equal society. It was necessary, radicals and socialists alike believed, to emancipate, as one fervent democratic republican, Cérutti, expressed it, prior to the French Revolution, in 1788, the *classe populaire* from the slavery to which they are subjected by the *classe dominante*.[66] Thus far, the two trends comprehensively converged; but there the parallels and partial correspondence between the rival opposition blocs ended.

For the two rival camps' respective analyses of humanity's general state of oppression, and the remedies required for ending humanity's misery, differed substantially. For socialists, mankind is exploited, impoverished, and wretched because the economic system is geared to exploit them, to their systematic disadvantage; the way to emancipate humanity, accordingly, is to capture the economic system and transform it fundamentally, to usher mankind into the new age of fairness and equality. For radical enlighteners, by contrast, the *classe populaire*, most of humanity, live exploited, repressed, unnecessarily impoverished lives due to their own ignorance, credulity, and "superstition," their trust in priests along with perverse laws and institutions nourished by prevailing wrong beliefs and assumptions. Men are wretched, as Condorcet expressed a notion he shared with this entire tradition, because "they are deceived with regard to their true happiness and how to attain it," their minds being filled with "phantoms, fables, *réveries*, and mysteries."[67] For radical enlighteners, human emancipation, ameliorating the world fundamentally, ending the oppression of the *classe populaire*, is accomplished not by mass action, and not principally by capturing and transforming the economic system, but through the enlightened underground spreading on all sides and conquering ignorance, prejudice, "superstition," "priestcraft," the allure of aristocracy, and the mystique of monarchy, by enlightening men's minds sufficiently for them to be able to grasp genuinely enlightened modes of thought, the armament required to reform society, education, morality, culture, and the law.

A proven, valuable historiographical concept, the "Radical Enlightenment," most contributors to it (myself included) were unaware, prior to Frederik Stjernfelt's May 2013 Brussels lecture on the usage of the term, reaches back much earlier than Margaret Jacob's *The Radical Enlightenment* of 1981. First introduced into scholarly debate in an innovative and comprehensive fashion by the conservative German Jewish philosopher Leo Strauss (1899–1973) in the 1920s,[68] his "Radical Enlightenment" rightly viewed the phenomenon as emerging from an older, more variegated social and cultural underground, especially Epicureanism and late medieval Averroism. *Radikale Aufklärung* [Radical Enlightenment] in his view amounted basically to "atheism," an intellectual tendency that by the commencement of the early Enlightenment era had already existed in rudimentary form for many centuries. Strauss

[66] Cérutti, *Mémoire pour le peuple* (1788), 15. [67] Condorcet, *Bibliothèque* vi. 69.

[68] On the origins of the term "Radical Enlightenment" see Stjernfelt, "Radical Enlightenment: Aspects," 95–8.

envisaged *Radikale Aufklärung* as not just a rival to, but also as preceding the "Moderate Enlightenment" chronologically and outlasting it. For him, there was a less profound divide between Radical Renaissance and *Radikale Aufklärung* than is argued for in this volume. Contending that the Enlightenment possessed two main and in part contrary strands, moderate and radical, with only the latter being anti-religious and genuinely secular,[69] Strauss presented a philosophical bifurcation of the Enlightenment subsequently further developed by Strauss himself and then Günter Mühlpfordt,[70] Henry May, Giuseppe Ricuperati, Margaret Jacob, Silvia Berti, and Wim Klever.

Strauss introduced the category *Radikale Aufklärung* as part of a general reinterpretation of the Enlightenment on which he embarked while researching Spinoza's Bible criticism.[71] To him *Radikale Aufklärung* was the Enlightenment's veritable core; but because his label signified above all "atheism," he chiefly identified what by 1928 he already termed "moderate Enlightenment" in terms of the latter's theistic premises and willingness to compromise with ecclesiastical authority.[72] From the late seventeenth century, "Moderate Enlightenment" may have been the principal reforming project in the eyes of governments, churches, and educators, and have remained so in the minds of most philosophers and historians ever since, but beneath the surface, in terms of effective arguments, contended Strauss, the radical impulse proved sturdier philosophically and culturally, and in the long run, despite its long clandestine and inconspicuous beginnings, emerged as the "real" or principal Enlightenment, not least in shaping the Enlightenment's troubled legacy, the intellectual paradoxes and dilemmas of post-1800 modernity.[73] As well as essentially "atheistic," Strauss unhesitatingly pronounced *Radikale Aufklärung* the "true Enlightenment" while casting Locke, Leibniz, Voltaire, Montesquieu, Moses Mendelssohn, and other apparently committed "moderates" as cautious compromisers who ultimately, with their unworkable philosophical "fixes," weakened rather than strengthened their to many hard-to-defend dualist philosophical contrivances harmonizing reason with faith—and philosophical critique with kings and courts. Strauss also laid particular emphasis on Radical Enlightenment's embracing an exclusively naturalistic conception of science, philosophy, and knowledge, a naturalism radicals, not unlike Nietzsche later, in his middle period, deployed to ruthlessly strip out all *supernaturalia. Radikale Aufklärung* thinkers, he stressed, considered their standpoint more objectively true, more demonstrably verifiable, than alternative philosophies and

[69] Strauss, *Spinoza's Critique of Religion*, 35; Smith, *Spinoza's Book of Life*, 191; Nicolas Dubos noted, in 2009, that when writing my earlier Enlightenment volumes I was, as yet, unaware that the radical–moderate dichotomy first originates with Strauss in the 1920s; see Dubos, "Hobbes et les Lumières radicales," 38–41.

[70] For republished articles of Mühlpfortdt's from the 1970s and 1980s, see Günter Mühlpfordt, *Halle-Leipziger Aufklärung: Kernstuck der Mitteldeutschen Aufklärung* (Halle, 2011).

[71] Israel, "Leo Strauss," 18–20.

[72] Pangle, "Light Shed on the Crucial Development," 59–63.

[73] On America' Radical Enlightenment, see May, Stewart, Nash, Cotlar, Wilentz, and my *Expanding Blaze.*

creeds, being more concretely open to verification by reason and scientific observation than the views of Lockean moderates, like Voltaire, or of counter-enlighteners, Christian or Jewish.

There is much in Strauss's reasoning that has proved insightful. But although eliminating religious authority must necessarily have far-reaching political and social consequences, Strauss hardly broaches this dimension at all. He did not attach any specific political character to *Radikale Aufklärung*. By contrast, the first scholar to introduce the "Radical Enlightenment" debate into English was again not Jacob (as the "negative critique" regularly misinforms readers), but Henry F. May (1915–2012), who in several publications of the 1970s presented the "moderate Enlightenment" as crucial to American developments and 1775–6 as the point where the radical tendency first directly challenged "moderate Enlightenment" to become a major American Enlightenment ideology. May's American Enlightenment displayed an abiding split between radicals and moderates, but he projected this rift chiefly in terms of support for or against the democratizing tendency; he did also link the tendency to critique of religion but only secondarily, in rather vague terms.[74] Hence, neither Strauss nor May, the two main coiners of the concept "Radical Enlightenment," considered how exactly the two primary components, rejecting religious authority and espousing democratic republicanism, connect and interact. Strauss's and May's "Radical Enlightenment thesis" still left a yawning gap, an important historiographical analytical step yet to be taken: both hinted at, but neither underlined or explained the inherent, close, and abiding linkage of the tendency's secularizing and democratizing tendencies here identified as Radical Enlightenment's core characteristic.

The argument of this volume is essentially an amalgam of intellectual, social, and political history, but one clashing with the kind of "sociability" and cultural-turn arguments most historians employ to explain the advent of the revolutionary era and the "invention" of universal and equal rights. Although the statesmen and legislators of the era were often hard-headed men of the world uninterested in intellectual matters, during the revolutionary era so much hinged on fundamental constitutional and other public issues projected in the press, theatre, and debating and reading societies, that political leaders and statesmen like Franklin, Jefferson, Adams, Mirabeau, Sieyès, Brissot, Mounier, Frederick the Great, Catherine the Great, Napoleon and his brothers, and later Miranda, and Bolívar, in Spanish America, could not afford to remain detached from the ideological discussions bearing on the political scene, and these figures all impressively immersed themselves in the literature and debates surrounding the theoretical and constitutional issues. Equally, key *philosophique* publicists and theorists—Paine, Price, Priestley, Burke, Filangieri, Condorcet, Lafayette, Cérutti, Brissot, Volney, Destutt, Von Humboldt, Constant, and, later, Bentham and Auguste Comte—often acquired formidable political weight, merely through being effective ideologues.

[74] May, *Enlightenment in America*, 88; Meyer, *Democratic Enlightenment*, pp. xiv–xxvi; Kloppenburg, *Toward Democracy*, 755 n. 51.

Philosophically charged ideologies during the revolutionary era helped reshape reality not because ideas shape reality but because reality is differently refracted, illustrated, and impacted on, by contrasting ideas diffused via newspapers, pamphlets, posters, books, cartoons, debates, banquets, toasts and public ceremonies, the law courts, theatres, and the arts, and also processions, mass meetings, and demonstrations, all these being channels whereby the public could participate in the ensuing struggles. The process pulled in the wider public, but with the theorists and ideologues, not ordinary men and women, or commonplace lawyers, professionals, military commanders, or purely pragmatic statesmen, exerting the main impact on the intellectual input colouring and infusing the political process. Intellectuals formulated and disseminated the ideals that inspired, motivated, armed, and empowered the various revolutionary vanguards acting as managers furnishing the rival ideologues and theorists with the meetings, newspapers, and publicity machines that procured them some mass support, albeit this was usually fitful and sporadic. Modernity, one might say, was forged by the masses on one level, and by intellectual, media-controlling elites interacting with them in a complex fashion on another, but with the former the main factor in generating grievance, dissatisfaction, instability, and upheavals, while usually in the more passive role as regards shaping ideology and agendas, and the latter playing the main active role only as regards guiding principles and legislative programs, without prevailing attitudes among the general population, commonplace notions, having remotely the impact on the great revolutionary declarations and enactments, or the rise of "universal and equal rights" some historians attribute to them.

Overall, it is hard to overstate the Radical Enlightenment's overriding centrality for any proper grasp of the revolutionary era starting in 1775, or for understanding the rise of "universal and equal human rights" and the process of world secularization—hence for the entirety of modern history. Since the 1990s, it has increasingly been recognized as of central significance relevant to all modern philosophy, politics, and moral and social thought as well as higher education, scholarship, and general awareness. Throughout its nearly two centuries of sustained impact, "Radical Enlightenment" fought to improve human existence generally, extend universal benevolence, and emancipate oppressed sections of society above all by transforming the way men think. It strove to replace what it denounced as credulity, "ignorance," "superstition," prejudice, and "fanaticism" with a fundamentally new conception of the individual as a free, educated and enlightened citizen participating on an equal basis in society and politics.

Broadly, the radical tendency began to weaken from the 1820s onwards and from the 1830s was more and more displaced by socialism. But while it was the rise of socialism in the early nineteenth century that actually displaced it from its position as main systemic opposition to the status quo, overwhelmingly the principal reason for its failure, we shall see, was Radical Enlightenment's continuing inability to sufficiently close the gap between the concepts it offered and the loyalist thinking and religious assumptions of the great majority. It viewed education as the answer to the central contradiction in its general position and posture, but its educational reach never extended as far, or as rapidly, as the radical predicament demanded, and probably, in the circumstances could not have done. Initial successes between 1775 and 1793 were followed by successive heavy defeats during the ensuing later revolutionary era down to the 1848 revolutions. Following the failure of the 1848–9 revolutions, and armed clashes in Paris between socialists and radicals leading to the demise of the French Second Republic, Radical Enlightenment was finally and definitively marginalized. Opposed by most of society from the outset, the "Enlightenment that failed" remains vehemently contested today.

Part I

The Origins of Democratic Modernity

2

The Rise of Democratic Republicanism

2.1. ENGLAND AND THE "DUTCH WAY" (1688–1720)

Early nineteenth-century radicals decidedly preferred republics to monarchies. But merely preferring a "republic," as such, far from sufficed to meet the exacting requirements of democratic republican "modernity." Weighing the history of the Swiss republics in 1824, the eminent Genevan economist and (since 1814) philosophical radical, Jean Charles Leonard de Sismondi (1773–1842), was decidedly scathing in his judgment of the old Swiss republics.

Earlier, in the 1790s, Sismondi had been an Anglophile moderate opposing the French Revolution in most of its aspects. He was so disgusted, though, by Restoration Counter-Enlightenment rhetoric and reaction, the general reversal of values the conservative "Allies" of the Holy Alliance sought to impose on Europe from 1814–15, and especially with the Allies' brutal demolition of the modernized federal republic Napoleon established in his homeland in 1802–3 that, like Bentham, he switched to a forthrightly radical outlook to which he adhered undeviatingly from 1814. In itself, simply establishing a republic, the Swiss experience taught him, much as Italian experience in the late 1790s had previously convinced many Italian radicals, is to accomplish practically nothing regarding the common good, given that most republics, including all the eighteenth-century Italian, Swiss, and Dutch republics, were conservative, oligarchic "aristocratic republics."[1]

Early Modern republicanism needs urgently to be assessed simultaneously as a social and intellectual phenomenon. From the seventeenth to the nineteenth century, Britain was dominated by aristocratic and gentry elites exercising a high degree of cultural and intellectual primacy. Hence, while many post-1650 English political writers and activists presented a "moderate" undifferentiated "republicanism" offering little or no real distinction between the aristocratic and democratic forms, conceiving this as a valuable continuing tradition, critics urging a more democratic society, as a few "Levellers" and Commonwealthmen already did during the 1640s and 1650s, made little headway against the dominant trend. There was also at least

[1] Fruci, "Democracy in Italy," 27–8, 42; Koekkoek, "Waare en vrije," 240; Israel, *Expanding Blaze*, 489–91; Romani, "Republican Foundations," 19–22.

one major, open, public confrontation—the Putney Debates of 1647—between England's democratic and aristocratic tendencies, revealing the depth of the rift. In writings such as *A Call to All the Souldiers of the Armie, By the Free People of England* (n.p., 1647), by the lifelong conspirator and radical John Wildman (*c.*1621–93), the men of the New Model Army were urged to rise against Cromwell's emerging tyranny and all "crafty politicians and subtill Machiavellians" and especially the principle of monarchy: "beware that yee be not frighted by the word ANARCHY, unto a love of Monarchy, which is but a gilded name for tyranny."[2] But at the climax of the English Revolution, the public controversy was decidedly more about the rights and nature of the Parliament and parliamentary sovereignty, and England's supposed pre-Norman freedoms, than the merits of "kingless rule" and the values of republicanism whether as a classical or democratic tradition. Though doubtless less malicious and "Machiavellian" than radical republicans contended, Cromwell did favour "mixed government," a "settlement with somewhat of monarchical in it."[3] The Putney debates had much to say about "every true Englishman that loves the peace and freedom of England," but little to add about the universal principles of citizenship.[4]

Adopting a revolutionary democratic republican stance, Wildman, Lilburne, and other Commonwealthmen charged Cromwell with renewing the "tyrannie and oppression" of the Stuart monarchy under false pretense of championing the "Laws, Rights and Liberties of England." They accused him of being driven by like "pride and ambition," and insidiously furthering his appetite for power with "high professions of Godliness, simplicity and integrity" and "hypocritical prayers and days of fasting." All true Englishmen they summoned to take up arms against Cromwell "in the great contest for right and freedom," to combat political tyranny allied to systematic abuse of religion and the churches.[5] That such Commonwealthmen were, to a degree, democratic republican revolutionaries, is indisputable; but Lilburne, Wildman, and their ilk produced no extended or coherent theory of democratic republicanism justified in terms of society's needs or explaining what they meant by "free-born" and "right and freedom." Moreover, in the writings of the main English republican theorists of the mid- and later seventeenth century, Harrington, Sidney, and Needham, the incipient, tentative confrontational aspect of seventeenth-century English republicanism, urging a more democratic format, rather than gaining ground, inexorably receded.[6] A seventeenth-century democratic republican tendency, sporadically sparked and glimpsed, it failed to produce a more robust and lasting tendency or enduring theoretical construction, never amounting to more than a few rhetorical flourishes. Bruno Bauer, in 1843, aptly described the English Revolution of the 1640s as a search for freedom perverted by "religious fanaticism" and a fruitless search for

[2] BL 102 b 37: [Wildman] *A Call to All the Souldiers*, 3, 6–7; Worden, "Republicanism," 318, 320, 324; Rees, *Leveller Revolution*, 204–11.

[3] Quoted in Worden, "Republicanism," 317, 319.

[4] Worden, "Republicanism," 324, 327; Robertson, *The Levellers*, pp. xxix–xxxi, 59.

[5] [Lilburne], *A Declaration of the Free-born People* (1654), 1; Rees, *Leveller Revolution*, 210–11.

[6] Villaverde Rico, *Ilusión republicana*, 99–101, 106–9; Houston, *Algernon Sidney*, 4, 7–8.

justification of men's "rights" in the "yellowed parchments" of ancient precedent, a fight for liberty unable to free itself from religion or precedent.[7] Consequently, neither the constitutional outcome of the English Revolution of the 1640s, nor that of the so-called "Glorious Revolution" of 1688, readily lent themselves as international models, or to formulation of clear, enduring, or universally influential forms of democratic republicanism as such.

If English republicanism nevertheless remained a potent and, for many, inspiring social and political reality with a pervasive impact in Britain, America, and Ireland, the "Glorious Revolution" of 1688–9 only rendered English republicanism—decisively for subsequent British, American, and European developments, and for the eighteenth century—a still "tamer or softer body of ideas than before" and "in some ways," as it has been put, "a more difficult one to define and identify."[8] The Glorious Revolution diluted republican tradition especially in two respects— by lessening the tension between monarchy and republicanism with a robust and viable constitutionally limited monarchy, and, secondly, by firmly entrenching the aristocratic and gentry elites in power with an assuredness that long eased the friction between the democratic and aristocratic republican tendencies in the British context. Both developments, Condorcet, followed by Destutt de Tracy, later pointed out, were assisted over the long term by a predominantly willing and submissive public conditioned to venerate monarchy and aristocracy and to treat social superiors with deference.[9] This prolonged muting effect, already discernible before 1688, the Glorious Revolution reinforced and extended to America, another development of fundamental significance.

These trends mitigating tension between monarchism and republicanism, smoothing the friction between aristocratic and democratic republicanism, caused the "English republicans of the seventeenth century" to be, as one historian put it, "conventionally presented as being more inclined to aristocracy than to democracy."[10] They are trends well illustrated in the republican legacy of Algernon Sidney (1622–83) which was sturdy to an extent, especially in its anti-monarchism, his republicanism contributing to the aristocratic conspiracy to emasculate Charles II's absolutism in 1683, the so-called Rye House Plot. But, though partly inspired by the Dutch republican example, Sidney's republicanism relied, unlike that of the Brothers De La Court which was grounded in Hobbes's pessimism about human nature, on appeals to the citizen's "virtue" and "reason." During the crucial 1770s, around the onset of the American Revolution, Sidney's republican legacy helped reinforce the previously rather loose, undefined republican surge of sentiment in America. But no more than Locke did Sidney represent a ""threatening radicalism" or

[7] Bauer, *Christianity Exposed*, 2.

[8] Worden, "Revolution of 1688–9 and the English Republican Tradition," 241–2; Zurbuchen, "Republicanism and Toleration," 48.

[9] Condorcet, "Réflexions sur la Révolution de 1688," 1–3; Destutt de Tracy, *Commentaire*, 137–8, 141.

[10] Hammersley, "Rethinking the Political Thought," 355–6.

advance "democratic ideas" premised, as has been wrongly suggested, on "a shared commitment to the Christian ideal of mutuality."[11] Rather, Sidney's "classical republicanism" of virtue, if forthright in curtailing monarchy, proved decidedly unspecific in its social implications and consequences, sufficiently vague to be equally useful to "moderates" and "radicals"—and especially for papering over the gap between them.

During the American Revolution, consequently, Sidney's republicanism signally failed to cut a clear path to democratic republicanism. Rather it appealed equally to radicals and moderates and even to some "Tory" Loyalist opponents of the Revolution, leaving it firmly stranded on the moderate side of the great republican rift.[12] Thus, John Adams (1735–1826), a leading "moderate" of the American Revolution and stalwart anti-democrat (as well as foe of Franklin, Condorcet, and Paine), remained a lifelong Sidney enthusiast, evincing a republican zeal which he could perfectly consistently combine not just with resolute support for American Independence, but deep veneration for the post-1688 "British constitution," the "British model" as a structure buttressing aristocratic dominance of society, Although Sidney was read by radical republicans in late eighteenth-century France, his arguments no longer seemed relevant.[13]

Adams's first book, *Novanglus* (1775), the "New England man," eloquently sketched the ideology of what became the American Revolution's "republican" mainstream. Before 1776, he believed, the colonies already possessed "a constitution," by which he meant shared in the 1688 Glorious Revolution constitution, and this, in his eyes, remained the precious legacy British ministers irresponsibly and unjustifiably violated. In 1775, Adams still thought of America as sharing in the existing "British constitution" under the king even though the "nature of the encroachment upon the American constitution is, such as to grow every day more and more encroaching." Certainly, vigorous, openly revolutionary, steps were called for.[14] "If we enjoy the British constitution in greater purity and perfection than they do in England as is really the case, whose fault is this? Not ours."[15] A convinced aristocratic republican and Glorious Revolution ideologue using his posting as American envoy to the United Provinces in the closing years of the American revolutionary war to mobilize opinion against the pro-American Patriot democrats battling the Orangist pro-church and pro-British faction there, Adams allied exclusively with Dutch enlighteners who were moderates like his pro-oligarchy ally Jean Luzac (1746–1807), owner of the *Gazette de Leyde*, the foremost European paper backing the American cause, who likewise firmly rejected democratic principles. Luzac backed the American Revolution only in its "aristocratic" mode, as championed by Adams and Morris. Because of its democratic

[11] Kloppenberg, *Toward Democracy*, 138.

[12] Scott, "Classical Republicanism," 68–71; Houston, *Algernon Sidney*, 7–8, 257–8, 261–6; Miquieu, *Spinoza, Locke*, 163–6, 309.

[13] Hammersley, *English Republican Tradition*, 74, 163–4.

[14] Adams, *Novanglus*, 26–34; Pocock, *Machiavellian Moment*, 531, 546.

[15] Adams, *Novanglus*, 91; Bonwick, *American Revolution*, 2–4, 134; Nelson, *Royalist Revolution*, 159–60.

proclivities, he vigorously opposed the Genevan democratic revolution of 1782, publicly supporting the oligarchies ruling the Bernese and Zurich republics which Sismondi later came to detest. Both Adams and Luzac likewise urged an "aristocratic" outcome also for the bitter ideological struggle dividing the Dutch Republic during the 1780s, viewing the democrats as deluded ideologues misconstruing American developments, seeking to transfer a profoundly mistaken, falsely democratic image of the American Revolution to Europe.[16]

Adams's *Defense of the Constitutions* (1787–8) includes a discussion of the Swiss, Italian, and Dutch republics that was the mirror reverse of Sismondi's 1824 analysis: the democratic tendency was always destabilizing; the more "aristocratic" and like (most) American states, the Swiss republics stayed, the more stable, prosperous, and better governed they would be.[17] Mainstream English and American republicanism in the eighteenth century simply did not, at least not until the American Revolution, mirror the yawning divide between aristocratic and democratic republics. Yet, already long before 1775, this was the overriding issue already embryonically in the Putney Debates and more emphatically in the Netherlands and Switzerland, and hence potentially all Europe. Where British republicanism, from 1688, increasingly strove to circumvent the crucial—and increasingly challenging—question, the clash between aristocratic and democratic republicanism (except tangentially, at a few heated moments), those immersed in Dutch and Swiss developments became increasingly aware of the profound theoretical implications of this clash. This lasting, fundamental ambiguity, bridging the gap between aristocratic and democratic republicanism much as Anglicanism bridged the gap between Catholicism and Protestantism, became a major factor in forging the dual character, the unresolved tension between aristocratic and democratic republicanism, at the heart of the American Revolution.

Anglo-American non-engagement with the most decisive issue relating to Enlightenment era republicanism, the divide between aristocratic and democratic republics, ceased, from 1775–6, with the rise of a distinct radical tendency in the circles around Thomas Young, Ethan Allen, and Tom Paine, and the sporadic success of the radicals within a few key segments of the Revolution, especially their promoting universal male suffrage in Pennsylvania and Vermont in 1776. Their rhetoric and slogans, and especially Paine's sensational pamphlet *Common Sense* (1776), an unfettered, vehement attack on the "British model," the British constitution and aristocratic republicanism, thoroughly antagonized Adams, Morris, Hamilton, and all America's "aristocratic" republicans, and helped stir what from the 1780s became a wholly new and more divisive Anglo-American ideological context than existed previously.

Aristocratic republics, held Paine, represented an entirely different kind of phenomenon from democratic republics. The two opposed categories had all along been at war with each other, in theory and practice, but this circumstance had for so long remained veiled in Britain and America that one rarely encountered there much

[16] Israel, *Expanding Blaze*, 242. [17] Ryerson, *John Adams's Republic*, 284–6.

understanding of the rift. That aristocracy and clergy, with what radicals saw as their cunning alliance, deliberately exploited public ignorance about this fundamental duality for their own gain, appeared evident to very few onlookers. As priests and priestcraft had often abused Christianity to further their particular interests, contends Paine, in *The Rights of Man* (1791–2), so it became integral to the "political craft of courtiers and court-governments to abuse something which they call republicanism" while rendering the concept as vague and innocuous (to them) as possible.[18] Where many Anglo-American and European contemporaries joined Adams in venerating Sidney, and enlisting Locke and Montesquieu too in aligning America's newly born republicanism behind Europe's aristocratic republics and "mixed government" systems, radicals like Paine resoundingly broke ranks. To them, much the same sliding back into degradation, reverting to aristocratic republican status that Holland experienced in 1787, had occurred earlier at Geneva, in 1782, after the French crown crushed the democratic revolution there.

Aristocratic republics, contended Paine, like the Dutch democratic republicans of 1795,[19] and Destutt and Sismondi later, were not really republics at all. These counterfeit "republics" since September 1787 now again included the United Provinces where the first sustained democratic upsurge, the *Patriottenbeweging*, had, by 1785, seemed to be gaining the upper hand, transforming the land from oligarchy into a democratic entity, but had then been abruptly suppressed by the Orangists with Prussian help, partly at British instigation. "It is true that certain countries, such as Holland, Berne, Genoa, Venice etc. call themselves Republics," remarked Paine, writing to the French revolutionary democratic republicans, Condorcet and Bonneville, in June 1791, "but these countries do not merit such a designation. All the principles upon which they are founded are in direct contradiction to every republican sentiment, and they are really in a condition of absolute servitude to an aristocracy."[20] Destutt de Tracy, writing under Napoleon, likewise highlighted the vast gulf separating "aristocratic republics" like those of Berne or Venice from the democratic republican model he admired and advocated. Venice Destutt considered especially pernicious in this connection: for, to maintain their ascendancy, the Venetian nobility had conceded much power to the Inquisition, ecclesiastics, and "superstition," rendering religion the key tool of their domination, reducing ordinary Venetians to a servile "canaille dépravée et misérable."[21] Aristocratic republics, held Europe's *Radicalen*, exhibited the same tendency as monarchies to keep their subjects "superstitious" and "ignorant," and therefore the same willingness to endorse religious authority.[22]

[18] Paine, *Rights of Man*, 178–9; Worden, "Revolution of 1688–9 and the English Republican Tradition," 242.

[19] Koekkoek, "Waare en vrije," 245.

[20] Paine to Condorcet, Bonneville, and Lanthenas, Paris, June 1791, in Paine *Writings* ii. 1317.

[21] Destutt de Tracy, *Commentaire*, 65, 82.

[22] Destutt de Tracy, *Commentaire*, 82–3.

In the Americas, as Europe, the two warring strands of republicanism, democratic and aristocratic, fundamentally divergent and irreconcilable, remained separated by an immense rift and, from 1775, were continually in conflict. Despite this reality having been largely masked by the distinctive Anglo-American republican tradition before 1775, the abiding significance of the clash increasingly impressed itself on the public's consciousness during the late Enlightenment. The ideological struggle steadily intensified from 1775 and, to explore this now crucial duality in broad theoretical terms, Anglo-American observers had to direct their intellectual gaze increasingly toward France, Holland, Germany, and Switzerland rather than their own political traditions. Hugely antagonized by Paine's analysis, Adams, Morris, and Hamilton were perfectly right in insisting that such notions had nothing whatever to do with authentic, mainstream English republican tradition which was rooted in the thoroughgoing Glorious Revolution papering over of the central clash. Stung by Paine's accusations of "abuse," contemporaries confined to the English-language context showed little appreciation of whence Paine's unprecedented and, for many, shocking, warring dichotomy, pitting democratic against "aristocratic" republicanism, derived, of how the new American radical republicanism and its wide trans-Atlantic resonance had suddenly burst on the scene.

2.2. A NOTABLE PUBLIC CONTROVERSY (1706–1710)

Paine, Price, Priestley, Barlow, and other American and British writers embracing democratic republicanism in the late eighteenth century shattered the post-1688, pre-1775 Anglo-American mold. But already well before 1775 several noteworthy public controversies had occurred that provided hints of the intellectual origins of the post-1775 ideological rift. The masking effect and deep implications of English fusing of aristocratic republicanism with Italian civic republicanism are strikingly illustrated, for example, by the noisy controversy, commencing in 1706, over one of the most fiercely contested early eighteenth-century English texts, *The Rights of the Christian Church Asserted* (1706), the "most infamous book," as some styled it at the time,[23] of the recalcitrant Oxford don, Matthew Tindal (1657–1733).

Fellow of All Souls College since 1678, Tindal was a secular-minded eclectic and erudite legal scholar of declared anti-Trinitarian views who, during the Glorious Revolution and for some time afterwards, frequented republican circles.[24] His innocuous-sounding publication provoked a bigger furore and livelier efforts to get it banned (and those associated with publishing it punished), than almost any other publicly vilified text of the English "deists." It was a landmark case, the exceptional

[23] Wigelsworth, "God can require nothing from us," 147; Brown, "Theological Politics," 195.

[24] Hudson, *English Deists*, 108; Hudson, *Enlightenment and Modernity*, 5–6; Wigelsworth, *Deism*, 17, 20, 60; Wigelsworth, "God can require nothing of us," 140.

indignation it aroused stemming partly from the subtle insolence critics detected in its tone and variously styled "villainous," "fallacious," "disingenuous," "dangerous," and "blasphemous" insinuating suavity evident not least in his title, that Tindal gave his camouflaged subversive message. His method was to promote his political vision by engaging in lengthy digressions into ecclesiastical history and the Church Fathers richly punctuated with cutting remarks about the Anglican and Presbyterian as well as Catholic (and Jewish) churches.

Not only do churchmen of all stripes appropriate privileges, influence, and power to which they are not entitled by Scripture or law, contends *The Rights*, but "priests" of all religions universally abuse the power they usurp to pervert the moral and legal order. This "wolf" in "shepherd's clothing," protested one adversary, and his allies "love to give their books contrary titles, like *The Rights of the Christian Church*."[25] The anonymous author, whose name remained less than wholly unknown to his adversaries throughout the ensuing huge public controversy, suggested that "priests" of all confessions are driven by more or less identical motives in building their relentlessly oppressive sway over mankind, all employing the same tried and trusted techniques for deceiving the superstitious, credulous, and ill-informed.[26] In a sermon preached in London, in October 1708, Robert Moss, Dean of Ely, designated the anonymous author of *The Rights* "a more disingenuous caviller perhaps, and more scurrilous scoffer, than ever was Julian the Apostate".[27] Anglican churchmen demanded Parliament suppress Tindal's text, as indeed, in 1710, eventually happened.

The controversy dragged on at an exceptional level of polemical heat for five years with over thirty full-length rebuttals, supplemented by court proceedings, hostile sermons, and newspaper reports. Some had expected the uproar to blow over quickly, that the "blazing meteor, what noxious influence so ever it had for a while" would soon decay and in a "short time die into utter darkness and contempt" like those "false lights that amused the world before." Had not earlier schemes of atheism soon lost appeal as fresh ones displaced them, asked Samuel Hill (d. 1716), Archdeacon of Wells, in 1708, in his *A Thorough Examination of the false Principles and fallacious Arguments, advanc'd against the Christian Church, Priest-hood, and Religion*? "So we have seen Hobbs, Spinoza, Blount and Toland, etc. with others of lower form in impiety, blaze for a while, and then go out in disesteem and neglect."[28] But others realized that the political and religious subversion plied by this eventually banned but far from effectually suppressed text, burnt by the common hangman in March 1710,[29] represented a challenge that needed guarding against in the future with great vigilance. The consternation it aroused stemmed almost as much from the book's far-reaching political implications as its aspersions on Christianity—from its impugning

[25] *The Second Part of the Wolf stript of his Shepherd's Cloathing*, 14.
[26] *Dangerous Positions: or, Blasphemous, profane, immoral and Jesuitical assertions*, 29.
[27] Moss, *A Sermon Preach'd at the Parish Church of St Laurence-Jewry, London*, 8.
[28] Hill, *A Thorough Examination*, p. A4v.
[29] Brown, "Theological Politics," 196; Wigelsworth, *Deism*, 59–62.

the 1688 revolutionary settlement with its solidly aristocratic outcome. All too obviously, while pretending to champion Glorious Revolution principles, the unknown writer insinuatingly defamed these as deception and betrayal.

Nor did this widely execrated author seem at all daunted or displeased that "*The Rights* made a great noise throughout England." Readers must carefully consider, he defiantly retorted, in a follow-up pamphlet pouring scorn on Oxford's "highflying clergy" who are "for allowing the Prince an unlimited power in civil matters,"[30] "why they, who are reckoned the most famous combatants of the Church-militant, batter'd *The Rights* with their heavy artillery from the press, while 10,000 random shot have been made at it from pulpit blunderbusses."[31] Imagining "themselves in a state of persecution, while they are ty'd up from persecuting others," England's sinister "highfliers," plotting "ever since the death of the late king [i.e. William III], assisted by the profess'd Jacobites and Papists," sought "to disturb the growing quiet of the nation, and to set all things in confusion, in hopes of breaking in on the sacred Act of Toleration." Nor was it only Highfliers who designed to wreck England's hard-won toleration: all churchmen everywhere threaten the basic freedoms "since the generality of the ecclesiastics in most places, by the Church, seem to mean only themselves, and by religion only their own power and dominion" so that in effect churchmen oppose not just toleration but "charity, benevolence, moderation, mutual forbearance, and all other Christian virtues." For Tindal, churchmen with their competing theologies were the "cause of Christians treating one another with so much barbarity" as they had in the sixteenth and seventeenth centuries.[32] True virtues are scorned by all clergies "and their contrarys cry'd up as the only virtues."[33] "Certainly "twill never be well with us," Tindal charged his adversaries of dreaming, "till something like to the Spanish Inquisition be in England."[34]

Such outrageous remarks, retorted opponents, are not just unacceptable in any "Christian" society, but turn everything upside down, subordinating faith to individual preference, and utterly destroying ecclesiastical sanction, privilege, and status. "Our assertor is pleased to make this reflection on the clergy," protested one adversary: "that where [the churches'] interest, power, and authority are at lowest ebb, there men are more angelical, and less diabolical, immoral, lewd, vicious, debauch'd and irreligious."[35] For tactical purposes, Tindal avowed that his aim was to conserve the Protestant Reformation's basic gains against the ravages of priestly ambition. But few doubted that behind this screen, Tindal was among the most articulate and systematic advocates of the early eighteenth-century "religion of nature." He was one of those who helped turn the young Benjamin Franklin into a convinced "deist" already at the age of 17.[36]

30 [Tindal], *A New Catechism*, 16.
31 [Tindal], *A Defence of The Rights*, 72, 267; Champion, *Pillars of Priestcraft*, 97–8.
32 [Tindal], *The Rights*, 23. 33 [Tindal], *The Rights*, 144.
34 [Tindal], *A New Catechism*, 20.
35 *Dangerous Positions: or, Blasphemous, profane, immoral and Jesuitical assertions*, 44.
36 Champion, *Pillars of Priestcraft*, 98; Walters, *American Deists*, 12, 15.

While the outrage he provoked stemmed above all from Tindal's contempt for clergymen and theology, his accusing the world's churches of fomenting immorality instead of morality, considerable indignation sprang too from the purely political side of his argument, his subversive views on crown and constitution. Tindal's antagonists quickly identified his coupling rejection of church authority with democratic republicanism as the essential frame of his assault. Several tracts highlighted his political argument: starting from something resembling Hobbes's "state of nature," the malefactor established a list of basic freedoms, claiming, in highly unHobbesian fashion, that these then remained fundamentally intact in civil society, being rights no prince or church had any power to infringe or alter. Where in Hobbes the freedoms of the state of nature are "made over" to the prince, under civil society, by means of contract, Tindal denied all contract: "men are still in the state of nature, without any sovereign representative to determine for them, what they shall believe or profess," leaving every individual wholly free to believe, or not believe, whatever he likes with no church or state possessing authority to interfere in his or her free choice.[37] For Tindal, who rejected all mysteries out of hand, it is every person's duty to use his or her reason to examine the arguments of others, and determine for themselves what is true and what is not. Tindal's conception of the individual's untrammeled freedom to judge all matters relating to religion and morality for himself proved an especially provocative challenge for his age, even in England and America. "Tis a gross inconsistency, and an intolerable imposition upon the world," complained one adversary, "for *The Rights* to assert independency in religion, among the Natural Rights of mankind which can't be made over to Prince or Priest."[38]

The two prongs of Tindal's subversion, the anti-church and the democratic republican, noted several commentators, were, rather unusually, closely bracketed together. For the English, this theological-political challenge was bafflingly unfamiliar and hard to grapple with. While traditionally scholars stress Tindal's debt to Hobbes, and also his friend Locke,[39] in reality it was impossible to proceed from a radical standpoint more contrary to Hobbes and Locke, or contrary to Locke's limited toleration. The author constructed civil society and the state, from the state of nature, not just differently from Hobbes, transferring power and authority to sovereign governments only to a limited extent, and leaving churches without any authority or power of censorship, but failed to introduce any violable "contract" in the manner of Locke, "any compact between those who govern and those who are governed," as Paine expressed it.[40] Instead, Tindal lodged sovereignty and ultimate say in the

[37] *Dangerous Positions: or, Blasphemous, profane, immoral and Jesuitical assertions*, 3; Wotton, *Rights of the Clergy*, 2, 15; Stewart, *Nature's God*, 402; Hudson, *English Deists*, 108–9.

[38] *Dangerous Positions: or, Blasphemous, profane, immoral and Jesuitical assertions*, 3; Zerbuchen, "Republicanism and Toleration," 58–9.

[39] See, for instance, Wigelsworth, "God can require nothing from us," 145.

[40] Paine, *Rights of Man*, 70.

people itself without designating any general transfer of power and authority, either automatic or by contract![41]

"The authority of government," holds the author of *The Rights*, as Le Clerc summed up the political content in his lengthy review, in his *Bibliothèque choisie*, in 1710, "arises not from hence, That people have given an Absolute power of life and member, but from the natural Right every one has to preserve himself, and to prefer his own Good to any other person's." Consequently, "God, in giving Man this one innate principle inseparable from his nature (i.e. to seek his own Happiness, and endeavor to live as conveniently as Nature permits) has given him the right, or rather has enjoin'd it as his duty, to do all that is proper to attain that end."[42] Individual rights were proclaimed equal, very extensive, and in matters of conscience absolute. Not only was the text's political subversion distinctly "republican" but it exuded an unmistakable democratic tendency, erecting society's collective will as the true sovereign with an influence all the more insidious, according to most, in that the book "has been so much talk'd of, and by some applauded for one of the best books this age has produc'd."[43]

Especially outrageous to moderate Whigs as well as Tories and High Churchmen, was that in *The Rights* civil and church authority, as constituted by Parliament after the Glorious Revolution of 1688, were "assaulted" together.[44] "Kings and Queens," complained one detractor, "are but their [i.e. the people's] creatures, made by 'em and for 'em . . . " with the consequence that "noblemen and gentlemen, deriving their honours from Kings and Queens, are but creatures of a creature from the people; for were the people made for noblemen and gentlemen, any more than for Kings and Queens?"[45] Tindal's political creed plainly repudiated Locke's focus on "property" as the basis of civil rights and spurned his *supra rationem. The Rights* pronounced it impossible for two independent sources of authority, material and spiritual, to exist, as there can never be any independent power over others in religious matters. Since there can be only one authority in society, "nothing can be plainer than that all ecclesiastical power has no other foundation than the consent of the society."[46] Studying past and present human societies proves the "grievances and miseryes they labour under are chiefly, if not wholly owing to the abuse of power, by their governors either extending it to such things as they were not, or cou'd not be intrusted with, or else employing it [. . .] contrary to the end for which they were entrusted: and that Christians besides having their share in the common clamitys, have been miserably harassed by a new pretense of two independent powers [church and state] in the same society."[47]

41 Champion, *Pillars of Priestcraft*, 137; Wigelsworth, "God can require nothing from us," 146–8.
42 *Mr Le Clerc's Extract and Judgment*, 6–8; De Vet, "Spinoza en Spinozisme," 9–10.
43 *The Villanous Principles of* The Rights, 3.
44 Oldisworth, *A Dialogue Between Timothy and Philatheus* i, dedication, pp. A1v–A2.
45 *Dangerous Positions: or, Blasphemous, profane, immoral and Jesuitical assertions*, 49.
46 [Tindal], *The Rights*, 80; Hudson, *English Deists*, 111.
47 [Tindal], *The Rights*, 1, 19; Champion, *Pillars of Priestcraft*, 97, 136–7.

It was "plain how happy human societys would be, did not their rulers usurp more power than they could be invest'd with by their subjects, who would not oblige themselves to assist 'em with their force, except in such cases only as themselves had a right to use in the state of nature." Instances where rulers unjustly mobilize their subjects for war or other emergencies "cannot well be mistaken in; and, consequently, the commands of a tyrant are so far from justifying or excusing their assisting him either in unjustly invading their neighbours, or injuring their fellow-citizens, that they are oblig'd by the common ties of humanity to assist one another in opposing tyrants, who by betraying the highest trust, become the greatest and basest of traitors." Had men, "instead of becoming the cursed instruments of tyranny, assisted one another in defending their natural rights by whomsoever invaded, as by the Law of Nature they were oblig'd, the greatest part of mankind wou'd not for so many ages have groan'd under an insupportable slavery."[48] A classic "Spinozist" in the late seventeenth-century sense of perceiving royal absolutism as heavily vested in false theology: it was "at the instigation of priests, too many of whom have been everywhere active in enslaving their country," as Tindal put it, that tyranny had advanced so vigorously during the seventeenth century, leaving society now "reduc'd to a most miserable slavery."[49]

It is immoral to shirk responsibility for combating tyranny at home and abroad, contended Tindal, making sure readers grasped that "despotism" here has a double-barreled theological-political sense—meaning political oppression tied to "ecclesiastical tyranny and priestcraft." It is unworthy to disdain (as most Englishmen did) "those few but brave nations, which are happy as yet to be free" and have been "at so great expense of blood and treasure in maintaining their libertys, for which those who at present reap the mighty advantage, cannot without monstrous ingratitude condemn the conduct of their ancestors, or the noble principles which thus animated them."[50] In short, it was disgraceful to be ungrateful to the Dutch for their revolt against Spain, opposing Cromwell and the House of Orange, and helping engineer the 1688 Revolution. Tindal's explosive book not only disparaged the post-Glorious Revolution settlement and maligned the public church, but claimed the entire world languished in an unnecessarily wretched condition due to the inadequacy of most people's beliefs, mankind's generally defective understanding of morality, and lack of political activism against tyrants allied to churchmen. This was quintessential Radical Enlightenment. The world needed improving, from bottom to top, by reforming men's ideas and turning their thoughts to fighting the tight alliance of monarchy, aristocracy, and religious authority.

Men's duty to their fellows, as well as prime involvement with the state, is to ensure government adheres to its obligation, that all understand that the "chief end of it is to protect men in all such actions as may be done without prejudice or injury to one another," safeguarding their freedoms as if men are still in the state of nature. It was

[48] [Tindal], *The Rights*, 25–6; Hudson, *Enlightenment and Modernity*, 130–1.
[49] [Tindal], *A New Catechism*, 10. [50] [Tindal], *The Rights*, 26–7.

never compacts, agreements, or associations which they enter into with one another that "put them out of the State of Nature, but that political union only which they engage in for the defence of themselves and propertys, and where they oblige themselves to assist the magistrate in punishing all such injuries, as the good of the whole will not permit to go unpunish'd." Hence, the state of nature is "much wider than is generally imagin'd, since not only whole nations with respect to one another are still in it, and every one in the same society, [. . .] but all men are born in it, and always continue to be so in all such things as they may practice without injuring one another."[51] Since the "authority of government arises [. . .] from the natural right every one has to preserve himself, and to prefer his own good to any other person's," furthering the individual's and society's "happiness" is the state's sole function and obligation.[52]

Sovereignty of the people Tindal championed by condemning monarchy, aristocracy, and ecclesiastical pretension, and the entire system of despotism in his view rendering mankind unhappy. The present "deplorable state of mankind" Tindal attributed less to external force or direct oppression than the circumstance that the English, like "most nations have been enslav'd by their own governors, in not either soon enough perceiving the fetters design'd for 'em, or not daring to refuse wearing 'em."[53] The whole edifice of human delusion, misery, and wretchedness is therefore theological-political, resting on men's false beliefs; the sole remedy lies in changing how men think, and precisely here the churches were the prime obstacle: "since ignorance is the mother of devotion, not to God, yet to the priests, who are in a manner ador'd where the people are thoroughly ignorant, 'tis unreasonable to expect that they shou'd in earnest endeavor to make those whose education is intrust'd with 'em, so learned or wise as to be above priestcraft."[54] Tindal's Radical Enlightenment hence pivoted on freedom of judgment and conscience, including unrestricted freedom to criticize church and state in speech and publications. "If it be the liberty of the press (as all thinking men agree) which secures our other libertys, will not that be in a great measure restrain'd, if such men as are against all liberty civil and ecclesiastical (as 'tis notorious the railers of *The Rights* are) shall enter into a conspiracy to worry booksellers, and carry on malicious prosecutions?"[55]

Several of Tindal's detractors noted the rigorous coherence and unsettling novelty of his emphatically unHobbesian and unLockean political theory, and centrality of the assault on churchmen, churches, and theology in his political thought. The author of *The Rights* obviously despised most men's beliefs and was a republican democrat of a highly unusual and systematic kind, tightly interconnecting his rejection of monarchy, conventional notions, faith, priests, and all churches. The author invoked "the

[51] [Tindal], *The Rights*, 11; Hudson, *English Deists*, 110–11; *Mr Le Clerc's Extract and Judgment*, 9–10.
[52] [Tindal], *A Defence of The Rights*, 306; Wigelsworth, "God can require nothing of us," 141–2.
[53] [Tindal], *A Defence of The Rights*, 169.
[54] [Tindal], *The Rights*, 223; Wigelsworth, "God can require nothing of us," 149.
[55] [Tindal], *A Defence of The Rights*, 93–4.

Natural Rights of the People" but his approach had no connection with what most people believed: no doctrine could have been more foreign to English republicanism's mainstream tradition. From where did this disconcertingly militant doctrine of popular sovereignty, and curtailing of all ultimate transfer of sovereignty to government from the people, derive and whence his notion of the universal responsibility of all to oppose tyranny, aristocracy, ignorance, intolerance, and priestcraft? It seemed thoroughly but mysteriously extraneous.

Alternately labeling him "atheist" or "deist," adversaries reguarly associated Tindal's attack on religious authority and theology with Hobbes. Among the full-scale rebuttals that of the London editor William Oldisworth (1680–1734), an Oxford-educated Tory son of a Hampshire vicar, remarks that the author "has thought fit to found his whole hypothesis upon Mr Hobb's state of nature." Yet the core of his doctrine, Oldisworth also noted, his claiming the "state of nature" is "much wider than is generally imagin'd," and his discarding compacts and contracts to transfer legitimate power,[56] diverged markedly from what readers normally gathered from Hobbes and Locke. Especially unHobbesian, noted Oldisworth, anxious to ensure no political faction ever took root in England fed on such appallingly subversive principles, was that the author's "state of nature" was less "quarrelsome" than Hobbes's, indeed by comparison "very peaceable," without that brutal war of all against all for which Hobbes was notorious.[57] The reason for entering into civil society—to defend, stabilize and protect natural rights—according to this disturbing new doctrine was the sole legitimating principle in politics and its effect is to delegitimize and render secondary and derivative monarchy, nobility, ancient constitutions, existing law and all precedent, laws, institutions, and churches.

Unlike Hobbes, Harrington, Sidney, or Locke, this author showed no more reverence for gentry and aristocracy than for kings and priests. Rather he "crowded the overthrow of dukes, treasurers, speakers, deans, doctors, and other his subordinate-powers all into one paragraph," recasting everything "as a prey to the giddy licentious multitude." If the essence of the 1688 settlement and constitution was moderation, balance as between rights and monarchy, people and aristocracy, representation and authority, *The Rights* advocated the "supreme power of the mob," the "lowest defect", insisted Oldisworth, in his second volume on the controversy, dedicated to the Bishop of Winchester, "and most remote extream that ever deviated from the Golden Medium of legal liberty."[58] Not least, *The Rights* brazenly trampled on the restrictions on freedom of conscience in the Toleration Act (which Locke respected) "by removing the public fence and throwing open the bounds and limits of our indulgence and letting in the whole herd and spawn of ranters and enthusiasts."[59] The book's subterfuges, including its title, were obviously aimed at evading the "laws penal and

[56] *The Second Part of the Wolf stript of his Shepherd's Cloathing*, 19–20.
[57] Oldisworth, *A Dialogue Between Timothy and Philatheus* i, Preface, pp. xii–xiii.
[58] Oldisworth, *A Dialogue Between Timothy and Philatheus* ii, Dedication, p. A3.
[59] Oldisworth, *A Dialogue Between Timothy and Philatheus* ii, Dedication, pp. A8 and B6v–B7.

mulctuary, for securing the interests of religion and preserving the great mysteries and primary notions of Christianity, sacred and inviolate," namely the blasphemy laws. Hence, it was far from a purely academic question to unmask precisely whence such comprehensively malicious and malignant ideas derived. The author said nothing of his sources. "To avoid the vengeance due to such enormities, *The Book of Rights* (Prodigious irony)", complained Oldisworth, "skulks in obscurity".[60]

2.3. *SPINOZA REVIV'D* AND THE *CERCLE SPINOZISTE*

Plainly, the anonymous miscreant was perpetrating outrageously foreign influence: he "has advanced a set of notions that are without precedent: and therefore he ought to stick to his own principle of despising the authority and judgment of other writers; and yet he is not ashamed to refer himself to the opinions of foreigners." In places, Tindal cited Grotius; but this struck critics as just another ploy rather than an authentic derivation (though Grotius *was* actually a significant source for republican "carry over" of the basic freedoms from the state of nature into civil society).[61] The anonymous offending author had backed his claims with the testimony of those "most unfit to write of our Constitution, for which the author of *The Rights* professes himself an advocate; had he thought himself equal to the work he engaged in, he ought to have produced as many evidences in behalf of his notions, as those who opposed him, did in defence of theirs. This would have been agreeable to his doctrine of a majority: and yet in the excess of his modesty, he has contented himself with only one or two of a different communion and government than the English."

Following the Dutch "invasion" of 1688 and subsequent military occupation of London (1688–91) which had helped shape the constitutional outcome of the 1688 Revolution, antipathy to the Dutch nation, state and religious, commercial and political system among the English, unsurprisingly, had welled up strongly. Such antipathy became a marked feature of the English domestic scene,[62] with anti-Dutch sentiment seething especially among Tories and Jacobites. During Queen Anne's reign (1702–14), it remained commonplace for Anglican stalwarts and the conservative-minded to deplore the effects of "Dutch Toleration" and republican attitudes. One tract in this vein published shortly after William III's death, in October 1702, celebrated the aborting of the schemes of Wildman, that "cursed agitator with the Army, in procuring the murder of our royal martyr [i.e. Charles I]" that recalcitrant who "with much hazard [. . .] escap'd Cromwell's clutches, when he ap'd the monarch." "So professed a Common-wealth's man" was Wildman that, on returning from Holland, in 1688, he had tried to impart a republican twist to England's

[60] Oldisworth, *A Dialogue Between Timothy and Philatheus* i, p. A3v.
[61] *The Judgment and Opinion of Hugo Grotius Concerning the Principles and Notions of* the Rights, 3–5.
[62] Israel, "Dutch Role in the Glorious Revolution," 120–62.

Revolution, a tract of his of January 1688 claiming the "people may set up what government they please, either the old, or a new; a monarchy absolute, or limited; or even an Aristocracy or Democracy," and that the "way of doing it must be Great, Awful and August, that none may be able to quarrel it." He had proposed a "National Convention made up of representatives of the community: that the Convention may be truly national, and represent the community, it must be larger than a house of Commons ordinarily is." This "Grand Council of the Nation" should "have more power than a Parliament" and be "the Creator" of the new Body Politic.[63] Thankfully, agreed most, Wildman's democratic republicans secured nothing of the proposed "Foundation laid by this Convention" that no Act of Parliament "can be strong enough to move."[64] Wildman failed to influence the 1688 Revolution "which when settled, his confidants of the Republican Gang, upbraided him for betraying their cause: never could there be such an opportunity of setting up a Commonwealth, according to the Dutch way, and making the Prince head thereof."[65]

The "Dutch way" dreamt of by the handful of English radicals in Holland meant in essence usurping Parliament's sovereignty to substitute a republic for monarchy and curtail the powers and privileges of the public Church while eliminating the sway of aristocracy. The United Provinces were widely perceived during the early eighteenth century as the Western world's most prosperous and successful, as well as most republican, society. In Britain, France, and other lands, this often encouraged radical critics of the status quo to contrast their own country with the United Provinces as a way of sharpening their denunciations of the state of affairs at home. This was plainly the case with Louis XIV's France where many detested the advance of an intolerant, arrogant absolutism. For this reason the argument, leveled against the "Radical Enlightenment thesis," that because Dutch democratic republican writers belonged to an intellectual thought tradition so different and so strikingly unrepresentative of most of Europe at the time, they could have no real impact abroad can be seen to be fundamentally mistaken. That most of Europe differed so markedly from Holland, for some, served precisely to heighten, not dampen, the attraction of the "Dutch way," as the 1706–8 "Rights of the Church" controversy so vividly illustrates.[66] Abhorrence of absolutism rendered the "Dutch way" everywhere a highly effective subversive politico-philosophical strategy.

Most of British and European society after 1688 indeed remained impervious and fiercely hostile; but it was precisely dissidents, intellectuals, and academics like Tindal, countering commonplace notions from the republican side, who, though relatively few, discovered in "the Dutch way" an effective means with which to rationalize and consolidate a path toward a new kind of democratic republican polity shorn of noble dominance, "priestcraft," and royalty. According to Toland, in his *Anglia Libera* (1701), the Stuart dynasty from 1660 "sought to subvert our laws and liberties" as

[63] Wildman, *A Letter to a Friend*, 14–15. [64] Wildman, *A Letter to a Friend*, 16.
[65] BL C.108 bbb 33 (2): *Separation and Sedition Inseparable* (31 October 1702), 8–9.
[66] See the rebuttal of Lilti in Israel, "L'Histoire intellectuelle," 211–17.

well as "extirpate the Protestant religion," in response to which "the free people of this kingdom invited over the Prince of Orange, under whom they put themselves in a posture of defense and successfully recovered the just rights of themselves and their posterity."[67] Alignment with Holland proved indispensable for recovering the people's rights and "the union of England and Holland," the "two most potent and flourishing commonwealths in the universe," also remained requisite, held Toland, for retaining them.[68]

While humanity is mostly a picture of misery, tyranny, and persecution with much of English, Scots, and Irish society lured into Jacobite modes of thinking, venerating despotism, intolerance, and theological sway, even as the world currently existed, held *The Rights*, some societies were incontrovertibly "happier" than others. "Is not Holland, from being one of the most beggarly provinces in the world, become, the most flourishing and most populous spot upon Earth?" Freer and more prosperous than neighbouring lands, there "we see the power of the clergy at so low an ebb, that they are not able to set on foot persecution, or any other of their darling methods by which a nation is render'd thin, poor and miserable;" the chief reason England, "next to Holland and the other United Provinces," was the best and most flourishing of lands was that England too was "most jealous of the clerical usurpations," the land that next to Holland keeps the "clergy most in subjection."[69]

If the contagion propagated by *The Rights* was essentially foreign, the most resolute effort to uncover the sources of Tindal's radicalism was that by an Irish ex-priest converted to High Church Anglicanism, William Carroll (dates unknown), reinforced by his mentor and ally, George Hickes (1642–1715), a former High Anglican Dean of Worcester compelled to resign, in 1690, for refusing to recognize William III's enthronement.[70] Carroll and Hickes entitled their joint refutation *Spinoza Reviv'd or, A Treatise proving the Book intitled* The Rights of the Christian Church [. . .] *to be the same with Spinoza's Rights of the Christian Clergy* (London, 1709). Actually, Carroll and Hickes wrongly inferred that the 162-page anonymous radical text published in 1665 that they highlighted—*De Jure Ecclesiasticorum*—issued from Spinoza's pen.[71] It was a common misattribution encountered earlier in Bayle's *Dictionnaire*, and in subsequent eighteenth-century histories of thought like Giambattista Capasso's *Historiae Philosophiae Synopsis* (Naples, 1728),[72] though some early eighteenth-century authorities disagreed with this attribution given this text's distinctive Latin style and reference to God as "Deus optimus maximus," a term

[67] Toland, *Anglia Libera*, 22–3.

[68] Toland, *Anglia Libera*, 4–5, 26, 150–1; Toland, *Art of Governing By Partys*, Dedication.

[69] [Tindal], *The Rights*, 254; Hudson, *English Deists*, 111.

[70] Champion, *Pillars of Priestcraft*, 179–80; Brown, "Theological Politics," 195; Brown, "Locke as Secret 'Spinozist'," 217.

[71] The full title is *Lucii Antistii Constantis, De Jure Ecclesiasticorum, liber singularis: quo docetur, quodcunque divini humanique iuris ecclesiasticis tribuitur, vel ipsi sibi tribuunt, aut falso impieque illis tribui* (Alethopoli [Amsterdam], 1665).

[72] Capasso, *Historiae Philosophiae Synopsis*, 396.

Spinoza never uses. The most common alternative attribution, to Lodewijk Meyer (1629–81), Spinoza's Amsterdam physician ally, or Pieter de La Court, was also rejected by the great mid-eighteenth-century German bibliographer Baumgarten; but he could suggest no convincing alternative.[73] Still, the important point is that like Bayle and Baumgarten, Carroll and Hickes rightly identified the text's political theory as quintessentially Spinozist;[74] Carroll and Hickes showed, by comparing parallel passages, that *De Jure* was indeed the primary source from where Tindal derives his argument.

Claiming the ecclesiastical estate neither possesses, nor can possess, any inherent authority, superiority, privileges, or separate status,[75] *De Jure* is closely linked to Spinoza's legacy. Applauding Carroll for "discovering the mysteries of iniquity" behind Tindal's insidious anti-ecclesiastical republicanism, Hickes too stressed the affinities between *The Rights* and *De Jure Ecclesiasticorum*. Several chapter headings and other key passages of Tindal's *The Rights* conspicuously paralleled key passages of *De Jure*. In fact, "having examined the late misnamed book *The Rights of the Christian Church Asserted*", Carroll and Hickes could announce that Tindal had followed *De Jure* so closely his text amounted to "Spinoza's *Rights of the Clergy* translated and made worse than the atheist himself made it." Tindal's primary concepts—"God," "soul," "Christ," man, "spirit of Christ," "spirit of God," state of nature, "natural rights of mankind"—all stemmed directly from the one-substance doctrine expounded in *De Jure Ecclesiasticorum*.[76] Carroll not only denounced *The Rights* for propagating Spinozism but also Le Clerc, for reviewing it favourably, pronouncing him a concealed "Spinozist." Le Clerc was no "Spinozist" but in warming to this unprecedented assault on all ecclesiastical coercion had perhaps been somewhat incautious.[77]

According to *De Jure*, all political, legal, and religious power without exception originates from the sovereignty of the whole people acting as a collectivity. Authority begins, but also remains, democratic in its legitimate operation as well as origin. Who did write *De Jure* remains still today unknown. Sometimes attributed to Meyer, it undoubtedly sprang from the *cercle spinoziste* and was printed clandestinely, by an unknown publisher employing fictitious details on the title-page, with the place of publication given as "Alethopolis" [i.e. Eleutheropolis or "Freedom-city" (hence Amsterdam)].[78] Its illicit doctrine later attracted a few connoisseurs of such material, including Anthony Collins in whose remarkable library, auctioned at his death, on 18 January 1731, it was inventoried.[79] As the source of Tindal's revolt against

[73] Baumgarten, *Nachrichten* iii. 26–7.

[74] Brown, "Locke as Secret 'Spinozist'," 232 n. 79; Krop, "Secularism of Spinoza," 96–7; Israel, "Intellectual Origins," 14; Bordoli, "Monopoly," 126; Lavaert, "Lieutenants," 151.

[75] *De Jure Ecclesiasticorum*, 52, 55; Skeaff, *Becoming Political*, 18–19.

[76] Carroll, *Spinoza Reviv'd*, 1–4; Brown, "Locke as Secret 'Spinozist'," 232 n. 79.

[77] De Vet, "Spinoza en Spinozisme," 22; Marshall, *John Locke*, 565–7.

[78] *De Jure Ecclesiasticorum*, title-page; Lavaert, "Lieutenants," 149–51; Bordoli, "Monopoly," 126–8.

[79] *Bibliotheca Antonij Collins, Or A complete Catalogue of the Library of Antony Collins, Esq., Deceased* (n.p., 1731), part 1, no. 17.

England's crown and church, *De Jure*, reasoned Hickes, proved his extraneous, subversive republicanism was essentially Spinoza's bolstered by the latter's teaching concerning God, the universe, matter, and motion.[80] Tindal's principles "are only Spinoza's principles," insisted Carroll, "grounded upon that atheist's hypothesis."[81]

De Jure relies heavily on the claim that all inequality of status, authority, and privilege, including all ecclesiastical establishment, stems exclusively from human rather than divine government, that "aequalitatem omnium hominum naturalem status civilis constitutione in privatis non mutari"[82] which Carroll rendered as the "natural equality of mankind is not in private persons chang'd by the institution of a commonwealth." Since all institutionalized "inequality betwixt man and man, in the civil society, is descended or deriv'd from the vice-gods [i.e. those men speaking for the gods]" and as there cannot be two independent powers in the same society, all differentiated status is exclusively man-made and men's rights in the state of nature remain intact after formation of the state.[83] It is from the secular power alone, contends *De Jure*, that the delegated authority of the representatives of the gods presiding over civil society, that is the clergy's status "deriv'd, no less, nor otherwise, than that of the other civilians;" as Carroll renders the passage, hence, "there is no difference between the latter and the former."[84]

Neither in the Old Testament nor the New does one find any statement delegating jurisdiction over others to priests. Here as with their "universal, impartial, inviolable toleration in matters of religion," notes Carroll, "you see all this is bottom'd upon those men's favourite principle, to wit, That as to matters of conscience, or religion, mankind is actually in their state of nature, wherein every man has an equal natural, inalienable, inherent right, to believe, or not believe whatever he pleases."[85] Individuals are free, there is only one source of legitimate power in society, and churches have no divinely-given independent authority over anyone. As "all power is originally in, and immediately from the people," as Carroll summarizes Tindal, "they are the unappealable judges, judges in the last resort," so that the individuals constituting society remain "in a state of nature with relation to religious matters," everyone having a natural "inalienable right to chuse, believe, profess, etc. whatever religion they please," while retaining the right to take up arms to defend their natural rights, equality, and liberty in whatever respect these are infringed by any authority

[80] Hickes, "A Preliminary Discourse," in Carroll, *Spinoza Reviv'd*, pp. A5–6.

[81] Carroll, *Spinoza Reviv'd*, 150.

[82] *De Jure Ecclesiasticorum*, 38, 42–3, 154–5; Krop, "Secularism of Spinoza," 97; Lavaert, "Lieutenants," 157.

[83] *De Jure Ecclesiasticorum*, 38; Baumgarten, *Nachrichten* iii. 29–30; Carroll, *Spinoza Reviv'd*, 8–9; Bordoli, "Monopoly," 128–9.

[84] "Omnem inaequalitatem ecclesiasticorum non minus aut aliter, quam caetorum civium a solis prodiis procedure: nec ullum illorum et horum discrimen esse," in *De Jure Ecclesiasticorum*, 52; Carroll, *Spinoza Reviv'd*, 9.

[85] Carroll, *Spinoza Reviv'd*, 72; Baumgarten, *Nachrichten* iii. 31–2; Bordoli, "Monopoly," 129–30.

whatsoever. In the *statu civili* the basic equality reigning among men in the state of nature is conserved only now in a more orderly, structured way than before.[86]

These principles apply generally throughout the world, affirms *De Jure*, without special reference to any particular society; they are the quintessence of all societies. Crystallizing during the early 1660s as a group of enthusiasts debating Cartesianism, before long, as The Hague Cartesian physician Bontekoe noted, the *cercle spinoziste* had become an intellectual pressure group initially preoccupied with undermining and displacing Cartesianism and academic philosophy more generally.[87] With its roots in Amsterdam, Leiden, and The Hague, the network soon percolated to Utrecht, Rotterdam, and other places. Its founding members, apart from Spinoza, were Franciscus Van den Enden (1602–74) who in some respects was more emphatically radical and democratic than Spinoza and was later executed in Paris by Louis XIV for conspiring against his crown, Meyer, Johannes and Adriaen Koerbagh, the Collegiant Jarig Jelles (*c.*1620–83), Johannes Bouwmeester (*c.*1630–80), the prolific translator Johan Hendrik Glazemaker (1620–82), Abraham van Berckel, Abraham Cuffeler (*c.*1637–94), and—crucial for the evolution of the group's political thought—Johan and Pieter de La Court. The De La Courts likewise rejected religious authority per se though their views may have originated more in an anti-Calvinist, radical Arminian rather than a wholly secular stance; De La Court judged *De Jure Ecclesiasticorum* an "excellent" and "irrefutable" book.[88]

Van den Enden inculcated good Latin style into his pupils, getting them to perform the plays of Seneca and Terence in the original, and certainly helped Spinoza master Latin. It was also his practice, until ugly rumours spread, to insinuate atheistic ideas into those in his charge.[89] Koerbagh too, observed Goeree, "through contact with this man did not imbibe anything good [. . .] as is plain from all those offensive entries in his Dictionary, or stinking *Bloemhof*."[90] We do not know anything definite about the ex-Jesuit Van den Enden's views prior to 1660,[91] however, and, in any case, Spinoza's thought issued not from solitary, detached reflection, but group effort,[92] from a heterodox network that persisted after these individuals' deaths into the early eighteenth century,[93] a milieu characteristically Dutch but one noticed outside the Netherlands by the principal thinkers of following decades. The distinctive feature of their collective endeavor in the sciences, arts, scholarship, and philosophy as well as political thought was their eliminating religious authority from morality, social

[86] *De Jure Ecclesiasticorum*, 131, 139, 154; Baumgarten, *Nachrichten* iii. 32; Van Bunge, *From Stevin to Spinoza*, 88.

[87] Van Bunge, *Spinoza Past and Present*, 42; Israel," Spinoza as an Expounder, Critic," 41–53.

[88] Weststeijn, *Commercial Republicanism*, 297–8, 313–14.

[89] Akkerman, *Studies in the Posthumous Works of Spinoza*, 3, 18 n. 12.

[90] Goeree, *Kerklyke en Weereldlyke Historien*, 665; Meinsma, *Spinoza et son cercle*, 192, 381–2; Israel, *Radical Enlightenment*, 168.

[91] Mertens, "Franciscus van den Enden," 729.

[92] Mertens, *Van den Enden en Spinoza*, 63–78; Krop, *Spinoza*, 707, 711.

[93] Israel, *Radical Enlightenment*, 307–27; Wielema, *March of the Libertines*, 9–17, 103–32; Wielema, "Een onbekende aanhanger," 23–40; Wielema, "Ongeloof en atheïsme," 332–53.

theory, and politics, and combining this with a fundamentally unHobbesian and unLockean democratic tendency in political thought.[94] Late seventeenth-century Dutch "democratic republicanism" Van den Enden rightly believed to be a fundamentally new conception of profound significance for the entire world.[95] Little acknowledged by historians and philosophers, the point needs emphasizing due to its crucial importance for understanding the history of the Radical Enlightenment, representative democracy as political theory, and the origins of Western modernity.

If Spinoza's philosophy was assuredly largely his own individual achievement, and while he clearly influenced others in their collective intellectual formation, his legacy was nevertheless also partly a collective outcome forged by all these personages in dialogue. "It would seem that by the late 1650s," writes one scholar, "Van den Enden, Spinoza, Meyer, Bouwmester, Van Berkel and possibly the Koerbagh brothers had embarked on a common quest."[96] Without entering here into a continuing disagreement about whether Spinoza was initially a disciple of the Antwerp ex-Jesuit, art-dealer, schoolmaster, and atheist, Franciscus Van den Enden, as sometimes claimed, following seventeenth-century Dutch reports, and therefore someone seeking to "elaborate the ideas of Van den Enden,"[97] as the Cartesian–Cocceian preacher, Salomon van Til (1643–1713), expressed it, or, alternatively, as an anonymous notebook discovered in the Utrecht University Library affirms, Koerbagh and Van den Enden "fuerunt praecipui discipuli Spinosae" [were Spinoza's principal disciples], the truth seems likeliest to lie somewhere between these two extremes: the relationship of Van den Enden and Spinoza was a two-way process.[98]

Dutch democratic republicanism was much indebted to Machiavelli, Descartes, and Hobbes, but the impetus and distinctive stamp of this group's political thought with its stress on elimination of religious authority, including its conspicuously unHobbesian and unLockean features, stemmed principally from their immediate predicament—the political and confessional crisis confronting the Dutch Republic. The *cercle spinoziste* formed a semi-clandestine early Enlightenment literary, as well as philosophical and medical, rebellion against established academic culture and theology, grappling also with issues of sexual repression and emancipation (a feature prominent in the writings of the Koerbaghs, Hadrianus Beverland, and Goeree), that the authorities deemed fundamentally godless and illicit. For these reasons, as well as their incisive criticism of the Republic's existing structure, all the group's principal works, including Spinoza's *Ethics* (1678) and *Tractatus Theological Politicus* (1670),

[94] Klever, *Mannen rond Spinoza*, 11, 31–3; 61–2, 245–6; Krop, *Spinoza*, 94–102; Van Bunge, *Spinoza Past and Present*, 60–4, 195–8.

[95] Israel, "Intellectual Origins," 16.

[96] Van Bunge, "Introduction" to Wielema (ed.), Adriaan Koerbagh, *A Light Shining in Dark Places*, 8.

[97] Van der Wall, "*The Tractatus*," 216.

[98] Steenbakkers, Touber, and Van de Ven, "A Clandestine Notebook, 286–7 n. 92; Mertens, "Franciscus van den Enden," 733–5; Israel, "Dutch Golden Age Politics," 48.

were banned and actively suppressed in the United Provinces until well into the eighteenth century.[99]

An underground opposition culture simultaneously political and anti-church, that developed in the 1670s into a "sect" rooted both in big cities and universities, it spread among persons exposed to academic culture, an aspect reflected in the philosophical novel *The Life of Philopater* (published in two parts in 1691 and 1697) recording the embattled intellectual odyssey of a young theology student (Philopater) who, through discussion with competing intellectual factions, wrestling with issues of faith within himself, transfers first from Calvinism to Cocceian liberal Calvinism, then from faith to skepticism, and finally from skepticism to Spinozism. Participants in the post-1670 extended *cercle spinoziste* were in their different ways all political, religious, and social dissidents and often rebels against the sexual norms of their time—overtly so in the cases of Koerbagh, who died in prison in 1669, and Beverland, expelled from the Republic in 1679.[100] Furtive, publishing their most challenging works only anonymously, the *cercle* nevertheless became conspicuously embroiled in virulent public controversies starting in the mid-1660s. A huge uproar greeted publication of Meyer's *Philosophia S. Scripturae Interpres* (Eleutheropolis [Amsterdam], 1666), a book championing primacy of philosophical "reason" in interpreting Scripture that arguably "caused a greater shock among the Calvinist divines" than even Spinoza's *Theological-Political Treatise.*[101] Subsequent major controversies provoked much anxiety at the supposedly catastrophic effects of "Spinozism" on society, that over Bekker's *The World Bewitched* (1691–4), trumpeting doubts about the reality of sorcery, satanic influence on individuals and witchcraft, and that surrounding Van Leenhof's *Den Hemel op Aarde* (1703), worries about how far *Spinozismus* had surreptitiously invaded theological studies and the Reformed Church ministry.

2.4. DUTCH DEMOCRATIC REPUBLICANISM (1650–1700)

No real equivalent existed in pre-1688 England, France, or Germany to these Dutch writers' democratic republicanism, not even in Switzerland, and this significantly added to the factors elevating the United Provinces to a unique and unparalleled position in the process of generating the Radical Enlightenment during the late seventeenth century. In political thought, it was a process fed not only by using local intellectual resources but also Machiavelli and Hobbes, whose concepts were intensively reworked and recycled, in particular by the Brothers De La Court and the author of *De Jure Ecclesiasticorum*, as well as Spinoza, to produce what one scholar termed "republican reinterpretations."[102] The specifics of the Dutch republican

[99] Hollewand, *Banishment of Beverland*, 52–68, 101–6.
[100] Mertens, "Spinoza's Amsterdamse vriendenkring," 73.
[101] Van der Wall, "The *Tractatus*," 218; Mangold, "Salomon van Til," 341.
[102] Laerke, "Anthropological Analogy," 22.

predicament between 1650 and 1672 were not the sole reason for the special character of this new phenomenon in Western history. Another fundamental reason why the West's "Radical Enlightenment" found its initial sources and roots in the Republic rather than elsewhere was that the Radical Reformation of Servetus, Castellio, Socinus, and Coornhert acquired, through the Dutch Revolt of 1572, deeper roots and a far wider early following there than, for example, in England, Germany, or Scandinavia.[103] By the 1650s, only a few in England consciously preferred what one writer called the "free Ayre" of Holland "where all religions are permitted" to the imposed, coercive Puritan conformity of New England.[104]

Nevertheless, the political drama unfolding in the mid-seventeenth-century Netherlands was, in the end, the crucial factor: for it was this that drove the first great wedge between oligarchic republicanism and an ideological opposition to oligarchic control that became the key feature of republican debate in the later eighteenth century in America and continental Europe. In direct opposition to Machiavelli and, still more, Hobbes, the *cercle spinoziste* transferred and institutionalized the state of nature's freedoms as basic human rights in political society and the "common interest." In claiming the collective power of the state is the greater the more it protects and equalizes the "natural rights" of its individual members, Spinoza expressed the main political thrust of the entire group.[105] Yet Van den Enden, whether or not he led in asserting one-substance monism, was unquestionably first among the Amsterdam group to follow the De La Courts in combining democracy with claiming that enlightening and educating the people against "superstition" is the sole and exclusive means to overcome political and religious tyranny; and maintain that a social system spurring everyone to improve their ideas, and discard "superstition," can only effectively pursue the "common good" where based on a democratic form of republicanism.[106] The form of government exalted by the *cercle* they identified as that which best defends the "common good" and is least apt to be captured by private interests infringing it.[107] Their political theory was a strategy rooted in their need for an activist, uncompromising anti-Orangist recipe capable of widening the support for the "True Freedom" and abolishing ecclesiastical direction of morality, society, and education.

Dutch democratic republicanism as such, it should be noted, first arose as a coherent political thought system neither in Van den Enden, Meyer, Koerbagh, or Spinoza, but in the *oeuvre* of Johan de La Court (1622–60) followed by his more

[103] Buys, "Without Thy Self," 363–8; Coffrey, "Toleration Controversy," 53–4; Israel, "Spinoza and the Religious Radical Enlightenment," 181–90.

[104] Coffrey, "Toleration Controversy," 54.

[105] On this point see also Ursula Goldenbaum's paper "The People Have the Power': Spinoza's Argument for Universal Inalienable Rights" given at the International Political Science Association's annual conference held at Atlanta, Georgia, 29–30 April 2005; Van Bunge, "Modernity of Radical Enlightenment," 141–2; Schnepf, "Enlightened Radicals," 103.

[106] Van den Enden, *Free Political Propositions*, 191, 194.

[107] Van den Enden, *Free Political Propositions*, 156–60.

famous but less original brother, Pieter de La Court (1618–85). If none of these, aside from Spinoza, were thinkers of the first order, they engineered a group breakthrough of pivotal importance in political thought that exerted a masked but crucial underground impact on English thought during the critical years from 1688 (followed by publication of the English version of the *Tractatus Theologico-Politicus* in 1689), down to Parliament's burning of Tindal's *The Rights* in 1710, in particular through Blount, Toland, and Tindal. Its innovative thrust should be regarded less as a purely intellectual reaction than a political response to the prolonged political and social crisis gripping the United Provinces in the third quarter of the seventeenth century, a crisis endemic in the very structure of the loosely constructed federal republic forged in the 1570s by rebellion against Spain.

While the Dutch Revolt had earlier produced several texts reflecting an incipient shift toward a republicanism based on humanist enquiry into Greek and Roman antiquity,[108] with ardent expressions of republicanism recurring sporadically during the 1570s and 1580s (also among English volunteers, like Sir Philip Sidney (1554–86), helping fight "Spanish tyranny" in the Low Countries), such flurries, though not unimportant, hardly amounted to a distinctive republican tradition capable of exerting a significant influence on the wider Western world. The Revolt retained symbolic significance as a classic instance of rebellion against despotism and persecution; but, for a theoretical corpus suited to grounding a comprehensive political, moral, and social democratic republican ideology, contemporaries had to wait until the aftermath of Stadholder William II's assault on Amsterdam, in 1650, and the mounting difficulties facing De Witt and the "True Freedom" in the 1660s. While the rivalry between the stadholders and the most powerful Dutch representative assembly, the States of Holland, was already intense much earlier with major clashes between Prince Maurits and Oldenbarnevelt during the Twelve Years' Truce (1609–21), an episode still fresh in the collective memory of the *cercle*, it was the renewed conflict in and after 1650 that revealed the extreme precariousness of the freedoms which the Republic had since fostered and the immediate urgency of finding a political formula and set of values capable of rallying wider support on behalf of those besieged freedoms.

As political observers, the brothers Pieter and Johan de La Court matured in an unusual position. Offspring of a prosperous family of Flemish Protestant exiles, their father's successful textile manufacturing business afforded sufficient means for them to live comfortably without needing to work for their living, ample leisure to study, debate, and write while simultaneously locking them into an unprivileged, marginal, immigrant social milieu, and hence into exclusion from participation in the tightly oligarchic republican politics presided over by the seventeenth-century Dutch urban "regent" ruling class. Their marginal situation combined with their status as full-time amateur observers fostered a carefully crafted, long pondered oppositional attitude.[109]

[108] Van Gelderen, *The Dutch Revolt*, 177–8.

[109] Weststeijn, *Radikale Republiek*, 19, 39–40.

Exclusion from the corridors of power, and marginal social status combined with wealth, ease, and long years of intensive study, explain their rare ability to construct a political theory geared to actualities, innovative, and far from academic, but yet also closely tied to existing scholarship and erudition, a republican political theory based on close observation of one particular polity, their own, but yet consciously generalized, and universal in scope. Eager political observers since the 1640s, their first major publication, the *Consideratien en Exempelen van Staat* (Amsterdam, 1660), appeared, at a decidedly late stage in their development, after Johan's death (Pieter was then 32). Although from a public perspective this marked the starting-point, the text forcefully expressed ideas that had evolved in the private, unpublished writings of Johan over many years. Johan had long prevaricated about publishing his work; he knew his merciless analysis of oligarchic republican body politic and church would prove explosive and possibly entail unpleasant consequences for family and friends.

On his deathbed, dying at barely 40 in 1660, Johan instructed his brother that his political theory should not appear, but be destroyed. Pieter ignored his brother's directive, but did tone down some of his more vehemently anti-oligarchic and anti-ecclesiastical rhetoric. The unremittingly anti-oligarchic flavor of Johan's insights Pieter often softened by changing the wording in places to mean simply that republics are better than monarchies rather than provocatively pronouncing the democratic republic superior to monarchy *and* the aristocratic republic. But he by no means removed the democratic emphasis to the extent sometimes suggested. Even with this dilution, it still emerged plainly from their principal works (published anonymously and usually just signed with their soon notorious code "V.D.H."), that they not only conceived the democratic republic they extolled to be inherently superior to aristocratic republics like Venice, Genoa, Lucca, Zurich, Geneva, and the other Swiss cantons they discussed, but a political creed in unending and implacable conflict with the hitherto dominant form of republicanism.

The democratic republic the Brothers De La Court declared the "naturlijkste, redelikste, vreedzaamste en voordeligste voor de ingezetenen" [most natural, rational, peaceful, and most advantageous for the inhabitants] form of state.[110] This they proclaimed in sharp distinction to the "True Freedom" creed, the mainstream republicanism, of the ruling Johan de Witt faction, the familiar form of Dutch republicanism envisaging each of the Seven Provinces as a separate sovereign republic, governed in Holland and Zeeland by entrenched urban patriciates, an ideology strong on religious toleration and freedom of expression, and also individual liberty, but providing little scope for non-elite participation in the political sphere or criticism of the regime. De Witt's "True Freedom" contrasted favourably with the historic Venetian or Genoese model in key respects, especially by allowing greater freedom of expression and religious freedom, and by rejecting the hereditary principle by parading De Witt's central political maxim that in "a free republic no one has any right by

[110] V.H. [De La Court], *Consideratien en Exempelen,* 292; Weststeijn, *Commercial Republicanism,* 151–4.

birth to the high dignities" and offices of the state,[111] that all office-holders should be chosen purely for their abilities by representatives of the cities and countryside. In theory, De Witt even accepted that the hereditary principle is always an imminent danger to a "free state," as the histories of the Visconti at Milan, and the Medici at Florence, abundantly illustrate. But De Witt's purportedly non-hereditary, non-noble representatives were in practice an entrenched privileged stratum of affluent urban regents, an informal oligarchy of families monopolizing political power, a narrow, exclusive semi-hereditary elite.

The Brothers De La Court considered it scandalous that not only in the United Provinces from Oldenbarnevelt down to De Witt, but all Europe's "northern" republics, including the leading Swiss cantons, Zurich, Berne, and Geneva, and principal German Imperial Free Cities, practically no serious effort had been made thus far to study the republicanism all these entities ostensibly acknowledged to be a precious asset benefiting their societies. Prior to themselves, no one had attempted to develop and perfect Europe's most valuable corpus of political theory, or clearly identify its basic principles. Consequently, all those republics had failed to consolidate and fortify their republican credentials as they should have done.[112] The brothers aimed to fill the gap both locally and more generally, in Europe, for which reason they theorized on a broad European level, in a relentless quest for the true foundations of the freest, most stable, prosperous, and enduring republic conceived as a benefit for everyone. Europe's medieval republics originated in what the Brothers deemed an instinctive, natural movement of resistance to the pretensions of the Visconti and other princes and feudal lords, an idea Sismondi would later revive in the 1820s. These late medieval Italian republics being small entities had all had to grapple uninterruptedly, like the seventeenth-century Dutch Republic, with their own obvious vulnerability and instability to defend their independence against grasping larger neighbours; they survived by forming leagues or federal unions like those of the Swiss and Dutch.[113]

De La Court republicanism was the first in the modern West systematically to assert as its central principle that the representative democratic republic is intrinsically the best form of government for all, contrasting it with aristocratic republicanism which it declares defective and inferior in every respect, a feature not encountered in England, Switzerland, or America, until much later. They dismissed the aristocratic republic whether on the Venetian–Genoese, Swiss, German Imperial City, or Dutch model, even if hitherto invariably more prevalent, as invariably intrinsically inferior. They also provided a clear explanation of how it was that no one had ever preceded them in attempting their kind of unprecedented and unparalleled theoretical break with all existing Italian, Swiss, German, Dutch, and English republican theories by claiming that studying politics systematically, and especially expressing views like theirs, had been strictly discouraged over the centuries, blocked from evolving into a

[111] [De Witt], *Deductie ofte declaratie* (1654), 121, 180; Weststeijn, *Radikale Republiek*, 37–9.
[112] De La Court, *Politike Discoursen* i. 2.
[113] De La Court, *Politike Discoursen* i. 196–7; Weststeijn, *Commercial Republicanism*, 164, 214, 219.

fully-fledged representative democratic republican theory by dominant vested interests. Political thinkers before themselves had always succumbed to pressure to reiterate feeble, scholastic arguments against the democratic republic, a disastrous state of affairs ensuring what is best for society and all mankind had remained hidden from view, a deep secret concealed over the centuries behind a mass of obscurantist academic verbiage and mystification generated by manipulation, intimidation, and scholars' own vested interest. Since no rewards or favors can be obtained from the masses, political theorists invariably looked to princes, commanders, and especially grasping tyrants for remuneration and emoluments, rewards deriving only from them. Since writers lose rather than profit from speaking out in favor of the "common good," or championing the collective interest, speaking out against rulers and oligarchic oppression as the De La Courts did had been a perennially thankless and risky undertaking. Scheming, ambitious men waste no time expounding the will of the majority, or the common people's rights; they rush to extol princes, oligarchs, aristocracy, and ecclesiastics. Hence, the universal trend since ancient times had been to condemn democracy by greatly exaggerating its faults, "making elephants out of mice," as the brothers expressed it.[114]

Johan's *Consideratien* launches straight into a ferocious denunciation of monarchy in all its forms. So pernicious is hereditary monarchy that virtually all monarchs focus their ambitions in dynastic concerns, warlike rivalry, and acquiring territory, always placing their self-seeking, avaricious goals ahead of any concern for their subjects. Children of monarchs are raised to esteem themselves as belonging to a different species from everyone else, to care nothing for the people's interest; they seek only their own interest. Queens—in many respects even worse than kings—usually rule only in appearance, devolving effective authority to favorites and courtiers who, eager to retain their confidence, take care to cultivate only the royal interest along with their own, prioritizing their own gain and families even more brazenly than do monarchs and always wholly ignoring the needs of the populace. Since men only become courtiers through flattery and corruption, courtiers are usually baser than everybody else.[115]

While monarchy is always abysmal, what chiefly matters in the De La Courts' republicanism is that they likewise denounced all "mixed government." As "democracy" was the original form of state in their eyes, as well as the most natural and the best,[116] monarchy and aristocratic republicanism are both conceived by them as essentially perversions from an earlier state of "democracy," a view reaffirmed afterwards by Spinoza (and, following Spinoza, in the early 1840s by the young Marx). It was why the aristocratic republics were supposedly still governed, according to their constitutions, by both small and "great" councils "like for example most of the

[114] V.H. [De La Court], *Consideratien en Exempelen*, 283; V.H. [De La Court], *Aanwijsing*, 8–9.

[115] V.H. [De La Court], *Consideratien en Exempelen*, 8–18, 36–7, 63–5, 260; [De La Court], *Aanwijsing*, 2–3, 7–8.

[116] V.H. [De La Court], *Consideratien en Exempelen*, 259–60, 279–80.

cantons of Switzerland" but with the "great" councils now always a mere rubber-stamp and real power pertaining to the oligarchic "small" councils. Since everyone, however he or she presents their views, is governed by the laws of nature and pursues only his own quest for happiness, or what the De La Courts with their Hobbesian psychology call an "inborn drive and necessity to seek his own conservation, advantage and ease," formal aristocracies like those of Britain, France, Genoa, and Venice, and informal oligarchies like those running the "republics" of Switzerland, the German Imperial Free Cities, and so forth hardly differed in their contempt for the "common good." Aristocracies formal and informal always divide into rival cliques wrestling for power, striving to restrict the number of those exercising effective control. Regents of a closed oligarchy in a republic are just as reliant on corrupt methods in pursuing private advantage, and favoring family and friends, as any foreign prince or aristocrat. Informal oligarchy like the Dutch was hence no less harmful to society than monarchy, mixed government, and formal aristocracy.[117]

This point was later expanded on by the controversial Reformed preacher Frederik van Leenhof (1647–1713), a writer who extensively absorbed Spinozistic concepts into his "theology." Van Leenhof's writings, published in 1700–3 and widely influential in early eighteenth-century Germany, reaffirmed the Dutch Spinozistic tradition of democratic republicanism for the first decade of the new century. Everyone has the same needs, and right to security and opportunity, so there is no reason to accept claims that inherited wealth, rank, or position bestow rank and privilege above those of the common people. Just as kings possess no inherent right or worthiness to rule (and are usually worthless), men boasting social rank and offices are highly unlikely to be those who most deserve to exercise power on society's behalf, given that social rank is achieved more through power-seeking, favoritism, and nepotism than by reason.[118] Because high-ranking men normally disdain the common people, it is quite wrong, held Van Leenhof, for those of humble origin with virtue and intellect to be excluded from high office due to their humble origins; history teaches that from the humblest backgrounds derive princes, kings, and popes excelling all predecessors in achievement.[119]

The brothers soon found their recommendations for strengthening the Dutch polity opposed by De Witt's faction, as well as by Orange and the preachers. Pieter de La Court's last book, the *Aenwysinge der heylsame politique gronden ende maximen vande Republique van Holland* (1669), where he again avows that few of the Republic's citizens grasped the superiority of democratic republics over monarchy and aristocratic republics,[120] recommends curbing religious authority, and praises *De Jure Ecclesiasticorum* as an "irrefutable" book, spelling out the measures needed to widen support for the Republic, was immediately banned by the States of Holland, at

[117] De La Court, *Politike Discoursen* i. 120–1, 124–5; Scott, "Classical Republicanism," 67–8.
[118] Van Leenhof, *De Prediker*, 156, 292.
[119] Van Leenhof, *De Prediker*, 292.
[120] [De La Court], *Aanwijsing der heilsame politique gronden*, 9.

De Witt's insistence, on 28 May 1669, for assailing the preachers "with very harsh, offensive and insulting expressions" and making highly unflattering remarks about monarchs who were the Republic's neighbors, risking royal allies becoming alienated from their alliances and engagements with the Republic.[121] Yet while De Witt's republicanism fell short in the eyes of all the *cercle spinoziste*, they still saw grounds to defend the "True Freedom" from its internal and external foes. Its broad toleration and respect for individual freedom still deserved their every effort to help conserve and defend it against the encroachments of Orangism and the public church. Since the "True Freedom" was chiefly vulnerable, in their view, because most people were insufficiently educated, informed, and aware to see through the Calvinist preachers' admonitions that their great men, Oldenbarnevelt, Grotius, and De Witt, were godless traitors and heretics, it was precisely that fatal defect representative democratic republican theory must devise methods to overcome.

Viewed from a radical perspective, De Wittian deference to kings and clergy only placed "True Freedom" toleration and individual freedom even more immediately at risk, as the events of 1672 and De Witt's overthrow soon demonstrated. De Witt's regime was simply too fragile to withstand the pressures threatening it. The Republic could survive only if popular support was broadened and popular support could not be broadened without two vital preconditions being met: the Republic had to become more representative of the "common good" while the people's veneration for religious authority and the clergy had to be drastically reduced. Here, for the first time, we find at the heart of political debate, tightly linked and constantly interacting, the two vital components of Radical Enlightenment—representative democratic republicanism tied intrinsically to rejection of religious authority.

In contrast to contemporary English republicanism, Johan vilified the aristocratic republic just as much as he did monarchy. The De La Court Brothers' approach meant publicly recognizing, as had no one before, that the universal principle grounding *all* monarchy and *all* aristocratic republics is "pure force and deceit" so that both are equally malign. Only through time, deception, and the people's passivity had these two generally accepted but universally pernicious forms become seemingly legitimized.[122] Both everywhere enjoyed enormous popular support—but only due to ignorance, superstition, lack of appropriate education, and credulity. The "democratic or popular form of government," by contrast, is not "founded on force but natural and rational and inherently possesses integrity: what could be more natural than to live under one's own judgment, order and laws?"[123] Democratic republicanism's superiority is doubly reflected in that whereas under all other forms of government *salus populi*, the people's welfare, the common good remains just a mask [*dekmantel*] for self-interest, in democracies it is the supreme law, the highest injunction. Given

[121] BL Dn 2/4 (24): decree of the States of Holland, 28 May 1669; Weststeijn, *Commercial Republicanism*, 314.

[122] V.H. [De La Court], *Consideratien en Exempelen*, 246–8.

[123] V.H. [De La Court], *Consideratien en Exempelen*, 248–9, 252; Kossmann, *Political Thought*, 180.

that everyone seeks his own welfare, and strives for that, it follows necessarily that the voices of all together, decisions by majority vote, embody "het beste van 't gemeen" [the welfare of the whole].[124] With office holders and magistrates chosen "yearly," by majority vote, candidates (despite privately favoring their personal interest like everyone else) find themselves boxed into serving their fellow citizens "with all care and courtesy." Accordingly, the "democratic or popular form of government" does not thrust unnecessary wars and taxation on the people like monarchies and aristocratic republics (and England more than most).[125] The brothers' antipathy to ancient Roman bellicosity and all wars of expansion was one more striking contrast between their new brand of republicanism and Harrington's and Sidney's gentry republicanism with its unwelcome Spartan leanings.[126]

That all other forms of government are inherently likelier to initiate and prolong wars than democratic republics became a characteristic feature of the new Spinozist sect. Republics are uniformly preferable to monarchies, held Van Leenhof, because they avoid war except where the state's security and basic interests are at stake, while monarchs habitually embark on war for glory, dominance, and aggrandizement. Van Leenhof followed Spinoza not least in holding that the ancient Israelites became hugely more afflicted with burdens, wars, and devastation of war after ill-advisedly opting for monarchy than they had been previously, under the Hebrew republic: when the biblical kings gained sovereignty over Israel, wars were no longer fought, as before, for peace and freedom but for glory—"non amplius, ut antea, pro pace et libertate, sed pro gloria"—entailing a massive trampling on the collective interest. All Israelite kings, except one, initiated damaging wars, the sole exception, Scripture recounts, being Solomon (equally eulogized by Spinoza and Van Leenhof) "cujus virtus, sapientia scilicet, melius in pace quam in bello constare poterat" [whose virtue, wisdom of course, could be better demonstrated in peace than war].[127]

2.5. REVISING THE "POCOCK THESIS" ON REPUBLICANISM

Since society's well-being is best assured by promoting security, tranquility, and peace, the collective interest was linked by the *cercle* to the conditions under which the human individual most thrives and finds happiness. The essential purpose of political society being to provide safety, protection, order, and heightened opportunities for co-operation for all, and bring "a thousand advantages and services" to every individual, laws need crafting that serve that end but also guarantee the "same security and advantages for all."[128] Throughout its two centuries from the 1650s down to the 1848 revolutions, Radical Enlightenment, unlike socialism later, focused

[124] V.H. [De La Court], *Consideratien en Exempelen*, 253; Scott, "Classical Republicanism," 69–71.
[125] V.H. [De La Court], *Consideratien en Exempelen*, 254–5, 282; Stern, *Orangism*, 109, 112.
[126] Weststeijn, *Commercial Republicanism*, 165, 218–19.
[127] Spinoza, *Opera* iii. 196–7.
[128] Van Leenhof, *De Prediker*, 50, 228; Israel, "Spinoza, King Solomon," 313.

primarily on the individual not in isolation, like the ancient Stoics and Epicureans, but in broad social context, a drive for political reform focusing on the quest for a collective consciousness enhancing individual "happiness" and freedom, individual and collective quality of life to the highest degree attainable via enlightenment and education. His principal book, *Hemel op Aarden* (1703), Van Leenhof dedicates to "alle slag van menschen" [every sort of person], omitting no persons, sex, age-group, or other category from consideration because no one group enjoys a greater right to happiness in this world than others and because the peace, tranquility, and happiness of everyone crucially depends on the tranquility and security of the whole, so that enhancing each individual's scope for happiness is inseparably tied to promoting collective happiness and swaying as many as possible to support the democratic republic.[129] The political context is duty bound to confer equivalent benefits on everyone as everyone has equally pooled his or her individual will in the collective will of the whole, and is equally motivated by nature to seek happiness and strive to avoid sadness.

Yet, while the democratic republic is always "absolutelijk de beste" [absolutely the best] form of state,[130] all types of government have their particular weaknesses and dangers with the democratic republic no exception. The De La Courts' democratic theory hinges on the idea that in a properly ordered society, the "laws must be so drawn up that all the citizens, seeking their own advantage and to avoid disadvantage, respect the general well-being."[131] But their own social psychology taught that individual drives and passions usually outweigh the individual's rational judgment.[132] They laid such stress on how self-centered monarchs and aristocrats deceive everyone aided by preachers that, like Van den Enden and Spinoza subsequently, they bequeathed a seeming contradiction that proved difficult to erase. The democratic republic they declared the best form of government for all, while at the same time the common people, being ruled by prejudice, "appearances," and passions, represent the principal threat menacing it. Democratic republicanism clearly confronted three perennial political foes according to the De La Courts—monarchy, aristocracy, and, thirdly, "het dumme graauw" [the stupid mob]. How then could locating sovereignty in the people be reconciled with their fundamental principle that reason is, and remains, the guiding principle and foundation of the democratic republic?

A happier society was their goal. The seventeenth century had proved an exceptionally violent, gloomy, dispiriting time for nearly all Europe. Among Pieter's closest associates at Leiden was the clandestine Catholic writer and translator Jean Nicolas de Parival (1605–69), who rendered parts of the De La Courts' *oeuvre* into French and shared many of Pieter's anti-clerical, republican views. Passionately lamenting the often man-made miseries and enormities of their age,[133] I.N.D.P. [Parival] tells his

[129] Israel, "Spinoza, King Solomon," 310, 313–14; Van Bunge, *From Stevin to Spinoza*, 137.
[130] V.H. [De La Court], *Consideratien en Exempelen*, 282.
[131] De La Court, *Politike Discoursen* i. 95. [132] De La Court, *Politike Discoursen* i. 105.
[133] I.N.D.P. [Jean Nicolas de Parival], *Le Vray l'Interet* [*sic*] *de la Hollande*, "au lecteur."

readers in the French preface to one of his De La Court renderings that he agrees with V.D.H. that the republic exists to serve the interests of the people, to benefit "tous les habitants, sans en exclure aucun" [all the inhabitants, without excluding any], as even the most wretched remain part of the republic's citizenry, but pointed out that this presents serious difficulties. If the Dutch Republic was indeed a gleaming exception where peace, stability, and prosperity reigned, an oasis of peace enjoyed by all its citizens amidst a sea of devastation and misery, these advantages, noted Parival in his earlier *Abrégé de l'Histoire de ce Siècle de fer* (1655), were almost completely lost during the Twelve Years' Truce when the people became so incited that theological ire and popular fury, stoked by the clergy, gained irresistible force, almost destroying the Republic.[134] The Republic's greatest vulnerability, then, and both the De La Courts and Spinoza adopted this principle, is that the common people understood little of the political and nothing of the theological issues involved, having no inkling when taught to yell that the Arminians were "traitors" that they were being "deceived." Duped by princes and churchmen combining to exploit their simplicity, the populace invariably vent their frustration in the wrong direction, fomenting division, uproar, and tumult.[135]

Thus, the "multitude" became the central theme, and difficulty, of Radical Enlightenment political theory: the people's good is the highest objective but the people possess no understanding, at least not under existing circumstances, as to what their interest is. The people possess every right to express their dissatisfaction; but doing so on the basis of ordinary, commonplace notions and prejudices spells disaster for everyone. Infuriated by high taxes caused by war and dynastic rivalries, the people of Naples revolted, in 1647, led by a simple fisherman, Masaniello; but failing to understand their situation, pitifully yelled "Vive le Roy, le Diable détruise le mauvais gouvernement" [Long live the King; the Devil destroy bad government].[136] No matter how detrimental to men are monarchy, aristocracy, and churchmen, the greatest threat to the democratic republic are the ill-informed and least educated: popular "superstition" and ignorance menace the stability and "happiness of the people" more than anything else, an idea that remained basic to the Radical Enlightenment throughout. The democratic republic's dependence on "reason" and emancipating men from "superstition" in the end makes the people the prime menace also to those who frame its goals, its "politieke reformateurs" [political reformers]—the radical enlighteners spreading the new secular gospel whom the least educated are constantly instructed by their preachers to revile as "atheists."[137]

The people remained a deeply worrying dilemma to Spinoza, the De La Courts, and the *cercle spinoziste*. Had not the events of 1618 and 1650 proven that in struggles between the States of Holland and the Orangist faction, with the latter having the support of the preachers, the common people mostly align with intolerance and theological ire, against their own interest? In 1672, when De Witt and the "True

[134] I.N. de Parival, *Abrégé*, 119–20; Stern, *Orangism*, 150.
[135] Parival, *Abrégé*, 121–2, 429–30.
[136] Parival, *Abrégé*, 431–2.
[137] De La Court, *Politike Discoursen* i. 2–5, 8; Stern, *Orangism*, 147–9.

Freedom" were overthrown by a successful Orangist coup mounted by the young William III and his faction, Orangism was again backed by unruly mobs demanding vengeance on their supposedly "ungodly" leaders. Leading republicans among the regents were then ruthlessly purged from the States and city governments. Like Spinoza afterwards, both Pieter and, at least on his deathbed, Johan realized that nothing harms society more than a deeply divided potentially unruly state: all three, by the late 1660s, had become acutely aware of the vast difference between regular consultative, constitutionally regulated, meetings of the people's chosen representatives where "moderate" well-meaning and responsible people do the talking and passionate, spontaneous, irregular popular gatherings of crowds where "angry, highly emotional, or very ignorant, persons" deliver the speeches and decide what happens.[138]

According to the *cercle*, men must eventually learn the true causes of the prevailing general ignorance about reality and how things occur, the clergy's false pretensions must be exposed, the machinations of royal and princely propaganda uncovered.[139] In a democracy, making decisions contrary to the common interest occurs continually but only through ignorance and prejudice and these barriers, they maintained, can ultimately be overcome by public instruction and education. Indeed, nothing proved more characteristic of Radical Enlightenment as a tradition of intellectual opposition spanning two centuries than claiming the people's susceptibility to priestcraft, to the wiles of kings and nobles, and courtly pomp, can be conquered, albeit only slowly and with great difficulty, by changing how men think.[140] That was the essence; but of necessity it was a long-term strategy. One reason for the noticeable retreat from Johan's more forthright democratism, characteristic of Pieter de La Court's early works, including his 1661 reworking of the 1660 *Consideratien*, the new version appearing under the title *Consideratien van staat, ofte Politijke Weegschaal*,[141] was the challenge posed to all the Dutch radicals by the failure of English republicanism. The 1660 Restoration and the triumph of Charles II was widely considered proof in Holland, as elsewhere, that republicanism does not work, though it was also a brutal challenge demonstrating the need for a more powerful—but, at the same time, more cautious—theoretical formulation of democratic republicanism.[142]

Democracy offers no easy way to prevent unruly gatherings, and the hopes vested in re-educating the people, and weaning them from superstition and veneration for princes, could easily be viewed more as wishful thinking than the hard realism the De La Courts and Spinoza prided themselves on imbibing from Machiavelli and Hobbes. The French Revolution and rise of Robespierre and the Montagne would demonstrate further that democratic republicanism's exponents, starting with the Brothers De La

[138] V.H. [De La Court], *Consideratien en Exempelen*, 282–4.

[139] V.H. [De La Court], *Consideratien en Exempelen*, 259.

[140] V.H. [De La Court], *Consideratien en Exempelen*, 258–9; [De La Court], *Aanwijsing der heilsame politique gronden*, 9.

[141] Weststeijn, *Radikale Republiek*, 41–2.

[142] Helmers, *Royalist Republic*, 264.

Court and the *cercle spinoziste*, despite being vividly aware of the threat, had still underestimated the menace posed by intolerant, militant authoritarian populism, the kind all too readily turned against intellectuals, dissidents, and religious minorities, no less than political leaders vying with princes and churchmen.

Spinoza and the Amsterdam circle, unlike seventeenth-century English republicans and Locke, focused on how best to promote the collective "common good" as Spinoza calls it in his last work, the *Tractatus Politicus* (1676–7), when this is defined in exclusively worldly terms, on the basis of a moral theory rooted in the principle of equality and equal justice for all. Classical example, owning land, and possessing arms and a military bearing were all wholly irrelevant to the urban, mercantile republicanism of the Brothers De La Court, Van den Enden, Koerbagh, Meyer, and Van Leenhof no less than Spinoza—even while these remained central to the gentry republicanism of Harrington and Sidney. Indeed, English republicanism and its gentry attitudes—Pieter had lived for a time in England and knew English—were an integral part of what Dutch republican writers consciously criticized and rejected. The democratic republican format urged by "Spinozists" was a system that, contrary to Hobbes, leaves the natural freedom of the individual as intact as representative government can secure, and, contrary to Locke, eschews all contract and conditional transfer of power, indeed transfers to the sovereign, whether crown or legislature, unlike Locke, only absolutely.

By 1662, seven or more editions of the two distinct versions of the *Consideratien* had already appeared, and the De La Courts' ideas, as Van den Enden remarks, had diffused widely in the Netherlands and beyond. Inspired at least in part by them—though he also criticized them for not being inclusive enough in their concept of democracy—Van den Enden enthusiastically responded to their call for democratic republicanism.[143] Their common quest, as Van den Enden expressed it, was to "inquire, how in a collection of people the common best shall be most surely and safely pursued, promoted, and freed from, and protected against, all violence within and from outside so that at all times it will be able to grow and flourish toward an invincible well-being."[144] Here was the commencement of the secular, naturalist, as opposed to theological and Platonic, "general will" concept in modern political thought, a "general will" that achieves expression in assigned basic rights.[145] A regime will be the more stable and secure, held Van den Enden, Spinoza, and later followers like Van Leenhof, the more the private interests and concerns of those who govern are constrained and laws are framed and enforced for the benefit of all impartially and even-handedly. The more government is exercised for the "common good" in the *cercle spinoziste*'s strictly anti-religious sense, the less the people need to be coerced and the more they will respect their government. The more based on the "common good", the sturdier the republic becomes. "Everyone is by nature free,"

[143] Weststeijn, *Radikale Republiek*, 42, 45, 245–6.
[144] Van den Enden, *Free Political Propositions*, 148–9; Israel, "Dutch Golden Age Politics," 51–2.
[145] Miquieu, *Spinoza, Locke*, 478, 494–8, 502–7.

reiterated Van Leenhof later, "and prefers to be ruled by rational benevolence than compulsion."[146] In this sense, every regime, monarchy, aristocracy, and democracy, should be considered more or less democratic, with nearly all falling deplorably short.

Van den Enden sounds distinctly more optimistic that the "general well-being and common best" can indeed be advanced by enlightening the common people than does Spinoza. While "one people is better disposed to it, from nature or other circumstances, than another, I still take it that all of them (except the Hottentots at the Cape of Good Hope, if what is written about them, that they are more like an unconscious mass of flesh than humans, is true) can and also must be conducted to their common best by reason, without deceit."[147] Where Van den Enden developed theories of education, and Meyer and the Brothers Koerbagh published "books to educate the people," Spinoza, it has been argued "did nothing comparable."[148] But this is best explained as a difference of strategy. Van den Enden's expulsion from Holland and execution in Paris, and Adriaen Koerbagh's early death in prison, can only have confirmed Spinoza's notion that an overly bold activism, provocatively running schools on unacceptably new lines, propagating forbidden ideas in the vernacular, and organizing revolutionary conspiracies, was more likely to prove self-defeating than a more cautious strategy. Popular zeal for Orangism soon wrecked prospects for a more democratic system in the Netherlands, indeed gravely undermined and destabilized the "True Freedom." Following their overthrow by the Orangists in 1672, the De Witt brothers were caught by the mob in the streets of The Hague and literally torn in pieces, an atrocity that utterly horrified Spinoza but also strengthened his and his circle's conviction that the common people possess hardly any understanding of their own interest. Enlightening society must proceed more systematically but also more cautiously, slowly and securely, behind the scenes.

Aware that any direct challenge to the status quo will quickly be crushed, Spinoza opted for the clandestine approach, and the long haul. The lesson of the 1640s English Revolution, for Spinoza, was that if you let the people take the revolutionary initiative the only result is abject failure, replacing the old with "a new king" (Cromwell) under another name.[149] The one method of enlightenment that might eventually succeed was that presented to his mind by the experiences of his own family and other crypto-Jews facing the Inquisition in Spain and Portugal, a strategy pursued over centuries: forge a forbidden hidden underground of the enlightened like-minded creating networks that quietly and cautiously spread the message by clandestine means, cultivating chosen potential sympathizers unseen by vigilant as well as oppressive authorities. Clandestine networks might one day grow to the point of becoming formidable enough to undermine the grip of tyrannical monarchs, nobles, churches, and ordinary

[146] Van Leenhof, *Het Leven*, 168.
[147] Van den Enden, *Free Political Propositions*, 155; Schnepf, "Enlightened Radicals," 95–6.
[148] Schnepf, "Enlightened Radicals", 96–7, 102.
[149] Spinoza, *Theological-Political Treatise*, 235–7; Israel, *Radical Enlightenment*, 167.

thinking all lumped together—as indeed they did. Beating the Inquisitors allied to the ordinary requires immense patience, caution, and discretion.

Unlike the ideology of the Montagne in the French Revolution during 1793–4, Dutch Golden Age democratic republicanism did not and could not, appeal directly to "the people;" for in the eyes of the De La Courts, Van den Enden, the Koerbaghs, and Spinoza ordinary folk were the essence of the problem, not the solution. Radical Enlightenment was democratic in the sense of seeking to promote the collective "common good" on the basis of representative democracy but it was also, from the outset, vigorously anti-populist in the sense of fiercely contemptuous of popular ideas. When a theory of democratic representative government first emerged as a major plank of political theory in Britain in the revolutionary era, and then after 1815, with the democratization of the philosophic radicalism of Bentham and James Mill, much the same argument was heard as one encountered earlier among the Dutch *cercle spinoziste*: the pursuit of the "general happiness" in society can be pursued by democratic political means not because each individual seeks the general interest—each seeks only his own interest, and mostly from ignorance—but because such a democratic framework broadens and organizes the collision of individual interests in the direction of the greatest good; but only—leading advocates again still added the old proviso—if a certain educational level and degree of literacy is reached first.[150]

Yet "the people" were central to the Spinozist understanding of the purpose and benefits of republican forms of government. This was the first seed of the distinction so vital to the late Enlightenment (and also Hegel) between "the people" as a generalized democratic concept and the revolutionary crowds or *sans-culottes* viewed negatively, as in Naples in 1647 or at The Hague in 1672, as dangerously misguided spontaneous pressure-groups, the unruly multitude. The people were the reason why the *cercle spinoziste* developed a technique of subversion, using bookshops and the printing-press, that operated neither from top down nor from bottom up, but rather in clandestine fashion, sideways, horizontally, via the networks of like-minded dissidents that they created and which evolved into the Radical Enlightenment.

It has been suggested that Locke provides a sturdier principle of justified resistance than does Spinoza because Spinoza, like Hobbes, supposedly transfers the entire "natural right" of men to the sovereign with the forming of the state. But this is a major misconception. Spinoza accepts that no one has the right to disobey or resist the law, whether the laws are good or bad, so that in this sense the individual does transfer his natural right to the sovereign and cannot challenge the transfer. The very idea that there are illicit or illegal laws appears wholly self-contradictory, makes no sense in Spinoza's system. But the "natural right" of all is restored whenever the power of the multitude does successfully challenge or overthrow the sovereign, as the people broke the power of Philip II in the northern Netherlands, and that of Charles I in England. Natural right has no moral standing in Spinoza and basically amounts to

[150] Burston, *James Mill*, 203–5.

"might is right." If the multitude can overthrow the tyrant that happens whether the subsequent outcome is good or bad. Meanwhile, part of the individual's "natural right," contends Spinoza, the power to think independently, write and criticize, and discuss in groups, cannot be transferred to the sovereign and always remains intact however hard oppressive regimes try to censure thought and speech. Consequently, Spinoza's strategy of resistance, through philosophizing, discussion, and forming private groups with the ultimate aim of elevating and steering the multitude, actually provides a more democratic and less violent, if less direct, path for resistance than Locke's justified armed resistance which must always be entrusted to those prominent in rank. Spinoza insists, in contrast to Hobbes, that his aim is to protect and conserve as much of the individual's "natural right" and freedom as is possible and that this is the essence, as he (and Van den Enden) understood it, of the "common good" of society as a whole. Whenever the "multitude," as in medieval Aragon or in sixteenth-century Holland, successfully deters or strikes back at despots, it gains Spinoza's applause.

A glowing inspiration for Tindal, Mandeville, Radicati, and other republicans, in England and elsewhere, in the early eighteenth century, the United Provinces no longer served as an uplifting, enviable model by Montesquieu's time, due to economic decline and loss of power and prestige during the 1730s and 1740s, when the "decline of Holland" first became internationally evident.[151] If less fossilized and obviously an oligarchic tyranny in 1748, when Montesquieu's *L'Esprit des Loix* was published, than Venice or Genoa, the Dutch Republic, not least owing to the 1747 Orangist coup which greatly strengthened the powers of the Stadholder and formalized a court nobility at The Hague, lost its former capacity to inspire, becoming, rather, an example of the dangers and costs of an opulent commerce and of oligarchization.[152] But the tension between democratic and aristocratic republicanism did not lose its central relevance, even if the significance of this has been unfortunately glossed over and obscured by quirks of the historiography.

Pocock's and Skinner's thesis about the role of Machiavellian republicanism in English format as background to the American Revolution deservedly has been, and remains, fruitful and influential, but suffers from a particular defect that, once perceived, is hard to overlook: it largely misses the centrality of the split between democratic and aristocratic republicanism in the development of seventeenth- and eighteenth-century Western political thought. For the most part it has become accepted practice,[153] among political scientists and historians of political thought, and among early modern historians, to view the history of republicanism as a story with classical origins, an Italian Renaissance middle, and an Anglo-American culmination in the seventeenth and eighteenth centuries bearing fruit in a supposedly relatively homogenized American republicanism, leaving the basic rift between democratic and aristocratic republicanism the real heart of the early modern republican drama (not least in the United States as the German immigrant journalist Francis

[151] Israel, *Dutch Republic*, 1002–18, 1067–82. [152] Kapossy, "Neo-Roman Republicanism," 227–8.
[153] Villaverde Rico, *Ilusión republicana*, 85–132; Albertone, "Democratic Republicanism," 108, 112.

Grund emphasized during the 1830s and 1840s),[154] papered over and hidden from view.

Pocock's argument resembles "an express international and boat service," remarked one historian humorously, that "between departure from Florence, refueling in England, and arrival in America" made "relatively few stops." As he watched this remarkable engine thunder past from a disused railway siding (Amsterdam), Ernst Kossmann, "could not help wondering if the driver were not missing something." He chose this playful wording to raise an important objection that probably needs formulating more forcefully. For what emerged was a wrongly constructed intellectual process of republican transition clarifying which requires a more adamant *rompedor de mitos* [breaker of myths] to dispel and reconstruct. Acutely aware though he was, of the De La Courts' and Spinoza's distaste for Spartan values and military zeal, and the sharp contrast between Dutch commercial republicanism and the Pocock–Skinner Machiavellian "Atlantic model,"[155] Kossmann failed to bring out sufficiently the Dutch (and soon Swiss) focus on the fundamental incompatibility and clash of aristocratic with democratic republicanism and the highly unfortunate and misleading absence of this clash, forming the principal political thought arena of the post-1775 revolutionary era, from the standard pre-1775 English republican texts.

The "limits of the present-day historiography of republicanism," as they have been aptly called,[156] represent an enduring, formidable barrier to an accurate appraisal of the history of modern political thought, and require extensive modification of a kind impossible without deviating somewhat from the standard historiography's relentless Anglocentricity, that is without paying more attention to the Dutch, Swiss, and pre-1789 French republican contexts. Pocock was right that English republicanism dominated the development of an "Atlantic republican tradition" that proved formative for the American Revolution, but wrong in thinking this constituted "the Atlantic republican tradition" representing the main thrust of early modern republicanism in Europe and America more generally. Recognizing the error, and modifying the thesis along the lines here suggested means not just shifting some of the emphasis from Harrington and Sidney, but more generally lessening the old stress on "classical republicanism," for "classical republicanism" was very far from being at the root of the "democratic republicanism" that became the real basis of trans-Atlantic democratic modernity. In fact "classical republicanism" is broadly irrelevant to Radical Enlightenment. The effect of making this substitution is to remove much of the stress given to pre-Enlightenment traditions, and re-cast the republicanism of the American Revolution as actually a protracted and unresolved conflict of two opposed currents of post-1660 Western republicanism, the democratic and aristocratic, with only the latter having its philosophical origins in the English context.[157]

[154] Grund, *Aristocracy in America*, 18–21.
[155] Kossmann, *Political Thought*, 181, 187, 191; Scott, "Classical Republicanism," 62.
[156] Mijnhardt, "The Limits," 75–7.
[157] Israel, *Expanding Blaze*, 22–3, 51–2, 55, 75–9, 132–3, 186–7, 321–5.

3

From Radical Renaissance to Radical Enlightenment

3.1. REDISCOVERING LUCRETIUS

The existence of forbidden clandestine anti-religious intellectual networks spread across the Western Europe by no means began with the *cercle spinoziste* in the 1650s and 1660s. During the European Renaissance, the fifteenth and sixteenth centuries, philosophical anti-Christianity, atheism, and forms of anti-fideist skepticism and eclecticism preceded Radical Enlightenment as an underground intellectual culture furtively aspiring to establish alternative structures of belief, morality, authority, and education. Very slowly but perceptibly, the impact of these various corrosive and subversive currents gained momentum during the course of the fifteenth, sixteenth, and early seventeenth centuries.

Even though the teaching of Epicurus of Samos (341–270 BCE) and the great poem *De rerum natura* of Lucretius (99–55 BCE) were not in fact altogether forgotten during the Western Middle Ages,[1] no real debate about Epicureanism began until the mid-fifteenth century. Epicurean materialism, naturalism, and ethics were long sunk in oblivion until, during what today we call the Renaissance era, mankind's slow philosophical progress, as d'Holbach later expressed it, edging toward intellectual rationalization, resumed thanks to Lucretius, before accelerating, and proceeding more broadly and confidently, in the seventeenth century, with Hobbes, Spinoza, and Bayle.[2] Although during the early fifteenth century references to Lucretius and Epicureanism were few, the rediscovery of Lucretius' great poem, in 1417, by the humanist Gian Francesco Poggio Bracciolini (1380–1459), an eager searcher for ancient manuscripts in monastic libraries, led to ancient Epicureanism being revealed as a moral and philosophical system challenging the existing order *in toto*, opening a debate about the meaning of Epicurus' world-view and moral system that gradually developed into a wider intellectual ferment of profound significance for the

[1] Brown, *Return of Lucretius*, 1; Passannante, *Lucretian Renaissance*, 12, 36, 63–4; Fubini, *Humanism and Secularization*, 149.

[2] Paul-Henri Thiry d'Holbach, *Le Bon Sens*, in Paul-Henri Thiry d'Holbach, *Œuvres philosophiques*, ed. Jean-Pierre Jackson, iii (Paris, 2001), 339; Paganini, *Introduzione alle filosofie clandestine*, 149.

Renaissance era. Epicurean ideas circulated in Italy (as later in France), developing into a testing intellectual challenge to the existing moral order, belief, and tradition.

Poggio, though hostile to Epicureanism as such, was fascinated by features of the Epicurean system, and conscious of the attraction it exerted on some, as demonstrated by the dialogue *De voluptate* (1431) by Lorenzo Valla (1407–57), which Poggio condemned for boldly championing a philosophical sect "wiped away and almost buried centuries ago and condemned by all philosophers."[3] By the 1440s, the text had entered into a phase of creeping manuscript proliferation and, in 1473, for the first time was printed. Inconspicuous to begin with, this Epicurean underground showed signs of spreading and becoming more entrenched during the late fifteenth century, prompting the Church's ban on the Epicurean and Averroist philosophies for denying immortality of the soul and postulating the eternality of the world, in 1513.[4] From 1515, *De rerum natura* ceased to be printed in Italy.

In 1517, a papal synod condemned Lucretius as profoundly dangerous and contrary to Christian teaching and faith, and from then on, though not officially placed on the papal Index until 1559, the text's use was strictly forbidden in Florentine schools.[5] While an influential line of Renaissance studies, associated with Otto Kristeller, denies a revived Epicureanism, or any form of materialism or atheism, could in that era truly challenge the accepted beliefs of the age, and disagreement continues as to how far the "Lucreziani" officially condemned by the ecclesiastical establishment, from 1513, genuinely reflected the presence of Epicurean thought and Epicurean radicals in Italy,[6] most scholars today accept that a radical "naturalism" rejecting notions of creation, miracles, supernatural entities, and revelation did take root, an intellectual underground initially encountered chiefly in Florence. In his *Platonic Theology* composed between 1469 and 1474 and printed in 1482, Marsilio Ficino (1433–99), the greatest humanist thinker of the early Renaissance, vigorously assailed Lucretius, especially his and Epicurus' denial of immortality of the soul, to counter the local Florentine Epicurean "attack on religion." Ficino viewed his project as a continuing dialogue, an unfinished battle with contemporary "Lucretiani."[7]

What we might term Radical Renaissance slowly evolved into a varied mix of diverse strands featuring a radical skepticism and eclecticism, but with Neo-Epicureanism playing a central role,[8] into a tradition of *libertinage érudit* during the sixteenth and seventeenth centuries, that almost certainly reached back further than 1400 to the late medieval Averroist underground, even though Christian Averroists of the later Middle Ages mostly countenanced the possibility of "double truth," permitting Christian theology and philosophy seemingly to contradict each other,

[3] Fubini, *Humanism and Secularization*, 102–4, 149.

[4] Davidson, "Unbelief and Atheism," 61, 65; Brown, *Return of Lucretius*, 77–8; Mulsow and Schmitz, "Eigennutz, Statuserhaltung," 60–2.

[5] Palmer, *Reading Lucretius*, 36; Landon, "Bridging the Supposed Chasm," 67.

[6] Palmer, *Reading Lucretius*, 36–7.

[7] Brown, *Return of Lucretius*, pp. ix–xi, 5, 11; Palmer, *Reading Lucretius*, 37–8; Greenblatt, *The Swerve*, 221.

[8] McKenna, "Épicurisme et matérialisme," 77–9.

being unaware this was the opposite to what the medieval Andalusian philosopher Averroes [Ibn Rushd] (1126–98) himself actually taught. A forbidden "Aristotelian" philosophical freethinking underground, teaching the eternity of the world and mortality of the soul, already existed in the medieval Islamic and Jewish world, that was strengthened by Ibn Rushd, and subsequently seeped into Christendom and the Renaissance Jewish world. One prominent Renaissance Jewish writer steeped in crypto-Averroism, Elijah Delmedigo (1458–93), a Cretan active in Venice, Padua, and Florence during the 1480s, can be shown to have had a certain direct impact on Spinoza himself. During the age of conscious openness and philosophical and geographical enquiry characterizing the early Renaissance, a dose of Averroism assuredly featured too in the forbidden, clandestine philosophical mix.[9]

Condemnation of Lucretius' poem as a "lascivious and wicked work, in which every effort is used to demonstrate the mortality of the soul,"[10] stopped the text being taught and read in Florentine schools but only encouraged Lucretius' increasingly pervasive influence within the widening clandestine "Radical Renaissance" philosophical underground. Clandestine Neo-Epicureanism, especially Lucretius, may well have exerted a greater influence on Niccolò Machiavelli (1469–1527) and his political thought than historians usually acknowledge. The great Florentine rarely quotes Lucretius in his political works and never mentions him by name; yet we know he personally transcribed the whole of Lucretius' text as a young man, in 1497, whilst studying the various philosophical traditions intensively, imbibing a range of influences, at a time when it was particularly advisable to mask preoccupation with such ideas. For the fervent religious frenzy associated with the Florentine dictatorship (1494–8) of Girolamo Savonarola (1452–98), a popular movement as fierce and intolerant as it was short-lived, to which Machiavelli was deeply averse, was then at its height.[11] Struck by how a massively popular leader "acts in accord with the time and colours his deception [of the people] accordingly,"[12] Machiavelli's *filosofia*, his radical this-worldliness, "materialism," notion of how readily men are led by theological "lies," conception of *virtù*, and conception of Christianity as a force rooted in fear and superstition, all resonate with hints of Neo-Epicureanism.

The "acutissimus Machiavellus" [the very penetrating Machiavelli], as Spinoza calls him in his *Tractatus Politicus*,[13] did not, of course, unlike Epicurus, Lucretius, and Spinoza himself, dare explicitly deny divine Revelation and providence, immortality of the soul, miracles, or the principle of religious authority; however, there are numerous insinuations in his thought that can be read as oblique criticism of Christianity and the papacy, as exposing what he considered the negative effects of religious belief on politics and society.[14] The great Neapolitan thinker Giordano

[9] Leibniz, *Theodicy*, 80; Fraenkel, *Philosophical Religions*, 26–7, 208; Tamamy, *Averroes, Kant*, 74, 98, 203–4; on Delmedigo and Spinoza, see Fraenkel, "Reconsidering," 216, 223, 230.

[10] Brown, *Return of Lucretius*, 14.

[11] Brown, *Return of Lucretius*, 113–15; Greenblatt, *The Swerve*, 185; Morfino, *Temps de la multitude*, 203.

[12] Landon, "Bridging the Supposed Chasm," 65–7.

[13] Spinoza, *Tractatus Politicus*, 138.

[14] Davidson, "Unbelief and Atheism," 56, 67; Landon, "Bridging the Supposed Chasm," 76–8.

Bruno (1548–1600), an ex-friar, once a Dominican in Naples, ventured further still. A longstanding admirer of Epicurus and Lucretius, he was publicly burned alive in Rome, by the papacy, for "heresy," in 1600, among other things for asserting the eternity of the universe, denying Christ was God, and rejecting the Trinity along with Mary's virginity. His most "atheistic" text, according to his accusers, was *Spaccio della bestia trionfante* [Expulsion of the Triumphant Beast], a work written in England and published in 1584, much admired later by Toland, in which, careful readers perceived, "triumphant beast" referred not just to ignorance and vice but also to Christianity. All Bruno's works were comprehensively banned by the Inquisition in August 1603.[15]

Bruno's long-drawn-out trial and terrible end demonstrated how deeply entrenched but also how risky, during the Counter-Reformation era, steeping oneself in clandestine underground philosophy had become. Bruno is especially noteworthy among the Radical Enlightenment's precursors because he, more clearly than others, as Toland saw, conflated body and mind into a form of materialism tempered by Copernican astronomy and geared toward scientific discovery, rendering the universe infinite but also unitary based on minute units of being or monads, while also defending the principle of intellectual freedom. What separates him from the Radical Enlightenment is that all remains on a clandestine and also individual level—there is no element of republican activism or democracy in his philosophy, while his "materialism" possessed a distinctly vague ontological status not "unmixed with magical elements," being not yet consistently framed by a rigorous mathematical conception of reason, the principle of verifiability, later fundamental for the radicals.[16] Despite his clear affinities with Spinoza (and Toland), the differences remained substantial until the hermetic element was removed, most decisively by Spinoza, and the principle of mathematical-scientific verifiability more consistently applied.[17]

The *libertins érudits* of early seventeenth-century France, men such as Gabriel Naudé (1600–53) and, the most philosophical of them, François de la Mothe le Vayer (1588–1672), however, stood still further from Radical Enlightenment being less pantheist and Epicurean than Bruno, and more intensely skeptical, indeed verging on a fideism that was anti-intellectual, and hostile to science, more completely precluding any basis for a science-based naturalism than Neo-Epicureanism and Bruno's thought.[18] Like early French deism, the pre-1650 *libertinage érudit* cultivated in Richelieu's France by the circles of Naudé and La Mothe le Vayer, was either non-political or else inclined to royal absolutism and political conservatism.[19] Meanwhile, the strain of skepticism in sixteenth- and seventeenth-century clandestine philosophical literature remained a powerful current down to the early eighteenth century, as

[15] Paganini, *Introduzione alle filosofie clandestine*, 6; McClure, *Doubting the Divine*, 123–43.

[16] Wilson, *Epicureanism*, 97, 167; Dagron, *Toland et Leibniz*, 196–8; Passannante, *Lucretian Renaissance*, 10, 158; Gatti, *Ideas of Liberty*, 59–62.

[17] McClure, *Doubting the Divine*, 139–42.

[18] Wilson, "Epicureanism," 268; Popkin, *History of Scepticism*, 90–4.

[19] Mulsow, *Prekäres Wissen*, 122–3.

did eclecticism and, of course, deism.[20] Certainly, by the late seventeenth century, there existed several examples of clandestine manuscripts merging radical skepticism with quasi-Spinozistic rejection of miracles and conceptions of "God," and the immutability of the laws of nature; Renaissance skepticism too made its contribution to the rise of Radical Enlightenment.[21] But strictly viewed in themselves skepticism, eclecticism, *prisca theologia*, fideism, and deistic belief in a Creator God especially when accompanied by immortality of the soul were not, and could not be, precursors of the Radical Enlightenment to the extent Neo-Epicureanism was in several significant respects.

Lucretius no less than Spinoza inspired Goethe's uncompromising anti-Newtoniansm in the 1770s and 1780s. "Along with Spinoza, Lucretius," explains one scholar, "provided the eighteenth century with one of its main models for a rigorously naturalistic explanation of all reality, and the radical Enlightenment with one of its weapons against teleological and Providential views of nature and human history. Lucretius' arguments against established religion, immortality and the fear of death are continually cited by deists as well as radical *philosophes* with the line [. . .] 'tantum religio potuit suadere malorum' where Lucretius deplores the superstition that prompted the sacrifice of Iphigenia, becoming the line of Lucretius most resonant among both atheists and deists, not least Tindal, Radicati and Voltaire, and perhaps the most frequently quoted."[22] Only through embracing Lucretius and Spinoza, held Goethe and Lichtenberg, can human history be fully merged with natural history. This seemed incontrovertible to thinkers who were arguably "Lucretians" as much, or more, than "Spinozists"—in being unwilling to embrace the activist political and social agenda Spinoza invokes at the conclusion of the *Tractatus Theologico-Politicus* and in which the full-blown Radical Enlightenment came to invest so heavily. For Spinozists, unlike Epicureans, wherever popular notions and superstition are successfully combated, great benefits for society and a general re-ordering of our social, moral, and political universe in a more benevolent direction follow.

Lichtenberg typified the Neo-Epicurean syndrome of the late eighteenth century. A quietly radical thinker wholly committed to materialism, determinism, and rejection of religious authority, he plied his path, however, strictly only in private. Bold amid his thoughts and books, he remained withdrawn and timid in practice, refraining from all effort to realize radical principles in the intimidating world of power, religion, policing, and politics. But passively quiescent though such types were, the ideas of irreligious private "Epicureans" concealed from sight over the centuries nevertheless had a profound effect. More actively revolutionary spirits might dream of comprehensive change but even the most ambitious in thought could achieve

[20] Paganini, *Introduzione alle filosofie clandestine*, 88, 92–4; McKenna, "Épicurisme et matérialisme," 76; Gawlick, "Epikur bei den Deisten," 325.

[21] Paganini, "L'Apport des courants," 93–5, 99.

[22] Radicati, *Succinct History*, 21; Nisbet, "Lucretius in Eighteenth-Century Germany," 99–100; Gawlick, "Epikur bei den Deisten," 337–9; Baker, "Lucretius in the European Enlightenment," 285–6.

nothing in the real world until sufficient cracks in the wall of repression and conventional thinking appeared to afford some prospect of opening a breach, until favorable circumstances presented the opportunity. Until then, philosophers roundly repudiating the sway of the publicly accepted, despising conventional ways of viewing reality, either persevered inconspicuously underground or else sought truth for its own sake out in the open, which meant, as with Bruno and Vanini, doing so largely isolated from others, in a fashion requiring suicidal courage.

Meanwhile, strands of continuity linked ancient and Renaissance Epicureanism with Spinoza to a greater extent than to revived Stoicism, late medieval Jewish Averroism, or any other past tradition of thought. Spinoza shared the Epicureans' suspicion of the Stoics, rejecting what he considered the Stoics' "confused" and imaginary doctrine of the soul. Although Stoics conflated God and the world, like Epicurus and Lucretius, stressing God's immanence in nature, they retained divine providence and intention, teleology, final ends, enabling men to attune themselves to God through their souls.[23] These "errors," as Spinoza called them, especially concerning providence and the soul, originated in what he saw as Stoic failure to rely on clear inference from actual things perceived, causing them to be misled by their imagination.

Not the least of the strands connecting Epicureanism with Spinoza was their common rejection of asceticism and claim that joy, friendship, and happiness are the object of philosophy as well as of human life more broadly, and that the individual is happiest leading a thrifty life and eschewing ambition.[24] A reference in Spinoza's *Letters* together with his generally good grounding in Roman literature suggests he knew Lucretius, to whom he was probably introduced in the mid or later 1650s by Van den Enden, as he was to classical philosophy and literature more generally.[25] A possible echo of the *De rerum natura* occurs in the third paragraph of the preface to the *Tractatus Theologico-Politicus* (1670), where Spinoza writes "tantum timor homines insanire facit" [to so much madness fear drives men],[26] a passage invoking the vast damage caused by religious superstition: "fear is the root from which superstition is born, maintained and nourished."[27] For exactly in this connection Lucretius' wrote his similar-sounding "tantum religio potuit suadere malorum."[28] In any case, this passage of *De rerum natura* and possible echo in the *Tractatus* reflect a fervently shared doctrine—that of the appendix of Part 1 of

[23] K. H. E.de Jong, "Spinoza en de Stoa," *Mededelingen van wege het Spinozahuis v* (Leiden, 1939), 2, 5; Brooke, "How the Stoics became Atheists," 391.

[24] Mignini, "*Een Ligt schijnende*," 200; Tatián, *Spinoza: filosofía terrena*, 121.

[25] Klever, *Spinoza classicus*, 10–11; Tatián, *Spinoza: filosofía terrena*, 108.

[26] Spinoza, *Tractatus Theologico-Politicus*, 5; Samuel Shirley translates "tantum timor homines insanire facit" as "To such madness are men driven by their fears": see Spinoza, *Tractatus Theologico-Politicus* translated by S. Shirley (Leiden,1989), 50; in the edition used here, prepared by Michael Silverthorne and myself, it is rendered: "It is dread that makes men so irrational" (see p. 4).

[27] Spinoza, *Tractatus Theologico-Politicus*, 5.

[28] Lucretius, *De rerum natura*, book 1, line 101.

Spinoza's *Ethics* stressing the harm inflicted on mankind by commonly received beliefs rooted in fear.[29]

Prior to Spinoza, only the "Epicurei" altogether eliminated divine providence from our world scene or, as the seventeenth-century Dutch humanist scholar, Vossius, expressed it, "autem in totum tollebant providentiam divinam."[30] Peter Gay erred, though, in suggesting "the men of the Enlightenment found themselves completely at home in [Lucretius'] *De rerum natura*—that poetic rendering of the most unpoetic of philosophies, Epicureanism."[31] For if Voltaire possessed at least six editions and translations of Lucretius in his library, and privately scoffed at Cardinal Polignac's *Anti-Lucretius*,[32] for him, with his providential deism, belief in fixity of species, fervour for Locke and Newton, and commitment to the idea that morality is divinely delivered, Lucretius was no friend, but a challenging, disturbing complication, philosophically and politically, no inspiration but a menace with respect to final ends and divine Providence that he felt driven to combat.[33] Without demolishing Lucretius, Voltaire could not counter the anti-deist critique of Diderot, d'Holbach, and the other eighteenth-century materialists.

If the Radical Enlightenment too viewed Lucretius as the vital bridge connecting ancient Greek materialism with the Renaissance, and Spinozism, where Diderot and d'Holbach applauded, Voltaire, in his last years, furiously demurred. Loudly invoking the same Memmius, the patron and friend to whom Lucretius addresses his great poem, in his *Lettres de Memmius à Ciceron* (1771), when replying to d'Holbach's *Systeme de la nature* (1770), Voltaire tellingly directs his attack simultaneously against Lucretius *and* Spinoza. By merging his two targets into one he underlined his argument that his Enlightenment combats only priests, and not priests and kings together, like his wrong-headed unnamed Radical Enlightenment adversaries, while also discreetly pointing to the partnership of Diderot and d'Holbach, his target behind the scenes. Voltaire had no difficulty with their offensive against religion and priestcraft, it was Diderot's, Raynal's, and d'Holbach's denouncing the alleged alliance of priests and kings, a strategy bound to mobilize all the world's courts and monarchs against the *philosophes*, that deeply alarmed him. The *philosophie moderne* proselytizing materialist atheism that he opposed, held Voltaire, threatened to wreck the *philosophes*' standing and (his) reputation where it counted most—at court in Berlin, Petersburg, and Versailles, and in aristocratic circles everywhere. Modern materialism's advance Voltaire deemed a catastrophe for the *philosophes*' future, though it would damage him less than the rest, he joked sourly, as he expected to die shortly and would soon discover who was right concerning the

[29] Akkerman, *Studies*, 33 n. 7; Klever, *Spinoza classicus*, 67 and Pina Totaro's notes in Spinoza, *Tractatus Theologico-Politicus*, ed. Pina Totaro (Naples, 2007), 501, 585–6, 621.

[30] G. J.Vossius, *De Theologia Gentili, et Physiologia Christiana sive De Origine ac Progressu Idolatriae* (new edn., 2 vols., Amsterdam, 1668), i. 38.

[31] Gay, *The Enlightenment: An Interpretation*, i, *The Rise of Modern Paganism*, 99; on this point see also Barbour, "Moral and Political Philosophy: Readings of Lucretius," 161–2.

[32] Haskell, "Religion and Enlightenment," 198.

[33] Pomeau, *Religion de Voltaire*, 290–1.

soul's composition and immortality—Plato or Spinoza, Saint Paul or Epictetus, Christianity or Confucianism.[34]

Closely coupling Spinozism with Epicurus and Lucretius was a central feature of Voltaire's late stance but, by the 1770s, also typified the stance of those, like Lichtenberg, the Göttingen scientist and *litterateur*, among the great prophets of self-emancipation of the *Aufklärung*, who, while pronouncing Lucretius and Spinoza the twin towering heroes of the human spirit, kept their rejection of the political and social status quo strictly private. While circumventing the Spinozists' scheme to transform society and politics, Goethe and Lichtenberg endorsed Spinoza's non-providential, evolutionary, and self-creating conception of reality, the stance Voltaire consistently, and in many writings from the late 1760s onwards, expressly repudiated. Even if, for those following Diderot and d'Holbach in opposing Voltaire's one-front war against priestcraft, Lucretius' philosophy was insufficient, *Spinosistes* at the time could readily agree with Lichtenberg that it was Spinoza who "den grössten Gedanken dachte der noch in eines Menschen Kopf gekomen ist" [thought the greatest (system of) thought that has yet entered a human head].[35]

Eighteenth-century French theological *antiphilosophie* too often viewed eighteenth-century philosophical atheism and materialism as a single philosophical tradition with a high level of inner cohesion reaching back to ancient times, albeit not to Stoicism (which retains divine Providence), and still less Platonism or Aristotle, but specifically Epicurus and Lucretius. To Counter-Enlightenment thinkers, no less than Voltaire and the radicals, the continuities of Epicureanism with Spinozism seemed manifest, reflected in biology as well as metaphysics. For Epicurus and Lucretius denied that a knowing benevolent God had designed men, animal, and plant species or directed Creation generally. Human, animal, and plant organs, it was axiomatic for Lucretius, cannot be explained as things designed to perform their functions. His poetry grounded a conception of naturalism abolishing all teleology wholly distinct from most schools of philosophy and during the Enlightenment one wholly incompatible with Newtonian physico-theology and "argument from design", as well as Locke, deism, and Rousseau, the entire moderate as well as the "religious" Enlightenment. Coupling the names of Lucretius and Spinoza thus seemingly made eminently good sense and became a stock feature of the culminating attacks on philosophical materialism in France and Germany during the 1770s and 1780s, before the Revolution. To Aimé-Henri Paulian, professor of physics and mathematics at Avignon, son of a Protestant minister and a convert to Catholicism, originally from Nîmes, author of *Le Véritable Système de la nature* (2 vols., Avignon, 1788), where he tries to refute d'Holbach's *Système de la nature* (1770) comprehensively, d'Holbachian materialism was essentially a recapitulation of ancient materialism.

[34] Voltaire to marquise Du Deffand, 21 Oct. 1770, in Voltaire, *Correspondence*, xxxvii. 40; Naville, *Paul Thiry D'Holbach*, 113.

[35] Lichtenberg, *Schriften und Briefe* i. 705.

The *Système* did contain some modern ingredients, Paulian recognized; it relied on views of biology only recently developed by Diderot. By conjoining science and social theory closely together, the *Système de la nature* (1770) capped all previous efforts to overthrow existing structures of authority, religion, and the state by maintaining that promoting men's worldly happiness is the sole valid criterion in evaluating the legitimacy of laws and government.[36] With this synthesis, the *Système*, held Paulian, distilled into one malignant concoction all that is most contrary to God, faith, piety, and morality encountered in "Diderot, Voltaire, Bayle, Spinoza, Hobbes, Epicurus and Lucretius."[37] Philosophic roots of great antiquity fed the entire process, a tradition based partly on ancient thought, especially Lucretius, and partly modern ideas, especially "the Jew Spinoza," "le premier impie," asserts Paulian, echoing Bayle, who dared openly present atheism "d'une manière systématique."[38] As for the anonymous authors of the *Système* and daughter texts it spurned, it was an outrage that these "Apôtres du mensonge," the book's authors, had not been arrested and severely punished.

3.2. EPICUREANISM VERSUS SPINOZISM

From the 1670s onwards, the close affinities between Lucretius and key elements of Spinozism were routinely commented on by observers. Fear and superstition moved men to believe in divine intention, Epicurus and Spinoza both agreed, but this harms mankind and morality, making men divide along religious lines, with every individual thinking up "from his own temperament," as Spinoza puts it, "different ways of worshipping God, so that God might love them above the rest, and direct the whole of Nature according to the needs of their blind desire and insatiable greed."[39] Men naturally assume nature does nothing in vain and that final ends characterize all that happens around us. Final ends explain men's way of viewing things and seemingly justify enforcing beliefs, dogmas, and divisions, helping organize power relations and allocation of rank, possessions, and wealth. Human misery, consequently, is universal but distributed unevenly, structured by dogmas of belief and notions of rank even though all the rival theologies are fed exclusively by ignorance, aided by religious authority, credulity, and fanaticism. Human betterment is achievable but only by defeating credulity and religious authority, a truly uphill task. The way to counter this evil, according to Epicureans, is to found a hidden proselytizing movement that draws individuals into "the Garden," a clandestine movement, creating a hidden underground—a clear affinity between Epicureanism and Radical Enlightenment, at

[36] Paulian, *Le Véritable Système* i, preface, pp. 1 and p. 179 and ii.162.
[37] Paulian, *Le Véritable Système* ii. 162, 271–84, 300, 325, 382.
[38] Paulian, *Le Véritable Système* i. 57–60, 263, 335 and ii. 149–50, 325–7.
[39] *The Collected Works of Spinoza* ed. and trans. Edwin Curley, vol. 1 (Princeton, 1985), 439–42.

least as the latter developed in its earlier stages, down to the 1770s.[40] In their respective ethical schemas, both Epicureanism and the underground culture of the *cercle spinoziste* placed a special emphasis on the importance and value of friendship. Here, then, was a cluster of affinities subsumed later by Diderot, d'Holbach, and Helvétius in what came to be called "la nouvelle philosophie," *la philosophie moderne*, or *philosophisme*, that segment of the Enlightenment that evolved into the ideological motor of the Brissotin "Revolution of reason" in 1789.

Yet, what was not common to Epicureanism and Radical Enlightenment was perhaps even more threatening to defenders of religion and the status quo. For no aspect of the new eighteenth-century materialism seemed more menacing to theologians and the conservative-minded, before 1789, than the promise resounding in d'Holbach's and Helvétius' mature works, and the notorious radical text the *Histoire philosophique* (1770), calling for rectification of what they alleged was mankind's unnecessary wretchedness and the distress of the poor.[41] Here, we encounter the greatest difference between Epicureanism, including Early Modern Neo-Epicureanism, and Radical Enlightenment: Epicureanism was unsuited to form the basis of a revolutionary subversive philosophy like Diderot's, d'Holbach's, and Raynal's aiming at overturning how society as a whole manages the most important issues, at challenging the existing social and political status quo, whereas Spinozism was so adapted. For Epicureans, what is principally wrong with society can be corrected by human effort but only discreetly, on a permanently unseen, inconspicuous, and tranquil individual or minority group basis. Their stance implied the possibility of a secluded, localized revolution changing how a few view the universe, enabling hidden groups to form that transform how these elect conduct their lives. But the scope of emancipation offered did not stretch far, scarcely reaching beyond the isolated small group or individual. Epicureanism thereby left the bulk of mankind to their delusions and their misery.

What was needed to ground a Radical Enlightenment nurturing a wider revolutionary impulse was a system equipped with a more combative political thought apparatus, more political and revolutionary in character, less willing to leave the delusions of the majority unchallenged, geared to society as a whole, offering a wider recompense to those whom the status quo render deprived and unhappy, and a more combatative stance toward official theologies and presiding philosophical systems. In his *Pantheisticon*, Toland equates his own "Pantheism with Spinozism," while countering Lipsius' reconciliation of Christianity with Stoicism, contending that authentic ancient Stoicism equated God with nature, removing all notion of divine providence as a benevolent guiding force.[42] Tolandists and "Spinozists" hence both resorted to underground methods, like the Epicureans, but aimed to work toward goals offering tangible prospects of amelioration to all. By 1770, their subversive

[40] Brown, "Politics and Society," 190–1; Springborg, "Hobbes and Epicurean Religion," 175–6.
[41] Polignac, *L'Anti-Lucrèce* i. 288.
[42] François, *Observations* ii. 157, 159; Leask, "Stoicism Unbound," 238.

activism, and promise to help the wretched, was starting to worry theologians, deists and conservative atheists alike.

The *Système de la nature* (1770) exerted a huge impact, acknowledged Voltaire, writing to Madame Du Deffand, in October 1770, chiefly due to its power to attract the socially aggrieved. Due to its ominous, beguiling promise, the *Histoire philosophique,* with its unmistakable revolutionary rumblings, resembled, in Voltaire's view, the bogus financial schemes of John Law (1673–1729), the Scottish adventurer whose grandiose project for issuing bank-notes in France had crashed sensationally in 1720, causing vast loss, despair, and scandal. The new political and social doctrine propagated by Diderot, d'Holbach, and Helvétius which Voltaire and even his atheist ally d'Alembert firmly rebuffed, promised much, including alleviation of the suffering and drudgery of the poor, which according to Diderot and d'Holbach is an avoidable consequence, the malignant outcome of ignorance, deception, fanaticism, imposture, priestcraft and vested interest preying on humanity at large, a poisonous mix concocted by theologians allied to kings and courtiers.

The affinities between Epicureanism and Spinozism, then, were striking; but equally there existed concrete differences between the Spinozist and Epicurean accounts of how and why "error" prevails in the world, and how to rectify the harm. Lucretius' explanation of why men trust in the supernatural power of the gods to direct human affairs, in Book Five of *De rerum natura* (lines 1160–1240), focuses squarely on the origin of belief in supernatural forces. But the cultural, social, and political circumstances of Lucretius' age differed vastly from those of Early Modern Europe. In the war-torn, divided Roman republic in which he dwelt, Lucretius needed to be particularly discreet concerning the possible political implications of an imported Greek philosophy that might attract the suspicion of the Roman Senate and authorities, as the philosophy of Epicurus indeed did. Due to its originally suspect, marginal status in Rome, Epicureanism, unlike other ancient Greek schools of thought, actually increased its emphasis on passivity, non-participation in the public political sphere, preaching withdrawal from mainstream society so as to safeguard its veiled "garden," a protected reserve for the hidden sect of adherents sharing convictions contradicting those of the multitude and living together in *amicitia*, a shuttered off harmony and friendship, forming the greatest divide between early modern Neo-Epicureanism and Spinozism.[43] Roman circumstances reinforced this tendency; in the sixteenth and seventeenth centuries so did Inquisition repression and the Counter-Reformation.

While both Epicureanism and Radical Enlightenment stress the ubiquity and power of "superstition," sharing a common detestation of tyranny, state militarism, and war,[44] superstition's ability to mobilize religious authority and dogma to control belief, restrict freedom of thought and expression, utilizing dogma, theology, inquisitions, indexes, church councils, and formal condemnations of heresy as instruments

[43] Brown, "Politics and Society," 179–80, 188–90, 196.
[44] Salem, "Peut-on définir les principes," 39–40.

of public condemnation and humiliation together with law, education, moral exhortation, and politics, and not least to dominate higher learning and restrict "freedom to philosophize," had, by Spinoza's time, vastly expanded its capabilities since ancient times. By 1650, "superstition" hence needed analyzing to a greater extent in terms of social and political thought than in Lucretius' day. New forms of persecution had directly impacted on Spinoza's own family and Jewish associates in Portugal and Spain. The persecuting fanaticism of the Inquisition and a Europe of pitiless confessional strife during the Wars of Religion were viewed by Spinoza as far more grotesque, more menacing deformities of humanity, morality, and good governance than Roman imperial administration and justice in Lucretius' time. The prevailing belief system of his day hindering the "happiness" of the individual and of society was now a far more powerful, larger, and more damaging apparatus than anything known in the ancient world. State power allied to what the ill-informed and uneducated think had become a more elaborate, organized, and institutionalized belief-control system than existed even in Renaissance Italy, an apparatus capable of penetrating and breaking up every private philosophical "garden" and crypto-religious network of the kind Spinoza's Sephardic parents and relatives cultivated underground in Portugal and France. Absolute monarchy joined to ecclesiastical sway, being now a system harder to escape from than formerly, had become a doctrinal colossus that it was no longer feasible simply to evade: it needed to be intellectually and practically massively assailed.

Spinoza's account of the hegemony of "error" and fear, and its rule over the empire of misery, became both broader than that of Epicureanism and more geared to confronting a wider range of intrusive and intolerant forms of credulity and dogmatism. Rejecting final ends and teleology consequently came to be more directly associated with Spinoza than Epicureanism or Averroism, as did active pursuit of toleration, freedom of thought and expression, and promotion of the "common good," and hence more connected too to political activism and reform, resisting tyranny and calling for a secular state. In his *Ethics*, Spinoza not only affirms unequivocally that "Nature has no end set before it and that all final causes are nothing but human fictions," but that this crucial dimension of truth remains altogether hidden from most men. If he too presents "truth" as a masked, underground tradition, a reality long clearly grasped since ancient times but only by "very few," the price we pay for our fears and for delusion preventing men's grasping the truth—the fact that most are disposed to reject and violently suppress the truth—had escalated so that its destructive effects amounted to a more complex, more structured oppressiveness and general blindness than prevailed in ancient times, a universal disposition toward unreasoning irrationality damaging humanity more broadly, encouraging war and inequality, hindering science and education, promoting fanaticism, strife, ecclesiastical authority, and tyranny—oppressive power relations constantly feeding greed and thirst for power, drives equally hegemonic in ancient times, but now possessing a much wider reach so that the institutions sanctioned by religious authority constrained men everywhere and could no longer be contemplated with equanimity.

Neither Lucretius nor Spinoza supposed they could persuade more than a handful of their fellow men. But Lucretius follows Epicurus in deriving all human ills directly or indirectly from fear, especially fear of death, focusing markedly more than Spinoza on urging men that death is not to be feared and that plagues such as crime, lust, and envy are all aggravated by fear of death. This tendency lent primacy to the quest for security and stability, helping affix Epicurean political thought, as with Hobbes, to the need for a strong, stable state and an indifferent, pragmatic attitude regarding the specifics of law and governance, besides quietly segregating the Epicurean moral order, their "garden," from the public sphere rather than fusing moral striving with political commitment and participation.[45] Where Epicurus and Lucretius identify anxiety and apprehension as the prime source of superstition, Spinoza's *Ethics* provides a broader psychological analysis of credulity, hatred, and prejudice, leaving more scope, especially for the natural drive for ascendancy and advantage over others. Epicureanism in short was subversive intellectually and religiously but not socially or politically. Where both Epicureanism and Spinozism reject religious authority, the first did so inconspicuously without publicly challenging and offending the priesthood, whereas the latter sought ways to grow more vocal, effective, and public, striving to challenge and topple rather than simply disregard religious authority.

Hence, one does not find in Lucretius the same preoccupation with discrediting censorship, heresy-hunting, and forms of despotism utilizing belief as their justification as one encounters in Holland's great philosopher.[46] Spinoza's thought represents a more urgent, explicit spur to intellectual subversion allied to political engagement than did the other strains of clandestine philosophy flourishing in the seventeenth century, so that only Spinoza's framework was fit to serve as a durable, operative basis for a Radical Enlightenment not just wholly rejecting religious authority but also promoting equality of the right to be "happy" by forging political rights and democratic republicanism. Epicureanism could not fulfill such a function, and here Hobbes stood decidedly closer to Epicureanism than Spinoza or the radical underground.[47] Shaftesbury, no Spinozist but a radical enlightener in tendency, considered Hobbes a firm adherent of Epicureanism, expressing hostility to both Hobbes and Epicureanism especially because of their passive, evasive view of civil society and the public sphere.[48] Admittedly, the principle that *homo homini lupus* [man is a wolf to man] is less prominent and fundamental in Early Modern Epicureanism generally than in Hobbes while the idea of natural sociability as the foundation of the state is less alien to Epicureans; but the Epicurean strand interested in establishing a strong state to act

[45] Paganini, "Hobbes, Gassendi," 113, 123–4; Brown, "Politics and Society," 179–80, 190, 196; Springborg, "Hobbes and Epicurean Religion," 163–4, 175, 184.

[46] Lucretius, *De rerum natura* iii. 40–93, 830–977.

[47] Paganini, "Hobbes, Gassendi," 113, 121, 124; Springborg, "Hobbes and Epicurean Religion," 208–13.

[48] Tortarolo, "Epicurus and Diderot," 386; Israel, "Leo Strauss," 24–6.

as a shield protecting the community still implies a political sphere that is "radically individualist," withdrawn and non-participatory.[49] By contrast, Spinoza's political thought stems from the idea that general amelioration is possible and actually occurs, via a gradual rise from despotic forms of society based on fear, to forms allowing freedoms closer to the "state of nature," climbing, where the difficulties are surmounted, towards the republic based on "freedom," a process that involves gradually replacing "fear" as the prime instrument of statecraft with "reason" and the "common will": "for a free people is led more by hope than fear, while a subjugated people is led more by fear than by hope; the former seeks to engage in living, the latter simply to avoid death."[50]

Meanwhile, there were also other major, fundamental differences between Epicureanism and Spinozism as underground sects rendering the latter again more active and better equipped to promote Radical Enlightenment. It is striking that Neo-Epicureanism, like ancient Greek Epicureanism itself, was far less concerned with analyzing and studying nature than Spinozism: it lacked the commitment to scientific enquiry and mathematical precision paramount for Spinoza and his circle. Here especially Bayle's judgment seems valid: "I believe," he wrote in his *Dictionnaire*, "that Spinoza is the first to reduce atheism to a system, and turn it into a body of doctrine, tied together and integrated according to the maxim of the geometers: but beyond that his system is not new," he added, pointing to the similarity of Spinoza's doctrine that "God and the world are just one being" to the Stoic conception.[51] Epicurus' philosophy, after all, stressed pursuit of *ataraxia*, that state of inner tranquility and detachment assiduously cultivated by both Epicureans and Stoics which they conceived as stemming from the philosophical life and, in the Epicurean case, from abandoning delusions about the gods. In Lucretius it is not gradual collective progress in knowledge and science, nor pursuit of mathematics, nor any cumulative development or new criteria impacting on the world of culture and philosophy, that expands their grasp of basic truth for the enlightened few withdrawing from society to their sheltered retreat in "the Garden." What ameliorates our world for the Epicurean philosophical outcast elite, favoring a successful quest for individual happiness for some, was the philosophical breakthrough of one particular genius, Epicurus, who with unparalleled insight, and unmatched grasp, all at once revealed everything necessary to men.[52] Remaining above active politics, "Lucretianism" was later one source, notes Charles Taylor, of Nietszchean and other nineteenth-century atheistic "immanent Counter-Enlightenment" reacting to the collapse of the 1848 revolutions by becoming wholly disillusioned with society and its prospects.[53]

The centrality of *ataraxia* in Epicureanism meant this tradition ultimately lacked any sense of mankind possessing the power to "shape and fashion our world, natural

[49] Paganini, "Hobbes, Gassendi," 124, 126–7, 131–3.
[50] Spinoza, *Tractatus Politicus*, 62–3; Williams, "Spinoza and the General Will," 118–19.
[51] Bayle's judgment circulated widely during the eighteenth century, being quoted verbatim for example by Jean-Baptiste Gaultier, in 1746, in his book against Pope's *Essay on Man*, Gaultier, *Le Poëme de Pope*, 100.
[52] Lucretius, *De rerum natura* i. 62–79.
[53] Taylor, *A Secular Age*, 599.

and social," as it has been put, "actuated by some drive to human beneficence."[54] Epicurean "friendship," unlike Spinoza's, was strictly non-political. Real "Lucretians" during the early modern age, observed Taylor, were figures like St. Evremond, Fontenelle, or Temple, standing aside from both religious faith *and* awareness of any need to forge a beneficent new order. The Anglo-Irish Epicurean Sir William Temple (1628–99) perfectly combined early modern drawing on Epicurean moral philosophy with turning his back on research into the sciences.[55] La Mettrie, despite zeal for science and his eschewing the atomism of the Epicureans, also belongs to the category of non-radical Neo-Epicureanism rather than Radical Enlightenment. While his anti-Stoic moral philosophy and view of the individual in relation to society were Epicurean, the reason he is excluded from the Radical Enlightenment's ranks is his political passivity and conservatism. His Epicurean outlook exuded a static quality, offering no prospect or project of reform promising to ameliorate the world or make it a more hopeful place than it was in his day for most. Rather, La Mettrie's writings reflect Epicurean aversion to active involvement in the public sphere, recommending those adhering to his recipe for individual happiness to avoid accepting public offices and functions as far as possible. While striving to influence those who rule, he had no wish for a broader impact via the press.[56] He broke with Epicurean tradition only in one respect—his impatience with ruses and stratagems to conceal one's philosophical as distinct from political views. He was unEpicurean in urging fellow *philosophes* to revolt against the prevailing system philosophically, urging true *philosophes* to be free in their actions as well as their writings: "montrons y la fière indépendance d'un républicain" [let's show there the fierce independence of a republican].[57] But this was his sole genuinely "republican" propensity.

3.3. METHODS OF SUBVERSION

Leibniz, writing around 1680, concluded that "there are two sects of naturalists fashionable today that have their sources in antiquity," one "revives the opinions of Epicurus;" the other, which he contrasted with the Neo-Epicureans, proclaimed "a mechanical necessity to all things" and a single "God who "has neither understanding nor will." This rival modern philosophical stream he calls "nouveaux stoïciens" [new Stoics], according a prominent place in it to "Spinoza's views," though, like Bayle (who likewise linked Spinoza to the Stoics rather than the Epicureans), he also noted a significant link between *Spinozisme* and Averroism."[58] The differences between the two kinds of "naturalists" Leibniz considered essentially philosophical; yet, arguably

[54] Taylor, *A Secular Age*, 27, 248, 267–8.
[55] Wilson, *Epicureanism*, 34–5; Springborg, "Hobbes and Epicurean Religion," 176.
[56] Thomson, *La Mettrie et l'épicurisme*, 373, 378.
[57] Thomson, *La Mettrie et l'épicurisme*, 380.
[58] Leibniz, *Philosophical Essays*, 281–2; Laerke, *Leibniz lecteur*, 977.

more fundamental than any metaphysical differences was that neither ancient Epicureanism, nor Averroism, nor Italian Renaissance Neo-Epicureanism, nor Italian Renaissance political thought generally, fought to transform the political and social system. Here, his first stream, Radical Renaissance, differed fundamentally from his second, which was in fact Radical Enlightenment.

It was typical of Averroism and Neo-Epicureanism to adopt a quiescent political stance and eschew confrontation. Humanists of the pre-Machiavelli era, it has been importantly remarked, mostly "avoided confrontations over constitutional forms, preferring to direct their reforming energies at improving the virtues of the ruling class. Their reforms were generally about governors, not governments." The one notable exception, the sole Italian Renaissance political writer before Machiavelli to contrast republicanism and monarchy at any length, expressing far-reaching dissatisfaction with the prevailing political order, was Aurelio Lippo Brandolini (1454?–1497), whose book of political theory he submitted to Lorenzo de Medici in manuscript around 1494, but never published. No writer, correctly observed Brandolini, ancient or modern, had, prior to himself, attempted to study and compare republics and monarchies systematically. But he was the exception that proves the rule: the Renaissance saw no way to combine republicanism with general amelioration: his unique study led him to reject republicanism in favor of monarchy, claiming autocrats and monarchs protect the poor and weak more effectively than oligarchic republics like Florence.[59]

That profound divergences between Renaissance anti-Christian philosophical underground and post-1650 Radical Enlightenment were no less crucial historically than the affinities is well illustrated by the *Theophrastus Redivivus*, among the most important mid-seventeenth-century Western clandestine manuscripts. Dating from 1659 and composed seemingly in France, this clandestine text offered a non-Spinozist Neo-Epicurean subversive outlook, rooted in a pre-Spinozist "philosophical atheism" encompassing some elements of the subsequent radical tradition but not others.[60] It comprehensively denies all the dogmas of religious faith, a process it terms "throwing off the yoke" [*iugum excutere*].[61] Although the ancient philosopher Theophrastus (*c.*371–*c.*287 BCE), Aristotle's successor as the director of the Peripatetic School in Athens, was not actually an Epicurean, he influenced Epicurus' views on cosmology and was a professed atheist.[62] What is radical, or rather "radical Aristotelian," in *Theophrastus Redivivus* is the strict separation of morality from belief in God and religion, elimination of divine providence, and rejection of all religious authority. But the text is patently Epicurean rather than quasi-Spinozist in evincing little interest in scientific enquiry (unlike the real Theophrastus) so that here the text is *not* radical. Where the real Theophrastus was a true Aristotelian scientific researcher, seeking the causes of natural phenomena by examining evidence, Epicurus and Lucretius—despite being strict naturalists, viewing thunder, lightning, meteors, and

[59] Brandolini, *Republics and Kingdoms*, 4–5; and Hankins's introduction to this text.

[60] Paganini, *Introduzione alle Filosofie clandestine*, 8–24; Palmer, *Reading Lucretius*, 42.

[61] Paganini, "Early Modern Atheism," 28.

[62] Taub, "Cosmology and Meterology," 121–2.

all potentially frightening natural phenomena as of purely natural origin, and not the work of gods, and providing lists of all possible plausible natural explanations—showed scant interest in discovering which plausible explanation actually pertained in each case. What mattered to them was alleviating anxiety and fear, not investigating the specific cause.[63] Unlike the real Theophrastus and the *cercle, Theophrastus Redevivus* adheres to a skeptical approach not just to belief and theology but also scholarship and science. Far from presenting nature's laws as revealed by science as our chief verifying principle, *Theophrastus Redevivus*, like William Temple afterwards, sought to downplay, even discredit pursuit of science and "philosophy."[64]

Very different was Spinoza's approach to "superstition." Especially where religious authorities claim "the judgments of the gods" far surpass men's ability to understand, for him they are propagating an elaborate political as well as metaphysical deception. This kind of delusion alone, held Spinoza, "would have caused the truth to be hidden from the human race for all eternity, if mathematics, which is concerned not with ends, but only with essences and properties of figures, had not revealed to men another standard of truth. And beside mathematics, we can assign other causes also [. . .] that were able to bring it about that men—but very few in relation to the whole human race—would perceive these common prejudices and be led to the true knowledge of things."[65] Enhanced awareness of the power of science and philosophical reason based on science was therefore among the factors in the later seventeenth century causing the *cercle spinoziste* to part ways with Lucretius and the Epicureans in key respects: science made it more plausible that the web of deception could be successfully punctured and discredited as "deception." But for Spinozists, unlike Epicureans, there were also urgent political and social considerations affecting the well-being of all requiring the prevailing general body of delusion to be more actively challenged, even if challenging and attempting to undermine imposture, something Epicureans purposely avoided, entailed great individual risk and could proceed only surreptitiously.

Theophrastus Redivivus locates the roots of the "true" moral order exclusively in Nature and society, like both Neo-Epicureans and the post-1650 Radical Enlightenment, pronouncing its social values superior to those proclaimed by religion. Here it is radical. But while insisting injustice reigns on Earth, and using this as an argument against belief in God and religion, and identifying religion as essentially a political instrument, *Theophrastus Redivivus* remains chiefly concerned with the individual's moral development and attitudes without explicitly denouncing the prevailing social hierarchy and political order.[66] Here, *Theophrastus* diverges in the usual manner of the Neo-Epicureans from the radical tendency initiated by the *cercle spinoziste*. It manifests nothing like the confrontational republican and reformist tendencies of

[63] Taub, "Cosmology and Meterology," 122–4.

[64] Gengoux, *Un athéisme philosophique*, i. 135–55; McKenna, "Épicurisme et matérialisme," 77–8.

[65] *The Collected Works of Spinoza* ed. and trans. by E. Curley, i. 441–2.

[66] Paganini, *Introduzione alle filosofie clandestine*, 10–12, 14; Gengoux, *Un athéisme philosophique* ii. 767–9.

Johan and Pieter de La Court, Van den Enden, Bouwmeester, Meyer, and Koerbagh, or even, to take a later example, Helvétius, reflecting rather the political passivity of Hobbes. The *Theophrastus*'s Averroism and Neo-Epicureanism hence neither challenged absolute monarchy's pretensions nor demanded liberty of expression and toleration. Nor, like Averroism and Neo-Epicureanism more generally, does it evoke any real sense of philosophical "reason" being an advancing, cumulative, and investigative force attacking and eventually gaining the power to vanquish "superstition," ignorance, and tyranny.[67] Liberty of thought and expression do not figure as political goals to be doggedly fought for.

Admittedly, by the seventeenth century early modern Epicureanism had evolved from what has been dubbed fifteenth-century *individualethischen Epikureanismus* [individual-ethical Epicureanism] to an Epicureanism more orientated toward society and with a political face, culminating in Hobbes.[68] But even there, post-Renaissance Early Modern Epicurean tradition with a political dimension constituted a partly concealed and wholly quiescent underground, expressing dissatisfaction with the existing social and political order but adjusting to it via Epicurean quiescence, and the double truth affectations the latter gave rise to. During the age of Greek philosophy and ever since, noted d'Holbach, there existed some enlightened men but such was the tyranny of ignorance, credulity, and superstition that until recently even the "most enlightened" could communicate only in veiled terms and "by a cowardly complaisance" often shamefully mixed "lies with truth."[69] "Universal prejudices" [*les préjugés universels*] so powerfully repressed even the finest minds, over such long spans of time, that many despaired utterly of humanity; very few could or were bold enough full-frontally to combat "les erreurs universelles." Far from being overly optimistic, as twentieth-century critics often allege, pre-1775 Enlightenment radical thinkers often tended to be tentative, even pessimistic about the future—like Voltaire, Frederick, and Hume, on the moderate side.

"What does it matter," if a thinker "has particularly daring ideas", asks one critic of the Radical Enlightenment thesis, where "he or she shrinks from implementing them in practice?"[70] Such a view ignores both the ploys and ruses resorted to, to oppose religious, political, and cultural repression, and the deeply intimidating realities coercing those who, like Toland's early eighteenth-century "pantheists," saw little alternative but to embrace two doctrines, a private one concerned with truth and an external, public one necessary to placate the authorities and the people, the one "internal, or philosophical, altogether conformable to the nature of things and therefore to the truth itself," the other concealing a "truth" so unpalatable and intolerable to most people that it had to remain under wraps.[71] This kind of double-speak, apparent

[67] Gengoux, *Un athéisme philosophique* i. 69–84, 104, 112; Paganini, "Hobbes, Gassendi," 136–7. Paganini, *Filosofie clandestine*, 149-67; Paganini, "Enlightenment before the Enlightenment," 186–7.

[68] Mulsow and Schmitz, "Eigennutz, Statuserhaltung," 53–4.

[69] D'Holbach, *Le Bon Sens*, 316; Mori, *L'Ateismo*, 30.

[70] Chisick, "Interpreting the Enlightenment," 50.

[71] Toland, *Pantheisticon*, 96, 110.

conformity to the ordinary, decried by d'Holbach, was profoundly characteristic of the Epicurean tradition and arguably also Hobbes.[72] Those making no effort to undermine the system formed the underground networks fomenting quiescent, hidden abjuration of the sort inspired by Epicurus and Lucretius. But by the early eighteenth century, these rubbed shoulders with more conspiratorial, active elements often in the same clandestine philosophical "societies," those of the sort Toland conjures up in his *Pantheisticon* (1720), where he designates his thought "pantheism," equating it with Spinozism as a "secret philosophy" but one diffused only among minuscule numbers of adherents exceptionally fervent for truth and to philosophize, adherents gathering solely in "their private assemblies and societies where they feast together," hidden from the great mass of mankind which they see as sunk in ignorance, and from the "scrupulously pious," from the "lying and superstitious fictions of men" and "spirit-haunted enthusiasts," above all sheltering together from the fury and violence of the "superstitious" multitude.

The atheistic philosophical undercurrent, abjuring belief in a divine providence governing men's affairs, prevalent in Italy and France before 1660, was hence predominantly Neo-Epicurean and avoided challenging the prevailing status quo. Pure Neo-Epicureanism pervaded the clandestine philosophical literature until the 1650s, but rapidly receded during the late seventeenth century as the systems of Spinoza and his following became the clandestine intelligentsia's prime tools and reference points. It was the *cercle spinoziste* in Holland that first forged a republican system systematically undermining religious authority and all teleology, openly challenging these belief systems in society and linking underground philosophy to reformist activism and propagating democratic values. Removing miracles and divine providence more comprehensively than Hobbes, Spinoza and his circle stepped beyond ancient and early modern Epicureanism and Averroism by tying the assault on religious authority to political engagement, a combination largely lacking previously, and adopting Galileo's decidedly non-Epicurean mathematical science as the overriding, exclusive verifying criterion, the sole authority for deciding what is and is not "true," while fusing this with Descartes's revolutionary principle that all physical reality is governed by a single coherent set of physical laws.

These crucial structural innovations explain why "Spinoza" and "Spinozism" became more central to the subsequent development of the Radical Enlightenment than Epicurus or Lucretius and why Spinoza's name retained a stronger negative resonance and rhetorical menace in Enlightenment controversies than those of Epicurus, Lucretius, Averroes, Machiavelli, Bruno, Vanini, Hobbes, Sidney, or Bayle, from the 1660s right through to the 1848 revolutions, after which Radical Enlightenment was displaced by socialism as chief opponent of the prevailing status quo. Sporadically, "Epicurus" and "Hobbes" played a not dissimilar rhetorical role as generalized foes of God and man in anti-radical polemics, but only Spinoza and "Spinozism" were

[72] Springborg, "Hobbes and Epicurean Religion," 208–13.

routinely invoked by theologians and moderate enlighteners to fight irreligious foes of the existing order everywhere and continually down to the mid- nineteenth century.

Radical Enlightenment defined as rejection of religious authority and the supernatural linked to rejection of the existing order and promoting an active democratizing republicanism was not especially optimistic regarding the future. Its adherents mostly eschewed short-term perspectives when expounding expectations for human amelioration. Conscious of the density of the "darkness" everywhere gripping humanity since Lucretius' time, the coterie of Diderot and d'Holbach, unlike Marxism, in the next century, issued no guarantee of general salvation or amelioration even for the long term. It is this that kept the Epicurean dimension relevant. Thus, Lichtenberg deemed Spinozism the only correct philosophy but was by no means sanguine about the chances of elevating philosophy, morality, and higher learning sufficiently to ameliorate humanity. Rather, he viewed the much trumpeted "improvements" and supposedly enhanced "humanity" of his own time, including "unser Eifer in der Philosophie aufzuklären" [our zeal in philosophy to enlighten] as mostly superficial and ineffective, more empty bombast and fashion than reality. Yet Lichtenberg and the radical-minded of the late eighteenth century also saw something ultimately compelling in what they perceived as their legacy to the future—higher, truer, and more reliable criteria of verification than those of the churches, universities, and academies—a body of philosophy with its methodology rooted in science. Despite the slowness of our steps, concludes d'Holbach at the close of his *Système social* (1773), the evidence proves there is a gradual progress of "la raison humaine." If several ancient and modern philosophers found the courage to embrace reason and experience alone to frame their thought, rejecting all theology, breaking free from "des chaines de la superstition," it was Leucippus, Democritus, Epicurus, and Strato who first lifted the veil of prejudice and delivered "la philosophie des entraves théologiques." Unfortunately for mankind their systems were too devoid of mystery, wonders, and marvels, "trop simples, trops sensibles," for most men so that everything long remained befogged in the "conjectures fabuleuses des Platons, des Socrates, des Zenons."[73]

Lucretius built a bridge between Hellenistic Greece and the eighteenth century that materially contributed to overturning the premises of the *ancien régime*. But basic human rights, sweeping social reformism, and the ideology of the "Revolution of reason" derived predominantly from the Radical Enlightenment or what the French Revolution (prior to Robespierre and the Terror) called simply "la philosophie moderne." A close linkage between materialism and radical political and social reformism needed to be introduced before Radical Enlightenment could gather momentum; for only a materialism negating divine providence and final ends tied to an activist democratic republicanism could account for how and why human society had become fundamentally disordered, wrongly organized to the disadvantage of the majority, while claiming this could be rectified, converted into a state of

[73] d'Holbach, *Système social*, 551–64.

happiness for all, by philosophy. If Voltaire considered the materialist philosophies of Diderot, d'Holbach, and Helvétius just weaker echoes of Spinoza's system, they had, he also recognized, become distinctly more dangerous. "La nouvelle philosophie," if not defeated quickly, he assured Grimm in a letter intended also for the eyes of d'Alembert and Condorcet, of October 1770, would result in "une révolution horrible."[74]

Epicureanism then both contributed to and remained a recognizable later strand of the Radical Enlightenment. By injecting a strenuous reformist activism, including crypto-republican thought, Helvétius, despite his moral philosophy being steeped in Epicureanism, later became one of the main sources of the radical tradition.[75] He was not alone in doing so. "I too am an Epicurian," Thomas Jefferson, a self-declared "materialist," assured William Short (1759–1849), in October 1819.[76] A fellow Virginian who had been his deputy and protégé while Jefferson served as United States ambassador in Paris in the late 1780s. In his reply, Short too professed to being an "Epicurean." Having participated along with Jefferson and Lafayette in the Paris discussions preceding the drafting of the French "Declaration of Rights of Man and the Citizen" in 1789, unlike Jefferson Short adhered consistently to radical views also with respect to race, being a founding member of the *Amis des Noirs*, the abolitionist society Condorcet, Lafayette, and Brissot established to advance the cause of black emancipation, in 1788. An ardent admirer of Franklin and Lafayette, whom Jefferson later designated his "adoptive son," Short continued sending Jefferson detailed private reports about French developments after the latter left France, returning to America, in October 1789. Jefferson and Short both deemed individual and collective "happiness" to be what Jefferson called "the aim of life."

In line with ancient Epicurean tradition, Jefferson and Short rejected Revelation, miracles, atonement and *supernaturalia* of every sort, viewing what happens on earth not as the will of any god but the outcome of human deed and effort. However, neither was genuinely Epicurean in viewing the American and French Revolutions as closely linked parallel movements that constituted the great leap forward in the history of humanity (until Robespierre and the Montagne in their view utterly perverted the French Revolution). To them, the Montagnard phase of the French Revolution (1793–4), with its intolerance and rampant populism, was a catastrophe, popular madness rooted in deception of the kind Machiavelli condemned in the Savonarola movement. Short was quicker than Jefferson to condemn Robespierre and the Terror. But Jefferson too, like all enlighteners, eventually denounced Montagnard intolerance, authoritarianism, and populism emphatically. The Montagnards Short loathed for their suppression of free expression and freedom of the press, and

[74] Voltaire to Grimm, 10 Oct. 1770, in Voltaire, *Correspondance* xxxvii. 112; Pecharroman, *Morals, Man, and Nature in the Enlightenment*, 20 n.; Robinet, *Dom Deschamps*, 79.

[75] Force, "Helvétius as an Epicurean," 107–9.

[76] Jefferson to Short, Monticello, 31 Oct. 1819, in Thomas Jefferson, *Writings*, 1430; Scherr, "Thomas Jefferson," 92.

systematic violation of all human rights; to him, as to Jefferson, they were the Revolution's great betrayers. The concepts that powered America's and France's great leap forward, the two self-declared Virginian "Epicureans" concurred, sprang from a particular tendency in Western thought and sub-category of the Enlightenment—a stream of thought combining rejection of religious authority in the public sphere with a passionate democratizing republicanism and stress on universal and equal human rights. Where the two Virginians were more strictly Epicurean was in their joint need to conceal certain features from the public, their unwillingness to carry their common anti-Scripturalism into the open.

Jefferson possessed at least five different Latin editions of Lucretius' great poem, *De rerum natura*,[77] and, like Spinoza, professed to have little time for Plato's "foggy conceptions" and "mysticisms incomprehensible to the human mind." He harshly rebuked the Stoics and Cicero, despite some good things in their thought, especially disapproving of "their calumnies of Epicurus and misrepresentations of his doctrines." For Epicurus' moral and metaphysical doctrines, however, America's leading radical voice evinced only praise. "I consider the genuine (not the imputed) doctrines of Epicurus as containing everything rational in moral philosophy which Greece and Rome have left us."[78] For the revolutionary age beginning in America in the 1770s, infused with its Jeffersonian quest for universal and equal human rights, there was indeed much in Epicurus' teaching of lasting value. Unlike Aristotelian virtue and other pre-Hellenistic ethical systems, Epicurus' moral doctrine not only focused on the worldly self, and pursuit of happiness in this world, but was universalist, strictly separate from the city state and all religion, offering salvation on an equal basis to all, something seemingly capable of being shared by everyone, including slaves, women, and barbarians.[79] Recognizing this, Jefferson joined a line of French High Enlightenment thought reaching back to Diderot, d'Holbach, and beyond.

By undermining accepted notions of reality, encouraging views of "God" as identical to nature, demolishing the sphere of the supernatural, and basing its moral philosophy on the principle of "happiness" to which all are equally entitled, Radical Renaissance contributed to the heterodox ferment from which *spinozisme* as a broad tendency in Western thought followed by late Enlightenment egalitarian ideas-and eventually universal and equal rights, arose.[80] By helping corrode privilege, "divine right of kings," and ecclesiastical sanction of the existing social order, Radical Renaissance extensively contributed to the groundwork from which democratic republicanism was to emerge. But at the same time, Radical Renaissance lacked several key ingredients indispensable for what has been called the *rupture irrévocable* that so fundamentally transformed Western thought in, and from, the 1660s and 1670s.[81]

[77] Greenblatt, *The Swerve*, 262–3.

[78] Jefferson to Short, Monticello, 31 Oct. 1819, in Thomas Jefferson, *Writings*, 1430–3.

[79] Salem, "Peut-on définir les principes," 30–2.

[80] Paganni, "L'Apport des courants," 99; Wilson, "Epicureanism," 280; Force, "Helvétius as an Epicurean," 105, 116–17.

[81] McKenna, "Épicurisme et matérialisme," 75.

4

From Radical Reformation to the *cercle spinoziste*

4.1. SOCINUS AND THE SOCINIAN REVOLT

Tying rejection of religious authority to democratizing republicanism in the wake of the Dutch *cercle spinoziste* undoubtedly provided a broader, more lasting platform for social, moral, and ecclesiastical reformism and activism (beside scientific enquiry) than existed earlier. It was better adapted for making and following through a comprehensive challenge to the existing order than the earlier clandestine mix, or any of the separate strands, of Epicureanism, skepticism, eclecticism, and the Averroist, Machiavellian, and Hobbesian legacies, or any of these trajectories separately. For in 1650, the biggest insufficiency, or gap, in the armory of the philosophical–theological underground viewed as a challenge to the existing order was still the absence of a clear strategy for comprehensively discrediting and replacing the dogmas, arms of authority, and hierarchies of the past. Radical Reformation rejecting Luther and Calvin as well as Catholicism did offer a counter-culture of group subversion undermining the prevailing religious, social, and legal status quo in a way that Neo-Epicureanism did not: a vigorous activism, the appeal to equality, and a recipe for attacking the sway of kings, hierarchy, and priests. Even so, Radical Reformation of itself proved an inadequate basis for comprehensive change especially through being unable to free the moral order, law, education, and politics from theology, theocracy, and divine providence.

During the sixteenth century but continuing patchily in part of Europe through the seventeenth, Radical Reformation, the second main foundation upon which the Radical Enlightenment eventually arose, exerted a wide impact. Radical Reformation constituted, just like Radical Renaissance, a generally decried and despised fringe movement; but it proved much more willing and able to engage in direct confrontation with the existing order owing to its deep religious motivation. Attempting to translate belief into action and concrete outcomes, its advanced strains of "Protestantism" broadened and supplemented the impact of Radical Renaissance by greatly intensifying and expanding rejection of the dogmas of the medieval church along with the entire dogmatic Christology, Trinitarian theology, and intolerance of Luther,

Calvin, and the Anglicans, in this way becoming (and remaining) a key source of inspiration and reinforcement for many. Radical Reformation included the Socinians, a resilient, defiant fringe where the Christian ideal stood almost entirely free and independent of institutionalized ecclesiastical authority; it demanded a "divine truth" based on "reason," universal peace and tolerance, offering a sturdy Christian utopianism rejecting ecclesiastical sway that was essentially social and moral. Those segments of the Radical Reformation that championed "rational faith," virtually excluding mysteries and largely disregarding miracles, proved ready to fight every obstruction, demanding a broad irenicism while remaining inimical to all "priestcraft" and persecution.

Certainly aversion to the authoritarianism and political conservatism of Luther and Calvin (as well as the Catholic Church), reaction greatly encouraged by the Radical Reformation, did lead directly here and there to such intense disillusionment with religious tradition generally as to generate a renewed, intensified turn to Epicureanism and rejection of a knowing creator God, revelation, and immortality of the soul. In the case of the Lyon-based humanist Bonaventure des Periers (*c.*1510–*c.*1543), author of the atheistic text *Cymbalum mundi* (1537), for example, and the "sect of atheists" reportedly thriving in Lyon, in France, in the 1530s and 1540s, we see a direct convergence and overlapping of Radical Reformation and Radical Renaissance.[1] Even so, only a more systematic and philosophical call to refashion the world by altogether repudiating religious authority such as the Radical Enlightenment offered, eliminating the supernatural, ending theocracy, secularizing government, extending toleration, and basing social and legal principles on a secular morality of reciprocity and equality, grounded in the politics of republican democracy, could fully meet the necessary conditions for a comprehensive emancipation simultaneously freeing men from religious authority and monarchy tied to aristocracy and social hierarchy.

Although the term "Radical Reformation" itself was first coined only in 1957, by Harvard theologian and Unitarian minister George Huntson Williams (1914–2000), the topic as such emerged earlier and has been studied at least since the 1890s. A general picture began to appear with the first trans-Atlantic history of the Anti-Trinitarian tradition, *Socinianism and its Antecedents* (1952), and other studies, by another Unitarian minister, Earl Morse Wilbur (1866–1956). Williams followed up with his comprehensive survey of the topic, *The Radical Reformation* (1962), depicting the category as a mix of diverse fringe groups and free spirits, including the circle of Thomas Müntzer (1489–1525) and the revolutionary Anabaptists who, summoning the poor to rise and redistribute the wealth of the rich, seized Münster in 1534–5, groups already earlier prominent in Marxist accounts of the sixteenth century, and renowned among those interested in the origins of the modern revolutionary traditions. But Müntzer's and the armed Anabaptists' militancy, a fervent millenarianism calling on artisans and peasantry for support, and adhering to Trinitarian doctrine,

[1] Mothu, "Athéisme et politique," 99–104, 116–18; for a helpful discussion of the range and significance of the term "Radical Reformation," see Eire, *Reformations*, 250–64.

placed no particular value on "reason" or tolerance and assumed an ideological hue very different from that of the irenicists and proclaimers of peace and toleration who converged with the Radical Renaissance as contributors to and precursors of the Radical Enlightenment.

Müntzer and the Münsterites were revolutionaries certainly and avid for action. But they were also theocratic in orientation, given to violence and harshly dogmatic in their reasoning. Unlike the Radical Reformation relevant to our story, Müntzer's creed stemmed from a shrilly aggressive, darkly chiliastic, fanatical theology proclaiming the immanent end of the world, strongly sanctioning immediate mass action and force, including extermination of recalcitrant princes. Where, for Marxist historians, Müntzer, mobilizing the poor for armed action, splendidly expressed the quintessential "Radical Reformation,"[2] the strands that contributed to Radical Enlightenment had little connection with the revolutionary Münsterites, but comprised rather reformers defying the main churches on the basis of a "Christian truth" focused on reason and irenicism, a call to moral transformation and rejection of violence, intolerance, and persecution shunning all mystical as well as militant millenarianism. The trend relevant here is that of those shunning mysteries, militancy, and intolerance, the trend of rationalist Socinianism and, in the English-speaking world, Unitarianism, with other Christian "free spirits" joining the Socinians in exalting irenicism and "reason."

Once the early Anabaptist groups' armed militant chiliasts, the Münsterites and Batenburgers, were suppressed by the authorities in the borderlands between Germany and the Netherlands, in the years 1535–8, Anabaptist currents in the Low Countries, Switzerland, and Germany developed mainly as pacifist clandestine communities using preaching, books, and concealed networks to stabilize their movement.[3] Not only Catholics and Lutherans but also the first Calvinist missionaries were appalled to find so many independent-minded Anabaptists, David-Jorists, insurgent ex-Lutherans, Nicodemists, "Libertines," and confirmed indifferentists, refusing to conform to any of the main confessions.[4] The religious crisis gripping the fringe groups in the Netherlands, parts of Germany, Poland, and Switzerland during the 1530s and 1540s was shaped by the need to escape official persecution on the one side, and internal doctrinal fragmentation on the other. Many adherents of the fringe movements were in fact eventually absorbed and "confessionalized" into the "Lutheran," "Zwinglian," or Calvinist blocs, and eventually brought under ecclesiastical authority, direction by the clergy, and the sway of dogma. But some Anabaptist and "Libertine" groups stalwartly resisted all catechisms, elaborate doctrine, and clergy, continuing to reject ecclesiastical supervision of any kind, pushing Luther's maxim "sola Scriptura" to extremes he would not have dreamt of.

[2] MacCulloch, *The Reformation*, 161, 552; Biagioni, *Radical Reformation*, 10–12.

[3] Mellink, *Wederdopers*, 334–6; Duke, *Reformation and Revolt*, 85–9; Israel, *Dutch Republic*, 87–95.

[4] Braekman, *Guy de Brès*, 95–6; Kaplan, *Calvinists and Libertines*, 96–9.

Sebastian Franck (1499–*c*.1543), who joined the Reform party in 1525 and began propagating his vision of an invisible spiritual universal church from 1530, was among the earliest and purest examples of the type. He abhorred all theological polemics and rejected heresy-hunting.[5] Guided by the "light" emanating from the Holy Ghost, he rejected all dogmatic theology, fomenting a religiosity based on a free conscience, heresies that resulted in his expulsion from Strasbourg, in 1531, and Ulm in 1539. Since Radical Reformation leaders were everywhere unremittingly persecuted and oppressed, their plight encouraged clandestinity and elaborate evasion, an ethos of belonging to a small group needing to conceal its attachment to "the truth" from a persecuting majority whose views were deemed false, a disposition with clear affinities with the later Radical Enlightenment.[6] Nicodemism, ultra-irenicism, spiritualism, and indifferentism became typical responses to the Reformation's characteristic harshness, violence, and severity. All these factors contributed to the making of a clandestine underground that eventually helped generate the post-1650 philosophical Radical Enlightenment. The "Radical Reformation" that chiefly contributed, in other words, was the anti-Trinitarian irenicist, egalitarian, humanistic-rationalistic Reformation of the "spiritualists" and Socinians, but in a less specific sense all the thwarted theological offshoots of Luther's revolt against Rome contributed something through their undeviating repudiation of the medieval church, their generating a vast post-1520 spectrum of religious fragmentation, and growing plethora of theological offshoots advancing passionately-held rival, incompatible truth claims, their creating a perfect cacophony of conflicting theologies that, in a dialectical sense, by way of reaction, also contributed to the growth of underground opposition to the prevailing status quo by encouraging the rise of late sixteenth-century skepticism, Neo-Epicureanism, and deism. The strife and divisions themselves inevitably caused a strongly negative reaction in the minds of some,[7] a revulsion stimulated by the very harshness of the unremitting rival theological claims.

The fate of the Aragonese heretic Michael Servetus (1509–53) perfectly illustrates the relentless pressures driving both the theological fragmentation and the intense antipathy it generated. A remarkable theologian, polymath, and physician of partly Jewish descent who studied at the universities of Toulouse, Paris, and Montpellier, disillusioned by the pomp and pretensions of Charles V's court and Catholic hierarchy, Servetus joined a Reformation group in Basel in 1530, putting out a series of publications, beginning with his *De Trinitate Erroribus* [On the Errors of the Trinity], in 1531. Servetus showed there is no biblical basis for the doctrine of the Trinity, a notion originating, he came to believe, in Greek philosophy. Yet, while abjuring the Orthodox, Catholic, and Protestant notion of the Trinity, and later considered by Polish and Transylvanian Unitarians the first founder of their movement, he never fully rejected Christ's divinity but devised an intermediate position as a "subordinationist," that is, he demoted Christ to the lesser status of a divine logos. Denounced

[5] Roeck, *Morgen der Welt*, 787; Vasoli, "Contestazione," 28–9.
[6] Weeks, *Valentin Weigel*, 4, 20.
[7] Gregory, *The Unintended Reformation*, 368–73; Weeks, *Valentin Weigel*, 183, 186–8.

chiefly for his Anti-Trinitarianism and rejecting infant baptism, Servetus also denied Predestination and much else. His heresies were not of a sort likely to be dealt with lightly: Catholic and Protestant leaders both moved to crush what Calvin termed his "execrable blasphemies." Condemned in June 1553 by the Catholic authorities at Vienne, two months later Servetus was apprehended for "heresy" in Geneva. On 27 October 1553, he was burnt alive there at the stake, his execution endorsed afterwards by the Lutheran establishment at Wittenberg as well as the Catholic and Calvinist authorities, and the influential theologian, Heinrich Bullinger (1504–75), who had successfully stabilized the Reformation at Zurich following Zwingli's death, the author of Protestantism's best-known guide to marriage.[8] Banned, Servetus' major work, *Christianismi Restitutio* [Restitution of Christianity], became exceedingly rare.

Servetus' execution was sanctioned by all the main rival churches, but outraged the clandestine underground of so-called "libertine" independents and adversaries of theocratic power. Particularly appalled and disgusted were Bernardo Ochino (1487–1541), a Siennese estranged from Catholicism who fell foul of Calvin and, after being expelled for Anti-Trinitarian leanings and other heresies from Zurich in 1563, died a hounded outcast in Moravia; David Joris (*c.*1501–56), a Dutch ex-Anabaptist estranged from Menno besides Calvin and Luther who spent his last years at Basel as a "spiritualist" rejecting all external conformity; and Sebastian Castellio (1515–63), a Savoyard whom Calvin had brought to Geneva to head the municipal college and who became one of the established churches' most learned and resolute foes. For Castellio, Catholics and Protestants were equally remote from the truth; the true guide for mankind lies nowhere in theology or church doctrines but exclusively in following Christ's example. A humanist deeply influenced by Erasmus and Franck's "spiritualism," Castellio upheld freedom of conscience, vigorously discounted everything ecclesiastical from doctrine to hierarchy, and, not unlike Spinoza later, presented Christianity as essentially just justice and love; his *De Haeretecis, an sint persequendi* (1554) comprehensively abjured the very concept of "heresy," wholly denying the right of the Calvinist Church, or any church, to persecute.[9] No one more clearly represents the suppressed legacy of the Radical Reformation that later resurfaced in the seventeenth century and helped generate the Radical Enlightenment. All Castellio's writings, needless to say, were banned by Catholics and Protestants alike. Even so, something of his legacy lived on and, fostered in particular by Dirk Volckertsz. Coornhert (1522–90), established lasting roots, especially in the Low Countries.[10]

Hence, alongside the Reformation's unrelenting confessionalization process, pulling the great bulk of Europe's population into disciplined, increasingly closely

[8] MacCulloch, *The Reformation*, 244–5, 660; Weeks, "From Radical Reformation," 97–8.

[9] Biagioni, *Radical Reformation*, 30–1, 38; Roeck, *Morgen der Welt*, 841; Vasoli, "Contestazione," 30–1; Greminger, *Sebastian Castellio*, 18–19.

[10] See BL Tracts 2243/4 [Coornhert], *Opera Sebastiani Castellionis* [. . .] *waer in crachtelijck bewesen wordt* (Haarlem, 1613), 1–2; Buys, "Without Thy Self," 363–8; Vermij, *Geest uit de fles*, 33–4; Eire, *Reformations*, 308–9, 672.

supervised, and catechized blocs, Lutheran, Calvinist, and Catholic, the Reformation also generated a powerful anti-dogmatic reaction reviling all pressure for conformity and ecclesiastical guidance. It was this that potentially served, as hardened "philosophical" Socinians later showed, as a bridge between de-theologized Christianity and non-Christian humanists, indifferentists, and freethinkers.[11] Menno Simons (*c.*1496–1561), who did more than any other to stabilize and reinvigorate Low Countries Anabaptism after the crushing of the chiliastic militants, arguably the foremost figure of the Dutch Reformation, had several toes in the Radical Reformation, being strongly committed to irenicism and toleration. Like other Mennonite leaders, he agreed governments should confine their attention to purely human affairs and not concern themselves with consciences.[12] However, he laid greater stress than the hard core Radical Reformation of the so-called "libertines" on the congregation as a force for discipline, and the need for submission to creed and communal norms.[13] It was those who rejected all strict congregationalism, including the Mennonite and Remonstrant creeds, as well as all Trinitarian theology, formal clergy, and intolerance, like the flock of Hubert Duifhuis (1531–81) at Utrecht, and Caspar Coolhaes (1536–1615) at Leiden, that strove hardest to keep the various strands of opposition to the main blocs "a-confessional," forging a strand of "Radical Reformation" especially apt to contribute to the milieu from which Radical Enlightenment sprang.

Coolhaes, a highly influential anti-Calvinist "libertine" preacher, active in the 1570s and 1580s, was a former monk of German background, holding a pulpit in Leiden until 1581 when he was removed by the Reformed Church's National Synod (meeting at Middelburg) for irenicism, Erastianism, and opposing Calvinist theology. His pamphlets explained why he and his followers avoided confessional labels and theology, preached no catechism sermons, and called themselves simply "Christians": "our office is to preach Christ, not Calvin."[14] Coornhert, for his part, firmly rejected Original Sin and Predestination, conceiving man as free and capable of improvement. Son of an Amsterdam merchant, he remained nominally within Catholicism but preached toleration and individual liberty of conscience while pouring reproaches on the David-Jorists, Schwenkfeldians, and other liberal Anabaptist groups seeking converts and influence within the Dutch, German, and Swiss Radical Reformation, as well as on Calvinists, Lutherans, Zwinglians, and Catholics, wherever these seemed to him too hierarchical and fixated on the personalities and teachings of their spiritual leaders.[15] His campaign against intolerance, the tyranny of religious persecution, and dividing Christianity into mutually hostile churches, sects, and factions, was unrelenting and second in impact to none.

If moralizing, irenicist, "unchurched" radically anti-theological Christianity flourished most, after 1600, in the Netherlands, while in Germany the confessionalization

[11] Mulsow, *Enlightenment Underground*, 26–7, 55, 61, 186.

[12] Kolakowski, *Chrétiens sans église*, 157–9; Van Gelderen, *Political Thought of the Dutch Revolt*, 240–2.

[13] Israel, *Dutch Republic*, 92–3.

[14] Kaplan, *Calvinists and Libertines*, 98–100.

[15] Hamilton, *Family of Love*, 72, 106–7; Van Gelderen, *Political Thought of the Dutch Revolt*, 243–53.

better succeeded in cutting back the radical tendency,[16] the earliest roots of the Radical Reformation, reaching back before Servetus, were to be found, as with Radical Renaissance, in Italy rather than Germany or the Low Countries. Socinus—or, to give him his full name, Faustus Sozzini (1539–1604)—from Siena, first began preaching that Christ was not divine and rejecting immortality of the soul whilst at Lyon and Geneva a decade after Servetus' execution, in the early 1560s. The latter part of his life, from 1579, Socinus spent disseminating his anti-Trinitarian doctrine in Poland where he established a sect that became known as the "Polish Brethren." Before long, others appeared offering a still more radical stance. One who went still further and whose notion of a true Reformation led to his being denounced as an outrageous neo-Pelagian by Jesuits, Lutherans, Calvinists, and liberal Protestant opponents of Predestination alike was the "Florentine beast," as Erastus called him, the Italian humanist Protestant and early ally of Socinus, Francesco Pucci (1543–97).[17] Horrified by the St. Bartholomew's Day massacre of the Protestants in Paris, in August 1572, Pucci abjured Catholicism and, from then on, devoted his energies to what he understood as the true Reformation of Christianity which both the "Anti-Christ in Rome," he believed, and Luther and Calvin, were obstructing. He strove to secure theological reconciliation among Christians and universal peace through political action—a program for which he tried to enlist the French king, Henri IV, while the latter struggled to reunite France amid the French Wars of Religion.

If all Christian independents within the seventeenth-century Radical Reformation, rejecting dogmatic theology, devoted their efforts to searching for universal truth and human betterment, and defended intellectual freedom, appealing to all *omnibus veritatis studiosis* [searchers for the truth] to reduce Christianity's basic *fundamenta fidei* to as few and as rational doctrines as possible, Pucci boiled Christianity down to just one: rational belief in a God, creator of the universe, who is infinitely merciful toward all men. This, together with his extreme Pelagianism, entailing the immortality of all souls, and the doctrine that "natural reason" alone suffices for Christian salvation without any sacramental or priestly intervention, proved too much even for Socinus. Anxious to rally especially Italian humanist exiles driven abroad by religious or political persecution, alongside the residual dissident crypto-Protestant underground in Italy itself (found especially in Venice), Pucci published (in England) his *Informatione della religione christiana* (1580) in Italian. But, for him, mobilizing Italian dissent was just an initial stage of the true universal Reformation.[18] With friends and supporters in several lands, between 1578 and 1585 he conducted a prolonged dispute with Socinus, initially at Basel, later largely at Cracow, but with the two unable to reconcile their differences. Salvation, concurred Socinus, is closely tied to reason, knowledge, and observance of Christ's word; but he could not accept that salvation and the soul's immortality ultimately remain wholly independent of

[16] Weeks, "From Radical Reformation," 90–1.
[17] Caravale, *Italian Reformation*, 1–2, 4; Salatowsky, *Philosophie der Sozinaner*, 58, 378.
[18] Biagioni, *Radical Reformation*, 50–6.

Revelation and all supernatural intervention, procedure, or operation of "divine grace." He refused to go the last step with Pucci in acknowledging "true Christianity" to be a moral philosophy allied to immortality of the soul, not a faith in a revealed creed.[19]

Allying with other foes of autocracy and anti-Medici exiles from Florence, Pucci represented a variant of Radical Reformation that showed how Christianity could become conjoined with a basically philosophical and political standpoint. After several restless years in Poland, he was arrested in Salzburg when returning to Rome to try to persuade the pope to change his mind. Tried and condemned for heresy, he was executed by the Papacy three years before Bruno, in the Tor di Nona in Rome on 5 July 1597; his body was then burned by the papal authorities, as befitted so fearsome a heretic, before the public in the Campo dei Fiori. Radical anti-theological Christian universalist rationalism of which Pucci was such a striking example, the tendency later encompassing the Dutch Collegiants, developed gradually into a pan-European underground which, though very different in some respects from the underground Neo-Epicureanism of the sixteenth century, was equally a founding element of what, after 1650, developed into the "Radical Enlightenment."[20]

Radical Reformation was soon ruthlessly stamped out in Italy and Switzerland where it briefly flourished, besides France and Germany, but gained a securer footing for a time in Poland-Lithuania from where it later fanned out via Hungary-Transylvania, Germany, and Holland to again become a pan-European and American trend. Among the chief adherents and heirs of the Radical Reformation, defined as rejection of mysteries and Trinitarian theology, an uncompromising stress on "reason," and a demand for full freedom of conscience, were leaders and adherents of several Socinian strains. The post-1620 Collegiant movement emerging in Holland was a movement continually reinforced by outcasts from different main churches as well as defecting Arminians and liberal Anabaptists appalled by the splits and relentless polemics embroiling mainstream conservative and progressive Mennonites. If all Collegiants were "unchurched Christians," rejecting clergy and ecclesiastical authority and adhering to an open form of congregationalism, many or most remained indifferent or hostile to "philosophy"; during the third quarter of the seventeenth century only a small but crucial fringe among them, combining abjuring clergy, congregational discipline, the Trinity, and sacraments with liberty of conscience and unrestricted theological rationalism, entered into alliance with Spinozism. By the 1650s and 1660s, the combination of individual freedom of conscience and expression with stripping away congregational discipline and traditional theology had coaxed a handful of remarkable Socinian Collegiants, inspired by Cartesianism, to the view that philosophical and theological "truth" is and must be identical,

[19] Biagioni, *Radical Reformation*, 82; Caravale, *Italian Reformation*, 11–12, 56–7.

[20] Caravale, *Italian Reformation*, 4, 9; Salatowsky, *Philosophie der Sozinaner*, 367–8; Gatti, *Ideas of Liberty*, 50.

leading them into eager debate with members of the *cercle spinoziste* and alliance with Spinoza.[21]

Collegiants convened on the basis of no clergy, no catechism, no congregational discipline and every individual free to express their own personal views and conscience.[22] Full freedom of conscience inevitably meant Collegiants accommodated a wide variety of viewpoints, some of them retaining belief in the Trinity and other "mysteries."[23] The vehement criticism directed against them by Calvinists, Lutherans, Catholics, Zwinglians, and strict Mennonites and the mainstream Remonstrant Church nevertheless chiefly highlighted their collective Anti-Trinitarianism and eventual rejection of virtually all traditional Christian theology, including immortality of the soul.

4.2. GROTIUS AND THE RADICAL ENLIGHTENMENT

A key difference between Radical Reformation, including the Christian millenarianism implicit in Pucci's scheme, and Radical Renaissance, was the close link it established between utopianism and political activism—its exhortation to action. But here too "action" where undisguised and open could too easily end at the executioner's block or the stake. Hence, by no means all adherents of the Radical Reformation combined theological radicalism with an open summons to resist and resort to political action. There flourished also a Nicodemite tendency that everywhere remained pronounced in these circles: the same understandable evasion of persecution and concern for self-preservation that generally blunted the impulse to propagate opposition by clandestine means within underground Neo-Epicureanism, and the Radical Renaissance generally, reappeared in no small measure in the Radical Reformation too. If, as Machiavelli uniquely showed, there are concealed ways Neo-Epicureans could intervene effectively both politically and intellectually in the public sphere, to question the prevailing norms, without fully revealing the motivation and deep subversion lurking beneath, this was equally true of the Radical Reformation Nicodemites. No one more skillfully demonstrated this than Grotius.

Hugo Grotius (1583–1645), the sometimes bold, sometimes timid, heir of Erasmus, was a crypto-Socinian who accomplished much by way of denting the pillars of theocracy and sway of miracle-based theology while renewing the Christian ideal on the basis of unity and the universalism of the Christian message. A victim of the persecution unleashed by the Calvinist Counter-Remonstrant triumph over the Dutch Arminians, in 1618, he set out to prioritize Christianity's moral content, in justice, and render its theology subordinate, problematic and secondary.[24] That

[21] Van Slee, *Rijnsburger Collegianten*, 383–4; Hunter, *Radical Protestantism*, 42–6; Erdozain, "Heavenly Poise," 19.

[22] Van der Wall, *Mystieke Chiliast*, 201–2; Fix, *Prophecy and Reason*, 23–56.

[23] Van Bunge, *Johannes Bredenburg*, 5, 10–11.

[24] Van Miert, "Janus Face," 106.

Grotius' intellectual legacy fed into the foundations of the Western Enlightenment is a historical truism no one will dispute. But two salient aspects of Grotius' intellectual and political legacy to the Enlightenment—his Bible hermeneutics used by some of the most radical post-1700 *anti-Scriptuarii*, and his role in rigorously rationalizing the strain of the philosophically inclined wing of the Socinian movement—acquired a particular significance for the later "Christian" wing of the Radical Enlightenment, that tendency sufficiently libertarian, naturalistic, tolerant, and rationalist to ally with the one-substance materialists of the later eighteenth century to forge the universal democratic egalitarianism of the revolutionary era. Grotius' Bible criticism was sweepingly innovative, his Christian vision unreservedly universalist and opposed to moral skepticism; both exerted a profound impact for generations until deep into the eighteenth century.

Deists found Grotius' approach appealing and so did some radical Socinians and crypto-Socinian Arminians. The German "translator" of the Wertheim Bible, Johann Lorenz Schmidt (1702–49), belonged to a notable line of "naturalists, deists, Socinians and Arminians" who, according to the author of the most detailed history of the Wertheim Bible controversy that shook the German Lutheran, Catholic, and Calvinist theological worlds in the years 1735–8, Johann Niklaus Sinnhold, all scandalously misinterpreted Scripture thereby proving themselves *Glaubens-genossen* [fellow believers] of "Spinoza, Grotius and Le Clerc."[25] A professor at the Lutheran university of Erfurt, Sinnhold took the view that the Socinians and Arminians, inspired by Grotius and Le Clerc, had eroded belief in mysteries and miracles, theology's sway, and the redeeming power of sacraments no less insidiously than Spinoza and his followers. Likewise, the devastating anti-Christian Bible criticism of the great German philologist Hermann Samuel Reimarus (1694–1768) adopted Grotius' Bible research as its principal starting-point. In the footnotes and text of his secret anti-Christian *Apologie* which he began composing in the late 1730s and 1740s in the aftermath of his own encounter with Schmidt and the Wertheim Bible, Reimarus cited Grotius more frequently than any other source, more than Spinoza, Collins, or any of the English so-called "deists."

Grotius had shown Collins the way, held Reimarus in his *Apologie*, in explaining obscure points of Scripture in a serious, searching [i.e. naturalistic] manner, treating the text almost as one would any ancient text, except that Grotius at the same time strove not to appear to be undermining institutionalized Christianity but trying to iron out difficulties and reconcile the Old and New Testaments' irreconcilable messages. Having eroded the New Testament's integrity, Grotius feebly sought to paper over the cracks with ridiculously inappropriate arguments.[26] Yet, his fumbling

[25] Sinnhold, *Historische Nachricht*, 8; Israel, *Enlightenment Contested*, 25–6, 114, 188–92.

[26] "wer sieht aber nicht, dass Grotii Erklärungsart eine gantze fremde und wider alle Deutung andere Schriftsteller lauffende, und daher nur eigentlich zur Rettung des N. T. erfundene Regel voraussetzt?" Reimarus, *Apologie oder Schutzschrift* i. 61; Israel, "Philosophical Context of Hermann Samuel Reimarus," 187; Groetsch, *Hermann Samuel Reimarus*, 127–9.

retreat in no way detracted from Reimarus' admiration for the impressively innovative naturalistic hermeneutic method he introduced, the invaluable fresh path he had opened up, that Grotius' disciple Le Clerc later developed into his *ars critica*, or science of true text criticism. Reimarus had met Le Clerc, in Holland, as a young man, and conversed with him at length, and from this he dated his own awareness of Grotius' researches as a radical new departure. What especially appealed to Reimarus and Collins in Grotius' hermeneutics was his systematic discarding of supernatural explanations, his continually implying that whatever is valid and true in the Bible, and in religion, is natural and rational without any supernatural element intervening.[27]

If Schmidt's Wertheim Bible vividly reflected the drift toward deism, contended Ernst Friedrich Neubauer (1705–48), in his 1736 annotations on Johann Jakob Rambach's commentary on the Old Testament, the "translator" [i.e. Schmidt] of the Wertheim Bible merely reflected the seventeenth-century Dutch tendency to marginalize and reject the miraculous, a tradition originating in the hermeneutics of Grotius and, following him, Le Clerc.[28] Not the least disturbing and for true Christians unacceptable consequence of Grotius' humanistic Bible hermeneutics was his receptivity to Jewish and other arguments denying that the Old Testament prophecies do point to the coming of Christ. Where authentic Christian theologians claim that the Old Testament announces that coming; strict textual criticism, following Grotius' naturalistic principles, shows that it does not, a stance thoroughly concurred with, of course, by Collins and Reimarus as well as Spinoza.[29]

Grotius' undermining of established Lutheran and Calvinist *philologia sacra*, moreover, extended well beyond issues of hermeneutics. Indeed, the Arminian–Grotian current came to form a vital part of the backcloth to the Western Socinian–Unitarian tradition which full-frontally attacked and undermined Lutheran and Calvinist theology not least by referring "back to the *Consensus veterum sapientium*" and subtly absorbing "in a humanistic sense a pre-Christian 'natural' theology." If Grotius' naturalism and boiling down Christian dogmatics to a few *fundamenta* appealed to Le Clerc,[30] Schmidt, and Reimarus, it horrified Lutheran, Catholic, and Calvinist commentators precisely because it marginalized the miraculous and removed the supernatural, erasing the redeeming power of sacraments and theology. For Grotius, Christianity is true and verifiable in the sense that it remains an urgent necessity for men to extract its unifying, essential principles; for him these principles had in some fundamental way to be grounded in the wider doctrines of natural law, natural theology, and *consensus omnium*.[31] This Grotian doctrine of an underlying

[27] Groetsch, *Hermann Samuel Reimarus*, 128–9, 138–9.

[28] See Neubauer's notes to Johann Jakob Rambach, *Collegium historiae ecclesiaisticae Veteris Testamentii*, ed. E. F. Neubauer (Frankfurt and Leipzig, n.d. [1736]); Israel, "Early Dutch Enlightenment as a Factor," 222.

[29] Schröder, *Ursprünge des Atheismus*, 96; Sorkin, *Religious Enlightenment*, 50.

[30] On Le Clerc's espousal of Grotius' conception of Christian truth, see Van Eijnatten, *Liberty and Concord*, 167–8.

[31] Blom, "Styles of Heterodoxy," 66–71.

general legal truth that pre-dates sovereignty and the state was to become a powerful element in the Brothers De La Court's, and Spinoza's, breaking of Hobbesian doctrine of sovereignty and their replacing it with the irreversible "carry-over" of basic democratic rights and freedoms into the state.[32] It was a stance that wholly skirted round Christological interpretations and "justified the veracity of the Bible by the natural rationality of its account," avoiding the miraculous and the doctrinal.[33] In his *De veritate religionis christianae* (1627), Grotius endeavored to combine this reductive Christology and natural theology with apparently repelling Socinus and retaining the Trinity as the basis of a minimalist Christology, but in a way, noted the Socinian leader, Johannes Crellius (1590–1633), in 1623, that looked pitifully feeble in the context of his own sweepingly powerful hermeneutical approach.[34]

Grotius' theological naturalism and rejection of skepticism, like the rationalizing of the Socinians more generally, presented a special challenge in relation to God's justice.[35] Abjuring all voluntarism, Grotius denied God is an absolute master over his creatures. They remain subject to His commands in a weak sense, but he answers the question how God should be thought of in relation to natural justice by stating that God is a "rector" or "princeps" presiding over the moral community. When God punishes he is not enforcing His own will but that of the community, upholding the moral order that men naturally embrace from the natural law. There is nothing arbitrary in his judgments of the kind one expects from a "dominus absolutus." "In this life," as Jeremy Bentham later echoed this idea, "there are laws of nature which the Deity cannot or will not interrupt."[36] For Grotius, as for Bentham, Natural Law would be valid "etsi Deus non daretur" [even if God did not exist].[37] God, of course, is not subject to the law like a human judge but rather the ultimate supervisor, adjuster, and guardian of that law. But here lay a troubling dilemma from which Grotius could never really extricate himself: if God punishes wrongdoers not because they have offended Him but the Natural Law, a universal natural law is implied that exists beyond and independently from, and even in some sense above God. It was a stance differing significantly from that of Pufendorf and Locke who viewed natural law as binding on men expressly by virtue of God's command.[38]

Calvinist divines suspected Grotius' tract *De Satisfactione Christi* (1617), supposedly rebutting Counter-Remonstrant charges that his theology was unorthodox and veered towards Socinianism, was a bogus refutation really designed to salvage the arguments of the Socinian "adversary."[39] Yet, it was not the hints of Anti-Trinitarianism, or dissolving ties between the Old and New Testaments, that

[32] Weststeijn, *Commercial Republicanism*, 152–3, 160–1, 346.

[33] Schmidt-Biggemann, "Edifying versus Rational Hermeneutics," 62.

[34] Kühler, *Socinianisme in Nederland*, 86.

[35] Mortimer, "Human and Divine Justice," 75–6.

[36] Bentham, *Influence of Natural Religion*, 42, 60.

[37] Schröder, *Ursprünge des Atheismus*, 162; Taylor, *A Secular Age*, 126.

[38] Kühler, *Het Socinianisme*, 82–3; Kolakowski, *Chrétiens sans Église*, 252–3; Taylor, *A Secular Age*, 126; and especially Blom, "Grotius and Socinianism," 122, 124, 132–4, 145–6.

[39] Blom, "Grotius and Socinianism," 131; Mortimer, "Human and Divine Justice," 84–92.

Socinians sufficiently radical to join ranks with Spinozism in the seventeenth and eighteenth centuries principally found appealing in Grotius, but rather insistence on the contiguousness and ultimate oneness of reason, natural theology, natural law, and Revelation. By unifying all reality and morality in this way, Grotius proved subversive with respect to all churches and even the Radical Reformation itself as a distinct religious bloc. Claiming Christianity's fundamental core consists of just a few principles acknowledged by all churches, with the residue of Christian doctrine being secondary and dispensable, powerfully reinforced the trend to marginalize all theology in favor of moral and political philosophy. His was a universalism drawing pagan and Christian justice, and pagan and Christian piety, ultimately together, here once again sharing kinship with Socinianism and Anglo-American Unitarianism.[40] His stance worked divisively, though, both within and without. Subsuming theology in philosophy and legal thought was not approved by the entire Socinian–Unitarian movement, much of which subsequently resisted associating with the Radical Enlightenment's broadly secularizing and revolutionary democratic tendency.

As the philosophical-rationalist tendency associated especially with Descartes and Spinoza gained ground as a defining framework within Dutch Socinianism in the second half of the seventeenth century, philosophical Socinianism correspondingly became increasingly divisive and controversial among the Radical Reformation as a whole. Furious divisions developed not just because some Collegiants, like the "spiritualist" theologian Petrus Serrarius (1600–69), retained the Trinity and belief in other "mysteries," but also because some committed Anti-Trinitarian Collegiants judged the new philosophical tendency a threat to congregational unity and piety. While all Socinians identified the "light of reason" as Man's principal guide in matters of faith and Bible interpretation, for most this remained primarily just a hermeneutical principle, a method of explaining Scriptural passages from other Scriptural passages consistently. Only a minority fringe, much as among English Unitarians later, in Joseph Priestley's day, pushed their rationalizing principle to the point of merging of theology and philosophy, blending the light of reason in Bible criticism with the philosophical-scientific explanations of nature's laws, and philosophical reason.[41]

Prime representatives of this latter "philosophical" Collegiant current were Spinoza's friends Pieter Balling (d. 1669), author of *Het Licht op den Candelaar* [Light on the Candelstick] (Amsterdam, 1662), the translator who rendered much of Spinoza's early work into Dutch, Jarig Jelles (*c.*1620–83), Spinoza's longstanding ally of over twenty years who composed the Preface to the *Opera Posthuma*, in 1677, and Jan Rieuwertsz (*c.*1616–87), publisher of all Spinoza's books. Balling may have diverged markedly from free-thinkers like Meyer in remaining zealous about winning his

[40] Blom, "Grotius and Socinianism," 137; Schröder, *Ursprünge des Atheismus*, 179, 203; Zagorin, *How the Idea of Religious Toleration Came*, 174–5.

[41] Bietenholz, *Daniel Zwicker*, 272–7; J. Sadler, "The Collegiants," in L. Hunt, M. Jacob, and W. Mijnhardt (eds.), *Bernard Picart and the First Global Vision of Religion* (Los Angeles, 2010), 66–7.

readers for the *light*, and pursuing spiritual truth and a pious life, but that does not make his abjuring dogma, rejection of "mysteries," comprehensive tolerance, and veneration of "reason" any less subversive.[42] Such men, and later also Jan Bredenburg (1643–91), who wrestled long and hard with the implications of Spinoza's philosophy, shaped a dissident wing of the Collegiant movement that before long found itself openly at war with the more conventional mainstream. "Philosophical" Collegiants found themselves under siege by the many Anti-Trinitarian Bible fundamentalists attending Collegiant meetings and amidst Socinianism generally. In the 1680s and 1690s, prominent Collegiants like the influential preacher Frans Kuyper (Franciscus Cuperus, 1629–91) began denouncing philosophical "unchurched Christians" as a veritable plague, blighting the true Socinian Anti-Trinitarian movement. Proclaiming the reality of supernatural entities, spirits, devils, and satanic (as well as benign magical) powers, Kuyper denounced Bredenburg and his supporters as a disruptive Spinozistic betrayal from within.[43] This anti-philosophical trend tended to prevail in the end: most late eighteenth-century American Unitarians followed the latter tradition in taking the Bible narrative, supernaturalia, and miracles more literally than the philosophical independents; in Britain too Priestley's version of Unitarianism tied to science, philosophy, and political emancipation was hastily abandoned after 1800.

Only one particular narrow offshoot from the Radical Reformation ended up directly fusing with the Radical Enlightenment by erasing all distinction between theology and philosophy and reducing the miraculous and belief in *supernaturalia* practically to nothing. Nevertheless, the wider Socinian movement in varying degrees encouraged this development and all late seventeenth- and eighteenth-century Socinians were continually accused of replacing theology with philosophical reason. The prevailing objection to the Socinians, remarks Bayle, in his 1697 *Dictionnaire*, is that by refusing to believe whatever seemed "opposé aux Lumières philosophiques et de soumettre leur foi aux mystères inconcevables de la religion chrétienne" [opposed to philosophical reason, and submit their faith to the inconceivable mysteries of the Christian religion] they opened the door to "Pyrrhonisme, au Déisme, à l'Athéisme." Bayle doubtless meant this in his usual subversive, ambiguous manner, but rightly stressed that by denying mysteries and the miraculous "on renverse toute la Révélation, ensuite de quoi tout n'est que Dispute de Philosophes" [Revelation is overthrown and after that everything is just philosophers' disputes].[44] Anti-Trinitarian Socinians like Kuyper agreed except that to their mind such admonitions applied only to philosophical Socinians, Unitarians like Balling, Jelles, and Bredenburg, not to the bulk of Socinians in their day.

[42] Kolakowski, *Chrétiens sans Église*, 208–17, 220–25; Van Bunge, *Johannes Bredenburg*, 151, 184, 188; Hunter, *Radical Protestantism*, 44–5; Israel, "Dutch Golden Age Politics," 44, 48.

[43] Kolakowski, *Chrétiens sans Église*, 261–5, 271–2; Van Bunge, *Johannes Bredenburg*, 87–98, 192–6.

[44] Bayle, *Dictionnaire historique et critique* (1740), iv. 236–7; Ogonowski, "Sozinianismus und die Aufklärung," 83–4.

Grotius has often been deemed a vital link between "the Erasmian tradition" of the Renaissance and the Enlightenment.[45] But he was a crucial link also, the evidence shows, between Reformation and Radical Enlightenment. The connecting thread was a demythologized Christianity, shorn of theological doctrine that focused on a core of moral precepts compatible with pagan-classical natural-law ethics. In this respect, Grotius was among the first movers, followed by Hobbes, Spinoza, and Bayle, of the seventeenth century's transfer of primacy from theology to philosophy, and modernity's subordination of religious authority to individual liberty, freedom of thought and expression, and the common good of the human community understood in a secular, moral sense.

4.3. POLISH BRETHREN, MORAVIAN BRETHREN, RESCUING ANTI-TRINITARIAN THEOLOGY

Before leaving Italy, late in 1575, Socinus too was a Nicodemist keeping his heretical theology to himself. He abandoned concealment only during his Swiss refuge at Basel (1575–9), and especially afterwards during his exile in Poland (1579–1604) where he emerged prominently in late Reformation polemics. Even then, he disavowed any intention to found a separate sect. His followers, though, formed a lasting dissident movement which, before long, came under intense pressure. Many features of the Polish Brethren as a sect developed during the opening years of the seventeenth century from their need to resist the intolerant dogmatism and authoritarianism of the Calvinist Reformed Church there, followed by the post-1600 Polish–Lithuanian Catholic Church's militant Counter-Reformation. A prime focus of opposition to the encroaching tide of unrelenting confessionalization was Raków, a Polish new town in south-central Poland, near Kielce, founded in 1569 by a semi-Calvinist local nobleman connected to a group of nobles in north-eastern Poland and Lithuania championing toleration and coexistence of churches. Raków, like some other Polish towns, acquired a remarkably mixed religious population comprising Arians and Socinians besides Calvinists, Lutherans, Jews, and Catholics, though in this respect it did not rival Vilna which in addition boasted substantial communities of Muslim Tartars, Karaites, and Greek Orthodox.

Raków remained unique, however, in attracting a large mass of the *Bracia Polscy* (Polish Brethren) who for a time precariously held out as the dominant segment there. The renowned Socinian Racovian Academy, founded in 1602 by a son of the founder, and its function as a center of religious printing, reflected Socinianism's roots in theological revolt against Calvinism and Lutheranism as much as Catholicism. Johannes Crellius, a refugee from Franconia, rector at Raków in the years 1616–21, openly promoted Socinian views in his writings, printed at Raków. An

[45] See, for instance, Beiser, *Sovereignty of Reason*, 91–2, 130.

important later rector, from the late 1620s down to 1631, was Joachim Stegmann the Elder (1595–1633), a former Lutheran pastor expelled from his pulpit in Brandenburg for Socinian propensities, whose two internationally influential posthumously published books appeared in 1633 and 1644, at Amsterdam, both pushing Socinian rationalism to the limit, toward an uncompromising rationalizing stance, well beyond where Socinus himself had dug his trenches, the second denying the dogma of Original Sin outright.[46] For Socinus, Revelation remained the indispensable ground of what we know of God. Stegmann did concur with Socinus, though, with respect to the miracles related in Scripture that, without Revelation, human reason on its own is insufficient. Among Stegmann's other projects, collaborating with Crellius, was the publication in 1630 of the Socinian New Testament, in German. Raków reformers eroded but did not finally remove this final barrier impeding the hegemony of pure reason.[47]

For decades, from the expulsion of the Socinians from Cracow, in 1591, down to the mid-seventeenth century, links between Socinians in Poland and the Socinian fraternity in Holland figured centrally in their efforts to counter the mounting persecution of Socinianism in central and east-central Europe[48] A key role in this interaction was played by a grandson of Socinus on his mother's side, Andrzej Wiszowaty (Wissowatius, 1608–78), who figured among the foremost leaders of seventeenth-century Polish and European Socinianism. Active initially in Poland, and only much later in the Dutch Republic, Wiszowaty helped establish, consolidate, and define Socianism in the West, playing a notable part in our story by erecting the most durable, meaningful barrier separating mainstream Socinianism from Radical Enlightenment. Born in Filipów, a new town some fifteen miles north-west of Suwalki in the extreme north-east of present-day Poland, he was formed intellectually at the Raków academy. After ten years at Raków (1619–29) he travelled widely, meeting Grotius in Hamburg and studying for a time, in 1632, at Leiden besides also later visiting England and France before returning to Poland in 1637. The following year, Raków became the focus of a major upheaval after the Polish Catholic episcopate denounced a band of Socinian students for desecrating a Catholic cross, whipping up popular anti-Protestant fervour and precipitating the culminating stages of over half a century of intensifying repression. The academy was closed by order of the Polish Sejm, and afterwards demolished. Eventually, in July 1658, at the instigation of the church, Poland's national assembly, dominated by nobles and bishops, decreed the expulsion of all Socinians from Poland, although it was only after the war of 1655–60, during which the Swedes devastated much of the country, wrecking Warsaw, that it fully took effect, propelling the final wave of Polish Socinian emigration westwards, and to Transylvania.[49]

[46] Salatowski, "Socinian Headaches," 175–9.
[47] Ogonowski, "Der Sozianismus und die Aufklärung," 88–9.
[48] Tazbir, "Die Sozinianer," 9–10; Wrzecionko, "Sozinianer und die Sozinianismus," 249.
[49] Tazbir, "Die Sozinianer," 16–39; Spruit, "Introduzione," p. xxvi.

Wiszowaty remained in Poland–Lithuania as long as he could, maintaining ties with the Socinian remnant there and the Socinian exiles in Transylvania, a country under Turkish rule following the collapse of the Hungarian kingdom in the 1520s and for a time a uniquely secure haven for Calvinists, Lutherans, and radicals of every stripe, especially Socinians, the place where Stegmann spent the last phase of his life (1631–3) ministering to the German Unitarians in exile there. Transylvania was so exceptional as a secure refuge from the religious persecution convulsing the Western world that some viewed it as part of God's plan for the better future of humanity, a new Israel and potential base for religious revolution elsewhere, until a decidedly unholy mix of zeal and war devastated that principality too in the late 1650s.[50]

Abandoning Poland for good in 1660, Wiszowaty settled in Amsterdam, where he edited and, in 1668, published the complete works of Socinus in two folio volumes, and reissued Crellius' works together as the renowned Socinian compilation, *Bibliotheca Fratrum Polonorum* which he helped guide through the press. With Wiszowaty as chief editor, this soon notorious major collection of Socinian writings came to be regarded throughout Europe as the summation of Socinian doctrine and among the foremost challenges to Christian belief in existence; it was quickly banned by the Dutch States General, at the demand of the Reformed Church. When in 1678 the city government of Utrecht reissued the earlier (1655) States of Utrecht ban on all "Socinian, Arian, blasphemous and entirely pernicious books," it listed those most powerfully menacing religion in their province as the *Bibliotheca Fratrum Polonorum*, Hobbes's *Leviathan*, the *Philosophia Scripturae Interpres* [of Meyer], and the *Tractatus Theologico-Politicus* [Spinoza] along with B.D.S[pinoza], *Opera Posthuma*.[51]

As the editor responsible for the version printed, Wiszowaty also revised and defended the 1609 Socinian creed, the "Catechism of Raków" (Katechizm Rakowski), which appeared in Amsterdam in 1666, in the same year Lodewijk Meyer published his *Philosophia* (1666), a book Wiszowaty singled out for special rebuke. As well as being a skilled leader, spokesman, and editor, Wiszowaty was also among the foremost Socinian controversialists of the day, his *De Sancta Trinitate objectiones quaedam* (1665), an attack on the Trinity, and Christ's divinity, being answered by none other than Leibniz in his *Defensio Trinitatis contra Wissowatium* (1669), a debate later re-examined by Lessing in the mid-eighteenth century.[52] Another of Wiszowaty's publications that was much discussed was a slender treatise, *Seu de rationis judicio, in Controversiis etiam Theologicis, ac religiosis, adhibendo, Tractatus* that appeared several years after his death, at Amsterdam in 1684 (not 1685 as usually stated), a text later published in German in 1703, under the title *Die vernüftige Religion*.[53]

[50] Wilbur, *History of Unitarianism*, 124; MacCulloch, *The Reformation*, 457–63.
[51] Israel, *Dutch Republic*, 916; Israel, "Andrzej Wiszowaty," 84.
[52] Lessing, "Des Andreas Wissowatius Einwurfe," 489–535; Salatowsky, *Philosophie der Sozinianer*, 20, 222.
[53] Kühler, *Socinianisme in Nederland*, 229–30.

Wiszowaty's *Religio rationalis* became a principal target of Bayle's trenchant critique of Socinianism.[54] Bayle had long criticized Socinians for holding that reason must underlay faith while inconsistently applying their chosen principle. Wiszowaty's stance, later that of Le Clerc, Locke, and other rationalizing theologians and philosophers, was to gain foundational significance in the building of the post-Lockean moderate mainstream Enlightenment. *Religio rationalis* staked all on the basic distinction, crucial to the early Enlightenment, between what is "au-dessus de la raison"—"above reason"—and what is contrary to reason. Precisely this distinction, which Stegmann had eroded, was reinforced by Wiszowaty's theology and later Locke's philosophy, but rejected as false and dangerous by Bayle who, like Spinoza and Toland, roundly denied the possibility of any such distinction.[55] Ostensibly assailing Socinianism because it rejects Fideism and Pyrrhonism (according to Bayle, the only philosophical positions compatible with Calvinist orthodoxy), Leibniz and others at the time suspected that Bayle's real objective was to steer the reader, with artful circumlocutions, round to something else.[56] Recent scholarly research and discussion has tended to confirm his stance as one of deliberate Nicodemite evasion, siding with the anti-Scripturalism of Meyer and Spinoza while pretending not to do so.[57] When Bayle pronounced Wiszowaty's, Le Clerc's, and Locke's "above reason" invalid what he really meant was that there exists no theological truth, or moral universal, apart from what is demonstrated by philosophical reason.[58]

That the Dutch Republic became the prime center for publication of all Radical Reformation and Christian fringe literature in the seventeenth century, for the Brownists and, for a time, the Quakers, besides the Polish and Moravian Brethren, only further reinforced the special status of the Dutch Republic, rather than England, as first seedbed of the Radical Enlightenment. Socinianism's viability as a defense against radical thought, meanwhile, came progressively into doubt, not least due to Lodewijk Meyer's philosophical challenge to the rationalizing Left Socinians. The term *Religio rationalis* was plainly being deployed by Wiszowaty and his following to mean something decidedly different from philosophical or deist "natural theology" as understood in the eighteenth century. Where Deist "natural theology" sought justification by reason alone, Socinian *Religio rationalis* acknowledged "reason" only up to a point and thereafter the guiding principle of divine Revelation and the reality of miracles—albeit, as in Locke and Le Clerc, only where confirmed by concrete historical "evidences" considered certain.[59] While Wiszowaty, like Koerbagh and Meyer, repudiates the Trinity, Incarnation, divine Grace, and other "mysteries" because such dogmas violate the principle of right reason, Socinians, differently

[54] Jean Le Clerc to Pierre Bayle, Amsterdam, 16 Aug. 1684, in Bayle, *Correspondance* iv. 41–2; Mori, *Bayle philosophe*, 172.

[55] Schröder, "Deismus," 15; McKenna, "Norme et la transgression," 128–9; Salatowsky, *Philosophie der Sozinianer*, 20, 186, 222–3; Salatowsky, "Socinian Headaches," 178–9.

[56] Israel, "Meyer, Koerbagh," 204.

[57] McKenna, "Norme et la transgression,", 119–20.

[58] McKenna, "Norme et la transgression," 129, 134; Pitassi, "Bayle, the Bible," 266–7.

[59] Jelles, *Belydenisse*, 1–3; Kuyper, *Bewys*, 3–4; Fix, *Prophecy and Reason*, 148–50.

from the radicals, held that one can nevertheless have faith in theological doctrines rendered clear by reason where reason exonerates them from being inexplicable mysteries.[60] Wiszowaty affirms the undeniable truth of the Resurrection, for example, but, like Locke and Le Clerc later, held that the certainty of this truth derives from the testimony of witnesses to the event; it is the event's evident historical veracity that places it beyond reasonable doubt.[61] Such reasoning formed the core of Wiszowaty's theology, enabling him to claim Christ's supernatural status as man's redeemer,[62] ensuring eternal reward for the saved and torment for the wicked, and even the existence of angels and demons, thereby permitting him and the younger generation of mid-seventeenth-century Socianians, like the Danzig physician Daniel Zwicker (1612–78), to supersede the limited, rigid literalism of Socinus and early Socinianism, on the one hand, and, simultaneously, permanently fence off Socinianism from Meyer and Radical Enlightenment on the other. But was the distinction between *contra rationem* (contrary to reason) and *supra rationem* (above reason) a real one, was it "assent founded on the highest reason"? Meyer and Bayle pronounced it wholly lacking in cogency.[63]

Wiszowaty helped lay the cornerstone of a Lockean enlightenment where theology, miracles, and mysteries all securely have their place, grounded not on tradition, authority, faith, or Scriptural literalism, but exclusively on rigorous, supposedly factual, proofs presented as the guarantee that nothing is sanctioned *contra rationem*. On this basis, Jesus is held to have been procreated by the Holy Ghost, to be the Messiah and Man's Saviour, leaving an unbridgeable gap between Wiszowaty's Socinian theology and the freethinking naturalism of a Koerbagh or Meyer eradicating all distinction between theology and philosophy.[64] Leibniz recognized Wiszowaty as among the most learned and formidable of his sect,[65] but refused to concede his objections to the Trinity, following Meyer (and preceding Bayle) in claiming a basic contradiction in Wiszowaty's reliance on *supra rationem* that urgently needed exposing and correcting, as Wiszowaty's argumentation, in his view, was more subversive, and destructive of Christian truth, than even Catholic doctrine. Where Catholics worship one God, he contended, Socinians worship God *and* Christ while defining the latter as "a creature" who is not part of the one God but someone distinct in his essence from God. "Therefore, they have two Gods. They worship a man" whereas true Christians worship God inhabiting a man.[66] Leibniz accepted, though, that Wiszowaty was not insidiously abolishing faith in favor of "reason", or making it supreme judge and expositor of religious controversies and the Bible, like the anonymous expositor of the vile anti-Scripturalism systematically and malignly subordinating Bible criticism to the supremacy of philosophical reason. Meyer's

[60] Wiszowaty, *Religio rationalis*, 16, 18, 33–5. [61] Wiszowaty, *Spooren der Deugden*, 134.
[62] Wiszowaty, *Religio rationalis*, 82–3; Wiszowaty, *Spooren der Deugden*, 31, 42, 69–70, 91–2, 94.
[63] Wiszowaty, *Religio rationalis*, 82–4; Krop, *Spinoza. Een paradoxale icoon*, 88–9; Ogonowski, "Der Sozianismus und die Aufklärung," 90; Mori, *Bayle philosophe*, 241; Spruit, "Introduzion," p. xxxv.
[64] Van Bunge, *Johannes Bredenburg*, 95, 251. [65] Laerke, *Leibniz lecteur de Spinoza*, 117–19, 121.
[66] Antognazza, *Leibniz on the Trinity*, 40.

notorious book, the *Philosophia* (1666), subsequently remained for decades, Leibniz recalled in 1716, in his *Theodicy*, the subject of intense controversy in Germany, provoking great disputes among the theologians.[67]

Meyer specifically targets the Raków Catechism of which Wiszowaty was editor. When the question arises: "whence comes such a difference of opinion concerning the understanding of Scripture," Socinians answer, "this is because men read Holy Scripture carelessly, or do not bring to it a heart sincere and free from all impediments and desires, or do not implore divine help—that is the grace of the Holy Spirit—which God has promised to all who call on Him for it night and day."[68] Here we clearly see, complained Meyer, their inconsistency: sometimes Socinians follow Wiszowaty in interpreting Scripture exclusively in terms of reason, "sometimes they require in addition the grace and assistance of the Holy Spirit."[69] "What is necessary to know for salvation is presented and expressed," they contend, "so clearly in the Holy Writings that anyone of sound mind and free from prejudice and passions can immediately understand it." Anything that remains obscure is not necessary.[70] Yet, the Socinians abandon this principle the moment difficulties arise. Even so, where orthodox Calvinist, Lutheran, and Catholic theologians are "the enemy" of free, independent rational philosophy which all lovers of truth must fight, Socinians support "our party and are, though not totally, on our side, not differing much from our position, as far as can be gathered from their writings."[71] Wiszowaty did not go quite far enough and failed to eliminate all the Socinians' residual distinction between theology and philosophy, held Meyer, but was nevertheless a vital ally against a hostile world.

4.4. FUSING RADICAL REFORMATION WITH RADICAL ENLIGHTENMENT

A principal function of the *cercle spinoziste* was its role as a debating ground and meeting-point, for extreme radical Socinians (and Collegiants) with radical philosophy and Spinozists.[72] The eagerness of Collegiants such as Jelles, Balling, and Rieuwertsz to fuse theology into philosophy, and support and, from the late 1650s, congregate around, Spinoza, proved highly divisive in Collegiant circles and posed an eventually alarming challenge to Socinian leaders striving to defend their movement as a theological sect. But this development, and the ensuing Socinian rift, also raises the question of how exactly Radical Reformation finally fed into what became the Radical Enlightenment.

[67] Leibniz, *Theodicy*, 82–3.
[68] Meyer, *Philosophy as the Interpreter*, 207, 216.
[69] Meyer, *Philosophy as the Interpreter*, 207.
[70] Meyer, *Philosophy as the Interpreter*, 210–11.
[71] Meyer, *Philosophy as the Interpreter*, 206; Israel, *Radical Enlightenment*, 204.
[72] Krop, "Secularism of Spinoza," 75, 78–9.

Some scholars discern a blurring and rapid diversification within the late seventeenth-century Socinian movement, as well as its growing impact due to the migration of many key Socinians across Europe from Poland to Transylvania, Germany, Holland, and Britain from the mid-seventeenth century onwards, characterized by a growing strain of skepticism in place of dogmatic denial of the Trinity. This blurring both encouraged receptivity to various strands of contemporary philosophy, Cartesian, Spinozist, and Lockean, and helped harden the more theological tendency. "The new Socinians not only consist of a mixture of identities," argues Mulsow, "they also illustrate the tendency toward a new unity and commonality," convergence reflected in the growing stress on reason as the key to understanding Scripture and increasing appeal to individual conscience and freedom of thought. "From them, came many deists and so-called early Enlightenment philosophers shortly thereafter."[73]

But if late seventeenth-century Socinianism became a stepping stone to fragmentation, deism, and Enlightenment in general,[74] it also strikingly formed a stepping stone to radically enlightened thought. A key strand of the Radical Enlightenment that the Radical Renaissance with its philosophical elitism wholly missed and first appeared on the European scene via Radical Reformation specifically was the principle that since reason is the exclusive path to truth and to a universal morality of equality, "reason" as opposed to "superstition," dogmatism, and intolerance needs urgently to be inculcated, by new techniques and methods of education, into society as a whole, that is into the minds of all. In this connection, the Moravian reformer Jan Amos Komensky, or Comenius (1592–1670), stands among the foremost figures of Radical Reformation and chief precursors of the fusion of Radical Reformation with Radical Enlightenment: for no one else, certainly in the seventeenth century projected a broader, more impressive vision of how to improve human life and society universally through education than this remarkable Czech contemporary and interlocutor of Descartes. A revolutionary figure in his vision of the social purpose of philosophy, his innovativeness in education theory derived directly from rootedness in the Radical Reformation. A fervent Christian, man of faith and believer in the Trinity to the extent of getting into long and arduous debates with Socinian preachers in Poland, Transylvania, Holland, and elsewhere over the true nature of Christ and Christianity, he had no wish to subordinate enlightened reform to religious authority, churchmen, and traditional theology. Rather, he always remained a sworn foe not just of Catholicism but all major churches and all clergies, and all religious authority and theology in the sense understood by Calvinists and Lutherans. He was as uncompromising in championing toleration, freedom of conscience, and freedom of expression as any Socinian.

Comenius' family belonged to the Moravian Brethren, or *Unitas Fratrum*, a sect surviving persecution in the Czech lands largely underground, whose founder, Jan

[73] Mulsow, "The "New Socinians," 51; Mulsow, *Radikale Frühaufklärung* i. 112–15, 134, 139–40.
[74] Ogonowski, "Sozianismus und die Aufklärung," 80–1.

Hus (*c*.1369–1415), was burnt at the stake for heresy in 1415 and whose followers, following the Protestant defeat at the Battle of the White Mountain in 1620, found themselves fiercely persecuted throughout the Austrian Habsburg empire. Like other radical Protestants, the Moravian Brethren wanted religion proclaimed and taught solely in the vernacular, not Latin; but went much further than most in equating religion with pious conduct rather than belief in doctrines, insisting on the purely pastoral role of religious leaders, and abjuring the use of theology to forge confessional allegiances with churches, or alliances with rulers.

Comenius studied and taught in Moravia, Germany, Sweden, Poland, Transylvania, England, and Hungary beside the Netherlands. For a seventeenth-century savant his learning and experience were broad and exceptionally cosmopolitan; and all this he deployed to counter everything denominational, dogmatic, sectional, and national. Though strongly attracted to the Socinian–Unitarian conception of rational religion with "reason" as the supreme and only decisive criterion of truth and a strong adherent of "kritischer antikirchlicher Antidogmatismus" [critical anti-church anti-dogmatism], he also believed Christianity's unity as an undogmatic, enlightened religion required unifying symbols. He sought to retain the Trinity as an emblem of spiritual inspiration, his thoughts on the topic reflecting his conception of the world's unity and oneness, his idea that theology and philosophy must fuse into a single entity comprising all knowledge and awareness of reality, that men must learn to steep themselves in the essence of things instead of lose themselves in the vastness of detail, polemic, and diversity.[75] He offered a moral universalism that stemmed from his religious background merged with an unprecedented emphasis on education instead of belief, sacraments, or Church discipline, rendering education and pious conduct the true path to universal salvation.

Education, not belief, he proclaimed the sole effective means to elevate mankind to a higher level, promote peace and end persecution, fanaticism, and intolerance, advances without which mankind cannot rise morally. By redefining religion as pious conduct and education, not faith or belief, rejecting confessional theology and a professionally-trained separate priesthood claiming religious authority over the community, while demanding that education be universal and linked to rejection of intolerance, he foreshadowed such eighteenth-century Unitarian democrats as Richard Price and Joseph Priestley (1733–1804), who likewise sought to combine a rationalized, de-theologized Christianity with one-substance philosophy and universalism in morality. It became a defining feature of this type of "Christian Radical Enlightenment" that it refused to employ faith or doctrine as grounds for hostility against even freethinkers and unbelievers. "Though steadfastly attached from his earliest years to the Christian religion", noted Price's first biographer, and his "own opinion as to its nature and design, he indulged no evil passions or prejudice against

[75] Kuchlbauer, *Johannes Amos Comenius' anti-sozianistische Schriften*, 70–5.

those who entertained different opinions or even who rejected it altogether. His candour and liberality in this respect were indeed truly exemplary."[76]

What for the Protestants was the disaster of the White Mountain, and consequent flight of most leaders of the Moravian brethren from their native country, turned Comenius into a political as well as religious and educational revolutionary.[77] Without a comprehensive overturning of the thought-patterns, oppression, and persecution imposed by monarchy in alliance with theology and churchmen, the exile, persecution, and marginalization of the Moravian Brethren, the Polish Brethren, and groups like them, would prove unending. The world needed a revolutionary transformation and this revolution he planned with tireless energy and hope, turning it in basic respects into an Enlightenment program: only by extricating men from their fatal ignorance—ignorance that supports and justifies oppressive government allied to theologically-based religious authority—can men be redeemed and enter the realm of universal justice and charity presided over by a universal college of the learned functioning as a higher spiritual court designed to adjudicate and ensure harmony and peace between countries and states.

Despite his theological irenicism, Comenius was no pacifist, and no follower of Castellio or Coornhert: he believed, rather, in just revolution by the sword, convinced his revolution's prime enemy, the Catholic Church, would be overthrown by divine providence acting through zealous princely warriors. This moved him to support the Elector Palatine's election as king of Bohemia in 1618, the spark that ignited the Thirty Years War, and back the Swedish monarch and prince of Transylvania in invading Poland in the 1650s, again with ruinous consequences for Protestantism throughout east-central Europe, and not least for his own sect, the Moravian Brethren.[78] Bayle, detesting all religious war as well as all Reformation millenarians and chiliasts, later scathingly condemned this aspect of Comenius' efforts: especially Comenius' espousal, infused with millenarianism, of kings and political alliances.[79] But despite this, Comenius' general program made him one of Europe's pre-eminent reformers and visionaries especially in the field of education, and a great social philosopher. Education, promoting all knowledge including the latest findings in science, was the fittest tool for elevating and propagating what is best in humanity. His ideas entailed an even more stunning leap in the progress of the human mind—what Enlightenment thinkers called the *l'esprit humain*—than Rousseau's ideas on education later. For Comenius' educational theory represents the first comprehensive rejection of the medieval conception of education as specialized knowledge, especially theology and mysteries, reserved for small elites of society couched in a restricted language—Latin—and terminology accessible only to those specially trained in it. If education

[76] Morgan, *Memoirs*, 93.

[77] Denis, *Comenius*, 20, 123–4; Mulsow, *Enlightenment Underground*, 56, 271.

[78] MacCulloch, *The Reformation*, 463–4.

[79] Kuyper to Bayle, The Hague, 5 June 1692 (Letter 871), *CPB* VIII. 576; Laursen, "L'Anti-millénarisme de Bayle," 196–8, 207.

is to fulfill its potential as a generator of moral truth and human dignity, promoting a universal irenicism, contended Comenius in his educational writings, the essence of human learning must be taught to everyone, male and female, everywhere and in the same way, must be universal in the sense that no national, ethnic, or theological denominational forms of discrimination intervene, and taught not just in the vernacular relevant to each country but using familiar terms current in society.[80]

In his one prolonged discussion with Descartes which took place at Endegeest, near Leiden, in 1642, Comenius denied that "reason" must be defined in Cartesian fashion as purely abstract or that knowledge can be effectively transmitted to children in an abstract manner. For Comenius, using illustrations, pictures of all kinds, symbols, and diagrams was fundamental to didactic technique at all stages of children's, and, later, men's development. The visual *and* sensual in all their dimensions he considered basic to knowledge and inherent in reason itself. Against Descartes's pure abstract reason, he urged a conception of reason based on a dialectic of rationality working with the sense-experience infusing all our perceptions, inferences, and conclusions. Envisaging the mind as a dual mechanism responding to everything, as reason dialectically interacting with sense-experience, he clashed with Descartes, and posthumously also Locke who viewed the mind as an empty slate, a *tabula rasa*, filled by experiences from which valid inferences are subsequently to be derived via reason. For Comenius, there can be no such process as sense-experience first and reason making inferences afterwards. Experience and inference, he maintained, operate together and are inseparable.[81] He came close to rejecting all dualism of mind and body separating thought from the connected sensual arena of feelings and impulse.

As Radical Reformation buttressed the educational universalism and egalitarianism of Comenius so the Unitarianism of Priestley, Price, Benjamin Rush, and Jebb would later connect their embrace of democracy and political egalitarianism and engagement with one-substance, monist philosophy. Although there are significant differences between the democratizing political stance of Price and that of Priestley with Priestley eventually the fiercer of the two in their shared anti-monarchism, both, like all radical enlighteners, were, by definition, nevertheless distinctly hesitant about involving the illiterate and ignorant in the active political process, and noticeably reluctant to enfranchise the illiterate. Both dwelt on the need for universal education to raise the level of the illiterate while insisting that the freedoms of civil society must mean equal legal status for all. Priestley was even more emphatic than Price in insisting that the purpose of the state is exclusively to promote the worldly "happiness" of all equally, and the "common good."[82] Despite lingering differences between their respective political views that were by no means unimportant, this brought the

[80] MacCulloch, *The Reformation*, 683, 696–7; Kuchlbauer, *Johannes Amos Comenius' antisozianistische Schriften*, 72–4; further on this see Pavel Floss, "The Problem of Comenius' Sensualism," and the other papers in the *Symposium Comenianum 1982. The Impact of J. A. Comenius on Educational Thinking and Practice*, ed. M. Kyralova and J. Privratika (Uhersky Brod, 1984).

[81] Floss, "The Problem of Comenius' Sensualism," 103–5.

[82] Duthille, "Right of Resistance," 419–20 and n. 53; Sakkas, "Joseph Priestley, 104–16."

Christian Radical Enlightenment of Jebb, Price, and Priestley equally into immediate and close proximity with the atheistic Radical Enlightenment, and to a surprising level of convergence in the sphere of morality and politics, as John Jebb (1736–86), a Cambridge don converted to radical Socinianism after studying Scripture in the original Hebrew and Greek and who wanted Cambridge undergraduates to become versed in Grotius' writings in favour of Christianity, natural law, and toleration as well as the Greek text of the Gospels, abundantly recognized. A warm admirer of d'Holbach's books, or at any rate of their moral content, his burning sense of the injustices of the world turned him into a leader of political radicalism and of the incipient Anglo-Irish democratic movement in the 1770s.[83]

During the 1790s, the bulk of the British public may have been aroused to dogged antagonism to the French Revolution but a substantial segment of the English, Scottish, Welsh, and Irish intelligentsias were not. Tiny minority though they were, the distinguished group of British intellectuals who believed a revolution was needed not only in America and France but also other places, including Britain and Ireland, identified by the French revolutionary journalist Camille Desmoulins, in his *Révolutions de France et de Brabant*, as "les Price, les Williams, les Priestley, les Horne-Tooke, les Payne,"[84] vividly illustrates the convergence at this point of freethinking radical thought with "Christian Radical Enlightenment" stemming from the Socinian tradition. David Williams (1738–1816), a friend of Jebb, a Welsh democrat and universalist egalitarian born near Caerphilly to a Methodist family, later adopted uncompromisingly Unitarian views verging on deism, imbibed whilst studying at the Carmarthen Academy, in the years 1753–7. His *Letters on Political Liberty* (1782), appearing also in French, translated by Brissot, revealed another fully radical dissenting minister strongly committed to universal toleration, universal education, and abolition of all articles of religion; like Price, Priestley, and Jebb, he also became thoroughly estranged from the British Parliament and constitutional system. Chosen, like Priestley, an honorary French citizen, in September 1792, he moved to Paris and undertook to assist the French National Assembly's *Comité de constitution* chaired by Condorcet, in its deliberations, formally presenting his democratic constitutional recommendations on 29 April 1793.

The doctrine of *volonté générale* Williams judged precious and truly *philosophique* but only when properly understood and applied with precision. Rousseau's brilliant imagination had caused the French to waste much time and effort on illusory notions of *volonté générale*, his concept being weak especially in providing too few platforms for debate at intermediate levels. Genuine *volonté générale* would improve on Rousseau by embracing, among other things, women's right to vote and become active citizens, and ensuring their equal access to education; women should compose half the members of juries dealing with cases involving both sexes. It was strange, even absurd, averred Williams, that in Britain the idea of equality was generally rejected,

[83] Page, *John Jebb*, 67–76, 100, 134.
[84] Hammersley, *French Revolutionaries and English Republicans*, 157.

while in France it possessed immense weight but was so inconsistently applied. A [revised] *Declaration of Rights*, couched in the language of republicanism was needed but would be of little use among a populace unused to hearing democratic republican language unless there first took place an organized campaign of public education to render such concepts clear and familiar to ordinary folk.[85]

Among late eighteenth-century British radicals, Jebb was the most passionate, even more than Price and Priestley, in tying democratization to the right of "the people of England" to an "annual election of their representatives, and to equal representation." Unfortunately, the "contagion of corrupted doctrine," as he expressed it, in March 1772, spread "by the craft and cunning of a designing and despotic priesthood," had ruined not only Catholicism but the greater part of Protestantism.[86] For Jebb, who agreed with d'Holbach that "natural rights" are not "created, but only secured by society,"[87] "true religion, the religion of the Gospel," is exclusively "founded on the solid basis of sound reason and uncontroverted fact."[88] Superstition and ignorance had tragically betrayed the people into the hands of designing men: "by subjugating your understanding to the dominion of the priest, you open the door to mystery, and the worst species of despotic power."[89] Only by eradicating the "mysterious doctrine of the Trinity, the mysterious doctrine of Original Sin, the mysterious doctrine of Justification by Faith and not by works, and those other mysteries, which, with envious breath, you have raised as clouds to veil the meridian splendours of the Gospel from the sight of men," can mankind progress.[90]

Jebb recognized the close proximity of his own views to [d'Holbach's] *Système de la nature*. There are no theological mysteries. Justice and good works are the only true religion. Jesus had been a true "'théiste, dont la religion a été peu a peu corrompue' [theist, whose religion had little by little been corrupted]. Our duty to our neighbor is the sole basis of true religion. [D'Holbach] conceives this to be the voice of nature. I only differ from him in thinking it is the voice of God."[91] "Reason," Jebb, like the radical *philosophes*, proclaimed the exclusive path to a better future for humanity: "deprive the priest of his favourite power of creed-making, and of creed-imposing, and reason re-assumes her throne, and true religion beams, with unclouded lustre, on the mind; the virtues follow in quick succession, and all is light, tranquility and joy."[92]

Priestley's democratic credentials too were beyond doubt: his insisting that the illiterate should enjoy equal civil rights but should not participate actively in politics while society works to eliminate illiteracy, striving toward the goal of all being equally represented, was entirely typical of the Radical Enlightenment. His writings likewise acknowledged close proximity to the materialism, determinism, and monism as well as the moral thought of Collins, d'Holbach, and Diderot. Though certainly a

[85] *La Chronique du Mois, ou Les cahiers patriotiques*, ed. J. Oswald, L. S.Mercier, et al. (Paris, 1791–3), v (Feb. 1793), 39; Gauchet, *Révolution des pouvoirs*, 114; Page, *John Jebb*, 101, 225.

[86] Jebb, *The Works* iii. 161.

[87] Jebb, *The Works* ii. 180.

[88] Jebb, *The Works* ii. 206.

[89] Jebb, *The Works* iii. 178.

[90] Jebb, *The Works* iii. 186.

[91] Jebb, *The Works* ii. 165–9.

[92] Jebb, *The Works* iii. 178.

"Christian" in his own rarefied sense and later, in the United States, clashing with Volney over the latter's atheism (but not his materialism), he was a writer whose ideas clearly embodied the Radical Enlightenment's key elements—revolutionary democratic politics tied to determinist-materialist metaphysics and the principle that human morality and law are best built on the principle of equality.[93]

Finally, there is a need to comment on the argument that the "structural dependence of secularization literature upon sectarian religion" is so pronounced that in reality "Spinoza and Bayle personify the organic relationship between morality and theistic commitment that they were supposed to be destroying."[94] "To engage the Christian underworld of the radical Reformation is to discover striking prototypes of ideas considered 'fully secular' and resolutely 'natural' in Spinoza and Bayle."[95] Here is an approach that can seemingly be employed to undermine the "Radical Enlightenment" thesis and claims about Western modernity by holding that the core of Spinoza's "liberating stance" was, in reality, its combining faith and intellect, God and rationality, that Spinoza's intimate connection with the piety of Collegiant friends like Jelles and Balling led not to secularization but to a conception of philosophy that fused the Radical Reformation's Christian piety with reason: for Spinoza "it was only with Christ, "the supreme philosopher", that philosophy made a decisive entrance, eclipsing the "servitude" of superstition and the treadmill of religion," for Spinoza, Christ is the "way of salvation [via salutis]."[96]

A marked degree of convergence there certainly was. But one must bear in mind that Spinoza's circle consisted of two somewhat disparate groups, Collegiants like Jelles, Balling, and Rieuwertsz on the one side, and freethinkers sharply critical of even the most radical Collegiant fringe for being inconsistent in their rationalism, headed by Meyer, Koerbagh, and Van den Enden, on the other. The details of his life and letters show Spinoza went to considerable pains to mediate between, and bridge, these two not quite identical impulses which Meyer and Koerbagh identified as close allies but which did not entirely converge as regards "reason" and "faith."[97] For Koerbagh, the spiritualists, Quakers, and Brownists were sometimes on the right track, like the most rational Socinians, but, equally, "are often simple, foolish people" who failed to embrace reason comprehensively enough.[98] Jelles undoubtedly considered Spinoza's system a "Christian" philosophy,[99] while Koerbagh states that "only the Socinians are free of religious fallacies,"[100] and Spinoza pronounces Christ "the supreme philosopher." But one must also remember that, for Spinoza, Scripture was intended only to teach the common people "obedience" to the moral and religious law and not correct their superstitious beliefs, which, according to Spinoza and his following, Christ and the Apostles made no effort to do. All Scripture is adjusted to the ignorant and

[93] Israel, "Spinoza and the Religious Radical Enlightenment," 191–3.
[94] Erdozain, "Heavenly Poise," 76. [95] Erdozain, "Heavenly Poise," 77.
[96] Erdozain, "Heavenly Poise," 81; Hunter, *Radical Protestantism*, 183–5.
[97] Israel, "Meyer, Koerbagh," 198–205; Israel, "Andrzej Wiszowaty," 87–8.
[98] Koerbagh, *Light Shining in Dark Places*, 244–5. [99] Hunter, *Radical Protestantism*, 94.
[100] Koerbagh, *Light Shining in Dark Places*, 322–3.

superstitious notions of the Jews of antiquity, contends Spinoza, while the teaching of Christ and the Apostles is so tuned to the understanding of ordinary folk of their age that its miraculous, supernatural, demonic, and revelatory dimensions possess no truth value whatever; for Spinoza, Scripture contains no truths except as regards moral content.

This is not to deny that the Radical Reformation in its seventeenth-century Dutch Collegiant legacy converged closely with and handsomely contributed to the rise of Radical Enlightenment, which, as the crucible of trans-Atlantic Western secular "modernity," first began in the Netherlands. But in drawing this conclusion a measure of caution and some strict definitions concerning radical Christian piety and "secularization" remain necessary. It must be remembered that in late seventeenth-century Holland, the Collegiants themselves split between those who saw no danger in fusing religion with monist philosophy and eliminating the supernatural and those who argued that if you eliminate miracles, the supernatural, demons, and angels there is no more religion, that Koerbagh's "reason must be judge in everything" will extinguish all revealed religion.[101] "Secularization" begins where the "unchurched" reach the point, as a few of them did, of not only eliminating all religious authority and theological dogma but the supernatural as such so that there is no longer any divine revelation separate from natural processes, and no miracles, sacraments, resurrection, angels, or demons. At that point philosophical reason's claims to be "judge of everything" can no longer be contested. If the saving of a man's soul becomes, as Koerbagh expresses it, "salvation by which someone who is ignorant is guided through instruction to understanding, knowledge and wisdom, and through reason to the truth,"[102] then we have crossed the line from Radical Reformation to pure Radical Enlightenment. If "to write inspired by the Holy Ghost is to write while endowed with an enlightened mind, in accordance with reason and unchangeable laws"[103] then the Holy Ghost has effectively vanished, and been secularized.

The contention that "Spinoza's religious thought remains closer [...] to the Christians who rejected him than to the atheists of the Enlightenment who adopted him as their own"[104] superficially presents a paradox enticing to some but hardly one that is cogent. For Spinoza there are no miracles, and have never been, and the reason one finds so many narrated in the Old and New Testaments is simply that "it is not the intention of the Bible, as we have shown, to explain things in terms of natural causes but only to speak of things that commonly occupy people's imaginations, and to do so in a manner and style calculated to inspire wonder about things and thus impress devotion upon the minds of the common people."[105] In other words a great

[101] Koerbagh, *Light Shining in Dark Places*, 498–9; Fix, *Prophecy and Reason*, 225–31; Van Bunge, *Johannes Bredenburg*, 243–5.

[102] Koerbagh, *Light Shining in Dark Places*, 118–19.

[103] Koerbagh, *Light Shining in Dark Places*, 242–3.

[104] Hunter, *Radical Protestantism*, 187; Cliteur and Gordon, "Enlightenment in Contemporary Cultural Debate," 311.

[105] Spinoza, *Theological-Political Treatise*, 90.

part of what one finds in Scripture, not least when we encounter blind men being healed by faith, or great empires collapsing due to sins, is entirely false in terms of facts and causes, since Scripture is not a guide to truth in any sense but exclusively to what impresses the ignorant, and superstitious. Such a stance, ruling out all possibility of revelation and divine providence in the sense of interruption of the normal laws of nature, is wholly incompatible with any meaningful conception of religion, as is Spinoza's eliminating faith and belief as conditions for salvation. "Miracles could not demonstrate to [the ancient Hebrews] that God cares equally for all men: only philosophy can teach this."[106] In Spinoza's thought whether one believes in Christ or not is simply irrelevant to salvation and "blasphemy" is redefined as what is "contrary to reason." Far from essential, beliefs and faith are just guides to men's misconceptions, biases, and delusions.

The claim that in Early Modern times, there was no "secularization," that "no such process was taking place,"[107] though intriguing, in particular by consigning the entire secular thrust of the Enlightenment as recognized by a vast tradition of historiography to the waste-paper bin, is nevertheless profoundly misconceived and even distinctly disturbing, given that the Enlightenment, and especially Radical Enlightenment, is the intellectual foundation of modern secularism. One can term Spinoza's "God or Nature" a religious idea if one wishes, and indeed he himself did; but this is to redefine "religion" and the "religious" to mean upholding justice and charity, an exclusively moral stance without reference to either revealed or divined truths accessed by mystical processes that is assuredly equivalent to "secularization." By this definition, one can be secular and Christian in a moral and cultural sense, and equally well secular and Jewish.

[106] Spinoza, *Theological-Political Treatise*, 88.

[107] Hunter, "Secularisation," 12.

5

English "Deism" and its Pre-1700 Roots

5.1. RIVAL "DEIST" IDENTITIES (1700–1740)

For the Early Modern world, including the Americas, "atheism" and "deism" represented menacing challenges of a scale and depth hard for us today fully to comprehend. Circumstances differed strikingly from those of the Western Middle Ages when "atheism" and "deism", where they existed at all, were either academic abstracts deployed as targets in university debates, or so well masked behind walls of secrecy that concrete instances practically never intruded on theological and philosophical debate, or the general consciousness.[1] Anxiety in this regard escalated dramatically with, and especially after, the Renaissance and Reformation due to the growing intellectual challenge to religious authority, rising numbers of heresies identified and heretics tried, and also the now much more elaborate, more forcefully imposed, confessional system interweaving theology at every level with society, education, politics, and culture.

The sixteenth and early seventeenth century was an age of systematic and intensifying "confessionalization" and insistent punishment of confessional disobedience. In dramatic contrast to these dominant realities of the age, deism and atheism both dared to imply the total irrelevance of all confessional systems, and hence the breathtaking spuriousness of theology's oppressive dominance over culture, education, and society, the superfluous character of theological arguments, of theology's sacraments and churchmen themselves. "To a deist it is all the same," explained one commentator, "whether he takes the path to heaven via Rome or Geneva, Wittenberg or Raków, or Constantinople."[2] As the drama intensified after 1650, universal alarm and indignation was kept at boiling point by a ceaseless ringing of solemn pronouncements, ecclesiastical councils and academic rulings condemning the heinousness of the great theological crimes of "atheism" and "deism."

Rejecting the beliefs of the great majority, "atheism" seemed to denote denial of all the basic tenets of morality, law, and natural law. Hence, the "atheist" and "deist" continued to be generally perceived, at all levels of society, with unmatched horror, special categories of public foes outlawed by state and church together, betrayers of

[1] Schröder, *Ursprünge des Atheismus*, 58–60.
[2] Löwe, *Dogmatische und Moralische Einleitung*, 47.

the entire social, moral, and legal order, corrupters of all structures of authority and duty, enemies of the most fundamental rules of social and political life and education. What contemporaries labeled "atheism" became everywhere an immense source of anxiety, controversy, investigation, and recrimination universally perceived as a towering menace.

While freedom of expression in England, after the Glorious Revolution of 1688, certainly stretched further than in virtually all Continental countries, nevertheless, in England too, with the Anglican Church and Parliament mobilized against the irreligious threat, and the "Blasphemy Act" of 1698 in place, such freedom was undoubtedly more circumscribed than was once supposed. If neither Toland, Collins, Tindal, nor any of those routinely designated "deists" at the time, and often since, ever admitted to being "atheists" in print, none admitted to being "deists" either, as was hardly surprising given that contemporaries understood "deism" as the product of a great "prejudice against the Christian faith," a horrendous offence closely related to "atheism."[3] No declared, public "atheist," but today considered to have been an atheist even so, Collins never unambiguously rejected allegiance to theism.[4]

Arguably not one of these was really a "deist" in any real, meaningful theistic sense. To complicate matters further, even the most subversive "deists", Blount, Toland, Collins, and Tindal, remained sufficiently steeped in Protestant tradition and theology to enable them to dress up some of their insinuations in misleadingly sounding innocuous ways, which has proved a help to those modern scholars arguing, implausibly, that the non-providential "deists" were "not radical."[5] In any case, all deists before the mid-eighteenth century had a good deal to hide, even when it was genuine "deism" rooted in theism they were concealing or, at least, obscuring. Hence, in revisiting the English "deists" it seems best, or most likely to clarify matters, to divide the "deists" considered into two broad but fundamentally separate categories: on the one hand, "déisme réel" [real deism], entailing a benign divine providence that is truly a creative force, should be clearly distinguished from "déisme nominal" [nominal deism], masking atheism.[6] In accordance with this classification, Toland and Collins were not really "deists" but Spinozist atheists.

Plainly, the ambiguities and evasiveness would be easier to negotiate, had "deists" masking their private views kept personal notes recording their underlying real views, indicating how these differed from what surfaces in their published writings. It is exceedingly rare, though, to encounter an eighteenth-century "deist" self-exposure, like that of the "greatest *Systematiker*," as he has been called, among the deists, Hermann Samuel Reimarus (1694–1768).[7] An authentic, classic deist, Reimarus' private journal of his spiritual odyssey, his *Apologie*, composed for no eyes but his

3 Jacob, *Newtonians*, 202–3; Gawlick, "Epikur bei den Deisten," 329, 337; Hudson, *English Deists*, 2–3, 79.
4 Hudson, *Enlightenment and Modernity*, 15.
5 See, especially, Wigelsworth, *Deism*, 4, 7–8, 204–7.
6 On these categories, see Jaffro, "Qu'est-ce qu'être déiste?," 273.
7 Gawlick, "Epikur bei den Deisten," 326.

own, helps map precisely the forms and extent of the evasion and imposture infusing his published writings and ascertain the exact nature of his subversive intent from the 1730s onwards. A highly skilled and innovative Bible critic indebted for his critical methodology to Grotius and Le Clerc as well as the German philological tradition, no fiercer early and mid- eighteenth-century foe of the Christian Gospel (in private) or adversary of the notion that Scripture is divine revelation could be found. Behind the scenes, he was a vehement and implacable adversary of all Christianity (and Judaism, albeit expertly using Jewish polemical texts to demolish Christian arguments). Yet Reimarus, the evidence shows, was no atheist but unquestionably a true "deist" who extolled the Almighty and divine providence and attributed to animal and plant species a benignly intended fixity accompanied by divinely intended drives and characteristics. A thoroughgoing deist embracing divine creation of the universe and the deity's continuing intervention in the world's day-to-day governance, he was in no way part of the Radical Enlightenment.[8]

Firmly excluding Reimarus from the ranks of the Radical Enlightenment is not just an academic issue of categories, or result of his being fiercely anti-Spinozist. For Reimarus' deism was embedded in undeviatingly conservative positions as regards social hierarchy, education, and politics, and deep reserve even as to whether most people should ever be permitted to learn what he considered the truth about Christianity's allegedly false character and bogus origins. No reformer, let alone revolutionary, Reimarus' overall *Weltanschauung* was by no means a fully secularized one despite his antipathy to all current theology. A leading intellectual light of early eighteenth-century Hamburg, and ardent Newtonian fervently proclaiming physico-theology and the "argument from design," Reimarus neither sought elimination of religious authority in society (however much he sapped its foundations in secret), nor advocated anything remotely like a democratizing republicanism. Due to his furtiveness, his sweeping inner rejection of belief and religious authority remained totally unnoticed for decades, from the 1730s to the 1760s wholly screened from the public. Only with the *Fragmentenstreit* [Fragment struggle] of 1774–8, when Lessing published and discussed several anonymous "fragments" by him claiming the "fragments" were the thoughts and conclusions of someone thinking very differently about the issues concerned than he himself did, did Reimarus' critique suddenly become massively disturbing.[9]

Providential "real" or "strong" deism of the kind Reimarus (and later Rousseau) manifested, like the deism broadcast in England by Wollaston and Morgan, was indeed generally permeated by Newtonian physico-theology, especially the "argument from design," a style of argument immensely successful in bridging the gap between authentic deism and traditional religiosity thereby helping narrow the distance separating the Christian and non-Christian dimensions, or sides, of the

[8] Israel, "Philosophical Context," 188–97; on Reimarus' critical use of Jewish sources, see Klein, "Reimarus, the Hamburg Jews," 159–82.

[9] For the *Fragmentenstreit* see Israel, *Democratic Enlightenment*, 314–25.

"moderate Enlightenment."[10] If strict Newtonianism ruled out "particular providence," all notion of a divine providence that could suspend what the Cambridge-educated Staffordshire teacher and deist William Wollaston (1659–1724) called the "prodigious scheme" of the normal laws of nature, denying the divinity intervenes in human life with any frequency, Newtonian general providence remained an all-knowing, all-encompassing and benign supervisor. Although this kind of deism, that of Wollaston and Thomas Morgan (d. 1743), eliminated "supernaturalism" from the picture, it still venerated a knowing, transcendent God and envisaged human social organization and the existing moral order, like species development, as the outcome of what is divinely planned and intended, the design of what Morgan called the "one supreme, universal, independent, contriver, designer, and disposer of all things."[11] The overriding difference between deists and atheists, correctly affirmed Wekhrlin, in 1788, is over the issue of whether a knowing, intelligent divine Providence guides the world, or, as Spinoza and his followers held, does not.[12]

But if a wide intellectual gulf separates "real deism" from atheism and Spinozism, in principle, general usage, and contemporary intellectual culture, in practice the gulf between "deism" and "atheism" was continually being obscured and hazed over. During the early and mid-eighteenth century, "nominal deists" everywhere produced highly convoluted strategies designed to protect themselves and others while promoting a range of disruptive moral, political, and social attitudes. On a purely abstract, theoretical level, atheism and deism sound fundamentally different, and in the cases of Morgan, Wollaston, or Reimarus, were actually wholly distinct. But this was much harder in other cases. For on a practical level, the question was not whether God exists, or any abstract difference between deism and atheism, but whether God reveals truths to men, delivers moral systems, performs miracles, sends saviors, inspires prophets, rewards and punishes, and can suspend the normal course of nature. If there are no miracles, prophets, saviors, or resurrections, no divine interference in the normal course of things, then there exists no religious authority and the difference between deism and atheism is—for social, moral, educational, and political purposes—voided. What matters in practice is whether God desires a particular outcome and delegates His authority to churches and churchmen, or does not.[13] As the French revolutionary Camille Desmoulins observed in his stirring revolutionary pamphlet *La France Libre* (August 1789) what chiefly mattered for advancing revolutionary democratic republicanism in the world—for rejecting monarchy and ecclesiastical authority along with aristocracy—was not whether the universe's ultimate design and immutable laws do or do not derive from some remote divine presence, but whether divine intervention and governance of the world is sufficiently conscious, real, and effective to shape and sanction the existing political and social order or not.

[10] Feingold, "Partnership on Glory," 304–5; Israel, *Radical Enlightenment*, 519; Israel, *Enlightenment Contested*, 202–3.

[11] Morgan, *Physico-Theology*, 140.

[12] Wekhrlin, *Hyperboreische Briefe* iii (1788), 40–1.

[13] Camille Desmoulins, *La France Libre* (Paris, August, 1789), 11, 23–5, 31–41.

In many instances commentators like the Cambridge vice-chancellor Daniel Waterland (1683–1740), in the 1730s, were not mistaken in claiming that "what atheism chiefly aims at is, to sit loose from present restraints and future reckonings; and these two purposes may be competently served by deism, which is a more refined kind of atheism."[14] Within this perspective, the furtive non-providential "deism" propagated by Blount, Toland, Tindal, Collins, Franklin, Gordon, Paine, Palmer, and Jefferson closely conjoined with atheism to produce freethinking and libertarian, social, sexual, and emancipating political consequences. Such a position was very different from the positive deism of Wollaston and Reimarus as well as the "rational Christianity" of Newton and Clarke.[15] Hence, in the early Enlightenment British context, it makes excellent sense, since it is effectively impossible wholly to separate them, to treat atheism and anti-Scriptural, non-providential deism as merging, conjoined phenomena. All atheism and deism removing divine providence from the affairs of the world, and negating religious authority, sitting "loose from restraints," was apt for fomenting Radical Enlightenment. In practice, where deists erase active, knowing divine providence, removing all reason for prayer and penitence, criteria excepting the ardent Newtonian and Arian "Christian deist" Morgan from the black list but possibly not the late Chubb, virtually nothing, agreed Bishop Berkeley, distinguishes such unbelievers from "atheists."[16] Denying immaterial forces or supernatural entities and actions exist, denying Nature's laws can be suspended, or that miracles are possible, brought "deists" of the ilk of Toland, Tindal, Collins, Jefferson, and Paine close to determinism, materialism, and necessitarianism beside "atheism."[17]

During the first half of the eighteenth century, "atheism" and "deism," wherever obtrusively, or forcefully, expressed, continued to be vigorously repressed by the secular and ecclesiastical authorities, in Britain and America no less than continental Europe, by government decree, public opinion, the pulpit, and magistrates' courts. "Atheism" overlapping with non-providential "deism" earned fierce public condemnation at every level, including the universities where academic theses denouncing "deism" and atheism, and particular "atheist" thinkers and strands of "atheism" proliferated spectacularly from the late seventeenth century onwards. When, in 1706, Tindal demanded: "have not even atheists such as Vanini and Effendi"—the latter the unbelieving Turkish model of honesty and integrity, the legendary atheist of Istanbul portrayed as an iconic virtuous "atheist" by Bayle—"dy'd martyrs for their opinions?"[18] contemporaries were more likely to be shocked by Tindal's calling them "martyrs" than by their being hauled to the stake and scaffold and dispatched for "atheism."

The "Toleration Act" of 1689 explicitly excluded Catholics, Socinians, deists, and other anti-Trinitarians and provided no protection for Jews (already then again present in Britain) or Muslims; with the subsequent "Blasphemy Act" further curbing freedom of expression, it was clearly understood that atheists and deists not only

[14] Force, "Newtonians and Deism," 43.
[15] Force, "Newtonians and Deism," 60–2.
[16] Hudson, *Enlightenment and Modernity*, 14–15; Wigelsworth, "God always acts suitable", 159, 170.
[17] Hudson, *Enlightenment and Modernity*, 110–13.
[18] Tindal, *The Rights*, 184–5.

possessed no established rights but, unlike Jews and Unitarians, were not even tacitly tolerated. Consequently, openly refusing instituted religious authority and Revelation's divine character, given that it was on these that moral, legal, and social legitimacy rested, hardly seemed advisable to radical "nominal deists" rejecting divine governance of men, in the manner of thoroughgoing skeptics like Hume or Gibbon later, or to atheists proclaiming conservative social and political attitudes, like La Mettrie or Goethe. Neither "atheism" nor "nominal deism" could work unambiguously toward expurgating religious authority from government and legislation to produce the religiously neutral, secular state geared to the "common best" in a purely worldly sense. But wherever a "deist" did reject operative divine providence and governance of mankind, and demanded sweeping reforms, he was apt to belong to the Radical Enlightenment; for him too, confessional conformity, intolerance, priestly intercession and teaching represented obstacles to the desired changes, obstructive manifestations of imposture and deception, a barrier to be overcome, encouraging a combative attitude to "priestcraft," apt to be openly exhibited in a way Reimarus' antipathy was not.

For advocates of freedom of conscience, the 1689 Toleration Act was, of course, a huge and welcome advance on previous levels of toleration. But it was also, for many, a highly divisive, disturbing, and controversial upset. Tories and High Church ecclesiastics staunchly opposed the Act, sometimes disparagingly terming it "the Dutch Toleration." During the Dutch invasion of Britain, in November 1688, and its immediate aftermath, especially in the months London lay under Dutch military occupation and the Houses of Commons and Lords had their arms twisted by the Stadholder backed by a foreign army, foreign pressure (William III and his army) to all appearances, despite the extensive English (Whig) support, forcibly coerced Parliament into accepting the Revolution settlement, proclaiming William and Mary joint king and queen in place of the banished legitimate monarch, James II. Hardly had the Revolution begun than William's chief agent in England, Everard van Dijkvelt, "gave privately great assurance to the Nonconformists," as one observer put it, "that they should find great respect from the Prince when occasion offer'd; and that they might be satisfied that he was no friend to rigour and severity in religious matters, but a great friend to liberty of conscience."[19] In fact, William III never had the slightest respect for the Church of England except as a purely political construct, and little desire to uphold that church's traditional authority and privileges. Undeniably, the Toleration *was* the direct result of foreign intervention and deep indifference to the presiding church. Nonconformists received a limited toleration, aimed at accommodating Presbyterians, Congregationalists, and other dissenters while still excluding the universally prohibited and execrated categories, a considerable change from before 1688.

[19] BL C.108.bb 33 (2): "Separation and Sedition Inseparable," 11; more generally on Dijkvelt's role in the 1688–9 Revolution settlement, see Israel, *Anglo-Dutch Moment*, 116, 130–4.

Philosophically, early eighteenth-century English and American toleration was at best a hybrid, stop-gap measure, a political "fix" lacking inherent logic, devoid of principle. Britain received a limited toleration largely on the Dutch model, apart from two not insignificant differences: first, from 1689 there were two churches sanctioned by public authority instead of one—the "Anglican" in England, Wales, and Ireland and the Presbyterian in "North-Britain" (i.e. Scotland); secondly, and still more loathsome for many, given the influence of king and court, it became noticeably harder than in the United Provinces to shut out those not belonging to the "public church" from office-holding, political and diplomatic roles, and military command. "Since our nation is become an Amsterdam of religions," complained one anonymous critic of "the Dutch Toleration" imposed on England in 1689, "'tis requisite, we should have so much of the Amsterdam government, as not to let the Tolerated be our governors."[20] A vigilant guard against evasion, "imposture," and the real or alleged deliberate concealment of subversive heresies continued to figure among the characteristic features of cultural life and theological debate, injecting a strong dose of political animus into the swelling stream of theological repression, a social and cultural milieu aggressively besieging early eighteenth-century English "deism" throughout.[21]

The Early Modern world was formally a culture of strict limits and active repression. Powerful structures of authority invaded every realm of human existence—philosophy, the arts, novels, and sexual life no less than education, local government, foreign policy, and the military. At the same time, in both Holland and England surged a ceaseless intellectual commotion of a most disturbing new kind, in the universities, churches, and in general culture alike, striving with difficulty to determine where and how to implement the widely supported demand for tougher surveillance, censorship, and repression. When the deist earl of Shaftesbury published his *Letter Concerning Enthusiasm* in 1708, a text making no open avowal of deism, and still less atheism, but urging a wider toleration, and scoffing at zealotry, he provoked a major national furor, drawing furious indignation from Dissenters no less than Anglicans, all the main Protestant churches insisting on strict application of the 1689 Toleration Act's provisions, and repression of Anti-Trinitarianism together with deism and atheism. Britain and the Netherlands remained striking exceptions to the continuing quest of the age for confessional uniformity but only to a limited extent. Everyone seriously averse to religious persecution remained unavoidably at war with existing authority, society, law, and institutions and needed to express their thoughts in the contrived, devious, guarded manner Michel Onfray dubbed "penser sous le manteau."[22]

Orthodox endeavors to uncover the "atheism" supposedly lurking behind Cartesian, Leibnizian–Wolffian, and Lockean masks often appear contrived and paranoid

[20] BL C.108.bb 33 (2): "Separation and Sedition Inseparable," 29.

[21] Heyd, "Limits of Toleration," 155–6.

[22] Onfray, *Ultras des Lumières*, 28–31; Klein, *Shaftesbury*, 160–9.

to the modern reader. Yet, from their standpoint, the tireless worries and stringency of the orthodox were justified. Study of the late seventeenth-century clandestine philosophical literature circulating in limited circles, and copying, lending, and diffusion of forbidden manuscripts, shows these texts operated not just by borrowing from Epicurus, Hobbes, Spinoza, and Bayle but often also by highlighting, reworking, and drawing flagrantly subversive conclusions, from problematic features and formulations found in Machiavelli, Descartes, Malebranche, Gassendi, Leibniz, and Locke too.[23] As with Continental clandestine philosophical literature, one of the thorniest problems besetting study of early Enlightenment English "deism" is that concealment, evasion, and imposture, often assuming highly contrived and ingenious forms, everywhere abounded.

Careful sifting, then, is needed, between conservative real deists upholding "general providence" in the strong sense, designating the benevolent divine force planning and directing the natural and social order, and those rejecting divine governance along with existing forms of society, condemning the latter as oppressive, despotic, and corrupt. Radical "deist" critique of "superstition" and ecclesiastical "imposture," whenever we find it, was unlikely to be confined solely to issues of belief as the latter remained closely tied to constitutional questions, education and the laws, marriage practices, family ties, and a repressive sexual code. Those deeming prevailing systems of church government and dogma despotic found the entire social system, its laws and institutions, oppressive, corrupt, and couched in deceit. Hence, an integral feature of "radical deism," as we shall characterize it, was an unremitting attack on "priestcraft" as the prime source of the allegedly false consciousness blinding men to their being fundamentally deceived and misled to their own great disadvantage by authority generally.

Militant "deism" integral to Radical Enlightenment seethed underground in the universities, aristocratic retreats, London's coffee-houses, and frequently featured hints of democratic republicanism, but its principal attack was against theology, "priestcraft," and the practices and social, educational and moral strictures of the churches. Deeply characteristic of the radical "deists"—Shaftesbury, Tindal, Toland, and Collins—was the notion that the churches and priesthood had, from an early stage, betrayed their trust, parading their own "grandeur and authority (both in spirituals and temporals) absolutely repugnant to the spirit of the Gospel," everywhere seeking power and securing their corrupt goals by promoting a tyranny built on credulity, superstition, and ignorance.[24] Hardened "deists" lurking in small groups sought inspiration from each other and the past, from abroad, and from Jewish sources. Among the boldest of the Early Enlightenment radical "deist" sect in England were Continentals with strong English connections like Beverland, Mandeville, and the Piedmontese "deist" Alberto Radicati di Passerano (1698–1737).

[23] Paganini, *Philosophies clandestines*, 35–40, 60–78.
[24] Cavalho, "Atheists or Deists," 184, 188; Klein, *Shaftesbury*, 169.

Radicati flatly denied Hobbes, Spinoza, Bayle, or any other great thinkers were "atheists"—a term employed only "by the vulgar and those whose interest it is to decry them" since all such thinkers proclaim a First Cause under the name of "God", Nature or Matter, or Eternal Being. He went further than any English "deist" in calling for sweeping social and political change and in proclaiming "democratical government" the "most ancient and agreeable to the natural and free condition of men."[25] If he knew Spinoza from his Piedmontese days, and had long savored Hobbes and Vanini, developing a materialism that has been termed "Epicurean" rather than Tolandist, Radicati also enthusiastically imbibed Blount, "l'ingénieux Mr. Toland," Tindal, whom he called a "savant auteur de notre parti," and "that great and good man Mr. Collins."[26] He admired and absorbed them, and it was in the freer atmosphere of England, during the 1730s, that he fully developed the uncompromising republican and "deistic" ideas, and anti-Scripturalism (and Islamophilia) he outlined earlier in Piedmont.[27]

Motion, contends Radicati, in his *Philosophical Dissertation upon Death* (1732), rendered from Italian by a certain "Joseph Morgan," and published in London in 1732, is inherent in, not external to, matter; Newtonianism he rejected as a system; "divine providence" he repudiated outright, instead affirming the unalterable character of Nature's laws while rejecting all notion of absolute "good" and "evil." Good and bad he deemed purely relative to what benefits or damages society, like Spinoza, Shaftesbury, and, later, Helvétius.[28] The book provoked uproar, one royal minister styling it the "most impious and immoral book I ever read."[29] Arrested and briefly imprisoned, Radicati was released on bail and fled to Holland, where he died in 1737.

5.2. CONSERVATIVE "DEISM": WOLLASTON, MORGAN, AND CHUBB

Anglo-American "deists" who conformed to the basic "Radical Enlightenment" template as it evolved in the 1660s and 1670s, such as Toland, Tindal, Trenchard, Gordon, and the young Benjamin Franklin, were not necessarily those most pursued and persecuted at the time. A striking paradox of the "deist" phenomenon was that the more moderate one's deism, and closer to the teaching of Protestant revealed religion, the easier it was to challenge accepted opinion publicly and provocatively.

[25] Radicati, *Twelve Discourses*, 203; Venturi, *Alberto Radicati di Passerano*, 200, 205; Sutcliffe, *Judaism and Enlightenment*, 196–7; Israel, *Radical Enlightenment*, 68–9, 71–4, 273.

[26] Tarantino, *Scrittoio di Anthony Collins*, 128–9.

[27] Venturi, *Alberto Radicati di Passerano*, 41, 138, 191–3; Berti, *Anticritianesimo e libertà*, 334, Betz, *After Enlightenment*, 28–9.

[28] Radicati, *Philosophical Dissertation*, 5–6, 8, 11, 29, 60; Alberti, *Alberto Radicati*, 28, 151; Israel, *Radical Enlightenment*, 69.

[29] Venturi, *Alberto Radicati di Passerano*, 157–9; Berti, *Anticristianesimo e libertà*, 89–90, 321, 325.

Wollaston's *Religion of Nature Delineated*, for example, featured among the great publishing triumphs of the age. Appearing in eight editions between 1722, and 1759, and also in French (1726) and German (1728), its popularity and wide diffusion reflected its moderate tone and character. Arriving in England, for the first time, at barely 18, from Philadelphia, in December 1724, the young Franklin for a time worked in a London print-shop employed on the third edition; Wollaston's text stimulated the aspiring young intellectual to disagree with his claims for "natural religion" and draft a more radical and incisive tract of his own, *A Dissertation on Liberty and Necessity, Pleasure and Pain* (most copies of which he later destroyed). Extolling reason and science, Franklin followed Collins (and hence Spinoza) in expounding philosophical necessitarianism eliminating free will and predicating God so minimally as to amount to virtual "atheism," not deism.[30]

For Wollaston, among the most widely-read English "deists," it made perfect sense to consider the soul a separate spiritual entity, defend divine providence, and pray to God much like the ancient Stoics.[31] He showed no tendency toward sweeping reformism or social revolt. Widely read in Ireland and America too, Wollaston presented himself publicly neither as a "deist," nor opponent of Christianity, but, like Reimarus, an exponent of natural religion firmly championing "particular providence" as well as general providence. He belonged, plainly, with the moderate, not the Radical Enlightenment,[32] his stance remaining perfectly compatible with outward conformity to whichever church one nominally conformed to, without in any way undermining faith in a Creator and governor of the world. Nevertheless, his "moderate" stance, being openly propagated and more apt to blur confessional difference than more furtive incursions, incurred the furious disapproval of preachers, denunciation noisier and more noticeable, because more widely announced, than condemnation of philosophical "deism" ruling out meaningful divine providence. Hence, while Wollaston's stance remained closer to the majority's religious outlook, and was more supportive of the existing order than Radical Enlightenment positions, it was no less prone to fall foul of the censorship and suffer persecution. The Northamptonshire semi-Christian Anglican "deist" Thomas Woolston (1670–1773), Fellow of Sidney Sussex College, Cambridge, swayed by Collins to an extent and convinced churchmen should interfere less in politics, was dismissed from the University in 1721, for publicly denying Christ's miracles and the Resurrection and using irreverent language about sacred topics; arraigned for blasphemy in 1725, he was tried again in 1729, receiving a one hundred pound fine and one year's imprisonment.[33]

Deists made an example of, like Woolston, were the most outspoken in defying public norms and respectability, rather than the most radical intellectually and

[30] Franklin, *The Papers* I. 57–8; Walters, *Revolutionary Deists*, 62–5; Stewart, *Nature's God*, 184–5; Lyons, *The Society*, 30–1.

[31] Lucci, "William Wollaston's Religion," 132–5.

[32] Schröder, *Ursprünge des Atheismus*, 82–6; Hudson, *Enlightenment and Modernity*, 39; Israel, "The Philosophical Context of Hermann Samuel Reimarus' Radical Bible Criticism," 183–200.

[33] Lucci, *Scripture and Deism*, 167–9; Burson, *Rise and Fall*, 232; Herrick, "Blasphemy," 105–8.

politically. This leads us to back to the Postmodernist distinction, introduced by Lilti, against the Radical Enlightenment thesis, between those enlighteners more willing outwardly to defy, provoke, and challenge contemporary opinion, rhetorically and emotionally, like Rousseau (who was nevertheless a champion of strong providence), and furtive types adopting philosophically more radical, less traditional, positions but doing so less publicly and conspicuously. Cautious concealed subversives were likely to go further philosophically while keeping their heads below the parapet, like Diderot after his early three-month incarceration in 1749, at Vincennes, resolved to avoid further repression and punishment. Such a reclassification is not entirely without logic. What some deemed Rousseau's attention-seeking posturing did attract more hostile (as well as adulatory) attention than Diderot's camouflage and caution.[34] Conservative deism boldly expressed could outrage the public sensibility more than radical deism heavily camouflaged and surreptitiously diffused. But positive deism challenged only superficially, not the basic doctrines, and had far less sweeping implications for social and political change and the future.

Steeped in the Latin, Greek, and Hebrew sources, Wollaston immersed himself, like many deists, in rabbinic commentaries and Talmud, beside Al-Farabi, Ibn Sina (Avicenna), and Ibn Rushd (Averroes). He concocted a compelling vision of "natural religion" as a universal creed independent of all revelation and confessional theology, viewing the world as governed by laws under which natural causes act and the "constitution of things is preserved." "By the providence of God I mean His governing the world by such laws."[35] He subscribed too to "particular providence" but, by this, chiefly meant the endowing of special characteristics, strengths, and advantages to species, groups, or individuals, rather than what was normally meant, namely "innovations" or interruptions in the regular course of nature. Wollaston's "particular providence" followed from his "general providence" in denying the miraculous and supernatural. It was the general design of nature and course of history that, to his mind, stemmed from the benign purposefulness of the divinity. The reality of things broadly corresponds to God's plan, he urged in typical Moderate Enlightenment vein, as does the scheme of human conduct and the social order. The suffering of the innocent, and profits of the unjust, arise from the unalterable general character of social organization he considered an integral part of the divinely planned order of nature.[36]

Two other early eighteenth-century English "deists" of moderate to conservative stamp were Morgan and Chubb, both ardent, thoroughgoing Newtonians. Thomas Morgan (d. 1743), had been a dissenting preacher, then a Quaker healer. Converted to "natural religion" and a notion of divine providence incompatible with belief in Holy Scripture and Christianity, he became a vehement critic of the Bible, especially hostile to Judaism and the Old Testament, which he impugned for most of what he deemed

[34] Lilti, "How do we Write the Intellectual History of the Enlightenment?," 12–13.
[35] Lucci, "William Wollaston's Religion," 133.
[36] May, *Enlightenment in America*, 17, 25; Lucci, "William Wollaston's Religion," 134.

wrong with Christianity. But he eschewed denouncing Christianity as such, and deemed Christ's role indispensable for those lacking understanding, hence the majority. His main work, *The Moral Philosopher*, appeared anonymously; in 1737; it ruled out miracles and particular providence as it would be unworthy to suppose the "Deity or universal Cause and Agent, ever suspends or alters the mechanical properties of matter, the laws of communicating motion, the forces and directions of the heavenly bodies," or "any of the general laws of nature." For Morgan and Chubb, God is the universal "Preserver and Director" as well as "Cause" of Nature, ensuring permanent divine concurrence for preserving the forms of species, rhythm of life, and the institutions of men.[37] Like Wollaston's, Morgan's was a knowing God directing and sanctioning the existing social hierarchy, legal system, and natural and moral order.[38] "Ascribing," as did Toland and Collins, "the universal force and energy by which the whole material world is incessantly acted upon and moved to the mere passive matter, as the inherent essential powers and properties of the bodies themselves," is to abjure Newtonianism and shock all authentic deists. He abhorred their pseudo-deism operating "in effect to exclude the Deity out of the universe."[39]

For a time, no other deist so ardently recommended prayer and praying, to commune with the deity, and elevate one's thoughts, as Thomas Chubb (1679–1747). Keen observer of the latest scientific developments, living much of his life in Salisbury, Chubb admired Samuel Clarke's Newtonianism as a way of grounding the rationality of immaterial forces, but went beyond Clarke's Christian Arianism to embrace a deism hardly distinguishable from conservative Socinianism. A loyal churchgoing Anglican, Chubb invoked Christ while rejecting the teaching of the Apostles, and eventually all Christology and Christian theology. "A passionate physico-theologian," close to rejecting "particular providence," he grew reluctant to acknowledge miracles and began to question prayer as something that could be heard and responded to; like other "deists," he recognized no process of divine redemption, no need for divine mercy or grace, no divine aid to individuals. But while his "general providence" sufficed to operate the universe on its existing benevolent lines, he did not deny miracles altogether. God had simply not created a universe requiring instances of "particular providence" to sustain Nature, or the moral and social order.[40]

As a public adversary of theology Chubb evolved in stages, in the 1720s penning controversial pamphlets defending the deists' right to be heard and their moral integrity while reviling clergy relying on coercion and ecclesiastical authority rather than rational argument. In the 1730s, he assailed more specifically Christian doctrines, the Trinity, immaculate conception, divine revelation, Original Sin, and

[37] Wigelsworth, "God always acts suitable," 160–3, 172; Lucci, *Scripture and Deism*, 187–96; Hudson, *English Deists*, 8.

[38] Force, "Newton's God of Dominion," 94–5; Wigelsworth, *Deism*, 190–3.

[39] Morgan, *Physico-Theology*, 59–60; Young, *Religion and Enlightenment*, 38–9, 188–9.

[40] Löwe, *Dogmatische und Moralische Einleitung*, 36, 41; Porter, *Enlightenment*, 115–16; Hudson, *English Deists*, 8–9.

efficacy of sacraments; his pillorying Anglican "high-flyers" grew more vehement. God, he insisted, had sent Christ to redeem men not least by rescuing them from the unworthy morass of priestcraft and superstition in which they were sunk. The Gospels were not divinely inspired, contended his *Enquiry Concerning the Books of the New Testament* (1734), but penned by upright reformers offering accounts of Christ's career and moral significance that were not strictly accurate but true "in the main." Paul strayed even further from authentic Christianity than the Apostles.[41] Christ is not, he asserted in *An Enquiry Concerning Redemption* (1743) in any doctrinal sense mankind's redeemer but rather an inspiring symbol and model. Believing Christ was sent by God is simply unprovable.[42]

Their relative conservatism does not mean Wollaston, Chubb, Morgan, and Woolston contributed nothing to radical thought. There is the dialectical aspect to consider. Their arguments were deeply challenging for most while at the same time, the young Franklin found, for some, annoyingly tentative, half-baked, and unconvincing in a way positively provoking reaction against their studied moderation. Here again the insights of Leo Strauss seem relevant. Although Strauss knew that the stream he was the first to label "moderate Enlightenment" proved crucial to separation of state and religion, and forging the modern religiously neutral, legal, and legislative context, he nevertheless considered the kind of philosophical harmonizing and mediation offered by Locke, Le Clerc, Reimarus, Mendelssohn—all the moderate enlighteners (even Hume and Voltaire)—too obviously flawed philosophically to underpin a stable, durable truly viable Enlightenment "moderation." Often their arguments degenerated into an under-the-counter, discreet surrender to philosophical "atheism" of a kind bound to lead to socially, morally, and religiously disintegrative consequences.[43] It is an argument valid to a degree, though he certainly overstated his case in claiming such harmonizations (*Vereinbarungen*) always "work as vehicles of the [radical] Enlightenment, and not as dams against it; for the radical Enlightenment, the moderate Enlightenment is the best friend."[44]

Meanwhile, multiple ecclesiastical, educational, judicial, and social pressures to conform to officially endorsed structures of belief remained intense. So formidable was the apparatus of repression, so vigorous the calls to suppress "atheism," ostracize "deism," vilify anti-Trinitarianism, marginalize Judaism, and discriminate against Catholicism, compelling one and all to submit to legally-defined, accepted ways of understanding not just revealed religion but the world, foreign policy, and politics, that subversive thoughts tending toward "atheism" and radical "deism" had to be elaborately dressed as something else. Here, Holland and Britain differed only marginally from the rest—as did the post-1776 United States where Blasphemy

[41] Hudson, *Enlightenment and Modernity*, 88–9; McKown, *Behold the Antichrist*, 248; Wigelsworth,' "God always acts suitable," 160–6.

[42] Lucci, *Scripture and Deism*, 196–8; Hudson, *English Deists*, 8–9, 17.

[43] Smith, *Reading Leo Strauss*, 72–3, 127.

[44] Quoted in Ranieri, *Disturbing Revelation*, 20; see also Hudson, *English Deists*, 17, 20–1.

Laws were incorporated into the legal codes of the new state constitutions so that anyone associated in the public mind with "atheism," blasphemy, or unbelief down to the 1830s, continued in theory, and not infrequently in practice, to be excluded from meeting halls, public office, and teaching, and subject to heavy penalties as well as condemned by press and public.[45]

The difficulty with Strauss's claims regarding the inevitability of Early Modern subterfuge, and need for the modern reader to read between the lines, of course, is that disagreement over how to interpret particular passages in any author suspected at the time of "atheism" becomes hard to avoid. Where does such evasion begin and end? This applies to Hobbes, with some urging his assertions of belief in God and Christ the Savior should be taken seriously, others labeling these a "charade;" Bayle is still more contested. All too easily this produces an inconclusive, frustrating deadlock. Up to a point one might go along with the view that the resulting complexities, wide range of nuance, and "philosophical, theological, and sociocultural permeability of the first half of the eighteenth century makes it difficult to distinguish the Radical Enlightenment, Moderate Enlightenment, and Counter-Enlightenment."[46] But one cannot on that ground dispense with the need for broad, general categories since the logic and ramifications of these distinctions permeated and shaped the entire contemporary scene, with the battle lines slowly emerging more clearly with time, as the masking faded.

While both theistic and atheistic categories of "deists" seemed menacing, the need to distinguish was nevertheless often insisted on since one category, the radical deists, struck more discerning theological minds as decidedly more perverse than the theistic alternative. The early eighteenth-century French court preacher Jean-Baptiste Massillon (1663–1742)[47] underlined the significance of this distinction much like the Lutheran pastor Johann Caspar Löwe at Gotha. The latter described the difference at the start of his 448-page book on the German theologians' disputes with *Naturalisten* and *Deisten*, in 1751, as a rift between those seeing God's guidance as being exclusively through the regular processes of nature while still upholding the majesty and benevolence of a divine providence emanating from a separate divine being, versus *Deisten* merging "God and Nature," conceiving God's existence and the World as one and the same, so that these "are also called *Pantheisten*, like Spinoza, Toland, Collins, Tindal and Johann Christian Edelmann".[48] Though often termed "deism," the "deism" of Toland, Collins, and Tindal for conservative real "deists" represented nothing remotely like genuine "deism." To many at the time it seemed obvious that Toland's stance simply replicated that of Spinoza, "the most celebrated patron of Atheism in our time," as the Newtonian philosopher Samuel Clarke (1675–1729) called him, the thinker "who taught there is no difference of substances, but that the whole and every part of the material world is a necessarily-existing Being; and that

[45] Sehat, *Myth*; Israel, *Expanding Blaze*, 88–9, 420. [46] Burson, *Rise and Fall*, 9.

[47] Massillon, *Pensées*, 292–3; Israel, *Radical Enlightenment*, 63–4, 90–1.

[48] Löwe, *Dogmatische und Moralische Einleitung*, 9.

there is no other God, but the universe" [praeter Deum nulla dari neque concipi potest substantia].[49]

5.3. SHAFTESBURY'S RADICALISM

Distinguishing between conservative deists who were true "deists" and radical deists depleting "deism" of authentic theist content, inevitably carried political implications. Those, like Morgan, acknowledging a benevolent, knowing divine providence that governs the world accordingly sanctioned the existing moral and legal order as the evident outcome of the divine will, while those denying divine guidance, supernaturalism, miracles, redemption of individuals, immortality of the soul, and reward and punishment denied divine intention too, facilitating the embrace of republican attitudes.[50] Among the most notable early eighteenth-century formulations of radical "deism" denouncing superstition, persecution, and all stirring of collective fury against victims using theological notions, figured the *Letter concerning Enthusiasm* (1708) by Anthony Ashley Cooper, third earl of Shaftesbury (1671–1713), a work tending to outright rejection of all previous philosophy and theology.[51]

Shaftesbury chose ridicule as his favored device for attacking institutionalized theology along with what he saw as its crutches—obsolete metaphysical and moral philosophy.[52] First and perhaps profoundest of the philosophical influences on Diderot, Shaftesbury's secular philosophical cult of "moral sentiment" proved attractive to several later eighteenth-century French and other freethinkers.[53] Like the Dutch *cercle* of the 1660s, but unlike Hobbes, Locke, and the "Christian deists" including Chubb, Shaftesbury offered a purely natural morality wholly independent of Revelation and religion.[54] Where La Mettrie and Helvétius identified the self-seeking quest for pleasure as the key to understanding human conduct, sympathy, and morality, Diderot and d'Holbach followed Shaftesbury in viewing pleasure as an inadequate basis for explaining human aspirations and morality. His non-Epicurean conception of "virtue" Shaftesbury viewed as central to, and inherent in, absolute universal truth, in his eyes something quite separate from theology and religion, Christian or otherwise. It was a striking philosophical departure, exalting a "virtue" like that of the ancient Stoics, as a worldly necessity for all men, something universal, essential to happiness and vital for a sound politics.

Seeking to detach morality from religion, Shaftesbury moved to dismantle Locke, for whom, as Jefferson too later objected, Revelation and morality were closely linked,

[49] Quoted in [William Carroll], *Remarks upon Mr. Clarke's Sermons preached at St. Paul's*, 3.

[50] Israel, *Radical Enlightenment*, 471.

[51] Lucci, *Scripture and Deism*, 13.8.

[52] Herrick, "Blasphemy," 106, 116; Tarantino, *Scrittoio di Anthony Collins*, 60–2.

[53] Furbank, *Diderot*, 25.

[54] Champion, *Pillars of Priestcraft Shaken*, 209–18; Pagden, *The Enlightenment*, 68–73; Furbank, *Diderot*, 26.

and ultimately inseparable.[55] Here Shaftesbury shared common ground with Bayle, whom got to know personally during the nine months he spent in Rotterdam down to April 1699. Nevertheless, although these two highly gifted savants appear to have discussed philosophy during their conversations in Holland, and while Bayle had a high regard for the English lord, whom he addresses, in the surviving letters between them, with great deference, there is no indication that they proceeded far together, as regards serious dialogue. Despite agreeing about "virtuous atheists" and being equally keen to separate morality from faith, Shaftesbury seems to have felt that he shared few points of view with the exiled Huguenot. Bayle's letters to Shaftesbury, after 1699, mostly concern recommended rare and expensive volumes, often classical works offered at Rotterdam book auctions, apt for the earl's library at his splendid rural retreat near Salisbury.[56]

Following publication of Diderot's rendering of the earl's first treatise, *An Inquiry Concerning Virtue* of 1699, in early 1745 (the copy presented to Rousseau is dated 16 March 1745), Shaftesbury's moral philosophy entered the mainstream French High Enlightenment, and became integral to it. In 1745, appreciable risk still attached to confronting French readers with the notion that morality is inherent in nature's design, and human life, and does not stem from faith or religious authority, but is solely accessible through reason with nothing requiring explanation by divine revelation or churchmen. According to false details on the title-page (where neither Diderot's, nor Shaftesbury's, name appears), the book was published "at Amsterdam" although it was probably produced in Paris.[57] Though he translated rather freely, Diderot had vested much effort in the task, and was confident he had accurately rendered Shaftesbury's philosophy along with his own numerous addenda and editorial "reflections."[58]

Shaftesbury acknowledges that "design" proclaims divine intention and purpose; and it is here that he diverged furthest from Spinozism and showed himself a neo-Stoic. Nature was Shaftesbury's "God"—a rationalist naturalism with a Platonist tinge, steeped in ancient Greek Stoicism, with which Shaftesbury claimed close affinity, formed his creed.[59] *An Inquiry Concerning Virtue* views the world as a unity organized under a single set of principles. Passions as such, for Shaftesbury, are never intrinsically "good" or "bad" but all relatively good or bad depending on their social effects and consequences in different contexts. Thus, "*Kindness* and *Love* of the most natural sort" can be harmful if "immoderate and beyond a certain degree,"[60] while feelings like envy or malice, however despicable, originate in excesses of better passions. Morality hence possesses no existence outside nature and society. It

[55] Shaftesbury, *Characteristics*, 164 n.; Carey, "Two Strategies on Toleration," 60–1; Scherr, "Thomas Jefferson," 80–1.

[56] See Voitle, *Third Earl of Shaftesbury*, 239.

[57] See Wilson, *Diderot*, 50–1.

[58] Diderot-Shaftesbury, *Essai sur le mérite et la vertu*, 24.

[59] Voitle, *Third Earl of Shaftesbury*, 402–3; Champion, *Pillars of Priestcraft Shaken*, 210, 212; McNaughton, "British Moralists," 205–6; Israel, "Shaftesbury, an Early Voice," 90–1.

[60] Shaftesbury, *Inquiry*, 64.

cannot be cultivated in a solitary individual and never depends on, or is revealed by, a divine being independent of nature.[61] Politics and morality align at a fundamental level and one cannot possess a proper notion of virtue without grasping that the "publick Interest" is the measure of what is "admirable or blameable," right or wrong.[62] Men's passions, all human life, must attune to "the good" in general: the standard of good and bad in our world is how well human actions conform and contribute to "the publick Good, or good of the Species." What is "disserviceable or contrary to that main End" is bad, "corrupt and *ill*."[63] Shaftesbury's "main end" lends his ethical philosophy a universalist quality and cohesion, binding politics, society, and morality together and directly clashing with Locke's notion of the coexistence of radically different moral systems. Where Locke asserts moral diversity, and irreducibility of cultural differences, the impossibility without religious authority of grasping the moral core of the Gospel's teaching, Shaftesbury dismisses this as error rooted in his former private tutor's perusing too many extravagant traveler's tales and inability to see irrational conduct, corruption, and barbarism as lapses from universal moral norms.[64]

Another feature of Shaftesbury's moral thought contradicting Locke paralleled Bayle in viewing "the atheist" as no more prone to violate basic morality than others. "Atheists" could be good while, in Shaftesbury, priests, fanatics, and Jews, his three most morally corrupt categories, are always more inclined to pervert truth than others. (Unlike Toland, but like some eighteenth- and early nineteenth-century radicals, Shaftesbury nurtured marked anti-Semitic prejudices.)[65] He also fiercely resented the Epicurean tendency in ancient and modern thought (which in his schema included Spinozism). All philosophical moralists of the ancient and modern world, he classified, like Leibniz, "in two broad categories," Stoic and Epicurean. The first cultivate virtue, the "common good," and public-spiritedness and are "real deists" while the latter, irretrievably "egotistical, hedonistic, and dismissive of virtue" in his Stoic sense, are hence mere "nominal deists."[66]

By assailing the despicable league of "Superstition and Enthusiasm" tied to political authority that buttressed the despotic structures of the Early Modern world, the Epicurean sect was not wholly devoid, he concedes in one letter (*Letter* 328 [18]), of beneficial consequences: Epicureanism does help banish the deities "out of the Universe and Nature of Things," and dismantle ecclesiastical authority as well as discredit the obsession with saving souls Shaftesbury ranked among society's worst defects.[67] Basically, though, Shaftesbury viewed Epicureanism, including Hobbes,

[61] McNaughton, "British Moralists," 205–6; Dedeyan, *Diderot et la pensée anglaise*, 290–1.

[62] Shaftesbury, *Inquiry*, 68–70; Israel, "Shaftesbury, an Early Voice," 91.

[63] Shaftesbury, *An Inquiry*, 64–5.

[64] Prince, *Philosophical Dialogue*, 94–6; compare Carey, "Two Strategies on Toleration," 61; Jaffro, "Toland and the Moral Teaching," 84.

[65] See Champion, "Men of Matter," 120–2.

[66] Shaftesbury, "Pathologia," 232–8; Klein, *Shaftesbury*, 61; Jaffro, "Qu'est-ce qu'être déiste?," 284; Israel, *Radical Enlightenment*, 626; Pagden, *The Enlightenment*, 61–2.

[67] Shaftesbury, *Moralists*, 140; Prince, *Philosophical Dialogue*, 206 n. 17.

distinctly negatively, attributing to them the idea that "it was only *Force* and *Power* which constituted *Right*," that there was no natural justice, "no such thing in reality as *Virtue*; no Principle of Order in things above, or below; no secret *Charm* or Force of Nature, by which every-one was made to operate willingly or unwillingly towards publick *Good*, and punish'd and tormented if he did otherwise."[68] Rejecting Epicureanism and Spinozism in this manner lent Shaftesbury's thought a moralizing, optimistic gloss that appealed especially to his Huguenot protégé, Pierre Desmaizeaux (1673–1745).[69]

Morality for Shaftesbury is simultaneously a social phenomenon and fact of nature, shaped by human needs, passions, and social impulses, and quintessentially disinterested, a rising above, a transcending of egoism and selfishness, and rejection of the other malignant emotions, or "perturbations" as he calls them, like cruelty, ruthlessness, and brutality, in the interest of the whole, a principle Diderot imbued from him.[70] Where Locke's morality required a divine lawgiver meting out reward and punishment in the hereafter, such an approach struck Shaftesbury as not just ungrounded but unethical, being crudely self-centered—a restraining of inner impulses to please higher authority in the hope of attaining an ultimate reward. For Shaftesbury, neither fear of Hell nor hope for redemption can be virtuous emotions. The virtuous man's reward lies solely in the enjoyment of virtue itself (as with the Stoics—but also Spinoza), like the reward of the elevated person who, through striving to refine his or her taste, savors the universal laws of good taste, the sublime, and of beauty.[71] The idea that disinterested virtue and pursuit of "the Good" are more likely consistently to prevail in the collective drives or impulses of societies than in individuals and their passions no doubt helped Diderot formulate his later pivotal idea of the *volonté générale*, which is indeed closely related to Shaftesbury's as well as the *cercle spinoziste*'s general good, or "publick Interest."[72]

Shaftesbury and the young pre-1746 Diderot both seemingly claim the moral philosophy they extol presupposes a benevolent God. Both claim to uphold a genuine *théisme* or deism. Although for Shaftesbury these terms were practically interchangeable,[73] he sometimes professed to distinguish between them—whereas "the *Atheists*" fail to do so.[74] Ultimately, though, a troubling swirl of ambiguity, or "imposture," envelops Shaftesbury's benevolent all-knowing God—as with the Stoic "God" more generally. Shaftesbury's divinity, or rational order of nature, is undoubtedly benevolent, yet "He" is far from omnipotent, indeed turns out to be not just powerless to judge men fit for Heaven or Hell but no regulator of the laws of nature or author of the principles of ethical life either. Divine providence in Shaftesbury is simply drastically curtailed, carrying no implication of divine governance of the course of

[68] Shaftesbury, *Sensus Communis*, 58. [69] Hammersley, *English Republican Tradition*, 44–5.

[70] Shaftesbury, "Pathologia," 232, 238; compare Ehrard, *L'Idée de nature en France*, 370; Quintili, *Pensée critique de Diderot*, 56–9.

[71] Porter, *Enlightenment*, 164; Taylor, *Secular Age*, 268, 314; Israel, "Shaftesbury, an Early Voice," 92.

[72] Shaftesbury, *Inquiry*, 156. [73] Jaffro, "Qu'est-ce qu'être déiste?," 276, 285.

[74] Shaftesbury, *Moralists*, 126; Israel, "Shaftesbury, an Early Voice," 93–4.

affairs and history. His Providence merely lends men their physical and emotional character and attributes while exercising no more sway over their preferences, choices, and actions than over events.[75] The classes of modern philosophy Shaftesbury expressly repudiates (those of Descartes, Hobbes, Locke, and Spinoza) denied divine providence, he argued, by refusing to recognize that the "Order or Harmony of Things in general" includes moral, political, and aesthetic dimensions that are eternal and inherent in that order.[76] His stress on the common good—which some scholars, pointing to his identification of Nature and God, deemed Spinozistic—while representing a parallel strand of Radical Enlightenment that was discreet, conversational, super-tolerant, and gentlemanly, diverges from Spinoza's system by firmly vesting divine virtue in nature itself.[77] In this respect, he struck out on a path from which Toland, reverting in his moral theory to the Spinozist format, notably diverged.[78]

Divine providence is the rational and benevolent order of the universe and, for Shaftesbury, what lends meaning and moral perspective to men's lives. His ethical principles are fixed, universal, and eternal, leaving no room for changes in the relationship of what he calls the "publick Interest" to virtue. By contrast, in "Epicurean atheism," including Spinoza, nature possesses "no Intention at all, no Meaning or Design."[79] Even so, detaching moral truth from religious authority is Shaftesbury's no less than Spinoza's or Bayle's aim, a separation he resolutely embedded in his republican politics. His hostility to all religious authority, and eliminating divine direction of the course of affairs, place Shaftesbury firmly among the prime moral and philosophical architects of the "Radical Enlightenment." A vehement streak not just of anticlericalism but revolt against religious authority pervades the entirety of his *oeuvre.* For this reason, Shaftesbury felt drawn to unbelieving freethinkers like Toland, Collins, and Tindal, and his texts helped turn Franklin, the American Radical Enlightenment's first major figure, into a "real doubter in many points of our religious doctrine."[80]

Shaftesbury's morality is inherently closely linked to politics, law, administration, and power. A principal function of any valid moral scheme, concurred Diderot, is to enable us to evaluate and judge the conduct of peoples and governments.[81] Such a view of morality and virtue, spurred by Shaftesbury, entailed a wholly new, unifying, approach also to history and historiography, elevating history into what it became for Condorcet later—"l'histoire du genre humain." Here too, though conventionally receiving less attention in studies of English "deism" than Toland or Collins,

[75] Shaftesbury, *Moralists*, 206.

[76] Shaftesbury, *Miscellaneous Reflections*, in *Characteristics*, 60; Dupré, *The Enlightenment*, 120–4.

[77] See Porter, *Enlightenment*, 160; the perceived parallels with Spinoza and Spinozism (which I myself consider exaggerated for reasons explained above) have been especially stressed in Stewart, *Nature's God*, 65, 140, 143, 153, 163, 169, 281–2, 292–3, 297–9, 301, 304.

[78] Jaffro, "Spinoza and the Moral Teaching," 78–9.

[79] Shaftesbury, *Moralists*, 206; Jaffro, "Qu'est-ce qu'être déiste?," 286.

[80] Franklin, *Autobiography*, 64; Furbank, *Diderot*, 26.

[81] Diderot-Shaftesbury, *Essai sur le mérite et la vertu*, 100–1.

Shaftesbury arguably stands as the most quintessentially Enlightenment-orientated, the most fully enlightened and enlightening, as well as most radical of the early English Enlightenment's principal figures: "To love the Publick, to study universal Good, and to promote the Interest of the whole World, as far as lies within our power," he writes in his 1707 *Letter Concerning Enthusiasm*, is "surely the Height of Goodness, and makes that Temper which we call *Divine*."[82] This distancing of the moral order from organized religion, linking it to human advancement in politics and social organization, is a recurring theme in Shaftesbury's thought, clasping virtue to his fervent republicanism. Here was radical thought attired in uplifting, beautiful words, the poetic touch Montesquieu acknowledges in his *Pensées* when accounting Plato, Malebranche, Montaigne, and "milord Shaftesbury" to be philosophy's "quatre grands poètes."[83]

The universal character of Shaftesbury's moral criticism is striking. Abjuring contractarian political thought in the manner of Hobbes and Locke, he broke with conventional thinking and underlined the systematic quality of his cosmopolitanism of virtue and moral universalism. His mankind was a moral unity in characteristics, aptitudes, and needs in an age of rapid European expansion overseas, trends with which his grandfather, the first earl, had been closely associated. The latter's secretary, Locke, had contributed projects and plans to promote colonial settlement in North America, and while it is doubtless true that some scholars have significantly overstated Locke's complicity in justifying slavery, and in propagating unflattering perceptions of the different, the exotic, and the unchristian, he was at best ambivalent about black slavery and seizure of land formerly belonging to Native Americans; equally, while Locke did not advocate outright intolerance of Catholics and Catholicism, he certainly heavily circumscribed and qualified that toleration.[84] By contrast, the third earl roundly rejects all suggestion that Europeans possessed superior rights or virtues arising from their beliefs or Protestant commitments. Mocking the contemporary public's thirst for whatever was "most unnatural and monstrous," deriding the "credulous Mr Locke's willingness to believe wild stories about savage tribes of the New World,"[85] Shaftesbury combined rejection of moral relativism with aversion to arrogant Eurocentrism in travel literature, and all suggestion that savage, exotic peoples were morally of a lower status to those who pass as "Christians."

Shaftesbury's quest for moderation and "*Proportion*" as a universal moral and aesthetic norm in no way detracted from his radicality as an uncompromisingly subversive moral reformer; his "virtue" remained a species of universal harmony detached from theology, reflecting the harmony of music and symmetry and

[82] Shaftesbury, *Letter concerning Enthusiasm*, 352.

[83] Montesquieu, *Mes Pensées*, in Montesquieu, *Oeuvres Complètes*, 1073.

[84] Brewer, "Slavery, Sovereignty," 1038–78; Marshall, *John Locke*, 687–90.

[85] Shaftesbury, *Correspondence*, 405; Pagden, *The Enlightenment: And Why It Still Matters*, 171–2; Daniel Carey deals with this aspect in detail in his "Contesting Diversity: Shaftesbury's Reply to Locke," in *Locke, Shaftesbury and Hutcheson: Contesting Diversity in the Enlightenment and Beyond* (Cambridge: Cambridge University Press, 2006), 98–149; Brewer, "Locke, "Slavery, Sovereignty," 1038–78.

proportion found in nature; but it also possessed bite. Despite his gentleness of temperament, precarious health, and respect for the other, his cosmopolitan conception of virtue committed him to what he perceived as a vast struggle of rival political and moral systems. The Marxist social theorist and historian Neil Davidson claims the War of the Spanish Succession (1702–13) was, for Shaftesbury, the "latest instalment in the inter-systemic conflict between England, centre of the still insecure capitalist order (with some support from the declining United Provinces), and France, the dominant feudal absolutist power."[86] What transpired during the closing years of the seventeenth century and opening years of the eighteenth in Shaftesbury's eyes, was indeed an inter-systemic struggle, but not between rival economic and social systems. Rather than a struggle between capitalism and feudalism, the ideological war into which he threw himself aimed to thwart Louis XIV's "universal monarchy," and prevent monarchy buttressed by organized religion frustrating hopes for republican emancipation of society, and free mankind from overweening absolutism, intolerance, "superstition," and ecclesiastical tutelage of the individual.

The conflict between the rival powers stemming from the Glorious Revolution, Shaftesbury viewed as a political and social conflict certainly, a conflict of world-systems and institutions, but especially a war of philosophy on ignorance and superstition, freethinking versus bigotry, human dignity versus servility, piety, and fanaticism, Enlightenment against Counter-Enlightenment. If less openly confrontational than his conspiratorial grandfather, the first earl, Toland, or Collins, Shaftesbury was no less contemptuous of monarchy, conventional religiosity, and everything broadly accepted. He was a classic radical enlightener in tying rejection of religious authority to democratizing republicanism. Urging "frequent parliaments," like Toland, he felt dissatisfied with the Glorious Revolution, shocked by the court influence and corruption that flourished under William III and subsequently. "He saw so many of those, who were zealous for the Revolution so much pervert the design of it," remarked Toland, "and so willfully endeavouring to frustrate the chief ends of it, that he could attribute it to nothing but court-influence, which at length turn'd his stomach at times against the court itself."[87] This could not estrange him from 1688 as such, but did lead "him to a hearty contempt and detestation of many Revolutioners."[88]

The aim of his *A Letter Concerning Enthusiasm* was not to persuade readers that organized religion breeds rigid severity, intolerance, mass devotion, superstition, and a destabilizing zeal menacing everyone: all this Shaftesbury considered too obvious to require explanation. He aimed to convince rather that the menace collective religious passion and dogmatism pose to society and individual must be fought by the virtuous for social and political reasons, and combated in the appropriate manner—gently, without fanaticism, without repression or persecution, with a tolerant eye deploying

[86] Davidson, *Discovering the Scottish Revolution, 1692–1746*, 105–6; Hammersley, *English Republican Tradition*, 34–5.

[87] Toland, "A Large Introduction," p. xv.

[88] Toland, "A Large Introduction," p. xvi.

reason alone and all reason's critical tools—not least ridicule and laughter. The latter was a resource reason had too often neglected hitherto in mankind's ceaseless and unremitting war against the ferocity and stupidity of collective religious fervor.[89] In this conflict of values, Britain and Holland were thankfully gaining ground: "there is a mighty Light which spreads its self over the world," he assured Le Clerc, in March 1706, eighteen months after the Anglo-Dutch victory at Blenheim (August 1704), thanks to "those two free Nations of England and Holland; on whome the Affairs of all Europe now turn: and if Heaven sends us soon a peace suitable to the great Successes we have had, it is impossible but Letters and Knowledge must advance in greater Proportion than ever."[90]

5.4. TOLAND REVISITED

Steeped in Bayle, Locke, and Spinoza, John Toland (1670–1722), the "Lucian of our times" as one contemporary dubbed him, presents an enduring puzzle. A bizarre mix of discreet evasiveness and provocative flamboyance, apt to "raise against him the clamours of all parties," highly adroit at subversive manipulation of the theological debates of his time, his elusive and convoluted texts trumpet by turns "multiple deisms and diverse heterodoxies," beside pantheism and atheism. They swirl dizzyingly in all directions. Much that he wrote was so thickly veiled that it is hardly surprising one expert went so far as to state that "despite a considerable scholarly literature on the subject, no one knows what he really believed."[91] Even great erudition, avers Toland when researching his hero, Bruno, can leave key issues shrouded in darkness, "even the great Bayle can lead one into error."[92] Yet, one conviction we know for certain Toland adhered to throughout, a belief profoundly characteristic of the Radical Enlightenment: that the bulk of what men take to be true, including their most cherished religious convictions, is false and dangerously so; the chief menace facing mankind is neither Pope nor Catholicism, as Protestants believe, but Bruno's "Beast," as he called global ignorance in 1709, "the multifarious superstition which (as he claims) everywhere holds sway over credulous men, in all places and at all times" [Bestia haec sit multifaria Superstitio, quae credulis (ut vult) hominibus, omne loco et tempore, late dominatur]."[93]

Born at Ardagh, in north-western Ireland, Toland converted from Catholicism to Presbyterian Protestantism at 16. Conventionally, scholars locate the roots of his thought in his English and Irish background, especially Locke's philosophy. Over time, the insistence on Locke has been constant and unrelenting; but recent research

[89] La Vopa, "A New Intellectual History?," 733.
[90] PRO Shaftesbury papers: 30/24/22/2, fo. 175r.
[91] Hudson, *Enlightenment and Modernity*, 5, 15–16.
[92] Begley, "John Toland's On the Manner," 108.
[93] Begley, "John Toland's On the Manner," 109.

shows the need for a very different perspective. Originally destined to become a Presbyterian minister, Toland studied at Glasgow, Edinburgh, and for two years (1693–4?) at Leiden where he became acquainted with clandestine circles and free-thinking, and the Spinozistic influences, that were to shape his life as a philosopher, deist, naturalist, republican, and cosmopolitan. During 1707–10 he again resided principally in Holland while also spending time in Germany. His first and most noticed text, *Christianity not Mysterious* (1696), scandalized by claiming there are no true mysteries in the Bible, that all valid dogmas of true "faith" are found by philosophical reason by investigating "natural religion." Condemned in England and burnt by order of the Irish Parliament,[94] this work provoked general uproar leading to trial by a grand jury in London which taught him the need for greater caution in future. It was a work no more Lockean in basic inspiration than Shaftesbury's texts.

Toland first met Locke in August 1693 and remained on friendly terms with him for around four years until the latter broke off relations, following publication of *Christianity not Mysterious*, in 1697.[95] Conventionally considered a "founding text" of an entire new stream in Western thought, a foundation of something fundamentally new, in reality it merely shadows Spinoza's main points regarding God, Nature, substance, and motion along with the latter's discussion of methodology of Bible criticism,[96] and treatment of ceremonies, miracles, and almost everything else. Far from representing a generic *spinozisme* so elastic as to bear no real relation to Spinoza's philosophy, as the Lilti school and the "negative critique" affirm,[97] it is a precise, cutting *spinozisme* evincing a consistently close relationship to Spinoza's thought in his Bible criticism, moral philosophy, and rejection of religious authority. Toland undoubtedly had Locke centrally in mind when composing *Christianity not Mysterious*, but his objective was not to build on, but systematically, if deviously, undo Locke's system, which argues for a non-denominational core Christian doctrine presenting Christ as the Messiah, Scripture as infallible, and the universe as actively and benevolently governed by God, insisting on the need for faith.[98] Where Locke had encountered Spinoza's *Tractatus Theologico-Politicus* first in the period 1672–5, and invariably diverged from his (and all other) challenges to the divine inspiration of Scripture thereafter, Toland diverged from Locke in viewing Christ as an essentially ethical teacher and detaching Christianity's moral core from its dogmas, observances, ceremonies, and subservience to churches and churchmen.[99] The "divine law which

[94] Taylor, *Secular Age*, 223; Gillen, "Radical Enlightenment and Revolution," 244; Brown, *Irish Enlightenment*, 15–16, 20.

[95] Champion, *Republican Learning*, 73–5; Young, *Religion and Enlightenment*, 27.

[96] Simonutti, "Deism, Biblical Hermeneutics," 51–3; Leask, "The Undivulged Event," 78–9; Israel, "'Radical Enlightenment': A Game-Changing Concept," 36–7.

[97] Dagron, *Toland et Leibniz*, 192–3.

[98] Locke, *Reasonableness*, 172–5, 191–2; Nuovo, "Locke's Proof," 57–9; Nuovo, *John Locke*, 4–5, 147; Lucci, "John Locke on Atheism," 239–43.

[99] Nuovo, "Locke's Proof," 57–8; Jaffro, "Toland and the Moral Teaching," 82–3, 89, Mori, *L'Ateismo*, 148–50.

makes men truly happy and teaches true life, is universal to all men," a law not taught by any church, or found anywhere in instituted observances and ceremonies like "baptism, the Lord's Supper, feast-days, public prayers and any others" common to Christianity, which "if they were instituted by Christ or the Apostles (which is still not clear to me) were instituted only as external signs of a universal church and not as things that contribute to happiness or have any sanctity in them." No one is bound by such "ceremonies," and those Dutchmen in Japan "where the Christian religion is forbidden and where the Dutch residing there must refrain from all external worship, by command of the East India Company," he noted (echoing Spinoza), are no more prevented from living true Christian lives than anyone else.[100]

Toland, deemed by Reimarus the most incisive anti-Christian commentator prior to himself, urges his contemporaries to keep abreast of the most up-to-date hermeneutical approaches to Bible criticism since failure to do so encourages those "grosser errors, which have been too commonly advanc'd into fundamental Doctrines, administering fuel for endless contentions, but neither reforming men's manners, nor informing their understandings."[101] His stress on strict "historical contextualization" of biblical passages combined with close philological analysis echoed Spinoza, as did his conclusions. Toland's discussion of ceremonies, mysteries, miracles, institutions based on religious authority, and concern with what he construes as the clergy's abusive adoption of ceremonies and dogma to deceive men, "authorize" theological doctrines, and build an illicit sway over society, like his lifelong conflation of God and Nature, and elimination of metaphysics, are all broadly the arguments of the *Tractatus Theologico-Politicus*, rather than those of Locke.

"Reason" in Toland and English radical "deism" generally serves as an emancipating, liberating force freeing men from servitude to theology and the authority of preachers and tyrants. This contrasts fundamentally with Hobbes's political theory and hermeneutics which were intended to bolster the state, and ecclesiastical authority as an arm of the state, broadly in an anti-libertarian direction. But equally Toland distances himself from Locke. His "deistic" reason strives to liberate, "assert freedom of thought," and reform politics.[102] His deepest "secret philosophy" is that which "acknowledgeth," as John Leland characterized it, "no other God but the universe."[103] In *Christianity not Mysterious*, Toland's prime philosophical goal is to break Locke's pivotal distinction between "supra rationem" and "contra rationem" as reasonable grounds for faith and religious authority. This radically *antimétaphysique* stance left no room for any reality that is immaterial or arises from the mystical secrets of hermeticism.[104] For Toland, the Gospel cannot be "above reason" and Locke fails to establish grounds for believing anything beyond the strictly observable.[105] It was a

[100] Spinoza, *Theological-Political Treatise*, 75; Israel, *Radical Enlightenment*, 613.

[101] Hudson, *Enlightenment and Modernity*, 11–13; Groetsch, *Hermann Samuel Reimarus*, 111.

[102] Jaffro, "L'Ecclésiologie," 18–19; Lucci, *Scripture and Deism*, 43.

[103] Leland, *A View* i. 62.

[104] Iofrida, "Matérialisme," 49–50.

[105] Leask, "The Undivulged Event," 66–70; Leask, "Personation," 209–30; Champion, *Republican Learning*, 68; Hudson, *English Deists*, 85.

conclusion expressly rejected by Leibniz, who, in a text of 1701, reaffirms "above reason" vindicating the Christian mysteries in part like, and in part differently from, Locke.[106]

Where Locke's thought is Arminian and Latitudinarian in spirit, proximate to Le Clerc and Van Limborch regarding belief, authority, salvation, and atonement, Toland's assails the Arminian approach, as all religious authority, on every level. "Spinozism" Toland systematically injected into his *Letters to Serena*, *Pantheisticon*, and other writings including his deeply insinuating *The Primitive Constitution of the Church of England*, where he not only demolishes all church authority, as Tindal had, insisting on a huge gulf between true Christian doctrine and the teaching of the churches, but reduces true Christian doctrine to just a very few basic moral precepts, essentially just peace and union among men.[107] Toland's Christ is in all essentials Spinoza's Christ.[108] "In a word, much the greatest part of the inhuman barbarities, controversies and divisions of Christians with nine parts in ten of the religious volumes they have written, owe their being to the opposite factions of priests and to their various forms of church government," all a vast fabrication which has nothing to do, held Toland, with Christ's true doctrine.[109] Toland's thought is steeped in Spinozism with respect to Christ, God, and Nature, and the non-existence of theology, but also to "ceremonies" and the nature of church–state relations. In effect, he forged a materialist ideology substituting (Spinozist) philosophy for religion as man's principal guide in the universe while denying intelligence and reason are separate from matter. It was an "atheism" claiming God remains conceptually distinct from the universe, being the creative dimension of intelligence (as in Spinoza). This scarcely veiled philosophical engine was the Trojan horse he dragged mercilessly into the Anglican, Dissenter, and Catholic worlds.[110]

Modern scholars frequently claim the "Spinoza" Toland introduces in *Letters to Serena* and elsewhere is so remote from the real Spinoza that "Spinoza arguably would not recognize himself in it at all;" but differences of style and context need approaching with a cautious but also constructive critical eye given Toland's creed, though distinctive, was regularly pronounced indistinguishable from Spinoza's system in essential points in eighteenth-century Germany, just as he was generally deemed "a true Spinoza," from at least 1709, in Enlightenment France.[111] The "pantheism of Toland is indeed a Spinozism," concludes one scholar, even if Toland pretends to repudiate Spinoza in his *Letters to Serena*; the relation between Toland's "Spinozism"

[106] Leibniz, *Theodicy*, 106; Antognazza, "Natural and Supernatural Mysteries," 29–30, 38–9; Laerke, *Leibniz lecteur*, 145, 163 n., 323, 326–7.

[107] Toland, *Primitive Constitution*, 142; Jaffro, "L'Ecclésiologie," 61–2, 66, 68; Laerke, *Leibniz lecteur*, 355.

[108] Jaffro, "Toland and the Moral Teaching," 80–4; Jaffro,"L'Ecclésiologie," 61–2; Iofrida, "Matérialisme," 39, 49.

[109] Toland, *Primitive Constitution*, 143; Jaffro, "L'Ecclésiologie," 17–18, 59.

[110] Leask, "Undivulged Event," 79–80; Leask, "Stoicism Unbound," 238; Hudson, *English Deists*, 93–4.

[111] Laerke, "Anthropological Analogy," 16; Kors, *Naturalism and Unbelief*, 98, 122.

and Spinoza's philosophy is everywhere primary.[112] Leibniz in his *Annotatiunculae* of 1701 on Toland's *Christianity not Mysterious*, noting his excluding all possibility of miracles and Revelation, observes that he argues for this conclusion on precisely the same basis as Spinoza.[113] Toland and Collins, following Spinoza and Bayle, both strove to counter Locke's dualism of body and soul, stress on primacy of individual communion between the individual and God rather than collective worship, and separation of material reality from holy mystery.[114]

Locke, for his part, had resolutely defended dualism of body and spirit, always asserting the primacy of the individual's quest for Christian salvation through faith and prayer. Other prominent deists beside Toland and Shaftesbury, familiar with Locke but likewise conflating body and mind, and deploying Spinoza and Bayle to demolish Locke's characteristic positions, were Collins and also Bolingbroke, who consistently propagated a monist view of mind and behavior in his exchanges with Samuel Clarke, a philosopher-theologian and Anglican clergyman vigorously promoting Newtonianism, immaterial substance, immortality of the soul, and religious mysteries against the determinism and necessitarianism of the Spinozistic onslaught.[115] Bolingbroke later became a major influence on Jefferson.

Nor must we forget that Toland considered himself an expert in the use of esoteric "contradiction" as a clandestine strategy.[116] At one point, assuredly, Toland insistently claims to diverge from Spinoza. Spinoza, objects Toland, in his *Letters to Serena* (1704), Letter IV, declares "motion and rest" to be the "causes of all the diversitys among bodys"—quoting his Lem.1 ante Prop. 14. Part 2: "corpora ratione et quietatis, celeritatis et tarditatis, et non ratione substantiae ab invicem distinguuntur"—but "did not hold motion to be an eternal attribute of matter," citing this as a clear contradiction. Not allowing God as first mover, Spinoza "neither proving nor supposing motion to be an attribute (but the contrary) nor indeed explaining what motion is," objects Toland, "he cou'd not possibly show how the diversity of particular bodys is reconcilable to the unity of substance, or to the sameness of matter in the whole universe; wherefore I may safely say that his system is intirely precarious and without any sort of ground, indigested and unphilosophical." This reasoning is sometimes assumed to point to a real gap in Spinoza's argument uncovered by Toland, and enabling him to develop a fresh, more dynamic form of monistic pantheism, placing more emphasis on force and motion, and at least one scholar thought this enough to

[112] Leask, "Personation," 246; see also Laerke, "Anthropological Analogy," 16–17.

[113] Laerke, *Leibniz lecteur*, 310, 323, 326.

[114] Leask, "Undivulged Event," 63; Lucci, *Scripture and Deism*, 13–15; though there is also a dissenting view proposed especially by Klever and Stewart—though commencing with William Carroll—whereby Locke is reconfigured as really more radical than moderate, and closer to Spinoza, than at first appears; according to this hypothesis, Locke deployed "above reason" merely as a cover, to mask his own alleged crypto-Spinozism; for this view, see Stewart, *Nature's God*, 4, 147, 229–33; also [William Carroll], *Remarks upon Mr. Clarke's Sermons preached at St. Paul's*; Miqueu, *Spinoza, Locke*, 35–6, 412–13.

[115] Klever, *Mannen rond Spinoza*, 231, 235, 237; Stewart, *Nature's God*, 232–5.

[116] Melzer, *Philosophy between the Lines*, 314–16; Thomson, *Bodies of Thought*, 119.

justify speaking of "l'antispinozisme de Toland"; but this hardly seems cogent in the wider context of Toland's writing. If there is any difference between Spinoza's and Toland's positions on rest and motion in substance, between their two doctrines of "conatus," it is extremely hard to specify what it is.[117]

When the German thinker and associate of Leibniz, Walther Ehrenfried von Tschirnhaus (1651–1708), raised the issue of matter and movement directly with Spinoza personally, in a letter, noting the difficulty of conceiving how motion and diversity can arise from extension considered by itself, Spinoza answered, as Toland (and Leibniz) report, that it is not just difficult but impossible to conceive how motion, or particular bodies, can arise from "extension" as Descartes conceives it, that is whenever matter is represented as an inactive and passive bulk. For matter at rest will, of itself, stay at rest; on this ground, Spinoza pronounced Descartes's principles of natural things altogether useless. Spinoza's first principle of science is that matter is built of "motion and rest" and motion is inherent in "extension" (his main reason for rejecting atomism). From the Tschirnhaus–Spinoza exchange which Tschirnhaus discussed with Spinoza at the time, Toland later claimed to deduce that the latter's system "is built on no certain or probable foundation, but on gratuitous suppositions, from which he deduces what he and his followers call demonstrations."[118] But this looks like a sleight of hand, another instance of Toland's style of convoluted imposture, given he denies "matter is or ever was an inactive dead lump in absolute repose, a lazy and unwieldy thing," and affirms the impossibility of "absolute rest," claiming "action is essential to matter, that matter cannot be rightly conceived nor consequently be rightly defin'd without it, that nothing can be accounted for in matter without this essential action." Here he appears to be deliberately muddying the water by attributing to Spinoza the opposite of what he actually maintains.

Of course, it was Newton, not Spinoza, who follows Descartes in conceiving matter as wholly inert and for whom the dynamic factor can only derive from outside immaterial forces, from the First Mover. In Spinoza's thought, from the earliest writings onwards, it is fundamental that "differences between one body and another arise only from the different proportions of motion and rest, by which this one is so, and not so, and this and not that."[119] Making motion-and-rest inherent in "extension," one of the infinite modes of substance, entrenches the principle that the laws and rules of nature, under which all things occur, and change from one form to another, remain always unchanging and are lodged within nature itself.[120] Toland was right that Spinoza had insufficiently explained and developed this crucial point. But his real aim in the *Letters to Serena*, where he pretends to dispute with a fervent Dutch disciple of Spinoza and assert that while Spinoza had "several lucky thoughts" his

[117] Toland, *Letters to Serena*, 145; Clarke, *A Demonstration*, 19; Gurdon, *Pretended Difficulties*, 156–99; Dagron, *Toland et Leibniz*, 199–201.
[118] Toland, *Letters to Serena*, 153–5; Dagron, *Toland et Leibniz*, 202–3; Laerke, *Leibniz lecteur*, 366–7.
[119] Spinoza, *Collected Works* I. 91; Israel, *Radical Enlightenment*, 612.
[120] Della Roca, *Spinoza*, 72–3.

system overall was "not only false, but also precarious and without any sort of foundation," was to push readers to focus on his actual arguments, and circumvent the "vilifying epithets" Spinoza's innumerable adversaries "bestow on his person for the sake of his opinions."[121] He did so without acknowledging his subversive purpose, to consummate Spinoza's dynamic materialism and produce a "Spinoza perfected" as one scholar expressed it. All Toland does when discussing motion in matter, remarked the Buckinghamshire rector William Wotton (1666–1727), a skilled Latinist and controversial theologian and classicist, who, if often drunk and pursued by creditors, was nevertheless an acute critic, is restate Spinoza's thesis. "Mr Toland... makes matter to be self-moving, whereby we may suppose that he intends to supply all the defects of Spinoza's thesis: i.e. make the world without a God."[122] Toland teasingly misrepresents the Dutch thinker, not to formulate an *antispinozisme*, but as a contrivance to evade condemnation by pretending to assail Spinoza while mocking those who are assailing Spinoza, underlining the very doctrine underpinning Spinoza's one-substance metaphysics. Here was imposture designed at once to affirm Spinoza's doctrine, and promote Toland's own role in disseminating it.

For Toland, divine providence is just realization of the natural order through its laws, laws remaining eternally the same.[123] There was no obvious incursion of Lucretius, or of Epicurean atomism as there was in Radicati's materialism, albeit Bruno may have been an additional source.[124] Toland's dismantling of Locke's "supra rationem" [above reason], his concluding "there is nothing in the Gospel contrary to reason, nor above it," is then specifically Spinozist.[125] Without saying so, Toland simply underwrites Spinoza's refusal, challenged subsequently by Locke and Newton, to "acknowledge any difference between something contrary to Nature and something above nature."[126] Of course, there were other methods of dismantling Locke's dualism and endorsement of miracles, and with greater philosophical acumen than Toland evinced, as Hume showed later, but Hume's skepticism did not attack or reject religious authority, in Spinozist fashion, as a moral, political, and social safeguard, or prompt a sweeping program of republican political reform.[127] Eliminating "supra rationem" and rendering reason the sole tool for evaluating "mysteries," Toland distanced himself from Locke and Newton along with Descartes, Hobbes, Malebranche, Van Limborch, Le Clerc, and Leibniz, aligning philosophically with the *cercle spinoziste* and its heirs. Dismantling Locke's philosophy of body and soul

[121] Toland, *Letters to Serena*, 116–17; Leask, "Introduction," 26–7.

[122] Wotton, *Letter to Eusebia*, 47–8, 53; Moniglia, *Dissertazione* [...] *Materialisti* i. 48–55; Lurbe, "Spinozisme," 44; Jaffro, "L'Ecclésiologie," 63; Leask, "Stoicism Unbound," 235–6; Leask, "Introduction," 26.

[123] Leask, "Introduction," 23; Laerke, *Leibniz lecteur*, 145, 714.

[124] Berti, *Anticristianesimo e libertà*, 334–6.

[125] Simonutti, "Deism, Biblical Hermeneutics," 46–50; Leask, "Undivulged Event," 67; Mori, *L'Ateismo*, 149.

[126] Spinoza, *Theological-Political Treatise*, 86–7; Israel, "Introduction," pp. xv–xvi; Simonutti, "Deism, Biblical Hermeneutics," 46–7.

[127] Simon, "Hume et les 'Lumières radicales'," 383–4; Israel, *Democratic Enlightenment*, 222–3.

dualism in this way remained a cornerstone of Radical Enlightenment subsequently, almost a defining feature.

Until a few years before, admitted Priestley, in 1777, in his *Disquisitions relating to Matter and Spirit* (London, 1777), he had unquestioningly believed, like most of his countrymen, "that man had a soul distinct from his body," holding this "soul to be a substance so intirely distinct from matter, as to have no property in common with it." Only via "a slow and laborious investigation," both personal and part of a wider process characteristic of the age, had he slowly emancipated himself from this millennia-old theology-empowering belief along with "'many gross corruptions' and 'vulgar prejudices,' as I now deem them." To Priestley, it seemed "unaccountable in Mr Locke" after acknowledging, as he does, that there is no clear evidence of two substances in man," that he yet deemed "it more probable" that the faculty of thinking "inhered in a different substance" from the body, namely an immaterial soul.[128] Perceiving "no real inconsistency between the known properties of the body, and those that have generally been referred to the mind," Locke had nevertheless refused to infer, as a true philosopher should, "that the whole substance of man, that which supports all his powers and properties, was one uniform substance" and that, hence, man does not consist "of two substances" as academic philosophers and divines maintain, but only one.[129]

For radical enlighteners, Locke's "confusion" regarding soul, body, and substance, free will and necessity, and the colossal muddle he lent his name to, to underpin theology, urgently needed sweeping aside, and precisely this was accomplished by Collins in his *Philosophical Inquiry concerning Human Liberty* (1717), a treatise brought to Priestley's attention by the deist schoolmaster Peter Annet (1693–1769); it was a work Priestley judged "sufficiently methodical and concise to give intire satisfaction to every unprejudiced person."[130] Much the same qualities characterized Collins's materialism and necessitarianism more generally. Collins, though traditionally included among the "English deists," has, ever since the publications of David Berman in the 1970s and 1980s, more accurately been considered an "atheist." Recent studies confirm this reading as do Collins's unyielding insistence on the exclusive criterion of reason for judging truth and here, unlike Priestley later, detaching "virtue" completely from religion. By contrast, Richard Price, who, according to Lindsey, "though an Arian, is one of the firmest Unitarians I know,"[131] while breaking with Locke's political thought, persisted, unlike Priestley and Jebb, in contending for free will and Locke's separate immaterial soul. Price denied that Socinianism inevitably leads to a universal materialism but nevertheless still found Lockean dualism so awkward that, in practice, he too eschewed it.[132]

[128] Priestley, *Disquisitions*, 31. [129] Priestley, *Disquisitions*, 32, 73, 218–20.

[130] Priestley, *Disquisitions*, 266, 288–9; Hudson, *Enlightenment and Modernity*, 115; Priestley, *Doctrine*, Preface, p. xxx.

[131] Webb, "Price," 162.

[132] Webb, "Price," 334; Porter, *Enlightenment*, 411–12; Hampshire-Monk, "British Radicalism," 671.

Eighteenth-century historians of philosophy saw no difficulty in coupling Toland's name with Spinoza. A review in the *Bibliothèque angloise* of 1720 simply classifies Toland's thought as "le spinozisme tout pur."[133] Genovesi, in his five-volume *Elementa Metaphysicae* (Naples, 1743–5), squarely equates Toland's thought with Spinozism.[134] But this creates a considerable problem for modern Enlightenment historiography which traditionally insists on the Englishness of the Enlightenment's origins. Contending that Toland did hold a significantly different position from Spinoza on "motion and rest," though a relatively trivial matter in itself, has thus become integral to the efforts to shore up the long hegemonic idea that the essential starting-point and foundation of the Enlightenment, this great development in world history, was surely laid in England. Margaret Jacob introduced the idea that Toland was the founding-figure of the Radical Enlightenment as such, representing him as a highly creative and influential thinker who forged a new path by tying republicanism to an irreligious philosophy and anchoring his supposedly new creed in a branch of freemasonry. Along with tirelessly plying ambiguity and signification slippage, Lilti adds that attributing the Radical Enlightenment's origins to the 1660s *cercle spinoziste* and the Dutch milieu involves an unacceptable underestimation of the universally agreed primacy and centrality of English developments at the Enlightenment's inception. At stake is whether, as historians have long insisted, English deism was really the Enlightenment's effective starting-point, or whether, on examination, English deism's central and most challenging and subversive claims in philosophy, Bible scholarship, comparative religion, general philosophy, moral thought, and republican political discussion of law and institutions, as argued here, were in no way startlingly original, and mainly derivative from earlier Dutch and Dutch Huguenot sources.

This disagreement is reflected not least in the German historiography of the early Enlightenment. To prop up the longstanding, deeply-entrenched view, endorsed by many Marxists, that the Enlightenment *must* have originated in England because that is where economic change and the dynamic of class-warfare were centered, a trend emerged, from the 1970s over several decades, firmly denying the radical tendency in Germany can have originated in Spinoza and the *cercle spinoziste*. But Marxist insistence on the "English" origins of the Enlightenment also entailed diverging from a long-established much earlier German vision of pre-1730 German pantheistic deism: eighteenth-century German histories of philosophy, including Jakob Brucker's *Historia critica philosophiae* (1744), always identify such early radicals as Theodor Ludwig Lau (1670–1740) and Johann Christian Edelmann (1698–1767), as "Spinozismi suspectus." Lau, author of the clandestine text *Meditationes philosophicae* (1717), and Edelmann counted among the foremost freethinkers of the *atheistische-pantheistische* stream in early eighteenth-century German lands, the latter a product of nine years of study at Königsberg, and Halle (1685–94), and three more at Leiden

[133] De Vet, "Spinoza en Spinozisme," 28. [134] Genovesi, *Elementa Metaphysicae* I. 105.

(1695–8). Twentieth-century historians, Marxist and non-Marxist, playing down the "Spinozist" factor because England, not Holland, must have been the source of Early Enlightenment "deism" generally, circumvented this historiographical hurdle by claiming Toland, not Spinoza, was Lau's true *spiritus rector*. Despite calling God "natura naturans" and himself "natura naturata," Lau, a victim of fierce persecution, supposedly rightly disavowed the appellation *Spinosista*. For he was definitely a follower of Toland, readers were assured, and hence no "Spinozist." Among the evidence adduced for this was that Lau adopted "Toland's doctrine" that "all the phenomena of nature must be explain'd by motion" by the "action of all things on one another."[135]

Although it has since emerged that Toland's influence on Lau was in any case secondary,[136] it remains a stubbornly-defended last-ditch contention that while eighteenth-century German commentators like Lilienthal, Zedler, and Thorschmid uniformly classify Toland's thought as "Spinozism," they were distorting the evidence and greatly exaggerated Spinozist influence on early eighteenth-century German underground thought: the real source of the German underground intellectual tradition *had* to be English. In reality, of course, claiming Toland, not Spinoza, was Lau's veritable intellectual mentor, even were this more exact than it is, scarcely changes the position at all because Spinoza's influence on Toland has been seriously underestimated by almost all modern Enlightenment scholars (myself included). Although Toland undoubtedly *was* a significant spur to radical thought and attitudes in the British, Irish, American, French, and German contexts, his was far from an original mind and not remotely the founding architect of the Radical Enlightenment.

"For Toland, as for all pantheistic materialists," notes Jacob, "God and nature are effectively one, and this position was stated most clearly in *Letters to Serena* (1704) and the *Pantheisticon* (1720)." Her mistake was to suppose Toland's pantheism played a pioneering role in the development of the Radical Enlightenment either intellectually or as an international clandestine network.[137] To claim d'Holbach was heavily indebted to Toland, which he was,[138] merely confirms d'Holbach was a philosophical *spinoziste* in the specific sense central to the "Radical Enlightenment thesis," a *philosophe* conflating body and soul, rejecting all *supernaturalia*, and merging matter and movement into one, while deeming movement undeviating in its rules and rejecting Epicurean ontology and the Epicurean swerve. She was right, though, contrary to experts such as Hudson, Champion, Wigelsworth, and others, that Toland *was* an essentially radical enlightener and explicitly so in most of his writings, not least in his *Pantheisticon* where he expressly teaches a "Pantheistic

[135] Lau, *De Deo, Mundo, Homine*, 9; Pott, "Einleitung," 30, 40; Schröder, *Spinoza in der deutsche Frühaufklärung*, 124, 128–9; Schröder, *Ursprünge*, 490 n. 3; Rumore, *Materia cogitans*, 43–50; Groetsch, *Hermann Samuel Reimarus*, 310.

[136] Pott, "Einleitung," 40; Rumore, *Materia cogitans*, 23–30, 47; Mulsow, *Prekäres Wissen*, 67–70, 88.

[137] Jacob, *Radical Enlightenment*, 151–72.

[138] Jacob, *Radical Enlightenment*, 20, 154; Lurbe, "Matière, nature," 53–6; Iofrida, "Matérialisme," 50; Borghero, *Interpretazioni, categorie*, 32.

philosophy," that "all things are from the whole, and the whole is from all things," equating God with nature,[139] characterizing this as a "secret philosophy," an ecclesia of pantheists, disseminated through hidden "assemblies and meetings," something forced on Pantheism's adherents by the prejudiced multitude's implacable and unreasoning hostility. Those boldly resisting the multitude's pernicious beliefs formed a clandestine philosophical underworld that had to remain clandestine until Pantheists "are at full liberty to think as they please, and speak as they think"—in other words, Toland was a mirror of the *cercle spinoziste.*[140]

Throughout the *Pantheisticon* the threat posed by the multitude to the defiant culture of underground coteries of Spinozist cells that began in Holland in the 1660s and that Toland himself had encountered in the Netherlands in the 1690s, now also infiltrating London coffee-houses, is vividly invoked. It is quite wrong to suppose, as several scholars maintain, that "beyond a rather unexceptionable use of the language of the 'ancient constitution'," it "would be difficult to characterize Toland's political thought as radical."[141] Concern with "ancient" constitutions never has the slightest relevance to Enlightenment radical thought (whatever mid-seventeenth-century English revolutionaries believed). Claiming Toland or any early Enlightenment thinker was not "radical" because he spurned "pure democracy" on the model of ancient Athens,[142] or supported the Hanoverians, is equally misconceived: by definition radical enlighteners, from Spinoza to the 1830s, always abjure "direct democracy."

Toland's aversion to vulgar notions and ordinary people's prejudices, arising from the deep menace from which the clandestine radical enlighteners must hide, should not be mistaken for aristocratic disdain for the populace, or lack of concern for the common interest. In his *Anglia Libera* (1701), for instance, he not only endorses the Glorious Revolution of 1688 but went far beyond any stance pro-Revolution Whigs could normally contemplate. Parliament, or any legislature, he argues, is "only the fiduciary power to make laws for the good of society, and since no people can be suppos'd to intend their Liberty and Property shou'd be destroy'd by the authority they delegated to their representatives, 'tis plain that whenever these neglect to fulfil their Trust, or that they use it to contrary ends from those design'd by their principals [. . . the people] may not only defend themselves against their Legislators (as well as from all others attempting to inslave or destroy them) but may likewise place this power afresh in such persons, and after what manner or form they shall think most conducing to their security, welfare and felicity."[143] The essence of Toland's radicalism—as with the "Spinozists" generally—was his tight linkage of rejection of religious authority with a democratizing republicanism denying sovereignty to crown and legislature. Among the Glorious Revolution settlement's serious defects, he

139 Toland, *Pantheisticon*, 15, 61, 85; Leask, "Stoicism Unbound," 230, 235–8.

140 Toland, *Pantheisticon*, 97, 108; Jaffro, "L'Ecclésiologie," 27; Thomson, "Lumières radicales," 246; Mori, *L'Ateismo*, 157–8.

141 Champion, "John Toland: The Politics," 276; Wigelsworth, *Deism*, 77, 125–7, 204.

142 Champion, "John Toland: The Politics," 276.

143 Toland, *Anglia Libera*, 4–5.

believed, were the corruption of elections by "private entertainments, publick feasts, and bribes" so that "our representation is very unequal." New towns like Manchester, Leeds, and Halifax should now be accorded appropriate status and equal representation.[144] The Anglican Church's continuing influence was a hindrance. Deplorably, the "holy religion of Jesus" by Julian the Apostate's time had "metamorphos'd into faction, superstition, hypocrisy, and a mere worldly policy,"[145] and worse was to follow: "how often and in how many parts of the world have the wicked priests contributed to enslave their country, by preaching up the absolute power of the prince over the subjects, that in return he may become their subject."[146]

Margaret Jacob was quite right to characterize Toland as a quintessential "radical," wrong to view him as the architect of a new edifice. Not without justification Toland has been designated the "most important deist thinker of the eighteenth century;"[147] but there are no grounds for presenting him as a thinker deriving his inspiration essentially from an earlier, seventeenth-century English context or portraying him as particularly innovative in his main conclusions.[148] Rather, those eighteenth-century English, French, and German observers viewing the writings of Toland, Tindal, Collins, and the whole English anti-providential "deist" tendency as being grounded on "Spinozerian atheism," as Carroll expressed it, were the commentators who had hit on the correct perspective.[149]

Against this, Roche and Lilti maintain that the term "Spinozist", although indeed very frequently used in eighteenth-century Britain, as in France, Germany, Spain, and Italy, carries no special significance, being used to cover multiple meanings, a term lacking coherent signification and applied to a wide range of different things, a term referring to a faction that was really mythical. Insistence on "signification slippage" will doubtless continue to be immensely admired by many, but for all that remains totally incoherent, inconsistent with the evidence, and staggeringly untrue. Far more accurate was Brampton Gurdon's affirmation, in 1723, that since "Spinoza is the only person among modern Atheists that has pretended to give us a regular scheme of Atheism [. . .] I cannot act unfairly in making him the representative of their party, and in proving the weakness and absurdities of the atheistick scheme, by shewing the faults of his."[150] Whilst assailing the "Spinozists" in England, Gurdon recognized that Shaftesbury, propagating a different conception of substance and God from Spinoza, was not strictly of the "Spinozist" party;[151] and hence, needing a more complete "Spinozist," aimed his shafts, aptly enough, at Toland.[152]

144 Toland, *The Art of Governing by Partys*, 76–8.
145 Toland, *An Appeal to Honest People*, 17.
146 Toland, *An Appeal to Honest People*, 46.
147 Lucci, *Scripture and Deism*, 14.
148 Dagron, "Néo-spinozisme ou anti-Spinozisme?," 325–6.
149 Miqueu, *Spinoza, Locke*, 35–6, 412–13; Leask, "The Undivulged Event," 64.
150 Gurdon, *Pretended Difficulties*, 86.
151 Gurdon, *Pretended Difficulties*, 104, 268.
152 Gurdon, *Pretended Difficulties*, 156–99.

6

Great "Moderates" and the Temptations of the Radical

Montesquieu and the Forbidden

The attitudes and strategies of the rival moderate and radical camps toward each other changed over time as regards diffusion, broadening and elaboration of their respective intellectual standpoints and in response to altered social and political circumstances and pressures. Major public controversies and public intellectual strategy inevitably involved appreciable jockeying for position and regard for public realities and tactics. The Radical Enlightenment thesis is nothing if not intellectual history synthesized at every level with social, economic, and cultural history. A cautious ally of Diderot and the d'Holbach circle during the great controversy over the *Encyclopédie* initially, until the late 1750s, and more cautious, more distant ally from then until the late 1760s, Voltaire became an outright ideological opponent only during the final decade of his life, as documented in this tetralogy in considerable detail.[1] Shifting context, alliances, and degrees of polarization, means a sequence of many stages.

Furthermore, great moderates like Voltaire, Montesquieu, and Hume, being as they were immersed in Enlightenment debates in both their reading and conversation, could not avoid becoming familiar with, and at times, and especially privately, drawn to aspects of radical thought. Given that we are discussing the Enlightenment, the era of sociability and intellectual debate par excellence, how could it be otherwise? Formidable public pressures and considerations profiled their public stance in a way that sometimes failed fully to overlap with these individuals' private views. Thus, Hume was always at considerable pains to conceal the full extent of his religious heterodoxy so as not to give offence to churchmen and the public in general, but, equally, had no wish to alienate the "sensible gentlemen," the common sense of the gentry and aristocratic class, the landed elites around which his entire political philosophy and social philosophy of politeness, sociability, and common sense revolved and whose domination of the British body politic he was keen to reinforce.[2] Classifying

[1] Israel, *Democratic Enlightenment*, 654–78.

[2] Finlay, *Hume's Social Philosophy*, 23–9; Merrill, *Hume and the Politics*, 9–11, 26–7.

Hume as an essentially conservative thinker, it has been argued, fails to do justice to his antipathy to colonialism while classifying him as "moderate" opposing the Radical Enlightenment requires further nuancing.[3] But if there is always more room for nuancing, at the end of the day Hume made no effort whatever to join the radicals in rejecting religious authority openly and publicly, or questioning monarchy or aristocracy as such, quite the reverse, and none to present an argued systematic, public rejection of colonialism in the manner of Diderot, d'Holbach, Paine, Raynal, and Condorcet. What he was concerned to do politically was reinforce the sway of the gentry. As for Montesquieu, he undoubtedly felt attracted to and imbibed aspects of radical thought, indeed did so evidently from an early stage in his career, and, as a consequence, in the years around 1750 was accused by ecclesiastical opponents, not without some justification, of "Spinozism."[4] Temptations and dangers were many and complex, and shifted significantly over time as the different stages of the long-drawn out process of the Radical Enlightenment's evolution proceeded.

If, until the 1740s, Radical Enlightenment remained wholly forbidden and clandestine and hence hidden from the general public, locked into prolonged marginality (1660–1750), Diderot and his allies engineered their break out from marginality, rupturing the constricting frame in part by means of one of the greatest Enlightenment enterprises, the *Encyclopédie*, a camouflaged *machine de guerre*, with subversive elements carefully buried, often inconspicuously, amidst a large mass of innocuous-seeming material. With this they created a whole new intellectual context from the end of the 1740s. Their innovative subversive strategy entailed a good deal of outward echoing of conventional notions and compromise with the authorities and the status quo, and hence with the "moderate Enlightenment," not just in terms of textual content, but also public statements, contacts with officials, and partnerships with moderate semi-allies like Voltaire. Diderot's strategy was less than entirely successful and, from 1759, the *Encyclopédie* was comprehensively banned in France as well as Spain and Italy, but proved effective enough to help Radical Enlightenment emerge fully from its former marginality and become part of the main forum of open, mainstream public discourse and debate.

The battle of the *Encyclopédie* inevitably had complex implications for Voltaire and Montesquieu. During Radical Enlightenment's purely clandestine phase until the late 1740s, and intermediate emerging, semi-clandestine phase from around 1747 to 1770, the age of Diderot's *Encyclopédie*, devices of surreptitious philosophical subversion, imposture, and innuendo still everywhere predominated over direct, outright ideological challenge and debate.[5] Still a fringe phenomenon when the *Encyclopédie* was officially suppressed, Radical Enlightenment did not yet seem the direct, immediate menace to the aristocratic-courtly status quo it more obviously became later. Voltaire

[3] Baumstark, "End of Empire," 254–7; Merrill, *Hume and the Politics*, 120–1, 164.

[4] Israel, *Enlightenment Contested*, 268–9, 271–2, 685–7; Israel, *Democratic Enlightenment*, 330–2; Villaverde, "L'Abbé Raynal," 244–5.

[5] Duflo, "Diderot et la fin," 32–3.

had for many decades been conscious of the radical "underground" prior to 1770, and intermittently had attacked it behind the scenes, but until the late 1760s did not yet consider it *the* overriding, comprehensive, threat to the Enlightenment he aspired to lead and did embody in the last phase of his life. Early in the 1760s, for instance, he still detected no immediate public threat from materialism and atheism tied to attacking kings and aristocracy of the kind he encountered in the *Testament* of Jean Meslier (1664–1729), among the pre-eminent clandestine texts of the early eighteenth century. Exclaiming furiously against Rousseau, in a letter to d'Alembert, of July 1762, Voltaire devoted several remarkable lines to this now long dead and obscure Radical Enlightenment atheist priest.

Though relatively little known today, Meslier belatedly achieved prominence in late eighteenth-century French debates, during the French Revolution, as a pre-eminent foe of Christianity and the church. Indeed, during the 1793 de-Christianization campaign, Meslier's name was proclaimed far and wide, notably by Anarcharsis Cloots who wanted a statue of him erected in Paris, preferably in the Jacobin Club.[6] Not only was Meslier's assault on organized religion, theology, and ecclesiastics, finalized around 1720, exceptionally vigorous but he fused it more systematically and vehemently than Toland or Radicati with an equally explicit and furious attack on the existing social and political order, especially the nobility, which he denounced in every respect but also, if less severely, kings. Those of no use [*d'aucune utilité*] to society, meaning nobles, and "accomplices to the rule of the nobility," meaning lawyers and ecclesiastics, held Meslier, represented an odious burden on the people "as they live off the work of others" and one day should be properly dealt with, that is "severely punished."[7] If we designate the Radical Enlightenment the "left wing of political thought emerging from the second half of the seventeenth century," as the point has been expressed, "who better to symbolize the movement than Jean Meslier," the atheist priest of the Champagne region later much admired by Marxist historians and "often interpreted as one of the earliest advocates of communism?"[8]

However, we must be exactingly careful with our categories, and the Marxist view of Meslier as a proto-communist never made sense given Meslier has no conception of a proletariat, rejected notions of class-warfare and placed relatively little stress on economic factors. Classifying him as Radical Enlightenment makes much better sense. Voltaire's attitude to Meslier remains of particular significance for refining the categories and subdivisions within the Enlightenment, because Meslier unquestionably represents one of the clearest, late seventeenth- and early eighteenth-century examples of "Radical Enlightenment" in action. "Meslier's anticlericalism pushed him towards an anti-monarchist critique" and "preferring," it has been noted, "a more equitable form of government wherein all have an equal say in the affairs of the

[6] Mori, *L'Ateismo*, 242; Israel, *Revolutionary Ideas*, 484.
[7] Devellenes, "Radical Atheism: Jean Meslier," 167–8; Mori, *L'Ateismo*, 113.
[8] Devellenes, "Radical Atheism: Jean Meslier," 160.

common thing, or republic."[9] Early in life, he had entered the seminary and become a priest, he confessed (at least to himself), "pushed by his parents," principally to gain "a state of life softer, more peaceful and more honourable in the world than that of the common man."[10] The oppressive system, or alliance of aristocracy and the priesthood, constricting society all around him, he felt he must resist and oppose with all his being, but he also understood he could not oppose it effectively by coming out openly. Church, state, and social oppression were a co-ordinated system far too powerful at the turn of the eighteenth century for open defiance to survive for one moment: but church, monarchy, and nobles could be resisted, he believed, by surreptitious, privately avowed adversaries in a veiled manner, with infinite prudence, so as not to bring crushing reprisal down on their heads. Consequently, Meslier fought the fight of his life, his lifelong passionate crusade against injustice, totally unnoticed by those around him. It was a real but submerged contest partly fought by constantly striving to mask the great drama going on in his thoughts and private jottings from fellow priests and parishioners.

Aware of what it would mean for himself if any inkling of his materialist and atheistic views got out, and knowing the impossibility of his thoughts being openly expressed, he kept his main text, his *Testament*, entirely secret, almost wholly unread during his lifetime, while ensuring it survived after his death in just a tiny number of manuscripts.[11] The stock of manuscripts of his explosive text increased only very slowly through the 1730s and 1740s, remaining extremely scarce, as did references to them, until the 1750s. One of those few surviving references affords some inkling of the shock and horror such material produced in the minds of most contemporaries: "it is a monstruous text, horrible, abominable, worthy only of the hell that produced it."[12] If to the reading public it remained wholly unknown, in the Enlightenment underground, surviving in extreme marginality, Meslier's hidden counter-attack lived on with growing vigor as a handful of select readers, moderate and radical, discovered it: Voltaire, d'Alembert, Diderot, and d'Holbach all read it; Frederick kept a copy at Potsdam.[13]

Appalled by the 1762 Calas case at Toulouse, which struck him as an outrageous example of superstition mangling lives, Voltaire embarked on the most militantly anti-ecclesiastical and pugnacious phase of his career as a philosophe at that time. The July 1762 letter to d'Alembert referred to above rails furiously against the French clergy, Protestant and Catholic alike, but at this point Voltaire felt no qualms about enlisting (at any rate, a neutered) Meslier to support his own agenda: "the *Testament* of Jean Meslier seems to me to make a great effect. Everyone who reads it becomes convinced," a comment to which he appended an astounding rebuke to the now growing *philosophe* community at Paris: "Jean Meslier should convert the earth. Why

[9] Devellenes, "Radical Atheism: Jean Meslier," 161, 173; Kors, *Epicureans and Atheists*, 183–97; Israel, *Enlightenment Contested*, 716–17, 725–7.

[10] Devellenes, "Radical Atheism: Jean Meslier," 163.

[11] Artigas-Menant, *Du secret des clandestins*, 328, 363–4.

[12] Artigas-Menant, *Du secret des clandestins*, 186, 189, 308.

[13] Devellenes, "Radical Atheism: Jean Meslier," 163.

is his evangelism in so few hands? How lukewarm you are at Paris! You leave the light under the bushel."[14] Even though assailing monarchy and aristocracy, or the churches' grip over the lower classes, was anathema to Voltaire, he saw nothing distasteful or worrying, from his own standpoint, as would-be leader of the international Enlightenment, in exploiting Meslier's more radical approach for his own purposes at this point, and even urged allies to diffuse it more widely. Still, when reworking selected extracts of Meslier for wider propagation by himself he took scrupulous care not just to twist, but totally pervert, Meslier's ideas into a much gentler, non-insurrectionary deism wholly unlike his authentically militant stance but closely resembling Voltaire's.[15]

The obscurity enshrouding Meslier's message that frustrated Voltaire in the early 1760s was soon to end; but equally about to end abruptly, indeed be totally reversed, was Voltaire's former frustration that such ideas as Meslier's had remained little known. If Voltaire never coupled attacks on the church with assailing kings and aristocrats, fusing irreligion with radical republican politics, he saw no reason during the early 1760s not to work at raising Meslier's standing in the general estimation. But before long occurred a dramatic change, one of the great shifts in Voltaire's biography. The last part of his astounding career as the Enlightenment's most enduring and celebrated figure, from the late 1760s, precisely when his passionate philosophical campaign for justice and law reform and his insisting on his philosophical deism, his God without religion, was at its most intense,[16] until his death in 1778, was, more than any previous phase, overshadowed, his correspondence proves, by what he now viewed as a highly disturbing, rapidly widening rift among the *philosophes*.[17]

The intellectual crisis Voltaire felt caught up in from 1770 was precipitated by several anonymous, incisive, highly subversive French publications, of which the most menacing, in his eyes, was the *Système de la nature* (1770), internationally one of the Enlightenment's most subversive books, which only later, during the Revolution, was identified as chiefly the work of d'Holbach. What Voltaire and those drawn to his court-orientated enlightened world-view found impossible to stomach in this tide of publications was their simultaneously attacking religious authority and what they claimed it was tied to, the prevailing political and social order, their alleging the system of kings and aristocracy buttressed by clergy formed an alliance devised to prey on the majority. He could not accept that the *philosophes*' assault on religious authority should in any way be tied to attacking kings and courts and felt driven to highlight the widening rift as an urgent public issue to which attention needed to be drawn internationally.

[14] Voltaire to d'Alembert, aux Delices, 12 July 1762, *Voltaire's Correspondence* xlix. 101–2; Artigas-Menant, *Du secret des clandestins*, 311, 313, 316; Stalnaker, "How does Enlightenment End?," 47.

[15] Benítez, *Foyer clandestin*, i. 404; Artigas-Menant, *Du secret des clandestins*, 364.

[16] Dagen, "Quel besoin Voltaire a-t-il de Dieu?," 213–15.

[17] Israel, *Democratic Enlightenment*, 658–75.

Attacking theology and kings together, arguing these were allies in oppressing the people and that a close connection existed between tyranny foisted on society by theology and tyranny allegedly imposed by kings, was the old legacy of Meslier (and Spinoza), but one, since the late 1760s, suddenly broadcast on a more public level and on a much vaster scale than in the past—indeed diffused widely enough to produce a profound shock throughout Europe. If the basic recipe, tying together the attack on religious authority and kings and aristocracy, the claim that kings and churches, aristocracy and clergy collaborate to mystify ordinary men and women and plunder them, was identical in 1770 to that proclaimed by Meslier in 1720, and Spinoza in 1670, in the changed circumstances the effect on Voltaire's relations to the radical fraternity was dramatically different. He now assigned urgent priority to countering the threat that the rift represented from his own standpoint, and that of Frederick's and Catherine the Great's courtly Enlightenment. What chiefly made the difference, changing Voltaire's response to the thought-world embodied in Meslier's *Testament*, was the extreme rarity and marginality of Meslier's legacy until the late 1760s as against the rapid proliferation and wide impact of radical publications and their suddenly achieving a wide distribution throughout the trans-Atlantic world in the 1770s. The former, with scarcely even a handful of people having the slightest whiff of it, seemingly represented no challenge to Voltaire's outlook and leadership; the transformed situation of the 1770s plainly did.

Like the *Histoire philosophique des Deux Indes* (1770), which appeared in the same year and was to run through even more clandestine editions, reaching a still wider readership either side of the Atlantic, the *Système* had a considerable impact everywhere and caused a further proliferation of anonymous subversive printed texts provoking controversy, discussion, and rebuttals in print and person by numerous respondents. The dual assault against churchmen and theology, *and* against kings and aristocracy, in the manner of Van den Enden, Spinoza, Toland, Radicati, and Meslier, was palpably gaining momentum. As one might expect, what chiefly antagonized Voltaire was not the irreligion but these texts' anti-monarchical and anti-aristocratic orientation; nevertheless, as part of his vigorous counter-attack, he also needed forcefully to condemn their denial of any providential hand guiding the processes of nature and creation of species, to rebuke the uncompromising naturalism engineering, following Spinoza, the total elimination and exclusion of the supernatural. Voltaire was already an avowed if not necessarily altogether sincere "deist" but now needed to become a publicly more emphatic "believer" in God, divine providence, intended fixity of species and the "argument from design." Whatever his private thoughts about God, God was now more essential than ever to the overall logic of what he called his "system."[18]

Where Meslier had been a "light kept under the bushel," unnoticed for decades except by Voltaire and a few others, the unseen Diderot's and d'Holbach's double

[18] Dagen, "Quel besoin Voltaire a-t-il de Dieu?," 213, 226–7; Mori, *L'Ateismo*,121, 214–18, 236–40.

attack, rejecting organized religion *together* with the social-political order, seconded by Helvétius and soon also Naigeon, Raynal, Condorcet, and Paine and many others, scandalized the entire Western world, stoking general uproar in intellectual circles, and splitting Parisian *philosophique* opinion down the middle as neatly, complained Voltaire sourly, as any "minuet at Versailles."[19] Basic content always separated the two camps, but had decidedly different implications for relations between them depending on changing circumstances.

Responses to Montesquieu's political thought and legal reformism offer a similarly illuminating category marker for all interested in the shifting nuances and intricacy of the interaction of Radical and Moderate Enlightenment during these crucial decades. For throughout his intellectual career Montesquieu was a thinker who absorbed a wide range of influences, including radical and libertine tendencies, and one continually at pains, perhaps even wrestling with himself, to keep up his guard against atheism and subversive republicanism. Although he was only marginally indebted to Spinoza,[20] and publicly consistently rejected his views, his *Pensées* pronouncing Spinoza dangerous for society,[21] Montesquieu was steeped in Bayle and Machiavelli and, from his first stay in Paris (1709–13), on amicable terms with Fontenelle, Boulainvilliers, and likewise Fréret with whom he also interacted later on.[22]

Montesquieu's early period when he was more open to radical influences than later, or at least had less reason to be as exactingly cautious, also coincides with the period, strikingly, when he seems to have been more favorably inclined toward republics than monarchy, and most drawn to the cause of sexual liberation.[23] If his lifelong penchant for religious toleration, as prominent in the *L'Esprit des Lois* as the *Persian Letters*, owed much to Bayle, Montesquieu's recalcitrance toward radical tendencies discernibly heightened during his maturity. In the *Esprit des Lois,* he took pains to counter the "paradoxe de Bayle," the latter's contention that it is less dangerous for society and morality to have no religion, and for men to be atheists, than be "idolators," meaning accept a false faith. The Christian faith, answered Montesquieu, had rendered the princes of Christendom more moderate, gentler, and "less cruel" than Muslim and other Asian princes following non-Christian religions.[24] "It is poor reasoning against religion to gather together in a large work, a long enumeration of all the bad things it has produced, if one does not do the same with the benefits it has brought."[25] Refusing

[19] Israel, *Democratic Enlightenment*, 658–75.

[20] Volpilhac-Auger, "Une modération radicale?," 390–1.

[21] Montesquieu, *Pensées*, in Montesquieu, *Oeuvres complètes*, 902; Oudin, *Spinozisme de Montesquieu*, 69, 119.

[22] Shackleton, *Montesquieu*, 10–13, 55–6; Volpilhac-Auger, "Une modération radicale?," 391; Bianchi, "Modération non sans tentations," 344–5, 347–8.

[23] Villaverde, "L'Abbé Raynal," 244–6.

[24] Montesquieu, *L'Esprit des Lois*, Book XXIV, sections 2–3; Bianchi, "Modération non sans tentations," 350–1.

[25] Montesquieu, *L'Esprit des Lois*, Book XXIV, section 2; Ewald, *Über Revolutionen*, 240–1.

Bayle's "paradox," he insisted on the essential usefulness of religion for the maintaining state and society on a stable basis, albeit without appealing to theology.

While Montesquieu's relations with the radical tendency remained highly complex and, like Voltaire's, shifted with changing circumstances, his "moderation" became the dominant feature. He belongs overall in the "moderate" camp, though there were sufficient radical strands in his thought for the charge of *Spinosisme* to become a serious threat to him. Moreover, the correct inference from these shifting tensions and periodic "tentations" is not that the binary moderate/radical establishes lines that are rigid and simplistic, as the "negative critique" claims, but that the manifold complexities and nuances of relations between the moderate and radical tendencies can only be understood and mapped accurately by more comprehensively as well as carefully applying the moderate/radical dichotomy. What the evidence shows is the very reverse of what several contributors to the "negative critique" contend—rather than being too rigid, the dichotomy helps clarify the tensions within a great Enlightenment thinker steeped in the debates and conflicting pressures of the age, seeking to order his thoughts and balance his system so as to make the most plausible and convincing case he could for his method of classifying political and moral systems and religions.

Simply affirming Montesquieu's thought was complex and multifaceted without using the dichotomy moderate/radical is neither saying much nor particularly helpful in unraveling the complexities of Montesquieu's situation and thought, its distinctive flavor, shifting role in Enlightenment debate, or the sharply varying responses of later Enlightenment theorists. To make sense of the complex, deeply-divided reception his work received, precise categories and a clear typology are indispensable. No theologian, Montesquieu set out to understand the role of religion in the politics of different societies not justify particular beliefs. Here one finds a decided element of naturalism, a potential radical tendency in the way he portrays moral systems and religion as fulfilling natural social and political functions, without concerning himself with whether true as well as untrue religion exists. Necessary relations deriving from the nature of things, climate especially, determine Montesquieu's social and moral systems much as the laws of nature determined physical reality. The question why one religion, rather than another, dominates a given land, and why other faiths fail to establish themselves, Montesquieu explains in essentially naturalistic terms, in terms of laws of nature, deeming it less in their dogmas and beliefs than their social and moral consequences that religions shape political realities and Christianity reveals its superiority.[26]

Hence, in *L'Esprit des Lois* one finds no claim that Christianity is inherently superior theologically, by revelation, or morally, to other faiths, a feature that particularly displeased ecclesiastical readers. Hardly surprisingly, there erupted a five-year public controversy (1748–52) over the underlying naturalism and implications of *L'Esprit des Lois*. In October 1749, several ecclesiastics launched a public campaign against Montesquieu attacking *L'Esprit* in the French Jansenist journal

[26] Gaddo and Tortarolo, *Secularizzazione*, 73–4.

Nouvelles Ecclesiastiques, founded in 1728, labeling it a subversive work permeated with naturalism and *Spinosisme*, wholly unfitting for a Christian society.[27] What Montesquieu calls the "esprit general" of a people not only becomes the prime agent of social change but is shaped by blind, necessary forces, often climatic, a conjunction of relations fixed by natural laws evincing an overriding and unalterable character. Unknowing natural forces govern a universe in which God, or at any rate the God of the Bible and revelation, plays no role.

Nor was his naturalistic approach to religion the sole hint of openness to radical insights. Another "Spinozistic" or Tolandist trait pervading Montesquieu's thought was his distinctly anti-Cartesian, and anti-Newtonian, conflating of matter and motion.[28] Montesquieu's usually reliable biographer, Shackleton, wrongly assumed that "in the eighteenth century the word *Spinoziste* was mainly a term of abuse, and often of unthinking abuse" and that this is what it was also here.[29] But there was a radical dimension to Montesquieu's thought and temptation for radicals to move closer to him (and perhaps for him to move closer to radical thought) that was never greater than in the immediate aftermath of *L'Esprit*'s appearance when he found himself under attack from Jansenist and other ecclesiastical critics. His being classified as a "Spinosiste" was partially justified insofar as he was attributing the particular dominance of particular religions and moral systems to purely physical causes.[30]

In his *Défense de l'Esprit des Lois*, anonymously published at Geneva in February 1750, Montesquieu angrily rebutted the charge of *Spinosisme*, which, far from being a mere polemical label with no real meaning, as Shackleton too supposed, defined the entire controversy and entailed a very specific significance, menacingly implying he was eliminating divine providence from human existence. "Necessity" lies at the heart of "spinozisme," he retorted, but was not the essence of his system—indeed some of his points were objections to *le spinosisme*.[31] Where Spinoza's God cannot change the established order of things, Montesquieu postulates divine creation of the universe and the possibility of divine intervention to change the order of things. Where Spinoza conceives morality as not divinely revealed but purely a social contrivance, he claimed to recognize the existence of justice prior to all social life.[32] Meanwhile, during these months he collaborated closely with the radical Huguenot, Laurent Angliviel de La Beaumelle (1726–73), whom we shall meet again later in this volume, an early advocate of equality between the sexes,[33] and a staunch republican opponent of Dutch Orangism who, in 1751, published the continuation, or *Suite*, of Montesquieu's *Défense* in collaboration with his hero. In fact, during the 1748–52 public

[27] Oudin, *Spinozisme de Montesquieu*, 64–5; Shackleton, *Montesquieu*, 261–4, 360; Volpilhac-Auger, "Une modération radicale?," 394–5.

[28] Bianchi, "Modération non sans tentations," 349; Craiutu, *Virtue for Courageous Minds*, 262 n. 7.

[29] Shackleton, *Montesquieu*, 261.

[30] Oudin, *Spinozisme de Montesquieu*, 131; Shackleton, *Montesquieu*, 264.

[31] Oudin, *Spinozisme de Montesquieu*, 132–3.

[32] Oudin, *Spinozisme de Montesquieu*, 66, 68–70, 75.

[33] La Beaumelle, *Suite de la Défense*, 16–17.

controversy over *L'Esprit des Lois*, La Beaumelle emerged as Montesquieu's most fervent supporter and eulogist.[34] Montesquieu cheerfully joined forces with him but only briefly since this, it soon transpired, threatened to drag him deeper into trouble.

La Beaumelle returned to the debate as to whether Montesquieu was, or was not, a *Spinosiste*, devoting several pages to this issue in his *Suite de la Défense*.[35] He did so not because *Spinosisme* was a *un scandale, la figure extrême de l'hétérodoxie*, a vague corpus without specific meaning denoting different things to different people—here Roche, Lilti, Negri, and co. could not be more mistaken—but, on the contrary, because it possessed all too specific a meaning, a significance around which not only the international polemic surrounding Montesquieu's masterpiece, but also much other serious mid-eighteenth-century investigation and debate, swirled. Far from meaningless, *Spinosisme* remained a towering cultural preoccupation of the age, signifying a determinism and materialism, often termed *fatalisme*, that abolished all *supernaturalia* and all religious authority and denied all divine governance of the world, miracles, and Revelation. It was a total abjuration not just of Christianity, Cartesianism, Lockeianism, and Newtonianism, but also all positive deism; it meant tying one's entire account of nature and humanity into a single interlocking mechanistic system, or *méchanisme totale*, built around denial of divine governance and all teleology, rendering all moral and political values purely man-made. It invariably meant that "reason," understood as mathematical scientific "reason," is the exclusive tool of verification mankind possesses, the sole criterion of what is true; it meant not just toleration and liberty of conscience, but "freedom to philosophize" in the sense of rendering philosophy and science wholly independent of all religious sanction, control, or censorship and allowing criticism of all religion and politics. It meant intellectual revolution.

Part of La Beaumelle's defense of Montesquieu against the charge of *Spinosisme* proved somewhat too ingenious: although Montesquieu held similar views on toleration and freedom to philosophize as Spinoza, and while Spinoza undeniably initiated the Enlightenment's philosophical plea for full toleration preceding and going further than Locke and Bayle in this respect, these characteristics needed to be detached from *Spinosisme* proper because in themselves they imply no atheistic denial of divine providence and Revelation, or the exclusive hegemony of reason.[36] Spinoza mainly defends comprehensive toleration in his *Tractatus Theologico-Politicus*, argued La Beaumelle, when not yet the atheist or *fataliste* he became later, before he became a *Spinosiste*. This Spinoza only became when composing his *Ethics*. More uncompromising in championing toleration and more partial to republicanism than Montesquieu, La Beaumelle sought to vindicate, and build on, his hero's naturalism, which he did by arguing that Montesquieu's views certainly overlapped with Spinoza's but only

[34] Shackleton, *Montesquieu*, 365, 376, 390–1; Lauriol, *La Beaumelle*, 184–96.

[35] La Beaumelle, *Suite de la Défense*, 48–50, 63; *Pièces pour et contre* L'Esprit des Loix (1752), 119–22, 135–6.

[36] La Beaumelle, *Suite de la Défense*, 48; *Pièces pour et contre* L'Esprit des Loix (1752), 119.

as regards some aspects of naturalism, insofar as moral categories are explained in purely naturalistic terms. Wherever Montesquieu does embrace Spinoza's views his position should not be thought atheistic, or to involve *fatalisme*. Here La Beaumelle was being excessively bold and Montesquieu soon angrily drew back.[37]

The presence of radical strands in Montesquieu's thought, and his radical contacts, besides the fact that the *L'Esprit des Lois*, once firmly established as a masterpiece by the early 1750s, could be used to mask, not least in the *Encyclopédie*, more radical ideas, does not blur, but rather underlines the reality of the tension between radical thought and philosophical moderation, and helps explain why Montesquieu thrust himself firmly onto the moderate side.[38] The "temptation of the radical" and his contacts does not change the fact that Montesquieu outwardly opposed atheism and irreligion and consistently argued for the superiority of Christian societies over other societies, linking this to his defense of monarchy and aristocracy. Given the manifold influences at work in the evolution of his thought, and extent of his interaction with radical intellectual approaches, the dichotomy moderate/radical proves indispensable to explaining the overall direction and goals of his system, and why his European and American reception developed as it did, with radicals soon drifting away from his support and conservatives increasingly espousing his viewpoints. Precisely his interaction with the likes of Fontenelle, Boulainvilliers, Fréret, and La Beaumelle clarifies how and why he intertwined the most startlingly innovative strands of thought together in the way he does. But his preference for monarchy and mixed government also explains why, during the late eighteenth century, Montesquieu's political ideas—the most widely cited, applauded, and discussed of any political philosopher's during and immediately after the American Revolution—came to be championed exclusively by moderate enlighteners, anglophiles, and constitutional monarchists, by publicists deemed by radicals to be defending aristocracy, division of powers, and constitutional monarchy, and "moderate" monarchy on the French model, even if, as some American revolutionaries pointed out, especially in his early work, he also tentatively supports republican ideas.[39]

Incipient radical antagonism to Montesquieu's political theories was already discernible as early as the 1760s. Whereas in the 1750s, the young directors of the *Encyclopédie* were keen to associate the great Montesquieu with their project and capitalize on his high standing among the progressive-minded, their attitude had changed markedly by the mid-1760s. D'Holbach preferred representative, constitutional monarchy to absolute monarchy, and here differed significantly from Voltaire and Helvétius, who preferred royal absolutism (though Helvétius was even more hostile to Montesquieu's climate classification).[40] But after returning to Paris from

[37] Lauriol, *La Beaumelle*, 193; Israel, *Enlightenment Contested*, 836–9.

[38] Blom, *Enlightening the World*, 146; Villaverde, "L'Abbé Raynal," 244–6.

[39] Imbert, *Destutt de Tracy critique*, 24; De Dijn, "Montesquieu's Controversial Context," 69, 81; Israel, *Expanding Blaze*, 81–2, 228–9.

[40] Romani, "All Montesquieu's Sons," 223.

England in 1765 much disillusioned with the British "mixed government" system, some of d'Holbach's fierce criticism of the English system not unnaturally rubbed off onto Montesquieu; and he sufficiently swayed his ally Diderot in the same direction, so that he too began expressing derogatory remarks about Montesquieu's political outlook.[41] For the remainder of his life, d'Holbach abjured "mixed government" on the British model, as championed by Montesquieu and Hume, his visit to England having convinced him the British constitution was irretrievably "corrupt."[42]

Of course, swayed by Montesquieu, most opinion considered England's constitution the "greatest effort of the human spirit," but this famed model with its inherent proneness to ally aristocracy with monarchy against the common people, a bias further reinforced by episcopal presence in the upper House, was in reality, held the post-1765 d'Holbach, alarmingly defective. Britain's Lower House, the Commons, suffered from the fatal defect of infrequent elections (under the Septennial Act), enabling the people's *représentants*, once elected, to forget their accountability to the people and "without incurring any risk betray the people's true interests and sell their liberty to the monarch."[43] Equally indicative of the defects of Montesquieu's political schema, held d'Holbach, was the insidious role of the British monarch. Bloated with prerogatives, the crown remained sole dispenser of the nation's public funds, a corrupt arrangement facilitating government vitiation of the electoral process.[44] In sum, "English liberty" was not remotely what most commentators hyped it up to be, nor were its deficiencies at all mitigated by the absurd veneration of the Magna Carta, an obscure medieval charter extorted from King John.[45] Such veneration was just another ridiculous instance of "political superstition," of the way many cherish old charters without evaluating their rationality, supposing them valid and venerable simply because they are ancient.[46]

For d'Holbach, perfection in government consists in steering men's passions toward the common good and "le bien public" and is always based on virtue, and nothing else.[47] Hence, Montesquieu's categories struck him as fundamentally false. He had erred greatly by exaggerating climate's role in determining the moral and political character of different societies, though he accepted that an identical form of government would not suit all peoples and climes and that, to some extent, different circumstances do necessitate differences in laws and forms.[48] But these differences are marginal: the state's essential purpose and moral guidelines should always converge

[41] Strugnell, *Diderot's Politics*, 106–7; Wilson, *Diderot*, 232–3, 518.

[42] Naville, *D'Holbach*, 389; Strugnell, *Diderot's Politics*, 106.

[43] D'Holbach, *Système social*, 295–6; d'Holbach, *Politique naturelle*, 72–3; Goggi, *De l'Encyclopédie à l'éloquence républicaine*, 399–400.

[44] D'Holbach, *Politique naturelle*, 89; d'Holbach, *Système sociale*, 297–9; Sandrier, *Style philosophique*, 310.

[45] D'Holbach, *Système social*, 429; Peña, "Lumières radicales," 317.

[46] D'Holbach, *Politique naturelle*, 322.

[47] D'Holbach, *Politique naturelle*, 81; Devellennes, "D'Holbach radical," 321; Di Domenico, *Natura, Uomo, Dio*, 189.

[48] D'Holbach, *Politique naturelle*, 76, 314–17; Wolloch, *History and Nature*, 108.

and be equivalent everywhere. About this, he differed too from d'Alembert, and profoundly from Hume, as well as, again, from Voltaire. Montesquieu's basic preference for monarchy and aristocracy sufficiently proved, for d'Holbach, as for Condorcet, Volney, and Destutt later, that his schema must be rejected. "Honour" is not the special principle of "monarchy" as the latter argued in the *L'Esprit des Lois*, held d'Holbach, neither is "virtue" the distinctive underlying principle of republican government. Considered carefully, Montesquieu's separating "honor" from "virtue" as he does is so baffling that it makes one suppose, as there would otherwise be no explanation for so absurd a conclusion, that Montesquieu, like Aristotle, is insinuating that there exist no real kings, only "tyrants" (d'Holbach did hold this view).[49] If one takes Montesquieu seriously, and republics are grounded by nature in "virtue" while monarchy rests on "puerile vanity, frivolous distinctions depending on the caprices of a single master," then monarchy must needs be generally despised.

During the late eighteenth century, radical *philosophes* shifted still further from sympathy for Montesquieu, chiefly owing to his conservative aristocratic preferences, *noblesse de robe* agenda, and ardour for intermediary powers in the hands of aristocracy.[50] Nor could they ignore the fact that *L'Esprit des Lois* had been adopted by prominent apologists for slavery as a bulwark against abolitionism.[51] The shift to growing radical hostility toward Montesquieu's characteristic positions became especially marked after the onset of the American Revolution in 1775. Montesquieu, having eulogized the British model, came to be extensively utilized in both France and the United States during the revolutionary era precisely to defend and uphold the hegemony of monarchy and "aristocracy."[52] In America and France alike, *L'Esprit des Lois* inevitably became an ideological battleground between the rival ideological factions as attitudes toward Montesquieu polarized further still, with revolutionary moderates aiming to salvage monarchy and aristocracy during 1789–92 defending Montesquieu and democratic republicans demolishing him.

No matter there were some radical ingredients in his system, hard-core republicans in both France and America turned more and more against Montesquieu's political thought, especially harsh criticism being directed against it by Condorcet, Filangieri, Thorild, Volney, and Thomas Paine, followed by Jefferson, Say, and Destutt de Tracy, all political writers abhorrent to conservative theorists such as Burke and American "aristocratic" republicans like the "openly Montesquieuan Anglophile" John Adams.[53] Condorcet's journal, the *Bibliothèque de l'Homme Public* (1790–1), established to promote awareness of political science and government more widely, in 1790 included a critique by the revolutionary journalist and diplomat Philippe-Antoine Grouvelle

[49] D'Holbach, *Éthocratie*, 600; Doyle, *Aristocracy*, 141.

[50] Romani, "All Montesquieu's Sons," 199.

[51] Condorcet, *Réflexions sur l'esclavage*, 90; Loft, *Passion, Politics*, 202; Fergus, *Revolutionary Emancipation*, 59–60; Rahe, *Montesquieu*, 157–8, 60; Romani, "All Montesquieu's Sons," 200–1.

[52] [Condorcet], *Bibliothèque de l'Homme Public* vii (1791), p. 6, reviewing Philippe-Antoine Grouvelle.

[53] Levy, "Montesquieu's Constitutional Legacies," 132.

(1757–1806), analyzing Montesquieu's influence specifically on the French Revolution. Son of a goldsmith, Grouvelle was a founder member of the "Club de 1789," a republican serving as the Revolution's envoy in Denmark–Norway during 1793–9. Styling Montesquieu a "benevolent genius" who taught men to reflect on the differences between different systems of laws, Montesquieu should also, contended Grouvelle (like Condorcet), be considered a "culpable genius insofar as he defended aristocracy." Unlike his friend, Jefferson, Condorcet had never admired Montesquieu,[54] any more than Rousseau, but was especially exasperated by Montesquieu's undeviating preoccupation with "moderation" in monarchies and republics alike: it is not "moderation," countered Condorcet, agreeing with d'Holbach, but justice that is the principle of every state, justice being one and universal.[55]

An academic thesis submitted at Uppsala in 1787 by the Swedish radical poet and Spinozist, Thomas Thorild (1759–1808), was followed in March 1788 by a public disputation on Montesquieu, at Uppsala, in which Thorild vigorously criticized *L'Esprit* in the presence of the Swedish king.[56] An expanded version of Thorild's thesis reappeared in French, at Paris, during the Revolution. Pronouncing Montesquieu always "great and ingenious" but "rarely interesting or true," Thorild reproached him especially for offering humanity a variety of very divergent types of political system—absolutist, aristocratic, and republican—whereas, like d'Holbach, Condorcet, and Filangieri, he insisted that he should be advancing just one—whatever is best for mankind.[57] Democratic republicanism alone, urged radical enlighteners, promotes equality and the majority's well-being and this applies universally irrespective of whether countries are large or small. Conversely, after 1789, ideologues like the German apologist of Joseph II and Frederick the Great, Ewald, defending enlightened despotism as the sole viable way to promote Enlightenment, eulogized Montesquieu for emphasizing the indispensability of religion to monarchical rule and indispensable role of Christianity in rendering absolutism generally, including enlightened absolutism, human, gentle, and non-despotic.[58]

Radicals writing during the revolutionary and Napoleonic era, while aware Montesquieu had once been targeted for bold innovation and what to some seemed "Spinozist" tendencies, and while usually still acknowledging his greatness—though even that often rather grudgingly—were increasingly antagonized after 1775 by his being mobilized by moderate reformers and publicists, like Saint-Méry, Malouet, and John Adams to reinforce the fences of their aristocratic "moderation." What had

[54] Badinter and Badinter, *Condorcet*, 537.

[55] Levy, "Montesquieu's Constitutional Legacies," 127–8; Romani, "All Montesquieu's Sons," 233; Craiutu, *Virtue for Courageous Minds*, 56–7, 249; Williams, *Condorcet and Modernity*, 206.

[56] Hoeckermann, "Thomas Thorild," 27.

[57] Thorild, "Critik over Montesquieu," in Thorild, *Samlade Skrifter* ii. 279–85; Carrithers, "An Appreciation," 13; see also A. Hoeckermann, "Thomas Thorild, der skandinavische Lessing," *Greifswalder Tageblatt. Sonntags-Blatt* viii (1883), 26–7.

[58] Ewald, *Über Revolutionen*, 240–4.

formerly been tentative reservations now turned into vehement criticism.[59] Of course, on occasion Montesquieu was harshly criticized by moderates too—but then with a very different critical thrust. Voltaire objected not to Montesquieu's preference for monarchy and aristocracy, for Christian societies and semi-defense of slavery, but to how he applied his climate relativism and way of depicting national character.[60]

On an individual level, radical rejection of Montesquieu manifested itself in the intellectual development of several prominent figures. Once a youthful admirer of Montesquieu, prior to the American Revolution, when Montesquieu's readers were mostly less aware of his bias toward monarchy, and discreet indictment of republicanism, than after 1775,[61] later in life Jefferson's perspective changed markedly. "Every man who reflects as he reads," he commented, in August 1810, writing to William Duane, after reading Destutt de Tracy's manuscript analysis of Montesquieu's political thought, "has considered [*L'Esprit*] a book of paradoxes, having, indeed, much of truth and sound principle, but abounding also with inconsistencies, apocryphal facts, and false inferences."[62] Destutt's effort he welcomed as "a correction of these." Among the "false inferences" Jefferson believed totally "exploded by experience, with some other brilliant fallacies accredited by Montesquieu," was of course, for the American revolutionaries, Montesquieu's inconvenient thesis "that small states alone are fitted to be republics."[63] Writing to Destutt himself a few months later, in January 1811, concurring with his call for "a radical correction," Jefferson remarked that his own view of Montesquieu had been growing more negative and derogatory for some time, specifically since 1789–90.[64] "I had, with the world, deemed Montesquieu's work of much merit, but saw in it with every thinking man, so much of paradox, of false principle and misapplied fact, as to render its value equivocal on the whole. [David] Williams and others had nibbled only at its errors. A radical correction of them," like that of Destutt, was therefore, "a great desideratum."[65] Another leading Radical Enlightenment commentator of the Napoleonic era, Jean-Baptiste Say (1767–1832), even claimed Destutt's highly critical *Commentaire* on the *L'Esprit des Lois*, rebuking Montesquieu at every turn for belittling democracy, a text wholly unpublishable in Napoleon's France, was of greater worth to humanity than the *Esprit des Lois* itself.[66] Adams firmly disagreed but conceded that Destutt was at any rate "a sensible man and easily understood," and "not an abstruse, mysterious, incomprehensible Condorcet."[67]

59 [Condorcet], *Bibliothèque* vii. 4, 6–7; Lutz, "Relative Influence," 189–97; Jolly, "Introduction," 14–15.

60 Romani, "All Montesquieu's Sons," 206–9.

61 Levy, "Montesquieu's Constitutional Legacies," 121–2.

62 Jefferson to Duane, Monticello, 12 Aug. 1810, in Jefferson, *Writings*, 1230; Carrithers, "An Appreciation," 3–4.

63 Jefferson to Francois d'Ivernois, Monticello, 6 Feb. 1795, in Jefferson, *Writings*, 1024.

64 Albertone, "Thomas Jefferson and French Economic Thought," 133.

65 Jefferson to Destutt de Tracy, Monticello, 26 Jan. 1811, in Jefferson, *Writings*, 1242; Levy, "Montesquieu's Constitutional Legacies," 127.

66 Jolly, "Introduction," 7; Imbert, *Destutt de Tracy critique*, 14, 17–18; Carrithers, "An Appreciation," 40.

67 Adams to Jefferson, 2 Feb. 1817, in *The Adams–Jefferson Letters* ii. 506.

It was certainly not owing to one or another particular strand of his thought that post-1789 democratic republicans increasingly opposed Montesquieu's system, but the overall framework, a typology of forms of government declaring the most "moderate"—a pivotal term in Montesquieu—the most stable, favorable to liberty and resistant to tyranny, corruption, and degeneration, and most easily maintained without excessive stress. But these most "moderate" regimes were decidedly the aristocratic governments, especially the Christian monarchies.[68] In Montesquieu, types of government needed to be appropriate to their setting, moral milieu, and geographical context. Often, he appeared to be using his schema to urge readers that their government "should remain such" unchanged, simply because that was how it was;[69] he offered justifications for different kinds of government boasting very divergent legal systems, according to different environments, climates, and moral systems, forging a cultural and moral relativism that stretched even to a certain ambivalence regarding slavery.[70]

Praised for the comprehensiveness of his approach by conservatives, the striking inadequacy of Montesquieu's discussion of republics and republicanism only became fully evident from 1789. When discussing republics, Montesquieu almost exclusively focuses either on ancient democracies or else modern aristocratic republics such as Venice and Genoa, which he disdained, omitting all analysis and imagery relating to the representative or democratic republic radical theorists prized, and all discussion of how democratic republican constitutions and legislatures might function. He had nothing to say about republics of the sort a good many in Geneva, the Dutch Republic, and elsewhere, with La Beaumelle prominent among them, already in his time aspired to see, and wanted to turn all existing republics into. The result was that in all three of the pressure-points where democratic republican modernity broke through late in the eighteenth century—North America, Switzerland, and the United Provinces, Montesquieu provided scarcely one word of any use or relevance to the ideologues leading the revolutionary movements.[71] In *L'Esprit des Lois* Book IX Montesquieu does briefly touch on confederate republics like the Dutch, Swiss, and Hanseatic confederacies but begins, hardly encouragingly, by affirming that "si une république est petite, elle est détruite par une force étrangère, si elle est grande, elle se détruit par un vice intérieur" [if a republic is small, it is destroyed by a foreign force, if it is large, it destroys itself by an interior vice], claiming this applied both to "les démocraties et les aristocraties."[72] Montesquieu grants the greater resilience and

[68] Rahe, "Forms of Government," 76–82; De Dijn, "Montesquieu's Controversial Context," 69, 87.

[69] [Condorcet], *Bibliothèque* vii. 12; Carrithers, "An Appreciation", 14–15; Carrithers, "Democratic and Aristocratic Republics," 147; Levy, "Montesquieu's Constitutional Legacies," 133.

[70] [Condorcet], *Bibliothèque* v. 5 and vii. 11–12; Benot, *Diderot*, 206, 210; Vyverberg, *Human Nature*, 90–1; Larrère, "Montesquieu and Liberalism," 290.

[71] Carrithers, "Democratic and Aristocratic Republics," 128; Krause, "Freedom, Sovereignty," 149, 151, 153.

[72] Montesquieu, *L'Esprit des Lois*, Book IX, chapter 1; Villaverde, *Ilusión republicana*, 170–1.

durability of federal as compared to city republics,[73] but says nothing whatever about their councils, legislatures, and representative arrangements.

It was indeed a yawning gap, as was Montesquieu's striking failure to bring European colonialism and colonial empires into the picture. Paine acknowledged that, at some level, Montesquieu had once been "inclined to republican government."[74] Montesquieu, after all, affirms that where "l'esprit de la monarchie" is war and aggrandizement, the spirit of republics is "peace and moderation."[75] But Paine too found Montesquieu excessively prone to moderation, timidity, and even obscurantism, especially in promoting the "absurd dogma" that republics are fit only for small countries: "for he had always the Bastille before his eyes when he was speaking of republics, and therefore pretended not to write for France."[76] In the eyes of radicals like Paine, d'Holbach, Condorcet, and Destutt, all varieties of political system in the world boil down in the end to just two kinds—those of the "intriguers," as Condorcet decried the prevailing forms of government, built on vested interests instead of popular sovereignty, rejecting *volonté générale* and befogging the "common good," using specious arguments to dupe those whose discernment, dimmed by religious piety is sufficiently feeble as to cause them to venerate kings, aristocracy, and ecclesiastics, and, on the other hand, democratic republics, or "gouvernements nationaux," founded on "l'interêt général", as d'Holbach and Destutt call it, based on reason and natural right.[77]

Democratic republicanism rejecting all religious authority alone can legitimate a political and moral system, held Thorild, publicly rebuking Robespierre and the Montagne in a pamphlet of 1794. While different climes and contrasting legal and moral traditions may explain why different moral and political systems exist, only one kind can be universally valid and fitting from a genuinely enlightened standpoint—the kind that best promotes the "common good."[78] This ran flat against Montesquieuan relativism and moderation which make no provision for states based on institutionalized equality and revealed a deeply-rooted bias toward social hierarchy and institutionalized inequality.[79] While he too occasionally employs the term "general will" in the *L'Esprit des Lois*, believing the Venetian Republic was based on an aristocratic "general will" and that ancient classical republics had been based on a broader "general will," Montesquieu resolutely opposed the Spinozist idea, renewed by Diderot and d'Holbach, that there exists an overriding common will that is best for

[73] Montesquieu, *L'Esprit des Lois*, Book IX, chapter 1.

[74] Paine, *Rights of Man*, 93; Imbruglia, "Civilisation and Colonisation," 861–2.

[75] Montesquieu, *L'Esprit des Lois*, Book IX, chapter 2; Spector, *Montesquieu et l'émergence*, 92–3.

[76] Paine, *Complete Writings* ii. 598–9; Nicolet, *L'Idée républicaine*, 120–2.

[77] Condorcet, *Bibliothèque* ii (1791), vol. 3, pp. 71–2; Destutt de Tracy, *Commentaire*, 68; Imbert, *Destutt de Tracy critique*, 35–6; Jolly, "Introduction," 39.

[78] *Le Conservateur des Principes des Républicains* ii, no. 7 (Paris, 20 Messidor Year II), 3–8; Israel, *Revolutionary Ideas*, 335–6, 698.

[79] Larrère, "Montesquieu on Economics," 337.

everyone viewed collectively, a will that society must work towards by subordinating to it all particular individual and group interests.[80]

After 1789, on both sides of the Atlantic, the breach between moderates and radicals was open and unmistakable. Acutely aware of their inherited intellectual baggage, the *Radicalen* knew perfectly well who were their chief contemporary publicists. Radical Enlightenment's twin goals—overthrowing religious authority along with the prevailing socio-political order—inherently linked philosophically *and* politically, suffused the entire stepped-up rhetoric about "ignorance," "priest-craft," "imposture," and "superstition." In America by the 1790s, enthusiasts and opponents alike filled their libraries with the works of Raynal, Condorcet, Paine, Beccaria, Volney, Godwin, Wollstonecraft, and "some Rousseau," knowing this was where the radical, democratizing message lay.[81] The blind leader of the New York radical "deists," as they called themselves, around 1800, Elihu Palmer (1764–1806), exalted Paine as "probably the most useful man who ever existed on the face of the earth,"[82] but publicly revered also Condorcet, Volney, Helvétius, d'Holbach, Godwin, Price, and Bentham. Montesquieu had no place in his list even though "philosophy," anchored in naturalism and materialism, urged Palmer, was the universal liberating force that had already "destroyed innumerable errors," advanced science and technology, repulsed theological ire and arrogance, and devised "those moral and political systems, which have softened the savage and ferocious heart of man, and raised the ignorant slave from the dust, into the elevated character of an enlightened citizen."[83]

Among the chief objections of the "negative critique" is the claim that the binary moderate/radical underpinning the general schema of the Radical Enlightenment interpretation ranging Voltaire and Montesquieu among the "moderates," and Diderot and d'Holbach among the radicals, creates an overly simple dichotomy, a forced polarity, with the lines drawn, contend Casini, Bianchi, and Paolo Quintili "trop forts et trop rigides" [too strong and rigid].[84] Needless to say, numerous specialists heartily concur. But given that considerable space has been devoted in this series to the shifting interactions and tensions, as well as agreements and disagreements, determining the relationship between "moderates and "radicals," it hardly seems what has been described can fairly be deemed a simple bifurcation. Rather the rift was a dynamic, highly complex set of tensions constantly modifying at the edges, so much so that much of the usefulness of the categorization follows precisely from its enabling us better to appreciate the hindrances, clashes, and difficulties, the shifting play of "temptations," concurrence, overlap, and rapprochement.

[80] Krause, "Freedom, Sovereignty," 153–8; Williams, "Spinoza and the General Will," 125.

[81] Lundberg and May, "Enlightened Reader in America," 270–1.

[82] Foner, *Tom Paine and Revolutionary America*, 256; Carrithers, "Democratic and Aristocratic Republics," 113.

[83] Palmer, *Principles of Nature*, 159; Keane, *Tom Paine*, 497–500; Walters, *Revolutionary Deists*, 204.

[84] Quintili, "Diderot dans les Lumières radicales," 279–80; Quintili, "Note critiche," 268–71; Bianchi, "Modération non sans tentations," 345.

The lines dividing the categories moderate and radical were partly intellectual and ideological stemming from differences of view, perception, and argument. But the evolving relationship between the two was also one of dialogue and interaction. This interplay between what eventually, from the 1770s, became openly clashing tendencies was by no means shaped solely by ideas. Both sides' terminology, the growing friction between the divergent tendencies, and the dash of imposture pervading pre-1770 radical thought were all shaped also by social taboos and inhibitions, laws, government pressures, ecclesiastical intervention, and public reaction. Society and its priorities, consequently, played a large part in separating and defining the rival factions as well as alternately quietening or intensifying, softening or sharpening the friction between them. The classification, then, must be understood as being as much social, political, and religious as intellectual, highly intricate and always dynamic, never simple.

7

D'Holbach against Voltaire and Rousseau

A Triangular War of Political Thought Systems

7.1. OUR "VALE OF TEARS"

Enlightenment writers allied to kings and courts, like Montesquieu and Voltaire, took good care not to offend their patrons more than necessary. For decades, Voltaire was the publicly declared ally of Prussia's Frederick the Great and Catherine the Great of Russia in particular. Paul-Henri Thiry, the Baron d'Holbach (1723–89), by contrast, assures readers that "there still exists no well-ordered political constitution on earth" [il n'existe point encore de constitution politique bien ordonnée sur la terre],[1] because "to govern is to maintain, protect and guide a society to happiness" [gouverner, c'est maintenir, protéger et guider au Bonheur une société] which cannot happen without obliging everyone to contribute to "l'utilité générale." Sadly, in his own time, tyranny, violence, and unreason dominated the political scene everywhere, tarring all existing governments and their legislation. Accordingly, d'Holbach's denunciation of the status quo was hardly likely to fit any view of politics that was not sweepingly radical. And indeed, his political thought was both consciously revolutionary and embedded in a programme for far-reaching crypto-republican, crypto-democratic, and universal rights transformation of society and politics.

"Error, religious and political," held d'Holbach, "has transformed our world into a vale of tears."[2] Humanity needs nothing more urgently than salvaging from the dismal edifice of ignorance, superstition, persecution, and despotism oppressing it, oppression so vast and pernicious that most of humanity is kept in chains, plunged in misery and destitution, as it has been for millennia. This morass of "political and religious error" rendering mankind downtrodden and wretched was reflected in what d'Holbach considered the highly defective political theories prevailing in his time. Eighteenth-century political thought prior to his own, he maintained, was not just imperfect but a gigantic mass of error, stemming from the same pernicious mix of "ignorance" and "superstition" as kept mankind in general needlessly wretched. Not

[1] D'Holbach, *Système social*, 259–60, 271.

[2] D'Holbach, *Système de la nature* i. 365–6.

only were all peoples ignorant about politics but "those who govern men are, just like their subjects, dupes and victims of an infinity of prejudices" to which kings and subjects alike sacrifice their own happiness. Since the veritable maxims of politics "are entirely unknown to most princes . . . "[3] the regimes of his day had little prospect of ceasing to be despotic and wreaking more harm to their societies than good—or being aided in degrading men by religious authorities. In d'Holbach's eyes, it despicably encourages tyranny to assure princes their power comes from God, deceit which had become one of the chief props of despotism.[4]

Practically all existing political theory being false: "the simple and natural principles of morality and politics remain still to be found."[5] Like Helvétius, d'Holbach derived his political doctrines from a tightly integrated materialist system in which human conduct and morality function as a kind of moral physics. With fixed laws of cause and effect, d'Holbach's principles of society and politics grounded a universal and single moral order, basically the same secular universal moral order defined by the pursuit of happiness underpinning the republicanism and democratic egalitarianism later infusing the revolutionary ideology of Condorcet, Volney, Cérutti, Naigeon, Gorsas, Garat, Lanthenas, Destutt, and other key intellectual figures of the (democratic republican anti-Montagnard) Revolution subsequently.[6] The challenge of politics, for d'Holbach, was not how to check and constrain government, but how to steer it toward the general amelioration of society and individual life.[7] This in turn begged the question: how could any worthwhile restructuring of regimes transpire if, as yet, practically no one had any grasp of correct political principles? If peoples possessed scant understanding, princes and aristocrats equally clung to the "most false ideas about happiness, power and glory; the truth practically never enlightens them."[8] It is hard indeed to imagine Montesquieu or Voltaire writing thus.

Misery arising from credulity and ignorance afflicted all mankind, in d'Holbach's view, a fact devastating for every state, society, and individual; prejudice and error vitiated legal and political practice enabling injustice and oppression to reign supreme everywhere.[9] Needless wretchedness was the ubiquitous result, with nothing done to "find the means to prevent those who have no part in the government becoming the prey of those who govern them."[10] When composing his series of political writings, during the 1770s, religion, morality, and government seemed to d'Holbach all fundamentally wrongly constituted, to "have combined their power to obstruct the

[3] D'Holbach, *Politique naturelle*, 387, 414–15, 466.

[4] D'Holbach, *Politique naturelle*, 303–4; Devellennes, "Fourth Musketeer," 472.

[5] D'Holbach, *Système de la nature* i. 337–8, 351–2, 377–8; d'Holbach, *Système social*, 17–18; d'Holbach, *Politique naturelle*, 412.

[6] Israel, *Revolutionary Ideas*, 132; Vyverberg, *Human Nature*, 13, 42–3, 47.

[7] D'Holbach, *Politique naturelle*, 411–13; Gaddo and Tortarolo, *Secularizzazione*, 76–7.

[8] D'Holbach, *Système social*, 160, 202; d'Holbach, *Morale universelle* ii. 53; d'Holbach, *Éthocratie*, 600–1.

[9] D'Holbach, *Système de la nature* i. 340.

[10] D'Holbach, *Politique naturelle*, 80–1; d'Holbach, *Système social*, 276; d'Holbach, *Éthocratie*, 653–4; Israel, "Rousseau and d'Holbach," 157–8.

goal of human association and set up obstacles to the happiness of nations."[11] Through ignorance, a false "science du politique" [science of politics] ensured governmental power is everywhere "usurped by force, by conquest and tyranny or confided without reserve to men who abuse it" turning it into an affliction of humanity no less "cruel than anarchy."[12]

But mankind's universal destitution, misfortune, and misery, avows d'Holbach, stems not from mankind having degenerated, or strayed from the purity of the state of nature, as the deluded Rousseau imagined, but from human reason remaining stunted in its infancy, in unknowing immaturity regarding society, morality, and political theory. In short, d'Holbach, dropping hostile allusions to Rousseau at every turn, fervently denounced the political culture of his time, and not least its veneration of classical republicanism and what he dismissed as the oppressive morality of ancient Sparta and Rome.[13] Existing political thought seemed to him so retrograde that mankind had not yet even begun to hit on sound principles, except perhaps, in some degree, in China where government was tightly conjoined to morality and philosophy (Confucianism), and traditional "religion" supervised by priests had (supposedly) lost all hold over the governing class, with "superstition" and belief in the supernatural purged from morality and the state. There, no one could participate in administration unless "exempt from popular religion," thereby enabling general improvement to set in. The court at Peking rewarded merit and achievement rather than deferred to pretensions of noble lineage.[14]

Hereditary nobility d'Holbach condemned outright, deeming noble arrogance toward those beneath them especially reprehensible.[15] Hereditary nobility cannot be regarded as anything but an *abus pernicieux*, fit only to "promote social friction and indolence, laziness and general incapacity to become citizens, to the detriment of everyone."[16] If the education of Europe's princes was abysmal, so universally was that of the aristocracy.[17] Nobles in every land "seem to condemn themselves not just to the profoundest ignorance but from childhood on to devote themselves to the most complete corruption."[18] Distinctions of nobility might be legitimate where awarded on merit, but this has nothing to do with hereditary right and separate legal status. "It is education" not birth or blood that shapes citizens capable of serving the state.[19] Deriding those priding themselves on ancient noble lineage, and the "puerile art" of heraldry, d'Holbach believed such unreasoning haughtiness detached the nobility

[11] D'Holbach, *Système social*, 208; Israel, *Democratic Enlightenment*, 811.

[12] D'Holbach, *Système social*, 21, 215, 274.

[13] Hammersley, *English Republican Tradition*, 133; Spitz, "From Civism to Civility," 108–12.

[14] D'Holbach, *Système social*, 313–14, 321; Lough, *Essays*, 226; Israel, "Diderot, D'Holbach et la question de la Chine," 185–99.

[15] D'Holbach, *Morale universelle* ii. 108–11; Peña, "Lumières radicales," 318.

[16] D'Holbach, *Politique naturelle*, 191; Devellennes, "Fourth Musketeer," 467.

[17] D'Holbach, *Politique naturelle*, 143–5; d'Holbach, *Morale universelle* ii. 36–8 and iii. 67–9, 74–7.

[18] D'Holbach, *Système social*, 512.

[19] D'Holbach, *Politique naturelle*, 190–1; Vyverberg, *Human Nature*, 43.

from the interests of all other citizens.[20] Aristocracy displays many vices but the worst assuredly was their "vanity": "the noble believes himself to be really a being of a higher order than the rest of the citizens" despite lacking all justification for such presumption. Alas, it was still to "social rank alone that belongs the right to be unjust and oppress others with impunity."[21]

Central to d'Holbach's political philosophy was the principle that government should be the "sum of society's collective force deposited in the hands of those it judges best equipped to lead it to happiness" [la somme des forces de la Société deposés entre les mains de ceux qu'elle juge les plus propres à la conduire au Bonheur];[22] hence, the "best government is that that distributes well-being with the greatest legality possible to all the members of society."[23] This exactly fits our definition of "democratic" in the Radical Enlightenment in which two key elements combine—the state's responsibility is to promote the happiness of all of society, everyone equally, requiring some form of "common good" or "general will" thesis, and government by elected representatives representing this "general will."

To his key term "happiness" d'Holbach linked equality before the law, equality of opportunity and status, and the need for society to provide secular education for all classes of the population and organize an improved distribution of property and wealth. Where states function as they should—which, he regularly repeats, is practically never—citizens will cherish and support the state. When referring to d'Holbach, the "negative critique"—Hunt, Jacob, and Chisick especially—grant his atheism, materialism, and determinism but fail to include his severing all legitimate morality and legislative responsibility from religion and the divine, a separation bound to have far-reaching consequences.[24] Morality, where genuine and useful, is always purely social and secular, held radical enlighteners, d'Holbach not least, and was hence necessarily at war with all theology and teaching of churches.

Rare exceptions notwithstanding, kings, princes, and royal ministers could scarcely be more detrimental to society, morality, and reason than they are. Being, strangely, often mistakenly denied by modern scholars, the passion behind d'Holbach's antimonarchism needs stressing. "A good king is such a rare outcome, there is no room for peoples to flatter themselves they will see one often."[25] In d'Holbach's political science, there exists no such thing as legitimate authority not subject to the consent and final sovereignty of the people; that is laws based on equity. The usual goal of monarchs, however, is "le pouvoir arbitraire, le despotisme," power to twist nations to their wishes and fantasies.[26] Royal authority, wherever legitimate, must, if better times are to come, adhere to the basic purpose of the state: pursuit of the people's greatest happiness even where this is in direct conflict with the interests of king, aristocracy,

[20] D'Holbach, *Système social*, 381–2; d'Holbach, *Politique naturelle*, 67–8.

[21] D'Holbach, *Politique naturelle*, 181–5; Doyle, *Aristocracy*, 141.

[22] D'Holbach, *Système social*, 235.

[23] D'Holbach, *Système social*, 204, 268–9.

[24] Domenech, "D'Holbach et l'obsession," 111–12; Duflo, *Diderot philosophe*, 397.

[25] D'Holbach, *Système social*, 253–5.

[26] D'Holbach, *Système social*, 263–4; d'Holbach, *Morale universelle* ii. 34; d'Holbach, *Éthocratie*, 603.

and court. The will of one man, however great the king, must never rival the wills of all merged as the "general will."[27] Whether constitutions and fundamental laws exist in a given society or not, kings do not make nations, nations make kings. "A nation can be very well governed without a king;" a king cannot exist without a nation.[28] Monarchs, where societies have them, must be "citizens"—the "first of citizens."[29] Unfortunately, "nothing is rarer than kings who are magistrates or citizens."[30]

Utterly remote from Voltaire, d'Holbach was no "monarchist" in the ordinary sense of the term: rather, he considered monarchs, both in principle and practice, appallingly defective and in need of correction.[31] Monarchy's shortcomings include not just the usual abysmal quality of kings themselves and the oppressive power structures they create, but the entire mystique and social aura they foster. Royal ceremonial demands an "admiration stupide" from ordinary folk, ridiculous frivolities that merely compound the obstacles to good government.[32] Not the least deplorable feature is that the "ignorance and incompetence" usual "among princes, especially when they enjoy absolute power" attaches them to the "pompous minutiae of etiquette": reigning over men, they think, means making themselves adored, being treated like "gods" whose exalted rank distances them from all other mortals. Courts and courtiers, and the pomp they stage, are pernicious not just because royal opulence lays onerous fiscal burdens on society but because from royal courts emanate affected manners, disdain for the common man, and all the "impertinences that sometimes render an entire people contemptible in the eyes of strangers."[33]

"In nearly all part of our globe, the sovereign is all, his nation nothing." Wherever peoples embrace the hereditary principle, imagining birth and descent confer status, and confirm the glory of dynasty (something worthless), tyranny and oppression advance.[34] In addition, monarchs are mostly inappropriately educated for their role and perversely susceptible to flattery. Being free of constraints only feeds their arrogance. Monarchy, placing vast power in the hands of a single man, by its nature tempts rulers to abuse their position, look down on laws, and "exercise that despotism and tyranny that are the most terrible scourges of nations." To curb royal education of princes in a constitutional monarchy, ensuring respect for the public good, constitutions must stipulate how the king's children should be educated to ensure the people's interest, not the king's, infuses their schooling.[35] Nearly all kings are malignant, and given that "religion, for princes, is just an instrument for pushing peoples more firmly

[27] D'Holbach, *Politique naturelle*, 89–90, 118.
[28] D'Holbach, *Système social*, 246; D'Holbach, *Morale universelle* ii, 50–1; Charbonnel, "Futurologie politique," 452.
[29] D'Holbach, *Système social*, 153; d'Holbach, *Politique naturelle*, 113.
[30] D'Holbach, *Politique naturelle*, 395.
[31] D'Holbach, *Système social*, 375–7, 391, 490–1, 493–4; d'Holbach, *Politique naturelle*, 200–2.
[32] D'Holbach, *Système social*, 374, 484–5.
[33] D'Holbach, *Morale universelle* ii. 43–7; d'Holbach, *Éthocratie*, 646.
[34] D'Holbach, *Système social*, 319; Di Domenico, *Natura, Uomo, Dio*, 182–5.
[35] D'Holbach, *Système social*, 306; Frederick the Great, *Oeuvres philosophiques*, 372–4.

under the yoke,"[36] most promote tyranny by allying throne and altar. But worst of all are "devout kings" who sacrifice society's stability and security for pious goals. No one should be surprised "to find so few good princes on earth."

"Under a monarch's rule," some suppose, "nations are governed by a father, like families;" but actually, these "fathers" of peoples, history teaches, normally replicate the Saturn of Greek fable—they are gods who devour their own children. Royal courts "nearly always form cliques of influential persons working against the public good" as harmful to their nation as to monarchs, so that it is among monarchy's worst features that merit rarely presents itself at court.[37] In theory, a genuinely enlightened monarch could "make a huge difference for the better;"[38] but such rulers are exceedingly rare (Frederick decidedly did not count in d'Holbach's or Diderot's eyes). Most are "princes injustes" desiring *pouvoir absolu*, corrupting their subjects' morality, dividing them, blinding them with "superstition," rewarding only vices promoting the monarch's interest, always striving to convert subjects into "slaves."[39] Also, while monarchs are too remote to comprehend their subjects' needs, their courts and courtiers conceive their own particular interest to reside in steering rulers still further away.[40] Monarchy is thus "a real conspiracy against their peoples".[41] Hence the misfortunes of nations, from which monarchs continually suffer also themselves, originate in false notions which a false politics assigns to their own interests, kings being betrayed especially by the "flattery of vile courts that poison them," the "fatal councils of the unenlightened men who surround them."[42]

Courts and courtiers encourage kings to be malign as it is in the courtier's interest that their prince should be "foible, inappliqué, indolent, vicieux;" only through bad kingship can courtiers and *les grands* amass more power and wealth for themselves.[43] Royal courts thus foster great aristocrats whose "arrogance insultante," emulated by those beneath them, propagates those ridiculous caprices shared by most inhabitants of lands dominated by a *noblesse*. Unfortunately, monarchy remains also the governmental form likeliest to encourage luxury, a malaise less frequent in republics where ordinary men are less under the sway of superiors. "Republican government," among other precious advantages, affirms d'Holbach, when assailing aristocratic republicanism in *La Morale universelle* and elsewhere, "supposes a strong equality among citizens who are equally subject to the laws."[44] While exalting its own superiority over everything else, even a monarchy that is stable and curbs monarchy's worst excesses cannot prove its "superiorité sur le government republicain."[45]

[36] D'Holbach, *Le Bon-Sens*, 164–6; Kors, *D'Holbach's Coterie*, 324.
[37] D'Holbach, *Morale universelle* ii. 72; Frederick the Great, *Oeuvres philosophiques*, 370–1.
[38] D'Holbach, *Essai sur les préjugés*, 74–5.
[39] D'Holbach, *Politique naturelle*, 372; Devellennes, "D'Holbach radical," 326–7.
[40] D'Holbach, *Politique naturelle*, 424–5. [41] D'Holbach, *Système social*, 332–4.
[42] D'Holbach, *Système social*, 414. [43] D'Holbach, *Système social*, 320–3.
[44] D'Holbach, *Morale universelle* ii. 48; Curran, *Atheism, Religion, and Enlightenment*, 38.
[45] D'Holbach, *Système social*, 256; d'Holbach, *Éthocratie*, 646–8; Hulliung, *Autocritique*, 140–1.

"To monarchy, despotism, and tyranny," argued d'Holbach, "succeeded the form of government that is called republican" which is decidedly an improvement.[46] Frederick the Great and Voltaire rightly noted that d'Holbach and his following were, as Voltaire put it, no *royalists*, in fact deeply hostile to absolutism and aristocracy (as well as churchmen).[47] While acutely aware of the danger of faction and instability in republics, d'Holbach never opposed soundly-based representative republicanism (which he discreetly advocated); nor does he suggest—as the "negative critique" wrongly claims—that he preferred monarchy and aristocracy in the manner of Voltaire to republicanism of the type he endorses. Needing to be discreet about this, d'Holbach remained a crypto-republican who considered republics inherently superior to monarchy. Consistently, he was, however, always averse to aristocratic republics, considering these inherently malignant, as vicious and repugnant as monarchies.[48] The "puerile vanity" of nobles rendered the aristocratic republic a form of government that is universally pernicious; unsurprisingly, the ancient aristocratic republics of Greece and Rome "usually degenerated into true tyrannies."[49] Constitutional monarchies, if less good than genuinely representative republics, are at least better, he maintains, than aristocratic republics.

Was d'Holbach then a "democrat"? "Clearly," contend Chisick, Spitz, Peña, and the "negative critique," "d'Holbach is no admirer of democracy and this he has in common with Voltaire and most other Enlightenment thinkers."[50] Even "the most enlightened and best administered peoples show us at every moment very marked vestiges of their ignorance and the most savage unreason." "While sound government requires the application of reason," in his eyes, asserts Chisick, democracies "are generally lacking in this quality." With respect to two categories of republic, this was indeed d'Holbach's view. Scorning kings, courtiers, and aristocrats, and the hereditary principle, d'Holbach naturally rejected aristocratic republics out of hand. Likewise, he rules out direct democracy. "De toutes les tyrannies, la tyrannie démocratique est la plus cruelle et la moins raisonée" [of all the tyrannies, democratic tyranny is the cruelest and least rational].[51] But in dismissing "pure" or direct democracy, the baron was merely decrying what all radical enlighteners rejected, not least Paine, Cérutti, Condorcet, Destutt, and Volney. This does not alter the fact that, like these others, he warmly endorses representative democracy, a point that needs to be heavily underlined.[52] For the "negative critique," in its usual fashion, is simply misrepresenting and

[46] D'Holbach, *Politique naturelle*, 65.

[47] Naville, *D'Holbach*, 109, 370; Duflo, *Diderot philosophe*, 470.

[48] D'Holbach, *Politique naturelle*, 432; Hulliung, *Autocritique*, 6, 140.

[49] D'Holbach, *Politique naturelle*, 67–8, 325; d'Holbach, *Morale universelle* ii. 47–9, 69–70.

[50] Chisick, "Of Radical and Moderate Enlightenment," 63; Peña, "Lumières radicales," 312–13; Hammersley, *English Republican Tradition*, 123–4.

[51] D'Holbach, *Système social*, 17–18, 251–2; Peña, "Lumières radicales," 313–14.

[52] D'Holbach, *Politique naturelle*, 170; Devellennes, "D'Holbach radical," 326; also Cérutti, *Mémoire pour le peuple* (1788), 49, 52, 59; Spitz, "From Civism to Civility," 110, 112–13; Koekkoek, "Waare en vrije," 249–50.

thoroughly muddling when arguing the Radical Enlightenment thesis fails because d'Holbach dismissed "direct democracy" and holds "a democratic people is a tyrant that is deceived and a slave that is flattered."[53]

Fortunately, the "negative critique" unwittingly helps clarify matters by undermining its own stance itself. D'Holbach, notes Chisick, consistently asserts that the "people are sovereign. This was perhaps primarily a way of calling into question the legitimacy of monarchy and aristocracy," though also consistent with his utilitarian "conviction that the objective of government was the greatest degree of well-being of the greatest number."[54] Or indeed both: both being true exactly fits the Spinozist conception of popular sovereignty; d'Holbach "called into question the legitimacy of monarchy and aristocracy" *and* pushed for the "greatest degree of well-being of the greatest number."[55]

No eighteenth-century thinker did more than d'Holbach to profile the basic distinction, decisive for democratic revolutionaries like Condorcet and Destutt, between representative democracy and "démocratie pure, ou anarchie," as Destutt calls it. Where direct democracy, "la démocratie originelle," as he also terms it, is contemptible, something mankind, they thought, must at all costs avoid, a quagmire inevitable at the lowest level of Destutt's three stages of "civilization," totally different is "démocratie de la raison éclairée" [Enlightenment rational democracy] typifying Destutt's third and highest level of civilization. Representative democracy, the sole legitimate form of "gouvernement réprésentatif" for d'Holbach, therefore has nothing in common with monarchy, aristocracy, or "démocratie pure."[56] What compounds much of the confusion characterizing the "negative critique," including the mistaken view that d'Holbach was a "moderate" enlightener opposed to "democracy," is simply failure to grasp that for d'Holbach and his legacy, pure democracy and representative democracy were not just different but virtual opposites: where the former is destructive, "insupportable," representative democracy is the only form capable of affording liberty, stability, and men's rights and conserving the "general will."

Like Spinoza and Toland earlier, and the *Idéologues* later, d'Holbach loathed royal courts and despised aristocrats, but dreaded even more the irrationality of the masses.[57] What has been said of Destutt de Tracy, writing in the later 1790s and under Napoleon, that his political theory sought "a balance between principles of democracy and enlightened leadership,"[58] fully applies to the entire Radical Enlightenment, remaining a defining feature down to the 1840s. Where, for d'Holbach, ancient Athens abundantly demonstrated the instability, follies, and vulnerability to faction and popular passions of "pure democracy," no direct government by the people can ever amount to more than an unstable, priest-ridden, fleeting

[53] Cérutti, *Mémoire pour le peuple* (1788), 73; Urbinati, "Condorcet's Democratic Theory," 56; further on the muddle, see Kim, "Volney and the French Revolution," 236.

[54] Chisick, "Of Radical and Moderate Enlightenment," 63–4.

[55] Forsyth, *Reason and Revolution*, 64; Lough, *Essays*, 136–7, 226.

[56] Destutt de Tracy, *Commentaire*, 96, 74–5, 91, 94, 158–9, 162–3, 172–3; Jolly, "Introduction," 41–2.

[57] Kors, *D'Holbach's Coterie*, 323.

[58] Head, *Politics and Philosophy*, 305.

phenomenon given its inherent tendency to defer to the dictatorship of demagogues capturing the citizenry's unquestioning allegiance by exploiting their prejudices and "superstition."[59] In direct democracy, the "people, sovereign in appearance, is generally the slave of perverse demagogues who flatter them and incite their passions, and thereby become tyrants."[60] This was one of d'Holbach's many premonitions of what became the *Robespierriste* "ultra-democratic project." On seizing the leadership, demagogues easily tyrannize over the republic, or if an unsteady, turbulent limited monarchy, over king and people, in the name of the people.[61]

Radical enlighteners never had much good to say about ordinary people's beliefs and opinions, as distinct from their needs, moral capacity, and rights. Arguably, one detects here a deep-seated contradiction and one that perhaps contributed more than anything else to the ultimate failure of the Radical Enlightenment. But while d'Holbach, like all radical enlighteners, scorns regimes characterized by what to him were the ignorance and prejudices of the multitude, he (and they more generally) also believed "the duties of morality and precepts of reason" are intrinsically within the common people's reach, or can be made accessible to the masses, where government and education act to propagate sound values among the people. This can only happen, though, where responsible representative government emerges first and state-supported education flourishes. Error, contends d'Holbach is not an "innate malady of the human race;" but curing the malady is extremely difficult because authority, and political and ecclesiastical censorship, are usually geared to obstruct diffusion of truth, preferring deception and propagating false notions the more easily to reduce mankind to being their "prey," while rewarding only those who "poison" men with superstition and priestcraft.[62] This was a point where d'Holbach's atheism closely entwined with his political thought: the greatest hurdle in his own time, and for millennia past, was that government and education, both tied to religion and clergy, are inherently unable to communicate what d'Holbach considered sound moral and political ideas to the masses.[63]

While, like radical enlighteners after him, d'Holbach abjured all democracy stripped of the guidance of reason, that is "pure democracy," or what Paine called "simple democracy," he warmly advocated representative government by a legislature equipped for positive political decision-making under a rational constitution.[64] Yet, even the better forms of government, representative democracies and drastically limited monarchies, can all too easily derail, particularly in the latter case, where the king's power is insufficiently curtailed. In representative democracies, the chief

[59] D'Holbach, *Politique naturelle*, 275–6; Condorcet, *Bibliothèque* vi. 89.

[60] D'Holbach, *Politique naturelle*, 275, 430–1.

[61] D'Holbach, *Politique naturelle*, 428.

[62] D'Holbach, *Morale universelle* ii. 50–1 and iii. 82; Romani, "All Montesquieu's Sons," 228–9; Chisick, "Of Radical and Moderate Enlightenment," 62.

[63] D'Holbach, *Essai sur les préjugés*, 33; D'Holbach, *Politique naturelle*, 225, 239–40; Naville, *D'Holbach*, 308; Devellennes, "D'Holbach radical," 338.

[64] D'Holbach, *Politique naturelle*, 65–6; Israel, *Democratic Enlightenment*, 813; here Minchul Kim fell into the same confusion as Chisick: see Kim, "Volney," 236.

danger is that the principle of "equality" is pushed beyond its legitimate limits, the sphere of equal rights, toward equality of influence in administration and decision-making, thereby rendering ordinary opinion and prejudices dominant, in d'Holbach's eyes an inevitable recipe for disaster.[65]

7.2. REJECTING ROUSSEAU'S "EQUALITY"

D'Holbach, note several scholars, "was very concerned with the conditions that kept the poor in subservient conditions in society, fiercely criticizing the great inequalities of wealth in *ancien régime* France."[66] But correcting such imbalances, he also recognized, requires a particular type of state based on principles that existed nowhere in his time. Like Spinoza, d'Holbach believed Nature endows people with very different strengths and weaknesses both mental and physical so that nothing is more illogical than averring, as Rousseau does, that people are equal by nature. The "rights of mankind" which d'Holbach deploys so effectively for the first time in the history of modern political thought, and on which Brissot, Condorcet, Volney, Destutt, and the rest built during the Revolution, are essential to empowering the law to offset the natural inequalities of wealth, strength, and intellect. Common rights, the common good, and the "general will" become the collective force that corrects the imbalances natural inequality would otherwise accentuate.

Individually, men are "always unequal," as Condorcet expounded d'Holbach's view.[67] It is because people are fundamentally unequal by nature that laws designed to equalize by formalizing equal rights are needed to enable the democratic republic based on popular sovereignty and the common good, or what Condorcet called the "bien général de tous," to properly function, doing so by evening things up. People being always and inevitably naturally unequal, the principle of citizen equality becomes essential to any state genuinely seeking the common welfare in Spinoza's, d'Holbach's, and Condorcet's sense. One contributor to the "negative critique" managed to confuse the issue three times in one short paragraph by insisting that d'Holbach does not belong in the "Spinoza-based Radical Enlightenment" category because he "does not endorse the transfer [of natural rights]" whereas, he mistakenly suggests, Spinoza does; he then doubled the confusion by assuming d'Holbach's "defense of natural rights" was not inspired by any "radical" thinker at all.[68]

The category "Radical Enlightenment is not "Spinoza-based" but defined by combining rejection of religious authority with a democratizing tendency (defined as representative democracy based on the "general will"); but, relevantly here, Spinoza

[65] D'Holbach, *Politique naturelle*, 70–2.

[66] Naville, *D'Holbach*, 376; Devellennes, "Utility contra Utilitarianism," 200.

[67] Condorcet, *Bibliothèque* vi. 69–70; Spitz, "From Civism to Civility," 115–16; Thomson, *Bodies of Thought*, 237.

[68] Edelstein, *On the Spirit of Rights*, 88.

emphatically distanced himself from Hobbes's comprehensive transfer of "natural right" when men move from the state of nature to civil society: "I always preserve the natural right in its entirety," as he himself put it," and I hold that the sovereign power in a state has right over a subject only in proportion to the excess of its power over that subject," as is "always the case in the state of nature."[69] The formalized "rights" and freedoms that men enjoy in society, where equal, are always the artificial, political creation of the (democratic) republic itself which is why monarchies and aristocracies are innately inferior to the democratic republic. D'Holbach's doctrine is thus identical to Spinoza's,[70] while Rousseau's innate, natural equality and unmediated "general will", d'Holbach, like Diderot and Condorcet, who both also dismissed Rousseau's natural, inalienable equality as destabilizing and dangerous, scorned utterly.[71] Where Rousseau views men as equal by nature, and Robespierre later expressly rebuked Condorcet for proceeding, when discussing rights of mankind, as if the eternal laws of nature were less inviolable "que les conventions des hommes" [than the conventions of men], d'Holbach "condemns inequality before the law," that is man-made inequality, here once again diverging widely from Voltaire, who simply sanctioned social inequality,[72] as well as from the Abbé Henri Grégoire, the revolutionary Catholic churchman who, on his deathbed, was refused the last rites by the Archbishop of Paris owing to his near radical views, a clergyman strenuously advocating emancipation of blacks and Jews, certainly, but claiming that men's equal rights derive from their Maker and can be justified only within the context of Revelation.[73]

While in its early stages the French Revolution sought to anchor its "universal and equal" rights in nature, declaring "natural rights,, a concept Bentham firmly opposed, during the transition of 1795 in revolutionary debate, the neo-Brissotin leaders, Danou, Sieyès, Louvet, and others shifted equal rights from being anchored in Nature to *l'état social*, the needs of society. With this the Rousseauist view of universal rights gave way to the (Spinozist) Diderotian and d'Holbachian approach.[74] Where man's individual will is passionate, unreasonable, violent, and precipitate, the "general will" or "l'intérêt général de la société," as d'Holbach also dubs it, is calm, dispassionate, and intent on forging a "balance of power" out of the everyday clashes of individual wills. Where each individual "in the savage state," according to d'Holbach's anti-Rousseauist viewpoint, is a "brutal, ignorant animal, a wicked and ferocious beast, like bears and ourang-outangs," society, guided by Enlightenment, social science, and the state, can become a "community of citizens, united by fraternal sentiments, and reciprocal wants, turning their respective strengths into one common force," a

[69] Spinoza, *Letters*, 258; McShea, *Political Philosophy of Spinoza*, 138, 142; Harris, "Spinoza's Treatment of Natural Law," 70–1.

[70] Edelstein, *On the Spirit of Rights*, 47–9, 145 n. 122.

[71] D'Holbach, *Politique naturelle*, 24–5; d'Holbach, *Système social*, 153; Citton, "À quoi servent les Lumières radicales?," 139–40; Lord, "Spinoza on Natural Inequality," 138–9.

[72] Bosc, "Liberté et propriété," 66.

[73] Naigeon, *Adresse à l'Assemblée nationale* (1790), 13; Lehner, *Catholic Enlightenment*, 209–11.

[74] Gauchet, *Revolution des droits*, 279–82, 290; Goggi, "Spinoza contre Rousseau," 182–3.

"bank of interest," where love of one's neighbor infuses the whole.[75] It was on the basis of these characteristically *Idéologue* social and moral principles that Volney and Destutt initiated moves in the National Assembly, in 1789–90, to ban all dynastic, royal, and colonial wars and warfare and later renewed Raynal's war on the great colonial trading companies, including the French Compagnie des Indes (for which Destutt earned a public rebuke from Edmund Burke).[76]

The "inequality that nature interposes between individuals," holds d'Holbach, far from being the source of misfortune, is the "true base of their happiness." Only through "entire dependence" on society, explains Condorcet, does d'Holbach's individual attain the "happiness" that is his main object in life.[77] D'Holbach was actually among the very first to deploy "universal and equal rights" as a political construct designed to correct the state of nature where society functions in pursuit of the common good. Despite men being wholly unequal by nature, society's legislation can correct this: "des loix impartiales et inflexibles commandent également à tous: c'est en cela qu'elles établissent une egalité très-réelle, la seule à laquelle les hommes aient le droit de prétendre" [impartial and inflexible laws command equally to everyone, it is there that they establish a very real equality, the only one men have a right to claim].[78] Condorcet warmly endorsed d'Holbach's analysis, deeming it the sole correct philosophical foundation of the French Revolution's universal and equal rights and the "general will." Natural inequality between individuals, physically and in their talents, being irreducible for d'Holbach and Condorcet (as for Spinoza), only through becoming members of society "are men invited and compelled to join together to lend each other mutual help. Inequality of strength and talents obliges them to rework in common, for the good of all, what nature assigns each individual in particular."[79] No genuine liberty exists where some men enjoy rights or privileges that others lack. D'Holbach's logic was so compelling, suggested Condorcet, during the Revolution, that he and his fellow architects of public policy should now altogether abandon the "fictive equality believed [by Rousseau] to have originally existed among men." Government by representatives of the people, whether constitutional monarchist or republican, being innately superior in d'Holbach's eyes to all other forms of government, he firmly rejected Rousseau's "illusion" that "a people ceases to be free" from the moment it chooses "representatives" just as he did Rousseau's natural equality.[80]

[75] Condorcet summarizing d'Holbach, Condorcet, *Bibliothèque* vi. 72; Hammersley, *English Republican Tradition*, 130; Devellennes, "Fourth Musketeer," 474–5.

[76] Volney, *Abridgement*, 3, 6; Renauld, *Antoine Destutt de Tracy*, 84, 88–9; Cook, "Great Society," 309–28.

[77] D'Holbach, *Politique naturelle*, 27, 30, 36, 56–7; Condorcet, *Bibliothèque* vi. 66, 72, 83; Goggi, "Spinoza contre Rousseau," 177.

[78] D'Holbach, *Politique naturelle*, 280; Peña, "Lumières radicales," 317–18.

[79] Condorcet, *Bibliothèque* vi. 69; Devellennes, "Fourth Musketeer," 474–5.

[80] Condorcet, *Bibliothèque* vii. 27 n.; Lord, "Spinoza on Natural Inequality," 130–2; Hulliung, *Autocritique*, 135.

Rousseau was never a "moderate"; but after 1757 he abandoned the radical stance of his early phase and developed an immensely influential but idiosyncratic political thought that in the 1790s has often been considered the most formative intellectual influence on the Revolution—though it caused intractable difficulties for the revolutionary leadership. A key consequence of the clash between the rival human rights and "general will" systems of d'Holbach and Rousseau is that whereas in Rousseau, as in Montesquieu, only small countries, like the Swiss cantons, are fitted for the republican form of government, in d'Holbachian political thought, it is the reverse: small republics do not depend on elected representatives, and large councils, as much as big ones, and hence are more "popular" and populist, nearer to direct democracy, and thus more irrational, anarchic, and vulnerable to faction. Big republics require fixed constitutional rules, elections and representation and hence remain inherently more stable and rational.[81] Diametrically opposed to Rousseauism in key respects, d'Holbach's political thought here again offered valuable resources to the democratic republicans. Whether it is a large republic or a constitutional monarchy being considered, d'Holbach (and Condorcet and the others) countered Rousseau, representation remains the key to good government.

In constitutional monarchies, the "fundamental laws" should establish a fixed assembly of representatives, chosen from amongst the most upright, enlightened, and public-spirited, charged with setting out lines of policy in accord with the common interest, hear the citizens' voice, and guard against courtiers' flattery and lies. But to achieve this the obstacle presented by corruption and cheating that d'Holbach thought (after 1765) disfigured eighteenth-century British parliamentary politics had to be overcome. Simply emulating the English was inadvisable: such a course would merely encourage candidates to bribe voters and buy votes, an outcome worse than useless as venality of office vitiates all administration. Legislators must ensure, through careful supervision, that elections remain free and undisturbed. "To acquire representatives worthy of upholding the interests of the country, venality, corruption, license, cabales and intrigue must be rigorously banished from elections."[82] "Every man found to have obtained his place [in the assembly] via unworthy means should be excluded forever from the right of determining the interests of his country."[83]

In constitutional monarchies, d'Holbach's "représentants" needed "prerogatives" and "droits" [rights] recognized as "inviolables," as a rock, resistant to the monarch whose capacity to goad, influence, and corrupt must be effectively curtailed; but equally, while impervious to royal interference, they must be dependent, lacking all capacity to diverge, when voicing the interests, needs, and will of the people.[84] Who

[81] Condorcet, *Bibliothèque* vii. 27–8.

[82] D'Holbach, *Politique naturelle*, 166–7, 427–9; d'Holbach, *Système social*, 278; d'Holbach, *Éthocratie*, 601; Charbonnel, "Futurologie politique," 459–60.

[83] D'Holbach, *Éthocratie*, 601; Spitz, "From Civism to Civility," 117.

[84] D'Holbach, *Politique naturelle*, 166–7.

then should the nation's representatives be? Those best-placed to know and express the people's complaints, needs, and "rights." Some object that the people are not "competent" to judge the "candidates" who put themselves up for election to the national assembly; but "the people is rarely deceived," answered d'Holbach, here giving way to questionable optimism, in evaluating the degree of enlightenment and integrity of persons known in their localities who present themselves as candidates.[85] His ideal electoral candidate facing the electorate would be "riche et bon" (like himself). But special care was needed to ensure representatives did not become, or come to represent, a particular social group or economic stratum. Along with being self-supporting and having a stake in society, integrity, talent, and enlightenment are the essential qualifications and most likely to converge in persons owning some land. What he proposed was what a Marxist would despise as an elusive bourgeois idyll for prominent urban and rural proprietors.[86]

Different groups within society must not be separately represented as "orders" in the national assembly, as in the existing French Estates General. This was a key objective of d'Holbach's reformism which the Abbé Sieyès noted as far back as 1775.[87] Basic to his anti-aristocratism, opposition to "orders," and his and Sieyès's insistence on the unity of the common interest of society without regard to rank or the hereditary factor, d'Holbach's theory of representation was thus "national" in precisely the manner adopted by the National Assembly of 1789. The constitution must uphold men's equal rights, stipulated as essential objectives of society and the state, guaranteeing personal liberty, defined as the "right to do for one's own happiness or interest everything not contrary to the happiness or interests of others,"[88] including the right to property and personal security.[89]

The most crucial requirement in well-constituted republics and constitutional monarchies, for d'Holbach, was to prevent the emergence of a new "aristocratie," a clique with interests opposed to those of the citizenry. Representatives must not become either a dominant or a distinct "class" with their own agenda for building an ascendancy that crushes the peasant farmer and extorts levies from commerce. D'Holbach's preference for landed property and agriculture over commercial and financial wealth, like his preoccupation with increasing population, clearly reflects, as with many French writers at the time, a physiocratic bias. Agriculture is good, commerce, industry, and finance suspect. Finance, especially, he deemed harmful by damaging agriculture, retailing, and other main preoccupations.[90] Additional absolute priorities were preventing separate representation for ecclesiastics, and removing religious influence from education. A "sane politics" forging good government means ensuring churchmen cannot direct the citizenry's views in any way, that enlightened writers remain free to say whatever

[85] D'Holbach, *Politique naturelle*, 169.
[86] D'Holbach, *Politique naturelle*, 168; Benot, *Diderot*, 284.
[87] D'Holbach, *Politique naturelle*, 169–70; Sieyès, *Des manuscrits*, 221.
[88] D'Holbach, *Éthocratie*, 602.
[89] D'Holbach, *Politique naturelle*, 42–4.
[90] D'Holbach, *Politique naturelle*, 363; Wolloch, *History and Nature*, 118.

they wish including against churches, clergy, and religion.[91] Separation of churches from, and subordination to, the state is hence crucial.

In limited monarchies it is vital too that the king should *not* possess the sole right to summon, or not summon, the representative assembly. Rather, the people's representatives must retain the power to convene whenever they see fit, irrespective of the monarch's wishes and those of his courtiers. Yet even these restraints hardly suffice to correct the mass of defects "fatal experience" continually manifests—arising from the ruler's interest being "often" so remote from that of his people that conflict becomes unavoidable. To sufficiently emasculate royal power, ensure monarchical interests do not gain primacy over the people's, and render kings truly subordinate to the general interest, more stringent curtailment is required. Above all, royal power should be bound by the representative assembly's possessing the right to meet at frequent fixed intervals, and ensure government is transparent, that honest laws are made, discussed, corrected, and rescinded exclusively in the "councils of representatives of the nation."[92]

The convergence between d'Holbach's doctrine of representation and that of Sieyès was reflected in the work of the revolutionary National Assembly's *Comité de Constitution*, in 1789, when the committee's leading figures, Sieyès and Thouret, drew heavily on earlier French Enlightenment thought expressly endorsing d'Holbach's doctrine as expounded in the article on "Representatives," in the *Encyclopédie* (and later work), that "it is possession of property which makes a man a citizen."[93] For d'Holbach, elected representatives gathered in a national assembly constitute the supreme safeguard against ordinary people's irrationality, ignorance, and "superstition," and are the means to organize government for the people without the people being able to "command."[94] This was all the more essential where men had previously lived under monarchy, aristocracy, and theocracy, for then, as in any tyranny, men are wholly "blinded by ignorance and superstition." D'Holbach excludes the propertyless from participating as candidates, his English observations having taught him that the impoverished and moneyless are all too readily corruptible. "Remove corruption and the choices of the people will be mostly very sensible."[95]

Pursuit of "happiness" being natural to men individually and collectively, finding the means to further man's happiness, and carry over and institutionalize the freedoms of the "state of nature" to the maximum under the state, as far as possible removing obstacles, is, for d'Holbach as for Spinoza, what ensures everyone possesses a vested interest in politics, debate, and discovering truth and exposing error.[96] A vital function of free debate and publication in a well-governed society is to stimulate

[91] D'Holbach, *Politique naturelle*, 375–6.

[92] D'Holbach, *Politique naturelle*, 129; d'Holbach, *Système social*, 280; d'Holbach, *Éthocratie*, 601.

[93] Forsyth, *Reason and Revolution*, 64; Devellennes, "D'Holbach radical," 327; Crook, *Elections*, 31.

[94] D'Holbach, *Politique naturelle*, 171–2.

[95] D'Holbach, *Politique naturelle*, 169; Hope Mason, *Irresistible Diderot*, 339 n.

[96] D'Holbach, *Essai sur les préjugés*, 5; d'Holbach, *Morale universelle* i. 44–5; Lord, "Spinoza on Natural Inequality," 134–5.

awareness and active involvement by all the citizens. Apathy and indifference to the quest for "le bien public" are virtues only among slaves.[97] "It is I repeat, to the nation, the unique and veritable source of all legitimate authority, that it belongs to judge whether it is well or badly governed, well or badly represented, whether its laws are useful or harmful."[98] The laws should always strive to subordinate society's elected representatives "à leurs constituants" [to their constituents]. In a well-ordered government no one, whatever rank he possesses (including the king), should be exempt from fear of punishment by the people for their misdeeds. Where abuse prevails, electors must retain the right to revoke the election of any representative and dismiss him with ignominy.

The path to human happiness requires that the state be adequately organized, which, in turn, requires departing from the "state of nature" in the right way. "Government" d'Holbach defines as the combined force society as a whole employs to oblige its members to adhere to the terms of the "pacte social" that rescues men from the "state of nature."[99] His "state of nature" was a halfway-house between the "monstruous constraint" of Hobbes's *Leviathan*, on one side, and Rousseau's "imaginary" natural equality on the other.[100] This principle, so proximate to Spinoza's, tied d'Holbach's utilitarian ethics to his political theory. For d'Holbach morality underpins, or should underpin, politics and government, and "true morality is universal: it is the "same for all the inhabitants of our globe."[101] It grounded his revolutionary concept of the "rights of men," he averred, in 1776,[102] rights being the free usage of men's wills and faculties to pursue their own happiness in their own way, subject only to reason as enforced by society through its laws, much as Jefferson asserted likewise in America's *Declaration of Independence*, earlier that year.[103] Every citizen has an equal right to be protected in his rights by society.

7.3. CONTESTING VOLTAIRE'S COURT "ARISTOCRATISM"

To speak of the "shared assumptions" of d'Holbach and Voltaire, and even their "broad similarities in outlook," to claim the "differences between d'Holbach's materialism and Voltaire's deism do not seem that great,"[104] conflates and confuses two fundamentally divergent political and moral theories. In his inmost thoughts, Voltaire's views on religion may not have differed much from d'Holbach's; but his public

[97] D'Holbach, *Système social*, 281–2; d'Holbach, *Éthocratie*, 604.
[98] D'Holbach, *Système social*, 284. [99] D'Holbach, *Morale universelle* ii. 22.
[100] Naville, *D'Holbach*, 372–3; Devellennes, "D'Holbach radical," 337.
[101] D'Holbach, *Système social*, 71; Devellennes, "D'Holbach radical," 321.
[102] The *Mémoires secrets* announced the appearance of *La Morale universelle* on 4 October 1776, see Vercruysse, *Bibliographie descriptive*, p. 1776, A4, A5, A6.
[103] D'Holbach, *Morale universelle* i. 81, 87 and ii. 21; Charbonnel, "Futurologie politique," 453–7.
[104] Chisick, "Of Radical and Moderate Enlightenment," 68.

stance, the political implications he attached to it, differed profoundly. Where d'Holbach, like Condorcet, Volney, Naigeon, and Destutt, held the science of nature, meaning basic physics, conceived as a comprehensive philosophy of materialism, affords the necessary tools for explaining society's principles and the workings of politics to all,[105] Voltaire flatly disagreed. He did not believe most of society could be enlightened. In his estimation, the idea of God remains absolutely necessary for both princes and peoples making it necessary for most to remain under the churches' moral guidance, a view d'Holbach totally rejected.[106] Hence Voltaire's remark that if God does not exist we shall "have to invent Him." In this way, the efficacy of untruth, of political lies and pious frauds, became a further point of dispute between Voltaire and d'Holbach, as afterwards between Voltaire and Condorcet.[107]

Where Voltaire defended the principle that it is necessary to employ lies in politics to stabilize society, d'Holbach countered that, far from promoting the happiness of the people, religion promotes only discord, tyranny, and slavishness; "ignorance and lies" are the "true sources of the ills," as Condorcet reports his position, "with which we see human societies afflicted."[108] It was assuredly this contrast between Voltaire's and d'Holbach's opposed positions that was at stake in the debate, promoted during the 1780s by the Berlin Royal Academy, over whether untruth was, as Voltaire professed, indeed indispensable to society.[109] Where governments deceive or block access to the truth, argued d'Holbach, "forbidding [their subjects] to cultivate reason, by substituting phantoms, fables, reveries and mysteries," they prevent men understanding what is most vital to them, blocking their knowledge of how to secure their own happiness; perverse social institutions were the inevitable result.[110] "Happiness" in d'Holbach's political thought loomed to the point that it wholly usurped divine providence's role in more conventional systems.[111]

Although meritocracy is "opposed to aristocracy and old-regime monarchy," in d'Holbach's system, "it is not, and is not intended to be," contend Chisick and Peña, "democratic." But what d'Holbach proposed *was* meant to be "democratic" in the specific, novel, and compelling sense that government must be based on the common interest and society's welfare, which, in d'Holbach's eyes, was precisely what *ancien régime* governance failed to be. Herewith, d'Holbach expressed the quintessence of the Radical Enlightenment stance: "to convince *concitoyens* they were obeying [the monarch] too blindly, to help them perceive the full extent of their rights, help them reject a force that burdened, deprived, and insulted them all at the same time," d'Holbach reverted to the very origin of society and its essential purpose.[112] Birth,

[105] Boulad-Ayoub, "Voltaire et Frédéric II," 59–60.
[106] Gay, *Voltaire's Politics*, 264–5; Di Domenico, *Natura, Uomo, Dio*, 190–2.
[107] Condorcet, *Bibliothèque* vi (1790), 4–5; Sandrier, *Style philosophique*, 256–61.
[108] Condorcet, *Bibliothèque* vi (1790), 69; Sandrier, *Style philosophique*, 261–2; Mori, *L'Ateismo*, 239.
[109] Condorcet, *Bibliothèque* vi (1790), 5; Boulad-Ayoub, "Voltaire et Frédéric II," 60.
[110] Condorcet, *Bibliothèque* vi (1790), 10, 26–7, 69.
[111] Wolloch, *History and Nature*, 46; Spitz, "From Civism to Civility," 115–19.
[112] Condorcet, *Bibliothèque* vi (1790), 62–3.

wealth, or favoritism should never determine the selection of those placed in charge of the enlightened state based on popular sovereignty; the true principle was to choose those for whom "utility to society" in the sense of advancing the "general will" is the guiding principle.

D'Holbach covertly and not so covertly espoused a democratic republicanism tied to rejection of religious authority. After 1770, Voltaire grew increasingly alarmed by the encroachment of Diderot's and d'Holbach's radical views among the *philosophique* elite, indeed during his last years worried more about this than any other issue. Far from their not differing much, something like a mini civil war erupted among the *philosophes* over Voltaire's and d'Holbach's opposed positions, with Diderot and d'Holbach considering "Voltaire's compromises with existing political institutions intolerable." While d'Alembert stayed loyal to Voltaire, even he expressed distaste for Voltaire's "pandering to *les grands*."[113] During the autumn of 1770, the young Condorcet gained first-hand insight into the rift between Voltaire's moderation and the *philosophique* faction of Diderot and d'Holbach whilst lodging for a fortnight, with d'Alembert, at Voltaire's residence at Ferney. The conversation turned on what Voltaire considered the threat posed by d'Holbach's system. Thus Condorcet witnessed, from the front row, at 27, the start of what "marked the definitive break," as it has been put, "between the two wings of the philosophic movement."[114]

Certainly, Voltaire, like d'Holbach, scorned "priestcraft", superstition, and intolerance; but given that he wanted the church to retain guardianship over what he saw as the irredeemably ill-informed majority, by which he meant nine-tenths of the population, his stance only marginally connected with the deeper issues of religion's political role, the nature of monarchy, and legitimacy of the existing social order. Spreading atheistic doctrines among princes, Voltaire objected, would also be harmful by rendering royals less subject to moral restraint than they were already.[115] Where d'Holbach wanted religious authority curtailed in every respect, believing priestly guidance always damages both the majority and the enlightened minority, Voltaire, as Condorcet summarized his stance, felt "obliged to accommodate one of mankind's enemies [monarchical tyranny], in order to possess the right to attack the other [religion] with impunity." Thus, he fought "superstition but does not oppose despotism," ignoring its crimes and leaving "peacefully reposing in royal hands the power to commit them."[116] A much better and wittier stylist than d'Holbach, Voltaire was far less ambitious, innovative, and radical as a political thinker and considerably less of an adversary, averred Condorcet, of the *ancien régime* social and political order.

"D'Holbach was pragmatic enough," it has been claimed, to encourage monarchs he considered enlightened and "whom he believed would work for the well-being of

[113] Loft, *Passion, Politics and Philosophie*, 30–1, 101; Zaretsky, *Catherine and Diderot*, 208–11.

[114] Baker, *Condorcet*, 18, 28; Badinter and Badinter, *Condorcet*, 65–6; Trousson and Vercruysse, *Dictionnaire général de Voltaire*, 625; Curran, *Atheism, Religion and Enlightenment*, 93–4.

[115] Trousson and Vercruysse, *Dictionnaire général de Voltaire*, 626.

[116] Condorcet, *Bibliothèque* Year I, ix (1791), 58 and III, no. 4, 3.

society." Yes; but since he considered these so rare as to be practically non-existent that is not saying much. Unlike Voltaire, Diderot and d'Holbach excluded Frederick from among monarchs sufficiently "enlightened" to serve the Enlightenment cause; rather, the "opposition between d'Holbach and Frederick was total."[117] "Despotism," states d'Holbach's *Essai sur les préjugés*, is a dreadful, destructive factor in human life; Frederick quickly grasped that d'Holbach was alluding to him. Not only did royal government impede "l'esprit humain" by permitting churchmen to control education, it hinders too by failing to advance the sciences, merit, useful knowledge, and basic morality. Frederick patronized La Mettrie the atheist; Lucretius' *De rerum natura* counted among his favorite books; but d'Holbach's strictures in the *Essai sur le préjugés* and *Système de la nature* were another matter; his "overt challenge to political and religious authority" incurred the king's intense wrath.[118]

Among the worst factors causing humanity's universally wretched predicament, held d'Holbach, was the "indifference sovereigns show for the education of their subjects"—and to their talents and virtues.[119] "Government everywhere," reprehensibly "allied to superstition, supports [religion's] sinister projects with all its power." Of all categories of men, everything shows priests are the "least fitted to educate fathers of families, statesmen, magistrates, citizens, and enlightened, reasonable beings," a d'Holbachian doctrine afterwards fully imbibed by Brissot, Condorcet, Destutt, and Volney.[120] Monarchs entrusted education to the "ministers of superstition;" hence royal supervision of education infected the human spirit with "unreasonable opinions, shocking absurdities, and oppressive terrors."[121] Despite periodic rows with Frederick, Voltaire broadly endorsed his enlightened despotism. No believer in Christianity, Frederick nevertheless agreed with Voltaire that the masses need religion and in his realms scrupulously maintained the church's grip, whether Catholic hegemony in Silesia (conquered in 1740), Calvinism in Cleves-Mark and at court, or Lutheranism in the rest. Frederick was indeed widely criticized by Mirabeau and other radicals for his education policy. If churchmen are pernicious teachers, in d'Holbach's eyes, it was due to the "negligence of sovereigns" (including Frederick) that there was "no country where the education system was appropriate for producing statesmen, magistrates and *citoyens utiles*."[122] Such views infuriated Frederick; d'Holbach's implying his education policy rendered things worse than "superstition" already made them especially angered him.

Maintaining that "on important social and political questions d'Holbach and Voltaire did not differ much" is thus to hopelessly confuse d'Holbach's views on monarchy and ecclesiastics, and obfuscate his attack on aristocracy and the church. In monarchies and aristocratic republics, wherever government operates chiefly on

[117] Strugnell, *Diderot's Politics*, 131; Niekerk, "Introduction," 16.
[118] Curran, *Atheism, Religion and Enlightenment*, 101.
[119] D'Holbach, *Système social*, 512–13; d'Holbach, *Politique naturelle*, 328–31.
[120] D'Holbach, *Système social*, 507; d'Holbach, *Politique naturelle*, 331–2; Loft, *Passion, Politics*, 90–1.
[121] D'Holbach, *Essai sur les préjugés*, 10.
[122] D'Holbach, *Système social*, 510.

behalf of vested interests and the wealthy, "the poor and weak are perpetually crushed by the injustice of the powerful" whom they see prosper; this harms the whole of society because the poor then become the foes of the rich and, through crime, revenge themselves for the government's "partiality in distributing benefits only on the fortunate of the land while totally forgetting the unfortunate."[123]

For d'Holbach, the correct principle is that citizens should be equal in rights but not equal in influence or status. Those contributing most to the advantages society affords, society's wisest, most useful members, should be the best recompensed and receive the most tokens of distinction; but no meritocratic elite can or should ever be hereditary.[124] It was a political theory that became dear to the heart of Bolívar in Spanish America during the 1820s. Where Marx preached class-warfare, d'Holbach preached class harmony; but deemed his plans for basic political restructuring impossible until the aristocracy changed its ways—or were made to change them. Among the foremost historians of Marxism, George Lichtheim acknowledged that Marx's thought was "profoundly rooted" in the ideas of d'Holbach, Helvétius, and Condillac but claimed Marx understood, where they did not, that "their determinism was at odds with their humanism" by rendering man the "passive object of corrupting influences which could scarcely prepare him for the task of reshaping institutions that had moulded him." But mankind is far from passive in d'Holbach's account; rather he slowly gains capacity to revolutionize social institutions through "reason."[125]

If Voltaire and Frederick abominated d'Holbach's attack on monarchy, they denounced his assault on aristocracy too. Pernicious though kings and churchmen were, nothing is more prejudicial to society, held d'Holbach, than "aristocracy." If aristocratic republics are malign, "aristocracy" flourished most widely and damagingly in his day as monarchy's partner: it was especially in monarchies that noble "vanity" swells into a domineering component of the social system to "infect royal courts with the same vices of which they are the dupes."[126] Aristocracy harms society not least because *la noblesse moderne* adds "ignorance" and "l'oisivité fastidieuse" to its other vicious habits.[127] Among medieval kings' worst features was that often they were just "phantoms" delegating real power to a grasping *noblesse* occupying all important posts and offices. Feudal practices, institutions, and courts were deserving only of abolition.

The "negative critique" invokes d'Holbach's emphatically-expressed reservations about popular insurgency to claim he opposed "revolution," once more thoroughly confusing matters.[128] The baron's antipathy to violence ran deep, as even Frederick acknowledged; he sought to mobilize armed force against neither priests, aristocrats, nor kings. The *Système de la nature* deliberately reworks Locke's theory of resistance,

[123] D'Holbach, *Morale universelle* ii. 54; Schechter, *Genealogy of Terror*, 74–5.

[124] D'Holbach, *Essai sur les préjugés*, 63; d'Holbach, *Système social*, 153, 269, 310, 378; d'Holbach, *Morale universelle* i. 84 and ii. 68–9, 85–6; d'Holbach, *Éthocratie*, 705–6.

[125] Lichtheim, *Marxism*, 252; Sandrier, *Style philosophque*, 90–3.

[126] D'Holbach, *Politique naturelle*, 450.

[127] D'Holbach, *Morale universelle* ii. 94.

[128] Peña, "Lumières radicales," 315.

to minimize justification for armed, violent opposition to unjust monarchs while transferring responsibility to the level of institutionalized resistance, refashioning it into a theory of institutional revolution.[129] D'Holbach disdained what he understood by "revolution," a negative term in his vocabulary, because his powerful revolutionary thrust sought to avoid mobilizing the masses and encouraging violence. Here the distinction between violent revolution via the masses, the Marxist conception, and revolution not initiated by social forces but generated from within society by underground intellectual networks, or what we have termed Spinoza's alternative revolutionary strategy, is what matters. The prospect of mass insurgency filled d'Holbach (like Spinoza, Bayle, and Toland) with revulsion, but this did not preclude far-reaching, sweeping structural change guided by "reason." Since no radical enlightener trusted in the rationality, unschooled good sense, or unguided political propensities of spontaneous masses, radical enlighteners mostly avoided sanctioning revolution of the sudden, violent kind. As a category they remained extremely cautious regarding armed resistance to whatever regime, even the most detested, and especially condemned violent risings simply for vengeance, or to express grievances or resentment. Violent protest, to them, was wasted energy causing unnecessary bloodshed and disruption. Reviling social turmoil, strife, and war, they preferred peace and social harmony. What they conspired to engineer was another kind of revolution altogether—sweeping structural change plotted and instigated by their underground fraternity of reason.

Yet armed resistance to repressive government, however dubious its effects, was sufficiently expressive of the people's misery for d'Holbach carefully to nuance his rejection of popular rebellion as a path to far-reaching change. When complimenting the English, Dutch, and Swiss on escaping part of the misfortune and "superstition" the church had heaped on mankind during the Middle Ages, their escaping some of the obfuscation and "préjugés politiques" underpinning "despotisme" sanctioned by churchmen, he remarked that some would doubtless object to his presenting the Reformation in a positive light and point out that it was achieved partly via popular disturbances and "revolution." "Revolution" in this latter sense is indeed bad; but since it was the persecuting "esprit tyrannique" of princes, priestly fanaticism, and the ambition of the powerful and wealthy that provoked the violence, "which would have been less considerable had the peoples been more educated and their leaders more reasonable," the bloodshed was reprehensible only in part.[130] What was wrong with popular "revolution," held d'Holbach, was not the quest for revolutionary change per se but the undirected, unreasoning, fitful ways the masses seek the profound revolutionary changes society requires. Hence, contrary to the "negative critique," d'Holbach *was* a revolutionary in stark contrast to Voltaire, and of a characteristically Radical Enlightenment type.

[129] Frederick the Great, *Oeuvres philosophiques*, 367; Goggi, *De l'Encyclopédie à l'éloquence républicaine*, 392, 412–13; Devellennes, "Fourth Musketeer," 462.

[130] D'Holbach, *Essai sur les préjugés*, 35.

No form of government is perfect, held d'Holbach, in and of itself.[131] It is a vain and idle pastime to speculate whether monarchy, aristocracy, democracy, or "gouvernement mixte" is theoretically best since the goal, and hence character, of all government (directly contrary to Montesquieu) remains, as with Condorcet and Thorild, always identical—namely, the "conservation and happiness of the society governed."[132] "Despotism" or rule in the interest of vested interests is far more usual and always malign. Christianity, by teaching submission, instead of active resistance to tyrants, reprehensibly makes things worse.[133] If government, be it monarchical or republican, does not follow the essential rules maximizing the well-being of society, ruling instead in the interest of a privileged group, clique, or the king himself, then the people have every justification to intervene and change the government.[134] There is no such thing as legitimate obedience to sovereigns rooted in anything other than securing the advantages everyone has a right to expect from and for society.[135] Every prince ignoring men's yearning for "equitable laws," that is virtually every prince, "invites his subjects to revolt against him."[136] The republican maxim "salus populi suprema lex" [the well-being of the people is the highest law], as Cicero expressed it, d'Holbach embraced wholeheartedly. Every enlightened regime which functions "à l'aide d'une législation éclairée" [that works with the help of enlightened legislation] is good, every unenlightened regime is malign irrespective of how it is structured.[137]

D'Holbach was *not* against but for profound structural "revolution," political, social, secularizing, and educational, to secure the fundamental changes needed, especially revolution securing these goals without excessive violence and disorder. Monarchies generally needed to be fundamentally restructured.[138] "Si tous les peuples veulent être heureux et ont le droit de songer à leur Bonheur, tous les peuples de droit sont libres, quoique souvent esclaves dans le fait" [if all peoples desire to be happy and have the right to think of their happiness, all peoples are free by right although often slaves in fact].[139] Only madness, avers d'Holbach, could lead anyone to renounce "this right;" only ignorance fails to recognize it; only injustice can suppress it.[140] "Revolution" in the sense of long-term, fundamental change, rather than mass action, was not just desirable but essential and urgent. For society requires legislation and laws enabling state and citizenry to secure the "conservation and well-being of all," or what Toland called the "common good of mankind."[141]

[131] D'Holbach, *Politique naturelle*, 75; Hammersley, *English Republican Tradition*, 132.

[132] D'Holbach, *Politique naturelle*, 70; d'Holbach, *Morale universelle* ii. 23–4; d'Holbach, *Éthocratie*, 599; Larrère, "Montesquieu and Liberalism," 290–1.

[133] D'Holbach, *Le Bon-Sens*, 160.

[134] Naville, *D'Holbach*, 385.

[135] D'Holbach, *Système social*, 154.

[136] D'Holbach, *Système de la nature* i. 364; d'Holbach, *Morale universelle* ii. 59, 63.

[137] D'Holbach, *Système social*, 416; d'Holbach, *Politique naturelle*, 84–5.

[138] D'Holbach, *Système de la nature* ii. 240–1; d'Holbach, *Politique naturelle*, 301–2.

[139] D'Holbach, *Politique naturelle*, 294–5, 465–6.

[140] D'Holbach, *Politique naturelle*, 295.

[141] D'Holbach, *Système social*, 235; Toland, *Pantheisticon*, 100.

"Revolution" to emasculate monarchy, aristocracy, and the clergy is everywhere necessary according to d'Holbach's political science. Every monarch's power is illegitimate the moment it departs from promoting the "general will" through legislation and statecraft to serve the particular interest of monarch and court—in other words, nearly always.[142] Legitimate monarchical power, in d'Holbach's sense, was always extremely limited in executive power as "society remains always mistress in fixing the rules for those she charges with exercising her authority." Peoples never lose their right to limit or revoke the powers they delegate to their sovereigns. Rather, "la volonté de la société est toujours la loi pour le souverain comme pour le sujet" [the will of society is always the law for the sovereign as for the subject].[143] Hence, the "sovereign is not the master but minister of society, charged with fulfilling his responsibilities toward the citizens," upholding the true moral order. "Le souverain n'est que le gardien et le dépositaire du Contrat Social; il en est l'exécuteur; il ne peut point acquérir le droit de l'anéantir ou de le violer" [the sovereign is only the guardian and depositary of the Social Contract; he is its executor; he cannot acquire the right to abolish or violate it].[144]

The chief reason d'Holbach opposes popular movements, unrest, and "revolutions," then, is less because they are violent, though that is part of it, than because through ignorance, prejudice, and defective understanding, they usually end up going badly wrong, pursuing incorrect goals, failing to do their job. Given that there are three great social and political sources of oppression that need eradicating, kings, churchmen, and aristocracy, most human error, maintained d'Holbach, stems from trying to counter one pillar of oppression while mistakenly allying with another (the accusation he and Condorcet leveled at Voltaire). Thus, in 1660, the Danes blundered by embracing unlimited monarchical power when trying to escape the clutches of their landowning aristocracy; it was "evidently to get away from the tyranny of their insolent nobles that the Danes conferred on their monarch more extensive power than he had before." The successful coup, in 1772, by which Gustav III smashed the power of the noble-dominated Swedish Riksdag, which had previously curtailed his authority, flowed from the resentment felt toward the pre-1772 oppressive sway of Sweden's magnates and "senate": thus, noble oppression was the cause of the "last revolution" in Sweden that restored royal absolutism there.[145]

Most revolutions d'Holbach appraised as just wasted effort, to be condemned not because they might overthrow the existing order but because whenever revolts occur among the downtrodden, oppressed, and ignorant, the insurgents, being mostly ignorant, follow the lead of all manner of "charlatans politiques et spirituels" promising to end the people's misery while, in reality, exploiting men's naivety and

[142] D'Holbach, *Politique naturelle*, 92–4.
[143] D'Holbach, *Politique naturelle*, 96–7 112–13, 154–5.
[144] D'Holbach, *Système social*, 235; Devellennes, "D'Holbach radical," 321.
[145] D'Holbach, *Système social*, 242; d'Holbach, *Morale universelle* ii. 93; Goggi, *De l'Encyclopédie à l'éloquence républicaine*, 622–3.

"superstition" to forge a fresh tyranny even crueler and more "superstitious" than that they rebelled against. "Voilà pourqui les revolutions, loin de rendre les peuples plus heureux, ne font communément que redoubler leurs misères" [That is why revolutions, far from rendering peoples happier, commonly only redouble their misery].[146] Revolutions normally bring back the same abominable yoke of oppression as before, or usher in a still worse one.[147] Where Diderot's view of the first English Revolution of the 1640s was slightly more positive, d'Holbach's *La Morale universelle* echoes Spinoza's highly unflattering judgment: the English had no idea how to make a revolution and when executing Charles I merely put another despot (Cromwell) in his place. The same judgment recurs in Condorcet: "the death of Charles I was of no benefit to the English people, their king was replaced by Cromwell who was a tyrant."[148] Revolutions regularly fail due to ignorance and religion. Yet revolution is an inevitable response to despotism and despotism reigns almost everywhere. "Les révolutions sont au monde politique ce que les tempêtes et les orages sont au monde physique: ils purifient l'air et rétablissent la sérénité" [revolutions are in the political sphere what tempests and storms are to the physical world: they purify the air and restore serenity].[149]

D'Holbach rejected peoples' "revolutions," then, primarily because they were not revolutionary enough as regards demolishing tyranny, oppression, superstition, and bad laws and replacing the existing moral order with his purely secular "ethocratic" order. What was needed was removal of everything that is wrong. When critics deny d'Holbach developed a positive theory of revolution, or consciously willed a revolution,[150] they are mistaken, forgetting that what Spinoza, Toland, and d'Holbach, here again in parallel, aimed at was not a violent rising without a prior thought-out program, which they thought worse than useless, but a non-violent transformation through infiltrating the institutions of government by mobilizing opinion, criticism, intellectual pressure, representation, elections, and the press. Enlightenment (and hence justified revolution) for d'Holbach meant simultaneously combating "the interests of the great and the stupidity of the people;"[151] this was the essence of his radicality and revolutionary intent.

Every government failing to procure the advantages of nature, the happiness and freedoms society should give its members, breaks the social pact whether possessing a charter or constitution or not.[152] No king, parliament, aristocracy, or theocracy, or combination of these, should be permitted to rule society in its own interest rather than that of the whole. The right to elect representatives belongs to all "vrais citoyens"

[146] D'Holbach, *Essai sur les préjugés*, 40; d'Holbach, *Système social*, 258; Kors, *D'Holbach's Coterie*, 310.

[147] D'Holbach, *Système social*, 260–1.

[148] Spinoza, *Tractatus Theologico-Politicus* xxvi. 236; d'Holbach, *Système social*, 260 n.; Condorcet, *Bibliothèque* vii, "Pièces extraites," 8; Goggi, *De l'Encyclopédie à l'éloquence républicaine*, 397–8, 525–7.

[149] D'Holbach, *Politique naturelle*, 297.

[150] Chisick, "Of Radical and Moderate Enlightenment," 73.

[151] D'Holbach, *Essai sur les préjugés*, 30.

[152] D'Holbach, *Politique naturelle*, 461; Condorcet, *Bibliothèque* vi. 67.

[true citizens], as d'Holbach and Diderot first affirmed in their article "Représentants" for the *Encyclopédie*, written between 1762 and 1764; by "true citizens" d'Holbach meant settled inhabitants with a stake in society: the right to vote should be withheld from vagabonds, mercenaries, and criminals.[153] He who owns nothing, or is a vagabond, held d'Holbach, lacks ties to his country. In a well-governed state, tying the sovereign to the "general will" includes responsibility for aiding the poor economically.

Divergence between the political views of Voltaire and d'Holbach, then, was as fundamental as between d'Holbach and Rousseau. These core differences, not least the issues of representation and "general will," and d'Holbach's insistence on the need to enlighten the common people versus Voltaire's and Frederick's view that the majority cannot be enlightened, as well as Rousseau's rejection of representation and his divergent "general will," matter greatly, and mattered not least during the Revolution. Where Voltaire, concurring with none of d'Holbach's goals, opposed neither kings, courts, nor aristocrats, nor promoted the "general will," nor aspired to enlighten or represent the masses, nor aimed to remove ecclesiastical tutelage of the majority, d'Holbach's 1770s publication contradicted Voltaire along all these lines, "shocked the public and," notes one scholar, "exposed the [moderate] *philosophes*' inability to deal with radicalism within their own ranks."[154]

"By a vice common to all government," contended d'Holbach, very differently from Voltaire, "the most numerous part of nations is usually the most ignored; it would seem that it is only for princes, the rich, for *les grands*, that societies are formed;" one might say the people only come into the social arrangement to spare those who are already the happiest the trouble of working for themselves. A truly enlightened government would do the reverse to all existing governments and rule in the interest of the whole, especially the most numerous part, instead of for small elites. It was a question of promoting and spreading economic well-being, certainly, but, still more important, of extending education and enlightenment to raise the level of society's moral awareness and enable men to understand the reality of things.[155] It is often hard to judge whether "superstition," incompetence of kings, adulation of courts, noble arrogance, or ignorance looms largest in buttressing a particular oppressive regime. But with respect to the universal hegemony of despotism, d'Holbach tended to opt for ignorance and "superstition" as more damaging and anti-social than anything else—albeit all of these malignant factors share responsibility, operating together to produce the general drudgery compounding human misery.[156]

Hence, an essential restraint on all government is freedom of thought and freedom to criticize, since "free communication of ideas" is the only means to combat popular

[153] D'Holbach, *Système social*, 279; Tortarolo, *L'Illuminismo*, 137; Israel, *Democratic Enlightenment*, 813–14.

[154] Curran, *Atheism, Religion and Enlightenment*, 144.

[155] D'Holbach, *Politique naturelle*, 174–6.

[156] D'Holbach, *Système social*, 417; d'Holbach, *Politique naturelle*, 336.

ignorance. No regime can be allowed to obstruct freedom of the press: "liberty of the press is worrying only to tyranny which is always suspicious and nervous."[157] Since every good citizen owes his enlightened ideas to his co-citizens, in a well-governed state "man has the right to think, speak and write" as he sees fit and this must always prevail as an indispensable barrier against tyranny and intrigue. By this criterion, the outcome of the British "Glorious Revolution" of 1688–9 was insufficient to satisfy d'Holbach's revolutionary zeal. The British model so admired by Hume, Montesquieu, and Voltaire struck d'Holbach, like his assistant, Naigeon, in his revolutionary pamphlet addressed to the French National Assembly in 1790, as far from deserving the exorbitant praise Montesquieu and other political writers famously heaped on it, the famed post-1688 British constitution being in reality "très vicieuse à un infinité d'égards" [very vicious in an infinity of respects].[158] Until royal prerogative and aristocratic hegemony were further drastically curtailed, there was scant prospect the British constitution could be satisfactory. In fiercely criticizing the "British model," d'Holbach was to be followed by Paine, Condorcet, Brissot, Volney, and Destutt, as well as Barlow and Jefferson.[159]

A well-governed state suffers no disturbance from political debate or publications. It was d'Holbach's argument, still more strongly affirmed, that his former collaborator Naigeon asserted, in 1790, declaring that "in a free and enlightened government, one where the sacred rights of man and the citizen are known, declared, established and respected, everyone should possess the right to say everything and print everything, even personal satire."[160] Calling for "la liberté absolue de la presse," Naigeon was perfectly conscious that he and other pamphleteers demanding this were simply reiterating what his former mentor and employer had demanded in the early 1770s.[161] What Naigeon could affirm openly, in 1790, that only by reducing the monarch's power to zero can it be made compatible "with just government," d'Holbach himself had more cautiously and discreetly insinuated in print a decade and a half earlier.[162]

7.4. IMPROVING SOCIETY INCLUDES ECONOMIC REDISTRIBUTION

Not remotely a complacent "monarchist" d'Holbach wanted royal ministers chosen by society's representatives, not the king. To minimize royal power (and popular passions), the constitution should include a law "permanent" and "irrevocable to that effect." Another vital bar, to help curb wars of aggression, was forbidding seizure of

[157] D'Holbach, *Politique naturelle*, 288–94; d'Holbach, *Éthocratie*, 604.
[158] Naigeon, *Adresse à l'Assemblée Nationale* (1790), 65–6.
[159] D'Holbach, *Système social*, 301–2; Renauld, *Antoine Destutt de Tracy*, 155–7.
[160] Naigeon, *Adresse à l'Assemblée Nationale* (1790), 86.
[161] Naigeon, *Adresse à l'Assemblée Nationale* (1790), 71, 81.
[162] Naigeon, *Adresse à l'Assemblée Nationale* (1790), 122.

lands and assets belonging to other peoples. Kings liked to embark on conflict abroad. Though often admired by "le vulgaire stupide," nothing more damages society's true interests than royal wars for extending power and wealth, conquest, ambition, colonization, and glory. As the "esprit militaire" causing so much harm in the world is fomented chiefly by monarchs seconded by aristocrats, here was yet another way in which d'Holbach considered republics preferable to monarchies.[163] Wars desolating our world would be less frequent if princes took up arms only when obliged to by necessity or safeguarding their subjects. Unlike Voltaire, but like Spinoza and Meslier, d'Holbach viewed royal ambition in international politics and war as the supreme threat to the common good.[164] A striking feature of his crypto-republican cosmopolitanism is his claim that the world's wars and militarism should be viewed as just an integral part of the wider defectiveness of governments and political systems, the inherent viciousness of monarchy, aristocracy, and religion, and proof that no divine providence guides human affairs: "is not the unjust and cruel way that so many nations are governed here on earth manifestly among the strongest proofs, not just of the little effect produced by fear of another life, but of the non-existence of a providence concerning itself in the fate of the human race?"[165]

D'Holbach's political ethocracy was a "universal morality founded on the universal needs of the human race."[166] International relations and supervising those relations, for him, focused chiefly on conserving peace but included other aspects. For peaceful relations and trade "may enshrine and foster inequalities," as one scholar put it, and sustain slavery and oppressive colonial rule of a kind d'Holbach, like Raynal and Diderot, condemned, while "a fairer distribution of wealth would bring about additional safety" internationally especially for individuals within countries.[167] "A virtuous sovereign should renounce forever any personal claims on distant states," knowing that pressing such claims must mean strife detrimental to his subjects' interests. "Distant possessions diminish the forces of a nation and serve merely to distract the monarch's attention," not least from better distributing property and wealth within his own kingdom.[168] D'Holbach frequently reiterates his militant anti-militarism and anti-colonialism, views characteristic of the Radical Enlightenment, but untypical of Voltaire. Like individuals in society, each state must yield some of its sovereignty "for the good of the society of states as a whole."

If governments, monarchical and republican, were generally abysmal, among monarchy's most reprehensible features was its tendency to ignore the responsibility

[163] D'Holbach, *Politique naturelle*, 397; Frederick the Great, *Oeuvres philosophiques*, 370, 373–4.

[164] Devellennes, "Utility contra Utilitarianism,"192; Devellennes, "Radical Atheism," 167.

[165] D'Holbach, *Le Bon-Sens*, 159; Goggi, *De l'Encyclopédie à l'éloquence républicaine*, 218.

[166] D'Holbach, *Système social*, 137; Israel, "Rousseau and d'Holbach," 158–9; Quintili, "Diderot," 274–5.

[167] Condorcet, *Bibliothèque* vi. 76; Devellennes, "Utility contra Utilitarianism," 195; Espinosa Antón, "Proyectos," 9.

[168] D'Holbach, *Système social*, 346–8; d'Holbach, *Politique naturelle*, 122–3, 347, 391–8; d'Holbach, *Éthocratie*, 605; Blank, "D'Holbach on Self-Esteem," 449–50, 452.

of "a wise government" to ensure "wealth does not become concentrated in the hands of a small number of citizens." Monarchy and aristocratic republics had created a context "in almost all countries, where more than three-quarters of the subjects have nothing while all the riches and property are concentrated in the hands of a small number of men who seem to attract all the care of the government."[169] Preventing polarization by asserting the unity of the "general will," of society's common interest, and the "national" common good as the ground on which the democratic republic functions, became the greatest divergence between the mature Radical Enlightenment of d'Holbach, Condorcet, Volney, and Destutt and those early nineteenth-century strands of socialism preaching class-warfare. Diderot and d'Holbach's doctrine that legitimate government pursues the good of the people, the *volonté générale*, in everything, including the state's economic policy, later endorsed by Condorcet, meant pulling all sections of society into a common "good" that introduced its leveling effect also into the economic sphere. Inequality of wealth, education, and status represents the greatest blight on human societies, held Destutt; the democratic republic's task is to minimize the subservience, servility, and impoverishment that inequality creates by every just and equalizing fiscal and legal means available.[170]

Equally, d'Holbach's aim was to spread wealth more evenly and harmonize: there was no sense of the different social classes being in some fundamental fashion structurally separate and in conflict. Basic to d'Holbach's "bonheur national," which violent revolutionary upsurges rarely secure, is combining political freedom with economic well-being.[171] Here lies a great part of d'Holbach's revolutionary radicalism and originality. "A better distribution of property," remarks one scholar, "seemed to [d'Holbach] worth aiming at."[172] But it was more than worth aiming at. Excessive economic inequality in his system results from a malign politics and inevitably means a bad social and moral order. To d'Holbach it was a characteristic problem of the English constitution and social system that crime remained so prevalent and, due to highwaymen, England's roads so insecure. Since three-quarters of society, in existing monarchies, possessed nothing, and an electorate comprising only property-holders would be too small, d'Holbach's "revolution" required society to be fundamentally reshaped by government: the "interest of society demands that the greatest number of its members possess something."[173] Most should own enough to subsist on, giving sufficient security to enable them to vote, and be included in the political process.

D'Holbach and Condorcet rejected "community of goods," or communism, as "imagined" by Morelly and one or two other eighteenth-century utopians. Such a concept was "impracticable among unequal beings" as men irreversibly are,

[169] D'Holbach, *Politique naturelle*, 352–3; Wickwar, *Baron d'Holbach*, 180.

[170] Imbert, *Destutt de Tracy critique*, 149–57.

[171] D'Holbach, *Politique naturelle*, 299–300.

[172] D'Holbach, *Morale universelle* ii. 183; Wickwar, *Baron d'Holbach*, 178, 196–203; Devellennes, "D'Holbach radical," 325–6.

[173] D'Holbach, *Politique naturelle*, 352–3.

individually and by nature. What society needs to become wisely and properly ordered, avoiding undesirable economic inequality, held d'Holbach, was to prevent citizens making any "dangerous usage of the inequality of their power and resources against one another," or dominating one another through the "general will."[174] Those paid salaries by the monarch should all be deemed "suspect" and "by law excluded" from speaking for the people. Properly curbing court power also forbade exemptions, immunities, and privileges for favorites, especially anything exempting them from obligations applying to other citizens.[175] Since taxes were among the usual causes of friction between kings and their subjects, removing such tension is essential for a happier, better society. Though hard to achieve, on a theoretical level the answer is simple: no king should be permitted to decide the taxes imposed on society; these must be determined by councils of representatives and always be "progressive" according to a *cadaster*, or general property register, setting down each citizen's possessions "with exactitude" to ensure taxation is rendered fairer by ensuring the rich pay more and the poor less.[176]

Among the chief responsibilities of the state serving the common good is restraining the influence of the rich and ensuring taxation is genuinely proportionate to means. No royal court, and no favored clique, should have any say in the fiscal system. The best proof of a "free people" living under an enlightened government is possessing the right to decide the tax system itself, and preclude royal exactions, aristocratic levies, church tithes, and "arbitrary taxes," ensuring all taxes are collected impartially and solely for the common good, with all citizens contributing in proportion to means, "suivant des justes proportions."[177] An especially "just" and socially desirable form of taxation, d'Holbach suggested, is the laying of heavy duties on unnecessary luxury (to which he harbored a particular antipathy). Swingeing taxes should be levied especially on "sumptuous palaces, gardens, large parks, and teams of valets intended for show," besides anyone keeping more than a given number of horses.[178] Any enlightened mind appreciates that "la politique est intéressée à enricher ses subjets avec le plus d'égalité qui est possible" [the political system has an interest in enriching its subjects with the greatest degree of equality possible]. Taxes figure among the key tools enlightened government possesses not just to foster social harmony and uphold a fair balance of fiscal pressure but to correct imbalances of wealth, prevent military adventurism, and adjust social inequality.[179]

Ignorance, superstition, and fanaticism, Voltaire could readily concur, generate the prejudices and error vitiating our world. But by no means would he agree with

[174] Condorcet, *Bibliothèque* vi. 79.

[175] D'Holbach, *Politique naturelle*, 353–4; d'Holbach, *Système social*, 386–7; Rosanvallon, *Democracy*, 131.

[176] D'Holbach, *Politique naturelle*, 343; Devellennes, "Fourth Musketeer," 474.

[177] D'Holbach, *Politique naturelle*, 282–3, 344–5.

[178] D'Holbach, *Éthocratie*, 644–5; d'Holbach, *Système social*, 472–4; d'Holbach, *Politique naturelle*, 345, 433–9, 441–3; Wolloch, *History and Nature*, 223.

[179] D'Holbach, *Éthocratie*, 604, 642–3; Wickwar, *Baron d'Holbach*, 185; Onfray, *Ultras des Lumières*, 262–3.

d'Holbach's insistence that ignorance and prejudices are also the main cause of the misery and poverty everywhere afflicting mankind, and that eliminating misery and destitution by tackling ignorance at all levels, especially dismantling church power, and enforcing equal rights, is the first duty of government (and the *philosophes*).[180] The latter is a revolutionary Radical Enlightenment claim, the former a "moderate" stance. Whatever the particular form of government in a society, it "will be good," asserts d'Holbach's *Politique Naturelle* (1773), "when it will bring happiness to the greatest number." Since "virtue" in d'Holbach is not defined as "other-regarding" or "self-less," but evaluating and acting according to a true understanding of things, steering self-esteem in an enlightened direction, as "internalization of common interest as part of self-interest," in Devellennes' apt words, d'Holbach's moral theory is always closely connected to the social and the political sphere, producing a particular view of the political. Opinions and values, he argues in the *Essai sur les préjugés* (1770), should be judged not only under the yardstick of reason and their role in the past, but also by whether they are "really and constantly advantageous for the greatest number."[181] Those running the state, whether monarchical or republican, remain accountable to society, and must follow the basic rules of this social utilitarianism if they are to be said to rule reasonably and be viewed as administrators, not appropriators of public revenues, funds, treasuries, and other resources.[182]

Much as the individual surrenders part of the "freedom of nature" on entering society not just for the sake of safety and stability but also—contrary to Hobbes and Locke[183]—to better conserve those core freedoms (NB: as with Spinoza, *not* contrary to Spinoza as has been claimed) so, in d'Holbach's universalist ethical politics to achieve a better future for humanity, peoples must surrender part of their national sovereignty in favor not only of their own equal rights but of the "right of all other nations taken collectively." Here too, unlike Voltaire, d'Holbach was radical in foreshadowing the spirit of 1789. Among the worst abuses aiding oppression that practically all kings and princes foster is their using precedent, history, the way things have been in the past, their prestige and glory, to justify established ways and practices when, nearly everywhere, these require sweeping away. Conventional accounts of constitutional practice, d'Holbach felt, were often written in a spirit of subservience and flattery toward egocentric sovereigns, or dictated by fear. When judging what is just and unjust in politics, consequently, the enlightened onlooker must ignore constitutions, charters, fundamental laws, and precedents. It is the "rights of nations," reason, and *la justice éternelle*, that constitute the supreme law, not anything from the past. What is true justice? The equal spreading, as far as possible, of the opportunity for "happiness."[184]

[180] D'Holbach, *Essai sur les préjugés*, 13–14.

[181] Devellennes, "D'Holbach radical," 332–5; Blank, "D'Holbach on Self Esteem," 441–2; Thomson, "French Eighteenth-Century Materialists," 252.

[182] D'Holbach, *Système social*, 277; Naville, *D'Holbach*, 381; Onfray, *Ultras des Lumières*, 252.

[183] D'Holbach, *Politique naturelle*, 15.

[184] D'Holbach, *Système social*, 241; Blank, "D'Holbach on Self Esteem," 449–52.

It is characteristic of d'Holbach's political theory that the focus is on the whole but simultaneously on the individual, that individual liberty and the "general will" become tightly interlocked: "le bien de la société totale doit donc être la mésure de la liberté de ses membres" [the good of society overall is then the measure of the liberty of its members].[185] Liberty without reason and enlightenment is mere destructive license.[186] "The true privilege of the free man is to see his rights guaranteed by all his fellow citizens."[187] Hobbesian negative notions of liberty, for d'Holbach, are worthless. It is the combined force of society collectively, when properly governed, that assures the individual his and her freedoms, security, property, and education. This is the essence of d'Holbach's radicalism and what sets his political thought not only directly at odds with Hobbes, Locke, Montesquieu, Rousseau, and Voltaire but also renders it proximate to, an after-echo of, Spinoza. D'Holbach makes only one explicit mention of Spinoza's political thought where he rebukes him for following Hobbes too closely; otherwise, he does not refer to him, so we do not know if the parallels and affinities between the two political theories, striking as they are, were conscious in d'Holbach's mind, though it is hardly unreasonable to presume they were.[188]

7.5. RIGHTLY AND WRONGLY INTERPRETING D'HOLBACH

D'Holbach's maxim, "every legislator is the organ of the *volonté générale*," laws are good and just only when they conform to the interest of society, he applied indiscriminately to monarchies and republics, but its spirit is radical, republican, democratic, and revolutionary. His revolutionary summons was urgent: "que l'on cesse donc de regarder comme un chimère l'amélioration du sort des hommes" [let us cease to regard the amelioration of the human condition as a chimera]. Men can engineer a better society, albeit not by popular action but by application of reason through representation and pressure. The only valid criterion is "conformity with the rights of the human race" [ce qui est conforme aux droits du genre humain].[189] For d'Holbach morality underpins, or should underpin, politics and government, and "true morality is universal: it should be the same for all the inhabitants of our globe."[190]

Hardly surprisingly, many at the time recognized d'Holbach's ideas as a dire menace to the prevailing status quo. When the French Assembly of the Clergy convened in mid-March 1770, at the Grands Augustins in Paris, the Archbishop of Toulouse, Loménie de Brienne, admonished the gathering that the *Système de la nature* disseminated a "pur athéisme" "with an audacity Hobbes, Vanini, and Spinoza

[185] D'Holbach, *Politique naturelle*, 271, 278; Wickwar, *Baron d'Holbach*, 183–4.
[186] D'Holbach, *Politique naturelle*, 275. [187] D'Holbach, *Politique naturelle*, 281.
[188] Goggi, *De l'Encyclopédie à l'éloquence républicaine*, 401–3.
[189] Domenech, *L'Éthique des Lumières*, 118–19.
[190] D'Holbach, *Système social*, 71; Devellennes, "D'Holbach radical," 321.

would never have condoned." But the book also entailed great political danger as the assembly needed to impress on the royal court.[191] Voltaire and Frederick the Great intervened early on in the controversy, denouncing the book less for its religious subversion than because they too considered it politically dangerous: Frederick was indignant, reported Voltaire, that the "philosophes ne soient pas royalistes" [*philosophes* are not royalists].[192] All this vindicates the analysis of 1790s commentators seeking to identify which philosophical stream contributed most to shaping the French Revolution. The sweeping revolutionary crypto-democratic character of d'Holbach's thought, and its hidden role in determining key themes of the Revolution, was recognized among others by the *philosophe* turned *antiphilosophe* Jean-François de La Harpe (1739–1803) and by one of the Revolution's most discerning Voltairian "moderate" royalist opponents, the Swiss publicist Jacques Mallet du Pan (1749–1800).[193] The wide-ranging legal and penal reforms Europe needed, in 1789, could have been accomplished, Mallet believed, by the active reformist tendency operative in the 1770s and 1780s at many princely courts. How and why, then, did the French Revolution occur? For the Revolution to happen, there needed to exist a system of thought overturning all accepted political, social, and moral premises. That key revolutionary impulse Mallet, like La Harpe, located in the tide of publications initiated by the *Système de la nature* and the *Histoire philosophique*, locating the vital root especially in Diderot and d'Holbach.[194]

Condorcet, discussing that "excellent ouvrage," d'Holbach's *La Politique naturelle* (1773), in 1790, in his revolutionary journal *Bibliothèque de l'homme publique*, omitted citing the author's identity, regretting he still "could not make known its author, promote recognition of his merit, or express the admiration he so well deserved." His unprecedented "boldness of his principles at a time when it was a crime to be a *philosophe*, had made him fear the fury of despots who like birds of the night grow irritable when anyone shows them the light."[195] Condorcet pronounced *La Politique naturelle* an excellent work and "one of those we believe did most to prepare minds for the Revolution which has regenerated France."[196] Politics until recently had been an entirely obscure, problematic science, "un chaos impénétrable," dominated by the imaginary interests of princes and "metaphysical ideas of theology." If "ignorance and lies are the true sources of the ills afflicting human societies," *La Politique naturelle*, the "precious work of which we speak here, is one of those that we

[191] Charbonnel, "Réquisitoire de Séguier," 19–20.

[192] Strugnell, *Diderot's Politics*, 131; Boulad-Ayoub, "Voltaire et Frédéric II," 45–6; Borghero, *Interpretazioni, categorie*, 198, 357.

[193] On Mallet du Pan see Israel, *Revolutionary Ideas*, 18, 33, 46, 132, 152, 225, 548, 723.

[194] Borghero, *Interpretazioni, categorie*, 214; Israel, *Revolutionary Ideas*, 18.

[195] Condorcet, *Bibliothèque* vi. 62; Lough, *Essays*, 119–22.

[196] Condorcet's analysis of *La Politique naturelle* in *Bibliothèque de l'Homme public; ou Analyse raisonnée des principaux ouvrages françois et étrangers, Sur la politique en général, la Législation* [. . .] *et sur le Droit naturel et public* vi (Paris, 1790), 62–226, here p. 62.

consider most relevant for preparing minds for the Revolution which is regenerating France."[197]

D'Holbach's recipe for salvaging mankind from what he saw as the universally oppressed state of humanity was crucial in the history of political thought but one hardly ever recognized as such by modern scholars.[198] That d'Holbach's texts proved highly pertinent not just to Condorcet and Naigeon but also other leading revolutionary intellectuals of the 1790s needs to be more widely noted. The case of *manifeste brabançonne*, discussed in Chapter 15, is striking; so is the Italian case. When the young Napoleon, still posing as a republican, defeated the Austrians in northern Italy, in 1796–7, groups of Italian democratic republican revolutionaries seized control of the political press in Milan and neighboring cities, among them political refugees from Naples. These Italian "democratic republicans" of the late 1790s, together with the Dutch and Swiss democratic republicans of the 1790s among the most radical political groups in Europe,[199] conscious of being a small, isolated coterie among a populace lacking all notion of what republicanism and democracy were, aspired to transform the situation by re-educating the public. Among their revolutionary propaganda texts were several invoking d'Holbach's revolutionary republican message, including one addressed to the region's "free workers and artisans," the *Catechismo repubblicano ad uso de' lavoratori ed artigiano liberi d'Italia* (Milan, 1797), by a local professor, Girolamo Rostagni, which turned out to be mainly a summary of d'Holbach's *Politique naturelle*, and another, the *Catechismo repubblicano ai Giovanni della repubblica*, partly inspired by Rousseau but switching to d'Holbach to convey two crucial points where Rousseau hardly served: one was the gulf between representative democracy and pure democracy, the need for the people to guide the state, and exert legislative power, through representatives; second was the need to end overconcentration of wealth in too few hands, to spread wealth more equitably.[200]

Among the foremost radical social and political thinkers of the pre-socialist age, d'Holbach pulled no punches. The first theorist to follow Spinoza and Diderot in proclaiming in direct opposition to Hobbes, Locke, Montesquieu, and, above all, Rousseau that neither security, property, spiritual care, "virtue," nor "freedom," but "le bonheur de la société est la fin de tout gouvernement" [the happiness of society is the goal of all government], he was also the first systematically to proclaim the "droits de l'homme" [the rights of man] to be universal, *éternels*, everywhere always equal and "inaliénables."[201] Universal and equal rights should be recognized and understood as

[197] Condorcet, *Bibliothèque* vi. 62, 69; Israel, "Rousseau and d'Holbach," 157.

[198] Devellennes, "Fourth Musketeer," 459, 476.

[199] Philp and Posada, "Liberalism and Democracy," 183–5; Fruci, "Democracy in Italy," 26, 28–30, 32–4.

[200] Guerci, "Catéchismes républicains en Italie," sections 8, 16–19; Cremona, *Catalogo delle edizioni*, 62–3, 274, 325–6; De Francesco, "How not to Finish a Revolution," 68–9; Devellennes, "Fourth Musketeer," 465; Israel, *Revolutionary Ideas*, 643; Israel, "Rousseau and d'Holbach," 153, 156–61, 174.

[201] D'Holbach, *Système de la nature*, i. 354–5; d'Holbach, *Politique naturelle*, 39–40; Goggi, "Spinoza contre Rousseau," 176–9.

deeply rooted in man's quest for happiness, and needs, and hence his unalterable nature. D'Holbach who, of all the major eighteenth-century thinkers, has been the one most routinely sidelined, ignored, and marginalized by the general historiography, was actually among the most revolutionary of eighteenth-century political thinkers, a thinker intent, Frederick recognized, on overturning the whole established order [*tout l'ordre établi*].[202] Frederick was right.

Behind the scenes, without the public knowing it, d'Holbach's political ideas played a formative role in the French Revolution, much as Condorcet claimed, albeit not directly among the public but rather in a private more subtly subversive fashion, among the top vanguard of the democratic republican intellectual leadership. Especially those gathering in the entourages of Mirabeau and Sieyès, and at Auteuil in the salon of Madame Helvétius, the front line of French democratic republicanism, judged his political ideas a crucial resource. Meanwhile, the dense haze of mystery and concealment d'Holbach deliberately fostered around himself and his activities from the end of the 1760s down to 1789, during which his anonymously-published books were widely propagated in Europe (principally from Holland), only partially lifted during the Revolution. No doubt this was principally owing to his being a wholly unknown quantity among the general public as a result of the longstanding, masked, illicit way his influence had diffused earlier.

Yet modern scholarship has lamentably failed to draw attention, let alone do justice, to his crucial innovations. The lingering anonymity and secrecy shrouding his authorship of key subversive works during the 1770s, and contributions to political articles in the later volumes of the *Encyclopédie*, and continued semi-anonymity still after 1789, no doubt help explain why, despite his extensive revolutionary significance, he has long languished among the most underestimated, marginalized, and ignored of the revolutionary age's major political theorists. Even so, his almost complete subsequent eclipse, in the nineteenth and twentieth centuries, still remains hard to explain. That what was once an official and concerted taboo should linger on down to today as an unquestioning, tacit, general consensus among scholars to preclude d'Holbach from the front rank of political thought is curious and unsatisfactory. Even d'Holbach's most oft repeated political doctrine, derived originally from Boulanger—that organized religion has always allied with monarchy and aristocracy to oppress and pilfer from everyone else is almost universally ignored. In the Oxford *Encyclopaedia of the Enlightenment* (2003), the d'Holbach entry offers just one solitary sentence on his political philosophy, stating, needless to say, that it should be considered an entirely secondary aspect of his thought.[203] The *Historical Dictionary of the Enlightenment* (2005), edited by Chisick, provides no information at all about d'Holbach's social and political ideas.[204] The otherwise generally excellent 900-page survey *The Cambridge History of Eighteenth-Century Political Thought*,

[202] D'Holbach, *Politique naturelle*, 51, 465; d'Holbach, *Système social*, 429; Condorcet, *Bibliothèque* vi. 83; Frederik the Great, *Oeuvres philosophiques*, 368–9; Di Domenico, *Natura, Uomo, Dio*, 186–7.

[203] Kors, *Encyclopaedia* ii. 214.

[204] Chisick, *Historical Dictionary*, 210–11.

published in 2006,[205] yields only passing references, making no attempt to explain d'Holbach's political and social doctrines. Everywhere, he remains a marginal figure assumed to have made no significant contribution to political ideas. Not a single reference to him is to be found in the index of the major volume *The General Will: The Evolution of a Concept* (Cambridge, 2015) when, by any reasonable assessment, d'Holbach figures among the most important "general will" and human rights theorists of the Enlightenment. Yet d'Holbach, the figure the "negative critique" maintains was no radical political thinker, followed up the *Système de la nature* with no less than four full-scale works of political theory.

Admittedly, a few scholars note in passing that d'Holbach's "general will" differs significantly from that of his longstanding rival, Rousseau's, d'Holbach's version being the collective thrust of the laws when these extend the advantages for which society was set up to the greatest number of citizens possible;[206] nevertheless, d'Holbach's "general will," fundamental in the history of Western political thought though it is, attracts hardly any attention. Scholars commenting on the profound differences between the two rival "general will" theories acknowledge d'Holbach's concept is more fixed and universal, more tolerant, cosmopolitan, and firmly tied to promotion of man's happiness and the good of society,[207] but then revert to the old view that, as far as the *Declaration of the Rights of Man and the Citizen* of 1789 is concerned, "Rousseau is the only source that really matters," naturally without giving any reason for a judgment, the erroneousness of which should be obvious to anyone who reflects. For it was not Rousseau, but d'Holbach, who was on the right track, as far as Diderot, Condorcet, Volney, Destutt, Naigeon, and other key democratic republican late Enlightenment "general will" theorists and adversaries of Rousseau's and Robespierre's ideas were concerned.[208]

D'Holbach, affirms the author of the classic account of his life and work in French, Pierre Naville (1903–93), son of a Protestant Swiss banker and friend of André Gide, successively a Stalinist, Trotskyist, and finally a founder of the French New Left, "did not want and did not foresee a revolution." Of course, d'Holbach was not thinking of a socialist revolution brought about by the proletariat; but Naville also claims d'Holbach was not a "republican" or a "democrat."[209] He hugely misled many. Daniel Roche agreed that the Revolution revealed what he too saw as the basic contradiction between d'Holbach's "philosophical radicalism" and his "political moderation," further befogging the issue by insisting d'Holbach was an unremarkable "moderate" and "monarchist" not very different in general outlook from Voltaire (a revived familiar theme nowadays) in no way propagating advanced ideas. For many, Marxists and

[205] A volume otherwise expertly edited by Mark Goldie and Robert Wokler.

[206] Di Domenico, *Natura, Uomo, Dio*, 87–8; Devellennes, "Fourth Musketeer," 474–5.

[207] Swenson, *On Jean-Jacques Rousseau*, 164; Hulliung, *Autocritique*, 135, 170–1; Blank, "D'Holbach on Self-Esteem," 444, 449.

[208] Swenson, *On Jean-Jacques Rousseau*, 164–5; Blank, "D'Holbach on Self-Esteem," 443–4.

[209] Naville, *D'Holbach*, 373.

Postmodernists alike, there cannot be any direct link between "l'athéisme de salon" and the politics of the Revolution.[210] Both are greatly mistaken.

In other words, a wrong-headed historiographical tradition misconstruing d'Holbach's political thought has come to be subsumed into the body of the "negative critique" which at times seems eager to seize on just about any nonsense it thinks helps its criticism of the Radical Enlightenment thesis. Despite its obvious erroneousness, the old originally Marxist error is now hailed by the Postmodernist approach and the "negative critique," and enjoys a notable revival with Lilti, Jacob, Ferrone, and Hunt all endorsing Roche's untenable stance:[211] Roche was on "firm ground," agrees Chisick, in "citing Robespierre's denunciation of the moderation of d'Holbach's circle." (Of course Robespierre's particular notion of "moderation" did encompass Condorcet, Brissot, Desmoulins, and many another committed democratic republican revolutionary.) "The view of d'Holbach and his circle as radical and revolutionary," agrees Margaret Jacob, "is not tenable." [212] The contention that the "differences between d'Holbach's materialism and Voltaire's deism do not seem that great" is so wildly incorrect, though, that there is no chance at all it can be salvaged. Most astonishing of all, this astounding tale of confusion and error is nowadays repeatedly praised in reviews as "incisive" and "convincing," which is the very last thing it is.[213]

"The question is," writes Chisick, "whether metaphysical materialism implies and results in social and political radicalism." Actually, this is not the question, but rather confuses everything further by misreporting the Radical Enlightenment thesis which does not claim metaphysical materialism necessarily results in political radicalism as the cases of La Mettrie and Goethe show. But one perceives what he is trying to say: the Radical Enlightenment thesis claims such a necessary connection exists, "the case of d'Holbach would indicate otherwise."[214] Not the least bizarre feature of the negative critique's morass of confusion regarding d'Holbach is that its adherents do much of the work of demolishing their argument themselves. "D'Holbach's political

[210] Roche, *Républicains des Lettres*, 247–51.

[211] Chisick, "Of Radical and Moderate Enlightenment," 74.

[212] See Chisick, "Of Radical and Moderate Enlightenment," 69; Peña, "Lumières Radicales et démocratie," 304, 312; Jacob, *Radical Enlightenment*, 20, 286; Jacob, "Radical Enlightenment: A Heavenly City," 56.

[213] See Chisick, "Of Radical and Moderate Enlightenment," 61–79; Jacob, "Radical Enlightenment: A Heavenly City," 56; see also Julian Swann's review in *H-France Review* 17 (Dec. 2017), no. 222, p. 2, where he writes: "... Chisick probes the alleged dichotomy between radical and moderate enlightenments, via the emblematic figure of baron d'Holbach, who as a materialist and an atheist, is usually placed firmly in the radical camp. By looking closely at d'Holbach's attitudes towards concepts such as democracy, equality, slavery and revolution, Chisick challenges a simple binary approach towards the Enlightenment. He proposes instead a more fluid, and for this reviewer convincing, model in which d'Holbach, Condorcet, Diderot, Voltaire and others were not wedded to a 'moderate' or a 'radical' stance. Chisick also seems on firm ground when he challenges Israel's argument that those whom he identifies as radical were seeking to overthrow the existing order and were ultimately the principal cause of the French Revolution."

[214] Chisick, "Of Radical and Moderate Enlightenment," 69–70.

writings, although hostile to courts and the abuse of monarchical authority," holds Jacob no less "incisively," "should not be described as republican."[215]

"Harvey Chisick," writes one commentator, with still more exquisite "incisiveness," in *French Studies*, "shows, quietly but devastatingly, that there is really little difference between the 'moderate' Voltaire and the 'radical' d'Holbach, and that, far from advocating popular democracy, Enlighteners, including d'Holbach and Diderot, distrusted the 'people' and denied equality. It is ironic," this critic added, referring to Ducheyne's volume in which Chisick's critique features, "that the first sustained examination of Israel's radical Enlightenment should leave the concept in shreds."[216] Here is irony indeed. With scholarly "incisiveness" at this level who can doubt that Enlightenment studies are on a sound path?

[215] Jacob, *Radical Enlightenment*, 284; Jacob, "Radical Enlightenment: A Heavenly City," 56.
[216] See the review of Ducheyne's volume in *French Studies* 72 (2018), 284–5.

8

Revolution without Violence

The Nordic Model

8.1. ENLIGHTENED REFORM IN SWEDEN–FINLAND

D'Holbach was decidedly unimpressed with the English Revolution of the 1640s and also with the Glorious Revolution. To his mind, the other revolutions in Europe since the Reformation seemed equally dismaying in outcome. Notable among these were what to him, and other radicals, were the failed revolutions of Denmark–Norway and Sweden–Finland. In 1660, trying to escape the "tyranny of their insolent nobles," the deluded Danes had surrendered to unlimited monarchical power, conferring on "their monarch a more extensive power than he had had before." In his own time, the Swedes, resenting the pre-1772 oppressive sway of Sweden's magnates and "senate," blundered no less, backing Gustav III in overpowering the noble-dominated Swedish Riksdag that had previously confined his authority. Noble sway and ambition, he observed, caused the "last revolution" in Sweden no less than the intensification of Danish–Norwegian tyranny, in 1660.[1] The kind of revolution Europe needed, held d'Holbach, was one toppling all three main pillars of tyranny—nobles, kings, and clergy—employing non-violent methods and forging a more equal society organized for the common benefit and employing better social models.

Yet, arguably, as if learning the lesson, it was Scandinavia, from the late eighteenth through the nineteenth century, that came closest to achieving the kind of "revolution of reason" d'Holbach had in mind. By moving gradually toward constitutionalism, toleration, freedom of expression and the press, legal equality, and reduced economic inequality, Scandinavian societies laid the first foundations of what later came to be known as the "Nordic Model." Stemming from the Enlightenment which vastly expanded horizons, this gentle "revolution" created what eventually became a new form of Scandinavianism, a new global format for human society. As European writers began comparing their own societies with others, in other parts of the world, Britain, the Netherlands, China, and North America all emerged as relevant

[1] D'Holbach, *Système sociale*, 242; d'Holbach, *Morale universelle* ii. 93; Goggi, *De l'Encyclopédie à l'éloquence républicaine*, 622–3l; Hallberg, "Translation on Trial," 5–6.

models in selected contexts; but soon there were also others. European observers from elsewhere on the Continent began comparing the striking progress the Enlightenment registered in Scandinavia with what was being achieved elsewhere. Such evaluations are of interest both in themselves and for what they tell about the distinctive characteristics of the Nordic Enlightenment as a sub-category of a whole; eventually the "Nordic model" emerged as one of the most admired plans for humanity of modern times.

During the eighteenth century's middle decades, mainstream Enlightenment achieved impressive advances in Scandinavia and was widely acclaimed at court and among the upper classes, including broad sections of the clergy, throughout the region's two multiple kingdoms. Indeed, by 1750 the Scandinavian elites were sufficiently permeated with the values and attitudes of the moderate, religious, pro-aristocratic Enlightenment to conceive themselves as a quintessentially "upplyst," as already constituting a model "enlightened" society.[2] This emerges nowhere more clearly than from the language of administrative and public rhetoric, science and learning, the newspapers, published periodicals (the Enlightenment's favorite means of expression), and growing appetite for religious, legal, and social reform.

If earlier, until the mid- eighteenth century, Enlightenment in Scandinavia had gone largely unrecognized abroad, during the second half of the century it attracted growing attention. As with any enlightenment process, scholarship, science, and publicly debated schemes for reform led the way. By mid-century, the Royal Swedish Academy of Sciences, founded in 1739, on the initiative of the Hat party in the Riksdag, already ranked among the foremost European academies promoting the sciences.[3] Denmark's "Royal Academy of Sciences and Letters," opened in 1742, added to the momentum, as did the "Royal Society of Science and Letters," prompted by Bishop Johan Ernst Gunnerus, founded at Trondheim in 1760.[4] Enlightened cosmopolitanism nurturing science and technology boosted interest in applying new discoveries to newly conceived commercial and industrial goals. Although Wolffian philosophy continued to hold sway in Scandinavian universities from around 1740 down to the 1780s,[5] and German cultural influence remained strong, interest quickened also in recent developments in French and British thought.

Among eminent foreign visitors, the Veronese diplomat, Michele Enrico Sagramoso (1720–91), a disciple of Scipio Maffei, recorded, while undertaking an exacting six-year (1746–52) tour of northern Europe (having earlier toured southern Europe), considerable ferment in many fields. He conferred with Ludvig Holberg (1684–1754), Denmark–Norway's s leading literary figure, contacted the Danish royal librarian, Hans Gram (1685–1748), and inspected the vast sixty-thousand volume Copenhagen

[2] Skuncke, "Jean-Jacques Rousseau in Swedish Eyes," 103; for Norway, see Naess, "Holberg and the Age of Enlightenment," 54–75.

[3] Bonnet, *Mémoires autobiographiques*, 163.

[4] Sharpe, "Scandinavia," 21.

[5] Tore Frängsmyr, *Wolffianismens genombrott i Uppsala* (Uppsala, 1972); Tore Frängsmyr, *Sökandet efter Upplysningen* (n.p., 2006), 128–41; Israel, *Radical Enlightenment*, 59–61, 556.

library of Otto Thott, the largest private library in Europe. In Sweden, he stayed nine months conferring with Linnaeus, then Europe's most celebrated naturalist, and most admired and eminent figure, beside meeting the naturalist Olof Celsius (1670–1756), the Wolffian philosopher Samuel Klingenstierna (1698–1765), and others. Delighted to discover his mentor, Maffei, and other Italian savants were familiar names, he made a point of also visiting new laboratories, harbours, and mines. In April 1748, acknowledging his role as a mediator between the Italian and Swedish worlds of learning, Sagramoso was made a foreign member of the Swedish Royal Academy of Sciences.[6] After leaving, he long remained in contact with Linnaeus.

Carolus Linnaeus (1707–78), son of a rural Lutheran pastor, professor of medicine and botany at Uppsala in succession to Lars Roberg from 1741, emerged from the early 1740s as Uppsala's most celebrated scientist and the pre-eminent icon of Sweden's Enlightenment. Visitors were routinely shown how he had enlarged and developed the university's botanical gardens as an integral part of his wider botanical project. Engrossed in a great range of activity, Linnaeus forged a vast network of correspondents and ex-students adept in natural history, ranging right across Europe and the world. For decades, he continued refining his celebrated system of natural history classification first expounded in his *Systema naturae* (1735), becoming the Western world's leading exponent of the kind of discursive natural history that predominated in eighteenth-century Europe. Baconian, rooted in observation and description, but also firmly aligned with natural theology, his outlook reflected many core features of the moderate mainstream Enlightenment. Exhibiting scant interest in the forming and development of life forms, or generally in biology's dynamic dimensions, he strove to continually enlarge his static binomial classification, using two labels for classifying each plant—its genus and species—categories he deemed divinely ordered and fixed. His physico-theological leanings and classificatory system envisaged the categories of plant life as eternally distinct rungs composing the hierarchy of nature centering around his doctrine of fixity of species in animal and plant life, placing man firmly at the apex, as "lord of the animals."[7] His leading apostle in Denmark was the Norwegian, Martin Vahl (1749–1804), who studied in Uppsala in the years 1769–74 and became a leading figure of the "Danish–Norwegian" Enlightenment. Prime authority on botany at the Copenhagen Natural History Society, or Naturhistorie-selskabet, founded in 1788-9, loyally adhering to Linnaeus's classificatory system and "argument from design," Vahl long remained the incontestable chief mentor of natural history studies in Denmark–Norway.[8]

Impelled by a deep sense of calling, viewing himself almost as a second Luther, Linnaeus fused fervent physico-theology with zealous Lutheran religious commitment

[6] Mazzolini, "Linnaeus and Michele Enrico Sagramoso," 69–70.

[7] Dupré, *The Enlightenment and the Intellectual Foundation*, 37; Quintili, *Pensée critique de Diderot*, 297–8; Trousson, *Denis Diderot*, 72.

[8] Helge Kragh, *Natur, Nytte og Ånd, 1730–1850* (Aarhus, 2005), 128–30; Ballstadt, *Diderot: Natural Philosopher*, 131.

into numerous intellectual contexts. Most of Europe's savants warmly applauded; but his static, physico-theological conception of botany, and biology, also drew Linnaeus, chief prophet of botanical physico-theology, into a prolonged feud with Buffon, Diderot, and Daubenton, and the *encyclopédistes* more generally. For the radical *philosophes* (and La Mettrie), unlike Rousseau and Voltaire, rejected his system, openly deriding his methodology, mania for classification, "sexual" system, and doctrine of fixity of species, scorning the natural theology underpinning his science. In his *Interpretation de la nature* (1753) Diderot dismissed physico-theological, descriptive classifiers in the mode of Linnaeus, Vahl, and Réaumur as mere *méthodistes* lacking any proper conception of what they were studying. Emphasizing especially the harmony and balance of a nature supposedly rooted in intelligent design, Linnaeus retaliated by dismissing Buffon as a naturalist without system or method, the scientist who "has erred the most."[9]

This rift between the two rival Enlightenment conceptions of botany and biology, with the radical approach far more focused on the dynamic and adaptive development of life forms detached from any fixed classificatory system and hostile to Linnaeus' physico-theology, not only permeated the entire field of eighteenth-century natural history, but became an enduring split fundamental to the whole history of scientific endeavor and debate, a continuing underlying tension between moderate and radical Enlightenment in eighteenth-century Scandinavia and beyond. His providential outlook led Linnaeus to view the researcher in natural history not just as a scientist but as a social and cultural teacher, a pious God-fearing moral exemplar, staunch in combating freethinking and libertinism,[10] even though (not unlike Newton, one of his principal heroes) he was not actually a particularly prepossessing individual, being notorious among those familiar with him personally for his greed, stinginess, and arrogance.

Prominent Scandinavians, growing increasingly eager to leave behind them the sense of being ignored and marginal to the rest of world, consciously used the Enlightenment as a way to accelerate their becoming a topic of interest. The first issue of the *Dänische Bibliothec*, published at Copenhagen in 1738, complained of the striking lack of notice and publicity given to Danish–Norwegian erudition in Europe, particularly since the demise of the Lübeck *Nova Literaria Maris Balthici et Septentrionis* (1698–1707) and aspired to rectify this. But at cross purposes with this goal, the *Dänische Bibliothec* simultaneously sought to promote awareness of wider European developments, intellectual and scientific, in Denmark–Norway and, to this end, contemplated publishing its debates and reviews of foreign books in Danish.[11] But publishing in the vernacular, however relevant to the Enlightenment propagation locally, would inevitably hinder efforts to spread awareness of local developments

[9] Koerner, *Linnaeus*, 28; Duflo, *Diderot philosophe*, 158; Hope Mason, *Irresistible Diderot*, 68–9.

[10] Koerner, *Linnaeus*, 16, 23.

[11] *Dänische Bibliothec oder Sammlung von Alten und neuen Gelehrten Sachen aus Dänemarck* i (Copenhagen and Leipzig, 1738), 2.

beyond Scandinavia. Some urged publishing the journal in Latin as the best means to escape the trap of parochialism, but this would mean confining debates purely to the academic sphere, creating an unwelcome separation from society more generally that enlighteners were anxious to avoid. Finally, the editors settled for publishing Denmark–Norway's premier journal in German.[12]

By 1750, Sweden especially was being frequently commented on for its contributions to the sciences. But it was also being noticed for increasingly renowned aristocratic republicanism, this aspect having already attracted attention from Doria and others earlier. Surveying Europe from a mid-eighteenth-century perspective, Mably did not hesitate to pronounce the Swedish constitutional settlement of 1720–1 the "masterpiece of modern legislation."[13] Among the more literate sections of Sweden's population, resentment against the extremely costly failed militarism and absolutism of Charles XII (reigned: 1697–1718) lent the 1720 "Constitution" impressive local as well as international prestige. Reputed an immense benefit by many, even a work of unique excellence that was divinely sanctioned,[14] the constitution of 1720 drastically limited monarchical power, transferring most authority to Sweden's legislature. By doing so it had inaugurated what became known at the time, and has been called since, Sweden's "Age of Liberty." But two rival noble factions, "Hats" and "Caps," alternately dominated the post-1720 Riksdag, constantly quarreled with great vehemence at all levels as they pursued a ceaseless rivalry for influence and power.[15]

This bitter rift pervaded all spheres including university politics and higher learning where the rivalry deeply affected especially appointments and practical and organizational matters. Philosophical realignment in the Swedish universities during the later 1730s and 1740s, with Wolffianism conquering first Uppsala, then Åbo and finally, in the mid-1740s, Lund, was more bipartisan, pulling in all the prominent figures of Swedish science and scholarship. Linnaeus, once a Cartesian, and during his years in Holland (1735–8) a proponent of Newtonianism, on returning to Sweden combined devotion to physico-theology and ardent allegiance to the "Hats" with Wolffianism. The astronomer Anders Celsius (1701–44), another "Hat" celebrity, having defected from Cartesianism, led the Wolffian drive at Uppsala. Another Wolffian "Hat" was the prominent mathematician and physicist Samuel Klingenstierna (1698–1765), trained under Wolff at Marburg. But Wolffianism proved equally attractive to the Uppsala philosopher Petrus Ullén (1700–47), a leader among the academic "Caps."[16]

[12] *Dänische Bibliothec* i (1738), 3–4; Israel, *Northern Varieties*, 18.

[13] Wright, *Classical Republican*, 162, 232 n. 39, 239 n. 1; Mastellone, "Italian Enlightenment and the Swedish Constitution," 112–14.

[14] Roberts, *Age of Liberty*, 59–62.

[15] Lindroth, *History of Uppsala University*, 95; Skuncke, "Jean-Jacques Rousseau in Swedish Eyes," 89.

[16] Evan M. Melhado and Tore Frängsmyr (eds.), "Enlightenment Science in the Romantic Era: The Chemistry of Berzelius and its Cultural Setting," *The British Journal for the History of Science*, 166–7; Elis Malmeström, *Carl von Linné's religiösa åskådning* (Stockholm, 1926), 68, 80–9.

But it was the Hat faction that made a point of encouraging expansion of science and new fields of erudition as a way of building cultural and academic prestige. Theirs was a policy closely linked to their economic protectionism and drive to stimulate Swedish–Finnish agriculture, commerce, industry, and the mechanical arts, an agenda aimed at regenerating Sweden–Finland after its defeat in the Great Northern War (1700–21). Hats favored the establishment of new disciplines and academic chairs including professorships in physics, economic practice, and constitutional law; chairs of chemistry were established at Uppsala in 1750, Lund in 1758, and Åbo in 1761; another characteristic innovation was the founding at Uppsala of the first chair of *oeconomia publica* [public economics].[17] By the early 1770s, the number of permanent professors at Uppsala had risen to twenty-four. Money was also found under the Hat aegis during these years for construction of impressive new buildings, libraries, and gardens at Uppsala, Lund, Åbo, and Greifswald; at Uppsala, these comprised such new facilities as Anders Celsius' Observatory, a chemistry laboratory, and Linnaeus' orangery.[18]

The "Caps" responded by pointing out that the four Swedish universities, Uppsala, Lund, Greifswald, and Åbo, were churning out too many scholars for the shrinking empire's requirements, a surfeit of science, erudition, and academic training costing too much and bound to create disturbing social problems. A leading exponent of this view, on retiring from the Uppsala rectorship, in 1749, delivered a speech claiming Sweden's universities were producing twice as many graduates as there were vacant posts, and calling for retrenchment, and cutting back output of graduates to more realistic proportions. Along with many of Europe's leading universities in the later Enlightenment era, Uppsala's student body did in fact significantly contract from its mid-century peak, falling back from nearly 800 during the 1750s to between five and six hundred during the later 1760s and 1770s, a phenomenon closely connected with a gradual shrinkage of theology training and output of pastors.

Gaining a pre-eminent place in national self-esteem, and attracting foreign praise, the 1720 Swedish–Finnish Constitution achieved a comparable stature with the widely hailed Glorious Revolution settlement of 1688–9 in Britain. There were indeed striking affinities—the establishment of a stable constitutional monarchy with a regularized sharing of power between the royal house and the legislature—but also crucial differences. Curtailment of monarchy and, for the first time, the advance of a de facto republicanism in a large European realm were undoubtedly striking developments, a weakening of the principle and practice of monarchy that went even further than did the Glorious Revolution. Where the British outcome was incontestably a constitutional monarchy, the Swedish "result was the sovereignty of the Estates," the primacy of the legislature.[19] Where the British monarch still appointed and dismissed his ministers, could dissolve Parliament when he saw fit, appoint peers when so minded, and directly participated in all legislation—as d'Holbach

[17] Malmeström, *Carl von Linné's religiösa åskådning*, 96, 124–5; Skuncke, "Jean-Jacques Rousseau," 91, 97.

[18] Koerner, *Linnaeus*, 102.

[19] Roberts, *Age of Liberty*, 62.

complained, the drastically curtailed Swedish–Finnish monarch between 1720 and 1772 found himself altogether stripped of comparable powers.

Despite—and in Montesquieu's and Voltaire's cases, because of—its severely oligarchic character, Sweden–Finland's parliamentary political system during the half-century, the so-called Age of Liberty (1720–72), was looked on with warm approval by the *philosophes*. Mably, Doria, Voltaire, and Rousseau all expressed enthusiasm for Sweden's new liberty. Closer to the scene, the Huguenot Laurent Angliviel de La Beaumelle (1726–73), Denmark's most radical and subversive journal editor and no friend of kings, nobles, or clergy, observing Sweden from Copenhagen around 1750, pronounced Sweden's constitution not just exceptional but truly "admirable." Royal power was effectively curtailed while the king, differently from in England, found himself totally without funds to corrupt either ministers or representatives; meanwhile, the Swedish–Finnish nobility he supposed too weak, of itself, to seriously oppress the people, while the people were insufficiently strong to "désobéir," so that the three powers in Sweden's "mixed government" held each other wondrously in check. La Beaumelle pronounced "la république de Suède" the European land that, more than Britain or any other, most happily eluded both monarchy and "la servitude."[20]

Post-1720 Sweden–Finland, the republican-minded La Beaumelle did not doubt, was dedicated to peace and altogether more beneficial to its citizens than either the warmongering monarchical Sweden of the past or the Denmark–Norway of his day. Sweden had definitely replaced the Dutch Republic as Europe's freest, most open society, in his estimation particularly since the Orangist revolution of 1747–8, with which the now abject Dutch, reinstating the stadholderate, had finally succumbed to princely ambition, scheming, and dynastic calculation.[21] However, this new and uplifting Swedish reality still manifested one major, conspicuous flaw: the Riksdag maintained a large professional army to protect Swedish Pomerania and Finland (and keep the nobility employed), a large slice of it garrisoning the huge new fortifications of Sveaborg, constructed to guard Helsinki against the Russians. This potentially fatal entity could one day be utilized by Sweden's seemingly emasculated, powerless king as the means to overthrow the Riksdag's pre-eminence and, as in Denmark in 1660, bring the people once again firmly under royal absolutism.[22]

Sweden–Finland served as a unique model for many of Europe's self-proclaimed enlightened for decades. Even so, the eulogies heaped on the new constitution increasingly jarred with the reality of a distinctly stale, old-fashioned conception of the state. Sweden's political reformism in the mid-eighteenth century was not untouched by traces of Sidney and other English republican thinkers, or of Locke; but the 1720 revolution was chiefly justified as the restoration of a supposed historic but partly fictive "authentic" constitution, without any mention of inherent rights of

[20] La Beaumelle, *Mes Pensées*, 259; Israel, "Northern Varieties," 27–9.

[21] La Beaumelle, *Mes Pensées*, 235, 258; on the Orangist coup of 1747–8, see Israel, *Dutch Republic*, 1067–78.

[22] La Beaumelle, *Mes Pensées*, 180, 430.

mankind. It also exhibited other characteristically *ancien régime* features.[23] Liberty of the individual in religious, intellectual, and sexual matters remained strikingly limited and truncated by the standard of the "universal and equal rights" republicanism that the Radical Enlightenment, with d'Holbach well to the fore, began generating either side of the Atlantic during the 1770s. Though scarcely representative of the population generally, the Riksdag deemed itself a fully sovereign body not to be criticized by press or public, indeed as presiding to an even greater degree than the British Parliament. Both forbade public criticism of their proceedings; but the Riksdag went further in constraining press and general political debate.[24]

In Sweden–Finland before the 1760s, there was nothing resembling liberty of the press, no freedom for non-noble individuals to participate in political (or religious) discussion, and no right to criticize. Riksdag power remained absolute. Of the four Estates constituting the Rikdag, the Nobility were always much the most influential, exercising a stranglehold over appointments to high civil and military offices, professorships, and the diplomatic service.[25] Sweden–Finland, together with Swedish Pomerania, was, for all practical purposes, an aristocratic republic. Nevertheless, the two most striking features of Swedish society around 1750, the country's institutionalized anti-monarchism combined with aristocratic monopoly of power and the widely-acknowledged, impressive progress in scientific enquiry and debate, interacted in ways that continually fomented discreet discussion of the need for freedom of debate, expression, and publication.

In the 1720s and 1730s, few reforms to speak of emerged other than the new constitution itself. By 1750, by contrast, Sweden's quasi-republic, under the Hat party's direction, had become a major innovator in the Enlightenment's quest to restructure society and culture, spurred by subdued but growing resentment at the restrictions hemming in enlightened debate, and in one remarkable case, that of Peter Forsskål (1732–63), a former theology student and disciple of Linnaeus, philosophical radical protest going well beyond that of La Beaumelle. Gifted philosopher, naturalist, and orientalist, a clergyman's son raised in Finland and trained at Uppsala, Forsskål completed his studies at Göttingen, where, from 1753, he studied Arabic, with the great orientalist, Michaelis. An unusually broad Enlightenment outlook he combined with a questioning scientific approach and mounting dislike of the narrowing, intellectually stifling effect of the Wolffian ascendancy. He provoked a scholarly furore in Sweden, with his Göttingen thesis, *Dubia de principiis recentioris* (Goettingae, 1756), which by 1760 had appeared in three different editions, by urging more toleration and freedom to philosophize and venturing some wide-ranging, penetrating "doubts" about "recent philosophy," picking holes in the Wolffian philosophy.[26]

Forsskål's text, composed with Michaelis's support, included unmistakable hints of a subversive, oppositional attitude. On returning to Uppsala, where he aligned with

[23] Roberts, *Age of Liberty*, 60–1, 66; Skuncke, "Jean-Jacques Rousseau," 87, 103.
[24] Roberts, *Age of Liberty*, 104–5; Hirschfeldt, "Freedom of Speech," 55.
[25] Roberts, *Age of Liberty*, 69.
[26] Goldberg, "Who was Peter Forsskål?," 17–18.

the "Caps," he soon found himself in the midst of a theologico-philosophical uproar, loudly denounced as a libertine especially by Niels Wallerius and the "Hats."[27] He responded by broadening his observations into a more general critique of Swedish culture and society, a tract published in 1759, in Swedish, under the title *Tankar om Borgerliga Friheten* (Stockholm, 1759), with a second version in Latin, summoning readers to awaken and firmly reject Sweden's excessively curtailed pseudo-freedoms. He proclaimed an urgent need to fight for the "true Swedish freedom," liberty of thought being indispensable to progress of the sciences and philosophy,[28] and freedom of the press and expression to political progress and awareness. "A wise government will rather let the people express their discontent with pens than with guns, a freedom which enlightens on the one hand, appeases and prevents disorder on the other."[29]

Commencing with incisive remarks on the liberty-curtailing character of aristocratic republics in general, "such as the Polish and Italian ones, which take pride in the hallowed name of freedom" but where "most people are bondsmen of the high ranking notwithstanding,"[30] Forsskål lambasted the restrictive, privileged "aristocratic" character of access to high offices and positions in the Swedish state, resulting in the country's highest posts coming into "unworthy hands." In China, by contrast, high offices were assigned according to merit, not noble status.[31] "Each and every inhabitant," held Forsskål, "should have a reasonable share in public benefits. For society is common as should liberty be also."[32] This principle he combined with a plea for progressive taxation laying the heaviest burden on the wealthy and taxing the poor least. Echoing Helvétius especially, Forsskål's tract shocked the university and was banned outright by the aristocratic government, albeit only after all 500 privately printed copies had been distributed so that most were never recovered.[33] Denounced as a disciple of Spinoza and Bayle, Forsskål was debarred from an academic career in Sweden–Finland. Scandinavia's first noteworthy post-Wolffian enlightener thus found himself obliged to resume his scholarly career abroad. On Linnaeus' recommendation, he accompanied the ill-fated Danish-sponsored Niebuhr expedition to Arabia. After researching botany and Arabic dialects for three years in the Middle East, he tragically died from fever, in 1763, at Jerim, near Sanaa, in the Yemen, aged only 31.[34] Linnaeus commemorated his former pupil by labeling a new variety of nettles he had found in Arabia, *Forsskålea*.

[27] Frängsmyr, "Enlightenment," 169; Frängsmyr, *Sökandet*, 127, 139–41; Sörlin and Fegerstedt, *Linné och hans apostlar*, 82–3; Oittinen, *Peter Forsskål*, 144–6; Frängsmyr, *Sökandet*, 139–41.

[28] [Peter Forsskål], *Tankar om Borgerliger Friheten* (Stockholm, 1759), 4–5.

[29] [Forsskål], *Thoughts on Civil Liberty*, 17; Oittinen, *Peter Forsskål*, 145; Goldberg, "Who was Peter Forsskål?," 20.

[30] [Forsskål], *Thoughts on Civil Liberty*, 14–15, 22.

[31] [Forsskål], *Tankar*, 6.

[32] [Forsskål], *Thoughts on Civil Liberty*, 18–19.

[33] Frängsmyr, *Sökandet*, 163–4; Oittinen, *Peter Forsskål*, 144.

[34] Sörlin and Fegerstedt, *Linné och hans apostlar*, 13, 65; Goldberg, "Who was Peter Forsskål?," 21; Vermeulen, *Early History of Ethnograph*, 166–7.

If Forsskål was ahead of his time, parliamentary disagreement and debate, and attempts at reform, generated a growing and lively critical dialectic of its own. A notable change set in from 1766 when the Caps gained the upper hand. After the political shift, a carefully-worded ordinance for the "Liberty of Printing" was passed by the now Cap-dominated Riksdag that was largely a response to the changing intellectual climate. Influenced in part by Forsskål and the Finnish clergyman, scientist, and savant, Anders Chydenius (1729–1803), a young Cap pressing for reforms from within the Riksdag, this decree was a striking instance of gradualism in reform. It specifically declared "unrestricted mutual enlightenment in various useful subjects" to be its goal and it to be the Riksdag's obligation henceforth to render a wide range of public, administrative and judicial documents accessible to the public.[35] However, landmark though it was, the 1766 Swedish *Ordinance for the Liberty of Printing*, while abolishing the general requirement for prior censorship of works intended for publication, exempted from the new freedom everything concerning religion, theology, and current political debate in the Riksdag and government.[36]

Prior censorship on publications ended except for works touching on theological issues where the clergy retained their traditional stranglehold: [37] the rule remained that anything deemed damaging to (the Lutheran) "religion" remained forbidden, together with criticism of the constitution, the Estates, and the aristocracy's monopoly on power.[38] Nevertheless, the measure, and the public debate surrounding the reform, for the first time acknowledged as a general principle that freedom of expression and the press are a benefit for society and made clear that some contemporaries wished to go further.[39] Other liberalizing measures, or at least efforts, followed. In 1769, the Estates set up a committee to draft procedural changes aimed at ending arbitrary arrest and imprisonment without trial along with judicial torture. This initiative failed for the moment, narrowly rejected by the Nobility (and more comprehensively by the Burghers and Peasantry). Even so, by the late 1760s, the enlightened constituency among Sweden's elite were clearly a growing force in society.

8.2. ENLIGHTENED REFORM IN DENMARK–NORWAY

By contrast, until the 1760s the Danish–Norwegian "Enlightenment" looked distinctly less promising to opposition-minded enlighteners like La Beaumelle. Under both an autocratic monarchy and powerful aristocracy, its sporadically repressive court remained firmly allied to the Lutheran clergy, as was demonstrated by the banning of

[35] Hirschfeldt, "Freedom of Speech," 57–60; Nordenstreng, "Freedom of Speech in Finland," 72–3.
[36] Roberts, *Age of Liberty*, 106, 166; Arvidson, *Thorild*, 211; Hirschfeldt, "Freedom of Speech," 55, 57–8.
[37] Roberts, *Age of Liberty*, 106, 166; Holm, *Nogle Hovedtræk*, 3.
[38] Holm, *Nogle Hovedtræk*, 9–10, 91.
[39] Holm, *Nogle Hovedtræk*, 3; Frängsmyr, *Sökandet efter Upplysningen*, 202.

the deistic Wertheim Bible in 1737.[40] Tindal and other English "deists" of the early eighteenth-century tended to blame the extinguishing of the old Danish constitution and installing of royal absolutism, in 1660, chiefly on the machinations of the Danish–Norwegian clergy.[41] Yet Denmark–Norway was also in several respects untypical of the wider monarchical Enlightenment. Ironically, and rather paradoxically, the "deist" responsible for the Wertheim Bible, Johann Lorenz Schmidt (1702–49), hounded across Germany, sought refuge that same year under Danish jurisdiction and protection, in Altona.

It had become a commonplace remark by the 1760s that even though the Danes lagged behind the Swedes and Germans in their Enlightenment, Denmark–Norway too had registered substantial progress during the last twenty years.[42] Where Prussia's Enlightenment derived its momentum and specific characteristics from the fertile brain of its authoritarian soldier-king, Frederick the Great, and Austria's from the personal reforming zeal of Joseph II, the prime characteristic of mid-eighteenth-century Danish royal enlightened reformism, due to the inertia and passivity of Denmark's absolute monarch, was his dependence on aristocratic reform-minded courtiers and advisers. Proud absolutists in theory, the Danish monarchs of this period, Frederik V (reigned: 1746–66) and Christian VII (reigned: 1766–1808), had no capacity to govern personally. The royal cabinet of ministers and heads of the administration, mostly moderate enlightened aristocrats, firmly presided over the process.[43] There was perhaps no greater encouragement to the Enlightenment's steady progress in post-1746 Denmark than the feebleness of its kings.

La Beaumelle remained decidedly more critical of monarchical Denmark–Norway than of Sweden–Finland. Danish improvements in politics, religion, society, and culture were too few and too slow for his taste, while intellectual life remained too narrow. Copenhagen with its court, university, merchants, theatres, and foreign communities overwhelmingly dominated the literary and intellectual scene. But for decades its leading figure had been the erudite, patriarchal Norwegian Ludvig Holberg (1684–1754), who, according to La Beaumelle, owed his pre-eminence to a plagiaristic tendency nourished by wide reading which chiefly reflected the narrow conventionality and general poverty of the Scandinavian cultural scene.[44] Born at Bergen, an essayist, moralist, playwright, historian, and, since the age of 30, professor at Copenhagen University, Holberg had traveled widely in France, Italy, the Netherlands, and England as a young man, lingering in Paris and staying nearly two years at Oxford (1706–8). He possessed an excellent knowledge of French, German, and English beside Greek and Latin, and was keenly interested in Old Norse and Icelandic sagas. Created a baron in 1747, he prided himself on not using elevation in rank as an

[40] Israel, *Radical Enlightenment*, 554.

[41] Tindal, *A New Catechism*, 9–10; Laursen, "Censorship in the Nordic Countries," 102; Israel, *Enlightenment Contested*, 107.

[42] *Anekdoten eines reisenden Russen über die Staatsverfassung, Sitten und Gebrauche der Dänen, in Briefen an seine Freunde* (Lübeck, 1771), 69, 71–2.

[43] Frängsmyr, *Sökandet efter Upplysningen*, 190.

[44] Lauriol, *La Beaumelle*, 154.

excuse to abandon study or cease submitting reform proposals and promoting the public good.[45] Holberg's witty and refined essays, especially his popular comedies, ridiculing common prejudices and prevailing opinion, gave him a wider readership than any other Scandinavian.

For his part, Holberg disdained La Beaumelle's proneness to assume the cultural superiority of everything French. La Beaumelle's short-lived Copenhagen journal, *La Spectatrice danoise* (1748–50), launched in September 1748, initially in collaboration with Holberg, briefly succeeded, selling sixty-four copies to the court alone, and hundreds more among the ministries, the capital's wealthy homes, and the university, beside another 200 copies in Hamburg and Altona. He could count on selling 1,000 copies in French and another 1,000, he and Holberg conjectured, with the Danish version they briefly planned to launch together. Remarkably, the two editors counted on selling 600 copies of the latter in Copenhagen as against a mere 400 in all the rest of Denmark–Norway.[46] This Danish version never materialized, however, despite a translator setting to work and translating parts, due to difficulties with the censorship and Holberg's suspecting La Beaumelle was plotting against him.[47]

La Spectatrice danoise stands out for its incisive critical and egalitarian spirit and many disparaging remarks about the nobility and clergy. Highly significant is the manner La Beaumelle treats, as if it were a matter of common knowledge, the largely veiled struggle between deism and Christianity within Danish court society, which he viewed as a battle provoked by the advance of "philosophy," a battle he discusses, furthermore, in surprisingly neutral tones without pretending to denounce and vilify irreligion: "there has never been a more interesting war than that the Deists have declared, since a century ago, against the Christians."[48] He even remarks that in this fight over men's salvation, highest good, immortality of the soul, divine providence, and whether Christ was an envoy of God or an impostor, the chief spokesmen on either side were thus far admirably evenly balanced in genius and ability. One was continually caught up (in certain unrepresentative Danish circles), observed La Beaumelle, in a debate in which "Hobbes, Bayle, Collins, Tindal, Mylord Shaftesbury, [and] Woolston" were pitted against "Grotius, Abbadie, Pascal, Ditton, Turretini, [and] Huet."[49] But if many authors had helped foment a context in which Danish–Norwegian "deists" abounded among "les gens d'un certain rang" [persons of a certain rank], he assured his brother, in France, in April 1748, it was Bayle who exerted the greatest impact. Bayle's profound knowledge and "génie transcendant" were highly esteemed in Copenhagen, "mais le prétraille le croit fort dangéreux" [but the clergy consider him very dangerous].[50] Among nobles seeking out Bayle's books and studying him avidly, the count of Rantzau, to whom he was close, discussed that philosopher obsessively every time he saw him.

45 Holberg, *Memoirs*, 260. 46 Lauriol, *La Beaumelle*, 151–3.
47 Israel, "Northern Varieties," 28.
48 La Beaumelle, *Spectatrice danoise* i. 465; Israel, *Enlightenment Contested*, 87.
49 La Beaumelle, *Spectatrice danoise* i. 466. 50 Lauriol, *La Beaumelle*, 139.

Holberg too immensely admired Bayle, as he had demonstrated in his highly successful *Moralske Tanker* [Moral Thoughts] (1744) and five volumes of *Epistler* [Essays] (1748–54).[51] But the "Bayle" Holberg esteemed was the erudite skeptic and proponent of toleration, not the more philosophical and radical Bayle of the *Pensées Diverses* and the late works. Even Holberg's plea for toleration really amounted to just dislike of dogmatic rigidity and zeal rather than a principled advocacy of personal liberty and freedom of expression. Morality's true foundation, Holberg concurred with Bayle and La Beaumelle, is "reason;" but his "reason" amounted to little more than a plea for orderly lifestyle, healthy living, avoiding excess, and adhering to the mainstream. "I do not approve of customs, however prevalent," he remarked toward the end of his life, "when I do not find any justification for them."[52] If Holberg's respect for Natural law led to a certain dislike of social inequality generally,[53] and aversion to noble privilege, the only respect—albeit a crucial one—in which Holberg evinced a forthright radical tendency was his willingness to promote gender equality, his suggesting women might well make better administrators, judges, and lawyers than men.[54] Claiming the "weakness we impute to the female sex is derived solely from education,"[55] Holberg pre-echoed the condemnation of gender inequality leveled later by Diderot and Condorcet. Otherwise, Holberg's "reason" was of a middle of the road, common-sense sort, blended with a typical bias definitely not shared by Bayle or La Beaumelle—genteel skepticism not least about the value of philosophers and philosophy.[56]

Another leading moderate still more alarmed by the invasion of intellectual irreligion was Erik Pontoppidan (1698–1764), a prominent Pietist court preacher and Copenhagen University professor (1735–48) who later became bishop of Bergen (1748–55). Once chaplain to a duke, he had composed an account of parish life on the Island of Als, off Jutland, complaining of the frightening tenacity of superstition, Satanism, and belief in witchcraft, among Jutland's simple villagers. Typically for moderate Enlightenment, Pontoppidan saw no reason for any change in the hierarchical social system of his time even with respect to black slavery. Defending the Royal Danish West India Company, which shipped black slaves from West Africa to the Danish West Indies (St. Thomas, St. Jan and St. Croix), from where most of the slaves were then re-exported elsewhere, he pronounced heathendom a far worse scourge than even the most debased Christianity (Catholicism). Slavery is justified when by this means slaves will "get to know God and His kingdom better, thereby becoming liberated in Christ, though servants of men."[57] By the time Pontoppidan transferred to Norway, his chief worry was the progress of "atheism" and deism in his homeland.[58] Among declared "deists" who especially worried him was La Beaumelle's

[51] Mitchell, "Age of Enlightenment," 136–7. [52] Holberg, *Memoirs*, 275.
[53] Rossel, "Holberg and his Times," pp. xviii, xx, xxii.
[54] Fitting, "Buried Treasures," 95, 99, 101–2. [55] Fitting, "Buried Treasures," 102.
[56] Holberg, *Memoirs*, 255, 257, 266. [57] Parker, *Agony of Asar*, 41, 164.
[58] Pontoppidan, *Abhandlung von der Neuigkeit der Welt* i. 13–14; Israel, *Enlightenment Contested*, 176.

closest ally among the aristocracy, Woldemar Hermann, count von Schmettau (1719–85), who during 1750–1 avidly read a stream of subversive French books including *La Lettre sur les Aveugles* and others by Diderot which La Beaumelle procured for him.[59] Later, anonymously, Von Schmettau published subversive deistic works of his own, notably his remarkable *Auch Fragmente* published at "Philadelphia" [i.e. Altona] in 1783.[60]

After residing many years in Copenhagen, La Beaumelle fell into disgrace at the court, as well as among the University's Lutheran professors, and in October 1751 was ordered to leave Denmark.[61] On departing Copenhagen, he stayed briefly, contemplating his future, at the Von Schmettau *Schloss* at Itzehoe in Holstein, from where his noble friend strove, in vain, to get him recalled to the capital.[62] Transferring to Hamburg, in late 1751, La Beaumelle not only ill-advisedly spoke "with contempt" of the Danes, noted the poet Klopstock, but openly disparaged their monarch and court.[63] Arriving in Potsdam shortly before La Mettrie died of food-poisoning on 11 November, he received a letter from Von Schmettau, eulogizing La Mettrie and urging him to seek the Berlin Academy position La Mettrie had just vacated: "this position is right for you and you are right for the king [Frederick the Great]." At this point began the soon epic quarrel between La Beaumelle and Voltaire, a clash in which Von Schmettau vigorously supported the former: "what a pity that so much talent is to be found in such a monster."[64]

If Sweden was ahead of Denmark around 1760, during the 1760s enlightened reforms, administrative, judicial, economic, and penal, gathered pace also there. The founding of a Royal Society for Agricultural Science (1769) to promote improvement of agriculture by spreading new scientific knowledge, encouraging debate among noble landowners and officials, and facilitating consultation at different social levels, also prompted an official review of serfdom. Serfdom was still more formalized and legally-defined in Denmark than in Sweden, though manorial ties and obligatory labor dues remained extensive in both kingdoms. Although no measures were taken as yet to lessen peasant labor dues or other forms of bonded obligation to noble landowners, government proposals initiated some standardizing of forms of peasant subjection.[65] More concretely, Beccaria's famous treatise on crimes and punishment precipitated a decisive shift of opinion, as in much of Europe, regarding the penal codes.[66] While the University's theologians held the biblically-prescribed death penalty to be rightly mandatory in all cases of murder, reforming officials urged the need to adapt penalties to the nature and social circumstances of crimes.[67] The general reform of Danish law relating to murder, introduced in 1767, was plainly based on Beccaria. This law marked the point in Scandinavian legal history where automatic

[59] Lauriol, *La Beaumelle*, 234.
[60] Lauriol, *La Beaumelle*, 116.
[61] Lauriol, *La Beaumelle*, 161.
[62] Lauriol, *La Beaumelle*, 281–2.
[63] Lauriol, *La Beaumelle*, 256, 300.
[64] Lauriol, *La Beaumelle*, 266, 280.
[65] Munck, "Danish Reformers," 248–50; Barton, *Northern Arcadia*, 106.
[66] Holberg, *Memoirs*, 189–90.
[67] Tamm, "Beccaria et le climat de réformes," 189–90.

imposition of the death penalty in murder cases, as stipulated under customary law and the *Code Danoise* of 1683, formally ended. From the perspective of 1800, the measures of the late 1760s were seen as the first of three vigorous bouts of late Enlightenment Danish legal, institutional, and cultural reform.

The second round of substantive changes, more radical in character, dominated the brief but spectacular ascendancy as chief minister (1770–1) of Johann Friedrich Struensee (1737–72). A Halle-trained German physician who became the Danish monarch's chief physician early in 1769, Struensee's most far-reaching reform, curtailed afterwards but not fully reversed until 1799, was his royal proclamation of 4 September 1770, proclaiming unrestricted freedom of the press [*eine uneingeschränkte Freyheit der Presse*] and free expression throughout Denmark and its dependent territories (Norway, Schleswig-Holstein, Greenland, Iceland, the Faroes, and the Danish Antilles). Struensee persuaded King Christian and publicly justified his sweeping, revolutionary 1770 proclamation on grounds for which he had been arguing for many years: freedom of thought and expression greatly benefit society, promote the "common good," and encourage scholarship and science as all impartial search for truth inevitably suffers from the intrusion of censorship.[68] Denmark–Norway thereby became the first Western country to proclaim full, unrestricted freedom of the press, extending this to religion, morality, and politics, and institutionalizing it as a fundamental right and principle of an enlightened society—a universal right benefiting humankind both collectively and individually.[69]

This Danish decree, made "after ripe consideration," caused an international sensation. Voltaire greeted it with unqualified enthusiasm, penning in gratitude to King Christian an *Épitre à sa majesté le Roi de Danemarc, sur la Liberté de la Presse accordée dans ses États*, printed in Copenhagen in both French and Danish versions that included the words: "I throw myself at your feet in the name of the human race."[70] Unaware that it was not the mentally unstable Christian but a hitherto unknown German "deist" physician upon whom the ailing monarch felt a strong personal dependence who was the decree's author, Voltaire lavishly eulogized the king.[71] But when communicating his enthusiasm to d'Alembert, in February 1771,[72] Voltaire also expressed concern: certain ideas were gaining too much ground (especially those of Diderot and d'Holbach); his chief ally, Frederick the Great, was displeased. Perhaps the Danish king, worried Voltaire, was going too far in permitting a wholly unrestricted press freedom.

[68] Winkle, *Struensee und die Publizistik*, 81–7; Laursen, "Spinoza in Denmark," 190–1, 195; see also Laursen, "David Hume and the Danish Debate," 167–72.

[69] Laursen, "Spinoza in Denmark," 190–1.

[70] Winkle, *Struensee und die Publizistik*, 82; Grashoff, *Johann Friedrich Struensee*, 40–1.

[71] Voltaire to d'Alembert, 13 Feb. 1771, in Voltaire, *Correspondence* xxxvii. 256.

[72] Voltaire to d'Alembert, 4 Feb. 1771, in Volaire, *Correspondence* xxxvii. 244; Holm, *Nogle Hovedtraek*, 27.

Requirement to obtain official approval before printing books and pamphlets ended at once.[73] During 1771–2, no less than twenty-seven new weekly and monthly journals began publication, and for the first time Denmark–Norway was inundated with printed criticism, debate, and satire.[74] A collection of this mass of press ephemera was made at the time by Bolle Willum Luxdorph (1716–88), historian, poet, *maître des requêtes* in the Danish Chancellery from 1753 to 1771, and co-signatory of many of the reforming edicts issuing from Struensee's office, a collection preserved today in the Danish Royal Library in forty-five volumes comprising around a thousand items, amounting to some 30,000 pages. (Luxdorph was also afterwards a member of the commission that sentenced Struensee to death for treason.)[75] Beside different religious views and pleas for new approaches to government and taxation, and more toleration, the flood of tracts appearing under Struensee's press freedom expressed dissatisfaction of many kinds. But dominating the picture was a torrent of criticism of a kind Struensee had not anticipated—furious attacks on himself. Numerous tracts denounced him and his policies as destructive of religion. Freshly arrived at the helm, reputed a "deist" and foe of religion, the new royal chief minister was already deeply unpopular and every additional sweeping reform only rendered him more so. The outcry against Struensee's "atheistic" proceedings inspired attacks on him of unprecedented vehemence. By October 1771, Struensee had decided that press freedom must, after all, be limited by legal safeguards to protect persons scurrilously reviled by hostile authors. Modifications followed, requiring either author or publisher to be named on every publication, and the printer to record who the author was, so that responsibility in libel cases could be less easily evaded.[76]

The mass of anti-Struensee pamphlets appearing in Denmark between 1770 and 1773, *Luxdorphs Samling af Trykke-frihedens Skrifter*, helps chart the character of the opposition political, religious, and cultural, to Struensee's radical reformism. The outcry was fueled especially by allegations of religious and moral pollution and complaints about the disorientating effect of this sea of printed matter.[77] One detractor conjured up a nightmarish vision of proliferating published material since "freedom of the press": Denmark had become a stinking heap of texts on every imaginable topic, financial writings, "project writings," and "Machiavellian, Spinozistic writings," of which there were many, and from which the "stench was so dreadful," the author could not bear it.[78] Danes were becoming lost in a madhouse of ideas "from which no one could find the exit."[79] Denmark's new German chief minister was wrecking morality and religion, one pamphlet, the *Nye Prøve af*

[73] Winkle, *Struensee und die Publizistik*, 81–2; Glebe-Møller, *Struensees vej til skafottet*, 25–6.

[74] P. M. Mitchell, "The Age of Enlightenment," in S. H. Rossel (ed.), *A History of Danish Literature* (Lincoln, NB, 1992).

[75] Laursen, "Luxdorph's Press Freedom Writings," 62–3.

[76] Laursen, "Luxdorph's Press Freedom Writings," 90–2; Holm, *Nogle Hovedtræk*, 6.

[77] *Anekdoten eines reisenden Russsen*, p. A3.

[78] *Luxdorphs Samling af Trykke-frihedens Skrifter* xv, no. 6, p. 14.

[79] *Anekdoten eines reisenden Russsen*, p. A3v.

Skrive-Frihed, pronouncing him the new "Haman."[80] "Freedom of the press" for some meant Denmark–Norway's religious and moral collapse.

Protest, though, by no means emanated solely from reactionary circles. Many objectors actually welcomed the broad general impact of Enlightenment "philosophy" on Danish society since the 1740s. If belief in demons and sightings of the Devil were still encountered more often among Denmark's common people, in Jutland and Norway especially, than practically anywhere else in Europe, the Lutheran clergy had all but ceased condemning theological dissidents as "Socinians" and no longer claimed, as they once had, that salvation occurs exclusively within the Lutheran Church.[81] The Enlightenment offered much that Christians could accept as good. The problem with Struensee's approach, insisted one pamphlet, the *Alvorlige Betragtninger over den almindelige Tilstand* [Serious Observations on the Common Condition] of 1771, while parading its own "enlightened" standpoint, was his overreaching what was acceptable due to certain kinds of "philosophy." The "Christian" philosophy of "Grotius, Pufendorf, Leibniz, Wolff, Locke, Newton, Boyle, Boerhaave, Haller, Hoffmann, Sulzer," this tract lauded enthusiastically; these geniuses had demonstrated the workings of nature much better than "the materialists." But philosophy submissive to religious authority, and embracing the "argument from design," was under threat. Vanini's and Bruno's attacks on "true religion," occurring in "dark times," had caused little stir and amounted to nothing that needed worrying about. But a more dangerous far-reaching attack had now developed under the mask of "philosophy" and the sciences, issuing chiefly from "Tindal, Spinoza, Collins, and Bolingbroke."[82]

Here and there, mixed in with the mass, one detects even hints of radical ideas. One tract stressing the huge impact of "philosophy" on Denmark, *En Grønlaenders Beskrivelse over Kiøbenhavn* [A Greenlander's Description of Copenhagen], is strikingly mild in condemning the unbelievers in Copenhagen who had "torn themselves from and denied all religion," convinced the world has existed as it is since all eternity. These, explains this anonymous text, adopt as their hero a certain Dutch Jew called Spinoza who, in a thick, tedious book of metaphysical Latin, attempts to "prove all of nature is only one substance and that all Nature's parts are only just so many modifications of it, so that all that one sees in the whole of nature, is equally as divine, as royal, as grand, so that the writer and his pen are equally important, both just modifications of nature's whole."[83] While deriding this doctrine, this tract nevertheless also observed that while these "Spinozists" recognized no sin, nor any punishment for sin, nevertheless, usually "they live better and show more charity than the rest [of society] who pretend to be true to and follow their heaven-sent book [the

[80] *Luxdorphs Samling af Trykke-frihedens Skrifter* xiv, no. 2, p. 14; Holm, *Nogle Hovedtræk*, 59, 76.
[81] Holm, *Nogle Hovedtræk*, 69.
[82] *Alvorlige Betragtninger*, 16; Laursen, "Spinoza in Denmark," 196.
[83] *En Grønlaendes Beskrivelse*, 5.

Bible]," their integrity being "something they have in common with their originator [i.e. Spinoza]."[84]

Such literature addressed the ordinary reader, not the savant, hence its special value. One might object that this singling out of Spinoza as the leader of the sect of philosophical unbelievers in Denmark, noticeable in several tracts, simply mirrored the earlier, pre-1720 phase in France, Germany, and England when Spinoza had been generally acknowledged the head of the underground philosophical "sect" of atheists. Yet it is still of considerable significance that in the Denmark of 1770, even semi-illiterate and largely ignorant people knowing nothing of other thinkers had heard, and acquired a lurid picture, of Spinoza and his allegedly fatal influence on mankind. Spinoza charged the *Grønlandske Professors* [...] *Betragtninger over Maanen* [Greenlander Professors' Observations about the Moon] "negtede al Guddom" [denied all Divinity].[85] *Ole Smedesvends Begraedelse over Rissengrød* [Ole Smedesvend's Complaint over Rice Porridge] ridiculed the "Dutch Jew, reputed learned, who wanted people to believe the world had made itself," something as wrong-headed as maintaining that doors could lock themselves. "This fellow was called Spinach or Spinos" and is not alone: another of his kind is the "French fool" La Mettrie.[86]

Struensee's reformism was rooted in a utilitarian morality which, as in Spinoza, Helvétius, and d'Holbach (but not La Mettrie), conceived moral concepts as existing solely in relations between people, real "nur insofern sie für die Gesellschaft Folgen hätten" [only insofar as they had results for society].[87] Aside from his decrees, little survives from Struensee's own pen. But after his downfall, in 1772, the "enlightened" Lutheran theologian Balthasar Münter (1735–93), an admirer of Newton's views on religion and miracles, charged with tending Struensee's soul, in prison, records him as confessing, following their first interview in 1772 that, whilst he exercised power in Denmark, he was "no Christian." Miracles he deemed impossible and had never believed "man consists of two substances," body and soul; he "considered himself and all men to be pure machines" with nothing surviving after death. This hypothesis he had not acquired from La Mettrie, "whom he had never read," however, but worked it out for himself.[88] Rousseau was among his favourite authors, along with Voltaire, Bonnet, and Reimarus. Another who impressed him, and helped shape his radical outlook, was Boulanger, whose *Antiquité devoilée* he had read carefully.[89] At Paris in 1768, accompanying the king, he had had the opportunity to converse with several *philosophes*, notably d'Alembert. It was Helvétius, however, who had exerted the greatest influence on his intellectual and political outlook.[90]

84 *En Grønlaendes Beskrivelse*, 5.

85 *Luxdorphs Samling af Trykke-frihedens Skrifter* xv, no. 21, p. 6; Laursen, "Spinoza in Denmark," 199.

86 *Luxdorphs Samling af Trykke-frihedens Skrifter* xv, no. 9, p. 7; Laursen, "Spinoza in Denmark," 198.

87 Laursen, "Spinoza in Denmark," 198; Glebe-Møller, *Struensees vej*, 74–5.

88 Münter, *Bekehrungsgeschichte*, 10; Glebe-Møller, *Struensees vej*, 57.

89 Münter, *Bekehrungsgeschichte*, 132–3.

90 Münter, *Bekehrungsgeschichte*, 133; Amidsen, *Til nytte og fornøjelse. Johann Friedrich Struensee*, 48, 67, 154.

Struensee was a Helvétius disciple, a materialist attempting to extend the principles governing his own personal philosophy to Danish–Norwegian society.[91] Opposition to his sweeping reformism arose from both moderately enlightened and reactionary sources rallying behind the headline accusation that his ideas about society and politics derived from "atheism," naturalism, materialism, and Spinozism."[92] A German-language anti-Struensee pamphlet appearing shortly after his downfall condemned him as a "naturalist born out of Spinoza's school," an atheist and lust-maddened sensualist scorning the true God and thoroughly corrupting the court. Despite royal support, ecclesiastical, noble, and burgher opposition grew so intense that after little more than a year his position became untenable. Having no power base apart from a few like-minded courtiers and German immigrants, and the royal favor of a half-demented drop-out,[93] his authority (and the queen's reputation) rapidly withered.

Increasingly antagonistic to radical thought, and Struensee, Frederick the Great willingly lent his backing to the organizers of an aristocratic coup, staged in January 1772. Arrested together with the queen at a ball, at Christianborg Castle, Struensee found himself stripped of his offices and arraigned for high treason. King Christian would have saved him, had he been able to, but such was the backlash this proved impossible. In March 1772, Frederick wrote to Voltaire suggesting he should share his outrage that, in league with the queen, the Danish king's physician-chief minister had vilely turned that pitiable monarch into their tool by administering regular doses of opium under the guise of "medicine," enabling them to do with the kingdom as they pleased. Fortunately, Struensee and the queen had been thwarted, "ont été prévenues par bonheur."[94] But Struensee's overthrow disturbed Voltaire. "Votre Dannemark," he wrote, in July 1772 to d'Alembert, who had been impressed by Struensee, and was another enthusiast for the Danish reforms, "has supplied a scene that makes one shrug and shudder."[95]

Tried for high treason, put to judicial torture, and found guilty of irreligion, immorality, and betrayal, Struensee was publicly executed together with his closest accomplice, Count Enevold Brandt (1738–72), on 28 April 1772. In defiance of Beccaria, the two men were publicly mutilated, having their hands cut off prior to beheading; their corpses were afterwards drawn and quartered to reflect the full gravity of their "crimes." According to most of the public, and clergy, God's justice had been done. Radicals, by contrast, were disgusted then—and for long after. Mary Wollstonecraft, who visited Sweden, Norway, and Denmark, in that order, during the summer of 1795, found much to criticize in the ignorance and prejudice prevailing in Scandinavian lands, not least the servility of the poorest paid and men boorishly "oppressing the women. The most menial, laborious offices were left to these poor

[91] Amidsen, *Til nytte og fornøjelse*, 177; Glebe-Møller, *Struensees vej*, 30, 72–5.
[92] Laursen, "Spinoza in Denmark," 192.
[93] *Luxdorphs Trykke-frihedens skrifter* xiv, no. 10, "Teutsches Echo," 6–7.
[94] Frederick to Voltaire, 1 Mar. 1772, in Voltaire, *Correspondence* xxxviii. 271.
[95] Voltaire to d'Alembert, 13 July 1772, in Voltaire, *Correspondence* xxxviii. 456.

drudges," the females. Participating in several discussions about Struensee whilst in Copenhagen she concluded that "as the king's conduct had always been directed by some favourite," Struensee and the Queen strove to govern him, from a principle of self-preservation and a laudable ambition; but, underestimating the prejudices they had to encounter, "the system they adopted displayed more benevolence of heart than soundness of judgment. As to the charge, still believed, of their giving the king drugs to injure his faculties, it is too absurd to be refuted."[96]

8.3. SCANDINAVIAN ENLIGHTENED DESPOTISM AFTER 1772

Struensee's overthrow was greeted with jubilation by the Danish man in the street and ushered in a period of sustained reaction in many areas of society and culture. Of his various reforms, some were cancelled outright, one key reversal under an edict of 12 August 1773 halted the review of government supervision of peasant–lord relations he had initiated. Noble privilege was strongly reaffirmed. But while almost no one spoke out in Struensee's defense, the alliance of reaction and moderate Enlightenment that brought him down and reversed his reformism was hardly likely to remain intact after his overthrow; rather it left a growing tension between traditional royal absolutism allied to Lutheranism and the new enlightened despotism that soon bordered on antagonism. If all Struensee's detractors appealed to the king to counter impiety and irreligion many also demanded that the king steer Denmark–Norway toward genuinely needed reforms rather than more traditional, distinctively Danish values.[97] Consequently, many changes were retained in part and, in the longer run, after a period of quiet retrenchment, during the 1780s the process of reform resumed, albeit now on a more stable and permanent basis as well as more moderate lines.

The pamphlet *Til Kongen* [To the King] (Copenhagen, 1772), by Peter Frederik Suhm (1728–98), notably contributed to the pressure for resumed but modified reform. A well-known critic, journalist, and historian residing in Norway in the 1760s, he had edited a critical journal at Trondheim, the *Trondheimske Samlinger* [Trondheim Collections] during 1761–5. A central figure of the Danish–Norwegian moderate Enlightenment, Suhm denounced Struensee for attacking religion and virtue, and associating only with foreigners, wanting a more traditional style of monarchy serviced by native Danes and Norwegians;[98] his forceful intervention partly stemmed from conservative, patriotic reaction against unacceptable foreign radicalism, yet his pamphlet, a text still referred to in Germany in the late 1780s, also expressed far-reaching criticism of absolutism, appealing for constitutionalism and

[96] Wollstonecraft, *Letters Written during a Short Residence*, Letters III and XIV.
[97] Munck, "Danish Reformers," 250; Grashoff, *Johann Friedrich Struensee*, 89–90, 93.
[98] Mitchell, "Age of Enlightenment," 153.

much else. Not least, Suhm demanded Struensee's freedom of the press be retained and wanted the monarchy to better curb ministerial corruption.[99] He urged the monarch to change his cultural habits, speak Danish, and create a court with a more "national" flavor, employing responsible, dutiful, and conscientious ministers and administrators. An admirer of Holberg, Suhm had long sought to expand the stock of good Danish–Norwegian books and theater, and widen the habit of reading among the populace. Convinced a better-read public would help strengthen the common good, in 1775 he opened his large private library to the Copenhagen public on a regular basis.[100]

Denmark's nobility and church recovered some ground in 1772. Coming under the control of a group of aristocratic Lutheran traditionalists surrounding the royal stepmother, Juliane Marie (1729–96), the court also encouraged the chauvinistic tone of some of the post-1772 reaction against the German and French cultural presence, and use of the German and French languages in public life. Ove Høegh Guldberg (1731–1808), the presiding figure in Danish political life after Struensee's removal, was virtual "prime minister," from 1772 until 1784, but presided in a far less energetic manner than Struensee. A historian and professor, he was a commoner, son of a modest Jutland merchant, who took scrupulous care to defend aristocratic and ecclesiastical privilege, while courting wider popularity by encouraging popular reviling of Struensee. In 1776, the court produced a law restricting major state appointments to natives of the kingdom in terms that seemed absurd to some enlightened visitors, including the Venezuelan *Libertador*, Miranda, who visited in 1787.[101] Guldberg approved the new xenophobic impulse, encouraged *Danskhed* (Danishness), and firmly backed Lutheran religious authority;[102] but since Denmark–Norway was a multiple monarchy including German-speaking Schlewig-Holstein, it was by no means only foreigners who scorned the changes.

During the 1770s, the effort to combine moderate Enlightenment with reaction generated irresolvable tension but had a stimulating effect on the intellectual and literary scene. For the Danish–Norwegian stage, the 1770s and 1780s were a golden age with dozens of plays by famous authors translated from German, French, and English being published and performed in Danish.[103] Some of the material proved controversial, though, and none more so than Lessing's dramas, which soon acquired an unrivalled status not just as plays but a prophetic voice of special appeal to aspiring social critics and reformers. By 1775, Lessing's *Emilia Galotti* was performed no less than fifty-four times in Denmark, including five times at Copenhagen's court theater.[104] However, publication of the Reimarus *Fragmente* in the late 1770s awakened the public to the radical tendency lurking within Lessing's *oeuvre*, suddenly bringing his ballooning

[99] Peter Suhm, *Til Kongen overleverer Suhm et Brev* (n.p., 1771), 3, 6; Wekhrlin, *Graue Ungeheuer* vi (1786), 113.
[100] Mitchell, "Age of Enlightenment," 152.
[101] Barton, *Northern Arcadia*, 8, 39.
[102] Munck, "Danish Reformers," 252; Sharpe, "Scandinavia," 24.
[103] Mitchell, "Age of Enlightenment," 165.
[104] Mitchell, "Age of Enlightenment," 161–2; Bohnen, "Lessing und Dänemark," 306.

Danish reputation under acute pressure. In Scandinavia, there was a marked proclivity to equate the contents of the vehemently anti-Christian Reimarus *Fragmente* with Lessing's own views, causing a mounting backlash against his theatrical *oeuvre*,[105] reaction led by the "Danish Goeze," the theologian H. Chr. Schønheyder, one of Lessing's "silly fools" who did not shrink from mobilizing political contacts at court to vilify him as a foe of Christianity,[106] and try to get him dismissed from his librarianship at Wolfenbüttel. Lessing's polemical writings against Goeze and other theological opponents, already banned in several German states, were suppressed also in Denmark–Norway, which further contributed—until the coup of 1784—to Denmark's faring badly compared with Sweden–Finland, on Wekhrlin's swingeing 1779 "philosophical map of Europe."[107]

The drive against Struensee's legacy, Lessing, and Spinozism inevitably entangled *Nathan der Weise*, Lessing's classic play which could be easily construed as an extension of Lessing's theological-polemical writings. In 1779, Schønheyder urged the Danish Literary Society, *Det danske Litteraturselskab*, to offer a prize for the best refutation of the *Parable of the Three Rings*, a blatantly Spinozist theme attracting widespread Danish and Swedish condemnation. They succeeded in bringing this quintessential Enlightenment play under a general ban throughout Scandinavia. But the intolerance of the broad public at the same time also ensured Lessing important recruits for his radical conception of toleration and religion, especially among students and professors, so that an increasing number now resented the repression and attitudes of the ordinary public led by the clergy. Knud Lyne Rahbeck (1760–1830), editor of *Minerva*, the pre-eminent Danish periodical of the later 1780s and 1790s, a well-known republican-leaning literary figure, began translating *Nathan der Weise* into Danish in the early 1780s but abandoned the project on realizing the impossibility of staging it at the time. The controversy surrounding Lessing reflected post-1772 Scandinavian conservative reaction, but also reinforced the polarizing tendency in society, creating a rift over Lessing's significance which persisted into the early nineteenth century. The first performance of *Nathan* in Danish was delayed until 1799.[108]

Danish reaction and retrenchment were dominant themes for over a decade from 1772, as was true in some degree also of Sweden–Finland, where weariness with the Riksdag's ascendancy, noble sway, and government corruption helped prepare the ground for the absolutist "revolution" of that year. Commencing with the revolt of the garrison at Helsinki's Sveaborg, the largest and costliest fortress in eighteenth-century Europe, Gustav's conspiracy gained him first absolute control of Finland, then Sweden. He triumphantly suspended the constitution of the "Age of Liberty" and restored unrestricted monarchy. With Gustav's successful monarchical-aristocratic *coup d'état* of August 1772 following hard on the heels of Struensee's overthrow, all

[105] Bohnen, "Lessing und Dänemark," 309.
[106] Bohnen, "Lessing und Dänemark," 305–14, here p. 308; Yasukata, *Lessing's Philosophy of Religion*, 54.
[107] Wekhrlin, *Chronologen*, 8; Bohnen, "Lessing und Dänemark," 309.
[108] Bohnen, "Lessing und Dänemark," 307; Israel, "Toward the Nordic Model," 38–40.

Scandinavia again seemingly conformed to the familiar European monarchical, ecclesiastical, and courtly aristocratic mold. Convening the Riksdag was now at the king's sole discretion. If Denmark's new ruling faction was a mix of moderates and reactionaries, Gustav, a professed disciple of Voltaire, proudly championed enlightened despotism.[109] He prayed to God daily, he assured Voltaire a few months before the coup, to prolong the latter's days, "so precious to all humanity" was he, and "so useful to the progress of reason and true philosophy."[110] Initially, Gustav professed to favor press freedom and approve of the American Revolution. But this quickly changed: he opposed the American cause from the late 1770s and after a few years cut back Swedish liberty of the press substantially.[111] Raynals' *Histoire philosophique* was among the key radical texts banned. Sweden's output of books, pamphlets, and periodicals declined from the late 1770s, just as in Denmark until 1784.[112]

Gustav's coup was concerted by army officers. But he acted with the support of much of the Swedish population—besides that of Voltaire and d'Alembert, who were eager to show Europe's kings they were loyal royalists not to be confused with Diderot, d'Holbach, and their ilk. Voltaire dubbed Gustav's coup "la belle revolution de Suede," congratulating all concerned on the "prudence" and "firmness" with which the monarch had seized the reins of power, adding enthusiastically that the event "donne envie de vivre."[113] Veneration for monarchy in Sweden–Finland ran deep. Restoring full princely control and court dominance, as in Holland in 1747–8, was rapturously greeted by ordinary folk. But it was endorsed also by much of the nobility and even the professorate, including Linnaeus.[114] A new constitution, drawn up by Gustav and his advisors, praised by Filangieri as part of a "universal revolution in the constitution of government," supposedly restored a perfectly balanced "mixed government" regime with power shared between king, council, and estates.[115] Sweden's monarch presented his rule as a justified return to a more balanced constitution, with noble privilege and the Riksdag remaining significant elements but with the people now better protected against aristocratic exploitation.[116] Only Mably loudly condemned Gustav's coup, deploring the loss of Sweden's "age of liberty."[117]

Gustav reigned as absolute king of Sweden–Finland for twenty years (1772–92), tightening his grip, weakening the nobility as an independent force in society, and ending their monopoly of high office. He further reduced the Rikstag's role with his emergency "Act of Security" of February 1789. But he took good care to leave the nobility's social ascendancy intact. In his way, Gustav was sincere in becoming a true

[109] Roberts, *Age of Liberty*, 183.

[110] Gustav III to Voltaire, Stockholm, 10 Jan. 1772, in Voltaire, *Correspondence* xxxviii. 212.

[111] Nyman, *Indragningsmakt*, 259.

[112] Jarrick, *Back to Modern Reason*, 90; Hallberg, "Translation on Trial," 6.

[113] Voltaire to Frederick, landgrave of Hesse-Cassel, 15 Sept. 1772, in Voltaire, *Correspondence* xxxix. 63; Wright, *Classical Republican*, 162.

[114] Koerner, *Linnaeus*, 31; Mastellone, "Italian Enlightenment and the Swedish Constitution," 115.

[115] Filangieri, *Scienza* I. 144. [116] Wolff, *Noble Conceptions*, 123.

[117] Wright, *Classical Republican*, 162–3, 195.

"enlightened despot." Many of the Riksdag's projected reforms of the 1769–72 period were actually implemented in the early years of the new king's reign.[118] Among his early measures was a law, emulating that of the Danes, abolishing judicial torture. He introduced a formal religious toleration so that his reign marked the founding of Sweden's Jewish, Catholic, and Moravian communities. With a nod to the French *économistes*, he lowered import duties and freed the grain trade of most restrictions. At the same time, though, he reversed other liberalizing tendencies. "It was not only political liberty," remarks one historian, "that fell a victim" to Gustav's coup, so did all prospect of opposing noble dominance of society and ending serfdom.[119] In fact, a fundamental contradiction infused the 1772 monarchical restoration in Sweden: for while Gustav's coup was popular with Stockholm's artisans and servants, with a people weary of a constitution bolstering aristocratic domination of society and control of its institutions, restoration of full monarchy relied on the support of many nobles who, with a better-informed realism, expected the revived monarchy to end their internal splits, expand the armed forces, and reinforce noble domination of society and culture.[120] Since this is exactly what it did, new tensions began to surface.

For a time, ostentatious display and lavish patronage of the arts helped paper over the cracks. Gustav encouraged scientific research, penal reform, economic innovations, and the establishment of new literary and scholarly institutions like the *Svenska Academien*, the Swedish Academy of Belles-Lettres, founded in 1786, primarily a device for furthering the ascendancy of French literature and fashion in Sweden–Finland. An eager collector, impatient to display the ancient sculptures and paintings he had acquired in Italy,[121] Gustav also prepared the way for the Stockholm Kungliga Museet (The Royal Museum), though it was not formally inaugurated until the next reign, in November 1792. For these and like measures, the monarch received international approbation. Until the early 1780s, Sweden was rated very highly as an "enlightened despotism" on what the German radical journalist Wilhelm Ludwig Wekhrlin (1739–92) called the "philosophical map of Europe" and, once again, higher than Denmark, especially for state-supported science, research institutes, and industrial projects.[122] During the 1770s, although general publishing contracted, the founding of new erudite and scientific journals and periodicals in Sweden–Finland proceeded noticeably faster than in the 1760s.[123] But though an ardent patron of court science, arts, and architecture, Gustav did little to expand education and literacy more generally or reverse the universities' decline. Uppsala in the 1770s and 1780s continued withering in student numbers and international prestige, proving a distinct disappointment to foreign visitors venerating Linnaeus and expecting an impressive memorial to his legacy.[124]

118 Roberts, *Age of Liberty*, 207; Jarrick, *Back to Modern Reason*, 24, 146–7.
119 Roberts, *Age of Liberty*, 207.
120 Kirby, *Northern Europe*, 385.
121 Olausson and Sõderlind, "Nationalmuseum," 198–9.
122 Wekhrlin, *Chronologen* I (1779), 9.
123 Hirschfeldt, "Freedom of Speech," 56.
124 Barton, *Northern Arcadia*, 36–7.

The most striking difference between Danish and Swedish developments after 1772 was that where Denmark passed from a reactionary phase to a progressive one, especially from the mid-1780s, Sweden moved emphatically in the reverse direction. From the mid-1780s, Gustav became increasingly despotic, militaristic, reactionary, and geared to personal glorification, heightening the negative impact his rule exerted from the outset on press freedom, publishing, and reading. Total book production fell from 864 titles in 1772 to only 378 in 1773, the decline continuing uninterruptedly in subsequent years, to 264 titles by 1777.[125] The revised Swedish press law of 26 April 1774 professed to embrace the principle of press freedom as a socially useful institution and, in theory, a residual freedom of expression persisted (albeit less than in Denmark–Norway), but from the later 1780s additional restrictions were introduced, and royal control grew increasingly intrusive, provoking growing opposition, not least from one of Sweden's leading literary personalities, its foremost opposition-minded intellectual, Thomas Thorild (1759–1808). In response, several publications and journals were suppressed for using "revolutionary" language or sounding anti-monarchical. A few being made examples of sufficed to cause publishers and printers to exercise greatly increased self-censorship; publication rates fell further From December 1791, the restrictions included a comprehensive ban on publishing reports of the French Revolution.[126]

8.4. SCANDINAVIA'S GRADUAL REVOLUTION (1784–1820)

The thirteen-year reactionary phase in Denmark–Norway ended with a palace coup in April 1784, orchestrated by counts Bernstorff and Reventlow, which removed the now much hated Queen Mother from the scene and sidelined Guldberg (assigned a post as a provincial governor). Power was nominally transferred to the 16-year-old crown prince, Frederik, standing in for the now hopelessly deranged king. But Bernstorff, effectively chief minister until his death in 1797, and "universally celebrated for his abilities and virtue," according to Mary Wollstonecraft,[127] became the real power behind the throne. With Count Christian Ditlev Reventlow (1748–1827), he guided the country's new course. This mid-1780s victory of the Danish reformers brought in its wake some of the most far-reaching reforms achieved by enlightened despotism in Europe before 1800. A moderate press freedom was restored. Law reform resumed; executions subsequently took place only for the crime of murder and the entire penal code began to look mild by comparison with that then prevailing in Britain and elsewhere. Rather paradoxically, what evolved into Europe's most

[125] Nyman, *Indragningsmakt*, 281; Barton, *Northern Arcadia*, 91.

[126] Thorild, *Om den almindelige forstands frihed*, 56; Nyman, *Indragningsmakt*, 24, 59, 85, 180, 278–9; Wolff, *Noble Conceptions*, 118; Hirschfeldt, "Freedom of Speech," 56, 60.

[127] Wollstonecraft, *Letters Written during a Short Residence*, Letter VII; Jones, *Agricultural Enlightenment*, 150.

spectacular non-violent revolution of the era culminated during the 1790s just when most states were pushing reform onto the back burner: it produced a wave of agricultural improvements and innovation, and land reform entailing introduction of many new techniques and products borrowed from Britain and elsewhere. The most important feature was the drive to abolish manorial obligations and labor services.[128]

Reventlow had earlier been experimenting with commuting labor services and changing the system on his inherited estates in Lolland. It had become a commonplace among reformers as well as enlightened foreign visitors that under modern conditions Danish serfdom was counter-productive, not least for the landowner since the best, most fertile, and potentially productive areas were often also the most serf-ridden and poverty-stricken. The continuing prevalence of manorial ties and obligations on the peasantry had thus become a major issue for those seeking to foster economic prosperity and growth. Despite Struensee's efforts, forms of feudal obligation still widely predominated, having been reaffirmed and strengthened by the *stavnsbånd*, or Adscription Law, of 1733, a measure aimed at tying male peasants of military age to their registered districts but which effectively bound them from their fourth to their fortieth year to the manors where they were raised, supposedly for the advantage of their noble landlords. By the 1780s, in the wake of the American Revolution, such feudal servitude was generally deemed degrading and enervating for the kingdom as a whole, an "unfortunate" mark of "former preponderancy and injustice," as one traveller called it, that urgently needed removing. Despite considerable noble resistance, the *Store Landbokommission* [Great Agrarian Commission] chaired by Reventlow, set up in August 1786, on 20 June 1788 decreed the general abolition of the *stavnsbånd* and residence obligations for all peasants under 14 and over 36 immediately, with a twelve-year limit for the rest so that all feudal dues would lapse definitively from 1800. The military conscription system had to be completely reorganized simultaneously. Further measures, in 1791 and subsequently, provided for renegotiation of all remaining labor dues, and conversion of tenancies in freehold farms, on the basis of conversion to annual payments arbitrated by the crown, and here too rapid progress was achieved. Having also initiated the setting up of a land credit bank, in 1786, Reventlow used it to hasten emancipation from feudal dues by helping peasants purchase their own freehold plots.[129]

In 1792, Denmark joined France to become one of the first two European nations to announce their intention to suppress the slave trade to their Caribbean colonies, with provisions to phase it out over the next ten years.[130] The 1788–92 reforms marked a significant broadening of the social application of Europe's Enlightenment. Where formerly Danish peasants had been "lethargic, characterless, downtrodden, and dehumanized," according to observers, by the 1790s, amid rapid changes, they

[128] Jones, *Agricultural Enlightenment*, 147–54.
[129] Munck, "Danish Reformers," 257–8; Jones, *Agricultural Enlightenment*, 150–1.
[130] Munck, "Danish Reformers," 259.

were now reportedly more "cheerful, industrious and active."[131] They were visibly drawing closer to their more fortunate Norwegian counterparts. "Norwegians appear to me," commented Wollstonecraft during her Scandinavian tour, "to be the most free community I have ever observed."[132] Too rosy a picture should not be drawn of the changes, as these also eliminated large areas of Danish common grazing land, village commons, reducing many previously semi-independent cottagers to landless status as paid laborers on landed estates, or for more substantial peasant farmers. The Danish and Swedish "gradual revolutions" of 1784–1820 were both essentially moderate Enlightenment reform programs steered through by reforming aristocrats. Although of far-reaching and enduring significance, the Danish reforms of 1788–92 were still "moderate Enlightenment" in character being essentially a state arbitrated compromise between the aristocracy and the peasantry.[133] But Enlightenment had now become part of the fabric of state and society to a greater extent than almost anywhere else, which of itself meant accommodating a strengthened radical "equal rights" tendency.

But the changes inevitably meant intensifying the battle between the conflicting Enlightenment wings. As society changed, newspapers, books, pamphlets, and the theater increasingly became the central sphere of clashing philosophies and lively public debate. In both monarchies, a court-sponsored Enlightenment, based on a moderate reform agenda seeking a "mixed government" balanced constitution on Montesquieuan lines, law reform, science based on Newtonianism and "argument from design," and resolving mounting rural unrest, had consolidated a largely uncontested predominance over government and law, that was fiercely contested, however, by fringe intellectual networks associated with literature, science, and higher education. The underlying challenge of unresolved social and cultural problems intensified as the various literary-philosophical controversies and quarrels over intrusive foreign influence demonstrate. Responding to criticism and unrest, the growing political and intellectual repression in Sweden–Finland was already in full swing by 1788—and hence not a reaction to the French Revolution per se, though it did intensify further after 1790, and still more between 1800 and the coup of 1809.

Consequently, from 1784 to 1809, Denmark–Norway again eclipsed Sweden as much the freer context, and Sweden–Finland was again viewed internationally as the more repressed land. Press restrictions throughout the revolutionary era remained markedly stricter in Sweden than in Denmark. As a result, Copenhagen became a crucial cultural channel linking the intelligentsias of Denmark–Norway and Sweden–Finland, the headquarters of networks of opponents of the restored Swedish monarchy striving to revive Sweden's now emasculated freedoms. During the later 1780s and early 1790s, Denmark emerged too as chief provider to Scandinavia (and

[131] Barton, *Northern Arcadia*, 105–6; Israel, "Toward the Nordic Model," 37.

[132] Wollstonecraft, *Letters Written during a Short Residence*, Letter VII; Moseng et al., *Norske Historie*, 284–5.

[133] Munck, "Danish Reformers," 260–1.

Germany) of German translations of French and English radical literature, including Paine's *The Rights of Man*. Stringently banned in Germany, Paine's text appeared in German at Copenhagen, in 1793, at the very moment the Swedish version, and French versions of it, were banned in Sweden.[134] Even so, compared to Germany, Italy, Ireland, and even Britain, the position in Scandinavia, even if especially Denmark–Norway, remained relatively benign and tolerant and would soon become more so.

By the 1780s, it was more evident in Scandinavia than perhaps anywhere else in the Western world that the Enlightenment was transforming the face of society by eroding traditional social hierarchy. Copenhagen, Stockholm, and Helsinki were all surrounded by fortifications and built on waterways and small islands, giving them, as also St. Petersburg, a more planned, organized look than London or Paris, cities which had already been large centers long before 1700. William Coxe (1748–1828), an Anglican divine and Cambridge don who traveled widely in northern Europe as tutor to young English nobles, compared Copenhagen, which he visited in 1779 and 1784, with the Russian capital by noting that while the latter was more magnificent in imperial and aristocratic palaces, the Danish capital "does not display that striking contrast of meanness and magnificence [found in Petersburg], but in general exhibits a more equable and uniform appearance."[135] The devastation caused by the burning down of Christiansborg Palace and much of Copenhagen city center with the great fires of 1794 and 1795 left visitors, Wollstonecraft among them, horrified; but recovery was remarkably rapid. An English visitor in 1799 found Copenhagen "risen with renovated splendor from her ashes; a great improvement being visible in the streets, and many magnificent houses substituted in place of antiquated mansions, that wanted repair and had been burned."[136]

Greater press freedom assured Copenhagen's position as the headquarters of political opposition and critical thinking throughout Scandinavia. But with many underlying tensions evident in Scandinavia where absolutism confronted a recently defeated but still dogged constitutional tradition—where the works of Paine, Volney, and Thorild in the vernacular were banned in Sweden—both crowns faced tenacious opposition from several quarters. The nobility felt caught between conflicting rural models, a besieged and illogical coexistence of serfdom with a largely free but resentful Swedish (and Norwegian) peasantry, while the Lutheran Church faced a ceaseless upsurge of impiety, libertinism, and skepticism among nobles and academics. In Norway, a country with few noble estates mostly "divided into small farms which belong to the cultivator," as Wollstonecraft put it, but where lingering resentment against noble domination was acute in some areas, a sporadic peasant rebellion broke out in October 1786. Initially, Reventlow and Prince Frederik responded positively to the grievances presented by Christian Jensen Lofthuus (1750–97), a Norwegian proprietor and farmer of illegitimate birth whose father

[134] Munck, "Troubled Reception," 173; Åhlén, *Censur och tryckfrihet*, 104.
[135] Barton, *Northern Arcadia*, 24. [136] Barton, *Northern Arcadia*, 000.

had been of high social status but who had become a foe of nobility and social hierarchy. In early 1786 Lofthuus had secured two meetings with the prince. But after the October 1786 rising, the crown began rebuffing Lofthuus's complaints and petitions and, from 1789, with the French Revolution looming ever more as a menacing spectacle, became increasingly guarded. By 1792, as the general situation in Europe grew more confrontational, a sense of crisis gripped both courts, and both opted for outright repression. Lofthuus was sentenced to penal servitude for life in Akershus Fortress in Christiania (Oslo) where he died in 1797. There were innumerable signs, observed Wollstonecraft, that the "French Revolution has not only rendered all the crown heads more cautious, but has so decreased everywhere (excepting among themselves) respect for the nobility, that the peasantry have not only lost their blind reverence for their seigniors, but complain in manly style of oppressions which before they did not think of denominating such, because they were taught to consider themselves as a different order of beings. And perhaps, the efforts which the aristocracy are making here, as well as in every part of Europe to secure their sway, will be the most effectual mode of undermining it."[137]

A dramatic full-scale crisis erupted with the assassination of Sweden's monarch. Gustav had received repeated warnings of serious "fermentation" among the population during the late 1780s, that the "populace here in Stockholm is said to be, and is, agitated."[138] He responded by intensifying repression, which only proved further that Gustav was flagrantly violating his own 1772 constitution. On 16 March 1792, he was shot, and grievously wounded, at a masked ball. He died twelve days later convinced Sweden was falling victim to seditious "republicans" with French revolutionary ideas.[139] The king's assassination was actually planned by a group of some eighty aristocrats, many with narrow, self-seeking class motives. But several were actually authentic democratic republicans. The man who fired the fatal bullet, an officer named Jacob Johan Anckarström (1762–92), a former court page who had come to detest courts and monarchy, had joined the conspiracy at least partly from disgust over Gustav's plans to support Louis XVI against the French Revolution. He genuinely believed Gustav had become the "enemy of the realm" and that he was sacrificing himself for the people's "happiness."[140] Stripped of his aristocratic privileges and estates, Anckarström was publicly flogged, before being beheaded and having his corpse quartered.

Nine months later, in December 1792, the leading light of Sweden's literary intelligentsia, Thorild, "Sweden's Tom Paine," an out-and-out radical, followed up his second edition of Peter Forsskål's *Tankar*, issued earlier that year, with his pamphlet (which provoked a considerable political scandal) *On Everyone's Liberty of Understanding, presented to the Swedish Regent and Nation*, denouncing the suppression of Paine. Since 1779, when only 21, Thorild had been steeped in d'Holbach's

[137] Wollstonecraft, *Letters Written during a Short Residence*, Letter III.
[138] Jarrick, *Back to Modern Reason*, 28–30. [139] Wolff, *Noble Conceptions*, 119.
[140] Wolff, *Noble Conceptions*, 120.

Système de la nature, and subsequently Spinoza. Championing one-substance monist philosophy, he also demanded sweeping social and political renewal on the basis of a fiercely anti-aristocratic and anti-hierarchical agenda.[141] Securing the people's happiness, contends his 1792 pamphlet, denouncing monarchy, aristocratic oppression, and the clergy,[142] means embracing democratic republicanism. By the time Gustav IV's officials seized the stocks of this "incendiary text," several thousand had already been distributed. The crown did prevent Thorild's subsequent pamphlet lambasting royal press restrictions from appearing in Sweden, but it appeared nevertheless, in 1793, at Copenhagen, in Danish.[143]

Notorious at Uppsala for his undisguised Spinozism, antipathy to Montesquieu's monarchism and relativism, and his democratic leanings, Thorild was dragged into court in Stockholm, on 8 January 1793. But to the dismay of the authorities, a noisy crowd forced their way in, demanding to witness the proceedings. Every time Thorild spoke, the crowd cheered. When he was dragged away, a noisy demonstration erupted with loud shouts of "Long Live Thorild! Long Live Liberty!" Troops had to be deployed around the courthouse and in central Stockholm to silence the "badly intentioned." The capital's garrison was reinforced, guard patrols doubled, and a curfew imposed on inns and taverns from nine in the evening.[144] Condemned for sedition, Thorild was banished from Sweden in perpetuity; he never returned, spending the remainder of his life in northern Germany, at Greifswald, where the painter Caspar David Friedrich was among his pupils.

The new Swedish monarch, Gustav IV Adolf (1792–1809), proceeded with greater caution and less severity than his father, trying again to rally the people behind the crown. In July 1792, he introduced a new law easing the press censorship. Still, in the main, he continued his predecessor's post-1788 reactionary and repressive stance. Simmering domestic discontent, growing alienation of the Finnish elite, and reimposition of the earlier eased restrictions on the press and freedom of expression during the period 1800–9, followed by his ill-advised and disastrous war against Russia during 1808–9, led to the definitive loss of Finland, chronic state indebtedness, and a renewed crisis which patently weakened the monarchy. This was followed by a revolutionary intervention by the Riksdag, Gustav's deposition and the end of absolute monarchy, this time definitively, in March 1809.[145] The coup permanently dethroned the royal dynasty, excluding all his heirs from the royal succession. At the time, Denmark–Norway and Sweden were at war, and the officers who moved troops to Stockholm to effect the coup acted in collusion with subversive fellow officers in Norway, who were simultaneously rebelling against Copenhagen. Among the rebels'

[141] Arvidson, *Thorild*, 73–89; Jarrick, *Back to Modern Reason*, 6.

[142] Cramer to Klopstock, Kiel, 22 Feb. 1793, in Klopstock, *Werke* VIII. 1; Åhlén, *Censur och Tryckfrihet*, 93, 100, 104; Goldberg, "Who was Peter Forsskål?," 21.

[143] Thorild, *Om den almindelige forstands frihed*, title-page.

[144] Girey-Dupré, *Patriote français* 1269 (1 Feb. 1793), 129; [Feller], *Journal historique et littéraire*, 1 Feb. 1793, 195–6; Forster, *Sämtliche Schriften* x. 289, 388; Israel, *Revolutionary Ideas*, 335–6.

[145] Hirschfeldt, "Freedom of Speech," 56, 60–1; Nordenstreng, "Freedom of Speech in Finland," 73–5.

aims was a scheme for the union of Sweden and Norway which the Norwegian dissidents helped promote even though this was far from conforming to the general sentiment of Norway's population.[146] Gustav IV Adolf, expelled from Sweden, was replaced with an aged and heirless uncle, Duke Carl. The heavily revised new Swedish constitution ensured full control over taxation, the treasury, and the national bank by the Rikstag.[147] To protect individual liberty, the constitution also provided, innovatively, for an "ombudsman," an independent official authorized to keep all levels of government and administration under surveillance in the public interest. Under a fresh press law of 1810, supplemented by a second measure in 1812, it became a cornerstone of the new Swedish constitution that all censorship of books and other printed matter prior to publication was forever abolished.[148]

Royal collections and the royal museum in Stockholm were detached from the court and assumed the character of a national, public collection permanently open to the public, under the care of professional curators, though this profound organizational transition was only fully completed in 1845 when, after years of discussion, the Riksdag finally decided to construct a new, much larger museum building to house the National Museum's now vast collections.[149] Briefly, Sweden entered the orbit of Napoleonic France, receiving Western Pomerania and the Isle of Rügen back from Napoleon, and agreeing to form part of the Continental System against Britain and the reformed European state system alongside other Napoleonic satellite states. To secure the succession, in 1810, the Riksdag elected and invited one of Napoleon's ablest and most regal-looking field marshals, Count Jean-Baptiste Bernadotte (1763–1844), to become Sweden's crown prince, under the title Prince Karl Johan. He later succeeded to the throne, reigning from 1818 in Sweden and Norway as King Karl XIV Johan.[150]

The French founder of the present Swedish royal dynasty, a lawyer's son and already a revolutionary colonel by 1792, Bernadotte's career, despite spending much of it in Napoleon's shadow, was remarkable. Once considered Bonaparte's militarily most obvious and gifted French rival, during the 1796 campaigns, he suffered multiple defeats at Austrian hands, in Germany, whilst Napoleon won his stunning successes in Italy. In 1797, during the coup of Fructidor, Bernadotte had hesitated to support the conspirators whereas Bonaparte, with whom his personal relations were always tense, did not, strengthening the then prevalent, but incorrect, impression that Napoleon's republican credentials surpassed Bernadotte's.[151] Later a decidedly different "republican" myth about the two began to circulate. Where the victorious "Army of Italy" under Bonaparte in 1796–8 was supposedly corrupted by pillage and ambition, Bernadotte's troops, according to Germaine de Staël at least,

146 Kaartvedt, "Some Reflections," 51.
147 Barton, *Scandinavia*, 286–90; Sjöström, *Karl XIV Johan*, 7.
148 Åhlen, *Censur och tryckfrihet*, 13; Hirschfeldt, "Freedom of Speech," 60–1.
149 Olausson and Sõderlind, "Nationalmuseum," 209, 211 n. 47.
150 Booth, *Almost Nearly Perfect People*, 355.
151 Dwyer, *Napoleon*, 311; Roberts, *Napoleon the Great*, 145–7.

conserving their republican austerity far better, offered an edifying contrast to Napoleon's.[152] This later myth also fitted better with the reputation for honesty and fairness Bernadotte acquired in the Baltic region, subsequently, when posted to the Hanseatic cities. Among French generals—apart from Napoleon—who made France great between 1795 and 1812, Bernadotte alone, held de Staël, united the "qualities of a statesman and distinguished soldier." By 1798–9, relations between Napoleon and Bernadotte had cooled markedly and it seemed that Bernadotte alone remained "wholly devoted to the republican party, someone who would no more approve the subversion of the [French] Republic than would royalists subversion of the throne."[153] Napoleon's Consulate struck Bernadotte's as just a thinly disguised dictatorship; he also abhorred Bonaparte's 1801 Concordat with the papacy.[154] Despite regaining military prominence by crushing the Austrians at Austerlitz, where he won the title of "Prince of Pontecorvo," a former papal enclave, subsequently he fell into deep disgrace in Paris.

Publicly disavowing absolutism and traditional monarchy, Bernadotte staged his ceremonial entry into Stockholm on 2 November 1810. Abjuring Catholicism, and converting to Lutheranism, on 5 November, he vowed to uphold Sweden's constitution and rule together with the Riksdag. He at once confirmed the new freedom of the press law, recasting it, in 1812, in a form that then remained in force until 1949![155] The consequence was a notable surge in periodical and book publications in Sweden.[156] When de Staël came to visit Sweden, in September 1812, she eagerly renewed the alliance she had with him around 1802 when she had first learnt to trust his libertarian and republican sentiments. She spent eight months in Stockholm and helped plant in Bernadotte's mind the idea that he could perhaps become a "new William III," a compromise constitutional monarch for France, a kind of half-way house between the republican Revolution and threatened return of the Bourbons. She became Bernadotte's behind-the-scenes European publicity agent; in return, he found positions for her sons, Auguste and Albert, the first in his diplomatic service, the second in the Swedish Hussars.[157]

Although Sweden, like Denmark–Norway, was expected to remain allied to France, following the brutal British bombardment of Copenhagen, in 1807,[158] when the Grande Armée began preparing to invade Russia, in 1812, Bernadotte prevaricated. Disliking the pressure to enforce the anti-British embargo, and more interested in annexing Norway than Finland, which Napoleon offered, Bernadotte eventually refused, out of "hatred for tyranny," commented De Staël whom a furious Bonaparte blamed for the "corruption of Bernadotte."[159] Instead, the former republican general

[152] De Staël, *Considerations*, 393, 405.
[153] De Staël, *Considerations*, 424, 428; Palmer, *Bernadotte*, 94, 96–7; Höjer, *Bernadotte*, 195–6, 210.
[154] Winegarten, *Germaine de Staël*, 146; Palmer, *Bernadotte*, 106, 111.
[155] Nyman, *Indragningsmakt*, 253–6, 262, 288.
[156] Nyman, *Indragningsmakt*, 263, 276, 281, 287–90.
[157] Winegarten, *Germaine de Staël*, 234–5.
[158] Schroeder, *Transformation*, 429.
[159] Jordan, *Napoleon and the Revolution*, 5, 51, 254; Palmer, *Bernadotte*, 186; Barton, *Scandinavia*, 317.

allied with Czar Alexander. Under the terms of the Russo-Swedish alliance of April 1812, negotiated in the Finnish university town of Åbo (Turku), in exchange for Bernadotte's joining offensive operations against Napoleon, Norway was transferred to Sweden. By leading Sweden into the anti-Napoleonic coalition, Bernadotte secured a prominent place among the Allies' military leaders and recast Scandinavia politically.

Following Napoleon's defeat at the vast battle of Leipzig (October 1813), to which the Swedish army, led by Bernadotte, crucially contributed, Bernadotte reached the peak of his career. He now had his chance to match, or even surpass, Napoleon and his brothers among early nineteenth-century prominent Enlightenment reformers. For several months, until April 1814, some talked of making him constitutional monarch of France, guarantor of a continuing moderate Enlightenment in France, as well as Sweden, an "enlightened" alternative to the Austrian and British preference for full-scale Bourbon restoration. Bernadotte tried to make the idea palatable to the Czar and it appealed to those loathing Napoleon but lacking stomach for a Bourbon return. Benjamin Constant, Europe's leading intellectual adversary of Napoleon's "vast prison" [Europe], strove to promote Bernadotte's prospects of becoming a new "William III" ready to transform France, as the Williamites had Britain and Ireland with the Glorious Revolution of 1688–9.[160] Constant traveled to Hanover to offer his services to Bernadotte while completing his *De l'esprit de la conquête et de la usurpation*, published at Hanover in January 1814, a blistering attack on Napoleon, whose tyranny he styled the heir to the Montagnard legacy of demagogy, and political corruption, and linked to Rousseau's "general will" viewed as the idea that had perverted the Revolution and destroyed individual liberty. In particular Napoleon, like Robespierre before him, had authorized everyone in society to spy on and interfere with everyone else.[161] Between bogus political legitimacy counterfeited "in England by Cromwell and in France by Bonaparte" and Sweden's crown prince "called to the throne by the wish of a people," Constant perceived a mighty contrast.[162] William of Orange's revolt against the Spanish crown in 1572, and William III being "invited" to be king of England in 1688, proved, held Constant, that "no authority which is established by national will can be suspected of usurpation" and that the "people know perfectly well when they are governed by a usurper."[163]

Bernadotte, returning to Sweden in March 1814, capitalized on his reputation as an enlightened reformer and constitutionalist first by encouraging the mounting unrest in Norway, where the movement to dissolve the union with Denmark was gaining momentum.[164] Outraged by the terms of Sweden's entry into the Allied coalition, Denmark, in the spring of 1813, had renewed its alliance with Napoleon, and now had to pay the price—the splitting of Norway from Denmark and eventual transfer to

[160] Constant, *Spirit of Conquest*, 101, 158; Winegarten, *Germaine de Staël*, 242–3; Fontana, *Benjamin Constant*, pp. xii, xiv.
[161] Fontana, "Introduction," 11–12, 35; Wood, "Benjamin Constant," 13; Vincent, *Benjamin Constant*, 164.
[162] Constant, *Spirit of Conquest*, 90.
[163] Constant, *Spirit of Conquest*, 158–9.
[164] Moseng, Opsåhl, et al., *Norske Historie*, 375.

Sweden (despite the Norwegians' preference for independence).[165] When Norway's transfer by the Allies, under the terms of the Treaty of Kiel (14 January 1814), was announced, a revolt broke out in Norway in protest and defiance. But after a brief three-week war (July–August 1814) in which Bernadotte strove to minimize damage and casualties, Norway had to submit. The transfer proceeded, albeit it was less Norway's annexation to Sweden that proved historically significant than the form in which the transfer occurred. What followed was a development that dug a gaping hole in the agenda of Metternich and the Holy Alliance. For it occurred solely on the basis of a personal union via the crown and was only meaningfully effective in military and foreign policy. Otherwise, the king accepted that his power was confined to just a suspensive veto on legislation. The Norwegians had drawn up a new national constitution, finalized on 17 May 1814, using French translations of the American state constitutions and *The Federalist* as well as copies of the 1791 French constitution and the recent Cádiz constitution of 1812, to devise a particularly egalitarian form of constitutional monarchy borrowing elements from all of these, especially the 1791 French "moderate Enlightenment" constitution which Sieyès had helped shape. Opting to dramatically diverge from his fellow European monarchs, Bernadotte willingly accepted and endorsed this historic new 1814 Norwegian constitution, which, remarkably, still stands today as the second oldest surviving written constitution in the Western world after that of the United States, and Europe's sturdiest monument to compromise between radical and "moderate Enlightenment;" inspired by the American, Swiss, and Dutch revolutions as much as the French, and abolishing the principle of nobility in their land, the Norwegians had pulled off a remarkably egalitarian republican coup.[166]

Bernadotte kept his promises: the contract of union solemnized by the Riksakt of 1815 stipulated that the two realms would each retain their own separate constitution and institutional framework.[167] Not only the parliaments and constitutions, but the armies, currencies, and legal systems remained entirely separate. By accepting this schema, Bernadotte became a king reigning over two separate constitutions both exceptional when compared to the few others then current elsewhere and standing in glaring, undisguised contradiction to the Restoration ideology of the Holy Alliance and Congress of Vienna, a severe slap in the face for the reactionary values Austria, Prussia, Russia, Spain, and Britain then strove to impose on the world. In Sweden, the king could balance the Riksdag with his absolute veto; in the Norwegian assembly, emulating the 1791 French constitution, the king possessed only a "suspensive" (temporary) veto. After being tightly integrated into the Danish monarchy for 434 years, Norway was now virtually an independent country in domestic affairs, a status the new king studiously respected.[168]

[165] Aaslestad, *Place and Politics*, 295–6.

[166] Forsyth, *Reason and Revolution*, 221; Billias, *American Constitutionalism*, 143; Barton, *Scandinavia*, 343–8; Seip, "Revolution of 1848," 313–14; Nilsen, "Republican Monarchy," 39–41, 46–9.

[167] Kaartvedt, "Some Reflections," 52; Palmer, *Bernadotte*, 220, 222.

[168] Sjöström, *Karl XIV Johan*, 4.

Bernadotte gave a boost to constitutionalism in the post-1815 West and likewise displayed his disdain for the principle of aristocracy. Norwegian society differed from most of the Continent in its social composition, consisting almost entirely of free small tenant farmers with a level of de facto socio-economic egalitarianism found hardly anywhere else in Europe. Barely still extant by 1815, aristocracy in Norway, with Bernadotte's agreement, was abolished by law in 1821.[169] Bernadotte did try to delimit Norway's newly-won autonomy by exploiting ambiguities in the constitution, but his efforts to strengthen the monarch's position were firmly resisted by the Norwegian assembly (*storting*) and were soon abandoned.[170] The king contented himself with touring his dual kingdom continually initiating far-reaching projects, and evidently became genuinely popular despite the fact that he never managed to learn to speak either Swedish or Norwegian.[171]

His reign represented a decisive stage, however imperfect, toward a Western world where the purpose of government was recognized as being to promote the welfare of society as a whole on the basis of greater equality, enlightened values, and shared participation.[172] Law reform resumed, bringing Sweden's penal code into line with the more liberal Danish pattern, among other changes, with the law relating to murder and infanticide being thoroughly revised and use of the death penalty drastically cut back.[173] Bernadotte also vigorously backed efforts to emulate the earlier agrarian reforms in Denmark. Former grazing lands were enclosed, and the area of arable land expanded, while productivity, spurred by innovation, increased too. The 1811 Swedish Académie Royale d'Agriculture [Kungliga Landtbruksakademien], established as a government arm entrusted with experimenting with seeds and animals to identify the strains most suited to Sweden's harsh climate, was followed in 1813 by the establishment of economic societies [*hushållningssallskap*] in all twenty-four Swedish counties. Food production, especially output of cereals, markedly increased.[174] By the end of Bernadotte's reign, cultivated land was reported to have grown by 40 per cent in Sweden due to drainage projects, clearances, and other improvements. In some years the rise in production even provided a surplus for export. Potato production reportedly increased by five times in the twenty years 1810–30.

Admittedly, these trends went hand in hand with a rapid growth in numbers of landless laborers and unemployed; the segment subsisting on low wages and in poverty significantly increased due partly to population increase but, as in Denmark, also to consolidation of farms and peasant freeholds at the expense of small tenant farmers and village common lands. Aristocratic dominance in the traditional sense was curtailed but a new underclass of landless laborers was created. Meanwhile, several measures, notably the setting up of the Poor Relief Commission in 1839, made a start in creating the welfare net which would one day become the most

[169] Kaartvedt, "Some Reflections," 52. [170] Kaartvedt, "Some Reflections," 52–3.

[171] Sjöström, *Karl XIV Johan*, 6, 9; Alm and Johansson, *Scripts of Kingship*, 148.

[172] Palmer, *Bernadotte*, 238; Alm and Johansson, *Scripts of Kingship*, 46–7, colorplate 1.

[173] Jarrick, *Back to Modern Reason*, 11. [174] Jones, *Agricultural Enlightenment*, 141.

distinctive aspect of the "Nordic model;" but it was only due to large-scale emigration to North America in the late nineteenth century that the worrying increase in landlessness and poverty was eventually reversed.[175] It was in Scandinavia, towards the end of her life, that Mary Wollstonecraft made her prophetic remark: "England and America owe their liberty to commerce which created new species of power to undermine the feudal system. But let them beware of the consequence; the tyranny of wealth is still more galling and debasing than that of rank."[176]

By the 1830s, despite mounting problems of poverty and landlessness, there was a sense in which Scandinavia and what was then starting to be called "Scandinavianism" was beginning to create a new kind of Europe, a de-militarized society no longer dominated by crown, aristocracy, or ecclesiastical authority, or entangled in royal ambitions of acquisition and conquest. No Scandinavian state was any longer a military and territorial power outside the Scandinavian peninsula. Having won the Allies' respect at Leipzig and contrived the union of Norway and Sweden, Bernadotte switched to a policy of immovable neutrality that was to last until today. "Neutrality" in European great power rivalries, remaining at peace for the good of the people, henceforth became a cornerstone of the emerging "Nordic model." Post-1815 expansion and lifestyle improvements in Scandinavia were impressive in many areas, most of all educational reform, the very core of the Western Enlightenment. Especially expansion of secondary education was remarkable: in 1823, there were only 183 *lycées* in Sweden; by 1840, the equivalent figure was 1,400. Book production, which fell by about a quarter in the 1780s, and stagnated between 1790 and 1810, rose steeply thereafter.[177] The contraction of Sweden's universities during the later eighteenth century was vigorously reversed: Uppsala boasted 1,197 students in 1819, and Lund 600, making them, at a time when Heidelberg had only 363, Giessen 241, Marburg 190, and Halle had sunk to under 500, two of Europe's largest universities.[178]

Visiting Scandinavia in 1796, Mary Wollstonecraft, despite cutting criticism of certain aspects of Scandinavian society, did not fail to notice the signs of a general amelioration, signs already suggesting the "Nordic model" might one day evolve into something of real significance for mankind. Thankfully, the grip of intolerance and the church, she noted, had drastically weakened; the rise in "freethinking" was unmistakable. "The happiness of the people is a substantial eulogium," she notes in her VIIth Letter, "the inhabitants of Denmark and Norway are the least oppressed people of Europe. The press is free. They translate any of the French publications of the day, deliver their opinion on the subject, and discuss those it leads to with great freedom, and without fearing to displease the government."[179] During the 1848 revolutions in Europe, political reform societies sprang up and rioting briefly broke out in Stockholm in March, fueling a growing demand to finally do away with

175 Trägårdh, "Swedish Model," 571; Barton, *Scandinavia*, 326.
176 Wollstonecraft, *Letters Written during a Short Residence*, Letter XIV.
177 Jarrick, *Back to Modern Reason*, 90–1.
178 [Jullien] *Revue Encyclopédique* 2 (1819), 372.
179 Wollstonecraft, *Letters Written during a Short Residence*, Letter VII; Barton, *Northern Arcadia*, 39.

old-style Swedish representation based on estates (Nobility, Clergy, Burghers and Peasants) and replace it with Norwegian-style unicameralism based on universal male suffrage. Although conservative opponents successfully resisted then, the Swedish parliament finally abolished separate representation of estates in 1866, a time of many progressive reforms equalizing the status of religious minorities, secularizing aspects of the law including the introduction of civil marriage, and admitting women to public offices.[180] By then, the Scandinavian lands had decidedly edged ahead of the rest in turning the radical vision into a conceivable European vision.

[180] Nilsson, "Sweden 1848," 334–5.

Part II

Human Rights and Revolution (1770–1830)

9

Parallel Revolutions

America and France (1774–1793)

9.1. BREAKTHROUGH TO "MODERNITY": THE TWIN AMERICAN AND FRENCH REVOLUTIONS DOWN TO JUNE 1793

Compared to all earlier revolutions the American and French revolutions had an unprecedented international impact well beyond the geographical regions in which they occurred. This reflected the fact that they were quite different from all earlier revolutions: they "polarized along new dividing lines;" no longer rifts "between elite factions or religious groups, these were global conflicts between rival world views," that both systematically rejected the previous political, social, and cultural order.[1] Hence, they belonged to a fundamentally new category of revolution, less defined by social forces or strata than by the Enlightenment, something the emerging modern world had not witnessed before.

Both royalist opponents of the Revolution and sympathizers, looking back from the mid and late 1790s, agreed the principal reason for the French Revolution differing so markedly from anything witnessed before, was what they called "la philosophie moderne" [the modern philosophy], setting the grievances and motivations for change driving the revolutionary process within a wholly new framework of argument, rhetoric, and justification.[2] However, the competing factions, as an inherent part of their rivalry, construed "la philosophie moderne" decidedly differently. A key contrast between royalist anti-revolutionary definitions and pro-Revolution commentators, noted Pierre-Louis Roederer (1754–1835), a revolutionary leader from Metz, in his 1799 book on the topic, apart from royalist outrage at the modern philosophy's "destruction de toute religion" [destruction of all religion], was that royalist theorists like Antoine de Rivarol (1753–1801) and the Marquis Adrien Lezay (1769–1814) interpreted the revolutionary doctrine of "equality" to mean imposing equality on everyone "without restriction," while

[1] Osterhammel, *Transformation*, 515; Clark, *Thomas Paine*, 12.
[2] Roederer, *De la philosophie moderne*, 2–5.

pro-Revolution commentators understood the doctrine adapted by Sieyès (from earlier democratic philosophes) to mean the need for society to counterbalance the natural inequality of men, in abilities and means, using the guarantee of "equal rights" to protect the weak against the strong,[3] in other words apply the "rights" doctrine Diderot, Raynal, and the d'Holbach circle had introduced in the early 1770s. Concerning religion, responded Roederer, *la philosophie* had reunited to its own domain the spheres of politics and morality, removing these from the hands of theologians and clergy, spheres religion has always tried to annex—but without condemning religion as such, or seeking to eradicate any religion.[4]

Since the post-1775 revolutionary outlooks or scripts in collision were only marginally influenced by local particularism or loyalty to faith or dynasties, ethnic allegiance, the kinds of allegiance dividing societies in the past, they stood in dramatically different relation to tradition, custom, and established practice than earlier great upheavals and conflicts. Moreover, the American and French revolutions undeniably were closely conjoined, indeed widely considered parts of a single, much larger process. "Car, de même que la révolution Américaine a fait naître la nôtre," commented Brissot characteristically, in his *mémoire* on press freedom, in June 1789, "la nôtre entraînera sans doute celle de l'Europe entière" [For just as the American Revolution gave birth to ours, so ours will no doubt entail that of the whole of Europe].[5] Spain would follow, as would Germany, "which would feel more vividly the feudal chains on seeing us free and happy," while Britain would surely blush at possessing her lamentably "defective constitution" while the nation she considers her rival acquires a far better one.[6]

What set the American and French revolutions hugely apart from anything that went before, then, had little to do with long-term changes in general "culture" or reading habits. Nor did these vast upheavals derive from class conflict or new economic forces, certainly not directly. Rather, they were predominantly shaped by revolutionary new concepts and sets of principles emerging from Enlightenment debates and widely diffused through public declarations and propaganda, assemblies, societies, salons, and theatres, concepts enshrining revolutionary social and political policies and principles substantially drawn from public controversies, "philosophy," social science, and political theory. Principally rooted in new ways of viewing society, morality, law, education, and the political process, these revolutions—albeit decidedly not the turmoil that triggered them—originated in intellectual vanguards that latched onto real but longstanding social and economic grievances, resentments, tensions long generating underlying frustration and friction but in the past mainly immobile, passive, and static. Revolutionary principles operated like an anti-aristocratic, anti-monarchical, and anti-ecclesiastical bottle-opener suddenly allowing enormous motive social force and power to escape, unleashing momentum capable of swiftly overturning hitherto seemingly stable, deeply-rooted political and social systems. To

[3] Roederer, *De la philosophie moderne*, 6–7.
[4] Roederer, *De la philosophie moderne*, 7–8.
[5] Brissot, *Mémoire aux États-Généraux*, 70–1.
[6] Brissot, *Mémoire aux États-Généraux*, 71.

gain a proper grip on the revolutions, it is essential to distinguish between the massive, longstanding, and fairly passive social pressures, the brute power of social grievance long pent up and ubiquitous, and the dynamism of newly diffused, destabilizing ideas powerfully releasing long-contained resentments.

Jointly, the two revolutions constituted an unprecedented transformative landmark in world history. While concepts of class and class warfare are routinely employed by Marxist scholars to impart a sense of overall unity to the processes of revolution from the Dutch Revolt of 1566–1609, through the English Revolution (1640–7), to the Russian Revolution of 1917, a better, more genuinely applicable formulation emerges from a classification that firmly separates pre-1770 revolutionary visions, or "scripts," from the new post-1775 Enlightenment-based revolutions, from viewing revolutionary upheavals prior to 1775 as predominantly backward-looking cultural phenomena, aimed at restoring supposedly foundational constitutions grounded in tradition and religion. Thus, the Dutch Revolt and English Revolution of the 1640s, and also the 1688–9 Glorious Revolution, invoked pre-Enlightenment notions of how society and politics had supposedly once been and should again be, defined in considerable part by religious commitment. Enlightenment era revolutions, from 1775, proceeded on a quite different basis.

But a third distinct phase was to follow—the revolutions postdating 1848–9. Though no less prone to invoke "the people" than those of 1775–1848, later revolutions, like 1917 or 1933, were powerfully authoritarian and quasi-religious, based on fundamentally undemocratic socialist, populist, and Fascist ideological constructs. Only the interposing trans-Atlantic revolutionary wave commencing in 1775, which the American revolutionary poet Philip Freneau termed the "Expanding Blaze,"[7] ending with the 1848–9 revolutions, stemmed from the Enlightenment. Only these upheavals offered democratic republicanism, constitutional liberty, freedom of expression, and, crucially, universal and equal rights, as the indispensable and veritable ground for humanity's progress to a higher level of development.

Their common Enlightenment base of itself offers a striking and fundamental affinity tying the two great upheavals together into a combined global force which was indeed much more widely recognized at the time as a single trans-Atlantic process powerfully infusing the entire revolutionary era (1775–1848) and affecting the entire known world than it came to be subsequently, whether by Marxist, other socialist, or other modern scholarship. Contrasting sharply with the pre-1775 and post-1848 revolutions, the closely linked American and French revolutions became the new primary template guiding the modern Western world's overarching "grand narrative": rejection of all previous systems of authority, replacing *ancien régime* structures with wholly new, purportedly reason-based forms and concepts.

This is not to deny that a rival contemporary narrative also arose, especially, a dogged, pervasive myth which became importantly entrenched in the later 1790s, first

[7] On Freneau see Israel, *Expanding Blaze*, pp. v, 1, 3, 17, 88–9, 93, 96–7; Wilentz, *Rise of American Democracy*, 49–50, 53, 80, 95.

in the United States, contending that the American and French Revolutions were fundamentally different in character, a view afterwards inherited by generations of historians and philosophers sympathetic to the conservative tradition of Anglo-American hostility to the French Revolution.

Some historians still incline to the view that the American Revolution was essentially "moderate" in character (which is only partly true), and a political rather than a social revolution (likewise only partly true), while the French Revolution, by contrast, was supposedly a more destructive, ideologically dogmatic upheaval, a failed social as well as a political revolution that allegedly sprang from significantly different and distinctively French intellectual traditions. Some French scholars too embrace this approach. "Republicanism in France," averred Patrice Higgonet, in his 1988 book *Sister Republics: The Origins of French and American Republicanism*, "failed as a doctrine of social and ideological consensus, and its failure occasioned frightful civil war."[8] Yes, but the American Revolution too was in key respects an unremitting, bitter civil war that violently scattered large groups of white, red, and black émigré exiles in all directions—to Nova Scotia, Ontario, Britain, the Caribbean, and the American West—a civil conflict in which segments of North America's population of often passionately committed (and today frequently underestimated) Loyalist sympathy, along with many Indians and blacks, fought the revolutionaries in the name of more traditional and conservative principles, and different interests and traditions.

In reality, both revolutions, and both sets of revolutionaries, remained deeply divided in the same fashion over closely parallel ideological issues of social, political, and constitutional principle.[9] As many contemporaries observed at the time, when the two revolutions are compared closely, for the period down to June 1793—that is, before the Montagnard *coup d'état*—what is most striking is their close proximity and affinity, both upheavals being in essence dual phenomena, in ideological terms basically unresolved clashes between moderate and radical Enlightenment tendencies. The vital difference between the revolutionary era of 1775–1848, and the earlier and later revolutionary batches, was its anti-authoritarianism combined in part with egalitarianism, and the centrality of universal, generalized "human rights" and also the ways in which theories of equality, popular sovereignty, and individual "rights" dislodged, or sought to unseat, traditional elites, gentries, ecclesiastical sway, and aristocracy and fought (with very mixed success) to integrate ethnic and religious minorities into the social mainstream. If we consider the great enactments of the two revolutions—the *Declaration of Independence* (1776), the revised state constitutions especially those of Virginia and Pennsylvania, the American Federal Constitution (1787), *Declaration of the Rights of Man* (1789), the various freedom of the press and expression statutes, the August 1789 abolition of feudalism, the June 1790 elimination of aristocracy and aristocratic titles from public life, secularization and equalization of the marriage laws (1792), emancipation of the Jews, the 1792

[8] Higgonet, *Sister Republics*, 278. [9] Israel, *Revolutionary Ideas*, 694–708.

French decree encompassing free blacks in universal male suffrage, the curtailing of ecclesiastical authority and (in 1795) full separation of church and state, together with France's first democratic constitution (Condorcet's Constitution of February 1793), beside the French and American Northern states' slave abolition decrees down to the mid-1790s—the ideological parallelism of the two great revolutions becomes striking.

The parallelism holds equally compellingly if we focus on the principal actors and articulators, the individuals and groups leading the two revolutions, down to June 1793. For, again undeniably, those legislators, publicists, and constitution-framers shaping the overall outcome in its democratic, universal rights-based, libertarian aspects were "republicans" in a profoundly new sense, that is democratic republican protagonists hostile to all tradition and religious authority. Correspondingly, efforts to stem the radical tide in America and France with limited suffrages, constitutions entrenching aristocratic republicanism, reinforcing constitutional monarchy, and compromise with ecclesiastical authority plainly all derived from the common trans-Atlantic moderate Enlightenment stream. Of course, this is to depict the French Revolution minus the Terror, *robespierrisme*, and the Revolution's counter-revolutionary populist and authoritarian tendencies, movements that until a late stage, well into 1792 never professed to be "republican." For these constituted a quite distinct non-libertarian revolutionary current, a wholly separate phenomenon.[10] Genuine "republicans," remarked Constant in 1797, were never anything but the Terror's "victims."[11] He was right. "The Terror established itself in France after the fall of the democratic republican leadership (the Brissotins), and the flight, imprisonment and proscription of their friends. One must not therefore confuse the central principles of the French Revolution (as so many do) with Marat, Robespierre, and the Terror, conflate authoritarian populism with free expression and equal rights, confuse democratic republicans with their executioners."[12]

Inevitably, the Terror provided fresh fundamental disagreement between royalist and pro-Revolution commentators in their conflicting interpretations of *la philosophie moderne*. Where publicists like Lezay, Rivarol, and Da Costa later, portray the Terror as the direct outcome of *la philosophie moderne*, pro-Revolution publicists passionately rejected this slur. "The Terror was a veritable Counter-Revolution," held Roederer typically for the Brissotin intelligentsia, "and not a consequence or accompaniment of the Revolution."[13] Likewise the young Constant denounced Lezay's intervention as pernicious myth-making.[14] For radicals, the "ferocious and brutal violence of the *Terrorists*," rooted as it was in popular ignorance, was not just a catastrophe, ruining the Revolution but, being built on "consecrated" populist principles, would, as Constant put it, "be eternally dangerous." The Terror was the work of a "ferocious tyranny" that seized power in June 1793 by an organized coup, taking

[10] Constant, *De la Terreur*, 340.
[11] Constant, *De la Terreur*, 349; Fontana, *Benjamin Constant*, pp. xii–xiv.
[12] Constant, *De la Terreur*, 350. [13] Roederer, *De la philosophie moderne*, 29–30.
[14] Constant, *De la Terreur*, 337–8.

advantage of the weakening of the revolutionary regime by military defeat abroad and financial collapse. For Europe's and America's radical enlighteners, Robespierre was, as Mary Wollstonecraft put it, "a monster," the destroyer of the Revolution's core values, the factor that made her "sicken at thoughts of a Revolution which costs so much blood and bitter tears."[15]

The American Revolution's prime theorists and ideologues were Franklin, Paine, Jefferson, Adams, Hamilton, and Madison—all renowned enlighteners; but of these Adams and Hamilton stood firmly on the "aristocratic" side, while the others adhered to the radical side. The key formative figures, theorists, publicists, and legislators of the democratic, egalitarian French Revolution of 1789–1800 were assuredly those who were already unequivocally "republicans" prior to 1789, namely Sieyès, Mirabeau, Brissot, Pétion, Condorcet, Desmoulins, Lafayette, Bonneville, Cérutti, Kersaint, Fauchet, Volney, Chamfort, Robert, Barnave, and the playright Chénier. Historians sometimes claim Mirabeau, who wished to retain king and crown, was not a "republican;" but by any meaningful criterion he indubitably was: he aimed to emasculate the royal executive, deprive it of practically all its power, and ensure the education of the heir to the throne, the Dauphin, was wholly controlled by the nation's "représentants" and not by court or king.[16]

But the essential point in both cases is that leading orators and spokesmen, several of whom like Brissot had emerged through journalism to the front rank of the revolutionary leadership,[17] exerted the impact they did only thanks to backing from a formidable phalanx of publicists and newspaper and journal editors. "What made the Revolution in the United States," demanded Brissot in his *Mémoires*: "the gazettes." In the French case, the key publicity men were headed by Carra, Gorsas, Louvet, Cérutti, Giret-Dupré, Cerisier, and Prudhomme. On the American side, none exerted a greater sway than Paine. "The celebrated pamphlet entitled *Common Sense* [of Thomas Paine]," explained Brissot, "only had the prodigious effect that it did because it was cited and reproduced a hundred times in the [American] papers and devoured with avidity by the artisan, the farmer, by men of all classes. What prevented Canada from taking part in that glorious revolution? Lack of newspapers."[18]

None of these republican publicists, Anglo-American and French, championed traditional monarchy, pre-1789 constitutional precedents or traditions, or religious authority. Both revolutionary vanguards comprised ardent devotees of "philosophy" in the sense of being passionate republicans, tolerationists, and secularists steeped in Enlightenment literature. Among those most politically effective as well as eloquently parading democratic republican views in France, in 1789, were precisely Robespierre's chief Jacobin rivals during 1791–2—Brissot and Jérome Pétion de Villeneuve (1756–94)—both of whom loudly abjured monarchy, aristocracy, and ecclesiastical

[15] Wollstonecraft, *Collected Letters*, 254; Barton, *Northern Arcadia*, 45.

[16] Baczko, *Éducation pour la démocratie*, 14–15.

[17] Brissot, *Mémoires* ii. 275.

[18] Brissot, *Mémoires* ii. 81.

power and privilege, expressing republican attitudes, before 1789,[19] as we see, in Pétion's case, from his pamphlet *Avis aux François sur le salut de la Patrie* (1788), published some months before the onset of the Revolution proper.

Pétion, mayor of Paris in 1792, figured briefly among the leading figures opposing the rising menace of Jacobin populism. An egalitarian republican and addict of "philosophy," vehemently opposed to religious authority, in 1788 he answered adherents of Locke and Montesquieu demanding revised constitutional monarchy and "aristocratic" republicanism, and those clamoring, like Rousseau, that republics are impossible in large states by pointing out that the "United States of America" consisted of republics that "encompass immense territories but there is no government in the universe where liberty rests on more solid foundations than theirs."[20] "If a universal revolution in the political principles of the entire globe" seems an insane dream, contended Pétion, unrealizable for now, it will materialize one day; and while we await this "fortunate epoch for the human race," men everywhere must strive to "reform the abuses and, by diffusing *philosophique* ideas, eradicate the fanaticism, ignorance, and prejudices that oppress men" and obstruct humanity's path to liberty and happiness. Success will come when we enlighten mankind.[21] Exactly that was the common American–French Radical Enlightenment recipe.

Although revolutionary "rights of mankind" were bitterly contested and achieved lasting concrete results only in sporadic, incomplete fashion in America, in 1775–83, the program itself derived from the radical *philosophique* tendency that prepared the way for the two revolutions. Despite their electrifying novelty, these foundational concepts were never presented as something specifically or characteristically "American." Rather "rights of mankind" were proclaimed by Paine, Franklin, Jefferson, Young, and others (as by Raynal, Diderot, d'Holbach, Condorcet and Gorani and other Europeans earlier) as a universal creed lately "remembered" and "perfected" rather than newly devised. Consequently, the American and French upheavals alike were heavily disrupted from the outset by internal splits on every side that reflected social divisions in many respects, with large New York and Virginia landowners, for instance, tending to the "aristocratic republican side" and Irish immigrants in Philadelphia preferring the democratic republican creed, but drawing their rhetoric, logic, and principles from the underlying ideological rift. Colonial Virginia, New York, Massachusetts, Maine, the Carolinas, and New Jersey were all just as divided by class antagonism as was French society, the splits between wealthy "aristocratic" landowners and poor white tenant farmers, and between white and black, just as socially divisive in America (and bloody) as social rifts in France.

Projecting essentially the same internal conflict of ideologies, the two revolutions generated comparable quarrels over basic rights and identical dilemmas around the complexities of press freedom, religious toleration, organizing electorates, designing suffrages, and restructuring the tax system. Both sought rationalization and

[19] Brissot, *Mémoires* ii. 274–6; Tackett, *Becoming a Revolutionary*, 103, 105, 177, 303.
[20] Pétion, *Avis aux François*, 65. [21] Pétion, *Avis aux François*, 69–70.

universalization on an Enlightenment basis while entangling social hierarchies either side of the Atlantic in irresolvable conflict with "universal and equal rights."[22] Sharing the same basic aspirations and intellectual traditions, the American Revolution and the French Revolution prior to the June 1793 Montagnard *coup d'état*, together dominated Western consciousness at the close of the eighteenth century and start of the nineteenth. Both were deeply entwined with the other even before 1789, given the crucial importance among the intellectual vanguard of pre-1789 French revolutionary republicanism, the republicanism of Condorcet, Brissot, and Pétion, firmly grounded in American experience and example.[23] However insightful in other respects, Hannah Arendt, seriously misread the logic of the situation when claiming Condorcet's *L'Influence de la Révolution d'Amérique sur l'Europe* (1786), asserting the centrality of the American Revolution for France and the world, published three years before the Bastille's storming, marked the "end, not the beginning, of an Atlantic civilization."[24] The historical reality was exactly the reverse. Beside Brissot and Condorcet, it was Jefferson, Paine, and Lafayette who were most inclined to stress the common identity and goals of the two revolutions.

Contemporaries active in both revolutions were not just acutely aware of the interaction and these affinities, but frequently discussed and felt inspired by them. Thirteen or fourteen senior French officers who served in the American Revolution were elected to the French Estates-General of 1789, only three of whom were conservative royalists. Most, including Lafayette, the Brothers De Lameth, Custine, Biron, Noailles, Dumas, and Broglie, gained prominence either within the moderate or the radical Left revolutionary factions together with many other close observers of the American Revolution.[25] Lafayette was merely the most renowned lifelong advocate of and enthusiast for the American model. Another key bridging figure was Franklin's chief ideological collaborator in Paris, the duke de La Rochefoucauld-Liancourt (1747–1827), who translated and published the American state constitutions in France, together with the state bills of rights and *Declaration of Independence*, texts that powerfully infused French republican political thought during the 1780s prior to the outbreak of the French Revolution, as well as subsequently. Among revolutionary nobles abjuring separate estates and, in June 1789, defecting to the Third Estate, while soon emerging also among the National Assembly's foremost orators (until 1792), La Rochefoucauld sat on no less than nine National Assembly committees and hosted at home numerous policy meetings with Condorcet, Lafayette, and other key champions of universal rights.[26]

Radicals of the American Revolution associated with, admired, and supported radicals of the French Revolution. About the French Revolution's prospects and role

[22] Allen, *Our Declaration*, 22.
[23] Israel, *Revolutionary Ideas*, 35, 70–1, 97, 110, 167; Israel, *Scripting*; Israel, "'Radical Enlightenment': A Game-Changing Concept".
[24] Arendt, *On Revolution*, 217–18.
[25] Cloquet, *Recollections*, 39, 151, 153; Jourdan, "Alien Origins," 189.
[26] Badinter, *Condorcet*, 293, 328, 344; Billias, *American Constitutionalism*, 67–70.

in the world, Jefferson remained optimistic long after leaving France, in October 1789. Exhilarated, he returned to America, in the fall of 1789, Adams recalled twenty-three years later, convinced the French "would succeed in establishing a free republican government" in key respects resembling that of the United States. It was the "first time," he recalled, "that you and I differed in opinion on any material question." During the years 1790–3, Jefferson regularly reaffirmed his confidence. "The event of the king's [i.e. Louis XVI's] flight from Paris," he assured Adams, from Philadelphia, on 30 August 1791, "will have struck you with its importance." "I confess I have not changed my confidence in the favorable issue of that revolution, because it has always rested on my own ocular evidence of the unanimity of the nation, and the wisdom of the Patriotic party in the National Assembly." Despite intensely disliking Mirabeau, the French Revolution's most prominent early leader on the Left, Jefferson stuck to his unabashedly positive view of the French democratic republican wing, especially the coteries headed by Brissot, Condorcet, and Pétion, the Girondin faction, until June 1793, remaining hopeful his ideological allies would prevail in what had by then become a ferocious, life and death struggle pitting the democratic republican faction against the tyrannical intolerance, virulent anti-intellectualism and Counter-Enlightenment populism of Marat, Robespierre, and the Montagne. From August 1792 until May 1793, much to his satisfaction, Jefferson's republican friends dominated the French national legislature; from early 1795, their heirs regained control but only precariously.[27]

During these years, the specter of a trans-Atlantic "General Revolution" was as dear to Jefferson's heart as to Paine's, Price's, Thorild's, Gorani's, or Priestley's. Jefferson and his American and other non-French radical friends and allies, including the Polish hero Kościuszko, were justified, moreover, in viewing French developments as the trigger of a wider General Revolution beyond America and France, for which the American upheaval remained the primary template but which, by the 1780s, had, in their eyes, now lost its initial momentum on the American side, and come to require re-invigoration, needing in fact, as Jefferson and others saw it, to be recharged by the French experience, something for which these men ardently hoped. Nothing pleased Jefferson more than to see the Revolution spilling over into Belgium, Holland, Switzerland, Italy, and Germany. The Prussian king in Berlin "was terrified," he cheerfully reported to Philadelphia, before leaving France, dreading the "contagion of the same principles gaining his own subjects, as they have done those of the Austrian Netherlands, Liège, Cologne and Hesse-Cassel."[28]

Like Jefferson, Paine, Condorcet, and Brissot, numerous revolutionary enthusiasts felt inspired by the close affinities between the two revolutions. Many an ideological opponent of the French Revolution, like Rivarol and the veteran Swiss patrician champion of French aristocracy and royalism, Mallet du Pan, were equally struck by the parallels, blaming the American Revolution's ideology for instigating the

[27] Jefferson to Adams, Philadelphia, 30 Aug. 1791, *Adams–Jefferson Letters* I. 251–2; Halliday, *Understanding Thomas Jefferson*, 113, 135; Philp, *Reforming Ideas*, 196, 198–202.
[28] Jefferson.

revolutionary tendency in Europe. It was the American Revolution that spawned the "swarm of fanatics," complained Mallet du Pan, responsible for European democratic republicanism and rejection of religious authority, their abjuring not just monarchy but all social privilege, including both formal aristocracy in monarchies and old-established oligarchic "aristocratic republicanism," dominating his native Geneva and the rest of Switzerland. It was the likes of Franklin, Paine, and Jefferson who sought to push America in the democratizing direction stalwartly opposed by America's "moderates"—Adams, Hamilton, and Morris seeking to defend monopolization of power by small established state elites. In America and Europe alike, "moderates" battled in parallel to defend Montesquieu, "aristocracy," and "mixed government."[29] America's *Declaration of Independence*, snarled Mallet, had outrageously proclaimed popular sovereignty and equal rights not just for the United States but all humanity, the entire world, dragging behind it all the later French, Dutch, Swiss, German, Irish, and Italian declarations.[30]

Until the mid-nineteenth century, viewing the American and French Revolutions and the latter's sister revolutions in Belgium, the Netherlands, Germany, the Ionian Islands, Ireland, and Italy as components of a single democratic republican and "human rights" revolutionary trajectory hence typified the entire trans-Atlantic Left intelligentsia. Whether Paine, Condorcet, Jefferson, or the Italian Gorani, the German Forster, the Dutchman Paape, or the Irish secularizing, irreligious revolutionary leader Wolfe Tone was the spokesman, all proclaimed the same universal human rights message rooted in democratic republican theory, anti-aristocratism, and resolve to curtail religious authority and the clergy drastically, all employing the same basic concepts and rhetoric.

9.2. "DEMOCRATICAL PRINCIPLES" VERSUS ARISTOCRATIC REPUBLICANISM

Much impressed with Paine's pamphlet *Common Sense* (1776), Brissot was deeply struck by the huge impact it exerted throughout the United States in forming, expanding, and mobilizing public opinion behind the Revolution at the decisive moment, in early 1776. Witnessing this phenomenon heightened his confidence that *la philosophie* disseminated by writers like himself, Condorcet, Mirabeau, Carra, Pétion, Cérutti, and Sieyès, the French equivalents of Paine, could likewise energize and steer French sentiment forcefully and effectively.[31] And, undoubtedly, it was publicists such as these who provided both the intellectual leaders organizing the political movement in Paris and the provinces, and who successfully propagated the message in print on all sides. British diplomats in Scandinavia during the 1790s who registered mounting unease over the upsurge of Jacobinism and pro-French

[29] Acomb, *Mallet du Pan*, 97–8. [30] Acomb, *Mallet du Pan*, 98.
[31] Loft, *Passion, Politics*, 150.

sentiment knew perfectly well that it was never among the (enthusiastically royalist) laborers, peasants, or artisans of Denmark and Sweden that conservatives should fear active agitators and trouble-makers, but among the students and professors of Uppsala and Copenhagen, among the booksellers and addicts of book- and coffee-shops.

France's National Assembly's radical enlighteners, in 1789, were assuredly a small group; but, despite the untiring efforts of Barnave, the Brothers De Lameth, Bailly, and other "moderates," and the initially "republican" Lafayette—who during 1790–1 abandoned Condorcet and Brissot and joined the moderates—it was the Brissotins rejecting constitutional monarchy on the British model who fixed the Revolution's terms, concepts, principles, and general direction. They did so by exerting a stronger pull than could moderate leaders, being more able than their rivals to use newspapers, pamphlets, books, meetings, and the theater to mobilize longstanding social grievances and resentments and secure the support of the masses—temporary and sporadic though this proved. As the new United States ambassador who replaced Jefferson in Paris, an aristocratic republican and vehement foe of Paine, Gouverneur Morris (1752–1816) noted reporting to President Washington (who by no means agreed with Jefferson's positive estimate of the French Revolution), on 30 September 1791, the newly elected French Legislative Assembly "as far as can at present be determined is deeply imbued with republican or rather democratical principles."[32] Morris was right but was referring to Brissot, Pétion, Condorcet, and the radical *philosophique* elite: nothing could have been less true, in 1790–2, of French society generally, the broad world of cultural trends and sociability.

In France, the democratic republican, universal rights "principles" so detested by the new American ambassador, Morris, had begun to take root a decade earlier. The process had been discernible ever since a group of French sympathizers, including Brissot, became caught up in the longstanding conflict between "aristocrats" and "democrats" during the Genevan revolution of 1781–2. This erupted as a local democratic revolution within a traditionally oligarchic republic, in no small part inspired, scholarship has shown, by events in America.[33] Aided by Berne, Zurich, and the French crown, the Genevan "aristocrats" eventually gained the upper hand and crushed Geneva's democratic revolution, but not without scattering exile groups, angry, highly articulate Genevan republicans, across France, Switzerland, and the Low Countries, stoking up the friction between aristocratic and democratic republicanism throughout Western Europe. Interaction between the two great revolutions was thus by 1781–2 already in the making as became still more plainly evident with the vigorous republican surge gathering momentum in Holland during the 1780s. The result was the rise of a consciously international republican, universal rights ideological network that had gathered considerable momentum throughout western Europe by 1789. August Wilhelm Rehberg (1757–1836), a Humean conservative and key

[32] Morris, *Diary* ii. 275. Morris to Washington, Paris, 30 Sept. 1791.

[33] Brissot, *Philadelphien à Geneve*, 47, 50–2, 178, 146–7.

German intellectual figure, correctly identified the phenomenon as a direct outcome of the American Revolution of which the stirring principles and heroic allure stoked up French enthusiasm for the Revolution of 1789 even before it actually began, crucially encouraging democratic republican sentiment despite the fact that most participants in the American drama, being "moderates," had been "entirely shaped by English concepts and ways of viewing things."[34]

Among France's large, zealous, and erudite band of republican enthusiasts for the American Revolution on the eve of the French Revolution, none was a more powerful orator than Mirabeau, who, during the elections for the Estates-General, over the winter of 1788–9, reportedly "electrified" the French with his talk of America.[35] Brissot's enthusiasm, widely diffused already with his 1783 text *Le Philadelphien à Genève*, was afterwards powerfully reiterated in his *Plan of Conduct for the Deputies of the Estates-General* (April 1789).[36] Indeed, the authors of all the most influential French revolutionary pamphlets of 1788–9, Rehberg pointed out, citing Sieyès, Pétion, Kersaint, and Brissot by name, were unmistakably democratic republican and egalitarian in tendency, all denying the basic legitimacy of the 1789 States General as originally constituted by the French crown on the basis of estates, religion, and precedent, because its delegates were not democratically elected and because the whole did not express popular sovereignty.[37] The likes of Brissot and Pétion, observed Rehberg, shared nothing of the liberal monarchism, or veneration of Montesquieu and the British model, characteristic of all ideological allies of Adams, Morris, Hamilton, Jay, John Quincy Adams, and the conservative bloc in the new American polity, or the moderate monarchist factions seeking to steer the French Revolution until August 1792.[38] Rehberg was right; but then neither did Franklin, Jefferson, Paine, or Madison look favorably on monarchy, or Montesquieu's Anglophilia, apology for nobility, and plea for separation of powers.[39]

Much as the Struensee reform drive in Denmark–Norway, in 1770–1, was undercut by the advent—for the first time in world history—of full, unrestricted press freedom operating on the principle that this constituted a benefit for society—so, equally, noted Rehberg, the Versailles court reformers, deferring to Necker, undermined their own position—and the entire edifice of social hierarchy, constitutional monarchy, and religious authority bundled together—by disastrously (for them) conceding full press freedom. For they thereby ignited an explosion of anti-aristocratic republican political pamphlets and rhetoric that fundamentally transformed the French scene in 1788–9. Press freedom opened the door to "philosophy," meaning Radical Enlightenment, that is the egalitarianism, secularism, universalism, irreligion, and democratic republicanism of Mirabeau, Brissot, Condorcet, Desmoulins, Lafayette, Pétion,

[34] Rehberg, *Untersuchungen* i. 57; Israel, *Democratic Enlightenment*, 745–6.
[35] Mejan, *Collection complète* i. 10–11; Israel, *Expanding Blaze*, 77, 122.
[36] Rehberg, *Untersuchungen* i. 98–9; Billias, *American Constitutionalism*, 84–5.
[37] Rehberg, *Untersuchungen* i. 57, 84.
[38] Rehberg, *Untersuchungen* i. 99.
[39] On Madison's critical stance toward Montesquieu's division of powers doctrine, see Sheehan, *James Madison*, 58–9.

Bonneville, Carra, Kersaint, and Sieyès, generating an international revolutionary tide, a gigantic extension of precisely what had surged up so menacingly for aristocracy in Geneva in 1782 and the Netherlands in 1782–7. Post-Bastille French press and theater freedom loudly amplified exaltation of the American Revolution's core principles, proclaiming that revolution the guiding model, example, and inspiration for the entire world. Though still nominally a monarchy until September 1792, at a deeper level, as many understood at the time, between July 1789 and August 1792, when the last vestiges of monarchy were swept away, France was a monarchy in name only. It was then in reality already a virtual republic in its core values, or rather those of the guiding faction of the revolutionary leadership. But paradoxically, while French republicanism grew progressively more radical during the years 1787–92, in the United States, Franklin, Jefferson, Paine, and the radicals steadily lost ground during the late 1780s, leaving the United States a better base than France for Montesquieu, enthroning landed and mercantile wealth and clawing back of universal rights, hence for oligarchy and political "aristocracy."[40]

Edmund Burke (1729–97), abandoning his earlier Whiggish tendencies and becoming a hard-core conservative, from 1787 when Dutch democratic republicanism was suppressed by Anglo-Prussian intervention with his support, remained from 1789 onwards wholly unsympathetic to the French Revolution. But it is often missed that he had earlier been equally averse to the democratic dimension of the American Revolution (and its resonances in Britain, Holland, and Ireland). During the Dutch political crisis of 1787, Burke abruptly abandoned his former Whig stance and connections, displaying what for some was a baffling unwillingness to support the Dutch anti-Orangist democrats. Permanently breaking at that point with Mirabeau, Cloots, and other radical friends, including—after a curiously long delay—with Paine, he began denouncing universal democratic causes and equal rights as absolutely not for the British or Irish.[41] He totally disagreed with the anonymous English democratic republican who penned the *History of the Internal Affairs of the United Provinces from the Year 1780* predicting, before the 1787 crisis, that "a new Republic of the purest kind is about to spring up in Europe, and the flame of her liberty, which was first excited in America, and has since communicated itself in a manner more or less perfect to so many other countries, bids fair for the production of consequences, not less extensive than salutary."[42] Rather, like Rehberg, Mallet, and Morris, he considered those principles anything but salutary. From 1789, he denounced the French Revolution continually but did so without condemning the American Revolution which many still today incorrectly suppose he had earlier championed. Moreover, he condemned the French Revolution while making no attempt to contrast and compare it with the American, or compare their political theories and doctrines. This has

[40] Rehberg, *Untersuchungen* i. 126–7, 146, 150–2.
[41] Lock, *Edmund Burke* ii. 142–4; Israel, *Democratic Enlightenment*, 88–96.
[42] BL [William Godwin?] *History of the Internal Affairs of the United Provinces from the Year 1780, to the Commencement of Hostilities in June 1787* (London, 1787), 345.

prompted some historians endorsing the myth of fundamental difference between the two great revolutions to "regret" that Britain's greatest conservative ideologue drew no clear contrast between the two revolutions. They assume that in 1789–93 a meaningful contrast really existed and fail to grasp that Burke's denouncing the French Revolution without contrasting it with America—except for what he viewed as the French revolutionary leadership's more blatant irreligion—is actually entirely consistent with his earlier stance, his unceasing opposition to the democratic tendency and (discreet) rejection of the (Jeffersonian) American Revolution.

Even suggesting the French Revolution was more irreligious than the American[43] hardly amounted to a real contrast given the deistic, anti-theological, and anti-Christian views of Franklin, Jefferson, and most American Founding Fathers, including such "aristocrats" as Morris and Hamilton. During a bitter exchange across the floor of the Commons, in 1790, the English parliamentary leader Charles James Fox, having earlier, during the American struggle, been Burke's parliamentary ally in opposing the British government's war policy, cited lines from Burke's own speeches to show how wildly inconsistent he was supposedly now being in denouncing the French Revolution.[44] But Burke was not being inconsistent; he had simply come to fear the American democratic tendency more since it had gained added momentum in Europe. Meanwhile, where Burke made no effort to contrast the two revolutions, Adams most decidedly did. While Jefferson remained approving and confident throughout the French Revolution until well after Robespierre's coup, Adams repudiated its democratic republican tendency from the outset. But then he equally condemned the American democratic tendency, considering the essentially new dimension fostered by Franklin and Paine (both of whom he loathed), as well as Jefferson, a towering threat to the America his revolution aspired to build. Adams believed passionately in the uniqueness of the American Revolution. Even a republic based on a non-democratic, heavily oligarchic constitution with a limited suffrage, like that adopted in 1780 by his own state of Massachusetts (most of which he had written himself),[45] would be excessive, he thought, in France.

All republicanism, not just democratic republicanism, Adams deemed wrong for France. A "project of such a government" for "over five and twenty millions of people, when four and twenty millions and five hundred thousands of them could neither write nor read, was as unnatural, irrational, and impracticable as it would be over the elephants, lions, tigers, panthers, wolves, and bears in the Royal Menagerie at Versailles." If British "mixed government" with a president instead of a king was right for America, as he thought, it was even more essential—especially retaining the king—for France. As in other respects, the respective "moderate" wings of the American and French revolutions, and democratic wings of the two revolutions,

[43] Burke, *Reflections*; Clark, *Language*, 222–3.

[44] Bromwich, *Intellectual Life of Edmund Burke*, 308–13; Lock, *Edmund Burke* ii. 264; Himmelfarb, *Roads to Modernity*, 85.

[45] Israel, *Expanding Blaze*, 94–5, 212–14; Ryerson, *John Adams's Republic*, 214, 223, 415.

almost exactly mirrored each other in their respectively contrasting *pro et contra* attitudes to the British constitution. America being a confederacy of states and France a unified monarchy did entail some significant organizational differences and differences of emphasis within each revolution; but with respect to Montesquieu and his robust apology of mixed government, eulogizing or attacking "aristocracy," and extolling or deriding the British model, one encountered only parallels with both revolutions harbouring powerful lobbies for and against. Where Franklin and Jefferson were Francophiles, Adams, a lifelong Francophobe, kept steadfastly to his (moderate) Enlightenment creed, denying "multitudes of ignorant people" could ever become materials for constructing a viable democratic republic on the basis of utopian dreams. Nor was it only in America and France that he doggedly fought the democratic republican tendency—he sought to discredit it internationally, especially whilst in the Netherlands.[46] Along with Morris, Jay, and Hamilton, Adams detested French, Dutch, *and* American democratic republicanism; like them, he remained implacably hostile to the Jeffersonian democratic faction convulsing the legislatures of Pennsylvania, Vermont, New York, Maine, and Massachusetts.

Later, when public perceptions of the French Revolution became tied to Robespierre and the Terror, it became more plausible to credit Adams with good judgment in maintaining that the American Revolution from the outset possessed a wholly different character from the French. By 1793, many had become convinced like him of the need to distinguish between pernicious French "ideology" and Anglo-American solid good sense. But in reality Jefferson's and Paine's judgment remained the more accurate perception of the situation: during 1789–93, and again from 1795 onwards, the French Revolution to which Franklin, Jefferson, Madison, Monroe, Short, Barlow, and Paine all materially contributed was the American Revolution's twin in both its "aristocratic" and opposing democratic republican guises.[47] Indeed, many American revolutionaries—Monroe, Barlow, Madison, and the poet Freneau, no less than Paine and Jefferson—committed themselves to advancing the two great democratic republican transformations jointly in the international sphere and to recognizing what they hoped would prove a stable and close correspondence between the parallel revolutions. No American observer, it has been claimed, was "more committed to the concept of the Revolution in France as an extension of the one in America than was Madison."[48]

On arriving as US envoy in Paris, in March 1794, James Monroe (1758–1831), later fifth president of the United States, and John Quincy Adams's immediate predecessor, a Virginian *protégé* of Jefferson's, though himself likewise of the planter class, defended the republican credentials and integrity of the American Revolution on the same basis as the French. To Philadelphia, he reported that the horrific, widely-reported Paris prison massacres of September 1792—atrocities assiduously publicized on all sides by European monarchists to tar the Revolution's reputation—were

[46] Grund, *Aristocracy in America*, 19, 195; Israel, *Expanding Blaze*, 211–41.
[47] Grund, *Aristocracy in America*, 19, 85, 351; Mattes, "Tocqueville and Grund," 29, 46.
[48] Words of James Morton Smith quoted in Wood, "Is there a James Madison Problem?," 428.

actually the work neither of the republican democratic faction then dominating the National Assembly, Brissot and his friends, nor of the common people. The ugly truth, reported Monroe (correctly), was that the September massacres of 1792, highly damaging as they were to the French Revolution's international reputation, were the work of unscrupulous conspirators and agents of the Montagne working for Marat and the populist authoritarian faction. The *septembriseurs*, as those who ushered in the criminal regime of the Terror became known, were groups diametrically opposed to freedom of expression, basic rights, and all democratic freedoms.[49] (It is untrue that both sides, Brissotins and Montagnards, blamed each other for the September massacres, as one contributor to the "negative critique" has claimed; only the Brissotins accused the Montagne of the atrocity.)

Especially during 1791–3, the French Revolution generated a fervent internationalism among sympathizers across Europe, but also across America. "Peuples de tous les climats," exclaimed Gorani, the Milanese revolutionary of aristocratic background, close to Mirabeau and Condorcet, "levez-vous, secouez les chaines de la crédulité, de l'erreur, de la superstition, et du despotisme. Connoissez vos droits et vos forces" [peoples of all climes, rise up, shake the chains of credulity, superstition, and despotism. Know your rights and your power].[50] "Let us no longer tolerate," he urged, that a batch of "princes and nobles take advantage of nations, enslave them, oppress them and pillage them; perish royalty and the nobility!"[51] Hesse-Cassel, noted a former leader of the Illuminati, Adolf Freiherr von Knigge (1752–96), writing to friends in June 1792, had suffered devastating social consequences from Britain's intensive recruiting for her almost half German North American army during the American war. Numerous officers and men had returned to Hesse, Württemberg, and other regions, from America, changed men, disgusted with Germany's venal princely court system, brimming with their American experiences and perspectives. They lost no time in introducing the new ideals in Germany. From 1776, it was not just a few intellectuals and professors who viewed central Europe's politics as a battleground where *Aristocraten* and *Democraten*, princes and popular sovereignty fought for supremacy. Army veterans were beginning to too.

In Hesse-Cassel, a new subversive organization, the *Deutsche Union*, succeeded the Illuminati and began pervading the reading societies and clubs. Awareness of the American Revolution, derived from direct experience beside books and pamphlets, fused, from 1789, with the subsequent stimulus of the French Revolution, particularly in university towns like Marburg, Tübingen, and Giessen and among student organizations, bookshops and reading societies.[52] By *Aristocratismus*, pro-Revolution intellectuals and students in Germany during the early 1790s meant not just the

[49] Monroe to Randolph, 6 Mar. 1794, *The Writings of James Monroe*, ed. S. Murray Hamilton (7 vols., New York, 1898–1903), ii. 222–6; this letter is wrongly interpreted in Davis, *Revolutions*, 104 n. 10; see also David Bell's error here in Bell, 'A Very Different French Revolution'.

[50] Gorani, *Lettres sur la Révolution*, 53.

[51] Gorani, *Lettres sur la Révolution*, 53; Trampus, *Naissance du langage*, 107.

[52] Haug, "Weibliche Geselligkeit," 178, 183–6.

hierarchical social order prevailing throughout central and eastern Europe but also tyrannical princely rule and the newly intensified censorship and persecution of dissidents, the entire new Counter-Enlightenment intellectual apparatus, imposed since 1789 by the courts of Berlin, Vienna, Cologne, and Petersburg.[53]

The risk of sliding back into repression, despotism, and intolerance grew throughout the period of Brissotin ascendancy over the Revolution, driven by what Condorcet considered the two most powerful factors in French society and public affairs at the time—ignorance and crude economic motive. To the unrelenting populist menace, Condorcet and Brissot could find no immediately effective answer. Planning for the future required consensus, orderly constitutionalism, and time; and Liberty was directly at risk. The tragedy of the First French Republic for radical enlighteners was that, following Louis XVI's flight to Varennes, the democratic republicans simply lacked enough time, and support, to consolidate their leadership, principles, ideology and reforms. It is one thing to draw up a new constitution and establish institutions capable of sustaining liberty, a despairing Condorcet realized in early 1793, quite another to conserve them on a stable basis, to viably maintain a democratic republic. To prevent slipping back into tyranny, oppression, and intolerance, France had to move closer to the kind of general equality of individuals and cults prevailing in the United States and embodied in the American Declaration of Independence.[54] Unfortunately, the only effective way to make the Revolution viable and stable was via universal secular education and what Brissot called "wise laws" and "taxes well distributed to divide property, and distribute more economic ease [*aisance*] among the citizenry;" for these were too slow to save the Revolution's core values being negated and blighted by their populist foes. Every day, commented Condorcet in 1791, he felt "we are working for our great-nephews."[55]

The 2 June 1793 *coup d'état* brought populist authoritarianism, militant *Rousseauisme*, and *anti-philosophisme* to power in France in the shape of Robespierre and the Montagne. The Montagnard victory spelt dictatorship, Terror, and suppression of all criticism, dissent, and freedom of expression. Within months most newspapers were shut down and the theater gagged by strict controls and surveillance. Even though the ruthlessly anti-rights and anti-Enlightenment regime lasted only just over a year, the Terror powerfully took hold, impressing its image on the Revolution, extending its murderous grip over the entire French and European political scene, wrecking the institutions and legislation of the democratic republican Revolution. The Terror (June 1793 to July 1794), whose principal initial target was precisely the democratic republican radicals, the *gens de lettres*, who had conceived, formulated, and led the Revolution, came near to obliterating the revolution of republican democracy, *critique*, and freedom of thought and expression. Robespierre and his Montagnard colleagues went all out to liquidate not just the persons of their democratic republican ideological opponents—Brissot, Condorcet, Pétion, Carra,

[53] Zaunstock, *Milieu*, 286. [54] Allen, *Our Declaration*, 22–3.
[55] [Condorcet], *Bibliothèque de l'Homme Public* ii (1791) issue 5, p. 255.

Louvet, Gorsas, Cloots, and all the Revolution's other principal intellectuals, orators, and journalists—but their entire Radical Enlightenment legacy. Anyone publicly criticizing Robespierre, or the Terror, or daring to defend press freedom and other aspects of democratic republicanism, including such ardent revolutionaries as Desmoulins, editor of *Le Vieux Cordelier* (1793–4), Girey-Dupré, editor of the *Le Patriot français*, and Proly of *Le Cosmopolite*, were persecuted, seized, denied all rights, and summarily tried and guillotined. During 1793–4, the Revolution was utterly perverted by the brutally repressive authoritarianism and Counter-Enlightenment attitudes of the Montagne. Foreign "Jacobins" committed to genuine enlightened values, like Gorani, Thorild, Forster, and Knigge, were thrust into a terrible crisis, emotional as well as political, being at once disgusted and profoundly disillusioned. Nothing seemed more terrible than the capsizing of the democratic republican Revolution, and triumph of unenlightened populism and authoritarianism, that traumatized France during 1793–4. Wollstonecraft, like many another, felt utterly sick at heart; a despairing Knigge, like many German former "Jacobins," seeing America as now the only hope, dreamt of emigrating there.[56]

The Terror sought to extirpate radical *philosophie* and the republican Revolution. All the Brissotin leaders were guillotined, imprisoned, or forced into hiding. Condorcet, the Revolution's greatest theorist, was outlawed and driven to suicide. France's playwrights came under a strict censorship, leaving those with anything critical to say about the new social and political reality subject to a merciless persecution that drove Beaumarchais abroad, Laya into hiding, and Dubuisson to the guillotine. Jean-Louis Laya (1761–1833), an ardent republican revolutionary, dared stage *L'Ami des Lois* at the Theatre-Français in Paris in January 1793, a few months before the Montagnard takeover, a play in which Robespierre appears as "Nomophage" [Eater of the Law], a total hypocrite, impostor, and "tartufe de civisme" who ceaselessly spouts about "virtue" while flattering the least informed purely for his own advantage.[57] In the play, "Nomophage" assumes ordinary folk understand nothing whatever and can easily be led to liquidate those who most ardently champion their true interests. Another victim of the purge of democratic republicans was Paine, whom the dictatorship also came close to guillotining, but hesitated to liquidate owing to his proximity to America's revolutionary leaders, the United States being the only power recognizing the now hopelessly mutilated and emasculated French Republic.

Denouncing the *philosophes* as a new "aristocracy," the Montagne succeeded not in wholly erasing but temporarily crushing and permanently weakening the French Revolution's veritable Left. Executing their leaders, the Montagne also aborted the Old World's first democratic constitution as finalized by Condorcet and his colleagues, in February 1793, albeit after briefly retaining it in an amended version for a few weeks, as a modified showcase constitution, to mask the regime's unconstitutionality and hasten the Brissotin defeat. Robespierre formally suspended the constitution in

[56] Von Knigge, *Ausgewahlte Werke* iv. 13, 45.

[57] Israel, *Revolutionary Ideas*, 297.

August 1793. But even the Montagne's unrivalled ruthlessness could not eradicate Radical Enlightenment allegiance to democracy, criticism, freedom of expression, and the core values of the "real" French Revolution within France or from the wider European scene. For all its anti-intellectualism, brutality, intolerance, and violation of rights, for all its unremitting populism, the Terror and Robespierre's railing against the Enlightenment could not compel total conformity to their anti-*philosophique* Counter-Enlightenment. After Thermidor (July 1794) and Robespierre's execution, remnants of the democratic republican Revolution revived during 1795 (as again in 1830 and 1848), to resume the fight for humanity's democratic progress on the basis of Radical Enlightenment in conjunction with America's now equally besieged Paineite–Jeffersonian radicalism.

American radicals disavowed every strand of Robespierre's and the Montagne's unbendingly authoritarian and debased Rousseauist ideology equating the "general will" with dictatorship of the people to justify dictatorial government and remove all limits to its sway.[58] That Robespierre was repudiated unreservedly by all enlighteners is a point that needs stressing since it is often obscured by historians of the Revolution and directly contested by the "negative critique," especially Hunt, Bell, and Jeremy Popkin. Scarcely a single American, British, Irish, German, Italian, Belgian, Dutch, Swiss, or Scandinavian intellectual of prominence known for publicly championing the French Revolution of 1789–93 endorsed, aligned with, or in any way supported Robespierre and the Montagne. No declared democratic republicans failed to loudly and publicly condemn them unreservedly—even if it took Thorild somewhat, and Jefferson more than somewhat, longer than the rest to do so.[59] There are no significant exceptions to this rule: every prominent radical enlightener embracing *philosophisme* in the sense proclaimed by Diderot, d'Holbach, Condorcet, Volney, and Destutt—that is, commentators sympathizing with the democratic republicanism of the Revolution of 1789–93—publicly denounced Robespierre, as well as Marat and the Montagne generally for their crimes and for wrecking the veritable French Revolution.

Paine and Barlow enthused over the French Revolution but never had a good word to say for Robespierre or the Montagne, and always condemned the Terror, aligning consistently with Condorcet, Brissot, Bonneville, and the other republican democrats extolling enlightened values. Paine's ten months' imprisonment during the Terror with the threat of death hanging over his head, despite the efforts of Barlow and other Americans in Paris to extricate him, not unnaturally embittered him. If the Swedish radical, Thorild, labeled Robespierre "an all-consuming crocodile," Paine for the rest of his life deemed Marat and the Montagne the greatest criminals on earth, though Montagnard Thermidorians prominent in toppling Robespierre in July 1794, such as Billaud-Varenne and Vadier, he thought no less dishonest, politically as corrupt as the "incorruptible" himself, and rightly afterwards sentenced to life banishment in the

[58] Bates, "Rousseau and Schmitt," 281.
[59] Israel, *Expanding Blaze*; Cruise O'Brien, *Long Affair*, 310.

tropical penal colony of Cayenne. But Paine, Barlow, and Jefferson felt a parallel bitterness against those American aristocratic republicans who sought to exploit the Robespierre episode at the expense of radical opponents. Paine felt outraged by the American minister in Paris during the Terror, Monroe's predecessor, the New York "aristocrat" Morris, who, with the United States the only power maintaining normal relations with the French Republic, made no effort to rescue Paine (whom he despised) from his Montagnard prison cell. "Soon after I was put into arrestation, and imprisonment in the Luxembourg," recalled Paine later, "the Americans who were then in Paris went in a body to the bar of the Convention to reclaim me. They were answered by the then President Vadier, who has since absconded, that *I was born in England*, and it was signified to them, by some of the Committee of General Security, to whom they were referred (I have been told it was Billaud-Varenne), that their reclamation of me was only the act of individuals, without any authority from the American Government." Yes, indeed; Morris and Washington appear to have ignored the repeated requests for the US government to intervene.[60]

Washington made no move to extricate Paine and seems to have deliberately chosen Morris as ambassador to France in place of Jefferson, much as he selected Adams's son, John Quincy, for the Batavian (Dutch) Republic, with the deliberate aim of furthering aristocratic republicanism and the British model, against democratic republicanism. Morris and Quincy Adams could be counted on, he knew, to oppose democratic tendencies and radical ideas, Brissotin egalitarian principles no less than those of Franklin, Jefferson, and Monroe.[61] Consequently, it was not Morris alone that Paine and Barlow accused of cynically shelving them. The entire Federalist leadership they charged with conniving at their near destruction. After his eventual release, in November 1794, Paine did not shrink from accusing Washington himself of complicity, launching a personal vendetta against the President. "It was no more consistent with the policy of Mr Washington," he protested, in 1796, than "with that of Robespierre or of Pitt, that I should survive. They have however, missed the mark, and the reaction is upon themselves."[62]

Montagnard Counter-Enlightenment and the liquidation of leading *Américanistes* like Brissot and Condorcet, America's republican friends, was deeply distressing for democratic republicans everywhere, including the United States. The outcry against the Terror was universal. But there was an important difference in reaction between the United States and the rest. Initially, in the mid-1790s, so stubborn was the deeply-entrenched sympathy for the French Revolution among most Americans—as well as the radical fraternity—that a habit of making allowances and not condemning the Montagne too severely conspicuously took hold. France after all was besieged by numerous powerful enemies, as America had been until 1783. "Even in America," commented the English (and then Paineite) radical Thomas Cooper (1759–1839),

[60] Buel, *Joel Barlow*, 114, 179–80; Clark, *Thomas Paine*, 322, 325, 328.
[61] Wilentz, *Rise of American Democracy*, 33, 35, 823 n. 14.
[62] Paine, *Letter*, 189; Keane, *Tom Paine*, 388–9, 429–31.

recently expelled from Britain for political radicalism, the "close of the war [in 1783] was a period extremely unpleasant for a stranger to fix his residence. Violent political prejudices, impatience of differing opinions, private and personal animosities, ferocious manners, insecurity of rights, individual and national poverty, incessant political contentions, all men dividing into parties" introducing all the evils of "unsettled government were for some time prevalent in the United States." Happily, he wrote in 1794, "at present little or nothing of this kind is perceived;"[63] hopefully, the outcome in France would be similar. Certainly, the Montagne's proceedings *were* sometimes despicable, granted Cooper; "their execrable accusation of the unfortunate [Queen Marie] Antoinette, whose crimes were the crimes of the age and the nation rather than the individual; their whole system of proceeding against female delinquents, without allowing the political rights of females" was detestable from any perspective; but none of this prompted him, any more than it did Wollstonecraft or Paine, to repudiate the French Revolution as such.[64]

Ejected from Britain, Cooper had only just arrived in Pennsylvania and was actually ahead of most American opinion in expressing reservations about the Terror in his *Some Information respecting America* (London, 1794). On the American side of the Atlantic, he was also ahead of the rest in recognizing *Robespierrisme* as a total perversion of genuine democratic revolutionary values, something that had to be conceptually detached from the veritable joint legacy of the American and French revolutions. Acknowledging that as far as theory of government and society was concerned, he had been and still was an outright zealot for the French Revolution, something then totally unacceptable in Britain but perfectly usual in the United States, it was nevertheless "impossible for me to approve the ferocious injustice of many of the [Montagnard] practices." "The vague, loose, declamatory, prejudging style of their accusations; their denial of a full and fair hearing" appalled all who knew of it, as did the Robespierre dictatorship's "total disregard to past character and services, to genius and learning; their evident accusations from motives of robbery and plunder, against persons whose only crime appears to be their possession of property, the compleat and absolute despotism they have established not only over the words, actions and writings of men in France, but almost over their very thoughts, amounting to a perfect annihilation of the liberty of the press, and the liberty of speech." All this was atrocious by any standard and their "exciting every man to become a spy upon the words and actions of his acquaintance" negated the true French Revolution in every respect. For Cooper, as all authentic radicals—whether Jefferson, Paine, Priestley, Barlow, Freneau, Coram, Knigge, Paape, Gorani, Miranda, Forster, Volney, Constant, Say, Wedekind, or Thorild, the Terror meant the total unraveling, not the culmination, of the French Revolution, and consequently further raised expectations of post-revolutionary America for rescuing "universal and equal rights" and democracy.[65]

[63] Cooper, *Some Information*, 77.
[64] Cooper, *Some Information*, 75.
[65] Cooper, *Some Information*, 75.

Unlike British public opinion and the press, their American equivalents, highly significantly, remained broadly sympathetic to the French Revolution throughout the early and mid-1790s, only growing noticeably cooler from 1796.[66] Initially, the American public, like America's radical intelligentsia, condemned only the Terror and the atrocities perpetrated by Marat, Robespierre, and the Montagne, and not the democratic republicans or the Revolution. In 1796, it remained unusual in the United States to encounter the kind of blanket hostility to the French Revolution prevailing in Britain and Germany. Where one did encounter sweeping rejection and ardent alignment with Britain, this was, until around 1796, almost entirely confined to the topmost Federalist elite, and tied to the ideological antipathy to democratic republicanism of Adams, Quincy Adams, Hamilton, Jay, and Morris. Benjamin Rush, after defecting from the radical cause in Philadelphia (in the late 1770s), likewise became a convinced opponent. Nothing in this stance had changed much since the late 1770s except they now believed the Terror vindicated their unremitting hostility to all (democratic republican) revolutionary principles.

John Quincy Adams (1767–1848), America's future sixth president, on reading the first major political pamphlet, *De la force du gouvernement actuel* (1796), of the young Benjamin Constant (1767–1830), indignantly rejected his claim that the horrors of the Terror, and stifling of basic freedoms, in no way derived from the Revolution's basic principles and values. He pilloried Constant's argument that the perverseness lay wholly in the aberration of *Robespierrisme*. In later life, Constant shifted to a more "moderate" stance, but in the 1790s he remained a strong supporter of the (Brissotin) Revolution and, after Thermidor, ally of the neo-Brissotin revolutionary elements striving to salvage the Revolution by reversing the legacy, despotism, anti-intellectualism, and populism of Montagnard dictatorship. John Quincy, scion of the Federalist social elite, turned his ire on Constant, no less than Paine, for claiming the basic unity of the American and French revolutions and insisting on the oneness of the revolutionary values proclaimed by the democratic Enlightenment of the American and French (and Swiss, Irish, Dutch, and Vonckist Belgian and Dutch) radical intelligentsias.

Constant's perspective John Quincy termed "depravity."[67] For John Quincy, like his father, the atrocities of the Terror *were*, on the contrary, the direct, logical consequence of the democratic and anti-religious principles and ideology that had forged the French Revolution.[68] John Quincy and his father were outraged too by Paine's suggestion that a majority of the British people opposed monarchy and the existing British constitution, and would do well to follow the French example. Commenting on John Quincy's scathing review of Paine's *Rights of Man* in the Boston press, in 1791, Jefferson remarked scornfully that the French Revolution's

[66] Wilentz, *Rise of American Democracy*, 53–65.
[67] Palmer, "Two Americans," 406; see John Quincy Adams, *Writings* ii. 213.
[68] Vincent, *Benjamin Constant*, 32–8; Israel, *Revolutionary Ideas*, 697–8.

detractor was attacking "Mr. Paine's principles" which were the "principles of the citizens of the U.S."[69]

Conservative counter-revolutionary and Counter-Enlightenment writers all over Europe had a vested interest in destroying Constant's analysis. For conservatives, it was essential that the public should accept that the Terror *was* the fruit of *la philosophie moderne*, the direct consequence of its anti-religious universalism, secularism, democratism, and *philosophisme*. For them, this was a vital point: Condorcet had been forced to take poison, as one royalist publicist put it, not by hopelessly ignorant ordinary folk and anti-intellectuals but by "his brothers in philosophy."[70] French counter-enlighteners like De Maistre, while agreeing Marat was a criminal and murderer, and approving of the neo-Brissotin removal of his remains from the Paris Panthéon, on 8 February 1795—a mere five months after the Thermidorians, trying to shore up their sagging support, had put him in[71]—denied this sufficed to repair the Panthéon's moral integrity. De Maistre gleefully quoted a then current conservative witticism: "I understand very well how one can de-pantheonize Marat, but I shall never conceive of how one can de-Maratize the Panthéon."[72]

From 1789, both radicals and *ancien régime* defenders regularly interconnected the American and French revolutions, perceiving the latter as the direct outcome of the former. From the mid-1790s onwards, by contrast, observers and commentators increasingly divided into progressives identifying "an identical spirit at work in both America and France," insisting, like Paine and Cloots, that the "cause of France is the cause of mankind," and conservatives seeking to "play one revolution against the other."[73] The Terror, held Constant, in 1796, issued not from the Revolution's authentic values but the illiberal, anti-Enlightenment reaction permeating Montagnard Jacobinism.[74] Constant's urging all Europe's enlightened intellectuals to support the new post-Montagnard French revolutionary government, the *Directoire*, in proclaiming Robespierre "le chef" of the Terror, a dictator who was neither a republican nor follower of *la philosophie moderne* but the Enlightenment's antithesis, precipitated a furious trans-Atlantic ideological quarrel at the time, which has continued, eventually involving Marxist theory and then Postmodernism, to this day.

When Adams tried to persuade Anglophone radical opponents like Price and Priestley that the American Revolution differed fundamentally from the French, they answered that he was mistaken.[75] Where Adams's contrary classification proved persuasive was among Europe's reactionary monarchists (though he disliked these), and conservative foes of "philosophy," like the Dutch anti-democrat Orangist,

[69] Jefferson to Adams, Philadelphia, 30 Aug. 1791, *Adams–Jefferson Letters* i. 250; Unger, *John Quincy Adams*, 73–80.

[70] Rivarol, *De la philosophie*, 68–72, 75; Roederer, *De la philosophie*, 29; McMahon, *Enemies*, 95–9.

[71] Israel, *Revolutionary Ideas*, 597, 601.

[72] [De Maistre], *Considérations sur la France*, 7.

[73] Schulte Nordholt, *Dutch Republic*, 277; Bevilacquer, "Conceiving the Republic," 560.

[74] Constant, *De la Terreur*, 349–50; Spitz, "Républicanisme," 29–30, 44; Craiutu, *A Virtue*, 216–17.

[75] Grant, *John Adams*, 363; Wilentz, *Rise of American Democracy*, 97, 123.

Gijsbert Karel Van Hogendorp (1762–1834), an acute observer of Europe and America who concurred with both Adamses, Hamilton, Morris, and Jay that America's Revolution was about law, order, separation of powers, and protecting property. By contrast, the deluded French had overthrown monarchy, social hierarchy, and religion, the indispensable pillars of modern society. The veritable American Revolution, American and European conservatives agreed, was not about equal rights, secularism, installing democracy, or promoting society's general welfare in Condorcet's or Jefferson's sense: it was about revolution as authorized by Locke, Montesquieu, and Burke, sanctioned above all by the triumph of informal aristocracy over democratic republicanism. Adams's "American Revolution" was irrelevant to reviving monarchical absolutism of the kind proclaimed by Charles X of France in the mid and later 1820s; but it warmly approved of conservative aristocratic monarchies boasting limited constitutions and suffrages like the British monarchy prior to the Great Reform Act (1832), the post-1814 Dutch monarchy, and the "liberal" monarchy of Louis Philippe (1830–48).

America's second president, and the first major theorist and enlightener to claim the two great revolutions were profoundly different, Adams held that the French Revolution differed fundamentally from the American—and was heading for disaster—from its commencement. Like Franklin, Jefferson, Madison, Monroe, Paine, Rush, Freneau, and most Founding Fathers, Adams too felt deeply committed to the Enlightenment. "The nations of Europe, appeared to me, when I was among them, from the beginning of 1778, to 1785, i.e. to the commencement of the Troubles in France, to be advancing by slow but sure steps towards an amelioration of the condition of man, in religion and government, in liberty, equality, fraternity, knowledge, civilization and humanity. The French Revolution I dreaded; because I was sure it would not only arrest the progress of improvement, but give it a retrograde course, for at least a century, if not many centuries. The French Patriots appeared to me like young scholars from a college or sailors flushed with recent pay or prize money, mounted on wild horses, lashing and speering, till they would kill the horses and break their own necks."[76] In 1813, he reminded Jefferson how all the Enlightenment's hopes had subsequently been blighted. "Let me now ask you very seriously my Friend, where are now in 1813, the perfection and perfectability of human nature? Where is now, the progress of the human mind? Where is the amelioration of society? Where the augmentation of human comforts? Where the diminutions of human pains and miseries?"

Adams knew perfectly well that "rights of mankind," the trans-Atlantic democratic tendency, was an American as much as European Enlightenment invention and that Jefferson, now a friendly correspondent, was the chief patron of the idea that the American and French democratic republican revolutions were one joint enterprise, and a longstanding ally of Condorcet and Paine. Like his son, John Quincy, he blamed

[76] Adams to Jefferson, 15 July 1813, *Adams–Jefferson Letters* ii. 357.

not only the French but just as insistently the parallel radical American legacy propagated by a phalanx of democratic writers and journalists headed by Paine, Barlow, Priestley, Freneau, Duane, Coram, Cooper, Callender, Lyon, and Benjamin Austin (1752–1820), a republican publicist who during Adams's presidency (1797–1801) unsparingly derided Massachusetts' chief politician in the Boston papers. The stable American republic he had helped found, contended Adams, was being pushed into confusion and disorder by a ruinous democratic and radical republican ideology. "When? Where? And how? Is the present chaos to be arranged into order?" "There is not, there cannot be, a greater abuse of words than to call the writings of Callender, Paine, Austin and Lowell or the speeches of Ned. Livingston and John Randolph, public discussions. The ravings and rantings of Bedlam merit the character as well; and yet Joel Barlow was about to record Tom Paine as the great author of the American Revolution! If he was, I desire that my name be blotted out forever, from its records."[77]

Not all of those Adams deemed disruptive were radicals. The Virginia planter, John Randolph of Roanoke (1773–1833), nominally a Congress "Jeffersonian" (until he broke with Jefferson, in 1803), and lifelong opponent of slavery, championed states' rights mostly to promote conservative positions. But those Adams chiefly blamed for America's domestic ideological deadlock were out and out radical enlighteners. Personal relations between Adams and Paine had long been vitriolic. But their decades-long quarrel, while personal, also reflected the profound ideological rift intrinsic to both the American and French revolutions. Paine considered Adams "one of those men who never contemplated the origin of government, or comprehended anything of first principles," vilifying him as an ally of hereditary government, monarchy, and aristocracy whose main concern was to find "some sinecure for himself, and a provision for his descendants. He did not go so far as to say, also, that the vice-presidency should be hereditary in the family of John Adams," but it was no secret he wanted his son, Paine's prime public enemy, John Quincy, to follow him. "He prudently left that," added Paine snidely, "to stand on the ground that one good turn deserves another," insinuating that Adams counted on his own unstinting support for Washington's presidential pretensions to secure his help for his son.[78]

9.3. MOBILIZING THE MASSES; FORGING CONSTITUTIONS

Revolutions, including the English Revolution of the 1640s, usually manifest a tense, ideologically complex relationship between political leaders and the common people, especially society's "lower ranks." But only rarely, at moments of chronic breakdown

[77] Adams to Jefferson, 15 July 1813, *Adams–Jefferson Letters* ii. 358; Wilentz, *Rise of American Democracy*, 95.

[78] Paine, *Letter*, 184.

in law and order, do the people themselves become the prime actor or agent shaping events. Except for brief moments, during the most spectacular *journées* of the French Revolution, the "people," though constantly invoked, rarely presided. It was hence another key affinity between the American and French revolutions, that, against the backcloth of an often largely uncomprehending population, all revolutionary factions claimed to want to raise the general level of "happiness," promote amelioration of society, to be recommending the course that most favored the "common good," rhetoric first introduced by the Enlightenment. All contemporary contenders vying for control of the French Revolution—Robespierre too—agreed the Revolution was primarily prepared and initiated by *philosophes* and "la philosophie," leaving the common people, whether as beneficiaries, victims, or prime obstacle, dangling at the receiving end, rather than participating as prime actors.

The least informed were also seen as more volatile in their allegiances than other groups, more likely to shift from one faction to another, from one extreme to another, suddenly and unpredictably. The illiterate and less literate were also more likely than other groups to embrace vivid myths and heed reactionary voices, often religious authority, directing them to support all kinds of authoritarian indoctrination, and especially the aristocratic–ecclesiastical system of faith and deference, and reject revolutionary values. Many barely literate men joined the royalist Vendée revolt of 1794–5, much as they did the "Church and King" riots against the French Revolution's supporters in Britain and likewise the pro-Orangist reaction against democrats in Holland; the same is true of the popular pro-Church, pro-aristocracy, *Vandernootiste* rising of 1787–90, in Belgium. Disagreeing about everything else, the sole point on which Robespierre Jacobins, Hébertistes, Girondins, moderate monarchists, right-wing constitutional monarchists, and outright ultra-royalist counter-revolutionaries could agree unreservedly was that the common people were readily swayed, continually misled, utterly divided, and profoundly baffled throughout. If those sections of modern historiography claiming the different political ideologies identified with different social interest groups were correct, the common people would have actively shaped and promoted those programs. But neither the American nor French Revolution was, or could have been, impelled in its general direction and ideological contours by social groups. Rival elites mobilized and directed the ordinary man's aspirations using rival highly complex ideologies and revolutionary scripts.

While the common people were continually affected and caught up in the process, all the revolutions were organized and directed by "Founding Fathers," leaders often commencing as publicists, newspaper editors, and orators gaining national profile by forthrightly promoting either "moderate" or explicitly republican, constitutionalist, and egalitarian positions. Democrats and egalitarians claiming that representative democracies promised most were almost invariably universalists considering such republics best for all mankind, the right framework for promoting freedom of thought, expression, and the press, eliminating institutionalized hierarchy and aristocracy, and eradicating ecclesiastical authority. This quest for a universally superior constitutional framework based on democratic republicanism arose with equal force in America and Europe and was always inherently anti-Lockean and anti-Montesquieuian. Despite a few genuinely unique features, such as adoption of a strong, one-person executive in the American Constitution of 1787 (opposed by Paine and Jefferson), the constitutional schemes devised to uphold "universal and equal rights" either side of the Atlantic possessed a good deal in common.

Correspondingly, leading figures of the broad coalition of conservative and liberal monarchists in France, the "moderates," including Mounier, Lally-Tolendal, Barnave, the Brothers Lameth, Malouet, Maury, Clermont-Tonnerre, and Jean-Nicolas Démeunier (1751–1816), who, like La Rochefoucauld, was a renowned expert on American state constitutions, paralleled their American "moderate" counterparts by likewise seeking constitutional safeguards designed to block democracy and buttress informal aristocracy. Meanwhile, there was also some shifting between the rival blocs. From June 1791, this "moderate" group also comprised Lafayette, who, though earlier, in 1789–90, an ally of Jefferson and friend of Condorcet proclaiming himself a "republican," chiefly strove to bridge the gap between radicals and moderates, eventually choosing the latter. Earlier, before 1789, Démeunier had collaborated closely with Jefferson in producing articles and books on America, culminating in his *L'Amérique indépendante, ou les différentes constitutions des treize provinces qui se sont érigées en républiques sous le nom d'États-Unis de l'Amérique*, published at Ghent as part of the Belgian revolutionary upheaval in 1790.[79]

The American Revolution, then, like the French, was in part a product of the moderate mainstream Enlightenment opposing absolutism, mercantilism, fiscalism, and ecclesiastical authority, on the one hand, and, on the other, a rising radical tendency ensconced at its core originating in Franklin's, Paine's, Jefferson's, and Madison's publicly proclaimed democratic principles. Franklin during his last months and weeks certainly entertained anxieties about the French Revolution but, until he died, remained hopeful that his and Jefferson's principles would finally prevail, especially after hearing Jefferson's detailed report of his experiences and observations at Versailles. "The convulsions in France," noted Franklin on 4 December 1789, "are attended with some disagreeable circumstances; but if by the struggle she obtains and secures for the nation its future liberty, and a good constitution a few years enjoyment of those blessings will amply repair all the damages their acquisition may have occasioned. God grant that not only love of liberty, but a thorough knowledge of the Rights of Man may pervade all the nations of the earth, so that a philosopher may set his foot anywhere on its surface and say 'This is my country.'"[80]

Enlightenment, then, for both main factions either side of the Atlantic, formed the fiercely contested core. Here is the central theme without which no discussion of either revolution makes much sense. Of course, hardly anyone's stance was wholly consistent in every respect. In Jefferson's case, the radical construct sat uneasily and ambiguously with his status as a leading Virginia "aristocrat" and slave-owner, and

[79] Palmer, *Age of the Democratic Revolution* i. 251.

[80] Franklin, *Writings* x. 72; Cruise O'Brien, *Long Affair*, 6; Wilentz, *Rise of American Democracy*, 38–9.

most of all with his status as president (March 1801–March 1809).[81] During the 1790s, though—and this was doubtless the reason for his prolonged reluctance publicly to repudiate the Montagne—he viewed the French Revolution not just as deeply akin to the American Revolution but as an indispensable antidote to what he saw as the Federalist tendency to surreptitiously edge away from, dilute, and betray the values of' 76. Recognizing the American and French revolutions as an indissoluble joint enterprise seemed to him essential to upholding what he considered the veritable values of the United States, something necessary for fending off the growing threat of a reversal of principles in America, engineered by a landowning-mercantile "aristocracy" championed by Adams, Hamilton, and Morris, a menace he deemed allied to British interests and high finance. If Jefferson "hated" England, as several commentators complained, what he reviled was the "aristocratic" Britain striding the world as an unrelenting antagonist of the joint cause of the American and French revolutions as he understood them, as chief co-ordinator and paymaster of the forces of reaction, monarchy, aristocracy, and religious authority everywhere which he viewed as vying with true revolutionary principles for domination of the world. Which enlightenment, then, would the new United States actually promote domestically and in the wider world? That of Montesquieu, the "British model" and America's "aristocracy," or that of the democratic radicals? The first and original revolution, as Mirabeau put it, "qu'avoue la philosophie" [that philosophy acknowledges], it was far from obvious which of the two divergent Enlightenment ideological streams that engendered them would be prime driver and beneficiary, becoming prime generator of the wider Western series of revolutions in their collectivity.[82]

With universal and equal human rights crucial to their common duality, and both main revolutions undergoing marked oscillations in direction depending on where and when moderates or radicals presided, another striking shared feature illustrating the parallelism of the American and French revolutions, and marking them off from all previous revolutions, were the public intellectuals who first enthusiastically publicized democratic republican revolutionary values but then, for whatever reason, grew disillusioned, changed course, and emerged as reverse-direction ideologues vehemently attacking and seeking to overturn revolutionary principles. A notable instance was Jean-François de La Harpe (1739–1803), dramatist and disciple of Voltaire and who, as a publicist during 1789–93, like Marie-Joseph Chénier (1764–1811), passionately supported the Revolution, not least freedom of the press and theater. The Terror, though, which left him languishing for four months in the Luxembourg prison in Paris in 1794, overturned his earlier perspective: he now vigorously repudiated the Revolution and especially its democratic tendencies. In particular, in his two-volume *Philosophie du Dix-Huitième Siècle*, mostly composed in 1797 albeit not published until later, he denounced that strand of Enlightenment

[81] Wright, "Thomas Jefferson," 74–7; Dahl, *On Political Equality*, 19.
[82] Mirabeau, *Considerations*, 1.

"philosophy" that had given birth to the joint trans-Atlantic Revolution, a malign ideological current, he believed, that originated with Diderot.[83]

A notable American parallel illustrating this switching of sides was Noah Webster (1758–1843), a leading education theorist and America's chief lexicographer. All revolutionary turmoil, observed Webster, a leading commentator on the French Revolution who published an extensive analysis of it, in New York in 1794, creates unwanted difficulties, disruption, and trouble. Difficulties arise especially "when tumultuous meetings of people, unknown to the laws and unrestrained by legal modes of procedure, undertake to direct the public will." The result, held this former radical turned conservative, is faction and "faction begets disorder, force, rancorous passions, anarchy, tyranny, blood, and slaughter."[84] As in the French Revolution, so "at the beginning of the late revolution in America, the people of this country had recourse to a similar mode of combining all parts of the continent into a system of opposition to the existing government." To counter royal oppression, revolutionary "leaders found it necessary to call in the aid of the great body of the people, to rouse their passions, inflammatory publications were circulated with great industry, and to unite, condense, and direct the opinions and passions of an immense people, scattered over a great extent of territory, associations were formed under the domination of committees of safety, which had a correspondence with each other, and molded the proceedings of the people into uniformity and system. The first Congress grew out of the same system; and then followed union, concert and energy in prosecuting the Revolution."[85] Elated initially, it took Webster much longer than his friend Benjamin Rush (1746–1813), a leader of the Philadelphia Enlightenment who, from 1779 onwards, repudiated the revolutionary ideals he had embraced in 1774–6, until he too reversed and declared against democratic republicanism. Rush especially deplored how the American Revolution initiated democratization, weakened religion, and changed the "principles and morals" of the people.[86]

It seemed amazing in the America in 1775–6, remarked Webster, that "such a number of illiterate men should be prevailed upon to resist tyranny in principle, and risk the evils of war," when the "effects of the British claims were but slightly felt by the mass of the people." Yet, it was the common people who impelled and sustained the Revolution, enabling the leaders to secure the *Declaration of Independence* even though most ordinary folk participating showed little grasp of the issues, and needed to be shepherded toward the declared goals. In this respect—the temporarily successful mobilizing of the unaware and barely literate by revolutionary vanguards as an ill-informed motor of revolution—the two revolutions either side of the Atlantic, it struck Webster, seemed particularly closely akin. In France, in July 1789, a protesting, upstart fringe of democratic republican orators, journalists, and *philosophes* captured the Revolution precisely as happened earlier in America, but captured it only

[83] Israel, *Revolutionary Ideas*, 18–20.
[84] Webster, "Revolution in France," in *Collection*, 31.
[85] Webster, "Revolution in France," in *Collection*, 31–2.
[86] Wood, *Radicalism*, 366; Wood, *Empire of Liberty*, 14, 487.

precariously, and thanks to their ability to incite, diffuse incendiary ideas, and organize agitation in the streets. Social forces thus animated both revolutions in a peculiarly passive and unknowing way as far as goals were concerned. To gain ground, France's democratic republican leadership required a host of café orators, theater habitués, theatre men, and journalists, as well as the phalanxes gathered in local revolutionary associations and clubs. Outside the main cities, though, these assets were of little help in mobilizing the endemic discontent and everywhere the resentment of the illiterate proved difficult to control. The Bastille's fall, in July 1789, was followed by weeks of rural unrest in parts of France, including, disquietingly, unplanned attacks on noble *châteaux* involving murder and pillage, even though popular fear aroused by sensationalizing reports greatly outstripped reality.[87]

The National Assembly expressed outrage and dismay at this anarchy, but having been propelled into government by the people, as one observer put it, the Revolution had no way of disciplining the people.[88] In America and France alike, a peculiar mix of skills was required to manage and manipulate popular sentiment and disturbance with the consequence that revolutionary rhetoric and exhortation more and more veered toward exaggeration, crass distortion, and lies. "The truth is discernment and talents were necessary to form and direct the system, but the multitude" were managed far more by prejudice and passion than reason. "The committees of safety were the instruments of union, and the passions of the populace the instruments of action." The printing presses teemed with publications sensationalizing the "horrors of slavery;" those "who wrote, intended when they wrote, to exaggerate real facts for the purpose of rousing the passions of resentment and dread of evils, which reason told them were not to be expected." The most worrying and enduring parallel between the American and French revolutions, suggested Webster, was that "in a popular government, it is not difficult to inflame the passions of a people with imaginary as well as real evils."[89]

In France, in July and August 1789, fear fed by sporadic peasant violence precipitated a wave of emigration (the first of several) of nobles from the countryside, including members of some of the most illustrious lineages—Condés, Contis, Polignac, and Breteuil—from the environs of Paris.[90] By 1794, tens of thousands of nobles, clergy, writers, intellectuals, and wealthy commoners had fled the country. Nevertheless, when compared with the huge exodus of Loyalists from the United States between 1775 and 1783, estimated at around 60,000, frequently chased from their homes in Philadelphia, New York, Boston, and elsewhere by unruly demonstrations and intimidation, *émigrés* taking some 15,000 slaves with them, one can hardly claim the aristocratic-ecclesiastical exodus from France from 1789 down to 1793 represents a contrast with the American pattern. Rather, in proportion the exodus of *émigrés* exiled by the American Revolution was much larger than the exodus caused by the French Revolution. America's *émigrés*—white Loyalists, escaped blacks, and

[87] Fontana, *Venise*, 320. [88] Dumont, *Mémoires de Mirabeau*, 94–5.
[89] Webster, "Revolution in France," in *Collection*, 32. [90] Furet, *Revolutionary France*, 69.

resentful Native Americans allied to the British—were forced to flee in large numbers to Canada, East Florida, the West Indies, and Britain: some 6,000 whites to the Quebec area, 5,500 to Jamaica and the Bahamas, and around 5,000 whites and 6,500 blacks to British (and then from 1779–81 Spanish) West and East Florida (today the states of Mississippi, Alabama, and Florida, all reconquered by Spain at that time).[91]

The unrest and intimidation driving the exodus was more explicitly an assault on entrenched social elites in France than was harassment of Tories in America; but the assailing and pillaging of the aristocracy in (parts of) rural France were no part of any program proclaimed by any legislative faction competing for control of the Revolution from 1789 down to June 1793. Pillaging the aristocracy as such did not form part of the revolutionary agenda, or at least not until late 1793 when the Revolution was derailed by authoritarian populism. Many or most nobles, clergy, and other refugees fleeing France between July 1789 and June 1793 departed in much the same spirit of dread and despair at the chaos and disorder, hence the same reasons, as American Loyalists between 1775 and 1783: they left abjuring the Revolution and its principles, refusing to accept the loss of privilege and influence entailed. Often, like their American Tory counterparts exiled abroad, they expected to participate in the reconquest and ideological purging of their homeland from without.

One apparent difference between the revolutions was American preference for two-chamber legislatures and separation of powers, versus French preference for a single chamber and primacy of the legislature. But, here too, what at first looks like a contrast when more closely examined turns out to be a parallelism. Heady debates over bicameral versus unicameral arrangements played out on both sides of the Atlantic. Many American democrats, including Franklin, Jefferson, and Paine, harbored serious doubts about two chambers; and in Pennsylvania and Vermont, the only states to adopt genuinely democratic constitutions, in 1776–7, the original choice was not actually for two chambers but, as Franklin preferred, a single chamber (as remained the case in Pennsylvania until 1790).[92] The French revolutionary leadership opted for a single chamber in 1789, and continued to until 1795; but this preference ended with Thermidor and was never conceded by Mounier's and Lally-Tollendal's liberal monarchists. In France, from 1788–9 onwards, there were always numerous "partisans" of the British Constitution, especially among constitutional moderates who, like many Americans, considered the two-chamber system, each balancing the other, "the masterpiece," as Pétion sarcastically styled it, "of modern politics."[93] Under the 1795 French Constitution, a two-chamber system was introduced by the neo-Brissotin revived "real Revolution" and this remained the pattern until Napoleon's consolidation of dictatorial power in 1799.

[91] Jasanoff, *Liberty's Exiles*, 6, 354–7; Clark, *Thomas Paine*, 11.

[92] Palmer, *Age of The Democratic Revolution* i. 219, 231–2; Wilentz, *Rise of American Democracy*, 805 n. 31.

[93] Pétion, *Avis aux François*, 92; Appleby, "America as a Model," 270–2.

Discussing bicameralism, in 1788, Pétion did not doubt that it would appeal to many French political leaders. In theory, an upper house could function as a useful and valuable check on the lower.[94] But if bicameralism suited America, it remained inappropriate, he thought, for a still hierarchical society like France: being accustomed to languish under a dominant aristocracy and privileged clergy, an upper chamber in France was apt, like the House of Lords serving England's aristocracy and bishops, to be an instrument of entrenched social elites placing the two houses, in terms of the interests they represented, eternally at loggerheads. Viable in America, two chambers would be as harmful in France as in Britain. But, like most European observers at the time, he was still under the spell of the myth of American equality and imagined there were no American equivalent of France's domineering seigneurs presiding over the United States. Every American householder supposedly enjoyed an admirable independence, leaving less to divide the two legislative chambers; from which he inferred that two American chambers would work together harmoniously, debating freely and enlightening each other.

Mounier and other moderate leaders summoned the French to turn their backs on "philosophy" and embrace British experience and common sense. They clashed outright with Condorcet, Pétion, and Brissot, who all, like Paine, had already before 1789 dismissed the British Constitution as corrupt, "unenlightened," and defective. Here they exactly paralleled the summons of America's aristocratic republicans that Americans should sidestep "reason" and adhere to solid traditions inherited from England.[95] During the early revolutionary years, France's National Assembly resounded just as fulsomely to eulogies affirming the superiority of the British constitutional model as the American legislatures. If, early on, Mounier and Lally-Tollendal abandoned the fight by fleeing abroad, their place was taken by Barnave and other centrists striving to check the tide of republicanism and democracy. Until late 1791, there was good reason to suspect that "mixed government" devotees championing two chambers, separation of powers, and Montesquieu would preside over both revolutions.

Both revolutions debated which citizens should be represented and how representatives should be allotted. A pre-eminent principle of the French Revolution, in 1789, was the idea that a legitimate representative system assigns an equal number of voters and family dependants to each elected representative. Approximately the same number of mouths to feed should be represented by each National Assembly deputy. For this reason, late in 1789, Mirabeau, Sieyès, and the National Assembly's other leading reformers abolished the old French provinces with their different sizes, local institutions, and legal systems and established the new framework of "departments" all identically constituted, with cantons of equal population, able to organize elections based on genuine equivalence of representation. Very different was the American system both in state elections and electing the Congress, where representation

94 Pétion, *Avis aux François*, 93–4.

95 Arendt, *On Revolution*, 68; Whatmore, *Republicanism*, 67; Lefer, *Founding Conservatives*, 305.

remained on a spectacularly unequal basis. While in Massachusetts there were between three and four hundred representatives in the state legislature's lower chamber, in Pennsylvania, with virtually the same size of population, there was "not more than one fifth" of that number. "New York, whose population," in Madison's words, "is to that of South Carolina as six is to five, has little more than one third of the number of representatives. As great a disparity prevails between the states of Georgia and Delaware, or Rhode-Island."[96]

Where Pennsylvania provided one representative for every four or five thousand people, Rhode-Island boasted one for every thousand, or even slightly less. These were huge disparities which were then in turn reflected and magnified in the Federal Senate where every state had two senators despite state populations varying greatly, giving Delawarians and Rhode-Islanders, for example, many times more Senate voting power per person than pertained to inhabitants of New York or Virginia. Democratic radicals in the American Revolution, commencing with Franklin and Jefferson, worried about these discrepancies. When copies of the American Constitution first arrived in France shortly before the Revolution, Condorcet, for one, expressed marked disquiet: "I see with pain," he admonished Franklin, in July 1788, that the "aristocratic spirit seeks to introduce itself among you despite many wise precautions."[97] Yet the divergence between American and French revolutionary practice was less a question of principle than force of existing circumstances. In principle, Franklin, Jefferson, and Madison concurred with their French allies.

A key divergence between the respective revolutionary governments was the great power of the executive under the American Constitution and, especially, its being vested in one person rather than committees. "There is an idea," commented Hamilton, in March 1788, "which is not without its advocates, that a vigorous executive is inconsistent with the genius of republican government." Indeed, there was; and this objection became widespread after 1787 in the United States as well as France, not least in Franklin's mind and that of Jefferson. If Hamilton disdained those who "regard the servile pliancy of the executive to the prevailing current either in the community, or in the legislature, as its best recommendation," many believed subservience to the legislature and Constitution was precisely the quality that should be required of a republican executive. The same argument demonstrating the need to separate the powers of government, contended Hamilton, "teaches us also that this partition ought to be so contrived as to render the one independent of the other. To what purpose separate the executive, or the judiciary, from the legislature, if both the executive and the judiciary are so constituted as to be at the absolute devotion of the legislative? Such a separation must be merely nominal and incapable of producing the end for which it was established."[98]

[96] *The Federalist* 55 (Madison, 13 Feb.1788), 269–70; Fenimore Cooper, *Notions of Americans* i. 261.
[97] Quoted in Billias, *American Constitutionalism*, 81, 409 n. 116.
[98] *The Federalist* 70 (Hamilton, 15 Mar. 1788) and 71 (Hamilton, 18 Mar. 1788), 341, 349–50.

From 1788 down to the Montagnard coup of June 1793, few French revolutionaries argued for a strong executive independent of the legislature. But there were some who did, notably in the early stages, when Mounier and the moderate royalists sought to retain extensive powers in the monarch's hands in emulation of the British royal (and American presidential) example. From 1791, urging a strong executive was chiefly characteristic more of Marat and the Montagnard faction, who took to calling for a dictatorship and scorned genuine debate. After June 1793, in the hands of the Montagnard group dictatorship the pressure to defer to ideological orthodoxy steadily intensified with extreme intolerance of dissent and criticism becoming the defining feature. Repeated purges took place at the center of power in Paris, and constant purges and a sustained drive to eliminate dissent also in the provincial Jacobin clubs, or *sociétés populaires* as they were called. "So, while the base of the Jacobin clubs was broadened socially," as one historian expressed it, it became "extremely narrow politically by the time Robespierre was overthrown."[99] Orthodoxy, authoritarian censorship, and conformism wholly displaced freedom of thought and expression.

After Thermidor, the French Revolution reverted to the concept of a carefully circumscribed group executive (the Directory), supposedly subordinate to the legislature though the system never attained much stability or efficiency and Jefferson grew distinctly critical of it.[100] The French Revolution ended (for the time being) with Napoleon's *coup d'état* of 9 November 1799 [18 Brumaire An VIII]. Jefferson, Madison, and many another American expressed profound dismay that France should thus depart from the previously shared global revolutionary platform, leaving the United States alone on the world stage, as the solitary remaining republican model.[101]

The parallels and affinities between the American and French revolutions, then, are arguably far more lastingly significant than the differences. Moreover, there is an important sense in which both revolutions ended in the 1790s but yet both in a certain sense also lived on as a continuing inspiration at home and abroad.

The French Revolution no more ended in Napoleon's dictatorship, in 1799, held Auguste Comte (1798–1867), the most eminent French philosopher of the early nineteenth century, than the American Revolution ended in 1783. Among the founders of sociology and modern political science, Comte maintained in 1848, in a lengthy report to his Positivist Society in Paris "on the nature and plan of the new revolutionary government of the French Republic" set up that year,[102] that France had been continually "in revolution" for over sixty years since the "decisive explosion" of 1789 "began to transport the mutation that had already taken place in thinking into the political sphere." The mutation in ideas that caused the French Revolution *qua* revolution had had a generalized effect in society and should be studied as a continuing, irreversible process. To this he added yet another blistering attack on

[99] Wolloch, *Jacobin Legacy*, 8, 10. [100] Welch, *Liberty and Utility*, 127.
[101] Jourdan, *La Révolution*, 357.
[102] BHVP Printed 14086/6: Comte, "Rapport à la Société," 5–6; Muglioni, *Auguste Comte*, 84.

the British model (and Montesquieu), a system which, he thought, had failed utterly "in France and Spain" before, as after, 1814, and would prove equally irrelevant to the majority in Italy.[103] The French Revolution viewed as a long-term process would conclude, reaching viability and stability, only on the basis of philosophy allying with democratic republicanism. Hence, it was essential, he added, to finally win over the working populace, the *prolétaires*, to the cause of the democratic republic. While this required studying history with a scientific eye and evaluating social circumstances by means of the new science of sociology, it was only by immediately conceding the principle of universal suffrage and creating a network of political clubs to guide and educate the workers in true political principles that the democratic republic could be built.

[103] BHVP Printed 14086/6: Comte, "Rapport à la Société,", 13–14; Muglioni, *Auguste Comte*, 86.

10

"General Will" and the Invention of Universal and Equal Human Rights (1750–1789)

10.1. "GENERAL WILL" AND THE RISE OF EQUAL RIGHTS

Central to the American Revolution's significance in 1789, and its global significance today, was the advent of universal and equal "human rights."[1] At the point the *Declaration of Independence* was thrashed out, in 1776, crucially important changes had just occurred, during the third quarter of the century, in the trans-Atlantic debate about "rights." Diderot in his article "Droit Naturel" (1755) in the *Encyclopédie*, setting aside the natural right jurist tradition of Grotius, Pufendorf, and Barbeyrac (in a manner subsequently rejected by Rousseau), redefines man as a rational animal who, through his nature, inevitably prioritizes his own happiness above everything else and can only civilize and rationally seek and consolidate his natural right by institutionalizing and equalizing this unalterable impulse of nature within society, by fixing, stabilizing, and universalizing the pursuit of happiness as an irreducible general equity of "natural right."[2]

A disciple of Diderot and d'Holbach, Cérutti echoed this idea that "general right" or "general will" is the "right of each individual becoming the general right" after the fall of the Bastille, in a pamphlet on the general lines of the future French constitution urging French people and their revolutionary leadership to emulate the American Revolution in avoiding all atrocities and internal splits within their Revolution and, also, to be just to other peoples, remembering that the Helots were the "crime impardonable" of Sparta, as black slavery remained the "crime impardonable of Europe."[3] With Diderot's and d'Holbach's intervention began a new stage in the Enlightenment's evolution, one precipitating a general intellectual upheaval that was to be closely followed by a political revolution that, before long, gripped North America and Europe.

[1] Arendt, *On Revolution*, 147.

[2] Diderot. "Droit naturel," in Diderot, *Oeuvres* (Versini), iii. 46–7; Wokler, "Influence of Diderot," 68, 75, 103, 107; Goggi, "Spinoza contre Rousseau," 156–7, 159, 162; Riley, "Kant on the General Will," 340–1.

[3] Cérutti, *Vues générales sur la constitution*, 21, 29.

In that seminal article, Diderot renders the "human race" itself judge and arbiter, through reason (not sensibility or feeling), of what constitutes true universal and fundamental equity, the "common will." It is to the *volonté générale* that the individual must address himself to know what it is to be a "man, citizen, subject, father, child and when it befits him to live or die."[4] In this way, (non-Rousseauist) "General Will" theory and "universal and equal rights," not just in contradistinction but very much in conflict with Rousseau, became two sides of a single coin together with "universal and equal rights," both crucial to the complex, slow, and arduous process of forging a genuinely democratic republicanism. From the mid-1770s, under the stimulus of the American Revolution, this powerful new intellectual–political concoction, "general will" grounding "universal and equal rights," predicated on the democratic republic, rapidly matured as an active agenda for revolutionizing the world either side of the Atlantic. Diderot, Rousseau, d'Holbach, Raynal, Cérutti, La Rochefoucauld, Condorcet, Volney, and Destutt de Tracy all lent their particular insights and energy to steering French pre-1789 republican "universal rights" revolutionary political reformism in this direction. Radical Enlightenment *volonté générale* was thus a particular tradition, commencing with Spinoza, the first to declare that the best and freest state is that "so established that all men, both rulers and ruled, whether they so will or not" find themselves obliged to "do what is in the interest of their common welfare" [*salus communis*], that is, "all live as reason prescribes."[5] If he was not the first to introduce the "general will" into the European political thought tradition, Spinoza was the first, as it has been aptly put, "to understand and employ the notion in an explicitly political fashion."[6] It was a tradition that tirelessly stressed the primacy of reason and the universal as the basis of the state and always diverged fundamentally from Rousseau's in recent times more famous, but narrower, less universal conception. Rousseau's was "a great deal more *particulière*," as it has been put,[7] though it is very possibly true that Rousseau must have borrowed his idea that whoever refuses to obey the general will "shall be compelled to do so by the whole body"—and hence "forced to be free"—from Spinoza.[8] In any case, based on Diderot's and d'Holbach's *morale universelle* [universal morality], *volonté générale* in the radical tradition, from Diderot down to Volney and Destutt, regularly and expressly abjured Rousseau, Sparta, Rome, and all domination of one people by another. It was a fiercely secular ideology proclaiming the kind of universal morality to which Spinoza, Bayle, and Shaftesbury had aspired earlier, a *morale universelle* originating in the state of nature but carried over into the state, and fixed and institutionalized by the state, and which, according to Diderot, will always remain fixed and the same.[9]

4 Diderot, "Droit naturel," in Diderot, *Oeuvres* (Versini), iii. 46.

5 Spinoza, *Tractatus Politicus*, 64–5.

6 Williams, "Spinoza and the General Will," 129.

7 Riley, "Kant on the General Will," 341–2; Villaverde, "Spinoza, Rousseau," 179.

8 Villaverde, "Spinoza, Rousseau," 87–8; Villaverde, "Rousseau, lecteur," 118–19; Israel, *Democratic Enlightenment*, 636–7.

9 Diderot, "Contributions," 587, 628; Goggi, "Spinoza contre Rousseau," 170–3; Peña, "Lumières radicales," 315.

Diderot employed the term *volonté générale* eight times in just this one four-page article, as well as many times elsewhere, most strikingly in his sections of the *Histoire philosophique*, tying "general will" inseparably to universal and equal human rights. Despite being much less often referred to today, Diderot's conception of *volonté générale* was nevertheless substantially more relevant and historically more formative than Rousseau's rival notion, which, as both Diderot and Rousseau themselves were aware, was in several respects a strikingly different conception.[10] For it was precisely the universality, equality, and inalienability of universal rights, in Diderot's and d'Holbach's concept, that was to dominate usage of the main concept "*volonté générale* as we find it becoming widely diffused in the immediate pre-revolutionary and revolutionary eras via the works of d'Holbach, Condorcet, Cérutti, Sieyès, Destutt, and likewise Volney, who derived his *philosophique* system from Helvétius as much as Diderot and d'Holbach and was indebted also to Boulanger and Fréret, but was even more contrary and antagonistic to Rousseau and his thought than were Diderot, d'Holbach, and Condorcet.[11] When the French revolutionaries declared in Article VI of the *Declaration of the Rights of Man*, in August 1789, that the "Law is the expression of the general will" it was decidedly not Rousseau's conception that underlay a usage introduced by Mirabeau, Sieyès, La Rochefoucauld, and Cérutti, the radical vanguard of France's National Assembly.

What Radical Enlightenment *volonté générale* did have in common with Rousseau's *volonté générale* was its being conceived as the sole and exclusive source of legitimacy in politics: everything else, divine authority, ancient charters, dynastic ambition, conquest, hereditary rights, belonging to a particular caste, is relegated by General Will to total redundancy. But while the two divergent notions had this vital thread in common, the two kinds of *volonté générale* otherwise differed fundamentally, above all in their republican consequences. In mainstream secular democratic republican systems postulated by the Radical Enlightenment, Man is envisaged as incapable of attaining fulfillment, of being as happy and long-lived in isolation or trapped in "savage "society; Man can attain his highest happiness only in enlightened civilized society, with General Will providing the basis not just for particular republics but linking all rationally organized societies together. Non-Rousseauist *volonté générale*, unlike Rousseau's, indissolubly ties the concept to legislative supremacy, representation, the nation's legislature, and each nation's constitution, legally fixed fundamental "rights" being deemed attainable only at the highest levels of civilization, under fully rational government which is, by definition, inherently incompatible with monarchy, nobility, religious authority, and the hereditary principle.[12] Mainstream revolutionary doctrine was explicitly anti-Rousseauist in addition in being closely linked to denunciation of war and conquest, rejecting Rousseau's (and Robespierre's) adulation of the

[10] Wokler, "Influence of Diderot,"100–5; Riley, "Kant on the General Will," 340–2.

[11] Rosso, "De Volney," 349; Deneys, "Volney, Auteuil," 108, 115, 117, 120.

[12] Cérutti, *Vues générales sur la constitution*, 33–5, 74; Destutt de Tracy, *Commentaire*, 68, 157; Jolly, "Introduction," 46.

"Spartan" as well as abjuring all dynastic ambition in statecraft, recognizing, as Condorcet expressed it in 1782, that the "true interest of a nation is never separate from the general interest of the human race." Hence, mainstream General Will championed an international order of justice.[13] For Condorcet, and his followers, Volney and Destutt, only two kinds of government exist in the world, those based on *volonté générale*, that is legitimate regimes serving the interest of all on the basis of equality, and those based on minority vested interests, or what Destutt termed "gouvernements spéciaux."[14]

Radical Enlightenment *volonté générale* thus differed fundamentally from Rousseau's notion, and not least in being an entity expressed via elections wherever the method of representation, of electing representatives, was "véritablement nationale" [truly national], as Volney put it, speaking before the National Assembly, in Paris, on 18 September 1789, that is where private individual interests are balanced and checked by "l'intérêt general."[15] The national legislature "depends on the General Will," agreed Cérutti, and this is "represented" by the nation's "delegates."[16] During the September 1789 National Assembly debates over the future French constitution's outline, and whether, under the new "mixed government" system, the monarch should possess an absolute, or temporary, veto over legislation, La Rochefoucauld, repeatedly asserted, like Cérutti and Volney, that the future "national assembly must be permanent," being "l'expression de la *volonté générale*" and that the king must remain subordinate to the "volonté générale de la nation"; the principle he also invoked to justify establishing a single rather than two-chamber legislature.[17] Among Condorcet's circle debating constitutional theory at the height of the Revolution, in 1792–3, figured, beside Brissot, Pétion, and Paine, all members between October 1792 and February 1793 of the National Convention's "Comité de constitution," several others who likewise contributed to developing revolutionary "General Will" theory, "devising a real institutional foundation for the General Will." Serving alongside Condorcet and Brissot in a more advisory capacity, these included Delmotte, Debry, Daunou, and Pierre Guyomar (1757–1826), one of Condorcet's staunchest supporters against *Robespierrisme*, a veteran republican democrat since the 1770s and now also promoter of women's rights.[18] Jean Debry (1760–1844), who in 1795 was a leader of the neo-Brissotin come-back in the Convention, envisaged universal rights in a broad sense, as also did Department Du Nord deputy François

[13] Condorcet, *Oeuvres* i. 398; Imbert, *Destutt de Tracy*, 87, 114; Cook, "The Great Society," 309–28; Devellennes, "Fourth Musketeer," 474–5.

[14] Imbert, *Destutt de Tracy*, 35–6.

[15] BL 7R 74/16: "Motion de M. de Volney, deputé d'Anjou,"18 Sept. 1789, p. 4; Cerutti, *Vues générales*, 74, 82.

[16] Cérutti, *Vues générales*, 58.

[17] BL 7R 74/24, "Opinion de M. le duc de la Rochefoucauld," 7 Sept. 1789, pp. 5, 7, 12, 18–19.

[18] Gauchet, *Révolution des droits*, 214, 298; Davidson, "Feminism and Abolitionism," 106; Israel, *Revolutionary Ideas*, 361–2.

Poultier Delmotte (1753–1826), all being implacable foes of Robespierre, popular Rousseauism, and the Montagne both before and after 2 June.[19]

These National Convention constitutional theorists defined *volonté générale* as the participation of all in the *force publique* understood as a system of rights, including the right to subsistence, allowing the majority no right to mistreat, impoverish, or intimidate minorities.[20] Poultier Delmotte wanted it stipulated in the Constitution "that the allegedly General Will voted by the majority cannot bind the minority when it evidently violates the *Rights of Man*. The minority always remains free to remind the majority of their true sovereign—*la raison universelle* [universal reason], the sovereign that dictated those rights."[21]

Poultier Delmotte, among the Convention's most colorful personalities, once a priest and later a soldier, was too independent-minded to align politically for long with any faction. A revolutionary journalist and *littérateur*, author of a book on Condillac's epistemology and another on the Polish partitions, he viewed the history of revolutions generally as a dismal story. To him it was a tale of how readily the common people are misled and deceived by impostors. Ambitious men directing "the sovereign's will" in ways conducive to their own interests and sway generally substitute their own private will for that of the people they dupe. In addition, the majority's will itself often involves unjustly subjecting the weakest to the strongest and hence becomes the gateway to a new tyranny. *Volonté générale*, taken in its *Rousseauiste* sense untreated, he thought, actually facilitates subjection to tyranny and oppression, blighting everyone's rights. "Let us assert, then, that reason is the only veritable sovereign among men; and that to reason alone belongs the right to make laws. Laws not dictated by reason are never obligatory, even when sanctioned by the majority." "Let us begin, then," he urged colleagues, "by recognizing this great truth: that among men there exists no other legitimate sovereign on earth than *la raison universelle* and that this truth constitutes the most fundamental principle on which we base the majestic edifice of our Constitution."[22] Here was the true language of encyclopedism, Diderot, d'Holbach, Raynal, and Radical Enlightenment, a rhetoric that unrelentingly presupposed a republican and democratic form of government.

This anti-Rousseauist mainstream tradition of French revolutionary *volonté générale* political thought culminated in the *Idéologues* and especially Volney and Destutt de Tracy, classic late Radical Enlightenment thinkers. When the questioner in Volney's revolutionary "catechism" for French citizens asks why Rousseau identified the "state of perfection" with the "savage state," he answers that this is because the vulgar often award the title "philosophers" to whimsical, extravagant geniuses, who, from moroseness, wounded vanity, or disgust with the vices of society, dream up "for

[19] Taillandier, *Documents*, 76; Urbinati, *Representative Democracy*, 176–87; Israel, *Revolutionary Ideas*, 346–8.

[20] *Archives Parlementaires* lxvii, p. 289 (24 June 1793); Gauchet, *Révolution des droits*, 294–6.

[21] Poultier Delmotte, in *Archives Parlementaires* lxvii, p. 383 (24 June 1793).

[22] Poultier Delmotte. in *Archives Parlementaires* lxvii, p. 382 (24 June 1793).

themselves chimerical ideas of the savage state contradictory to their own system of a perfect man." In reality, he added (echoing d'Holbach), "man in the savage state" is a "brutal ignorant animal, a wicked and ferocious beast, like bears and ourang-outangs."[23] For Destutt too, the decisive, overriding factor in political science is "Enlightenment." Where Volney pronounced "ignorance" the real "Original Sin" that perverts mankind, for Destutt it is only a given society's level of enlightenment, its "degré de civilization", a notion concerned with education, awareness, and moral attitudes, and appropriate ways of behaving toward women, that determines the "forme de gouvernement" apt for that society.[24] Tension always intervenes between real circumstances and the ideal conditions for liberty, and attainment of *volonté générale*, and this led Destutt to place less emphasis on declarations, and lists of universal rights, than Sieyès, Mirabeau, or Condorcet, and more on the social mechanisms helping society attain higher levels of respect for individual liberty, minority rights, women, freedom of expression, and freedom of the press.

Universal and equal rights are the mark of the best societies, held Destutt, but merely proclaiming lists of rights, and devising formulae to itemize them, is no way to achieve them. Struck by the lack of enthusiasm of most of French society for the constitution of 1795 despite its specifying "rights" in the most explicit manner, Destutt concluded that the best institutions and laws *absolument*, in abstract terms, are not necessarily the best *relativement*, in a given historical context, that "institutions can only improve in proportion to rising levels of Enlightenment among the mass of the people."[25] It was studying history in his, Condorcet's, and Volney's[26] sense, and the conditions that fit particular laws and institutions, that enables us to learn the basics of political science, and understand the mechanisms enabling a society to graduate to higher levels of respect for universal and equal rights. Chief among these auxiliary mechanisms, for Destutt, were eliminating the hereditary principle, a principle he proclaims perennially in opposition to *volonté générale*, eradication of nobility, slavery, and despotic attitudes toward women, along with minimizing religious authority's influence, curbing economic inequality, and, most urgent of all, lessening inequality of "enlightenment" by raising the educational level of the population generally.

"Before the tribunal of philosophy and reason," avers Diderot, in the *Histoire philosophique*, "morality is a science the aim of which is the conservation and happiness of the human race."[27] For Diderot and d'Holbach, this is the justifying criterion of all laws, institutions, duties, and rights.[28] There exists no other valid moral criterion. By introducing and binding together in the 1750s the two new concepts of "rights of mankind" and *volonté générale*, re-conceptualizing all rights

[23] Volney, *Abridgement of the Law of Nature*, 3; Walters, *American Deists*, 202–3.

[24] Jolly, "Introduction," 40.

[25] Destutt de Tracy, *Commentaire*, 135.

[26] "Volney soutient que la seule histoire utile doit comporter l'universalité, faire abstraction des moeurs et des traditions d'un pays, et viser l'humanité toute entière," Rosso, "De Volney," 346, 348.

[27] Diderot, "Contributions," 629.

[28] Diderot, "Contributions," 587–90, 629–33; Goggi, "Spinoza contre Rousseau," 175–7.

and justice as equity and reciprocity of basic freedoms universalized, Diderot and the *encyclopédistes* transformed the discourse of "rights" from Locke's fragmentary, occasional "rights" differing in different lands and contexts, into a newly invented universal and revolutionary conceptual apparatus that underlay the American and (democratic republican) French Revolution. Re-conceptualizing mankind as a totality based on a world-wide, uniform "enlightened equity" opened the door to universal and equal human rights, and to proclaiming the essential unity of mankind whatever men's color, creed, or social status, laying the intellectual basis for the democratic republican constitutionalism and revaluation of all values of the revolutionary era (1775–1848). It was a development which tied the destinies of North America and Western Europe closely together in the most dramatic fashion for three-quarters of a century.

That the newly independent United States in 1776 offered their revolutionary principles as an example to follow to the rest of the world has, of course, frequently been denied.[29] Most Founding Fathers evinced very little interest in establishing new universal concepts of government and the *Declaration of Independence* itself was intended, by most Founders, less as a profound innovation of universal significance than to pave the way for a lasting confederacy uniting the colonies and prepare for "forming foreign alliances."[30] For most American revolutionaries, and most Founding Fathers, the Revolution was simply a revolt against the British crown and Parliament intended to consolidate "mixed government" and the Revolution principles of 1688 on a firmer basis, perfecting an inheritance derived from England. Practical realities, not ideals and theory, were what mattered. But, for some, the American Revolution assumed a much broader significance, challenging the most essential values of *ancien régime* Europe and America. Coupling the revolt against the British crown with democracy and the "universal rights of man" was what chiefly lent the Revolution global significance, as Paine and Price forcefully pointed out, precipitating a vast and highly complex development transpiring on both sides of the Atlantic across a wide terrain during the 1770s. America's *Declaration of Independence* on the basis of natural, universal, and equal rights precipitated a massive unsettling wave of subversive debate throughout the trans-Atlantic Enlightenment.[31]

The American Revolution's legitimacy was challenged and denied from the outset by all the European monarchies then dominating the international arena, including the United States' allies in the war against Britain, Spain, and France, a situation that confronted the revolutionaries with an urgent need to justify their revolutionary claims and establish their theoretical credentials. In Germany, pro-prince conservative enlighteners and "moderates" were as emphatic as Britain's Parliament and the Dutch Orangists in pronouncing the American Revolution unjustified and illicit, an attack on legitimacy, crowns, and churches everywhere, no universal example and platform for human amelioration but a crime against God, authority, and all order, a

[29] Wills, *Inventing America*, 318, 350–1.
[30] Wills, *Inventing America*, 319–27; Herzog, *A Short History*, 181–2.
[31] Ferrone, *The Enlightenment*, 152.

going astray to be comprehensively condemned. If the American "colonies had acted without deception," admonished the Berlin Lutheran pastor Andreas Riem (1749–1807), in his widely-read pamphlet *On Enlightenment* (1788), expounding a firmly moderate Enlightenment standpoint, they would not now be an anarchic state that "subsists unsteadily through weak bonds without any majesty, a state whose constitution is without true inner greatness and without the force that a well-ordered entity ruled by a sovereign must have. Every state [of the American Union] is sovereign, and so every state is by itself powerless! There is no spirit of harmonious unity, and everywhere there are false concepts of freedom!"[32] Universal democratic principles, redefining what is good in society, law, institutions, and politics exclusively in terms of "l'interêt général et commun" as expounded by Diderot, d'Holbach, Raynal, Jefferson, Paine, Price, Priestley, Brissot, Condorcet, Volney, and Destutt, were entirely illicit in the eyes of the Western world's courts, churches, aristocracy, and most contemporary theorists.

Radical-minded republicans, by contrast, not only fervently sympathized with the joint American and French Revolutions, predicting their triumph despite the immense concentration of courtly power and monarchical–aristocratic systems ranged against them, but sought to accelerate that triumph by mobilizing support and propagating egalitarian principles on all sides. In promoting the new United States' propaganda war in Europe, no publication intervened more effectively than the *Histoire philosophique* of Raynal and Diderot. In the ninth volume of the hard-hitting 1780 revised edition, Diderot (anonymously) denounced Britain for treating the Americans as their "serfs," expressing confidence that the Revolution would succeed and exert an immense influence on the world. American agriculture and industry, he predicted, and the law, arts, and sciences would all prosper; the United States would prove a great example: "may all tyrants and oppressors, either political or religious, know that a place exists in the world where people can cast off their chains; where persecuted humanity has raised up its head again; where the harvest grows for the poor, the laws are no more than the guarantee of happiness, religion is free and conscience no longer a slave; where nature, finally, wishes to be justified in having created man; and government, for so long guilty over all the earth, finally makes good its crimes." According to radical enlighteners like Paine, Price, Priestley, Jefferson, and Condorcet, the American Revolution was the commencement of the General Revolution, a universal leap forward, forging a government that for the first time functions on behalf of the people in their great majority. Such a sanctuary, predicted Diderot—who became more and more anti-monarchical and subversive as well as openly atheistic in his last years—would "frighten the despots" and restrain their tyranny; for even though kings are by long habit indifferent to the happiness of mankind, they readily yield ground when fearful—when afraid, that is, like the aristocracy and clergy, of losing their power and wealth.[33]

[32] Riem, *On Enlightenment*, 177.
[33] Diderot, *Political Writings*, 204; *Histoire philosophique* (1780), ix. 375–9.

Diderot and d'Holbach forged a social philosophy in which "man," as Mirabeau expressed it after two years of the American Revolution, in 1777, "in all the countries of the world, has the right to be happy; that is the first of laws, the first of entitlements."[34] It was a foundational law of society that tied the individual to the collective in a fundamentally new manner. The world's peoples were summoned by Mirabeau and many another French republicanizing *philosophe* electrified by the American Revolution to "learn from the Americans the art of being free, of being happy, of turning social institutions to the profit of all the individuals who compose society." That art was the new art of revolution, underpinned by the "right to revolt" to recover human liberty, end slavery, and establish collective and individual "happiness."[35]

An earlier rhetoric of "rights" and "liberties" employed by publicists and pamphleteers around the time of the "Glorious Revolution (1688–93) and during the eighteenth-century prior to 1776, in English, was abundantly in evidence still and historians long supposed the frequent references to "rights" encountered before 1776 belonged to a long, gradual, venerable, almost natural progression toward the conception of universal "human rights" enjoyed equally by all humans. Americanists once argued endlessly whether Locke or the English gentry republican tradition reaching back to the seventeenth-century author James Harrington (1611–77) was the prime source for the genesis of modern "human rights." In reality, neither Locke, who had no conception of "General Will," nor the English gentry republican tradition, participated in the advent of universal and equal "human rights" which was the central principle at issue in the American and French revolutions. Locke anchors his theory of "rights" in protection of property and conformity to Christianity, creating a hierarchy placing nomads, native American Indians, and the landless in some sense beneath proprietors, and libertines, Catholics, Jews, atheists, and homosexuals beneath Protestant believers, that severely qualified or restricted "rights" to civil liberties and empowered the people to participate in the political process, and scrutinize and criticize government, only in a limited, tentative manner.[36]

There is a basic discordance and divergence, then, between the "rights" discourse of the early mainstream Enlightenment and "the rights of mankind," the universal and equal rights discourse promoted by Paine, Price, Mirabeau, Condorcet, and Volney, as well as by American radicals like Franklin, Jefferson, Young, Allen, Freneau, Coram, and Palmer, in that effective protection of natural and inalienable rights becomes conceivable, possible, and immediately attainable only when the people examine, judge, and participate in the political process. With respect to "rights of mankind," Paine quite rightly dismissed the principles of the British "Glorious Revolution" of 1688–91 as something quite distinct, and far less significant, than the new principles lending universal significance to the American and French

[34] Mirabeau, *Avis aux Hessois et autres peuples de l'Allemagne*, 314.

[35] Mirabeau, *Avis aux Hessois et autres peuples de l'Allemagne*, 317, 326, 329.

[36] Dickinson, *Liberty and Property*, 68–9, 240–1; Marshall, *John Locke*, 695–6; 702, 712–18; Brewer, "Slavery, Sovereignty," cue 107; Wills, *Inventing America*, 229–31, 295, 310.

revolutions. Analysis of the "architecture" of "rights" as a concept and cultural entity, and the objectives sought, demonstrates that neither the ubiquitous pre-1776 talk of "rights" nor the theory of "natural right" deriving from early modern "Natural Law" concepts is really linked to post-1776 universal human rights as a conceptual construct designed to transcend particular national traditions and legal systems, and all religious authority, while equalizing the status of all individuals, peoples, and social classes.

"Natural rights" discourse was basic to teaching of Natural Law theory in the seventeenth and eighteenth centuries. But the "rights" that ensued, including the right of authorities "to punish," mostly served to bolster existing systems of government and privilege, and hence of repression, to promote virtue and piety according to responsibilities and duties imposed by the divine plan. Unlike his predecessors, the Huguenot exile Jean Barbeyrac (1674–1744), among the leading commentators on Pufendorf and Natural Law theory, active in Switzerland, Germany, and Holland, did adopt freedom of conscience, the right to toleration, as a fundamental inalienable "natural right" that no government could justifiably infringe or withdraw, coupling this, following Locke, with the right of resistance to sovereigns who break the social contract. But it remained unclear whether even Barbeyrac's progressive reformulation of the doctrine applied to non-Christians; and it most certainly did not apply to non-believers, deists, and outright atheists.[37] Like Locke's still more restricted semi-toleration, which militated also against Catholics, Jews, and those belonging to other non-Christian faiths, Barbeyrac's toleration remained severely limited.

In any case, Barbeyrac fails to link freedom of conscience to other conceivably inalienable rights that governments or social classes might violate. "Natural Law theory," however pivotal in the history of law and philosophy, was not particularly focused on individuals but aimed rather to define and clarify the divergent "rights" pertaining to different status groups and levels of authority when viewed as derivative from, and secondary to, duties emanating from a divinely imposed universal moral law.[38] Adam Smith, who delivered a series of lectures on "natural rights" at Glasgow in 1762–4, building on the tradition of Grotius, Pufendorf, and Barbeyrac, specified an impressively broad range of "natural rights" including the right to reputation, property, to engage in commerce, and to obtain justice. But none of his "natural rights" presupposed universal equality of political and legal status, universal freedom of expression, or a generalized right to amend or rewrite political constitutions that fail to uphold universal human rights such as is affirmed in the American *Declaration of Independence*.[39]

A staunch "moderate," believing the aristocracy should remain the governing class in Britain, Adam Smith undoubtedly promoted "natural rights" but remained highly antagonistic to every egalitarian, democratic conception of "rights". Conventional

[37] Haakonssen, "German Natural Law," 254–5.
[38] Haakonssen, "German Natural Law," 259; De Bolla, *Architecture of Concepts*, 72.
[39] Moore, "Natural Rights." 301–2, 308–9; Allen, *Our Declaration*, 145–6, 183.

eighteenth-century "rights" viewed as "civil liberties" and universal and inalienable human rights as a universal political principle simply constitute two disparate and in some ways antagonistic intellectual traditions and value systems. For this reason the "jusnaturalist" tradition, as it has been called, was generally treated cavalierly and set aside with an ironic nod not just by Diderot and d'Holbach,[40] but likewise by Condorcet and the whole radical *philosophique* tendency. Grasping the difference between the two distinct traditions is less a question of terminology, or particular phrases, given that the expressions "human rights" and "rights of mankind" did appear occasionally in English-language texts before 1776, as we see in the case of Tindal, but rather a question of grasping the basic change in meaning, and patterns of thinking, driven by the festering contradictions of a socially and culturally highly stratified society where the status and "rights" of different groups and classes, and of kings in relation to their subjects, previously sharply and hierarchically distinct, and resting on divine sanction, came to be full-frontally contested. The older framework's continuing prevalence, and incompatibility with the new universal and equal rights doctrine, helps explain the vehemence of Smith's and Burke's hostility to the democratic, universalist doctrine of the Welsh dissident preacher Richard Price—whom "I have always considered a factious citizen," remarked Smith, in December 1784, "a most superficial philosopher and by no means an able calculator."[41] Another leading Scots enlightener, Ferguson, likewise scorned Price's universal human rights while expressing his preference for historically evolving specific "rights," especially the right to property.[42] Inherently antagonistic though Natural Law "natural rights" and the universal and equal rights of revolutionary democratic republicanism were, the swift demise of Natural Law theory in European universities in the years around 1800, precisely when universal and equal rights were gaining ground, seems to have been accelerated by fears, at universities and in government, that "natural rights" were in some dialectical way, perhaps now just their evident flimsiness, helping to disseminate and mobilize support for universal "human rights" theory.[43]

Pre-1776 usages of the "rights" concept, in short, lacked all the basic characteristics of modern universal and equal human rights—universality, equality, a generalized right to understand and insist on their application, eradication of theology and religious authority from their sanction, participation of everyone in upholding them politically, and the "constitutional priority" of rights over everything else: all are either wholly absent or else not present as a tightly interlinked and integrated package. The concept of universal human rights was to an extent pre-echoed, it has been suggested, in *A System of Moral Philosophy* by the earlier Scottish moral philosopher Frances Hutcheson (1694–1746); but, while one or two universal criteria do permeate Hutcheson's "rights of men," most of the above criteria remain

[40] Goggi, "Spinoza contre Rousseau," 166. [41] Smith, *Correspondence*, 290.
[42] Dickinson, *Liberty and Property*, 139–40, 297; Hamoury, "Scottish Thought," 369–73.
[43] Moore, "Natural Rights," 315.

conspicuously absent and the general concept is anyhow expressed only very tentatively.[44] All considered, neither the pre-1770 general discourse of "rights" nor the philosophical–legal tradition of Natural Law, often used to bolster institutionalized slavery and monarchical sovereignty, the latter especially in Germany and Denmark,[45] nor the legacies of Harrington, Sidney, or Locke, afforded an adequate conceptual basis for the universality and inalienability of the "rights of man" proclaimed by revolutionary America and then revolutionary France.[46] No continuous thread of "rights" evolving toward universal "human rights" within the mainstream Enlightenment occurred in the eighteenth century, no preparatory work, or clearing of the path for universal rights, is found in Locke, Harrington, the Scots philosophers, or Natural Law theory.

10.2. WHY THE "CULTURAL" EXPLANATION OF THE INVENTION OF HUMAN RIGHTS IS WRONG

Separating pre-1776 uses of the term "rights" in English from the sudden emergence of "human rights" in the 1770s is supported not only by analysis of the divergent structures of ideas but also digitally collected data recording usage of the expression "rights" where linked to "mankind," all men," or "citizens."[47] The pre-1770 conception invested "rights" in authorities, institutions, groups, castes, or churches, and in divine command; the new conception, very differently, operated without theological sanction, vesting equality of rights in everyone and in all peoples universally. Nothing could be more fallacious than claiming the equality invoked by Paine and Jefferson, in 1776, was "very similar" to the civil liberties derived from Locke's "Arminian enlightenment," or regard the "conviction that all men possessed natural and inalienable rights" as an outcome or derivation of Enlightenment "rationalism" as such.[48] The decisive change reflects the irruption of a revolutionary consciousness in the Western world during the 1770s. Confirmed by both intellectual history and digital book history methods, the abruptness of the upsurge of universal "human rights" rhetoric in English and French, from around 1770, solidly disproves not just traditional Harringtonian and Lockean accounts of the 1776 American *Declaration of Independence*, and all invoking of the jusnaturalist tradition, but every generalized explanation of the rise of human rights in terms of Enlightenment rationalism and rejection of tradition as such. One could be as rationalistic and skeptical about norms and tradition as Voltaire, Montesquieu, Hume, Smith, Gibbon, and Bentham, as committed to the idea of progress as Joseph II or Turgot, without moving one jot toward universal "human rights."

[44] Wills, *Inventing America*, 231–9; De Bolla, *Architecture of Concepts*, 114–15.
[45] Haakonssen, "German Natural Law," 256–8.
[46] De Bolla, *Architecture of Concepts*, 53, 67.
[47] De Bolla, *Architecture of Concepts*, 82–3.
[48] Dickinson, *Liberty and Property*, 243; Wills, *Inventing America*, 173–5.

The divisiveness and suddenness of the change to comprehensive theories of equal "human rights" also contradict the new cultural history's attempt to explain the "invention" of "human rights" as a consequence of gradual cultural shifts, social practice, or reading novels. The pre-eminent exponent of the "cultural" thesis, Lynn Hunt, acknowledges that "before 1789, 'rights of man' had little cross-over into English,"[49] yet insists that the underlying sentiments behind "rights of man" discourse should be conceived as a new commitment to autonomy and empathy that "had deep roots." Gradually, the people were transformed into morally and socially independent agents less tied to communities and churches than earlier, and this broad social–cultural process, she contends, was reflected in the art and especially the epistolary novels of the era. "My argument depends," writes Hunt, "on the notion that reading accounts of torture or epistolary novels had physical effects that translated into brain changes and came back out as new concepts about the organization of social and political life."[50] Reading novels might well heighten empathy and sensitivity toward others but is far too vague a factor to explain a dramatic conceptual shift in terminology so far-reaching as to pull together in an integrated package the essential elements of the revolutionary doctrine arising abruptly during the 1770s; it also signally fails to account for the continuing deep divisions over the question in both America and Europe.

Hunt's explanation is indeed "wide of the mark" in being unable to explain either the abruptness of the advent of "universal and equal rights," or the subsequent deep divisions they provoked; neither does it distinguish between principles and readers (who in most cases were white, European, and upper class); but in any case, no account of the "invention" of modern human rights assuming universal rights became an uncontested commonplace (least of all in the French National Assembly of 1789) can have any real analytical value.[51] One scholar reviewing the debate since the 1980s saw that Hunt's thesis is untenable, and that Samuel Moyn's claim that post-1948 modern "human rights" are based on different principles from the universal and equal rights of the *philosophes* is likewise fallacious and misleading. The new concept of human rights is directly linked to post-1948 "human rights" and cannot have derived from novels, Locke, or the jusnaturalist tradition. But he then produced an argument as untenable and misleading as Hunt's and Moyn's, attributing the invention of universal and equal rights to the French *philosophes* as an undifferentiated group and tradition, suggesting Voltaire's contribution was as substantial as Diderot's, and that their intellectual intervention suddenly spread widely, becoming a generally accepted commonplace owing to "sensibility" and cultural diffusion so that no particular intellectual vanguard was needed to persuade the French National Assembly to embrace the "Rights of Man and the Citizen" in 1789. They supposedly all or mostly agreed on it. The "cultural shifts" approach is thus only half discarded in this

[49] Hunt, *Inventing Human Rights*, 24; De Bolla, *Architecture of Concepts*, 48.
[50] Hunt, *Inventing Human Rights*, 33.
[51] De Bolla, *Architecture of Concepts*, 143–67, 245; Hunt, *Inventing Human Rights*, 33–4.

curious piece of revisionism, which remains just as unhelpful as the approaches he dismisses for explaining the deep rift over universal and equal "human rights" in late eighteenth-century society, politics, and intellectual life. If there is little reason to assume "new kinds of reading (and viewing and listening)" created "new individual experiences (empathy)" or generated the "new social and political concepts (human rights)" from within society and general culture, and no reason to think cultural shifts explain either the timing of Jefferson's adoption of the new "rights" concept, or the bitter post-1775 divisions over that concept; then neither is there reason to suppose moderate *philosophes* vaguely referring to "rights" provide any sort of explanation either.[52] All these approaches are evidently wide of the mark.

Far from most of France and Europe embracing universal rights, which is what one would expect if the "cultural shifts" argument, the appeal to sensibility and sentimentality, were valid, the concept remained extremely divisive and was widely rejected for many decades. The prolonged and bitter controversies over applying the new principle in key instances, such as emancipating the Jews, clearly arose neither from "cultural shifts" nor the writings of the moderate *philosophes*. Most people in Alsace-Lorraine, where the largest Jewish community in eighteenth-century France lived, as well as (initially) a majority of the National Assembly, vigorously opposed full Jewish emancipation in 1789–91; only a tiny, resolute fringe advocated it, not because the great majority had failed to read enough novels, were devoid of sensibility, or had forgotten their Voltaire, but because most opinion, guided by churchmen, remained, like the papacy, fiercely hostile, culturally, intellectually and religiously, not just to granting Jewish rights, but to the very principle of universal and equal rights.[53] And since "cultural shifts" cannot explain the profound divisions in society and the National Assembly during 1789–91, strife over whether the principle of human rights should be adopted, how could an appeal to the moderate *philosophes* do so more convincingly?

Only a minority of *philosophes* were abolitionists, urging an end to slavery, in the late eighteenth century and those who did were the radical *philosophes* invoking universal and equal rights. In America too, opponents of democracy broadly rejected universal and equal rights, among them many staunch republicans of a more traditional type, anchored in seventeenth-century English gentry (or "classical") republicanism. Thus, the foremost adversary of the new American order of Cincinnati, Aedanus Burke (1743–1802), though incontestably an ardent republican antagonistic to monarchy and nobility, opposed abolitionism, resolutely defending slavery, on the basis of state rights and Lockean sacrosanctity of "property." For Burke rejecting "universal and equal" rights mattered every bit as much as abjuring kings and aristocratic privilege. Aedanus had little time for the propertyless in general, not

[52] Edelstein, *On the Spirit of Rights*, 196, 202–3, 297 n. 6; on this point, see also D. Edelstein, "Enlightenment Rights Talk," JMH 86 (2014), 530–65.

[53] See Jonathan Israel and Lynn Hunt, "Disputations: Was Louis XVI Overthrown by Ideas?," *New Republic*, 31 July 2014.

just slaves, and was later notoriously unsympathetic toward the Pennsylvania "Whiskey Rebels" of 1794 whom he dismissed as "silly, mischievous Yahoos."[54]

At the same time, it is vital not to slide into a logic, like Furet's, envisaging the "French Revolution" as a single revolutionary consciousness unfolding, as a single revolutionary language, born suddenly under the stress of intense pressure, in an emergency situation heightening the political involvement of a comparatively large mass of individuals.[55] The Revolution *did* arise out of revolutionary consciousness but did so well before 1789, through the 1770s and 1780s, and stemmed from intellectual innovation, not any cultural shift. When Paine's pamphlet *Common Sense* (1776), dated Philadelphia, 14 February 1776, accuses Britain of offending all mankind by brutally attacking a particular country, thereby "declaring war against the natural rights of all mankind, and extirpating the defenders thereof from the face of the earth,"[56] he was invoking a new style of political thought rooted in Diderot, d'Holbach, Raynal, and the radical standpoint.[57] The American transmitters of this change in doctrine, rhetoric, and tone, Paine, Young, Lee, Mason, Franklin, Jefferson, and others who engineered this conceptual mutation on the American side, were assuredly drawing on the widely-diffused and vigorous pre-1776 French radical discussion of universal "rights." There was no "rights of mankind" ideology directly infused among the population under pressure of the 1774–6 American drama itself. American and subsequent British usage borrowed the pre-existing French radical doctrine of "universal rights" as expounded in Diderot, Raynal's *Histoire philosophique*, d'Holbach, Helvétius, and their followers, a trans-Atlantic transmission aided by the intensity of Jefferson's profoundly Francophile attitudes. This is confirmed by the fact that it is exclusively in the French radical literature of the early 1770s that we first encounter an uncompromising emphasis on universality, equality, inalienability, and the priority of the "rights of mankind" over each and every particular constitution.

French radical thought on the eve of the American Revolution was suffused with *volonté générale*, crypto-republicanism, rejection of religious authority, and universal and equal rights. In d'Holbach's *Politique naturelle* (1773), Diderot's and his radical coterie's characteristic doctrine that rights of peoples and individuals are universal is powerfully reaffirmed. All laws not democratic in the sense of serving the "common benefit," the interest of society as a whole, "are disavowed by reason." Hence, upholding the people's "rights" essentially means ensuring governments do not prey on the majority, or serve minority interests, but are obliged by the people (the true sovereign) to promote the interest of society as a whole, *l'utilité générale*, "general utility" defined as the worldly interest of the greatest number, which d'Holbach pronounces the only just and rational basis of the law.[58] "Rights" of peoples are defined by nature but can only be fixed by rational, good laws. "Rights" here orbit in close proximity to equality, the interest of the majority, blocking the selfish initiatives

[54] Meleney, *Public Life*, 187–90.
[55] De Bolla, *Architecture of Concepts*, 196–7, 202.
[56] Paine, *Common Sense*, 63.
[57] Stewart, *Nature's God*, 7, 19–20.
[58] D'Holbach, *La Politique naturelle*, 26–9, 44, 47.

of kings and vested interests, rejecting bellicose ambition to conquer and colonize, ending militarism and war, rejecting colonialism, suppressing slavery, and promoting the freedom the individual enjoyed in the state of nature insofar as the "common good" or *volonté générale* permit these to be transferred into society. The notion that individual and group freedoms and autonomy are carried over directly from the state of nature is a prime radical doctrine common to Diderot, d'Holbach, Raynal, Helvétius, Condorcet, Cérutti, Volney, and Destutt. But it was clearly an older concept, one Diderot—and initially Rousseau too, until after 1755—derived directly from Machiavelli and Spinoza and that remained as a marker, constituting the prime difference between Hobbesian and Spinozist political theory.[59]

Laws not operating in the interest of the greatest number are, for these political thinkers, unreasonable and cannot embody, be based on, or protect any "rights," being products of tyranny and violence. Such laws lack legitimacy. Pressure and publicity of various kinds, even force, may legitimately be used to secure rights, but exclusively where these conform to equity and justice, a rule applying to peoples no less than individuals. Since men always are entitled to enjoy the "rights of nature" grounded on reciprocity and justice, the "rights" of peoples and individuals are "eternal and inalienable." Societies can adopt laws that vary; but insofar as laws are worthy of respect, durable, and apt to contribute to the "happiness" of society, all laws without exception, contended these thinkers (but with Rousseau opposing this view), must conform to the principle of equity, which in itself never varies.[60] This conception of the "rights of mankind," when replicated, as for example in the thought of Rhigas Velestinlis (1757–98) in the 1790s, could also be deployed to peaceably resolve troublesome ethnic and religious divisions in regions like Greece or the Baltic lands. It was an ideological remedy reducing such distinctions to secondary status while forging, conceptually at least, unitary republics in place of the discarded war-torn, hate-filled context prevailing hitherto. The true republic is feasible but only on the basis of multi-ethnic and multi-religious citizenship, eliminating religious authority and caste, discounting faith as nothing, and according equality to all.[61]

"Let us conclude," d'Holbach summed up, in 1773, "that there cannot be any legitimate rights except those which are founded on nature, justice, utility, and the true interest of society."[62] Unfortunately for mankind, he added, "princes, aristocrats and the rich seem only to be occupied with finding ways to appropriate the fruits of labor of others," thus infringing most men's basic rights. Privileged groups, being all too often "useless and harmful" members of society, "usurp whether by acquiescence or force the advantages which nature or industry made the property of their fellow citizens": they abolish their liberty, violate their persons, and appropriate their possessions. They claim the incontestable right to be unjust, oppression that is unchallenged wherever it "continues for long and ignorance, prejudice, feebleness,

[59] Wokler, "Influence of Diderot," 83–4, 87; Israel, *Democratic Enlightenment*, 633–40.

[60] D'Holbach, *Politique naturelle*, 34–5; Wokler, "Influence of Diderot," 105–7.

[61] Kitromilides, "Enlightenment Perspective," 472.

[62] D'Holbach, *Politique naturelle*, 36–7.

and inertia have prevented their subjects resisting or complaining." In short, "le Bonheur de la Sociéte est la fin de tout gouvernement" [the happiness of society is the goal of all government] and the *volonté générale* the general drive in society towards securing the common universal and equal rights of mankind. The "rights" all governments must respect are never the "rights" of specific groups, or strata, or individuals (though they protect individuals) but the "rights of society," and these are by nature eternal, inalienable, and "sacred" in a way the "rights" and privileges obtained by plundering, aristocratic violence, and vested interest can never be.[63]

"Rights" within the post-1770 radical conceptual framework are also a measure by which to evaluate and criticize governments, enabling every reader, through the journals, newspapers, and debates, to participate in local and international politics, criticism being, as d'Holbach repeatedly stresses, a regulatory tool for imposing an invariable moral order on relations between nations and peoples and making judgments about rulers, laws, and constitutions. "Universal rights" implies a measure of critical, cosmopolitan oversight and—contrary to Rousseau—also of subordination of popular sovereignty to a higher universal standard, indeed all forms of sovereignty to an overriding international code.[64] The good citizen has pressing, unavoidable international as well as national obligations. Here was the conception of "human rights" eternal, anti-colonial, and inalienable, underpinning the principles of the American *Declaration* of 1776, the earlier, epoch-making Virginia *Declaration of Rights* of June 1776, and the Vermont state constitution of July 1777, beside the August 1776 Pennsylvania Declaration of Rights, the French Declaration of 1789, and Paine's *Rights of Man* (1791).

Virginia, in June 1776, became the first of the revolutionary American states to revise its constitution fundamentally. In the state legislature, Jefferson and his colleagues ensured their new constitution was prefaced by a comprehensive *Declaration of Rights*, a document drafted in May 1776, principally by George Mason (1725–92) of Gunston Hall, a wealthy planter and magistrate raised amidst a large library. Much esteemed by Jefferson and Madison, Mason entertained no ambition to be a political leader; but in aptitude for political theorizing he outshone the rest of the drafting committee (which did not include Jefferson or Madison) entrusted with the task by the Virginia legislature.[65] Among the foremost proponents of republican ideas and basic human rights among the Founding Fathers, Mason maintained, noticeably more energetically than his neighbor and friend, George Washington, that slavery was wholly unjust and incompatible with "inherent natural rights," despite being himself a slave-owner. He accepted that it was inadvisable to move too rapidly to abolish slavery. But the slave trade, he thought, should end forthwith. Ill-health and a retiring disposition account for his lack of subsequent prominence and renown: during the French Revolution, though, the 1776 Virginia Declaration became well-known,

63 D'Holbach, *Politique naturelle*, 48.
64 Blank, "D'Holbach on Self-Esteem," 449–50, 452; Cotlar, *Tom Paine's America*, 50–1, 69.
65 Mason Rowland, *Life of George Mason* i. 229–30, 236–8; Lutz, *Origins*, 120–1.

playing a notable part in the 1789 French legislative deliberations, albeit usually assumed to be chiefly the work of Jefferson.[66]

Virginia's came first among the world's declarations of human rights, breaking new ground by proclaiming that "all men are born equally free and independent, and have certain inherent natural rights, of which they cannot, by any compact, deprive or divest their posterity; among which are, the enjoyment of life and liberty."[67] "This was the first thing of the kind upon the continent," Mason observed with pride, in October 1778, "and has been closely imitated by all the states."[68] His text certainly went beyond Congress's subsequent 1776 *Declaration of Independence*—which appears to have borrowed some of his phrases.[69] For Mason, unlike Congress, stressed not only the natural equality of all men but also, following the French radicals, that the object of government is the "common benefit, protection, and security of the people," capturing the essence of *volonté générale* in Diderot's and d'Holbach's anti-Rousseauist sense. Massachusetts and many other states at least partly adopted Mason's terminology when subsequently drawing up their own state declarations of rights. Strikingly, while the *Declaration of Independence* itself asserts that the purpose of government is to protect inherent natural rights, it failed to match Virginia's affirmation that the point of doing so is to secure the "common benefit," thereby detaching "general will" from the universal rights it had given rise to.[70] If only a brief outline sketch, the 1776 American *Declaration* did establish a universal discourse of "rights of mankind" broadly in line with radical rather than with Voltaire's moderate Enlightenment principles.

The 1776 *Declarations*, then, discarded Natural Law theory, abandoned the hitherto hegemonic rhetoric of the special "rights of Englishmen," eschewed references to the Glorious Revolution, and all contract, precedents, charters, or mixed government, and notably avoided invoking religion, providence, and the Christian God, speaking instead of the "God of nature." Rights were now universal, equal, and abstract, drastically widening traditional notions of liberty so that, among other things, the "people have a right to freedom of speech and of writing," as the Pennsylvania Declaration put it, "and publishing their sentiments."[71] According to the *Declaration of Independence*, "all men are created equal" and are endowed by their Creator "with certain unalienable rights, that among these are Life, Liberty and the Pursuit of Happiness." Such wording not only subordinated Locke's preoccupation with property and, no less important, deleted all reference to contract, but nullified his denial of toleration to certain groups, his truncating Catholic and Jewish rights and those of "atheists." Starkly unLockean, especially in replacing Locke's "right to property" in the list of basic human rights with the "pursuit of happiness," the new revolutionary

[66] Lafayette, *Mémoires* ii. 305; Billias, *American Constitutionalism*, 89–90.

[67] Nash, *Unknown American Revolution*, 211.

[68] Mason Rowland, *Life of George Mason* i. 239.

[69] Mason Rowland, *Life of George Mason* i. 249–50; Peterson, *Thomas Jefferson*, 89, 101.

[70] Hunt, *Inventing Human Rights*, 25, 121, 126; Wood, *Empire of Liberty*, 66; Moyn, *Last Utopia*, 24.

[71] Lutz, *Origins*, 120; Rosenfeld, *American Aurora*, 286; McCullough, *John Adams*, 121.

approach embodied the supreme good of the *cercle spinoziste*, Spinoza having pronounced equality and equity, the common welfare [*salus communis*], rather than property, the overriding principle, much like Diderot, d'Holbach, Raynal, and Helvétius later. This generalized equality based equally on individual and collective pursuit of happiness and stabilizing the relationship between these through customs and laws, applied to the state of nature and to man in society, all peoples possessing an "equal station" given to them by the "laws of Nature and Nature's God." Whatever Jefferson's stance owed to earlier intellectual sources, his doctrine of equality ensured this privileged Virginia planter and slave-owner, owning over a hundred slaves at the time,[72] subsequently embodied—more clearly than any other prominent figure of the his age—the irresolvable tension lodged within the American Revolution between radical (democratic) and "moderate" (aristocratic) principles, between equality versus property tied to stratified social hierarchy.[73]

This radical thrust within the American Revolution materialized first in Pennsylvania and was also strongly reflected in Vermont's constitution-drafting convention held, in July 1777, under the influence of Ethan Allen and Thomas Young. In terms of political theory, the independent republic of Vermont was as much a haven of radicalism, early on, as was Pennsylvania. The 1777 Vermont constitution not only stressed sovereignty of the people and that government exists for the "common benefit" but held that "all men are born equally free and independent and have certain natural, inherent and inalienable rights." The first state formally to abolish slavery, and to propose voting rights for adult black males, Vermont, though not yet constitutionally part of the United States, for some years remaining an independent entity, was also the sole other American state to emulate Pennsylvania in adopting universal adult male suffrage and the idea of a "Council of Censors" to keep a watchful legal eye on the processes of government, both executive and legislative. Vermont's "General Assembly" originally had only one chamber, the state senate being added by amendment later.[74]

At the heart of the *Declaration of Independence* stands the contention that "governments are instituted among men, deriving their just powers from the consent of the governed" and that "whenever any form of government becomes destructive of these ends, it is the right of the people to alter or to abolish it," and establish a new government, "laying its foundation on such principles and organizing its powers in such form, as to them shall seem most likely to effect their safety and happiness." Adopted on 4 July 1776, with Jefferson, Adams, Franklin, Rush, Witherspoon, and Sam Adams among its principal signatories, the Founders introduced a revolutionary ideology swiftly seized on and trumpeted on all sides, across the Atlantic, and steadily resounding louder through the 1780s, not least in Mirabeau's ringing rejoinder to the Anglo-Prussian suppression of the Dutch democratic revolution, in September 1787,

[72] Foner, *Story*, 32–3. [73] Bonwick, *American Revolution*, 125–6.

[74] Thompson, *History of Vermont* ii. 108–15; Nash, *Unknown American Revolution*, 281–4; Stewart, *Nature's Law*, 20, 200, 375–6, 434; Billias, *American Constitutionalism*, 25.

when he wrote that "tous les hommes sont nés libres et égaux" [all men are born free and equal], that they are "equal and free by the intention of Nature," and that to attain the "happiness for which government is instituted the people has the inalienable right to reform it, correct it or change it totally whenever its happiness so demands."[75]

According to Condorcet, one of those radical thinkers who most fully developed universal human rights theory prior to 1789, America's *Declaration of Independence* set a great example for all peoples. "The Act declaring [America's] independence is a simple and sublime exposition of these rights so sacred and so long forgotten."[76] America's success in founding a republic which comprehensively proclaimed human rights, he contended, in his first openly republican essays, composed in the mid-1780s, inevitably exerted a broad beneficial effect, eroding tyranny and oppression and extending understanding of human rights, democracy, and republicanism across the Atlantic.[77] In no other nation had natural rights been conserved with such a perfect integrity as the nascent United States. Condorcet then listed the four most essential natural and inalienable universal rights as those to security, property, justice, and to participate in the passage of laws and the political process.[78] Already then a convinced republican and democrat, Condorcet continually reaffirmed that the democratic republic is the best form of government and most apt for preserving and extending universal human rights. But he stressed also that the democratic republic can only function where ignorance and superstition are overcome and the people become enlightened. If the people remained devoted to religious prejudice rather than Enlightenment values then they have to be provisionally excluded from the political process.[79] Black slavery, unfortunately, survived "in some [American] states," but "all the enlightened men there feel the shame of it," he added optimistically, and "this blot will not long soil the purity of American laws."[80] His disparagement of the far more tepid pro-Americanism of Mably and Necker (whom he detested) was also fierce. By 1786, Condorcet's universalism and republicanism, rejection of France's existing power structures and the *parlements*, emphasis on the universality of Franklin's and Jefferson's "rights," his plans to emancipate blacks, women, and religious minorities, was so uncompromising, if always well-mannered and delivered in a quiet voice, and his insistence on the American Revolution's global significance so relentless, that he was already then known as "le mouton enragé" [the enraged lamb].[81]

Reminding the world of the centrality of universal human rights for the happiness of society, held Condorcet, was the American Revolution's prime lesson for Europe. The only way to ameliorate and elevate human societies is by enlightening populations and extending respect and understanding for universal human rights. The basis

[75] Mirabeau, *Aux Bataves,* 117, 120.
[76] Condorcet, "De l'influence de la Révolution," 11, 30.
[77] Condorcet, "De l'influence de la Révolution," 13; Grimm, *Correspondance Littéraire* xiv. 79–80.
[78] Condorcet, "De l'influence de la Révolution," 11–12; Condorcet, *Lettres d'un Bourgeois*, 280.
[79] Condorcet, "De l'influence de la Révolution," 12.
[80] Condorcet, "De l'influence de la Révolution," 11.
[81] Grimm, *Correspondance Littéraire* xiii. 145, 193 and xiv. 79–80, 161.

of human rights is equality; and although most men did not realize it, he added two years later, in 1788, eventually women must also share equally with men in the benefits of universal rights. Women need to escape the unrelenting oppression of men and in a truly enlightened democratic republic would eventually escape it. Women's happiness and interests would one day be treated as of equal value and their participation in the political process, he predicted, become a reality.[82] Equally vital for all humanity, propagating republicanism and respect for human rights must and will drastically cut back the lamentable curse of war, which many enlighteners, Kant included, agreed was a plague operating virtually always directly contrary to the "general will." Democratic republicanism would enable peoples to respect and benefit from, rather than rival and fight each other.[83]

The 1776 Declaration embodied the American Revolution's radical legacy but also underlined the Revolution's central paradox—its subsequent retreat from equality and universal human rights. For invoking the "rights of man" in 1776 came to be replaced, in 1791, by a Bill of Rights that largely reverted to the pre-1776 discourse of "rights," a document specific to America that meticulously avoided universal claims, creating a tension and paradox implicit in the structure of the Revolution itself.[84] The radical tendency that erupted in 1776, above all in Philadelphia where Paine was active and Franklin had his base, eventually came to be checked by more traditional gentry republican principles already in the ascendant in all the other nascent states except Pennsylvania and Vermont. Only part of the American Revolution, and only part of the French, ushered in "a new era for all mankind," as Hannah Arendt put it, but as such they were "events which would concern all men *qua* men, no matter where they lived, what their circumstances were, or what nationality they possessed."[85] None could deny the Revolution was buoyed at crucial moments by the radical tendency; yet Congress and most state legislatures continued to be controlled by conservative oligarchs and big proprietors.

The clash between the two enlightenments in America, between democratic and aristocratic republicanism, from the outset permeated and complicated the indispensable business of converting the now obsolete colonial charters into state constitutions. The process began at the prompting of Congress, which was anxious to remove references to the British crown, royal authority, and other now incongruous features from all the state constitutions. But the unavoidable reconsideration and revising of the constitutions served only to intensify disagreement over basic principles and aggravate the Revolution's central paradox, leading to growing theoretical and constitutional disarray and months of often unproductive wrangling. The first wave of revisions in 1776, commencing with New Hampshire, which came up with the shortest as well as the first of the new state constitutions (only eighty-eight lines

[82] Condorcet, *Lettres d'un Bourgeois*, 281–7; Grimm, *Correspondance Littéraire* xiv. 80.

[83] Condorcet, "De l'influence de la Révolution," 26–7; Riley, "Kant and the General Will," 343–4; Stuurman, *Invention of Humanity*, 362.

[84] De Bolla, *Architecture of Concepts*, 202–3.

[85] Arendt, *On Revolution*, 47.

long), was not submitted to a popular vote for approval. Some states, like South Carolina, adopted only minimal changes, retaining their pre-1776 "aristocratic" systems largely unaltered.[86] Even so, some innovations of note were introduced also outside Pennsylvania and Vermont, most notably Virginia with its declaration of rights.

The first among the newly revised state constitutions submitted to popular vote for endorsement, that of Massachusetts, was ready in draft by February 1778, but rejected overwhelmingly by 9,972 to 2,083 votes, the electorate objecting less to the draft's archaic features, recognition of black slavery, and denying black freemen the right to vote, than to its being a poorly drafted jumble widely criticized for incoherence during the public debate. In 1780, Massachusetts' constitutional convention agreed to end the now five-year deadlock in their state by allotting their foremost constitutional theorist, Adams, a free hand to draft it himself. A Harvard-educated Massachusetts lawyer, Adams knew his Grotius, Pufendorf, and Barbeyrac, but Sidney and Locke remained his favorites, the sources that shaped his central doctrine of justified resistance. Reviling Franklin's and Paine's far-reaching influence on the Revolution, he believed, like Locke, that armed resistance to authority is justified only when not led "by the people, the vile populace or rabble of the country" but by the "greater and more judicious part of the subjects of all ranks." Where radical enlighteners, like d'Holbach, Raynal, and Condorcet, saw the people collectively as possessing the right of resistance,[87] justified resistance, for Adams, derives exclusively from the higher ranks while the tyranny against which they rebel "must be so notorious and evidently clear, as to leave nobody any room to doubt of it."[88] Certain observers, including Ferguson, labeled the American Revolution a "revolt," terminology Adams roundly rejected. He designated the uprising legitimate, justified "rebellion" in answer to the crown's tyrannical conduct—"open, avowed resistance by arms, against usurpation and lawless violence." Only "resistance to lawful authority," he contended, echoing Locke, "makes rebellion." "Hampden, Russell, Sidney, Somers, Holt, Tillotson, Burnet, Hoadley, etc. were no tyrants nor rebels, although some of them were in arms [against the king] and others undoubtedly excited resistance against the Tories."[89]

A Founding Father devoted to the principles of Locke, Sidney, British "mixed government," and the Revolution of 1688, Adams was a model advocate of "moderate Enlightenment." He lost no time in endowing his new Massachusetts constitution with the constitutional checks and balances, and anti-democratic safeguards, he deemed essential for the American body politic generally, notably by swelling the numbers excluded from voting, adding numerous additional, disqualified white voters to those already denied the vote, and by lodging far-reaching powers in the hands of the state governor. Such checks were an essential part of the "mixed,"

[86] Lutz, *Origins*, 101–4; Meleney, *Public Life*, 39–40.
[87] Hammersley, *English Republican Tradition*, 132.
[88] Adams, *Novanglus*, 64–6; Nash, *Unknown American Revolution*, 424–5; Ward, *Politics*, 386, 410.
[89] Adams, *Novanglus*, 38; Grant, *John Adams*, 65, 67; Staloff, "John Adams," 38, 43.

British-style "aristocratic" constitution he aimed for, characteristics firmly rejected by more committed republicans stressing collective participation like Jefferson and Mason.[90] Far from easing tension between "classical republican" gentry rule and the democratic tendency, Adams's intervention rendered the conflict more open, confrontational, and explicit. While concurring with Jefferson and the radicals that "that form of government which communicates ease, comfort, security, or in one word happiness, to the greatest number, and in the highest degree, is the best," and that no good government exists that is not "republican," he repudiated democracy and equality, and (with particular vehemence) Tom Paine.[91]

Locke and the Glorious Revolution of 1688 were immensely revered in America, as in Britain. But where Locke solidly buttressed Adams's undemocratic project, for Adams, Price, and Priestley he posed a problem. His own principles, avowed Price, were the "same with those taught by Mr Locke;" but to anyone with Adams's theoretical acumen, this was obvious nonsense: for Price maintained not just that the people were sovereign when setting up the original contract, like the "radical "Whig tradition, but, like Diderot, Helvétius, Paine, and the *Histoire philosophique* (and here also Rousseau), that government is a mere agency for executing the will of the people in the interest of the majority at all times—a doctrine dispensing with any contract with a sovereign distinct from the people—something altogether divergent from Locke. In reality, Price's stance was not Lockean at all. Rather, representative democracy and the Raynal–Dragonetti–Paineite principle that the aim of government is to serve the best interest and welfare of the majority, the ideology of Diderot and d'Holbach, underpinned his system,[92] negating Locke's key political (and religious) doctrine that the people must obey those to whom they entrust government as long as the latter abide by the terms of the entrustment, or contract, by which authority was originally delegated, irrespective of its effects. Like Condorcet's, Price's pro-Americanism was quintessentially unLockean, at odds with the main Anglo-American political thought tradition, something reflected, Adams observed, in Price's negative attitude towards England's existing political, religious, and legal institutions. (Between 1688 and 1848, moderate enlighteners, almost by definition, exalted the existing British Constitution, radical enlighteners denounced it.)

Far from viewing the British constitution as the "perfection of government," in his pamphlet of 1776 Price adopted a stance resembling Paine's and that of John Jebb (1736–86), deeming Britain "a state so sunk that the majority of its representatives [in the House of Commons] are elected by a handful of the meanest persons in it," a mere few thousand out of a population of seven million, constituting an electorate far too restricted to be representative in any meaningful way, an abuse that helped the crown

[90] Morison, *First Massachusetts Constitution*, 16–18; Higgonet, *Sister Republics*, 181, 195; Richards, *Shay's Rebellion*, 70–1.

[91] Morison, *First Massachusetts Constitution*, 18; Arendt, *On Revolution*, 164–5; Zilversmit, *First Emancipation*, 112.

[92] Price, *Political Writings*, 20; Thomas, "Introduction," 20; Dickinson, "Friends of America," 14.

corruptly manipulate the legislature. Jebb, Price, and Paine, like d'Holbach, all dismissed the British constitution as deeply corrupt.[93] The crown tyrannized over its colonies, observed Price, taking this to lengths Adams and most Founding Fathers—apart from Jefferson and Franklin—could by no means endorse. If many Americans in and out of Congress disliked Parliament's "Quebec Act" for according equal rights to Catholics in Canada and extending Canadian jurisdiction over large tracts coveted by American investors and colonizers between the Ohio and the Mississippi, radical theorists like Price and Jebb opposed it very differently. To them, the Quebec Act meant collusion with a small, entrenched, partly noble, partly ecclesiastical Canadian elite, a transparent ploy to render the king heir to the ousted French monarch as untrammeled executive, rendering him "a despot over all that country."[94]

Only the 1776 Pennsylvania and 1777 Vermont constitutions introduced universal suffrage for white adult males: the remaining American states all interposed property qualifications of varying stringency governing the right to vote. Pennsylvania and Vermont were also alone in discarding bicameralism, which many theorists in the 1770s, Turgot and Price among them, considered essentially a mechanism for informal aristocracy operating by restricting access to the state upper chambers via higher property qualifications than those applying to the right to vote for the houses of representatives.[95] Two chambers, explained La Rochefoucauld, "renders the expression of the *volonté générale* more uncertain and even sometimes causes the opinion of a minority of the nation's representatives to prevail over that of the majority."[96] Equally deplorable in radical eyes, none of the new state constitutions emerging in 1779–83 (apart from Vermont) abolished slavery, or included free blacks and mulattoes in the citizenry and the franchise, or for that matter peacefully residing Indians. Nor were these the only slights to the "rights of mankind" and popular sovereignty, or sole restrictions on the suffrage and office-holding. Nearly all the state constitutions retained "religious tests" for office-holders, adding a theological tinge to the mounting pressure to elevate Locke and property into the American constitutional principle par excellence.

If Adams found Price's hostility to British institutions and Paine's stress in *Common Sense* on the "constitutional errors in the English form of government" abhorrent,[97] he and Paine clashed also over commercial freedom. Adams did not object to Britain conserving its imperial ascendancy outside North America. With his marked anti-French bias, he had never been against Britain's imposing its imperial hegemony on large stretches of the world. That Britain "has confined all our trade to

[93] Price, *Political Writings*, 25, 43; Dickinson, "Friends of America," 18.

[94] Price, *Political Writings*, 43; O'Shaughnessy, *Empire Divided*, 124–5; Grant, *John Adams*, 128, 140, 168.

[95] Turgot, *Lettre à Monsieur Price*, 88–9; Stalof, "John Adams," 38.

[96] BL 7R 74/24, "Opinion de M. le duc de la Rochefoucauld," 7 Sept. 1789, p. 7; Zurbuchen, "Religion and Society," 784.

[97] Bailyn, *Ideological Origins*, 288–9; Foner, *Story*, 16–18; Nash, *Unknown American Revolution*, 190, 202–3; Kramnick, "Introduction," 30.

herself" was disagreeable to some, including Paine but, until 1776, did not bother Adams: "we are willing that she should [monopolize trans-Atlantic trade]," he wrote prior to independence, "as far as it can be for the good of the empire."[98] Like many Americans, before 1775, Adams had no objection to the empire as such, approving of both British aristocracy and its overweening global mercantilism. Where Paine espoused Diderot's vehement anti-colonialism, Adams's objection to the imperial format of the 1760s and early 1770s was simply that Britain refused, in return for America's economic subordination to the metropolis, to grant its colonists adequate local autonomy or their "rights" as regards consenting to taxation.

During the American crisis of 1774–6, Adams and the "moderates" had no choice but to compromise with Jefferson and the Anglo-American radicals. There had to be an agreed Congressional *Declaration* and the rebels needed to rally support at home and in Britain and elsewhere. It meant much to Adams that there was at least some support for America in Britain. But British mainstream enlighteners, publicists, and journalists of conservative and "moderate" stamp all invariably boycotted the American cause. Rebellion against the British crown in the name of universal and equal human rights found no favor among enlighteners wedded to Locke and sympathetic to the empire. Ferguson expressed his unshakable belief in the "undoubted right of England" to require from America some share in the taxation "necessary to support the Imperial Crown and the Empire of Great Britain," urging the colonies to eschew "civil war" and work instead for "reunion of the Empire," since "no nation ever planted colonies with so liberal or so noble a hand as England has done."[99] England had colonized America "on the plan of those very charters, statutes and precedents which are now to be set aside." The colonists boasted their English legacy of constitutional freedoms; but Britain "having done so much for her colonies" was a most unfavorable basis "from which to infer the right of her colonies to do nothing for her."[100]

It bothered Adams considerably that all British commentators of stature publicly endorsing the American Revolution and its proclamations were, without exception, radical democrats like Price, persons deemed outrageous dissidents and outcasts with wholly illicit views, by Burke, Smith, Ferguson, Hume, Gibbon, and the British Enlightenment intellectual mainstream generally. There were no exceptions to the pattern. Despite his courageous criticism of the British ministry on previous occasions, and willingness to denounce the war in North America, even Burke, it turned out, sweepingly rejected democracy, republicanism, "human rights," and hence the American Revolution's core principles. Price and Priestley, Adams had to acknowledge, were also widely read in North America and valuable allies.[101] But their undeniable Unitarianism, rejection of the existing British constitution, and undisguised democratic preferences, turned the entire British Moderate Enlightenment (at that point including Bentham) vigorously against them, threatening to entrench the nascent ideological conflict at the heart of the new American polity deeper and deeper.

[98] Adams, *Novanglus*, 37.
[99] Ferguson, *Remarks*, 31–2.
[100] Ferguson, *Remarks*, 27.
[101] Bonwick, *American Revolution*, 53.

10.3. THE "SIXTH BUREAU" AGAINST UNIVERSAL HUMAN RIGHTS

The fact that the American Federal Constitution drafted and signed in September 1787 was not preceded by a Declaration of Rights cast in universal terms offended Mason and distinctly worried Jefferson, Madison, and some others. George Mason emerged among the draft Constitution's most dogged opponents. He objected to Congress's sordid compromise in refusing to ban the slave trade outright, permitting it to continue for twenty years, the conservative scheme for division of powers, and what he considered the excessively strong one-man presidency. But most of all he objected because it lacked a declaration of universal human rights. "This government will set out a moderate aristocracy," he protested in his manuscript circular "Objections to the Constitution," adding that "it is at present impossible to foresee whether it will, in its operation, produce a monarchy, or a corrupt, tyrannical aristocracy; it will most probably vibrate some years between the two, and then terminate in the one or the other."[102] Mason's proposal to add a "declaration of rights," drafted by himself, was voted down on 12 September 1787. The entire document he considered "highly and dangerously oligarchic."[103] The "general will" factor had been excised. In addition, the strong presidency risked encouraging a powerful, non-elected inner circle of government congregating around that one person. His biting criticism provoked a complete rupture with his former friend Washington.[104]

Universal and inalienable "human rights" had made a vigorous entry onto the American stage in 1776, and in France and Britain subsequently, and dominated the political discourse of much of continental Europe from 1789 to 1799. The idea that the United States was born on a declaration which introduced to the world a new conception of liberty that was egalitarian and universal, giving hope to the world and a special responsibility to America, making "universal and equal rights" the measure and criterion of true legitimate government throughout all humanity, could now reasonably be dismissed as nothing more than empty and hypocritical rhetoric since the concept was not embodied in the 1787 American Constitution.[105] But the "human rights" launched in 1776 comprised much more than an illusory "myth" for many Americans and Europeans, at the time and later. And if the American Revolution and the state legislatures remained deeply divided in the 1770s and 1780s, and subsequently, over the issue of universal and equal rights, exactly the same holds true for the French National Assembly and the French press.

Whilst chairing the Sixth Bureau of the National Assembly, whose "minimalist" draft of the "Declaration of Rights" served as a basis for the final phase of the Assembly's debate over the *Rights of Man and the Citizen*, in Paris, in August 1789,

[102] George Mason, "Objections to the Constitution" (MS in Chapin Library, Williams College; see www.constitution.org/gmason.

[103] Mason Rowland, *Life of George Mason* i, p. ix.

[104] Hirschfeld, *George Washington*, 174–6.

[105] Wills, *Inventing America*, pp. xviii–xix.

the Bishop of Nancy, Anne-Louis Henri De La Fare (1752–1829), primarily aimed to restrict equality, human rights, and freedom of speech and, especially, limit freedom to criticize church, theology, and the clergy. His goal was to curtail substantially, in the interest of crown and church, the "American" principles Mirabeau, Sieyès, Volney, and a minority of the Assembly tenaciously championed. Here was a classic clash between Radical Enlightenment propounded by Mirabeau, Sieyès, Brissot, and the Left and its "moderate" Enlightenment adversaries. A subtle defender of ecclesiastical sway now under siege to a greater degree than ever before, Bishop De La Fare battled long and hard especially to limit freedom of expression and freedom of the press as these related to the church and religious authority—as far as it was in the now increasingly besieged church's power to do so.

Designed to modify the draft *Declaration of the Rights of Man and the Citizen* by diluting equality of rights and freedom of expression, the Sixth Bureau's minimalist draft for the "Declaration of the Rights of Man" drawn up under De La Fare's chairmanship failed in large part; but the final outcome was not wholly a success for the radicals either. In the Declaration's final version, the Assembly adopted the "rights" urged by Mirabeau and Brissot in the main but with several restrictive qualifications.[106] The tensions and contradictions in the National Assembly's attitude to universal rights, as the radical *philosophes* understood these, was likewise reflected in the majority of the legislature's opposition to Jewish equality and rights, opposition by several legislative factions comprising aristocrats, constitutional monarchists, and churchmen, prominent among whom, once again, was the bishop of Nancy. Having, in August 1789, led the unsuccessful attempt of the Assembly's Sixth Bureau to cut back the "universal and equal rights" advocated by Mirabeau, Sieyès, and Brissot, it was likewise De La Fare especially who led the "moderate" opposition to Jewish equality.[107]

While acknowledging some Lorraine Jews had performed services to the state, including in his own diocese of Nancy, De La Fare rejected Jewish equality on the grounds that Mosaic and Talmudic religious law effectively segregates Jews from the rest of society. Above all, the common people loathed the Jews, those of his own diocese "les a en horreur" [hold them in horror]. Eternally "étrangers" [strangers], the bishop predicted "de grands désastres" should this universally detested group be accorded full equality and civil rights against his and his ecclesiastical colleagues' advice: "les préjugés du peuple contre les juifs ne sont que trop connus" [the prejudices of the people against the Jews are only too well-known].[108] A decree bestowing citizenship on France's Jews "pourrait allumer un grand incendie" [could

[106] Israel, *Revolutionary Ideas*, 78–85.

[107] For the significance of the historiographical controversy over the Sixth Bureau's role in the *Rights of Man* debate, and what I termed the "Baker–Bell–Edelstein error," see *H-France Forum* vol. 9, Issue 1 (Winter 2013), no. 5, section replying to Baker.

[108] BL FR 170/17: *Opinion de M. L'Evêque de Nancy Député de Lorraine sur l'admissibilité des Juifs à la plénitude de l'état civil* (Paris, 1790), 12–13; Loft, "Mirabeau and Brissot," 615; Trigano, "French Revolution and the Jews," 180.

cause a great conflagration].[109] If less "medieval" and estranged from the Enlightenment mainstream than the historian Arthur Hertzberg claimed, De La Fare *was* indeed an adamant monarchist and foe of liberty of expression and democratic principles as well as implacable opponent of Jewish rights. Later, in January 1791, he became an *émigré* counter-revolutionary. Opposing Jewish rights in December 1789 was directly linked to his earlier opposition, and that of monarchist, pro-church allies like Maury and Mounier, to full human rights generally. Recognizing his stubborn resistance if not to moderate revolution then certainly to universal and equal human rights, and Jewish emancipation, under the Restoration he was rewarded by crown and church for opposing the Revolution, and raised to the rank of Cardinal-Archbishop of Sens.[110]

Not that every prominent advocate of equal Jewish rights was a radical enlightener. In the National Assembly, the motion in favor of Jewish rights was moved by an aristocratic moderate, Comte Stanislas de Clermont-Tonnerre (1757–92), a proponent of British-style constitutional monarchy and of the American as well as British "aristocratic" "mixed government" approach. But while opposing "universal and equal rights" elsewhere, and despite usually championing "moderate" views, the arguments Clermont-Tonnerre deployed to advance Jewish equality *were* uncompromisingly radical. On this topic he was won over especially, seemingly, by the arguments for Jewish equality advanced by the Polish Jewish publicist and Metz Academy Prize Winner, Zalkind Hourwitz (1751–1812).[111] Following Grégoire's and Thiery's Metz prize essays, Hourwitz's was the last to appear in print, but the first to be widely reviewed. The influential *Mercure de France*, in January 1790, drew attention to the unusual phenomenon of an erudite, unafraid Jew stepping forward to "défendre sa nation" and "réclamer pour elle ces droits imprescriptibles et communs à tous les hommes" [claim for it these imprescriptible rights common to all men].[112]

Deep divisions and doctrinal rifts over universal and equal human rights, especially full freedom of expression and freedom to criticize political and religious authorities, pervaded both the American and French revolutions and by no means proved short-term. Rather, these splits remained fundamental, continuing to be fiercely contested, for decades after 1789. Only a minority faction in the legislatures, in both cases, endorsed and supported "universal and equal human rights." This makes it imperative for historians, social scientists, and philosophers, concerned to identify and understand the roots of democratic modernity, to move away from the muddle of "cultural shifts," sociability, reading novels, and diffusion of new sensibilities, and focus more specifically on the hard reality of the intellectual rifts and debates, the clash of philosophical categories, and the competing interests driving them.

[109] Badinter, *Libres et égaux*, 141.

[110] Badinter, *Condorcet*, 289–90; Hertzberg, *French Enlightenment and the Jews*, 297; Badinter, *Libres et égaux*, 141–2, 152–3.

[111] Sorkin, "Count Stanislas," 34–5.

[112] Girard, *Révolution française et les juifs*, 105–6.

11

Emancipating Women

Marriage, Equality, and Female Citizenship (1775–1815)

11.1. GENDER SEGREGATION AND REPRESSION

Emancipating those groups early modern European society most discriminated against—blacks, Jews, homosexuals, and women—advanced only excruciatingly slowly on all sides despite the arguments in favor being forcefully set out by the 1770s and a rising awareness of the systematic injustice. It would take another ninety years, from 1775 to 1865, before the greatest social injustice in the Western world was nominally corrected, before universal and equal rights, the prime principle of modernity, reached the point in the United States where, with the thirteenth amendment to the Constitution, of December 1865, the institution of slavery finally lapsed. With that major milestone attained, "disabilities of women," John Stuart Mill cuttingly admonished the editor of the New York Anti-Slavery Society's journal, the *National Anti-Slavery Standard*, in July 1867, "are now the only remaining national violation of the principles of your immortal Declaration of Independence."[1]

By the mid-eighteenth century, signs of progress, over recent centuries, toward greater gender equality were perceptible, or so some late Enlightenment writers believed. It was true, the Scots radical John Millar averred, that advances since the most primitive, hunting and gathering stage of society had regularized marriage and benefited women.[2] But it did not seem to Diderot and d'Holbach that civilization's advance thus far had changed the situation vastly: the dismal abuse and oppression of the past persisted everywhere: "in all the lands of the earth the fate of women is to be tyrannized over."[3] Natural equity, they argued, condemns all such usages and laws "comme evidémment usurpés" and one day men will abolish them in accord with the basic rules of equity and humanity. These rules enjoin husbands that the authority

[1] Quoted in Capaldi, *John Stuart Mill*, 328.

[2] Miller, *John Millar*, 68, 210–13; La Vopa, *Labor of the Mind*, 280–1.

[3] D'Holbach, *Système social*, 523, 525; Williams, *Condorcet*, 158–71.

allocated by nature to man, far from assigning him the power to mistreat or reduce his wife to the status of a slave, obliges him to love, defend, and protect her.[4] It may be that everywhere in the world the husband is considered the head of "la société conjugale," grants d'Holbach, but neither can it be doubted that virtually throughout the world a mixture of "unjust laws" and "usages peu raisonnables" accords husbands unlimited sway. In effect, men have arrogated to themselves the right to exercise absolute authority over their wives and daughters.

Before the 1780s, only the most radical philosophes, Diderot, Helvétius, and d'Holbach, and a few British and other radicals, demanded systematic reform of the marriage laws—ousting arranged marriage and the dowry system, equalizing inheritance rights, and introducing civil divorce. "Women are not dealt with justly by the laws of the land," complained Jebb: "all laws of inferiority should be repealed. Compact supposes equality."[5] Radical Enlightenment had pushed in this direction since Fontenelle's time and did so vigorously from the late 1760s.[6] By contrast, even the most liberal Dissenter religious groups, though often more liberal than mainstream Protestant and Catholic society, evinced relatively conservative attitudes concerning women's place in society.[7] On the French Revolution's eve, women's social and moral equality was beginning to be widely broached, but chiefly by Mirabeau, Brissot, Bonneville, the Auteuil circle, and the Condorcets, hence decidedly the radical fringe.[8]

Condorcet, his wife, and a few others also proposed women's eligibility for equal political and voting rights and did so already well before 1789. During the early Revolution, Condorcet reaffirmed his arguments for woman's political emancipation in a journal article of July 1790, *Sur l'admission des femmes aux droits de la cité*: though unequal in physical strength, women are men's equals in intellect and moral stature, even if this becomes evident only where men make a special effort to push aside rooted prejudice formed by the long entrenched "inequality with which the sexes are treated by the laws, institutions, custom, and prejudice."[9] The blatant injustice of laws reducing women "to the condition of slaves," compelling a mistreated wife to remain under her husband's tyranny (unless she can prove her life in danger), contended Condorcet and his circle, must be ended and a more rational marriage system instituted.[10] But there was little progress with this feminist agenda prior to the monarchy's end and the advent of the Republic, in August 1792.[11]

Woman's subordination to man was no longer as "barbaric" as it had once been. Montesquieu's *L'Esprit des Lois* suggested women's status was linked to different forms of government and moral systems, imparting fresh impetus to the widening

[4] D'Holbach, *Morale universelle* iii. 2–3, 25. [5] Jebb, *The Works* ii. 180.

[6] Démeunier, *L'Esprit des usages* i. 77–133; Hollewand, *Banishment of Beverland*, 246–8.

[7] MacCullough, *The Reformation*, 658. [8] Portalis, *De l'usage*, 226.

[9] Condorcet, *Tableau historique*, 898–901; Condorcet, *Political Writngs*, p. xxix; Kates, "Powers," 172; Leeuwers, *Robespierre*, 146; Larrère, "Women, Republicanism," 15 5n.; Wolin, "In Praise of *Philosophie*," 103.

[10] *Chronique de Paris* ii/xxxv (4 Feb. 1790), 137; Corno, "Loi révolutionnaire," 62, 65.

[11] *Chronique du mois* ii (Mar. 1792), 86; Fauré, "L'Exclusion des femmes," 166–72.

Enlightenment debate about women's social position.[12] Among the few points where Hume wholeheartedly concurred with Diderot, Helvétius, and d'Holbach was his conviction that in savage and barbarous societies, females had been subjected to "the most abject slavery" and that, over the centuries, the civilizing progress had slowly nurtured an appreciable improvement.[13] Yet segments of European society stoutly resisted further progress and were encouraged, argued radical enlighteners, by the legacies of the Protestant Reformation and Catholic Counter-Reformation with both reinforcing gender subordination in marriage, family law, and other ways. In the Reformation's wake, a progressive hardening of the theological culture of shame and sin had generated an intensified drive to institutionalize social prejudice, further curtailing women's personal freedom and freedom of dress, penalizing pre- and extra-marital intercourse differently for women, and further stigmatizing birth out of wedlock.[14]

Females are physically weaker than men and "in almost all countries," commented Diderot," the cruelty of the civil laws is allied against women with the cruelty of nature."[15] Admittedly, conditions were worse, much more degrading in primitive societies, but that did not change the fact that men continued their abominable tyranny over women in supposedly "civilized" societies too, with nunneries, to his mind, the very acme of gender tyranny, a theological apparatus of ceaseless psychological torture intensified by hypocrisy and excruciating boredom.[16] The "servitude"" imposed on women, legal, social, and institutional, remained appalling. A point where Diderot notably anticipated the Revolution's emancipating reforms was his urging Catherine the Great to introduce civil divorce to afford more individual freedom to men and women alike, to "remove" Russian marriage law to the secular sphere from the superstitious gloom of ecclesiastical authority. Although Diderot felt Helvétius discussed divorce, and how to accommodate the children of divorced parents, too cavalierly, suggesting a suppressed impulse to deprive women of proprietorship over their own bodies, a program for modifying female servitude without genuinely ending it, he still concurred with Helvétius' conclusions in the main. Especially, he and d'Holbach agreed on the urgent need to render civil divorce a right generally available.[17]

Theologically grounded forms of repression undoubtedly had intensified during the Reformation era and in the mid-eighteenth century still showed scant sign of abating. There were signs of change, though, and, not coincidentally, by the late eighteenth century, a rising chorus of protest. Wekhrlin, in 1791, lambasted the "harshness with which unmarried girls bearing children, and prostitutes, were treated

[12] Larrère, "Women, Republicanism," 140–2.

[13] Sebastiani, "Race, Women and Progress," 76–7, 79, 83.

[14] MacCulloch, *The Reformation*, 612; Loft, *Passion, Politics*, 41–2.

[15] Diderot, *Sur les femmes*, 21; Diderot, *Réfutation d'Helvétius*, 791.

[16] Diderot, *La Religieuse*, 53, 60–4.

[17] Diderot, *Réfutation d'Helvétius*, 911–12; Diderot, *Mélanges pour Catherine II*, 329–30; Dessertine, "Le Divorce," 206.

in German and Austrian society."[18] Assigning heightened prominence to sexual and marriage offenses, Protestant reform in Germany and Switzerland from the 1570s had elaborated procedures of control and penalization generating a widening spiral of recrimination and shame, degradation of the illegitimate, and, consequently, also dismaying levels of infanticide, in turn provoking redoubled official retribution. In 1574, following other Protestant German and Swiss cities, Frankfurt am Main closed its brothels, previously flourishing for centuries, labeling prostitution a crime for the first time, a change due to Reformation theology mixed with fear of syphilis.[19] Giving birth out of wedlock was increasingly dealt with by rigorous lifelong social ostracism, marginalizing both the mother and the illegitimately-born. Exclusion of illegitimate boys from city guilds became usual in Lutheran cities, and, despite the difficulties in investigating such matters, proceedings against females suspected of fornication, marital infidelity, sodomy, and blasphemy remained a constant preoccupation of magistrates until well into the Enlightenment era. The only tangible proof of guilt, not infrequently, in "fornication" as in blasphemy proceedings, was hostile testimony, hearsay, or pregnancy out of wedlock—the direst threat to a woman's reputation, dignity, freedom, and status. Bars to individual and group freedom, penalizing disapproved-of lifestyle manifestations, affected everyone to an extent, but social repression rooted in institutionalized discrimination affected women and homosexuals, and Jews, far more than most heterosexual males.

Under existing laws, gender inequality prevailed at all levels aided by theological antipathy to divorce—absolute in Catholic lands but formidable also in Protestant lands—as did subordination of woman within marriage and persecution of homosexuality, sodomy, and suicide actual and attempted. Censure by pastors and magistrates, institutionalized stigmatization of unmarried mothers and condemned behavior, often had a devastating effect on those lower down on the social scale. The vulnerability of menial status, especially for disadvantaged single women, frequently left no way out of the *ancien régime* trap of social-theological repression. A Frankfurt domestic maid who committed suicide in 1690 after killing her illegitimate baby won no sympathy from the city magistrates: they had her corpse dragged to the gallows, symbolically hanged her, placed her severed head on a pike, and stretched her torso on a wheel.[20] Legal constraints, social pressure, and prejudice blighted lives by discriminating against entire segments of the population, generating, as Mary Wollstonecraft described with deep pain in the 1790s, a vast sea of church-supervised misery and deprivation. The sway of repressive pressures was furthered everywhere by the near total absence of individual rights of those from lower social strata.

Female suicide was the frequent consequence of public censure. In January 1779, an unmarried Genevan servant, Françoise Dupont, abused by her master and pregnant for the second time, facing severe punishment and unbending condemnation,

[18] Wekhrlin, *Paragrafen* 1 (1791), 143.
[19] MacCullough, *The Reformation*, 632, 634.
[20] Boes, "'Dishonourable' Youth," 361.

drowned herself in the Rhone, at the age of 22.[21] Pregnancy out of wedlock and illegitimacy, whether the result of disorderly sexual behavior or not, stirred a burgeoning public debate, as did the surging problem of infanticide, a controversy tinged seemingly with a collective guilty conscience. Unease was evident in the ubiquitous wrangling over foundlings' institutions, orphanages, and alarmingly rising rates of suicide among unmarried female servants and employees. Growing awareness of the extent of misery linked to sexual repression, retribution on homosexuals, and stigmatizing illegitimate birth stirred among some the realization that infanticide was less a perverse than a desperate crime committed mostly by devastated young women who knew that the shaming penalties menacing them ended all chance of respectability and marriage—leaving prostitution, entailing perpetual humiliation and scorn, vagrancy, or suicide the sole available options. Novelists took to empathizing with the plight of young women yielding to importuning suitors or bullying employers, from love, weakness, or subservience, and then being abandoned to the unforgiving consequences of giving birth out of wedlock on their own. In July 1780, over 400 essayists submitted entries to a prize competition initiated by the *Rheinische Beiträge zur Gelehrsamkeit* enquiring: "What are the best and most practical means to suppress infanticide?"[22]

Fads for novels and sentimental empathizing no doubt furthered reaction against the drastic penalties and public humiliation prescribed by law. As realization dawned as to why desperate young females felt driven to kill their own infants, the law increasingly began to look defective and blameworthy. Obviously, it maintained a blatant double standard, unrelenting toward the offending female and her infant born or unborn while making only perfunctory efforts to trace or punish the father. Far from deterring transgression, such imbalance unjustly penalized the weaker party and thus actually encouraged both bullying and infanticide. With advancing Enlightenment, the drive to abolish penalties for fornication became a regular feature of calls for legal reform. Nevertheless, in Frederick the Great's Prussia, it was not until 1765 that "fornication" ceased being a legally punishable offense for unmarried pregnant women. While simultaneously reinforcing noble privilege in Prussia and widening disabilities on Jews, the Prussian crown abolished all *Hurenstrafen*, shaming penalties for female fornicators of all types, stipulating that women were longer to be punishable for intercourse outside marriage, nor subject to public shame or recrimination.[23] But here Prussia was way ahead. In Denmark–Norway and Schleswig-Holstein, removal of *Hurenstrafen*, initiated by Struensee in 1771–2, remained fiercely controversial, the clergy's vociferous objections only heightening his surging unpopularity; hence, the Danish measure was revoked along with the general reaction against Struensee's reforms in 1772–3. A measure comparable to those in Prussia and Denmark was contemplated but not adopted in Hanover in 1772; lesser compromise

[21] Watt, "Suicide, Gender and Religion," 144. [22] Hull, *Sexuality, State*, 112, 280.

[23] Hull, *Sexuality, State*, 127; Stoicea, "When History Meets Literature," 217–20.

measures stopping well short of decriminalization of female fornication passed in Bavaria in 1781, and Saxe-Weimar in 1786.

Outside Brandenburg-Prussia these tentative reforms rarely abolished fornication penalties altogether. In Austria in 1769 the law was modified but not fundamentally changed, the rule henceforth being to punish less severely and now behind closed doors rather than publicly. The Hanover draft law of 1772 proposed abolishing fornication penalties for both genders except where a male servant seduced his master's daughter or intercourse was procured by promise of marriage. Baden, in 1773, mitigated penalties but retained the principle that extra-marital intercourse is a criminal offense. Court officials in Bavaria resumed their push for reform in 1779–81, but the Elector demurred, anxious not to prejudice his status as protector of the church, and prime enforcer of moral rectitude, causing a tussle at Munich which, in 1780, resulted in two overlapping and contradictory Bavarian edicts, one removing shaming penalties for "first-time fornication" where due to weakness rather than corrupt character, the other reaffirming traditional corporal punishments (*Leibstrafen*) and monetary penalties for fornication offenses requiring local magistrates to punish first-time instances without leniency. The deadlock long continued: fornication was not wholly decriminalized in most German states until after the 1848 revolutions.[24]

In France, laws against whoring and lewdness were equally draconian but *ancien régime* enforcement, research shows, was sporadic and inconsistent. This left the poorest, least protected, especially unattached women and prostitutes, at the mercy of local or seigneurial authority, unequal application of the law, and merciless stigmatization. Any girl deemed a vagrant, whore, or kept woman was automatically debarred from registering charges of abduction and rape and deprived of legal recourse against abusive, violent, tyrannical, or dishonest males.[25] In early eighteenth-century England, standard procedure for disciplining petty crimes by females—small thefts, disorderly behavior, vagrancy, and prostitution—included confining miscreants for periods in houses of correction. Much sentencing and correcting was supervised by "Reformation of Manners" societies set up under the Anglican Church's direction to strengthen theologically-driven enforcement of society's stern moral code. In theory, the societies targeted gaming houses, theaters, music houses, and other rowdy establishments beside brothels and bawdy houses; but in practice, after a certain point, the focus was mainly on curbing disapproved-of sexual conduct, especially single women acting too freely (an acute problem in London), homosexuals, and births out of wedlock. While, around 1700, London societies "for the reformation of manners" also initiated numerous prosecutions for sabbath violation, swearing, drunkenness, and other predominantly male offenses, by the 1720s males were being largely left unmolested and prosecutions becoming more narrowly focused on "loose" women and girls arraigned for whoring, vagrancy, or lewd behavior.

[24] Hull, *Sexuality, State*, 123–4.
[25] McManners, *Church and Society* ii. 285–6.

Until 1789, antiquated laws ruled gender relations to a far greater extent than any drive to advance individual dignity and liberty, or the rights of the unprivileged. Nowhere was this clearer than with *ancien régime* society's obsessive concern with preventing elopement and seduction and equating these with abduction and rape. Where the crucial criterion in modern legal definitions of rape, whether or not the woman consented, is primary, this had scant relevance for pre-1789 legal practice, since consent had little bearing on the gravity of the affront to the father, husband, or brother, especially where of high social standing. Existing statutes, often medieval in origin, were still weighted to reflect notions of rape as essentially stealing something valuable belonging to husbands, fathers, or betrothed men, a crime robbing husbands of their wives' or future wives' reputations for chastity and purity, and prospective husbands of hopes for sizeable dowries. Stealing an unmarried woman's virginity, hence her honor, was major theft of her father's possessions, and harm to her family, deeply damaging to social standing.[26] Elopement and seduction were hence widely equated with rape and abduction, which were deemed to have occurred irrespective of whether or not the woman consented, or even whether intercourse occurred. What mattered was "reputation," honor, and what others would presume.

Far from being equal individuals in the eyes of the law, women were legal dependants of fathers before marriage, and husbands after, across the board. Marital permission was needed before a married woman could undertake any legal proceeding, business transaction, deed of responsibility, or financial contract. Female authors required their husbands' (or, if unmarried, father's) consent to publish books and settle publication rights. Deprivation and humiliation resulting from property and assets inherited by married women coming automatically under their husbands' sway was endless. Wives had little scope for countering spendthrift husbands' high living, banqueting, or gambling, or otherwise irresponsibly wasting their inheritances. In France, a married woman could obtain a physical separation legally (*separation de corps*) but only where she could prove her husband's mistreatment was life-threatening.[27]

11.2. RADICAL THOUGHT AND THE ORIGINS OF MODERN FEMINISM

Supporters of the "negative critique" might object that all enlighteners sought to improve women's lot so why distinguish between moderate and radical Enlightenment? But there was a considerable difference between a moderate stance aiming at compromise with theology, viewing women's situation in terms of current practicalities, and defending the basic norms of current society, and championing universal and equal rights. Certainly, for moderates too there was plenty of scope for

[26] Rudolph, "Rape and Resistance," 171–8. [27] Hesse, *Other Enlightenment*, 60.

amelioration with respect to better education, countering "superstition," and modifying moral guidelines. Kames, never afraid to offend what most people thought, noticed opportunities for the "progress of the female sex" but, characteristically, only in terms of moral earnestness and piety; otherwise, typically for most of the Scottish Enlightenment, he kept females in a permanently subordinate position, this to his mind being the indubitable, universal, and timeless proper order of things justified by "what we feel," by "Common Sense": "the man as a protector, is directed by nature to govern: the woman, conscious of inferiority, is disposed to obedience." Having always been so, this was decreed by providential design and divine intention. "The intellectual powers correspond to the destination of nature: men have penetration and solid judgment to fit them for governing; women have sufficient understanding to make a decent figure under good government; a greater proportion would excite dangerous rivalship."[28]

Cultural shifts, sensibility, and moderate Enlightenment came nowhere near breaking the mold, only the underground force of "la philosophie moderne" could. It was "as a philosopher," recalled Wollstonecraft, that the opportunity came to her to respond with force and indignation to the subordinate status to which women were everywhere confined, to protest at their being denied all opportunity to develop their minds and reason. It was "as a philosopher" she had discovered that "if there be but one criterion of morals, but one archetype for man," women for the moment found themselves consigned to a strange limbo, being apparently not included in that archetype. Far from being encouraged to pursue a life of reason, they were taught that they "must not aim at respect, lest they should be hunted out of society as masculine."[29] That woman was either, as Wollstonecraft put it, "naturally weak," or else systematically "degraded by a concurrence of circumstances," reduced to "slavery," to put it bluntly, was undeniable.[30] Yet it remained impossible for any writer or thinker subscribing to religious authority or tradition, or according legitimacy to the established order of rank and dependence, for anyone adhering to either moderate or Counter-Enlightenment concepts, to accept that woman had been unjustifiably tyrannized over throughout the centuries any more than it was to concur with *la philosophie moderne* that most men had been too. Radical ideas were the exclusive intellectual basis on which one could accept that the basic indictment was true and that the only way to emancipate woman and restore her to her proper place was to overturn the entire system of moral, religious, and educational as well as social and political principles and prejudices on which Western society rested. Hence, Wollstonecraft's *Vindication* and Scandinavian *Letters*, as much as any Radical Enlightenment texts, unrelentingly deplore ignorance and superstition, and assail kings, nobility, and tradition.

28 Kames, *Six Sketches*, 194–5; Ahnert, *Moral Culture*, 98–9.
29 Wollstonecraft, *Vindication of the Rights of Woman*, 106, 133; Vega, "Feminist Republicanism," 169.
30 Wollstonecraft, *Vindication of the Rights of Woman*, 107–9; Ferguson, "Mary Wollstonecraft," 131–3.

While all European societies boasted heaps of post-Reformation legislation repressing fornication, adultery, improper dress, pregnancy out of wedlock, homosexuality, prostitution, and, in Catholic lands, infringing ecclesiastical celibacy, this undeviating obsession betrayed what radical *philosophes* considered society's scandalous lack of genuine moral concern for more substantial, deeper social problems. Obsessed with combating "sin," society seemed utterly blind to the real misery and despair generated by ill-matched marriages, domestic cruelty, wife-beating, workplace exploitation, victimization of children, abuse of servants, and tyrannizing over soldiers and sailors by officers. Nothing was clearer than that Europe's obsolete, archaic legal systems were not intended to protect individuals, or promote human "happiness." Rather, the law remained the abject instrument of authority allied to prejudice, obscurantism, and theology. And if churchmen allied to princes were the chief culprits, pre-Enlightenment Stoic, Neoplatonist, and Aristotelian philosophers, held d'Holbach, had worsened the dismal picture by continually summoning the individual "to detest oneself," abase oneself in one's own eyes, feel disgust at all pleasures, stifle desires of one's heart, and flee from all thought of worldly felicity. Individuals taught to view their lives as a holy pilgrimage of self-mortification are tailored for misery. Lessons "so contrary to those of nature" might be ignored by those given to dissipation, but were more often piously deferred to, thereby generally fomenting sullen, misanthropic, unsociable attitudes.[31]

It was not easy to get such views across. Shutting up unwanted daughters in convents, widespread in Catholic lands, had been portrayed as despicably cruel and increasingly denounced in *philosophique* circles particularly since Helvétius' *De l'Esprit* (1758).[32] Opposing forced "taking of the veil" family decisions to cloister girls had developed since the mid-century into something of a behind-the-scenes concerted movement, especially among Helvetius' admirers, among them Giambattista Biffi (1736–1807), one of the "coterie de Milan" associated with Beccaria, alongside whom he stands, elegantly attired, in a famous group portrait of the Enlightenment "society" Accademici dei Pugni, by Antonio Perego, painted in 1766. But scope for progress under *ancien régime* conditions remained extremely limited. When Biffi proposed an article for the Milanese journal, *Il Caffé*, urging that young girls should no longer be confined in convents by their families, Pietro Verri, the Milanese enlightener editing this spectatorial periodical but who believed social reform must be highly cautious to avoid offending princes and clergy, refused to publish any piece obviously echoing Helvétius' message on the ground that Italians were not yet ready, or sufficiently "enlightened," for a writer to be able publicly to call it a bad thing to "bury" a girl in a convent.[33]

The campaign Helvétius initiated peaked in Diderot's *La Religieuse*. Diderot began writing his *La Religieuse* [The Nun], a devastating indictment of nunneries and nuns, around 1760, but it remained unpublished until Naigeon brought it out in 1796.

[31] D'Holbach, *Essai*, 173; Spitz, "From Civism to Civility," 109, 112.

[32] Helvétius, *De l'Esprit*, 131.

[33] Capra, *Progressi della ragione*, 190, 220.

Unpublishable under the *ancien régime* laws, it became publishable and was approved only under a non-Jacobin neo-Brissotin revolutionary government. Reading it made it hard to judge whether society's cruelty, sadism, and exploitation were worse in, or outside, the convent. Recounting the story of a young woman whose parents, aided by nuns, browbeat her into the most abject psychological, moral, and personal submission, it raised the question of girls' status in society in a distinctly innovative fashion. Yet hardly anyone knew anything of it during Diderot's lifetime. Against the claim that Diderot was genuinely radical in gender matters, some scholars maintain that ambiguity pervades the alleged "feminism" of his texts.[34] *La Religieuse* has been adduced as evidence confirming the Postmodernist view that Diderot viewed women as intrinsically dependent and weak.[35] "His biologically essentialist materialism," some argue, "made women's intellectual capacities innately inferior to men's."[36]

In his writing on women, Diderot did suggest the female organs cause women's minds to be less steady and more prone to hysteria and upset (including unhealthy religious devotion) than those of men. But he counterbalances averring women's greater frailty of mind by claiming intelligent women are also intellectually often freer and more "original" than men. Girls should receive instruction in anatomy from the age of 16 or 17, he recommended, to help steady their minds, organize their lives, and, after marriage, run their households.[37] But his depiction of the abominably repressed and bullied nun, like his comments on the Jews in his late writings, is chiefly concerned with showing how egoism, self-interest, and power-seeking create generalized tyranny stiffened by religious doctrine and the church, producing social structures and institutions that unjustly oppress particular groups. The abject misery of Suzanne, the young nun who discovers she is the offspring of her mother's infidelity, reflects the dishonesty, hypocrisy, cruelty, and systematic legalized injustice with which society universally humiliated innocent women and the illegitimate.[38] Entirely against her own will, she is intimidated into the step that darkens the whole subsequent course of her life. Browbeating Suzanne is justified by a twisted morality portraying the real evils bedeviling her existence, and that of other girls, as theological benevolence, suffering as good adduced supposedly by God to test, and the Devil to tempt, us.[39]

If women, as was then usually the case, *were* more ignorant than men, Diderot did not doubt this was because society had rendered them so. The prevailing ignorance and superficiality of women he attributed to their being obliged to focus on trifles, to a society and education that fashioned them thus.[40] Catharine Macaulay and later Mary Wollstonecraft similarly expressed anger and dismay at how existing social practice

[34] Steinbrugge, *The Moral Sex*, 44–53; Rosenblatt, "Rousseau, the 'Traditionalist'," 632; La Vopa, *Labor of the Mind*, 259–60.

[35] Mortier and Trousson, *Dictionnaire de Diderot*, 195; Pečar and Tricoire, *Falsche Freunde*, 25.

[36] La Vopa, "A New Intellectual History?," 728–9; La Vopa, *Labor of the Mind*, 266–7, 275–85.

[37] Diderot, *Mélanges pour Catherine II*, 256–7, 260, 323–4; Offen, *Woman Question*, 88–9, 103, 124.

[38] Diderot, *La Religieuse*, 47, 68–9, 71–3, 87; Wilson, *Diderot*, 385.

[39] Diderot, *La Religieuse*, 58, 152–3.

[40] Gardner, "Catharine Macaulay's Letters," 127–8.

and education fitted women only for preoccupying themselves with the latest fashion, trifles, and "foibles."[41] But while women were less accustomed to the world outside the home, more gullible and often taken advantage of, contended Diderot, when mistaken assumptions are explained to them, they also frequently grasp the truth faster, more intuitively than males.[42] Dialogue reflecting gender equality in debate was not just a literary quirk for Diderot, but a key ethical and methodological procedure. In *Le Rêve de d'Alembert* (1769), one of his principal texts, Diderot awards pride of place to Mlle de Lespinasse, placing her at the center of the philosophical debate with d'Alembert and the Montpellier physician Théophile Bordeu, underlining the inherent connection between monist one-substance materialism and general equality while promoting respect for women. In his *Entretien d'un philosophe avec Madame la Maréchale de*... (1774), he recounts a dialogue with a woman wholly lacking higher education who scarcely reads anything but yet is perfectly able to fence verbally with the *philosophe* about morality, religion, and sexuality. If one grants Diderot "made philosophy a collective, dialogic human enterprise—most famously embodied in the *Encyclopédie*," one must accept that his alleged "pseudo-feminism" in fact exhibits an egalitarian character.[43]

The depressed Suzanne, reduced to an "automate,"[44] reflects not female intellectual inferiority but a much wider system of oppression through legally backed family hierarchy and unequal marriage that Diderot full-frontally assails: males seeking pliant and submissive wives exploit an unremittingly repressive theology and law to institutionalize oppression and enforce submission within marriage.[45] "What need has the human race of so many victims?" Among the revolutionary changes society requires, contends Diderot, is elimination of nunneries and monasteries.[46] "Chacun songe à soi dans ce monde" [each thinks of himself in this world], and injustice and oppression will always reign supreme until laws and institutions are designed to compel tyranny and self-interest to recognize the freedom, independence, and equal right to happiness of each and every member of society.[47] If society's natural condition prior to the state, according to Hobbes, is one of conflict and war, replacing this with a general state of union, peace, and the convergence of all individual wills toward what maximizes the individual well-being of all (*volonté générale*), as the basis for general "happiness," can follow only from instituting the best kinds of state and law codes.[48]

Whether men and women will eventually achieve emancipation on an equal basis, whether or not genuine *volonté générale* will eventually triumph, securing universal

[41] Gardner, "Catharine Macaulay's Letters," 126–7.

[42] Diderot, *Sur les femmes*, 27–8; Diderot, *Réfutation d'Helvétius*, 811–12, 906.

[43] See my reply to Helena Rosenblatt's objections in "Rousseau, Diderot, and the Radical Enlightenment": A Reply to Helena Rosenblatt and Joanna Stalnaker," JHI 77 (2016), 649–77.

[44] Diderot, *La Religieuse*, 84–5; Duflo, *Diderot philosophe*, 439–40, 442–3.

[45] Diderot, *La Religieuse*, 69; Quintili, *Pensée critique*, 454–6.

[46] Diderot, *La Religieuse*, 151.

[47] Diderot, *La Religieuse*, 66; Duflo, *Diderot philosophe*, 444–5.

[48] Diderot, *Political Writings*, 123.

and equal rights for all, depends, or so Diderot, d'Holbach, Helvétius, Condorcet, Brissot, and Volney argued, on theology and churchmen becoming sufficiently discredited in the eyes of public and authorities alike that the sway of churchmen ends. Such a transformation could occur only via a thoroughgoing reform program and revolution in ideas and attitudes that Diderot, by the early 1770s, no longer expected from the policies of the enlightened despots. His earlier hopes, focusing especially on Catherine and her reforms in Russia, had come to naught. Tying his materialism to his changed post-1770 revolutionary impulse, he envisaged the generalized happiness of men as conceivable only in a society that formalizes *volonté générale* through good and equal laws with the interests of all being equally represented. Disillusionment with supposedly enlightened rulers did not alter his confidence that sweeping transformation of institutions and laws was possible. From Diderot's post 1770 perspective, a revolution of attitudes and principles led by his underground was the effective, and only, way "for men to regain their usurped rights."[49]

The American Revolution convinced the circles of Diderot, Helvétius, and d'Holbach and their intellectual heirs that there was indeed an alternative to enlightened despotism, a plausible general path to legal and social revolution. When the Americans began their Revolution, averred Condorcet, in 1788, they convened their representatives in a Congress permitting no distinctions between orders, no ecclesiastical presence, and no hereditary privileges.[50] Congress's effectiveness during the revolutionary war proved an assembly of representatives of the people can act more decisively than a single ruler, or small aristocratic group, that it is a fallacy to think either monarchy or aristocracy functions more efficiently than a democratic republic.[51] The structures of law, privilege, and authority distinguishing France's three orders—clergy, nobility, and Third Estate—needed erasing; in the forthcoming meeting of the French Estates-General, the privileged orders should merge with the Third to create a genuinely "national assembly." Once the Revolution began, Condorcet, like Volney, Destutt, Cabanis, and others, threw all his energies into advancing the revolutionary cause, laboring for constitutional, social, and educational reform across a wide front but with improving women's legal status and working toward women's eventual equality figuring among his, and his wife's, prime objectives.

Rejecting religious authority was crucial to any broad conception of female emancipation and to sexual liberation, which remained a characteristic feature of the radical stance. Adultery, though, held d'Holbach, does wreck esteem, confidence, and true friendship between husband and wife and hence the basis of marriage.[52] Unlike Diderot, Helvétius, and Condorcet, d'Holbach feared sexual freedom for women, and also sexual freedom in general, a factor playing an almost obsessive part in his treatment of personal morality and education. Frequently expressing

[49] Diderot, *Mélanges pour Catherine II*, 265, 268–72; Strugnell, *Diderot's Politics*, 217; Benot, *Diderot*, 46–8.
[50] Condorcet, *Sentiments d'un républicain*, 4–5, 8, 18–19.
[51] Condorcet, *Seconde Lettre d'un citoyen des États-Unis*, 21–2.
[52] D'Holbach, *Système social*, 26–7.

antipathy to the culture of flirtatious *galanterie* so prevalent in European courtly and aristocratic milieus, which he, like Rousseau, considered an abomination, he believed gallantry, coquetry, seduction and infidelity, and prostitution, should be condemned and universally despised along with sexual libertinism and promiscuity. On the other side, few went as far as Brissot in dismissing *ancien régime* laws relating to sexuality and marriage as an unmitigated, comprehensive assault on basic liberty and natural feeling.[53] Oppressive marriage laws and sexual frustration were so widespread that prostitution and informal concubinage in numerous forms had become indispensable, the "triste resource" of masturbation hardly sufficing to offset the deadening culture of repression. To threaten the *fornicateur* with eternal damnation and burning in hellfire, as theologians did, he labeled a terrible intrusion into private life, an assault on nature itself. Its ceaseless concern with repressing extramarital sexual activity, at least for women, prompted his condemning *le Christianisme* as the first sect in human history where laws and institutions are mobilized against the very passions nature "has inscribed in the souls of men and against the remedies she provides to satisfy them."[54] Instead of being despised, concubinage should be honored, as should the unfortunate women made to sacrifice reputations and happiness to ease the frustration of dissatisfied husbands, unmarried men, sailors, and clergy, beside their own, and check homosexuality.[55] Where married women cherished by husbands are free "when obeying nature," unmarried girls, widows, women abandoned or neglected, and with disabled, impotent, or inactive husbands, possessed no such recourse. It was easy for females satisfactorily married to be virtuous whereas extra-marital female offenders faced unrelenting opprobrium and scorn all their lives. Were respect at all proportionate to the difficulty of performing services useful to society "how much then should a prostitute be honored!"[56] A general reform of prostitution, by gathering ladies of the street in state-administered brothels where sexual services could be taxed for the public benefit and medical care provided, was needed especially to curb the spread of venereal disease.

11.3. ENLIGHTENMENT AND GIRLS' EDUCATION

In the minds of most contemporaries nagging questions remained. Were women really men's equals in abilities, intelligence, and potential? Only radical enlighteners, including Rousseau during his early, radical phase,[57] embraced the idea that they were. After breaking with Diderot and d'Holbach's radical coterie, in 1757, Rousseau,

[53] Brissot, *Lettres philosophiques*, 116.
[54] Brissot, *Lettres philosophiques*, 106–7; Loft, *Passion, Politics*, 40.
[55] Brissot, *Lettres philosophiques*, 112–13; Loft, *Passion, Politics*, 40–2.
[56] Brissot, *Lettres philosophiques*, 113.
[57] Botting, "Early Rousseau's Egalitarian Feminism," 732, 739, 744.

beside claiming basic differences in the moral qualities and the public and private status of men and women, became "infamously skeptical about the mental capacities of women." At the same time, he insisted on the need for gender difference in education.[58] Where, for Diderot and Condorcet, woman's intellectual capacity as such is not inferior, for Rousseau, as for Kames and Kant, "female reason does not," as one scholar expressed it, "develop to the same extent as man's" and girls' education should be intellectually more restricted than that of boys.[59] Where the late Kant mostly reacted against his earlier, pre-1780 enthusiasm for Rousseau, this does not apply to his view of women, where he remained deeply influenced, following Rousseau, in regarding women's mental make-up as inherently different from men's and intellectually inferior.[60]

If Condorcet's stance was that of democratic republicanism at its most developed, Rousseau's startlingly different position was that of "classical republicanism"—men and women are not at all equal. Rousseau construed the maxim that it is a crime to stifle the voice of nature quite differently to Helvétius, Diderot, d'Holbach, or Brissot. Trampling on a sentiment deeply natural to her sex, every immodest woman is "coupable, est dépravée" [culpable and depraved], an admonition that more strongly appealed to most readers (including Wollstonecraft until a certain stage in her life), than those of Helvétius or Diderot.[61] No aspect of radical thought was more roundly deplored by Rousseau after his break with the *encyclopédistes* in 1758, than Diderot's and Helvétius' support for sexual liberation for women, no less than men. Equality of sexual satisfaction, held Rousseau, was a cynical, artificial notion wholly contradicted by nature itself. Women naturally feel less sexual desire than men, seek sexual intercourse less, naturally prefer "modesty," the virtue most natural and characteristic of them. Where women prefer not to reveal themselves to men's eyes, men feel a stronger urge for the opposite sex. The veritable traits of feminine nature must be respected.[62] For Rousseau, gender barriers, the code of social difference, needed reinforcing, not diluting,[63] prompting Condorcet's sarcastic remark that "now Rousseau has earned [women's] approbation," he could hardly "expect them to pronounce in my favor."[64]

Condorcet was alluding not least to Germaine, Baroness de Staël-Holstein (1766–1817), who in her *Lettres sur les Écrits et le Caractère de J. J. Rousseau* (1788) fulsomely applauds Jean-Jacques from a female perspective. Rebuking Rousseau for

[58] Williams, *Rousseau's Platonic Enlightenment*, 110; Gauthier, *Rousseau*, 42–3; Greentree, "Writing against Sophie," 74–5; Taylor, "Rousseau and Wollstonecraft," 213, 216.

[59] Diderot, *Réfutation d'Helvétius*, 811–12, 845; Steinbrugge, *The Moral Sex*, 46–7, 65; O'Hara, *The Enlightenment*, 90; Davis, "Radical Enlightenment and . . . Women's Equality," 296–7.

[60] Shell, "Kant's "True Economy," 202, 211; Stoicea, "When History Meets Literature," 212.

[61] Rousseau, *Lettre à d'Alembert*, 172; Taylor, "Rousseau and Wollstonecraft," 217.

[62] Rousseau, *Lettre à d'Alembert*, 168–71; La Vopa, *Labor of the Mind*, 241; Nennon, "Gender in Rousseau's *Julie*," 246–9, 259.

[63] Zerilli, *Signifying Woman*, 18, 31; Larrère, "Women, Republicanism," 148, 155.

[64] Quoted in Larrère, "Women, Republicanism," 140; Offen, *Woman Question*, 30.

subordinating woman, and Mme de Staël and flocks of women for venerating him, Wollstonecraft (who could never wholly free her mind from Rousseau's captivating effect either) deployed arguments directly stemming from the radical critique. The principle of aristocracy and the established order, she pointed out, contemporaries justified by claiming the "mass of mankind cannot be anything, or the obsequious slaves who patiently allow themselves to be driven forward would feel their own consequence, and spur their chains." Men "submit everywhere to oppression when they have only to lift up their heads to throw off the yoke; yet, instead of asserting their birthright, they quietly lick the dust, and say, let us eat and drink, for tomorrow we die." "Women," protested Wollstonecraft, "from analogy, are degraded by the same propensity to enjoy the present moment; and, at last, despise the freedom which they have not sufficient virtue to struggle to attain." In Scandinavia, the narrowness, emptiness, and simple piety of women's lives filled her with despair.[65]

There was not (and cannot) be a theory of female emancipation, in other words, not anchored in a Radical Enlightenment general critique of society, morality, education, religion, and politics, stressing the power of "reason" to deliver improvement in human life by uncovering the truth.[66] It is evident how and why radical ideas specifically, and not some other current, spurred the trans-Atlantic movement for male and female equality and for sexual liberation during the eighteenth century and early decades of the nineteenth. Nothing could be clearer than the growing momentum of this surging movement of sexual emancipation, the social pressures behind it and the need for it. Philosophy had opened up a vast psychological can of repression and self-denial, releasing a torrent of talk and writing about sex, sexuality, sexual pleasure, adultery, illegitimacy, and female and male erotic contentment.

As part of this wider shift, female education was transformed into an urgent concern, and pressing social responsibility. Radical *philosophes* placed girls' education at the heart of their schema for the better society of the future. Ignorance, frivolity, capriciousness, love of vain amusements, and contrariness should in no sense be regarded as innate attributes of the female make-up, held Diderot and Helvétius, but rather unfortunate accoutrements foisted on them by a perversely immoral society, the dismal outcome of morally deforming, defective education. Conforming to a late seventeenth-century tradition reaching back to Poulain de la Barre (and Van den Enden), d'Holbach attributed most frailties of mind habitually imputed to women in his day to the ridiculous flimsiness of the education provided for them. Reading mounds of novels might refine a woman's sensibility, but, Wollstonecraft suggests in her story, *Mary*, composed on the eve of the French Revolution (1788), this was not necessarily the chief result. Mary's anti-social, insensitive, and ignorant mother constantly reads sentimental novels while "dressing her hair, and she could turn her

[65] Wollstonecraft, *Vindication of the Rights of Woman*, 185–6; Taylor, "Rousseau and Wollstonecraft," 216.
[66] Wollstonecraft, *Vindication of the Rights of Woman*, 127; Wollstonecraft, *Letters Written during a Short Residence*, Letter III.

eyes from the glass;" but with scant consequence as regards deepening understanding or heightening empathy.[67] Only raising women's intellectual and moral level through a different and better education, held radical authors, and here also d'Alembert, could enable women to attain their potential, be better appreciated by men, and figure in society for more than just looks and chaste reputations. Only thus could they gain more equal status and be respected in middle and old age.[68]

If boys' education was unsatisfactory, that of girls, complained d'Holbach, was barbarous and rudimentary in the extreme.[69] The existing system of education, he claimed, produced upper-class ladies who were not just intolerably vain, but dissipated, frivolous, and excessively prone to sexual adventure.[70] Upper-class women were as spoiled as princesses, and consequently remain ignorant of the requirements and duties of social life: the abysmal "manner in which they are raised would make one think that what is feared most is their becoming reasonable beings."[71] Especially bad in Catholic lands was entrusting girls' education to nuns, that is recluses devoid of knowledge of the real world. What could be more nonsensical than assigning instruction in matrimony and motherhood to females consecrated to celibacy? Correctly revolutionizing women's education could ensue, as with that of boys, only by adopting a wholly new conceptual framework detached from tradition, repression, and theology. Rousseau's *Émile* became a prime target not only of Diderot and d'Holbach but all writers seriously committed to gender equality. Catharine Macaulay, in her *Letters on Education* (1790), dismissed Rousseau's doctrine of basic gender difference as rife with "contradiction and absurdity."[72] Wollstonecraft's disciple, the much-scorned and derided (by men and women) Mary Hays (1759–1843), likewise stressed the need for women to reach the same goals in education as men, insisting on women's equal capacity for reason, erudition, and abstract thought, and equal capacity for science and philosophy, while indignantly rejecting Rousseau's contrary view.[73]

Nuns may administer lessons in morality, admonished d'Holbach, but, as a rule, their morality is hideously disfigured by "rêveries superstitieuses" converting female virtue into petty, superstitious, fastidious practices "totally alien to the interests of society."[74] The education ordinarily provided for girls served only to fill female minds with vain scruples, terrifying panics, and an obsessive religiosity fit for unsettling one's whole life, doubtless, but not for teaching the control of the passions that life demands. Educating girls for a meaningful life of equality in society could happen only through fundamentally revolutionizing attitudes to sexuality and marriage, but this in turn raised fresh moral quandaries. He in no way wished to be considered an apologist of debauchery and dissipation, protested Helvétius, at the end of his chapter distinguishing "virtues of prejudice" from "true virtue," but believed his proposed

[67] Wollstonecraft, *Mary*, 2.
[68] D'Holbach, *Morale universelle* iii. 102–5; Helvétius, *De L'Esprit*, 190; Offen, *Woman Question*, 123.
[69] D'Holbach, *Morale universelle* iii. 98–100.
[70] D'Holbach, *Système social*, 524.
[71] D'Holbach, *Morale universelle* iii. 99.
[72] Greentree, "Writing against Sophie," 76.
[73] Greentree, "Writing against Sophie," 80–3.
[74] D'Holbach, *Morale universelle* iii. 101.

revolution in moral thought the only means to end the confusion regarding the true criteria of right and wrong, the contradictions propagated by "moralists" over the ages.

D'Holbach presented a vigorous, impassioned defense of monogamous marriage, and fidelity within marriage, on the husband's as much as the wife's part, urging legislators and rulers to ensure the institution of marriage remained vigorously defended by education and law.[75] Condemning the Muslim *harem* as "un abus tyrannique," and polygamy in Christian lands justly forbidden, he scorned Plato's idea that women should be shared in common, but, in accord with his wider emphasis on equality, regularly added that masculine infidelity must be "également condemnable" as unfaithfulness in wives.[76] D'Holbach countenanced greater sexual freedom in certain respects, but chiefly aimed for equality and more honesty. How should we judge the vast mass of exhortations lamenting woman's fickleness, "falsity," and untrustworthiness given the deceitfulness of men, given that deception follows inevitably from the absurd contradiction between woman's natural desires and the austere humility and acquiescence that prevailing education, laws, and the chastity rules compels them to feign? In Malabar and Madagascar, women were perfectly straightforward and truthful because allowed to satisfy desire, their wants and fantasies, without scandal. Allowed lovers before marriage, they do not opt for a husband until after "repeated trials;" there, they have no interest in being false or hypocritical so no false or hypocritical women are to be found.[77]

Others went further. There is nothing unfeminine or shameful about fornication or adultery, proposed Brissot, these are natural occurrences, part of people's lives.[78] Diderot's and Helvétius' notion that the female modesty assiduously cultivated in society and tradition was mere social convention, the effect of upbringing without any basis in nature, Rousseau disparaged as a profoundly damaging, despicable myth.[79] To support his claims about the innateness of female modesty, Rousseau invoked the ancients, their rigorously separating the schooling of boys and girls, deeming this more relevant than any *encyclopédiste* argument for girls and boys being educated together and receiving the same lessons. Among the ancient Greeks and Romans, women were strictly confined to the household. In ancient Athens they attended the theater but stayed in a separate seating area well to the rear.[80] How they are raised is not the cause, as Diderot and Helvétius argued, of women's timid modesty, for remote rural women, such as unschooled, only slightly educated Swiss rural womenfolk, were more, not less, prone to lower their eyes, eschew male gaze, and avoid speaking in men's presence, than fine ladies raised in big cities.[81]

Not a few continued, even long afterwards, to laud Rousseau's *Lettre à d'Alembert* for censoring everything worldly and *philosophique* detrimental to woman's special

[75] D'Holbach, *Morale universelle* iii. 3–6, 8–11.
[76] D'Holbach, *Système social*, 527–9; Spitz, "From Civism to Civility," 115–17.
[77] D'Holbach, *Morale universelle* iii. 148.
[78] Brissot, *Lettres philosophiques*, 117.
[79] Rousseau, *Lettre à d'Alembert*, 168, 173, 175; Offen, *Woman Question*, 122–3.
[80] Rousseau, *Lettre à d'Alembert*, 177.
[81] Rousseau, *Lettre à d'Alembert*, 173–4.

charm, everything detracting from distinctively feminine virtue.[82] But virtues Rousseau eulogized and thought should be prized by educators, like prowess and forthrightness, he identified with masculinity and ancient bellicose societies like ancient Sparta and republican Rome. "Virtues" he despised (especially those cultivated in eighteenth-century Paris) he associated with effeminacy and supposedly quintessentially feminine traits like elaborate courtesy and vanity.[83] Rousseau's "notorious misogynist utterances" are compensated for, some argue, by his ecstatic eulogies of women's special virtues. Yet the very fact that for Rousseau, unlike the radical *philosophes*, there existed characteristic feminine virtues wholly different from those of men entailed a doctrine of comprehensive gender difference expressly repudiated by Macaulay, Wollstonecraft, Hays, Olympe de Gouges, Sophie Condorcet, and every feminist and advocate of universal and equal human rights adopting the radical equality of Diderot, Helvétius, d'Holbach, and Condorcet.[84] "Rousseau has often been singled out," comments one scholar, "as the Enlightenment's most eloquent defender of women's subjection to men,"[85] and not without reason. If no "traditionalist" in some segments of his thought, he decidedly *was* backward-looking as regards social morality, especially, like Robespierre and Napoleon, with respect to girls' education, marriage, and sexuality. In *Émile*, he offers a "theory of the essential difference between the two sexes, and advocates a political programme which would not only reinforce that difference, but would embody it in relations of radical inequality."[86] The same applies to his educational model. Contrasting sets of values and systems of "virtue" for men and women shape the divide in Rousseau's education theory, determining the divergent paths of Émile's and Sophie's upbringing in *Émile*.[87]

Republican liberty, for Rousseau, is the preserve of men, not a sphere shared between the sexes on an equal basis. The insistent Counter-Enlightenment stream among the French revolutionaries emphatically agreed. For it was Rousseau's virtuous and secluded wives and mothers, tucked away from the public arena of the male citizenry's political freedom, who were the publicly applauded model of female behavior during the ascendancy of Robespierre's revolutionary ideology. Rousseau's doctrine that women belong in the home, scorned by radical *philosophes*, for a time became public policy, along with his urging that education for boys and girls be kept separate because girls must chiefly absorb the domestic skills needed to prepare them for tending husbands and families, a principle expounded especially in the *Letter to d'Alembert* (1758) and *Émile* (1762). Rousseau's stance on the sexes'

[82] Ginguené, *Lettres*, 55, 61–2; Greentree, "Writing against Sophie," 75; Pečar and Tricoire, *Falsche Freunde*, 158–9.

[83] Zerilli, *Signifying Woman*, 37; Garrard, *Rousseau's Counter-Enlightenment*, 50.

[84] Parry, "*Émile*: Learning to be Men, Women and Citizens," 261; Greentree, "Writing against Sophie," 76.

[85] Kates, "Powers," 176; Vogel, "'But in a Republic, men are needed'," 214.

[86] O'Hagan, *Rousseau*, 181; Taylor, "Rousseau and Wollstonecraft," 217, 225; Israel, "Rousseau, Diderot," 656.

[87] Vogel, "'But in a Republic, men are needed'," 213–30; Taylor, "Rousseau and Wollstonecraft," 223–5.

disparate social roles and characteristic virtues, in 1793–4, was used to justify Robespierre's and the Montagne's halting female involvement in political societies and the reversal of Condorcet's and the Brissotins' campaign to educate boys and girls together.[88] Consequently, nearly all feminist theorists and female revolutionary spokespersons—Olympe de Gouges, Etta Palm, Sophie Condorcet, Charlotte Corday, Mary Wollstonecraft, Germaine de Staël, Claire Lacombe, and Helen Maria Williams, an author vilified in England for eulogizing the French Republic (until June 1793)—were vehement foes of Marat, Robespierre, and the Montagne.[89] Mme Roland did admire Robespierre (until she joined the Terror's innumerable victims); and did embrace Rousseau's doctrine of a natural division of tasks and duties between genders, albeit supporting expanding women's rights regarding divorce and ending primogeniture.[90] Early in the Revolution Olympe de Gouges vociferously opposed and denounced Robespierre as a dishonest hypocrite; she was guillotined too.[91]

No one else had nearly so great a literary and cultural impact on the late eighteenth century and beginning of the nineteenth—or the intellectual and general culture of the French Revolution—as Rousseau. But the different strands of his thought combined in an often highly idiosyncratic—and according to *philosophe* opponents—incoherent manner, and were utilized by rival revolutionary and anti-revolutionary groups and networks in markedly divergent ways. The only great thinker adulated by Left and Right simultaneously due to his unrivalled impact everywhere, he long remained a baffling mass of paradox. But his moral philosophy, "relying on the ordinary person's feelings, remained broadly traditional" and conservative, and eminently serviceable to *Robespierriste* authoritarian populism. During the Revolution, leaders antagonistic to both moderate and radical Enlightenment, like Marat, Robespierre, and Hébert, authors of the systematic intolerance and repression of 1793–4 and the Terror, not only ardently venerated Rousseau but created an organized public cult of "Rousseau" in a manner quite different from how the Revolution prior to June 1793 treated his legacy. Rousseau's voice, historians stress, was the loudest heard in France in 1789; yes, much the loudest, but equally many key revolutionary leaders quietly shunned his ideas, including Barnave moderates, Brissotins, Jefferson, who scorned Rousseau, and Condorcet, who practically never mentions him.

11.4. REVOLUTION AND DIVORCE

Radical Enlightenment aimed to reform marriage, inheritance, sex, and the family fundamentally, end subordination of women, decriminalize extra-marital sex (and by implication homosexuality), and equalize the legal status of the illegitimately-born,

[88] Israel, *Revolutionary Ideas*, 390–1; Offen, *Woman Question*, 127–8, 268.
[89] Franklin, "Romantic Patriotism as Feminist Critique of Empire," 551–64, here p. 554.
[90] Kates, "Powers," 169–71; Israel, "Rousseau, Diderot," 657.
[91] Israel, *Revolutionary Ideas*, 94–5, 123–6, 361–3, 508–9; Ferrone, *The Enlightenment*, 166.

but not, except perhaps in the case of Helvétius, depart from or abolish the traditional family as such. Sexual satisfaction is an indispensable component of compatibility within marriage, held Helvétius, and the point of marriage is to offer the best possible prospect of happiness for a partnership of man and woman. Hence, mere availability of divorce, he argued, hardly sufficed for ensuring optimal prospects of harmonious long-term relationships. Society should permit different forms of marriage to suit different individual, group, and social requirements. Why should a man and woman's living together for several years before formal marriage—what he termed "African marriages"—not be deemed respectable and useful by society?[92]

Helvétius, d'Holbach, and Brissot, like Macaulay, Wollstonecraft, and Hays, all strike a distinctly modern note in calling for more equality within marriage—all pronouncing it indefensible, as had Fontenelle earlier, that so many women remained chained to marriages "rendered indestructible by religion." All radical enlighteners condemned that "strange jurisprudence" which accords to husbands the license to commit the same "injustice" the law allows him to punish with the greatest severity should his wife permit herself the same freedom.[93] Indissolubility of marriage Condorcet designated an appalling blight on society and prime cause of prostitution, bastardy, wife-beating, and emotional misery.[94] Treatment of homosexuals occasioned yet another collision between traditional moral codes and Radical Enlightenment morality as propounded by Diderot, Helvétius, and d'Holbach. In much of Europe, treatment of homosexuals in the early and mid-eighteenth century remained fearfully punitive. In the Dutch Republic, in an exceptional wave of repression, hundreds of men were imprisoned and executed as *sodomieten* during the years 1730–1.[95] When Christian apologists charged Helvétius with encouraging corruption of morals, and subversion of religion and the law, his comments on homosexuality were cited as incontrovertible proof against him. Much as he deemed extra-marital intercourse to be not "incompatible" with a people's well-being and decidedly not to be criminalized, neither did he think "crimes against nature" incompatible with the well-being and good of the state. "From his principles," admonished one *antiphilosophe*, it follows that, for Helvétius, such crimes are not "contraires à la vertu."[96]

Refusal of divorce, absolute in Catholic lands, was difficult to obtain also in some Protestant countries, notably England, where dissolution of marriages, though theoretically available by law, required cumbersome procedures before an ecclesiastical court, to establish proof of adultery, the only acceptable grounds, followed by a private Act of Parliament, so that in practice recorded legal divorce remained highly inaccessible and affordable only for the wealthy. In England, too, divorce, like marriage, remained a closely-supervised church-directed procedure. Bickering, harassment, even shocking abuse and violence, remained entirely inadmissible as

[92] Helvétius, *De l'homme* ii. 736–7.
[93] D'Holbach, *Système social*, 525; d'Holbach, *Morale universelle* ii. 16–17; Helvétius, *De l'homme* ii. 736.
[94] Williams, *Condorcet*, 168.
[95] Diederiks, *Land van justitie*, 53, 59.
[96] Hayer, *Religion vengée* vii. 148–50.

grounds for escape from unwanted or detested husbands, according to the church, the sole arbiter.[97] Such laws, denying readily accessible divorce, d'Holbach termed laws "guided by barbarous prejudices." To force a girl to marry someone she hardly knows, often much older and who might well disgust her, and then remain indissolubly tied to that person, was a moral abomination.[98] Most marriages were contracted according to choices governed by "imprudence" and considerations of convenience (particularly of the parents), for which d'Holbach felt only indignation. If mere physical attraction is a flimsy basis for a hoped-for lifelong attachment, how much worse are motives of interest and dynastic pride, the impulses chiefly shaping upper-class marriages in his day? Nobility marry only to perpetuate their pedigree so that, among them, husbands and wives often treat each other on a personal level with the most perfect indifference, supposing it bad form to betray signs of affection. Concerned chiefly with status, reputation, and transmitting their name to posterity, "they seem to forget everything else for vain chimaera." Bad marriages generating only resentment and unpleasantness should, like any other association, be dissolved, as is plainly evident, held d'Holbach, from the nature of all human compacts.[99]

Although he modified his early stance later, the young Brissot's perspective on gender relations remained noticeably biased toward a masculine perspective. With availability of divorce, wives would be less likely to be pitiless harpies nagging husbands to pieces, would respect and love their husbands more; fear of divorce would help deter female infidelity within marriage.[100] Availability of divorce would also help diminish male resort to prostitutes and debauchery, by rendering the prospect of marriage less forbidding to younger men and encouraging earlier marriages. "Philosophy," asserts Brissot in his *Lettres philosophiques sur Saint Paul* (1783), composed at a time when he had repeated meetings in London with Bentham, requires every enlightened nation to adopt a comprehensive divorce law because an enlightened society refuses to chain together "irrévocablement" husbands and wives who make each other unhappy.[101] But Brissot, whose most supportive ally during his attempts to establish himself as a writer in England in 1782–4 was none other than Catharine Macaulay, consistently and throughout viewed lack of divorce as yet another illustration of religion's tyrannical grip on society.[102] Should indissolubility of marriage end, he did not think the actual incidence of divorce would be particularly large. Its mere availability, by easing anxieties, would alleviate the sense of being trapped that existing laws fomented. Marriage under prevailing conditions was truly "le tombeau de l'amour" [the tomb of love].[103] More equitable laws, more in conformity with nature, would release vast numbers of victims from bonds that "serve

[97] Langford, *Polite and Commercial*, 582–3.
[98] D'Holbach, *Système social*, 525–6; Loft, *Passion, Politics*, 46.
[99] D'Holbach, *Morale universelle* iii. 5, 25.
[100] Brissot, *Lettres philosophiques*, 120; Loft, *Passion, Politics*, 123–4.
[101] D'Holbach, *Morale universelle* i. 229; Brissot, *Lettres philosophiques*, 116, 119–21.
[102] Loft, *Passion, Politics*, 45–7; Davidson, "Feminism and Abolitonism," 104.
[103] Brissot, *Lettres philosophiques*, 116; Green, "Catharine Macaulay's French Connections," 65.

only to bind the unfortunate."[104] If peace and happiness are the goal of marriage, asked Brissot, why compel a person withering under its yoke eternally to bear its chains? If love is the essence of marriage why perpetuate bonds after indifference or aversion displace love?[105]

For this reason, Brissot condemned Jesus's teaching that "le marriage est indissoluble" except in cases of adultery as a *doctrine pernicieuse* against which all true *philosophes* must rebel. Only *la philosophie* could conquer indissolubility and virtual indissolubility of marriage, he remarks in his *Lettres philosophiques sur Saint Paul*, because—in opposition to the laws of Moses and the Pharisees—indissolubility of marriage had indeed, for most believers, been introduced by Christ himself. But *philosophes*, he pointed out, must also accept that while "prejudice" remained deeply entrenched in society there was no immediate prospect of achieving the requisite changes.[106] Rejected by most, there was assuredly no other way modern secular divorce could have been adopted, as it was in 1792, than by a revolutionary democratic republican intellectual vanguard driven by Radical Enlightenment ideas. Equally, it was specifically the work of the philosophical radicals—the Brissotins—and decidedly not the authoritarian populists (Robespierre, Marat, etc.). After 1792, stubborn resistance to civil divorce, stiffened by the Catholic and Protestant churches, continued even though many no longer believed that heaven especially approved of lives devoted to religious austerity, or that vows of perpetual virginity were anything but an assault on nature and human happiness.

During the Revolution, the most enlightened views of woman's place were those permeating the democratic republican journals, progressive Paris salons, and the *Cercle social* or *Amis de la Vérité*. The *Cercle social*, founded in early 1790, but a political club only from October that year, was an organization originating in the continuing fight over democracy within the Paris city assembly. Established by Fauchet and Bonneville, it soon drew in Condorcet, Lanthenas, and other Paris Commune republican democrats, becoming a movement for re-educating the broader public. A *littérateur* long steeped in *la philosophie* and initially allied with Sieyès, Bonneville proved an unyielding republican stalwart even before the convening of the Estates-General: he advocated a complete recasting of France's political institutions and laws on the basis of radical ideas. The *Cercle*'s leaders sought ways to bridge the gap between Commune and city sections, and enlighten the common people. Enlightened ideas combined with "excellent works" would "defeat hypocrisy, charlatanism, and tyranny forever."[107] The Revolution's key social reform proposals—including reform of marriage laws, and emancipating women legally and politically—lay, like dissolving religious orders, integrating "free blacks," emancipating Jews, and abolishing slavery, so far beyond the bounds of conventional

[104] D'Holbach, *Morale universelle* iii. 25; d'Holbach, *Système social*, 530–1.
[105] Brissot, *Lettres philosophiques*, 119.
[106] Brissot, *Lettres philosophiques*, 115–16, 120–2; Blanc, "Une humaniste," 28–9.
[107] Kates, *Cercle social*, 21; Monnier, "Républicanisme," 99.

notions and received thinking that initially they met with utter incomprehension and a broadly unsympathetic response. This was what "philosophy" had to change; the *Cercle*'s bookstore offered texts by Condorcet, Brissot, Bonneville, Mercier, Auger, Paine, and Lanthenas.

Liberating men and women by re-educating them meant overcoming conventional, majority ways of thinking and propagating revolutionary concepts which had little immediate connection with popular awareness, preferences, and concerns. In the republican leadership's view, everything "de plus philosophique" regarding law, religion, government, and moral principles had to become more familiar to the electorate before real, substantial changes could occur. To build the necessary momentum, revolutionary democratic republican journals regularly carried references to, and extracts from, *philosophes* "of the first order," especially Raynal, Diderot, d'Holbach, Mably, Condillac, Boulanger, Condorcet, and Paine beside Rousseau and Voltaire.[108] If the *Cercle*'s antipathy to the constitutional monarchist "moderate" center aiming to exclude the multitude from the political process led to their being viewed unfavorably by most National Assembly deputies before August 1792 and, while the monarchy lasted, by the court,[109] the *Cercle* nevertheless won extensive support in Paris and beyond.

Civil marriage and divorce, and abolishing the dowry system, regular topics of public debate from the summer of 1789, figured among the *Cercle*'s principal goals.[110] The Revolution would exert a "grande influence" on women's lives, announced the *Chronique de Paris*, a paper closely aligned with Condorcet, Brissot, and the *Cercle*. The Revolution's most outstanding women, Sophie Condorcet (1758–1822), Olympe de Gouges (1748–93), and the Dutch exile Etta Palm d'Aelders (1743–99), participated prominently in the *Cercle*'s work. Through its efforts, civil marriage, divorce, equality within marriage, a national education scheme for girls, and legal majority at 25, became stock themes among the revolutionary vanguard. Condorcet's wife had already become a noted figure before 1789, her Paris salon attracting among others Adam Smith, Jefferson, Morellet, Suard, Beaumarchais, Lafayette, Ginguené, and David Williams (1738–1816), the ex-Unitarian turned deist, and, during 1789–90, democratic radical. During the early Revolution, her salon, like that of Mme Helvétius at Auteuil, served as a regular focal point for leading democratic republicans, an arena where the social thought of Helvétius, Raynal, Diderot, and d'Holbach was reaffirmed in more revolutionary guise by her husband together with Brissot, Garat, Ginguené, Chamfort, Volney, Chénier, Lafayette, Paine, Cloots, and the materialist Cabanis, who later married Sophie's sister, Charlotte de Grouchy (1768–1844).[111] Another regular was Claude Fauriel (1772–1844), professor of literature, critic, historian, and philosopher who, after Sophie was widowed in 1794, became her lover.

[108] *Chronique de Paris* xlvi (Oct. 1789), 181.
[109] Halévi, "Girondins," 151–2. [110] Kates, "Powers," 163–80.
[111] Bouissounouse, *Condorcet*, 113; Staum, *Cabanis*, 293, 298–9; Deneys, "Volney, Auteuil," 108.

A famed beauty nicknamed the "belle Grouchette" after her maiden name (Grouchy), Sophie Condorcet won a commanding place in her own right among the Revolution's democratic leadership. Despite noble extraction and a provincial convent education, she had become, not long after arriving in Paris, in 1784, an ardent atheist and democratic republican. Fervent for *la philosophie* and equality, she and Condorcet married, with Lafayette present, in December 1786. Their salon, gathering in their apartments on the Quai Conti, in the Hotel des Monnaies, became a principal meeting point for all the "troupe philosophique" which, from 1788, as the United States ambassadors in Paris, Jefferson and Gouverneur Morris, both noted, but from contrary vantage points (one enthusiastically, the other scornfully), effectively led the Revolution as a movement for thoroughgoing social reform. The translator of Adam Smith's *Wealth of Nations*, zealous for the American Revolution, like her husband, she exerted her spell over the entire *philosophique* sect, albeit in a quieter, less dramatic fashion than Mme Roland. Along with Catharine Macaulay, De Gouges, Palm, and Wollstonecraft, Sophie powerfully contributed to the birth of modern feminism albeit, like Wollstonecraft, confining herself to a less activist, more distinctly *philosophique* role than her sister revolutionary leaders, Roland, De Gouges, and Palm d'Aelders.[112] Since women possess the same moral and intellectual capabilities as men, anything but equality for women, she argued, is by definition incompatible with the *Rights of Man* and discriminatory. After the Terror, and her husband's death, she remained steadfastly loyal to Condorcet's *philosophique* legacy, her salon resuming in Paris and at her summer residence, the suburban chateau La Villette, where she continued championing the Revolution's core principles, a focus of *philosophique* criticism and discreet opposition also after Mme Helvétius' death in 1800, and Napoleon's consolidation of power.[113]

Only stupidity and barbarism could sustain a code as "impertinent as that contemporary society applied to women," exclaimed another ally of the *Cercle*, in the *Chronique de Paris*—Charles-Michel du Plessis, Marquis de Villette (1736–93), a homosexual nobleman whose mother, an aunt of the marquis de Sade, had been a close friend of Voltaire. According to some, Villette, who renounced his former noble status (publicly burning his certificates of *noblesse*) early in the Revolution, was actually a natural son of the *philosophe* of Ferney. Most of the public and most revolutionaries, lamented "Charles de Villette," took no interest in women's rights. Persuading ordinary folk was an extremely arduous task but much of that could follow later; for now, those agreeing must sway all those of discernment and understanding, the *philosophes*, journalists, and revolutionary leadership; only this could win women's right to equality. Reason, morality, the progress of the sciences and arts had all transformed the female segment of society no less than the male. For centuries, women had been subjected to senseless "feudal servitude;" "our legislators" should now accord France's twelve million females "the rights they possess from nature."

[112] D'Abrantès, *Salons*, 44–5, 51, 61–2; Badinter, *Condorcet*, 385; Pagden, *The Enlightenment*, 22–3.
[113] Rothschild, *Economic Sentiments*, 216–17.

Refusing to waste time on "fools and the ignorant," Villette championed women's right to attend the primary assemblies and participate in their decisions. Was any contradiction more "revolting" than that great sovereigns like Catherine II and Maria Theresa, acknowledged by Europe's powers, would be excluded, under present rules, from "our political assemblies" and organizations?[114] Later, he became a prime target of the *anti-philosophique* Montagne.

From January 1790, the Condorcet circle initiated a series of motions in the National Assembly to accelerate amelioration of women's lot.[115] Where even the foremost radical spokesmen in America, Franklin, Jefferson, and Paine, made scant attempt to broach women's causes, the French Revolution during 1792–3 undertook an epoch-making promotion of woman's equality and rights and, given the fraught circumstances, achieved no small success especially as regards marriage, divorce, married women's property, and schemes for universal secular education. The March 1790 law abolishing primogeniture in noble lineages, a legal device conserving large estates and properties intact in aristocratic hands, marked an initial gain for women's rights by ending prioritizing of male inheritance rights in disposing of noble properties.[116] In April 1791, the National Assembly prohibited unequal divisions of inheritances according to gender in cases of intestate inheritance. To reduce paternal control of grown children, female and male, paternal authority was curtailed in September 1792, when the age of majority was reduced to 21.[117] But although the 1791 "moderate Enlightenment" Constitution rendered marriage a civil contract, it failed to equalize married women's property rights and status in marriage, or permit divorce.[118]

Philosophically, the case for viewing divorce free from ecclesiastical interference essential to human freedom is unanswerable, asserted the *Chronique de Paris*, reviewing a forty-page text on *La Necessité du divorce*, on 6 January 1791; yet civil divorce and treating men and women equally continued to be opposed by most French men and women and most of the legislature.[119] France's marriage laws needed reforming, insisted the *Cercle*, especially via a comprehensive divorce law according women equal rights with men in obtaining divorce.[120] But support for civil divorce invariably went hand in hand with democratic republican views and rejecting religious authority, with everyone opposing radical thought or following the clergy resisting such ideas. Their campaign was not the result of a broad cultural shift. During the Revolution, there was no surge of public sentiment or conventional sensibility pushing for civil divorce.[121] "Divorce is forbidden by the Christian religion," exulted the Abbé Royou following the National Assembly's rejection of the draft divorce law proposed by *Cercle* leaders and democratic journalists on 25 February 1792. Virtually

114 *Chronique de Paris* ii/206 (25 July 1790), 822; Israel, *Revolutionary Ideas*, 124–5.

115 *Chronique de Paris* ii/5 (5 Jan. 1790), 17–18.

116 Kates, "Powers," 168–70, 174–5.

117 Hunt, *Family Romance*, 40–1; Gross, *Fair Shares*, 203; Darrow, *Revolution*, 7, 11, 14, 66, 70, 78–9.

118 Desan, "Politics of Intimacy," 632.

119 *Chronique de Paris* vi (6 Jan. 1791), 21.

120 [Bonneville], *Bouche de fer* i. 107–12, *Lettre XI (*Feb. 1790) "de Marseille" au cercle social.

121 Royou, *L'Ami du roi*, 16 Oct. 1791, p. 1; Norberg, "Love," 40–1.

nobody in France wanted civil divorce, declared Royou (with only slight distortion), apart from *philosophes*, *déistes*, Protestants, and Jews.[122]

Backed by Condorcet, Bonneville, Brissot, and Villette, the Revolution's leading women—De Gouges, Palm, and Sophie Condorcet—raised the banner of a sophisticated, politically organized feminism capturing an incipient but real enclave in the public sphere.[123] As a public champion of women's rights, Sophie was decidedly eclipsed by the flamboyant De Gouges and also by Etta Palm d'Aelders (1743–99), an emancipated lady from Groningen close to Brissot, resident in Paris since 1774, translator of Mirabeau and Condorcet into Dutch. Angered by the prevailing refusal to take women's rights seriously, the fiery Olympe, once a high-class *courtisane* and later a dramatist, in September 1791 published her *Declaration of the Rights of Women* where, to underline her satirical purpose, she arranged her ringing exhortation in seventeen articles, like the *Declaration of the Rights of Man*. Her first article reads: "woman is born free and lives equal to man in her rights. Social distinctions can be based only on the common good;" her fourth: "liberty and justice consist in restoring all that belongs to any, to all. Thus the only limits on the exercise of the natural rights of woman are perpetual male tyranny. These boundaries are to be reformed by the laws of nature and reason."[124]

An effective and fearless orator with highly-placed lovers in both France and Holland, Palm d'Aelders delivered a resounding discourse, in December 1790, before a crowd of thousands gathered under *Cercle sociale* auspices denouncing French law for discriminating against the female population. Her *Discourse on the Injustice of the Laws in Favor of Men, at the Expense of Women*, subsequently published by the *Cercle*, pulled no punches.[125] "Our holy Revolution we owe to the progress of philosophy," she averred; but now "philosophy" must initiate a second revolution, this time in social practice so that discrimination against women, condemned by *la vraie philosophie*, yields "to a gentle, just and natural order."[126] A "women's circle" with its own *directoire* was established at the *Cercle*'s offices in the Paris Théâtre-Français section, its first gathering convening in March 1791. In her inaugural speech as "president," Palm d'Aelders expressed hopes that their group would secure concrete advantages for women—in Paris first, then France, and finally everywhere. She spoke optimistically, lauding the *Cercle* as "the first organization in France to admit women to political meetings."[127] The inaugural meeting agreed to establish a women's society with local branches, admission cards, and a vetting system for excluding undesirable types, ensuring the *Cercle*'s women's circle featured only "excellentes

[122] Royou, *L'Ami du roi*, 28 Feb. 1792, p. 1; Israel, *Revolutionary Ideas*, 124.

[123] Blanc, "Une humaniste," 27–8; Hesse, *Other Enlightenment*, 81–2; Tackett, *Coming of the Terror*, 89–90.

[124] Israel, *Revolutionary Ideas*, 125–6.

[125] Palm d'Aelders, *Appel aux françoises*, 1–3; Vega, "Feminist Republicanism," 164; Kates, "Powers," 163–5.

[126] Palm d'Aelders, *Appel aux françoises*, 9–12; Marand-Fouquet, *La Femme*, 120–1.

[127] [Bonneville], *Bouche de fer* 1791, no. 39 (6 Apr.), 43; Hufton, *Women*, 23.

patriotes" of proper character.[128] Each Paris section should have its own local affiliated *société patriotique de citoyennes* gathering weekly and sustained by a small entry fee. Women's section associations, it was envisaged, would spread enlightenment, assist the destitute, help vagrant girls, run nurseries for unmarried women's offspring, and help fend off the "people's enemies," meaning aristocrats, royalists, and theologians.[129] Charity schools, presently entrusted to ignorant beings "nourished on prejudices of all kinds," should come under their supervision. In Paris, and soon also provincial centers like Caen and Bordeaux where local patriotic societies likewise set up women's circles, political feminism was for the first time consolidated as an organized revolutionary movement.

Palm d'Aelders continued delivering speeches defending women's rights, many subsequently printed by the *Cercle*. To develop a sound moral sense in women, society must provide education equivalent to that for men, and not impose unequal restrictions and penalties. The law should protect women and men equally and promote equality within marriage. She mocked the National Assembly's new police code, with its Article XIII stipulating that adultery charges could be brought only by husbands against wives, and that women convicted of adultery could, unlike men, be imprisoned. She denounced the highly unequal laws concerning marriage settlements, labeling the corpus of supposedly revolutionary marriage law so far approved by the Assembly's constitutional committee an affront to human rights, because of its blatant inequality, making women men's slaves.[130] "Moderate" monarchist papers, like the *Gazette unverselle*, vilified d'Aelders as a violent democrat, *contre-révolutionnaire* (for opposing the moderates), high-class courtesan (which she had been), and agent of the Prussian court in "criminal correspondence with France's enemies" (she had some involvement in complex espionage intrigues).[131] Publishing a hard-hitting retort in Bonneville's *Bouche de fer*, she accussed the Assembly's moderates and Rousseau admirers of abasing women with barbaric rules drawn up in deference to "theologians instead of *philosophes*."[132]

Rousseau admirers were indeed infuriated by d'Aelders's feminism, which to many seemed rooted in *philosophique* ideas and "masculine" activism. A prominent female revolutionary journalist, Louise-Félicité de Kéralio-Robert (1757–1821), collaborating with her husband in editing the Paris *Mercure National*, furiously attacked Palm d'Aelders and her feminist cohort for trying to upset traditional gender relations under the banner of the Revolution, which should more vigorously impose Rousseau's vision of liberty, including gender difference and woman's passivity. The *Cercle* should concentrate on improving morals, and brushing up their Rousseau, rather than establishing women's political clubs, making activist speeches, and encouraging

[128] [Bonneville], *Bouche de fer* 1791, no. 36 (29 Mar.), 572, 575.
[129] Palm d'Aelders, *Apppel aux françoises*, 25–8.
[130] Palm d'Aelders, *Apppel aux françoises*, 38–40, 46; Israel, *Revolutionary Ideas*, 126–7.
[131] *Chronique de Paris* 201 (20 July 1791), 813.
[132] [Bonneville], *Bouche de fer* 1791, no. 39 (6 Apr.), 43.

female political involvement. Instead of drawing a "crowd of idle and curious women," the *Cercle* should adulate Jean-Jacques and exhort women to chastity, staying at home, avoiding meetings and public affairs, and tending their children and husbands.[133]

First to propose civil divorce in the Assembly, and the most active member of the legislature on women's issues, Mirabeau had many female admirers, including a former abused wife married off at 13 to a drunken gambler who abused her dreadfully; she deeply regretted her political hero's untimely death, in April 1791, which she thought deprived society, especially womanhood of "all the good he wanted to do."[134] Only with the monarchy's collapse, in September 1792, did resistance crumble and the marriage laws finally come to be fundamentally reformed. On 20 September 1792, with the Brissot faction now at the helm, the legislature enacted civil divorce along with an impressive list of permissible grounds for terminating marriages, including incompatibility of temperament.[135] The high point of the campaign for women's equality and rights, at odds with Enlightenment "moderation," populist intolerance, Catholic doctrine, and Rousseau admirers alike, Brissot's law declared divorce a pillar of individual and collective liberty, expressly denying marriage to be an indissoluble commitment. Still more remarkable, Brissot's law established equal rules for husbands and wives applying for divorce and, in theory, equal rights for mothers and fathers raising children after divorce.[136]

Over the next decade, research in local archives reveals, more than twice as many women as men filed for divorce under the new law, usually on grounds of male tyranny, violence, and wife-beating. In addition, divorce was resorted to much more frequently in Paris than anywhere else, even Marseille and Lyon, though even these large cities had much higher rates of divorces than smaller towns and villages. At Paris, between 1 January 1793 and 17 June 1795, 5,987 divorces were registered, 71 per cent initiated by female petitioners, chiefly on grounds of incompatibility of temperament.[137] Once equal rights to divorce were secured, however, the campaign for equality of women's rights slowed markedly, then rapidly receded as the Brissotin position weakened and Montagnard authoritarian populism with its strongly *anti-philosophique* agenda and powerful biases gained ascendancy. With regard to women's political and voting rights, expanding scope of the women's societies, and Condorcet's and the *Cercle*'s general agenda of female freedom, full emancipation, it soon became clear, remained a distant ideal.[138]

[133] Palm d'Aelders, *Appel aux françoises*, 34; Geffroy, "Louise de Keralio-Robert,"18; Censer, *Prelude*, 16; Desan, "Politics," 640; Offen, *Woman Question*, 126–7.

[134] *Chronique de Paris* 22 (22 Jan. 1792), 86–7; Desprat, *Mirabeau*, 673–5; Darrow, *Revolution*, 3–5.

[135] Hunt, *Inventing Human Rights*, 63; Kates, *Cercle social*, 120–4; Scott, *Only Paradoxes*, 40–50.

[136] Kates, "Powers," 167; Hunt, *Family Romance*, 41–2; Wolin, "In Praise of *Philosophie*," 104.

[137] Godineau, *Citoyennes tricoteuses*, 52–3; Dessertine, "Le Divorce," 211; Kates, "Powers," 167–8; Darrow, *Revolution*, 177, 203.

[138] *Chronique du mois* ii (May 1792), 33; Godineau, *Women*, 278; Israel, *Revolutionary Ideas*, 478, 509–10.

11.5. MONTAGNARD, NAPOLEONIC, AND POST-NAPOLEONIC REACTION

"Woman, be a *citoyenne*!" hence remained exclusively the cry of republican *philosophisme*, of the radical tendency, resisted by most of the public and especially the intolerant populism of Marat, Robespierre, Saint-Just, and Hébert. Vilification and scorn, observed Villette, was the typical response of the majority of both sexes to the *Cercle social*'s campaign for women's rights. But Mary Hays, in England, had no less reason to complain of the torrent of contempt for her views. Hays, De Gouges and Palm d'Aelders, according to traditionalists, were brazen men-chasers who appeared not to agree that society should rigorously enforce chastity on females. The clash between traditional and radical ideas intensified with the ongoing conflict between democratic *philosophisme* and populist *Rousseauisme*. Radical Enlightenment stress on equality meant not just that women should enjoy equal personal liberty with men, and equivalent political rights, but admitted no reason in principle why any professions, or sphere of business or politics, should remain closed to women. But such notions clashed directly with tradition, *Rousseauisme*, and also *Robespierrisme*, which here, especially, proved unbendingly traditional. Activist female involvement in the Revolution, the mounting female participation during 1792 not just in the Paris section meetings but in major *journées*, including the 20 June processions and the 10 August attack on the Tuileries ending the monarchy, was eyed disapprovingly by most of the public.[139] Battling across a wide ideological front and many different issues, feminism from 1792 became one more arena where Robespierre's militant *antiphilosophisme* combated Radical Enlightenment.

In practice if not intention, theological Counter-Enlightenment and Montagnard attitudes powerfully converged in curtailing freedom of the press and expression, and individual liberty, and imposing traditional morality with respect to women. The *philosophes* acquired their ability to influence society, admonished the Counter-Enlightenment propagandist, Feller, chiefly by appealing to young and pretty women. As the *philosophisme* driving the Revolution advanced, women served as "instruments of their power," endorsing the *philosophes'* arrogance, spreading their pernicious *tolérantisme*, and freeing men's lust, dissolving the very fabric of society.[140] Protest stemmed not least from among Faubourg Saint-Antoine working men, chief focus of Marat's authoritarian populism. On returning from a hard day's work, working men wanted their dinner, not to find their wives were out busy at political meetings.[141] Putting women in their place became a key objective of the Montagnard Rousseauist agenda, as of the Counter-Enlightenment's unrelenting war on *philosophisme*. Insisting woman's place was in the home and women's "virtues" different from men's, and essentially domestic whereas men's belonged to the public

[139] Levy and Applewhite, "Women, Radicalization," 83, 89–90, 100.
[140] Feller, *Journal historique* 1792 (1 Jan.), 23.
[141] Proly, *Le Cosmopolite*, 123 (16 Apr. 1792), 394.

sphere, together with belief in woman's greater moral fragility and corruptibility, foreshadowed the still greater insistence on re-differentiating masculine and feminine roles, "virtues," and levels of corruptibility, following Restoration Catholic discourse during the 1820s.[142]

With the Montagnard triumph of June 1793, the gains achieved thus far by the revolutionary feminist movement were rapidly reversed in whole or in part. While none of the autonomous revolutionary societies, for men or women, long retained the temporary influence they briefly attained during late 1792 and early 1793, women's societies in particular and first of all became the target of Montagnard repression. As authoritarian populism gained ground, in 1793, so correspondingly women's causes all receded. Organized repression commenced in the late summer of 1793, when Pierre Gaspard Chaumette (1763–94), a leading voice of prejudiced male street populism and the Montagnard campaign to confine women to the home and debar them from political activity, denounced De Gouges as the epitome of the unnatural revolutionary virago, as a dangerous, sexually immoral man-woman.[143] The likes of De Gouges, d'Aelders, Sophie Condorcet, and also Wollstonecraft (who was then in France and enjoying the favorable reception of the early 1792 publication of the French version of her *Rights of Woman*) were declared to contravene Nature and Rousseau's teaching that a life "domestique et retirée" is woman's proper role, that morally upright female lives stay within the domestic and family sphere.[144]

During the summer of 1793, numerous women still crowded into the galleries of the political clubs, section assemblies, and popular societies. Their activism led to a number of dramatic incidents. On 31 July 1793, the actress Claire Lacombe (dates unknown), "president" of the *Société des Citoyennes républicaines révolutionnaires*, an activist society formed in May by her and Pauline Léon, two renowned pike-bearing female protagonists of the 10 August 1792 uprising (in which Claire was wounded)—a group linked to the Cordeliers Club and Hébertiste faction—appeared as spokeswoman before the Convention leading a *citoyennes*' delegation drawn from all forty-eight Paris sections. The *citoyennes* complained of the Convention's tardiness in erecting an obelisk commemorating Marat whose popular cult was cultivated with great passion by working-class women.[145] Lacombe and Léon proclaimed women's right to bear arms, participate in politics, and make their voice heard. Close to the *Enragés*, aligned especially with Jean-Théophile Leclerc (1771–96), one of the "Patriots" expelled from Martinique by white monarchists in 1791, an *enragé* championing women's, black, and *sans-culotte* rights and who loudly denounced Robespierre's shelving of the Constitution and muzzling of the section assemblies, Lacombe soon found herself clashing with the Montagnard

[142] Hesse, *Other Enlightenment*, 51–2; Mills, "Negotiating the Divide," 30–2.

[143] Scott, "Woman who has Only Paradoxes," 104, 106, 115; Blanc, "Une humaniste," 31, 33–4, 36.

[144] Rousseau, *Lettre à d'Alembert*, 168, 175; Botting, "Wollstonecraft," 511, 513, 515.

[145] Levy and Applewhite, "Women, Radicalization," 102–3; Tackett, *Coming of the Terror*, 88–9; Clarke, *Commemorating*, 182–4; Jarvis, *Politics in the Marketplace*, 142, 144, 149.

dictatorship. Summoning *sans-culotte* women to demonstrate, Lacombe and Leclerc publicly deprecated several of the more corrupt Montagnard leaders, notably Chabot and Bazire, as worthless hypocrites "oppressing the people."

On 16 September 1793, François Chabot (1756–94), Claude Bazire (1761–94), and Jean-Pierrre Amar (1755–1816), all key architects of the Terror, and three of the most misogynist, *anti-philosophique*, and intolerant of the Montagnard leadership,[146] launched a concerted campaign against Lacombe's women's society in the Jacobins and before the *Comité de Sûreté générale*. Lacombe and her circle had to be firmly dealt with, being persistent protesters and trouble-makers; they denounced them as *contre-révolutionnaires* who "spoke contemptuously of M. Robespierre." Following a scuffle caused by her trying to address the Jacobins from the galleries, Lacombe was overpowered and dragged out by furious Montagnard market women yelling "Down with the new Corday!"[147] The *Comité de Sûreté générale*, declared the Jacobins, must compel the Revolution's womenfolk to purge their leadership and membership of trouble-makers. On 30 October, after a debate using Rousseauist gender tropes to justify women's exclusion from politics, and blaming recent unrest among Paris market women on "Brissot and his accomplices," led by the Grenoble lawyer, Amar, among Robespierre's closest, most *anti-philosophique* and corrupt aides—an ally of Caribbean slave-owners and a personage co-opted on to the *Comité de Sûreté générale* by the group dictatorship following the coup in June—the National Convention, rallying the least-informed on the marketplaces, including many illiterate women, dissolved all French revolutionary women's associations "under whatever name they may exist."[148] Republican women henceforth could only attend male *sociétés populaires*, all of which were now increasingly bridled to prevent expression of any views like those of Lacombe, Leclerc, Roux, and Varlet—independent and critical of Robespierre.[149] In January 1794, Robespierre again rebuked the societies for being insufficiently "patriotic," too readily penetrated by undesirable counter-revolutionary elements, pervaded especially by Brissotins and "aristocrats."[150]

The "popular societies" [*sociétés populaires*] were bridled with watchdog committees charged with identifying and ferreting out "monarchists," "aristocrats," "moderates," food hoarders, and *fédérés* [Brissotins], while keeping a suspicious eye on grocery and bakers' stores, cafés, theaters, gambling locales—and not least activist, independent-minded women and prostitutes. As the Montagne crushed the democratic Revolution's core values and principles in more and more of France, the drive

[146] Aulard, *Société de Jacobins* v. 506 (11 Nov. 1793); Lapied, "Absence," 309; Jarvis, *Politics in the Marketplace*, 160, 162–3.

[147] Aulard, *Société de Jacobins* v. 406–7 (16 Sept. 1793); Levy and Applewhite, "Women, Radicalization," 92; Roessler, *Out of the Shadows*, 151–3, 163; Guillon, *Notre patience*, 154–5.

[148] Godineau, *Citoyennes tricoteuses*, 172–3; Hufton, *Women*, 37; Scott, "Woman who has Only Paradoxes," 104; Roessler, *Out of the Shadows*, 156–61; Offen, *Woman Question*, 30, 90, 148, 268.

[149] *Journal de Perlet* vii, no. 243 (31 Oct. 1793), 404; Godineau, *Women*, 165–70; Hunt, *Family Romance*, 153; Slavin, *French Revolution*, 326–7; Jarvis, *Politics in the Marketplace*, 161–3.

[150] Slavin, *French Revolution*, 334–7; Israel, *Revolutionary Ideas*, 510, 584–5.

to curb prostitution, commencing in the late summer of 1793 in Paris and soon extending to other major cities, grew into an astounding mania.[151] Following the Brissotin defeat at Bordeaux, the "filles publiques" were treated in the most outrageous fashion, noted a local diarist, as if the Montagne aspired to establish "Spartan morals" throughout all France. With the Brissotins beaten, a similar crackdown followed in Lyon. The very antithesis of the Rousseauiste ideal of womanhood, a corrupt vestige of the *ancien régime*, street whores were declared an affront to revolutionary morals, a symbol of everything Rousseau and "virtue" sought to eradicate in the name of revolutionary austerity. Reacting to the conspicuous rise in prostitution caused by growing economic distress, Jacobin surveillance seemed intent on not just suppressing the girls, but eradicating every indulgence and "vice," forbidding the erotic itself.[152]

The Montagnard-dominated National Convention stipulated that girls caught soliciting should be shut up in public hospices and put to useful work. Street whores were locked in prisons—but sometimes their fate was worse. The fanatically puritanical Montagnard leader (privately a highly active homosexual), Chaumette, obsessed with the alleged threat from forward women of all descriptions, assured the Convention, in November 1793, that street whores were among the Counter-Revolution's principal agents and recruiters along with *dévôt* women and priests.[153] Two prostitutes, Catherine Alboury and Claire Servin, arrested in the Tuileries section for uttering counter-revolutionary remarks, were guillotined in December 1793, along with several other courtesans.[154] A woman forgetting the "virtues pertaining to her sex" became regular Jacobin parlance not just for females accused of sexual forwardness, but, as Mme Roland discovered, for unwomanly fondness for intellectual debate, exhibiting activist republican militancy, and, above all, for criticizing Montagnard leaders.[155]

Olympe de Gouges, vilified in the populist press, figured among the first victims of Montagnard persecution of feminism. Arrested on 23 July for defying the March 1793 edict forbidding counter-revolutionary writings, after posting up an *affiche* around Paris urging a general referendum to enable the people to choose between republican and constitutional monarchical government, she was tried for her life.[156] Republican laws promised that no illegal authority would oppress the citizenry, she admonished her judges, "yet an arbitrary law worthy of the Inquisition, that even the *ancien régime* would blush to implement, imprisons the *esprit humain* and has taken my liberty from me in the midst of a free people." "Is not liberty of opinion and the press consecrated as the most precious patrimony of Man in Article VII of the Constitution? Your [the regime's] arbitrary acts and atrocities must be condemned before the

[151] Marand-Fouquet, *La Femme*, 328–32.

[152] Brochon, *Un Bordelais*, 36; Scott, *Terror*, 131; Cobb, *The French*, 105; Hunt, *Family Romance*, 159.

[153] *Journal de Perlet* vii, no. 382 (9 Oct. 1793), 71, and vii, no.429 (25 Nov. 1793), 448; Lachapelle, *Considérations*, supplement, p. lxx; Higonnet, *Goodness*, 200–1.

[154] *Journal de Perlet* viii, no. 449 (15 Dec. 1793), 117.

[155] Godineau, *Women*, 275.

[156] Blanc, "Une Humaniste," 30–1.

whole world." Where Rome burned under only one Nero, *la France libre* today suffers under a hundred.[157] Sentenced to death for "counter-revolutionary writings," she was guillotined shortly after news of Brissot's execution caused Wollstonecraft, more and more shaken by these developments, to faint with horror. The Revolution's greatest feminist apart from Wollstonecraft met her end, on 3 November, reportedly with great calmness.[158]

Wollstonecraft's depression lasted right through the Terror, lifting only after Thermidor. "The liberty of the press will produce a great effect here," she reported, hopefully, from Paris, on 1 October 1794, thanking God that "some monsters" were already got rid of: "the cry of blood will not be in vain! Some more monsters will perish—and the Jacobins are conquered. Yet I almost fear the last flap of the tail of the beast." [159] Only from early 1795, as Neo-Brissotin elements gradually regained control of the National Convention from the now shattered, loathed remnants of authoritarian populism, did genuine revolutionary principles begin to revive. As the ludicrous myths of Marat the "friend of the people," Jacobin integrity, and Robespierre the Incorruptible disintegrated, an explosive emotional reaction surged everywhere. Plaster busts of Marat, the false *Ami du people*, were smashed by the hundred. On 8 February 1795, only five months after his entombment, "Marat" was ceremonially *dépanthéonisé* amid rapturous public applause. Soon, in provincial towns, crowds were routinely stamping on images of Marat and Lepeletier, and insulting their accursed names. Early 1795 witnessed a vast and passionate psychological and cultural reaction against *Maratisme*, Montagnard repression, and Robespierre, not least against their xenophobic and misogynist prejudices, a revulsion against Robespierre's "tout populaire" that generated a craze for replacing Jacobin Rousseauist "virtue" with anti-austerity, finery, elegant fashion, fine food and drink, low-cut dresses, and flirtatiousness. Women's fashions, also in official circles, suddenly changed spectacularly. Austerity was replaced with overt elegance and frivolity with erotic allure. Fashionable restaurants proliferated as never before; so did prostitution.[160]

Josephine de Beauharnais, released from prison after Thermidor, Juliette Récamier, and Térésa Tallien (1773–1835) emerged among the most glamorous of the fashionable ladies leading the anti-Montagnard revolution in Parisian and provincial fashion, eroticism, and gender relations. The scene was soon awash with Greek-revival-style flimsy dresses, flaunting the female bosom with astoundingly low necklines, plus jewelry.[161] No beauty, Wollstonecraft found it harder than most to lay aside the "melancholy mood" gripping her during the Terror. The undisguised eroticism displacing *Robespierriste* puritanism also troubled her, especially as there was no real improvement in women's situation. "You know my opinion of men in general,"

[157] De Gouges, *Oeuvres*, 126; McPhee, *Robespierre*, 138.
[158] *Journal de Perlet* vii, no. 408 (4 Nov. 1793), 276, and no. 409 (5 Nov. 1793), 284; Wollstonecraft, *Collected Letters*, 232.
[159] Wollstonecraft, *Collected Letters*, 268–9.
[160] Peyrard, *Jacobins*, 292; Spang, *Invention*, 138–9, 143–4; Lajer-Burcharth, *Necklines*, 191.
[161] Apt, *Louis-Phillipe de Ségur*, 91; Lajer-Burcharth, *Necklines*, 259.

she wrote to her companion, Gilbert Imlay, at the end of 1794, "you know that I think them systematic tyrants," and that a "man of sufficient delicacy of feeling to govern desire" is the rarest thing in the world.[162]

Under the Directory, women's limited gains through the Revolution remained broadly in place, but were largely dismantled, from 1804, by Napoleon, who was, in any case, something of a Jacobin misogynist, regarding women as mere "machines for making babies," in a series of calculated compromises with traditional thinking. The struggle between the Revolution and religious authority ceased, on an official level, with the Concordat with the Papacy of July 1801, and, at Easter 1802, Napoleon, as First Consul, formally ended the rift between France and the Papacy, restoring the old episcopate and recognizing its power to control the lower clergy and exercise spiritual authority over French Catholics and much of primary education. At the point revival of the church's influence in France began, the 1792 divorce law remained still formally in place and there were still divorces. The impoverished nobleman, disciple of Condorcet, and revolutionary social theorist Count Claude-Henri de Saint-Simon (1760–1825), who, in his first published work, *Lettres d'un habitant de Genève* (1803), argued that scientists and social scientists should henceforth assume the former place of priests in society, in June 1802 divorced the daughter of a former military colleague, after only ten months of failed marriage.[163] But the Concordat, and reviving ecclesiastical authority, rendered divorce less readily available and less in demand.

Having married Josephine de Beauharnais in a republican-style civil wedding, in March 1796, Napoleon subsequently remarried her, at the pope's request, in a religious ceremony the day before the First Consul was crowned Emperor of the French, on 2 December 1804. On 18 May 1804 (24 Floreal An XII), the senate formally transformed the French Republic into an empire with articles stipulating that the imperial dignity would henceforth be hereditary and pass by legitimate line of descent, from Napoleon, by order of primogeniture exclusively via the male line. Josephine's and Napoleon's remarriage eloquently symbolized the resurgence of Catholic influence, reintroduction of heredity, primogeniture, and male dominance, and the receding of civil marriage and the right to divorce. At Toulon, divorces, having averaged 10 per cent of the number of marriages in the late 1790s, rising to around 18 per cent by 1802, plummeted drastically to less than 2 per cent following the 1804 revision of the marriage laws curtailing the freedom to divorce that the 1792 law conceded to aggrieved wives.[164]

Bonaparte's compromises reconciled Catholic opinion to a degree, and brought the Papacy to a more neutral stance. According to Madame de Staël, the First Consul assured Cabanis that his church policy would prove the "vaccination of religion," a way to weaken it permanently.[165] But though he did seek to limit the revival of ecclesiastical influence, Napoleon also fully concurred with Rousseau and Robespierre

[162] Wollstonecraft, *Collected Letters*, 276. [163] Manuel, *Utopian Thought*, 592, 596.
[164] Crook, *Toulon*, 201; Roberts, *Napoleon the Great*, 157–8, 278, 281.
[165] De Staël, *Considerations*, 454.

that girls should be educated differently from boys and confined to the home, and that women should be excluded from the public sphere. His bias extended even to salon society and culture, driving a particular antipathy to intellectually gifted women like Madame de Staël, whom he accused of promoting society's effeminization along similar lines to those familiar under the *ancien régime*.[166] Among *philosophes*, ideologues, and medical men, friction between Rousseauist–Bonapartist insistence on natural difference in temperament and abilities and the radical conception of women's intellectual and general equality persisted unresolved. But materialist atheists were encountered on both sides, Cabanis, like Fichte, remaining a vigorous proponent of male/female difference and separate gender roles and capabilities through the 1790s.[167] Destutt, by contrast, held that the male and female mind is everywhere essentially the same. More favorably disposed than most to women's emancipation in professional and sexual life, and to their having more say in choosing their marriage partners, he also advocated readily available divorce. But, unlike Condorcet, De Gouges, and Lacombe, he judged women unfitted for political rights.[168]

After 1814, the church in France recovered some of its former power, property, and prestige. Among key revolutionary enactments cancelled, aligning France again with the rest of Catholic Europe, was the divorce law, half reversed in 1804 by Napoleon. Post-1814 French marriage again subjected wives legally to their husbands, removed protection against personal abuse within marriage, and left married women again with no right to dispose of inherited property, or any effective control over their property at all. But if the great Revolution's laws ameliorating women's rights ceased to apply, appreciation and longing to see them restored did not. The 1820s Restoration did little to dampen this aspiration and, for feminists, the disappointing "moderate" outcome of the 1830 revolution, which merely replaced conservative monarchy with a less conservative one, did little either to satisfy it.

Radical demands, including sporadic pleas for the divorce law to be reinstated, eventually revived. Among radicals publicly railing against the betrayal of egalitarian principles in 1830 and Louis-Philippe's decrees, petitioning the legislature for restoration of the divorce law, was Flora Tristan (1803–44), an ardent feminist who only narrowly survived a dreadful marriage to a drunken, tyrannical gambler. When her *Peregrinations of a Pariah* (1838), recounting her horrifying marital experiences appeared, it so enraged her husband that he publicly shot and wounded her in a Paris street, prompting a sensational trial which finally secured her freedom.[169] Of course, relatively few women shared the feminism, revolutionary outlook, and radicalism of a Tristan. Frequently at the fore of resistance to de-Christianization in the provinces during 1793–4, under the Restoration women were continually admonished by France's bishops and priests to continue taking the lead, in home and church,

166 Franklin, "Romantic Patriotism," 555; Davidson, "Feminism and Abolitionism," 108.

167 Cabanis, *Oeuvres complètes* ii. 400–2, 488; Staum, *Cabanis*, 215–16; Staum, *Minerva's Message*, 100–1; Kenkel, "Personal and the Philosophical," 280–1, 288.

168 Staum, *Minerva's Message*, 101.

169 Desanti, "Flora Tristan", 276–7, 281.

as agents of Restoration, piety, royalism, and re-Catholicization, especially by ensuring children were raised as loyal Catholics.[170] This further accentuated the growing imbalance between male and female attendance at mass and the confessional, piety increasingly being considered a characteristic female bias. Where, on the eve of the Revolution, male clergy had outnumbered the nuns by roughly two to one, with a numerous regular clergy (monks and friars), socio-economic change and the crown's inability to restore most of the regular orders' property after 1815 drastically altered the balance. In 1830, France had approximately 45,000 male clergy as against 31,000 nuns; by 1861, numbers of male clergy had climbed to 75,000, but nuns' numbers swelled to no less than 90,000.[171]

More so than in the 1790s or the Napoleonic period, the notion that the church dominated much of society by exerting sway over female parishioners, intimidating wives and daughters, became deeply entrenched in mid-nineteenth-century French republicanism. Where many Frenchmen were hardened republicans, women, disappointingly, as some saw it in the 1830s and 1840s, Michelet among them, remained politically blind, ignorant, superstitious adherents of an oppressive theocracy, leaving it to their menfolk to embrace science and "progress." A paradoxical consequence during the Third Republic (1870–1940) was the male electorate's stubborn resistance to female enfranchisement. Republicans, having once stood for universal and equal rights and a universal suffrage, were precisely those who most obstinately opposed votes for women later, a new prejudice rooted in the post-1815 perception of French womenfolk as the clergy's prime obedient flock. Women continued to be denied the vote in France until April 1944!

[170] Mills, "Negotiating the Divide," 41–2.
[171] Mills, "Negotiating the Divide," 44; McMillan, "Religion and Gender," 57.

12

From Classical Economics to Post-Classical Redistributive Economics (1775–1820)

12.1. BEGINNINGS (1748–1776)

The Enlightenment era gave birth to a large number of new sciences—ethnology, anthropology, paleontology, archaeology, geology, and also economics. The eventual emergence of social economics as distinct from classical pure economics figures among the central intellectual dramas of modernity and most enduringly relevant aspects of the Western Enlightenment. Classical economics, historians agree, arose during the eighteenth century's third quarter, especially during the two decades or so between the appearance of Montesquieu's *L'Esprit des Lois* (1748)[1] down to the 1770s, evolving internationally, especially in France, Italy, and England, with its basis laid by three foundational works—François Quesnay's *Tableau Économique* (1759), Turgot's *Reflections on the Formation and Distribution of Wealth* (1766), and Adam Smith's magnum opus *Inquiry into the Nature and Causes of the Wealth of Nations* (1776).[2]

Jefferson, keenly interested in the topic, eloquently summed the matter up in 1816: "Political Economy, in modern times," he observed, "assumed the form of a regular science, first in the hands of the political sect in France called the Economists. They made it a branch only of a comprehensive system, on the natural order of societies. Quesnia [i.e. François Quesnay] first, Gournay, Le Trosne, Turgot, and Dupont de Nemours, the enlightened, philanthropic, and venerable citizen now of the United States, led the way in these developments, and gave our enquiries the direction they have since observed." These figures all shared in pioneering how to analyze production, expansion, and circulation of wealth, and demonstrate how economic development follows from creating a surplus or net product, providing the wherewithal for improvements and expansion of production, refining techniques, and stimulating commerce, resources becoming the engine of further wealth creation.[3]

[1] Rather than just the decade 1765–75 as I wrongly stated in *Revolution of the Mind*, on this see Larrère, "Montesquieu on Economics," 336.

[2] Sismondi, *Nouveaux Principes* i. 39–40; Groenewegen, *Eighteenth-Century Economics*, 20; Muceni, "Mandeville," 97.

[3] Quoted in Albertone, "Thomas Jefferson and French Economic Thought," 130.

Despite unmistakable earlier hints that democratic republicanism, combating "aristocratic" republicanism, implied far-reaching changes in attitudes to wealth, property, and distribution of wealth, during the era of classical economics such concerns remained largely segregated from the newly-born science of economic theory. A striking early instance of the democratic impulse exhibiting clear economic implications was Radicati's account of "democracy" in his *Twelve Discourses* (1734): "democratic government then is that, where the whole authority is in the hands of the People indistinctly, and where Men are equal in nobility, power, and riches. To which end all possessions must belong to the Republic, which like a good mother, must distribute them to every Man, according to his necessities; so that no Man must be reduced to beggary, and no Man must enjoy superfluities."[4] But militant egalitarian leanings were not as yet linked to any systematic analysis of economic processes and did not at first penetrate the sphere of the economic theorists, even though Quesnay and the first *économistes* did embrace Montesquieu's notion of "commerce" as a form of economic activity generating wealth by concentrating acquisition in fewer and fewer hands and furthering luxury and inequality, and saw this as a problem.

Montesquieu pointed out that wealth accumulation through trade creates difficulty for republicans who must remain wary of "commerce," but nevertheless, being basically a defender of monarchy and aristocracy, he tended to view "commerce" favorably, offering no general objection to the increase in inequality he assumed "commerce" to be building. By contrast, François Quesnay (1694–1774) and the *économistes*, though absolutists and royalists in politics, at the same time believed one of monarchy's benefits was its ability to rise above conflicting economic interests and curb divisive tendencies like increasing wealth inequality, in the interest of the whole.[5] Their suspicion of commerce and finance arose from a belief that these did not benefit society overall, or the economy generally, but merely heightened inequality, promoting destabilizing divisions. Beyond this, pre-1790 French *économiste* preoccupation with economic issues, with Quesnay first, while rejecting the protectionism and regulatory mania of pre-1750 mercantilism, and discarding what their new economics disparaged as mercantilism's obsessive hindrances and restrictions, essentially transmuted older state mercantilist fixation on promoting society's prosperity by supporting policies to encourage economic expansion through shifting the emphasis away from international exchange, by boosting internal production, and favoring agriculture over commerce. A central feature of Quesnay's economic theory was what he saw as the need to maximize export of essential foodstuffs while minimizing imports of essentials and encouraging the importing of unnecessary luxury items instead, to step up pressure to increase overall production of essentials and depress domestic output of unnecessary luxuries. This was their way to ensure the overall health and solidity of the domestic economy and secure self-sufficiency, an

[4] Radicati, *Twelve Discourses*, 204; Berti, "Repubblicanesimo," 169.

[5] Larrère, "Montesquieu on Economics," 338–9; Spector, *Montesquieu et l'émergence*, 458–9; Forget, "Jean-Baptiste Say," 206.

overriding goal for physiocrats as for Rousseau, as well as strengthen the military, administrative, and other arms of the state. One of the social benefits of such an economics, held Quesnay, was to reduce the share of the rich in the overall amount of national wealth, thereby lessening inequality.[6]

The new science began with Quesnay and Antonio Genovesi (1713–69), the latter switching from general philosophy to the less risky sphere of political economy in the early 1750s, being appointed to the world's first chair in economics, at Naples, in 1754.[7] The new field most obviously diverged from traditional mercantilist explanations by developing a more theoretical preoccupation with the internal workings of economies. The most "general and fundamental principle" of political economy for Genovesi, the son of a shoemaker, was that society's productive classes should form as large a proportion of society as possible, aided and balanced by state policy, while those not directly involved in agriculture, trade, navigation, manufactures, or some other productive aspect of economic life should constitute as low a proportion as possible; meanwhile, exporting raw materials should in some degree be discouraged by the state to avoid growing subordination to stronger productive economies (like Britain).[8] Admittedly, analysis of economic processes as a complex set of interactions conceivable as functions of nature, entirely detached from theological and moral considerations, had been presaged earlier, most strikingly in Mandeville's *Fable of the Bees* (1714);[9] but during the early eighteenth century there was as yet little sense of this topic being a new science ripe for intensive observation, study, and debate. The rise of the new study as a social science stemmed from a growing awareness in the 1750s and 1760s, spurred by Montesquieu, that laws of nature, analyzed and understood with mathematical precision, possessed a wider application than had been assumed hitherto and that such laws, as in medicine, underpinned the economic and social processes governing whole social bodies no less than individual bodies.

A peasants' son trained as a surgeon, it was when representing the Paris surgeons in dispute with the university-trained physicians, in the late 1740s, that Quesnay originally caught Diderot's eye. As lead editor of the *Encyclopédie*, Diderot was impressed by his call for theory and practice to merge into a single corpus of research, study, and practice. Personal physician of Madame de Pompadour, from 1749, Quesnay presided as resident medical authority and man of letters at Versailles, a capacity enabling him several times to perform small services for Diderot, Voltaire, and their associates at court. An innovative, highly talented man, he turned to economics around the same time as Genovesi, in the early and mid-1750s. Protective of his position at court, Quesnay felt obliged by the initial hesitant royal condemnation of the *Encyclopédie*, in 1752, to distance himself publicly from Diderot and the latter's great project; he did not openly acknowledge his contributions to Volumes VI

6 Sismondi, *Nouveaux principes* i. 39–40, 45; Sonenscher, *Before the Deluge*, 205–8, 213.

7 Robertson, *Case for Enlightenment*, 352–3; Skornicki, "Découverte de l'économie," 261.

8 Genovesi, *Lezioni di comercio* i. 61–2, 165; Pabst, "Political Economy," 596–7.

9 Muceni, "Mandeville," 99–102.

(1756) and VII (1757) even though these, including his article on "Evidence," were substantial. In this as other respects, Quesnay showed himself a classic adherent of moderate mainstream Enlightenment. Anti-determinist and anti-materialist, he championed "freedom of the will," "a first-cause proof of the existence of God," and divine providence, and followed Locke in maintaining that truth, as knowable to men, is dualistic, stemming from experience, on the one hand, and religious authority and faith, on the other.[10]

Approaching economics from his medical background, Quesnay was predisposed to view the existing social and economic order as in some sense a divinely ordered and ordained body; he showed no interest in changing the balance between rich and poor, but opposed policies he judged likely to increase inequality and in that way disturb the natural status quo. His *Encyclopédie* articles, on "Fermiers" and "Grains," his initial forays in economics, especially the latter, were of considerable theoretical significance. Men's needs, markets, and the financial clout of Paris and other large cities, held Quesnay, were sucking in wealth, activity, and skills from outside, causing the general condition of the French countryside to become depleted and impoverished.[11] Inadvisable fiscal and recruiting policies only aggravated the harmful general shift of men, energy, and resources from the countryside, ensuring rural demographic stagnation and decline, mounting destitution, and degrading of animal stock, and also causing undesirable retention of less up-to-date techniques and tools. Whatever policy best favored agriculture, he maintained, would ensure the greatest abundance of grain and accessibility to subsistence for the poor.[12] The best policy, he urged, was "un commerce libre des grains" [free trade in grain], with renewed emphasis on promoting agriculture, which Quesnay and his school always identified as the prime source of national wealth and well-being, and key resource of the crown. This rendered the question of how to advance the peasantry's well-being and tackle rural distress primarily an economic rather than a political and social issue. Quesnay's major and, for economics, foundational work, his *Tableau économique* (1758), was innovative in using statistical tables together with pure economic concepts and effectively made Quesnay founder of the so-called "physiocrats" or *économistes*.

By "physiocratie," he and his principal followers—the older Mirabeau, Mercier de la Rivière, Gournay in some respects but not others, and Dupont de Nemours, son of a Huguenot watchmaker and the writer who actually coined the term—meant the "rule of nature," removing obstructions to the free functioning of the physical laws of nature and society, a concept underpinning the first modern scheme of economics by claiming that removing obstacles to normality, to healthy economic activity, would of itself solve the difficulties generating different forms of economic malaise. Quesnay's chief economic argument was that a government policy of unrestricted commerce in

[10] Kafker, *Encyclopedists*, 322; Muceni, "Mandeville," 98; Hill and Montag, *Other Adam Smith*, 244.

[11] Quesnay, art: "Grains," in Diderot and d'Alembert (eds.), *Encyclopédie* vii. 812, 816, 825; Vardi, *Physiocrats*, 114–16.

[12] Quesnay, *Examen de l'Examen*, 81.

grain would stimulate producers to trade in and profit more from grain, and thereby boost production, which would ultimately serve the whole rural and urban population, including the poor, by keeping bread prices low and stable; this, in turn, he saw as the key to general prosperity.[13] It remained characteristic of Quesnay's and the *économiste* approach, as Adam Smith, who immersed himself in their work, observed, that their primary concern was always with increasing and provisioning the population overall, and improving revenues and their country's general economic condition by promoting one dimension, agriculture, specifically. Quesnay in fact had remarkably little to say about manufactures, employment, poverty, and inequality.

Enthusiasts for the new science, seeking to uncover the laws linking economic life with the rest of social and political existence, theorists such as Pierre-Samuel Dupont de Nemours (1739–1817), editor of the new French *Journal de l'agriculture* during 1765–6, regarded the infant new science as a specialized field genuinely based on mathematical rigor and precision. Far removed from everyday assumptions, and the "prejudices of general ignorance," to them it was a science offering valuable but far from obvious truths largely unfamiliar to society at large.[14] Strikingly, all three foundational texts of classical economics dwelt particularly on the inhibiting effects of hindrances to enterprise and production posed by familiar but outmoded restrictions, mistaken policies, privileges, monopolies, and wrongly-conceived tariffs and taxes.[15] Striving to improve economic efficiency and productivity, they urged unimpeded circulation of goods and services, emphasizing the role competition, cost-cutting, a wisely devised tax system, and innovation play in boosting productivity. Above all they aimed to break the mold of ingrained tradition and received methods by removing longstanding barriers to higher production and increased prosperity, considering this the most efficient way for the state to regulate the economy. When government and administrators mismanage the fixed laws of economics and tax regulation, Dupont admonished readers in 1768, the cost to society in lost ease and prosperity is extremely high.[16] Years later, he would be one of a group of courtiers who thwarted the revolutionary mob attempting to seize Louis XVI's person during the Paris uprising of 10 August 1792. Imprisoned, and under sentence of death during the Terror, Dupont was saved by Thermidor.

Anne-Robert-Jacques Turgot, baron de l'Aune (1727–81), emerged among the foremost economists and reformers of the *ancien régime*'s last quarter-century. Youngest son of a Norman noble family, and during the years 1761–74 the dynamic *intendant* of Limoges, Turgot attained the peak of his brief epoch-making career in 1774–6, as Controller-General of the royal finances, then the presiding government role, assisted by his energetic personal secretary, the physiocrat Dupont du Nemours, whom he appointed "inspector general of commerce." If Turgot's elaboration of

[13] Quesnay, *Examen de l'examen*, 81–3.
[14] Dupont de Nemours, *De l'origine et des progrès*, 10–11; Gusdorf, *Conscience révolutionnaire*, 395–6.
[15] Robertson, *Case for Enlightenment*, 30–2.
[16] Dupont de Nemours, *De l'origine et des progrès*, 39–40, 46–8.

Condillac's epistemology and article on "Existence" for the *Encyclopédie* represented a more formidable challenge to radical thought than anything *antiphilosophie* could adduce, his *Éloge de M. de Gournay* (1759) further refined the economic doctrines of his chief mentor, Jacques Claud Vincent de Gournay (1712–59), a royal *intendant du commerce* renowned for his antipathy to *bureaucratie* and excessive regulation whom Turgot, when young, during 1753–6, accompanied on provincial tours of inspection.[17] In his *Réflexions sur la formation et la distribution des richesses* (1766), a foundational work of European laissez-faire economics, Turgot developed a theory of economics that brilliantly summed up pre-Smithian eighteenth-century free market thought offering the most formidable rival approach to countering poverty and inequality to that offered by radical ideas. Turgot presented a dazzling array of arguments and innovative solutions aimed at promoting society's general wealth by removing obstacles to capital flow and enterprise, and especially by improving the legal framework of commerce, finance, and investment and demolishing guild-orientated restrictive, medieval ways of organizing economic activity.

Keeping his distance from, and wary of, Diderot,[18] Helvétius, and the materialist *encyclopédistes*, rejecting their atheism and materialism, Turgot emerged among the foremost examples in post-Montesquieuan France of a moderate mainstream *philosophe* believing in God (prior to 1751 he adhered to an emphatically Christian outlook), while seeking a broad toleration and many social and economic reforms but always within the existing framework of social hierarchy, primogeniture, nobility, and royalty. Like Voltaire, Turgot rejected the principle of equality categorically. Like Quesnay, after 1757, he refused to be further associated with the *Encyclopédie* to which he had previously contributed five articles at d'Alembert's request. But while disapproving of radical thought, and the economic ideas of the Diderot–d'Holbach faction, he remained on close personal terms, through the 1770s, with the young Condorcet. Fervent admirer of Locke, Newton, and Condillac,[19] Turgot was undoubtedly an economic genius and amongst the foremost minds of the moderate mainstream Enlightenment. Averse to all doctrinaire positions, he disclaimed being either an *encyclopédiste* or *économiste* in the physiocratic sense of the term.[20] Lifelong connoisseur of Voltaire's writings, and avowed providential deist, known for his haughty manner, his plans to reform France's monarchy were inspired by essentially British and Dutch models of urban, commercial society blended with strands of physiocracy. Like the physiocrats, he scorned practically all medieval and mercantilist economic practices and institutions,[21] his primary objective being to stimulate enterprise and foster entrepreneurial freedom and initiative. The great commercial fairs of Europe, like those of Leipzig and Lyon, he held, in his article "Foire" in the *Encyclopédie*, had been, and remained in his day, decidedly more

[17] Poirier, *Turgot*, 74–6; La Nuez, *Turgot*, 45–6; Orain, "Journal oeconomique," 566–7.
[18] Israel, *Enlightenment Contested*, 548 681, 788. [19] Poirier, *Turgot*, 30–4, 37, 39.
[20] Kafker, *Encyclopedists*, 376; Vardi, *Physiocrats*, 8–9.
[21] Turgot, art: "Foire," in Diderot and d'Alembert (eds.), *Encyclopédie* vii. 39–41.

detrimental than conducive to national and international trade.[22] Nearly all his theoretical and practical contributions aimed at bolstering activity by removing obstructions to the flow of capital, labour, and produce. He especially disparaged monopolies, fiscal exemptions, internal regional tariffs, ancient endowments, guild regulations, provincial fairs, and royal and municipal controls on the internal movement and pricing of grain and wine.

Although Turgot's and Dupont's presiding political role was of short duration (1774–6), it proved a crucial turning-point in French economic life and political development.[23] Turgot disavowed the label "physiocrat" and, in several respects, noted Jean-Baptiste Say later, was not one; but he shared their passionate anti-mercantilism, agrarianism, and tendency to prioritize landed property over other forms of ownership, and also their willingness to ally with landowners, and rank big landowners with capital intrinsically more "useful" to society than small ones.[24] From early on, Turgot harbored a markedly unsympathetic attitude towards the small peasantry and generally displayed scant interest in issues of wages, labour, equality, and inequality. Despite an abiding concern with individual freedom, security, and prosperity, Turgot's approach, much like physiocracy, easily slid into becoming an economics of elite government and the landowning aristocracy, showing scant inclination to question the existing social hierarchy. Dupont, Turgot's assistant, a Quesnay disciple and leader of the younger breed of *physiocrates*, even more vigorously tied physiocratic notions of economics to a *dirigiste*, anti-democratic, pro-landowner view of society, being fundamentally unsympathetic to the democratic tendency in the American as well as French contexts, a point where he notably diverged from his later American friend and correspondent, Jefferson.[25] In his early work, *On the Origin and Progess of a New Science* (1768), Dupont contended, in typical physiocratic fashion, that the undeviating regularity of the required government role, adjusting trade policy and taxes for the maximum prosperity of agriculture, fitted with absolutism and hereditary monarchy far better than with democratic or aristocratic republican systems.[26] What Dupont presented in 1768 as a "perfect community of interests" between the monarch and "his people"[27] turned out to be distinctly more of a pact between the monarch and large landowners.

Historians customarily stress the foundational role of Adam Smith (1723–90). But Smith only turned his hand to the new science in the 1760s, well after Quesnay, Genovesi, and Turgot; and his *Wealth of Nations* did not appear until 1776. But if far

[22] Turgot, art: "Foire," in Diderot and d'Alembert (eds.), *Encyclopédie* vii. 41; Poirier, *Turgot*, 70.

[23] Horn, *Economic Development*, 226–7, 235.

[24] Dupont de Nemours, *De l'origine et des progrès*, 42–8; Sismondi, *Nouveaux principes* i. 40–2; Kates, *Cercle social*, 117; Sewell, *Work and Revolution*, 128–31.

[25] Albertone, "Thomas Jefferson and French Economic Thought," 140; Longhitano, "Industry, Government," 192–3.

[26] Dupont de Nemours, *De l'origine et des progrès*, 64–7; Forget, "Jean-Baptiste Say," 206; La Nuez, *Turgot*, 180.

[27] Dupont de Nemours, *De l'origine et des progrès*, 68, 77; La Nuez, *Turgot*, 179–80.

from the first, he *was* the most thorough and comprehensive in conceiving economies to be intricate complexes of economic activity, bodies of interacting components of vast complexity subject to fixed rules, entities comparable to bodies in having different ways of being healthy but constantly exposed to dangers and "violent effects," especially from disruptive consequences of mistaken policies and types of regulation, most obviously "mercantilist" interventionism. On its appearance, *Wealth of Nations* was immediately recognized as the undisputed masterpiece of economic thought thus far, although on the Continent some observers, like Condorcet, initially viewed Smith's work, grudgingly, as merely elaborating theories advanced earlier by Turgot.

Quesnay, founder of the Physiocratic School of economists in France, Smith was well aware, was Turgot's and his own chief predecessor in introducing the idea of the economy as comprising, like bodies, a circular flow from which impediments needed removing; but he was critical of his and their approach and diverged from it in important respects. Quesnay's view of how economies function Smith considered too focused on agriculture and population, and too apt to encourage government intervention. Physiocrats showed insufficient concern with advancing economic activity generally and improving the overall functioning of the economy. Even so, Smith judged the French physiocrats' system "with all its imperfections [as] perhaps the nearest approximation to the truth that has yet been published upon the subject of political economy."[28]

Major elements of Smith's conception, especially elements of his free market doctrine, his laissez-faire conviction that the "system of natural liberty" is the best basis for every economy's health,[29] did broadly resemble those of Turgot, with whom he became acquainted and first discussed economic theory at Paris, in 1766;[30] like Turgot, and the latter's influential predecessor and mentor, De Gournay, Dupont, and others, Smith aimed to demonstrate how an environment that encourages individual effort improves collective efficiency and benefits society as a whole. Less reminiscent of Quesnay, Turgot, and Dupont was the particular strain of moderate Enlightenment "natural theology" underpinning Smith's conception of how economies function, his belief individuals strive only for their own gain but, "in spite of their natural selfishness and rapacity" are "led by an invisible hand to promote an end which was no part of [anyone's] intention," namely the "public interest" and to "divide with the poor the produce of all their improvements."[31] Here lay the foundational principle of a classical economics Radical Enlightenment came to comprehensively reject. Quesnay and Turgot were by no means radicals, but for them, unlike Smith, there is no easy natural convergence of conflicting interests but rather a constant hard

[28] Packham, "Physiology of Political Economy," 468; Phillipson, *Adam Smith*, 194; Vardi, *Physiocrats*, 10.

[29] Packham, "Physiology of Political Economy," 468–9, 475; Harrison, "Adam Smith," 47.

[30] Robertson, *Case for Enlightenment*, 364, 373; Poirier, *Turgot*, 150–1; Horn, *Economic Development*, 239.

[31] Harrison, "Adam Smith," 45–6; Rothschild, *Economic Sentiments*, 116–56, 288–316; Hill and Montag, *Other Adam Smith*, 55, 241, 251, 299–301.

tussle to conserve the natural order, care of which is entrusted by the divine architect to king and ministers but requires careful, expert management and supervision.[32] For Smith, economies are healthy when left to the natural laws of economic and social life, pure market forces; they should not be regulated by governments or administrators but work best when left to their own devices, sustained by a kind of general providence, which was by no means the message of the physiocrats or Turgot.

Disapproving of the legal and general institutions as well as economic regulations and practices of his time, Smith, like many Enlightenment writers, was especially troubled by the "expensive and unnecessary wars" of his age.[33] Occasionally, one also finds, from his pen, expressions of indignation over how law and institutions are exploited by the rich and privileged for their own benefit to the detriment of the majority, thereby intensifying deprivation and oppression of the poor. However, such remarks are found mostly in unpublished papers and remained marginal to the basic lines of his economic thought.[34] Neither Turgot, Beccaria, Quesnay, Dupont, nor Adam Smith proved particularly relevant to the wider Enlightenment concern regarding social problems ensuing from unequal wealth distribution and oligarchic control of institutions, exploitation, oppression, legal and political inequality, and poverty, the very same issues Montesquieu had shelved. Contrary to what has been suggested,[35] there was no hint of late Enlightenment "universal and equal rights" in the physiocrats any more than in Turgot or Smith.

12.2. ECONOMICS AND THE "GRAIN WAR"

The clash between moderate laissez-faire economics and the radical egalitarianism of the *philosophes anti-économistes* first became manifest with the pamphlet controversy over the "grain wars" in response to famine conditions during 1766–9.[36] The split became public five years after the crown—humiliated by its recent defeats in India, Canada, and the Caribbean by Britain, and weighed down by debts—first adopted physiocratic doctrines on a temporary, trial basis, in July 1764, decreeing free trade in grain, as advocated by the *physiocrates*, within France, and for export.[37] Unrestricted liberty to import and export grain, held Quesnay, was the sole efficient means to ensure stability and evenness of grain and bread prices, and the economic strategy best suited to keeping grain and bread prices adjusted to the incomes of the poor.[38] It was at that critical juncture too that Turgot's *Reflexions* appeared and when free trade theory was first powerfully challenged by texts decrying Quesnay's principle, notably

[32] Spector, *Montesquieu et l'émergence*, 458; Albertone, "Democratic Republicanism," 120–1.

[33] Rothschild, *Economic Sentiments*, 68–9.

[34] Rothschild, *Economic Sentiments*, .69–70.

[35] See Edelstein, *On the Spirit of Rights*, 78–85.

[36] Quesnay, *Examen de l'examen*, 75–6.

[37] Hochstrasser, "Physiocracy," 426–7; Gauthier, "Political Economy," 50–1.

[38] Quesnay, *Examen de l'examen*, 77–8.

the Abbé Galiani's *Dialogues sur le commerce des blés* (1769), composed with the hidden assistance of Diderot.

Comparing the economic circumstances of different countries and regions, Galiani, an admirer of Montesquieu, highlighted the problematic character of applying rigidly an abstract economic model without considering the specific circumstances rendering one country, or region, different from another. Britain, for instance, had a more complex, mixed economy than France or any other major country—part commercial, part manufacturing, part agricultural—as well as a more complex constitution, so that to start by examining Britain's economy is misleading.[39] To grasp the basic laws of economics accurately one must start by studying simpler instances. His text was especially effective in showing the discrepancy between Quesnay's and Turgot's generalized model postulating a notional equality of individuals offering and buying commodities in the market, and the actual reality of a powerfully entrenched social hierarchy buttressed by massive inequality in law and land ownership, cornering vast supplies of grain for sale. Large-scale producers had every incentive to manipulate, extort, engineer shortages, and force up prices, accentuating price oscillations, by withholding supplies, or delivering abroad. He showed how and why, in existing circumstances, regular government purchases of grain designed to regulate the market do benefit society by stabilizing bread prices and better ensure social stability among artisans and the poor.[40] The public were being misled, mystified, and cheated, in other words, by a system of economic theory proclaiming a "liberté entière et absolue" in grain applied wholly out of context. The physiocrats were unwittingly colluding in generating higher prices, shortages, poverty, and disturbance by applying an imperfect model derived from inadequate theorizing.[41]

Ferdinando Galiani (1728–87), a disciple of Genovesi and secretary of the Neapolitan embassy in Paris since 1759, frequented the *coterie d'Holbachique* but drew his ideas and general approach to social and legal issues from Montesquieu rather than the radicals; Turgot he considered honest but too abstract and philosophical to succeed in the real world.[42] A witty raconteur, popular in fashionable salons, according to Marmontel he possessed the scheming acumen of a Machiavelli. Diderot greatly respected both his vast erudition and mature reflection on the practical significance of what he read.[43] With the onset of the "grain wars," Galiani convinced Diderot and d'Holbach of the dangers and drawbacks of upholding free market economics in the real social and legal context of contemporary life, and the highly negative impact on bread prices, subsistence, and fairness. Directly witnessing acute distress due to high bread prices himself when visiting the Langres area in 1770, Diderot felt Galiani's rebuttal of physiocratic theory to be entirely vindicated.

[39] Galiani, *Dialogues*, 63–5.

[40] Galiani, *Dialogues*, 44–5; Faccarello "Nil Repente!," 529–30; Hill and Montag, *Other Adam Smith*, 274–5.

[41] Galiani, *Dialogues*, 219–20, 223–5, 235, 252; Hochstrasser, "Physiocracy," 427; Duflo, *Diderot philosophe*, 158; Vardi, *Physiocrats*, 145; Gauthier, "Political Economy," 62.

[42] Clark, *Compass*, 181–5; Faccarello "Nil Repente!," 545.

[43] Trousson, *Denis Diderot*, 325.

Quesnay's, Gournay's, and Dupont's free market doctrines were not inherently wrong, viewed from a purely economic theoretical perspective—the ensuing shortages, Galiani observed, little affected Holland, a basically commercial and industrial society; but Diderot, d'Holbach, and Helvétius came to reject physiocratic doctrines as dogmatically imposed abstraction, associating these with pernicious social consequences with regard to grain and bread prices.[44] It was morally wrong to risk the severe harm to the poorest and most vulnerable apt to materialize from permitting unrestricted dealing in grain, from giving a free rein to the profit motive in a commodity so essential to human subsistence.[45] Diderot and his circle herewith clashed openly with Turgot and the physiocrats.

In official circles, where physiocratic doctrines had made deep inroads, there was a predictably indignant response to Galiani's intervention causing him to withdraw from the scene and return to Italy. His Italian friend was being unjustly vilified, Diderot felt, by powerful adversaries among the Choiseul faction at court, Morellet among them, motivated by political and self-interested considerations rather than France's and its people's best interest. The public controversy affecting the vital interests of the whole nation was exactly of the kind that should be subject to unrestricted, freely expressed opinion.[46] Free market exchange was a valid principle up to a point. Often it was right to remove internal barriers and restrictions; but government and municipalities must maintain reserve powers and controls enabling them to intervene in the market when necessary to fight profiteering, speculation, hoarding, regional withholding, and other "friponneries." The *économistes* had forgotten about the social effects of unrestrained avidity and greed. No one has the right to exploit price rises in grain leaving his fellow man succumbing to famine and starvation.[47] Completing his hard-hitting pamphlet the *Apologie de l'Abbé Galiani* in January 1771, Diderot, grown cautious since his early spell in Vincennes prison, then had second thoughts about publishing it, and in the end withheld it.

As controller-general, Turgot again imposed the physiocrat remedy and deregulated the grain trade, in September 1774, which again had the unintended effect of pushing up grain prices, by the spring of 1775, to more than twice the previous year's level, causing serious discontent throughout France and bitter renewal of the pamphlet "flour war" [*guerre de farines*], the public controversy over what should be the correct policy. During April and May 1775, food riots, caused more, Condorcet believed, by the people being stirred up, deceived, and misled than by distress or hunger, erupted across much of northern France, including Versailles and Paris where flour markets and bread shops were pillaged by mobs.[48] None of this seemed to confirm the physiocratic view that "God had established a natural order that should

[44] Diderot, *Apologie de l'Abbé Galiani*, 89, 92–3; Hope Mason, *Irresistible Diderot*, 324–5.

[45] Quintili, *Pensée critique*, 480–4.

[46] Duflo, *Diderot philosophe*, 475.

[47] Hope Mason and Wokler, "Introduction," pp. xxv–xxvi; Hope Mason, *Irresistible Diderot*, 325–6; Quintili, *Pensée critique*, 482–3; Rothschild, *Economic Sentiments*, 20; Hill and Montag, *Other Adam Smith*, 276–8.

[48] Condorcet, *Réflexions sur le commerce*, 101–3, 152; Gauthier, "Political Economy," 54–6.

serve as a rule for society," as Dupont expressed his and Turgot's common creed,[49] but it also failed to dent physiocratic confidence. Condorcet recommended an intensified campaign to change public opinion and convince the people that it was full liberty of commerce in grain, and everything else, that is in the general interest.[50] In early 1776, Turgot further issued, as one of his so-called "Six Edicts," a broad decree suppressing France's craft guilds, though this also met with widespread resistance. In January 1776, Turgot further abolished the forced labour *corvées*, raised in the countryside to assist construction of roads and bridges, a measure his young ally Condorcet, and helper in defending his stance on free trade, had been vigorously pressing for.[51] Soon after his sudden dismissal, in May 1776, his decrees lapsed and the guilds were re-established albeit in a modified, less rigid form.

If Turgot scorned medieval forms of economic organization and craft regulation, together with forced labor, he also despised medieval prejudices against usury or notions that interest rates should be regulated by government: "the rate of interest ought to be fixed, as the price of every other merchandize, by the course of trade alone."[52] In Turgot's eyes, the "law no more ought to fix the interest of money than it ought to regulate the price of any other merchandizes which have a currency in trade."[53] For him, it is individual effort and enterprise that promotes society's wealth and "abundance of capitals that animates enterprise" so that a "low interest of money is at the same time the effect and the proof of the abundance of capitals," a key feature of his economics.[54] Society as a whole, he held, benefits from this abundance. It is precisely, he maintained, when circumstances oblige capitalists investing in enterprises to "reduce their undertakings" that the disadvantaged suffer most. It is in shrinking enterprise, leaving the "total of the labour" and total consumption, production, and revenue all "diminished, that poverty will succeed to riches, and that the common workman, ceasing to find employ, lapses into the deepest misery."[55]

Like Quesnay, Dupont, and Smith, Turgot had relatively little to say about alleviating poverty or improving the living standards of peasantry and artisans by direct means, via instruments of government; and when he does discuss interventionist methods of alleviating deprivation he tends to be disapproving. Among his most interesting *Encyclopédie* contributions is his article "Fondation," in Volume VII, where he offers a devastating critique of efforts to alleviate social distress through endowed pious foundations. Enabling the most destitute to subsist without working, for free, in Christian charitable foundations, soup kitchens, and "hospitals," he dismissed as a sure way to foment more destitution by creating a culture of supported idleness. It was no accident that those countries where a culture of charitable

[49] Dupont de Nemours, *De l'origine et des progrès*, 82; Vardi, *Physiocrats*, 21–2, 109–10.

[50] Condorcet, *Réflexions sur le commerce*, 143, 150–1.

[51] Condorcet, *Réflexions sur le commerce*, 52, 55–6, 59; Baker, *Condorcet*, 60–3, 70–1; Sewell, *Work and Revolution*, 72–5; Horn, *Economic Development*, 224.

[52] Poirier, *Turgot*, 89; Clark, *Compass*, 237.

[53] Turgot, *Reflections*, 90.

[54] Turgot, *Reflections*, 106; Sonenscher, *Before the Deluge*, 285–7.

[55] Turgot, *Reflections*, 76; Sewell, *Work and Revolution*, 72–3.

institutions feeding and sheltering the poorest was most developed, like Spain and Italy, were precisely where begging, vagrancy, and conspicuous deprivation were most prevalent.[56] Genovesi had earlier likewise fiercely criticized charities and foundations of the sort that discourage the impulse to work, to earn one's bread, such as abounded at the time in Rome.[57] Pious foundations, moreover, were usually inspired by the self-importance and vanity of their founders, and quickly degenerate from their pristine virtuous standards into unsupervised, neglected establishments where the poorest are sustained by indifferent carers in a distressingly despotic and uncaring manner.

Turgot felt no desire to render men insensitive to the distress and suffering of the impoverished, he explained, or weaken well-meaning generosity and true charity, or substitute for these base and self-centered preoccupation only with oneself. But pious social aid foundations providing basic subsistence, seeking to deflect deprivation through charity or municipal or ecclesiastical oversight, had proven an utter failure. He was fiercely critical too of how charitable and religious foundations locked up capital and labor in fixed, static, long-term arrangements operating in outright contradiction to his own central economic doctrine (which was remarkably similar to Smith's), namely that "le bien général doit être le résultat des efforts de chaque particulier pour son propre intérêt" [the general good ought to be the result of each individual's efforts in his own interest].[58] Every healthy person should provide for himself or herself through their own activity, since every individual fed without having to work effectively lives at the expense of others. What the state owes all its members is removal of such hindrances as impede their efforts, or obstruct communication of useful knowledge between them, hindering enjoyment of the fruits and products that are work's reward.[59]

Late eighteenth-century and early nineteenth-century Western preoccupation with the problems of poverty and deprivation as central concerns of society, consequently, emerged more as a general moral and philosophical issue (which indeed in many ways it remains)—and especially Radical Enlightenment moral philosophy and politics—than as a question of economic theory. The democratic republican impulse also first developed partly in opposition to prevailing economic theory, even though economics inevitably remained of the greatest relevance to whatever solutions were proposed. In Europe, during the 1780s, shortly before the French Revolution, Jefferson was much struck by the much greater prevalence of poverty and destitution evident in France and northern Italy than one witnessed (among whites) in America. This strikingly greater prevalence of European poverty he ascribed to entails, primogeniture, and legal forms encouraging concentration of land and wealth in the hands of a few, and royal policies designed to buttress aristocracy and milk the peasantry for purposes diverging from the interest of society as a whole, alongside outdated

56 Turgot, art: "Fondation," in Diderot and d'Alembert (eds.), *Encyclopédie* vii. 73.
57 Genovesi, *Lezioni di comercio* i. 176–7, 180–2.
58 Turgot, art: "Fondation," 74; Clark, *Compass*, 238–9.
59 Clark, *Compass*, 235, 237–8; Manuel, *Prophets*, 23–4.

mercantilist policies designed to expand trade and industry, the cities, rather than agriculture. Jefferson's Enlightenment became closely linked to a passionate agrarianism, a way of viewing economics much influenced by the physiocrats while wholly severed from monarchy and big estates. "I am conscious that an equal division of property is impracticable", he assured Madison in October 1785, "but the consequences of this enormous inequality [in France and Italy] produce so much misery to the bulk of mankind, legislators cannot invent too many devices for subdividing property."[60]

Championing French rather than English perspectives, Jefferson was among those who did most to extend, to the United States, the physiocratic approach of Quesnay and Dupont de Nemours, whom he got to know well after the latter emigrated there with his family in 1799.[61] However, like Condorcet and Paine, Jefferson always blended physiocracy with anti-monarchism, anti-aristocratism, and a radical stance regarding poverty and property, seeking to mitigate social distress through more egalitarian inheritance laws, progressive taxation, reducing burdens on small proprietors, insurance schemes, and the like.[62] Meanwhile, among the foremost French radical *philosophes* following Rousseau in his *Discours sur l'origine et les fondemens de l'inégalité parmi les hommes* (Amsterdam, 1755) [Discourse on the Origin and Foundations of Inequality among Men] in placing inequality of wealth near the top of the philosophical and reforming agenda was Helvétius in his *De l'Esprit* (1758). Beyond a certain level of luxury (which in itself he regarded as morally neutral), argued Helvetius, possessions cannot significantly increase any individual's or family's "happiness," whereas too extreme an inequality of wealth, or "trop grande inégalité de richesses entre les citoyens" [too great inequality of wealth among citizens], does ensure misery, or greatly diminished happiness, for the greater number.[63]

In economic and social theory, Helvétius figured centrally also by introducing the vital distinction, largely arising from his utilitarian moral system, between a nation's or kingdom's overall aggregate wealth and those economic features philosophers would deem relevant to rendering a society "happy," or "réellement respectable à ses voisins" [truly respectable to its neighbors]. This was also of political relevance, as the number, vigor, and well-being of a country's citizens directly affects their attachment to it, their "courage et leur vertu."[64] Helvétius' quasi-physiocratic theory sought to account for how and why those countries most flourishing in commerce and finance are especially vulnerable to rapid deterioration. His theory was illustrated, he believed, by the startling but instructive case of eighteenth-century Holland, where general affluence and wages remained higher than elsewhere in Europe, but the economy, since around 1720, had lost its dynamism to England. He and many others wrongly conjectured that eighteenth-century British prosperity, likewise chiefly based

[60] Jefferson to Madison, Fontainebleau, 28 Oct. 1785, in Jefferson, *The Papers* viii. 682; Albertone, "Thomas Jefferson and French Economic Thought," 127–8.

[61] Albertone, "Thomas Jefferson and French Economic Thought," 129–31.

[62] Bosc, *Terreur des Droits de l'Homme*, 247–8.

[63] Helvétius, *De l'Esprit*, 34–5; Soenscher, *Before the Deluge*, 278–9.

[64] Helvétius, *De l'Esprit*, 36.

on maritime trade, colonies, and finance, would soon recede along similar lines to the Dutch. A great commerce and finance, his economic theory, like Quesnay's, contended, will draw population and wealth to the chief cities, impoverish the countryside, favor arbitrary power, step up the scale of subsidies to foreign powers, and heighten capacity to incur war-related and other foreign debts while reducing constructive energy and activity overall. Like Quesnay, Helvétius viewed France's economy as unhealthily pushing toward the sway of finance, excessive taxes, depopulation of the countryside (as many then believed), and general deterioration in the health and robustness of the population, collective health being vitiated partly by indolent luxury, partly by deprivation. To this, Helvétius' added admonitions about war and expansionist and dynastic policies geared to monarchical glory. What use are maritime and colonial wars, such as those undertaken, especially by Britain, purportedly for the sake of commerce, to the humble farmer or farm laborer?

The anti-royal, anti-aristocratic, anti-ecclesiastical thrust of radical thought decidedly predisposed Diderot, Helvétius, and their following to abhor all concentration of wealth in the hands of vested interests in a way mainstream enlighteners did not. But in their suspicion of court-based finance their critique followed closely along the physiocratic lines. Most wealth accruing from commerce, held d'Holbach, is distributed among a small number of individuals "and does no good to the rest."[65] Resistant as they were to economic doctrines alleging the accruing of benefit to all via the expansion and circulation of wealth in society, Helvétius, Diderot, Raynal, and d'Holbach were struck also by the frequent incidence of appallingly harmful wars supposedly (or actually) fought to expand national commerce, industry, and colonial empires. As the ordinary revenues of the state rarely suffice to pay for such undertakings, royal government resorted to higher taxes and loans when amassing fleets and armies, and fighting rival crowns, enabling merchants, financiers, and affluent office-holders to lend to government lucratively, while creating deficits and debts on which the honest laborer then had to help pay the interest with no benefit whatever accruing to him or his dependants. Mercantilist wars for trade and colonies costing thousands of lives and vast sums merely end up imposing additional burdens on the laboring classes while enriching "without work, some merchants, some financiers," together with a handful of other specialists in such a system, like gun-manufacturers and those fitting out privateering vessels to scour the seas. International financiers possess few ties to any particular state, including the society that has enriched them and without hindrance "can leave after enriching themselves on what is produced by the laboring citizen."[66]

Institutionalizing "national debt," and long-term financing of such debt, as in the Dutch Republic and Britain, was much admired and envied by court officials and statesmen for its proven ability to enhance capacity to sustain armies, fleets, and war, but should be reckoned, held d'Holbach, among the most deplorable impoverishing mechanisms of modern times.[67] The economic consequences of this huge financial

[65] D'Holbach, *Système social*, 478–9.
[66] D'Holbach, *Système social*, 479.
[67] D'Holbach, *Système social*, 479–84.

innovation enabling nations to maintain larger armed forces, and fight more wars, than would be possible with a state's ordinary revenues, were to expand the role of finance and burden the laboring population with additional taxes even in peacetime, obliging them to pay interest on war loans, and the costs of standing armies and navies, permanently instead of intermittently. Given that the distribution of the tax-burden was highly inequitable in the first place, inflating it inevitably further unbalanced it in favor of the wealthy to the detriment of the weakest. The "national debt" in the end renders society still more unequal than it was before and, in response, provokes yet more tax evasion, smuggling, deception, and oppression. "Rien n'est plus destructeur pour les moeurs d'un peuple" [nothing is more destructive of a people's morality], held d'Holbach, whose social and philosophy was based on the idea that the state's purpose is to extend to the greatest number of citizens possible the advantages for which the state was formed, "que l'esprit de la *finance*" [than the spirit of finance].[68] Here he barely diverged from the physiocratic view.

Distinguishing between the aggregate size and strength of a country's commerce, finance, agriculture, and industry, on the one hand, and the well-being and prosperity of a country's citizenry on the other, commencing with Helvétius, offered a starting-point for a fundamentally divergent approach to that of classical economics. Poorer countries exhibiting greater equality than France or Britain, as Switzerland and the United States (then were), appeared to be societies where the small tenant farmer was more prosperous, healthier, and happier, relying on a simpler but more abundant and healthier diet than in France or Britain, where immense wealth was concentrated in the hands of relatively few, who, moreover, mostly resided in the principal towns.[69] In Helvétius' mind, like that of Rousseau, d'Holbach, Diderot, and Jefferson, it was a fundamental maxim of political science that where there exists greater equality of possessions, not only are men happier but political freedom is more secure and tyranny and slavery better resisted; contrariwise, where opulence reigns unimpeded and excessive inequality increases, oppression and despotism possess a free hand. Determinists rejecting freedom of the will as upheld by Locke, Condillac, Quesnay, and Turgot, such as Helvétius, Diderot, d'Holbach, Condorcet, and Volney, and later Say, Sismondi, and Bentham and the British philosophical radicals, claimed pursuit of the individual's own happiness and especially the pleasure-principle, the desire for pleasure, motivates all men's conduct: "si tous les hommes tendent continuellement vers leur bonheur réel ou apparent," held Helvétius, "toutes nos volontés ne sont donc que l'effet de cette tendance" [since all men continually strive for their real or supposed happiness, all our desires are nothing but the effect of this drive]. Since all human thoughts and actions are determined, whether individuals choose what is best for them or not, whether they possess the relevant knowledge or receive the advice leading to good decisions or not, desire for individual fulfillment and happiness determines each to choose the course "which seems the most conducive to his

[68] D'Holbach, *Système social*, 481–3; Di Domenico, *Natura, Uomo, Dio*, 88.
[69] Helvétius, *De l'Esprit*, 37–8.

interests, tastes, and passions to him, in short to what he considers his happiness."[70] For Helvétius and d'Holbach, clashing directly with Turgot and Smith, this meant that only the collective will of society, not the individual will left to his own devices, can produce a balanced, rational outcome.

The democratizing tendency in social and political thought was thus to a considerable degree a reaction to the actual economic practices of the age. Paine discovered the chronic effects of unrestricted market manipulation on the majority, from the chronic distress briefly prevailing in Philadelphia after the British evacuated the city, in June 1778. Philadelphia's storekeepers, anticipating a pending British retaliatory sweep through Virginia and the American South, raised prices of supplies across the board even before coastal routes to the South were disrupted. During 1778–9, contemporary letters, news-sheets, and pamphlets, echoing the earlier crisis in France, bitterly decried the profiteering of "combinations" of "monopolizers"—cliques of local merchants conspiring to drive up prices by exploiting flour and bread shortages, exacting a heavy toll on Philadelphia's artisans and poor. Paine later recalled his shock at having had to pay vastly inflated prices for goods. A favourite method of "monopolizing," known as "forestalling," was withholding newly arrived flour and other necessities, for weeks, on ships anchored in Philadelphia's harbor or nearby warehouses. Among leading "forestallers" notorious for short-changing fellow Patriots was Robert Morris (1734–1806), "our celebrated financier" as Rush called him, in 1784, who as "Superintendent of Finance" became a powerful figure in the fledgling United States government and stalwart of the anti-democratic faction aiming to quash the unicameral 1776 democratic Pennsylvania constitution.[71] Popular pressure for price controls and regulation, expressed in rowdy informal gatherings and town meetings, powerfully surged up.[72]

In grounding a social theory, from 1769, wider than and in part antagonistic to the free market economics of Turgot, Dupont, and Adam Smith, Diderot joined with Helvétius and d'Holbach—while Condorcet, who likewise published a controversial pamphlet on the grain trade, firmly aligned with Turgot's doctrine of wholly free domestic commerce, including grain, which in its hostility to political interference and regulation at times sounded even more vehement than Adam Smith.[73] For Condorcet, as Turgot, prices and supply regulated by interconnected markets have a natural balance best left to itself. A minimum of political regulation maximizes the freedom of sellers and buyers alike and this boosts competition all round. It is hence unrestricted, free competition that most favors the consumer. Absence of state regulation ensuring the fullest freedom of consumer and entrepreneur alike is what ultimately advances society's best interest.[74] Condorcet's particular contribution to

[70] Helvétius, *De l'Esprit*, 47.

[71] Rush, *Letters* i. 337; Smith, *Freedoms we Lost*, 178–9.

[72] Foner, *Tom Paine*, 145–6, 150–2, 161–2; Keane, *Tom Paine*, 192.

[73] Kates, *Cercle social*, 214; Rothschild, *Economic Sentiments*, 60, 158.

[74] Baker, *Condorcet*, 57–8, 60–1; Rothschild, *Economic Sentiments*, 160–1.

the new "science of man," including economics, was to give a further boost to its mathematization, to the use of statistics, averages, proportions, and percentages.[75]

Inequality, held Diderot and Helvétius, undermines the political order and, by stimulating crime and misanthropy, the moral order as well. The man possessing nothing, averred d'Holbach, "ne tient par aucun lien à la société" [is not bound to society by any tie].[76] How can one expect wretched, destitute workmen who have imbibed neither principles nor morality to remain tranquil spectators of opulence and exactions unjustly extorted by self-seeking, corrupt individuals controlling the grain trade with the assent of the royal court, to all appearance insulting the wretchedness of the many while only rarely helping ease their wretchedness? With what right does society administer the death penalty to a domestic who steals a trifling sum after witnessing his master engaging in the most outrageous speculation and exploitation, rapacious practices in the free grain and flour market amounting to the mass pillage of the public? How can the poor acknowledge the law's legitimacy when they see its provisions used to serve the rapacity of the rich and fleecing of the destitute? In such conditions, even the death penalty loses all efficacy as one only dies once and an impoverished laborer might well think it worth risking execution to evade endless backbreaking toil for a life of destitution.[77]

Where Condorcet fully converged with all other radical thinkers, though, was in asserting the ultimate unity and oneness of the general interest, the *volonté générale*. This was the logic underpinning his and their claim that the inevitable differentiation of occupations generated by economic life does not necessarily result in class conflict, as some supposed, in "des intérêts réellement opposés." If it did, all of society would continuously be "agitated by a silent war between antagonistic classes" which, to Condorcet's mind, is not actually the case. Society's different economic classes are not inherently each other's enemies albeit he granted that they do not realize this. If the notion of class war is "imaginary," if all classes have but one identical general interest, it followed, to him, that it suffices to prove this truth to the public to defeat the menace posed by the contrary view, the objections it offers to "la prospérité générale," threatening liberty and public stability.[78] The common interest—and this was its tragedy—is, however, neither obvious nor, as Quesnay had stressed, automatic: it needs to be demonstrated by experts, and consolidated, made clearly manifest as the basis of society, through education on the basis of universal "rights" and equality instead of privilege, manipulation, and despotism.[79]

Like the *Idéologues* and Jefferson later, d'Holbach declared many times that a sweeping, rigid, dogmatic equality, something he associated with Rousseau, is both unattainable and undesirable.[80] Men are unequal in talents and diligence by decree of nature so that the rewards accruing must and should remain unequal. But this is no

[75] Gusdorf, *Conscience révolutionnaire*, 406, 410, 416, 418–21.
[76] D'Holbach, *Système social*, 441; d'Holbach, *Morale universelle* ii. 181–2.
[77] D'Holbach, *Système social*, 440–3.
[78] Quoted in Bosc, "Liberté et propriété," 67.
[79] Bosc, "Liberté et propriété," 68, 72.
[80] Muceni, "Mandeville," 101.

justification for contending, like the physiocrats, Smith, and classical economics, that therefore the play of the market should decide how much wealth each person possesses, that commerce and finance should enjoy a free hand sanctioned by an entrenched laissez-faire attitude by the state, making the market the ultimate arbiter. Rather, d'Holbach reckoned it among society's chief priorities to impose curbs on commerce and finance, to prevent desire for riches acquiring a free rein, while also refraining from unjust, inequitable methods of coercion. It was government's responsibility to prevent what was actually the prevailing circumstance under the *ancien régime*—that over three-quarters of the population, almost everywhere, as he puts it, possess nothing while virtually all of a country's property and wealth reposes in the hands of a restricted elite subtly contriving to secure royal support and encouragement.[81]

12.3. ECONOMICS AND THE ISSUE OF POVERTY

When all society's citizens, through a reasonable assignment of work, secure a tolerable degree of ease, the state can justly call on all for their support; where, by contrast, a tiny proportion are encouraged to engross practically everything, an informal economic oligarchy becomes effectively master of the state which is then all but incapable of seizing back, out of their hands, the wealth they have contrived to corner for themselves. "L'humanité, l'équité, l'intérêt général de la société" [humanity, equity, and the general interest of society], as d'Holbach characteristically expressed it, in 1776, during the opening phase of the American Revolution, unite to cry out to sovereigns to stop multiplying and oppressing the poor, to show pity for the common people whose lives and happiness they cruelly disrupt, and whom they reduce to despair. Poverty, say some, complacently, is the mother of industry; but poverty, warned d'Holbach, when honest labor is discouraged, or rewarded only with mounting taxes to pay for armies, navies, and war, is also the mother of violence and crime. Free market economics, economic liberalism, what d'Holbach calls "commerce illimité" [unregulated commerce], Turgot's and Smith's creed, menaces the security and well-being of all society's members.[82]

That even skilled workers often earned wages too low to cover basic expenses, and dwelt in poverty, needing sustenance for their families from church charities, seemed distinctly shocking. With the commercial spirit, a free market stance the chief criterion of what is good and bad for society, harmful and destructive activities come to be justified in terms of national interest and the quest for profit. Unrestrained commerce generates rivalries, jealousies, and almost continual clashes. It was commerce, the commercial spirit, held d'Holbach, that drove the almost insane thirst for

[81] D'Holbach, *Politique naturelle*, 352–3; d'Holbach, *Morale universelle* ii. 242–5.
[82] D'Holbach, *Morale universelle*, ii. 182.

colonial expansion causing his century's leading powers to unleash terrible wars sometimes over mere stretches of desert, wasteland, or remote isles, expansion rooted in avidity detecting the promise of future wealth.[83] Entire societies, and their governments, were dupes of avaricious merchants, financiers, and ship-owners seeking to exploit colonies more ruthlessly, as with the mercantilist regime Britain had foisted on America and Ireland. Nations went to war, expending their treasure and blood, impoverishing the majority by heaping up taxes and sacrificing thousands, for the sake of riches accruing to a tiny number who alone enjoyed the superadded wealth continually drained from society by the proud folly of their co-citizens.[84]

Economic arguments advanced by radicals before 1789 formed the seedbed of the challenging new school of economic analysis developed after 1800 by revisionist economists like Jean-Baptiste Say and, after him, Sismondi, drawing on the legacy of the radical *philosophes* and Brissotin revolutionary tradition with its hostility to "mixed government" and the British model.[85] Radicals questioning the logic, and resisting the final conclusions, of classical economics as summed up, systematized, and completed by Adam Smith and subsequently David Ricardo (1772–1823) urged government intervention to mitigate untrammeled enterprise's detrimental effects on the less fortunate. Sismondi's *Nouveaux principes d'économie politique* (1819), where he criticizes the physiocrats, Smith, and Ricardo, can be seen as the culmination of this pre-socialist (and in some respects anti-socialist) tradition of revolt against laissez-faire economics, of radical economic interventionism designed to reverse the negative effects of economic and technological development on society.

Say and his fellow Protestant, the Genevan Jean-Charles Simonde de Sismondi (1773–1842), offered an economic analysis countering classical economics by demonstrating that continuing exploitation of the socially downtrodden was an unfortunate, unacceptable, and intrinsic component of the prevailing early nineteenth-century system of European, British, and American economic life and regulation. In his major work of revision, the *Nouveaux Principes d'économie politique* (1819), Sismondi sees his own approach as part of a fourth stage in economic theory's development, after mercantilism, French physiocracy, and Smithsonian classical economics. Smith was by far the pre-eminent author of the "third system of political economy," and Say and Sismondi both accepted the validity of much of his analysis based on the idea that work forms the basis of wealth, as far as the process of wealth creation itself is concerned.[86] What Say and Sismondi rejected in Smith's and Ricardo's economics was their conceiving wealth production "abstraitement" instead of in "relation to men and society," leading them to construct an edifice that was by no means necessarily conducive—in fact often unconducive—to promoting human happiness individual and collective. They refused to accept classical economics' preoccupation only with growth of national wealth overall without considering how this affects most people's

[83] D'Holbach, *Politique naturelle*, 354–5; Blank, "D'Holbach on Self-Esteem," 450, 452.
[84] D'Holbach, *Politique naturelle*, 355.
[85] Albertone, "Democratic Republicanism," 118.
[86] Sismondi, *Nouveaux Principes* i. 49–50, 53.

lives. Smith is solely concerned, objects Sismondi, with wealth creation and "seeing that all those that have an interest in increasing it" are encouraged to do so, assuming general improvement cannot be better promoted than by abandoning society to the free exercise of "les intérêts individuels" [individual interests]. Since the rich strive to become richer still, government, according to classical economics, should let them do so, adopting a policy of laissez-faire: the rich will enrich the nation by enriching themselves. For classical economics as represented by Smith, the sum of private wealth forms the wealth of the nation.[87]

Economic theory, as grounded by Rousseau's materialist critics, while criticizing Smith's approach in key respects, and much preoccupied with the social consequences of industrialization and economic growth, nevertheless remained heavily indebted to Adam Smith and his legacy. After 1789, the radical tendency certainly strove to fuse their republicanism, egalitarianism, universal and equal rights, and assault on nobility, primogeniture, serfdom, and slavery, with elements of classical economics. Rousseau's critics from the Left culminating in Say and Sismondi sought to rebalance wealth distribution but at the same time safeguard the consumer's and entrepreneur's economic freedom. Theirs was an innovation of considerable importance against which Marx and Engels later powerfully intervened. While acknowledging that their post-Ricardo approach to economic and social analysis "dissected with great acuteness the contradictions in the conditions of modern production," Marx dismissed the radical approach as a bogus "petty-bourgeois socialism" both "reactionary" and "Utopian" in seeking to rebalance but also conserve existing property relations and modes of production.

"Sismondi was the head of this school," declared the *Communist Manifesto* in 1848, "not only in France but also England."[88] But when Marx first plunged into economic theory, in 1844, as his theory of capitalism's inherent contradictions evolved, it was the ex-Protestant agnostic, Jean-Baptiste Say (1767–1832), an economist chiefly known as a commentator on Smith and public critic and adversary of the most renowned classical economist of the subsequent generation, David Ricardo (1772–1823) whom he was especially preoccupied with, Say being the first and principal advocate of the thesis that "production," as Marx put it, "is limited only by production itself."[89] Although Marx later dismissed Say as "insipid" and even "pitoyable" for contending that there can be no such thing as "overproduction" [*surproduction*], in the mid-1840s Say was an important internal dialogue partner for Marx, since his theory of production and claim of no inherent fatal weakness in capitalism directly contradicted Marx's own incipient theory that capitalist competition, bankruptcies, and periodic recessions and commercial crises are more indicative than anything else of self-negating inner contradiction. If modern economic analysts view the agricultural crisis of 1813–16 in England, followed by two commercial-industrial recessions of 1815–17 and 1819–20, as not constituting a real

[87] Sismondi, *Nouveaux Principes* i. 53–4; Jeandeau, *Sismondi précurseur*, 13–14.

[88] Marx and Engels, *Selected Works* i. 57; Stedman Jones, *Karl Marx*, 171–2.

[89] Tiran, "Karl Marx lecteur," 586, 596.

existential, internal crisis of the system in the way Marx did, but a series of distinct shocks, essentially "external" to the prevailing system, here they concur with Say. For a time, proving Say wrong became a key concern of the young Marx.[90]

Before Sismondi's 1819 *Nouveaux principes* the radical tendency in economics had evolved more tentatively, in the work of Say. Likewise imbued with a Genevan republican tradition, Say joined the editorial staff of Mirabeau's *Courrier de Provence* at the start of the Revolution, and the many French intellectuals already openly republican prior to 1789. During 1792–3 he was closely associated with Brissotin circles,[91] in 1794 becoming a founder and soon managing editor of the key journal *La Décade philosophique, littéraire et politique par une Société républicaine.* After Thermidor, this publication, expressly anti-Robespierriste, anti-Babeuviste, and against the *niveleurs* (levelers), remained firmly republican and universalist in preaching equal rights. It became the chief organ of *Idéologie,* the foremost strand of the post-1793 French late Enlightenment. *Idéologie* stressed the "scientific" character of the study of the human mind and behavior, the need to reorganize the study of society, including economic life and politics, as a corpus of interrelated sciences recognizing the interaction and ultimate unity of all branches of knowledge. *Idéologie*, unrelenting in rejecting religion, tradition, and popular notions as guides, sought to redefine pursuit of human happiness as a collective project based on cultivating the social sciences, collective happiness being indissolubly tied to a wide range of specific conditions, not least enjoyment of a well-distributed prosperity and ownership of property.[92]

Say and his wife were also active members from 1797 of the second Society of the "Amis des Noirs," the first, founded in 1788, having lapsed with the outlawing and suppression of the Brissotin faction by the Montagne in the National Convention, in June 1793. Its successor, in which Sonthonax, the former Brissotin commissioner on Haiti who had proclaimed the abolition of slavery there in 1793–4, and the Abbé Grégoire were presiding figures, emerged at a time when the Haitian revolution was plunged in chaos, and counter-revolutionary elements in France were pressing the *Directoire* to reconsider the Revolution's abolition of slavery.[93] Say's and the society's purpose was to reinforce the abolitionist cause in France and its colonies, and reconstitute the economic base of the French Caribbean, the plantation economy as it had operated since 1794, without slavery. Say, who sporadically acted as the society's secretary, not only believed passionately that slavery was unjust and indefensible but also economically inefficient, a proposition he showed much zeal in demonstrating.

Say hugely admired Adam Smith, always regarded him as the prime founder of the modern science of economics, and up to a point liked to present himself as his disciple. But he also subjected his overall conclusions and legacy to extensive

90 Davis, "Historical Context," 138–40, 148–9; Tiran, "Karl Marx lecteur," 596–7.
91 Bosc, *Terreur des Droits de l'Homme*, 228–9.
92 Whatmore, "Democrats and Republicans," 45–6; Bosc, *Terreur des Droits de l'Homme*, 230–5.
93 Gainot, "Republican Imagination," 285.

criticism, accusing him of failing to see the wood for the trees, and especially failing to formulate and infer from the fundamental laws of economics with sufficient precision and clarity.[94] This was partly a question of inadequate formulation of economic laws as such, especially the nature of production. But, still more, as a radical enlightener, Say disliked Smith's "Invisible Hand," the idea that the market by itself spontaneously balances economic forces, generation of wealth, and the impact of economic life on society. While, as a rule, the marketplace proper can be left to its own devices, and individuals do efficiently discern their own interest there, they are far less able to do so, held Say, in the wider social and political context. Thus, most individuals definitely need help from an enlightened administration to grasp that progressive taxes on incomes which lessen wealth inequality are in everyone's interest, including the wealthy, because the result is a more stable, secure, and less crime-ridden social context. When society is left to the "spontaneous order" Smith and conservative economists favored, there tends to prevail a primitive, unrestrained egoism rather than enlightened self-interest taught by a *philosophique* outlook. A person's true interest, urged Say, often diverges from apparent immediate self-interest of the sort rooted in ordinary notions, that is ignorance.[95]

In general, individuals do not sufficiently understand their own interests, and still less those of society generally, argued Say, unless they receive an enlightened education. As an ardent enlightener, he identified "ignorance" as the greatest barrier to the market operating smoothly on its own.[96] He also thought, leaving aside attitudes, that certain aspects of the economy are intrinsically better organized by public legislation and authority than private enterprise: in particular enlightened government and legislation he considered conducive and sometimes essential to encouraging investment in complex industrial and technological research and discoveries so as to make these more broadly available to society.[97] While Say considered it the aim of good government to stimulate production, rather than, like modern Keynsians, boost consumption, he always resisted Smith's "Invisible Hand" and the later claim characterizing conservative economic thought that the market is best left to regulate itself, functioning on the basis of "spontaneous order."[98] Consequently, he gives a much larger role in generating economic improvement than any previous economic theorist to legislation, administrators, and education.[99]

The clash between Say and classical economics thus lay in the divergent social, moral, and political goals underlying their respective attempts to formulate the laws of economics. In seeking to define those laws with greater exactitude, Say's objective was to adjust classical economics to a framework of social policy undermining the status of privilege and royalty, eradicating slavery, and creating a post-revolutionary

94 Say, *Traité d'Économie politique* i, pp. lv–lvi, 31–2; Rothschild, *Economic Sentiments*, 237.
95 Sonescher, *Before the Deluge*, 336; Forget, "Jean-Baptiste Say," 201–2.
96 Say, *Traité d'Économie politique* i. 42; Forget, "Jean-Baptiste Say," 198, 200–1.
97 Say, *Traité d'Économie politique* i. 42, 50–1.
98 Skousen, "Say's Law, Growth Theory," 100, 105.
99 Forget, "Jean-Baptiste Say," 193–5.

economic context such that "in this great [French] republic there will not be [. . .] one miserable person who could complain of being unable to earn, by work and good conduct, a decent living, and lead a life which the English would call 'comfortable.'"[100] Say aimed to discredit both luxury and poverty, by simultaneously expanding overall prosperity while shifting everyone to the economic level of "modest comfort." By better balancing individual liberty and rights, on the one hand, with the social protection that social science and the state can provide, and doing so more effectively and in a more stable fashion than the Republic had hitherto, the Revolution could be saved and the "common good" placed on a secure basis.[101] His doctrine deplored the idle rich and large landowners more vigorously than had Smith, while lauding entrepreneurship and the productive class of manufacturers and idealizing the virtues and attitudes of the "middle class," a favorite term of Say's. Here Say was seconded by Destutt, who, though a nobleman himself, disparaged both nobility and the *capitaliste oisif*, the idle capitalist living off rent, or interest on his capital, without contributing to productive processes.[102]

Say, Daunou, Destutt, and also Pierre Jean Georges Cabanis (1757–1808), like d'Holbach and Condorcet earlier, and later also Sismondi, viewed economic inequality not as an unalterable fact of nature, as most observers still tended to do, but an unjustifiable, oppressive burden needing to be tackled and corrected. But just as slavery and serfdom can be removed only by far-reaching political action, so adjusting chronic wealth and educational inequality, reducing inequality of skills and knowledge, can be achieved only by the sustained vigorous action of a republican state genuinely and systematically committed to the "general interest." Poverty stems from overconcentration of wealth in too few hands, these authors felt, and the republic's task is to reverse this injustice by imposing new, better-conceived laws. Cabanis, like Say, was acutely conscious that in the most industrialized country, Britain, poverty was actually increasing; he pondered the efficacy of state-backed workshops, or *ateliers de travail*, as a device for reversing this process but then rejected it.[103] "The number of poor in each country," held Cabanis, "depends on the number of huge fortunes, especially those not the fruit of useful industry, for these fortunes are unrealizable without reducing a proportional quantity of individuals to indigence."[104] Convinced a comfortable existence for all is conceivable, and practicable, when pursued with appropriate state economic and fiscal strategies and public education reducing inequality of knowledge, even though absolute wealth equality is impossible and undesirable, these radical coteries did not maintain that there was anything wrong with succeeding in business or commerce as such. Their demand was that the Republic proceed to correct chronic imbalances in society without curtailing

[100] Whatmore, "Democrats and Republicans," 39, 46–7; Schoorl, *Jean-Baptiste Say*, 20–1.
[101] Kaiser, "Politics," 148; Bosc, *Terreur des Droits de l'Homme*, 249–50; Jennings, *Revolution*, 140–1.
[102] Destutt de Tracy, *Commentaire*, 84–5; Head, *Politics and Philosophy*, 268–71, 276.
[103] Cabanis, *Oeuvres complètes* ii. 199–203, 206–7, 237–8, 240–1.
[104] Cabanis, *Oeuvres complètes* ii. 218–20.

individual economic freedom, in fact emancipate it by impeding excessive and restricting inherited, illicit, and corrupt gain while removing obstacles to genuine enterprise.

Adulating Helvétius,[105] Cabanis distinguished between "petites inégalités de la nature," natural inequalities of wealth arising from different individuals possessing different abilities and skills, hence inequalities morally unobjectionable and "equitable," and *inégalités* "injustes" and "monstrueuses" forged by laws, entrenched by political means and privilege, and by social and religious institutions. Unfortunately, the latter generally prevail in modern society. Hitherto, all societies had been depraved by malign laws because everywhere "the strongest, most able and richest" have instituted government and promulgated laws to bolster their own interests over the general interest. Most societies are consequently organized, aided by religion and ultimately contrary to the interest of all, to favor the specific interests of the rich and powerful against the "general interest." But what the state foments, the state can undo by breaking up large estates and fortunes, eradicating privilege, facilitating trade and production, and taxing in a more designing and equitable fashion.[106] Turgot and Smith were profoundly wrong to think society naturally works toward "le bonheur social": this can only happen where the Republic intervenes to curb the strongest and the richest and support the weakest.[107] If all the dues and revenues the laboring classes of Germany pay to their princely courts and "rich abbeys," commented Destutt, remained in the hands of those producing that wealth for just four years, it would be a nation vastly transformed for the better.[108]

In Say's, Cabanis's, and Destutt's radicalism, economic elites oppress the masses as much through sustaining "ignorance," aided by religion and priests, as by economic means, so that combating "ignorance" and superstition, for them, formed a key strand of their strategy for reducing social inequality generally. A great advantage of this approach was that class antagonism could be eroded and minimized via the Enlightenment's progress.[109] For Say, Daunou, Cabanis, and Destutt, the veritable interest of the poor thus coincides with that of "reason" and the "general interest" which requires wide-ranging laws to protect the weak.[110] Sismondi was less explicit about the allegedly malign role of political elites and religion but agreed that physiocracy reinforces the sway of the landed elite and, prior to 1789, propelled the economic dimension of Enlightenment thought in a way that was severely unbalanced. Europeans and Americans often supposed France brilliantly "civilized" at a time when four-fifths of the population could not read, the provinces were plunged in "une ignorance profonde," and the mass of the nation was "exposed to constant privation, cruel worries about their ability to subsist, to everything that could curb the

[105] Cabanis, *Oeuvres complètes* iii. 66. [106] Cabanis, *Oeuvres complètes* ii. 222.
[107] Cabanis, *Oeuvres complètes* ii. 218–22. [108] Destutt de Tracy, *Commentaire*, 110.
[109] Head, *Politics and Philosophy*, 271–83; Jennings, *Revolution*, 52, 143.
[110] Cabanis, *Oeuvres complètes* ii. 220; Minart, *Pierre Daunou*, 107–8; Head, *Politics and Philosophy*, 284–7.

individual will, degrade morality and impoverish its character." Enlightenment, held Sismondi, is the key not just to liberty and good government but an improved society in a much wider sense, with leisure and economic improvement for most being integral to the general "happiness" true Enlightenment seeks.[111]

A core challenge at the start of the nineteenth century facing all economists, as Marx too later emphasized, was the troubling paradox, confirmed by all evidence, including tax returns, that while the annual percentage increase in wealth outstripped population increase, in the most developed economies, growing inequality, despite productivity and technological advances potentially enabling society to achieve the opposite result, nevertheless caused the proportion of poor to those comfortably off continually to increase. In Britain, the system of war financing developed by the British government proved spectacularly successful in expanding loans and increasing government borrowing and financial activity, while protecting property and capital formation, but achieved this by piling on non-progressive taxes and forcing down living standards for the majority; it was a system of wealth transfer causing concentration of wealth whereby society as a whole subsidized the further enrichment of the elites, and the unskilled working poor were the most severely squeezed.[112] Reversing this seemed to many not only morally but socially and politically essential. Tackling economic inequality, contended the *Idéologues*, continuing along the track originally sketched by Diderot and d'Holbach in the 1760s and 1770s, is not just in the interest of the poor, but essential to the whole community.

Everyone deserves a decent living was their rule. After two years in London employed in the financial sector (1785–7), as a young clerk in commercial houses trading with the Caribbean and India, Say spoke English fluently but he could never find an exact equivalent for the, to him, indispensable English term "comfortable." The idea, though, he shared fully with Destutt, Cabanis, and Sismondi. Marx, scathing about the economic theories of Say, Destutt, and Sismondi in *Das Kapital* and elsewhere, suggested that Destutt, who looked favorably on both trade and industrial production, was flatly contradicting himself, reasoning crassly and "brutally" when claiming "les nations pauvres, c'est là où le peuple est à son aise; et les nations riches, c'est là où il est ordinairement pauvre" [it is in poor nations that the people are comfortable, in rich nations where they are generally poor]. But this was precisely the paradox the physiocrats had brought to light and that the *Idéologues*, the "soldiers of the philosophique party" as Roederer called them, strove to address.[113] Inequality," held Destutt, "under whatever form it presents itself, is the great misfortune of men."[114] If educational inequality was society's worst blight, economic inequality too was a curse and a plague.

No more than d'Holbach and Condorcet were these late Enlightenment theorists opening a path to class-warfare: rather they embraced Condorcet's doctrine that

[111] Sismondi, *Nouveaux principes* i. 4–5, 7–9. [112] O'Brien, "Impact," 382–3.
[113] Marx, *Capital*, 648; Forget, "Jean-Baptiste Say," 202–4; Stedman Jones, *Karl Marx*, 175.
[114] Quoted in Imbert, *Destutt de Tracy critique*, 155; Head, *Politics and Philosophy*, 291–3.

ultimately "all the classes of society have only the same interest,"[115] or, as Destutt expressed it, that the "general interest" makes both the *classe inférieure* and the *classe opulente* tend towards the *classe mitoyenne*.[116] Destutt focused especially on the political implications: seeing society as having both a duty and interest in curbing excessive wealth accumulation among narrow groups. Society must edge toward equality not by violence but by judicial and legislative means, by abolishing feudal rights and dues, legislating against primogeniture, titles, and privilege, precluding unequal marriage and divorce settlements, eliminating venality of office, and encouraging equal distribution of inheritances among children.[117] For them, inequality, economic as well as educational, was society's greatest defect—and resolving it society's greatest responsibility: "every society should reduce it as much as possible;" this, for the *Idéologues*, was the "ultimate goal of representative government." Pursuing equality through representative government means society "strives to open to every individual, equally, all paths to fortune."[118]

Robespierre had been an individual despot; but, in Say's eyes, the menace of *Robespierrisme* is an eternal one, rooted in "ignorance," society's greatest ill, in a mistaken conception of human rights, sovereignty, and equality.[119] Equally hostile to Robespierre and to Napoleon's "illiberal institutions," having broken with him, in 1803, more fully than his fellow *Idéologues*, even before Bonaparte became emperor, Say still more reviled the new post-1814 French Bourbon monarchy, which he designated "a feeble and idiotic government." [120] Anti-Robespierre, anti-Napoleonist, and anti-Bourbon, a republican *Idéologue* throughout, Say labored to fuse egalitarian republicanism with a new society-benefiting economic agenda. But what political economy theory could explain the basic mechanisms of economics so as to facilitate achievement of this goal? Between September 1814 and January 1815, prior to Napoleon's return to Paris and the Hundred Days, Say again resided in England, commissioned by the newly enthroned restored Bourbon monarchy to analyze and assess the commercial, industrial, financial, and technological progress of Britain during the crucial twenty-year span since regular commercial and other contacts between France and its island neighbor had been interrupted by war. He discovered a country whose commerce and industry had, in a short time, made a greater impact on the world than even its triumphant armies and navies, than even its huge subsidies to allies and subordinate powers. Britain had undoubtedly grown increasingly opulent as well as powerful, and envied by its neighbors, during the long war; and yet, all those who worked with their hands, those who generated England's wealth, had been pushed down more and more, both Say and Sismondi stressed, into misery and distress.[121]

[115] ". . . que toutes les classes de la société n'ont qu'un même intérêt," see Bosc, "Liberté et propriété," 65.
[116] Destutt de Tracy, *Commentaire*, 84–5; Kaiser, "Politics," 156, 159.
[117] Destutt de Tracy, *Commentaire*, 91–3, 109. [118] Imbert, *Destutt de Tracy critique*, 149–56.
[119] Bosc, "Liberté et propriété," 76–7.
[120] Minart, *Pierre Daunou*, 153, 172–3; De Champs, *Enlightenment and Utility*, 166.
[121] Say, *De l'Angleterre*, 18; Sismondi, *Nouveaux principes* i. 5; Jones, *Agricultural Enlightenment*, 17.

Much impressed with the steam-engines, latest applications of coal, iron, and steel, and blast-furnaces he inspected, Say also visited a wide range of factories processing textiles, glass, casks, and other products. He toured Edinburgh and Glasgow as well as Newcastle, Liverpool, Manchester, and Birmingham, all cities growing, he noted, at a furious pace, Manchester from a population of 81,000 in 1801, to 98,000 in 1811, and Liverpool faster still from 77,000 to 94,000 between 1811 and 1814.[122] It was during 1814–15, too, that Say first encountered the two contemporary economists with whose economic theories he was to clash most, Ricardo whom he met again in Paris in 1817 and 1822, and Thomas Robert Malthus (1766–1834), author of the *Essay on the Principle of Population* (1798) with whom he also fought running battles over the next few years. The laws of subsistence and demography, held Malthus, a Cambridge-trained Anglican cleric, are a divinely-imposed curb, precluding permanently rising living standards and increased levels of "happiness." During his second English stay, Say came to admire Bentham and, henceforth, served as Bentham's chief correspondent in France.[123]

Though fascinated by the new technical processes themselves, Say's primary concern was with the principles and mechanisms of expansion in manufacturing, transport, shipping, and trade and the diverse ways demand, innovation, labour costs, competition, fashion, and taxation all impact on economic growth, and the effects of rapid overall economic growth on society. Noting that in the England of 1815, manufacturing and agriculture were heavily taxed while trade and transport were not,[124] he was struck by the prevalence of very high prices and costs in general, the high cost of living for most, but accompanied by astoundingly low prices, compared to France, for certain now mass-produced utensils and items of pottery and metal goods, mass consumption accompanied by a noticeable drop in the quality of products.[125] The conclusion he drew was that rapid economic growth was expanding Britain's national wealth overall, as Smith had insisted, but was nevertheless impoverishing and increasingly oppressing the majority of the British population. Higher living costs and taxes much heavier than anywhere else were the inevitable result of the efficient war-economy and system of war finance the British government had undertaken, a system compelling nearly everyone below the aristocratic elite to keep furiously busy, without pausing for a moment, just to survive. Britain's working class he considered to be in "grande détresse" [great distress], with a high proportion receiving some form of public charity. But the people were being deprived and impoverished through industrialization, and war-related taxation, as Say analyzed it, not just in an economic sense, but also in terms of culture and Enlightenment. Unlike France, England boasted practically no cafés full of idle talkers and readers. Under growing economic pressure, people enjoyed less and less leisure for books, talk, or thoughts. Owing to lack of time and the strikingly high cost of books, he observed,

122 Say, *De l'Angleterre*, 8.
123 Guillaumont, *Pensée démo-économique*, 97.
124 Schoorl, *Jean-Baptiste Say*, 77–8.
125 Say, *De l'Angleterre*, 24; O'Brien, "Impact," 371.

the English of 1815 read far less than they had earlier.[126] In short, Britain's economic transformation "exercises a deplorable effect on Enlightenment, and makes the *philosophique* observer fear the native land of Bacon, Newton and Locke will soon be making rapid retrograde steps toward barbarism."[127]

Say was always eager to place his economic observations strictly within a broad Enlightenment context of intellectual analysis and ideas, perusing journals and periodicals, and discussing his results with key experts and theorists, especially Ricardo and Bentham. Overall, his tour increased his longstanding admiration for British innovation, technology, and commercial prowess, while simultaneously toughening his critical stance toward England's public finance and monetary policy and heightening his alarm at the negative social effects of industrialization.[128] During the revolutionary and Napoleonic Wars (1792–1815), the British government had offset the gigantic cost of its foreign subsidies by ensuring they helped pay for great quantities of British produced and processed supplies and manufactures purchased by Russia, Prussia, Sweden, Spain, Portugal, Naples, and Austria in devalued and deflating pounds sterling, creating a subsidized foreign demand within a rigid wartime trading system generating rapid expansion of net surplus value inside Britain—little of which had seeped down, however, to the laboring classes actually producing the goods. The proceeds, apart from what accrued to manufacturers, financiers, big landowners, and exporters, were continually skimmed off through high taxes to fuel the system of subsidies, and pay for the army and navy as well as service the fast-burgeoning national debt. Paradoxically, the same system of foreign subsidies and national debt that Paine had attacked in his *The Decline and Fall of the English System of Finance* (1796) as a sure path to national ruin—a text the *Directoire* diffused widely in French and German—in the end proved the key to exponential growth of the British state, empire, navy, and Britain's dominance of the seas and world markets.[129] Britain had become an enormously efficient political and economic machine with a rapidly expanding apparatus of state, empire, and armed forces that enriched the presiding elites while inexorably pushing most of the rest into hardship and poverty.[130]

Highly efficient in producing wealth and power, as regards the prime democratic goal, furthering human "happiness," concerning which Say concurred entirely with Sismondi, Destutt, and Cabanis, the British machine was hence highly inefficient. Say tried to explain how the over-mighty British colossus had come into being, how it functioned, and why it constituted an economic machine commercially and industrially superior to any other but worked socially contrary to the interest of most of its own people as well as most foreigners. Frenchmen and other Europeans wanted to know how and why so immense a commercial and maritime giant dominating the world's seas, markets, and diplomacy could so successfully uphold a conservative,

[126] Say, *De l'Angleterre*, 20–1. [127] Say, *De l'Angleterre*, 20.
[128] Schoorl, *Jean-Baptiste Say*, 82. [129] Keane, *Tom Paine*, 428; O'Brien, "Impact," 382–3.
[130] Schoorl, *Jean-Baptiste Say*, 82–3, 86; Jennings, *Revolution*, 151.

monarchical–aristocratic world order, disadvantaging most of its own populace while simultaneously preventing neighbors and other peoples sharing their wealth and liberties. By supporting reactionary monarchy everywhere, subsidizing alliances, and combating democratizing movements, Britain seemingly extended its own empire and prosperity while keeping its advantages confined to a small minority. Drawing on the observations of Diderot, Raynal, Helvétius, d'Holbach, Destutt, and Cabanis, as well as Constant, Saint-Simon, and Sismondi,[131] Say simultaneously lauded Adam Smith to the skies while de-emphasizing his debt to the physiocrats, which sufficiently irritated Dupont du Nemours for the latter to rebuke him, by letter, in April 1815, for his "fanciful attempt to disown us, which you do not hide sufficiently well, my dear Say; it does not stop you from being, by way of Smith, a grandson of Quesnay and nephew of the great Turgot."[132]

Say's reputation as a theoretical economist eventually rested on his *Traité d'Économie Politique* (1803)—afterwards heavily revised in its 1814 edition—which diffused rapidly, first on the Continent, with six editions in Spanish (from 1804), five in German (from 1807), and later editions in Italian (1817), Danish (1818), and Polish (1821), and later also in Britain, Ireland, and America with six English editions beginning in 1821.[133] With Malthus, and in no small part Sismondi, his disagreements revolved around "Say's Law" pertaining to the question of the possibility or impossibility of inherently harmful overproduction and gluts, a controversy culminating in his *Lettres à Malthus* (1820) that also became known as "the General Glut Controversy." Say's Law, or "Loi des débouchés," held that "supply creates its own demand," and contended that demand is generated by those who produce and supply; it became an intensely controversial doctrine from 1814 when Say refined his formulation of his law, in the second edition of his *Traité*, and with the advent of the post-Napoleonic economic depression (1815–22) affecting Britain.

Say and Sismondi were friends and shared a common republicanism and irreligious attitude, and both strongly identified with the values of the (anti-Robespierre, Brissotin) French late Enlightenment. Until the late 1790s, Sismondi had been an adherent of Swiss aristocratic republicanism, a keen Anglophile and firm anti-democrat;[134] he fully shifted to a democratic republican stance only after 1813, due to disgust with the Restoration and the Bourbons, and what he considered the ill-effects of the 1814–15 restoration in Switzerland, as well as the post-1815 growing distress and poverty in England.[135] It was government's duty to mitigate the effects of economic distress by supporting the weakest as far as could be done.

The disagreement between Say and Sismondi, continuing into the mid-1820s, had mainly to do with Say's doctrine that increasing production was the principal path out of depression as against Sismondi's view that falling production at certain stages of the economic cycle is structurally unavoidable and must be moderated by

[131] Longhitano, "Industry, Government," 184–5; Jennings, *Revolution*, 141–3.
[132] Vardi, *Physiocrats*, 10. [133] Schoorl, *Jean-Baptiste Say*, 102.
[134] Urbinati, "Republicanism," 196–7. [135] Say, *Lettres*, 152.

governmental regulation to mitigate negative social effects. Nevertheless, unlike the classical economists both were chiefly concerned with the effect of economic processes on society as a whole and on problems of equality and inequality in wealth, each clearly influenced the other, and, by the 1820s, the two men, both ex-Protestants rejecting religious authority, both veteran opponents of Napoleon and stern critics of the British economic model, tended to converge in their thinking to a greater extent than they had earlier.[136]

But Sismondi continued to take a more pessimistic view of overproduction and gluts than Say. Damaging downturns within economic cycles, with sharply negative consequences for much of the population, especially the poorest, he considered unavoidable. Gluts were an inevitable feature of industrialization, an unavoidable aspect of growing instability of supply and demand and of workers' vulnerability to recession and lay-offs, of the economic cycles and *crises violentes* that accompany modern economic growth.[137] Apparent gluts, conceded Say, were certainly a mounting problem. But, in analyzing the depression, he attempted to show that, in the long run, demand catches up with production which moves in sudden, big spurts in output.[138] Rising levels of wealth and comfort, argued Say, against Sismondi and Malthus, mean there are no natural limits on consumption and therefore not on production either; what was holding production, and hence consumption, back, to the disadvantage of most, between 1814 and 1820, he contended, were the protectionist and war-geared fiscal systems of the day, piling excessive taxes on production—obsolete semi-mercantilist attitudes conserved to promote minority interests, and pursue rivalries with other states, with Britain the worst offender.[139]

Not the cycles but a combination of a bad fiscal system and damaging poor relief procedures were the cause of the growing distress and steady impoverishment of the English working class.[140] For Say, noted Sismondi, increasing output and production are always good whereas in his own view increasing production could be either good or bad depending on social circumstances and government policies: what mattered were the specific effects on living standards and society.[141] Excessive taxation and barriers to learning and acquiring skills are restrictions on economic growth, agreed Say, that can be reduced by government action; but he saw no essential problem in the structure or organization of modern economic life as such. Sismondi accordingly advocated a wider range of direct government intervention in the functioning and processes of the economy itself, including large-scale public works when and where necessary to mitigate temporary unemployment.

Sismondi's eventual marked unpopularity in Britain had less to do with his role in the "General Glut Controversy," his critiques of Smith, Malthus, and Ricardo as such,

[136] Guillaumont, *Pensée démo-économique*, 10, 15, 100, 118.
[137] Sismondi, *Nouveaux principes* i. 369, 422–4.
[138] Say, *Lettres*, 17–19; Guillaumont, *Pensée démo-économique*, 15, 34; Schoorl, *Jean-Baptiste Say*, 112.
[139] Say, *De l'Angleterre*, 31–2; Say, *Lettres*, 14–17, 47, 98–9; Sismondi, *Nouveaux principes* i. 338–40.
[140] Say, *Lettres*, 92–4.
[141] Sismondi, *Nouveaux principes* ii. 370; Skousen, "Say's Law, Growth Theory," 100, 106.

than his producing an analysis of the state of British society in 1819 even more unflattering than Say's. By 1820, Britain had achieved spectacular advances in manufacturing, technology, and trade, as well as empire-building. Its landed, industrial, and commercial elites were richer and more powerful than any other in the world. National wealth, in Smith's terms, had expanded impressively. But in recent decades, as Britain's power and national wealth grew, living standards for the majority had receded instead of improved, and one eleventh to one tenth of English society, 516,900 individuals by his calculation, were now so impoverished as to depend on the parish poor relief system for subsistence.[142] Division of labor, the growing simplicity of many tasks in manufacturing, and inherent tendency of capital to maximize its own growth, had all contributed to this disastrous trend. The major factor depressing living standards for many or most was the impetus of unrestricted expansion in manufacturing and trade itself alongside a growing supply of labor. In the cotton industry, he asserted, wage rates had declined by half or more in recent decades. Marx liked this aspect of Sismondi's reasoning. "People forget," recalled Marx in his *Eighteenth Brumaire of Louis Bonaparte*, "Sismondi's significant saying: the Roman proletariat lived at the expense of society, while modern society lives at the expense of the proletariat."[143]

The paradox that Britain was becoming richer while most of its population were becoming poorer, and lived in unenviable, even wretched conditions, remained the central problem underlying Say's and Sismondi's economic thought. [144] But living standards were by no means their sole focus. Sismondi fully agreed with Say that behind the drop in living standards lay a wider crisis of the Enlightenment. In some respects, he was even more critical of American society, where the problem of gluts as such was less pressing than in Britain. While endorsing the uplifting Enlightenment ideals of the American Revolution, he entertained the gravest doubts about how American society had developed since 1783. Output everywhere in America was now expanding at an unparalleled rate. Yet Pittsburgh, the "Birmingham américain," chiefly reflected what he saw as the depleting cultural and intellectual as well as economic effects of capitalism as much as, and perhaps even more than, any British industrial city. The development of the United States economy had created a social ruthlessness, and inequality, of such proportions that in the freest nation on earth, "liberty itself has lost its value compared to profit." There was no American now, he asserted, not preoccupied with how to increase his fortune as rapidly as possible; profit had become "la première considération de la vie" [first consideration of life]. This spirit of gain, he alleged, was stifling "the progress of the mind, taste for the arts, literature and the sciences," and depleting Enlightenment values.[145]

[142] Sismondi, *Nouveaux principes* i. 4, 352 and ii. 368.
[143] Marx and Engels, *Selected Works* i. 244.
[144] Sismondi, *Nouveaux principes* i. 407 and ii. 360, 370.
[145] Sismondi, *Nouveaux principes* i. 430–2.

For Say, rising production is invariably beneficial because it is inseparably tied to rising consumption and enjoyment. Say's theory held that consumption rises automatically with lower prices except, that is, where official obstruction and fiscal rules inhibit production on the part of domestic and foreign consumers thereby impeding the processes of exchange, a principle he felt Sismondi and Malthus inadequately grasped. Now that sugar was much cheaper than formerly, European consumption of this commodity had risen to 24 million pounds annually, or three pounds per person; in Cuba, where sugar was much cheaper still, each person was consuming ten times this, thirty pounds of sugar annually.[146] The reason, he contended, for the apparent crises of overproduction and oversupply highlighted by Sismondi—why British manufacturers had to sell redundant stockpiles of manufactures, in Italy and Brazil, for example, at a loss—was simply British hostility and residual domestic obstruction to Italian and Brazilian production and efforts to export to Britain.[147] Reassigning labor and machines from one sector of an industrializing economy to another, Say considered relatively easy, and readily capable of expanding demand to the point that gluts are soon ironed out. Reducing taxes and other forms of government stimulation can accelerate the catching-up process. There are many obstacles to expanding consumption, and switching labor and machines from one segment to another, countered Sismondi and Malthus, so that overproduction in one segment of the economy will foment and spread recession.[148]

At the same time, Say conducted a prolonged, sometimes acerbic, debate with Ricardo, an Anglo-Dutch Jew whose father had made a fortune on the London stock exchange but with whom he had broken over religion, converting to Unitarianism. The clash between Say and Ricardo focused on issues of value and price. Ricardo's theory placed greater stress than Say's on the objective role of labor and labor costs in determining the value of a product, viewing costs of production as decisive where Say, adhering to his more relative and subjective approach, stressed rather the variable, oscillating nature of market prices principally determined in his view by demand factors. Ricardo's economics, could not, according to Say, explain how a society can grow richer when the value of its products drops sharply, whereas his own doctrine, afterwards ridiculed by Marx, did.[149]

Both Say and Sismondi were Radical Enlightenment economists whose approach diverged markedly from the schema of the socialists. Militant socialists, including Marx, later, while equally struck by the growth in inequality and how the triumph of British commerce and industry seemingly operated to the disadvantage of most, were often chiefly concerned to promote class awareness and mobilize the resentment of the underdog. Say and Sismondi, by contrast, were primarily concerned to ease potentially violent, revolutionary tensions and impart harmony and unity to society by focusing on what they saw as mistaken government social and economic policies,

[146] Say, *Lettres*, 106–7; Sonenscher, *Before the Deluge*, 340–2.
[147] Say, *Lettres*, 14–17, 19, 106; Sismondi, *Nouveaux principes* i. 339–40.
[148] Say, *Lettres*, 140, 152. [149] Marx, *Capital*, 607; Stedman Jones, *Karl Marx*, 412.

policies narrowly framed in the interest of privileged groups. Moreover, where militant socialists viewed the growing proletariat as a welcome development strengthening their hand, and, by promoting class-warfare, ultimately positive in its social consequences, Say and Sismondi urged government action to provide more opportunities for small producers, encourage economic independence, and break down big money into a more even spread of wealth. While Say alone advocated government action to boost production and consumption, both Say and Sismondi favored expansion of society's middling segment, converting the proletariat as far as possible into a "petty bourgeoisie." As they viewed matters, the state should represent the interests of all, intervene to help the unfortunate, prevent competition between employers depressing wages, and promote proliferation of many small fortunes at the expense of big money.

All radical enlighteners from Helvétius to Destutt were, in broad terms, striving to maximize the extent of human "happiness" in society by means of education, fiscal policy, and a balanced system of political economy, rendering their view of economic theory very different from that of Smith, Ricardo, and the British economists, and it was with this late Enlightenment ideology that both Say and Sismondi aligned.[150] Neither was concerned with merely guaranteeing "subsistence." Both demanded that economic activity support entire populations living at a "comfortable" level. In Sismondi's eyes the whole point of the new science of "political economy" was to help government ensure the physical well-being of man, and minimize friction as well as wretchedness and poverty.[151] All men are engaged in the pursuit of happiness, and the task of "political economy," for Sismondi, was to help achieve "la participation équitable de tous à ce Bonheur."[152] The rich as a group, they argued, ultimately shared the interest of society as a whole in preventing economic inequality from growing excessive as reducing inequality means a more stable, safer, and generally happier society.[153] Minimizing destitution and misery by attacking inequality would prevent society overflowing with vagrants and the destitute of a character likely quickly to become permeated with crime which nothing can then easily eradicate.

Destutt too wanted society to remain a system of "exchanges," a commercial arena where capital, production, and entrepreneurship remained fundamental but were balanced by the need to protect the weak and poor and forge a veritable general interest. Destutt, like Say and Sismondi, advocated a "general interest" in the sense of what was best for society as a whole, a solution guaranteeing economic freedom and private property but also welfare and help, prompting Marx later to label him a "fischblutige Bourgeoisdoktrinär" [fish-blooded bourgeois doctrinaire].[154]

Consequently, at the core of the radical tradition, stood d'Holbach's formulation: "l'intérêt de la société demande que le plus grand nombre de ses membres jouisse

[150] Forget, "Jean-Baptiste Say," 211, 215–16.
[151] Sismondi, *Nouveaux principes* i. 2–3; Guillaumont, *Pensée démo-économique*, 77–8, 99.
[152] Sismondi, *Nouveaux principes* i. 2. [153] Cabanis, *Oeuvres complètes* ii. 192.
[154] Kennedy, "Ideology," 367–8.

de quelque chose" [society's interest demands that the majority of its members possess something].[155] It is destitution and the propertyless class that must be eliminated by government and economic theory collaborating to achieve this together. Here, Say and Sismondi were at one with the Benthamites, radical enlighteners who, through analysis and policies of amelioration, sought to raise levels of contentment in contemporary society, with Bentham less an innovator than an heir to the established tradition of economic and social thought ensuing from Helvétius, d'Holbach, Condorcet, Say, and Sismondi.[156]

Sismondi expressly disassociated himself from the ideas of Fourier, Owen, and other socialist theorists who began setting out their theories in the second decade of the nineteenth century.[157] What socialists, especially Marxists, disliked in Say's and Sismondi's economics was that the root of wretchedness and exploitation, in their analysis, was always located in institutions, and in the policies and principles of government, and not in some identifiable class of men, or the class system. Big landowners, merchants, and manufacturers were merely, as it were, incidentally, not fundamentally at fault.[158] The urgently needed corrective policies, held Sismondi, should include removing most of the burden of poor relief from society as a whole and heaping it onto the big employers, a sure way of getting them to improve wages and conditions. Another key too, in his view, was using the law to break up the largest accumulations of wealth and disperse capital more widely, though he admitted all this would horrify the British upper class and prove very difficult to execute.[159] Applying Sismondi's remedies would mean that the great mass of the population would no longer be subject to the privations, destitution, and worries that the existing economic regime was subjecting them to and would instead find themselves raised to the highest level of human felicity that humanity is able to attain, affording both economic ease and leisure to pursue the life of the mind and become more enlightened; and this would be achieved not by eliminating any social class, or reordering the economic system, but by moderating the power of the market, restraining the negative aspects of economic growth, by government action.

Government, insisted Sismondi, "only exists to procure, in the name of everyone, the 'avantage commun.'"[160] Under the auspices of Sismondi's Radical Enlightenment everyone would live in egalitarian republics at ease, while individual economic freedom and self-interest would function entirely as before. Economic enterprise would remain an inherent part of liberty in general. What would change was simply that the negative effects of market forces would be curbed by government penalizing unhelpful attitudes and tendencies and rewarding more generous ones. The basic relationship between capital and labor would not be transformed: capital and labor under both Say's and Sismondi's recipes would remain as interdependent as before

155 D'Holbach, *Politique naturelle*, 353; d'Holbach, *Morale universelle* ii. 183.
156 Bosc, "Liberté et propriété," 71, 73.
157 Sismondi, *Nouveaux principes* ii. 364–5.
158 Jeandeau, *Sismondi précurseur*, 15, 29–31; Guillaumont, *Pensée démo-économique*, 51, 77.
159 Sismondi, *Nouveaux principes* ii. 361–4.
160 Sismondi, *Nouveaux principes* i. 2–4.

only now harmonized, with the friction causing hostility between classes eradicated by government action—which is precisely what Marx found distasteful and unrealistic in their schemas.[161]

Say and Sismondi readily agreed that "political economy" is an observational science, a science studying effects with a view to discovering the underlying universal laws. Say compared the science of economics to chemistry, even though it had been an independent science only since the 1750s.[162] When data are sufficiently amassed, sifted, and correctly analyzed, then the laws of economics will be better and eventually fully understood, as would the social and political implications of those laws. But Say and Sismondi were in no way proto-socialists. Rather, they insisted, quite unlike the socialists of the 1830s and 1840s, but entirely in the spirit of d'Holbach, Condorcet, and Bentham, on the compatibility of the laws of economics with individual interest *and* the collective interest where the latter is properly regulated and supported, concurring with Condorcet that equality should be perceived as the conjunction of rights and freedom. What Say and Sismondi rejected, again following d'Holbach and Condorcet, was the idea that the laws of economics are primary and the other social sciences, including politics, legislation, and morality, ultimately subordinate to them.

[161] Sismondi, *Nouveaux principes* ii. 18–19; Forget, "Jean-Baptiste Say," 202.
[162] Rothschild, *Economic Sentiments*, 3, 40, 224.

13

Reforming Europe's Law Codes

13.1. SOCIAL STRUCTURE, CULTURE, AND THE LAW

Reforming the laws on crime and punishment, inheritance and the family, debt and religious obligation, by the 1760s and 1770s seemed not just necessary and urgent, practically all enlighteners agreed, but also among the toughest challenges facing European and American societies at that time. The gradually intensifying clash between Enlightenment principles and the formidable inertia of legal tradition, entrenched custom, and usage reached its climax at that point.

On 1 July 1766, shortly before Beccaria's visit to Paris that year, occurred a notorious incident that scandalized "all the friends of reason and humanity," the execution by the Paris *Parlement* of the 20-year-old François Jean Lefevre, Chevalier de la Barre (1745–66), for blasphemy, impiety, vandalizing a crucifix on a bridge at Abbeville, genuflecting before Voltaire's *Dictionnaire philosophique*, and passing a religious procession without removing his hat. After months of imprisonment, following his original sentencing by a lower court, the sentence was confirmed and de la Barre's execution, or judicial murder, as the *philosophes* termed it, was ordered by the Paris *Parlement*, and expressly sanctioned by the Jansenists: "voilà la tolérance", commented an appalled Morellet, "la philosophie, les lumières de nos magistrats!" [the philosophy and Enlightenment of our magistrates!]. The episode permanently damaged the once venerable, many centuries-old *parlements* as the arm of justice, together with the entire legacy of French legal tradition, in the eyes of Voltaire and all the *philosophes*.[1]

What is justice? What is the law? How should it be reformed to accord with reason? The law's deficiencies were not just a question of obsolete procedures and excessive severity of penalties: the entire dysfunctional European system, as it seemed to many, was tied to unsatisfactory forms of governance and arguably even more fundamental defects, particularly excessive deference to social hierarchy and religious authority. The great difficulty was that the defects were more or less fundamental, far-reaching, and problematic depending on one's social philosophy and religious views, though

[1] Morellet, *Lettres* i. 57–8, 66 n. 20; *Correspondance inédite de Condorcet*, 38, 184, 202, 205; Lascoumes, "Beccaria," 109–10; Israel, *Democratic Enlightenment*, 126–7.

anything beyond the minimum that even the most conservative jurists acknowledged the need for—putting an end to judicial torture, penal mutilation practices, and witch trials (which by the 1780s were anyway mostly receding from view)—was bound to be difficult for Europe's antiquated judicial institutions and procedures to adjust to. "La plupart des nations européennes," charged d'Holbach, "sont aujuourd'hui tyrannisées par des loix anciennes qui luttent avec leur situation actuelle" [most European nations today are tyrannized by ancient laws that clash with their present situation].[2] He was right, but correcting what society's more far-seeing and outspoken critics considered core defects proved nonetheless formidably challenging, not just owing to the overwhelming bias towards protection of privileged property at the expense of the propertyless, lack of prisons, and restrictions on individual liberty emanating from a highly repressive sexual code, but also the deeply contested nature of the underlying assumptions behind much of the criticism. For some, the basic challenge was how to extensively restructure the entire corpus of European law away from the outmoded heavy-handedness of the past, toward safeguarding society on a more equitable basis, without overturning the prevailing social and political order—while precisely that was what others were striving for. All considered, what was at stake in the mounting controversies, and tension, surrounding reforming the laws was of breathtaking scope, legal, moral, social, political, and religious all at once.

The existing "administration of justice," some radicals felt, "is often even more barbaric and stupidly cruel than religion," as the German materialist and admirer of Diderot, Wekhrlin, expressed it,[3] in 1791, but reforming outmoded laws was anything but simple and straightforward, not just due to judicial inertia and government reluctance but also deeply-rooted public attitudes. Law remained everywhere based on custom, theological directives, and tradition and, consequently, was widely venerated by much of the general public, even though the law and its penal codes were geared chiefly to the protection of privileged property and privileged elites, and offered astoundingly little help, security, or protection to most. Thus, while awareness of the longstanding archaism, disarray, cruelty, and irrationality of the penal and sexual codes and criminal system had become deeply entrenched among the new enlightened intelligentsia, powerful conservative voices, those whose "opinions," to echo Mary Wollstonecraft, "I should have said prejudices, the generality approved of," remained unmoved.[4]

Modern regimes, argued d'Holbach, seemed to have preserved much of the savagery and barbarousness of the primitive as regards wrongdoing and crime, especially by showing scant concern for protecting the weak.[5] Criminal jurisprudence throughout Europe, averred Brissot, the future Girondin leader, in a pamphlet addressed to the Emperor Joseph II on law reform, in 1787, was marred, and had long been, by three great defects: a crudely intrusive judicial approach which instead of placing

[2] D'Holbach, *Politique naturelle*, 319.
[3] Wekhrlin, *Paragrafen* i (1791), 223–5.
[4] Wollstonecraft, *Mary and the Wrongs*, 1; Williams, *Condorcet*, 178.
[5] D'Holbach, *Système social*, 443.

accuser and accused on an impartial par was essentially intimidating and inquisitorial in procedure; lack of any reasonable balance, or "correspondence" between crimes and retribution; and, official "retaliation," that is continuing use of intimidation, torture, mutilation, execution, and other "atrocious" penalties.[6] A genuinely "enlightened" approach would replace these with "une égalitéé parfaite entre l'accusateur et l'accusé" [a perfect equality between accuser and accused], a just equilibrium between offenses and punishments, and forms of punishment for offenders useful to society, that avoid violating basic dignity, humanity, and equality.[7]

Even discrediting time-honored belief in the efficacy of draconian punishment, or its threat, was no easy task. When, in 1764, the Spanish monarch, Carlos III, wanted to renew a law originally issued by Philip V in 1734, imposing capital punishment for crimes of theft in Madrid, his council respectfully objected that that measure was both draconian and demonstrably counter-productive.[8] Theft in the Spanish capital had shown no sign of receding since the 1734 ordinance, partly because victims and witnesses of robbery, especially petty thefts, were often troubled by the prospect of culprits being publicly executed. With the death penalty supposedly mandatory for stealing goods worth over 50 *pesos*, even only moderately devout victims of theft frequently felt reluctant to denounce destitute persons or servants especially, even when convinced they had committed the thefts, lest exacting such a terrible vengeance, when the accuser was in easier circumstances than the culprit, and the thief forfeited his or her life, constitute a mortal sin in the eyes of the Lord. Capital punishment for fraudulent bankruptcy, commented one judicial official, supposedly mandatory too, was similarly ineffective despite the frequency of the offense, and the losses many honest persons suffered from it, because the prescribed penalty was too severe.[9] A culture of not denouncing small offenses, especially servants thieving from their masters, remained prevalent throughout Spain.[10]

By the 1770s, Carlos III and his council were as resolutely set on reforming the Spanish and Spanish American penal codes as any "enlightened" court. But a measure of official concurrence hardly sufficed to dispel the mass of difficulties, as was seen with the problem of how to replace the often excessive use of capital punishment with alternative forms of retribution. In this connection the famed Italian law reformer, Cesare Beccaria (1738–94), long remained the most frequently cited reforming voice, the focal point of a Europe-wide debate about how to reduce executions and the threat of execution, render punishment more "proportionate," and end sentencing of miscreants to the galleys.[11] But reformers quickly ran up against the constraining limits of the possible within the confines of *ancien régime* society. Reducing capital punishment and sentencing to the galleys was scarcely feasible without government

[6] Tamm, "Beccaria," 192–3; d'Holbach, *Politique naturelle*, 368–9.
[7] [Brissot], *Lettre à l'Empereur*, 7–8.
[8] Sarrailh, *L'Espagne eclairée*, 536–7.
[9] Lardizábal y Uribe, *Discurso*, 48–9.
[10] Lardizábal y Uribe, *Discurso*, 46–7; Garnot, "Peines corporelles," 216.
[11] Lardizábal y Uribe, *Discurso*, 197; Broers, *Napoleonic Mediterranean*, 90, 107, 114.

providing more and better facilities for imprisonment and better arrangements for penal forced labor. By and large, prison remained an unwanted or impracticable alternative owing to its comparatively high cost.

Before 1789, the guiding principle of the penal code in practically all of Europe was still to deter crime via the threat of fearful retribution, imposing the voice of authority by obliging everyone to collude in the intimidating, despotic character of political authority. It is typical of tyrants, commented d'Holbach, to adjust punishments they administer not to the real harm to society caused by a given offense but in relation to their own furious lust for vengeance. Suspicion alone often suffices for them to exact the most atrocious retribution. Yet none of this despotic conduct helps victims or functioned to protect the vulnerable and weak. The result of the deplorable prevailing procedures was not just rank injustice on the part of government and dysfunction, but a disruptive upsurge in retaliatory action lower down, people taking the law into their own hands, or themselves resorting to crime and brigandage, rendering all of society unsafe and insecure. In Italy, Spain and Portugal, for example, murders were decidedly more frequent than in northern Europe, observed d'Holbach, owing to justice there being especially hard to come by. "Les hommes se vengent eux-mêmes, quand la loi ne veut pas les venger" [Men revenge themselves when the law does not want to avenge them].[12]

England had been in the past, and during the eighteenth century still was, associated with excessive use of the death penalty, which was prescribed for a considerable list of middling and lesser as well as major offenses. These included robbery, smuggling, extortion, blackmail, counterfeiting, and going armed in disguise. The long-term trend was certainly for execution to be steadily less resorted to.[13] Unease over excessive penalties was as widespread as enlightened discomfort with the continuing use of archaic forms of judicial investigation, torture, and mutilation. But despite growing pressure for more, and better-organized houses of correction in which offenders could be incarcerated and put to enforced work serving socially useful purposes, there was little real progress toward this goal.[14] Efforts foundered on issues of cost, inadequate policing, and difficulties of administration. Detention behind bars in Britain, widely resorted to on a short-term basis against indebtedness, was nowhere relied on for punishing murder or discouraging serious crime.[15] Historically, prisons and gaols had not been considered appropriate for long-term punishment but fit only for brief confinement, especially holding people in detention pending trial,[16] even though herding together a wide range of offenders, hardened criminals with first-time delinquents, robbers and contrabandists with mere debtors, caused prisons, like hospitals, to be suspected of exposing society to greater hazards than they curbed, by encouraging corruption of less serious miscreants by hardened criminals,

[12] D'Holbach, *Système social*, 443.

[13] Langford, *Polite and Commercial*, 156–60; Hoppit, *Land of Liberty?*, 471–3, 481–2.

[14] Lardizábal y Uribe, *Discurso*, 197, 214–15.

[15] Langford, *Polite and Commercial*, 158, 490.

[16] Lardizábal y Uribe, *Discurso*, 211.

a process furthered, both traditionalists and reformers agreed, by the prisoners' enforced idleness.[17]

Earlier, during the early eighteenth century, extending the use of the death penalty had been a conspicuous trend everywhere but especially a marked feature of English and Irish legal development, tied to the surge of highway robbery during that period, as well as smuggling between Britain and the Continent, and political subversion under the banner of Jacobitism. At the close of the Seven Years War, in 1763, came another sharp spike in the incidence of highway robbery, rife especially among recently disbanded soldiers. Numerous culprits were hanged. The gallows was somewhat less sweepingly employed in Denmark–Norway, under the *Code danoise* of 1683, than in England; nevertheless, for burglary, highway robbery, and other kinds of armed robbery, besides murder, death by hanging remained mandatory, regardless of circumstances, until 1767.[18] Likewise, in the Netherlands counterfeiting, sodomy, and other crimes in principle, and not infrequently in practice, still carried the death sentence. Worse than the rest in some respects, England was regarded by radical *philosophes* as distinctly superior at any rate as regards refusing to exempt aristocratic delinquents from the common penalties. Where on the Continent, high-ranking nobles committing serious crimes were brought to the scaffold usually only for treason or conspiracy against the ruler, offenses against lesser mortals being customarily treated with great leniency, in England overlooking, or treating lightly, aristocrats' violent misdeeds, even where the victims were servants, was less usual. On his visit to London, in 1765, d'Holbach was much impressed by reports of the public hanging, a few years earlier, in May 1760, of the Honourable Lawrence Shirley, fourth Earl Ferrers (1720–60), for murdering his steward. Long remembered as the last British peer to be hanged, his execution enabled Ferrers's younger brother to inherit his seat in the Lords.[19]

England was exceptional too, albeit in a less positive fashion, in that, until the end of the eighteenth century, women continued to be executed by hanging. This practice had ceased in Amsterdam half a century earlier and in German cities like Frankfurt it had never been in force. To the horror of some, during the 1770s and 1780s, a number of teenage girls were hanged in England for relatively minor thefts of goods.[20] In Holland, female domestic servants caught stealing were punished by public floggings, banishment, branding, or periods of confinement. With rates of detection and apprehension generally dismally low, even where bolstered by offers of financial rewards for members of the public who assisted in apprehending posted criminals, hanging for a wide variety of crimes continued to be thought essential to deterring crime. Public execution of offenders before large crowds of onlookers, many still supposed, instilled welcome terror into the minds of persons of dubious integrity and the public generally, acting as a salutary check all round. Yet magistrates and juries,

[17] Lardizábal y Uribe, *Discurso*, 213, 214–15.
[18] Tamm, "Beccaria," 190–1.
[19] D'Holbach, *Morale universelle* ii. 121 n.
[20] Boes, "Women and the Penal System," 66; Diederiks, *Land van justitie*, 78–80.

along with the victims, often regarded the letter of the law as outdated, producing collusion in evading in practice what the law stipulated—especially to avoid too many hangings. Pardons, partial verdicts, and acquittals were often handed out to the guilty; so that while the letter of the law *was* harsher in England than elsewhere, and foreign visitors often departed supposing frequent hangings in both provinces and capital were fearsomely characteristic of the English scene, in reality English justice was often more lenient than elsewhere or at least more inconsistent and unpredictable.[21]

Especially unjust and exasperating for *philosophique* reformers was the entrenched bias toward protection of property, privilege, and authority rather than protection of individuals and the common good. Here a profound clash of ideologies unavoidably enveloped the topic, compelling every serious law reformer to engage in the escalating collision between rival "moderate" and radical intellectual strategies. A vast conceptual and moral inadequacy underpinning the pervasive archaism maintaining outmoded practices kept obsolete laws on the statute books, retained overlapping jurisdictions, and obstructed introduction of less unjust modes of investigation and less drastic penalties. While men and women of status were privileged by the law, protecting unprivileged persons, the poor, female, orphaned, or menial especially, but also often persons of middling status, from intimidation, bureaucratic oppression, legal extortion, abduction, military and police brutality, or outright discrimination against their persons, by those in authority, or by others, was more rudimentary or non-existent.[22] The draconian bias of the English law of debt remained a constant cause of complaint—and still more of misery and disruption of families' lives. It was manifestly unjust in assigning intrusive powers to creditors over the debtor's person as well as his or her property, and that of immediate relatives, while providing few safeguards against apprehension and incarceration.

Wives of miscreants, children in orphanages, vagrants and vagabonds, soldiers in regiments and sailors on ships, generally had no recourse against those in authority over them. In Frankfurt am Main, a substantial number of women, sometimes with children, were peremptorily expelled from the city by magistrates, with severe effects on families, for no other reason than that their husbands had committed crimes incurring banishment and the law could not envisage wives doing anything other than accompanying them.[23] Much of the basic injustice and disarray characteristic of Europe's legal systems stemmed, in Beccaria's view, from the deplorable custom of treating society as an agglomeration of families rather than individuals. Sanctioning primacy of families on the ground the husband possessed absolute rights over his wife and children seemed an ineradicable doctrine that despotically turned a society of 100, 000 individuals into one of twenty thousand autonomous persons and eighty thousand slaves. This vast lingering travesty served to justify what he regarded as the wholly indefensible practice of confiscating property of convicted criminals irrespective of the impact on children and female dependants. Assigning excessive sway to

[21] Mazza, "Hume's 'Meek' Philosophy," 221; Blamires, "Beccaria," 70–1.

[22] Hoppit, *Land of Liberty?*, 480.

[23] Boes, "Women and the Penal System," 67, 69.

heads of families, urged Beccaria, generated huge conflicts within society over basic loyalties and issues of morality.[24]

Rank and privilege were what chiefly counted in early modern law. Startlingly, in the sizeable portion of France under the jurisdiction of the *Parlement* of Dijon, where 728 persons were condemned to death (407 actually executed) in the eighteenth century, and a far larger number, 2,300, sentenced to mutilation, the galleys, or other severe corporal punishment, an astoundingly large majority, around 70 per cent of these 3,027 instances of severity, were for offenses against privileged property, the church, or royal authority, with another 15 per cent for murder. Only a mere 15 per cent of the total—despite severe penalties often being supposedly mandatory—were punishments for all other crime, everything from armed robbery, abduction, and assault to rape and extortion where directed against the ordinary individual, non-privileged person.[25] To be in a subordinate social position was, in effect, to be marginalized and virtually unprotected by law. Very little in the way of established legal recourse or procedure was available to deter wife-beating, assaults on servants, banishing and branding vagrants, violent abduction (even by the state in the case of military and naval impressment), maltreatment of inmates of houses of correction, victimization of orphans and prostitutes, and so forth. Forming a sizeable percentage of the total population in *ancien régime* society, 5 or 6 per cent in the Dutch cities, domestic servants were particularly exposed and vulnerable.[26]

Privileged property, rank, and authority being what the law chiefly aimed to protect, lack of protection for the individual and lack of equality before the law generated an immense ideological rift dividing enlightened criteria from traditionally prevailing legal culture. Excluded from protection, persons of unprivileged status—hence most people— were constantly vulnerable to being abused by the law itself. The fundamental flaw was then further aggravated by the constant pressure of church-driven behavior codes and attitudes relating to sexuality, family, marriage, and the upbringing of children, impinging especially on book censorship and the illegitimate, orphans, and prostitutes— the latter being harassed dreadfully in Vienna, noted Wekhrlin, by Joseph II's police.[27] Harsh, irrational laws, against their own interests though they were, were nevertheless venerated in the late eighteenth century by ordinary folk, being long accepted and sanctioned by usage so that unjust practices, devised by ignorant barbarians, complained d'Holbach, remained everywhere in force to oppress civilized peoples in his day. For him, as for Diderot, true justice is the equal right of all members of society arising from the basic needs common to all members of the human species, common needs lying at the origin and formation of society, as they understood it.[28]

[24] Beccaria, *Of Crimes and Punishments*, 60; Pii, "Republicanism," 269–71; Broers, *Napoleonic Mediterranean*, 100–1.

[25] Garnot, "Peines corporelles," 216–17.

[26] Diederiks, *Land van justitie*, 77.

[27] Wekhrlin, *Graue Ungeheuer* 5 (1785), 144, 188; Beales, *Joseph II*, 90–1.

[28] D'Holbach, *Politique naturelle*, 120–1; Blank, "D'Holbach on Self-Esteem," 443–4.

Continued use of the press-gang, or "l'infâme presse des matelots" as a French writer called it in 1789, to provide men for the Royal Navy was considered, in France and the United Provinces, a particularly infamous feature of English life. In the seventeenth century, the press-gang had been discarded as wholly incompatible with the "freedoms" of the Republic in the United Provinces.[29] By some, the press-gang was bitterly resented in England too; but nothing seemed to discredit "this notorious infringement on the dearest rights of men, and [. . .] infernal blot on the very face of our immaculate constitution," commented Wollstonecraft sarcastically in 1790,[30] noting that state and society themselves propped up the worst, most outmoded abuses with the full collusion of most of educated society. The *Histoire philosophique* pronounced England's laws the most irrational, entangled, and contradictory judicial corpus to be found anywhere on earth;[31] but among the general public there existed scant pressure to abolish the press-gang and still less to disparage the legal system as a whole. With the pressing of seamen, admitted Hume, "we continue a practice seemingly the most absurd and unaccountable;" nevertheless, boxed in by his unbendingly conservative social and moral philosophy, he could not condemn the practice. The contradictions inherent in all human life, and all social and political systems, he argued, remain indispensable to every society; they afford the flexibility enabling social systems to function. Unjustifiable in principle yes, but what counts in society, held Hume, is not reason or principle but tradition, practice, and popular endorsement. "While this power is exercised to no other end than to man the navy, men willingly submit to it, from a sense of its use and necessity."[32]

The great drawback of Hume's philosophy as a practical aid to civil society in the later eighteenth century was that he was unable, on his premises, to urge any broad reorganization of justice in terms of reason, due to his philosophical curtailment of the scope of reason and his attributing the effectiveness and validity of legal systems mainly to tradition, experience, and their perceived usefulness. Hume's envisaging the history of civil society as driven, in the first place, by economic need and desires, and justice as essentially a prop to the requirements of the economic process, hence the market, was not in itself a problem. "The motive that led people" to begin respecting property and contract, held Hume, was "enlightened self-interest."[33] Hume's theory of justice and law, like that of Adam Smith, featured a built-in, inherent emphasis on justice being primarily a mechanism for protecting private property and commercial contracts.[34] The difficulty here was Hume's primacy of practice over every formulation of fundamental principle. The harsh reality of eighteenth-century legal practice everywhere drew sustenance and encouragement in resisting the radical reformers from a Humean skepticism bolstering "anti-philosophical" moral and

[29] Israel, *Dutch Republic*, 717.
[30] Wollstonecraft, *Vindication of the Rights of Men*, 14; Mounier, *Considerations*, 47.
[31] *Histoire philosophique* (1780) ix. 209. [32] Hume, *Essays*, 374–6.
[33] Stewart, *Opinion and Reform*, 166; Finlay, *Hume's Social Philosophy*, 156–7.
[34] Stewart, *Opinion and Reform*, 160–2; Zarone, *Cesare Beccaria*, 68–75.

legal conservatism. Hume, Blackstone, Ferguson, and Burke exhorted the public to an almost mystical veneration for the law. But no matter how great the boundless reverence for a constitution deemed surpassingly excellent by most, for those pondering the issues with a more critical eye it was not easy to dissent from Wollstonecraft's judgment that this was mostly just deeply ingrained prejudice and ignorance driven by a deeply emotional but misplaced loyalism and patriotism. In Britain, concurred Bentham in 1776, prevailed an amazingly widespread but reprehensible inclination to "yield the same abject and indiscriminating homage to the Laws [as] is paid to the despot elsewhere."[35]

Despite profound respect for each other as philosophers and men of learning, and as personalities, d'Holbach styling Hume "a great man, whose friendship, at least, I know to value as it deserves," the divide between Hume and his Parisian philosophical friends steadily widened, resulting in a pronounced lack of respect for the other's viewpoints on issues of law reform and morality. Helvétius struck Hume, Ferguson, and Gibbon as utterly superficial and lacking in rigor; but Helvétius thought the same of Hume. According to an Irish Catholic army officer in French service, Daniel O'Connor of Belanagare, writing in 1764, Helvétius, with whom he had just been conversing, believed the "ideas of Hume are ill connected, that he never studied the all of anything, and that his treatise on the passions is a very superficial work."[36] In any case, the absence of any serious reform program in Hume amounted to a profound philosophical dilemma entangling his efforts to explain how virtue can be in the true interest of everyone when virtue in his, Smith's, and Ferguson's thought amounted to tenacious conformity to a justice system rooted in undeviating protection of property and established attitudes.[37]

Another key difference between Britain and the rest was the frequent use of transportation of criminals to the colonies.[38] Given the—for many—disturbing insufficiency of appropriate intermediate penalties on the scale between execution and public flogging, and the unwillingness of local authorities to invest in public prisons, workhouses, and houses of correction, transportation emerged in early and mid-eighteenth-century Britain as the preferred instrument of correction short of execution and prime factor in reducing the rate of executions.[39] Between the 1720s and the outbreak of the American Revolution, in 1775–6, some 36,000 English convicts, over 80 per cent men, were shipped at public expense across the Atlantic to the colonies by the crown and sold into convict servitude for often excessively long periods. Convicts in this way became a key tool of imperial expansion, even though the practice inexorably increased the stock of fatherless families in England and was resented in the colonies. Briefly, the American Revolution interrupted the flow. But the method

[35] Bentham, *Fragment on Government*, 12.
[36] Helvétius, *Correspondance générale* iii. 108; Mossner, *Life*, 475, 480.
[37] Stewart, *Opinion and Reform*, 122, 176–7.
[38] Langford, *Polite and Commercial*, 159.
[39] Hoppit, *Land of* Liberty?, 480–2.

resumed on a considerable scale in the 1790s, as the crown took to shipping out large numbers of convicts, including Irish, Scots, and other political dissidents, to Australia.

Social rank, reflected not least in the divergent forms of judicial investigation and corporal and capital punishment, dominated every aspect of legal practice and thought. Suspects of wealthy background were less likely to be subjected to judicial torture, flogging, or initial confinement and were generally treated differently from those of "inferior" status. By contrast, lower-class female offenders in a city such as Frankfurt am Main, were almost as likely to be judicially tortured as men.[40] For executing convicted commoners, different modes of execution were available to French and German magistrates, ranging from simple hanging, via prior mutilation preceding hanging, to dispatch by being bodily broken on the wheel. Nobles and high officials, despite Struensee's, de la Barre's, and Ferrers's experiences, mostly retained the privilege of not being tortured or mutilated, and, when convicted of capital offenses, including treason and highway robbery, of death by decapitation rather than hanging, though nobles too were hanged in cases of crimes deemed "ignobles."

There was an unmistakable tendency for all the more lurid and drastic forms of public retribution—such as cutting out the tongue and breaking on the wheel, public degradation and capital punishment for offenses less than murder—to occur progressively less during the seventeenth than the sixteenth century, and less still in the eighteenth. At Frankfurt, a significant proportion of women sentenced to capital punishment during the fifteenth and sixteenth centuries had been drowned in the river or buried alive.[41] From 1618, drowning was replaced by decapitation with the sword. The same trend to curtail violent, lurid forms of penalty and mutilation occurred likewise in corporal punishment more generally, though heavy flogging of juveniles and females, as well as adult men, remained widespread everywhere. But while society experienced a universal, silent, unconscious drift away from earlier practice, tacit aversion to outmoded penal codes, the slowness of such change often served to intensify the bizarre paradox that modern Europeans in the 1770s still lived amidst a vast heap of elaborate, professional, and expensive jurisprudence which, to radical eyes, was altogether contrary to reason, or, as d'Holbach expressed it, "ténébreuse, absurde, contradictoire."[42] Case-law tradition and Enlightenment did not always clash outright. In 1751, the British Parliament's Commons Committee, under the chairmanship of Sir Richard Lloyd, produced wide-ranging proposals to improve penal law in Britain, urging more extensive use of imprisonment and more compulsory labor in the royal dockyards.[43] But without great increases in spending on prisons, administration, police, and judiciary such schemes remained impracticable and crown and Parliament unwilling to consider either the reorganization or the cost involved, added to which many judges and churchmen remained unconvinced of the need for reform.[44]

[40] Boes, "Women and the Penal System," 64. [41] Boes, "Women and the Penal System," 65–6.
[42] D'Holbach, *Politique naturelle*, 320. [43] D'Holbach, *Politique naturelle*, 158.
[44] D'Holbach, *Politique naturelle*, 158; Rousseaux, "Doctrines criminelles," 231–3.

Broadly, it was not sociability, economic pressures, or governments, and especially not—here Foucault was wide of the mark[45]—magistrates or legal expertise that were the chief agent of change, even if, in Montesquieu's unique case, it is true that his professional legal background aided his role in stepping up reconsideration of the principles behind Europe's law codes and initiating the idea that legal authority should be raised in status as an arm of the state and given more autonomy from the executive power and the church.[46] In fact, not really surprisingly, the legal profession made only a startlingly minimal contribution to the campaign for change. Without doubt, it was Enlightenment criticism and "philosophy"—or at least anti-Humean *philosophie moderne*—together with intensifying social difficulties creating new pressures (as opposed to attitudes) that became the decisive tool among the intelligentsia and officialdom and that did the major work. "Philosophy" gained this scope for action not due to widely diffused supporting attitudes, but inherent difficulties with the legal system now so chronic that supporting the status quo came to be heavily eroded among the governing elites themselves. Hence, far-reaching, concrete legal reform from the 1760s mostly stemmed from rulers and high-level officials embracing, in relative isolation, but in the face of intractable social pressures, the urgent recommendations of the *philosophes*, albeit doing so only in part and highly selectively. In Prussia, where exceptional progress in redefining capital crimes and limiting the death penalty, removing ecclesiastical authority from ordinary justice, and systematizing the law, ensued under Frederick, commencing in the 1740s and 1750s, the key movers, apart from the king himself, were figures such as Samuel, Freiherr von Cocceji (1679–1755), one of Europe's leading advocates of the abolition of judicial torture, son of a Bremen Calvinist professor of politics at Frankfurt an der Oder and himself a professor in Natural Law, and Philippe-Joseph de Jariges (1706–70), an eminent Huguenot *philosophe* and member of the Berlin Academy, who succeeded Cocceji as Prussian *Grosskanzler* [high chancellor], on the latter's death in 1754.[47]

More generally, though, it was unsurprising that European governments were largely unsuccessful in rationalizing either penal codes or general legal principles and procedures before 1789. From Italy to Scandinavia, the problems were now far more pressing than before 1750, and the shortcomings of prevailing legal practice more obvious and widely discussed. But, as Catherine the Great discovered in Russia, this could not of itself lead to reconstructing the law and its procedures on the basis of equity and reason, to overcoming the self-seeking ignorance and philistinism of the nobility, or secure de-sacralization of legal principles and assumptions, disentangling codes from custom, prejudice, deeply-rooted theological stipulations, and ecclesiastical authority.[48] Resistance was three-dimensional—simultaneously professional,

[45] Foucault, *Discipline and Punish*, 80–1. [46] Felice, *Per una scienza universale*, 73–93.

[47] Hubatsch, *Frederick the Great*, 194–6, 212–14.

[48] Tamm, "Beccaria," 189–90; Pasta, "*Dei delitti e delle pene*," 128, 141–2, 147; Dixon, *Catherine the Great*, 182, 198.

theological, and popular—and abundantly justified by key sections of Enlightenment social criticism and philosophy itself, the entire corpus of moderate mainstream thought aiding the dominant culture of legal training, case-law, and practice in its resistance. The scale of effort, intellectual, political, social, and administrative, required to engineer a comprehensive, coherent, and effective program of law reform was, consequently, immense.[49]

As radical *philosophes* and some other, mostly highly-placed observers saw it, the foundations of society's legal structures were inextricably entwined with political, social, educational, and religious structures that were wrongly conceived, or at least sturdily entrenched, and that effectively restrained government reform initiatives or steered them in an undesirable direction, creating an unbridgeable gulf between the reforming enlightened despots themselves and the radical *philosophique* fraternity. The art of legislation in all European lands, complained Helvétius, usually consisted only "à faire concourir une infinité d'hommes au bonheur d'un petit nombre" [in making an infinity of men conform to the happiness of small number] while keeping "la multitude dans l'oppression" [the multitude in oppression], and in this way violating systematically "all the rights of humanity."[50] "Rien de plus commun," agreed d'Holbach, in his *La Politique naturelle* (1773), than to find the prevailing "Loix Civiles en contradiction avec celles de la Nature ou de l'équité [the civil laws in contradiction with those of nature and equity]."[51]

That both European and New World edifices of law remained fundamentally unreformed in terms of basic principles and attitudes consequently spurred radical enlighteners not just to redefine justice, equity, and criminality in wholly new ways but to integrate law reform in their wider program of sweeping transformation of social and political structures and institutions. Where for traditional-minded and theological opponents criminality remained a mark of innate perverseness, of possessing a corrupt nature, for thinkers like Diderot, Helvétius, d'Holbach, and Condorcet, and their German disciples, Wekhrlin, Wedekind, Forster, and Dohm, it was rather Europe's laws themselves that were perverse, "barbares" as Condorcet put it,[52] "depraved" because they sanctified the interests and privileges of those who had promulgated these laws bolstered by "la perversité des moeurs," the harmful "erreurs" infusing the great majority adhering to what these philosophers judged absurd prejudices about women, marriage, lineage, extra-marital intercourse, homosexuality, masturbation, illegitimate birth, suicide, sacrilege, blasphemy, heresy, penance, and much else. It was legislators' prejudices and ignorance, contended Helvétius, that had always resulted in "l'intérêt particulier" operating "en opposition avec l'intérêt général" [in opposition to the general interest], the "particular interest" always having priority in the framing of laws, ensuring the general irrationality and incoherence of all legal systems. By contrast, he and his allies had a straightforward, clear formula for addressing the problem of law reform: what does not harm society is not in the sphere of justice.

[49] Hoppit, *Land of Liberty?*, 477.
[50] Gauchat, *Lettres critiques* xii. 110–11, 212–13, 328–9.
[51] D'Holbach, *Politique* naturelle, 41.
[52] Condorcet, *Tableau historique*, 392.

Meanwhile, as some saw it, the "interest" of the abused, oppressed, and exploited individuals, systematically wronged by a colossal machine of inequitably conceived laws, intrusive theology, and viciously superstitious popular notions, avenged itself on those who maintained these inequitable laws by regularly rebelling against, evading, and infringing the system.

13.2. LAW, POPULAR CULTURE, AND RELIGIOUS POLICING

Among the most formidable obstacles was the intrusion of theological considerations into the judicial process—something ubiquitous and, to an extent, defended by moderate mainstream Enlightenment, although here Montesquieu was notably, if discreetly, critical and innovative by arguing that punishments for religious crimes should be limited to the ecclesiastical sphere—censure, excommunication, and so forth.[53] Ecclesiastical authority and theology being everywhere integrally linked to the functioning of society, religious obligations and restrictions relating to festivals, processions, Sabbath observance, sacrilege, heresy, and witchcraft, as well as adultery, divorce, fornication, illegitimacy, and homosexuality, remained integral to the civil law; added to which the church remained chief sponsor of a range of morally-improving drives, notably against prostitution and gambling and the German 1780s anti-masturbation campaign to which Kant lent his support.

Cultural trends assuredly assisted the long-term tendency towards secularization, a process well-documented and everywhere under way by 1700. Executions for witch-craft, where these still occurred, as in Jutland, north-eastern Italy, and Bavaria, finally ended in the mid-eighteenth century, in part because magistrates refused to handle such cases. But while it is true that such changes relegating old-established practice to obsolescence stemmed from shifts in attitude among a broad public, there was nothing new about these shifts by the late eighteenth century and they were now marginal to the main issues in legal reform. Growing secularization had slowly but fundamentally transformed society's attitudes toward heresy, sacrilege, and many other offenses. Thus, in the sixteenth and early seventeenth century, suicide was still viewed as due to satanic temptation, demonic possession, and induced melancholia. In Reformation Geneva, magistrates dealt harshly with suicides, denying those condemned for killing themselves a Christian burial and even confiscating their estates and desecrating their corpses, whereas imposing corporal and financial penalties in cases of suicide became rare after around 1650.[54] At Amsterdam, marking suicides for special condemnation was progressively slimmed down to a few symbolic gestures. But nowhere did altering the letter of the law keep pace even with the slow-moving changes in attitude, creating a growing gap between practice and theory. Suicides and their relatives remained subject to legal penalties and stigmatization in many

[53] Felice, *Per una scienza universale*, 105–8.

[54] Watt, "Suicide, Gender, Religion," 140, 150.

places; ignominy and humiliation continued to be heaped on attempted suicides and melancholics charged with contemplating suicide. Feller noted how diametrically opposed in Catholic lands were the strictures of religion and the materialists' notion that suicide is preferable to a life of unrelieved misery. Were it not for strict religious policing, he argued, anyone deeply hurt by disgrace, poverty, betrayal by friends, humiliation over a spouse's infidelity, or children's ingratitude might decide that acute distress justified renouncing one's life.[55]

Religious coercion, needless to say, disproportionately affected the poor and disadvantaged. Charitable institutions in the United Provinces regularly struck off their lists those of the needy whose religious observance and moral conformity failed to meet the exacting standard expected; Catholics remained excluded from major, and, in many places, even minor, public offices. Orthodox members of the Dutch Reformed Church transferring from one town to take up a post elsewhere needed attestations of confessional status and observance from the consistory of their former place of residence. Religious policing was often stiffened by popular pressure mobilizing against proposed changes. In 1778, demonstrations at Flushing, incited by local Reformed preachers, aimed at preventing the town's Catholics constructing a church to replace the shed they had hitherto been confined to.[56]

Religious obligation shaped the lives of everyone whether they were religious or not. The illiberal core of Locke's restricted toleration, excluding atheists and, at the discretion of governments, possibly Catholics and others, ensued from the fact that for him "articles of religion are some of them practical and some speculative." While those "purely speculative" were "required only to be believed, and cannot be imposed on any church by the law of the land" and therefore constituted the proper sphere of toleration, went Locke's theory, no such delimiting of judicial power applied to the "practical" articles of religion. Articles concerned "with the will and manners" remained within the sphere of the magistracy, teachers, and tolerated churches alike, all of which were duty bound to steer society away from vice, atheism, and dissolute living and assist individuals prepare their souls for the great challenge of salvation.[57] Locke positively invites the magistrate to intervene in daily life and the taverns to suppress prostitution, fornication, homosexuality, and propagators of unchristian notions as well as step up pressure on violators of Sunday observance.

In the 1780s, Mendelssohn meditated on some length on the problems Locke's toleration poses for an enlightened society both in its practical and theological aspects. Locke's goal, a limited toleration excluding atheists, leaving Jews in a subordinate status, and potentially justifying exclusion of Catholics, combined with his Arminian strategy for promoting toleration, his idea that the state exists mainly to advance the temporal welfare, and not, or mainly not, men's spiritual welfare, which should be assigned to church authority, created considerable difficulties in the broader Enlightenment context. It implied temporal authority must defer to the

[55] Feller, *Catéchisme philosophique*, 127.
[56] Van der Wall, "Geen natie van atheisten," 49.
[57] Locke, *Letter concerning Toleration*, 54–5.

spiritual authority in spiritual matters. By excluding the temporal authority from men's spiritual welfare, Locke's approach opened the door to the public church, or a consortium of churches, claiming precedence in education and the entire spiritual and cultural sphere, including the right to define the exact boundaries of spiritual welfare, liberty of conscience, and censorship. Though a zealot for moderation himself, Mendelssohn worried that Locke's formula simply concedes too much sway to the spiritual authority. Even if, as he agreed, free expression of atheistic ideas *is* detrimental to society, it would still be better, he argued, not to allow churchmen any jurisdiction over matters of conscience. It was a stance that left him stranded in unresolved ambivalence.[58]

More forthright, Mirabeau, writing in 1778, insisted the sweeping effect of *la tolérance illimitée* is generally beneficial provided it truly removes all vestige of ecclesiastical censorship, all zeal of the "fanatics," and power of "superstition" and hypocrisy.[59] But whether Mendelssohn's or Mirabeau's, a fuller toleration than Locke countenanced proved unacceptable to most. Moderate mainstream Enlightenment's very real hesitations and inconsistencies over whether atheists should be tolerated were readily exploited by Counter-Enlightenment *anti-philosophes*. With "atheism" still generally classified a "crime" punishable by death, Rousseau was warmly congratulated by several *anti-philosophes* for pronouncing "atheists" so pernicious for society that they should indeed be executed. Not only Locke and Rousseau, but Hume, Montesquieu, and Voltaire too, observes Feller with justification, could be construed as claiming "atheists" are society's enemies and that toleration should not be extended to such persons.[60]

Conceding a formally equal toleration to believers in Christian Revelation, in whatever form, and those denying and rejecting Christianity, as Bayle proposes, argued the Jesuit Gabriel Gauchat (1709–79), creates an entirely false equation and reciprocity, a weighting against Christ, "et telle est la tolérance des incrédules" [and that is the toleration of the unbelievers].[61] Comprehensive *tolérantisme*, or *la tolérance illimitée*, the anti-Lockean concept for which Mirabeau, in 1778, considered Amsterdam still the model, the fully comprehensive toleration demanded by Bayle, while professing to reconcile differences and help social stability, actually, complained opponents, represented a militant, aggressive dismantling of the entire Christian format and logic of society. Bayle, neither Protestant nor Catholic at heart, objected Gauchat, was a "fanatic" opposing not just the Revocation of the Edict of Nantes but all confessional coercion. Bayle alone wrought Christianity more harm, he alleged, in 1759, than all other *incrédules* put together, generating a vast arsenal from which the rest borrowed their insidious weaponry against church authority. It was not cogent argument that had wrought this harm but his cunning mixture of candor and duplicity, "of apparent moderation and real fury," "of pretended impartiality and of *partialité marquée*," justifying setting free, while pretending not to, people's most

[58] Arkush, *Moses Mendelssohn*, 116–21.
[59] Mirabeau, *Lettres* i. 226–8.
[60] Feller, *Catéchisme philosophique*, 134–5, 142, 152.
[61] Gauchat, *Lettres critiques* xiii. 115.

criminal innermost passions.[62] From Bayle's "système de la tolérance universelle," releasing men from confessional conformity and the apparatus of religious enforcement and policing, "follows necessarily the extinction of Christianity." Helvétius' advocacy of full freedom of thought, the right "de tout penser et de tout dire" [to think and say everything], then further extended this clandestine conspiracy of total rejection of existing society and its laws, of establishing principles "from which arises from all sides a general overturning." Non-Christian toleration stemmed neither from charity nor equity but a secret malicious design to demolish the edifice of religion, an evil maliciousness converted into a "secte philosophique.[63]

Everyone was expected to attend divine service regularly, keep festivals and days of special solemnity, and observe regulations upholding church ordinances concerning abstention from work on holy days. Every European land boasted mounds of legislation upholding religious policing. Under French *ancien régime* law, attestations of satisfactory lifestyle and morals, issued by the parish *curé*, were required of candidates for judicial functions, the profession of notary, taking up university positions, and qualifying as a physician. No less than fifty-eight out of a total of 344 articles defining current policing tasks in the mid-eighteenth century, listed in the *Dictionnaire de Police* (1756), a handbook for practical use summarizing the responsibilities of royal *avocats prosécuteurs* charged with enforcing royal legislation in the Bourbonnais, compiled by a judicial official La Foix de Fréminville, exclusively concerned religious norms obligatory in Bourbon France in theory for all individuals.[64] Throughout Europe, laws Protestant and Catholic regarding sanctification of the Lord's Day and major festival days forbade work, holding sales, auctions, or fairs, or mounting public entertainments on those days, imposing monetary fines for infringements which secular officers had to exact. Strict rules applied to baptizing newly-born infants—an obligation falling in part on midwives, where abandoned or separated mothers died in childbirth—that were strictly enforced. Where those at risk of dying hesitated to be duly reconciled with Christ, all staff occupied with the sick or injured shared responsibility for ensuring the last rites were administered in time.

Everywhere, cafés and taverns had to conform to Sunday observance rules and were everywhere closed during hours of divine service. Requisite at Christmas, Easter Day, and on the Days of the Assumption of the Virgin, All Saints, and other key holidays in Catholic lands was refraining from all inappropriate pastimes, frivolity, and enjoyments as well as abstaining from meat during Lent. Butchers were threatened with heavy fines for selling meat during periods of abstinence. Not only in France, but everywhere, including the American states after 1776 (down to the 1830s), the public was under obligation to assist repression of blasphemy and sacrilege.[65] If rarely fully enforced, the French laws against blasphemy were nevertheless draconian; those convicted of repeated blasphemy were supposed to have their tongues cut out from the root.

[62] Gauchat, *Lettres critiques* xiii, Preface, pp. ix–x. [63] Gauchat, *Lettres critiques* xiii. 284, 293.
[64] Peronnet, "Police et religion," 377. [65] Israel, *Expanding Blaze*, 89, 250, 420.

In Amsterdam, Frankfurt, Hamburg, Metz, Venice, and the other cities where Jews were tolerated, they remained excluded from most professions, vocations, and public capacities with little sign of improvement in their status until the revolutionary French National Assembly's legislation in 1789–91. Only after 1791 were they finally free to reside anywhere in France and, after Napoleon's conquest of northern Italy (1796–7), in the new Italian republics. A further pressure on individuals enforced by law was submission to confessional indoctrination. Weekly religious instruction of children at parochial catechism classes was obligatory, in France until the age of 14, a responsibility imposed on all parents.[66] Royal officials had to ensure parish priests were not negligent in their duties regarding catechism classes and preaching to their parishioners. Late seventeenth-century French royal legislation governing catechizing was formulated especially with a view to re-Catholicizing the Huguenot population; in the later eighteenth century, policing the catechizing of village and small-town children still affected everyone irrespective of confessional background. Rural schools were essentially tools of confessionalization and sustained as a religious obligation via exactions levied on localities. With regular attendance at religious services in theory incumbent on everyone, royal officials had to ensure Sunday sermons conformed to established rules of social and political as well as religious propriety. *Curés* were required by law not just to edify the people but eschew emotive language when referring to doctrinal or disputed questions, sensitive confessional or liturgical issues, and anything political. Upkeep of churches too came under the purview of the royal magistrates as did charitable institutions, collection of tithes and other church taxes, and ringing of church bells to signal fires and murders as well as summon the faithful to services.

Preachers thundering from the pulpit against *Aufklärungsgift* [Enlightenment poison] and against extra-marital "fornication" reinforced coercion based on traditional notions of marriage and family life, paternal authority, and ecclesiastical opposition to divorce, beside popular stigmatization of unmarried mothers and illegitimate children, and general condemnation of homosexuality, sodomy, fornication, suicide, and prostitution, and hence continued to shape major areas of legal practice. Theologico-legal barriers and restrictions frequently piled complications and contradictions high on the desks of the magistrates. Despite the disappearance of heresy trials and witch-burning, entrenchment of theological notions and theologically formed popular prejudices, Wekhrlin stressed, in 1791, powerfully lingered in society, legal practice, and local administration. He singled out the Imperial Free Cities, and, above all, Frankfurt am Main, where the Jews remained confined to their walled-in ghetto, for special rebuke.[67] Varying levels of disabilities on Jews remained in force throughout Europe—even in England and Holland—including their exclusion in much of Germany from direct ownership of houses, land, and other fixed property.

[66] Peronnet, "Police et religion," 382–3.
[67] Wekhrlin, *Paragrafen* i (1791), 223–5; Israel, *Democratic Enlightenment*, 280.

Book censorship, even where churchmen played no direct part in administering state censorship, remained fundamental to religious policing. All individuals were exhorted, and teachers and librarians expected, to assist with preventing the reading of erotic, skeptical, and impious works. "It is to begin to lack faith, as one author put it, to permit oneself to read impious books as well as contrary to the respect due to religious authority which firmly forbids such reading."[68] It was in the hope of strengthening the laws against printing and distributing irreligious books that France's national assemblies of the clergy, in 1775 and 1780, requested Louis XVI to revise France's censorship law; but their concern was not to soften the draconian penalties menacing offenders in this sphere but to tighten up surveillance and inspection and more effectively curb diffusion of such literature.[69] While Europe's cities, despite censorship, teemed with "livres absurdes et pitoyables" produced by the new "philosophy," complained Caraccioli, at least society could be confident that rigorous religious policing ensured that all libraries to which members of the public had regular access could not be "disfigured" by such literature.[70]

In Portugal, a country enjoying a wholly new prominence in European culture and debates since the Lisbon earthquake of 1755 and Pombal's sensational expulsion of the Jesuits in 1758–60 and his expropriation of that order's immense properties, dramatic changes in attitudes to sacrilege and heresy occurred during the middle decades of the century. But these amounted to a perceptible softening rather than full-scale reversal. Where Inquisition trials for heresy remained frequent in the 1720s, 1730s, and even the 1740s, these rapidly diminished after 1750. The last person burnt for heresy in Portugal, the Jesuit mystic, Father Gabriel Malagrida, who had written on the Lisbon earthquake explaining the catastrophe as the workings of divine wrath, died in the flames in 1761, though apparently his real crime was treason. At the same Lisbon *auto-da-fé*, one of the greatest Portuguese champions of toleration and rebels against ecclesiastical authority, Cabaleiro de Oliveyra, an exile from Portugal who converted to Protestantism in England, was publicly humiliated and burnt in effigy amidst vast popular acclaim. In 1768, the crown drastically curbed the Inquisition's powers of arrest and imprisonment and, in 1769, Pombal largely eliminated what remained of the Inquisition's autonomous judicial power including its control of book censorship, setting up instead the new *real mesa censoria*, or royal censorship board, a development that did not occur in Spain until 1812. Certainly, *autos-da-fé* ceased and the death penalty for condemned beliefs and heresy in Portugal ended at least on a practical level. But this scarcely modified the ban on uncatholic conduct or the severity of Portuguese censorship with regard to literature of many kinds. Nor was there much attempt to reform the rest of the penal code or change the often barbaric penalties still prescribed by law and regularly employed by the judiciary throughout the Portuguese empire.[71]

[68] Le Masson des Granges, *Philosophe moderne*, 261–2. [69] Peronnet, "Police et religion," 392.
[70] Caraccioli, *Langage de la raison*, 110–11, 215. [71] Maxwell, *Pombal*, 82–3, 91.

Although by the 1760s and 1770s many laws and prohibitions long gracing statute-books had become largely irrelevant, they remained on the statute books and one could never be quite certain whether they were wholly redundant or not, so that even where no longer enforced they still exerted a deterrent effect, especially where occasionally applied with severity. The comprehensive 1678 ban on the printing, selling, and distribution of Spinoza's books imposed by the States General and States of Holland long remained in force—growing somewhat obsolete in the fast changing world of the later eighteenth century but without entirely losing its effect. In January 1760, the Amsterdam magistracy informed the provincial high court, at The Hague, that they had just fined a local city bookseller, Gerrit Blom, 300 guldens, a laborer's wages for a year, for selling the *Ethics* "of B.D.S. or Benedictus de Spinosa."[72]

Before 1789, securing meaningful change involved winning over powerful ministers and a great administrative effort. If there were few regions where both judiciary and general public were so fervently and uniformly opposed to "enlightened" legal reform in the 1780s and 1790s as in the Austrian Netherlands,[73] the reaction of the Belgian people during the revolution there of 1789, their furious support of old legal structures, was just an extreme instance of the general position.

13.3. THE "LAW REFORM" CONTROVERSY OF THE 1760s AND 1770s

Amidst the pressure for law reform and the irremovable obstacles, the disputes over Beccaria's principles grew into one of the great public controversies of the late Enlightenment. Although reform accelerated markedly in much of Europe between the 1760s and 1789, decades when Enlightenment debate and enquiry were at their height, with Denmark, Russia, and Spain being clear instances, a great deal remained undone and even untouchable. This predicament only further intensified the mounting quarrels over law, not least in the Italian Enlightenment's principal centers—Florence, Milan, and Naples. The law, most agreed, was in urgent need of reform; the difficulties and prolonged disagreement arose from the split between moderate and radical reform. Tuscan savants such as Ferdinando Paoletti (1717–1801), a disciple of Genovesi among the leading physiocratic *économistes* in Italy, Giovanni Fabroni (1752–1822), physiocrat, agriculturalist, and enthusiast for the American Revolution, and Filippo Mazzei (1730–1816), physician, friend of Jefferson, and a key propagator of republican *Américanisme* in Europe, all manifesting fierce impatience with the immense corpus of stiflingly archaic customary law, rendered Florence once more a hive of European intellectual debate and innovation—but within strict limits.

The entire Florentine academy was suddenly seized by the conviction that the essence of law has nothing to do with the great heaps of received jurisprudence, the

[72] Knuttel, *Verboden boeken*, 110–11.

[73] Rousseaux, "Doctrines criminelles," 230–5.

long-accumulated mounds of the customs of nations; rather, it was based, as Paoletti expressed it, "on a few, simple, true and unalterable principles" grounded not on authority, but "reason alone." What were needed and wanted were legal principles grounded on the laws of human nature and society endowed with the same clarity and certainty as the newly discovered laws of the physical universe.[74] Italian thinkers and savants of the High Enlightenment engaging in this debate ranged far and wide and, despite the ringing clatter of prohibitions resounding from Inquisition and the pulpit, experienced little difficulty in imbibing the arguments of the impressive flow of radical texts in French, entering via the well-developed clandestine book trade routes focused on Milan, Rome, Florence, and Naples.[75] Despite having declined noticeably, not only economically and in artistic and intellectual vitality since Renaissance times but having become intellectually quiescent, suddenly Tuscany, and especially the academy in Florence, spurred by the Grand Duchy's enlightened Habsburg ruler Leopold I (ruled: 1765–90), evinced a feverish impulse to ameliorate society with all manner of new initiatives, among them, in November 1786, abolition of the death penalty.[76]

Foremost among those spurring debate about legal reform, in Italy and throughout the Continent, was the figure who became Italy's most celebrated legal reformer, the Milanese marquis, Cesare di Beccaria, who concludes his famous treatise on crime and punishment, composed in 1763–4, with a striking general axiom: "in order that punishment should not be an act of violence perpetrated by one or many upon a private citizen, it is essential it should be public, speedy, necessary, the minimum possible in the given circumstances, *proporzionata a' delitti* [proportionate to the offenses], and determined by the law." This principle was both rational and just but also "poco conforme all'uso, legislatore il piu ordinario delle nazioni" [little conforms to custom—the most common legislator among nations].[77] This qualification was justified, but immediately placed his legal philosophy on collision course with Montesquieu, one of his chief sources, and—in his own intellectual circles—the soon influential philosophy of Hume, whose robust social and institutional conservatism had made him chief philosophical hero of one wing of the *coterie de Milan*, the group of Italian reformers with whom Beccaria consorted, as well as other Italian conservatives rejecting the radical path. Beccaria's, consequently, became a notably paradoxical stance: the two vying enlightenments fought, so to speak, within as well as around him.

Beccaria was trapped in an inescapable dilemma because the principles on which he based his reform proposals called in question the entire basis of privilege, legal and fiscal, as well as existing penal practice. One of his recommendations was that "assaults upon persons," as distinct from thefts without violence (which should be punished by monetary fines), should always entail corporal punishment or

[74] Quoted in Cochrane, *Tradition and Enlightenment*, 215.
[75] Venturi, *Pagine repubblicane*, 132.
[76] Venturi, *Illuministi Italiani* iii. 1091; Broers, *Napoleonic Mediterranean*, 114.
[77] Beccaria, *Of Crimes and Punishments*, 113.

imprisonment and not monetary fines so that "the rich and powerful should not be able to put a price on assaults on the weak and poor."[78] The wealthy or powerful man should not be able to expiate his crime with a sum substantial in the eyes of a destitute victim but trifling for a privileged miscreant and out of proportion to the penalty he would want exacted were anyone to do the like to him. Beccaria's principles rested on a conception of equality before the law and in matters of punishment (without which his hero Helvétius' utilitarian moral philosophy made no sense and had no application to law reform), and that, as many recognized at the time, comprehensively clashed with the principles of nobility and with ecclesiastical authority and the upholding of privilege.[79] Much crime, suggested Beccaria, was really the fault of the powerful and exalted, of an unequal society that encouraged it, albeit he was by no means as direct and explicit in asserting this as d'Holbach in his *Système social* (1773) and other works.[80]

Beccaria's entire approach, broadly in line with Helvétius, Diderot, and d'Holbach, contradicted the drift of Hume, Smith, and Ferguson, as did his theory of human progress with its insistence that man's natural right in the state of nature carries over into society, and optimism that, even though still far in the distance, mankind could look forward to "a state of equality and happiness," in times to come.[81] As for punishments specific to the nobility, Beccaria rejected such a principle outright, holding that "punishments ought be the same for the highest as for the lowest of citizens." To those claiming it is unjust to inflict the same punishment on a nobleman as a commoner given the difference in upbringing and the greater shame brought on an illustrious house, he replied that the "criterion of punishment is not the sensitivity of the criminal, but the harm done to the public which is all the greater when perpetrated by those who are more privileged."[82] Beccaria's reformist vision was simply incompatible with the requirements of the *ancien régime*. Yet, at the same time, he belonged to a cautious, relatively timid reforming clique at Milan and, like Pietro Verri, author of the *Meditazioni sulla felicità* (1763), relied heavily on the principle of strong, unrestricted, absolutism to carry through his agenda.

The noisy publicity and disagreements surrounding Beccaria's book, while a spectacular display of the Enlightenment's public reach, at the same time highlighted its internal divisions and contradictions, not least those implicit in Becccaria's own Enlightenment stance. The resulting international controversy was further amplified by several academy prize competitions focusing on law reform, notably those held in the late 1770s at Berne and Châlons-sur-Marne. The much-discussed Berne competition commenced in 1776, promoted by the local *société économique* following the intervention of an eminent anonymous Frenchman (Voltaire), who was impressed

[78] Beccaria, *Of Crimes and Punishments*, 50.
[79] Tortarolo, *L'Illuminismo*, 162; Ferrone, *Società giusta*, 115.
[80] D'Holbach, *Systeme social*, 437–8.
[81] Beccaria, "Pensieri," 106–12; Venturi, *Riformatori Lombardi*, 15.
[82] Beccaria, *Of Crimes and Punishments*, 52.

with Beccaria's *Delle delitti e delle pene* [Of Crimes and Punishments]. By then Beccaria's work had been republished several times in Italy and France, with three editions at Livorno, in 1764, 1765, and 1766, and had come to exert a wide impact either side of the Atlantic. The last edition to which the author himself contributed—that today judged the fullest and most correct—was an Italian-language edition issued at Haarlem in 1766, precisely a decade before the Berne competition. Voltaire endowed a prize of 50 *louis d'or*,[83] for the best contribution on the theme of penal reform composed in the spirit of the celebrated author of *Delle delitti e delle pene*, a prize the value of which was then supplemented by Frederick the Great and other donors.

Voltaire had composed his laudatory *Commentaire sur le livre Des Délits et Des Peines*, a much-noticed text that, by fulsomely disparaging the "barbaric" processes of legal procedure current in France, had helped make Beccaria the focus of the Europe-wide furore over law reform a whole decade earlier, in September 1766. Voltaire's role underlined the topicality, urgency, and importance of the burgeoning controversy but contributed little to the debate about the basic principles of law and punishment as such.[84] More substantial was Condorcet's denunciation of crude "punishments by the wheel or by fire," "torture and other useless cruelties," in 1775, in his *Reflexions sur la jurisprudence criminelle*, a text that clearly absorbed much from Beccaria. Wise legislators must suppress cruel and irrational laws that barbarize the civil order and the law, and provoke onlookers' natural sympathies for the offender without effectively curbing crime levels. A glaring example were the French laws relating to suppression of salt-trafficking to evade the salt taxes, stipulating nine years of galley service for a first offense and hanging and strangling for the second, It was hard to comprehend, urged Condorcet, how any such penalties could be enacted by human beings against their fellows. Presumably, tax-farmers did not think salt-traffickers "human."[85] The *gabelle* legislation "barbarities," and whole swathes of *ancien régime* legislation rooted in feudal privilege and narrow fiscal and commercial interest, required close scrutiny on the basis of a proper appreciation of the claims of human nature and human rights. These should be the guiding principles in civil and criminal legislation but were being systematically ignored and abused.

The Berne prize was for the best analysis and evaluation of Beccaria's principles, a competition open to all and guaranteed by the Society's prize committee to be judged free from all outside or local political interference. Competitors had to formulate the principles of a complete system of legislation encompassing criminal justice, including the question of proportionate punishment, issues of investigation, evidence, and proof, and maximum protection of the public. Although the competition proved a great success in terms of further fixing attention on both Beccaria and Berne, evaluating and judging the forty-six entries, submitted mostly from France,

[83] Röthlin, "Société économique," 172; De Champs, *Enlightenment and Utility*, 59–60.
[84] Davidson, *Voltaire in Exile*, 144, 149, 151–2; Loft, *Passion, Politics*, 111, 117.
[85] Baker, *Condorcet*, 231; Williams, *Condorcet*, 179–81.

Germany, and Switzerland, proved so onerous, the clash of principles so troubling, and interference from outside in fact so obtrusive, that the business dragged on far longer than anyone originally anticipated.

Problematic for the Enlightenment from the start, Beccaria's epoch-making book found itself caught in the strange quandary of being neither fully permitted by Europe's secular and ecclesiastical authorities, nor generally prohibited. Voltaire lived to hear that Beccaria's book had been publicly burned by the Inquisition, in Madrid (as he informed Catherine the Great, in July 1777), but died, in May 1778, several years before the prize committee, wading through conflicting pressures, finally managed, after an immense delay, on 23 March 1782, to announce the winners. Likewise, at Châlons, the competition drew distinctly more interest than that relatively minor academy's activities normally attracted,[86] but mounting political and judicial pressure from outside again greatly complicated the process. Brissot exaggerated later with his remark that at this "faible et médiocre" academy *le despotisme* stifled all ideas, but Louis XVI's minister, Vergennes, in the early 1780s, certainly applied pressure both to reduce future publicity surrounding French provincial academies' prize competitions and ensure entries were not published without royal authorization.[87]

It had been a royal minister, Malesherbes, director-general of the French censorship, himself, who, behind the scenes, had originally encouraged Morellet to translate Beccaria into French, providing his own copy, freshly received from Italy, for the purpose.[88] Writing to Beccaria, from Paris, in January 1766, Morellet reported having discussed his ideas, at length, with Diderot, who had important observations to make, as well as d'Holbach, Helvétius, Hume, and Buffon, who all also supposedly thoroughly approved.[89] There was no alternative to the French version being published illicitly, though, given the need to avoid prohibition and suppression by the *parlements*. Malesherbes, however, ensured tacit permission for the work to circulate in France. All this, Morellet confided many years later, in 1802, on the publication of the first Greek version of Beccaria's treatise by the philologist, Adamantios Korais. Beccaria's appearing in French was thus originally the outcome of a part court and part *philosophe* collusion designed to foment criticism of the legal profession and the *parlements* but without directly implicating the French monarch or court. Endorsed by Malesherbes, Beccaria's masterpiece eventually came out in two different French editions, in December 1765, at Amsterdam and at Paris (with a title-page specifying "Lausanne").

Officially, Beccaria nevertheless permanently remained banned, in *ancien régime* France, due to its scathing, disrespectful criticism of the existing judiciary and laws.[90]

[86] Roche, "Diffusion des Lumières," 899–901.
[87] Roche, "Diffusion des Lumières," 907.
[88] Morellet to Korais, 19 Feb. 1802, in Morellet, *Lettres* ii. 328–9; Trousson and Vercruysse, *Dictionnaire général*, 225–7.
[89] Morellet to Beccaria, Paris, 3 Jan. 1766, in Morellet, *Lettres* i. 36, 39, 51.
[90] Venturi, *Riformatori Lombardi*, 18.

It had appeared also in English, in 1767, and in other editions, including a key version in Spanish, of 1774, translated by Juan Antonio de las Casas, banned by the Inquisition three years later, and in German, appearing at Ulm in 1778. While the reception was generally enthusiastic in French enlightened circles, Beccaria found himself vehemently attacked by conservative jurists and more than a few erudite moderate Enlightenment commentators, especially in Italy. His adversaries included the learned Milanese jurist, Paolo Vergani (1753–1820), who expressed profound unease especially over Beccaria's patently deriving his guiding philosophical principles neither from religion nor established legal texts but purely from the "suppositions" of the French *philosophes modernes*. Another prominent detractor was the highly competent Neapolitan jurist, Giandonato Rogadeo (1718–84), summoned, in 1777, by the Grand Master of the Knights of Malta to reform the laws of his order along firm Catholic Enlightenment lines, which he did with energy; Rogadeo similarly deemed Beccaria's book insidious and recommended that governments should ban it.[91] But if Beccaria's innumerable enthusiastic readers mostly had little grasp of its underlying implications, of his approach's connection with radical thought, his success still represented a coup for the radical perspective.

Unsurprisingly, Beccaria had more success in impressing some royal ministers than jurists and magistrates. The Austrian authorities in Milan secured him his professorship in "cameral sciences" and then, in 1771, a place on the government's economic council for Lombardy. European governments made little attempt to disguise the extent to which they were influenced by Beccaria when drawing up proposals for legal reform. Catherine II of Russia, spurred by Voltaire and Grimm, extravagantly praised his work and, in late 1766, invited him to Petersburg to help supervise a commission newly charged with drawing up the principles of the new Russian penal code. Beccaria declined, as d'Alembert advised, preferring to stay in Milan, due partly to his marked distaste for established legal terminology and the legal profession, but also due to his innate reserve and caution; still his influence on Catherine's ideas for legal reform in Russia undeniably proved extensive.[92]

The initiative of the Austrian administration in Brussels, in the late 1760s, to abolish judicial torture and branding in the southern Netherlands (Belgium), was patently inspired by his work, though here too the reform was partly blocked by a resisting local judiciary.[93] In 1767, the Danish king reformed Denmark's laws on murder along lines proposed by Beccaria and, in 1771, prompted by his radical-minded minister Struensee, abolished judicial torture together with capital punishment for theft and robbery.[94] During his visit to Paris, as crown prince, in 1770 the future Gustav III of Sweden met both Morellet and d'Alembert and discussed

[91] Vergani, *Traité*, Introduction, pp. xxv, xxxiv–xxxvi; Ciappara, *Enlightenment and Reform in Malta*, 64.

[92] Venturi, *Riformatori Lombardi*, 18–19; De Champs, *Enlightenment and Utility*, 59; Dixon, *Catherine the Great*, 157, 223; Zaretsky, *Catherine and Diderot*, 83, 86.

[93] Rousseaux, "Doctrines criminelles," 231–3.

[94] Tamm, "Beccaria," 190–1, 193.

Beccaria with them; later, as king of Sweden, he finally abolished judicial torture in Sweden–Finland, expressly citing Beccaria's influence on the measure.[95]

Figuring among the great literary successes of the Enlightenment, but deemed illicit in many quarters, Beccaria's book nevertheless infiltrated courts and officialdom and powerfully moved the enlightened general reader. In one fell swoop, he tarred the Western world's entire legal culture as backward, irrational, and unjustly vengeful, though this cut little ice with the unenlightened and those opposing the Enlightenment. It was plain from the outset, though, that "enlightened despotism" would adopt his recommendations at best in only a highly selective fashion and even then, as Catherine and her pro-Enlightenment supporters found in Russia, faced by intractable local judicial and noble resistance, had to cut back further.[96] The radical coterie in Paris, seeing little could be hoped for from "enlightened" circles in government and the *parlements* in France, concentrated on winning over public opinion. "Mon cher ami," Morellet assured Beccaria, in a letter of July 1766, railing against the obscurantism and fanaticism of France's *parlements*, "c'est sur l'opinion publique qu'il faut compter" [it is on public opinion that we must count]. Neither Voltaire, d'Alembert, nor Rousseau, nor Beccaria, nor any *philosophe* he averred, could directly influence those who govern; he and his colleagues must work with public opinion. As Morellet summed up the Diderot's group's strategy: "l'opinion publique subjuguera enfin les fanatiques et même les tyrants" [finally public opinion will subjugate the fanatics and even the tyrants].[97]

Yet the situation hardly looked promising from this viewpoint either. If, initially, radicals expected Beccaria to help swing the *coterie de Milan* behind the Diderot–d'Holbach circle in Paris, this expectation withered with the then 26-year-old Beccaria's Paris visit of October 1766, which proved a disappointing failure. Beccaria's timid, hesitant public stance, and deference to the church and enlightened despots, were not the only features, it soon turned out, Diderot found to criticize. Congratulating him on his "âme noble et généreuse," Diderot (who had spent months inside a Parisian prison himself) pronounced Beccaria's humanity and compassion for criminals awaiting punishment a fine thing but refused to agree it should outweigh the need to protect society from "des brigands et des assassins:" it was vital to avoid harming society via "une fausse compassion."[98] Beccaria rightly argued that a regular diet of brutal floggings and executions can only brutalize and barbarize the public, but his approach seemed too simplistic. The broad reaction to Beccaria, he suggested in the *Correspondance littéraire*, in August 1771, had been overly enthusiastic and in part perverse. Despite freely borrowing some of Beccaria's ideas himself, he was unconvinced his book "was as important or its fund of ideas as true, as was being claimed."[99] "I do not intend to remove from [Beccaria's] *Dei delitti e delle pene* the human

[95] Tamm, "Beccaria", 193–4. [96] Dixon, *Catherine the Great*, 198–9.

[97] Morellet to Beccaria, Paris, July 1766, in Morellet, *Lettres* i. 59.

[98] Morellet to Beccaria, Paris, July 1766, in Morellet, *Lettres* i. 59.

[99] Mortier, "Diderot and Penal Law," 210; Hope Mason, *Irresistible Diderot*, 334.

character which has brought it so great a success," he added, when commenting on the Russian *Nakaz* in 1772–4; he was as much concerned as anyone to aid the innocent, and thoroughly agreed that "there is no true sovereign except the nation." But Beccaria's recommendations risked losing the exemplary effect of harsh punishment. Fewer than 150 men were put to death each year in Paris, noted Diderot, while in all the courts of France scarcely that number were tortured, yielding 300 cases among a population of 25 million.[100] Beccaria had got the balance wrong. Corruption, bogus medicine, and other faults were wreaking far more havoc than a handful of executions and judicial torture. Sparing the life of a defendant is right in trials for murder where there is doubt but not otherwise.[101]

The weaknesses of Beccaria's principles, Diderot admonished the Russian empress, were serious and as yet had "not received any attention."[102] Despite Beccaria, capital punishment should be retained while restricting its use to a minimum and expanding confinement in cells and hard labor.[103] But Diderot's prime reservation was that in his view discussing crime and punishment made little sense without critically examining the wider social context. "A society should first of all be rendered happy;" and would be happy "if liberty and property were assured," if trade were unrestricted, if all orders of citizens were equally subject to the laws, if taxes are paid progressively, according to resources, well-distributed, and do not exceed the needs of the state—and "if virtue and talents are well rewarded."[104] Beccaria's precept: "do you want to prevent crimes? Spread enlightenment" prompted Diderot to respond that this is true but if one sincerely proposes to reduce crime, rendering a ruler's subjects happy would accomplish still more. "If crimes are committed today, is it through lack of enlightenment?" More crimes were committed in Paris in one day than in all the forests of a primitive people in some remote land in a year. From this Diderot, like d'Holbach, concluded "that a badly ordered society is worse than man's primitive condition." By the late 1760s, even Catherine was beginning to lose confidence in Diderot as she perceived the growing radicalization of his politics.[105]

The gap between the Diderot circle and the *coterie de Milan* became wider, the clearer it became that it was to "enlightened despotism" alone that Beccaria looked to undertake the task of clearing the legal debris of the centuries and reorganizing law and punishment on a principled, rational basis. For Beccaria and Verri, like Gorani at that time and the young Neapolitan legal reformer, Gaetano Filangieri, in his first book, of 1774, very differently from Diderot, Helvétius, and d'Holbach (and Mazzei) in the 1770s, there was a need for the unrestricted strengthening of monarchical power, which, Beccaria hoped, would overcome the opposition his proposals for law reform universally provoked among legal professionals and the privileged elites. "This

[100] Mortier, "Diderot and Penal Law," 209–10; Trousson, Denis *Diderot*, 393; Hope Mason, *Irresistible Diderot*, 334, 337.

[101] Diderot, *Political Writings*, 119.

[102] Diderot, *Political Writings*, 119; Bellamy, "Introduction," p. xxvii.

[103] Mortier, "Diderot and Penal Law," 209.

[104] Diderot, *Political Writings*, 124.

[105] Diderot, *Political Writings*, 123; Dixon, *Catherine the Great*, 225–7.

is the ground," he argued, "for enlightened citizens all the more fervently to desire that their [i.e. the enlightened despots'] authority will go on increasing."[106] While the young Beccaria aimed to diffuse enlightened ideas as widely as possible, agreeing enlighteners should establish clubs and their own journals, like the Milanese periodical *Il Caffé,* to forge a public arena of opinion and debate, the forum he and his friends actually established was distinctly narrow, just a handful of state functionaries, enlightened aristocrats, and affluent men of leisure.[107]

Beccaria, then, was decidedly among those "great artisans" of the Revolution, who introduced potentially revolutionary ideas, sweeping away all earlier structures, aided the vast mental revolution whereby "philosophy" prepared the ground for the French Revolution, as De Tocqueville later recognized,[108] but rejected the method of "revolution" by spreading intellectual subversion among the intelligentsia—Spinoza's, and later Diderot's and d'Holbach's, preferred method—in favor of enlightened despotism. The Berne prize competition only deepened the fissures rendering the entire topic chronically fraught. The Berne committee jurists loudly celebrated Beccaria's achievement and the stimulus given to law reform, but proved unable to embrace the principles at the heart of his legacy which were in essence egalitarian and radical, principles ultimately incompatible with the system of social hierarchy and enlightened despotism onto which the Milanese coterie around him, and Beccaria himself, wished to graft it. His ideas were bound to generate conflict between the need for far-reaching reform and existing social and political reality which he himself sought to paper over. Even Bentham, far less radical then than later, thought his Milanese predecessor had gone too far: Beccaria's treatise is not just openly egalitarian, he observed, but undermines prevailing laws relating to property, a feature the pre-1789 Bentham was by no means inclined to countenance.[109]

Among the prize competition competitors at Berne were two young *philosophes* later to figure among the front rank of the French revolutionary leadership—Jacques-Pierre Brissot de Warville (who also entered the Châlons competition), and Jean-Paul Marat. Brissot, whose Châlons entry, *Moyens d'adoucir la rigueur des loix pénales en France,* was published there under the competition's auspices in 1781, eventually gave up awaiting the long-delayed Berne result, and published his *Théorie des lois criminelles* himself. Crimes against property, he agreed, stemmed from gross inequalities of wealth; issues of crime and punishment could not be separated from their social context and certainly, following Beccaria, capital punishment should be abolished. To avoid the French royal censorship, he published his treatise in the Protestant Swiss town of Neuchâtel, also in 1781.[110] Marat brought out his *Plan de législation en matière criminelle* in 1785, in the same town.

[106] Beales, "Philosophical Kingship," 516–17; Ricuperati, *Frontiere e limiti,* 24–5.
[107] Venturi, *Riformatori Lombardi,* 3. [108] Rahe, *Soft Despotism,* 159.
[109] Blamires, "Beccaria," 80; Lascoumes, "Beccaria," 112–13.
[110] Loft, *Passion, Politics,* 120–1; Röthlin, "Societe économique," 172.

Brissot's anti-establishment *Théorie des lois criminelles* (1781) in the event deprived him of all prospect of a law career; but it built his international reputation as a reformer.[111] Eventually himself to die by public execution, he fervently denounced the death penalty for violating both natural right and society's well-being, a view rejected by the foremost Spanish jurist to enter the international debate, Don Manuel de Lardizábal y Uribe (1739–1820), a member of the royal council in Madrid and admirer of Montesquieu (whom he continually invokes), who regularly cites Brissot among Beccaria's principal disciples in legal reform.[112] Lardizábal borrowed several of Beccaria's arguments for his reform proposals and plea for proportional punishments, and wanted to remove the death penalty for fraudulent bankruptcy, non-violent robbery, and other lesser crimes, and hence shared some notions with radical writers like d'Holbach and Brissot while remaining hostile to their underlying conception of society, morality, and religion. Since study of philosophy, as well as morality and politics, he observed in 1782, had "enlightened minds more," moderating older attitudes and customs, men had learnt to know the "value of human life and human freedom substituting this for slavery and, likewise, humanity and gentleness for severity and rigor," making it everywhere necessary to reform the laws of crime and punishment.[113] From "philosophy" had arisen "una fermentación general" [a general fermentation], commencing in Europe, ushering in "una feliz revolución" [a happy revolution] of fundamental legal reform in Russia, Germany, Sweden, Poland, and Tuscany.[114] Among key participants Lardizábal cites the Habsburg Emperor, Joseph II, especially praising his efforts to abolish serfdom.

There was much to applaud—however, as a court official, Lardizábal was acutely aware that he had to oppose several of Beccaria's chief principles and cites Beccaria's book as much to rebuke as to praise him.[115] His own more conservative legal reformism, demanding abolition of judicial amputation and mutilation but by no means all flogging,[116] he pronounced better suited to royal absolutism and Catholic Christianity, the religion that best restrains, as Montesquieu showed, ill-conduct and despotism and which he had vowed to uphold.[117] Suspicious of Beccaria's and Brissot's egalitarian tendency, Lardizábal, later among the firmest ultra-absolutists among Spain's jurists during the Napoleonic Wars, roundly rejected Beccaria's (and Helvétius', Diderot's, and d'Holbach's) principle that sovereignty derives from every member of society individually and equally, via the social pact, and that this of itself justifies ending the death penalty and standardizing punishments for identical offenses for all.[118] Beccaria's, Helvétius', d'Holbach's, and Brissot's principle that harm to civil society or public order, and to individuals, constitutes the exclusive concern of the law, all else being devices of despotism or superstition,[119] he reviled as

[111] François-Primo, *Jeunesse*, 85–6.
[112] Lardizábal y Uribe, *Discurso*, 59, 182.
[113] Lardizábal y Uribe, *Discurso*, pp. viii–ix.
[114] Lardizábal y Uribe, *Discurso*, p. x.
[115] Lardizábal y Uribe, *Discurso*, 76, 99–102.
[116] Lardizábal y Uribe, *Discurso*, 188–90, 195–6.
[117] Lardizábal y Uribe, *Discurso*, 27–31; Sarrailh, *L'Espagne eclairée*, 537.
[118] Lardizábal y Uribe, *Discurso*, 167–9, 177, 180–1; La Parra, *Fernando VII*, 254, 267, 311.
[119] Lardizábal y Uribe, *Discurso*, 102, 140.

excessively secular, acceptable to neither church nor prince. Equally, he rejected Beccaria's and Brissot's principle that nobles, commoners, and slaves must suffer identical punishment for the same offenses. He espoused far-reaching legal reform up to a point, but would not budge from insisting nobles must continue to be punished and imprisoned differently from commoners.[120]

Beccaria's legal philosophy derived in particular from Helvétius' maxim that punishment and penal legislation should be grounded in reason, and stem from careful analysis. Endorsed by Filangieri in Italy, similar principles were subsequently taken up also, in Britain, in his *Introduction to the Principles of Morals and Legislation* (1781), by Bentham, who opens by signaling his opposition to theology as a criterion in ethics or legislation, and laying down the principle that "private ethics has happiness for this end; and legislation can have no other."[121] A central rule in Bentham's elaboration of the foundations laid by Helvétius, Beccaria, and the Brothers Verri was that the cost of a punishment to the criminal must suffice to outweigh the profit resulting from his misdemeanor. Beccaria's principle that certainty of punishment matters more than severity and that proportionality is essential in matching punishments to crimes, a principle he developed but in essence borrowed from Montesquieu,[122] Bentham considered correct, although he disliked his contractarian theory of society (actually one of its strengths). Bentham eventually succeeded in going considerably further in determining appropriate punishments and quantifying society's interest, and the social costs, in particular solutions for specific cases.

Bentham's doctrine of punishment revised Becccaria especially by reducing the entire topic of penal reform to four clear rules. First, the essential object must be to "prevent, in as far as possible, and worth while, all sorts of offences whatsoever," by "offences" meaning acts seeming to the sovereign "to have a tendency to produce mischief." Second, the aim must be to persuade those who offend "to commit an offence less mischievous, rather than one more mischievous," that is, to choose always the least mischievous of two offences either of which will suit one's purpose. The third rule was to seek to dispose the offender bent on offending "to do no more mischief than is necessary to his purpose: in other words to do as little mischief as is consistent with the benefit he has in view;" and the fourth, "whatever the mischief be, which it is proposed to prevent, to prevent it at as cheap a rate as possible."[123]

At Berne, perhaps inevitably, the eventual result of the prize competition proved profoundly disappointing, a thoroughgoing anticlimax. Deciding to play safe and timidly eschew the controversial general principles embedded in Beccaria, the committee ignored the *philosophes* and *amis de l'humanité* entirely, awarding the prize to two professional jurists from Saxony, Hans Ernst von Globig and Johann Georg Huster, for their legalistic *Abhandlung von der Criminal-Gesetzgebung* (Zurich, 1783). The prize committee's preference was for a text that said nothing at all about basic principles, society, religion, or the laws of marriage. The Berne prize was hence

[120] Lardizábal y Uribe, *Discurso*, 144–5, 214. [121] Bentham, *Principles of Morals*, 313.
[122] Felice, *Per una scienza universale*, 102–3, 105, 111. [123] Bentham, *Principles of Morals*, 178.

awarded, precisely to avoid facing the implications, blatantly contrary to the spirit of Beccaria's principles, which in effect boiled down to Helvétius' central principle, that the law and society's institutions exist for the greatest good of the greatest number. Inspired chiefly by Helvétius, but utilizing also Rousseau and Montesquieu, Beccaria contended that the goal of all good legislation is to guide men to their greatest happiness possible, or least unhappiness, taking into account all the blessings and evils of life, which means that all attempts hitherto employed in making criminal legislation had been misconceived or were "contrary to the proposed goal."[124] He based his argument on a particular conception of the social contract, conceiving each person as joining with every other to form the state specifically to protect themselves from disorder and unruliness, and their property from intruders and marauders; from this, he inferred both the state's protective role and his rule that no sovereign is ever justified in taking any person's life—which he shared with Brissot but not Diderot.

[124] Beccaria, *Of Crimes and Punishments*, 103; De Champs, *Enlightenment and Utility*, 58.

14

Unity of Humanity

Race Theory and the Equality of Peoples

14.1. ENLIGHTENMENT AND THE ADVENT OF RACE THEORIES

Declaring the basic unity and equality of all mankind, rejecting hierarchy, social and confessional but also racial, infused all the Radical Enlightenment's dimensions. The only kind of hierarchy admissible under its "universal and equal rights" criteria were cumulative "degrees of enlightenment," levels of civilization. Its basic egalitarian thrust ensured an inherent tendency towards anti-colonialism, a central feature of d'Holbach as well as of late Diderot, and Raynal.[1] By contrast, enlighteners identifying with the existing European and overseas colonial order on the basis of moderate Enlightenment principles were logically drawn to arguments legitimating empire and dominion of particular peoples over others. For moderates, in the fraught conditions of the revolutionary era, racial theory added a compelling means of reinforcing their generally hierarchical approach, supplementing older, more traditional, legalistic, and constitutional arguments for dominion, empire, and the status quo. Gradually, more explicit, supposedly scientific theories of racial differentiation and innate superiority of particular races over others surfaced, thereby more closely attaching race theory to justifications of imperial sway.

A rhetoric of race bias was also employed in a less argued, cruder fashion, by those indifferent to any kind of Enlightenment but strongly supportive of the existing order and, after around 1780, deeply alarmed by the advance of abolitionism and the new revolutionary pressures. But while apologists for black slavery often insisted on the alleged lower intelligence, initiative and dignity, and supposedly lower or "animal" character, and uninhibited sexuality, of African captives shipped to American shores, relying on mere assertion without pretense of "scientific" proof, moderate Enlightenment claims needed more sophisticated, reasoned arguments for maintaining the black race were "naturally inferior," as Hume put it,[2] or that other races were all

[1] Blank, "D'Holbach on Self-Esteem," 443–4, 450, 452.

[2] Berry, *Social Theory*, 81.

inferior to the whites. Rising against such claims, the *Histoire philosophique* and radical circles generally contended that the New World's black slaves were indeed abject and degraded but only owing to the barbaric, despicable treatment they had received, abasement that would last no longer than their being trapped in servitude to whites. Black degradation ensued from subjection, merciless exploitation by their captors and tormentors. Slaves were limited in outlook and often mean-minded, granted Diderot, but only because the vile despotism of slavery blights all natural energy and creativeness of the soul. Some black slaves could be found willing to acknowledge the supposed natural dominance and higher intelligence of the whites, a proclivity defenders of slavery sometimes sought to exploit, but only because white sway perpetuated their ignorance and unjust subjection.[3]

A war of ideologies focusing on the principle of equality naturally emerged against the backcloth of colonial expansion and the racially hierarchical character of the colonial social system in Africa, the Americas, and parts of Asia. Social pressures, exploitation, and resentment inevitably found expression in what by the 1770s was conscious, open intellectual warfare. Where Delisle de Sales, following the *Histoire philosophique*, bitterly condemned the cruel *sophisme* that blacks are of a lower order of intelligence than whites, the Jesuit father, Pierre-François-Xavier de Charlevoix, author of the four-volume *Histoire de l'Isle Espagnole ou de S. Domingue* (Paris, 1730)—or "roman" as Delisle derided it—held that all the blacks of Guinea "naissoient stupides" [were born stupid], that most could not count beyond three, and that lack of intelligence justified slavery, which Delisle dismissed as grotesque calumny.[4] In reality, black peoples, answered Raynal's following, are as gifted and intelligent as any. Admittedly, blacks do not compose *livres philosophiques*, but free them, provide education, and you will soon see Africans studying at university. The first book written by a black should, logically, be a "manifeste pour la liberté contre ses tyrans" [manifesto for liberty against his tyrants], but it would assuredly fail to make the stifled voice of truth heard and be viciously suppressed, doubtless burnt, in all Europe's capitals "pour s"épargner la peine d'y répondre" [to save the bother of replying].[5]

Earlier in the century, jurists had frequently sought to justify slavery in natural law and international legal terms, employing arguments for slavery afforded by Grotius, Pufendorf, Ulricus Huber, and Locke, natural law exponents also well-qualified to legitimate theories of empire. For these writers, slave-owners' property rights over slaves were more or less straightforwardly derived from their having been sold to slave-dealers, and then their owners.[6] Diderot, Raynal, Deleyre, Pechméja, d'Holbach, Delisle, Cloots, and Brissot dismissed such approaches as just one more

[3] *Histoire philosophique* (1780) vi. 203–7; Cherni, *Diderot*, 418–19; Muthu, *Enlightenment*, 92–3, 105, 108–9.

[4] Delisle de Sales, *Philosophie de la nature* iv. 191–2.

[5] Delisle de Sales, *Philosophie de la nature* iv. 193; Diderot, *Political Writings*, 176–7, 186.

[6] Delisle de Sales, *Philosophie de la nature* iv. 190–1; Davis, *Problem of Slavery*, 474; Thomas, *Slave Trade*, 449.

wretched *sophisme*: by what absurd logic, demanded Delisle, could anyone tolerate a jurisprudence claiming "a free man can sell himself?"[7] It has been claimed that "very few *philosophes* became abolitionists;" this is wrong, a substantial number did, from the 1760s onwards—but only those adhering to "universal and equal rights" following Diderot, d'Holbach, and Raynal. Among the abysmal features of existing legal systems, held radical thinkers, were the compilation of voluminous slave and racial codes devised by locally dominant British, French, Dutch, Danes, Spaniards, Portuguese, and, after 1776, the whites of the newly independent United States' southern states. Such codes were recent, systematic, drafted at the highest level, buttressed by theology, and within their own terms seemingly coherent, but according to radical principles abominably unjust.[8]

France's royal *Code Noir*, first enacted by Colbert, in 1685, fixed the regulations governing slavery and black status in the French Caribbean territories, defining the terms of the slave trade and master and slave relations, and requiring slave-owners to ensure their slaves' baptism and performance of religious duties, forbidding teaching of any religion other than Catholicism. Many of the eventually considerably expanded *Code Noir*'s provisions were elaborated much later though, during the early, mid, or late eighteenth century. The 1767 edition contained 446 pages. Conceived originally for the French Caribbean colonies, its provisions, trapping every child, legitimate or illegitimate, of a slave mother in lifelong slavery, later encompassed the vast Louisiana territory and, from 1709, also Quebec.[9] Such slave codes invariably stipulated draconian restrictions, severe whippings and floggings for infraction, especially forbidding unauthorized movement and assembly—secret meetings most of all—as well as possession or bearing of firearms or other weapons, and all Voodoo and other unchristian rituals, beside any sort of insolent or threatening behavior. Another regular feature were bans on mixed marriage and all sexual contact between whites and slaves. Despotic the *Code Noir* undoubtedly was; but it was by no means the severest of its kind. The Dutch and British, claimed the *Histoire philosophique*, were the two colonizing powers that treated their black slaves worst. Jamaica's black code gained the reputation of being the Caribbean's most oppressive, and that of South Carolina North America's severest.[10]

Such systems of legal oppression were a form of institutionalized violence seemingly bound to nurture retaliatory violence in their wake. What the Diderot of the late 1770s considered the inevitable response of black revolt would, one day, overturn the Caribbean supremacy of the Spaniards, British, French, Dutch, Portuguese, and Danes alike, he predicted, and spread to adjoining regions, a process already beginning, he believed, in the hills of Jamaica and interior of Surinam.[11] In Surinam, where,

[7] Delisle de Sales, *Philosophie de la nature* iv. 191.
[8] Diderot, *Political Writings*, 212–13; Benot, *Diderot*, 254–6; Furbank, *Diderot*, 417.
[9] Regent, *France et ses esclaves*, 64–5; Trudel, *Deux siècles d'esclavage*, 49–52.
[10] Morgan, "Black Experience," 475; Régent, *France et ses esclaves*, 64–5.
[11] *Histoire philosophique* (1780) ix. 470; Tarin, *Diderot*, 38–9.

in 1754, 33,000 slaves were owned by only 1,441 whites, by 1780 no less than 60,000 black slaves were to be found toiling mostly on the colony's now 430 sugar, coffee, cocoa, and cotton plantations, subject to a mere 2,824 slave-owners. Trying to counter the relative ease of escape into the interior, Surinam plantation-owners reportedly held their slaves in even crueler captivity than was usual elsewhere, but without this halting the seepage of sizable numbers of "ces déplorables victimes d'une avarice infâme" [deplorable victims of an infamous avarice] into the forests.[12] Dutch retaliatory raiding parties hunted these "maroons" (runaways) deep in the tropical interior without being able to suppress them.

A measure of maroon "independence" had had to be accepted. Some black fugitives adjusted to living peacefully in their own villages; others formed roaming brigand bands that mounted pillaging forays against white-owned plantations.[13] Differently from in Catholic lands, there was scant pressure in Surinam to Christianize the blacks and, among slave-owners, some disinclination to do so, as instruction in a faith laying such emphasis on reading and understanding Scripture as Calvinism must elevate the slaves' awareness, and render it harder to keep them subservient.[14] Unlike the German missionaries, sent by the Moravian Brethren, who actively missionized among the slaves of the Dutch colonies from the early eighteenth century onwards, the Dutch Reformed Church remained largely inactive in this regard. Highly negative, scornful assessments of black moral capabilities were then routinely justified by pointing to their lack of Christian belief and devotion. Religious and moral segregation helped bolster slavery by keeping the question of black subjection out of the public eye in the Netherlands where, unlike in Britain, France, and United States, there was remarkably scant public debate about slavery during the century's last quarter even when the Patriot movement and the Batavian Revolution (1794–1806) were at their height.[15]

Diderot's charge that the British treated the blacks worse than the French was seconded by Adam Smith: "as the profit and success of the cultivation which is carried on with cattle depend very much upon the good management of those cattle, so the profit and success of that which is carried on by slaves must depend equally upon the good management of those slaves; and in the good management of their slaves the French planters, I think it is generally allowed, are superior to the English." For insofar as the law "gives some weak protection to the slave against the violence of his master," it is "likely to be better executed in a colony where the government is in a great measure arbitrary, than in one where it is altogether free." When marginally protecting the slave, French royal officials were in some measure interfering with his master's property whereas in what Smith termed "a free country, where the master is

[12] *Histoire philosophique* (1780) vi. 402–3; Postma, *Dutch*, 185, 213.
[13] *Histoire philosophique* (1780) vi. 421–2.
[14] Oostindie, "Enlightenment, Christianity," 154–6, 158.
[15] Oostindie, "Enlightenment, Christianity," 150, 157, 159.

perhaps either a member of the colony assembly, or an elector of such a member, [the magistrate] dare not do this but with the greatest caution and circumspection."[16]

Revolt, violence, and eventually black individual and community independence, held radical enlighteners, was the natural, inevitable, and desirable response to the institutionalized legal tyranny Europe's empires had imposed—and was already beginning. As all peoples desire to be happy and possess the right to look forward to their future happiness, so all peoples "are free by right," as d'Holbach expressed it, "even if often slaves in fact."[17] If most men passively submit to misery and oppression, this was chiefly due to the continuing prevalence of "superstition," ignorance, and credulity that equip greed and rapacity to hold the majority in chains. Racial prejudice counted, in their eyes, among the vilest strands of an all-pervasive web of credulity and ignorance—the essential structure upholding tyranny and oppression everywhere. Condemning the contempt Europeans had always shown "for men of another colour," Condorcet took particular pride in the French Revolution's having, from an early stage, moved beyond the American Revolution in applying that Revolution's own principles—in repudiating tradition, prejudice, and social hierarchy.[18] It was *la philosophie moderne*—certainly not religion or the French judiciary—that led the way, and first and most comprehensively declared war on the crimes, greed and rapacity of colonial sway. It was "modern philosophy" alone that produced whites deeming it an honor to be called "friends" of the blacks whom their "stupides tyrans" scorned to include among the ranks of men.[19]

The British empire came to represent, for the Radical Enlightenment, unlike the moderate mainstream, a particularly reprehensible segment of the system of world oppression, a ubiquitous and pernicious extension of the ills spread by empire generally. It was an empire based on a dangerous imperial lust rooted in what Condorcet called "prejugés commerciaux" and the Englishman's "respect superstitieux" for a highly defective monarchical constitution and equally highly defective laws.[20] "L'Anglois, ennemi de la tyrannie chez lui" [the Englishman, the enemy of tyranny at home], remarked Diderot, in 1774, becomes "le despote le plus féroce quand il en est dehors" [the most ferocious despot when abroad].[21] If Diderot thought the blacks more wretchedly exploited and traded in by Britain than any other power, he saw the same ruthless avidity in the ascendancy of the Anglo-Irish aristocracy and London's merchants over Ireland.[22]

Fundamental to the Radical Enlightenment approach was the idea that humanity, for all its diversity, is one and that, despite immense differences in cultural level, in awareness and unawareness of "true" moral and philosophical principles, all peoples reflect the same psychological motivation, desires, rights, ability, potential, and basic

[16] Smith, *Wealth of Nations* ii. 165.

[17] D'Holbach, *Politique naturelle*, 294; Helvétius, *De l'Homme* i. 427–8; Blank, "D'Holbach on Self-Esteem," 450.

[18] Condorcet, *Esquisse*, 332.

[19] Condorcet, *Esquisse*, 205, 266, 277.

[20] Condorcet, *Esquisse*, 261–5, 267–8, 273.

[21] Diderot, *Réfutation*, 422.

[22] Diderot, *Réfutation*, 422.

talents. All peoples have, or will pass, through the same stages of natural development towards maturity. There may be some truth in Antoine Lilti's Postmodernist argument that behind Volney's assertion of the oneness of humanity, and thesis that all peoples form a single "great society," lurks an imperialist French impulse to view themselves as "legislators of the world."[23] "O nations!" declaimed Volney, "let us banish all tyranny and all discord! Let us form but one society, one great family; and since human nature has but one constitution, let there exist in future but one law, that of nature—but one code, that of reason—but one throne, that of justice—but one altar, that of union."[24] While firmly condemning European colonization, and issuing a strong plea for a "great society" of mankind dedicated to global peace, Volney at the same time viewed mankind's progress as primarily the result of Enlightenment, the work of *philosophes* culminating in the French Revolution, a path arduous and elusive particularly outside Europe and North America owing to most of the world's lack of printing and Enlightenment, and it is true that this radical "universalism of reason" could in certain contexts translate into a triumphalist Eurocentrism implying the need for authoritarian imposition of "civilization," enlightened European norms, everywhere. But while such a tension is implicit and perceptible in Volney's vision of human progress, it in no way abolishes the immense gap between radical and moderate Enlightenment positions. If different peoples find themselves at sharply contrasting stages of mankind's common path of development at any one time, primitive peoples and individuals remain in their own way as inherently worthy of respect as the most civilized. Equal rights remain always intact however much d'Holbach's and Volney's fiercely anti-Rousseauist vision might view primitive societies as less fitted to uphold them than post-Revolution "civilization." Volney's vision of history was rendered more fraught and complex, but not undermined by his notion of Europe's exceptionalism.

In some cases, given the arrogance of the conquerors, and excesses of colonizing powers, stressed Diderot, Raynal, and also Herder, primitive men should indeed be judged *more* upright and humane than Europeans. Already well prior to 1770 and Raynal's first edition, the young German philosopher, Johann Gottfried Herder (1744–1803), concluded that the new Enlightenment conception of equality means the "childlike religious feeling" of primitive peoples should be treated by philosophers with greater respect than had Helvétius or Voltaire.[25] If theology is the only way serious moral and metaphysical issues can be contemplated among the primitive-minded, primitive cult and religious leaders can hardly be mere "scoundrels."[26] A genuinely enlightened approach, grasped Herder, requires a much deeper, more variegated, and genuinely cosmopolitan history-writing than anything found in what

[23] Lilti, "Et la civilization deviendra générale," sections 18–22; Cook, "Great Society of the Human Species," nn. 81–3.

[24] Volney, *Ruins*, 75.

[25] Herder, *Philosophical Writings*, 385–6; Barnouw, "Eräugnis: Georg Forster," 330–2.

[26] Herder, *Another Philosophy*, 10–11.

he dismissed as the shallow efforts of Voltaire, Hume, and Robertson.[27] It meant adopting new philosophical principles in history-writing, discarding, as d'Holbach and later Volney did, all a priori assumptions regarding the supposed innate superiority of Christianity, and, as d'Holbach and Volney failed to do, of European civilization over other cultures.[28]

Herder's ingrained "Spinozism" and radicalism, stiffened further by the *Histoire philosophique*, fully emerged in his *Another Philosophy of History* (1774), where he adds his voice to those condemning the blatant inconsistency by which Europeans, in recent centuries, had abolished "slavery" and cut back serfdom within Europe only to treat, increasingly, the other "three continents as slaves," banishing their inhabitants to "silver mines and sugar mills" and exploiting them ruthlessly, claiming "these are not Europeans, not Christians," while as their reward for subjecting them receiving "silver, gems, spices, sugar—and secret disease."[29] Before one can measure human aptitudes, capacities, and the character of a people, held radical writers—above all Herder in his *Ideen zur Philosophie der Geschichte der Menschheit* (4 vols., Riga, 1785), one of the foremost works of the German Enlightenment—much more had to be taken into account than race, climate, and working conditions.

Buffon had conceived of humanity as comprising one race only, originating in northern, cold, and elevated climes, like Siberia and Tibet, originally entirely white, with mankind's subsequent "light variations, or degeneration as he also called it, [being] caused by the influence of climate and food."[30] His scheme could be developed to suggest racial hierarchy with the whites at the apex but, especially as relayed by Diderot, chiefly stressed the oneness of mankind, providing a horizontal schema for mankind's ethnic diversity which contrasted with Linnaeus' more obviously vertical, hierarchical schema.[31] Should Africans return to northern climes, he argued, then, however slowly, whitening would set in and eventually transposed blacks would revert to their primal appearance and look as white as Europeans. Egalitarian *philosophes* preferred a "one race" approach to the question of skin color as an obvious way to underpin and stress the oneness and unity of humanity. Differences between Russians and West Europeans, and French and Moroccans, declared Helvétius, in 1758, are purely outward differences due to variations in customs, forms of government, and law. Intellectual inequality, or "l'inégalité d'esprit," among the different peoples, sprang in his view (deemed altogether too simplistic by Diderot) from the differing characters of the governments under which they dwell, the education —more or less conducive to intellectual development—they receive, and

[27] Herder, *Another Philosophy*, 28; Muthu, *Enlightenment*, 266–9; Hallberg, "Johann Gottfried Herder," 510–11.

[28] Herder, *Another Philosophy*, 34, 36.

[29] Herder, *Another Philosophy*, 62–4; Herder, *Philosophical Writings*, 328; Berlin, *Proper Study*, 373.

[30] Buffon, *Époques*, 120; Fréron, *Lettres* iv (1752), 98–9; Bernasconi, "Who Invented the Concept," 19.

[31] Buffon, *Époques*, 120–1; Curran, "Buffon et l'histoire," 187–8, 190, 192, 198.

other cultural conditioning.[32] Differences of color between peoples, like those of culture, Herder likewise deemed purely external, peripheral physical factors.

A similar, if more complex, view was expressed in 1773, by d'Holbach, in his *Système social.* If man is everywhere identical and everywhere possesses the same nature, needs, leanings, desires, and ties with the rest of his species, then white, red, and black men must all form part of the same social and moral unity. Indians, Europeans, Chinese, blacks, and Japanese do indeed exhibit the same nature, he maintained, the apparent differences being just "modifications de cette même nature" [modifications of this same nature], produced by circumstances, climate, government, education, and opinions. "Men do not differ," he summed up, except in the ideas they develop "about happiness and the means they have imagined for obtaining it."[33] Morality is, hence, one and the same "pour tous les êtres de l'espèce humaine" [all the beings of the human species], the principles governing their conduct being universally fixed, with human reason grounded on experience universally the exclusive means to help individuals achieve "happiness," exactly the formula afterwards adopted by Volney.[34] All men seek happiness, in their own way, "happiness" being defined by Helvétius and d'Holbach as what the latter calls "le plaisir continue." The philosopher, legislator, and statesman genuinely committed to promoting the general welfare must perceive all men as equal in their interests and search for "happiness." All races are in fact equal in aptitude for "happiness." When discussing race in the fourth volume of his *Philosophie de la nature*, Delisle de Sales, following Diderot, discusses men of darker colors, especially "les nègres," in most detail because, he explained, the "enemies of philosophy and nature" have degraded them "from the ranks of men to justify in advance their depredations, tyranny and murders."[35] Exploitation and despotism, held radical *philosophes*, require false theological and philosophical justifications behind which to camouflage their atrocious depredations.

Racial theories rejecting Buffon's view, stressing innate differences of race, were inherently more supportive of cultural and ethnic hierarchies, slavery, and imperial sway over non-white peoples. Polygenesis as such, however, could be inflected both in a "moderate" and "radical" direction. How then should the philosopher or social scientist—the rise of the social sciences figuring among the foremost new developments of the later Enlightenment—conceive of racial and color differences? The indefatigable researches of the Scots enlightener, Lord Kames, a passionate devotee of the "science of man" and empirical study of the stages of evolution of human society, left a legacy running through much of the Scottish and other sections of the later Enlightenment, not least his question: "whether there be different races of men or whether all men be of one race, without any difference but what proceeds from climate or other accident;" this he viewed as a "profound question of natural history,

[32] Helvétius, *De L'Esprit*, 416–18.
[33] D'Holbach, *Système social*, 71–2; d'Holbach, *Essai*, 346; Blank, "D'Holbach on Self-Esteem," 443.
[34] D'Holbach, *Système social*, 71; Volney, *Ruins*, 202–5.
[35] Delisle de Sales, *Philosophie de la nature* iv. 174.

which remains still undetermined after all that has been said upon it."[36] Although Kames's polygenism, later rejected by Kant, has been praised as "particularly benign"[37]—and to an extent it was—it also offered justification of imperial dominance of Europe over the rest. The prominent German ethnologist and, later, revolutionary and egalitarian, Georg Georg Forster (1754–94), by contrast, though equally committed to polygenesis, drew strikingly different conclusions about the status of the races.

Divergent race theories hence underpinned widely divergent political attitudes. Like Ferguson, Kames opposed American Independence after 1776, and did so in part adhering to a colonial doctrine that assumed white men born in the tropics, or other supposedly less favorable climes, should remain, as a matter of course, subordinate to Europeans sent fresh from northern European climes to supervise them—and would become more dependent with the passage of time.[38] Climate, empirical observation proved to his mind, cannot be the decisive factor generating the different races of men which frequently coexist in the same or similar climates. Buffon, he thought, erred in supposing climate has a "commanding influence" and that man "white in Europe, black in Africa, yellow in Asia, and red in America, is still the same animal, tinged only with the colour of climate."[39] Buffon stays "totally silent upon a fact that singly overturns his whole system of colour," objects Kames, "viz. that all Americans without exception are of a copper-colour, though in that vast continent there is every variety of climate."[40] Equally, there have been "four complete generations of negroes in Pennsylvania, without any visible change of colour: they continue jet black as originally."[41] Climate does not determine one's race but does modify it. To his theory of distinct races, Kames added his sweeping, unremitting doctrine of racial degeneration, according to which Spaniards settling on the Caribbean littoral of South America "lose their vigour and colour in a few months" and move only languidly; while Dutchmen "born in Batavia soon degenerate. Scarce one of them has talents sufficient to bear a part in the administration. There is not an office of trust or figure but what is filled with native Europeans. Some Portuguese, who have been for ages settled on the sea-coast of Congo, retain scarce the appearance of men."[42] Chronic degeneracy of whites in the Indies Kames deemed proof of the God-given character of racial difference: God created different races of men to accommodate the variety of the world's climates and conditions.[43]

What Kames envisaged as his prime achievement, the *Sketches of the History of Man*, appeared anonymously in Edinburgh, in 1774, the culmination of thirty years of collecting "materials for a natural history of man." It was a hugely ambitious undertaking. Though no best-seller, it sold respectably with calls for subscriptions, interestingly, appearing in the Philadelphia press as early as May 1775, appealing to

[36] Kames, *Six Sketches*, 1; Phillipson, *Adam Smith*, 86, 88; Hill and Montag, *Other Adam Smith*, 97–8, 184.
[37] Kames, *Six Sketches*, 200; Berry, *Social Theory*, 82; Bernasconi, "Kant as an Unfamiliar Source," 155.
[38] Kames, *Six Sketches*, 13; Lehmann, *Henry Home, Lord Kames*, 75, 123–4.
[39] Kames, *Six Sketches*, 15.
[40] Kames, *Six Sketches*, 15; Berry, *Social Theory*, 81.
[41] Kames, *Six Sketches*, 16.
[42] Kames, *Six Sketches*, 12–13.
[43] Garrett, "Human Nature," 199–200.

"those gentlemen who choose to promote science in America" to assist with bringing it out there by subscription.[44] The American response proved grudging, however, and in the end the Philadelphia edition came out in 1776, the year the Revolution began, only as a drastically abridged version of the hefty two-volume work. Kames's study aims to uncover the underlying logic of the progression, the "progress toward maturity" as he calls it, among different peoples, examining social and economic development against the backdrop of morality, law, manners, learning, government, and the arts, convinced that where "man pursues happiness for his chief aim," as he put it, the Almighty bends "our self-love into the social direction."[45] His racial theory certainly greatly complicated his notion of progress. Yet it was possible, in Kames's schema, to speak of the moral and aesthetic, as well as technical and economic improvement of Man, progress potentially available to all men, with basic moral and aesthetic criteria of judgment being identical for all, being rooted in Common Sense, the primal knowledge vested in the soul.[46]

Claiming there are different races by origin, polygenesis, was one amenable route to asserting racial supremacy and inferiority. But Buffon's theories of climate and racial differentiation could also be adapted to buttress hierarchical no less than egalitarian approaches. Buffon's thesis "that all men are of one race or species," wholly irreconcilable though it was with Kames's claims "that there are different races of men fitted by nature for different climates," could just as readily be merged, as various writers showed, with a parallel theory of racial degeneracy when and wherever races were transplanted to what he, like Kames, deemed the wrong climatic milieu. A device regularly used during the High Enlightenment to construct racial hierarchies was that introduced by Cornelis de Pauw (an uncle of Cloots) in his highly contentious *Recherches philosophiques sur les Américains* (Berlin, 1768), a work which set off a major international and trans-Atlantic controversy. Arguing that everything naturally degenerates to a lower level in the environmentally and climatically different New World as compared to the Old, de Pauw went far beyond Buffon, whom he frequently cites, in applying this principle, extending it even to native American languages, which he considered innately inferior to those of Europe, indeed so destitute of concepts and vocabulary as to be virtually useless for expressing sophisticated metaphysical or mathematical ideas. In most Amerindian tongues, he claimed, one cannot count beyond three.[47] The *Histoire philosophique* and Delisle strenuously protested, defending the Amerindians' humanity, intelligence, and courage. In particular de Pauw and others had failed to grasp that the Amerindians are a traumatized people, whose "character" had been incalculably damaged by the "most unjust of tyrannies." The terrible "tyrannie des espagnols dans les Indes," beginning with the

[44] Sher, *Enlightenment and the Book*, 528–30.

[45] Sher, *Enlightenment and the Book*, 145; Lehmann, *Henry Home, Lord Kames*, 175.

[46] Makkreel, "Aesthetics," 548–9.

[47] Delisle de Sales, *Philosophie de la nature* (1780) iv. 244–5; Imbruglia, *L'Invenzione*, 317–22; Cañizares-Esguerra, *How to Write*, 26, 29, 283.

Conquest, held the *Histoire philosophique*, had reduced the former Incas, Maya, and Aztecs to a wretched and supine state. To this, Delisle added a remarkable outburst against Bishop Zumarraga, the "fanatique" who smashed down the temples and burnt all the books of the Aztecs, afraid lest there remain "on the ruins of their country any monument to their intelligence."[48]

Admittedly, the lives of the Amerindians were made more wretched than was necessary due to superstition and ignorance but that is the case with all men. Some had behaved badly. Those made "nobles," or *caciques*, by the Spaniards, had been elevated, argued the *Histoire philosophique*, as tools of exploitation of the rest; they were not genuine descendants of the Aztec, Maya, and Inca nobility of the pre-Conquest era, simply those "who seemed most attached" to Spanish interests.[49] If de Pauw was an extreme instance, his theory of degeneration and general approach to the natural history and ethnography of the Americas, commented Samuel Stanhope Smith (1750–1819), shared much with the scornful attitudes of Buffon, Robertson, and others who "seem to have conspired, as it were in unison with each other," to locate New World natives "among the lowest grade of humanity." Their conclusions about the New World, relying excessively on biased travelers' reports, "can hardly be read without contempt."[50] Neither did the researches of the famed Charles Marie de La Condamine (1701–74), who spent the decade 1735–45 in Peru collecting astronomical data and studying Inca ruins and legends, support the thesis that Spaniards and other Europeans steadily deteriorate in the New World environment, notes Delisle, adding sarcastically that it was from that inferior climate that Europeans received the Philadelphia scientific publications that caused Franklin to be everywhere acknowledged "le Descartes de l'électricité."[51] Decimated by European rapacity and tyranny and unjustly maligned, the Indian masses, agreed Herder, were innocent victims of an unparalleled oppression—and bound to feel deep hatred and resentment.[52]

Among the most comprehensive race theories developed on American soil during the Enlightenment was that of Stanhope Smith, a Presbyterian minister who became Witherspoon's son-in-law and later, in 1795, seventh president of the College of New Jersey (today Princeton University), but, having offended Calvinist orthodoxy, was obliged to resign in 1812, accused of Arminianism and rationalism. His race theory he presented to the American Philosophical Society in February 1787, publishing it the following year as *An Essay on the Causes of the Variety of Complexion and Figure in the Human Species* (Philadelphia, 1788). Elected to the Philadelphia Philosophical Society in 1786, Stanhope Smith shared with Rittenhouse and Jefferson "a scientific ideology" reflecting the "common position of the Philadelphia elite of the period, balanced, according to Henry May, between the left of the Moderate Enlightenment

[48] Herder, *Ideen* ii. 72; *Histoire philosophique* (1770) iii. 44–6; Delisle de Sales, *Philosophie de la nature* iv. 248.

[49] *Histoire philosophique* (1770) iii. 47.

[50] Smith, *Essay on the Causes*, 104–5, 108; Cañizares-Esguerra, *How to Write*, 179–80, 283.

[51] Delisle de Sales, *Philosophie de la nature* iv. 246–7.

[52] Herder, *Ideen* ii. 71.

and the right of the Revolutionary Enlightenment."[53] More liberal-minded than many other ministers, Stanhope Smith held that blacks are not innately inferior to whites; yet his race theory, and further career, decidedly veered more in a "moderate" than radical direction. While contradicting "advocates of different human species," especially Kames,[54] firmly denying polygenesis and every "hypothesis of several original species" of men, he argued that a "just philosophy will always be found to be coincident with true theology." Although to his mind men comprise "but one species from the equator to the Pole,"[55] Stanhope Smith resorted to Buffon's degeneracy theory to re-install a clear race hierarchy, with Europeans, especially "Anglo-Americans," at the apex and peoples dwelling in the harshest, most undeveloped milieus forming the human pyramid's base. These latter were the "Lapponian, Borandian and Samoiede races," which, he agreed with Buffon, "are Tartars reduced to the last degree of degeneracy."[56]

Radical enlighteners, by contrast, contended that color, complexion, hair, stature, and facial characteristics are all non-essential and secondary, with no relevance to abilities and aptitude. Color, asserts Delisle, is just a consequence of exposure to the sun's heat. Admittedly, nowhere are indigenous blacks found in South American equatorial regions; but this was because in the Peruvian viceroyalty temperatures were some fifteen degrees lower on average than in Senegal, as La Condamine demonstrated with his data. It was a difference due to the sun's rays being absorbed more by the Andes, and by the peculiar "American humus," by sea vapors with a high salt content, and Amazonia's immense forests.[57] Peoples inhabiting the equator, in the East Indies, were likewise brown rather than black, but again presumably because their islands were surrounded by sea, and constantly cooled by fresh breezes. Ceylon was supposedly the clearest proof of this theory, since those dwelling close to the sea were of a yellow copper color but the "Bedas" inhabiting the inland forests were of a striking whiteness like "the Swedes."[58]

Sustained efforts to place the idea of race on a supposedly "scientific" basis commenced in the 1770s, the same decade when "universal and equal rights" first powerfully impacted. But as in other areas of scientific controversy during the High Enlightenment, tensions pertaining to issues of human variety reached back to the longstanding clash between Buffon and Linnaeus and the latter's speculations as to how humanity's several categories might relate to his world-renowned classification of animals and plants. Mankind, he argued in the 1758 tenth edition of his *Systema naturae* (1735), comprises four main types, which he classified as *homo Europaeus*, *homo americanus*, *homo Asiaticus*, and indolent and negligent *homo Africanus*, alternatively labeled *Europaeus albus*, *Americanus rubens*, or brown man, *Asiaticus*

[53] May, *Enlightenment in America*, 214–15, 270.
[54] Smith, *Essay on the Causes*, 169–97.
[55] Smith, *Essay on the Causes*, 49, 164; May, *Enlightenment in America*, 215.
[56] Smith, *Essay on the Causes*, 60; Buffon, *Époques*, 122.
[57] Delisle de Sales, *Philosophie de la nature* iv. 179–80; Imbruglia, *L'Invenzione*, 309–10; Cañizares-Esguerra, *How to Write*, 17, 27–9.
[58] Delisle de Sales, *Philosophie de la nature* iv. 178–9.

fuscus, and *Africanus niger*, four human varieties differentiated in the first place by color but with color deemed to reflect deeper divergence.[59] Linnaeus' human taxonomy left it unclear whether or not there was any real natural hierarchy of abilities but asserted a divinely intended permanent fixity of types, colliding with Buffon's purely naturalist and dynamic approach.

Though unwilling to locate human categories in a rigid hierarchy, Linnaeus' schema did imply a racial hierarchy of sorts later adapted by Johann Friedrich Blumenbach (1752–1840), keeper of the university museum at Göttingen, to underpin his new science of physical anthropology, a field he developed over many years, giving special emphasis to skull shapes.[60] A mineralogist and general naturalist of international renown whose collection attracted visitors from all over Europe, Blumenbach, a close friend of Lichtenberg, wrote one of the principal handbooks on race, physical anthropology, and ethnicity of the Enlightenment era, the *De Generis Humani Varietate Nativa* [On the Natural Variety of Mankind] (1775).[61] Like many others, he considered Linnaeus' *systema populorum* [system of peoples] the most apposite foundation on which to build such a theory. Rejecting polygenism, claiming the varieties of mankind merge insensibly one into another, and comprise just one species, he viewed mankind as nevertheless profoundly divided by "race." His hierarchy of race, with the white race (European but in part also Asian) at the top, had four levels. His second race, based in southern Asia, was brown; the third, the black race, originated in sub-Saharan Africa; and his fourth were the New World's indigenous peoples. In his revised 1795 version of his handbook, Blumenbach adjusted his system by splitting Asian peoples into a yellow variety or Mongolian branch and a tawny-colored "Malay" branch. There were now five races of humanity—the Caucasian, Mongolian, Ethiopian, American, and Malay. The top level, the whites, now termed the "Caucasian" race, was deemed the original and purest branch; the brown, yellow, black, and red races had all degenerated from the primal form.[62]

14.2. KANT IN CONTROVERSY WITH HERDER AND FORSTER OVER RACE

Where Buffon's conception of race implied malleability and a close relation of human types to climate and natural surroundings, Blumenbach stressed the reproductive, hereditary factor, biological continuity, together with ease of racial mixing and natural human unity within contingent variety. Voltaire, on the other hand, had

[59] Withers, *Placing the Enlightenment*, 143–4; Vermeulen, *Early History of Ethnography*, 205, 208–10.

[60] Vermeulen, *Early History of Ethnography*, 230; Pagden, *The Enlightenment*, 137.

[61] Gall, *Wilhelm von Humboldt*, 45; Withers, *Placing the Enlightenment*, 145–7; Stuurman, *Invention of Humanity*, 309–10.

[62] Cousin, *Souvenirs*, 76; Stuurman, *Invention of Humanity*, 311–12; Hallberg, "Johann Gottfried Herder," 500.

presented during the 1750s, in most detail in his *Essai sur les moeurs* (1756), a version of polygenesis implying divine intention behind species formation, a thoroughgoing physico-theology involving fixity together with claiming the intellectual inferiority of certain races to others.[63] The tendency towards racial ethnological classification and hierarchy gathered pace in the early 1770s, with Kames's *Sketches on the History of Man* (1774) and the writings on race of Schlözer and Kant. By the early 1770s, the entire question of race classification was beginning to be discussed more insistently and study of peoples, ethnography, and anthropology began to emerge as a recognized social science, especially at Göttingen, Leiden, Uppsala, and other German, Dutch, and Scandinavian centers. August Ludwig Schlözer (1735–1809), professor of history at Göttingen, extolled Linnaeus as the "greatest of naturalists in the history of peoples," calculating in 1775 that with language among the prime criteria of differentiation there existed "between 150 and 200" peoples in the world needing to be researched and classified into groups.[64] Kant, who had, for many years, been lecturing on natural history and geography at Koenigsberg, was another who, at this time, introduced a formal "scientific" theory of race as a central principle of natural history, beginning with his essay "Von der verschiedenen Rassen der Menschen" [Of the Different Human Races] of 1775.

Kant had already earlier asserted the moral and intellectual inferiority of blacks. In an essay of 1764, he cited Hume's 1753 essay "On National Characters," commenting that "Mr Hume challenges anyone to cite a single example in which a Negro has shown talents, and asserts that among the hundreds of thousands of blacks who are transplanted elsewhere from their countries, although many of them have been set free, still not a single one was ever found who presented anything great in art or science or any praiseworthy quality, even though among the whites some continually rise from the lowest rabble, and through superior gifts early gain respect in the world."[65] Answering criticism of the 1753 utterance about different races being different species, and qualifying his statement about negroes being "naturally inferior to the whites," Hume had afterwards deleted his statement that "there scarcely ever was a civilized nation of any other complexion than white." But his revisions still reflected a belief in the reality of racial hierarchy and the innate inferiority of the blacks. In 1777, for example, he retained his notorious remark that "in Jamaica, indeed, they talk of one negroe as a man of parts and learning, but it is likely he is admired for slender accomplishments, like a parrot, who speaks a few words plainly."[66]

Kant sought to incorporate Buffon's explanatory system of biology while simultaneously restricting, or curbing, the materialist implications of his approach. For Kant, the problem posed by race studies was how to reconcile a genuinely scientific biology with elements of teleology and providential design while leaving the latter implicit in the background rather than dogmatically asserting divine intent as basic to his

[63] Lagier, *Races humaines*, 15. [64] Vermeulen, *Early History of Ethnography*, 199, 203, 228.
[65] Brown, "Social Sciences," 1079–80.
[66] Hume, *Essays*, 208; Brown, "Social Sciences," 1078–9.

argument. It was neither respectable science, nor easily defensible philosophy, to explicitly base one's case, like Voltaire, on divine intention; accepted scientific procedure now required explanation of nature's laws in purely natural terms. Rejecting polygenesis and adopting Buffon's common origin for humanity, Kant viewed mankind as a single species but replaced the radical notion of modification as inessential mutation mechanistically driven by climate and circumstances, substituting an ultimately teleological conception of racial sub-categories that are permanent and irreversible.

Like Schlözer, following Linnaeus, Kant postulated four basic categories of one species of humanity—Whites, Blacks, Hindustanic, and Kalmuck.[67] Outwardly distinguished by skin color, Kant's racial groupings were not, he argues, the product of mere contingency, or mechanistic laws, but intended by Providence prior to their formation and benignly planned. All human varieties contained seeds [*Keime*] of natural predisposition that develop, or are arrested, by climatic and other conditions. This "further development of purposive primary predispositions implanted in the line of descent," as Kant calls them, are what causes racial differentiation.[68] Once what Kant identified as four separate basic racial types—whites, blacks, Mongols, and Hindoustans (Indians)—emerged, they then remained permanently fixed as such and there could be no further evolutionary change due to different climatic or other conditions.[69] The component of Kant's theory postulating pre-existing seeds, implanted by the divine intelligence for divine purposes, derived from an innovation introduced into biology and medicine in the years 1758–62 by Haller and Bonnet, notably in the latter's *Considérations sur les corps organisés*.[70] An apparent empirical strength of Kant's race theory was that it could account for why peoples of different color, of plainly different races, inhabit identical climates and geographical conditions.[71] Once formed, racial characteristics remain fixed, their intended, purposive nature being demonstrated, Kant thought, by the unchangeable blackness of Africans, whose color and natural laziness and frivolousness were intentional deviations intended to adapt them to the hot and humid African climate. Whichever implanted racial character was actualized froze the other seeds into permanent quiescence, creating an unchanging hierarchy of race with the whites representing humanity "at its greatest perfection" and possessing a monopoly of the highest talents and capacity to govern, and the blacks the lowest level, a situation which in Kant's view rendered racial mixing through intermarriage and otherwise highly undesirable.[72] Another consequence of his race theory was the late Kant's uncompromising Eurocentrism,

[67] Lagier, *Races humaines*, 16–18, 20; Wood, *Kant*, 187–8; Zammito, *Kant, Herder*, 302.

[68] Kant, "On the Use of Teleological Principles," 44; Brown, "Social Sciences," 1080.

[69] Bernasconi, "Who Invented the Concept," 23; Lagier, *Races humaines*, 19; Zammito, *Kant, Herder*, 303–4.

[70] Zammito, *Kant, Herder*, 304–5; Lüsebrink, "Aufgeklärte Humanismus," 191; Guyer, *Kant's System*, 89.

[71] Lagier, *Races humaines*, 23.

[72] Lagier, *Races humaines*, 24–5, 125; Carey and Trakelhun, "Universalism," 261–2; Bernasconi, "Who Invented the Concept," 26; Bernasconi, "Kant as an Unfamiliar Source," 147–8, 154–5.

his notion that humanity's future progress would emanate exclusively from Europe, with the peoples of the other continents being left at a standstill owing to lack of equivalent talents and "spirit."[73]

While agreeing with Forster that natural history and social science must follow strict rules of empirical procedure (which he believed Forster failed to observe, lapsing thereby into dogmatism),[74] Kant's adherence to monogenesis at the same time neatly reconciled his own race theory with Christian orthodoxy. Combining fixity of species with modification, or rather deviation, under climatic stimulus, Kant's approach typified his favorite tactic of mediating between key strands of disagreement in the philosophical and scientific debates of the age so as to transcend and resolve them, reconciling opposed viewpoints broadly (if not always) in favor of "moderate" positions and against materialism and Spinozism. But to his critics, the outcome hardly seemed compelling. Kant's race theory was vigorously attacked by Herder, who denied the reality of race as an essential category not least in the second part of his *Ideen zur Philosophie der Geschichte der Menschheit*, published in August 1785, prompting Kant to reaffirm his racial theory in his *Bestimmung des Begriffs einer Menschenrasse* the following November.[75] Subsequently, in the 1790s, Herder reaffirmed his doctrine of the oneness of humanity and rejected Eurocentrism still more emphatically.[76] Kant was assailed too by Forster, in his "Noch etwas über die Menschenrassen" [Still More about the Human Races], a key essay published in *Der teutsche Merkur* for October 1786. Forster commenced his polemic with Kant respectfully, and genuinely held him in high regard, but later adopted a harsher tone which he afterwards came to regret.[77]An experienced explorer (who had accompanied Captain Cook's Second Voyage of 1772–5 to the South Seas, with his father providing the expedition's main scientific back-up), Forster had become an internationally renowned naturalist, and member of the London Royal Society at the remarkably early age of 22. A celebrated member also of the Berlin and Stockholm academies of sciences, he accused Kant of failing to detach his science from theological considerations.[78]

Familiar with Buffon's conception of man since translating the fifth and sixth volumes of his *Histoire naturelle* into German, in the late 1770s, whilst teaching at Kassel (where he also more generally familiarized himself with recent French radical literature), Forster evolved, from the early 1780s, under the inspiration of such texts, in a progressively more radical, materialist direction.[79] While emphasizing the great gaps between different South Seas peoples in terms of understanding, technology, and general development, and scathing about the "stupidity" of the most primitive,

[73] Shell, "Kant's "True Economy," 227 n. 50; Carey and Trakelhun, "Universalism," 263.
[74] Riedel, "Historizismus," 45–6. [75] Zammito, *Kant, Herder*, 344–5; Zammito, *Genesis*, 205–6.
[76] Herder, *Philosophical Writings*, 393–6; Carey and Trakelhun, "Universalism," 274.
[77] Kant, *Briefwechsel* ii. 179; Barnouw, "Eräugnis: Georg Forster," 333–5.
[78] Zammito, *Genesis*, 207–9; Pagden, *Enlightenment*, 176, 186; Edmond, "Encounter and Disease," 254, 259.
[79] Merz-Horn, *Georg Forster*, 22, 67–8; Sahmland, "Georg Forsters Werken," 180–1.

Forster and his father never tied attainment levels or skills to skin color or race.[80] While arguing for the reality of racial differences, Forster felt a strong moral antipathy to establishing anything like a racial hierarchy, which could then be employed to assert inferiority, subordination, and slavery.[81] Despite feeling isolated in distant Vilna (Vilnius) in Lithuania during the years 1784–7, he disposed of a uniquely broad perspective over the entire German controversy, having earlier taught natural history at the Kassel gymnasium, where he debated intensively with nearby Göttingen luminaries, including Lichtenberg, whom he had got to know in England in 1774, and the ardently Lockean "moderate" defender of courts and theology, Christoph Meiners (1747–1810). In 1787, Forster transferred from Vilna to Mainz, becoming University librarian. While his own personal library at Mainz reportedly contained all Kant's more recent writings and some of his earlier ones, Forster admitted to being too busy to immerse himself thoroughly in all aspects of Kant's thought.[82]

Before publishing his article criticizing Kant's race theory, Forster sent a draft to Herder, the implicit egalitarianism of whose *Ideen,* and passionate plea for "one and the same human species," for human diversity in oneness and the races' equal standing, appealed to him. At this point he forged something of a common front with him, against Kant's philosophy of Creation, Providence, and race, an alliance linking Herder, Lichtenberg, the anatomist Samuel Thomas Sömmering (1755–1830), an expert on the human eye, brain, and nervous system and a long-standing ally, and himself, albeit he disagreed with Herder's climate theory, according to which European culture could only have developed in Europe and generally felt Herder's approach lacked empirical detail and rigorous substantiation of the sort underpinning his own ethnology.[83] Lichtenberg, sickly, timid, and with a small-town reputation to protect, refused to be more than a closet radical, but behind the scenes secretly repudiated all conventional thinking, remaining an undeviating materialist infused with Spinoza's unrivalled cogency, a clandestine radical dreaming of being the "deliverer of his Fatherland," but too timid to take concrete steps.[84]

Besides Kant and Blumenbach, the new anthropology embracing hierarchy of race in German-speaking lands appeared most influentially, as well as emphatically, in Meiners' *Grundriss der Geschichte der Menschheit* (1786), and the work of Ernst Platner (1744–1818), both contributing to an intensifying clash with the egalitarian, universalist (and hence radical) approach, and the mounting quarrel between Meiners and Forster.[85] Scouring the corpus of extant travel literature to extract its significance for ethnology and anthropology, and producing more footnotes than any rival, Meiners, like Kant, acknowledged that all humans originally comprised a single species. But early on, our species had subdivided into two principal stems, the

[80] Edmond, "Encounter and Disease," 259–60; Niekerk, "Introduction," 27–8.

[81] Riedel, "Historizismus," 49.

[82] Kant, *Briefwechsel* ii. 179.

[83] Barnouw, "Eräugnis: Georg Forster," 331–2, 336; Riedel, "Historizismus," 44, 49.

[84] Lüsebrink, "Aufgeklärte Humanismus," 189; Merz-Horn, *Georg Forster*, 11; Stern, *Lichtenberg*, 54, 58, 60, 72–3, 183, 245, 251, 353–4 n. 44a.

[85] Zammito, *Kant, Herder*, 248–51; Carhart and Robertson, "Enlightenments," 133–4.

Altaic or Black (including the Chinese), on the one hand, and, on the other, the Caucasian (Europeans, Arabs, and Hindus) or White race, from which sprang a great plurality of "types," resulting from the mixing of the two fundamental races in different proportions and circumstances. Combining race theory with attachment to Locke, Meiners denied the existence of a single, unified, universal human nature, claiming the human essence is a *tabula rasa* worked on by external influences, mostly, as with climatic factors, absorbed through the senses—influences that could, however, become genetic, hereditary traits.[86] Thus the peoples of southern Asia represented all the shades of yellow, brown, and black, variations caused by local differences of heat intensity, shade, and moisture.[87] Human build mattered more than color to Meiners' typology, but most crucial, following Blumenbach, was skull shape. Hence, the "heads of the peoples of southern Asia had a quite different form from those of the European nations." He then specified several differences in detail, among them the broader, flatter faces of south Asians: the "eyes of these peoples of the East Indies vary a good deal" but were, as a group, nevertheless quite different from the eyes of white peoples.[88]

Through the 1780s Meiners steadily refined his *Kulturgeschichte* of humanity, emphasizing both race and sensitivity to physical conditions as factors determining the varying builds, capabilities, potentialities, and orientation of different peoples. "No other conclusion is so well-supported by facts and evidence," held Meiners, in his *Grundriss*, "than that humanity is descended from two original groups of people, Caucasian and Altaic; and that the Altaic peoples have less aptitude and are less creative and capable in both body and mind" than the Caucasian varieties, as well as being less able to produce great works of art and architecture. Equally, they supposedly lacked intellectual curiosity, talent to innovate in technology, or any capacity for science.[89] All this, Forster, a future leader of the egalitarian Mainz Republic of 1792–3, rejected as pernicious, a completely false and distorting hypothesis, contending that there is nothing innately inferior about Africans or Tahitians, as compared to Europeans. Herder, who largely avoided Kant's and Meiners' term *Rassen* [races],[90] likewise strenuously objected to Meiners' approach. The lack of cultural development, indolence, and other deficiencies highlighted by Meiners, were all attributed by Forster, as by Diderot earlier, to circumstantial factors, climate, social organization, and lifestyle. The massive inequality blighting Europe itself, argued Forster, proved that, excepting only a few patches of Enlightenment, most of the continent remained as superstitious and unenlightened as it had ever been, as was nowhere more plainly manifest than in his all too familiar Poland–Lithuania.[91]

86 Carhart, *Science of Culture*, 244–7.

87 Meiners, *Ueber die Natur der Völker im südlichen Asien*, 264–6.

88 Meiners, *Ueber die Natur der Völker im südlichen Asien*, 268–9.

89 Meiners, *Grundriss der Geschichte der Menschheit*, 29; Meiners, *Ueber die Natur der Völker im südlichen Asien*, 289–92; Stuurman, *Invention of Humanity*, 309–10.

90 Herder, *Philosophical Writings*, 393 n. 33.

91 Carhart, *Human Nature, Human Culture*, 260–5.

The feud between Forster and Meiners commenced in the late 1770s, with the latter's review of Forster's *A Voyage*, which annoyed Meiners with its Diderotian remarks about the rapaciousness and cruelty of European colonizers in Africa, Asia, and the South Seas, sentiments abundantly shared by Herder.[92] Impressed by the charm, graceful lifestyle, and physical beauty of the Tahitians, whom he regarded as living in a kind of earthly paradise, and other ethnic groups possessing exceptional qualities, Forster became less and less convinced, over time, of the inherent superiority of the Europeans and other Whites. Meiners too collected and preserved a great deal of ethnological material, but Forster considered his approach fatally biased, a theory based merely on a priori presumption of European and white superiority. Even encountering Maori cannibalism first-hand, at Ship Cove, New Zealand, in 1773, which had deeply unsettled the rest of Cook's crew, failed to shake Forster's stalwart commitment to the principle he later shared with Herder, postulating one universal human nature with minor variants, with all men possessing the right to be deemed and treated as equal.[93]

The clash over race between Meiners and Forster, as between Kant and Forster (and Herder), culminated in the late 1780s and early 1790s. With the revolutionary struggle between democratic republicanism and monarchy allied to aristocracy reaching its height in Europe, Forster published several critical reviews of Kant's and Meiners' investigations and conclusions. His anthropology reflected the stress on equality infusing radical thought, invoking Buffon, Herder, and Sömmering in denying all legitimacy to Lockean, Voltairean, and Kantian teleologies in science and philosophy—quite unreasonably, according to Kant: for Forster denied established basic differences between Whites and other races, reducing the differences to consequences of surface factors, especially climate, leaving skin color devoid of essentialist implications for disposition, aptitude, and intelligence. Kant detected a clear contradiction between Forster's ethnographic egalitarianism and his polygenesis, his conceding Blacks were distinct from other peoples, having originated separately, without being willing to acknowledge the essentialist implications of this separateness.[94] Polygenesis Forster certainly considered a more plausible option than Kant's notion that all men descend from a single pair, Adam and Eve, which he dismissed as just another instance of Kant's willingness to make wholly unwarranted compromises with tradition, conventional thinking, and theology.[95]

While noticeably avoiding direct references to Diderot, Helvétius, and d'Holbach, Forster certainly knew their works and his standpoint was plainly indebted to theirs. His radical standpoint is reflected not least in the hylozoic tendency permeating his account of Creation and the origin of life. In closing, he concludes, rather like the

92 Herder, *Philosophical Writings*, 381, 385–6, 412.

93 Herder, *Ideen* ii. 85, 89, 154; Zammito, *Kant, Herder*, 324; Barnouw, "Eräugnis: Georg Forster," 336–7; Pečar and Tricoire are mistaken here, see Pečar and Tricoire, *Falsche Freunde*, 94–5.

94 Kant, "On the Use of Teleological Principles," 44; Kuehn, *Kant*, 343–4.

95 Lagier, *Races humaines*, 35–7.

Histoire philosophique, a work that influenced him profoundly, that "die Schwarze unsere Bruder sind" [the blacks are our brothers], demanding slavery's abolition much in the *Histoire*'s defiant manner.[96] Where proponents of racial hierarchy assumed and exalted white superiority, considering miscegenation reprehensible and undesirable, a form of degradation from Providential design, Forster, again not unlike Diderot and, later, some French revolutionary egalitarians during the 1790s, considered miscegenation beneficial to humanity and aesthetically desirable, echoing the *Histoire philosophique* in declaring the mixing of white and black, producing mulattoes, or "Creoles," as Raynal calls them, a path towards a potentially superior form of human, the higher education of whom "in Europe" would be a great asset to them and all mankind.[97]

In his 1786 essay, Forster introduces a general table indexing skin color, arranging all the peoples in the zones from northern Europe to the equator and then from the equator southwards, arguing that the calibrations between white and brown and then from brown to black, and then, in the southern hemisphere, proceeding back again, in reverse shading, the entire double spectrum, are a purely mechanistic response to climate—entirely superficial and secondary with respect to human essence, aptitudes, and potentialities.[98] Replying to Forster and Herder in his *On the Use of Teleological Principles in Philosophy* (1788), Kant retorted that the evidence of the skin color of children issuing from interbreeding between Whites and Blacks, or Whites and Arabs, altogether invalidated Forster's race table. Mixed caste children's skin color simply blended characteristics of both in a diluted, but balanced, form irrespective of where born and raised. Forster's approach was further disproved, held Kant, by the lack of gradations in color seen in West Africa, where "nature instead makes a sudden jump from olive-skinned Arabs and Mauritanians to the blackest Negroes in Senegal" without passing through any intermediate rungs. Furthermore, no members of three racial groups, Whites, Blacks, and yellow-skinned (or East-Indian brown), had been found indigenously in the New World.[99] Grounds for distinguishing different races of men were additionally strengthened, and Forster's climatic argument further undermined, contended Kant, by the evidence of the gypsies. Originally an Indian people, gypsies had kept their original skin color so consistently over the generations that "no difference would, in all probability, be found between them and those born in India."[100]

Lurking behind Forster's opposition to his racial schema, Kant detected a philosophically defective hylozoic tendency envisaging all living beings, even mosses and lichens, as bound in kinship, forming a vast natural chain of organic being deriving

96 Lagier, *Races humaines*, 45–6; Lüsebrink, "Aufgeklärte Humanismus," 192–4.

97 *Histoire philosophique* (1780) vi. 264–7, 273; Gainot, "Republican Imagination," 287–8; Miller, *John Millar*, 165–7.

98 Kant, "On the Use of Teleological Principles," 45.

99 Kant, "On the Use of Teleological Principles," 45, 49; Lüsebrink, "Aufgeklärte Humanismus," 191–2.

100 Kant, "On the Use of Teleological Principles," 45.

from a single evolving process with everything living forming "part of a system of reproduction descended from a common line of descent." This was the naturalism of Diderot and the atheists. Evolution, naturalism, and rejection of divine providence lurked behind Forster's (and Herder's) thesis, nurturing anti-theological implications Kant sternly refused to countenance.[101]

[101] Kant, quoting Forster, in "On the Use of Teleological Principles," 51.

15

Unity of Humanity

Property, Class, and the Emancipation of Man

15.1. SCOTTISH ENLIGHTENMENT AND THE "SCIENCE OF MAN"

During the eighteenth century's middle decades, Enlightenment thinkers began contemplating human development as a historical process, envisaging mankind as driven by needs, climate, the impulse to dominate, and population pressure, moving through stages. Inspired in part by a remarkably influential passage in Book XVIII of the *L'Esprit des Lois* of Montesquieu,[1] Hume's ruminations, and Rousseau, Kames, Ferguson, in 1762 Adam Smith, in a series of lectures on jurisprudence, began developing the "Four-Stages" conception of "human development" in what soon became its characteristic Enlightenment format, presenting a historical process in which humanity evolves linearly through four main phases—those of "hunting-gathering, pasturage, farming and commerce." Kames, who dubbed Montesquieu "the greatest genius of the present age," and called the earliest phase "the first state of men, viz. that of hunting and fishing," his much younger friend, Adam Ferguson, Smith, and others all became abidingly fascinated by this topic.[2]

The first basic transition was essentially from a "savage state," or primitive society of tiny groups of hunters and gatherers to a society of pastoral nomads herding sheep and goats, a transition conceived as marking the commencement of class formation and government. Primitive societies that "entrust their subsistence chiefly to hunting, fishing or the natural properties of the soil," noted Ferguson, give "little attention to property", and scarcely any to "subordination or government."[3] The hunter and fisherman "finds so much difficulty and is exposed to so many hardships in procuring the mere necessaries," concurred the philosopher John Millar (1735–1801), who first learnt of the stadial theory of human development as a student from Smith's Glasgow

[1] Montesquieu, *Oeuvres complètes*, 634–5; Larrère, "Economics and Commerce," 345; Wood, "Natural History of Man," 104–12; Moore, "Montesquieu," 186, 190, 192; Rahe, *Soft Despotism*, 64.

[2] Lehmann, *Henry Home, Lord Kames*, 179, 184, 186; Berry, *Social Theory*, 93; Harris, *Hume*, 142, 252; Pitts, *Turn to Empire*, 26–40; Kloppenberg, *Toward Democracy*, 246.

[3] Ferguson, *Essay*, 123–4; Millar, *Observations*, 121; Garrett, "Anthropology," 82–3.

lecture course in moral philosophy, that "he has no leisure or encouragement to aim at the luxuries and conveniences of life. His wants are few and in proportion to the narrowness of his circumstances."[4] Weapons, utensils, and the clothes they wore were practically their only kinds of property. A direct consequence, noted Millar, regius professor of Civil Law at Glasgow from 1761 to 1800 and the principal radical among the Scots enlighteners, was that marriage rules were rudimentary and unstable and "women more degraded in savage society than later." Unsuited physically for combat or hunting, women were relegated to all the "inferior concerns of the household." "Nothing can exceed the dependence and subjection in which they are kept, or the toil or drudgery which they are obliged to undergo" in society's "first stage."[5]

Adam Ferguson (1723–1816), son of a Perthshire preacher and, from 1759 until 1787, an Edinburgh philosophy professor, evinced higher regard for the primitive, and society's early states, than was commonly found among the Scots group.[6] Why should modern man, he asks, in the work that made his fame, the *Essay on the History of Civil Society* (1767), look upon the primitive savage with disdain? "The savage who performs, however rudely, the several tasks of human life for himself, though greatly inferior to the scientific performer, may in fact be as much superior to the mere labourer, who is no more than a tool in the hand of a master artist."[7] Ferguson adopted a far more empirically and anthropologically orientated approach to primitive society than Rousseau and many other contemporary essayists on man's natural history,[8] his Common Sense assumptions and respect for *consensus gentium* having taught him to study Man historically, in context, to profile actual societies documented by solid facts, rather than contemplate Man's social development as a pure abstraction with the individual dwelling in imagined isolation. Man's true nature he consequently viewed as emerging more from the history of primitive groups, "troops" and "companies," than a conjectured sphere and psychology of isolated individuals. Disinclined to idealize either the primitive or the civilized, he preferred to see all stages and types of human development as integral parts of a divinely intended trajectory, leaving little room for different degrees of structurally-conditioned fulfillment, for any progression representing different levels human happiness.[9] Certainly, "the polished state" is reached only after traversing the "barbarous state" characterized by crude forms of social subordination like feudalism, and then further intermediate stages, but it had its own drawbacks; it did not represent a decisively improved, higher human condition.

Mankind's history, for Ferguson, is a progression and in some respects a progress; but with nothing mechanistic about the process. "When we say that the Author of

[4] Millar, *Observations*, 2; Meiners, *Historische Vergeleichung* i. 19–20, 28; Moore, "Montesquieu," 190.

[5] Millar, *Observations*, 18–19; Berry, *Social Theory*, 109–11; Wood, "Natural History of Man," 113.

[6] Pocock, *Virtue, Commerce and History*, 130.

[7] Ferguson, *Principles* i. 251; Pitts, *Turn to Empire*, 26–7.

[8] Broadie, *Scottish Enlightenment*, 80–1; Wood, "Natural History of Man," 114; Hill and Montag, *Other Adam Smith*, 230.

[9] Broadie, *Scottish Enlightenment*, 99–100.

nature, has projected a scene of discipline and progression for men; it is not meant to affirm any rate of actual attainment for this versatile being. The faculties are given to him, and the materials are presented for his use: but the effect is optional to him."[10] The history of civil society, for Ferguson, represents a progress in complexity, ease, and capacity, but one encompassing relatively little that can be considered moral or political progress, being driven essentially (as in Rousseau) by changes in property relations and growing inequality. Many features of "polished societies" possessed a distinctly ambivalent character, he suggested, or were decidedly undesirable with a dangerous potential for harm. In particular, following the Seven Years War, he warned against "the ruinous progress of empire," denouncing Britain's "admiration of boundless dominion" as a "ruinous error," a view he fulsomely shared with Hume.[11]

In the second stage, differently from the first, men, "having possessed themselves of herds, and depending for their provision on pasture, know what it is to be poor and rich. They know the relations of patron and client, of servant and master, and suffer themselves to be classed according to their measures of wealth."[12] In primitive societies, there exists a high degree of equality, with every individual struggling to find the means to subsist, thereby developing a high degree of all-round proficiency. As society develops, and inequality increases, however, the "members of every state are divided into classes; and in the commencement of this distribution, there is no distribution more serious than that of the warrior and the pacific inhabitant; no more is required to place man in the relation of master and slave. Even when the rigours of an established slavery abate, as they have done in modern Europe, in consequence of a protection, and a property, allowed to the mechanic and labourer, this distinction serves still to separate the noble from the base, and to point out that class of men who are destined to reign and domineer in their country."[13] Social hierarchy and structural inequality Ferguson, like the Scottish Enlightenment more generally, hence viewed as a natural phenomenon unavoidable in any society. Natural and unavoidable also was this institutionalized inequality finding expression in the political constitution of the state: "the members of any community have never been found in such a state of equality as not to have a distinction of ranks, to the safety of which it is required that they should have each a distinctive share in the legislature of their country."[14]

In the third formative phase, men give up their earlier nomadic wandering and migrations and become a society of sedentary dwellers focusing their efforts on raising crops in the fields. Supported by more ample food resources, population grows denser and also becomes what Meiners called "halb aufgeklärt" (half enlightened), being now capable also of developing the sciences, arts, and crafts; during this phase society further differentiates not merely now into roughly delineated rich and

[10] Ferguson, *Principles* i. 314–15.
[11] Ferguson, *Principles* ii. 500–1; Pittock, "Historiography," 275; McDaniel, *Adam Ferguson*, 40, 55–6, 62.
[12] Ferguson, *Essay*, 123–4; Meiners, *Historische Vergeleichung* i. 20.
[13] Ferguson, *Essay*, 230; Berry, *Social Theory*, 99–101.
[14] Ferguson, *Principles* ii. 498.

poor groupings but more precisely profiled, more rigorously separated classes, developing in a way that steadily strengthens the grip of what evolves into the nobility. "It must appear very evident," commented Ferguson, "that property is a matter of progress."[15] This was equally true of rank, legal institutions, and the principles developed to justify property, privileges, and rank. Ferguson traced the "progress of arts and of policy," but like Mandeville and Kames conceived most of this as unconscious, unintended, and incidental; he remained distinctly hesitant as to whether these ensuing stages represented real or moral progress in any comprehensive sense. There is a "progress of moral apprehension," as there is progress "in the pursuits of physical knowledge, or the practice of the arts." But progress in moral knowledge, he contends, is mainly expansion in the detail available on which to base judgments and from which to draw general conclusions. Since the basic "distinction of right and wrong is coeval with human nature: it is perceived without instruction, in acts of fidelity and beneficence, or of perfidy and malice," remaining essentially the same at every stage.[16]

Like Voltaire, Turgot, and Smith, Ferguson considered inequality, in essential respects, basic, part of the unavoidable mechanism of human development. For where "those who would emerge from the lower station," in nations that are "forward in the accumulation of wealth", strive to better themselves, it is owing "in a great measure, to the inequalities of fortune" that effort is applied by which the "sources of wealth are enlarged."[17] For further development, inequality of wealth hence becomes a positive factor like rank and the emergence of hereditary orders: "in these inequalities, we find the first germ of subordination and government so necessary to the safety of individuals and the peace of mankind; and in these also find the continued incentive to labour and the practice of lucrative arts."[18] In rivalry commercial, political, and national, competition, and even war, Ferguson discerned natural motives driving the engine of progress: "the trials of ability, which men mutually afford to one another in the collisions of free society, are the lessons of a school which Providence has opened for mankind, and are well known to forward, instead of impeding their progress in any valuable art, whether commercial, elegant, or political."[19]

Through each distinct stage, human society grows steadily more complex but also approaches closer, or drifts further from, liberty and civility.[20] Consequently, examining the social contexts of the four stages from every angle—their anthropology, ethnology, economics, and political theories—came to seem the very key to comprehending the moral and political, as well as social, development of mankind generally.

[15] Ferguson, *Principles* i. 20–2, 29–36; Ferguson, *Essay*, 124; Herder, *Ideen* ii. 202.

[16] Ferguson, *Principles* i. 300; Lehmann, *Henry Home, Lord Kames*, 191.

[17] Ferguson, *Principles* ii. 423, 462–3; Evans, *Debating the Revolution*, 110–11.

[18] Ferguson, *Principles* ii. 463.

[19] Ferguson, *Principles*, ii. 508–9; Meiners, *Historische Vergeleichung* i. 20, 25–6, 32; McDaniel, *Adam Ferguson*, 74–8.

[20] Porter, *Enlightenment*, 252–4; Pittock, "Historiography," 262; Withers, *Placing the Enlightenment*, 153.

In each stage, the role of property, extent of subordination, and complexity of administration and government increased, exerting manifold effects on human happiness, security, and freedom. The fourth and last stage, generated by commerce, termed "civil society" alike by Smith, Ferguson, and Millar, reflected a capacity, they agreed, to reverse or moderate, in some degree, the growth of inequality and process of stratification. Thus, a society dominated by a warlike nobility—still a vivid, living memory in post-Culloden Scotland—can yield, under benign circumstances, to a society where individuals seek their betterment in a commercial, non-warlike milieu.

For Smith, the benefits of the fourth stage were considerable. But the newly confident class of capitalist, the merchants and manufacturers, always thinking of their own interest, were not a class to trust with the public interest. Rather the capitalist class should be regarded by society as a whole with considerable suspicion.[21] Governance, held Smith, is best left in the hands of the landowning aristocracy.[22] Millar alone among Scots Enlightenment thinkers showed much inclination to search for the emancipatory potential of mankind's stadial development. Differently from the others, he identified a marked tendency towards greater liberty for men and women alike, and emancipation of the species as such, inherent in the very process of social development. For Millar, modernity cures the worst of the oppression characterizing the past, but in his day there was still an urgent need to complete the process. "In the history of mankind, there is no revolution of greater importance to the happiness of society than this which we now have occasion to contemplate. The laws and customs of the modern European nations have carried the advantages of liberty to a height which was never known in any other age or country. In the ancient states, so much celebrated upon account of their free government, the bulk of their mechanics and labouring people were denied the common privilege of men, and treated upon the footing of inferior animals."[23]

His overall optimism did not hinder Millar from being extremely scathing about the shortcomings of the American Revolution from the perspective of social progress. He left it to others to fully explore the irony that where the Quakers had led, others failed to follow, that the Revolution had in the end yielded nothing, or very little, for black slaves, former slaves, and their would-be benefactors to celebrate. Where Ferguson was hostile to the Revolution and Millar enthusiastic about its founding, or ostensible principles, both were equally scathing about the hollowness of America's rhetoric of "rights." Was it not astounding "that the same people who talk in so high a strain of political liberty," protested Millar, "and who consider the privilege of imposing their own taxes as one of the unalienable rights of mankind, should make no scruple of reducing a great portion of the inhabitants into circumstances by which they are not only deprived of property, but almost of every right whatsoever. Fortune

[21] Smith, *Wealth of Nations* i. 264; Phillipson, *Adam Smith*, 12–30.

[22] Smith, *Wealth of Nations* i. 264–5; Himmelfarb, *Roads to Modernity*, 56–7; Israel, *Democratic Enlightenment*, 240–1, 243.

[23] Millar, *Observations*, 232–3; Evans, *Debating the Revolution*, 152.

perhaps never produced a situation more calculated to ridicule a grave, and even a liberal hypothesis, or to show how little the conduct of men is at bottom directed by any philosophical principles."[24]

Most radical philosophes agreed with Ferguson about modernity's proneness to perpetuate toil and drudgery for most, and intensify the stultifying tendency generated by the increasingly specialized drudgery to which working people are subjected. But moderate Enlightenment utilized the new sciences of economics, ethnology, and social science not just to build a plausible, highly naturalistic theory of stadial social development but also, as in Ferguson and Turgot, to forge new ways of conceiving and legitimating class hierarchy and subordination. "There is one ground of subordination," held Ferguson, "in the difference of natural habits and disposition; a second in the unequal division of property; and a third, not less sensible, in the habits which are acquired by the practice of different arts."[25] The fact that some forms of employment "are liberal, others mechanic" explained why different strata not only developed different talents and skills, but divergent habits of mind according to whether their activities were broad and "liberal" or immersed in drudgery. It is entirely reasonable, concluded Ferguson, to "form our opinion of the rank that is due to men of certain professions and stations, from the influence of their manner of life in cultivating the powers of the mind, or in preserving the sentiments of the heart."[26] This approach came to be widely followed in the 1780s by those justifying and defending social hierarchy. Stanhope Smith claimed such differentiation of activity and pursuits, despite some "particular exceptions," is clearly manifested in men's complexion and physiognomy. "What an immense difference exists, in Scotland, between the chiefs and the commonalty of the highland clans? If they had been separately found in different countries, the philosophy of some writers would have ranged them in different species. A similar distinction takes place between the nobility and peasantry of France, of Spain, of Italy, of Germany. It is even more conspicuous in many of the eastern nations, where a wider distance exists between the highest and lowest classes in society."[27] Nobility as a class arose from specific circumstances, an effect of need, resources, and population pressure; but the consequence was that the nobility, beside possessing more property and wealth, behaved, looked, and contemplated at a higher, more sophisticated, and responsible level than the rest of mankind.

Political "progress" for Ferguson, was by definition hesitant, ambivalent, gradual, and marginal and this infused his conception of progress more generally. Overall, he did not believe there is ever much reason to change the form of government under which one lives, be it a hereditary monarchy, an elective monarchy, mixed monarchy, aristocratic republic, or democracy. Whatever the effects in the executive power, he argues, if the "collateral legislative and judicative" branches of government function reasonably well "there is greater danger from change than from any trivial

[24] Millar, *Observations*, 241–2; Pittock, "Historiography," 264; Berry, *Social Theory*, 108.
[25] Ferguson, *Essay*, 282; Jacob, *Secular Enlightenment*, 143. [26] Ferguson, *Essay*, 282.
[27] Smith, *Essay on the Causes*, 84–5.

inconvenience attending the actual order of things."[28] It should be adopted as a general maxim "under every establishment whatever, that the present order, if tolerable, is to be preferred to innovation" since the consequences of the latter, even in relatively small matters, can never be fully foreseen. The man who goes "forth in search of speculative amelioration, or improvement, not absolutely required to the safety of his country," he admonished, "is to be dreaded as a most dangerous enemy to the peace of mankind."[29] Thinkers like his radical French counterparts enthusiastically encouraging the American Revolution "unsettle the minds of men on a point on which it is highly expedient they should never be unsettled, to wit, the reality of an actual authority to which they are bound to submit in all cases that concern the peace and good order of their country."[30] Neither republicanism, nor democracy, nor the principle of equality held much appeal for him. Ferguson also fully shared the hesitant ambivalence of Hume, Kames, and Ferguson with respect to "right to resistance."[31]

A penetrating critique of the four stages of human development construct, the sway of which lasted decades in Britain, Germany, France, and America alike, was offered by Herder in his *Ideen zur Philosophie der Geschichte der Menschheit*. Herder rejected the prevailing classification as too mechanical and simplistic. Real societies, he argued, contain elements of all four stages blended in different ways, according to an infinite array of shifting circumstances, evolving through time, geographically, psychologically, and in terms of man's relationship with the animal and plant worlds, in far more complex ways than the model suggests.[32] Bedouin, Mongols, Laplanders, and Peruvian Incas are all herders, for example, but manage their herds in sharply contrasting styles, variously using camels, horses, dogs, llamas, and their own two feet for what are actually very divergent tasks. Such wide differentiation, in turn, has vast implications for power relations, the Spanish Conquest of the Aztecs and Incas, for example, being inexplicable without reference to the Europeans' use of horses and attitude to managing animals and people.[33] Rather than four stages, the key social science tool, the most appropriate concept for elucidating the character of particular human societies, urged Herder, is the continual close interaction of physical and spiritual conditions which he called "culture."[34] The distinct "character" of each people is the outcome of a whole range of physical, climactic, historical, and political circumstances, of how particular peoples internalize and manifest their deepest experiences in religion, arts, and poetry. Herder's was a vision of social science and history firmly rooted in a particular style of philosophy. Priestley and other materialists were right in averring that the "spiritualists" have imagined the existence of pure

[28] Ferguson, *Principles* ii. 498.

[29] Ferguson, *Principles* ii. 498–9; Skjönsberg, "Adam Ferguson," 110–11.

[30] Ferguson, *Principles* ii. 499; McDaniel, *Adam Ferguson*, 204–5.

[31] Hill and Montag, *Other Adam Smith*, 222–5; McDaniel, *Adam Ferguson*, 204–6.

[32] Herder, *Ideen* ii. 93–4, 189–93; Herder, *Philosophical Writings*, 386, 396; Barnard, *Nationality*, 124–5.

[33] Herder, *Ideen* ii. 197–8.

[34] Herder, *Ideen* i. 190 and ii. 39, 204; Barnard, *Herder*, 8–11, 145–6.

spiritual entities where none exist and that we have thus far not understood the true properties of the physical and of matter.[35] "Culture" reflecting the specific character of each people is above all an interaction of the physical and the human mind, the impact of the physical on emotions, sensibility, and understanding.

But the most urgent question posed by the schema of four stages, given that the moderate mainstream no less than radical *philosophes* agreed that vast inequality and social stratification were among the foremost consequences and effects, was whether the greater flexibility and emancipatory potential of the fourth stage, civil society and commerce, sufficiently offset the subordination, drudgery, and impoverishment, the prevailing condition of unhappiness, in other words, of the majority. On some issues, the split between moderate and radical Enlightenment could perhaps be a question of degree and emphasis. But the question whether or not what had been achieved corresponds to how things should be—and whether divine intention underwrote this outcome—entailed a sharp, unavoidable rift and polarization. What was revealed to readers everywhere by the *Histoire philosophique*, the controversies it spurred and the variations on its themes expounded by Delisle, Wekhrlin, Herder, Forster, Filangieri, Gorani, Millar, and others, was, as Diderot expressed it, "un théâtre éternel de désolation, de larmes, de misère et de deuil" [an eternal theater of desolation, tears, misery and mourning].[36] No radical work of the later eighteenth century did more than the *Histoire philosophique* to discredit the European empires and colonization by whites of non-European peoples. No other work of the age focused readers' attention on the entire tableau of colonial empires forged by Europeans in the Americas, Asia, Africa, or Oceania with such relentless force, critical acumen, and broad perspective. Finally, no work did more to pose the question of how the universal ascendancy of the noble or other military cliques, allied to kings and ecclesiastics, actually detracts from the freedom, happiness, and well-being of the great majority of mankind. Diderot and his circle, like Wekhrlin, Forster, and Herder, tried to steer readers into abandoning their prejudices and received ideas, and rising up against oppression in the world to join with the radical tendency in relieving the wretchedness of "so many victims of our cupidity."[37] Where the moderate mainstream with its providential outlook and cautious, incremental approach considered the world by and large something functioning as it should and was intended to, by Smith's "Invisible Hand," requiring only relatively marginal adjustments, the position was dramatically different viewed through radical eyes. Most of the world's peoples, held Diderot, Raynal, Deleyre, and their colleagues, "sont dans les fers" [are in chains], sacrificed "aux passions de quelques oppresseurs privilegiés."[38] A devastating critique of fanaticism, superstition, greed, despotism, and slavery, the *Histoire philosophique* undertook the defense of the oppressed everywhere,

[35] Herder, *Ideen* i. 294; Barnard, *Herder*, 147. [36] Duchet, *Diderot*, 172.

[37] *Histoire philosophique* (1780) vi. 215; Hope Mason, *Irresistible Diderot*, 346–7.

[38] *Histoire philosophique* (1780), vi. 212; Diderot, *Fragments échappés*, 451; Duchet, *Diderot*, 173.

exhorting them, most of all the slaves and Amerindians of the New World, to understand the causes of their poverty and exploitation, and to protest and revolt.[39]

There was no way of reconciling this distressing vision to the mainstream Enlightenment view that the world is benignly governed by a divine providence, with broadly satisfactory results, a principle to which most of the Scots Enlightenment continued to adhere,[40] and which trapped Catharine Macaulay in her own peculiar predicament. Radical Enlightenment demanded sweeping, revolutionary transformation, moderate Enlightenment sought marginal, piecemeal amelioration within a basically awe-inducing, satisfactory structure. When anyone asks what kind of government we should have, or "under what roof we should lodge," remarked Ferguson, explaining his perspective on the mounting ideological battle, the correct response is to advise staying under the existing government and system. Should that government have defects, "as the walls or roof of the building in which we lodge may be insufficient, or threaten to fall on our heads," one should proceed with the requisite repairs. "In respect to your dwelling, the walls may be renewed or rebuilt in parts successively; and, in respect to the administration of government, grievances may be redressed. But, in respect to the one, it is a wise maxim: Beware you take not away so much of your supports at once as that the roof may fall in; or, in respect of the other, Beware you do not overthrow so much of your government at once as that the innocent have no protection against those who may be disposed to the commission of crimes."[41]

15.2. SOCIAL SCIENCE, AND DIFFERENTIATING THE TWO ENLIGHTENMENTS

A leading German exponent of the new anthropology and ethnology within a moderate Enlightenment framework, Meiners, reacted vigorously to the sharp upsurge of anti-Enlightenment sentiment, religious and nationalist, after the outbreak the French Revolution in 1789. Spurning what he saw as the zealotry, irrationalism, and espousal of despotism and superstition of the Counter-Enlightenment, he insisted on the great benefits mankind derived from the Enlightenment, openly championing the English Revolution of 1688 and the American Revolution, in its moderate "aristocratic" format, of which he remained an eager admirer. But by no means did this induce him to relax his antagonism to radical ideas. Rather, he reconciled himself to the absolute inevitability of a two-front war. Meiners is especially helpful to the modern historian in his efforts to define precisely the differences between what he called "wahre Aufklärung" [true Aufklärung] and "falsche

[39] Duchet, *Diderot*, 170.
[40] Wood, "Natural History of Man," 102, 109; Ahnert, *Moral Culture*, 87, 89, 116–17.
[41] Ferguson, *Principles* ii. 496–7; Dickinson, *Liberty and Property*, 139–40.

Aufklärung"—the war, that is, between moderate and Radical Enlightenment, and between moderate Enlightenment and Counter-Enlightenment—clearly explaining the differences philosophically, practically, and in terms of social realities and political development. By forcefully asking "was ist wahre Aufklärung?" [what is true Enlightenment?], Meiners sought to draw readers closer to what he saw as the valid global models—above all aristocratic Britain and conservative America—while sharpening awareness of the common bonds, as he saw it, linking the best traditions of German Enlightenment with British thought and the British social and political model.[42] The greatest *Aufklärer*, held Meiners, an admirer of Condillac and Bonnet but especially Locke, were Galileo, Bacon, Boyle, Gassendi, Bayle, Clarke, Newton, Locke, Shaftesbury, Bekker, Leibniz, Thomasius, and Wolff.[43] Leibniz had a particular significance for him, as the thinker who placed the junction of reason and faith on the best, firmest, and most stable basis. The principal bonds linking these formative giants of thought to the corpus of "wahre Aufklärung" were acceptance of religion together with acceptance of the existing social hierarchy and political order.[44] Philosophically, the key points constituting "true Enlightenment" are opposition to "superstition," intolerance, mysticism, and despotism, acknowledgment of God as the Creator of nature, belief in the immortality of the soul and traditional Christian morality, and rejecting libertinism and paganism.[45] "Falsche Aufklärung" Meiners, like his mentor and close friend, Feder, defined as exclusively reason-based philosophy, basically that of the *Encyclopädisten* in France, admittedly rejecting all superstition and intolerance like "true" Enlightenment, and having nothing in common with Counter-Enlightenment, but denying the omnipotent and omniscient God who created nature and directs and regulates the universe and rejecting immortality of the soul and traditional Christian morality. False Enlightenment eliminates theology and falsely replaces God with "eine blinde Natur oder Nothwendigkeit" [a blind Nature or necessity]. "Spinoza, Hobbes, Helvétius, d'Alembert, Hume, and Frederick the Great" could not be said to have been themselves immoral men who did not extol virtue. But by postulating a pure naturalism based on unalterable laws of nature they created a framework destroying society's moral basis, calling in question the social order and encouraging sexual libertinism and political and social "Anarchie."[46]

By the 1770s, Meiners's "true Enlightenment" felt decidedly threatened, if not besieged, by the advance of the "false Enlightenment" that began with Spinoza. Delisle de Sales, writing in the mid-1770s, was one of the first revolutionary *philosophes* to contend that the Christian festivals should be replaced in the future by a new kind of public "religious" festival marking the great moments of human emancipation and the triumph of what he called the religion of nature, the new "religion universelle" of the

[42] Meiners, *Historische Vergleichung* iii. 465–6; Zammito, *Kant, Herder*, 248–9.
[43] Meiners, *Historische Vergleichung* iii. 448, 453–4, 486.
[44] Meiners, *Historische Vergleichung* iii. 486–7.
[45] Meiners, *Historische Vergleichung* iii. 469–70, 477, 486.
[46] Meiners, *Historische Vergleichung* iii. 466, 507–8, 546–7, 549; Carhart, *Science of Culture*, 289–91.

future. All existing saints' days and days marking "ridiculous miracles" should be abolished and replaced with days marking the great defeats of "fanaticism" and tyranny like the Edict of Nantes, rehabilitation of Calas, and recent emancipation, for the first time, of a portion of the slaves in the New World, by the Pennsylvania Quakers.[47] The charge of "Atheism," the regular weapon of the moderate Enlightenment against its Enlightenment adversary, he rebuffed, pointing out that these reputed "atheists" had accomplished an immense amount of good in the world. "Combien l'accusation d'athéisme est vague et arbitraire" [how vague and arbitrary the complaint of atheism is], he complained, defending Bayle against the charge.[48] Offering a general condemnation of "atheism," he defined the crime narrowly, citing an impressive list of atheistic and materialist figures, above all Bayle, qualifying or offering extenuating justifications diminishing the force of the denunciation. The teaching of the legendary Chinese teacher "Foé," who first established a real sect of "athées," approached "assez de notre Spinozisme" [close to Spinozism] and culminated in the work of the great legislator, Confucius;[49] Averroes, "head of a sect of atheists that still exists among the Muslims," was wrongly persecuted;[50] and as for their modern equivalent, Spinoza, "ce fameux athée tant cité et si peu lu" [this famous atheist so much cited and so little read], he too was unjustly maligned, being a man of virtue who fell only by degrees into atheism, from which he was still quite distant when he published his book on Descartes (i.e. in 1663). As with Bayle, Spinoza's *scepticisme* was a corrosive fluid that began by biting at errors and only afterwards attacked the truths of nature. "These heroes among the modern atheists," Delisle de Sales continued, he grants are excessively extolled in France, especially as Bayle had refuted Spinoza's system "d'une manière triomphante."[51]

Predicting all European colonies in the New World and the rest of the globe would eventually rebel and break free, the *Histoire philosophique*, most forcefully in its 1780 redaction, declared the basic equality and right to happiness of all men, and the oneness and purely social orientation of "la morale universelle."[52] It also declared this universal morality of the radical philosophes the only correct premise for social theory and exclusive basis of valid legislation.[53] The continuing vigor and robustness of the opposing social, moral, and political structures that nourish and sustain repression, exploitation, and misery, including slavery, held Diderot and his co-authors, arise from the immense power of human ignorance and prejudice. What d'Holbach called "les prejugés universels" [the universal prejudices] impose themselves on all peoples of the world with such tenacity and force, so thoroughly permeating even many of the best minds, that it is unsurprising philosophers often despair of mankind. "Wahre Aufklärung" and its opposite were indeed characterized

[47] Delisle de Sales, *Philosophie de la nature* vi. 478–9; *Histoire philosophique* (1780), ix. 10, 118.
[48] Delisle de Sales, *Philosophie de la nature* v. 244, 253, 263.
[49] Delisle de Sales, *Philosophie de la nature* v. 283–5; *Histoire philosophique* (1780), ix. 456.
[50] Delisle de Sales, *Philosophie de la nature* v. 286–7.
[51] Delisle de Sales, *Philosophie de la nature* v. 314–17; Mortier, *Coeur et la raison*, 381.
[52] *Histoire philosophique* (1780), ix. 448–50, 470–1.
[53] *Histoire philosophique* (1780), ix. 455.

by deep religious and philosophical differences, averred Meiners; in addition, they were inevitably antagonistic politically and socially. But it was moderate Enlightenment alone that offered genuine political and social benefits to mankind. One need only contemplate the unedifying legal, social, and constitutional practices of the Middle Ages to appreciate the vast benefits conferred by "true Enlightenment," ranging from toleration and a restricted, balanced press freedom to civilized, rational laws, security for all, and administrative responsibility.[54] "False Enlightenment" was not just egalitarian but anarchic, subversive in being apt to stir up violent revolution, whereas "Wahre Aufklärung" never produced "violent revolutions" except where prevailing abuses were intolerable "and those whose task it should be to eradicate such abuse, ignored warnings, obstinately insisting on upholding unacceptable, insufferable mistreatment."[55]

Few are courageous enough, contended Meiners's opponents, full-frontally to combat "les erreurs universelles." What the common people believe seems all but insuperable. It is only too understandable, remarks d'Holbach, that many resort to the maxim "il faut penser pour soi, et parler comme les autres" [one must think for oneself and speak like the rest] to shield oneself from persecution. But such an attitude is deeply damaging to the progress of *l'esprit humain* and a sure way to spread supine submission, indolence, and backwardness. Yet, all considered, there was reason even so to believe that the revolution of the mind accomplished by radical thought would one day engineer a successful revolution of fact and establish in the world a wholly new kind of society. Despite the slowness of our steps, concludes d'Holbach's *Système social* (1773), the evidence proves there is a progress of "la raison humaine." We are manifestly less ignorant, barbarous, ferocious than our fathers and they were manifestly less ignorant than their predecessors. Doubtless it was in ages when ignorance and superstition prevailed utterly that there was least disposition in society to accept the light of reason. But who can deny that this resistance has significantly lessened in recent times? The resistance remains formidable and yet human reason, he held, will eventually overcome the inertia of tradition and groundless belief, and make dramatic and inspiring progress. Emancipation of man, and life in a free society according protection to all on an equal basis, is not an impossible dream: if error and ignorance have forged the chains that bind peoples, "si le préjugé les perpetue, la science, la raison, la vérité pourront un jour les briser" [if prejudice perpetuates itself, science, reason, and truth will one day be able to break them]."[56]

What proves that a more general revolution against superstition and "le pouvoir arbitraire"—one assuring the greatest number of citizens possible the advantages for which society was established—is conceivable and possible is that local revolutions

[54] Meiners, *Historische Vergleichung* i. 461 and iii. 519.

[55] Meiners, *Historische Vergleichung* iii. 519; Carhart, *Science of Culture*, 291.

[56] D'Holbach, *Essai*, 92; d'Holbach, *Système social*, 558–9; Condorcet, *Esquisse*, 267–8, 338, 378; Mirabeau, *Considerations*, 22, 91.

have already achieved notable things in earlier centuries. Did not the English and Dutch first throw off the papal yoke during the Reformation and, following that, the yoke of political tyranny in 1572 and 1688?[57] The accounts of travelers who have visited China report that in that great empire courtesy has been taught even to the very lowest of the citizenry. Why then should it not be possible to teach the common man to think in terms of reason? It was a noble thought, and much passion as well as knowledge and research lay behind d'Holbach's words. But was he right? That became the burning question of 1789 and the 1790s.

[57] D'Holbach, *Système social*, 561.

Part III

Revolution and Competing Revolutionary Ideologies (1789–1830)

16

Robespierre *anti-philosophe*

The Battle of Ideologies during the French Revolution

16.1. THE ROUSSEAUIST ROOTS OF ROBESPIERRE'S *ANTI-PHILOSOPHIQUE* DISCOURSE

Among radical enlighteners, French and foreign, condemnation of the ruthless authoritarianism, populism, anti-intellectualism, antifeminism, and violations of basic rights of Robespierre and the Montagne was always vehement and universal. This was invariably true of the allies and disciples of Condorcet, the revolutionary *idéologuistes*, advocates of "universal and equal rights," and authentic democratic republicans whether Franklin, Paine, Jefferson, Price, Priestley, Gorani, Thorild, Destutt, or Wollstonecraft. From 1792, radical, democratic condemnation of Robespierre became a key theme of the revolutionary era, not just in France but everywhere, a marker of far-reaching international philosophical and historical significance in the past strikingly too little stressed and highlighted by historians,.

Contemplating the Terror, seven years later, in 1801, Daunou's fellow *Idéologue*, Destutt de Tracy, located the core tragedy of the people's Revolution in blind, unreasoning revolt against "reason" itself, in revolt against emancipating society from the yoke of prejudice. Unawareness brought on the catastrophe that blighted France and all humanity under the 1793–4 group dictatorship, by entrusting the revolutionary leadership and National Convention to ruthless, power-hungry men who enthroned an authoritarian populism proclaiming "reason hateful" and placing France in the hands of "fanatics, hypocrites, rascals, and *fourbes*."[1] The Convention wrecked the Revolution, he contended, by ushering onto center stage unschooled newcomers freshly donning the red bonnet, with little grasp of democratic republican values, eager to join the chorus accusing the *philosophes* of being *réformateurs timides*. Disastrously, they dismantled the Revolution's democratic gains, helped the dictator's henchmen devastate the "useful institutions" the *philosophes* had

[1] Destutt de Tracy, *Commentaire*, 144.

introduced, organize repression, and finally liquidate the *philosophes* themselves, threatening with annihilation everything good the Revolution had achieved.[2]

Ideologically, the French Revolution is best understood, our series maintains,[3] as a three-way stretch between moderate Enlightenment (constitutional monarchy), Radical Enlightenment (democratic republicanism), and populist Counter-Enlightenment (Montagnard dictatorship of the people). Victory for populist Jacobinism in the summer of 1793 entailed elimination of *démocratie représentative* as a centrally active concept in French revolutionary public debate.[4] After Thermidor, and the Montagne's subsequent defeat, on 2 and 3 April 1795, Pierre Daunou (1761–1840) took the lead in urging the National Convention to immediately reverse its condemnation of Condorcet and the pro-Revolution *philosophes*, publish his *Esquisse*, and reclaim *la vraie République* based on justice and "Lumières" [Enlightenment]. They did so; and he rallied considerable support albeit decidedly not from the remaining Thermidorians and Marat adherents. The Convention should collectively reject the bogus republicanism and hypocritical politics of a revolutionary regime that Daunou, like Roederer and many another, denounced as a veritable "*contre-révolution* powered by tumult and lies."[5] But in 1795 only a handful of legislators, few compared with earlier in the Revolution, took much interest in fully re-democratizing the Revolution—or, for that matter, rehabilitating Condorcet. The truth was that *robespierrisme* had succeeded in permanently weakening the democratic impulse.

After more than a year's incarceration (since 3 October 1793), Daunou, released on 24 October 1794, long among the Revolution's principal education reformers and general enlighteners, now also began to emerge among the most prominent legislators striving to revive and reinvigorate the Revolution. Henceforth, he stood in the Convention as an unrelenting "anti-Robespierre." In his eyes, Robespierre's *gouvernement révolutionnaire* had proved itself a criminal pact fortified in power by the undeniably blatant vote-rigging Robespierre had used, in the autumn of 1792, to exclude Condorcet, Pétion, Sieyès, Paine, Priestley, Guadet, and other key revolutionary intellectuals committed to democratic republicanism, from being elected as Convention delegates for Paris.[6] With their grip on Paris secure, the authoritarian populists hijacking the Revolution had systematically pulverized all human rights and, deeming "all the enlightened Patriots" their "natural enemies," succeeded in "reducing them to silence."

[2] Destutt de Tracy, *Éléments d'idéologie* i, p. xxvi.

[3] Israel, *Revolutionary Ideas*, 19–29, 695–6; Israel, *Expanding Blaze*, 246–84; Israel, "'Lumières radicales' comme théorie générale," 423–9; Israel, "'Radical Enlightenment': A Game-Changing Concept," 19–32.

[4] Fruci, "Democracy in Italy," 33.

[5] Taillandier, *Documents*, 56–8; Minart, *Pierre Daunou*, 64, 83–4, 95; Head, *Politics and Philosophy*, 23–4.

[6] Barrière, *Bibliothèque des Mémoires* xii. 417, 438; Robespierre, *Lettres* 2nd series, no. 4, 149–50; Israel, *Revolutionary Ideas*, 244, 273–4, 291, 358, 365, 439, 688–9.

Like all despots engineering mass repression of individual liberty and freedom of expression, the group dictatorship were greatly aided by endlessly repeating an overarching ideological slogan, a crass substitute, contended Daunou, for a rationale justifying their general persecution, a slogan well calculated to sway the least informed. The Montagne had hit on their "fable du fédéralisme," the accusation their Girondin opponents were "federalists" threatening the Republic's unity, a groundless, almost meaningless accusation but effective, which, during the summer of 1793, became one of those "expressions magiques" tyrannical oppression so effectively propagates among unschooled masses: "moins on comprend, plus on soupçonne: l'ignorance haït avec fanatisme, elle égorge avec fureur" [the less one understands, the more one is suspicious; ignorance hates fanatically, it cuts throats with fury].[7] The perverse rhetoric of "fédéralisme," plied by Chabot and Robespierre especially, rallied many, but Robespierre's choicest doctrinal innovation, held Daunou, was his refitting the term "people" to make the least literate and enlightened quintessential representatives of the status and rights of society as a whole. By tirelessly exalting the virtues and "justice" of the people, Robespierre deployed a tool he used with devastatingly ruthless effect against reason, Enlightenment, the Revolution, and "la liberté démocratique" itself.[8]

Between 1792 and 1794 the battle between *philosophique* democratic republicanism and despotic populism escalated and intensified, but in essentials was nothing new. After breaking with the Diderot–d'Holbach coterie in 1757, Rousseau had acquired a particular image among the Diderot, d'Holbach, and Condorcet circles, and later Mme Helvétius' Auteuil salon, which, after Rousseau's death but before the Terror, had grown into something, "le démocratisme rousseauien," a few had already come to recognize as a threat to freedom of thought, freedom of expression, representation of the electorate, and constitutional government.[9] These included not least Condorcet, Volney, Paine, Destutt, Daunou, and all the *Idéologues*. As Robespierre exalted Jean-Jacques as humanity's finest teacher, the *anti-philosophe* who at every point exposed the "aristocratic" ideological conspiracy seeking to steer public opinion, presenting Rousseau as the people's supreme hero attacking tyranny, priestcraft, *and* the "philosophical sect" plotting to usurp the traditional role of the priest, a sublime thinker extolling the Divinity with simple enthusiasm, defending immortality of the soul and reward and punishment in the hereafter, the threat became more menacing. For radical enlighteners at war with Montagnard ideology, here lay the doctrinal core of the anti-intellectual blight sapping the Enlightenment and destroying the Revolution. In his major speech to the Convention of Floréal 1794, afterwards published in the *Décade philosophique*, on the relation of moral and religious ideas to *principes républicaines*, Robespierre publicly denounced the atheism and materialism

[7] Barrière, *Bibliothèque des Mémoires* xii. 439, 444; Brissot, *Mémoires* ii. 234, 341; de Mathan, "Fédéralisme Girondin," 195–7, 199.

[8] Barrière, *Bibliothèque des Mémoires* xii. 452–4.

[9] Schandeler, *Interprétations de Condorcet*, 66–7; Rahe, *Soft Despotism*, 93–4; Jolly, "Introduction," 12.

of the *encyclopédistes* and *philosophes*, exalting Rousseau's greatness and what he termed his justified and "invincible" scorn for "les sophistes intrigants"—those usurping the name of *philosophes*—justified contempt to which Robespierre ascribed the supposedly unjust, implacable antipathy of Rousseau's rivals—Diderot, d'Holbach, and Helvétius.[10]

Had Rousseau witnessed the French Revolution of which, in Robespierre's eyes, he was by far the most important precursor and prophet, his "generous soul" would have ecstatically embraced the Montagne's justice and equality. What, by comparison, had Rousseau's *philosophique* adversaries accomplished? Vehemently denouncing Condorcet, he accused the *philosophes* of opposing the Revolution from the moment they feared it would raise up the common people. Some questioned republican principles, prostituting themselves to political factions like the Orléanist clique; others withdrew into cowardly inaction (Raynal, Naigeon) or else "federalism." Overall, the intellectual elite had indeed "dishonored themselves in the Revolution," leaving the "reason of the people" to carry the burden—to the everlasting humiliation and disgrace of the *philosophique* sect.[11]

Modern historians often seem blind to the fact that Robespierre was widely perceived from 1792 through the rest of the 1790s and the Napoleonic era as among the greatest *anti-philosophes* of the late Enlightenment era, and foremost foes of core Enlightenment values. Yet, much of his lasting historical importance, in late Enlightenment debates and controversies, arises from this. Once the bitter struggle within the Revolution between the *monarchiens* and the democratic republicans, the fight between moderate and Radical Enlightenment, ended in 1792, it was the political and moral status of the unschooled "ordinary man," the *sans-culottes*, that during 1792–3, first during the merciless ensuing conflict and then through the course of the Terror, defined the profiles of the two opposing blocs, democratic republicans (Brissotins) versus their rivals for control of the Revolution, the Montagne.

Robespierre's *anti-philosophisme*, destined to play so crucial a role in derailing the Revolution, was no recent development, however, being already a pronounced feature of his earliest efforts to attract public attention, including the essay he entered for the royal Academy of Amiens prize competition, in 1784–5. Robespierre's entry, entitled *Éloge de Gresset*, published, in 1786, was a eulogy of a minor poet and dramatist, Jean-Baptiste-Louis Gresset (1709–77), famous for a feud with Voltaire which dramatically highlighted his disdain for *philosophes* and *philosophisme*. Gresset, described by one modern scholar as "profoundly insignificant," in Robespierre's eyes was a towering hero of humanity, not for literary or intellectual qualities but his exceptional "moral worthiness." Contemplating the literary feud between Voltaire and his hero, Robespierre, bizarrely, exalted Gresset as the superior genius of the two, the more eternally resplendent, because his writing reflected "nature" and natural man, whereas Voltaire, for all his superior wit and prose style, represented base artificiality,

[10] Robespierre, *Discours du 18 Floréal*, 31–2; [Say], *Décade philosophique*, 1 (30 Floréal 1794), 188–91.
[11] Robespierre, *Discours du 18 Floréal*, 31–2; Crow, *Emulation*, 175–6, 178.

"culture" in Rousseau's allegedly profoundly insightful negative sense.[12] Gresset's superiority over Voltaire, explained the then still unknown Robespierre, lay in his viewing true "liberty" as something rooted in ordinariness, plainness, the straightforward thinking and living of ordinary folk.[13] Berating Voltaire, and *philosophes*, Gresset had wonderfully idealized "honest and pious souls," "sensible and virtuous people," perceiving them as morally above others. It was Gresset's "moral" rejection of Voltaire's *philosophisme*, his scorning his intellectuality and cleverness, his preferring Rousseauist, Spartan sensibility, and "patriotism," his zeal for Rousseau's "sublime science of simple souls," that Robespierre found so intoxicating. For him, Gresset's words sanctified the very essence of Rousseau's "persecution" by Diderot and the *philosophes*.[14]

Loathing Enlightenment and convinced of the moral decadence of Rousseau's foes,[15] Robespierre already expressed strong sentiments about society and the Revolution in the national legislature, and the Jacobins, prior to gaining prominence during 1791–2; but republican tendencies were emphatically not among his pre-1792 views. Neither before the royal flight to Varennes, in June 1791, nor subsequently, did Robespierre show any commitment to republican principles. Rather, such was his aversion to Brissot, explained Mme Roland, he automatically opposed him on every issue whether monarchy, republicanism, religion, foreign policy, war, or the colonies. Rejecting the republicans' talk of representation, he tirelessly reaffirmed Rousseau's strictures against "gouvernement réprésentatif absolu," urging the need for direct democracy.[16] As it evolved later, in 1792–3, the Montagne, in theory, did embrace direct democracy (which Radical Enlightenment always rejected); but in late 1791 and early 1792, the lawyer from Arras, and his following, still staunchly defended the 1791 monarchical constitution against the surging democratic republican ideas championed by Condorcet, Brissot, Carra, Gorsas, Pétion, Desmoulins, Paine, and other leading Left-leaning journalists and *philosophes*. Even as late as August 1792, on the eve of the 10 August rising, his little-read paper, *Le Défenseur de la Constitution*, established in April 1792, still aligned with populist royalism against republicanism, manifesting an almost Humean or Montesquieuian indifference to "forms of government."[17] Clinging to monarchism until the "second revolution" of August 1792, Robespierre complained of being maligned by the pro-Revolution democratic press: his adversaries were trying to hoodwink uncomprehending ordinary folk with their high-sounding talk of "republicanism," an abstraction incomprehensible to most people and opposed to ordinary thinking. Belatedly swimming

[12] Platon, "Robespierre's Éloge," 488; Leuwers, *Robespierre*, 53–4, 67; Clarke, *Commemorating*, 34.

[13] Platon, "Robespierre's Éloge," 490; Dingli, *Robespierre*, 40.

[14] Platon, "Robespierre's Éloge," 492, 502; McPhee, *Robespierre*, 40; Neidleman, "Sublime Science," 823, 830.

[15] Dingli, *Robespierre*, 39–41, 228–9.

[16] Robespierre, *Le Défenseur* v. 215, 217, 225–6, 240; Thompson, *Robespierre*, 235–7.

[17] Robespierre, *Le Défenseur* i. 1–2; Brissot, *Mémoires* ii. 325–6; Roederer, *De la philosophie moderne*, 29.

with the tide, he only finally dropped his previously staunch anti-republicanism to avoid risking still being ruinously labeled a "royaliste."[18]

"Sovereignty of the people" was a principle proclaimed by the national legislature and press, protested Robespierre, but was not being realized.[19] The "people alone is good and just, and magnanimous;" the people is always pure in its motives;"[20] "man is good arising from the hands of nature," went his interminable Rousseauist refrain, while corrupt attitudes are the preserve of *philosophique* types disdaining the ordinary.[21] In his speeches, he continually reaffirmed the for him fundamental cultural and moral duality underpinning his unremitting campaign against the Brissotins, stressing the purity, disinterestedness, and "moderation" of ordinary people and their being deceived by those insidiously designing to raise themselves above them. These malefactors oppressing the common person were the "writers" and intellectuals, "aristocrats" at heart, whom Robespierre accused of betraying the people by conspiring with Lafayette, Dumouriez, and foreign courts.[22] If Brissotins discoursed endlessly on republican principles and philosophy, these infinitely devious "aristocrates hypocrites," he explained with his own incomparably flexible logic, sought to "exaggerate the principles they want to destroy."[23]

Brissot, Condorcet, and their allies extolled *philosophes*, but despised the ordinary, the "good citizens" of Paris, whereas he, Robespierre, stood shoulder to shoulder with the common man, with "des hommes simples et purs."[24] A high-point of Robespierre's drive against *philosophes* occurred on 9 September 1792, at a gathering of the electoral assembly of the department of Paris. When a Brissotin speaker delivered a speech urging the need to erase "l'intrigue et la bassesse" [intrigue and baseness] from the Convention, and for the assembly to choose men who since the Revolution's commencement had proven "invariables" in the principles of liberty, Robespierre replied, as quoted in the Paris papers: "I know there is a coalition of philosophes; I know Messsieurs Condorcet and Brissot want to put philosophes into the Convention [. . .] but what need have we of men who have done nothing but write books? What we need are Patriots practiced in making revolution, who have fought body to body against despotism, who have been victims."[25]

Robespierre "was the *détracteur* of *la philosophie*," observed Roederer and Marchena, "the enemy of the *philosophes*, the avenger of the Eternal One," who, against them, championed immortality of the soul.[26] *Philosophes* and philosophy,

[18] Robespierre, "Exposition," 14. [19] Robespierre, *Le Défenseur* 11 (July 1792), 538.

[20] Robespierre, *Lettres*, 1st series, no. 6, p. 285.

[21] Robespierre, *Lettres*, 1st series, no. 2, pp. 49–50 and 2nd series, no. 1, p. 13: "La première chose que doit savoir le legislateur, c'est que le peuple est bon;" Kloppenberg, *Toward Democracy*, 512.

[22] Robespierre, "Exposition," 12–13; Scurr, *Fatal Purity*, 182, 184; McPhee, *Robespierre*, 91, 123.

[23] Robespierre, *Lettres*, 1st series, no. 6, p. 285.

[24] Robespierre, *Le Défenseur* i. 45 and iv. 174–7; Robespierre, *Lettres*, 1st series, no. i, p. 21 and no. 2, pp. 49, 54.

[25] Robespierre, *Oeuvres* vii. 463.

[26] Roederer, *De la philosophie moderne*, 36–7; Marchena, *Essai de théologie*, 12, 32.

declared Robespierre, in his key speech of 18 Floreal of the Year II, had undeniably initiated the Revolution, but were only its "preface," mostly just "ambitious charlatans" denouncing despotism while themselves receivers of pensions from despots. If they denounced courts, they hypocritically dedicated their books to kings. "With much zeal this sect propagated *matérialisme* which pervaded the aristocracy and the *beaux esprits*." Did not Brissotin leaders, Vergniaud and Gensonné, demand of the Convention that the name of the Supreme Being be omitted from the new constitution's preface? Ultimately, *philosophes* and literary men "all dishonoured themselves in this Revolution;" to the eternal shame of the intellectual life, "it was the reason of the people alone that bore the burden. Arrogant little men, blush with shame!" Prodigious accomplishments "immortalizing this epoch of human history have been achieved without you and in spite of you."[27]

"I know of no surer means of Counter-Revolution," remarked Benjamin Constant in 1797, "than to defame Condorcet and Vergniaud [...] and represent 31 May [1793] and the horrors that followed it, as the necessary consequence of overthrowing the monarchy."[28] This comment he meant as criticism of royalist publicists attacking the Revolution, but his words apply equally to Robespierre. Ideologically, the latter's goal was to exalt "the sublime Jean-Jacques," whom Condorcet ignored, and Volney and Destutt despised, but Robespierre extolled at every opportunity.[29] If, on becoming the Revolution's most powerful figure, Robespierre nevertheless proved reluctant to install Rousseau's remains in the Panthéon this was because, to him, it was an edifice mired with the remains of Voltaire, Mirabeau, and other *philosophes*, a monument "debased" by philosophy where Rousseau's remains had no place. To his mind mixing the sublime Rousseau with *philosophes* was simply sacrilege—"quel décadence de l'esprit public!"[30] However, within days of Thermidor, Jean Debry, a Brissotin, moved in the Convention that with the despicable personage blocking entombment of Rousseau's remains in the Pantheon, the man "who could not suffer an equal," finally out of the way, transferring Rousseau's mortal remains should at last proceed.[31]

Robespierre's proclaiming "revolutionary government" as new as the Revolution that gave birth to it, was admittedly not Rousseauist.[32] Nor indeed was the Terror as such. Nevertheless, at the heart of Robespierre's ideology lodged a populist anti-intellectualism firmly rooted in Rousseau's idea of virtue, or what Volney termed the notions of a whimsical, extravagant genius "who, from moroseness, wounded vanity, or disgust with society's vices, harbored chimerical ideas of the savage state contradictory" to his "own system of a perfect man."[33] Robespierre's educational policies

[27] Robespierre, "Discours," 30–2; Schechter, *Genealogy of Terror*, 184–5.

[28] Constant, *De la Terreur*, 352, 354; Fontana, *Benjamin Constant*, 14–15.

[29] Robespierre, *Le Défenseur* iv. 184–6; McPhee, *Robespierre*, 107–8; Cook, "Between the Old World and the New," 98–100.

[30] Robespierre, *Le Défenseur* iv. 186.

[31] [Say], *Décade philosophique* ii (Thermidor, 1794), 247.

[32] Imbruglia, "Illuminismo e rivoluzione," 69.

[33] Volney, *Abridgement*, 3; Villaverde, *Rousseau y el pensamiento*, 56–7.

firmly articulated the educational philosophy Rousseau expounds in *Émile* with its bias toward manual skills as opposed to reading, Enlightenment, and book learning. Rousseau's ideas indeed pervaded the ideological clashes over schooling and universities in 1793–5 at every level.[34] Against Condorcet's stress on teaching children to make judgments, prove assertions, imbibe history, geography, science, and civics, and acquire a republican consciousness, with primary and secondary education supervised by *philosophes* of the Institut de France, Robespierre's following aimed to eliminate guidance by academies and science, downplay books and learning, and shift the emphasis to manual skills, moral formation, gymnastics, and rural simplicity.

Robespierre's anti-intellectualism, loathing of *philosophisme*, and unbending populism were all closely linked in his political ideology, with Rousseau's name and thought playing a central role throughout. Robespierre graphically displayed his passionate *anti-philosophisme* also in symbolic actions. On 5 December 1792, at the Jacobins, vehemently denouncing the foremost figure of the early Revolution, the dead *philosophe*, Mirabeau, he incited those present to pull down and smash Mirabeau's bust together with that of Helvétius, busts hitherto presiding over the Jacobins' meetings. Helvétius Robespierre declared a *philosophe* whose presence should not be tolerated in the Jacobins' debating hall, being an unbeliever in religion and "one of the cruelest persecutors" of Jean-Jacques. Both busts were pulled down, smashed, and trampled underfoot, the signal for Jacobin clubs across France to topple Mirabeau and "philosophy," and intensify the offensive against Brissotin intellectualism.[35] Busts of Mirabeau and Helvétius were promptly destroyed in the "clubs populaires" of Dijon, Langres, Châtillon-en-Seine, and many other places. Mirabeau "is not a great man any more," sneered Feller's anti-Revolution journal.[36]

Aware the *philosophes*' heirs considered him "a narrow intellect [*un esprit étroit*], a man of prejudices, perhaps a fanatic," Robespierre possessed a sound feel for the depth of the rift separating his own creed, centering on "virtue of the people" and the natural "sacred rights of man," from d'Holbach's and Condorcet's *antipopulaire* vision of constructed rights of mankind and democratic republicanism binding the different segments of society closer together via education, debates, elections, and laws.[37] Before the Revolution, held Robespierre, in his major speech to the Convention, of 7 May 1794 (18 Floreal Year II), reviewing the Revolution's course and explaining his Supreme Being cult, only one thinker (Rousseau) showed true grandeur and purity of doctrine, drawing "virtue" and the Divinity from nature against the perniciously false creed of *la philosophie.* Robespierre had no problem in openly admitting that his *philosophe* foes had been "republicans" long before he himself and his following claimed to be "republican," indeed were republicans even before 1789. Condorcet, Brissot, Carra, Gorsas, and Lafayette (and many other *philosophes*) had

[34] Israel, *Revolutionary Ideas*, 374–95.
[35] Scurr, *Fatal Purity*, 218; Culoma, *Religion civile*, 191; Clarke, *Commemorating*, 174.
[36] [Feller], *Journal historique* (Maastricht, 15 Jan. 1793), 148; Krebs, *Helvétius en Allemagne*, 367.
[37] Robespierre, "Discours," 49; Bosc, "Liberté et propriété," 75.

been openly committed republicans whilst he was still vigorously opposing republicanism before the public. (Here Robespierre was being more accurate than many a modern historian.) Nevertheless, despite their professed republicanism, they had "stupidly defended" the royal cause (that is, opposed the king's execution without an *appel au public*), in 1793. It was ordinary good sense alone, without philosophy, education, or intrigue, that had brought France to perfection. How vastly preferable was the ordinary artisan with a robust understanding of the *Rights of Man* to *philosophes*! *Philosophes* were at every level ordinary people's enemies. There was an urgent need to purge doctrines and persons detrimental to the quick, sure sentiments of the ordinary person.[38]

In *Émile*, completed in 1761 and perhaps his greatest work, Rousseau seeks to establish "virtue" as innate in man, a sentiment that exists and flourishes prior to its formulation as an idea. But where, for Rousseau, true "virtue" is a sentiment foreign to self-interest that readily prompts the individual to sacrifice his or her own individual interest for the common good, a theme prominent in Robespierre's *Éloge de Gresset*, this entire construct grated on Diderot, d'Holbach, Helvétius, Condorcet, and Volney as a false, superficial sentimentality stemming from what they considered the defective "moral sense" philosophy of Shaftesbury, Hutcheson, and Adam Smith.[39] Catholic Counter-Enlightenment apologists, by contrast, esteemed Rousseau as a valuable ally against *philosophisme* as did Robespierre.[40] Where Diderot, d'Holbach, and Helvétius, following Bayle and Spinoza, presented a secular morality, or *morale naturelle* based on reason alone, Rousseau, whose *Émile* Bergier and Jamin quote approvingly in this connection, claims "virtue" cannot rest on reason but only sensibility and faith.[41] Exactly this was Gresset's—and Robespierre's—principal point.

Our morality, held the Diderot circle, is unconnected with metaphysical entities man knows nothing about. Where "virtue" is best fostered in primitive societies according to Rousseau, the radical *philosophes*, culminating in Condorcet, Volney, and Destutt, saw progress of *l'esprit humain*, knowledge and reason, as the exclusive engine of mankind's moral improvement. Moral and political progress advances via philosophy and science: lessening ignorance alone makes reduction of human misery and oppression possible. Robespierre and the *philosophes* were equally convinced that "education" is the key to fomenting good citizenship, but they interpreted "education" quite differently, Robespierre envisaging it as meaning the formation of character and sentiment by society, not the instilling of knowledge, independence of mind, and judgment. For Rousseau presents a totally contrary view to that of his *philosophe*

[38] Robespierre, "Discours," 31–2; Crow, *Emulation*, 175–6, 178.

[39] Helvétius, *De l'homme* i. 457–8, 470–1; Cherni, *Diderot: l'ordre et le devenir*, 433–6.

[40] Rousseau, *Social Contract*, 307–8; Rousseau, *Émile*, 239–40; Domenech, *L'Éthique des Lumières*, 91.

[41] Rousseau, *Lettre à Voltaire*, 18 Aug. 1756, in Rousseau, *Oeuvres complètes* (25 vols., Paris, 1826), xx. 307–33, 309–10, 328; Rousseau, *Émile*, 237–48, 254–7; Bergier, *Apologie* ii. 11, 22–3; Belaval, *Études sur Diderot*, 150.

adversaries of how the human mind progresses.[42] Affirming the inertness and inactivity of matter, Rousseau embraced a strict dualism of active and inactive substances coupled with a Lockean conception of mind. Conceiving "virtue" possible only for those heeding the pleas of the soul, especially conscience and remorse, he tied the threads of morality to God, comprehensively condemning "atheism."[43] The *anti-philosophe* Jamin was thrilled by Rousseau's espousal of the soul's immortality while declaring the *encyclopédistes* dogmatic, intolerant, arrogant, and dangerous.[44] Bergier exalted in Rousseau's proclaiming the *philosophes*' principles delusions from which he was happy to escape, identifying the "only error" the *philosophes* taught him as the stupidity of his former veneration for them. Rousseau's rupture with them Bergier applauded but, ever upright, he also felt obliged to add that where Diderot's and d'Holbach's personal morals were above reproach, unfortunately this was more than could be said for Rousseau.[45]

The *Contrat social* appeared a month after *Émile,* reaffirming Rousseau's thesis that our hearts, not our reason, govern our consciences. Consciences buttress the moral order and "at the bottom of our hearts" one finds "an innate principle of justice and virtue [. . .]."[46] The chapter on "civil religion," restating his conviction that the cosmos is ruled by a conscious and benevolent deity, recommends banishment of whoever opposes natural religion's principal dogma. It also expressly curtails toleration in other respects, even urging the death penalty for whoever professes belief in divine providence but then subsequently disavows this—to Rousseau's mind—invaluable doctrine.[47] The work also powerfully reflected Rousseau's fixation with ancient cults—Sparta and pristine Rome, their prizing collective unity of mind, collective thinking superbly adapted to uphold *volonté générale* in Rousseau's and Robespierre's sense with their vibrant civic cults, exhortations of a public virtue closely linked to martial discipline, masculine values, bellicosity, antifeminism, and xenophobia. They lacked only the principle of equality, a defect Rousseau set out to rectify.[48] What Boulanger deemed the ancient republics' worst aspect—fusing their republican politics with religious cults—was precisely the feature Rousseau, Mably, and Robespierre made the foundation of their "republicanism of virtue" in opposition to the secular polity based on reason and toleration of Diderot and Condorcet.

Conflict always arises, held the radical *philosophe*s, between despotism rooted in ignorance, and cultivation of the sciences generating moral and political amelioration, prompting Diderot, d'Holbach, and their heirs to dub Rousseau "l'apologiste de l'ignorance," a false prophet urging men to revert to their original state of misery, stupidity, and unreason.[49] What considerations, demanded Helvétius, prompted

[42] Rousseau, *Émile*, 233–7; Gauthier, *Rousseau*, 61–3.
[43] Rousseau, *Émile*, 243–4. [44] Jamin, *Pensées théologiques*, 88, 351, 353, 356.
[45] Bergier, *Apologie* ii. 49–50; Rousseau, *Rêveries du promeneur solitaire*, 38–9.
[46] Rousseau, *Émile*, 250–4; Domenech, "Éthique et révolution," 38, 42.
[47] Rousseau, *Social Contract*, 71–2.
[48] Lafrance, "Idée rousseauiste," 28; Riley, "Rousseau's General Will," 130; Borghero, "Sparta," 307–10.
[49] Edelstein, *Terror of Natural Right*, 89.

Rousseau "à prendre si hautement part pour l'ignorance"? [so forcefully to take the side of ignorance].[50] Deeply committed to science and erudition, they scorned Rousseau for disparaging the sciences, for envisaging them as negative in origin, goals, and moral effects. Where, for Rousseau, science and mathematics lure adepts into forgetting the basic duties of life and exploring false paths, true knowledge, according to d'Holbach in his *La Morale universelle*, summons us to our duties. Where Rousseau dismisses history as useless enquiries about princes and wars, diverting attention from more edifying topics, compromising "notre liberté naturelle" with false *politesse* and a thousand vices, radicals proclaimed history indispensable for demonstrating the true nature of society, tyranny, oppression, conspiracies, churches, and war, and grounding our search for escape from the plethora of man-made evils for which mankind pays so dearly.[51] Where, for Rousseau, sciences foment luxury and a desire to excel, encouraging arrogant contempt for the unschooled, moral decay, and corruption of authentic good taste, radical enlighteners urged society to acclaim those cultivating the sciences. What is truly "criminal," suggested d'Holbach, is to disavow learning, malign the arts, and seek to deprive humanity of knowledge, like Rousseau obstructing the quest for truth.[52] Philosophy and science, far from diverting from genuine integrity, except where given to vague speculation and objects inaccessible to experience, can only promote man's *Bonheur*. Far from being the fruit of idleness, the sciences and arts arise from Man's true needs and assist discovery of what best contributes to our conservation and happiness—not least by showing how misery and wretchedness are fed by ignorance and tyranny.[53]

Rousseau's *Social Contract* fuses Radical Enlightenment strands with strands of deism, cultism, eulogy of "natural" man, and censorship, to create a strongly authoritarian and particularist *volonté générale*. If his republican political radicalism approximated to that of the Radical Enlightenment in part, it was grounded on a markedly different cosmology, metaphysics, and moral philosophy. Its central feature was his fusing creation of the universe by a knowing and benevolent God with a political and (in some degree) social radicalism claiming existing society, law, and institutions were fundamentally corrupt. This combining of elements was highly unusual during the Enlightenment and, to Diderot and d'Holbach, masked a fatal contradiction. Among major eighteenth-century thinkers Rousseau alone fused the idea that divine providence governs the course of nature with the complaint that human laws and institutions were universally corrupt leaving most men in chains. It was a remarkable conceptual contrivance devised by rigidly separating "natural man" who is basically good from fallen and corrupt "man in society." Rousseau's delimiting divine providence's scope so that it retains no role in the sphere of law, government,

[50] Helvétius, *De l'homme*, i. 497; Zaretsky and Scott, *Philosophers" Quarrel*, 6, 24.
[51] Helvétius, *De l'homme* ii. 202–3; Starobinski, *Remède*, 166–70; Borghero, "Sparta tra storia," 286–96.
[52] D'Holbach, *Morale universelle* ii. 203.
[53] D'Holbach, *Morale universelle* ii. 205; Dent, *Rousseau*, 51–2.

and institutions, his envisaging man as being what the Deity intended only when beyond society's artifices, enabled him to weld together powerfully, but, for some, fatally, a genuine providential theism with a potent but passive, authoritarian, severely truncated republican stance.

16.2. ROBESPIERRE, ROUSSEAU, AND THE CULT OF THE ORDINARY

Decades after their deaths, the post-1757 epic feuding between Diderot and Rousseau still resounded in the public arena, albeit the significance of their unresolved clashes only fully emerged during the Revolution. Rousseau's isolation and separation of natural man from society, applauded by Robespierre, was repudiated by Diderot, d'Holbach, and Condorcet, as later by Volney and Destutt, and even revolutionary writers who were otherwise ardent Rousseauistes, like Claude Fauchet,[54] critics all envisaging man in society as the only proper natural state. The savage state or "state of nature" to which certain "spéculateurs chagrins" (i.e. Rousseau) seek to revert is actually, averred d'Holbach, echoed later by Volney, a condition of misery, imbecility, and *déraison*.[55] After Diderot's and Rousseau's deaths, the ideological battle continued and widened in the revolutionary public sphere, becoming an unrelenting contest between the Revolution of Mirabeau, Condorcet, Sieyès, Volney, Destutt, and Brissot, the Revolution of the great enactments at the foundation of modernity, and the repressive dictatorship of *robespierriste* authoritarian populists idolizing Rousseau and undermining the Revolution by claiming "virtue" lies exclusively in the people good and simple and not in enlightenment, sciences, and learning.

Ideologically, the Revolution is best understood, we have argued throughout, as a struggle between three warring, incompatible, and fundamentally different ideological streams, a triangular contest between democratic republicanism based on "universal and equal rights;" a precedent-based constitutional monarchism rooted in Montesquieu, the "British model," and mixed government, defending aristocratism and a restricted suffrage; and the authoritarian populism of Marat, Robespierre, and Saint-Just. Moderate Enlightenment fought the democratic republicanism of the Brissotins, the Radical Enlightenment, while both battled the intolerant, authoritarian populism of Marat and Robespierre aspiring to crush all dissent and impose the values of the supposed iconic ordinary citizen.[56] Rousseau loomed large as an ideological force from the outset, present in all three revolutionary ideologies. But it was the third of these, evolving into a major force within the Revolution only from 1791–2, that transformed Rousseau into an active, potent revolutionary cult lionizing

[54] Ravitch, "The Abbé Fauchet," 247–62.

[55] Diderot, *Réfutation*, 316–17; d'Holbach, *Système social*, 213; Goggi, "Spinoza contro Rousseau," 134–6; Cook, "Between the Old World and the New," 98–100.

[56] Israel, *Revolutionary Ideas*, 695–708.

but also in some respects simplifying his thought, especially by replacing his typical neutralism and passivity before the contest between aristocratic and democratic republicanism with an active dynamic and highly intolerant *robespierriste* pseudo-republicanism echoing his resentment against the *philosophes* with a fervor quite distinct from the guarded, qualified, and mostly receding admiration for Rousseau of revolutionary leaders like Mirabeau, Cérutti, Brissot, and Desmoulins.

Little known to the wider public, Diderot, d'Holbach, and even Helvétius, meanwhile, figured posthumously as curiously hidden, unseen participants in the mechanics of French revolutionary ideological feuding. On 2 December 1789, the ex-Jesuit revolutionary pamphleteer, republican ideologue, and educational reformer, Joseph-Antoine Cérutti (1738–92), published a notable piece justifying "un homme estimable" (d'Holbach) unjustly attacked by "un homme célèbre" (Rousseau). Cérutti charged Rousseau with impugning d'Holbach in his *Confessions*, in a cruel, outrageous manner. Rousseau detested d'Holbach and his atheism, and considered the *Système de la nature* "an abominable work."[57] In his article, Cérutti recalled meeting d'Holbach at the bath resort of Contrexéville in the Vosges, some years before his death, and hearing the latter's account of the quarrel and why he considered Rousseau a still powerful "homme anti-social" and "anti-littérateur."[58]

Diderot had originally introduced them, bringing them into regular contact; relations began to sour, explained d'Holbach, when he took to teasing, contradicting, and provoking Rousseau to lure him out of his habitual inactive taciturnity. But it was their "philosophie anti-thérésienne," their dislike of Rousseau's relationship with his unschooled woman companion Thérèse Levasseur (1721–1801) and efforts to break up what to their minds was an unsuitable union, that finally so antagonized Rousseau as to cause his permanent rupture with d'Holbach, Diderot, and their friend, the critic Grimm, Catherine the Great's chief literary and intellectual agent in the West.[59] Thérèse "they regarded," as one Rousseau biographer expressed it, "as stupid and narrow." Apparently she never "learnt to tell the time by the clock or remember the months of the calendar;" though literate, her spelling was bizarrely phonetic. Their relationship, Rousseau liked to imply, was merely one of convenience; he called her "the supplement I needed." Despite scandalously abandoning their children, Rousseau remained firmly attached to her.[60] Thereby, the most eloquent of men, held d'Holbach, became the most anti-intellectual, and "l'homme le plus sensible s'est rendu le plus anti-social" [the most sensitive of men, the most antisocial].

Addressing the revolutionary public, Cérutti saw a need to set the record straight while cautiously pointing to the ideological "danger" the dead Rousseau still represented. Rousseau zealots were ubiquitous and "will perhaps consider it a bad thing

[57] Curran, *Atheism, Religion and Enlightenment*, 139.

[58] [Charrière] *Eclaircissemens relatifs*, 29–30.

[59] Cérutti in the *supplément* to no. 336 of the *Journal de Paris* (2 Dec. 1789), 1567–8; Charrière (Belle van Zuylen), *Eclaircissements relatifs*, 30.

[60] Damrosch, *Jean-Jacques Rousseau*, 188.

that I dare to oppose their mania and even my own"—for he too had admired Rousseau. A strange *intolérance* characterized Rousseau enthusiasts, a fervor now so swollen up that challenging their "opinions fanatiques" resembled setting foot on a savage island. Still, exposing himself to being devoured by cannibals was an apprehension he had to surmount since a deceased friend needed rescuing from their hands, a key reputation needed defending from "leurs outrages." It was "horrible" that anyone, even a démi-god like Rousseau, should, on dying, immolate on his tomb, as he had in his *Confessions*, all the friends he had had in his life, and compel their plaintive ghosts to follow his in opprobrium through all posterity.[61] Several readers, male and female, vehemently protested, angrily retorting that Cérutti's intervention only reflected discredit and dishonour on Diderot, d'Holbach, and Cérutti himself, showing all three to be arrogant, hypocritical, and insincere.[62]

An impressive deputation of writers, artists, and others complained to the National Assembly, on 27 August 1791, pointing out that Mirabeau and Voltaire had received public honors, magnificent ceremonies of entombment in the Panthéon, while Rousseau had not. They demanded Rousseau's *panthéonisation*, a state pension for Rousseau's widow, Thérèse Levasseur, and implementation of a December 1790 decree authorizing a public statue for central Paris honoring the *Contrat social*'s and *Émile*'s author under the rubric "La nation française libre, à J. J. Rousseau."[63] Penned by the Breton reformer Pierre Louis Ginguené (1748–1816), an ardent Rousseau admirer and future member of the National Convention's committee of public instruction, this petition bore no less than 311 signatures including those of Chamfort, Clavière, Lanthenas, Roland, Mercier, Gorsas, Duroveray, Perlet, and Fanny Beauharnais. Voltaire had been installed for crushing fanaticism "under the feet of philosophy," clearing away the *débris* from the ground where "you [the legislature] have raised the edifice of our liberty," so how could the Revolution not discharge its debt to Rousseau, the "premier fondateur de la constitution française" [chief founder of the French constitution]? Admitttedly, conceded Ginguené, Rousseau's ideas did not always conform to the revolutionary legislature's principles: Rousseau taught that his "general will" cannot be embodied in a representative assembly and that republican forms suit only small states and were inappropriate for France, a doctrine raised as an objection to French republicanism especially by advocates of constitutional monarchism, like the Brothers De Lameth.[64] Still, key strands of the projected new Constitution, especially the principle of equality, did stem from Rousseau's ideas, "equality of rights" and "sovereignty of the people" being the *idées-mères* from which the Revolution arose, foundational ideas Rousseau laid down under the eyes of

[61] Cérutti in the *supplément* to no. 336 of the *Journal de Paris* (2 Dec. 1789), 1568.
[62] [Charrière], *Eclaircissements relatifs*, 193–4.
[63] *Archives Parlementaires* xxix (27 Aug. 1791), 755–6; Jourdan, "Culte de Rousseau," 62–3.
[64] *Archives Parlementaires* xxix (27 Aug. 1791), 756; Swenson, *On Jean-Jacques Rousseau*, 10.

despotism itself. If Voltaire championed Calas and "all the oppressed," he hardly matched Jean-Jacques as a "foe of oppression."[65]

If Rousseau's "war" on the *philosophes* was partly resentment at d'Holbach's and his friends' scorning his humble Thérèse, as the Contrexéville discussion implied, antipathy to their "philosophie anti-Thérèsienne," the *philosophes*' disdaining the views of the uneducated and illiterate more generally now infused the entire quarrel.[66] It was precisely their "aristocratic disdain" for the ordinary, held Ginguené, that rendered the *philosophes* inferior to Rousseau. Had not the Citizen of Geneva taught men to penetrate behind the mask of false social convention to understand man as he truly is, teaching contempt for vain titles and illusions of grandeur, fostering that preference for simple tastes, natural sentiment, virtue, and liberty permeating all his publications that inspired the Revolution?"[67] At the height of the Terror, in the same month Danton, Desmoulins, and their colleagues came under the guillotine, Thérèse Levasseur appeared in person before the National Convention accompanied by a deputation to demand, once again, that the "author of *Émile* and the *Contrat Social*'s remains be transferred to the Panthéon."[68] Although the Convention sanctioned their demand in principle, still nothing happened. Rousseau was not to be publicly honored at the Panthéon until after Thermidor, in September 1794.

Condorcet maintained that Rousseau's rejecting representation, his opposing representation of the "general will" through a legislature, was closely related to the fallacy persuading him that men lose their liberty on entering into the social state. Just as the individual surrenders part of a merely illusionary liberty on entering the social state, so by electing representatives he sacrifices a measure of purely illusionary independence but gains thereby in *liberté réelle*, real freedom.[69] Maintaining that republican re-education of society is necessary to make elections and representation work, to overcome ignorance, prejudice and superstition, and that Rousseau's, Gresset's, and Robespierre's praise of the natural state, *l'état sauvage*, by obstructing this, is harmful and misplaced, thus became central to the revolutionary Radical Enlightenment. Inherently and militantly anti-Marat and anti-Robespierre, Brissotin revolutionary doctrine in this way came to view Rousseau's doctrines as a basis for tyranny. According to d'Holbachian ideas, it was vested interests, namely "the two classes of civil and sacred tyrants," monarchical and ecclesiastical, working against the common good as a whole, that prevent men from becoming enlightened about their own rights and interests, the true ends of the social body that vested interests continually subvert so as to prey on the majority.[70] They do so by mystifying the public (especially with religion and the mystique of monarchy); the Montagne did so with a revised theology

[65] [Ginguené], *Petition to Assemblée Nationale*, in *Archives Parlementaires* xxix (27 Aug. 1791), 5.

[66] Ginguené, *Lettres*, 132. [67] [Ginguené], *Petition to Assemblée Nationale*, 756.

[68] [Say], *Décade philosophique* 1 (25 Germinal, 1794), 33–4.

[69] [Condorcet], *Bibliothèque*, 1st series (1790), vii. 27, Condorcet's note; Condorcet, *Bibliothèque* 2nd series (1791), vii. 29–30.

[70] D'Holbach, *Politique naturelle*, 119–21; Israel, *Democratic Enlightenment*, 612.

and authoritarian political mystique. Through education and representation alone can this "politique aveugle" can be defeated.

Key educational reformers of the Revolution such as François Xavier Lanthenas (1754–99), among the most active ideologues of education reform, press freedom, and anti-*esclavagisme*, in the *Cercle social* and reforming circles around Brissot and Roland, eagerly adapted the principles expounded in *La Politique naturelle* and the *Système social* in their efforts to form a new public civic consciousness through public primary education.[71] To denounce and seek to discredit learning and the sciences is to ensure men have no means to form sound judgments and distinguish what enhances our existence from what harms and curtails it.[72] The "natural man" invoked by the "eloquent sophist" [Rousseau], charged both d'Holbach and Condorcet, would be a contemptibly limited, ignorant creature lacking the means to safeguard his own well-being. Rousseau believed ancient Sparta and Rome were especially equipped to uphold the *volonté générale*, but his eulogizing the pristine "virtue," austerity, and prowess of the ancient Spartans and Romans was both morally and politically reprehensible, as well as absurd, the latter having been in reality aggressive oppressors toward all neighbors.[73]

Condorcet's, Volney's, and Destutt's "general will," like Diderot's and d'Holbach's earlier, differed fundamentally from Rousseau's particularlist "general will," standing in an entirely different relation to philosophical reason, being universal, unalterable, and designed to safeguard all men's and women's basic rights and freedoms., There exists, held this view, a constant danger that the majority's will itself can unjustly subject the weakest to the strongest—and, in Condorcet especially,[74] women to men—becoming a gateway to new-fangled tyranny. *Volonté générale* in its *Rousseauiste* sense seemingly facilitated subjection to despotism and oppression, blighting everyone's rights. Department Du Nord deputy François Poultier Delmotte (1753–1826) wanted it inscribed in the pending democratic republican Constitution of early 1793, "that the allegedly general will voted by the majority cannot bind the minority when it evidently violates the *Rights of Man*. The minority always remains free to remind the majority of their true sovereign—*la raison universelle* [universal reason], the sovereign that dictated those rights."[75] "Let us assert, then, that reason is the only true sovereign among men; and that to reason alone belongs the right to legislate."[76]

Rousseau's, Gresset's, and Robespierre's stress on the purity and goodness of the ordinary person, that "the people alone is good, just, magnanimous," as Robespierre expressed it in April 1792, "and that corruption and tyranny are the exclusive domain

[71] Israel, *Revolutionary Ideas*, 132. [72] D'Holbach, *Morale universelle* ii. 204–5.

[73] D'Holbach, *Le Bon-Sens du Curé Jean Meslier*, 177–8; Condorcet, *Tableau historique*, 377; Spitz, "From Civism to Civility," 109–12.

[74] Condorcet, *Tableau historique*, 897–8.

[75] Poultier Delmotte, in *Archives Parlementaires* lxvii, p. 383 (24 June 1793).

[76] Poultier Delmotte, in *Archives Parlementaires* lxvii, p. 382 (24 June 1793).

of all those who disdain them,"[77] and, finally, their common emphasis on the natural tendency of this exalted "moral purity" to generate unity in the "general will," together with Rousseau's doctrine of dictatorship, assuredly had nothing to do with any form of Enlightenment, or the triumph of reason in d'Holbach's, Brissot's, and Condorcet's sense. Rather, this set of principles—and Robespierre continually vaunted his unbending adherence to "my principles"—became in his hands a dire threat to all Enlightenment values.[78] The theme of the common people's "moral purity," constantly paraded by Robespierre in his major speeches, could be, and in an oversimplified and debased version was, massaged to promote the Counter-Enlightenment thrust of a ruthlessly intolerant and repressive populist authoritarianism.

16.3. ROBESPIERRE AND THE HISTORIOGRAPHY OF THE REVOLUTION: REVISITING THE "MARXIST INTERPRETATION"

Reinterpreting the French Revolution so as to draw attention to the intellectual sources of its democratic republicanism, and why its democratic republicanism fused with an attack on religious authority, brings us also to the profound disagreement among scholars in recent years, especially between the revived Jacobin–Marxist school of interpretation of the Revolution, originally formulated by Albert Mathiez, George Lefebvre, and Albert Soboul, and the interpretation that views "universal and equal rights" and democratic republicanism as the core revolutionary doctrines. While their work and that of their heirs deserves considerable respect, and while the French Revolution unquestionably did involve elements of class conflict given that its first and most consistent target was the aristocratic–ecclesiastical social system first systematically denounced by Diderot and d'Holbach, and preventing vested economic interests preying on the majority always remained a primary concern, the vigorous revival of their claim that the Montagne was the true core of the Revolution has to be comprehensively rejected. The powerful recent trend in much French historiography to reaffirm Robespierre's integrity and centrality in the Revolution, known as the "le retour de Robespierre" [the return of Robespierre], is not just a misconstruing of Robespierre but a fundamental misreading of the entire Revolution itself.

The Revolution, Marxist scholars rightly argued, swept away outdated restrictions and restraints on economic freedom, attacked all forms of "privilege," guild regulations, and mercantilist corporations, and sought systematically to disarm and disempower aristocrats and ecclesiastics. The evidence supports Lefebvre's demonstration of the autonomy and centrality of the great peasant movement of 1789 and subsequent peasant unrest and Soboul's path-breaking demonstration of the autonomy and

[77] Robespierre, *Le Défenseur* i. 45.
[78] Jaume, "Robespierre chez Machiavel?," 220, 223, 228; Stalnaker, *Unfinished Enlightenment*, 176.

divergent character of the *sans-culotte* movement. But while these and a range of other social forces and movements were fundamental to the Revolution, historical accuracy requires diverging markedly from their approach in key respects. Their great mistake was seeing social forces and movements, popular protest and unrest, as the Revolution's primary engine, the key to understanding the vast upheaval. Overall, the evidence clearly disproves the view that popular pressures shaped the Revolution's main ideological and policy concerns, battles, and shifts in any defining way. What the evidence shows, rather, is that social movements and popular expressions of discontent, on their own, no matter how furious and powerful, practically never possess sufficient direction, power to articulate concerns, cohesion and lasting motive power, durability or viability in themselves to become sources of revolutionary authority, or engines of systematic reform. Anger and grievance simply cannot expound and sustain revolutionary programs and scripts.

This applies, universally, to the American, German (1792, 1830, and 1848), and Russian revolutions no less than the French: however indispensable popular anger, resentment, and unrest were for precipitating the revolutionary process (in the American case provoked by the fiscal exactions of a foreign sovereign), there always remained a stubbornly wide gap between the impulsive, vacillating, hesitant, unguided impetus of the people and the shaping force of competing agendas, the priorities of rival revolutionary scripts produced by the vying intellectual vanguards striving to formulate, publicize, and carry out the Revolution's goals.[79] Consequently, the latter is where the primary focus of attention needs to be. Popular discontent and grievance, no matter how great, generate only fleeting and archaic varieties of political pressure, as indeed Soboul famously admitted, impulses not just inarticulate in terms of the rhetoric of revolutionary thought produced by the vying elites but also—which Soboul failed to stress—exceedingly unsteady, inconsistent, and volatile within themselves, subject to swiftly being captured and steered first one way and then another by competing revolutionary blocs. If the Paris crowds were constitutional monarchist one day, Brissotin another, Hébertistes another, and finally, in 1795, violently ultra-royalist, there was nothing at all inconsistent, surprising, or unusual in that. Quite the contrary. Crowd behavior easily absorbed by rapid turns all these conceptually opposed but emotionally and socially easily fused impulses. Rioters and demonstrators mostly possessed scant awareness of, or interest in, the ideological splits as such. They cared little for the books and pamphlets; their concerns were different. That does not strip the people of its dignity, or hopes for a better life, or the justice of their cause, but does highlight their uncertainty and apprehensions, the complexity of their predicament.

Lefebvre and Soboul themselves felt disconcerted by the need they recognized and long wrestled with to label the "popular" protest movements, both the peasant

[79] Israel, review of Keith Michael Baker and Dan Edelstein (eds.), *Scripting Revolution: A Historic Approach to the Comparative Study of Revolutions* (Stanford, 2015), in *H-France Forum.*

and *sans-culotte* movements they studied, and felt immense personal sympathy for, as in some sense retrograde social impulses opposed to "libéralisme économique," "l'agriculture capitaliste," "l'individualisme agraire," and what they conceived as the necessary social laws of progress, the logic of what Marxists define as a bourgeois revolution.[80] The interpretation presented here is in no way Marxist, but, paradoxically, in one respect perhaps more Marxist than theirs: for there can be no revolutionary movement without an intellectual vanguard providing a cogent revolutionary ideology or ideologies beforehand, intellectual systems overturning past assumptions and belief and needing to be previously diffused, albeit diffused less among the general population than among literary, scientific, professional, and academic elites. Of course, for authentic Marixists, and more important than anything else, there must also be a class structural shift in society, a new stage in the ceaseless class war, before a major transformation of conceptual parameters can occur—a social structural shift generating the profound change in consciousness and priorities.

It is far from clear that such a shift actually occurred prior to the Revolution. But whether it did or did not, in 1789, Europe (including Britain), despite the economic expansion of previous centuries, remained essentially an *ancien régime* aristocratic–ecclesiastical society. Late eighteenth-century social unrest did not differ in any obvious way from the social agitation which shook England, France, Ireland, Spain, Portugal, and Naples in the seventeenth century. Rather, the anger, grievances, and rebelliousness remained exactly the same as in the previous century. Hence, arguing that social unrest of whatever sort forged and shaped the revolutionary process is wholly unjustified by the evidence. All popular interventions in the French Revolution from 1787 to 1799, without any exception, whether violent or not, were short, hesitant, unstable, and highly volatile, apt swiftly to shift direction. No matter how important such interventions were in introducing, destabilizing, unseating, and strengthening factions, they invariably had little directly to do with the ensuing clash of revolutionary ideologies or the legislative outcome. What chiefly matters for understanding the vast innovations of the French Revolution are neither social forces, nor social structure, nor *mentalités*, nor popular interventions, but the bitter rivalry between competing revolutionary vanguards and their agendas—the primary factor in America, France, Germany, and likewise in Russia, in 1917.

Like Marxism, recent cultural history too has attempted to interpret the Revolution in terms of changing long-terms trends, but it is hard to see how any of the Revolution's great legislative achievements could have arisen out of mainstream society, general *mentalités*, and widely accepted ideas, because the legislation reveals dramatic novelty and popular culture does not. The claim that "la modernité" is not the result of some dramatic events, as one historian expressed it, and did not issue from a "rupture radicale," but from the slow impact of tradition working upon itself ("un patient travail de la tradition contre elle-même"), might be true for the

[80] Bosc and Gauthier, "Introduction à la réédition," 26.

eighteenth century as a whole but remains distinctly hazy, opaque, and hard to substantiate.[81] But whether there is any truth to claims about long-term trends or not, democratic modernity unquestionably burst on the scene explosively and abruptly via the Revolution with the explosion coming not from below, as *mentalité* practitioners believe, but via the powerful irruption during the 1770s and 1780s of anti-monarchical and anti-aristocratic ideologies closely linked to atheistic and radical deist rejection of religious authority. By 1789, the Radical Enlightenment's mature agenda of universal and equal rights, representative democracy, universal secular education, secularization of the constitution, law, and all public ceremonies, *volonté générale* (whether in the sense of Diderot or Rousseau), and, after the Bastille's fall, full freedom of expression, was already fully formed but also still broadly unfamiliar to most of the public.

The republican revolutionary faction, the radicals, "the authentic Left," led originally by Mirabeau and Sieyès but publicized and built up by such journalists as Brissot, Pétion, Cérutti, Condorcet, Roland, Desmoulins, Prudhomme, Bonneville, Manuel, Carra, Volney, M. J. Chénier, Cabanis, Louvet, Perlet, Daunou, and others, steered the Revolution toward these overriding and epoch-making goals not because they were particularly admirable men, as one exponent of the "negative critique" thought I am arguing (though Condorcet and Daunou indubitably were), but because they were publicly (if not always privately) steadfastly committed, by factional loyalties, to the principles of freedom of expression, equality, republicanism, democracy, universal education, and freedom to associate. Press freedom, declared Condorcet, in a speech at the *Cercle social*, on 12 July 1791, is not just a right but a means of preserving the people's liberty: populist tyrants [*tyrans populaires*] can only operate "under a mask" which succeeds only where there is no press freedom.[82] Cromwell's dictatorship in England in the 1650s, he ascribed to the English being too busy reading the Bible to bother with newspapers, pamphlets, and gazettes. On ideological grounds, and in their own political interest, the democratic republicans adduced universal human rights, international solidarity of peoples, and the other fundamentally innovative concepts of the Revolution. Hence, the term "radical" must strictly be reserved for these particular enlightened tendencies, whereas the social groups that Marxist and *mentalité* historiography associates with *radicalité*—rebellious peasants, *sans-culottes*, Montagnard agitators, especially when evincing intolerance, nostalgia for an imagined past, proneness to violence, and repressive, retrograde and authoritarian tendencies—should never be styled "radicals" by any historian seeking accuracy, being far more accurately designated "authoritarian populist."

It is quite wrong to state that the Brissotins and Montagnards "blamed each other" for the September 1792 prison massacres, one of the main flash points of the propaganda war between Brissotins and Montagnards—as the same contributor

[81] Lilti, "Comment écrit-on l'histoire intellectuelle," 206; Israel, "L'Histoire intellectuelle des Lumières," 173–225.

[82] Condorcet, *Pièces Extraites*, 5, 8.

to the "negative critique" who wrongly thought I was saying the Brissotins were particularly "admirable" incorrectly stated.[83] Rather, Robespierre and the Montagne, instead of blaming anyone, defended the (small, extensively manipulated) crowds that perpetrated the massacres, presenting what occurred as the work of "the people," and "necessary" in the dire circumstances; only the Brissotins, commencing with Brissot himself, among republican revolutionaries, denounced the slaughter as an indefensible and heinous atrocity.[84] For their part, Mathiez, Lefebvre, and Soboul, who explain the state-driven repression of the Terror (1793–4) as a necessary response to external threats—European monarchies and aristocracies resolved to overthrow the Revolution—along with internal betrayal, conspiracies, and intrigues undermining the Revolution from within, while seeking to disassociate Robespierre in some degree from the atrocities, portraying him less as a pillar of ruthless authoritarianism than the supposedly astute savior of the Revolution, its chief pillar of integrity,[85] approached the September 1792 atrocities in the same manner.

Eventually, new research proved Mathiez, Lefebvre, and Soboul mistaken in supposing unavoidable massive external and internal threats drove the Terror. Great historians though they were, by building their interpretation around the unsustainable myth that Robespierre and the coalition making up the Montagnard dictatorship of 1793–4 saved the Revolution, they engendered a potent but utterly false myth that rendered their overall class-based interpretation more vulnerable. For their error here greatly aided the briefly fashionable rival framework introduced by François Furet in his *Penser la Révolution française* (1978). Furet succeeded in massively derailing what had previously been the standard interpretation, transforming the entire debate through being right about this one crucial point: Robespierre and the Terror were in no way a necessary response to external and internal threats to the Revolution; rather, the repression and the Terror were the direct consequence of a powerful ideological strain within the Revolution and hence intrinsic to (elements of) the Revolution. Bronislaw Baczko followed Furet in stressing the inherent, ideological character of the Terror, and sweeping intolerance of Robespierre's autocratic "Rousseauisme." Baczko also rightly drew attention to Robespierre's being particularly active—and original—in devising the disgrace and persecution of prominent revolutionaries like Condorcet, Cloots, Paine, Marchena, Louvet, Proli, Barlow, and many others by spreading elaborately constructed lies and mobilizing against them chauvinistic prejudice and ignorance, thereby converting them into scapegoats as foreigners, traitors, or "aristocrats," and sometimes all three.[86]

Deliberate use of widely-publicized falsehood as a political and propaganda tool to justify outright repression became *the* speciality of the Montagne and of Robespierre personally. As a consequence, the world's then most famous democrat and defender

[83] Bell's review in the *New Republican* is inaccurate or misleading in most respects.

[84] Martin, *Violence et Révolution*, 143–4; Wahnich, *In Defence of the Terror*, 40–5.

[85] Ansart-Dourlen, *L'Action politique des personnalités*, 58, 60; Schechter, *Genealogy of Terror*, 198.

[86] Baczko, *Politiques de la Révolution*, 22–3.

of the "Rights of Man," Tom Paine, was hurled into prison in Paris along with dozens of other zealously republican publicists and deputies of the National Convention, including Volney, Destutt, Daunou, and Mercier, beside many other foreign democratic revolutionary leaders, among them José Marchena (1768–1821), leader of Spanish democratic atheist revolutionaries active in France during the Revolution. The ruthless repression led to the liquidation of virtually the entire Brissotin leadership, much to the distress of enlighteners everywhere, horrifying not least nearly the whole of what were then called the "Jacobin" fraternity in Britain and Germany. Mary Wollstonecraft "described to me, more than once," recalled Godwin, in 1798, "the anguish she felt at hearing of the death of Brissot, Vergniaud, and the twenty deputies, as one of the most intolerable sensations she had ever experienced."[87]

Equally misconceived, up to a point, the *furetien* (anti-Marxist liberal) and Marxist interpretations both shared a common misreading of Robespierre's politics, both tendencies classifying his outlook as Rousseauist "utopique et rétrograde."[88] In fact, though constantly invoking Rousseau, Robespierre shared nothing of Rousseau's hesitant neutralism, his rooted unwillingness to intervene in the ongoing battle between democratic and aristocratic republicanism in Switzerland and beyond. But the Furet faction were more accurate and realistic than the "marxistes" in identifying the true cultural and intellectual rootedness and significance of Robespierre's ideology. For it was by no means Marat's assassination, or the execution of republican intellectuals in the autumn of 1793 that so shocked Wollstonecraft, that marked the origin of the Terror. Rather, as Baczko and later Haim Burstin demonstrated, the mindset that generated the horrors of the Terror was indeed inherent in ideological trends shaping the Revolution from an early stage.[89] But Furet's reinterpretation succeeded only to a very limited extent because, apart from the rooted ideological character of the persecution of critics and dissidents during the Terror, he was badly mistaken about almost everything else.

Wildly fallacious, and fundamentally misleading, is Furet's claim that a single coherent dominant ideological strain infused the whole Revolution from the outset, focusing on *volonté générale*. In reality, it is quite impossible to identify any basic continuity running from 1789 to 1794, for the evidence, we have seen, shows at all stages a primal clash of three wholly irreconcilable battling ideologies. Furet mistook the *monarchiens* of 1789, led by Mounier and Lally-Tolendal, and later Malouet and the Abbé Maury, for a small, weak minority when the constitutional monarchists were actually the dominant bloc in the Assemblée nationale during 1789–91, the main contest then being between them and the democratic republicans, with the groups afterwards forming the Montagne still playing just a minor part. Obscuring the split rightly characterized by one scholar as one between "une majorité modérée" adopting a restricted, narrow conception of political representation, and "une minorité

[87] Godwin, *Memoirs of the Author*, 90.
[88] Belissa and Bosc, *Robespierre*, 446.
[89] Burstin, "Entre théorie et pratique," 45–7.

patriote" contending for universal male suffrage,[90] the *furetiens* then hopelessly muddled everything further by obscuring the chasm between the democratic republicans and authoritarian, Rousseauist–populist Montagne, reducing the entire French Revolution to a morass of confusion.

Although Furet did recognize that a "political and intellectual chasm" separated the constitutional monarchists (and followers of Montesquieu) from the democratic republicans, he wrongly supposed the latter represented the "overriding spirit of the Revolution" throughout the period between 1789 and 1794, while simultaneously postulating close affinities between the Brissotins and the Montagne, leading him to identify the Terror and Robespierre with the true spirit and meaning of the Revolution as a whole—"la Terreur, en quoi il faudrait voir non pas un dérèglement de la Révolution, mais sa vérité dévoilée" [the Terror, in which one should see not the disordering of the Revolution, but its true character unveiled].[91] Nothing could be more wrong-headed. His conflating the Revolution's eventual authoritarian tendency with the democrats' early insistence on the oneness of popular sovereignty and their rejection of Montesquieu and separation of powers resulted in an essentially negative, and totally untenable, stance toward the Revolution as a whole. In one respect, meanwhile, the "historiens furétiens" and the Montagne's Marxist apologists, opposed but equally mistaken though they are, remain virtual allies: for both historiographical streams cheerfully expelled the Brissotins to the margins, allowing Brissot to become "l'introuvable et l'invisible du bicentaire" [the missing, invisible figure of the Bicentenary] of 1989–94.[92] Hence, paradoxically, both dominant trends in French Revolution historiography at the time of the Bicentenary marginalized what, for the history of "modernity," secularization, and the roots of modern democratic republicanism, matters most, the Radical Enlightenment democratic republican tendency, the backbone of revolutionary "universal and equal rights."[93]

Neither *furetiens* nor *jacobine-marxistes*, then, ever focused on or acknowledged what matters most for correctly understanding the French Revolution—that there were three basic and sharply distinct main currents, three main ideological impulses within the Revolution, three mutually opposed revolutionary creeds competing to capture the Revolution: the "aristocratic-monarchical," the democratic republican, and the authoritarian populist. Thus neither tendency could possess real cogency or validity. If there was no open conflict between democratic republicans and the Montagne until 1792, the triangular tension made itself felt almost from the beginning and was clearly perceptible throughout to those surveying the scene with a discerning eye. Brissot picturesquely characterized the three main revolutionary blocs in his newspaper, the *Patriote Français*, in May 1792, as *modérés*

[90] Guilhaumou, *L'Avènement des porte-parole*, 123. [91] Belissa and Bosc, *Robespierre*, 234–5.

[92] Pierre Serna, "Le Pari politique de Brissot ou lorsque le Patriote Français, l'Abolitionniste anglais et le citoyen Américain sont unis en une seule figure de la liberté républicaine," *La Révolution française* 5 (2013), 3.

[93] Belissa and Bosc, *Robespierre*, 20.

"who, in their minds, place the 1791 constitution over the Declaration of the Rights of Man and the Citizen which they deem 'impracticable'"; *enragés* [meaning *sans-culottes* and *Montagnards*] who, in their minds, recognize only the Declaration, ignoring the restraints and duties of the constitution; and *patriotes*, the democratic republicans aiming to combine and integrate the Declaration with the constitution.[94]

Correctly interpreting the Revolution certainly requires paying close attention to crowd behavior and popular reaction not just in Paris but also Lyon, Marseille, Montpellier, Nîmes, Toulon, Bordeaux, Caen, Strasbourg, and in Brittany. Indubitably, the upsurge of male and especially female dread and emotion surrounding the funeral ceremonies for Marat, after his assassination in July 1793, helped stoke popular calls for violence and terror against the Revolution's foes. Far from being a "totally idealized and disembodied vision of the Revolution driven by combat of ideas," as some critics maintain,[95] the Radical Enlightenment interpretation holds popular grievance and discontent were a natural, predictable response to revolutionary circumstances—sometimes well-targeted but more often, as following Marat's assassination, fearfully misdirected and manipulated.[96] Popular pressure to prevent vested interests preying on the majority meant raucous denunciation of hoarding and demands for price controls. For many, this became the Revolution's highest priority. The role of the common people remained throughout absolutely decisive to understanding why "the first revolution" (moderate Enlightenment and constitutional monarchist), partially successful in 1789–92, failed to consolidate its grip, why "the second revolution" (democratic republican), that of the Brissotins and Dantonistes, gained ground until early 1793, and then, with the Montagnard *coup d'état* of 31 May 1793, collapsed, and, lastly, why "the third revolution" (authoritarian populist), so different from the first and second revolutions in character, momentarily triumphed. The people's role in breaking the political deadlock at the Revolution's crucial moments (as well as their economic distress) was unquestionably decisive in shaping all these shifts but generally misdirected and oscillating in its relationship to the revolutionary (and later also counter-revolutionary) elites, disaffection constantly fragmenting in different directions—which, in the fraught circumstances, was scarcely surprising. Popular support chiefly vacillated three ways behind the "second" and

[94] Gauchet, *Révolution*, p. xii.

[95] See the exchanges between David Bell, Jeremy Popkin, Lynn Hunt, Keith Michael Baker, Johnson Kent Wright, Samuel Moyn, and myself in *H-France Review* 15 (May 2015), no. 66; *H-France Forum* vol. 9 (winter 2015), the *New Republic* (27 June 2014 and 31 July 2014); Jonathan Israel, "The French Revolution: An Exchange. A Reply by David A. Bell, "'A Very Different French Revolution'," in the *The New York Review of Books* (10 July 2014 and 9 Oct. 2014); for the connected quarrel over the origins of universal and equal Human Rights, see *The Nation* (5 July 2010), *HNN History News Network* (27 June 2010), and Ann Talbot and David North, "The Nation, Jonathan Israel and the Enlightenment," *World Socialist Web Site* (9 June 2010).

[96] Wahnich, *In Defense of the Terror*, 21–31.

"third" revolutions, and also behind the ultra-royalist, Catholic fundamentalist bloc everywhere formidable in revolutionary France.

Consequently, the people's principal pro-revolutionary interventions, such as on 14 July and 5 October 1789, 10 August 1792, 2–5 September 1792, 31 May 1793, or mid-July 1793 and 5 October 1795 (Vendémiaire), were fitful, sporadic, and, most importantly, conspicuously hesitant until guidance (or firm manipulation) was provided by rival leadership groups. This is not to downplay, or belittle, the role of the masses, as the *jacobine-marxiste* school protest, but rather shows how Robespierre first used and then unhesitatingly cheated the *sans-culottes*—as the *sans-culotte* leaders Jacques Roux, Théophile Leclerc, and the upright Jean Varlet themselves loudly complained and as sections of nineteenth-century French socialism, such as the "variation blanquiste," vividly recalled.[97] Robespierre and his colleagues perversely betrayed and suppressed the *sans-culottes* and the Hébertistes, just as they did every other dissident and potentially rival group. This is not to downplay the people's role but urge sharpening our sense of the gulf between "the people" and the divergent revolutionary ideologies vociferously depending on, competing for, appropriating, and misusing their support.

Conservative Enlightenment publicists reviling the Revolution's democratic principles, like Burke and Gibbon, along with Gillray and the British caricaturists of the 1790s, claimed the vying revolutionary factions all embraced the same destructive and murderous principles. This was logical for them, since they were seeking to tar the Revolution as a whole, like the *furetiens* and many other commentators in more recent times. By contrast, radical enlighteners of the period broadly supporting the Revolution, from 1789, never shared this view and never thought there was little to choose morally and politically between Brissotins and the Montagne. Rather, imputing a wide moral gulf between them, and applauding the former for their firmer and more explicit commitment to representative democracy and legislature sovereignty while viewing the Montagne as directly invoking the city sections and the people,[98] became defining features of the Radical Enlightenment. Even Montagnards who, during the Terror, accepted the regime's pretexts for repression, sometimes afterwards admitted that the Brissotins were more educated, dedicated to principle, and genuinely cosmopolitan than their Montagnard opponents, that the Brissot–Condorcet faction were the genuine heirs of the *philosophes* in a way that the Montagne were not.[99] Labeling the Montagne a repressive Counter-Enlightenment tendency is rejected by champions of the "Retour de Robespierre" as a "critique caricaturale de l'histoire de la 'Terreur,'" caricature of Robespierre and his political project. But the highly negative picture of the Terror and of Robespierre that emerges

[97] Mathiez, *Réaction thermidorienne*, 150, 152, 181–2; Yannick Bosc, "Robespierre liberal," *Annales historiques de la Révolution française* 371 (2013), 95–114, here pp. 105–6; Israel, *Revolutionary Ideas*, 437–43, 505–7, 584–5.

[98] Jarvis, *Politics in the Marketplace*, 138.

[99] Desan, "Foreigners, Cosmopolitanism," 95; Israel, *Revolutionary Ideas*, 264–6, 320–4, 382, 429.

in this series of volumes is no "critique caricaturale;" but rather sturdy historical revisionism based on the vast stock of evidence Robespierre's detractors adduced both at the time and later to demonstrate his fundamental deceitfulness and betrayal of core revolutionary principles and key groups.

A great admirer of Danton among nineteenth-century historians of the Revolution, Alphonse Aulard (1849–1928), was as immersed in the Revolution's sources as anyone could be. Aulard considered Robespierre more "funeste" to the cause of republican liberty than any royalist *émigrés* in arms,[100] as did Michelet before him; these historians nurtured a view of Robespierre and his accomplices close to that affirmed here.[101] Today, unfortunately, one encounters a growing readiness to defend Robespierre and the Terror, and advance what is termed a "more balanced" picture, presented in particular by Marc Belissa, Florence Gauthier, Sophie Wahnich, and Yannick Bosc. Their approach certainly represents a striking development in French Revolution historiography, vigorously opposing the perspective of historians like Doyle and Whatmore claiming the Brissotins were the "true revolutionaries;"[102] but their thesis that the negative, hostile contemporary view of Robespierre and the Montagne was inherently "antirévolutionnaire" is wholly untenable given that Paine, Jefferson, Wollstonecraft, Gorani, Cloots, Marchena, Constant, Thorild, Wollstonecraft, and other radically enlightened foreign commentators were indubitably zealous revolutionaries and ardent supporters of the French Revolution, but vehement public detractors of Robespierre. Claiming the negative picture derived chiefly from testimonies of royalist contemporaries or Robespierre's "ennemis girondins et 'modérés,'" and especially "fables invented by the Thermidorians after the execution of Robespierre," is misconceived.[103] The Brissotins were by no stretch (except in Montagnard rhetoric) *modérés* or "antirévolutionnaire," while the approach of Belissa, Gauthier, and Bosc fails to reflect the views of the foreign Enlightenment writers supporting the Revolution's democratic, universal, and equal rights principles between 1789 and 1794, who practically without exception abhorred and repudiated Robespierre and the Montagne. All those genuinely committed to representative democracy, freedom of expression, and a radical attack on monarchical, aristocratic, and religious ideas, as well as universal secular education and women's rights, depicted the Montagne in extremely derogatory and unflattering terms before as after the Terror.

Those seeking to rescue Robespierre's reputation and centrality have recovered ground not least by persuading some readers that Robespierre was "largely hidden" during the "celebrations commemoratives" in and after 1989, that more work is needed on "le républicanisme de Robespierre" and on his supposedly elevated role

[100] Bosc, "Robespierre libéral," 103.

[101] James Friguglietti, "La Querelle Mathiez-Aulard et les origines de la Société des études robespierristes," *Annales historiques de la Révolution française* 353 (July–Sept. 2008), 63–94.

[102] Bosc, *Terreur des Droits de l'Homme*, 246–50.

[103] Belissa and Bosc, *Robespierre*, 255–68.

as a thinker, legislator, and in public debates.[104] But here again they wrongly maintain it was the *Thermidoriens* who heaped Robespierre with accusations of hypocrisy and dictatorial ambition, fabricating the tirade today stigmatized as "la légende thermidorienne." For the evidence is clear that Robespierre was never a genuine republican, least of all before the Terror, and that numerous independents as well as Brissotins, moderates, and even some Montagnards depicted his character highly negatively long before July 1794.[105] As we have seen, many sources confirm the so-called "incorruptible" long adhered to an openly non-republican stance, condemning French revolutionary republicanism as "contre-productive."[106] While the *Thermidoriens*, comprising many veteran Montagnards, included more than a few malicious calumniators, to assume a priori that their accusations against Robespierre were false simply because known malefactors helped publicize them proves nothing given that those republican and democratic revolutionaries cited as the most honest and upright, such as Condorcet, Daunou, Cloots, Destutt, and Grégoire,[107] figure among those most scathing in denouncing Robespierre's ruthlessness, hypocrisy, dishonesty, lust for power, and intellectual mediocrity.

When recalling the course of the French Revolution, in 1795, Wollstonecraft, a lady as passionate for the Revolution as Williams or Paine, labeled the Montagnards "a race of monsters, the most flagitious that ever alarmed the world by the murder of innocents, and the mockery of justice."[108] Her idealistic and upright Scots–Welsh fellow female author, Helen Maria Williams (1759–1827), imprisoned for six months in the Luxembourg by the Montagnard regime, kept her zeal for the Revolution and its values intact, while regarding Robespierre as "the ultimate betrayer," as one scholar expressed it, "of revolutionary ideals."[109] For Constant likewise, Robespierre and Marat were the two prime destroyers of "gouvernement républicain" in 1793.[110] Taken as a group, both French and foreign, all prominent Radical Enlightenment intellectuals accused the rising Robespierre, from late 1792, of betraying liberty and revolutionary core values in every conceivable respect. Condorcet and Daunou pronounced him an intolerant "esprit étroit" spouting endlessly about providence and God, a "preacher" at heart, heading, through the Jacobin club, a kind of "religious sect" devoted to denouncing *modérantisme* and exalting *gouvernement révolutionnaire* while spreading the fable of *fédéralisme*, all extremely harmful and perverse political lies infusing political reality with fictions that never existed.[111] Montagnard branding of committed revolutionists like Paine, Brissot, Condorcet, Louvet, Desmoulins, Carra, Marchena, and Cloots as "enemies of the Revolution" or, as they stigmatized Gorsas "un libelliste infâme," if consonant with Robespierre's

[104] Belissa and Louvrier, "Robespierre dans les publications," 73–4, 93.
[105] *Opinion de Cabanis sur les réunions s'occupant d'objets politiques* (Paris, n.d. [1795?]), 3.
[106] Belissa and Bosc, *Robespierre*, 447; Bosc, "Robespierre libéral," 105.
[107] Paine, *Letter to George Washington*, 699–700, 702–3.
[108] Mellor, "English Women Writers," 259, 267.
[109] Mellor, "English Women Writers," 262–3.
[110] Constant, *De la Terreur*, 340–2.
[111] Minart, *Pierre Daunou, l'anti-Robespierre*, 80, 83.

views, struck educated onlookers as more indicative of a highly insidious power-grabbing tyranny than any republican creed.[112]

Robespierre's *Rousseauisme* amounted to more than just a rhetorical tool for mobilizing and manipulating his following; as the *Éloge de Gresset* shows, it was a serious ideological stance buttressing a conception of *volonté générale* as the direct untutored, unspoiled collective will of the common people—a *volonté générale*, he declared in late 1792, mobilized for all-out war against "the enemies of liberty, aristocrats, royalists and intriguers [i.e. Brissotins]," all the *modérés* and *Feuillants*, all the "ambitious" types "who have appeared thus far on the theatre of the Revolution,"[113] in fact everybody who "conspires with the tyrants of Europe" using a kind of "aristocratic constitution [i.e. that of Condorcet]." "The soul of the republic is virtue;" hence all the "ambitious and corrupt men," all the "egoists" [i.e. everyone opposing Robespierre], are by definition enemies of *l'intérêt général*.[114] Among the foes of the *volonté générale* were all the editors and paymasters of France's most widely read journals, "who did not cease to deceive France and Europe about the revolution that had just toppled the throne," in August 1792, by giving Brissotins more favorable write-ups than Robespierre's supporters. It was a conception that was always counter-Enlightenment and profoundly damaging.[115] What Robespierre introduced as the true *cause publique*, in reality, was a *contre-révolution* both theoretical and practical, cleverly engineered with "des tumultes et des mensonges," as Daunou expressed it,[116] a *contre-révolution* reversing the Revolution's true gains by decimating political and legal rights, freedom of expression, and individual liberty—a view universal among radical enlighteners before, as after, Thermidor. Robespierre, held Daunou, made a "divinité" of the people, a "religion" out of patriotism, and from the revolution a "fanaticism" over which he himself exercised the supreme pontificate. His prolix declamations and "insignificant writings," noted the *Décade philsophique* just days after his overthrow, were characterized by their "sacerdotal" tone.[117]

Imprisoned by the Montagne, the only radical actively to participate in both the American and French revolutions, Paine was not released until the Montagnard tyranny finally collapsed several months after Thermidor (4 November 1794). Subsequently, Paine bravely continued defending the principle of equality and universal male political rights against those of the Convention like Boissy d'Anglas who (understandably, given the trauma of the Terror) had come to reject representative democracy. Curiously enough, despite Paine's experiences in 1793–4, a leading proponent of the post-2000 "retour de Robespierre," Bosc, asserted that "for contemporaries in Year III (1794–5)," there was, in reality, no difference between the ideas of two men, Paine and Robespierre that "the historiography sets in opposition to

[112] Barrière, *Bibliothèque des Mémoires*, 236–7.
[113] Robespierre, *Lettres*, 1st series, no. 10, p. 476.
[114] Robespierre, *Lettres*, 2nd series, no. 1, p. 6.
[115] Robespierre, *Lettres*, 1st series, no. 1, pp. 6–7, no. 2, pp. 50–1, and no. 6, p. 428.
[116] Taillandier, *Documents biographiques*, 56.
[117] [Say], *Décade philosophique* ii (Thermidor 1794), 114; Minart, *Pierre Daunou*, 98.

each other": "ils sont tous les deux des libéraux-égalitaires" [they were both liberal egalitarians].[118] Astonishing! If Robespierre mouthed some of the same phrases, he never respected individual liberty, universal suffrage, individual liberty, or championed a genuine republicanism like Paine's. Hence Paine, like all radical enlighteners, inevitably harbored an extremely negative view of Robespierre, whom he publicly denounced before the French Convention nationale as "my inveterate enemy, as he was the enemy of every man of virtue and humanity."[119] Robespierre was as much the betrayer of the Revolution's authentic principles and values as the post-Brumaire Napoleon, concurred Jefferson, the keenest of America's Founding Fathers to endorse the French democratic republican Revolution: "Robespierre met the fate," he assured Mme De Staël in May 1813, "and his memory the execration, he so justly merited."[120]

In early 1794 Sweden's most passionate supporter of the Revolution from 1789 to 1794, the radical poet and publicist Thomas Thorild, declared Robespierre an "all-consuming crocodile."[121] Condorcet's, Daunou's, Wollstonecraft's, and Paine's view of Robespierre was shared, in fact, by all eminent American and British supporters of the Revolution, not just Jefferson, Paine, and Wollstonecraft but also Monroe, Priestley, Cooper, Short, Palmer, Barlow, Helen Maria Williams, Bentham, and Godwin; equally, all the German radical enlighteners—Herder, Klopstock, Forster, Wedekind, Lux, Hölderlin, Hegel, Fichte, Dorsch, and Cramer beside the radical editor of the *Aachener Zuschauer*, Dautzenberg—condemned him unreservedly. Their judgment was shared too by the Dutch radicals—Irhoven van Dam, Daendels, and Paape—the Spaniards, and the Italians—key publicists and revolutionary leaders like Marchena, Gorani, and Pagano. Marchena, for whom "political equality" is the base of the "social contract" and the hereditary principle the greatest bane of human life, could see no greater corrupter of the body politic than the "execrable Robespierre" who admired Rousseau, assuredly, but "cordially detested the *philosophes*."[122] Every pro-Revolution enlightener viewed Robespierre with unmitigated loathing, before as after Thermidor, regardng him as the pernicious head of a populist authoritarian tendency, the patron of the "executioners of September" and "conspirators of 31 May," as Marchena expressed it, presiding over a culture of political corruption, lies, anti-philosophy, and viciousness first concocted by Marat, whose "hideous" remains he was gratified to see removed from the Panthéon amid "l'exécration universelle" in February 1795.[123]

Fear of unschooled *sans-culottization*, if partly arising from dread of ruthless economic leveling, among radical enlighteners was chiefly due to the resulting general persecution, dragooning of critics and dissidents and muzzling of freedom of the

[118] Bosc, "Le Conflit des libertés," 104; Bosc, "Robespierre libéral," 97; Bosc, *Terreur des Droits de l'Homme*, 243–50.

[119] Quoted in Keane, *Tom Paine*, 415.

[120] Jefferson to Mme De Staël, 24 May 1813, in Jefferson, *Writings*, 1271.

[121] Muschik, "Ideen der Französischen Revolution in Schwedisch-Vorpommern," 173–4.

[122] Marchena, *Essai de théologie*, 23, 27, 32–3; Fuentes, *José Marchena*, 23.

[123] Marchena, *Essai de théologie*, 15; Israel, *Revolutionary Ideas*, 601–2.

press and expression. The late nineteenth-century socialist leader Jean Jaurès (1859–1914), one of the socialists who battled hardest to restore Robespierre's reputation, believed that while stirring up the *sans-culottes*, Robespierre sought to "prevent them from embarking on a fundamental class-war against the bourgeoisie and against property;" in this way, Jaurès helped construct the modern myth that Robespierre was *au fond* "emblématique des contradictions de la bourgeoisie montagnarde" [emblematic of the Montagnard bourgeoisie's contradictions].[124] Jaurès's positive view of Robespierre as the sympathetic bourgeois liberal reaching out to the *sans-culottes* foreshadowed the later mainstream socialist and Marxist view of Robespierre culminating in the interpretation of Lefebvre and Soboul. Here, Mathiez diverged somewhat from the others: a lifelong adversary of Aulard's perspective and of "toutes les légendes thermidoriennes," a scholar who broke with the Russian Revolution and the Communism of the Third International because he considered them repressive and anti-democratic, he objected to the views of Lefebvre and Soboul, but substituted a still more positive and ill-founded view than the others: adoring Robespierre, he eulogized him as the defender of the weak and disadvantaged.[125] Lauding Babeuf and Buonarroti for identifying Robespierre as the champion of the people, democracy, and natural rights, Mathiez viewed Robespierre as a true advocate of social revolution, rejecting the less positive conception of Robespierre as the agent of the bourgeoisie pervading other Marxist accounts.[126]

Babeuf, Buonarotti. and the earliest socialists did indeed begin the work, so cherished later by Mathiez, of turning Robespierre into a *culte véritable*.[127] Advocates of the "retour de Robespierre" vaunt his "libéralisme-égalitaire," his plans for "démocratie économique, sociale et politique."[128] Yet even the most socially conscious, caring, and cosmopolitan friends of mankind championing the Revolution rarely viewed Robespierre as a genuine egalitarian or generous soul, any more than they saw him as a principled republican: there is no indication he supported efforts to improve conditions for women—quite the contrary—or backed Brissotin moves to abolish slavery in the French Caribbean in 1792–4. By November 1793, Olympe de Gouges, the apostle of female equality, fantasized about how much good she would do for France if she could emulate Corday and dispatch Robespierre at the cost of her own life.[129] Leading "independents" of the Revolution known for social conscience and readiness to criticize neo-Brissotins and *Thermidoriens* publicly, as well as the Montagne, like Henri Grégoire, Bishop Claude Fauchet, and Bonneville, nevertheless also invariably shared the vehemently negative view of Robespierre rife among the radical pro-Revolution intellectual elite. Cloots, an atheist *philosophe* who, unlike

[124] Bosc, "Robespierre libéral," 104–7. [125] Vovelle, "Robespierre," 178–9.

[126] Mathiez, *Autour de Robespierre*, 243–8, 257; Bosc et Gauthier, "Introduction à la réédition," 36–9; Bosc, "Robespierre libéral," 109–11; Gauthier, "Albert Mathiez, historien," 100–1.

[127] Mathiez, *Autour de Robespierre*, 242; Baczko, "Comment est fait un tyrant," 50–2; Jaume, "Robespierre chez Machiavel?," 230.

[128] Gauthier, "Révolution française et le problème," 179, 190; Wahnich, *In Defence of the Terror*, 80–6.

[129] Dingli, *Robespierre*, 437–8.

the others, broke with the Brissotins and sided with the Montagne (partly because he hated Brissot)—until he too was arrested and guillotined for criticizing the leadership—nevertheless scorned Robespierre throughout as a base, dishonest, despicable, and perverse "dictator," "the most vicious and corrupt of bipeds" whose *paralogismes* "would lead us to ruin, anarchy and slavery."[130]

This means, then, that all enlighteners, moderate and radical, two opposed widely-separated blocs though they were, equally repudiated the "tyrant" Robespierre, along with Marat and Saint-Just, for their intolerance, anti-intellectualism, bloodthirsty methods, and quashing liberty of expression and press freedom. Above all, their tyrannizing over everyone while exalting the "ordinary" over the educated and philosophically-minded was reviled by all enlighteners. Even Montagnard stalwarts, like Antonelle, unmoved by seeing innocent Girondins executed for imaginary crimes, deemed Robespierre's suppression of freedom of speech and expression insufferable.[131] The 1793–4 repression not only liquidated numerous leading intellectuals, scientists, and literary men, but drastically narrowed literary and intellectual activity by deepening suspicion of the intellectual elite as a whole, and causing a dramatic further reduction in output of publications per year, the total falling precipitately to a tiny fraction of what it had been during the early Revolution.[132] Montagnard exaltation of the "ordinary" abundantly substantiated d'Holbach's, Condorcet's, the *Idéologues*' (and Spinoza's) axiom that bloody tyranny and oppression feed chiefly off ignorance, illiteracy, and gullibility.[133] Pervading the Radical Enlightenment's entire history was a deep apprehension regarding the ignorant *multitudo*, as Spinoza called it, fear vastly intensified by Robespierre and the Terror. The only effective antidote to this menace, held Condorcet, Daunou, and Destutt, the only way to fortify civic values, respect, and toleration among the people, is universal secular education of all, including in civics, politics and morality, a difficult and risky path, however, being very slow, arduous, and uncertain.

Gracchus Babeuf (1760–97), no enlightener but the idol of numerous mid-nineteenth-century socialists and ally of Buonarroti, the veritable founder of the post-revolutionary pro-Robespierre cult (and vein of historiography), venerated Robespierre. But even he did so only after a curious volte-face, having earlier roundly condemned Robespierre in print for most of the year after Thermidor, demanding restoration of press freedom, praising the "honest and unfortunate Camille Desmoulins," and condemning *robespierrisme* as dishonesty, hypocrisy, and despotism.[134] Only later, after condemning Robespierre in the most unambiguous terms, did he change his mind to fit new circumstances, his own subversive agenda and antipathy to the Directoire. Even then, what Babeuf admired when lending his name to reviving

[130] Biard, *Liberté ou la mort*, 113–14; Labbé, *Anarcharsis Cloots*, 160; Israel, *Revolutionary Ideas*, 284–5, 292, 305, 500, 511.

[131] Serna, *Antonelle*, 218–20.

[132] Margairaz, *François de Neuchâtel*, 375.

[133] Israel, *Revolutionary Ideas*, 698.

[134] [Graccchus Babeuf], *Journal de la Liberté de la presse* no. 16 (4 Vendémiaire An III), 5–6 and no. 17 (5 Vendémiaire An III), 1–3.

Robespierre's reputation was precisely his ability to rally the people behind the Terror, the man of action venerated by the common people, rather than his principles.[135]

If the "Incorruptible" was not corrupt financially, he was the very epitome of corruption politically, as we see from his scornful public statements about revolutionary personalities whose republican and democratic credentials were incontrovertible and reached back much further than his own, former allies like Condorcet and Desmoulins, and most of all by his choice of managers, agents, police and militia chiefs, and Paris mayors. During the Montagnard dictatorship (1793–4), men like Jean-Nicolas Pache (1746–1823), "elected" mayor in 1792, and instrumental in eliminating the Brissotins,[136] the nobleman Claude-François Payan (1766–94),[137] Robespierre's Paris National Guard chief, François Hanriot (1759–94), and Jean-Baptiste Fleuriot-Lescot (1761–94), mayor of Paris in succession to Pache until Thermidor, were all hugely, notoriously corrupt, criminal, and ruthless figures. Fleuriot-Lescot, guillotined with Robespierre at Thermidor, was an obscure Belgian revolutionary from Brussels unconnected with Paris, whose sole qualifications for the post of Paris mayor were his total disregard for integrity and truth and subservience to Robespierre personally.[138]

Baser still was René-François Dumas (1757–94), ex-priest, lawyer, and small-town mayor from Lons-le-Saulnier in the southern Jura, near Geneva, who, in September 1793, was selected by Robespierre as vice-president of the Paris *Tribunal Criminel-Révolutionnaire* and, from April 1794, was its president. In his account of the "despotisme de Robespierre et ses complices" delivered before the Convention on 18 Ventôse Year III [8 March 1795], the revolutionary playwright Marie-Joseph Chénier (1764–1811), one of the Revolution's most passionate pleaders for press freedom, rightly listed Dumas, along with Hanriot, as among the foremost of Robespierre's *complices*. Guillotined with Robespierre and Hanriot, on 28 July 1794, Dumas was a particularly vicious mediocrity, specializing in manipulating perversely ritualized trials. It was purely through ruthless loyalty to the "Incorruptible" himself that he rose high in the regime. None could have more callously presided over the liquidation of the *Hébertistes* and dispatch of the *Dantonistes* or more reliably helped Robespierre tighten his grip over the Jacobins. Hanriot's bullying second-in-command of the Paris National Guard, Jean-Baptiste de Lavalette (1753–94), salvaged twice from prison, in July 1793 and May 1794, by Robespierre after incarceration for unruliness, insubordination, and rowing with powerful deputies, was another ardent *robespierriste* who met his end at the guillotine along with his boss.[139]

[135] Baczko, *Politiques de la Révolution française*, 160–1; Jaume, *Le Religieux et le politique*, 7–8.

[136] Biard, *Liberté ou la mort*, 77, 82; Mortier, *Anarcharsis Cloots*, 432; Israel, *Revolutonary Ideas*, 294–5, 420.

[137] Leuwers, *Robespierre*, 323, 350, 365; Martin, *Robespierre*, 262, 274, 291, 344.

[138] McPhee, *Robespierre*, 218–19; Dingli, *Robespierre*, 410, 491, 501.

[139] BL F 1259. 60/1: Marie-Joseph Chénier, "Discours (18 ventôse Year III), 2–4; McPhee, *Robespierre*, 192, 212, 215; Martin, *Robespierre*, 292, 295.

The Montagne defeated the Brissotins in 1793–4, independent commentators remarked, chiefly because they were more ruthless, manipulative, and dishonest than their rivals. That is assuredly true. Belissa's and Bosc's *Robespierre: La fabrication d'un mythe* makes no mention in its index of Payan, one of Robespierre's closest aides during the Terror and a self-proclaimed believer in liquidating innocent men whenever their elimination is "useful," described by one scholar as a "stringent moralist" but, more accurately, by another as having "fewer scruples than Robespierre."[140] Another telling case, recounted in detail in the Convention, after Thermidor, was that of Louis Jullien Héron, a former naval officer and a participant in the September massacres, wounded in the attack on the Tuileries, in August 1792. An associate of Marat charged, in December 1793, by the municipality of Versailles, with unjustly arresting undoubted republicans, he was defended at the Convention by Vadier, Bayle, and Couthon, three of the Montagnard leadership's most unscrupulous members. Robespierre vigorously defended him. Restored to prominence as a key agent of the Committee of Public Safety, it was he, in January 1794, who arrested the Dantonist Fabre d'Eglantine in this capacity.[141] Belissa, Bosc, and the neo-Marxist historiography powering the "Retour de Robespierre" say little about Hanriot, Pache, Dumas, Payan, or Fleuriot-Lescot. One recent biography omits practically everything concerning Robespierre's massively imposing gallery of disreputable characters manning his chief levers of power.[142]

The evidence is irrefutable too concerning Robespierre's manipulation of the Jacobins, and systematic vote-rigging in the Paris section elections for the National Convention in the autumn of 1792, designed to exclude everyone other than close allies from being elected. That Robespierre's corrupt tyrannical streak stemmed partly from a sincere creed, a *Rousseauisme* parading the doctrine that "la liberté peut être despotique, avec justice" [liberty can justly be despotic with justice], a quasi-religious exaltation altogether clashing with Enlightenment values, does not make it any less politically corrupt.[143] Of course, not all the blame for the Terror and repression lay with Robespierre. After Thermidor, for many months there was only a very grudging easing of the political repression. Antonelle, released from the Luxembourg on 10 Thermidor,[144] was among the first set free, but others were kept behind bars much longer. Because initially, through the autumn of 1794, it was still the Thermidorians who controlled the levers of power, many notable savants, *gens de lettres*, and enlighteners imprisoned as ideological enemies by the group dictatorship, but who had not yet gone to the guillotine when Robespierre fell, remained in prison for months afterwards, as did most political prisoners incarcerated in provincial capitals. On 26 August 1794 there was a total of 5,679 prisoners in the Paris prisons, including

[140] Hampson, *Life and Opinions*, 163, 276, 286–7; McPhee, *Robespierre*, 192, 218; Scurr, *Fatal Purity*, 279, 388, 305.

[141] *Archives Parlementaires* vol. 96, pp. 78–9, 29 August 1794; Dingli, *Robespierre*, 492.

[142] Leuwers, *Robespierre.*

[143] Jaume, *Le Religieux et le politique*, 46–8.

[144] Serna, *Antonelle*, 245.

737 in the Hôpital Bicêtre, 470 in the Luxembourg, many in the Abbaye, and 305 at Vincennes;[145] on 16 September, nearly two months after Robespierre's downfall, the total was still 5,141 political prisoners, with the numbers at the Hôpital Bicêtre, to the south-east of the city, having actually increased to 741 and with 398 still in the Luxembourg and 264 at Vincennes.[146] If halting the stream of executions saved the lives of such celebrities of the late Western Enlightenment as Paine, Volney, Destutt, Daunou, Sonthonax, and Roederer, few political prisoners regained their liberty promptly.

Placing all these developments in their proper light lends a whole new significance also to the notable speech, delivered shortly after Thermidor, on 29 August, by one of the few remaining Brissotins in the Convention, Jean-Antoine Debry (1760–1834). A neighbor of Mme Helvétius and Condorcet at Auteuil, Debry figured among Condorcet's principal backers and had been his colleague on the Convention's *Comité d'Instruction Publique* during late 1792 and early 1793.[147] Among the Convention's acutest political theorists, he was closely involved in the spring of 1793 debates over Condorcet's projected republican constitution and known for solid republican commitment.[148] Detesting the "execrable faction" who struck on 31 May and seized power in France on 2 June 1793, Debry had colluded with Condorcet's going into hiding that month when in imminent danger of arrest, trial, and execution. Like Condorcet, Debry was a committed "general will" theorist construing this key revolutionary concept as the *force publique*, the collective will of all, but not in Rousseau's sense; he saw it, rather, as a system of rights protecting all and permitting no scope for the majority to mistreat minorities "with justice."[149] Debry characterized the Montagnard ascendancy since June 1793 as a veritable "counter-revolution" stirring up the lowest motives of the common people "and all the jealousy of ignorance," a case of the blind striking those who see, of the people unknowingly betraying what best served their cause. Identifying envy as the root of Robespierre's moral perversity, even the delay in transferring Rousseau's remains to the Panthéon Debry blamed on his obsessive jealousy of others.[150] At an early point after Thermidor, Debry's rapidly emerged as a lone but incisive voice: ignorance, intolerance, authoritarianism, and anti-intellectualism acquired such momentum as guiding principles of terror, insisted Debry, that Robespierre's chief supporters, Hanriot, Dumas, and the like, would have gladly dragged Mably and Jean-Jacques himself to the scaffold for decapitation as a "republican" under any king whatsoever, while Algernon Sidney would have been liquidated by any committee chaired by Saint-Just.[151]

145 *Archives Parlementaires* vol. 95, p. 470, 26 Aug. 1794.

146 *Archives Parlementaires* vol. 97, p. 219, 16 Sept. 1794.

147 Badinter, *Condorcet*, 350 396, 490.

148 Badinter, *Condorcet*, 557, 569, 619–20; Dingli, *Robespierre*, 447.

149 *Archives Parlementaires* vol. 67, p. 289, 24 June 1793; Israel, *Revolutionary Ideas*, 348.

150 Baczko, *Ending the Terror*, 208.

151 *Archives Parlementaires* vol. 96, pp. 72–3, 29 Aug. 1794; on Debry, see Israel, *Revolutionary Ideas*, 348–9, 363, 372, 591, 596, 629, 716; Badinter, *Condorcet*, 454, 557, 582, 619.

The only meaningful antidote to *robespierrisme*, to the evil of Montagnard authoritarianism, and unenlightened populism, Daunou agreed with Condorcet, in a text drafted whilst he still languished behind bars, in August 1794, was a profoundly reformed education system.[152] By August, the heirs of the *philosophes*, then mostly confined to prison or in hiding, began to conceive that they might, before long, be able to recapture control of the Revolution. No sooner had Robespierre's head fallen than the "New Jacobins," betraying basic revolutionary principles such as unlimited free press and democratic political rights that even the Old Jacobins adhered to, found themselves under mounting pressure from some Old Jacobins as well as neo-Brissotin republicans. Among the weightiest verbal assaults on the Thermidorians, in August 1794, was the work of the Convention's most fiercely independent, non-factional individual and the only one still wearing ecclesiastical dress, Henri Grégoire.

Purportedly presenting a committee report on the damage to the country's historical monuments and cultural heritage caused by populist "vandalism" and excesses, on 14 Fructidor (31 August), Grégoire seized the opportunity to pronounce a devastating indictment of Jacobin anti-Enlightenment and philistinism, or what he aptly termed "*robespierrisme* of the arts." Grégoire delivered this key speech in the Chamber in the name of the *Comité d'Instruction Publique*. Denouncing the "New Jacobins," echoing Debry he blamed especially Montagnard "esprit contre-révolutionnaire" for the appalling setbacks to "liberty" and the Revolution under the group dictatorship. All the arts and sciences had suffered abominably, the damage to sculptures, paintings, friezes, libraries, and décor of churches, monasteries, palaces, and chateaux throughout France being incalculable, "dilapidations immenses" caused principally by popular ignorance aided by the cupidity of a few cunning agents and the malicious *esprit contre-révolutionnaire* of others.[153]

Saving the more remarkable medieval, Renaissance, and Baroque sculptures and other monuments from being vandalized, or pillaged from monasteries, would prove quite a challenge. When the French Constituent Assembly, in June 1791, ordered the storing, cataloging, and safeguarding of a selection of the best in the Paris Petits Augustins convent (today the École des Beaux-Arts), the archeologist Alexandre Lenoir (1761–39) had been appointed the store's "garde-general." During 1793–4, the flow became overwhelming with items seized from churches and aristocratic chateaux; but at the same time it remained closed to the public, just a repository. Opening the Musée de Monuments français as a national asset, a state-supported museum for the public, had to wait until October 1795. Like Grégoire, Lenoir strove to check the paroxysm of violence and vandalistic destruction while imposing a new order and meaning, endorsing the appropriation and redirecting of ecclesiastical splendor and noble privilege, hoping eventually to display what had been seized

[152] Dauteribes, "Daunou et le modèle," 132–3.

[153] *Archives Parlementaires* vol. 96, pp. 150–1, 29 Aug. 1794; Baczko, "Vandalisme," in Furet and Ozouf, *Dictionnaire critique*, 903.

from the clergy and aristocracy as a museum in a monumental setting.[154] He was to succeed for a time under the *Directoire* and Napoleon, but eventually his grandiose project was again cancelled, in 1814–16, with the Bourbon Restoration, the crown requiring him to return the bulk of his display to the religious orders, churches, and residences from which it had been taken. A remnant was transferred to the Louvre.

After recounting the "vandalism"—a revolutionary neologism probably invented by Grégoire himself—directed against churches and monasteries, Grégoire launched into a detailed denunciation of revolutionary anti-intellectualism more broadly, the deliberate attack on the Enlightenment, first by *sans-culotte* leaders and then, more specifically, that unleashed by Robespierre's speech of 7 May 1794 (18 Floréal Year II), the speech prompting the ensuing Convention decree asserting the Revolution's commitment to the cult of the Supreme Being, and belief in immortality of the soul. Robespierre's attack on the *encyclopédistes* and *gens de lettres* in that speech Grégoire identified as the signal for the subsequent wave of intensified vandalism and anti-intellectualism: Robespierre strove to discredit the *philosophes* among the French people as much as possible, for their irreligion, atheism, and scorn for ordinary folk.[155] Implementing his assault on enlightened projects and books with alacrity, his lieutenants initiated a new form of prejudice. If Chabot admitted disliking *savants*, echoing Robespierre's maxim about the Revolution's intellectual luminaries being a new "aristocratie," "Dumas used to say that it was necessary to guillotine all the men of intellect." The unruly Hanriot, Robespierre's most loyal supporter, and a key tool of the Montagnard coup of 2 June 1793 and of Robespierre's efforts to regain his grip, on the eve of his downfall, in July 1794, Grégoire accused of aspiring to "renew the exploits of Omar," the Caliph responsible for destroying the foremost library of the ancient world, that of Alexandria, burnt to cinders when Muslim forces captured Alexandria in AD 642.[156]

Dumas possibly never said anything of the kind and much of the rhetoric of anti-intellectualism so thickly laid on by Grégoire, Debry, Daunou, Chenier, and others in the aftermath of Thermidor may have been exaggerated. But if a lurid myth of rampant anti-intellectualism was deliberately fabricated, in the wake of Thermidor,[157] there was a substantial enough core of truth to the myth. The charges proved effective and long stuck precisely because they sounded plausible in a way they could not have been had the Jacobins said the same about the Brissotins. Grégoire denounced *robespierrisme* not just as a *contre-révolution* but a *contre-révolution* inspired specifically by anti-intellectualism and Counter-Enlightenment. "Pour consommer le project de tarir toutes les sources des lumières, il fallait paralyser ou anéantir les

[154] Martin, *Violence et révolution*, 179; Macgregor, *Curiosity and Enlightenment*, 83; Osterhammel, *Transformation*, 12.

[155] Leuwers, *Robespierre*, 331–4; Dingli, *Robespierre*, 469–74.

[156] *Archives Parlementaires* vol. 96, p. 153, 31 Aug. 1794; Baczko, *Ending the Terror*, 197–207, 214; Baczko, "Vandalisme," in Furet and Ozouf, *Dictionnaire critique*, 904–6; Tackett, *Coming of the Terror*, 273–4.

[157] Baczko, *Ending the Terror*, 200–4; McPhee, *Liberty or Death*, 280–1.

hommes de génie" [to consummate their project of drying up all the sources of Enlightenment, it was necessary to paralyze or annihilate the men of genius]. Part of this was a campaign to deny certificates of "civisme" to a range of intellectuals. "Défiez-vous de cet homme, car il a fait un livre" [Suspect this man because he has written a book] allegedly became a watchword of the regime.

The group dictatorship's chief ploy was indeed "to flatter the pride of ignorance." Robespierre did not want French children educated from home but schooled away from the parents, fashioning them into young Spartans,[158] following Rousseau's precepts and "Lepeletier's error" but with more sinister motives—to enhance the dictatorship's power. In this way, held Grégoire, an entire "système de persecution" arose to suppress men of talent and Enlightenment. During a catastrophic nine-month period, declared Grégoire, the regime unjustly imprisoned Volney, Laharpe, Ginguené, Thillaye, Cousin, François de Neufchâteau, Vandermonde, Oberlin, Boncerf, Laroche, Sage, Lametterie, La Chabeaussière, Beffroy, Mauduit, and France's celebrated Homer translator, the Calvinist pastor Paul Jeremias Bitaube (1732–1808), from Koenigsberg, author of the *Vie de Frédéric II, Roi de Prusse* published at Strasbourg in 1788. Jean-Baptiste Thillaye (1732–1822) was a prominent Paris surgeon, medical writer, and naturalist, Alex-Théophile Verndermonde (1735–96) a mathematician, chemist, musicologist, and, in the last year of his life, from 1795, professor of political economy at the École Normale. Jérémie-Jacques Oberlin (1735–1806), imprisoned in 1793, was a Strasbourg professor, an authority on biblical archeology and a philologist specializing in Alsace-Lorraine local traditions and language; Antoine-Rémy Mauduit (1731–1815) was another renowned mathematician, a professor at the Collège de France for over fifty years.

Marat and Robespierre, "under the pretext of making us Spartans, wished to make us Helots," as Grégoire aptly expressed it.[159] The Montagne cancelled Condorcet's, Danou's, and Lakanal's project of bringing the learned academies of France under a new national institute or super academy in Paris, to serve as a general directorate of the sciences, humanities, and social science. Where Condorcet and his accomplices planned a national senate of savants, independent of the legislature (and Jacobins) in attitudes and thinking, and in policy and appointments, creating a bench of experts and intellectuals guiding the vast edifice of French science, research, and education, enthroning the Enlightenment in a presiding position over French life and culture, and directing the *esprit public* via *la philosophie*, Marat and Robespierre intended a dictatorship proclaimed by the common people, or what the Brissotins called the "tyranny" of the galleries over the legislature, based on the "ordinary," the levelling sense of Rousseau's "general will," idealizing the common man as the gold standard of legitimacy and purity in patriotism and virtue. There was no need for either the people itself, or particularly talented individuals, to be elevated intellectually to higher

[158] Baczko, *Ending the Terror*, 208.
[159] Grégoire, *Rapport sur les destructions*, 13; Baczko, *Ending the Terror*, 208.

levels at public expense in the way Condorcet considered vital to the functioning of the democratic republic.

The Convention needed urgently to take emergency measures to safeguard France's cultural treasures, restore the sciences' prestige and the arts, and generally revive "Les Lumières" [Enlightenment]. What plans had the Convention for the mutilated monuments and vast store of paintings and other art treasures retrieved? Roughly twelve million books and manuscripts, its committee estimated, had accrued to the French nation and state from the Revolution; where should these be housed? Cutting back science, scholarship, and research had been basic to the Montagnard populist agenda and induced the plan, promoted by Marat especially, to extinguish all the former royal academies, including the art and military academies. They had all been abolished by decree by the National Convention on 18 July 1793. The Académie Française held its last meeting on 5 August 1793. Lakanal's and Grégoire's efforts to salvage at least the Paris Academy of Sciences, given its usefulness for military and naval technology and in developing chemical processes, beside its function, since 1791, in overseeing the reform of France's chaotic *ancien régime* system of weights and measures by introducing universal metric criteria, had been thwarted. The renowned chemist Antoine-Laurent Lavoisier (1743–94), despite help from friends, failed to rescue even a sadly reduced inner core. The Academy's rooms, archives, and equipment were sealed and bolted. Europe's foremost chemist had gone to the guillotine on 8 May 1794.

By the autumn of 1793, French public morality had been so "corrupted," contended Daunou, that to survive everybody felt obliged to feign fanaticism, dogmatism, and crassness. "La liberté démocratique," intellectual life, the arts and sciences were, so to speak, decimated together, hand in hand.[160] In one sense, Montagnard triumph and the sway of the authoritarian populists with their organized campaign against the Enlightenment proved short; it was over once the Thermidorians were removed from power over the winter of 1794–5. From 1795 onwards, Condorcet's ideas were back in favor with the now neo-Brissotin, anti-Montagnard regime and the Revolution was once again fervent for giving public support to science, research, higher learning, the social sciences, and the museums and gallieries with which to demonstrate to the public the results, and meaning, of collecting from all around the world. The national institute of arts and sciences Condorcet had envisaged at the apex of the national educational edifice was provided for in the new revolutionary constitution drawn up in 1795 and in Daunou's education laws. The Institut National was finally established in October 1795.

But in another, highly pertinent, sense Montagnard Counter-Enlightenment proved far from short-lived: the great danger to France and all humanity posed by Robespierre and the Terror, as the *Idéologues* saw it, persisted long after Thermidor; for it lay in the permanent menace of populist activism, ordinary thinking, mass

[160] Barrière, *Bibliothèque des mémoires* xii. 453–6.

direct participation in decision-making by the ignorant, and the propensity to despotism inherent in Rousseau's defective understanding of modern representative government, democracy, and the "general will." As Destutt de Tracy expressed it in his chief work, the *Éléments d'idéologie* (1801), the anti-revolutionary *fureur* that impelled *robespierrisme* transmogrified into a lasting impulse, among some, to tear down everything good the Revolution accomplished as well as the bad.[161] This *fureur* partly took the form of religious obscurantism and royalism and partly a thriving populism alive also in aspects of Napoleonism.

The educational and public culture policies of the *Directoire*, despite the efforts of Daunou, Lakanal, Destutt, Volney, Cabanis, and the rest, to restore what had been lost and stabilize the Revolution, in the later 1790s, broadly failed and were then in large part reversed by Napoleon, reversal symbolized by the abolition of the revolutionary calendar, and return to the western Christian calendar, in 1804. Even after being guillotined, on 28 July 1794, some maintained, Robespierre continued to eat away at the Revolution's foundations. Memories of Robespierre were continually being used by the Revolution's opponents, noted Constant, to insult the ghost of Condorcet and "assassinate Sieyès": "it is the frenzy of 1794 that makes feeble-minded and bitter men abjure the Enlightenment of 1789. The memory of the 'régime abominable' that authored the Terror today still serves the friends of despotism."[162]

Robespierre's impact on the corpus of Radical Enlightenment thought proved a lasting one, further accentuating the central tension running through its entire development from Spinoza to the 1848 revolutions. The doctrine that the uneducated and only rudimentarily educated masses cannot be expected to usefully contribute to legislative and governmental decision-making had now become an anti-democratic mechanism and dire threat to the Republic. How could one salvage the principled ideal that legitimate government must be based on universal and equal rights and (non-Rousseauist) "general will," laws must be for the people, government must be in the general interest and responsible to the people, intended for the "common good," and yet also stipulate that the direction of government must not be entrusted directly to the ill-informed? Was it perhaps a manifest contradiction, rather than a guiding truth, that government must be carried on by a highly educated elite? From 1794, the democratic republicanism of the Radical Enlightenment was a doctrine neither easy to affirm theoretically nor readily turned into a plausible and practicable politics.

Daunou's and Destutt's solution was to introduce a two-stage electoral process: the population as a whole should participate in the primary elections held at local level; these should produce worthy "electors" whose job it was, in the second stage, to choose the actual delegates to sit in the legislature.[163] Theirs was a political thought tradition contrasting with the so-called "liberal" political thought of Constant, Mme De Staël, Boissy d'Anglas, and later Guizot, seeking to ground representation on a restricted franchise defined by property ownership, though Constant entirely agreed

[161] Destutt de Tracy, *Éléments d'idéologie* i, p. xxv.
[162] Constant, *De la Terreur*, 347.
[163] Destutt de Tracy, *Commentaire*, 148–50; Head, *Politics and Philosophy*, 28, 30, 307–11, 322–3.

with the radicals regarding the dangerous, despotic character of *robespierrisme*, and that Rousseau's ideas had contributed to the disaster, that Rousseau's "general will" is a confusion rooted in failure properly to differentiate ancient direct democracy from modern representative republicanism.[164]

After 1794, radicals diverged among themselves as to how far to go in combining democracy with representative government and protection of the individual.[165] Radicals wanted a solution apt to concentrate political power in the hands of an elite of merit and intellect, rather than one based on wealth and property, and hence likelier to uphold the "common good". Although correct that their solution was less prone to generate class conflict than that of the "liberals," their proposed electoral system was bound to be unwieldy and fraught with disruptive disputes. It was too complex, an apparent contradiction in the eyes of many that ultimately condemned Radical Enlightenment to abiding failure. In a bitterly cruel sense, the Enlightenment that failed was in part Robespierre's vindication.

164 For an opposing view, see Bosc, "Conflit des conceptions," 102, 107.
165 De Luca, "Benjamin Constant and the Terror," 110–13.

17

Swiss Revolution

The Climb to Democratic Republicanism (1782–1830)

17.1. SWITZERLAND: "ARISTOCRATIC" VERSUS "DEMOCRATIC" REPUBLICANISM

Among the revolutions that shook the Western world between the 1770s and 1848, the two greatest upheavals, the American and French revolutions, have long been considered central to the history of the Western world. But there were other revolutions at the time of no small importance for the wider trans-Atlantic story that remain relatively little known and are usually left tucked away in the background—much to the detriment of our general understanding the "Age of Atlantic Revolution." For alongside the American and Dutch republican revolutions, the Swiss revolution of the 1780s crucially helped shape the intellectual horizons of the Western world's radical intelligentsia on the eve of the French Revolution and its democratic republican revolutionary consciousness.

The 1781–2 Swiss upheavals figured among the first and most important of the trans-Atlantic revolutions as regards shaping the basic theoretical and rhetorical format of "democratic" versus "aristocratic" republicanism in an explicit, public manner, with the accompanying emblems and symbols, and for presenting the clash of these two fundamentally different and rival forms of government as an overriding late Enlightenment debate. The Swiss revolutions, more than any others, laid down, at the most formative stage, the prime theoretical, philosophical schema, European and trans-Atlantic, for conceptualizing the wider European scenario from the early 1780s down to 1848. Both sides to the Swiss struggle labeled themselves "Republikaner" with equal justification, and both equally claimed to embody whatever was universally valid in the legacy of the American Revolution.[1] Along with the Dutch *Patriottenbeweging* (1780–7), it was the Swiss drama that first lent the struggle between "démocratie" and "aristocratie" its uniquely central role in late

[1] Condorcet, *Bibliothèque* series II (1791), v. 21–4; Maissen, *Geburt der Republik*, 442.

eighteenth-century European political theory commencing in the years immediately prior to the outbreak of the French Revolution.

Since the Reformation and Dutch Revolt, Switzerland and the United Provinces were the two middle-sized republics that diverged most from, and most offended, the prevailing monarchical, absolutist system of political, religious, and social values. In both countries, oligarchy prevailed, as in the Italian republics and German Imperial Free Cities, but the Dutch and Swiss oligarchies were looser, less stable and tightly defined than those of Venice or Genoa, and where tightest conspicuously stood in contradiction with what some saw as their founding traditions. Although the path toward democratic republicanism proved long and arduous, the Dutch and Swiss were the European entities that had proceeded furthest along the potential (but not inevitable or necessary) path to modern democratic republicanism. Meanwhile, there also existed fundamental differences between the two confederacies, most obviously the greater resistance in the Swiss case to the dominance of urban commercialism and primacy of trade over rural society and agriculture.

Also, fondness for the past, traditional values, and resistance to conceptual innovation, had remained decidedly more entrenched in Switzerland through the seventeenth century. Throughout the sixteenth, seventeenth, and eighteenth centuries, both republics sporadically and inconsistently but more than other lands provided safety for those fleeing intolerance in France, Italy, Germany, and the Iberian Peninsula, receiving both religious minority groups and numerous individual religious dissidents, like Bayle and Le Clerc, seeking a refuge. During the eighteenth century, both republics profited handsomely from pumping streams of religiously, politically, and philosophically illicit books into France, Italy, and Germany. But although both displayed a relatively high degree of religious plurality and toleration, confessional thinking, whether Protestant or Catholic, dominated locally to a greater extent in Switzerland than the Netherlands and repression of fringe churches and Cartesian philosophy was notably more determined and persistent in Switzerland than the United Provinces. Down to the 1770s freethinking fugitives from church oppression, and the Inquisition, like the Neapolitan encyclopedist and editor, Fortunato Bartolomeo De Felice (1723–89), found themselves under heavier pressure to conform to local religious orthodoxy, to convert to the locally dominant religion and a moderate Enlightenment frame of thought than in the Netherlands.[2]

But where the United Provinces signally lost much of their wider European appeal from around 1730, owing to their obvious economic decline and decadence, the very warning this seemingly offered the world, and political thought, regarding the corrupting effects of commerce on republics, lent fresh prestige and symbolic significance to the non-commercial poorer rural Swiss cantons. Starting with Montesquieu but gaining real traction with Rousseau and Mably, some commentators of the 1760s and 1770s concluded that it was in these rural portions of Switzerland especially that

[2] Tröhler, "Switzerland," 90, 94–5; Israel, *Democratic Enlightenment*, 349–50, 800; on the De Felice case, see also Ricuperati, "Scrivere dall'Europa del Disseno," p. LV.

classical republican principles of simplicity, equality, and public virtue were best conserved.[3] In particular, Rousseau took to projecting the Swiss cantons, notably in his Corsican "Projet" of 1765, as a working model for demonstrating the rightness of his own political doctrines. This high prestige of rural republics based on agriculture and virtue, and antagonistic to commerce, lingered for a time. While the fresh stimulus lent to democratic revolutionary awareness by the success of the American Revolution certainly helped stoke the growing Patriot democratic republican agitation in the United Provinces in the 1780s, this did not prevent some Dutch activists battling the Orangist establishment for a more democratic society from still continuing to pronounce "some of the republics of Switzerland," as Van der Capellen, the Dutch democratic movement's leader, expressed it, in 1781, a valuable model for other lands and peoples for showing how men can, in a responsible and disciplined manner, elect their own representatives on a broad suffrage.[4] In 1793, the Cambridge rebel William Frend still considered the "small democratical cantons of Switzerland" to possess the greatest claim to the title of "republican" in Europe.[5]

During the 1770s and 1780s however, it was not only the Swiss rural cantons that drew international attention. The progress of democratic republicanism was *not* impeded because "in order to be justified in the eighteenth century," it had to be "shown to be compatible with commercial society," a test, some claim, representing a real obstacle in the Swiss context.[6] For Dutch democratic commercial republicanism, we have seen, had already long overcome this obstacle; and although Rousseau and Mably did briefly raise the prestige of the Swiss rural cantons in a backward-looking fashion this had lost much of its relevance by the 1780s. By 1789–92, with the growing impact of American and French revolutionary democratic republicanism, the old Swiss linkage, renewed by Rousseau, of "democracy" with "virtue" and antagonism to commerce had become broadly irrelevant—in Switzerland as in the rest of Europe. Besides, over time some small rural Swiss cantons had themselves become not just conspicuously oligarchic but also too resistant to personal liberty and freedom of expression any longer to be taken seriously as models. "What could be more oppressive," demanded Wekhrlin in 1787, than the yoke the Venetian nobility imposes on that Republic's subjects? Where in all the world is there less freedom, more oppression, personal insecurity and general distrust, than in Venice? Where does greater ignorance, poverty, and enslavement of reason predominate than in Genoa? For the answer, he suggested, one must contemplate the "Swiss cantons of Glarus and Solothurn."[7]

From any genuinely enlightened perspective, it was now obvious that there was much to criticize in both the late eighteenth-century Helvetic confederacy's rural and urban cantons. In Sismondi's post-1820 democratic Enlightenment perspective, the profound inadequacies of the Swiss "enlightenment" had sunk the country in an utterly deplorable predicament, shot through with self-delusion and self-deception,

[3] Kapossy, "Neo-Roman Republicanism," 227–8.

[4] Van der Capellen, *Aan het Volk van Nederland*, 36.

[5] [Frend], *Account of the Proceedings*, 91.

[6] Whatmore, *What is Intellectual History?*, 93.

[7] Wekhrlin, *Das graue Ungeheuer* x (1787), 194.

that persisted down to the 1790s. Coaxed and deceived by the narrow oligarchies ruling the various cantons into ridiculously celebrating and exalting their age-old "Swiss liberty," most Swiss, without at all comprehending the reality of their situation, in reality enjoyed only a minimal, tightly curtailed "liberty." Eventually, powerful but inchoate resentment and frustration stemming from their relentless subordination and marginalization by oligarchs surged up, but owing to the prevailing lack of understanding of their country's malaise and how to correct it, little was accomplished until the revolutionary wave from outside bought in fresh ideas, crucially from France (and also, from 1796, Italy), in the 1790s.[8] As realization of their true position dawned on the Swiss, disturbances erupted in the cantons and districts of Basel, Vaud, the Grisons, and St Gall, and along the shores of Lake Zurich; to this Switzerland's oligarchs replied with their old methods, namely book-burnings and imprisonment or banishment of trouble-makers. Eventually, the French Revolution intervened and, in 1798, the old Swiss confederation finally collapsed to the applause of a great many, Swiss and foreign.

The most vital thing Sismondi gathered from the eighteenth-century Swiss experience was that it is a total waste of time discussing republicanism at all unless one has some inkling, some awareness (which most people do not, he thought) of the age-old collision between aristocratic and democratic republicanism, and what this means for humanity generally. This in turn signified, in his eyes, that no such debate can arise except in an "enlightened" context. Without *les Lumières* no liberty of discussion exists and, therefore, neither does any prospect of grasping the reality of things, or drawing up a meaningful program for reform: without the Enlightenment there can be no understanding, and no appreciation, of the difficulties and self-delusion blocking the path of whatever people sets out to achieve genuine liberty.[9] If most ordinary Swiss in 1820 still conceived their republics in a pious, traditional, particularist, and non-ideological manner—that is, as Sismondi viewed matters, without comprehending anything—the sporadic, intermittent Swiss revolutions of the 1780s and 1790s were observed and studied by democratic ideologues and *philosophes*, commencing with Mirabeau and Brissot, with special commitment and zeal.

Republican veneration of the thirteen core republics forming the Helvetic Confederation undoubtedly possessed a long history, stretching back to Machiavelli.[10] Admired and extolled for the rural simplicity of their morals and politics by Machiavelli as well as later by Mably and Rousseau, Rousseau taught modern readers to view the Swiss republics as a powerful counter-example to monarchical France and British mixed monarchy.[11] In the fifteenth and sixteenth centuries when nearly all Swiss had been poor, and more equal than later, the cantons had also been militarily and

[8] See Sismondi's remarks on recent Swiss history in the *Revue Encyclopédique* XXI (Feb. 1824), 317–18; Fruci, "Democracy in Italy," 27–8, 42.

[9] [Jullien], *Revue encyclopédique* XXI (Feb. 1824), 313.

[10] Kapossy, "Neo-Roman Republicanism," 229–30.

[11] Rousseau, *Projet*, 141; Rousseau, *Gouvernement de Pologne*, 226, 232; Wright, *Classical Republican*, 181.

politically more formidable than they subsequently became. Lamentably, held Mably, Rousseau, and some others, traditional agriculture and rural mores were later undermined by the vitiating effects of commerce and luxury. Most urban Swiss cantons had gradually fallen victim to corruption and moral decay; in their own time, Geneva and Basel especially were plainly commercial republics. Berne, however, remained a largely agricultural–military state and decidedly more resolute in adhering to the anti-commercial tendency, separating politics from economic life, and supposedly abjuring "luxury" in the name of virtue, than Basel, Geneva, or Zurich. Alluding to ancient Rome in its rhetoric and symbolism remained a distinctive feature of the Bernese republic—something not the case with the others.[12] But, however relevant to Rousseau admirers and Rousseauist idealization of the Swiss republics, Bernese republicanism possessed precious little relevance to the collision between Radical and Moderate Enlightenment: while Bernese patricians were mostly landowners rather than involved in trade and finance, strict oligarchy and lack of freedom predominated at Berne just as at Zurich, Basel, and Geneva.

If Berne, where Albrecht von Haller became a member of the governing council in 1745 and remained prominent in public business until 1773, exemplified for some the prosperous and tranquil, uncontested aristocratic republic based on the Roman model, resoundingly justifying aristocratic bias in the distribution of power, the poor Swiss republics, for Rousseau and his following, glowingly represented the acme of political wisdom, moral uprightness ,and republican virtue. Unfortunately for Rousseau's recipe, though, practically all the Swiss republics, whether Catholic, like Lucerne and Fribourg, or Protestant, like Zurich and Schaffhausen, had in recent decades evolved constitutionally more and more in an oligarchic direction, Berne most of all. Since acquiring lordship over the Vaud region, in the early fifteenth century, the Bernese had led the way in unremitting oligarchization, so that "notwithstanding they designed to settle a perfect democracy," originally, as Radicati described Switzerland's failure, they "were not able to succeed in it, because they did not establish it upon a proper foundation."[13]

At Geneva, Rousseau found himself a celebrated, popular figure for defending the city's special integrity, character, and traditions in his *Lettre à d'Alembert* (1757). Helping Geneva's citizenry "regain" their rights was a prime goal of Rousseau's *Contrat social* first published in 1762. His political texts were part of the very fabric of Genevan and Swiss politics from their first appearance. But the challenge they offered, the vision they put forward, was, in the Swiss context a distinctly limited one characterized by marked unwillingness to abandon his neutrality in the face of the intensifying battle between democratic and oligarchic republicanism; and if there was

[12] Rousseau, *Projet*, 110, 126; Rousseau, *Lettres écrites* ii. 42; Tröhler, "Switzerland," 92–3, 95, 101; Kapossy, "Neo-Roman Republicanism," 233–7.

[13] Radicati, *Twelve Discourses*, 205; in the 1734 translation from Radicati's French the translator instead of "settling a perfect democracy" renders this "setting up a popular government" (p. 46); on the difference between the 1734 and 1736 versions of the *Discourses*, see Canestri "Monoscritto," pp. lxxxviii and xcv–xcvii.

support among Geneva's population for his bridging republican principles, there was also fierce criticism of the unchristian, Deistic tendency in *Émile*, which, appearing almost simultaneously with the *Contrat social*, was immediately condemned by Geneva's pastors as destructive of the "Christian religion and all Revelation." At Geneva in June 1762 the *Contrat social* and *Émile* were publicly condemned together, "shredded and burned by the public executioner before the gates of the city hall."[14] Banning the *Contrat social* Geneva's conservatives followed up by targeting anti-oligarchy opponents complicit in the book's advent and distribution. On the advice of Jean-Robert Tronchin (1710–93), among the city's most learned as well as powerful men, for twenty years (1759–79) the republic's *procureur-général*, an admirer of Beccaria in penal reform, and fervent moderate enlightener, secret orders were issued for Rousseau's arrest and trial should he again set foot in the city. Prohibiting Rousseau's texts chiefly for political reasons, the oligarchs used the pretext of religion to justify suppression, guided by the adept Tronchin, who, in publicity matters, was the *Petit Conseil*'s [Small Council's] chief apologist or, as Brissot later put it, defender of the "système monstrueux d'usurpation du sénat" [the senate's monstrous system of usurpation].[15]

The eminent Genevan naturalist Charles Bonnet (1720–93), who wished to see the *Encyclopédie* of Diderot and d'Alembert suppressed owing to its subversive character, fervently hoped Berne would follow Geneva's example in expelling Rousseau after the latter sought refuge on Bernese territory. Although Berne's emulation of Geneva in actively suppressing *Émile* and the *Contrat social*,[16] and then, in July 1762, expelling Rousseau (then at Yverdon) himself from Bernese territory, angered some Bernese citizens, Bonnet and Haller approved and were most displeased to learn it outraged some Genevans. It was right too that the outcast was expelled from Berne for his anti-Christian and not (or at least not publicly) his political views.[17] That Rousseau, a declared foe of Berne's oligarchy, enjoyed some support in both cities, they did not doubt: should such a situation develop that Rousseau's ideas should wholly capture opinion at Berne, Bonnet and Haller feared its "aristocratie serait bientôt changé en pure démocratie" [its aristocracy would soon be changed into pure democracy].[18] Bonnet and Haller not only promoted a rigorously Protestant, anti-Diderotian and anti-materialist Enlightenment in Switzerland but equally an explicitly oligarchic, anti-democratic Enlightenment. For them the two went hand in hand together.

The Genevan *Petit Conseil* actually proved more energetic in banning Rousseau's *Contrat social* as seditious than any other government.[19] But if, since the early

[14] Mason, "Genevan Republican Background," 548; Whatmore, "Rousseau," 387; Trousson, *Rousseau*, 524–7.

[15] Brissot, *Philadelphien à Genève*, 24; Trousson, *Jean-Jacques Rousseau*, 524–5; Rosenblatt, *Rousseau and Geneva*, 269–73; Gauthier, *Rousseau*, 67–9.

[16] Trousson, *Jean-Jacques Rousseau*, 531.

[17] Rousseau, *Confessions*, 495, 541–2; Rousseau, *Gouvernement de Pologne*, 222; Rousseau, *Lettres écrites* ii. 42.

[18] Quoted in Trousson, *Jean-Jacques Rousseau*, 532.

[19] Rousseau, *Lettres écrites* i. 240.

eighteenth century, serious disturbances periodically occurred at Geneva (with a less vigorous but still noticeable opposition movement from the 1750s also at Zurich), if some Genevan citizenry abhorred Natural Law doctrines, like those of Barbeyrac, sustaining narrow oligarchy and government by tiny elites by venerating the past, precedent, the old constitution, and the Roman example,[20] it was not until late in Rousseau's own life, until years after his own personal encounter with Swiss reality, and not particularly owing to him, that the influence of new democratic republican doctrines fomented by the American example became a formidable force. When they did, Rousseau's distinctive perspective quickly lost much of its relevance—even during his own lifetime. Due to his own painful rebuff in Genevan politics, and to Voltaire's residing nearby at Ferney, the late Rousseau no longer felt the inclination to visit, reside, and participate in the politics of his native Switzerland that he had evinced in the 1750s and 1760s. Always basically neutral regarding the battle between aristocratic and democratic republicanism in Switzerland broadly (and everywhere), and Geneva in particular, his rebuff left Rousseau personally less engaged, more neutral than ever.[21] At Geneva, Berne, and throughout Switzerland, indignation over Rousseau's attitude to the Reformed Church and its doctrines also significantly dampened enthusiasm for his republican ideals.

Plainly, the culminating shift to full Swiss oligarchization had occurred only in the recent past, especially the period 1680–1713. Recovery of pristine Swiss "virtue" should be the essential Swiss agenda, held Rousseau and Mably; for these Enlightenment giants, oligarchization mattered much less than sustaining the myth of Geneva and Berne,[22] as havens of *la liberté*, toleration, and republican well-being. In this way Rousseauism in Switzerland became the virtual ally of the kind of moderation championed by Bonnet and Haller, even if such hardened moderate enlighteners were often much more emphatic. Berne was lauded by the Lockean, anti-egalitarian Göttingen savant, Christoph Meiners (1747–1810), as "perhaps the most perfect aristocracy that was ever to be found in the real world."[23] In any case, by the early 1780s aristocratic republicanism was decidedly an ideology under siege and with it so was the bridge-building Rousseau. Simplicity of lifestyle and customs had given the Swiss their freedom, acknowledged Condorcet, who, about this, as on most topics, fundamentally disagreed with Rousseau: but simplicity also served to obstruct entry of foreign ideas and hinder enlightenment, so that what had once been an advantage had in their time become a formidable obstacle to Swiss liberty.[24] With his withdrawal into complete neutrality, it was only Rousseau's emotional ties to Switzerland that henceforth remained of real relevance. His epistolary novel, *La Nouvelle Heloïse* (1761), the eighteenth century's biggest best-seller, probably did more to entrench the Swiss countryside, the appeal of the Alps, in the Romantic imagination than any other

[20] Mason, "Genevan Republican Background," 555–7; Rosenblatt, *Rousseau and Geneva*, 102, 109–11, 115–17, 130–5; Tröhler, "Switzerland," 99, 102.

[21] Ramat, *Sismondi e il mito*, 27–9.

[22] Meiners, *Briefe* i. 119, 167, 228 and ii. 203.

[23] Meiners, *Briefe* i. 163–4.

[24] Condorcet, *Bibliothèque* series II (1791), v. 12–14.

text. But however alluring for budding Romanticism and Counter-Enlightenment, Rousseau and Rousseauism receded into non-political isolation, at his north French hermitage.[25] If, in the early 1780s, Rousseau's views remained sufficiently attractive to trigger a petition of protest over the shabby treatment to which the Genevan Republic had subjected its most famous writer—a petition signed, reports Brissot, by around 700 sympathizers—Rousseau had precious little to offer the rising Swiss democratic tendency.[26]

Oligarchization, argued Brissot, had wholly blighted authentic republican awareness in Switzerland and many Swiss felt likewise.[27] Earlier, there had been little attempt to theorize the intermittent tensions to which the cantons became subject after 1700, and no conscious ideological battle. Even when Rousseau's political writings shook the scene, in the 1760s, there was, despite the apprehensions of Haller and Bonnet, still no serious democratic republican script available to would-be thoroughgoing critics of the Swiss status quo. In fact, Rousseau's texts lent support, via his distinction between sovereignty and government, whereby the Swiss oligarchic regimes' legitimacy and authority, including those of the Genevan *Petit Conseil* as reconstituted after the 1738 settlement, found themselves considerably reinforced. Even his *Lettres écrites de la montagne* (1764), which offered some criticism of the Genevan elite, basically endorsed Geneva's "aristocratic," oligarchic system, and the principle of "mixed government," since modern Genevans, being neither "Romans nor Spartans, nor Athenians," and preoccupied largely with acquiring private wealth, nurtured only severely truncated, inadequate notions of liberty.[28]

Rousseau, hence, was of only very limited help to aspiring Genevan democrats. Besides being far too timid and constrained from a democratic republican standpoint, argued Sismondi, at the end of the 1790s, Rousseau, lamentably, "did not seem to have felt the importance of liberty of the press." He hardly touched on this topic in his *Contrat social* and yet it is by that vital freedom that the people as a whole can truly be most genuinely "souverain et législateur," which they never were in ancient Greece or Rome.[29] Sismondi's massive *Histoire des républiques italiennes* (16 vols., Paris, 1815–18), completed just as he evolved into a radical enlightener and democratic republican, proved a major landmark not just in historiography but in the evolution of European democratic republican ideology, especially in Italy and Switzerland. His reinforcing the prestige of the late medieval Italian city states, as great centers of the highest human achievement as well as democratic republican culture, became a worrying challenge to and regular target of both nationalists and "moderates" in Italy

[25] Blanning, *Romantic Revolution*, 141–4; Gauthier, *Rousseau*, 156–7.

[26] Brissot, *Philadelphien à Genêve*, 23–4.

[27] Brissot, *Philadelphien à Genêve* 181; Kapossy, "Neo-Roman Republicanism," 235.

[28] Rousseau, *Lettres écrites* i. 238–40; Brooke, "Revisiting," 80–1; Whatmore, "Rousseau," 411, 413; Romani, "Republican Foundations," 21.

[29] Sismondi, *Recherches*, 118, 187; Craiutu, "Rousseau and Madame de Staël," 245–6.

during the nineteenth-century Risorgimento with both trying to demolish the alluring and powerful city-state republican historical myth he single-handedly revived.[30]

For centuries the vast majority of Swiss, over a million and a half by 1789, had languished altogether deprived of political and civic rights. In the only other sizeable federal republic in Europe, apart from the United Provinces, pre-1789 Switzerland, most of the population, concluded Sismondi, in reality enjoyed little in the way of liberty. In the Helvetic Confederacy, only thirteen cantons enjoyed full status, leaving several areas in a subject condition. And most of these thirteen cantons had become tight oligarchies so that of a total population of one and half million, mostly dwelling under a modified feudal vassalage cemented by religious authority, less than 50,000 people, according to Sismondi's calculation, actually qualified to participate in elections and share at all in political life down to the 1790s.[31] Certainly, the wealthy elite of old-established families controlling the Geneva *Petit Conseil*, while denying the lowest stratum, in terms of formal status, of the city's population, that is around 25,000 people, any rights whatsoever, also feared the ambitions of the bourgeois middling status group. But they still succeeded in constantly extending their grip over legislation and taxation and in reinforcing "aristocracy," subordinating the interests of both the middling and lower strata increasingly to their own interests.[32] Despite their wildly deluded notions to the contrary, eighteenth-century Swiss were not free at all, and not "citizens," insisted Sismondi, merely obedient serfs.

By contrast, Swiss moderate enlighteners followed Haller, Bonnet, Tronchin, and Meiners in endorsing moderate Enlightenment closely tied to religious authority and oligarchy, and rejecting both Rousseau (even though, in this context, he remained a near "moderate") and the radical democratic tendency. Many revered theorists, insisted Meiners, agreed "aristocracy" is the best form of state.[33] The difficulty for Genevan radicals in the 1780s was that the *Petit Conseil* was opposed not just by the small, committed democratic faction hoping to transform Geneva's institutional framework on the basis of a general good promoting the "happiness" of the whole populace, but also, and principally, by convinced "moderates," hard-headed businessmen, shopkeepers, and merchants, a far larger group who, by aiming for a businesslike, working compromise between the upper and middle strata, on a purely pragmatic—that is, unprincipled—basis, were entirely agreeable, if only they were brought in, to excluding the majority. Hence, not just the patrician oligarchy but, as at Zurich, also the middling group frequently showed a preference for Montesquieu when invoking philosophical authority in support of their views rather than Rousseau.[34]

[30] Romani, *Sensibilities of the Risorgimento*, 115–16, 120.

[31] See Sismondi's late comments on the Swiss, in [Jullien], *Revue encyclopédique* XXVI (Jan. 1824), 316–18.

[32] Leigh, "Le "Contrat social," 105; Rosenblatt, *Rousseau and Geneva*, 152.

[33] Meiners, *Briefe* i. 163.

[34] Whatmore, "Venturi," 444.

Yet it had long been obvious to many that the magistrates of Geneva's *Petit Conseil*, and its governing committees, represented only their own selfish, narrow, vested interests. Even the much vaunted sovereignty of the collectivity of the restricted citizenry possessing political rights in theory, represented at Geneva by the "General Council," could be considered chimerical, as had long been recognized in the cases of Venice and Genoa. During the early 1780s, an initially Genevan local crisis rapidly broadened into a general Swiss drama, one that soon escalated outside Swiss frontiers into an international intellectual and propaganda war. By 1780 the American Revolution, discussion of that Revolution's principles and constitutions, and related issues, including forced impressment of large numbers of Hessian troops to serve Britain's cause in America, was exerting a polarizing effect in Switzerland as well as Germany, the Netherlands, and Ireland. The European impact also began to rebound significantly back to America. It was in April 1780 that Albert Gallatin (1761–1849), among the leading Radical Enlightenment voices of early America, emigrated from his native Geneva to the newly-born United States. Already immersed in Rousseau, Voltaire, and the Enlightenment, he was later among the principal democratic republican opponents of the *Alien and Sedition Acts*—and one of its immediate targets. Trans-Atlantic democratic republican mutual assistance would always remain one of Gallatin's guiding ideals: later, as US ambassador to Bourbon France in 1816–23, he would figure among the leading advocates of US intervention in the Greek struggle for independence. Protesting against the Mexican War, in 1847, at the end of his life, it was Gallatin who reminded Americans: "your mission was to be a model for all other governments and for all other less-favoured nations."[35] Still, the Swiss situation needed more than just American inspiration, which was equally strong in Germany and Britain, to become a political crisis; it was the local clash of political factions in Geneva, in 1781–2, that imparted a whole new edge to the longstanding split pitting backers of traditionalism and the status quo against the agitators for constitutional reform, finally liquidating the patently fabricated and false Voltairean–Rousseauan idyll of Swiss republican solidarity, "virtue," and exceptionalism.

The 1782 revolution at Geneva followed months of disagreement about whether or not a particular category of "natives" should be made citizens. In April 1782, angry crowds of shopkeepers and workmen resenting the *politique aristocratique* of the *Petit Conseil* seized Geneva by force. Overwhelming the militia, crowds occupied the town gates, squares, arms depots, and town hall. Both councils were purged of "aristocrats," resulting in forty-three of the so-called *grandes perruques* of Geneva being confined, more or less prisoners, to their homes.[36] To maintain order, a *commission de sûreté* was established, under two democrat leaders, Clavière and Duroveray, which, to the evident satisfaction of many, began preparing a thorough revision of the constitution or, as Brissot called it, "réforme générale du gouvernement." All natives of the city whose families had resided for three generations in the republic were proclaimed full

[35] Wood, *Empire of Liberty*, 250; Israel, *Expanding Blaze*, 351, 353, 360, 506, 575.

[36] [Feller], *Journal historique* (1782), 358–60; Meiners, *Briefe* ii. 203.

citizens.[37] Berne and Zurich, however, thoroughly alarmed at these developments, refused point blank to recognize the new government and, in a declaration of 12 May, jointly condemned the revisions as contrary to Geneva's laws and constitution.[38] Zurich proved too divided to do more at this point. But Berne, spurred by Louis XVI's chief minister, Vergennes, delivered a menacing ultimatum which the Genevans, explained the pro-democrat *Tableau historique et politique des deux dernières révolutions de Genève* (1782), the subsequent principal radical account of the episode, flatly rejected.[39] The French court, guided by Vergennes, then resolved to intervene militarily, on the Genevan patrician oligarchy's side, to crush the democratic movement (as Prussia was to do, five years later, in the Netherlands).

French royal officials expressed their indignation at the "oppression" perpetrated in Geneva by scheming men employing "les idées de la démocratie absolue."[40] Vergennes opted to intervene militarily despite France being then still in formal alliance with the American rebels against the British crown and hesitantly supporting the pro-American republican Dutch Patriots against the pro-British Orangists in the Netherlands—a remarkable contradiction, according to many, in French foreign policy. The *Tableau historique* demanded how the very same minister guaranteeing the triumph of "democracy" in America, and aiding Holland's democrats, could send forces to demolish the new Genevan Republic and "*la Démocratie* tempérée which lent it its whole luster".[41] Berne and Zurich were both reluctant to see France gain extra leverage in Switzerland; but their oligarchies detested democratic republicanism even more than French royal influence, which moved Berne, despite its ancient republican tradition, and history of local pride in "liberty" and suspicion of outsiders, to join forces with France and Savoy in crushing the revitalized Genevan Republic militarily. The sprawling Berne canton with its French-speaking appendages Lausanne and Fribourg, also now troubled by serious unrest, thus became directly entangled in the conflict. Zurich, by contrast, stood aside, paralyzed by its own internal wrangles, and the notion that if Geneva and Zurich now reflected incompatible, warring conceptions of "republic"—democratic versus aristocratic, the *philosophique* versus tradition and religion—nevertheless something remained of their once shared republican identity that forbade alignment with foreign monarchs bent on decimating a fellow Swiss republic's independence.[42]

The contradiction between France's sponsoring revolutionary movements in America and Holland while backing Switzerland's *parti aristocratique* against democratic republicanism was widely commented on by radical publicists at the time.[43]

[37] [Brissot], *Philadelphien à Genève*, 38–9.

[38] Bénétruy, *L'Atelier de Mirabeau*, 23; Whatmore, *Against War and Empire*, 168.

[39] [Feller], *Journal historique* (1782), 200–2, 283; Kapossy, "Neo-Roman Republicanism," 237.

[40] [Brissot], *Philadelphien à Genève*, 34; [Feller], *Journal historique* (1782), 285–6.

[41] [D'Ivernois], *Tableau historique*, 179–80.

[42] [D'Ivernois], *Tableau historique*, 166–7, 171; [Feller], *Journal historique* (1782, 200–1); Lerner, "Radical éléments," 304, 306; Maissen, *Geburt der Republik*, 442–3.

[43] Dumont, *Souvenirs*, 7; [Brissot], *Philadelphien à Genève*, 47, 193.

Both sides embarked on a propaganda war in the international French- and German-language press to drum up support for and against the democratic republican tendency. The rift in Enlightenment ranks became increasingly bitter and vehement. Prominent among adversaries of the *démocrates* was the influential *Courier du Bas-Rhin*, published at Cleves, which afterwards endorsed the Prussian invasion of Holland to topple the democratic faction there, in September 1787.[44] If to Mirabeau, Brissot, and the compiler of the *Tableau historique*, François d'Ivernois (1757–1842), the French court seemed mired in contradiction, Berne's intervention against the new Genevan constitution struck some as still more outrageous and self-destructive.[45] Democratic republican *philosophes* charged Berne's "aristocrats," judges, and lawyers with utterly betraying the Helvetic Confederation's authentic traditions and their own republican liberty. Such abject intervention against Geneva's democrats, charged opponents, isolated Berne within Switzerland and blighted the oligarchy's prestige locally. Detractors, including the renowned educationalist Johann Heinrich Pestolozzi (1746–1827), a leading voice among those opposing the local patrician aristocracy,[46] a thinker who admired Rousseau but not his ambivalent influence in Switzerland, deplored the patriciate's monopoly of the magistracies and sway over councils from which most people were excluded. This wider Swiss criticism of the Genevan, Bernese, and Zurich *parti aristocratique*, together with growing signs of agitation, notably in Fribourg, encouraged radical sentiment over a wide area. A rising democratic outcry bolstered the Genevan revolution, while the simultaneous murmuring against oligarchy in southern Germany, notably against the patriciate at Augsburg, signally demonstrated, observed Wekhrlin in 1785, that not all peoples are so sunk in "ignorance" as to blindly submit to their nobles and priests; desire for emancipation from oppression was proving a stronger force in Europe, certainly in Switzerland, the Netherlands, and south-west Germany, than many supposed.[47]

All Europe observed in fascination as 12,000 French, Savoyard, and Bernese troops took up positions around Geneva, on 23 June 1782, including at Ferney, laying siege to the defiant democratic faction ensconced within. Brissot, recently arrived, eager to study the dynamics of "l'esprit républicain," hurriedly departed for Neuchâtel, just prior to the siege.[48] Despite efforts of most of Geneva's pastors to persuade the populace to give in and negotiate, most Genevans, he reported, women and children included, evinced a remarkable willingness to fight for their liberty. The same conclusion was reached by Meiners, arriving six weeks after the democratic revolution's collapse. Geneva's defenders worked fervently preparing their defense and strengthening the walls. But there was little hope of holding out for long and, after three weeks, the revolutionary committee, led by Clavière, Duroveray, and

[44] *Courier du Bas-Rhin*, no. 75, 19 Sept. 1787, p. 617; Beermann, *Zeitung*, 434–5.
[45] [Brissot], *Philadelphien à Genève*, 51, 143, 181, 220; Mirabeau, *Lettres* i. 184–5.
[46] Meiners, *Briefe* i. 236–7; Soetard, "L'*Émile*," 17.
[47] Wekhrlin, *Graue Ungeheuer* iii (1784–5), 184–5, 187.
[48] [Brissot], *Philadelphien à Genève*, 50–1.

a brother of Jean-Paul Marat, voted to capitulate, to prevent large-scale bloodshed. The revolutionary leadership absconded by night before the besiegers entered the city.[49]

Under the Edict of Pacification, finalized on 18 November, the old "aristocratic" magistracy was reinstated; twenty-one revolutionary leaders, including Duroveray, *procureur-général* of the Genevan republic in 1781–2, Clavière, and d'Ivernois were officially proscribed and banished, with their property seized. Although everyone else was promised amnesty, many other known democrats also felt it advisable to depart, with something like 500 political outcasts fleeing, totaling, with family members, around 2,000 political refugees.[50] Under the so-called *Édit noir* [Black Edict] of November 1782, Geneva's democratic leaders were all banished in perpetuity and the press permanently bridled; the General Council was drastically reduced in size. The repression proved unrelenting, the general mood becoming deeply dejected. Many observers blamed Berne especially for cynically backing the *parti aristocratique* instead of interposing responsible compromise proposals. Many attributed the severity of the repression to a growing fear of "l'esprit philosophique," the spread of which, observed Brissot, was now arousing dread in the minds of sovereigns and oligarchies everywhere. Many pragmatic, middle-of-the-road Zurich and Bernese patriots, deeply dismayed and perturbed by the calamity at Geneva, were likewise inclined to blame what Brissot called "l'enthousiasme de la philosophie."[51]

Geneva's democratic republicans were banished a few weeks before Britain finally recognized American Independence. Their leaders, including the co-authors of the 1768 compromise, gathered initially at Neuchâtel, a Swiss principality under the Prussian crown, near Berne, where, among other sympathizers, they were joined by Brissot and Mirabeau.[52] Discussion with Duroveray, Clavière, and Brissot at Neuchâtel marked Mirabeau's personal introduction to his own career in political activism and republicanism, and helped shape his Radical Enlightenment outlook.[53] Like Brissot, Mirabeau researched, consciously seeking to become an expert on the Genevan revolution, absorbing it into the surging new trans-Atlantic democratic republican ideology he aimed to collate and unify, and just a few years later would use to exert a huge impact in France. Mirabeau and Clavière became comrades from this point on; but it was especially Duroveray, a fine speaker as well as accomplished jurist and constitutionalist by all accounts, who became Mirabeau's Genevan republican mentor.[54] Thus Swiss exiles constituted a key component of what in 1789 became known as Mirabeau's *atelier* [workshop], meaning his high-powered anti-aristocratic crypto-republican French–Swiss propaganda machine. With these now

[49] Meiners, *Briefe* ii. 206; [Brissot], *Philadelphien à Genève*, 49; McNutt, *Calvin Meets Voltaire*, 264–7.

[50] [Brissot], *Philadelphien à Genève*, 73, 75–6; Bénétruy, *L'Atelier de Mirabeau*, 38–9, 44; *Réclamation des Genevois Patriotes*, Preface, p. v; Whatmore, "Neither Masters," 76–7; McNutt, *Calvin Meets Voltaire*, 266.

[51] Brissot, *De la Vérité*, 257; Whatmore, *Against War and Empire*, 10–12.

[52] [Brissot], *Philadelphien à Genève*, 52, 56, 75, 147; Blamires, *French Revolution*, 140.

[53] Lutrell, *Mirabeau*, 58–60; Desprat, *Mirabeau*, 261–2.

[54] Bénétruy, *L'Atelier de Mirabeau*, 38–9, 44, 74.

professional revolutionaries still together and fomenting debate, anxiety, and perhaps agitation in Switzerland, the Prussian crown stepped in, on behalf of the Bernese authorities, to eject them; the entire dissident group were expelled from Neuchâtel in the autumn of 1782, causing the outcasts to scatter to Holland, Britain, Ireland, and elsewhere, with a few migrating to America. Early fruit of the future collaboration between Brissot and Clavière was their jointly composed *Le Philadelphien à Genève* ("Dublin" [Paris?], 1783), a work thoroughly lambasting the "despotism" imposed on Geneva by royal France in league with Genevan and Bernese *despotisme aristocratique.*[55]

With the old *parti aristocratique* restored and former constitution reinstated, all the democrats' new laws were rescinded and full control reverted to the *Petit Conseil.* According to the *Tableau historique* this was a tragedy for all mankind, not just Geneva, since amidst the battle between "démocratie" and "aristocratie," Genevans had finally discovered the right way to reform their constitution and forge a democratic republic, and how to make the rich understand "the need to make themselves loved," curb "the inevitable inequality of fortunes," and overthrow the "édifice gothique" of the education system. Education had begun to be reformed "toward the needs of the people." "A wise reform would have balanced the inevitable inequality of fortunes while facilitating equality of enlightenment."[56] All these precious Genevan discoveries, mapping the way ahead for all humanity, now lay in ruins—except in the minds of the refugees. Rather than a model of "balance" and "liberty," Geneva had become a place of strict censorship on political publications with clubs and societies banned, the civic militia purged, and what Brissot termed "le tableau le plus complet du despotisme" reimposed. According to Meiners, ousting the democratic regime entailed considerable damage and interruption to the city's normal vitality and cultural life which the restored regime's efforts long failed to make good. Encouraging theatrical performances to divert attention from politics while simultaneously banning all other types of gathering had only a slight ameliorating effect.[57]

Crushing the 1782 revolution, or what democrats termed "l'exécrable liberticide" perpetrated by the French crown, Berne and Geneva's "aristocrates" failed to reduce either the heightened tension or the dread of *l'esprit philosophique* which the most acute onlookers considered the main engine of the new revolutionary awareness. Rather, Geneva became a unique symbol polarizing sentiment throughout Europe in a wholly new fashion. While many became enthusiasts for "les peuples libres" others became opponents of the joint principles of the American, Dutch, and Swiss democratic republican revolutions.[58] A trans-European war of words raged, in Germany, France, and the Netherlands besides Switzerland, with democratic exiles vividly recounting what had occurred in those journals ready to depict the Genevan

[55] [Brissot], *Philadelphien à Genève*, 31, 174, 181.
[56] [D'Ivernois], *Tableau historique*, 154–5; Whatmore, "Role of Britain," 196–7.
[57] Meiners, *Briefe* ii. 199–200; Godechot, *France and the Atlantic*, 55.
[58] *Réclamation des Genevois Patriotes*, Preface, p. xiii.

counter-revolution in uncompromisingly negative terms.[59] Crushing Geneva's democrats resonated most notably in the fierce polemical exchanges between Cerisier's pro-republican *Politique Hollandois* and Manzon's (since 1781) increasingly pro-monarchy, Orangist, anti-democratic paper, the *Courier du Bas-Rhin.*[60] The Genevan *parti aristocratique* responded to this Dutch–Swiss republican propaganda assault by tightening links with Berlin and London and feeding material to the Orangist press in the Netherlands, where the split between democrats and Orangists, paralyzing the nation's political life, deepened by the month. Among prominent foreign enthusiasts championing joint Genevan–American–Dutch democratic republicanism was Benjamin Franklin's Genevan ally in Philadelphia, du Simitière, who zealously collected every newspaper and journal article about the American Revolution he could find.

The notion that the Genevan "Aristokraten" had despicably murdered the reconstituted republic aided by other Swiss "aristocrats" and France's monarchy, brutally thwarting the will of the people, during the mid-1780s spurred the Dutch Patriot tendency to emulate the Swiss by borrowing their "anti-aristocratic" rhetoric. Wide adoption of this terminology in Switzerland and the Low Countries between 1782 and 1787 helps explain the force and suddenness of the subsequent flood of "anti-aristocratic" rhetoric and its successful propagation in France during 1787–8, a flood engineered by radical journalists like Mirabeau, Brissot, Clavière, and Volney, and the crucial French intellectual shift, well ahead of the general populace, to republicanism and anti-aristocratism during the 1780s well prior to the gathering of the 1789 Estates-General. Echoes of the 1781–2 strife between Geneva's *aristocrates* and *démocrates* also brought the latent antipathy of European and many American moderate enlighteners to democracy to the surface, intensifying their bias toward oligarchic republicanism of the sort striving to keep its hegemony in the United States, United Provinces, Venice, Genoa, and Poland, besides Switzerland.

America's intellectual leadership split as deeply as Western Europe's. "The late revolution," commented Jefferson, from Paris, in October 1785, "has rendered [Geneva] a tyrannical aristocracy, more likely to give ill, than good ideas to an American."[61] By contrast, the *Gazette de Leyde*'s alliance with the American envoy in Holland, John Adams, reflected European "aristocratic" support for the conservative side in the American Revolution, of which Adams was a leader, a proclivity determining its coverage of the Swiss no less than the Dutch democratic movement. Its editor, Johan Luzac, favored much the same Anglophile "classical" gentry republicanism Adams tirelessly championed against Franklin, Paine, and Jefferson in the United States. Adams and Luzac, pulling in the opposite direction from the American Revolution's democratic wing, abhorred radical *philosophes*, Genevan democrats, Irish republican leaders, and Dutch Patriots on the same basis as they reviled American democrats. Warmly approving the French royal intervention in Geneva,

[59] "Demofilus," *Zakboek*, 49. [60] Beermann, *Zeitung*, 436–8.
[61] Jefferson to Banister, Paris, 15 Oct. 1785, in Jefferson, *Writings*, 838.

Luzac's *Gazette de Leyde*, in 1783, turned soon afterwards against the rising Irish agitation.[62] Championing "moderation," the British model, and "aristocracy" in the Dutch, Swiss, Irish, and American upheavals equally, Luzac exalted the Revolution of Adams and America's state oligarchies, in contradistinction to Jefferson and the democrats, as the true American model for all the European republics.

The Genevan exiles' militant democratic republicanism adopted by Brissot and Mirabeau also stood in stark contradistinction to the austere "Spartan" republican perspective of Rousseau and Mably, and those *philosophes*' willingness to justify the Genevan and other oligarchies in part. During 1767–8, corresponding with d'Ivernois and several others, Rousseau had argued that, in Geneva's case, it was necessary to embrace "un gouvernement mixte" where the people remain free without being "master and where the magistracy commands without tyrannizing."[63] It was this stance that was now in shreds. The Genevan radical stance, including their democrats' distancing themselves from Rousseau, provided a real alternative, a far more comprehensively democratic and subversive republican approach, a politically and philosophically more radical syndrome disseminated now in French, English, and Dutch as likewise by Bahrdt, Wekhrlin, Knigge, and others in German. Wekhrlin, a writer much taken with Raynal and the *Histoire philosophique*, in 1787 eagerly looked forward to the future age of "happiness of peoples," "virtuous regimes," "human freedom," and "harmony of the laws." Aristocratic republics he denounced as a despicable category, with Venice (which he had visited in 1767) the most insidious, oppressive, oligarchic, and suspicious of its citizens, of all.

Not that the ruling oligarchies of the German Imperial Free Cities escaped Wekhrlin's scathing criticism more lightly. Ejected from Augsburg, in 1777, and Nördlingen, in 1778, Wekhrlin considered these city republics just as despicably oligarchic and stiflingly oppressive as the Swiss cantons. Augsburg in his eyes exemplified the most contemptible type of republic, one permitting no genuine toleration, or freedom of speech or the press while locking the citizenry into an absurdly contrived parity of equally bigoted Lutheran and Catholic establishments.[64] Berne, he conceded, due to its flourishing bookshops and book trade, was marginally superior and more enlightened than the rest of Switzerland.[65] But for "ignorance" and "enslaving human reason," as well as poverty, he maintained, starkly contrary to Rousseau and Mably, nothing was worse than the rural Swiss republics, especially Glarus and Söldthurn. His particular scorn for Glarus peaked in the summer of 1782 whilst the drama of the 1782 Genevan drama was at its height, that also being the moment when the last person tried and sentenced for witchcraft in Switzerland and perhaps Europe (outside Poland), the chambermaid Anna Göldi (1734–82), was tried and sentenced to death

62 Popkin, *News and Politics*, 158–9; Altena, *Gerrit Paape*, 188.

63 Whatmore, "Role of Britain,|" 195.

64 [Wekhrlin], *Reise durch Ober-Deutschland*, 67–8; Mondot, "Wekhrlin et la Revolution," 128, 130.

65 Wekhrlin, *Graue Ungeheuer* x (1787), 194; Wekhrlin, *Hyperboreische Briefe* i (1788), 88–94; Böhm, *Ludwig Wekhrlin*, 23, 208.

by an Evangelical court in Glarus, though at the point she was sentenced she was already dead, having committed suicide a month before. So scathing was his journal's judgment about Glarus's pastors and attitude to the Enlightenment that the entire Swiss Confederation permanently banned him from entering their territory as a *persona non grata*.[66]

An impressive reply to the surge of democratic rhetoric was Meiners's *Briefe über die Schweiz* (4 vols., Berlin, 1784–90), a work valiantly striving to rescue the prestige of traditional Swiss oligarchy and gentry republicanism on moderate Enlightenment lines. A longstanding adversary of the ethnographer democrat Georg Forster, Meiners judged Swiss oligarchy far preferable to what he saw as the anarchic, disorderly alternative, provided intolerance and oppression are minimized. Amidst the deepening Swiss crisis Meiners carefully refined his rejection of democratic republicanism and secularism. Berne's peasants and those of other Swiss republics, he argued, were actually admirably free of servile obligations and dues and broadly proud and contented. Yes, Berne's oligarchy of around eighty families, dominated by rural landowners, had made Berne the most aristocratic of the Swiss republics; but it was also the best-governed and most prosperous, indeed "one of the most perfect aristocracies, perhaps the most perfect ever seen in reality." Berne, far from contradicting every republican principle, as the wild revolutionary Brissot contended, was wisely administered, flourishing despite the dismal condition of its subject territory of Vaud and Lausanne, a republic offering far more freedom of speech and thought than Venice while also enforcing impeccably strict Christian morals. Berne exercised a rigorous censorship over people's personal lives, but this was a valuable additional benefit in his view.[67] If Berne followed Geneva in expelling Rousseau, in 1762, this resulted chiefly, he argued, from Rousseau's anti-Christian views.

Berne, observed Meiners, featured noticeably less organized internal opposition to the ruling patricians than other oligarchic cantons—except in the French-speaking territory Vaud where resentment at subjection to Berne was intense but voiced exclusively in the old-fashioned terms of specific lost historic rights. Zurich, where manufacturing activity and the guilds were strongest, was decidedly a more stratified and hierarchical society, and internally more divided than Berne, as was likewise, though rather differently, Lucerne. On this ground, Meiners styled Berne "eine demokratische Aristokratie," in contrast to Zurich, which he called "eine aristokratische Demokratie," meaning the former remained more caring and fairer than Zurich regarding the population as a whole.[68] Meiners's "moderate" stance emphatically sanctioned a very narrow distribution of political power, something Rousseau, if not Voltaire or d'Alembert, had deplored. But Meiners also accepted that Geneva's and Berne's citizenry enjoyed neither religious freedom, nor freedom of thought, nor press freedom, all of which struck Brissot as intolerable; and these were restrictions to

[66] Böhm, *Ludwig Wekhrlin*, 130.
[67] Meiners, *Briefe* i. 119, 122, 163; Carhart, *Science*, 13, 22, 255.
[68] Meiners, *Briefe* i. 164–7 and iii. 62; Kapossy, "Neo-Roman Republicanism," 238–9.

which Rousseau as well as Meiners—though Meiners was more insistent on the need to curb personal freedom—offered no objection in principle. Having begun as a Rousseau enthusiast, eulogizing traditional Swiss "liberty," Brissot, before long, with increasing direct personal experience of Swiss piety, neatness, deference, and conventional thinking, quickly grew disillusioned. Stifling narrowness characterized not least Geneva's religiously directed policing of sexual activity: far from condemning this, Rousseau and Meiners, with their philo-Spartan leanings, expressly endorsed it, Meiners ascribing Geneva's post-1760s growing divisions and troubles to a weakening of its post-Reformation rigid moral discipline, the clergy's slackening grip over behavior, marriage, and family life, exemplified by divorce becoming easier to obtain.[69] In the later 1790s, another who found Berne's limited freedom stifling, whilst employed as a tutor in one of the more reactionary of the oligarchy's households, was the then young philosophical revolutionary, Hegel.[70]

Triumphing with French royal and Bernese help in 1782, the Geneva *aristocrates* still had every reason to dread a fresh upsurge of democratic sentiment at a point where Berne and France might be less ready to assist. Leading Genevan exiles, together with their French allies, Mirabeau and Brissot, were effectively rendering the "horror" of the aristocratic tyranny and the dishonesty of "la nouvelle aristocratie de Genève" as something evidently shocking to readers right across Europe. The *Tableau historique* of François d'Ivernois achieved a notably wide impact and not just briefly: an astounding forty-six different editions of this harrowing account of the 1782 Genevan revolution have been recorded for the period between 1782 and 1850, in French and English, giving Swiss aristocratic republicanism a distinctly obnoxious reputation in some quarters. Duroveray and Clavière likewise bombarded Geneva's "usurping elite" with propaganda alleging the city's "aristocrats" treated their compatriots as a conquered people despite daily observing the inwardly undefeated suppressed fury on their fellow citizens' faces.[71]

Within a short time, a resentful, highly articulate, and ideologically sophisticated European ex-patriot, intellectual revolutionary diaspora, established by Genevan exiles and reinforced by fleeing Dutch exiles, from 1787, became established and active, linking Switzerland, Germany, and the Low Countries, to Paris, London, and Ireland, in a remarkable, unprecedented fashion. The publicity the exiles organized powerfully contributed to the build-up of revolutionary and *Américaniste* consciousness in western Europe and helps explain why Geneva's aristocratic counter-coup of 1782 acquired such a starkly negative, unsavory reputation among Left-leaning contemporaries, including Price and Godwin. A revolution favorable to the people, based on philosophical principles, was obviously brewing in Europe's reading-rooms, contended Clavière and Brissot in a text they jointly published in 1787, a process accelerated by enthusiasm for the American Revolution beside developments in the

[69] Meiners, *Briefe* ii. 220–5.
[70] Meiners, *Briefe* ii. 222; Leigh, "Le 'Contrat social'," 104–6; Pinkard, *Hegel*, 55–7.
[71] *Réclamation des Genevois Patriotes*, Preface, pp. iii–iv.

Low Countries and France.[72] Genevan refugee leaders of the democratic trend in Paris, headed by Clavière and Duroveray, became full-time professional democratic agitators, as did Étienne Dumont (1759–1829), later Bentham's close assistant, a talented writer, editor, and translator already privately opposed to radical republicanism but who gladly became one of Mirabeau's paid speech-writers and co-editor of the latter's revolutionary journal, *Le Courrier de Provence*. The "violent persecution" the Genevan *parti aristocratique* ruthlessly unleashed on the revolutionary faction in 1782 in this way rebounded on the perpetrators and also, contended Brissot, on Berne and the rulers of France and Savoy, who, blind to their own true interests, willingly became tools of aristocratic reaction against the common interest of all the Swiss.[73]

17.2. THE SWISS REVOLUTIONS OF THE 1790S

Understandably, the Swiss aristocratic republics grew still more profoundly uneasy over French developments during 1788–9. The mounting political drama in France (and Belgium) soon noticeably ratcheted up tension and wrangling over rival political theories in Geneva, Berne, Zurich, and adjoining regions. In Paris, revolutionary leaders and journals regularly acknowledged Geneva's and Switzerland's earlier role in guiding the budding French revolutionary impulse: the Genevan as well as the American Revolution had decidedly prepared the path for the French in raising before the European public the great questions of their Revolution.

But Switzerland equally fed the powerful moderate Enlightenment trend resisting the Revolution. At this point, one of Europe's most gifted journalists fighting democratic republicanism, Jacques Mallet du Pan (1749–1801), a Genevan and son of a Protestant minister of Huguenot descent, now editor of the Paris *Mercure de France*, emerged as one of the most widely read and influential counter-revolutionary publicists in France, and later in exile. A Swiss deist admirer of Voltaire and ardent disciple of Burke, Mallet du Pan was always a committed enlightener but one fervent for British style "mixed government" in Switzerland as in France. As an enlightener, he found himself, before long, perfectly detested equally by democrats and Counter-Enlightenment publicists. But no one surpassed Mallet du Pan in propagating up-to-date "moderate Enlightenment" political theory against the democratic republican tide within the French, German, and Swiss revolutions.[74] In January 1789, he published a highly favorable analysis of a key work of Genevan political thought, the *Constitution de l'Angleterre* (1771) by Jean-Louis de Lolme (1741–1806), now reaching its seventh edition since its original appearance. Warmly reiterating Montesquieu's eulogies of the English constitution,

[72] Clavière and Brissot, *De la France*, Preface, p. xxvii; De Luna, "Dean Street Style," 167–8.
[73] Livesey, *Making Democracy*, 147.
[74] Cottebrune, *Mythe et réalité*, 145; Israel, *Revolutionary Ideas*, 46.

de Lolme reworked the Montesquieuan perspective into a more emphatically aristocratic, monarchist and conservative doctrine, emptying the "British model" of such residual hints of subversion and republican sentiment as still lingered in Montesquieu, to provide a sharper, purer Swiss antidote to Rousseau, Mirabeau, Brissot, and the Anglo-American democratic fever of the Paineites and Jeffersonians.[75]

Later in the Revolution, Mallet's royalism forced him to retreat first to Brussels, then Switzerland, and finally, when the Swiss revolutionary tide engulfed Geneva, to England. From early on he grew deeply alarmed that the stream of Genevan exiles producing radical republican publicity seemed to be gaining ground. By February 1789, Geneva was positively seething with political unrest. In March 1789, spurred by high bread prices and economic distress among the poor, occurred a new "revolution," this time powered by demands for the recall of the exiles of 1782. A compromise outcome obliged the conservatives to abandon some and relax others of the *pouvoirs usurpés* of the so-called "Black Code" imposed with French help in 1782. D'Ivernois and some colleagues, together with the pastors, hoped for a rapid rapprochement, a period of reconciliation, harmony of principles, the happiest in Geneva's history, but this middle group failed to retrieve their dominance and positions.[76] The *parti aristocratique*'s grip not only over Geneva but also Berne, Lucerne, and Zurich had become highly precarious. Through the summer and autumn of 1789, according to Gorani, then residing at Nyon in Canton Berne, and among the French Revolution's chief sympathizers in Switzerland, Berne and Geneva were convulsed with frantic political debates.[77] "The Swiss living under the aristocratic republics," reported Brissot's paper, the *Patriote françsis*, from Switzerland, on 25 August, "do not seem far from wanting to overthrow this aristocracy and establish a perfect equality."[78]

Seemingly, only a slight push was required for the Swiss revolution to be back on track. If their hope of returning and restoring the Genevan democratic republic of 1781–2 accounts for the ardour with which Clavière, Duroveray, and Dumont rallied to Mirabeau and the French Revolution, Mirabeau explained Duroveray's assiduous frequenting of the debates in the French National Assembly as due to his championing universal and equal rights, his being a Swiss "citoyen de l'universelle fraternité des hommes libres."[79] The unfinished business of Geneva should be put right, many French revolutionaries, as well as Genevan exiles, agreed once France had consolidated its own liberty and constitution, and was again in a position to intervene in Switzerland, this time more positively. It was an expectation dear to Duroveray and Clavière that Mirabeau took care to foster as a guiding principle of his *atelier*.[80]

[75] Tillet, "Place ambiguë," 200, 204–5, 228.

[76] Dumont, *Souvenirs*, 41; McNutt, *Calvin Meets Voltaire*, 270–1; Whatmore, *Against War and Empire*, 261–2.

[77] Catalano, "Alcune lettere," 151–3.

[78] [Brissot], *Patriote français* xxv (25 Aug. 1789), p. 4.

[79] Desprat, *Mirabeau*, 462.

[80] *Chronique de Paris* ii/lxxxvii (28 Mar. 1790), 345–7; Desprat, *Mirabeau*, 459, 462, 498.

In deep alarm, all the Swiss elites resorted to some vigorous back-pedaling. At Berne, the ruling oligarchy offered to widen the category of families from which members of the Canton's great council and executive council were drawn, hoping to avert immanent trouble by mollifying some citizenry. Mostly, though, nervous patrician oligarchies responded by intensifying censorship and the political repression. Displaying French revolutionary cockades was banned in several cantons; in some, including Fribourg, importing French papers and journals was prohibited except for anti-revolutionary and constitutional monarchist publications like those of Mallet du Pan. Nothing, though, halted the rising agitation, now fueled also by a mounting propaganda campaign emanating from Paris.[81] The French *Declaration of the Rights of Man and the Citizen* of August 1789 inspired Geneva's exiled democrats to summon the French National Assembly to formally repudiate the three-power guarantee of the old Genevan constitution, announce that France no longer opposed the return of the exiles of 1782, and demand the Genevan republic, having violated the exiles' natural rights, make amends.[82] While France's constitutional monarchists were loath to interfere, the democratic republicans were eager to. On 28 December 1789, Brissot's journal summoned the French National Assembly to put right the crime committed against the Genevan republic in 1782. French royal ministers had clapped Geneva in chains; France must now break those chains, to right the wrong done and to proclaim herself "la protectrice des républiques opprimées" in general.[83]

On the 29 December 1789, the French National Assembly held a debate on Geneva which Volney and Mirabeau opened with scathing attacks on the Genevan patriciate; the Assembly ordered Volney's harangue denouncing the Genevan "aristocrates" rule as "la tyrannie la plus affreuse" to be published.[84] By early 1790, it seemed just a matter of weeks before the Genevan democratic revolutionary regime of 1781–2 was restored and other Swiss oligarchies toppled; but the question was would this happen abruptly and violently, or via negotiated and peaceful transition? Dumont, returning to Geneva, was among the principal negotiators; by March 1791, the 1782 imposed settlement had been wholly set aside and the Great Council, in regular contact with Paris, had recovered the upper hand. But many demanded more. There was a pressing need for an "Anarcharsis Cloots" in Geneva, declared the "brothers" there, appealing to the *Chronique de Paris* in August 1791—an "orateur du genre humain" ready to lead the future battle for full liberty by issuing a stream of ideological "briefs," "bulls," and "excommunications," "like the Pope from Rome," against a retreating but still despotic patriciate vitiating their republic, together with all the hypocritical oligarchs harassing Swiss democrats, scorning Rousseau and revolutionary democracy, and encouraging the "Raynals" to betray true liberty. Geneva's *oppresseurs* had violated every conceivable right and freedom, and were continuing to do so, concurred

[81] Brissot, *Patriote français* ccxxxvii (2 Apr. 1790), 4; Fontana, *Venise et la Revolution*, 452.
[82] Brissot, *Patriote français* xxix (29 Aug. 1789), 4–5.
[83] Brissot, *Patriote français* cxlii (28 Dec. 1789), 4; Loft, *Passion, Politics*, 186–8.
[84] Brissot, *Patriote français* cxlv (31 Dec. 1789), 1–2; Bénétruy, *L'Atelier de Mirabeau*, 163.

Cloots, but Geneva's democrats had muddled one aspect of their "missive patriotique": they were overrating Rousseau, whose errors "are just as dangerous as his genius is sublime." If Geneva's democrats championed Rousseau's ideal of small independent republics, preferring this to Cloots's "système régénerateur de la république unique"—a single large republic anchored in Paris—Geneva's revolution would inevitably miscarry again. Genevan democrats must acknowledge France's National Convention as the "corps constituant du genre-humain" and Paris as headquarters of a new universal republic in which all free peoples would collaborate and form "sections."[85]

During the autumn of 1792, French revolutionary armies overran Belgium, Savoy, and the Rhineland. France's annexation of adjoining Savoy greatly alarmed all the Revolution's foes in Switzerland. There was little sign of resistance to the occupying revolutionary army encamped within view, immediately across Lake Geneva, observed one of the Enlightenment's most conservative major figures, a deeply perturbed Edward Gibbon (1737–94), who kept the Savoyard shore opposite his residence under surveillance through his telescope. The occupying revolutionary army offered an astounding spectacle—"officers (scarcely a gentleman among them) without servants, or horses, or baggage," constantly mixing "with the common men, yet maintaining a rough kind of discipline over them." But he was unable to ascertain "whether the mass of the people" of Savoy was pleased or disgusted by being annexed to France. In any case, it appalled him that "my noble scenery is clouded by the democratical aspect of twelve leagues of the opposite coast, which every morning obtrude themselves on my view."[86] More and more Swiss, sighed Gibbon, no uncritical admirer of Swiss oligarchies, were becoming "infected with the French disease, the wild theories of equal and boundless freedom." Having "embittered and divided the society of Lausanne," democratic ideas might soon overwhelm Geneva. He dreaded having to flee his Lausanne home and abandon his beloved "library to the mercy of the democrats."[87]

In mid-October 1792, Gibbon was still confident the aristocratic party would retain its hold on western Switzerland and that there was plenty of will to resist. To head off Geneva's growing agitation, the patriciate there summoned the assistance of Berne, which promptly sent 11,000 troops to prop up the neighboring conservative oligarchy. The Swiss federal diet helpfully "declared that the first cannon fired [by France] against Geneva will be considered an act of hostility against the whole Helvetic body. Berne as the nearest and most powerful canton, has taken the lead with great vigor and vigilance." Even so, the position remained precarious: "some disaffection lurks in the towns," noted a worried Gibbon, while at Geneva, "malcontents are numerous within the walls and I question whether the spirit of citizens will hold out against a bombardment." The real effect of the new Bernese incursion, Gibbon soon realized,

[85] *Chronique de Paris* no. 216 (4 Aug. 1791), 871.
[86] Gibbon, *Memoirs*, 266, 270, 275; McNutt, *Calvin Meets Voltaire*, 273.
[87] Gibbon, *Memoirs*, 283, 289; Spurr, "Gibbon et la Révolution," 272.

was to alienate still more Genevan sentiment, creating a political hotplate now increasingly unstable: "it is much to be feared," he increasingly grasped, "that the present government of Geneva will soon be modelled after the French fashion."[88] Clavière had now broken with his former allies Duroveray and d'Ivernois, who, after several years in Britain, and repelled by the French Revolution's radicalization, had become zealots for "mixed government" and the British model reconciled with Geneva's "aristocratic" party; Clavière, by contrast, stayed loyal to Brissot and the nascent French Republic's democratic tendency.[89]

The Genevois, announced the French resident at Geneva, must, if they valued their safety and the French Republic's friendship, dismiss Berne's troops. Gibbon designated the move "precisely the fable of the wolves, who offered to make peace with the sheep, provided they would send away their dogs. You know what became of the sheep."[90] A treaty signed between France and Geneva in late October guaranteed Geneva would "be preserved inviolate" and no French troops would approach closer than ten leagues of the city, on condition, in Gibbon's words, that the "Swiss garrison, with the approbation of Berne and Zurich, be recalled before the first of December."[91] Conservatives were rapidly losing confidence: "the Jacobin missionaries are powerful and zealous, and the malcontents of this country," noted Gibbon, on 27 October 1792, "who begin again to rear their heads, will be surrounded with temptations, and examples, and allies."[92] Geneva's third revolution, and second with a democratic complexion, widely predicted since the French Republic's advent in September 1792 (and the naming of Clavière among six new Brissotin ministers of the revolutionary regime, in Paris), erupted two months after the Bernese pull-back, in December 1792. Geneva's *Égaliseurs*, so dreaded by Gibbon, Meiners, and Mallet du Pan, took to rioting on, or before, 28 December 1792, seized the city gates, disarmed the garrison, and toppled the stunned ruling oligarchy.[93]

The December 1792 Genevan revolution occurred, Gibbon commented "sooner than I expected." "Citizens of the best families and fortunes" not promptly imprisoned, Jacques Necker and his family among them, fled to Berne and other neighboring cantons, along with numerous *émigrés* from France who had temporarily lodged in Geneva. Three weeks sufficed wholly to dismantle Geneva's *ancien régime*. The *Grand Conseil* proclaimed the principle of political equality among the citizenry, erasing all the traditional distinctions between citizens, natives, habitants, and bourgeois. Sovereignty formally reverted to the people under a decree enacted by the *Grand Conseil*, on 12 December: all privilege and oligarchy were abolished and full rights of citizenship reverted to the entire citizenry, or, as Gibbon expressed it, "to all the rabble of the town and country."[94] There would be, over a period of time, a

[88] Spur, "Gibbon et la Révolution," 273.
[89] Whatmore, *Against War and Empire*, 254–7.
[90] Gibbon to Lord Sheffield, 5 and 11 Oct. 1792, in Gibbon, *Memoirs*, 270–2.
[91] Gibbon, *Memoirs*, 273. [92] Gibbon, *Memoirs*, 274.
[93] *Neue Mainzer Zeitung* no. 13 (29 Jan. 1793), 263; Spur, "Gibbon et la Révolution," 273.
[94] Gibbon, *Memoirs*, 286–8.

complete reconceptualization and rewriting of Geneva's constitution, it was announced, via a process to be decided by the new *assemblée nationale*. To ensure an orderly transfer of power, the democrats created, on 28 December 1792, a provisional *Comité de Sûreté* of thirteen leading citizens who entrusted the promised comprehensive revision of the republic's laws and constitution to a "national assembly" of forty shortly to be elected.

In one fell swoop, Geneva's revolutionaries annulled all the republic's political edicts of the past century including the ban on Rousseau and his books.[95] "Theory always proceeds well in advance of practice," commented one Genevan enthusiast in the Paris *Gazette nationale*: "les vrais principes sont dans les livres." The French had implemented what the *philosophes* had conceived and "Geneva, having received the lessons appreciably earlier than France, now finally followed France's example."[96] Genevans "are all for a pure and absolute democracy," Gibbon wrote to Lady Sheffield, on 1 January 1793, "but some wish to remain a small independent state, whilst others aspire to become a part of the republic of France; and as the latter, though less numerous, are more violent and absurd than their adversaries, it is highly probable that they will succeed."[97] By early February, Gibbon felt slightly calmer as "all spirit of opposition is quelled in the Canton of Berne" and the Helvetic Confederation's neutrality (despite its refusal to recognize the French Republic) seemed assured for the present. Should Geneva and then other Swiss cantons fall to the French revolutionary scourge, Britain would stand alone as the "last great refuge against the opposite mischiefs of despotism and democracy."[98]

News of Louis XVI's execution (January 1793), recorded a scandalized Gibbon, was received in republican Switzerland "with less horror than I could have wished." In fact, French noble *émigrés* in Lausanne now felt so insecure they showed no public signs of mourning at all, "do not wear black, nor do even the Neckars." Against his instincts, Gibbon too felt obliged to refrain from "going into mourning,"[99] while at Mainz, Meiners's adversary Forster and the other leaders of the newly erected revolutionary republic there, Dorsch, Metternich, and Böhmer, publicly approved the execution; other German radicals, including Cramer and Oelsner, like Paine, disapproved but from a republican standpoint.[100] "The new constitution of Geneva," noted Gibbon, in early February 1793, is "slowly forming, without much noise or any bloodshed; and the patriots, who have stayed in hopes of guiding and restraining the multitude, flatter themselves that they shall be able at least to prevent their mad countrymen from giving themselves to the French, the only mischief that would be absolutely irretrievable. The revolution of Geneva is of less consequence to us [in

[95] Spur, "Gibbon et la Révolution," 273.

[96] *Gazette nationale* 3rd series ii, no. 18 (18 Jan. 1793), 154; *Journal de Perlet* ii, no. 92 (22 Dec. 1792), 176 and no. 96 (26 Dec. 1792), 205; *Neue Mainzer Zeitung* xiii (29 Jan. 1793), in Forste, *Werke* x. 263.

[97] Gibbon, *Memoirs*, 286–7; Spurr, "Gibbon et la Révolution," 272–3.

[98] Spur, "Gibbon et la Révolution," 272

[99] Gibbon, *Memoirs*, 292.

[100] Cottebrune, *Mythe*, 186, 188, 194.

Lausanne], however, than that of Savoy; but our fate will depend on the general event [in Europe] rather than on these particular causes."[101]

Switzerland stayed quiet in 1793, with Berne and the Helvetic confederacy refusing to recognize the French Republic but no longer actively opposing revolutionary France in alliance with Austria, Prussia, and Britain, either. As horizons progressively darkened in France, *robespierrisme* cast a long shadow over Switzerland too since the Montagnard coup of June 1793 inevitably spelt the complete uprooting of democratic republicanism. Dumont, among the returned exiles of 1782, after briefly participating in the provisional regime organizing the new Genevan republic during 1791–2, abandoned the task in despair once the Brissotins found themselves deep in trouble, departing for England in March 1793, while the "general supineness of the inhabitants of Lausanne" (which Gibbon left for the last time in May 1793) deepened. As Geneva's Jacobin club gained momentum, intolerance and friction intensified. Sismondi and his family departed for London in February 1793.[102] In France, explained Mme de Staël, "the friends of liberty were more detested by the Jacobins than even the aristocrats, because they had been engaged in a closer struggle with one another, and because the Jacobins feared the constitutionalists, whom they believed to be still in possession of a very considerable influence over the mind of the nation."[103] Brissot was among those guillotined. The two best-known Genevan democratic republicans in France—Clavière and Duroveray—though now on opposite sides of the democratic–aristocratic chasm, were both immediate victims. After months of incarceration, Clavière committed suicide in prison, in December 1793 (on learning of his death, his wife poisoned herself).

Drafting the articles of the new Genevan constitution by committee, amid broad consultation, involved extensive borrowing from France as well as examining other constitutions. The final outcome, reached against the backcloth of the Terror, was extensively shaped by local debate and a considerable measure of real democratic consultation.[104] The result was a bizarre mix of elements, including a January 1794 resolution deferring to popular sentiment, that, to qualify as a Genevan citizen, one must be a Protestant.[105] At Geneva, celebrating Rousseau's birthday as a public festival occurred for the first time, on 28 June 1793. When celebrated for the second time in June 1794, a monument was erected in his memory consisting of a bust of him mounted on a tall column, commemorating the triumph of "democracy" thirty years after the great persecution and ostracism that had banned the *Contrat social* and *Émile* and driven him from the republic.[106]

Promulgated in January 1794, the new Genevan constitution stipulated election of the city's magistrates by all males over 21 submitting to the civic oath. For six months

[101] Gibbon, *Memoirs*, 292; Spurr, "Gibbon," 273.
[102] Ramat, *Sismondi e il mito*, 50; Minerbi, "Introduzione," 9–10.
[103] De Staël, *Considérations*, 367; McNutt, *Calvin Meets Voltaire*, 274.
[104] Whatmore, *Against War and Empire*, 261.
[105] Sorkin, *Religious Enlightenment*, 110.
[106] Waeber, *Sismondi*, 134.

or so, a period in which some of the exiles, including Sismondi's family, returned, hoping for stability, the republic briefly appeared to function viably on its new democratic basis; but the return of the "moderates" proved premature. *Robespierrisme* began to rear its head more strongly. Operating in Switzerland as a British agent, Duroveray was among those who, at this point, inspired an anti-Jacobin pamphlet of protest in Geneva entitled *Declaration des Citoyens de Genève Anti-Anarchistes*, condemning the threat to property and morality, and demanding Geneva remain "Christian, Reformed, independent and neutral."[107] But at Geneva, the worst bout of repression only began after yet another armed insurrection that took place during the night of 18–19 July 1794—only eight days before the coup that overthrew Robespierre in France. The local Genevan Club des Montagnards, "Robespierre's partisans," as Sismondi put it, launched their premeditated coup, suspended the constitution, purged the militias, and set up a *tribunal révolutionnaire* which promptly embarked on a far more ruthless purge of "aristocrats" than anything seen thus far endorsed by mass meetings. The Calvinist pastors were severely curtailed in their functions and stripped of control over education. The Montagnard coup at Geneva led to the arrest or proscription, according to Sismondi, of eventually around 1,600 persons, hundreds being imprisoned but with relatively few death sentences, only eleven actually being executed.[108] D'Ivernois was sentenced to death for treason, in absentia, on 5 September 1794.[109]

Several pastors lost their positions and were forced into exile. The so-called *Terreur genevoise* continued through August, when Sismondi and his father too were briefly imprisoned, into September, before easing later in the autumn. On their release, Sismondi's family fled to the Vaud where they stayed over the winter of 1794–5 with their friends, the Gallatins. In October 1795, he and his family left Switzerland, via Berne, for Tuscany, where they found refuge on a secluded farm during the later 1790s, returning to Geneva only in 1800.[110] For the rest of his life, one could find no greater and more ardent republican foe of Robespierre than Sismondi.[111] For some years, this abhorrence also permeated his general views on liberty and republicanism. Before his turn to a radical democratic republican perspective began, Sismondi still adhered to his family's oligarchic preferences and de Lolme, contending that democracy and popular sovereignty are the enemy of "true liberty," that liberty and equality were incompatible.[112] It was during his Tuscan exile in the late 1790s that Sismondi began to reconsider, though his full turn to Radical Enlightenment did not occur until 1813–14. In Tuscany, he began writing his *Recherches sur les constitutions des peuples libres*, completed in 1801, a work never published during his lifetime because it later came to seem to him

[107] Whatmore, *Against War and Empire*, 260.

[108] Sismondi, *Recherches*, 188–9; Waeber, *Sismondi*, 140–3; Grab, *Napoleon and the Transformation*, 113; McNutt, *Calvin Meets Voltaire*, 275; Sorkin, *Religious Enlightenment*, 110.

[109] Whatmore, *Against War and Empire*, 261.

[110] Minerbi, "Introduzione," 8; Romani, "Republican Foundations," 19.

[111] Sismondi, *Recherches*, 158, 188.

[112] Urbinati, "Republicanism," 106–7.

too moderate in its general approach. While accepting popular sovereignty and convinced that "every political society is only constituted with the aim of ensuring the happiness of its members," the work chiefly expressed Sismondi's wide-ranging rejection of Rousseau, especially the latter's views on broad representation, the principle Sismondi henceforth considered the core of any viable republican doctrine.[113]

17.3. NAPOLEON'S RECONSTITUTION OF SWITZERLAND (1802–1814)

With French power and influence expanding in Europe in 1795–7, there was no let-up in the collision of Switzerland's rival democratic and aristocratic tendencies. The friction remained especially acute in districts bordering French-occupied areas on the Rhine and in south-west Germany, with violent incidents occurring regularly in the Basel area, the Vaud, Aargau—a former Habsburg territory conquered in the fifteenth century, most of which was also under the domination of Berne—and Schaffhausen. The anti-French and anti-democratic militancy of the Berne oligarchy during 1793–6 landed the young Hegel, as an "enlightened" tutor in an oligarchic household, and at that time a "Brissotin" and foe of *robespierrisme*, in some unpleasant disagreements.[114] By 1795, the Vaud unrest had escalated to the point that the Bernese senate dispatched an army of 5,000 men to restore order, provoking the Vaudois to rise in open revolt. Repelling the Bernese, the Vaudois proclaimed the so-called *République Léman*, named after their largest lake, an entity which immediately secured French backing. Not long afterwards, in 1797, revolution broke out also in Basel where the "French party," headed by Peter Ochs (1752–1821), a veteran democratic revolutionary conspirator, and Frédéric-César de la Harpe, ousted the old oligarchy from the city hall, declared popular sovereignty, planted a liberty tree, and proclaimed liberty and democracy. The Basel insurgent revolutionary regime also at once renounced all allegiance to the existing Helvetic confederacy, instituting a people's republic sworn to eliminate oligarchy and achieve national unity with a democratically-elected assembly in alliance with revolutionary France.[115]

During 1797–8, one of the chief instigators, in Paris, of the *Directoire*'s growing interventionism in Switzerland was none other than Napoleon. It was at Napoleon's suggestion, in early 1798, shortly before embarking on his Egyptian adventure, that Peter Ochs, now mayor of Basel and leader of the Swiss pro-French democratic republican faction, prepared, under the *Directoire*'s supervision, a draft of what became the first general Swiss constitution. It envisaged a Switzerland under a five-

[113] Sismondi, *Recherches*, 93, 106; Romani, "Republican Foundations," 25; Craiutu, "Rousseau and Madame de Staël," 243.

[114] Pinkard, *Hegel*, 51–2, 54.

[115] Ochs, *Reden*, 167–9; Polasky, *Revolutions without Borders*, 255.

man executive, like the *Directoire*, and federal Congress embodying popular sovereignty, reducing the cantons to subordinate status and revising their boundaries to eliminate subject areas, like Aargau and the Vaud; the proposed constitution conceded freedom of expression and freedom of religious conscience, albeit the latter for "Christians" only. All servile, feudal, and guild restrictions would lapse; all adult men, except Jews and ecclesiastics, enjoy political rights and share in the new Swiss republic's government.[116]

As the *Directoire* began more energetically backing Swiss anti-patrician insurgency (and exacting cash contributions from Basel, Berne, and Zurich), French designs on Switzerland steadily expanded. Chief among other unresolved issues, the *Directoire* broached the long-standing dispute with the Helvetic confederacy over the French-speaking Vaud. "There is no doubt that the Pays de Vaud was entitled to claim an independence existence," acknowledged Mme de Staël, who, however, still felt that the Vaudois had no business summoning the "terrible assistance of the French," plunging all Switzerland into war. Napoleon dismissed her objections while discussing Swiss affairs with her in Paris shortly after first meeting her, through Talleyrand: the "inhabitants of that district were subject to the aristocrats of Berne," he maintained, adding what she considered a blatant pretext for intervention, "that men could not now exist without political rights."[117]

Where the Vaudois and Basel democrats, under Ochs, welcomed the French troops that invaded in February 1798, most Swiss vehemently demurred. De Staël later recalled how the "small cantons in 1798, nobly ignorant of this world, dutifully dispatched their quotas" of men and money to Berne. The pro-Allies Swiss army marched to encounter the French in battle, on 3 May 1798, at Morgarten, where in 1315 the Swiss had gained a legendary victory over the Austrians; this time, though, they were swiftly crushed. Two days afterwards French troops occupied Berne and looted its public revenues.[118]

On 12 April 1798, the first ever Swiss national assembly, convened at Aarau, proclaiming the establishment of the "one and indivisible" new Helvetic Republic with "freedom" and "equality" as its guiding principles, adopting the constitution largely drafted by Ochs. Switzerland's now eighteen cantons were stripped of their sovereignty and the new legislature proclaimed sovereign, with the Swiss republic's day-to-day government entrusted, as envisaged, to a French-style five-man executive. All the country's inhabitants were declared "Swiss" citizens for the first time, and the special rights and privileges of the old patriciates wholly abolished along with the subject status of their territorial dependencies.[119] The country's remaining ecclesiastical states (the prince-bishop of Basel had already lost most of his Jura territory to France, in 1792) were dissolved, the Basel prince-bishopric effectively disappearing on

[116] Maissen, "Erfinder," 32.
[117] De Staël, *Considerations*, 415–16; Polasky, *Revolutions without Borders*, 255–6.
[118] Kapossy, "Neo-Reoman Republicanism," 247; Clemens, "The Swiss Case," 134.
[119] Clemens, "The Swiss Case," 134–5.

the Swiss side of the border, along with the abbey-principality of St Gall, secularized, under pressure, in September,[120] the prince-abbot fleeing to Vienna. Geneva, however, was not included in the new Switzerland but, as Gibbon had dreaded, annexed to France in total disregard of local opinion and the city's proud republican and Calvinist traditions. Geneva's inhabitants at a stroke became French citizens, except for those French *émigrés* on the French Republic's proscribed list along with the three most notorious Genevan ideologues opposing the Revolution—Duroveray, d'Ivernois, and Mallet de Pan.[121]

This was decidedly the point at which modern Switzerland as a country came into existence. Where before 1798 all the cantons minted their own separate currencies, in 1798 a single currency, the Swiss franc, based on the Berne *Thaler*, was introduced. For the first time a unified penal code and centralized postal system were adopted. Orders were issued, in May, for the removal, throughout Switzerland, of all symbols, titles, coats of arms, and other heraldic signs associated with the "aristocratic" system of the Swiss *ancien régime.*[122] To an extent consolidation of the new republic was aided by the fact that many urban educated Swiss had for years been agitating for the reform of the ramshackle, illogical, patrician-dominated old Swiss Confederacy.[123] Berne and other Swiss cities, acknowledged the indefatigably "moderate" Mme de Staël, had "undoubtedly possessed unjust privileges, and old prejudices were mingled with the small cantons' democracy; but was it by force that amelioration was to be effected in the condition of a country accustomed to acknowledge only the slow and progressive operation of time?"[124]

Although the new centralized Helvetic republic enjoyed some support, this was insufficient in the fraught circumstances to secure stability or unity. Despite the French decisively crushing a counter-invasion, mounted by Austrians and Russians, in the autumn of 1799, bitter rivalry between different cliques and localities, and between Catholics and Protestants, and especially the ideological rift between "aristocrats" and "democrats" (which only partly overlapped with the new rift between federalists and "unitarists") completely undermined the new republic's viability, reducing it by the summer of 1802 not just to a severe internal crisis but open civil war.[125] The greatest stumbling block, apart from outside interference and heavy French exactions, was the combination of traditionalism and religion: the smaller cantons remaining altogether unwilling, as Mme de Staël put it, to "accept the republic one and indivisible—that metaphysical gift the *Directoire* offered at the cannon's mouth."[126] It proved totally impossible to reconcile the old "Swiss republicans" intoxicated with historic Swiss "liberties" and Wilhelm Tell, steeped in religious fervor and deference to patrician privilege (and sympathies for the French

[120] Lehner, *Enlightened Monks*, 77.
[121] Whatmore, *Against War and Empire*, 265–6.
[122] Maissen, *Geburt der Republik*, 468, 569–70; Grab, *Napoleon and the Transformation*, 115–16.
[123] De Staël, *Considerations*, 419; Maissen, *Geschichte der Schweiz*, 162.
[124] De Staël, *Considerations*, 418.
[125] Maissen, "Erfinder", 34; Clemens, "The Swiss Case," 135
[126] De Staël, *Considerations*, 419.

royalist cause in exile and the French Counter-Enlightenment), with Ochs's besieged minority of democratic "new republicans" championing the slogans and ideology of equality, universal and equal rights, and the French Revolution.[127]

Napoleon responded to the progressive crumbling of the Helvetic Republic of 1798–1802, and the deep gulf that opened up between federalists and "unitarists," by summoning over sixty delegates of the warring Swiss republican factions to Paris and confronting them with a draft compromise format for the Swiss confederacy as it now became, hammered out in September 1802, and eventually finalized as the First Consul's so-called "Act of Mediation" (19 February 1803), one of his most successful and important acts of European statecraft. Napoleon, relaxing tentatively between September 1802 and March 1803, from the usual rigors of war, for some months devoted a considerable proportion of his time to devising a viable solution for Switzerland that would also be strategically valuable to France. Pondering the failings of the new Italian republics, Napoleon aimed for a structure that would unify Switzerland, and render it a reliable French ally by securing passage via the Simplon Pass and other key passes, one that removed the blatant inequalities and privileges of the Swiss *ancien régime* without erasing attachment to local autonomy and the cantons.

To contrive a workable balance between local autonomy and unity, a viable federal solution, Napoleon proceeded as a classic late enlightener, wholly throwing aside all concern with precedent, Natural Law, religion, and the past, while employing key experts like Roederer and La Harpe and the leading French scholar of the American state constitutions, Démeunier, as well as Swiss reformers and republicans, to advise. Although Napoleon had no sympathy for either the Bernese or other cantonal "aristocracies," or the Swiss clergy whether Catholic or Protestant, he understood that it would be best not to abolish these entirely but weaken them, leaving them under pressure, thereby rendering them fully dependent on himself. He aimed to permit the people to menace the patricians while making sure the latter understood that their survival depended on his protection.[128] Where "federalists" previously opposing the French were largely reconciled, Ochs and the "unitarists," the weaker faction, and more dependent on the French, had little choice but continue to defer. A French army of 40,000 men, under General Michel Ney, entered Switzerland to restore order and enforce implementation. It was at this point that modern federal Switzerland may be said to have come into existence.[129]

While the old formal hierarchy of patriciates, privilege, and subordinated dependencies like Vaud and ecclesiastical territories was abolished, the federal principle of extensive autonomy for the cantons was strengthened, with Vaud, Aargau, Thurgau, St Gallen, and other former subject territories for the first time now elevated to the status of full cantons. These henceforth all had their own legislatures, albeit based on electoral systems marked by high property qualifications that left most male

[127] Maissen, *Geschichte der Schweiz*, 157–8. [128] Roederer, *Mémoires*, 191–2.
[129] Maissen, "Erfinder," 41–3; Grab, *Napoleon and the Transformation*, 117–18.

householders once again without any political role. Thurgau had been a shared subject territory jointly ruled by Zurich, Lucerne, and several other cantons. St Gallen emerged from the dissolved abbey-principality of St Gall with the addition of several other adjoining former lordships. The old urban cantons, Zurich, Berne, Basel, Lucerne, Schaffhausen, and Fribourg, kept their former oligarchic systems. In the new federal Swiss diet, the larger cantons, headed by Zurich and Berne, received two votes each, the remainder of the now nineteen cantons just one.[130] Political censorship in Switzerland was again tightened up, one of its main targets being Paul Usteri (1768–1831), a Zurich delegate and the leader of the radical republican and free press faction in Switzerland.[131]

The mini-republics of Geneva and the Valais remained associated but separate and attached to France, where, from 1801, Protestantism now for the first time stood on an acknowledged equal basis with Catholicism. The Canton Valais, a prince-bishopric before 1798, had been incorporated into the 1798–1802 Helvetic Republic but was now, in 1802, kept separate by a Napoleon anxious to retain the Simplon Pass and other key Swiss passes into the northern Italian Cisalpine Republic under his control. Accordingly, when the Federal Swiss republic commenced life in 1803, the Valais curiously remained a miniature separate republic known as the République Rhodanique, a status retained until 1810, when Napoleon suddenly incorporated it into the French empire as the *département de Simplon.* Only in 1815 did the Valais finally become a canton of the Helvetic confederacy.[132] Separate too remained the principality of Neuchâtel (Fürstentum Neuenburg), which stayed under the Prussian crown until 1807, when Napoleon reassigned it as an independent principality under one of his foremost generals, Louis-Alexandre Berthier (1753–1815), who had been prominent in suppressing the Vendéean revolt, in 1793–5, and the 1796 Italian campaign, and now became "prince of Neuchâtel."

The twelve years from 1795 to 1807, among the most crucial in the modernization of the Western world, especially Germany, Holland, Belgium, and Italy, were decisive also for Switzerland. From 1807–8, comparable vast major changes also engulfed Spain and Poland. Like these countries, Switzerland was to experience fundamental reorganization not once but several times—twice by Bonaparte and thirdly, following Napoleon's defeat, by the 1814–15 Restoration and Vienna Congress.

The collapse of the Napoleonic state-system and the Restoration was anything but a smooth process in Switzerland. Although Napoleon's Act of Mediation was officially suspended already in December 1813, what would replace it long remained wholly unclear. Metternich and the Austrian Emperor, favoring all such reactionary designs, encouraged Berne to aspire to recover mastery of Vaud and the Aargau. Zurich and most other main towns also preferred the pre-1798 *ancien régime* framework with

130 Müller, "Switzerland," 212; Schroeder, *Transformation*, 232–3; Clemens, "The Swiss Case," 137–8.
131 Moran, *Toward the Century*, 91.
132 Roberts, *Napoleon the Great*, 313–14; Sorkin, *Religious Enlightenment*, 110; Palmer, *Encyclopedia*, 148.

political control reverting fully to the urban oligarchies. There was pressure too, notably in the Catholic Jura territory south-west of Basel, for the return of the ecclesiastical princes. But the Vaud and Aargau wished to conserve their post-1803 status as autonomous full cantons, while most Swiss seemed content with the status quo. A meeting of the Austrian Emperor, Czar Alexander, and the Prussian king, at Basel in mid-January 1814 failed to provide any clarity. A gathering of all cantons, the so-called Long Diet, in session from 6 April 1814 to 31 August 1815, strove to reach agreement on policies that would enable the confederacy to negotiate with the Congress of Vienna from a united standpoint and define the terms of Swiss neutrality. However, many reactionary measures were blocked with the aid of Czar Alexander, who at this time wished to be seen as an enlightened despot rather than Counter-Enlightenment reactionary and who, partly influenced by his former tutor, La Harpe, prevented Berne recovering her former rights over Vaud and the Aargau. In partial compensation, the former prince-bishop of Basel's secularized Jura territory, the French-speaking region annexed to France between 1793 and 1813, was reincorporated into Switzerland as a new subject dependency of Berne.[133]

17.4. TOWARD DEMOCRATIC REPUBLICANISM

At Zurich and Vienna, the Swiss delegates seemed keener to restore the old system of privilege and restricted access to local government than shape Switzerland as a confederacy. It was the great powers, anxious to strip France of control of the Simplon Pass and strengthen Switzerland as a barrier to French ambition, who secured incorporation of Geneva, Neuchâtel, and the Valais into the new Helvetic Confederation and assigned full cantonal status to Vaud and Aargau, raising the total of Swiss cantons to twenty-two.[134] Oligarchic control returned; the schools reverted to the pastors, press censorship grew much tighter, the currency again decentralized. D'Ivernois returned to Geneva in 1814, resuming his role in his city's oligarchic politics, now helping to promote conservative reaction, as well as contribute to the 1814–15 Vienna settlement. Sharply at variance with his stance of the early 1780s, his goal now was an "aristocratic" Switzerland functioning as an ally of Britain in a post-Napoleonic world, and serving as an effective buffer against France. Sismondi, by contrast, was horrified by the reaction: the immediate post-Waterloo years were the unhappiest and politically most transformative of his life.[135]

There was no way to prevent ideological warfare promptly flaring up again. Geneva's hard-core republicans, including several converted former "aristocratic" *émigrés* like Sismondi, were so appalled by the anti-Enlightenment reactionary

[133] Ochs, *Reden*, 185–6; Schroeder, *Transformation*, 492–5.
[134] Maissen, *Geschichte der Schweiz*, 178–9; Clemens, "The Swiss Case," 140.
[135] Ramat, *Sismondi e il mito*, 114.

changes and decentralization that they rejected the proposed new Genevan constitution outright, agreeing with former radical opponents that it assigned excessive power to the small executive council whose members were elected for life and not enough to the revived Council of Representatives whose members were to be elected under a severely restricted franchise. The disagreements remained unresolved. The Allies kept the reversions in place. But if the dissidents could effect no concrete changes to the constitution, they certainly sapped respect for it. Another major voice in the renewed ideological furor after 1814 was that of Dumont, now a convinced "Benthamite" of a "moderate" variety interpreting Bentham's texts rather differently from Bentham himself after 1815. Bentham's ideas, he believed, offered a way forward for Geneva and other former oligarchies, by providing for a legal and constitutional reform agenda suited to defusing old tensions, fostering stability, and curbing democracy while re-instilling into Genevan political culture an austere Calvinist morality.[136]

Consequently, between 1815 and 1830, Switzerland was again a troubled land of unresolved discord. The wave of revolutions that swept Europe in 1830 found a ready audience and eager disciples on Swiss territory, causing many disturbances in that country. Where in Germany the unrest mostly expressed only immediate local social discontents rather than long-term, fundamental agendas, remaining generally chaotic and aimless,[137] the Revolution in Switzerland assumed a more coherent character, powerfully aided by the prolonged formative experience of 1782 to 1815. The upheaval focused at first chiefly on Zurich, where Usteri resumed his campaign for a stronger federal body to guarantee basic rights and with his paper, the *Neue Zürcher Zeitung*, founded in 1821, led the progressive press in demanding freedom of expression. He had already succeeded in breaking the old censorship system in the Zurich canton in 1829.[138] The wider struggle between the "aristocrats" and "democrats" for control of the Swiss federation erupted in full force in the summer of 1830, intensifying in November and December with large-scale popular demonstrations in Fribourg, Aarau, Schaffhausen, Basel, Lausanne, and many other places besides Zurich. As in the Netherlands, the revolutionary year 1830 in Switzerland was an exception to the general European pattern: unlike in most of Europe, it registered permanent gains.

Aided by their traditions, a rich, complex legacy of republican symbolism reaching back centuries, supplemented by recent democratic republican political thought and institutional experience, the very factor conspicuously absent elsewhere, sweeping democratic republicanism and secularism gained momentum. In all cantons, the Swiss "aristocrats," whom the radical journalist Ludwig Börne accounted "worse and more dangerous than the kings," resisted tenaciously, bolstered by the pastors, battling to stem the tide of republicanism and democracy. Everywhere, there was

[136] Whatmore, *Against War and Empire*, 268–70, 283.

[137] Aprile, "Des cantons suisses," 85–8; Wegert, *German Radicals*, 108–10, 112; Nipperdey, *Germany*, 324–7.

[138] Moran, *Toward the Century*, 95, 138.

furious discussion of political ideas, with Benjamin Constant and his friend Sismondi notable influences. The outcome was a hard-fought compromise by which the old elites lost part of their post-1815 restored grip. Under a key confederate resolution of 27 December 1830, popular sovereignty and the right of cantons to shape their own specific format were proclaimed. During 1831, no less than eleven cantons, including Zurich, Berne and Lucerne, adopted revised constitutions featuring substantial extensions of basic freedoms.[139] Zurich's new-found press freedom proved a major gain for all Europe and briefly filled Börne with hope that, before long, this would benefit Germany likewise, breaching the walls of censorship there too. In Hesse-Cassel and elsewhere censorship did effectively collapse for some months in 1830–1, only subsequently to resume with undiminished or even greater force. In the end, post-1830 Zurich's chief contribution to Europe's constitutionalism and freedom of expression was as a reception center for fugitive German exiles, who powerfully contributed to what proved a great turning-point for Switzerland. The injection of new intellectual resources alongside faster economic growth led, in 1833–4, to several new universities of secular stamp arising in Zurich and Berne and a wider general movement to lessen theological influence in education.[140] Yet the Swiss Revolution of 1830–1 was ultimately still inconclusive, particularly at federal level where the outcome of the constitutional debates of 1831–3 was deadlock, leaving a legacy of bitterness and strife, aggravated by tensions between urban and rural interests, ensuring further conflict in the future; in many areas, the reformers facing determined popular, as well as patrician, resistance to lessening religious authority. In Basel, opinion split over whether the city should keep its old disproportionate representation in the cantonal assembly or bow to calls for equality between town and country. The canton of Schwyz split formally in two in 1833, between a conservative "Innenschwyz" and a more democratic outer canton. At Lucerne, conservatives captured control during 1840 and 1841 and reintroduced a strong theocratic dimension into the cantonal government.[141]

If conflict between Swiss patrician oligarchies and *démocrates* had become a central theme of European political consciousness since the Genevan revolution against the local patrician oligarchy in 1782, this was more than ever true in the 1840s. The twenty-five sovereign Swiss cantons remained deeply divided—both over religion, pitting Protestant against Catholic entities, and oligarchy, which, strongly entrenched still in most cantons, once more pitted "aristocrats" against "democrats." The steady growth of Switzerland's population by around 40 per cent to 2.4 million inhabitants since 1800, and introduction of new industrial machinery, while accompanied by less deprivation and hardship than elsewhere, altered the base of patrician rule, tying it

[139] Börne, *Briefe aus Paris* i. 160; Müller, "Switzerland," 213–14, 221–2, 229.

[140] Börne, *Briefe aus Paris* i. 160, 175–6; Ohles, *Germany's Rude Awakening*, 96–7; Maissen, *Geschichte der Schweiz*, 186–7.

[141] Müller, "Switzerland," 215; Maissen, *Geschichte der Schweiz*, 189–90.

more closely to commercial, industrial, and banking interests. After 1830, more and more concessions to democracy had to be made.

Responding to these gains, and especially the secularizing tendency in the universities, colleges, and schools, which greatly antagonized both Catholic and Protestant clergy, seven conservative Catholic cantons (Lucerne, Fribourg, Valais, Uri, Schwyz, Untwerwalden, and Zug), incited by hard-core conservative voices backed by the Austrian chancellor, Metternich, attempted to oust the "democrats" and secularists, and secede. Armed clashes destabilized Berne, Zurich, Basel, and Geneva. A brief civil war lasting twenty-six days erupted in late October 1847 that ended with the capitulation of Lucerne (24 November) and surrender of the confederate cantons (the Sonderbund) to the democratic republicans. The Swiss democrats' swift victory sent unsettling ripples through France, Italy, and Germany. At a "democratic" banquet in Lille, on 7 November 1847, Ledru-Rollin loudly denounced "aristocrats" and "bad priests" everywhere, toasting the Swiss and Italian "radicals" and vigorously extolling the great French Revolution and the "Rights of Man," "proclaimed in principle by two glorious revolutions [i.e. 1789 and 1830] but artfully evaded in their application." Insidious miscreants had wrested control from the people, leaving the earlier revolutions "today nothing but a glorious and bitter memory."[142] At Dijon, a fortnight later, he repeated his exaltation of Swiss liberty, popular sovereignty, and the designation "radical," declaring a war of "liberty" against "tyranny," a fight to the death between the "oppressed" and the "oppressor" with a view to finally securing liberty's triumph, free expression, universal suffrage (*le suffrage universel*), and democracy.[143]

Menaced by Austria and the great powers in December 1847, and anxious to conciliate cantonal sovereignty with democracy within a sturdier federal framework, the delegates of the cantons gathered and began hammering out a new national constitution. They were soon to be helped by the collapse of Austria and other conservative powers around them. For with Switzerland now at the forefront of the democratic tendency in Europe, the great revolutionary eruption of 1848, commencing not, as older textbooks claim, in France but rather in Switzerland and the neighboring Grand Duchy of Baden, exerted a tremendous impact, initially spreading deep dejection in London and all the royal courts of Europe. By late 1848, everything was reversed and democratic revolution was collapsing elsewhere. However, in Switzerland, the revolution did not disintegrate. The radical democrats finalized the new federal Swiss constitution to their satisfaction, in 112 articles, on 12 September 1848, and this constitution has remained the basis of Swiss democracy ever since. With it, the Swiss introduced the federal republic that most distinctly echoed the American Revolution on the mid-nineteenth-century European scene.

The Swiss revolutionaries of 1848 embraced both federalism and bicameralism, leaving a limited sovereignty to the cantons insofar as this did not impinge on

[142] Ledru-Rollin, *Discours politiques* i. 328, 338.

[143] Ledru-Rollin, *Discours politiques* i. 340–3, 348–9; Rapport, *1848 : Year of Revolution*, 39, 56–7.

the newly defined powers of the federal authority.[144] Separation of Powers was proclaimed, leading to a separate federal court of justice to direct the judiciary and a federal council, under a revolving presidency, to function as the executive. On the model of the American Congress,[145] a two-chamber Swiss legislature was constituted, featuring a lower house, or *Nationalrat*, with 111 deputies each representing 20,000 inhabitants, and a smaller elected (at first indirectly) upper house or senate. Federal elections to choose deputies for the lower house were based on universal male suffrage, with every male citizen over 20 enjoying the right to vote.

144 Maissen, *Geschichte der Schweiz*, 202; Billias, *American Constitutionalism*, 192; Müller, "Switzerland," 235–7.

145 Maissen, *Geschichte der Schweiz*, 200–1; Hobsbawm, *Age of Revolution*, 364.

18

The Belgian Revolution (1787–1794)

18.1. AN "ADVANCED SOCIETY" ENGINEERS A "BACKWARD REVOLUTION"

Less crucial for the wider picture than the Swiss revolution, another major upheaval of the revolutionary era, the Belgian revolution of 1789–94, reflects the complex, multifaceted interaction of Enlightenment and Revolution and the pervasive role of Enlightenment ideas from yet another highly revealing social and cultural angle. Strategically situated at the heart of north-west Europe, the future Belgium, known since 1713 as the "Austrian Netherlands," was a small but densely populated and urbanized land comprising several provinces each with its own representative assembly, or "estates," and other longstanding local institutions, evincing a marked tendency to provincial particularism. Yet, despite this strong sense of local identity and the Dutch–French language divide (less divisive culturally and socially then than later), the country, with its population of around two and a quarter millions, already possessed a certain overall identity, with many educated people already calling themselves "Belgen" and aware of differing from both the Dutch North Netherlanders and the French.

Since the War of the Spanish Succession (1702–13), the southern or "Austrian Netherlands" served as the other powers' principal barrier against French expansionism in Europe, being viewed by Austria, Prussia, Britain, and the Dutch Republic as a crucial strategic bulwark of Europe's stability. More highly urbanized than most of the continent, the region was also of considerable importance economically, with an impressively rich history of commercial and craft development—in fact it was the only part of the continent where industrial activity, especially the many-centuries-old linen and woolen textile industries, had long constituted a major segment of the economy. By the late eighteenth century notable too were several new industries such as calico printing, centered in Ghent alongside that city's thriving glass, earthenware, paper, and sugar-refining enterprises.[1]

Even if most of Belgium's expanding industrial scene was serviced by a large semi-rural proletariat marked by low productivity and using outdated technologies,

[1] Mokyr, *Industrialization*, 19, 24.

subsisting on wretchedly low wages, in terms of industrialization, differentiation, and the forming of a modern urban bourgeoisie, Belgium stood well ahead of most of Europe, coming undeniably second after Britain. The Flemish and Brabantine linen and lace industries concentrated in Antwerp, Brussels, Mechelen, and Kortrijk, employing some 25,000 workers, mainly women, though of unparalleled scale for any industry by international standards at the time, remained organized on a cottage basis operating with tiny units of production.[2] Inequality and stratification by class in what was economically the most advanced and stratified part of continental Europe were hence extremely marked: interposed between the nobility and the laboring poor stood a uniquely large and dynamic urban commercial–industrial bourgeoisie.

During the early and mid-1780s, political and social tensions of various kinds intensified. From 1787, protest stirred especially in the two biggest provinces, Brabant and Flanders, both mainly Dutch-speaking. The agitation welled up during early 1787 in the form of numerous small local disturbances, originating in part in Belgium's principal university, Louvain (Leuven), where it was felt that Joseph II's educational reformism threatened that renowned academy with "subversion totale."[3] A mass of pamphlets in Dutch and French aimed at mobilizing the rising anger and frustration caused by this and other government innovations appeared. Backed by formal protests of the Estates of Brabant, the agitation was directed chiefly against the Emperor Joseph II's enlightened reforms, loudly denounced as "diverses infractions" of Brabant's ancient provincial privileges and constitution, the famous so-called *Joyeuse Entrée* [Blijde Inkomste]. The opposition also conspicuously featured protest on the part of bishops and other ecclesiastical authorities angry at new measures imposed by the Emperor under his 1781 Toleration Edict introducing religious toleration and at his attempts to reform the seminary system and dissolve monasteries as part of a general drive to subordinate the church more effectively to the Habsburg state. In May 1787, the most turbulent month thus far, furious protesting "Patriots" took to wearing insurgent tricolor, black, yellow, and red, anti-Austrian cockades.[4]

Plainly, opposition to enlightened absolutism and to reform was widespread. Criticism of and resistance to local elites and authorities, by contrast, remained conspicuously muted initially, indeed strikingly unobtrusive compared with the situation in neighboring France and Holland. Powerfully shaped by the country's deeply ingrained late sixteenth- and seventeenth-century Counter-Reformation legacy, the populace gave furious vent to intense discontent while still deferentially following the nobility and clergy. Business, banking, shopkeepers, and workshop owners counted for a great deal more and intervened more directly and vigorously in the subsequent unrest and turmoil in Belgium than in France or Holland during the revolutionary era, and to this extent the Marxist theory that social forces shaped

[2] Mokyr, *Industrialization*, 12, 16.

[3] *Courier du Bas-Rhin* for 1787, no. 89, p. 750, and no. 90, p. 757.

[4] Feller, *Recueil de représentations* ii. 44–6; Van Dam, "Spirituele revolutie," 15–16; Duerloo, "Kleuren en symbolen," 93–4.

by economic development determine the character of revolutionary impulses is correct. Yet, remarkably, while Belgium's business class mobilized their social power and influence vociferously against Joseph's reformism, and loomed larger as a social force than any other northern European middle class, they did not intervene or emerge as a separate class in political and legal terms but dutifully rallied behind their nobility and clergy. There was no sign of their moving against the traditional social and cultural elites, or existing structures of authority and institutions. In the one part of continental Europe where a rising middle class dominated the economy, urban and part of rural life as well as commerce, finance, and industry, they and their army of lawyers mobilized their now impressive revolutionary force chiefly to resist Enlightenment ideas and reform.[5] Much as in England, most of the populace subsequently consistently rallied behind aristocracy and church against innovation and new influences, and especially against toleration, modernized schooling, and secularism.

The situation developed into a full-blown political crisis when the States of Brabant, Flanders, and Hainault dramatically suspended all routine fiscal collection on the monarch's behalf, in April 1787.[6] Resistance to Joseph's reforms, especially changes to the judicial system, his marriage reform law (1782), abolition of pious confraternities, dissolution of officially deemed superfluous monasteries and convents (1783), reform of guild regulations and Louvain university, and the religious toleration decree (13 October 1781), against which Luxembourg's Estates had earlier submitted a particularly forceful protest in December 1781,[7] vociferous by the spring of 1787, grew tumultuous. By June 1787, the capital, Brussels, was gripped by a rising anti-Austrian frenzy rife especially among the artisan guilds. In January 1788, armed clashes broke out between dissidents and Imperial troops in Brussels, Antwerp, and Mechelen. The continuing turmoil was further added to by the political crisis since 1785 gripping the northern Netherlands. The mass flight of Dutch democratic dissidents forced to flee following the Prussian invasion of the northern Netherlands, and Orangist reversion to power, with British support, in September 1787, complicated matters in the southern Netherlands by injecting a large contingent of restless exiles of Protestant background, several thousand in Antwerp alone,[8] evincing scant sympathy for conservative Belgian attitudes and traditions, or Belgian–Luxembourgeois antipathy to the Josephine Toleration Decree, which was a vital recourse for them.

During early 1789, after a sustained campaign of obstruction, encouraged by prelates, magistrates, and elite groups, popular anger and frustration boiled over. The emperor had become enraged with the Brussels high bourgeoisie, the bankers, lawyers, and merchants residing in fine houses around the prestigious Grande Place, who were not just backing but obviously concerting the opposition.[9] The Belgian revolution, to a greater extent than the French, was in fact a socially driven and

[5] Ewald, *Über Revolutionen*, 76–86.

[6] Dhondt, "Conservative Brabantse ontwenteling," 428, 430.

[7] Feller, *Recueil de représentations* ii. 2–8.

[8] Altena, *Gerrit Paape*, 263.

[9] Polasky, *Revolution in Brussels*, 59–60.

concerted "revolution," reaching full fury in reaction to Joseph II's culminating reform, his abolition in June 1789 of the *Joyeuse Entrée* itself, the compilation of the historic liberties and privileges of the province of Brabant. The emperor's latest measures provoked a sustained armed rising commencing in and around Brussels that spread through the Belgian provinces from August 1789, an explosion of social and political indignation directed in particular by Hendrik van der Noot (1731–1827), a Brussels lawyer earlier commissioned by the States of Brabant to formulate legal objections to Joseph's reforms. Van der Noot took to publicly urging organized armed resistance while behind the scenes intriguing with senior ecclesiastics and nobles, as well as ministers in Paris, London, and Berlin, using every means to exploit Joseph's difficulties while gathering impressive support. Some dissident newspapers began comparing him to George Washington, others styled him "le Franklin des Pays-Bas," an epithet that appalled the German radical Georg Forster (1754–94) in Brussels when Van der Noot's adherents captured the city, late in 1789. Acclamation of Van der Noot as the Belgian "Franklin" was to play a continuing role in the Belgian revolution, but was a designation that in radical eyes he in no way merited.[10]

The revolutionary tide, massively popularly supported but led principally by magistrates, ecclesiastics, and aristocrats, continued receiving much inspiration from Louvain where the university, steeped in theology and reaction, seethed with resolve to reassert the primacy of privilege, corporations, and religious intolerance.[11] But it was the solid backing of the Antwerp and Brussels middle-class commercial element, the world of law, retailing, and business, that imparted to the Belgian revolution its unprecedented social motive force. Fury against Joseph II's reformism focused above all on his scheme to set aside the ancient Brabant constitution, and suspend a plethora of medieval and early modern charters and privileges. Besides Van der Noot, emerged several other energetic leaders and publicists with a broad following, notably Pieter Simon van Eupen (1744–1804), an Antwerp seminary professor turned general publicist for the ecclesiastical interest, and the ultramontane bishop of Antwerp, Jacob Wellens (1726–84), a former Leuven professor of philosophy and theology, both heroes of the rising Antwerp middle class as unremitting foes of Josephine innovation.[12] Another internationally noted publicist supporting the furious insurgency and warmly promoting the ecclesiastical interest, among Van der Noot's chief aides, was a veteran foe of the French radical *philosophes* as well as a theological-political foe of Josephism, François-Xavier de Feller (1735–1802), fiery editor of Luxembourg's *Journal historique et littéraire*, among the principal anti-*philosophe* journals of the age.

Feller, a Brussels-born ex-Jesuit, had taught for many years in Liège and Luxembourg. A learned man, he aimed to whip up maximum popular indignation against his favorite scapegoat, *la philosophie*, the insidious inspiration, as he saw it, of the

[10] Gorman, *America and Belgium*, 184–7; Polasky, *Revolutions without Borders*, 42.
[11] Ewald, *Über Revolutionen*, 79.
[12] Ewald, *Über Revolutionen*, 85–6; Vanysacker, "Verlicht ultramontaan," 97, 101–2.

entire anti-ecclesiastical and anti-noble reform campaign welling up in Belgium as in France and Germany. Among Feller's accomplishments was his collating all the formal protests and admonitions by Belgian estates, churchmen, and official bodies he could find, which he published in a series eventually totaling seventeen volumes, at Liège, entitled the *Recueil des Représentations, protestations et réclamations de tous les ordres de Citoyens, dans les Pays-Bas Catholiques*. Opposing kings and emperors, held Feller, must always be vigorously condemned except where religion is concerned, ecclesiastical authority being the sole source, as he saw it, that overrules royal authority, in support of which he adduced a resounding quote from the third book of Montesquieu's *L'Esprit des Lois*.[13]

The Enlightenment reform movement Joseph had initiated in Belgium, and which he opposed with all his being, Feller attributed chiefly to *philosophisme*, to his mind a socially and politically venomous effusion, deriving principally from the works of Raynal, Diderot, d'Holbach, Helvétius, Paine, and Price. Beside these targets, Feller's journal abounded with hostile sallies against Franklin, and the American Revolution, the principles of which he pronounced "false" philosophically and religiously. The American "rebels" had condemned themselves by opposing monarchy for reasons other than religious ones, a double outrage because the Americans were resisting the British crown just when it accorded equal status to the Catholic Church in Canada! Overt sympathy for the American Revolution, manifested in several Belgian newspapers, greatly offended him. Discussion of John Adams's Massachusetts state constitution, he noted, had persisted uninterruptedly in Belgium since 1781 when the French translation of that text and discussion of its provisions first featured in the local press. But the most incontrovertible proof of the American Revolution's generally perverse influence, held Feller, was *l'enthousiasme* with which French irreligious *philosophes* eulogized it in the years prior to the eruption of their own 1789 revolution.[14]

The radical tendency Feller identified as an unparalleled threat to society, authority, and faith, a menace emanating principally from America and France but perceptible also in the uneasy city of Liège, where he was active in the years 1787–9, and where one encountered an unmistakable current of sympathy for, and engagement with, the American Revolution spiced with zeal for "Raynal," several editions of whose *Histoire philsosophique* had appeared there as well as at neighboring Maastricht. In Liège, it had become modish, admonished Feller, predicting serious trouble ahead, to admire *philosophes* and deride princes, religion, "obedience and order." "Insolence philosophique" seriously affected not just that town but the entire prince-bishopric, menacing not just the local princely–ecclesiastical regime but, more broadly, the southern Netherlands within which the prince-bishopric was embedded. Liège's prince-bishop Feller urged, whilst there was still time, to crack down harder on the

13 Feller, *Recueil de représentations* ii, title-page; Van Dam, "Spirituele revolutie," 17, 21.

14 [Feller], *Journal historique* 1784, pp. 107–8 and 1792, pp. 21–6; Gorman, *America and Belgium*, 66, 68, 89, 125–7; Palmer, *Age of the Democratic Revolution* i. 264.

core threat, "philosophy": he must not rely on some Liège townsfolk's perfunctory assurances of religion and submission. Had not Boston's citizens erected a statue to King George III, a decade before the American Revolution, apparently exalting British monarchy, only to emerge before long as outright "rebels" dragging that very same statue of their monarch through the streets mutilated in the "most ignominious manner"? Liège's local intellectual subversion might look manageable but beneath the surface was dangerously subversive.[15]

Counter-Enlightenment attitudes overwhelmingly dominated the popularly backed opposition vilifying enlightened royal reformism, infidelity, and bureaucracy.[16] The revolution in Brussels and Antwerp, complained a leading Dutch exile, Gerrit Paape (1752–1803), unlike that destabilizing the northern Netherlands, was a movement of "stupid," priest-ridden Brabant *Patriotten* blindly resisting enlightened ideas, opposing a courageous, reforming Emperor, hence a mindless rebellion not a constructive revolution, one scorned by all "reason-loving democrats" and enlighteners.[17] Admittedly, this was not the whole story. At Liège, Ostend, Bruges, and Ghent, a few "Patriots" could be found acknowledging "Man's true rights" and seeking to "erect true freedom on its throne;" but this paltry fringe was all there was to admire in the Belgian protest movement, held Paape, who grew increasingly contemptuous of the typical middle-class Belgian dissident.[18] Meanwhile, the Emperor was assured of the backing of all enlightened "reason-loving" men, including the Dutch exiles, since anyone choosing on the basis of reason must detest *Brabantsch Patriottismus*, which consisted only of demands for the "old constitution" and "pure fanaticism which the artful priesthood knows how to cultivate."[19]

Pieter Vreede (1750–1837), another prominent Dutch anti-Orangist in Belgian exile, a Leiden manufacturer living in Antwerp initially who had transferred his textile workshop, employing eighty workers, to Lier, establishing a Protestant congregation under the terms of the 1781 Toleration edict, was equally appalled by the surging Counter-Enlightenment rhetoric. Once the Belgian Revolution gained full traction, in 1789, Protestantism was again officially suppressed and his factory and congregation had to close down. Deference to clergy and traditional elites so dominated the prosperous and successful Belgian entrepreneurial class as to fill the Dutch Patriot exiles with indignation and contempt.[20] A direct consequence of the Belgian protesters' rooted conservatism was the very limited scope that developed for revolutionary collaboration with the thousands of expelled and resentful Dutch exiles, anti-Orangist and often fervent for democratic ideas, refugees whom the crushing

[15] Droixhe, "Raynal à Liège," 216–18.

[16] Heirwegh, "La fin," 472; Polasky, "Success," 414–15.

[17] Rosendaal, *Bataven!*, 72–4; Paape, *Hollandse wijsgeer in Braband* iv. 140, 168, 202–3; Popkin, *News and Politics*, 192–3.

[18] Paape, *Hollandsche wijsgeer in Braband* iv. 75–7; Altena, *Gerrit Paape*, 264–73; Israel, *Democratic Enlightenment*, 879.

[19] Paape, *Hollandse wijsgeer in Braband* iv. 140, 168, 202–3.

[20] Dhondt, "Conservative Brabantse ontwenteling," 425–7.

of the Dutch democratic movement, in September 1787, left uncomfortably lingering in Belgium's towns for the next eight years.

Viewed geographically (and ideologically), the Belgian revolution of 1789–94 consisted of three principal thrusts. Foremost was the agitation in Brabant headed by Brussels; second, further west, the turmoil in Flanders, especially Ghent; but significant too, further east, was the turbulence in the prince-bishopric of Liège, a long strip of territory with around 340,000 inhabitants, extending right across the southern Netherlands, technically outside the Austrian emperor's jurisdiction, stretching south almost to Namur. Liège disaffection, unlike that gripping Brussels and Antwerp, and differently from the rest of Belgium, soon reflected, much as Feller had warned, a revolutionary tendency of unmistakably anti-ecclesiastical character. According to Christian Wilhelm von Dohm (1751–1820), the enlightened official sent by the Prussian crown to mediate, two-thirds of the prince-bishopric's land surface belonged to the clergy while the priesthood was "almost entirely" exempt from taxes.[21] In Liège, unlike the rest of Belgium, widespread opposition to prevailing institutional arrangements abounded. Since 1784 the prince-bishop, Constantijn Franciscus van Hoensbroeck (ruled: 1784–92), endeavoring to tighten princely-ecclesiastical authority, had espoused forceful Counter-Enlightenment policies while seeking control of more of the magistracies constituting the city government.

Although foreign observers, ignoring local causes, mostly assumed the furiously anti-clerical Liège insurrection, commencing in early August 1789, was simply part of a wider revolutionary contagion spilling over from France, the revolution there retained an essentially separate character from those in both France and Brabant. Its leading figure, Jean-Nicolas Bassenge (1758–1811), locally known as "le Mirabeau Liégeois," in the early 1780s had been based in Paris, had assisted Raynal, and become steeped in Enlightenment thought. Inspired by the Bastille's Fall and the *Declaration of the Rights of Man*, an ardent democratic republican and future Brissotin ally, Bassenge, distributing red and green revolutionary cockades on all sides, headed a disciplined agitation that steadily gained ground. His initial two main demands were full representation for the prince-bishopric's citizenry in a reformed provincial Estates and ending special tax privileges for the clergy.[22] He and his adherents compelled the Liège cathedral chapter and clergy to surrender their fiscal exemptions on 13 August 1789.[23] Bloodlessly overthrown by Bassenge's following, the reactionary prince-bishop abandoned his immense episcopal palace on 26 August, fleeing to nearby Trier where he placed himself under the Holy Roman Empire's protection. Controlling city and principality, the Liège revolution evinced marked pro-French tendencies from the outset and an equally clear antipathy to the Brussels movement, preferring the radical liberty and equality proclaimed by the democratic intellectual

[21] Droixhe, "Raynal à Liège," 478; Houtman-De Smetdt, "Het prinsbisdom," 420; Israel, *Democratic Enlightenment*, 878.

[22] *Mémoires véridiques de la Révolution de Liège*, 4, 14; Dohm, *Exposé de la Révolution de Liège*, 23.

[23] *Mémoires véridiques de la Révolution de Liège*, 5–6.

vanguard in Paris and the Dutch exiles.[24] Fighting erupted in the prince-bishopric as the Austrians briefly reversed Van Hoensbroeck's defeat, expelling the Patriots; but on being decisively defeated themselves in Brabant, the Austrians were soon in turn ousted by the Liège revolutionaries.

The Liège revolution, like the Paris ferment, rejected talk of charters and precedent: "all privilege," as the crypto-republican enlightener Dohm expressed it, historic rights and precedent were repudiated in favor of *la volonté générale* and the philosophical principles of the "Rights of Man."[25] With equality proclaimed, all ecclesiastical privilege and exemptions were abolished. As a distinct revolutionary phenomenon, this insurgency lasted a year and a half, interrupted by a brief interval when Prussian troops, ten battalions with artillery, occupied the bishopric in December 1789.[26] Reaction here was hampered by discord between Austria and Prussia and between the Prussian monarch and Van Hoensbroeck, who had no intention of negotiating with the new city government, or conceding ground to the Revolution. Together with distractions in Poland, this induced the Prussians to evacuate Liège, early in 1790, enabling the local *Patriotten* again to resume control. Only with the convention of Reichenbach (July 1790) did Prussia and Austria reconcile their differences and reconstitute a combined anti-revolutionary front.

The Belgian revolution's impressive impetus fascinated but also baffled revolutionary opinion at Paris. Would Belgian insurgency become a "heureuse révolution," anti-aristocratic and anti-ecclesiastical like the French model, asked the *Révolutions de Paris*, one of the revolutionary papers electrifying Paris since July.[27] By late August, the entire southern Netherlands were in the grip of a three-pronged revolutionary upheaval—turmoil as pregnant with significance for all mankind as anything witnessed thus far in France, Holland, or Switzerland, observed the *Révolutions de Paris*.[28] During the ensuing crucial weeks, numerous Brabançon activists rallied to the revolutionary cause also in Liégeois territory, where they could organize free from outside interference, under the very nose of the Austrians.[29] The collapse of Austrian rule was accelerated by an armed incursion by a rebel army of 3,000 volunteers, recruited in the southern Netherlands but gathered and prepared by Van der Noot, across the Dutch border. Banished by Joseph along with other dissidents, including Van Eupen, the Antwerp canon who since 1788 was his ideological right-hand man, Van der Noot, rather ironically, organized his conspiracy at Breda, virtually as the Stadholder's guest. When the Austrian authorities complained of overt subversion plied on Dutch soil, and the Dutch authorities' refusal to arrest the conspirators, The Hague retorted that the Emperor's officials had outrageously granted asylum and

24 Fontana, *Venise et la Révolution*, 326, 364; Houtman-De Smedt, "Het prinsbisdom," 420.

25 Dohm, *Exposé de la Révolution de Liège*, 19–22, 29.

26 Fontana, *Venise et la Révolution*, 364–5; Raxhon, "Révolutionnaires liégeois," 117–18.

27 [Prudhomme and Tournon], *Révolutions de Paris* VII (22/28 Aug. 1789), 45.

28 [Prudhomme and Tournon], *Révolutions de Paris* VI (16/22 Aug. 1789), 45 and VII (22/28 Aug. 1789), 45.

29 Raxhon, "Révolutionnaires liégeois," 116–17.

were openly tolerating thousands of anti-Orangist fugitives actively scheming and propagandizing against the Stadholderate in Belgium.[30] Given the reactionary views of most Brabant and Flemish *Patriotten*, there was little contradiction involved in the Prince of Orange assisting them against Joseph and his innovating, supposedly "legitimate" imperial hereditary authority.[31]

By late October, the French papers were reporting that a general armed insurrection in and around Brabant was already on a scale too massive for the Austrian garrison in the southern Netherlands to contain, with the abbeys, seminaries, cloisters, and the university the principal engine of revolution but the rich bourgeoisie of Brussels and numerous lawyers also deeply implicated.[32] On 24 October 1789, leaders of the key Brussels secret society *Pro Aris et Focis* [For Hearth and Home] joined Van der Noot and States of Brabant representatives, at Breda, likewise proclaiming the right of all Belgians to throw off the yoke of foreign of tyranny. Founded in the spring of 1789 by a group headed by a gifted bilingual lawyer, Jean-François Vonck (1743–92), with over a third of its membership jurists, *Pro Aris et Focis*, a select group with several businessman among its members, including the wealthy banker, Edouard de Walckiers (1758–1837), owner of the chateau de Belvédère, one of Belgium's finest, soon emerged as a rival strand to that of Van der Noot within the Belgian revolution.[33]

18.2. RADICAL CONCEPTS USED FOR CONSERVATIVE ENDS

A notable feature of the central thrust of the Belgian revolution, the *Brabantse ontwenteling* of 1787–90, was that the prime revolutionary manifesto, the most widely-distributed publication of the revolution, the *Manifeste du peuple brabançon* (1789), among the foremost revolutionary documents of the age, published by the insurgents on 24 October 1789, signed by Van der Noot, was couched in terms dramatically different from anything found in previous foundational documents relating to Belgium's past and present. For it was a text unquestionably republican and anti-monarchist in tone, an uncompromising product of the late Enlightenment—and not just the Enlightenment generally, but, rhetorically at least and in terminology, the Radical Enlightenment. Although its basic purpose was deeply conservative, to accomplish its insurgent goals it employed highly subversive concepts borrowed by the "Nederlandsche Franklin," Van der Noot, from 1770s radical French crypto-republicanism. Proclaiming Joseph stripped of his sovereignty by the Belgian people,[34] this key text claimed sovereignty resided in the people as a

[30] Gorman, *America and Belgium*, 12; Altena, *Gerrit Paape*, 265–72, 285–6.
[31] Paape, *Zaak der verdrukte Hollandsche Patiotten*, 2–4, 9–10.
[32] Coppens, *Chronique des révolutions Belgique*, 24–8.
[33] Polasky, "Démocrates bruxellois," 55, 57; Polasky, *Revolutions without Borders*, 41–2.
[34] [Van der Noot], *Manifeste du Peuple Brabançon*, 23–4; Judge, "Provincial Manifestes," 127, 130.

whole, royal authority being merely a derivative *pouvoir limité*, and that, by overstepping its bounds, "tyrannizing over the Belgian people, and reducing it to slavery," violating the "rights and privileges of the constitution," seizing ecclesiastical property and violating "the rights of the Church," Joseph had caused the people to take up arms against the crown and with every justification depose him.[35] In justifying armed rebellion against rulers, and summoning the people to rise, this text surpassed every other revolutionary manifesto of 1789 in insisting that legitimate sovereignty is always popular, always "founded on the consent of peoples," and that every people always possesses the right to take up arms the moment any prince or ruler defies popular sovereignty and acts against the popular will.[36]

Undeviatingly reactionary in intent, the revolutionary *Manifeste*'s political theory was undeviatingly radical in its rhetoric of justified revolt, especially in its account of "oppression," and deployment of *volonté générale* [general will]. The revolution's leaders, it turned out, for those sufficiently knowledgeable about subversive literature to recognize the source, had pilfered, without citing it—as was first pointed out in 1968, by J. Vecruysse and has been repeatedly noted ever since—entire passages lifted wholesale from d'Holbach's *La Politique naturelle* (1773), among the most widely-diffused compendia of *philosophique* radical political sentiment of the day. The *Manifeste du peuple brabançon* resoundingly confirmed the revolutionary potential of d'Holbach's theorizing—even if d'Holbach's logic, averring men's right to overthrow royal government by force, was being hijacked for purposes that would have scandalized d'Holbach and his circle, and were soon to scandalize Vonck and his fellow conspirators of *Pro Aris et Focis*: namely, to secure the unchallenged primacy of ecclesiastical and aristocratic privilege and restore Brabant's historic "liberties."[37]

Almost immediately following publication of the *Manifeste* and the Breda declarations, the Austrian forces battling to restore order in the southern Netherlands were defeated by the invading Patriot column from Breda, commanded by Jan Andries Van der Meersch (1734–92), a veteran officer of both the French and Austrian royal armies during the 1760s and 1770s, and now an ally of Vonck. Risking a full-scale battle, which ensued at Turnhout on 27 October 1789, Van der Meersch, aided by townsfolk, barricaded the streets, lured 2,500 Austrians into the city, ambushed them, exhausted them in five hours of arduous street combat, and drove them out in shattered disarray, leaving behind hundreds of dead and captured. The news stunned Europe and prompted an almost miraculously swift collapse of imperial power and authority throughout the southern Netherlands. Invasion by armed groups organized in Holland and Liège triggered the process, but it was the massive support for the rising among the middle and laboring classes, not the invasion as such, that clinched

[35] [Van der Noot], *Manifeste du Peuple Brabançon*, 2–4.

[36] [Van der Noot], *Manifeste du Peuple* Brabançon, 1.

[37] Coppens, *Chronique des révolutions Belgique*, 33, 45–6; Dhondt, "Conservative Brabantse ontwenteling," 433; Vercruysse, "Pamphlets," 323; Roegiers and Van Sas, "Revolutie," 232; Polasky, "Success," 416–17; Heirwegh, "La Fin," 477–8; Judge, "Provincial Manifestoes," 140–1.

the revolution's early success and shaped its special character. Guild-members, shop-keepers, artisans, laborers, and prosperous farmers lent the insurrection a genuinely national character arguably to an extent witnessed nowhere else. In Brussels partly organized by the *Vonckiste* leadership and *Pro Aris et Focis*, the rising received enthusiastic support from all parts of Belgium. Ghent, the first provincial capital "liberated," was freed on 16 November 1789; by late November, the Austrians had been forced to abandon Mons and much of the Walloon area. The surrounded remaining Austrian troops in Brussels surrendered on 2 December.

Commenting enthusiastically from Paris, in early November, Brissot appealed to the Belgian insurgents, now sweeping the entire country, to declare their independence immediately, and adopt the American Revolution and American "rights" as their inspiration. Belgians must be ruled by their own Congress, and not an individual master: "the American Revolution should serve as their model in every respect."[38] On 19 December, Van der Noot, Van Eupen, and the Breda committee staged their triumphal entry into Brussels. By this time Van der Meersch's Patriot army had cleared the Austrians from the entire southern Netherlands except the Antwerp citadel, which capitulated only in March 1790, and the formidably walled city of Luxembourg. By early January 1790, volunteers from Ghent, Brussels, and other places were already gathering to attack the latter.[39] Beyond Luxembourg's city walls, the revolution swept even rural Luxembourg where the duchy's German half, to the surprise of onlookers, proved even readier to defy the Emperor than the Walloon half. The Brabant Estates, assembling in December, immediately proclaimed an indissoluble union with Flanders. The press spread rumors that the southern Netherlands would form themselves into a "republic," adopting the title "United States of the Low Countries" [États-Unis des Pays-Bas].[40] The expected convening of the full South Netherlands States-General took place in January 1790.[41]

The people, to a greater extent even than in France, were solidly and unequivocally the revolution's driving force, acting more unitedly, unambiguously, and assertively to topple an abhorred regime than any other insurgent people of the revolutionary era.[42] While Van der Noot's *Manifeste* does not cite the American *Declaration of Independence* directly, it borrowed some of its language and there is little doubt that every leading participant in, and contemporary commentator on, the Belgian revolutionary movement had the American Revolution no less than the French drama firmly in mind from the outset. The Brabant manifesto's Flemish counterpart, the *Manifeste de la Province de Flandre* (Ghent, January 1790), does directly invoke America, even incorporating part of the *Declaration of Independence* into its text. That brochure had been preceded by an undated short account of the American

[38] Brissot, *Patriote français* xciv (10 Nov. 1789), 3; Coppens, *Chronique des révolutions Belgique et Liégeoise*, 31–2.

[39] *Chronique de Paris* ii/xii (12 Jan. 1790), 47; Gorman, *America and Belgium*, 8.

[40] Coppens, *Chronique des révolutions Belgique et Liégeoise*, 52, 127, 138–40.

[41] *Chronique de Paris* ii/xxxiv (4 Feb. 1790), 137.

[42] Dhondt, "Conservative Brabantse ontwenteling," 428.

Revolution, appearing at Ghent shortly before, likewise incorporating sections of the *Declaration of Independence*, both texts claiming that the Flemish people, through divine providence and following the American example, were regaining "our natural rights of liberty and independence, breaking the ties that united us to a prince belonging to a house whose rule has been continually detrimental to the interests of Flanders."[43]

Van der Noot's triumphal entry into Brussels, on 18 December, with an armed column, amid vast crowds, was a popularly endorsed triumphant revolutionary celebration. The estates of the various provinces assembled, and declared their sovereignty and independence from the "tyrannical" rule of the Emperor, signing an *Acte d'Union* forming themselves into a single federal body, backdated to 30 November, though not ratified by the Estates of Brabant until January 1790. In Brussels a "war department" and common administration for the new armed forces of the États-Belgiques-Unis was established. On 11 January 1790, Belgium's "Congress" of supposedly sovereign "states" issued their formal declaration of independence from the Austrian crown, officially creating the "United States of Belgium." The infant new republic was equipped with a notably weak executive authority whose powers were limited to defending the country and issuing money. The assembly created a national army and federal *Congrès souverain des États belgiques unis* to represent the sovereign unity of the new federal state. Choosing the "Brabant Lion" as its symbol, the new republic adopted the black, yellow, and red tricolour in use since May 1787 as its political and military banner. The new "United States" (on documents styled the États-Belgiques Unis or, alternatively, Verenigde Nederlandsche Staten) in theory consisted of eight supposedly sovereign "states" (without Liège)—Brabant, Flanders, Namur, Hainault, Mechelen, Guelders, Limburg, and Luxembourg, though as yet the Congress did not actually control most of Luxembourg, albeit hoping to incorporate it, and Liège, eventually.[44] These now formed the world's first federal republic expressly constituted on the American model.[45]

Despite enjoying the common people's united support, the Belgian revolutionaries, in their bid for independence, faced daunting odds. The great powers rejected the Belgian republic on grounds of monarchical legitimacy and dynastic rights but also because such an isolated, small, flat, boxed-in independent entity could hardly provide a reliable military barrier to French power in the way a well-garrisoned Austrian Netherlands could. Besides, as the French revolutionary press pointed out, if the monarchical powers allowed the new federal republic to survive, they could not exclude the possibility that Belgium's Patriots might one day side with the Dutch anti-Orangists and overthrow the stadholderate, establishing a united Low Countries republic allied to revolutionary France, a prospect totally unacceptable to Britain,

[43] Gorman, *America and Belgium*, 157; Dhondt, "Conservative Brabantse ontwenteling", 436; Judge, "Provincial Manifestoes," 127–8.

[44] Dohm, *Exposé de la Révolution de Liège*, 116–17; Judge, "Provincial Manifestoes," 128.

[45] Polasky, *Revolution in Brussels*, 134–8.

Prussia, Russia, and Austria.[46] Adamantly opposed by the great powers, at the same time, the Belgian revolution was, for the moment at least, wholly out of step with the neighboring French Revolution. Furthermore, incipiently divided internally at elite level, the apparently united revolution, it soon became clear, had a leadership formed of two competing, irreconcilable tendencies.

For the new "United States," the République des Provinces Belgiques-Unies and their "Congress," America served both rhetorically and ideologically as the acknowledged model.[47] This remained the case until the French invasion in the autumn of 1792. The statutes of union signed by the federated Belgian "states," on 11 January 1790, with Van Eupen, a pillar of *anti-Vonckisme*, as "secretary" [*secretaris der Verenigde Staten*], were closely modeled on the *Articles of Confederation and Perpetual Union* drafted at the commencement of the American Revolution, in 1776, and finalized as the United States' provisional first constitution in 1781. A new journal established at Brussels, in January 1790, eagerly acclaimed this second "United States," emphasizing in its introductory dedication both its American links and the veneration in which Belgium's leaders and people held the world's principal "heroes of liberty," listing these as Brutus, William Tell, Oldenbarnevelt, Franklin, "Wasington," Bailly, Lafayette, Van der Noot, and Van der Meersch.[48]

Belgium's revolutionary leadership invoked the American example, but emphatically preferred the conservative reading of the American Revolution, that of Adams, John Dickinson, Gouverneur Morris, and Alexander Hamilton, the construct justifying rebellion when royal despotism infringed historic rights and privileges, the revolution preserving existing elites intact, and emphatically not the radical, democratic American Revolution of Franklin, Jefferson, and Paine. The main Belgian insurgency sought independence from the Habsburgs and a federal solution safeguarding the status of the provinces, nobility, and church while entirely discarding—to the dismay of French revolutionary ideologues like Brissot, Condorcet, and Cloots—the common American and French republican revolutionary rhetoric of equality, universalism, and human rights.[49] Yet the Belgian revolution of 1789–91 was more obviously and authentically the work of the people than anything happening in France, Switzerland, and Holland. Aside from dissident fringes demurring, it evinced greater capacity, in town and country, to carry the entire populace with it than any other, and more obvious capability to attract the active support of women. The French Revolution at this point looked altogether more divided and confused in the main cities, and still more in the countryside and small towns. With the best claim of any late eighteenth-century revolution to be labeled an authentic people's rising, the one that most fully reflected the views of a rising commercial middle class, the

[46] [Prudhomme and Tournon], *Révolutions de Paris* II (1790), no. 35 (6/13 Mar. 1790), 4–6.

[47] Palmer, *Age of the Democratic Revolution* i. 352–3; Polasky, *Revolution in Brussels*, 148–9; Polasky, "Women in Revolutionary Brussels," 153; Jourdan, *La Révolution*, 359–60.

[48] Gorman, *America and Belgium*, 159; Dubois, *L'Invention de la Belgique*, 108.

[49] [Condorcet], *Bibliothèque de l'Homme Public* I (1790), part xi, pp. 207–9; Mortier, *Anarcharsis Cloots*, 187, 194 n. 5.

Continent's most developed commercial and industrial bourgeoisie,[50] while firmly supported by the laboring poor as well, the Belgian Revolution was, in a sense, socially more "advanced" as well as more the people's work than the American, French, Swiss, or Dutch revolutions, the outcome of urban middle class mass politics, the most genuinely popular and "modern" of the trans-Atlantic revolutionary insurrections.[51]

In Paris, Bordeaux, and Lyon, during the preparatory moves in 1787–9 and the initial stages of the Revolution in 1789, events were dominated by small groups of highly literate and articulate journalists, writers, liberal nobles, and clergy, with sometimes vigorous but usually only sporadic and localized popular support. Outside Paris, in France more generally, "the people" failed to assert themselves in any particular consistent direction. They did not forcefully determine the outcome to the extent witnessed in the Belgian cities and countryside. At the same time, the radical tendency in the Belgian provinces was rapidly marginalized except in Liège and Ghent. If the democratic wing remained a force to be reckoned with, this was due less to sporadic local strength in a few towns than the proximity of the French frontier and the neighboring Revolution.

Inevitably, the spread of revolutionary turmoil to Belgium attracted dissidents from all sides, especially drawing the attention of the international fraternity of roving, more or less professional, international insurgents inspired by the American Revolution, figures like Brissot, Lafayette, Desmoulins, Mirabeau, Miranda, Paine, Kościuszko, Paape, and Barlow. A leading figure of the Liège insurgency, Colonel Jean-Pierre Ransonnet (1746–96), like Lafayette and Kościuszko a veteran officer of the American struggle, had returned to Liège from the United States in 1784. At the head of opposition to the prince-bishop, he had adopted a subversive, republican stance from the moment the Liégeois disturbances commenced; it was Ransonnet who led the men who captured the prince-bishop's citadel and palace on 18 August 1789, a triumph that lifted the spirits of *Vonckisten* throughout Belgium.[52] In the early autumn of 1789, Ransonnet participated in the Breda talks, assuring Van der Noot's revolutionary committee he would move against the foes of Belgium's revolution like "Calvin au diable."[53] But later, displaying his democratic zeal, and growing distaste for the Belgian revolution's chief tendency, he had to go into exile, becoming a general in the French revolutionary army.

Until January 1790, the Belgian revolution maintained impressive internal unity. Only when the burghers of Brussels, Antwerp, Mons, Ghent, and Bruges sought to consolidate their revolution, late in the winter of 1789–90, did they begin dividing into two rival and irreconcilable warring blocs: a conservative majority wanting to cancel Joseph's reforms and revert to the "old constitution," restoring aristocracy and higher clergy to their former ascendancy in administration and politics, as against a minority, tentatively more "democratic," wing, headed by Vonck. Van Eupen, now

[50] Polasky, *Revolution in Brussels*, 264.
[51] Doyle, *Oxford History*, 162; Kossmann, *Lage Landen* i. 59; Roegiers and Van Sas, "Revolutie," 233.
[52] Raxhon, "Révolutionnaires liégeois," 116–17.
[53] Gorman, *America and Belgium*, 110–11.

bearing the title "secretary of state" of the États-Belgiques-Unis, vividly characterized the incipient split in a letter, of January 1790, to the editor of a journal that had dared express criticism of the clergy. Our people laugh *chrétiennement* at the *philosophique* "madness" presently in fashion among some; the "people believes that its piety sustained its arms;" the Belgian States General agree the Catholic religion is the only basis for *la prospérité publique*. The recalcitrant editor Van Eupen admonished to cease fomenting notions *anti-chrétiennes* or face serious consequences.[54]

Having helped orchestrate the rising against Joseph in Brabant, Vonck's following now revealed itself to be considerably more *philosophique* in orientation than Van der Noot's mainstream Belgian tendency. A democrat, Vonck, among the more brilliant philosophy students of his age-group, was indeed hardly a man of the people. Born to a family of minor nobles and *curés*, he had studied in Brussels with the Jesuits, and then at Louvain, just when, in the early 1760s, under the empress Maria Theresa, that ancient seat of learning began to stir from its age-old lethargy and some were urging the dropping of medieval scholasticism and adoption of a "catholicisme éclairé" [enlightened Catholicism].[55] In 1790, Vonck became leader of the democratic tendency, or *la démocratie*, in the Belgian revolution, not by representing "the people" in any way, by popular feeling, sociability, or cultural shifts, but by heading the underground opposition network or secret society, *Pro Aris et Focis*, comprised of lawyers and professionals,[56] prominence gained through his being a penetrating political analyst and effective orator and pamphleteer steeped in Montesquieu, Rousseau, Voltaire, Mably, Diderot, and Raynal.[57] Inspired by the principles of 1789 in France, the "cabale" of leading *Vonckistes* consisted mostly of bankers, merchants, and lawyers, including also a few progressive-minded noblemen.[58] The challenge Vonck faced was how to bridge the two enlightenments. The radical *philosophique* tendency within the Belgian revolution commanded some support at Liège and Ghent but was so weak generally that Vonck's prospects in the wider Belgian context relied for the moment on keeping his program and support inconspicuous, in a discreetly quiescent back seat.

Vonck's personal popularity never rivaled Van der Noot's. There was no greater contradiction and paradox in the Belgian revolution than that Vonck's supposedly democratic movement, unlike Van der Noot's, lacked resonance among the people, found little support among the laboring poor, and, unlike the Brissotin faction in France, attracted practically no support from women activists ardent for the revolution.[59] Aside from some backing in Brussels, including financial help from De Walckiers, Vonck's democratic wing remained unrepresentative throughout Brabant and most other provinces, though it did build a stronger following in

[54] Coppens, *Chronique des révolutions Belgique*, 130; Van Dam, "Spirituele revolutie," 11.
[55] De Clerck, "Vonck avant Vonck," 22–3.
[56] Polasky, "Women in Revolutionary Brussels," 149, 151–2.
[57] De Clerck, "Vonck avant Vonck," 26.
[58] *Relation exacte De ce qui s'est passé à Bruxelles*, 6–7.
[59] Polasky, "Démocrates bruxellois," 62; Polasky, "Women in Revolutionary Brussels," 158.

Flanders. Vonck's supporters opposing the conservative mind-set were found primarily at Liège and Ghent, observed Paape, with some also in Bruges and the smaller towns of western Flanders and in "Austrian" Limburg where antipathy to nobility and clergy was more marked than elsewhere.[60] Vonck had to express himself publicly in a more restrained manner than his more radical supporters would have wished, publicly offering no specific proposals for introducing democracy, or demand for a constituent national assembly, and veiling some of his enthusiasm for developments in France, though he did suggest doing away with voting by separate orders in the Brabant estates.[61] Least of all did he suggest weakening the church. But his *Considérations impartiales sur la position actuelle de Brabant*, published anonymously in January 1790, the first major pamphlet issued by his circle, reappearing in Dutch the following year, nevertheless created a considerable stir by protesting against the monopolization of power by the Brabant nobility and clergy and urging expansion of the Third Estate's role in the provincial assemblies and the new "Congress" of the "United States" of Belgium.[62]

Where Van der Noot embraced sovereignty of the people rhetorically, Vonck did so more concretely, consistently, and genuinely. "Since the people have taken up arms to uphold the [old] constitution," contended Van der Noot, the revolution "would fall into contradiction with itself should the people fail to recognize their former [aristocratic and ecclesiastical] representatives as their sovereigns." This the *Considérations impartiales* termed a ridiculous "sophisme."[63] The existing Brabant constitution and Estates were "une aristocratie monstrueusement exclusive" so that proceeding as Van der Noot and his colleagues proposed could only reduce the people to a "much harsher and more humiliating slavery" than overturning Austrian rule had just released them from.[64] Belgians rose, held the *Vonckistes*, to overthrow an oppressive, extraneous, "monarchical constitution" illegitimately imposed by Joseph II and Austria. Promoting the *bonheur* [happiness] of the "nation" meant changing the old ways and introducing changes to "our ancient constitution," especially converting the new Congress into something like the French National Assembly with no division into separate "estates" and no separate status for the nobility and clergy.[65] Nevertheless, until early 1790, hardly any Belgian pamphlets explicitly called for a thoroughgoing revision of the country's constitution on the French revolutionary model; Vonck grew increasingly cautious about drawing parallels with the French Revolution owing to the latter's increasingly unfavorable image in Belgium and *Vandernootiste* accusations that the *Vonckiste* movement drew its inspiration from France.[66]

[60] Paape, *Hollandse wijsgeer in Braband* iv. 75–7.
[61] Dhondt, "Débuts de la démocratie," 67–8; Illing, "Montesquieu's Shadow," 333.
[62] Dhondt, "Débuts de la démocratie," 77–9; Dhondt, "Conservative Brabantse ontwenteling," 440.
[63] Vonck, *Considérations impartiales*, 5; Delsaerdt, "Beatus populus," 128.
[64] Vonck, *Considérations impartiales*, 6; Vercruysse, "Pamphlets," 322.
[65] Vonck, *Considérations impartiales*, 6–8, 17, 21.
[66] *Relation exacte De ce qui s'est passé à Bruxelles*, 4–5; Dhondt, "Débuts de la démocratie," 72.

Rendering the proposed Belgian legislature truly representative of the "general will of the people" was the key *Vonckiste* demand, but there was more. Following America's example, Vonck insisted "Montesquieu and with him the most enlightened publicists [*les publicistes les plus éclairées*] taught, and proved from examples ancient and modern, that a well-constituted government must, above all, ensure the three separate powers, legislative, executive, and judiciary, stay in different hands."[67] At the height of the Belgian revolution, remarkably, Montesquieu was cited in Belgian pamphlets more frequently than Rousseau.[68] But it was beyond Vonck's power wholly to restrain the anti-clerical thrust of his own revolutionary militants, given their dislike of the Josephist reforms at Louvain being cancelled, and the States of Flanders suppressing the higher education college at Ghent, erected by Maria Theresa, in place of the Augustinian *Recollet* friars.[69] Those supporting the generalized attack on religious authority, property, and privilege, in France, were hardly likely to refrain from decrying the formidable press restraints, and tightening of ecclesiastical control over education, in the new États-Belgiques-Unis born of their own revolution. An anonymous piece appearing in several Brussels papers in mid-February 1790 warned that if the aristocratic faction continued to have their way, all those citizens "who are partisans of the French constitution" will switch back and support Joseph II since it is better to be "ruled by an iron scepter than subjected to religious despotism, the most outrageous of all despotisms among the human species." Those sharing this sentiment would go to any lengths to prevent Belgium being "plunged back into the darkness of ignorance and bonds of superstition."[70] "Partisans of the French constitution" would find the means to break "la tyrannie aristocratique," the new aristocratic–ecclesiastical hold, and institute the freedom presently lacking, the first rule of which was "la liberté indéfinie de la presse" [unrestricted liberty of the press]. "Monks," complained Brussels' more militant dissidents, were the epitome of tyranny and obscurantism, "artisans of slavery," the category of men "least sensible to the duties of justice and almost complete strangers to the rights of humanity." Objecting that forty-nine parts out of fifty of the Belgian population found themselves excluded from representation in Congress while all the high positions and offices of state were monopolized by the narrow aristocratic–ecclesiastical elite that had seized power backed by the bourgeoisie and laboring poor, swayed a few. The people, urged the radical militants, must open their eyes and understand that, as things stood, the États-Belgiques-Unis lacked any "barrier against the fanaticism of priests, or rapacity of nobles."[71]

Anti-*Vonckiste* literature streamed from the presses condemning the "malcontents," claiming expulsion of the last sovereign meant the ancient Belgian constitutions had

67 Vonck, *Considérations impartiales*, 21; Vercruysse, "Pamphlets," 322.
68 Vercruysse, "Pamphlets," 322; Illing, "Montesquieu's Shadow," 332.
69 Coppens, *Chronique des révolutions Belgique*, 180.
70 Coppens, *Chronique des révolutions Belgique*, 153.
71 Coppens, *Chronique des révolutions Belgique*, 156, 166–7, 178–9.

now lapsed and that a new constitution should replace it. *Vonckiste* sedition, conservatives hit back, posed a dire threat to Belgian unity and liberty, menacing religion and the state. Vonck allegedly diffused malicious rumors that Van der Noot was deceiving the people, lulling them asleep the better to secure his grip, and that Van der Noot, Van Eupen, and Van der Hoop were all "scélérats" [rascals]. "It seems," admonished one pamphlet, alluded to the German Illuminati, "that the serpent that Germany has for some years nourished in her bosom, and has poisoned France, wants to scatter the rest of her poison across Brabant."[72] Liberty is a fine thing, concurred one Brussels pamphlet, but the "manner and consequences of the two revolutions," those of Belgium and France, differ essentially. In the latter, everything went wrong and the church's property was confiscated. Belgians, by contrast, a "nation wise and moderate," eager to "profit from the errors of neighbors" blinding themselves by embracing "esprit de philosophie," eschew democratic ideas, loath philosophy, and adhere to religion.[73]

Henri Van der Hoop, Van der Noot's ideological aide helping to refute Vonck's *Considérations impartiales*, loudly invoked Montesquieu and Robertson on behalf of noble and ecclesiastical privilege. With unconscious irony, given the bourgeoisie provided the muscle behind the revolution, Van der Hoop reminded readers of Mably's (and Adam Smith's) doctrine that merchants and traders are "less patriotic" than other men, more inclined to further their own interests than the common welfare. The common good, society's welfare, held Van der Hoop, much like Hume and Adam Smith, is best entrusted to nobles and gentry rather than merchants and business people as Montesquieu too maintained.[74] Also adduced was the argument that God Himself introduced aristocratic hierarchy to society, as history and existing society abundantly prove; ordinary mortals should not interfere with a divine scheme everywhere sanctioned by the church.[75] Besides, the Brabant Estates had no mandate from the people to convene a "national assembly" or elected Congress on the French model, and it would be inopportune and unwise to solicit one: the Americans consulted the citizenry but were free from outside interference; the French did so only at the price of massive internal dissension.[76] Van der Hoop could count on the Third Estate, shopkeepers, manufacturers, and commercial class, to take little interest in the revolution's shape and form and devoutly shun "philosophy." In the *Réflexions d'un Belge patriote*, the Belgian common man is urged to remain always loyal to his "wise, moderate" self, aligning with the clergy and existing laws, determined to "profit from the errors" of his impetuous French "neighbors."[77] "Moderation," backing nobility and clergy, was the Revolution's true battle cry, the essence of both its popular and its *bourgeois* character.

[72] BRL VH 27139A/V, *L'Anatomie de la Cabale*, 3, 5, 13.

[73] *Reflexions d'un Belge patriote*, 26–7.

[74] Van der Hoop, *Réfutation des Considérations impartiales*, 5, 23–4; Illing, "Montesquieu's Shadow," 334.

[75] Polasky, "Women in Revolutionary Brussels," 149.

[76] Dhondt, "Débuts de la démocratie," 75–6.

[77] *Réflexions d'un Belge patriote*, 27.

The Belgian revolution predictably revived memories of the 1572 Revolt against Philip II of Spain.[78] The aura surrounding William the Silent, the heroic leader of Low Countries rebellion against despotism, reappeared, some of Van der Noot's supporters openly exalting the 1572 revolt, even talking of restoring the stadholderate in the southern Netherlands—a tendency lent added edge by the widespread antipathy to the Dutch anti-Orangist exiles abounding in their country. Where Dutch Patriot exiles in the south, reviling the dominant faction's Orangism and religious intolerance, sided mostly with the *Vonckistes* against the *Vandernootistes*,[79] the *Vandernootistes*, much to their disgust, frequently sported Orange cockades signaling alignment with the northern Netherlands princely conservative faction as well as the southern clergy and nobility, reminding onlookers that the Orangist court at The Hague loathed the "parti démocratique" in both parts of the Netherlands. The Orangist court likewise greatly preferred Van der Noot's "parti aristocratique," as Brissot's paper reported in Paris, to those elements the Paris radical press called "partisans" of "la liberté française." [80] Several Dutch exiles in Antwerp had their houses of plundered by populist *Vandernootistes* who also attacked the anti-Orangist Dutch Protestant colony at Lier; Paape at this point fled Antwerp for Brussels.[81]

By February 1790, the Belgian revolution was fundamentally split and its principal military hero, Van der Meersch, entangled in bitter dispute with the aristocratic–ecclesiastical leadership. Out of protest, some of the Brussels "parti démocratique" ceased sporting the Belgian revolutionary cockades of 1789.[82] The French National Assembly became seriously alarmed as well as perplexed by the divisions. While Louis XVI, still formally allied to Austria by marriage and treaties, refused to recognize the États-Belgiques-Unis; the radical Left urgently called for French recognition.[83] France's revolutionaries feared the obvious instability of the "great scene of the insurrection in the Low Countries" and formidable strength of the Belgian clergy and nobility. Many were disturbed that the Congress of États-Belgiques-Unis, unlike the French legislature, "does not seem to possess all the characteristics that stem from the power of the people." By mid-March 1790, talk abounded of pending "civil war" in the Belgian provinces. In Brussels, there were outbreaks of disorder with groups of militia volunteers, commanded by Walckiers, patrolling the streets yelling support for Walckiers and Van der Meersch, and "Vive la nation! Vive Vonck!" The States responded by cracking down on democratic dissidents, the "monks" by railing in their sermons against Belgian and Dutch *novateurs* betraying the "bien public" and leading prayers for the Almighty to save Belgium from the "impious National Assembly of France."[84]

[78] Dhont, "Conservatieve Brabantse ontwenteling," 435–6; Israel, *Dutch Republic*, 1117.

[79] Rosendaal, *Bataven!*, 80. [80] Brissot, *Patriote française* clvi (11 Jan. 1790), 4.

[81] Rosendaal, *Bataven!*, 80.

[82] Coppens, *Chronique des révolutions Belgique*, 179; Van Rossem, "Politieke prenten," 28.

[83] [Condorcet], *Bibliothèque* I (1790), part xi, "discours" (Mar. 1790), 208–9, 211; Coppens, *Chronique des révolutions*, 199.

[84] Coppens, *Chronique des révolutions Belgique*, 202–3, 212.

Dutch anti-Orangists in Brussels and Antwerp came under mounting suspicion; their houses were searched; there was talk of expelling them from the country. In both cities and at Ghent, several Dutchmen were detained for aiding *Vonckistes*, causing many of the Patriot community to hurriedly transfer to neighboring parts of France and the Brussels "Hollandsche Societeit" to close its doors. A pamphlet appeared in early April openly accusing Dutch Patriot exiles in Belgium of treacherously conspiring with *Vonckistes* and French republicans against the États-Belgiques-Unis and its Congress. According to Feller, Holland's exiled anti-Orangists, welcomed in the country due to the Belgian people's natural goodness, "have become our cruelest enemies."[85] Those leaving included their two most radical leaders, Willem Buys and Petrus de Wacker van Zon, who, in 1786 at Alkmaar, had published a pamphlet, *De Adel*, under a pseudonym, fiercely attacking the Dutch nobility, and nobility in general, as a privileged elite whose political status was in every way incompatible with the principles of equality and freedom.[86] These two were also the anti-Orangist exiles with the closest ties to the *Vonckistes*.

Given the rift within the American Revolution from 1775 onwards, both *Vandernootisten* and *Vonckisten*, in their pamphlets and newspapers, could justifiably claim American revolutionary principles as firm endorsement of their own irreconcilable creeds.[87] Where the main French revolutionary journals championed Vonck and Van der Meersch, pouring scorn on Van der Noot and the Brabant popular "revolution,"[88] French constitutional "moderates," following the storming of the Bastille and their Revolution's initial great enactments, undeviatingly backed the conservative "Congress of Belgian United States" against Vonck. French constitutional monarchists—including some Jacobins (who until July 1792 mostly espoused constitutional monarchy)—firmly disapproved of *philosophique* republicanism and saw no reason to antagonize Van der Noot.[89] If Dutch Patriots mostly backed "le parti démocratique du Brabant," everyone seeking to entrench the "parti aristocratique" prior, as they anticipated, to the eventual restoration of monarchy in Belgium preferred Van der Noot.[90] Worried lest the new Belgian federal republic become a base for counter-revolutionary intervention in the French provinces nearest Belgium, an agent of the "cause aristocratique,"[91] the French democratic republican Left pressed for a Belgian "revolution more favorable to democratic principles," as Lafayette expressed it, that would ally with the radical French revolutionary leadership and Dutch democrats against Britain, Austria, and Prussia.

85 Rosendaal, *Bataven!*, 82–3; Rosendaal, *Nederlandse revolutie*, 72.

86 Rosendaal, *Bataven!*, 83–4; Altena, *Gerrit Paape*, 317; Rutjes, *Door gelijkheid gegrepen*, 140.

87 Palmer, *Age of the Democratic Revolution*, i. 353.

88 Lafayette, *Mémoires* iii. 17.

89 [Prudhomme and Tournon], *Révolutions de Paris* II (1790), no. 35 (6/13 Mar.), 5–6; Lafayette, *Mémoires* iii. 13–14, 17.

90 Brissot, *Patriote français* clvi (11 Jan. 1790), 4.

91 [Prudhomme and Tournon], *Révolutions de Paris* II (1790), no. 35 (6/13 Mar.), 5–8.

18.3. THE *VONCKISTE* REVOLUTION OVERWHELMED

The main Belgian institutional bodies, Congress, the provincial States of Brabant, Flanders, and Hainault, and the city governments, divided over the nobility's privileges, magistracies, and ecclesiastical property. At a theoretical–constitutional level, the argument revolved mainly around the question of sovereignty: did popular sovereignty, a doctrine both sides ostensibly embraced, mean the people should be represented in Congress, as the *Vonckistes* claimed, or only that their sovereignty was vested in Congress without their being represented there? On a practical level, the issue was whether, and how far, to widen representation. Even though the Brussels guilds and common people had engineered the revolution, the States of Brabant ruled that effective sovereignty belonged not to the people but the States which alone should decide the new constitutional arrangements. This view prevailed, after some months even in "Austrian" Limburg.[92]

Eventually, with the simmering clashes unresolved and democrats resisting, the question was settled not by negotiation but by force. The constitutional struggle for the soul of the Belgian revolution culminated in March and April 1790, with most of the Brabant population, as one Dutch-language pamphlet described the struggle, proving to be *Aristocraten* and very few *Democraten*.[93] Once again, undeniably, it was the common people's vigorous intervention, peasants and urban populace both, that decided the issue. Van der Noot, posting up placards two days previously, summoned the Brussels populace to a vast gathering in the Grande Place, on 16 March; skirmishes ensued, several rich merchants' mansions were pillaged. Violence spread to other towns. [94] During these tense days, the streets of Brussels, Louvain, and other cities constantly echoed to cries of "Vive Henri Van der Noot! Vivent les États-Unis!"[95] Congress dragoons paraded through the streets carrying busts of their hero, shouting "Vive Van der Noot!" and playing loud martial music which did nothing to dispel the "inquietude" that had seized the capital, any more than the sporadic outbreaks of yelling in the streets with stones thrown through the windows of residences known for *Vonckiste* opposition to Van der Noot.

The "democratic" faction responded by boycotting the Congress; they were proclaimed public enemies and swiftly overwhelmed by a furious populace. The *Societé patriotique*, the main *Vonckiste* organization, was quickly routed after a few minor armed clashes in the streets. Denouncing the Belgian Congress as "purement aristocratique," the *Vonckistes* in desperation called on France to intervene and join them in the fight for democratic freedom and equality or what the anti-*philosophe* Feller termed "une anarchie parfaite." In the streets, fields, every corner of Belgium, exulted

[92] Heirwegh, "La Fin," 481; Polasky, "Success," 420–1.

[93] Polasky, *Revolution in Brussels*, 168.

[94] *Relation exacte De ce qui s'est passé à Bruxelles*, 28, 30–1.

[95] BRL MS 6/1332224 *Lettres de Luxembourg à l'Abbé Brosius*, 6.

Feller, South Netherlanders showed their worth, their loathing of "philosophy" and democratic revolutionary values, their undeviating faith, and loyalty to clergy, aristocracy, and the old order.[96] They rose up as one body and overwhelmed the *Democraten*, decisively crushing the foes of the old Estates.[97] According to Condorcet, a *philosophe* convinced popular ignorance always represents the greatest danger to liberty, the Brabant revolution, originating, he believed, in a revolt on behalf of Catholic seminaries, proved all too plainly that the common people are readily misled and persuaded to act directly against their own cause and interest.[98]

Thousands of *Vonckistes* (and Dutch Patriots suspected of assisting *Vonckistes*) fled over the border into France, many migrating to Lille, Dunkirk, Cassel, and Valenciennes, the same places that received the Dutch fugitives in 1787, besides Paris where De Walckiers sought refuge.[99] Van der Meersch, caught on 13 April before he could escape, was imprisoned in Antwerp citadel (the walls of which Van Eupen had reportedly rescued from demolition). Another close ally, "one of the most powerful leaders of *Vonckisme*,"[100] the duc d'Ursel, was caught at Alost, and imprisoned, while enraged mobs attacked and pillaged his several chateaux. Escaping via Dinant, in May 1790, Vonck himself settled in Lille. There was no way, though, given the proximity of France and torrent of writings entering from France, diffusing anti-aristocratic, anti-Montesquieu, and anti-ecclesiastical rhetoric and propaganda, that Vonck and Van der Meersch could be entirely crushed by the "aristothéocrates," as *Vonckistes* scornfully termed the *Vandernootistes*.

A key *Vonckiste* later to play a notable role in subsequent stages of the Belgian revolution, intensively searched for at this juncture, was the French actor and dramatist Pierre-Ulric Dubuisson (1746–94), who had dwelt in the Caribbean and Paris but, menaced with a *lettre de cachet*, having displeased Louis XVI's officials, since 1783 had spent much of his time in Belgium. His sick wife, Mme Dubuisson, likewise a zealous supporter of the French Revolution's radical wing, was at their Brussels home when it was ransacked by Congress soldiers who in their search pierced their mattresses with their swords. She retorted with an open letter to Van der Noot which she afterwards had printed and followed up with a second missive, also printed, denouncing the "injustices, horrors, and atrocities committed in the name of law and liberty," complaining of being victimized and reminding him she was the wife of an eminent man of letters with a pen accustomed to "frightening tyrants and breaking their scepter of iron by enlightening their slaves."[101] In early May followed a vigorous "arbitrary" crackdown on all the publishers and printers in

[96] [Feller], *Journal historique* 1793 i. 175–8 (15 April); Van den Bossche, *Enlightened Innovation*, 177–80.

[97] Dhont, "Conservatieve Brabanse ontwentteling," 441–2; Doyle, *Oxford History*, 162–3.

[98] Condorcet, *Oeuvres* ix. 173; Baker, *Condorcet*, 269.

[99] Van Rossem, "Politieke prenten," 30; Rosendaal, *Nederlandse revolutie*, 73–4.

[100] BRL MS 6/1332224 *Lettres de Luxembourg à l'Abbé Brosius*, 7.

[101] Coppens, *Chronique des révolutions Belgique et Liégeoise*, 244–5.

Brussels, their premises ransacked for subversive materials and printed protest sheets, resulting in at least two bookshop owners being imprisoned.[102] During June, with the "fureur du peuple contre les Vonckistes" and *Van-der-Meerschistes* unceasing, a *Vonckiste* conspiracy to forcibly set Van der Meersch free, organized at Menin, Courtrai, and Ostend, was crushed; at Ypres, the home of a well-known *Vonckiste* magistrate related to Van der Meersch was pillaged. More arrests followed in Brussels, Antwerp, and Ghent.

But while the *Vandernootistes* stamped out the last remnants of *Vonckiste* resistance, with Brabant witnessing groups of armed peasants roaming the countryside carrying crucifixes and portraits of Van der Noot, fervently vowing to eradicate the *Vonckiste* godless,[103] the Austrians were gradually recovering lost ground, advancing across Belgium's several borders and from their strongholds in Luxembourg. By July, the king of Prussia had resolved to assist the Austrians to restore their rule. To counter the threat, Congress raised fresh units of armed volunteers across the country. Thrown onto the defensive, the "Congress of Belgian United States" also appealed to the French revolutionary leadership, and contacted Lafayette, imploring their assistance in saving Belgian independence. But the Paris legislature was then still too entangled in its own internal crisis to respond. To succeed, answered Lafayette, proclaiming the same strategy that he advocated in Paris, the Brussels leadership must bridge the deep rift in their midst, and unify their contending factions, a scheme impossible without first releasing Van der Meersch from prison. To the exasperation of some French as well as Belgian revolutionaries, Lafayette in the end refused point blank to assist a revolution refusing to make meaningful concessions to Vonck, popular sovereignty, equality, or reform.[104]

At Liège, where the officially proclaimed revolutionary rhetoric differed markedly from that prevailing in Brussels, opinion was more inclined to solidarity with the French Revolution, and little inclined to sympathize with Van der Noot. The Liégois sent their own representative to Paris, to represent their revolution in the celebrations scheduled to mark the first anniversary of the Fall of the Bastille. Dohm's record of the Liège revolution and his role as *ministre plénipotentiaire* of the duchy of Cleves, published at Liège shortly afterwards, in August, was remarkable for how this "écrivain philosophe" [philosophic writer], and ardent enlightener, despite working for the Prussian crown with instructions to prevent Liège separating itself from the Holy Roman Empire, and revise rather than demolish the old constitution, strove for solutions that would discreetly secure most of the Liégois revolution's aims. Dohm's text presented the Liège revolution in a mostly favorable light, invoked *volonté générale*, harshly criticized the prince-bishop and clergy, and was reportedly warmly received by all "friends of reason and humanity"

[102] Coppens, *Chronique des révolutions Belgique et Liégeoise*, 249–52, 268–70.
[103] Coppens, *Chronique des révolutions Belgique et Liégeoise*, 27–1.
[104] Lafayette, *Mémoires* iii. 42–5; Robert, *L'Ami de la liberté*, 8.

sympathetic to the French Revolution.[105] The prince-bishop's staff accused Dohm of permitting himself to be seduced and misled by the "rebelles."[106]

Europe's war of newspapers and pamphlets pitted the *Brabantse ontwenteling* against the French, Dutch, Liégeois, and Genevan democratic revolutions, Belgian aristocratism against the *Vonckiste* democratic tendency. Belgium itself was inundated with revolutionary texts, altogether some 2,000 printed pamphlets appearing in connection with the Revolution between 1787 and 1791.[107] Joseph having died in February 1790, his younger brother and successor, Leopold II (1747–92; reigned: 1790–2), now declared himself prepared to restore the old constitution and the *Joyeuse Entrée*, in exchange for Belgian contrition and submission, and a joint front against revolutionary France and Liège. The Belgian people were summoned to reconciliation with the Emperor, reported scandalized opinion in France, merely in exchange for his unconditionally agreeing to restore the outmoded and rotten "constitution ancienne," with the result that many were now, in December 1790, on the point of abandoning the Revolution altogether. The people's true interest was being sacrificed for the old south Netherlands constitution of the fifteenth century guaranteeing the ascendancy of the nobility, clergy, and city magistracies! How should the French revolutionary press explain such a ridiculous fiasco to rural readers?[108] Because Belgium's *ancien régime* had always favored the "tyranny of bishops and monks," on receiving guarantees that privilege, rank, and the old order would be restored, these groups, under Van der Noot's lead, had without hesitation simply betrayed the Revolution and the people.[109] "A revolution led by monks and nobles," concluded *La Feuille villageoise*, must inevitably end in "slavery." With ecclesiastics in charge, it is easy to foist "slavery" on peoples by mobilizing "credulity and fanaticism," but such sway cannot last. With *la philosophie* and *la liberté française* firmly entrenched on Belgium's borders, the paper remained confident, "our good books will little by little chase out both superstition and the monks."[110] This proved a delusion. As a Belgian *Vonckiste* noted, some months later: "the example of happy France wrecked everything among a people readier for liberty than for philosophy."[111]

Still drawing striking comparisons between the American and Belgian revolutions at this late stage was the revolutionary pamphlet *Triple Parallèle de la Révolution*, published in Brussels in October 1790. This text compared the Revolution "of the Thirteen United States" with the 1572 Dutch Revolt and the new Belgian revolution, affirming major affinities between all three and an implicit contrast with the French

[105] Dohm, *Exposé de la Révolution de Liège*, 68–9, 90–1; Coppens, *Chronique des révolutions Belgique et Liégeoise*, 305.

[106] Dohm, *Exposé de la Révolution de Liège*, Preface, pp. lxii, 157.

[107] Vercruysse, "Pamphlets," 317.

[108] Dhont, "Conservatieve Brabantse omwenteling," 433–44; Van den Bossche, *Enlightened Innovation*, 44–6.

[109] *La Feuille villageoise* i, no. 10 (2 Dec. 1790), 183.

[110] *La Feuille villageoise* i, no. 10 (2 Dec. 1790), 183–4.

[111] Coppens, *Chronique des révolutions Belgique et Liégeoise*, 366.

Revolution. The tyranny of an oppressive and grasping monarch, ruling an immense empire and excessively taxing his subjects, was heroically overthrown by the efforts of ordinary folk in their masses, led by aristocracy and their clergy, in 1572 in the northern Netherlands and America in 1776–7, as well as Belgium in 1789–90. In all these cases, an innovative federal system of "United States" headed by a joint "congress" had emerged and the people rejoiced, elevated by the heart-warming and liberating outcome.[112] More than others, this pamphlet also drew attention to the prominent role played by women. Much as Boston's womenfolk gave up luxury and drinking imported tea during 1774–6 to assist the revolutionary movement, held the *Triple Parallèle*, and were emulated by women in the rest of America, so Belgian women loyally embraced their revolution while remaining unshakable in their Catholic piety and modesty. But it was precisely their piety above all, objected dissenting voices, that misled Belgium's women into supporting religion and fomenting the *anti-philosophisme* that had so damaging and deleterious an effect on their country and its populace.

A prominent Belgian republican journalist based in Paris, François Robert (1762–1826), at this point published a leaflet expressing solidarity with the Belgian revolution and rebuking the Paris National Assembly moderates, aligning with Louis XVI, as well as Lafayette and other powerful figures, for preventing the Assembly from "fraternizing" more effectively with the Belgian Patriots.[113] There was no hiding the increasingly gloomy circumstances, in Liège, Brussels, and Ghent. Nevertheless, until late September, a residue of confidence persisted in Brussels, Antwerp, and even Liège despite the fact that, by late August, the Austrians had recovered Limburg and moved troops close to the city. The celebrations marking the 18 August anniversary of the overthrow of the prince-bishop and capture of his palace proceeded as planned, even at Huy, right under the noses of the Austrian troops. In Liège city, great crowds gathered for the parades, artillery salutes, stirring ringing of bells, and martial music, with the entire city illuminated during the evening. This defiant mood persisted through October into November. With Leopold's offer to the Belgian people published via an imperial *manifeste*, large crowds gathered, on Congress's orders, on 6 November in the Brussels Grande Place, to witness the Emperor's manifesto being publicly torn up and burnt at the foot of a monumental "Liberty Hat" to yells of "Vive les Trois États! Vive Henri Van der Noot!"[114]

On 10 November 1790 orders were issued under the signatures of Van der Noot and Van Eupen for the states to raise 20,000 troops, for the common army, to resist the invading Austrians, each province according to a fixed quota, with the two largest provinces, Flanders, raising 8,000, and Brabant 6,000, providing nearly three-quarters

[112] BRL VH 27139/vii/2: *Triple Parallèle de la Révolution*, 3–5, 28–33; Gorman, *America and Belgium*, 167–8.

[113] Robert, *L'Ami de la liberté applaudissant*, 7–8; Israel, *Revolutionary Ideas*, 120, 142, 727.

[114] BRL VH 27139 A/17, *Le Vrai Belge*, 37.

of the whole.[115] But fresh Austrian reinforcements, arriving in late November, and evident unwillingness in France and Holland to assist in preserving the États-Belgiques-Unis, were by this point rapidly sapping morale. Dismaying rumors had been circulating for weeks suggesting Van der Noot himself was seeking a negotiated capitulation, rumors which during November, to the fury of many, were proved correct. In late November 1790, with Austrian forces advancing on Brussels from all sides, the republic's army disintegrated and Van der Noot switched to publicly urging Belgians to accept a very different compromise from that Lafayette had recommended. Reconciliation with the *Vonckistes*, as the French advised, was rejected out of hand as prejudicial to church and aristocracy. It was better to submit to Austria, the leadership assured the people, than to impiety and philosophy. As the drama neared its denouement, Belgium's radical enlighteners and *Vonckistes* openly accused the Belgian Congress of sacrificing the republic to "ignorance and superstition."[116]

What remained of independent Belgium collapsed during December. On 2 December, the same day that they recovered Mons, Austrian troops, displaying impeccable discipline, entered Brussels without resistance and without wreaking any vengeance on the inhabitants. Antwerp surrendered on 6 December, Ostend on the 14th. A large wave of Belgian revolutionary exiles headed for France, often taking their families and possessions with them. A general drive began to remove from sight all symbols, banners, and emblems associated with the independent États-Belgiques-Unis.[117] By mid-December, all resistance had ended, except at Liège, from which Prussia had now withdrawn its protection but where revolutionary defiance continued down to the arrival of a mixed Austrian and Munsterite force outside its walls on 28 December, and beyond. The city itself capitulated the next day. But Bassenge escaped to Paris, and subsequent reports from the two revolutionary capitals, Brussels and Liège, during January 1791, indicated a sharp divergence. While in Brussels the mood was so subdued that ardent republicans felt "our revolution is like a dream: all thought of liberty has disappeared," in Liège, despite the leadership having fled to France, the mood remained defiant and fraught with tension, sharpened by the return of the prince-bishop and his close supporters, and the lodging of Austrian troops in the villages around. As if to taunt the defeated populace, groups of "antipatriotes" began yelling "Vive Hoensbrouck!" in the streets. One young man sporting a sign reading "Vive le prince-évêque!" [Long live the prince-bishop!] was hurled off a bridge into the river.

Final assessments varied, but according to some even of Van der Noot's disillusioned former supporters, quite apart from *Vonckistes*, the 1787–91 Belgian revolution was widely thought to have been ruined by popular "fanatisme religieux," ignorance and intrigue, defeated in effect by lack of enlightenment. Autocratic princely rule was now vigorously re-established throughout the southern Low

115 BRL VH 27139 A/17, no. 29, Proclamation, 10 Nov. 1790.
116 Coppens, *Chronique des révolutions Belgique et Liégeoise*, 311.
117 Duerloo, "Kleuren en symbolen," 93.

Countries. Despite this, the *Vonckiste–Van-der-Meerschiste* revolution lived on beneath the surface. Throughout Belgium lingered regret that the vying of *Vandernootiste* and *Vonckiste* factions had been allowed to dominate the scene and sap and debilitate the revolution, despite frequent exhortations, not least from Paris, for reconciliation. In early 1791, at least one former member of the revolutionary Belgian Congress published a confession regretting having participated in the repression of the "parti démocratique" and repenting his having been the "accomplice of the scoundrel Vandernoot and the tartuffe Van Eupen."[118]

During 1791–2, the *Vonckiste* democratic revolution, like the Dutch democratic revolution in exile, remained alive in the minds of some in Belgium and especially among a considerable exiled fringe on French soil, and in the French revolutionary press. Louvain University reportedly stayed fiercely split, locked in a schism of a kind bound to damage a university's functioning.[119] Among leading *Vonckiste* democrats subsequently active in Paris was Pierre-Joseph Proly (1752–94), in December 1791 founder of the internationalist paper *Le Cosmopolite*, a revolutionary vehicle that strongly backed the subsequent French de-Christianization drive but also defended the concept of an independent, democratic, republican Belgium that would remain independent, and not be absorbed into France.[120] Like their Dutch counterparts, the Belgian exiles in France plotted and planned for the day the French revolutionary armies would finally move toward the Low Countries.

In January 1792, Walckiers formed the *Comité général des Belges et Liégeois Unis* to help coordinate revolutionary policy in the Low Countries with the French revolutionary leadership. In April 1792, by which time it was obvious a general revolutionary war would soon engulf all western Europe, Lafayette placed Ransonnet in command of a legion of exiled Belgians and Liégeois being prepared for the projected French invasion to liberate Belgium and the prince-bishopric alongside parallel Dutch and German revolutionary legions which Cloots, president of the Convention's diplomatic committee, played a notable part in forming. But the ferment of revolutionary conspiracy intensifying in France at the same time precipitated fresh ideological splits among the Belgian revolution in exile. Where Proly, Dubuisson, Robert, and Walckiers aligned with the French Jacobins, other Belgian exiles preferred rapprochement with the more amenable elements of the *Vandernootistes*. Vonck refused to negotiate with *Vandernootistes* but also rejected the atheism, secularism, and universalism of Proly, Bassenge, and Cloots as well as the unruliness of the French Jacobins; he kept his distance from Walckiers's *Comité général*.[121]

The initial outcome of the Brissotin-backed French declaration of war on Austria, on 20 April 1792, was disastrous for the French and *Vonckistes* alike. The humiliating repulse of the revolutionary army, by Austrian troops, from the Belgian border near

[118] BRL II 8122A, no. 2: *Confession authentique et repentir d'un membre du Congrès*, 6–7.
[119] BRL VH 27139/10, no. 25: *Lettre à un Ami touchant les articles prescrits*, 3–4.
[120] Mortier, *Anarcharsis Cloots*, 429; Israel, *Revolutionary Ideas*, 500, 539, 551, 659, 727.
[121] Polasky, "Démocrates bruxellois," 62, 64 n. 28.

Lille was followed by a surge of anxiety in French border towns as Austrian propaganda began stigmatizing French willingness to provide refuge for fugitive *Vonckistes* as an affront to royal legitimacy and the Emperor meriting severe punishment. Lille was besieged for a month down to 20 September 1792. It was at this point that the *Legion belge,* hitherto existing mainly on paper, became a real armed unit of *Vonckistes* organized by the French revolutionary regime. On 6 November 1792, commanded by Dumouriez, the army of the first French Republic with its foreign legions won its first stunning triumph over the Austrians at the battle of Jemappes, near Mons, leading to the swift collapse of the Austrian defenses and opening of the roads to Brussels, Antwerp, and Liège. The revolutionary army, with several leading Belgian revolutionaries present, entered Namur on 15 November, Ypres on the 18th and Antwerp on the 19th. Within hours a "liberty tree" was erected in Antwerp, and busts and emblems of rulers, princes, and noblemen removed or destroyed.[122] On 19 November 1792, the French Republic's Brissotin-dominated National Convention vowed "fraternity and assistance" to every people aspiring to throw off the oppressive yoke of Europe's princes.[123]

French revolutionary armies overran the southern Netherlands in November 1792, accompanied by Belgian and Dutch democratic legions marching under the *tricoleur* and to the sound of the Marseillaise, plastering walls with revolutionary posters, erecting Liberty Trees, and distributing leaflets on all sides. The invaders were vigorously supported by the returning *Vonckistes* and Liégeois activists, Bassenge among them. For the first few days, moreover, the revived revolution was joyfully welcomed. But no sooner did its anti-clerical and anti-aristocratic orientation become too blatant to be ignored, than it antagonized most of the populace, who stubbornly persisted in opposing its values, except at Liège where the French continued to be welcomed as liberators.[124] Seriously ill, Vonck lived just long enough to hear of the triumphs and inauguration of republican, democratic principles in his native land, dying, aged 49, on 1 December 1792, his demise practically unnoticed by the revolutionary press. But by this point, other influential Belgian democratic leaders, avowed republicans, had taken his place, Proly and Dubuisson not least, who were among the Revolution's *commissaires* in French-occupied Belgium during 1792–3.

The fortunes of war, though, soon again veered against the French Republic and its client states. Heavily repulsed by Austrian and Dutch Orangist troops at Neerwinden, 35 miles east of Brussels, on 18 March 1793, the revolutionary forces, under Dumouriez and Miranda, were thrown into headlong retreat. A new exodus of Belgian revolutionaries, Bassenge among them, returned to France. But this time it was just a small trickle from most of Belgium, albeit more of a flow from Liège.[125] A war against aristocracy on behalf of the Belgian villager, observed Dumouriez to the French Republic's Belgian *commissaires*, Proly and Dubuisson, who were with him, had

[122] Deseure, "Revolutionnaire geschiedenispolitiek," 33. [123] Israel, *Revolutionary Ideas*, 317.
[124] Raxhon, "Révolutionnaires liégeois," 116; Polasky, *Revolutions without Borders*, 236–9.
[125] Raxhon, "Révolutionnaires liégeois," 116.

become wretchedly transformed in Belgian eyes into a crusade of peasants allied to aristocrats and princes to rescue priests and religion. It was a moral and psychological disaster, as much as a military defeat, for the Revolution. Dubuisson, a close ally of Proly, had participated in the 10 August 1792 rising in Paris and become a prominent (anti-Brissotin) Jacobin, allied also to Hébert. The Belgian *commissaires* were the first to warn the Paris Convention of Dumouriez's growing exasperation, repudiation of republicanism, and pending treason. Fed up with republicanism, the general defected, taking six or seven hundred men and officers with him on 5 April 1793, treachery which in the Montagne's hands turned into a most effective tool for influencing French public opinion against the Brissotins who had supported him.

It became a major prong of Robespierre's anti-Brissotin propaganda to accuse the Brissotin faction and the Venezuelan revolutionary, General Francisco de Miranda, as well as Dumouriez, of having deliberately sought to alienate the Belgian people against "our revolution" as part of their "project to prevent the reunion of Belgium with France."[126] Brissot, generally opposed to territorial annexations, had been heard to say that the French should be happy the Belgians were not more pro-French since that would make it easier for France to make peace with the European powers.[127] The three Convention *commissaires* in Belgium, Proly, Dubuisson, and the Jewish republican, Pereyre, soon found themselves accused of complicity in Dumouriez's actual (and Miranda's alleged) treason and, at the same time, bizarrely, of being *ultra-révolutionnaires* conspiring to split the French Convention by promoting democratic ideas too energetically, to crush the Republic between the opposed forces of *modérantisme* and atheistic extremism. Arrested and imprisoned by the Montagnard regime, along with Bassenge, they were publicly vilified as embodying the double threat of the *citra* and *ultra*, of conspiring to thwart France's honest, ordinary folk supposedly championing Robespierre and the Montagne.[128] Ordinary folk are not atheists, Robespierre reminded the Convention, "l'athéisme est aristocratique."[129]

Descended from an Antwerp financial dynasty of Italian origin and rumored to be an illegitimate son of the former Austrian chancellor, Kaunitz, Proly, like Cloots, ranked in the Holy Roman Empire as a "baron." He had drawn many leading Belgian and Dutch democrats into his "cosmopolitan," fiercely anti-Catholic circle, a group loathed by Robespierre, and some sections of the Montagne. His Paris journal, *Le Cosmopolite*, urged peace with Austria and rejected Cloots's revolutionary universalism which he considered too unitary and authoritarian. In line with opinion in Belgium (albeit not all Liégeois opinion), Proly judged the plans for Belgium's annexation to the French Republic a disastrous and reprehensible misconception.[130] In Paris, he figured prominently in attempts to form a central committee of *sociétés*

[126] Robespierre, *Lettres*, 1st series, no. 10, pp. 502–3.
[127] Robespierre, Lettres, 1st series, no. 10, p. 514.
[128] Desmoulins, *Vieux Cordelier*, 89, 115; Hampson, *Life and Opinions*, 221, 234–6, 243, 245.
[129] Dingli, *Robespierre*, 465; Leuwers, *Robespierre*, 307.
[130] Mortier, *Anarcharsis Cloots*, 429; Israel, *Revolutionary Ideas*, 551.

populaires as a democratic pressure-group to counter the intolerant authoritarianism of the Montagne. With the Montagnard victory in June 1793, the championing of democratic principles, freedom of speech and expression, a free press, free theater, and radical Enlightenment values was ruthlessly suppressed. Expelled from the Jacobins for opposing Robespierre and the Montagne, and accused of being an Austrian agent, Proly was declared a treacherous agitator sowing disarray in Jacobin ranks.[131] Tried and condemned in Paris with Hébert and *Hébertistes*, he went to the guillotine together with Dubuisson on 5 Germinal Year II (24 March 1794), a few weeks before his reputed father died in Austria (June 1794).[132]

The Terror temporarily suppressed but did not entirely eradicate the democratic Belgian revolution and the Radical Enlightenment tendency that it spawned. Three months after Proly's execution, shortly before Robespierre's downfall, the French revolutionary forces, on 8 June 1794, won their greatest victory on the Low Countries border, defeating 80,000 Austrian, Dutch, Hanoverian, and British troops at Fleurus, near Charleroi. Over the next six months the French revolutionary army little by little reconquered the Austrian Netherlands. The "revolution" of the nobles, magistrates, and notables in the southern Netherlands of 1789–90, derided by Dutch Patriot exiles like Paape and Vreede, and scorned by the *Vonckiste* element, was no more. Now transmogrified into the Belgian "Jacobins," the latter came to power in Belgium as the French recovered their grip on the country. But mainstream Belgian sentiment refused to accept this outcome, remaining unbendingly loyal to a system, as Lafayette contemptuously expressed it, "essentiellement ecclésiastique et nobiliaire."[133]

As the *Vonckistes* and Jacobins returned, Van der Noot, van Eupen, and the spokesmen of the aristocratic revolution of 1789–90 fled. Ensconced abroad they heard the reports that at home they had been publicly condemned and burnt in effigy.[134] The Belgian provinces and the prince-bishopric were formally incorporated into the French Republic in October 1795. More importantly for Belgium's future role in the Enlightenment, the church was systematically striped of all control and influence over secondary schools and universities, many of the clergy being compelled to leave. From 1795, the French republican revolutionary government in Paris assumed undisputed mastery over the country's educational and publishing apparatus, theaters, museums, and local societies, an ascendancy lasting down to the advent of Napoleon's dictatorship, in 1802. But still the people remained solidly opposed.

[131] Dingli, *Robespierre*, 466–7.
[132] Hampson, *Life and Opinions*, 201–2, 211, 235, 238.
[133] Lafayette, *Mémoires* iii. 13.
[134] Deseure, "Ouvrez l'histoire," 32–3.

19

Enlightening against Robespierre (and Napoleon)

The écoles centrales *(1792–1804)*

19.1. CONDORCET AND THE RADICAL ENLIGHTENMENT'S CULMINATING PROJECT

As rivalry between Brissotins and the Montagne intensified during 1792, with mounting agitation in the Jacobins and Cordeliers in Paris, and political clubs across France, the struggle became a generalized ideological conflict penetrating every sphere. Beside meetings and speeches, politics and journalism, ideological war also engulfed education, theatre, social theory, and the arts.[1] Long-delayed proposals for far-reaching education reform, originally drafted by Mirabeau, were revived following the setting up of the National Assembly's *Comité d'instruction publique* on 14 December 1791. The concept of free, secularized, compulsory education for all, on a common basis, became the central doctrine of detailed plans forged by Condorcet conferring with Chamfort, Garat, Cabanis, and Talleyrand.

During the second half of 1793, and first half of 1794, Montagnard leaders, anxious to reverse Condorcet's policies and erase everything *antipopulaire* from the Revolution, and reorganize "public instruction" and education policy accordingly, ushered in an era of drastically curtailed intellectual activity and criticism, causing, among other consequences, a precipitous fall in the level of publications appearing per year in France, reducing the flows of newspapers, periodicals, scholarly works, and scientific publications alike to a mere fraction of the pre-1793 levels of the early Revolution. Condorcet's and the *Comité*'s principle that primary education should be compulsory and free—in his scheme from the age of 6 onwards—and that "educational inequality was one of the main sources of despotism," was retained however,[2] albeit the Montagnard conception of free and compulsory universal primary education diverged markedly from Condorcet's. The Montagnard approach was less concerned

[1] Israel, *Revolutionary Ideas*, 278–315.

[2] Baczko, *Éducation pour la démocratie*, 219, 304; Israel, "Natural Virtue," 10–11.

with book learning and the sciences, the heart of Condorcet's conception, than with producing a disciplined new people nurtured by Nature, geared for uniformity, conformity, and austerity. Beyond children learning to read, write, and count, education policy veered drastically away from Condorcet's turning out knowledgeable, independently-thinking individuals, toward instilling "virtue" in Rousseau's sense, a steely chauvinist, authoritarian Spartan outlook.[3] The goals had changed, but lack of resources and time meant that, during 1793–4, the French National Convention were hardly more successful in implementing the gigantic undertaking of providing elementary schooling for all than the Brissotin regime earlier.

At the secondary and higher levels, meanwhile, education during 1793–4 was dramatically cut back. The royal and ecclesiastical colleges of France, proclaimed a sweeping decree issued by the National Convention on 15 September 1793, had, for centuries, been nothing but "asyles de l'ignorance privilegiée" [asylums of ignorance and privilege],[4] as Joseph Lakanal, invoking Montaigne and Rousseau, called them. All twenty-two universities then existing in France (to which were added, from 1794–5, those in Belgium), including most medical, law, and arts faculties, were formally suppressed on the ground they were mired in the past, irredeemably monarchical, ecclesiastical, aristocratic.[5] Within days of the September 1793 edict, the University of Paris's thirty-eight separate colleges, which in 1789 had together accommodated around 1,500 students and hundreds of professors, clergy, and other teachers, were closed, locked, and bolted by revolutionary committees and the police.[6] In the provinces, closure was less abrupt and more sporadic. Several ancient universities clung to a precarious existence through the Terror into the post-Thermidor era, including Douai, which in 1789 had been second largest in France in student numbers. Also a famous bastion of Catholic zeal and orthodoxy, it closed officially only in 1795 before reopening in 1808.

Dissolving the entire French university system, the 1793 edict, originally closely linked to the de-Christianization campaign, was comprehensively implemented over time. From late 1794, following Robespierre's downfall, suppressing the *ancien régime*'s network of universities to eradicate pre-revolutionary educational forms and practices, and curtail the old religion's educational impact, continued under the post-Thermidor neo-Brissotin regime, but now with very different goals in view than during the Terror, and in a very different spirit. For the Brissotin legislators who resumed their seats in the National Convention in December 1794, the central question of the Revolution now was how to ensure the legislature conceived as the "sovereign will" of the people truly ruled in place of the recent "démagogie sanguinière" [bloody demagogy], as Marie-Joseph Chénier called it;[7] how could France's legislature permanently guarantee there would not be another systematic assault on

[3] Israel, "Natural Virtue," 14–15. [4] Lakanal, *Rapport* (23 Ventôse An III), 4.

[5] Verger, *Histoire*, 257; Doyle, *Oxford History*, 399, 408; Kennedy, *Cultural History*, 159, 376.

[6] Garrioch, *Making of Revolutionary Paris*, 22, 104; Kennedy, *Cultural History*, 159.

[7] BL F 1259. 60/1: Marie-Joseph Chénier, "Discours" (18 Ventôse Year III), 2.

freedom of the press, expression, and to philosophize, savage culling of the arts, science, and scholarship?

For radical enlighteners, the antidote to Montagnard tyranny, repression, and *vandalisme* was clear, indeed could not have been more obvious—enlighten society to a higher level. By late 1794, the overriding general political question of the day, how to salvage the Revolution from the ruinous consequences of Robespierre, was directly linked to the chaotic vacuum created by the vast upheaval in education. Montagnard blighting of the schools and suppression of France's *ancien régime* universities and colleges had marked the onset of a profound crisis in French education at all levels, a crisis now at the heart of the post-1794 Revolution and the European later Enlightenment as such: it was a matter of urgency that the Revolution should regenerate primary and secondary education, restore higher education and the specialized sciences, and reorientate "public instruction," reviving lectures, libraries, and museums, outside the schools. For it was not just education and schools but the nation's attitudes and general culture that needed reforming fundamentally from bottom up and at top speed. The original overriding objective—how to extricate society from the monarchical-aristocratic past, buttressed by ecclesiastical authority—remained, but alongside it now loomed a no less crucial priority: how to ensure the catastrophe of *robespierriste* anti-intellectualism never recurred,[8] guarantee France never again succumbed to a generalized campaign against her *gens de lettres*, scholarship, and the sciences, never again yielded to *robespierriste* repression, intolerance, and Terror.

Thermidor inaugurated a renewed revolutionary Enlightenment preoccupation with education, characterized by a crucial shift of emphasis: the principle of free universal and compulsory primary education slid, almost without discussion, to the sidelines,[9] as the focus shifted emphatically to secondary and higher education. Over the winter of 1794–5 and during the spring of 1795, the newly purged and reorientated Revolution, having broken the Montagne and ejected the worst "monsters," placed the National Convention's key committees, including the "committeee of public instruction," in the hands of Lakanal, Chénier, Destutt de Tracy, Grégoire, Sieyès, Roederer, Daunou, and also Garat (who had helped Condorcet go into hiding when outlawed in 1793), all veteran radical enlighteners and anti-*robespierristes*, several of whom had been imprisoned, or in hiding, during the Terror. This was ground from which it was hoped the authentic "veritable" French Revolution of 1789–93 could revive and the Enlightenment achieve its culmination.

Post-Thermidor revolutionary education, then, was part of a wider political and cultural drive to liquidate Montagnard thinking, attitudes, and cultural practices and redirect the energy the Montagne vested in the nation's political clubs into more constructive pursuits reflecting authentic Enlightenment desiderata without blocking genuine political debate and criticism. A notable aspect of this throughout the later

[8] Baczko, *Éducation pour la démocratie*, 25–6.
[9] Baczko, *Éducation pour la démocratie*, 15–16, 34–8, 178, 181, 218, 500.

1790s was hence the question how to reconstitute France's societies, clubs, and associations. The Jacobin clubs themselves were shut by the Convention, in November 1794. But under France's new constitution of August 1795, political clubs, associations, and gatherings deemed "contraire à l'ordre public" by the government were, in theory, banned and this became a considerable problem.[10] In principle, the five-man *Directoire*, heading the Republic in the late 1790s, was required under the new constitution to divide gatherings into two different categories, on the one hand encouraging enlightened societies, salons and learned meetings, while, on the other, curtailing political *sociétés populaires* of the kind that had undermined the Republic in 1792–3. Since closing all the political clubs in a nation accustomed to such gatherings was widely considered an affront to liberty, the policy, at times imposed too rigidly, resulted at other points in an easing that encouraged their resurgence in changed and sometimes clandestine form, rendering the entire problem of associations and gatherings unresolved.

The goal of the *Idéologues*, the intellectuals surrounding the *Directoire*, was to steer society's collective cultural energies away from political conspiracy and opposition into what were considered more constructive, less menacing channels. In his leaflet *Des Sociétés particulières telles que clubs, réunions, etc.* (Paris, 1794), republished in Year VII (1799), Roederer affirmed as a basic principle of the post-1794 French Republic that free political debate should be confined to official institutions, public halls of deliberation, meeting-places, and the press, while in society "il ne peut exister de sociétés particulières que pour deux avantages inséparables l'un d'autre, celui d'acquérir l'instruction au sein de l'amitié, celui de goûter l'amitié au sein de l'instruction" [there can exist no private associations except where dedicated to two benefits inseparable from each other—acquiring education in the bosom of friendship, and enjoying friendship in the bosom of education].[11] Roederer's contention, vehemently opposed by the remaining Jacobins,[12] was that all criticism, debate, and political functions hosted by the Jacobin and other clubs of 1792–4 should properly either be a "public function" belonging to the sphere of established assemblies, official committees, and magistrates, or an exercise of "individual rights."

Between duly constituted official bodies and individual citizens expressing their own views, held Roederer, there should be no secondary bodies or "corporations" wielding political influence and exerting pressure; for such bodies inevitably work against liberty and there were no grounds for claiming clubs are needed to represent or protect individuals or reform established institutions. The reform-minded should work through the established public channels. Club votes and resolutions should be prohibited together with collective political correspondence and manifestos, to prevent perversion of revolutionary vigilance and surveillance, false "exposure," and denunciation of alleged "counter-revolutionaries" generating flows of club petitions.

10 Roederer, *Des sociétés particulières*, 4.
11 Roederer, *Des sociétés particulières*, 8; Margerison, *P. L. Roederer: Political Thought*, 122, 138, 146.
12 Wolloch, *Jacobin Legacy*, 118–19.

For Jacobin club culture twists patriotism into a fabricated collective identity projected at gatherings, banquets, and celebrations that is easily manipulated by ambitious demagogues. Claiming the right to exclude people, denounce public officials, and undertake "collective correspondence" abroad should be banned by a free republic to prevent clubs becoming tools of intimidation and political pressure. But Roederer was pushing his campaign too far, objected some. Political societies, argued Cabanis, had their uses as well as dangers: it would be better simply to limit their size and bring them under better judicial and police surveillance.[13] He and his fellow "véritables républicains" were right to go all out to emasculate *robespierrisme*—the populist threat, the menace of a Jacobin resurgence of the *populaire* must be effectively countered. But it could be no part of a true republicanism to become politically vindictive or suppress populist opponents. An excessive repressive sweep against the Robespierre tyranny's supporters could only further divide society, extend mutual hatred, and aid France's enemies.[14]

But through the later 1790s rousing toasts at club gatherings were often subversive and pro-Jacobin in tone. Toasts "to the martyrs of liberty and victims of reaction" could well mean not victims of the Terror and Catholic counter-revolutionary reaction but *sans-culottes* killed, wounded, or persecuted during the anti-legislature mass risings in Paris of 12 Germinal and 1 to 4 Prairial (1 April and 20–23 May) 1795, the tumultuous *journées* of Prairial Year III, or, later, between February and May 1797. They could refer to co-defendants at the public trials of Babeuf and his fellow conspirators. Where "Vive les pierrons" unambiguously meant yelling support for Robespierre's partisans, toasts to "republicans who have remained inviolably committed to the principles of liberty and equality" carried a deeply and worryingly ambiguous resonance.[15] The *Directoire*'s moderation, interpreted by Marxist and Marxisant historians as stemming from the "parochial middle-class spirit of 1791," and Thermidor created a space for revived clubs up to a point, as also for a press supportive of the clubs and sympathetic to popular grievances while upholding the constitution and forbidding the extremes of organized subversion through clubs. The *Directoire* sought a middle course, oscillating rather than consistently aiming between permitting political clubs to function as they had before June 1793 and banning them outright. Keeping them under police surveillance and trying to closely regulate them, they also sporadically shut them down whenever they were found to be too vocal or menacing.

Meanwhile, Enlightenment societies and gatherings, "societies of friendship and education," all neo-Brissotin circles agreed, should proliferate and be encouraged throughout France. The *Directoire*'s strategy produced a calculated policy of sapping the political clubs and undermining *sans-culottisme* by promoting "public education" along with school and higher education reform as the highest priority of the Republic.

[13] BL f 358/13, "Opinion de Cabanis," undated [mid-1790s], 13–15.
[14] BL f 358/13, "Opinion de Cabanis," undated [mid-1790s], 7–8.
[15] Wolloch, *Jacobin Legacy*, 128–9.

Although the *Directoire*, throughout the fraught years 1795–9, remained always a compromise between rival factions competing for power, several of the directors were strongly and publicly attached to Radical Enlightenment principles. Gathering around them at the Palais du Luxembourg and other official locations, leading writers, scholars, and scientists whom the Montagne had repudiated and despised, directors such as Louis-Marie de La Revellière-Lépeaux (1753–1824) and Nicolas Louis François de Neufchâteau (1750–1828), holding resolutely republican, anti-Catholic, and meritocratic egalitarian views, expended much effort in reconnecting the revolutionary government to the world of intellectual endeavor and Enlightenment.

Restoring liberty of expression and press was central both to the new political culture of 1795–1800 and the government's ambitious education policy.[16] The *Directoire*, spurred by Convention delegate Joseph Lakanal (1762–1845), a former philosophy professor from Moulins, among the most energetic of the Republic's education and science reformers, along with Chénier, Daunou, Roederer, and Grégoire, strove to reconstitute the Revolution as the voice of Enlightenment and meritocracy rather than the *populaire*, in a more systematic, explicit fashion than envisaged by Condorcet and the Brissotins of 1791–3. To them, decisively ending the Terror, and emasculating the apparatus of tyranny mattered more than extending and secularizing primary education in the way pre-Robespierre Brissotins had attempted.[17] During the crucial transition Year III (1794–5), the shift from *robespierriste* tyranny to restored revolutionary integrity, Dominique Joseph Garat (1748–1833), a regular member of the Diderot–d'Holbach circle in the 1770s and close to Condorcet who, in October 1792, Brissot had selected as justice minister, together with Pierre-Louis Ginguené (1748–1816), former editor of *La Feuille villageoise*, a prominent literary personality incarcerated during the Terror, led the new legislature's committee for *l'instruction publique*.

Liberty is secured by the "powerful energy of the people" through revolution, Chénier urged the Convention, in his report of 23 December 1794 (1 Nivose Year III), speaking for the *Comité d'Instruction publique*. But liberty cannot be secured, consolidated, and stabilized, painful experience proved, without wise laws and without inculcating the right attitudes into society by eradicating "prejudices" from the popular mind. The greatest peril society faces comes from "idées mystiques" like those precipitating whole nations into disastrous civil war during the Wars of Religion, devastating strife fought for theology "that no one understands." But eradicating theological notions is insufficient to make a society based on reason: vital too is the elimination of ideas and "institutions tyranniques et antisociales." The Republic must replace deeply-rooted authoritarian populist beliefs with *philosophique* secularized debate and attitudes without which liberty cannot survive.[18] Government's number one responsibility is thus to follow *la philosophie*'s commands and assail the "dogmas, mysteries and, miracles" blocking its path, to "follow nature," as Chénier expressed it,

[16] Margairaz, *François de Neuchâtel*, 364.
[17] Margairaz, *François de Neuchâtel*, 375.
[18] Chénier, *Rapport* (1 Nivose, An III), 1–2.

echoing d'Holbach, Condorcet, and Volney, in disavowing every attempt to change its "immutable laws, or interrupt their eternal course," via unremitting assault on ordinary, traditional, and popular as well as religious beliefs. This must be done, though, while scrupulously maintaining freedom of expression and personal liberty, always bearing in mind that eradication of incorrect attitudes and ideas is unattainable through repression and violence in the manner of the Montagne: "la verité ne doit pas avoir des inquisiteurs, comme l'imposture" [truth should not have inquisitors, as imposture does].[19]

By early 1795, Condorcet's ideas were everywhere back in the ascendant.[20] Condorcet's philosophy of education, elaborated during 1791–2, exerted a profound impact on the late French Enlightenment, and, through figures like the Cantabrian reformer, Manuel José de Narganes (1772–1823), a keen disciple of Condorcet's who taught Spanish literature in a French border college, at Sorèze in the department of Tarn in the years 1801–8, came to exert a profound impact too on the Spanish late Enlightenment.[21] Narganes emerged in 1808 as a leading education reformer in Napoleonist Spain. If Mirabeau had been the first revolutionary leader to project a "national" structure of education directed by society and the revolutionary state, one aimed not least at eradicating "despotism," by 1792 and the end of the monarchy, the entire revolutionary leadership concurred that "la morale populaire" required urgent reform. Following Thermidor, Chénier and the neo-Brissotins resurrected Condorcet's campaign for a genuinely enlightened "public instruction" countering the Montagne's aggressive, intolerant populism in the schools and colleges, and at every level, from the theater to the decadal assemblies.

"Decadal assemblies," held throughout France, were the post-1793 Revolution's substitute for the old weekly sermon. The new revolutionary calendar adopted in October 1793 replaced the traditional "week" with ten-day "weeks" or *décades*, with each of the year's new months consisting uniformly of thirty days evenly split into three new ten-day "weeks." Sunday observance was discarded along with the old Holy Days and festivals, but replaced by a new secularized day of rest (*décadi*) and national festivals. Where, however, the Montagne used the public gatherings on the *décadi* and festivals to harangue the public with political propaganda,[22] the committee, explained Chénier, in another December 1794 report to the Convention, wanted the "fêtes décadaires" replacing the Christian Sunday to provide a mix of entertainment and improved public instruction, constructively drawing in and elevating the community. Tenth-day festivities should be organized throughout France by the local communes, in the open whenever the weather permitted, with the elderly prominently seated, and commence with a "moral" harangue, called "l'instruction," followed by brief summaries of the legislature's decrees of the past ten days, given by a local official or, in big cities like Paris, where each section had its own local fête, by the "president" of each

[19] Chénier, *Rapport* (1 Nivose, An III), 2. [20] Gros, *Lakanal*, 55–6.
[21] Baczko, *Éducation pour la démocratie*, 177–83; Ruiz Berrio, "Introdución," 16, 19–20.
[22] Israel, *Revolutionary Ideas*, 496–7.

section, after which everyone would join in singing Convention-approved "patriotic anthems" (several composed by Chénier). The tenth-day public gatherings would end with performing scenes "adapted to republican morality," dancing, and general jollification.[23]

From late 1794, leading roles in organizing the new general educational, cultural, and museum system were assigned Chénier, Destutt, Daunou, and above all Lakanal. The *comité*'s key report to the Convention about how it envisaged reforming the Republic's schools, of 23 Ventôse Year III (13 March 1795), was delivered by Lakanal, who, having sat with the Montagne and participated in administering that regime's cultural policies during the Terror, had discreetly tried to shield as much French science as he could. Aided by Louis Daubenton (1716–1800), Buffon's elderly former assistant at the old Paris Jardin du Roi, it was Lakanal, for instance, who drew up the 10 June 1793 statute reorganizing the former Jardin du Roi (today the Jardin des Plantes), where Buffon had been director from 1739 to 1788, conserving it as a key center for research. Lakanal greatly contributed to French science's impressive rebound from Thermidor onwards. Montagnard despotism, they all agreed, demonstrated how extremely dangerous for society it is to leave the illiterate and semi-literate multitude sunk in the "debasement of ignorance and brutal passions" in which they had been immersed by crown and church over many centuries. Destutt wholeheartedly endorsed his friend Volney's dictum: "ignorance is the real Original Sin;"[24] ignorance they considered foundational to a traditional system sanctioned by priestly sway that had turned theology into a mystery "science" based on fear and superstition instead of "observation," mystification that "oppresses and stifles all other" knowledge.[25]

Although he did help shape the new history courses from a distance, Volney had less impact on the 1794–6 arrangements and subsequent developments than other leading *Idéologues*, having left for a long stay in the United States in January 1795, hoping to recover from his feelings of shock and disgust at the persecution perpetrated by Robespierre and the Montagne as well as improve ties between French neo-Brissotin and American democratizing republicanism and strengthen the Republic's links with Jefferson and the Philadelphia academy.[26] Destutt de Tracy had been formed intellectually in the mid and late 1780s, partly in Sophie de Condorcet's salon where he rubbed shoulders with Cabanis, Garat, Lalande, Ginguené, Lafayette, and also Jefferson as well as Volney, and through the later 1790s was a regular among the renewed second Auteuil circle spearheading the French radical intellectual tendency. Only by redeeming society from its "ignorance" could the Republic be rescued, and the new order rendered stable and secure.[27] What Robespierre and the Terror signified for Lakanal, Chénier, Sieyès, and Daunou, as for Destutt, Volney, Cabanis,

[23] Chénier, *Rapport* (1 Nivose, An III), 6.
[24] Volney, *Abridgement*, 6.
[25] Destutt de Tracy, *Analyse raisonée*, pp. xxv–xxvi, xxx.
[26] Renauld, *Antoine Destutt de Tracy*, 118; Cook, "Between the Old World and the New," 89, 93.
[27] Harris, *Antoine Destutt de Tracy*, 235–6; Renauld, *Antoine Destutt de Tracy*, 37–40, 46–50.

and the second Auteuil circle, and, through them, several of the directors, was that the authentic democratic republic is impossible without enlightening the mass of society first, as their mentor Condorcet proclaimed, but that, equally, enlightening the mass of society is impossible without radically enlightening those in positions of power, the elites, first of all.

Lakanal presented a strategy that was subsequently to prove of great importance in the history of the post-Thermidor Revolution and later Enlightenment. Although universal primary secular education remained the ultimate first priority, in theory, for the present, higher and secondary education must have priority; every effort to revive it and extend it on a fundamentally remodeled republican basis was required. The illiterate mass could only be raised up by first creating an enlightened teaching and professional elite. Although it was not until his *Observations sur le système actuel d'instruction publique* (1801) that Destutt formally endorsed and expanded on the distinction between two separate classes in society defined by educational background, his two-class society placing the "classe savante" in the higher professions and administration above the majority, or the "classe ouvrière," this, in principle, was the schema underpinning the *Directoire*'s education policy and plans for science and the *écoles centrales* from the outset.

Scholarship and the sciences were henceforth to possess a preferential position in the nation's education policy and general culture. Among institutions assigned an expanded teaching and research as well as public role was Lakanal's reorganized Jardin des Plantes with its collections and gardens open to the public, now called the Musée Nationale d'histoire naturelle. Its leading lights included the taxonomist and radical enlightener who finally overthrew the Early Enlightenment biology categories of Linnaeus, Réaumur, and Bonnet, one of the great pioneers of evolution theory, Jean-Baptiste Lamarck (1744–1829). Having originally made his name, in the late 1770s, not as an exponent of *transformisme* or primitive evolution theory but as a botanical taxonomist, Lamarck, a former army officer retired early due to an accident, passionately interested in plants and their environments, and allied to Buffon, had long openly challenged Linnaeus' categorization, insisting on the need for a better framework.[28] During the early Revolution, he had still followed Linnaeus and Réaumur as regards "immutability of species,"[29] like Voltaire an "essentialist" convinced species are unchanging. But after Robespierre's downfall, in September 1794, he presented the Committee of Public Instruction with his revolutionary reconceptualization of biology, fiercely criticizing Linnaeus' system for its artificiality and proposing to undertake a complete new *Système de la nature* in eight volumes, a comprehensive total revision of natural history taxonomy.[30] Lamarck never wrote those volumes, but by the late 1790s he had developed a new philosophy of nature built around his revolutionary new evolution theory, a considerable advance on the evolutionist conjectures of de Maillet, Diderot, and d'Holbach. Having abandoned "essentialism"

[28] Cuvier, *Biographical Memoir*, 5–6, 8; Burkhardt, "Lamarck, Evolution," 279–80.

[29] Burkhardt, "Lamarck, Evolution," 279.

[30] Barsanti, "Lamarck, Taxonomy," 120–1.

after researching into fossils of mollusks which proved to him that transmutation of species does indeed occur over time, by 1799 he envisaged adaptations to creatures' organs originating in both inner capacity to adapt "through power of life" and external pressures from conditions and environment, a simultaneous internal and external dynamic causing mutations. When effectively adapted to circumstances, he conjectured, such mutations could then be passed on.[31]

On 11 May 1800 (21 Floréal, Year VIII), at the Musée Nationale d'histoire naturelle, Lamarck delivered the lecture where he first expounded his complete theory of evolution, a concept chiefly differing from Darwin's later theory of natural selection in identifying natural inheritance of acquired characteristics during the lives of individual animals as the driving motor. It was not yet Darwin's evolution, but Lamarck's evolution did mark a milestone in the history of the life sciences. Changing needs, he admonished his fascinated audiences, caused giraffes to stretch their necks, a successful strategy that rendered the giraffe's long neck hereditary. He publicly clashed with Georges Cuvier (1769–1832), another still more virtuoso researcher in fossils and skeletons, but a defender of divine "creation" using a sophisticated scientific defense admitting extinction of species and new phases of creation over time attuned to different climatic and geological phases. Cuvier ridiculed Lamarck's thesis as one whereby "pikes by dint of happening upon dry land changed into ducks,"[32] scorning what he considered Lamarck's spurious conjectures in geology and chemistry. Once Lamarck's principles are "admitted, it will be easily perceived that nothing is wanting but time and circumstances to enable a monad or a polypus gradually and indifferently to transform themselves into a frog, a stork, or an elephant."[33]

Government support for scientific research, and projecting science to the public, fueling national debates, was crucial to the *Idéologue* recipe for definitively crushing theology and *robespierrisme* through renewed Enlightenment, as was reforming primary education. But most essential of all was the reform of secondary education. In reports on the Republic's schools, Lakanal reaffirmed that without *lumières* [enlightenment] "man is always the victim of imposture." Every child in France must receive elementary education and the new *écoles primaires* he and his colleagues sought to make general across France must be compulsory, free, and at public expense. Though no friend of the *ancien régime* education system, Lakanal had for years deplored the systematic wrecking, depletion, and total disarray of France's primary school system. A national system of secular primary schools, he reiterated time and again, is indispensable if mankind is to be redeemed from populism and *l'imposture*.[34] The cost of providing one school for roughly every thousand inhabitants, based on the calculation that a France of 26 million

[31] Kennedy, *Cultural History*, 64, 70; Wulf, *Invention of Nature*, 272–3; Cohen, *Science, Libertinage*, 365.
[32] Burkhardt, "Lamarck, Evolution", 295–6.
[33] Gillispie, *Science and Polity*, 161.
[34] Lakanal, *Rapport* (23 Ventôse An III), 1.

inhabitants required around 26,000 primary schools, he estimated would not in reality be as prohibitively expensive as his anti-Brissotin opponents alleged.[35]

But the new chief priority, averred Lakanal, Destutt, and Cabanis, along with Garat, Lalande, Volney, Chénier, Roederer, Daunou, and the other French late Enlightenment leaders of the counter-offensive against *robespierrisme*, royalism, and religious authority, was to remove the Montagne's focus from primary education for now and fundamentally reconstitute secondary education first. The Republic must still edge toward Condorcet's free universal primary education for all to elevate the common people, but for the moment the primary emphasis must be on forming a secularized republican secondary education capable of churning out suitably enlightened teachers, professionals, and leaders.[36] To effectively eradicate Robespierre's *tout populaire* and *anti-philosophisme*, a philosophy and science nullifying Montagnard thinking, Christianity, and royalism all together was the only way. The Republic's new cult of the sciences and arts allied to free speech, expression, and criticism would provide the basic inspiration and framework for the new system of secondary education. Accordingly, the proposed new secondary colleges, or *écoles centrales*, would be tied to the wider public education drive. On appointed days in the year, non-pupils living nearby, and the local adult public interested in the sciences, would attend "cours publics," lectures and demonstrations offered by the schools, designed to expand the public's understanding of natural science, physics, and chemistry.

Destutt, while retaining core elements of Condorcet's general plan for public education of January 1792, had long pondered a comprehensive system of large secondary colleges, each in a principal town of every department, around one hundred or so *écoles centrales* in all. By 1800, there were in fact to be nearly one hundred of these remarkable schools.[37] Destutt, Lakanal, and the others envisaged secondary education as developing in three stages: the first, teaching boys from 12 to 14, would focus on their reading and writing French, on grammar and other linguistic studies, and achieving intermediate levels of Latin and Greek. The second, for 14- to 16-year-olds, would prioritize the natural sciences, especially mathematics, physics, and chemistry; the third would prepare boys of 16 to 18 for higher education and France's "special schools" by expanding horizons by teaching history, legislation, and civic values, and what the *Idéologues* called the moral sciences, as well as continuing training in languages and the sciences but with more choice of specialization.[38] Presented to the Convention's *Comité de l'instruction publique* by Lakanal, the committee's plans for secondary education were adopted for general implementation throughout France by Convention decree of 7 Ventôse Year III (25 February 1795), precisely seven months after Robespierre's removal.

With formal separation of church and state in France proclaimed by the neo-Brissotin National Convention also in February 1795, a whole new educational and

35 Lakanal, *Rapport* (23 Ventôse An III), 1–2.
36 Renauld, *Antoine Destutt de Tracy*, 124.
37 Head, *Politics and Philosophy*, 379; Karady, "De Napoléon à Duruy," 257, 263.
38 Mérot, "Écoles centrales," 797; Renauld, *Antoine Destutt de Tracy*, 122–3.

political scenario came into being. The *Directoire* and legislature moved ahead with the scheme as finalized by the committee and its spokesman Lakanal, in a set of articles drafted in March 1795 to which Garat, Ginguené, and Cabanis also contributed and that essentially reproduced Condorcet's ideas for combining secondary with higher education, plus a few adjustments, such as conceding ground to Lakanal's plan to teach Adam Smith and assign more emphasis to commerce and agriculture.[39]

The result was comprehensive replacement of the old secondary college and university system with a new network of *écoles centrales* combining secondary and the initial stages of higher education, generalized higher education preceding specialized vocational and professional training. For the most talented and astute boys, these colleges would then be followed by attending France's now rapidly expanding system of *écoles speciales*, specialized centers heavily centered in Paris and a few large cities, providing high-level training from 18 to the early twenties in professional disciplines such as medicine, mines, law, administration, military studies, and engineering. These colleges likewise projected and re-conceptualized by the Republic in February 1795 included military colleges, the École Normale and its branches for training the new elite of *professeurs* who were to teach in the new secondary schools, and the École de Services Publics (later the École Polytechnique for administration), several Écoles de Mines, France's now three Écoles de Medicine established in December 1794 at Paris, Strasbourg, and Montepellier using facilities of the former university medical faculties, and, finally, the Musée d'Histoire Naturelle, Paris Conservatoire des Arts et Métiers, the Observatoire, and the Conservatoire de Musique.[40]

Although France's former colleges and universities had all been suppressed, their locations, buildings, libraries, and endowments from aristocrats, ecclesiastics, and kings remained in abeyance conveniently at hand so that, supposedly, an entire new system of secondary schooling could be furnished not just without unmanageable expense, as with the projected primary schools intended for everyone, but, some optimistically imagined, no extra expense whatever.[41] Every department of France (now including Belgium) was directed to establish an endowed, properly equipped *école centrale* teaching the full stipulated range of languages, sciences, and other disciplines of a general character needed to form the civic outlook of boys prior to specialized training in administration, medicine, engineering, law, military technology, oriental studies, and other fields successful graduates moved on to. While it is true this entire proposed intermediate schooling for youths between 12 and 18 was intended chiefly for sons of officials, professionals, academics, and teachers, a quarter or so of the annual intake to the *écoles centrales*, stipulated the new law, must consist of talented boys from poor rural and artisan families provided with scholarships at public expense so as to provide opportunity more widely. Exclusion of boys from peasant or laboring class backgrounds from the *écoles centrales* was thus avoided to an

[39] Isaac and Sorgeloos, *L'École centrale du département de Jemappes*, 47–8; Staum, *Cabanis*, 164.

[40] Verger, *Histoire*, 257, 263; Grab, *Napoleon and the Transformation of Europe*, 56–7.

[41] Lakanal, *Rapport* (23 Ventôse An III), 4–7.

extent. But since allocation of free entrance places without payment of fees where "indigence" justified this was to account for no more than one quarter of the places at the colleges, pupils from the laboring classes, especially from peasant rural backgrounds, always remained a small minority.[42] Students from big-city backgrounds and professional families were undoubtedly specially favored. At the *école centrale* of the department of the Bas-Rhin, at Strasbourg, for instance, two-thirds of the gradually increasing, but usually 150 to 200 pupils, enrolled between 1796 and 1802 hailed from the departmental capital Strasbourg.[43]

Under the *comité*'s original plan, finalized in March 1795, each *école centrale* was required to teach for eight days out of every *décade*. New subjects like hygiene, gynecology, commerce, agriculture, and the economic theories of Adam Smith were for the first time declared obligatory, integral to the curriculum. Equally obligatory, no religion was to be taught. Each *école centrale* was required to maintain fourteen professorships—in mathematics, physics (with chemistry), languages, "arts et métiers" (arts and crafts), moral sciences, and also "history," a discipline radically distinct from traditional historiography following the approach inspired by Condorcet and Volney termed by Lakanal "histoire philosophique des peuples"—in effect the style of social studies and politics pioneered by Diderot and Raynal. Only "historical studies" useful for civic, political, and moral enlightenment and improvement, contended Volney, the key influence here—that is, "history" abstracting from the political and moral experiences of particular countries and peoples, enabling universal conclusions to be drawn, a history relevant to all humanity—was wanted.[44]

Holders of the fourteen chairs, to be called *professeurs* or *instituteurs*, were supposed to be academically outstanding personages chosen in each department by the local "jury central d'instruction publique" which consisted of three overseers entrusted with oversight over the functioning of the schools and their chairs. These unelected juries, appointed by the Convention's education committee, were the sole bodies that could, where appropriate, remove and replace professors found wanting.[45] Each "professor" had a defined extra-mural public function as well as a teaching role. Each of the roughly one hundred *écoles centrales* of revolutionary France was obliged also to possess a "bibliothèque publique" and place it at the disposal not just of the school's pupils but equally the adult inhabitants of the entire department; in addition, again for the general benefit as well as teaching, each was required to establish a botanical garden, cabinet for physics, facilities for chemistry demonstrations, and "machines et modèles" for the arts and crafts.[46]

[42] BL R 235/27, *Opinion de Du Vidal* (8 Floreal An X), 6; Mérot, "Écoles centrales," 798, 801–2.

[43] C. Simien, review of J. Buck, *L'École centrale du Bas-Rhin*, AHRF 374 (2013), 213–16.

[44] Gusdorf, *Conscience révolutionnaire*, 504–1; Guy, "L'Enseignement de l'histoire," 93; Rosso, "Volney," 346.

[45] Gros, *Lakanal*, 107; Merot, "La Fréquentation," 423.

[46] Lakanal, *Rapport* (23 Ventôse An III), 7, 9; Gros, *Lakanal*, 100–1, 107; Boulad-Ayoub, *Comités d'Instruction publique*, 57–8.

France's revolutionary new vision of a republican governing elite based on merit and solid instruction in civics and ethics, as well as history, languages, and science, under the plans of Condorcet, Destutt, Volney, Lakanal, Chénier, Cabanis, Roederer, and François de Neufchâteau, was thus most concretely embodied in the system of departmental *écoles centrales*. The system arose throughout France proper but also in conquered Belgium, Luxembourg, and, from 1798, the Rhineland, replacing hundreds of former Jesuit, Oratorian, and other colleges and universities suppressed by the French military occupation. In the Rhineland, four *écoles centrales* were established—at Mainz, Bonn, Cologne, and Trier.[47] Since the overriding aim was to combine secularism with preventing *robespierrisme* and the sway of the *populaire* ever returning, populism—the mobilized ignorance of the ordinary man—was obsessively targeted as the most dangerous foe of the Enlightenment and hence of society, more menacing even than churchmen and theology. If Robespierre could so swiftly and thoroughly stifle all enlightened values, and install a debased Rousseauism as France's political creed, every effort was needed to forge an enlightened elite sufficiently scornful of the ordinary to resist every populist pressure. The *sine qua non* for effective republicanization and democratization of France on sound principles, the same formulae and values were deemed necessary to advance world democratization and republicanization generally.

19.2. INAUGURATING THE *ÉCOLES CENTRALES*

The so-called "Loi Daunou" of 25 October 1795 (3 Brumaire Year IV), the guiding legislation of the Republic on education during the *Directoire*, was inspired by Condorcet but also departed from Condorcet's plans for education reform in several key respects. Instead of his plan to enlighten all of society by simultaneously forging a secularized primary school system teaching children the rudiments of the sciences and philosophy, Daunou, in particular and the *Idéologues* more generally, preoccupied with fighting the threat of *démocratisme rousseauien*, shifted the emphasis from primary education to the new system of secondary and higher education.[48] The *écoles centrales* under the direction of the newly-formed and *Idéologue*-dominated Paris Institut National des Sciences et Arts thus became the guiding institution at the heart of the Republic's education reforms, the means of ensuring adherence to secularism and republican values, use of prescribed textbooks, and appropriately high teaching levels on a uniform basis throughout greater France. Deemed central to the life of every department, the *écoles centrales* were not just schools, public libraries, and science demonstration centers but also regularly figured prominently in *fêtes civiques*,

[47] Guy, "L'Enseignement," 119.

[48] Baczko, *Éducation pour la démocratie*, 305–7, 500–1; Schandeler, *Interpretations de Condorcet*, 31–3, 36, 40–1.

the Revolution's civic festivals. Inauguration of the "central schools" accordingly featured large-scale public ceremonies, impressive processions though the town centers where they were established, accompanied by detachments of National Guard, with thousands of local citizens participating or looking on. All the *écoles centrales* were inaugurated with numerous officials present, in the celebratory, festive manner of the post-1794 Republic, with long and pompous speeches interspersed with bands playing patriotic marches, and speeches laced with republican and anti-ecclesiastical rhetoric.

These inauguration ceremonies presented the newly-appointed *professeurs* to the public, each in turn swearing his oath of office, promising to teach the regulatory eight days out of ten of every *décade* and uphold the highest principles of the Revolution and Republic. Inaugurating the *écoles centrales* hence has a special place in Enlightenment history, marking not just a drastic break with the *ancien régime* in terms of educational theory and assumptions but a bold new general initiative to present the Revolution as the embodiment of (radical) Enlightenment ideas staged in direct contrast and opposition to what Brissotins rejected as the criminal, barbaric "vandalism," repressiveness, denial of human rights, the unenlightened attitudes of Robespierre and the Montagne. Far from being an "almost impossible task," as one contributor to the "negative critique" mistakenly saw it,[49] distancing their democratic republican ideals from Robespierre's and the Montagne's creed was much the most convincing and effective part of the *idéologues*' political ideology. The inaugurations were staged by an elite of radical enlighteners aspiring to change the way French society thought about itself, and understood the wider world, science, and the past. It was a social and cultural phenomenon reflecting not social change, or tensions, or cultural shift, but a tenacious, far-reaching Enlightenment project. This was the message of the elaborate inauguration ceremonies which everywhere in France, Belgium, and the Rhineland shared a striking rhetorical and thematic cohesion.

At Bourges, in central France south of Paris, where Calvin had once studied and the university, founded in 1464, was closed in 1793, the *école centrale* was inaugurated on 13 June 1795 with twelve instead of ten *professeurs*, not in the former university premises familiar to Calvin, but the sober edifice of the town's early seventeenth-century Jesuit college, vacated in 1764, but still used by priests to teach Christian doctrine until 1793. The principal speech delivered reminded Bourges' inhabitants of the "cruelle experience" that had persuaded everyone that "tyranny" is the foe of enlightenment and vice versa, that tyranny relies on "ignorance" as its chief resource for holding mankind in bondage. The "revolution" of Thermidor freed all Frenchmen by casting off the false "mask of patriotism" used to trick and delude the people into slavery, reversing the "ideas so cruelly false that those vandals employed to dishonor virtue." Thermidor made possible the restoring of ideas and principles to their true meaning and significance, which the Jacobins had so basely perverted. The task now

[49] Bell, *Shadows of Revolution*, 170.

was to engrave in the hearts and minds of youth "les véritables principes de la morale républicaine, un vrai civisme" [the veritable principles of republican ethics, a true civic spirit]. What mattered now more than all else was to resume the fight against the "corruption of the partisans of the old aristocracy," the clergy and aristocrats, while with equal vigor reversing the "fureurs insensées de l'anarchique démagogie" [senseless rages of anarchic demagoguery] of Robespierre's tyranny. The essence of Robespierre's legacy was "ignorance, vandalisme et le crime."[50]

The public attending these inauguration ceremonies were fed, along with much else, a general review of human history, presented in Condorcet's terms as the progress of the human mind, "la marche de l'esprit humain," and hence enlightenment by stages. Civilization arose first in Egypt and Asiatic lands, where if one cast one's eyes today one encountered countries "once so brilliant" now sadly reduced to degradation and ruin. The Western Middle Ages were a misguided, dreary, hopeless era. In the fifteenth and sixteenth centuries, thankfully, "la lumière" [intellectual light] and science revived and moved westwards, savants escaping Constantinople's fall helping to generate the new movement that recovered the heritage of Greek and Roman antiquity and gave birth to the "science" of philosophy, that is of Galileo, Bacon, Kepler, Copernicus, and eventually Voltaire. Philosophy and science conflate in these addresses into a global force advancing on a broad front arm in arm with literature and the arts. It was not until one particular individual, Raynal, emerged among a circle "cruelly persecuted" by the *ancien régime* royal and ecclesiastical authorities that men begin to grasp the crucial interaction between the New World and Old World, the real relationship of Europe to the many colonies "Europe's ferocious brigands clapped in chains while massacring the wretched Indians." Bacon, Diderot, d'Alembert, Raynal, and Condorcet were the chief architects of this new secular vision of human history replacing the fictions and mythologies contrived by churchmen to exalt hierarchy and delude mankind.[51]

It was Raynal and his group, the inhabitants of Bourges were admonished, who first promulgated a call to liberty addressed to all the peoples of the globe. Friends of humanity had earlier shuddered at the cries of the unfortunate enslaved blacks; but only now with the Revolution and "abolition of slavery in France, and in the United States" were we on the verge of slavery's "extinction from the surface of both worlds." The American Revolution, headed by "Franklin et Vashington," was centered in "la tolérante Philadelphie" which subsequently opened its port to the vessels of all peoples, laying the foundation of modern liberty and human happiness which the French Revolution had now consolidated despite the appalling setbacks caused by the "vandals." All friends of the sciences and arts were summoned to cover their heads in mourning and figuratively throw flowers on the tombs of Condorcet, Lavoisier, Bailly, and Roucher, and festively celebrate the passing of that "fatal time," Robespierre's

[50] BL R 372/1: *Procès-verbal de l'inauguration solemnelle de l'école centrale d'instruction publique de Bourges*, 3–4.

[51] *Plan d'enseignement suivis par les professeurs*, 69.

detestable tyranny, the catastrophe resembling in the devastation it caused the relentless irruption of Huns and Goths which centuries before had likewise decimated all talent, all arts, and all virtues.[52] (Jean-Antoine Roucher (1745–94) was a poet, Voltaire disciple, translator of Adam Smith, and anti-Robespierriste revolutionary guillotined on 25 July 1794.)

The inauguration of the *école centrale* of the Aveyron department, at Rodez, north-east of Toulouse, on 29 Floréal, Year IV or 18 May 1795, equally reflected the closely-planned unity and consistency of emblems and propaganda framing these events. At the Rodez inauguration, the principal *discours* proclaimed France's new *écoles centrales* a "foyer de lumières" [foyer of enlightenment] forged to fight the "barbarie de l'ignorance" and criminal ambition driving Jacobin "vandalism." Only totally repulsing the "horde of vandals" could open the door to the "happy return of principles and resounding triumph of justice." "Cette grande révolution," that is, the post-Thermidor revival of the Brissotin faction driving enlightened principles and the education revolution, was projected as a renewal, dissemination, and social application of the sciences, philosophy, and ethics, a moral and cultural as much as political revolution elevating human life in diametrically opposite fashion to the trampling on human rights and degradation the Jacobin convulsions precipitated, driven "by the atrocities of the new Caligula [Robespierre]." Where Robespierre and his "ferocious agents" left rivers of blood and heaps of corpses, a frightful counter-enlightenment "atroce et arbitraire," overturning the authentic Revolution and its achievements, France now exulted in her new post-1794 revolution whose "empire c'est celui des lumières" [empire is that of enlightenment]. Robespierre's "immense chain of horrors" would no longer freeze men's blood with dread, having been decisively reversed by a "revolution of the human mind which has no other principle than philosophy, no other agent than thought, nor other motor than justice, or other support than the virtues." The Revolution's renewal had as its essential purpose to "rendre impossible, par la force de la raison, tout retour à les tyrannies révolutionnaires" [render impossible, by the force of reason, any return to the revolutionary tyrannies], any reversion to the "vandalism" of Robespierre and his criminal henchmen.[53]

Setting up of the *écoles centrales* required in addition a publicity drive explaining the point of the various new academic disciplines to the public; for the names and meaning of the new subjects were often unfamiliar and mystifying to parents. Indeed, the regime had to convince parents, as well as teachers, that the new pedagogic agenda was actually more relevant and useful to society than the now discarded but more familiar older disciplines. The professor teaching physics and chemistry at the Versailles *école centrale* vowed that "no part of chemistry will be neglected, the modern discoveries and the applications to be made of all of them will be expounded

[52] BL R 372/1: *Procès-verbal de l'inauguration solemnelle*, 28–9; BL R 372/9: *Inauguration de l'école centrale du département de l'Aveiron* (Rodez, 1796), 5.

[53] BL R 372/9. *Inauguration de l'école centrale du département de l'Aveiron* (Rodez, 1796), 5, 7–8.

in the greatest detail;"[54] but it was by no means entirely clear why. Children, parents discovered, were required not just to perfect their French and learn Latin, but understand the basic laws of nature and the universe governing all the movements and actualities, the rotations of stars and planets, and, following Buffon, Lamarck, and Cuvier, the basic structures of natural history and botany. Every boy was required to develop his critical judgment "contre les charlataneries de toute espèce" [against deceptive imposture of every kind], to fortify and safeguard himself against the two principal human defects obstructing republican well-being—"idolatry" and superstition. To maintain a republican form of government promoting the true interests and happiness of the people, youth must absorb the basics of political theory, the moral sciences, and legislation, learn to appreciate art and literature, and grasp what the *Idéologues* called "grammaire générale," or "anatomy of the mind" and epistemology, among the foremost new disciplines. "Grammaire générale" sought to uncover the underlying forms and inflections of language, the rules of human logic, the paths and movements of our minds, which, according to Cabanis and Destutt, was the "exclusive solid basis of the moral and political sciences."[55]

A problem overshadowing *Idéologue* pedagogy and the *écoles centrales* from the start was that some were established in departments where resources, premises, and teachers broadly sufficed, whereas a large proportion, often in more remote rural areas, suffered a chronic dearth of teachers, books, suitable premises, and everything else needed. Under the decrees, each *école centrale* had to provide suitable buildings to accommodate not just classrooms but the required public library, "cabinet d'histoire naturelle" [natural history cabinet], cabinet for chemistry and practical physics demonstrations, and space for the botanical garden, beside housing, close by, for boarders and what became—once the original plan for fourteen professors was abandoned—the mandatory minimum ten teaching *professeurs*. Possibly the most fortunate and favored *école centrale* of all was that of Seine-et-Oise department located at Versailles. Its lucky boys attended classes in outbuildings of Louis XIV's abandoned palace, including the Orangerie ("the most beautiful in Europe") and possessed a museum judged "the second of the Republic," while, in good weather, art lessons were conducted among the sculptures of the former royal gardens.[56] But for many departments finding and equipping suitable premises involved appreciable difficulties. At Nantes, the abandoned nunnery of the Ursulines seemed the best locale for the new establishment; it afforded the necessary space but only when abandoned, damaged, and pillaged buildings were repaired and furnished for their new role, requiring a considerable outlay of funds that were simply not available.[57] Some of the new institutions were earmarked for towns where no significant higher education

[54] BL 7 499/20: *Aux Pères et Mères de familie habitant le Département de Seine et Oise*, 20.

[55] Cabanis, *Oeuvres complètes* ii. 516–20 ; Destutt de Tracy, *Éléments d'idéologie* i, p. xxiii–xxiv; BL 7 499/20: *Aux Pères et Mères de familie habitant le Département de Seine et Oise*, 10–13; Jennings, *Revolution*, 310–11.

[56] BL 7 499/20: *Aux Pères et Mères de familie habitant le Département de Seine et Oise*, 5.

[57] BL R 372/32: "Rapport fait par Latournaux, séance 4 Brumaire, Year VIII," 2–3.

establishment had existed previously and scarcely any suitable accommodation existed. The *école centrale* of Toulon, crammed into inadequate, cramped premises, proved too small and distinctly a failure.[58]

New foundations in conception, the hundred or so *écoles centrales* established in France, Belgium, and the Rhineland, from 1795–6, in most cases found themselves, as intended under the terms of the founding decrees,[59] accommodated in the same locations, and using the same buildings, as the colleges and universities they replaced. They absorbed the facilities and other resources from their predecessor colleges, usually including the old library (minus most theology) and some former teachers. In the Rhineland, where, in 1798, the universities of Trier, Mainz, Bonn, and Cologne were all closed, these were immediately converted into *écoles centrales*.[60] Cologne, among Europe's oldest and largest universities, and Mainz, another renowned Catholic institution, both suppressed in 1798, displaced only temporarily by neo-Brissotin revolutionary style *écoles centrales*, nevertheless long remained closed. Cologne University failed to reopen until after the First World War; Mainz University disappeared until 1946; Trier until 1970.

In many cases, though, under the guiding principles, the old college buildings were judged inadequate. Medical teaching at Montpellier, renowned as one of the world's oldest, most venerable medical faculties, suffered few noticeable negative effects following the university's formal closure in 1793, its medical faculty simply continuing as before, integrated into the new framework. But what replaced the old university under the rubric *école centrale* was transferred to bigger and better premises, the former Benedictine monastery, later converted into the bishop's palace, from where all ecclesiastics had now been ejected. Paris acquired three *écoles centrales*, all inaugurated in 1796–7, the first, the École centrale du Panthéon located in the former grand Abbaye of Saint-Geneviève, beside the Panthéon. The others were the École centrale des Quatre Nations in the former college founded by Cardinal Mazarin in 1661 for the education of young noblemen, where d'Alembert had studied, fine premises today of the Institut de France, and, last to open its doors, the École centrale de la Rue Antoine, located in a former Jesuit college destined to become the Lycée Charlemagne under Napoleon, the name it still boasts today.[61]

In some *départements* prolonged controversies erupted over which town should enjoy the privilege, facilities, and public activities associated with hosting the *école centrale*.[62] Since suitable buildings, grounds, and good communications with the surrounding area were a priority, the new location need not coincide with where the most prestigious pre-1793 teaching establishment was located. When Douai University eventually closed, the town found itself relegated to marginality and

[58] Crook, *Toulon in War and Revolution*, 206.
[59] Merot, "La Fréquentation," 424.
[60] Frijhoff, "Patterns," 83–4, 89.
[61] [Say], *Décade philosophique* no. 36 (4th Trimestre, Year V, 16 Sept. 1797), 536.
[62] Taillandier, *Documents*, 69; Head, *Politics and Philosophy*, 380; Isaac and Sorgeloos, *L'École centrale du département de Jemappes*, 48, 173, 179.

insignificance because departmental officials decided Lille offered superior facilities, as also did another contestant, Valenciennes, with a better library. After some delay, the departmental *école centrale* was inaugurated there, on 30 December 1796, in a former monastery. As occurred also in other instances, Douai received no successor institution or resource of any sort to compensate for losing its once renowned university.[63] At Nîmes, the university closed in 1795, the loss compensated with an *école centrale* but only rather late, in 1798. As *écoles centrales* substituted for universities only in part, higher education in France's older university centers often remained permanently as well as severely blighted without prospect of comprehensive revival. Bordeaux University, founded in 1441 and closed in 1793, was re-founded only in 1896. Nice University, shut in 1793, was resurrected only in 1965. Nantes, founded in the fifteenth century and closed in 1793, reopened only in 1970. Perpignan, commencing in 1349 and closed in 1793, like Angers (closed the same year), reopened only in 1971.

Louvain's philosophy, law, and medical faculties had been earmarked for transfer to Brussels, where historically there had been no university, under the Emperor Joseph, before 1789; but no move occurred until the *école centrale* was established in Brussels in May 1797. The foremost academic reformer dismissed by Belgium's anti-Josephine revolution in 1789, Jean-Guillaume de Leempoel (1751–96), Joseph's rector of Louvain University, had already concluded early in the 1780s that breaking the conservative stranglehold of large ancient universities like Louvain over academic life, science, and culture meant transferring key faculties to the capital. Louvain, among the foremost of all European universities before 1789, was closed down in stages, being permanently shut by the revolutionary authorities only when the Brussels *école centrale* commenced activities, in 1797. At that point, most of Louvain's books deemed still relevant to teaching were transferred to Brussels, which, with 80,000 volumes by 1800, now possessed one of Europe's largest public libraries.[64]

19.3. ENLIGHTENMENT IN SECONDARY SCHOOL CURRICULA

As rector at Louvain, Van Leempoel, a Leiden-trained Dutch medical professor whose father introduced inoculation in the northern Netherlands, was the very symbol of uncompromising academic *josephisme*. Very much a government appointee, he was immediately dismissed once the *Vandernootistes* gained the upper hand in 1789. The entire Belgian episcopate denounced him as a heretic, unbeliever, and libertine poisoning Belgium's universities with enlightened reformism. Such

[63] BL R 372/8: "Deputés extraordinaires de la commune de Lille," 1, 3–4.
[64] Guy, L'Enseignement," 110.

"hommes à projects" [men of big reform schemes], held conservative opponents, were the root of society's troubles, having disastrously "seduced" the emperor with their base flattery, impiety, and "false zeal."[65] Contrasting with the usual pattern, with empty former ecclesiastical buildings affording continuity and consolidation, Brussels' "central school," like Versailles, found itself installed in a magnificent secular building—the former palace of the Austrian governors-general. This facilitated the subsequent incorporation of the *école centrale* into Napoleon's reformed imperial higher education system as the Brussels arm of the Université de France. Louvain University altogether disappeared from 1797 until several decades later, being revived by the newly contrived Belgian monarchy only in 1834.[66]

Democratic republicans championing Radical Enlightenment ideals and goals, culminating in the *Idéologues* of the late 1790s, had all along aimed to transform the structures of law, philosophy, classics, and theology found in *ancien régime* colleges, the entire edifice of pre-1789 academic culture, into a modernized, broader, secular higher education based on mathematics, science, social sciences, and modern languages. Hence, in Belgium, the 1795–7 educational revolution on *Idéologue* principles was in some respects a resumption of the ideological feuding provoked by Joseph II's reformism in 1787–9, which had entailed fierce controversies and the closure of numerous monastic establishments whose facilities were then utilized in the post-1795 reorganization. At Namur, the *école centrale* moved into the former College Therésien, itself successor to the former Jesuit college vacated when the Jesuit order in the Austrian Netherlands was suppressed in the early 1770s; at Mons, the new "central school" inaugurated in July 1798 was located, like many others, in a large vacated convent, that of the Ursulines (the nuns having been expelled shortly before).[67] At Liège, the former prince-bishop's grand college became the *école centrale*.

The mandatory ten *professeurs* for each *école centrale* supposedly included three for ancient and modern languages, one each for literature, drawing, philosophy, mathematics, and natural history, with one for ethics, politics, and legislation combined, and the last for "chemistry and physics" combined.[68] Given that most of these were optional some or most of the time, this meant, apart from religion and theology being altogether removed, that parents and students had a remarkably wide choice of courses: with "grammar," the sciences, mathematics, history, and philosophy including political theory and civics now forming the backbone of what was on offer. Although Condorcet's antipathy to steeping boys in Latin and Greek was only partially respected, leaving one of the ten mandatory professorships in each *école centrale* earmarked for "ancient languages," which hence continued to be taught in the new establishments, Latin studies were suddenly less important than studying

[65] BRB VH 27139/10 doc. 25, p. 5. [66] Frijhoff, "Patterns," 83.

[67] Isaac and Sorgeloos, *L'École centrale du département de Jemappes*, 60, 62.

[68] BL R 372/15: *Rapport fait par Roger Martin au nom de la commission d'Instruction public sur l'organisation définitive des Écoles centrales*, 10–11; Merot, "La Fréquentation," 423.

history, constitutions, and legislation,[69] while within Latin studies the focus shifted from old-style grammar and composition to studying key texts.

Although the ambitious breadth of early schemes for a wide range of new subjects like hygiene, gynecology, commerce, and agriculture quickly had to be curtailed, the pedagogic principles driving the new schools certainly differed dramatically from those of the past, not least in what was designated "philosophy" and "history." The content of their college libraries was transformed correspondingly. "Philosophy," redefined to exclude every category of disembodied entities whether souls, angels, devils, sacraments, or God, so that non-physical realities of whatever kind were removed, was now confined to what is perceived through the senses, with observation and impartiality prime principles, as presented by Condillac, its chief epistemological theorist. Philosophy's basic purpose in the new schema was to instill a critical spirit, creative skepticism, and independence of mind, and promote methodologies based on observation. Also basic to *Idéologie* was the notion that all the arts and sciences compose a single coherent whole— "la marche progressive des arts et des sciences"—which involved seeing all the sciences as forming a single Spinoza-style cohering unity governed by the unalterable laws of nature, an approach that lent a wholly new significance to the social and moral sciences, study of human behavior, including religion, and how to improve society, subjects differing from mathematics and the exact sciences in subject matter but not in epistemological standing or methodology. This drastically revised picture of the universe, knowledgeable readers could hardly fail to notice, was infused throughout by the same materialist monism underpinning the entire tradition of neo-Spinozist necessitarianism of Diderot, d'Holbach, Condorcet, Volney, Cabanis, and Destutt.[70]

Vast effort was invested in shaping the boys' attitudes and steering them toward the requisite secularized political and social outlook. Beside Voltaire and the *philosophes*, the intellectual heroes chiefly impressed on *écoles centrale* pupils were either scientists—"Bacon, Galileo, Kepler, Boyle, and Copernicus"—or political reformers. The world beyond Europe, insofar as dominated by colonial systems and the "brigands" of Europe, was presented as a world of oppression and misery justly denounced by Raynal, Diderot, and d'Holbach. Abolition of slavery "in France and the United States of America," meaning Haiti, the French Caribbean, and the northern states of the American union, as achieved by the late 1790s, heralded the "extinction totale" of slavery everywhere. Vital to this *philosophique*, global approach was the doctrine, shared by Paine and Jefferson, that the "American Revolution was carried on by the French Revolution." The teaching provided by the central schools undoubtedly generated a huge new demand for Radical Enlightenment literature of all types, schoolbooks produced for the *écoles centrales*, selected, edited, and produced, mainly in Paris, reflecting the preferences of Condorcet, Lakanal, Destutt, and

[69] *Plans d'enseignement suivis par les professeurs* (Doubs), pp. x–xi.

[70] *Plans d'enseignement suivis par les professeurs* (Doubs), pp. vi–viii, 29–31; Cabanis, *Oeuvres complètes* ii. 480–1 and iii. 35, 38, 383; Head, *Politics and Philosophy*, 85–9.

also François de Neufchâteau, who, though only for a short time one of the Directors, whilst at the helm during 1797–8 took a particular interest in this dimension. While old libraries were substantially transferred from the former colleges to the new, the *Directoire*, as a matter of policy, also wanted great quantities of new books and editions used in teaching. Library holdings at the *écoles centrales* were divided into three main categories—the sciences, literature and fine arts, and historical studies (encompassing also geography, politics, and legislation).[71]

A fervent enlightener, literary critic, poet, and writer on agriculture, Nicolas-Louis François de Neufchâteau (1750–1828), like Volney and Destutt imprisoned during the Terror, was as passionately averse to Jacobinism, Robespierre, and the Montagne as Catholicism and the *ancien régime*. Jesuit educated himself, François de Neufchâteau exalted secularizing middle and higher education and proved highly energetic in priming the *écoles centrales* of France, Belgium, and the Rhineland not just with literary works and Rousseau but the scientific and mathematical writings of Buffon, Linnaeus, Bonnet, Daubenton, and d'Alembert, beside political and philosophic authors like Mably, Raynal, d'Holbach, Helvétius, and Condorcet, along with the *Encyclopédie*. Raynal's *Histoire philosophique* became ubiquitous in the *écoles centrales*, as did d'Holbach's *Politique naturelle* and *Système social*, works hugely esteemed by Condorcet, Volney, and Destutt employed as standard texts in the colleges' civics and politics courses,[72] d'Holbach's *Politique naturelle* serving at the *école centrale* of Mons as a standard textbook in routine teaching of politics and republican morality.[73] Many *écoles centrales* possessed enormous libraries—over 200,000 volumes reportedly at the Doubs department *école centrale*, at Besançon. Accordingly, they also instituted courses in bibliography or "bibliologie," a new scholarly science teaching students how to use catalogs, and navigate their way through vast stacks of tomes, and paleography, while building a coherent overview.

For Condorcet, Volney, and Destutt, seconded by Lakanal and the other *Idéologues*, correct intellectual formation is vital to forming a suitable leadership for the democratic republic and ensuring society's well-being and stability. "Never will a people enjoy a constant, assured liberty," proclaimed Condorcet, in 1792, "if education in the political sciences [*les sciences politiques*] is not general, if it is not independent of all social institutions, if the enthusiasm which you excite in the souls of citizens is not directed by reason, if enthusiasm can be ignited by what is not the truth, if you do not prepare each, attaching him by habit, imagination, and sentiment, to his constitution, laws, and liberty, by a general education [*par une éducation générale*] . . . " It was a central principle of Condorcet that the "general education" each individual receives must centrally include politics and civics.[74]

[71] *Plan d'enseignement suivis par les professeurs* (Doubs), 64, 67, 69.

[72] Isaac and Sorgeloos, *L'École centrale du département de Jemappes*, 258, 277, 299, 516–17.

[73] Isaac and Sorgeloos, *L'École centrale du département de Jemappes*, 517; Staum, *Minerva's Message*, 57.

[74] Baczko, *Éducation pour la démocratie*, 195; Williams, *Condorcet and Modernity*, 166–7; Israel, "Natural Virtue," 11.

Disturbing recent episodes such as French royalist revolt in the Vendée and the Montagnard dictatorship demonstrated that, on its own, freedom of the press is insufficient to secure society's most essential goals and that, without an educational revolution such as theirs, society will inevitably fail to achieve an enlightened awareness of reality, life, and politics, without which the democratic republic, social stability, and man's common pursuit of "happiness" must inevitably fail. Despite the horrors of 1793–4 Condorcet's intellectual progeny still expected (or fervently hoped) universal literacy combined with secularized education and genuine freedom of thought would secure the decisive breakthrough to an enlightened society and finally vanquish ignorance, "fanaticism," prejudice, and "superstition," the eternal bastions of despotism, oppression, and church sway.

The ambitious, many-faceted higher education revolution the *Idéologues* sponsored and supervised advanced rapidly during the late 1790s, before long spilling over into the French-occupied parts of Italy, and various satellite states, including Switzerland. But it also quickly emerged that many difficulties hampered the *écoles centrales*. There were constant complaints that they were swallowing up resources urgently needed for the primary schools and purposes outside education. None could deny that the situation left an awkward gap between elementary education and the relatively demanding standards of the *écoles centrales*, and a second awkward gap between the latter and specialized higher education. A report drawn up by the legislature's *Commission d'Instruction publique*, in October 1797, suggested closing all the universities in one swoop, in 1793, had been "excessivement révolutionnaire," and entirely unhelpful to the cause of higher education, while basic primary education was not being extended and funded far and fast enough. The republic needed one primary school for every 3,000 of population.[75] To save costs, and redistribute resources, the commission at this point contemplated keeping the total of *écoles centrales* at just forty-two, the number—including several outside France's 1792 borders, among them those at Brussels, Ghent, Liège, and Nice—actually functioning at that point. Each *école centrale* should employ eleven professors, including one for "morale et la legislation" and one each for "dessein," geography, philosophy, physics, and natural history, with two for mathematics, two for languages, and a learned *bibliothécaire*.[76] But no cap was placed on the number of *écoles centrales* and the total continued growing.

By 1799, most *écoles centrales* planned actually existed and, up to a point, functioned smoothly under the *Directoire*'s *Conseil d'Instruction publique* set up to preside. But there was mounting criticism of their performance, and especially the failure to attract sufficient students.[77] Acknowledging difficulties, the *Idéologues* rallied round to defend their system. During 1799–1801, their house journal, the

[75] BL R 235/14: Rapport fait par Roger Martin (6 Brumaire An VI), 9, 21.
[76] BL R 235/14: *Rapport fait par Roger Martin* (6 Brumaire An VI), 18, 29, 32.
[77] BL R 235/27: *Opinion de Du Vidal* (8 Floreal An X), 3–4.

Décade philosophique, carried several lengthy articles eulogizing the best *écoles centrales*, rebutting traditionalist objections, and suggesting improvements, while vigorously championing the basic concept.[78] Destutt and his colleagues also compiled a comprehensive overall review of the system for the government, dated 5 February 1800, defending the concept and its implementation, their assumptions, and the existing framework. Destutt, a member of the *Conseil* in February 1799, also penned an outline of his own work in social science and philosophy, his *Projet d'Éléments d'Idéologie* (1801), to be used as a guiding textbook for the *écoles centrales*.

Departmental prefects, responding to instructions from Paris to send in reports, during 1801, divided into two distinct camps, but were mostly unfavorable.[79] There was a widespread and growing feeling that attempting to establish all the *écoles centrales* everywhere, at the same time, without first providing sufficient resources, had been a significant error. Many, like that at Toulon, were wrongly located in buildings too small to accommodate the facilities required.[80] Meanwhile, the overall concept seemed to many too ambitious and idealistic, there was insufficient "relation," not enough interaction between the different fields of study, the range of courses was too broad, too *philosophique*, and too demanding.[81] Basically, from the specific perspective of the *Conseil* and departmental heads, as well as from the First Consul's, Napoleon's, standpoint, the system was a failure, as it was also, in some respects, from that of Condorcet, Destutt, Volney, Lakanal, and the *Idéologues*.

French families, far from evaluating the possibilities with a *philosophique* eye, looked chiefly at the practical, vocational possibilities, whatever struck local sentiment as useful training for trade, business, and skilled artisan crafts. Where the overall aim of the planners was the well-rounded Radical Enlightenment revolutionary leader, teacher, or administrator steeped in d'Holbach, Diderot, Helvétius, Raynal, and Condorcet, someone highly literate, secular, and politically conscious, this, predictably, was not at all what parents and the general public wanted from the new colleges. Society attached some value to mathematics, writing French well, and especially "drawing," a discipline encompassing technical design, surveying, and planning widely deemed useful in commerce and various trades. These subjects attracted the bulk of course enrollments and far more interest than the moral sciences, historical studies, and exact sciences so ardently promoted by the *Idéologues*. Neither parents nor students particularly enthused over a revolution in education which introduced a range of unheard-of new academic disciplines and sciences, and showed even less appreciation for Condorcet's, Volney's, and Destutt's doctrine that religion and theology had perverted "all morality," and the basic principles of the social order,[82]

[78] Head, *Politics and Philosophy*, 391–2. [79] Head, *Politics and Philosophy*, 398.

[80] BL R 235/29 : *Rapport fait par Jard-Panvillier*, 13–15.

[81] Barruel, *Observations*, 7–8; Head, *Politics and Philosophy*, 391–5.

[82] Destutt de Tracy, *Analyse raisonée*, 146–9, 159; Baczko, *Éducation pour la démocratie*, 197.

or why this meant morality and civics should be taught as independent subjects wholly detached from theology. According to Destutt, "theology is the philosophy of the childhood of the world," and it was time theology gave way to the philosophy of our world's "age of reason;"[83] most families firmly disagreed. Why should their children be made to imbibe "moral sciences," philosophy, politics, legislation, physics, chemistry, *histoire philosophique*, or Destutt's *grammaire générale*? Here, then, was one of the fundamental contradictions underlying the ultimate failure of the Radical Enlightenment.

The system aimed to steer secondary education toward providing a specially formed educational elite with an encyclopedic, scientific outlook based on experimentation, observation, and critical judgment, a sound grasp of history and geography, and a generous dose of philosophy, political theory, and study of legislation. By and large parents and students resisted less out of religious objection to the *Idéologues*' militant secularism, though that played a part, than deeply-rooted preference for more obviously practical, useful knowledge, skills linked to vocational training. Earning a living mattered more to most than understanding the reality of things. From everyday concerns, families were proving increasingly averse to Enlightenment and its lofty demands in whatever format, and were prodding their children to steer clear, as far as they could, of moral sciences, politics, history, and ancient languages, and especially philosophy. Finding enough teachers of "legislation" and political science proved difficult in any case and this only aggravated students' lack of interest.[84] The government survey, directed from Paris, into the functioning of the schools, and attendance at courses, conducted in 1799, revealed an unsettling, stark pattern of course selection and attendance. Collected from all over newly expanded France, the government data showed that, in practice, students consistently flocked to commercial "drawing" (rather than drawing as preparation for natural science, or art), and to a lesser extent mathematics and French, while "history" and moral, social, and legislative sciences, the chief glory of the *écoles centrales* according to Destutt,[85] attracted only minimal enrollments.[86] The *Conseil*'s and the *idéologues*' proposed answer to what they deemed a chronically unsatisfactory balance of studies was a specialized school in Paris, of a kind first envisaged earlier, promoting general study in the physical and mechanical sciences by training teachers in the field. However, after the coup of Brumaire (9 November 1799), it was Napoleon and his ministers who were increasingly in charge, and Napoleon, it soon emerged, took no interest in this proposal.[87]

[83] Destutt de Tracy, *Analyse raisonée*, 158.

[84] Roederer, *Discours . . . relatif à l'instruction publique*, 2.

[85] Destutt de Tracy, *Éléments d'idéologie* i, p. xxviii.

[86] Guy, "L'Enseignement," 111–13; Head, *Politics and Philosophy*, 393–4; Mérot, "La Fréquentation," 414, 416–17, 422; Mérot, "Écoles centrales," 799–800, 803.

[87] Head, *Politics and Philosophy*, 397.

19.4. NAPOLEON REORGANIZES FRENCH SECONDARY AND HIGHER EDUCATION

Beside divergence of outlook between *Idéologues* and public, the general dislocation of middle and higher education stemming from closing the *ancien régime* colleges and universities, and the administrative challenge of replacing them with "central schools," despite some continuity of locations, buildings, and resources, also created considerable, sometimes insuperable, difficulties. Many pupils had had their education gravely disrupted at all levels by the successive upheavals of 1792–5, creating chasms hard to overcome. Even assuming qualitative improvements— which were not always obvious—as well as doctrinal reorientation, the quantitative drop represented a colossal setback to French education. The total number of pupils attending the *écoles centrales* within the 1992 borders of France, at the end of the 1790s, approximately 20,000, amounted, it is estimated, to only about one quarter to a third of the total, in the same age range, attending the 562 *ancien régime* colleges of France in 1789.[88] The great artist Jean-Auguste Dominique Ingres (1780–1867), 14 when Robespierre fell, figured among the vast number of young Frenchmen whose truncated, inadequate schooling during the Revolution remained a source of social embarrassment and inner discomfort throughout the rest of their lives.

Worst of all, too great an educational gap persisted between France's post-1795 relatively neglected, inadequate, and poorly funded primary schools, the *écoles primaires*, and the comparatively high levels of attainment required of 12-year-old boys applying to the *écoles centrales*. Partly due to disruption and bad planning, this also reflected the *Idéologues*' obsessive preoccupation with building a wall against any possible resurgence of *le démocratisme rousseauien*, by training a reliably enlightened and sophisticated elite to supervise their representative democracy.[89] Whatever one's reservations regarding Napoleon's scathing criticism of their educational goals, he was certainly correct in thinking that the basis for a meritocratic society the *Directoire* and the *Idéologues* provided was simply too narrow, too academic, and in career terms too unspecialized and restricted in practice for France's urgent requirements.

Napoleon's Concordat with the Papacy of July 1801 also rendered continuation of the *écoles centrales* in their existing form, with their militant secularism, unfitting, implausible, and inappropriate. By 1801 Napoleon's relationship with the *Idéologues* had become tense, and his dislike of their philosophy evident.[90] After carefully reviewing the situation, on 1 March and then again on 1 May 1802, the Napoleonic regime issued decrees for the general reform of secondary and higher education, which were now separated, with (supposedly) thirty to forty-five elite *lycées* being established as the backbone of the new system—a system from which *idéologie* was erased.[91] Napoleon and his officials' main objective was to replace the nearly one

[88] Mérot, "Écoles centrales," 802. [89] Schandeler, *Interprétations de Condorcet*, 40–1, 66–7.
[90] Staum, *Cabanis*, 281; Minart, *Pierre Daunou*, 170. [91] Head, *Politics and Philosophy*, 33–4, 47.

hundred *écoles centrales*, one in each department, with over thirty larger *lycées*, one in approximately every three departments, partly to cut down the cost of the *écoles centrales*' special facilities and libraries, and reduce the tax burden, but equally to remove the *philosophique*, republican element, with the deliberate aim of weakening the republican tendency characteristic of the *écoles centrales*, reducing teaching of civics, and marginalizing the materialist philosophy propagated in the works of d'Holbach, Condorcet, and the like.

Meanwhile, the regime also introduced a lower level of fee-paying secondary schools, of decidedly more limited scope and facilities than the *écoles centrales* now replaced by *lycées*, to teach mainly French, Latin, and mathematics.[92] The 1802 education reforms were one of the main factors bringing the three-year-old alliance between Bonaparte and the *Idéologues* to an abrupt and bad-tempered end. Napoleonic intent on refocusing the Enlightenment in France, substituting for republican and materialist textbooks non-republican materials fused with some Catholic input, and involving fewer and less "philosophical" disciplines, won the day.[93] The new *lycées* needed fewer professors than the *écoles centrales* though each should still have a minimum of eight professors;[94] and students would again compete for places through examinations. Like the *écoles centrales* before them, the *lycées* were mostly installed on sites of earlier colleges. At Grenoble, the town where Stendhal studied and which during the Revolution had been renamed "Grelibre" and was only now reverting to its original name, the *lycée* was installed in the former Jesuit college and chapel.

The 6,400 students attending the *lycées* at any one time were all to be boarded at the expense of the Republic, 2,400 of them chosen from the ranks of sons of the Republic's military and administrative personnel. Boarded free at the *lycées* for a maximum of six years, on completing their secondary education pupils would sit examinations and the best 20 per cent would graduate to the Republic's special schools. The latter meanwhile would be increased with the addition of three new medical schools, four specialized colleges for physics, chemistry, and natural history, and one for history, geography, and political economy. There would be four colleges of arts and design, three, at Paris, Dijon, and Toulouse, already existing and a fourth to be established. Professional training in law was reorganized and expanded, the new law colleges added to those already existing, raising the total to ten to twelve overall with five professors each, institutes scattered across the empire designed to turn out large numbers of state functionaries.[95] Under a law of April 1803, the medical profession was fully professionalized so that departmental administrations as well as the army and navy must henceforth employ only qualified state-trained doctors in medical roles and capacities.

[92] BL R 235/23: *Projet de loi* (27 Germinal, An X), 3.

[93] Roederer, *Discours ... relatif à l'instruction publique*, 8; Renauld, *Antoine Destutt de Tracy*, 149; Staum, *Minerva's Message*, 222.

[94] BL R 235/23: *Projet de loi* (27 Germinal, An X), 4.

[95] BL R 235/23: *Projet de loi* (27 Germinal, An X), 9, 12–13.

In his *Discours* of 24 Floréal, Year X (14 May 1802), defending the regime's striking change of course, Roederer, a key participant in the coup of Brumaire and the new regime, maintained that the "sciences properly speaking"—meaning mathematics and physics but also social science and political thought—"cannot and should not be common to everyone;" France needed less universalists, and more specialization. The plan now was for better social targeting: each science should train a requisite number of experts in that field, a "number of citizens in proportion to the needs of society."[96] Rather than developing the outlook of each individual as much as possible, as his *Idéologue* Radical Enlightenment associates wanted, the new regime's distinctly more authoritarian, and less republican, objective was to tighten bonds between individual and government, focus more on society's needs, and reconcile state-supported education with society's vocational preferences at large, including most people's desire for some religious education. It was a bad thing for society, he argued, that education should produce large numbers of individuals with a broad *philosophique* view, imagining themselves suited for everything. For society is thereby impeded in finding the experts it needs. In particular, explained Roederer, there should be less teaching of philosophical "history" and less study of legislation and law-making, a specialism for the few not the business of citizens generally.[97] There should also now be more room for private education and more balance between private and public education. It is a better investment for society to increase primary school numbers and raise general literacy levels while promoting more specialized fields of knowledge through higher education.[98]

Other speeches justifying the regime's change of course in the legislature made more of the classic moderate "Enlightenment" argument that "enlightenment" is assuredly not for everyone. The idea that Enlightenment is for all was disproved, it was claimed, by experience and the "indifference" of the great bulk of the citizenry.[99] If, on the one hand, "no state would be rich enough to achieve" the goals set by the planners of the *écoles centrales*, their aims, like their libraries, were simply of no interest to most students or the general public. Condorcet's vision, concurred Baron Louis-Alexandre Jard-Panvillier (1757–1822), a physician and revolutionary veteran who since Brumaire had proven a loyal Napoleonist, splendid no doubt in aspiration, and eminently worthy of an enlightened people, was a luxury item, a vision of education which on examination turned out to be almost impossible to realize.[100]

It was assuredly Napoleon's embrace of moderate Enlightenment in place of radical Enlightenment in the years 1801–4, his belief that religion alone can give the French state the firm, steady support it needed, his growing aversion to the "philosophy" of the *Idéologues* and the study of history, that underlay his ideological shift away from

96 Roederer, *Discours... relatif à l'instruction publique*, 5–6; BL R 235/29: *Rapport fait par Jard-Panvillier*, 5; BL R 235/30: *Discours... par Simeon, 11 Floreal An X*, 2.

97 Roederer, *Discours... relatif à l'instruction publique*, 3.

98 Roederer, *Discours... relatif à l'instruction publique*, 13–14.

99 BL R 235/30: *Discours... par Simeon, 11 Floréal An X*, 2.

100 BL R 235/29: *Rapport fait par Jard-Panvillier*, 2–3.

democratizing republicanism tied to rejection of religious authority. The Republic's First Consul in effect reoriented the late French Enlightenment toward a boldly reforming autocracy tied to a perspective lending society as a whole a more Catholic gloss while keeping only the education system's higher strata essentially secular. Destutt answered those supporting the changes by reissuing his 1799 *Analyse raisonée* of all revealed religions, reaffirming his portrayal of religious authority as a way of subjecting "philosophy and all higher knowledge" to the sway of ignorance and the priesthood, and laying the ground for political despotism.[101] By contrast, Chateaubriand expressed delight that Napoleon, though assuredly no believer, had ceased preventing the sale of his highly controversial anti-Enlightenment *Génie du christianisme*, and even wanted to use his text as propaganda to strengthen the common people's Catholic preferences.[102] Chateaubriand had written the book while seeking refuge from the Revolution in England during the 1790s, and originally planned to publish it in London. But, taking advantage of the amnesty Napoleon unexpectedly issued, in 1800, he actually published it, in April 1802, in France. The dramatic cultural, religious, and political shift away from republican values and from hostility to organized religion, under Napoleon's aegis in the years 1800–4, Chateaubriand termed Bonaparte's drive "to establish his power on the principal foundation of society," namely religion, a policy realignment beginning in earnest with his offer of compromise with the Papacy. If the Revolution Chateaubriand reviled he viewed as rooted in the republican principle of "equality," Napoleonic rule, something very different in terms of basic principles, he recognized as tyranny based on "force" and religion.[103]

The whole "empire voltairean," as he scornfully termed the edifice of irreligious Enlightenment merging the moderate and radical strands, the "enormous edifice built by the *encyclopédistes*," by the "Diderots, d'Alemberts, Duclos, Dupuis, les Helvétius, les Condorcet," rose up against him, exulted Chateaubriand, and his book. But with Napoleon's new direction, a whole new phase in the war between moderation and the "mouvement philosophique" had begun.[104] The change in ambience, in the general feel of France, Chateaubriand later recalled in 1801–2, was immediate and profound. On all sides, churches that had not been wrecked reopened. One felt a profound change everywhere, in the streets and cafés, with everyone picking up the "debris as if after a battle," taking stock of the damage and their personal loss. The opportunity to bring his book out in France, just as all this transpired, thrilled Chateaubriand with the feeling he was leading the intellectual and political revival of Catholic influence in France, "blowing the trumpet" at the entrance to the temple.

Though uninterested in primary schooling, and even less interested in women's education, Napoleon gave much thought to his *lycées* and special schools, being

[101] Destutt de Tracy, *Analyse raisonée*, pp. xv–xvi.
[102] Chateaubriand, *Mémoires* i. 527; Jennings, *Revolution*, 311.
[103] Chateaubriand, *Mémoires* i. 504–5; Jennings, *Revolution*, 87–8.
[104] Chateaubriand, *Mémoires* i. 525–6.

obsessed with the need to increase his stock of competent officers and state functionaries and continue the *Directoire*'s concern for raising qualifications for medical and other professionals. At the same time, he increasingly disliked and was suspicious of the avowedly intellectual, overtly republican legacy of those responsible for the educational revolution of 1795–1802. Research and higher learning remained for now under the purview of the Institut de France in Paris, still dominated by the *Idéologues*. But this materialist republican coterie of anti-Catholic heirs to Diderot and d'Holbach exerted a now much reduced influence which Napoleon felt eager to replace altogether with a more purely technocratic and politically neutral elite. Their republican, anti-religious legacy he increasingly rebuffed while absorbing the elitism and meritocratic character of the revolutionary *écoles centrales* into the newly projected system of *lycées* into which, from May 1802, the former central schools were increasingly subsumed. His objective in education reform was to forge a narrower, more disciplined secondary curriculum, with greater emphasis on Latin and traditional subjects, while expanding scientific and technical training at post-secondary level, eradicating republican rhetoric, and bringing the entire system more directly under centralized control. He made a point of ending teaching of civics and politics, along with materialist philosophy.

Napoleon's lack of sympathy for the *Idéologue*s soon became overt. Auteuil was placed under police surveillance. On 3 Pluviose, Year XI (23 January 1803), the Institut de France's previously influential *classe* of *sciences morales et politiques*, the section to which Destutt, Volney, Garat, and Cabanis belonged (and to which, ironically, they had elected Napoleon, back in December 1797), was permanently dissolved by merging it with the *classe* of languages and literature. Plainly, Napoleon was deliberately curbing the "republican" tendency and penalizing the *Idéologues* for opposing his dictatorship.[105] Of Condorcet's vision of widespread education in social sciences, political science, natural rights, the rights of peoples, little now remained.[106] An embittered Destutt, while working on his *Commentaire* on Montesquieu's *L'Esprit des Lois*, in 1806–7, retorted that "any government aiming to oppress, is attached to priests" and seeks to make them powerful enough to serve it efficiently by perverting public morality and stifling knowledge and the sciences.[107] As long as he ruled as emperor, Napoleon ensured Destutt's principal work of political theory remained unpublished.

Radical Enlightenment was displaced, in short, by a technocratic, militarized new variant of moderate Enlightenment following a *coup d'état* in which the *Idéologues* themselves had been directly complicit followed by a concentration of power in autocratic hands. A lasting result was Napoleon's transformation of the education system away from the ideals of Condorcet and Lakanal's plans of 1795. A body of

[105] Renauld, *Antoine Destutt de Tracy*, 145, 148–9; Imbert, *Destutt de Tracy critique*, 74; Gaulmier, *Grand témoin*, 266; Nicolet, *L'Idée républicaine*, 125.

[106] Renauld, *Antoine Destutt de Tracy*, 146–9; Karady, "De Napoléon à Duruy," 262, 266–7.

[107] Gusdorf, *Conscience révolutionnaire*, 322–8; Head, *Politics and Philosophy*, 120–3.

inspecteurs généraux was created as a tool to ensure uniformity of teaching, discipline, and milieu in the *lycées*. But while Napoleon's scheme for the nation's schooling marked a departure from a Radical Enlightenment project that had failed, it still retained from the *écoles centrales* the idea that a large elite with a broadly enlightened outlook, predominantly disdainful of traditional notions and theology, was required and must be turned out by the state educational system.[108] If the syllabus of the *écoles centrales* was replaced by teaching based on non-republican, less philosophical, and, to an extent, Catholic materials, the atmosphere prevailing in the *lycées* remained predominantly secular and freethinking. Napoleon's differentiation between secondary and university education, with both sectors successors to the *écoles centrales*, cleared the way for the *lycées*, which were eventually far more numerous than the "central schools," to proliferate purely as secondary schools and for the new university campuses, including Brussels, to expand on the basis of one per department but all belonging to a single imperial organization or University corpus.

By May 1802, Chénier, Say, Ginguené, and Constant had all lost favor with Bonaparte, or broken with the regime, while Destutt and Lafayette—whose son, Georges, married Destutt's daughter that year—were reduced, having never aided Bonaparte, to furtive resistance by word and pen. Volney, earlier a close advisor of the First Consul, but appalled by the papal Concordat and 1802 reintroduction of slavery into Martinique, Cayenne, and Haiti, finally lost all illusions and broke with Bonaparte over his elevation to "emperor," in 1804. Their rupture followed a flaming row in which Napoleon reportedly gave him a hefty kick; Volney too joined the ranks of the behind-the-scenes whispering radical opponents.[109] Roederer alone remained a firm supporter of the imperial regime. For disapproving, or rather showing disapproval, of his self-elevation to the title and status of "emperor," in 1804, Bonaparte, having privately dismissed them since 1801 as fourteen or fifteen "affreux metaphysiciens" daring to obstruct his plans, took to publicly insulting the former allies who helped him capture power in 1799. The *Idéologues*' journal, the *Décade philosophique*, whose editor Say was among the most resolute in distancing himself from the emperor, having been curtailed by Napoleon in 1804, was suppressed altogether in 1807.[110]

[108] Karady, "De Napoléon à Duruy," 263.

[109] Staum, *Cabanis*, 292–5; Gaulmier, *Grand témoin*, 260–3, 277; Cook, "Between the Old World and New," 89.

[110] Nicolet, *L'Idée républicaine*, 125; Head, *Politics and Philosophy*, 33–4; Minart, *Pierre Daunou*, 172–3.

20

Revolution and the Universities

Germany's "Philosophy Wars" (1780–1820)

20.1. ENLIGHTENMENT, REFORM, AND TRANSFORMING THE UNIVERSITIES

German lands in the 1790s were at a watershed, graphically confirming the basic rift, as has been noted,[1] between two separate, ultimately antagonistic enlightenments. The split pitted key enlighteners like Möser, Rehberg, Gentz, and also Biester, chief editor of the *Berlinische Monatschrift*, all sharing Hume's skeptical view of reason and admiring British mixed government and the "aristocratic" American Revolution of Adams and the Federalists, thinkers avowing the superiority of "experience" over "theory," rejecting universal rights, and espousing moderately reform-minded princes and courts, against advocates of universal and equal human rights, the French Revolution's basic principles, and Herder's doctrine that both individual existence and German national culture as a whole needed fundamental renewal through an autonomous drive for a deeper enlightenment.[2]

"The historian of the late Enlightenment, therefore," remarked one scholar rightly, "must not conflate the two movements."[3] Without firmly separating anti-revolutionary reform-minded moderates from radicals, *Revolutionsfreunde* [friends of the Revolution], the picture makes no sense. But among the latter, it is necessary also to differentiate clearly between *Jakobiner* who were *philosophique* radicals siding with the Brissotins against the Montagne and the few sympathizing with Robespierre and authoritarian populism (who had scant support in Germany). Even before the Terror proper, prominent *Jakobiner*, including veteran eyewitnesses of the Parisian scene like Konrad Engelbert Oelsner (1764–1828), were deeply apprehensive about the Montagne. During the September massacres, Oelsner personally attested, the great bulk of the Parisian crowds witnessing the scenes of barbarity were just

[1] Knudsen, *Justus Möser*, 164–9; Umbach, *Federalism*, 134–5; Gare, "Democracy and Education," 3, 17–19.

[2] Herder, *Another Philosophy*, 114–16; Himmelfarb, *Roads to Modwernity*, 95.

[3] Knudsen, *Justus Möser*, 165.

spectators, the few active perpetrators were organized agitators directed by the Paris Commune and the Montagne.[4] Germany's *Jakobiner* were basically Brissotins—and those among them explicitly embracing the Revolution in cosmopolitan rather than particularist terms, and inclined to recognize radical *philosophique* ideas, "die Philosophie," as chief motor of the authentic Revolution, like Oelsner, Forster, Dorsch, Matthias Metternich, Wedekind, Rebmann, Heydenreich, and Fichte, were mostly either professors themselves or acquired their radical ideas during their university student years. In this respect, being led and dominated by professors, Germany's *Revolutionsfreunde* [Friends of the Revolution] of 1792–3 paralleled the pre-1789 underground organization the Deutsche Union, many of whose former members were prominent among the *Revolutionsfreunde* of 1792–3 though prior to 1789 the latter was more of a mix of radicals and moderates.[5]

At Göttingen, in the duchy of Hanover, opposed moderate and radical factions could be traced back in a continuous line to the late 1770s, to factions for and against the American Revolution; it was at Göttingen too that the jurist Karl von Knoblauch (1756–94), among the more notable late eighteenth-century German radical enlighteners, developed his distinctive form of Spinozistic materialism and commenced his drive against all types of "superstition."[6] Later, it was from another university, Giessen, that he propagated his underground assault on tyranny and Europe's monarchs, or the "sultans" as he called them. At all the great central European universities, the rift ran deep: even the secret society of Illuminati divided at this juncture between enlighteners exerting a moderating influence on princes, and enemies of the princely courts adopting more obviously subversive strategies. Germany's greatest philosopher, Kant, sympathized with aspects of the Revolution but only in the most discreet terms and never abandoned his preference for court-inspired reform from above, over revolutionary pressure from below, even when emanating from universities.[7] From 1789, the growing ferocity of debates about the Revolution in the journals, reading societies, and universities drove the two opposed blocs ever further apart. The conservative press spurred further polarization in readers' minds by using emotive language denouncing every *Illuminat* and *Demokrat* as a bloodthirsty *Jakobiner*.[8]

During the early and mid-1790s, key works such as Fichte's *Concerning the General Concept of the Wissenschaftslehre* (1794),[9] and Kant's remarkable essay *Der Streit der Fakultäten* [The Conflict of the Faculties] (1794), warned of the grave peril arising from the growing gulf between university theology and philosophy faculties, between princely authority and universities, between existing law and universal ideas, and

[4] Cottebrune, *Mythe et réalité*, 166; Israel, *Revolutionary Ideas*, 270, 305, 331.

[5] Cottebrune, *Mythe et réalité*, 133–6; Mühlpfordt, *Halle-Leipziger Aufklärung*, 340, 343–9, 386.

[6] Mulsow, "Karl von Knoblauch," 94–5; Rumore, *Materia cogitans*, 205–8; Mühlpfordt, *Halle-Leipziger Aufklärung*, 347.

[7] Wilson, "Enlightenment's Alliance," 374; Cottebrune, *Mythe et réalité*, 140–2.

[8] Aaslestad, *Place and Politics*, 121.

[9] Fichte, *Early Philosophical Writings*, 114; Crouter, *Friedrich Schleiermacher*, 160–1.

between public opinion and philosophers. A thoroughly alarmed Kant, appalled by Robespierre, Montagnard tyranny, and the Terror, warned in his 1794 essay of the danger to everyone posed by superficiality and instability of ordinary opinion. But he also refused to be pushed into lining up for or against the Revolution. He was determined to stick to a bridging role, a tactful, mediating position connecting the two sides no matter how politically intellectually precarious his stance became. Previously always a pillar of moderation, in his tentative mediating role, after 1789, he remained anxious above all to defend and justify Enlightenment as a continuing program of moral advancement and general amelioration while deferring to the princes and simultaneously endorsing the general principles of the American and French revolutions. He felt scant sympathy for revolutionaries or revolutionary violence and kept his criticism of the courts within careful bounds.[10] Yet the Enlightenment, whatever mistakes had been made, signified the moral and social progress of mankind itself, and those statesmen and preachers opposing basic Enlightenment principles, he did not doubt, were opposing society's true interests. The French Revolution and Robespierre, he admonished, teach mankind that human amelioration moves not from bottom to top, which is impossible, but from top to bottom. Consequently, educational renewal is more basic in the broader frame of things than any violent upheaval can be. Philosophers, not ecclesiastics or courtiers, are best qualified to judge how the general frame and content of education should be reorganized, and the overall debate conducted.[11]

The now elderly Kant berated not only clergy and statesmen hindering human improvement, but equally the common man's notions and outlook. Statesmen boast of how pragmatic they are, insisting we must "accept people as they are, not expect them to be as some unknowing pedant or good-natured dreamer imagines they ought to be." But they prognosticate without reflecting that they themselves rendered the people what they are—"obstinate with a tendency to rebel, made so by unjust coercion." The clergy deplore religion's "complete decline while doing precisely what is required to cause this effect," showing indifference to universal moral principles "that would lead directly to moral improvement." Instead, they make "observances and historical faith an essential duty," outmoded props intended originally only to promote moral improvement indirectly, among the illiterate and ignorant. "From this arises a mechanical unanimity as in a civil constitution, but none in moral conviction." When denouncing men's failings, churchmen "complain of an irreligiosity they themselves have created." Kant believed a wider view reveals a natural sympathy for the ideals of the French Revolution that "can have no other cause than a moral capacity in the human race." The overriding difficulty continues to be that government, lawyers, preachers, and peoples, not least their princes, had everything hopelessly confused. Despite the obstacles posed by ordinary thinking and common assumptions, republicanism, constitutionalism, cosmopolitanism, and a

[10] Kuehn, *Kant*, 404–5; Ellis, *Kant's Politics*, 168–9; Höffe, *Kant's Cosmopolitan Theory*, 12.

[11] Kant, *Toward Perpetual Peace*, 155, 162; Kuehn, *Kant*, 405–6.

touch of anti-colonialism derived by Kant apparently from the *Histoire philosophique*, along with improvement in moral awareness and the lapsing of war, will ultimately raise the level of human life and happiness.[12] In his post-1789 mediating mode, steering between radical and moderate Enlightenment, Kant strove to offer a cautious revolution in thought tinted with optimism.

The unprecedented structural crisis in Germany's universities, of the 1790s and the new century's opening years, stemmed from huge pressures arising from the latest developments in science, scholarship, student aspirations, and teaching, powered by the Enlightenment itself. Universities were subject to new requirements that threatened to undermine not just existing academic traditions and syllabuses but the very existence of these institutions. Keeping up with the latest developments in science alone imposed massive pressure. Introducing into Germany's more ancient higher education facilities the "clinical, anatomical, and medical sciences insofar as they are of purely scientific nature, a library, Observatorium, botanical garden, and Natural History and Art collections,"[13] observed the great university reformer Wilhelm von Humboldt (1767–1835) in 1807, must mean vast expansion and reorganization entailing fundamental change. The recent growth of princely academies as a separate sphere of intellectual endeavor and debate further complicated matters by separating much modern enquiry and research from older academic entities geared to teach only longstanding disciplines, some of which were now less relevant to society's needs than formerly. Older structures in this way directly obstructed society's increasing need for better trained physicians, functionaries, professionals, and military officers, the requirements of expanding administrative and legal systems rapidly growing more complex. "Enlightened despotism," the growth of the state, and of armies and navies, all added to the pressure for expanding and restructuring the universities. Yet, anxiety to protect academic autonomy against church and state, one of Kant's chief concerns, at the same time produced calls for more autonomy and more autonomous procedures for academic appointments.

The 1790s crisis of the universities was indeed unprecedented. Over half the total, no less than twenty-one of the universities in Germany and Austria in 1789, had closed by 1818, with many, including recently established Stuttgart (founded in 1775, closed in 1794), and Ingolstadt, where the Illuminati began their underground movement in the 1780s, once southern Germany's largest university (founded in 1472, closed in May 1800), having disappeared by 1800.[14] But even more disorienting than closures was the fast-changing balance of disciplines displacing theology from its presiding role at a time when theology's prestige was in any case receding. For leading higher education reformers like Von Humboldt and Schleiermacher, the urgency of

[12] Kant, *Toward Perpetual Peace*, 155–6; Aramayo, "Radical and Moderate Enlightenment," 315–16, 322–3.

[13] Von Humboldt, "Antrag auf Errichtung," 145.

[14] Whaley, *Germany* ii. 522; Märker, *Geschichte der Universität Erfurt*, 76; Lemberg, "Universität Marburg," 224; Frijhoff, "Patterns," 83.

determining more clearly what the Enlightenment's impact meant lent "philosophy" and the humanities a heightened responsibility for keeping watch over the overall structure of studies. Philosophy alone, they believed, could assess the rapid proliferation of fields of scholarship, the meaning of new exact sciences and fast-changing terminology. "Philosophy" hence acquired unprecedented centrality in the increasingly fraught late Enlightenment academic sphere as thinkers battled to come to grips with the crisis—a centrality it would keep, Von Humboldt pointed out, only if they did effectively guide society's adapting to modernity and new knowledge.

The intellectual crisis assured Kantian Idealism an exceptionally formative role in the German late Enlightenment, but also made it an additional destabilizing influence.[15] As the turmoil of the revolutionary and Napoleonic wars swirled all around, idealization of the university as the "visible embodiment of the immortality of our human race," the summit of human aspiration and striving that peaked in Fichte's thought, also added additional layers to the universities' overall predicament.[16] Kant, Fichte, and Von Humboldt all maintained that philosophy must ensure the sway of free, rational critique of the assumptions and principles of all the other disciplines and sciences, including society's and government's expectations of the universities, and the theory and practice of education itself. If Kantians and Fichteans were decidedly more accommodating toward religious authority and princes than Condorcet, Volney, or Destutt de Tracy, in subjecting German academic tradition and conservatism to devastating critique, denouncing princely interference with academic freedom, and ridiculing commonplace anti-intellectualism, they contributed more than their share to the mounting intellectual turmoil.

Central Europe's enlightened despots hardly needed reminding of the need for urgent and far-reaching reorganization of their universities. Joseph II, advised by Austria's chief enlightener, Joseph von Sonnenfels (1732–1817), led the way, being the first to significantly expand, centralize and secularize, and adjust universities to the non-confessional framework of his 1781 Toleration Edict. Maria Theresa's elite academies for educating nobility separately from the rest of society, mostly in Vienna, closed in 1783.[17] To end academic status as a separate order of society, and as an ecclesiastical adjunct, Joseph in 1784 banned the use of special academic gowns throughout the empire.[18] From 1781–2, Prague University, lifting its bar on Protestant and Jewish students, rapidly expanded, by 1818 having 880 students on its rolls, not far behind Vienna with 957.[19] Budapest, formerly a Jesuit university, secularized and enlarged (albeit keeping Latin as its academic language), re-emerged as the Royal Hungarian University. Lesser universities, meanwhile, like Moravia's Olomouc, founded in 1570, and Graz, an Austrian Jesuit university founded in 1585, closed, each of these replaced, by 1782, with a local *lycée*. Twelve years after annexing

[15] Von Humboldt, "Über die innere und äussere," 156. [16] Sauter, *Visions*, 13.
[17] Rosa di Simone, "Admission," 754–5, 323.
[18] Ridder-Symoens, "Management and Resources," 207.
[19] [Jullien], *Revue encyclopédique* ii (1819), 168; Rosa di Simone, "Admission," 295.

south-eastern Poland to the empire, in 1784, Joseph closed Zamosc University (founded in 1594).

Joseph strove to widen academe's role, close smaller universities, and, to keep costs within bounds and ensure adequate facilities for research by gathering resources and personnel in fewer, larger, better-funded institutions, concentrate old and new disciplines together. Concentrating funding, student numbers, and teachers heightened the pressure on smaller universities while further diluting confessional barriers, introducing a whole array of new structural difficulties. Some central European universities, reflecting these contrary pressures, expanded and contracted by rapid turns. The eastern Galicia Theresianum, at Lemberg (Lvov), Joseph reformed and secularized, aiming to create a major university for a large region; but it soon ran down, nevertheless, and, by 1803, had to be closed. Marburg, billed for expansion, following the closing of the Collegium Carolinum in Kassel in 1786, acquired the latter's anatomical theater and botanical garden as well as a new "laboratorium chymicum," yet, suffering setbacks at the same time, faded steadily, reportedly sinking by 1804 into a deplorable state.[20]

It was no secret, observed Kant, that the Enlightenment wrought deep divisions in higher education everywhere. This was an inevitable state of affairs since Enlightenment concepts, by the 1780s, had formed many professors and students, which unavoidably meant the academy increasingly divided into vying ideological factions for and against fundamental far-reaching reform, polarizing the entire sphere. At Louvain, although in 1788–90 the conservatives briefly secured the upper hand, by the early 1790s, as we have seen, resumed feuding divided the university's professors and students "into two almost equal parties."[21] If their victory in 1789–90 had enabled the Belgian bishops and anti-Josephist conservatives to remove "unorthodox" professors opposing faith, church, and nobility this entirely failed to end Louvain's academic *schisme*.[22] When the Austrians regained control in 1791–2, the purged professors were simply reinstated by the Emperor Leopold. Enlighteners everywhere, meanwhile, felt outrage at Louvain's succumbing to Counter-Enlightenment reactionary pressure in 1789–90. Repeatedly purged again, following annexation to France in 1792–3 and again in 1794, by 1797 Louvain University had ceased to exist (it was re-opened in 1816).

Despite far-reaching reforms, and huge acquisitions of books by surviving universities from smaller colleges closing down and suppressed monastic and episcopal libraries, the general picture in 1789 was still predominantly of a conservative façade ill-adapted to accommodating new sciences, research, and learning. Anyone with a radical outlook in the 1780s could only react like Brissot visiting Harvard in 1788, which for immersion in theology and the past he pronounced "almost the same as at

[20] Lemberg, "Universität Marburg," 227–9.

[21] BRB VH 27139/10 doc. 25: "Lettre à un ami touchant les articles prescrits récemment à l'Université de Louvain" (Sept. 1791), 3–4.

[22] BRB VH 27139/10 doc. 25, pp. 17–18.

Oxford," making it "impossible that the recent [American] Revolution will not bring about a great reform. Free men must quickly cast off their prejudices and see they have above all else to be men and citizens, and that study of dead languages and tedious philosophies and theologies should occupy few hours of their lives which could be more usefully devoted to studies more suitable to the great family of mankind."[23] Yet quantitative analysis of American library holdings and editions in the 1790s and first years of the new century fully reflects the widening rift within the Enlightenment, with radical works by Paine, Raynal, Rousseau, Volney, Beccaria, Condorcet, Godwin, and Wollstonecraft being widely read.[24] Feuding over the moral, social–political, and religious meaning of the Revolution pervaded American higher education and the public sphere. The war of ideas also invaded sermons, rendering American colleges simultaneously moderate Enlightenment strongholds, bastions of public conservativism and religious allegiance, while at the same time nurturing-grounds behind the shutters for clandestine networks promoting radical critique. The post-Revolution changes in America's higher education colleges were much less sweeping than Jefferson, Madison, Barlow, and other enlighteners hoped for, but the penetration of radical thought nevertheless everywhere fomented an atmosphere of conflict and struggle.[25]

In Europe, the democratic republican trend pulsing from the Swiss, Rhenish, Belgian, Dutch, and Italian revolutions of the 1790s, as well as France, subverted academe to the point that an entire underground academic army existed ready to act on the most negative evaluations of the universities' character and role the moment opportunity knocked. The 1792–3 revolutionary enclave in the Rhineland, the Mainz Republic, was based in a city of around 25,000, predominantly loyal to its archbishop-elector. It enjoyed scant popular support, but vigorous backing from a phalanx of republican-minded academics and students which gave it considerable allure.[26] If the common people adhered to the exiled archbishop-elector, the revolutionaries were backed by the reading clubs and societies of Mainz, Speyer, and Worms, as well as Heidelberg and Mannheim, where organized revolutionary clubs had emerged well ahead of the French invasion.[27] Revolutionary exultation gripped a fringe of highly educated intellectuals and secularist university-trained professionals. The Mainz Jacobin club, boasting at its peak 492 members, and the local *Lesegesellschaft* [reading society], founded in 1782, were closely linked to the university.[28] However, academic (as well as Protestant and Jewish) involvement only further boosted popular aversion. A similar clash occurred at Aachen, which experienced its own separate internal revolution. Most Aachen citizens, observed Dohm, resented seeing Jews and Protestants

[23] Brissot, *Travels in America*, 95, 97.

[24] Lundberg and May, "The Enlightened Reader," 269–71; Morgan, "Ezra Stiles," 109, 117.

[25] Israel, *Expanding Blaze*, 103–10, 416–18.

[26] Forster, *Werke* xvii. 213–14, 216; Blanning, *Reform*, 276–8; Wegert, *German Radicals*, 19–21.

[27] Mühlpfordt, *Demokratische Aufklärer* i. 276–7; Voss, "Kurpfalz im Zeichen," 16–19.

[28] Klopstock, *Werke* viii/2. 970–1; Grab, *Norddeutscher Jakobiner*, 21; Schweigard, "Studentische Netzwerke," 331–5.

becoming equal to Catholics far more than they resented the principality's antiquated laws and hierarchical status quo.[29]

Prior to 1792 Mainz (founded in 1477) figured among the largest Catholic universities. Although by the 1780s Enlightenment ideas already exerted a considerable impact, with Protestants and Jews admitted as students to most faculties from 1784, under the short-lived Mainz republic, the university, like Louvain, split asunder, most professors and many students fleeing to the archbishop-elector's court across the Rhine. The rump that stayed formed the backbone of the Rhenish revolution, a democratic republican challenge to Germany's princes led by Professors Wedekind, Dorsch, Blau, (Matthias) Metternich, and Forster. The Mainz revolution's principal journal, *Der Patriot*, viewed republican revolutionary ideals as an ideology originating exclusively from the *Aufklärung* and the march of "reason," and the conspicuous refusal of most professors to embrace democratic principles as largely due to a combination of slavish service to princes and ecclesiastics and the fact that relatively few of them, as the archbishop's former physician, Professor Wedekind, now conspicuously radicalized, observed, could offset the loss of their extra-mural official and administrative salaries, and become independent.[30]

Wedekind, Dorsch, and Forster strove to mobilize local support for *Freiheit und Gleichheit* and establish a democratic rights-based society, upholding freedom of thought, press, and expression. They organized their following through the Jacobin *Gesellschaft der Freunde der Freiheit und Gleichheit* [Society of Friends of Liberty and Equality]. Backed by the French commander in the area, Adam-Philippe Custine (1740–93) (until tried and guillotined by the Montagne), and his German secretary, Georg Wilhelm Böhmer (1761–1839), a former professor at the Worms gymnasium, Wedekind, Dorsch, and Forster, with the mathematician Matthias Metternich (1747–1825), editor of the journal *Burgerfreund* [Citizen's Friend] dominated the nascent republic. Across Germany they unleashed a vigorous propaganda campaign, from Mainz, publishing in the ten-month span from October 1792 to July 1793, over 120 pamphlets, speeches, and other pro-Revolution texts, which certainly helped establish more underground cells of republican and "Jacobin" support including at several universities, among them the "Friends of Freedom and Equality" student club at Würzburg.[31]

The Rhineland Republic's professorial leadership remained convinced the Revolution sprang from the iron logic of the Enlightenment and that the answer to their lack of popular support was an expanded, mass enlightenment launched from the printing press.[32] *Der Patriot*, a weekly commencing in November 1792, and other pro-Revolution journals like the *Neue Mainzer Zeitung*, offered translations of discourses by prominent revolutionary ideologues like Cloots, Proly, and Gorani, chosen by

[29] Hansen, *Quellen* ii. 710–11; Rowe, "Tale of Two Cities," 125–6.
[30] Wedekind, *Der Patriot*, vol. 1/c, pp. 2–3; Grab, *Norddeutsche Jakobiner*, 21.
[31] Schweigard, "Studentische Netzwerke," 338.
[32] Wedekind, *Der Patriot*, vol. 1/A, p. 3; Blanning, *Reform*, 276–7.

Wedekind and Forster as apt for promoting the doctrines of "general will," equality, and Human Rights. They reminded the Rhineland's long beleaguered Protestant and Jewish minorities that revolutionary universal rights and free expression, under *representative Demokratie*, offered them far greater advantages than any grudging princely policy of *Toleranz*.[33] While the Brissotins remained in the ascendant in France, the Mainz professors' efforts were supplemented by propaganda for Germany issuing also from Paris. In an undated 1792 address *Aux Germains*, Condorcet predicted the victory of the "irresistible force of reason": the Enlightenment would triumph over "princely perfidy and the errors and feebleness [of understanding] of the multitude." Did Germany not possess precious reservoirs of "des hommes éclairés" [enlightened men]. The countrymen of Copernicus, Kepler, Bekker, and Leibniz would not refuse to march with France under the banner of reason! "Germans, the destiny of humanity is decided; but that of the present generation lies in your hands."[34]

Striving to propagate *Republikanismus* in collaboration with the French, Forster grew profoundly disillusioned with the unresponsive attitude of most Rhineland burghers and peasants who seemingly bent their ears only to the reactionary admonitions of the Catholic clergy.[35] Their deference to *Kaiser und Reich* Forster could explain only in terms of limited horizons. For centuries, princes, nobles, and priests had mercilessly exploited the people; now they must learn to understand the true nature of their misery and wretched subjection—that and that alone would enable them to end the oppression that abased them. With popular *Aufklärung*, sectarian and national hatreds would fade and the new *Universal-Republik* of the future would eventually become attainable providing a higher collective good for all, a beneficent universalism nurturing more elevated ideals of humanity strong enough to end war and promote human happiness.[36] The propaganda campaign heightened the nervousness of the princely courts, which mobilized every possible means to block further dissemination of revolutionary literature, inhibit discussion of contemporary events, and tighten restrictions on free expression. When Prussian troops temporarily ejected the French and extinguished the Rhenish Republic, in the summer of 1793, they at once closed *Der Patriot* down.

Between 1789 and 1792, while France remained a constitutional monarchy, there continued to be two separate camps of German enlighteners sympathetic to the Revolution, moderates and radicals. Joachim Heinrich Campe (1746–1818), for instance, editor of the leading pre-1792 pro-revolutionary paper in German, the *Schlewigsches Journal*, published at Altona, admired Sieyès and the 1791 Constitution, and approved the French Civil Constitution of the Clergy, but, like Klopstock and his young friend, the budding philologist, ethnographer and educationalist,

[33] Wedekind, *Der Patriot*, vol. 1/A, pp. 12–14.
[34] BL 643/4 Revolution Tracts: Condorcet, "Aux Germains," 6, 23–4.
[35] Forster, *Werke* xvii. 284–5, 308–10; Broers, *Europe*, 122.
[36] Wedekind, *Der Patriot*, vol. 1/A, pp. 5–20.

Von Humboldt, deemed the Revolution entirely compatible with limited monarchy.[37] Forster, Wedekind, Dorsch, and Metternich, like the Brothers Johann and Franz Dautzenberg, the former a professor at Aachen, the latter editor of Aachen's now openly pro-revolutionary paper, the *Aachener Zuschauer*, on the other hand, wholly repudiated princely rule, monarchy, and "mixed government," demanding fully-fledged democratic republican values and a comprehensive curbing of religious authority throughout Germany.

20.2. THE POLITICIZATION OF GERMAN PHILOSOPHY

Akin to Kant's mediating discretion was the creed of Wilhelm von Humboldt, later among Europe's foremost late Enlightenment thinkers. During his brief student experience, chiefly at Göttingen, he had commenced his lifelong exploration of historical studies with Schlözer, philology with Heyne, and natural science with Lichtenberg.[38] Much preoccupied with French revolutionary politics, and questions of constitutions and constitutionalism, by 1791 he was predicting the failure of the moderate Revolution's attempt at "mixed government" while warning against over-estimating republican "free constitutions." Deeply influenced by Herder and the latter's Spinozistic radical tendency, he was convinced that in the end what chiefly matters are the concrete advantages to individuals and society the state affords.[39] This led him to acquiesce in the necessity, under German conditions, of a moderate Enlightenment outcome at the princely state level while simultaneously subverting the *ancien régime* at what he considered the deeper level of intellectual and cultural life, steering society toward individual autonomy with academic autonomy and universities becoming the nation's true powerhouse. Thus, Von Humboldt followed Montesquieu on one level: constitutional monarchies constrict individual liberty and self-development less than republics; [40] and no one would fight harder for a Prussian limited monarchy and constitution during the closing years of the Prussian reform era (1814–19). But he followed Spinoza, Toland, and Herder in seeking to forge a new kind of guiding elite to steer society destined ultimately to subvert the primacy of princes and courts.

Shortly before the Rhenish Republic's advent, in 1792, Von Humboldt gave classic expression to the enlightener's difficulties in revolutionary times in his *Ideen zu einem Versuch die Grenzen der Wirksamkeit des Staates zu bestimmen*, a text known in English as *The Spheres and Duties of Government*, where he defines the functions, duties, and limits of the enlightened state and claims the moral uprightness the state

[37] Losfeld, *Philanthropisme*, 147–8. [38] Von Humboldt, *Briefe*, 460–1.

[39] Gall, *Wilhelm von Humboldt*, 66; Barnard, *Herder on Nationality*, 15; Gare, "Democracy and Education," 19.

[40] High, *Schillers Rebellionskonzept*, 75.

must foment is "in no way inseparably associated" with religious ideas. [41] Knowing he could not publish it without falling foul of the intensifying censorship system, he left it to gather dust as an unpublished manuscript (that appeared posthumously only in 1851). But already this early cry in the dark expressed his later famous ideas of *Bildung*, the modern state's prime responsibility being to create the conditions, promote the process, by which the individual can attain his fullest "inner force," self-formation, moral autonomy, and potential through understanding. The highest freedom means individual development optimally ripening in cultural and social conditions forged by the state in its responsibility to elevate society to the utmost intellectually and morally.[42] This was the direction of his future reform strategy. As it developed subsequently, in Berlin, not least at the evening salon of the Jewish enlighteners, Markus and Henriette Herz, the creed evolved exclusively in cultural rather than ethnic, religious, or any traditional terms, enabling Von Humboldt, at the close of the Napoleonic Wars, to become the foremost single defender of Jewish rights and equality in Prussia, and all Germany.[43]

Von Humboldt's status as a Prussian state official, if still a junior one, of high social rank, and capacity for bridging ideological divides and forming lasting friendships—most notably with Forster (with whom he became friendly at Göttingen), Jacobi, Schiller, Goethe, Fichte, and the Brothers Schlegel, as well as the conservative political commentator, Gentz—enabled him to combine, as did Dohm, the public, urbane face of moderate reformist Prussian officialdom with a private, more daring, clandestine streak, affording leverage in enlightened circles behind the scenes that few other Enlightenment champions of the era could rival. He proved a more representative figure than Forster in that most younger philosophical critics did not desire to conspire politically with the French revolutionaries, but, via discreet rebellion and immersing themselves in the humanities, quietly propagate their call for human improvement and self-formation. They aspired to elevate the people via the non-political, or only discreetly political, routes recommended by Kant, Herder, and Schiller. Their new secular religion of freedom, self-improvement, republican political virtue, rights, duties, and aesthetics suffused with Herder's Graecomania, however disdainful of conventional notions and tradition, they proclaimed to be in conflict with the old order less directly and physically than conceptually and emotionally. Nor did they see themselves as less pertinent and effective Enlightenment revolutionaries than their French counterparts; rather, they considered themselves profounder.

The only way an eventually "republican" outcome presided over by the princes could evolve, under Kant's schema, was through reforms proposed and implemented by princely courts in the face of the French challenge, prodded by the progress of their own peoples in moral awareness and enlightenment. But the younger thinkers, Fichte,

[41] Von Humboldt, *Sphere and Duties*, 76–8; Gall, *Wilhelm von Humboldt*, 65–71.

[42] Von Humboldt to Forster, Erfurt, 1 June 1792, in Von Humboldt, *Briefe*, 68–9, 461.

[43] Von Humboldt, *Briefe*, 459; Nipperdey, *Germany*, 218; Gall, *Wilhelm von Humboldt*, 188–92.

Schelling, Hölderlin, the young Hegel, and their circles, found Kant's fudging between conservatism and a pro-revolutionary sympathy unconvincing. The fight for the universities was a struggle between Enlightenment and reaction for control of the formatively most vital part of the public sphere, one that fomented bitterly warring ideological factions, straddling the divide between moderate and Radical Enlightenment within the ranks of the philosophical professoriate and all the philosophically aspiring. Fichte, having earlier adhered to a type of non-providential deism, identifying God with Nature, close to Spinozism, converted to Kantianism during his Leipzig stay in the summer of 1790. This inspired his move to Königsberg for a season to attend Kant's lectures and, from July to October 1791, enter into intense debate with Kant himself, who, at the time, warmly encouraged his young disciple. By 1793, still an itinerant tutor, he was starting to gain notoriety throughout Germany by boldly revising Kant's system.

Kant's *Critique of Pure Reason* transformed Fichte by freeing him from the "apparent consistency of my previous system" which he thought constricted him with its rigid determinism and necessitarianism. Kant offered escape from materialism into "absolute freedom" and the concept of duty.[44] Fichte then reworked and modified Kantianism in a similar direction to the cosmopolitan crypto-Spinozist "revolution friend" and equal human rights activist Karl Heinrich Heydenreich (1764–1801), at Leipzig, a local leader of the underground Deutsche Union, by whom he was probably influenced[45]—that is, by replacing Kantianism's ontological dualism with an essentially monist system and coming out more explicitly for revolutionary ideals. In 1793, Fichte published at Danzig—anonymously, to avoid public and princely displeasure—two works, *A Discourse on the Reclamation of the Freedom of Thought from the Princes of Europe who have hitherto suppressed it* and *A Contribution towards correcting the People's Judgment of the French Revolution*, both directly challenging Germany's princes and popular culture, by appealing for freedom of thought and expression and affirming the "General Will" as the well-being of all—and generally indicating his support for the Revolution.[46] With Fichte, as so often in Enlightenment history, philosophical monism, here expressly distanced from Kantianism, signaled close interaction with democratic republicanism.[47] Despite publishing the texts anonymously, it soon seeped out that philosophy's rising star was an ally of the French and Rhenish democratic republicans (i.e. the Brissotins). Drafted in 1792, the *Discourse* had originally been conciliatory in tone, but grew more acerbic in its final version, vigorously renewing Bahrdt's assault on princes and court censorship, deploring the entire "system of patronage and tutelage." Confronting the iron hand of princely repression, Fichte recognized,

[44] Hudson et al., *Rethinking German Idealism*, 39.

[45] Crowe, "Theismus des Gefühls," 571–2, 584, 587; Mühlpfordt, *Halle-Leipziger Aufklärung*, 344–5, 357–8, 374.

[46] Breazeale, "Fichte and Schelling," 143.

[47] La Vopa, *Fichte*, 100, 122–30; Morujão, "Controversias teológicas," 310.

was bound to be a formidable undertaking. He later styled Bahrdt one of those "unfortunate martyrs for the truth" who made the mistake of expecting "humanity and reason" from the countless "enemies of the truth." Fichte labored under no such illusion.[48]

Kant, he believed, had rescued morality and duty from Diderot, d'Holbach, Lessing, and—hovering behind them—Spinoza. "The influence this [Kantian] philosophy, especially its moral part (although this is unintelligible apart from a study of the *Critique of Pure Reason*), has upon one's entire way of thinking is unbelievable—as is the revolution occasioned in my way of thinking in particular." With Kant, he came to "believe wholeheartedly in human freedom and realize full well that duty, virtue, and morality are all possible where freedom is presupposed."[49] In his *Foundations of Natural Right* (1795–6), he pushed on with his quest to rebuild philosophy in a post-Kantian mold by circumventing the divide Kant imposed between the objective and subjective. Fichte's principal innovation was to redefine "reason" as the striving of the self to be conscious of both itself and the non-self. Reason is first consciousness, then self-consciousness in relation to the other, and finally synthesis through the self's grasping and encompassing the other, that is the world. Individual freedom and morality Fichte anchored in group freedom and morality, and natural right, or what the individual accords to others naturally when demanding freedom for himself. "It turns out that, in thought, each member of the community lets his own external freedom be limited through inner freedom, so that all others beside him can also be externally free. This is the concept of right."[50]

Fichte's, like Schiller's and Von Humboldt's philosophy, emphasized individuality, autonomy, activism, and moral development of the self, rather than mere negative liberty as with Hobbes or Locke, while avoiding pure subjectivism by wrapping morality and theory of "religion" in the responsibility of men to one another.[51] Kantian moral philosophy he fused with his own revolutionary social and political stance and a Spinozistic notion of individuality as striving for one's advantage (*conatus*).[52] His transcendental idealism sounding at times like the opposite of materialism, commented Jacobi later, but this was an illusion: for there exists a point where the two meet and become one—and that convergence was Fichte's system.[53] Driven by its monist materialist underlay, morality in Fichte is simply reason applied to mankind as a whole, for the benefit of society. During the 1790s he was a radical enlightener in the main but by no means entirely: while willing to concede that women are the equal of men in possessing "reason," it is striking that he was never willing to grant women full equality with men either in the public sphere,

48 Fichte, *Appeal*, 98–9; Israel, *Revolutionary Ideas*, 334–5.
49 Fichte, "Selected Correspondence," 357, 360.
50 Fichte, *Foundations of Natural Right*, 10.
51 Wittekind, "Retorsion des Atheismus," 64–7; Hudson et al., *Rethinking German Idealism*, 48.
52 Fichte, *Foundations of Transcendental Philosophy*, 71–2, 76.
53 Jaeschke, "Messias der spekulativen Vernunft," 149–51.

as political beings, or within marriage. And then there was the question of his deep and abiding if ambiguous anti-Semitism.[54]

Fichte's 200-page *Contribution* or *Beitrag zur Berichtigung des Urtheile des Publikums über die Französische Revolution* vigorously refutes the sweeping conservative critique of the Revolution and "universal and equal rights" by the Humean skeptic August Wilhelm Rehberg (1757–1836), a leader of a Göttingen circle of moderates defending aristocracy and British-style mixed government. The Revolution's deep significance for all mankind, powerfully reaffirmed by Fichte, is redefined in relation to modern philosophy. The Revolution's core principles, its attack on privilege and aristocracy and theory of "the general will," which, Fichte claimed, Rehberg misrepresented, were morally and philosophically all justified, with every "people" possessing the right to assert its freedom and change its constitution. Theorists, like Rehberg and Schlötzer, asserting the opposite, advocating social hierarchy and seconding Burke, he dismissed as mere trifling *Sophisten*.[55]

Extolling toleration and universal rights (for men), Fichte settled in Jena just a month before his soon-to-be friend, ally, and fellow passionate advocate of Enlightenment likewise much preoccupied with the implications of Kantianism, Von Humboldt. Appointed by Goethe and the Weimar court to succeed Reinhold in expounding the new critical Kantian philosophy, he arrived from Zurich, in May 1794, as a nationally-celebrated 32-year-old ardent "Kantian." His lectures caused a sensation. Attracting students from all across German-speaking Europe, he became one of Europe's most influential thinkers while still in his twenties. By 1795 he had come to believe he had truly supplemented Kant in moral and social philosophy, beside metaphysics, crowning Kant's achievement by fully liberating the reflective, imaginative, and moral self, thereby completing the task of the Revolution in the intellectual and moral sphere. "Just as France has freed man from external shackles, so my system frees him from the fetters of things in themselves, that is from those external influences with which all previous systems—including the Kantian— have fettered him."[56] He felt he had finalized Kantianism's triumph, following the uproar over Mendelssohn, Lessing, and the *Pantheismusstreit*, as the sole viable philosophical alternative to Spinozism for the serious-minded. Where Kant believed his philosophy is the only viable alternative to Spinozism due to the fundamental duality it creates between concepts and the thing-in-itself, Fichte believed he offered the only convincing alternative to this by replacing Kant's dualism and thing-in-itself with a modified, reconciling monism.[57]

Jena University typified the wider ferment of post-Mainz revolutionary Germany. Fichte arrived in an intellectual milieu already deep in turmoil, philosophically and

[54] Rose, *German Question/Jewish Question*, 117–25, 131–2, 149, 198, 234, 274; see also La Vopa, *Fichte*, 132–40.

[55] Fichte, *Schriften*, 64, 66, 70, 91; Israel, *Revolutionary Ideas*, 334–5.

[56] Fichte, "Selected Correspondence," 385–6.

[57] Beiser, *German Idealism*, 261–2; Solé, "Intervención de F. H. Jacobi," 454.

politically, with the great dramatist Schiller, and their common friend Von Humboldt, plunged in debates encompassing Kantianism, the university's future, and theirs and Herder's new conception of humanity as self-formation only reaching full potential where the political and cultural context upheld by the state conduces to this end.[58] Fichte's reputation as a "rights" radical had preceded him, and while this spelt early success with some students, it immediately antagonized many colleagues and courtiers, provoking growing local opposition to his pro-Revolution philosophy and teaching.[59] A rumor spread that he had predicted in his opening lecture that "in ten or twenty years there will be no more princes;" whatever the truth of that, he remained relatively discreet in the lecture hall, while expressing more radical notions in private letters. "No king or prince will grant a pension to the author [i.e. himself] of the *Wissenschaftslehre*," he remarks in one letter, "for one sees from this system's first principles that it is incompatible with kings and princes." The *Gelehrter* [scholar] has a special role in man's vocation and destiny, he explained in 1795, adding that should a prince offer him a pension, "he would not accept it," but would accept one from the French nation. Throughout the 1790s Fichte remained a fervent supporter of the Revolution, which "consists in the constant advancement of culture and the equal and continuous development of all of man's talents and needs." The professor's role was to "supervise" that collective progress.[60]

Combining philosophy and history with high-level literary criticism, Jena emerged at this time as the intellectual center of all the major new trends in German culture—Kantianism, academic renewal, and romanticism,[61] underpinned by nationally renowned journals, like the *Allgemeine Literatur Zeitung* and an underlay of radical, republican politics. Contributing prominently on all fronts were the brothers Friedrich and August Schlegel and their scintillating *salonnière* wives, the latter's, Caroline, having been an enthusiastic participant in the 1792–3 Rhineland Republic. Friedrich Schlegel (1772–1829), a leading literary critic, though only briefly Fichte's philosophical ally during 1795–6, was more enduringly a political ally, in 1796 publishing his "Versuch über den Begriff des Republikanismus" [On the Concept of Republicanism], openly championing, like Fichte, revolutionary democratic republicanism while criticizing aspects of Kant.[62] The general tendency of political development, held Kant, in his 1795 essay "Perpetual Peace," is ultimately toward a "republican" outcome finally resulting in a "perpetual peace;" but Schlegel, like Fichte, in his *Foundations of Natural Right* (1796), found Kant's *Republikanismus* stunted and insufficient, through failure to set republicanism and despotism sufficiently in opposition and tie republicanism to democracy and Spinozistic monism.[63] Kant offers no doctrine of the *allgemeine Wille* [General Will] and does not acknowledge that

[58] Gall, *Wilhelm von Humboldt*, 75–6. [59] Almeida Carvalho, "Introdución histórica," 78–9.

[60] Draft of letter, April or May 1795, in Fichte, *Early Philosophical Writings*, 385; Sauter, *Visions*, 131–3.

[61] Blanning, *Romantic Revolution*, 50. [62] Beiser, *German Idealism*, 438.

[63] Fichte, *Foundations of Natural Right*, 14–16; Höffe, *Kant's Cosmopolitan Theory*, 155.

"der Republikanismus ist also notwendig demokratisch" [Republicanism is therefore necessarily democratic]. The conditions needed for mankind to reach the common goal of "perpetual peace" were the *Polizierung aller Nationen* [politicization of all nations], leading to fraternity of all republicans, autonomy of every state, and *Isonomia* [political equality] of all states. Until then, war between states remains inevitable.[64]

Jena students were abandoning the *ancien régime* "old order" and embarking, admonished Fichte, Schlegel, and the philosophical radicals, on a new era of freedom, insight, and moral responsibility. Such cells were to be found at various universities, including Württemberg's renowned university of Tübingen, where Friedrich Hölderlin (1770–1843) and his circle, including Friedrich Wilhelm Schelling (1775–1854), who had similarly defected from theology to Kantianism, and now embraced Fichte's Idealism, likewise exalted the revolutionary war against Europe's princes, and the French Revolution's summons to peoples to rise, and assert their republican sovereignty and rights.[65] Hölderlin, soon to emerge as a celebrated poet, having discarded his early theological studies and by 1790 joined forces with Hegel and Schelling, belonged with them and another poet, Gotthold Stäudlin (1758–96), his revolutionary mentor, and another friend, a younger revolutionary enthusiast studying at Jena since May 1794, Izaac Sinclair, to the student faction spreading across Germany, blending Revolution with Spinozism and Fichte's philosophy.[66] Steeped in the Jacobi–Mendelssohn controversy over Lessing's "Spinozism," by late 1792 Hölderlin expressly combined Brissotin republicanism with Fichtean Kantianism.[67]

During 1795–6, Hölderlin joined Fichte, Schiller, and Von Humboldt at Jena. While steeping himself in Fichte's *Wissenschaftslehre* he continued his close interaction with Schelling and Hegel, in the south-west. Through the mid- and late 1790s, down to the rupture between Schelling and Fichte in 1806, all these young thinkers remained broadly philosophical–political allies adopting Fichte's approach, especially Fichte's new foundation of the "I" as the key step to transcending Kantianism, and when Schelling did begin to loosen himself from close alignment with Fichte, from 1797, with his developing *Naturphilosophie*, he still remained an ally for some years even more steeped in Spinoza than before—a phase of his development that lasted until Napoleon's conquest of Germany (1805–7), after which he increasingly distanced himself from Fichte, Spinoza, and all leftist republican positions.[68]

In the late 1790s, the Jena coterie aimed to reform philosophy itself from a static academic abstract into a dynamic force rooted in the thinking individual, a form of underground activism in Spinoza's sense fusing instinct with reason, an "I" picturing the world, interpreting it, and embracing it to secure the individual's place in it and

64 Schlegel, *Kritische Friedrich-Schlegel-Ausgabe*, 1st series, vol. 7 (1966), 11–25; Cousin, *Souvenirs*, 48.
65 Nauen, *Revolution, Idealism*, 25, 50, 53; Michel, *Leben Friedrich Hölderlins*, 60–9.
66 Michel, *Leben Friedrich Hölderlins*, 127–30; Schweigard, "Studentische Netzwerke," 327–31.
67 Nauen, *Revolution, Idealism*, 52, 54, 56; Josephson-Storm, *Myth of Disenchantment*, 88.
68 Guilherme, *Fichte and Schelling*, 139–40, 149, 157, 164–6.

his and her relation to everything else.[69] Individuals apply reason for their own benefit, in the world, with a continual impact on one another. Wherever the "goal of reason is secured through unification of the individual goals of individuals (the general will)," individual "physical force must be restrained so that they will not hinder one another," for otherwise individuals will constantly obstruct each other through their individual aspirations hampering collective reason. Contrary to the "general will" (*volonté générale*) of Rousseau, to whose thought, and "state of nature," Fichte was as hostile as d'Holbach, Condorcet, or Volney,[70] his "general will," like theirs, identified the constraining of individual freedom as the buttress of "rights." Toleration and individual and minority rights are safeguarded in his system in a way Rousseau's merged oneness of the citizenry's collective will cannot do.[71] Like Diderot, d'Holbach, and Condorcet, Fichte deplored Rousseau's educational theories, especially his claiming "cultural advancement is the sole cause of all human corruption."[72] For Fichte, the opposite is true: collective reason restrains individual appetite and seeks the order that affords optimal levels of freedom for all; "die Rechtslehre oder Naturrecht" [theory of right or natural law] is "what arises from enquiring into how this can be accomplished." Free constitutions securing optimal conditions for human freedom derive from the "joint efficacy of nature and reason."[73]

Exploring the subjective consciousness, its character, limitations, and potential, the transcendental Idealist philosopher revises the relationship of man to nature, contemplating the thread of history, the essence of morality and meaning of politics. Fichte's and Schelling's endorsement of the "general will" in Diderot's, d'Holbach's, Condorcet's, and Volney's sense as a universal impulse, implied too the gradual emergence of an eventual "universal constitution" or system of states supervising a collective law of nations.[74] Where Robespierre Jacobins were xenophobic in outlook, the Brissotins with whom Fichte, Hölderlin, Schelling, and all the radical enlighteners aligned, stressed the universal, cosmopolitan aspects of "rights of mankind." Fichte and Schelling felt, again like Condorcet, Volney, and Schelling, that the "sole true object of the historian" is the gradual emergence of the world political order. If universal history's object is gradual realization of the rule of law, the measure of human progress is man's slow approximation to a goal "whose final attainment, however, can neither be inferred from experience, so far as it has hitherto unfolded, nor be theoretically demonstrated a priori, but will only be an eternal article of faith to man as he acts and works."[75] History, the union of the subjective and objective, was the necessary fusion of freedom and necessity. Subsuming Kant's strictures regarding

[69] Fichte, *Foundations of Transcendental Philosophy*, 82, 112–13, 151–3;Vatar, "Introduction," pp. xvi–xvii.

[70] Fichte, *Early Philosophical Writings*, 177–84; Michel, *Leben Friedrich Hölderlins*, 142–3.

[71] Fichte, *Foundations of Natural Right*, 96–101, 134–7.

[72] Fichte, *Early Philosophical Writings*, 177–9.

[73] Fichte, *Foundations of Transcendental Philosophy*, 470–1.

[74] Schelling, *System of Transcendental Idealism*, 198–9.

[75] Schelling, *System of Transcendental Idealism*, 202–3.

the unknowability of what is in itself, Fichte retained Spinoza's *Natura naturans* and *naturata*, nature both creating itself and being created, as he put it, Nature "both organized and organizing."[76] Redefining "God" as the humanly-grasped "moral world order (this supersensible, divine realm that is infinitely superior to all that is transitory),"[77] Fichte strove to reaffirm individual freedom, collective freedom, and the reality of moral obligation. Fichte, Schelling, Hölderlin, and Hegel accordingly all scorned "vulgar Kantians," as they called academics defending theology and tradition by employing Kant's unknowability of the thing-in-itself to counter rejection of faith and "mysteries" on the ground of reason's fallibility and limitations. Spinozism, they insisted, required qualification rather than discarding, nuanced by a better ordering of Kant's innovations.[78]

Robespierre's dictatorship, the startling victory of the *sociétés populaires*, Counter-Enlightenment, anti-intellectualism, and Terror inevitably exerted a deeply disheartening, disorienting effect on Fichte and the entire fringe of revolutionary young philosophers and writers. Traumatized, Schiller fell into a profound silence on political and public issues.[79] Plunged in gloom, Hölderlin's revolutionary comrade, Stäudlin, committed suicide in September 1796, drowning himself in the Rhine. Gritting his teeth, Hölderlin, like Hegel and Fichte, at first remained fervent for the Revolution, renewing his zeal after Thermidor, still eager to see comparable changes sweep across Germany, much as, by 1797–9, they swept across Italy and Switzerland. For the rest of his active career down to his mental breakdown (1805), no one strove more ardently to perfect his circle's pantheist political radicalism amid Germany's increasingly reactionary mood and the populace's anti-philosophical solidarity with princes and clergy. Fichte searched for counter-measures to preclude anything as appalling as *robespierriste* tyranny ever recurring. Writing to Reinhold, in July 1797, he urged a higher "constitutional court," or "ephorate" to oversee the workings of every republican government's executive power, to ensure it does not violate "natural rights" or the dictates of the "general will." His popularly elected, independent, well-paid, incorruptible higher constitutional court, resembled Condorcet's proposal along similar lines, being likewise empowered to summon the citizenry, suspend the government, and restore the republic on a corrected basis.[80]

The gloom of 1793–4 following earlier exhilaration presented a profound spiritual challenge to thinkers and writers identifying the Revolution with mankind's progress, and the advance of science, scholarship, and "philosophy." Especially from 1795, as the Revolution overran Belgium, Holland, and the Rhineland, the atmosphere at Jena became increasingly fraught. Confronting a sharply divided student body, radical professors clashed with the conservative, traditional student fraternities which spread

[76] Fichte, *Foundations of Transcendental Philosophy*, 76, 460–1.
[77] Fichte, *Appeal*, 103. [78] Vater, "Introduction," p. xix.
[79] High, *Schillers Rebellionskonzept*, 123, 156–8.
[80] Fichte, "Selected Correspondence," 421–3, 434; Fichte, *Foundations of Natural Right*, 16–17, 151–9.

reports that Fichte was scheming to suppress them and "erect an order of Illuminates upon their ruins." Disconcerted by the mounting opposition to his views, Fichte persevered while feeling increasingly estranged from the mainstream academic arena. After he began delivering well-attended lectures on Sunday mornings when church services were in progress, provoking friction with the Weimar ecclesiastical Oberkonsistorium chaired by Herder, Fichte's position at Jena grew still more precarious.[81] Reaffirming his allegiance to the Revolution's values and goals, in a letter drafted in the spring of 1795, after the neo-Brissotin recovery and Condorcet's rehabilitation signaled the revival of Enlightenment and philosophy in France, he expressed his readiness to accept a position and state pension in the French Republic and assist with its recovery from Robespierre's tyranny. Where in early 1793 it had been the French nation's example and "valor that encouraged me and gave me the energy I needed for grasping my [philosophical] system," France should now "externally and publicly appropriate my system by supplying me with the wherewithal to develop it." He considered living "somewhere in Alsace or, some other German province of that republic, since I do not know the French language well enough to use it in ordinary conversation."[82]

Although for now the Schelling–Hegel–Hölderlin clique remained broadly aligned with Fichte against Kant,[83] closely pondering how to restructure a republican monism that transforms mankind,[84] by 1798, after several years tutoring, Schelling, summoned by Goethe and the rectorate at the age of only 23 to serve as Jena's adjunct professor of philosophy, beside Fichte, was already discarding some of his early revolutionary fervor. Suspected by the Württemberg authorities of being a ringleader behind Tübingen student agitation in 1794,[85] by 1798 Schelling associated rather with circles seeking a gradual, peaceful evolution of Württemberg's representative institutions toward a more genuinely representative and republican outcome. Intimate with Caroline Schlegel (whom he afterwards married) and in dialogue with Hegel, in 1800 Schelling still felt he had much in common with Fichte: "philosophy is the history of self-consciousness" in various epochs; it is via history that "one absolute synthesis is put together."[86] For both Fichte and Schelling, Spinozism remained at this time "das consequenteste Product" of "dogmatism" and Fichte's Idealism the means to circumvent it. [87] Philosophy, held Schelling, can say nothing about being and reality in itself, and all metaphysics disregarding this is "dogmatism," for which *being* is fundamental. However, "a consistent dogmatism is found only in Spinozism." [88] While their transcendental Idealism repudiated all "dogmatism," meaning all metaphysics and prior philosophy, with regard to Spinoza it was actually completing and finalizing a system otherwise uniquely relevant and "consistent."

[81] Ohst, "Fichte's Entlassung," 11.
[82] Fichte, "Selected Correspondence," 386.
[83] Nauen, *Revolution, Idealism*, 11–13.
[84] Nauen, *Revolution, Idealism*, 62–3.
[85] Nauen, *Revolution, Idealism*, 21.
[86] Schelling, *System of Transcendental Idealism*, 50.
[87] Schelling, *System of Transcendental Idealism*, 99.
[88] Schelling, *System of Transcendental Idealism*, 17.

For the "dogmatist" must learn that philosophy is possible only as a science of knowledge, with knowledge, not being, as its object. Its principle can be no principle of being "but only a principle of knowledge."[89] "Self-consciousness is the lamp of the whole system of knowledge, but it casts its light only ahead, not behind," that is, does not elucidate the objective reality of the self, but only *our* reality. Hence, it transforms reality into a fusion of the objective and subjective meaningfully explained only by Transcendental Idealism. Schelling ultimately adopted a more comprehensive, totalizing approach to man's relationship with nature than Fichte, a rigorous monism, as destructive of Revelation, divine providence, and final ends as Spinoza's but grounded not on "substance" or *Natura* but the free and unbounded human ego, the universal interaction of the perceived and the perceiving.[90] The problem with this was that it meant philosophy could ultimately say nothing about being, and nothing about God, divine providence, or Revelation. Where *Fichteanismus* represented, using Jacobi's term, an "umgekehrter Spinozismus" [inverted Spinozism], Schelling's more obviously constituted a full-blown monist, materialist conception of nature, always verging on, while neurotically striving to avoid descending into, Spinozism.[91]

The Jena philosophical coterie represented a powerful renewal of the "republic of letters" of Bayle's day, reshaping mankind not least through periodicals, literature, and international intellectual networks except now with a more active, imperious demeanor, and allotting universities a far greater role in concerting mankind's march toward "reason" than was conceivable around 1700. Where Leibniz operated outside academe and Kant emancipated philosophy from Germany's theology departments, Fichte, Schiller, Schelling, and Hegel strove to martial the main reforming impulse within the academic world, all progressive academic endeavor, under the commanding baton of "philosophy." Like Schiller, Goethe, and Von Humboldt, Fichte viewed Jena as the new nerve-center of German philosophy,[92] the flagship leading the universities not just to a higher understanding of the world of thought, criticism, and study but a new conception of the relationship of knowledge, science, and the universities to society, including religion and politics, a vision grounded in his philosophy of human autonomy and activism.[93] The university authorities, however, remained acutely sensitive to anything that could threaten the University's standing, since Jena was surrounded by formidable competitors—the nearby universities of Halle, Leipzig, and Wittenberg.

To complicate matters further, Jena did not rest under a single prince's supervision, like most German universities, but under joint jurisdiction of four petty princes (the dukes of Sachsen-Weimar-Eisenach, Sachsen-Gotha, Sachsen-Coburg, and Sachsen-Meiningen) with the first possessing the privilege of nominating the rector

[89] Schelling, *System of Transcendental Idealism*, 18–20, 31; Solé, "Intervención de F. H. Jacobi," 454 n. 28; Wood, "Fichte on Freedom," 125.

[90] Naeuen, *Revolution, Idealism*, 38.

[91] Beiser, *German Idealism*, 473, 504; Bowie, *Schelling*, 15–16; Naeuen, *Revolution, Idealism*, 33–8; Jaeschke, "De Messias der spekulativen Vernunft," 149.

[92] Cousin, *Souvenirs*, 143–5.

[93] Hudson et al., *Rethinking German Idealism*, 38–40.

but all four sharing selection of the board of government.[94] Colliding with the theologians and the right-wing students' "prejudices," feeling "maliciously persecuted, pursued and slandered," Fichte also soon felt threatened by the growing anxieties of nearby princely courts. Fighting for republican freedom and the revolutionary cause, gradually Fichte came to feel more and more boxed in and became more and more disillusioned with the German intellectual class in which he had vested his hopes.

What is the nature of one's "reciprocal interaction" with other men? One cannot think of one's own being and identity, and assign to oneself primacy toward inanimate things and feelings of precedence in the world without simultaneously and equally ascribing such "rights" also to all other men. "The conditions making individuality possible," he assured his predecessor, Reinhold, now lecturing at Kiel (another university plagued by clashing revolutionary and counter-revolutionary fervor) and with whom he regularly corresponded—a maxim he reiterated afterwards verbatim to Jacobi—are called "rights."[95] Yet, suddenly, "reason" at Jena found itself under siege. To Reinhold, in August 1795, he described Jena's situation as "not the silent progress of reason, but rather a flaring of passion." He was forced to become increasingly guarded: "I am not thinking of direct political action," he assured Reinhold, in July 1797; "I believe this would be harmful. The scholar must work indirectly." Professoriate and student body had to be transformed unobtrusively if they were to lead the intellectual revolution he and his allies envisaged. But since the Rhenish Republic's collapse, Germany's universities and cultural life could hardly claim to be moving in the right direction; indeed, everything struck him as unsatisfactory. "Science [i.e. scholarship] is in greater danger than ever before. Intellectual freedom will be easily suppressed despite the stupidity of the forces conspiring against it, because the scholars themselves are of so little use." Here was the rub. Yet, his "Idealism" still made inroads.[96] During 1796–9, persevering at Jena, Fichte further refined his system in lectures and his *Wissenschaftslehre, nova methodo*, known in English as the *Foundations of Transcendental Philosophy*.

Fichte's sense of helpless revolutionary isolation was nothing unusual. Heydenreich, sunk in alcoholism, drugs, and debt, abandoned his academic career at Leipzig in 1798; Hegel spent most of the mid-1790s (1793–6) in the aristocratic republic of Berne feeling estranged and isolated—albeit with ample time for systematic study of Kant and Fichte, and dialogue with Jena.[97] Hölderlin, polishing the final version of his great poem *Hyperion*, at Frankfurt in 1796, began, not unlike Fichte, Schelling, Schiller, and Von Humboldt, to picture himself less a spokesman for an actual political and social program than a remote, beleaguered educator stranded in a corrupt setting, tormented by the burden of having to transform society's cultural and intellectual

[94] Ohst, "Fichte's Entlassung," 11. [95] Fichte, "Selected Correspondence," 408–9, 411.
[96] Fichte to Reinhold, 4 July 1797, in Fichte, *Early Philosophical Writings*, 422–3.
[97] Pinkard, *Hegel*, 80–1; Mühlpfordt, *Halle-Leipziger Aufklärung*, 371–2.

attitudes.[98] Composed in 1797–1800, his most grandiose poetic undertaking, the tragedy *Empedokles*, features an ancient Sicilian Greek philosopher seeking the ultimate meaning of life, politics, and philosophy who throws himself into the crater of Mount Aetna to become reunited with Nature. Averse to suicide except in special circumstances Hölderlin could never decide how *Empedokles* should end. By 1800, creeping insanity effectively removed him from the pro-Revolution philosophical coterie.

20.3. THE *ATHEISMUSSTREIT* (1798–1799)

Central Europe's universities during the late 1790s remained deeply split between the rival philosophical as well as political factions. At Göttingen, students and professors alike hesitated before the rival blocs for and against Kant, or, as some put it sarcastically, whether to join the "Protestants or Catholics of the critical philosophy."[99] Fichte scorned most contemporary German philosophy and literature teaching as "universal confusion, stupidity and weakness" apt to foment still more catastrophic intellectual chaos than gripped the universities already due to reactionary rectorates and scheming conservative student fraternities. He sought to strengthen his hand by allying with Reinhold and Jacobi, but before long the uproar surrounding his teaching exploded into a full-scale national furor, an intellectual–political scandal known as the *Atheismusstreit* [Atheism controversy], a re-run of the 1780s *Pantheismusstreit* but with a different cast of characters and less explicit preoccupation with Spinozism.[100]

This new grand controversy commenced in 1798 when Fichte went a step too far in princely eyes, with his article *Über den Grund unseres Glaubens in einer göttliche Weltregierung* [On the Basis of our Belief in the Divine Governance of the World] claiming that a comprehensive "moral world order" can exist without requiring a conscious, benevolent deity to act as moral lawgiver, with philosophical reason fulfilling that role instead. Construed by the wider public as a battle of theism against atheism, on a more academic level there was never much doubt that Fichte, like Spinoza, believed in "God" in his own "philosophical" sense. But by 1798 the public was rallying increasingly behind the princes and becoming exasperated. What was at issue in the furious controversy that now ensued was, essentially, the question underlying the entire feuding between radical and moderate Enlightenment: is there, or is there not, a divine world-governance that creates, directs, and governs the world sanctioning religious authority and the prevailing social hierarchy? Defining God as the moral world-order placed "God," in Fichte's view, beyond speculation or doubt, rendering "God" the formative force of reality, the ground of all rational

[98] Nauen, *Revolution, Idealism*, 64.
[99] Lehmann to Kant, Göttingen, 13 Nov. 1799, in Kant, *Briefwwechsel* iii. 274.
[100] Winter, *Die theologische und philosophische Ausinandersetzung*, 287–8.

certainty about the world, politics, religion, and humanity.[101] His article on the issue of "Divine World-Governance," published in the autumn of 1798, triggered a soon vast commotion. In terms of basic principles he had expounded in lecture-halls for years, it said nothing new. But laying "before the greater philosophical public, for examination and mutual deliberation, the results of his philosophizing" about "divine world-governance"[102] precipitated at this point one of the greatest public controversies of the Enlightenment era.

There *is* a "wahre Glaube" [true faith], argues Fichte, a fath inherent in our self-perception and perceptions of our relationship to others. Fichte's "God" in short was the natural moral world-order. Appearing in the Jena *Philosophisches Journal einer Gesellschaft Teutscher Gelehrten*, of which he had been co-editor since 1796, his article reaffirmed Kant's contention that direct knowledge of God is impossible. "God" he identified rather, for human purposes, with the passive and unknowing moral world-order perceived only by men, to which our consciousness and conscience unerringly leads us. All sense of duty urging men to act morally requires acknowledging, in Kantian fashion, the reality of "God" as the essence of that morality: "that living and active moral order is itself God; we require no other God and can grasp no other."[103] "True atheism, genuine unbelief, and godlessness," explained Fichte, is unwillingness "to obey the voice of one's conscience." To opponents this was "atheism" because along with all attempts to justify religious coercion, ecclesiastical authority, theology, and church jurisdiction over men, Fichte expressly denied the independent being, will, benevolence, and substantiality of God.[104]

Accepting such ideas, protested adversaries, meant "we could then no longer speak of Christianity" let alone a public, state-endorsed clergy.[105] Many found it inexcusable that Fichte "teaches his atheistic principles to young people who wish to prepare themselves for the most important governmental and ecclesiastical positions," while dragging Kant into the mêlée by saddling him with spreading "confusion" about God and Christianity.[106] When the Saxon court at Dresden learnt of the uproar over the article, a ban was slapped on the journal issue and copies found were confiscated. Dresden also leaned on the duke of Saxe-Weimar and his education minister, Goethe, demanding they repudiate Fichte and forbid his philosophy being taught "at your University of Jena (and in the Gymnasium and schools)," threatening, otherwise, to debar Saxon students attending Saxe-Weimar's educational establishments. Hanover and Brunswick followed Dresden's example, confiscating the journal issue and threatening further steps should Jena's quadrilateral governing board fail to act.[107]

[101] Fichte, "On the Ground of Our Belief," 27. [102] Fichte, "On the Ground of Our Belief," 21.

[103] Fichte, "On the Ground of Our Belief," 26; Hösle, *Short History*, 99–100.

[104] Fichte, "On the Ground of Our Belief," 25.

[105] Estes and Bowman, *Fichte and the Atheism Dispute*, 57.

[106] Estes and Bowman, *Fichte and the Atheism Dispute*, 58.

[107] Ohst, "Fichtes Entlassung," 11; Breazeale, "Fichte in Jena," 40–1; Morujão, "Controversias teológicas," 310–11; Estes and Bowman, *Fichte and the Atheism Dispute*, 78–9, 81, 83.

Furious, Kant felt obliged to intervene too, as in the mid-1780s, to ward off suggestion that he was at fault.

Fichte, whose reputed "atheism" and pro-Revolution views had for some time been disconcerting Weimar, now conducted himself in a manner that prompted the duke's education minister, Goethe, alarmed by the clashes between conservative professors and radicals, to withdraw his support altogether. Goethe's prime concern amidst the uproar was to protect Weimar's and Jena's reputation and the latter's enviable but precarious primacy among Germany's universities. Gotha wished to be rid of Fichte, but Weimar initially preferred retaining him, if he toned down, a preference that ceased in January 1799, when the "Atheism controversy" sensationally escalated, due to Fichte publishing his *Appellation an das Publikum* [Appeal to the Public], appealing to "unprejudiced readers" against the electoral Saxon state church council and his being declared an "Atheist and enemy of all religion" by ecclesiastical authority. In this, the most notable text of the *Atheismusstreit*, Fichte demanded the public itself be judge of the Saxon court's ban and actions—that is, judge local princes as well as ecclesiastical authority and the University: he demanded that the public choose between a doctrine "that debases you" and "one that promises to elevate you indescribably."[108] He did not deny princely right to censure atheistic tendencies in universities, or that teaching atheism should be prohibited, merely that his own philosophy was subversive or conducive to atheism, asking the public to be judge of this. The enlightened court of Duke Ernst II Ludwig, lover of the sciences, herald of *Aufklärung*, friend of Goethe, and protector of Adam Weishaupt, he declared, could hardly treat him like a latter-day "Vanini." But his claiming "morality and religion are absolutely the same"[109] negated organized religion and all religious authority. Admitting he was a "democrat" who "regards democratically constituted government as the only legitimate one, and recommends it be introduced," he affronted all the courts and princes.

The 1798–1800 *Atheismusstreit* surged just when French revolutionary forces again advanced on the Rhine, threatening princes and religion and the entire German *ancien régime*. Under French occupation, Trier University was closed and replaced by a "central school (*école centrale*), while the prince-archbishopric of Cologne was abolished altogether along with its ancient university (founded in 1388, the Holy Roman Empire's fourth-oldest), now likewise replaced by a revolutionary *école centrale* like the already closed Mainz University. The same fate met the Kurkölnische Akademie Bonn, founded on tolerant, moderate Enlightenment lines only in 1777; it remained shut until replaced by the new University of Bonn founded by the Prussian crown in 1818.[110] Multiple university closures and French revolutionary propaganda together helped further stoke the Fichte furor. One French commander, General Louis-Marie Turreau, delivered a speech in April 1799 praising the views of "one of your greatest philosophers, Fichte," expressly linking him to support for the French

[108] Estes and Bowman, *Fichte and the Atheism Dispute*,124. [109] Fichte, *Appeal*, 104.
[110] Frijhoff, "Patterns," 83–4, 89; Rowe, "Tale of Two Cities," 127.

Republic.[111] Fichte was now widely presented as Germany's foremost "atheist" and tool of French occupation.

Whether or not his philosophy was "atheistic" is a totally false question, insisted Fichte, suspended senselessly between divergent worlds of thought and terminology, like asking whether a triangle is "red or green, sweet or bitter." But his *Appellation*, termed by Goethe a "feverish delirium," exuded an ill-advised vehemence: his critics he styled obscurantists, idolaters, liars, and persecutors. Electoral Saxony was banning so many books it was no shame to be prohibited there.[112] He even hurled the charge of "Atheism" back in his accusers' faces, suggesting theologians' misconceived notions of "religion" exerted a negative effect on public morality and individual development. "Poor Vanini" could not speak openly before the inquisitors burnt him; "I will do so before my funeral pyre is built."[113] Such language seized attention right across Germany, provoking a major cultural upheaval that no one with intellectual pretensions could ignore. The *Appellation* made rupture with Jena, Weimar, Goethe, and the princes inevitable. Meanwhile, Fichte summoned two of the most prestigious liberal Neologist theologians, Johann Joachim Spalding (1714–1804), a noted foe of dogmatic authoritarianism whose "Christian" inspiration he extolled, and the Dresden chief court preacher, the *Oberhofprediger* Reinhard, to support him publicly and by so doing champion freedom of expression and freedom to philosophize. "Among philosophers," he likewise appealed to Reinhold and his friend, "noble Jacobi."[114]

Coherent philosophizing, responded Jacobi, adhering to his *Pantheismusstreit* stance in an open letter criticizing the *Appellation*,[115] published at Hamburg, presents one with a stark choice—belief in a personal God or atheistic nihilism. For Fichte, as for Kant and Schelling, a personal God remained a respectable individual choice but, when presented as "truth," is just unprovable metaphysical dogma. In 1799 and again when reissuing the text in 1816, Jacobi avoided calling Fichte himself an "atheist;" it was nonsensical to term Fichte's Transcendental Idealism "atheism" since, in typically Kantian fashion, it rules out objectively certain knowledge of God. But for that very reason "it cannot in any sense be theist either." Hence there were grounds for designating his Transcendental Philosophy "atheist." From his writings, like those of Spinoza, one can easily derive "atheism,"[116] though Jacobi did not consider Fichte "personally, an atheist," "nor a godless man." Fichte's "God who is a non-personal God, who is not a non-entity," means that it is "not the being of God but only his name that would be denied." The same gulf between forms of words and inner conviction characterized Spinoza: "... may you be blessed for me, you great, yes

[111] See Breazeale's note in Fichte, "Selected Correspondence," 436 n. 8.

[112] Fichte, *Appeal*, 93, 98.

[113] Fichte, *Appeal*, 94–5; Landau, "Rechtsgeschichtliche Kontext," 29; Wittekind, "Retorsion des Atheismus," 61.

[114] Fichte, *Appellation*, 354–5; Solé, "Intervención de F. H. Jacobi," 449–50.

[115] "Jacobi to Fichte," in Jacobi, *Main Philosophical Writings*, 497–536.

[116] "Jacobi to Fichte," in Jacobi, *Main Philosophical Writings*, 500; Barth, "Pantheismusstreit, Atheismusstreit," 106; Jaeschke, "De Messias der spekulativen Vernunft," 149.

you holy Benedictus! For whatever you may say philosophically about the nature of the Supreme Being, and whatever verbal mistakes you make, His truth was in your soul, and His Love was your life."[117] By envisaging the moral world-order as "God," Fichte's Transcendental Philosophy is not atheism as such, but does subvert true theism and directly induce Spinozism. Fichte had forged a monism, excluding all dualism, that is an "inverted Spinozism," a trap of "necessity," from which the reader can exit only by the same *salto mortale* required to escape Spinoza's "necessity."[118] Equally unhelpfully, Jacobi concurred with Fichte's critics that a philosophy professor with clear Spinozistic leanings should not teach at a German university.[119]

Reinhold predictably seconded Fichte's denial that philosophy can provide absolute proofs for or against God's existence, Revelation, or providence. The whole affair, he agreed, had been blown up by the "half-philosophy of our dogmatists and skeptics to an absurd degree."[120] Kant proved that the "necessity of moral faith in the existence of God follows from the nature of practical reason"—and that alone. None could doubt the efficacy of Kant's demonstrations, or success of his intervention in the *Pantheismusstreit*. However, it now seemed far from clear that Kant had securely entrenched the "necessity of moral faith," and latterly, with Fichte's and Schelling's modifying Kantianism by dragging Transcendental Idealism into close conjunction with Spinoza's undeniable "consistency" on the status of mankind's fundamental relation to nature's laws, authority, society, and politics,[121] the issue of Kantianism's unresolved underlying relationship to Spinozism was being disturbingly reopened. "You have always nurtured the hope of using philosophy to improve mankind," Fichte reminded Reinhold, in April 1799, "and you still nurture this hope." Surely his former ally would not deny that he too had embraced Kantianism expecting beneficial practical and public results. He *had* attempted to employ philosophy to "convert men and to instruct them concerning their duties," conceded Reinhold, but he now realized, contrary to earlier expectation, that Kantianism and Fichte's "scientific idealism" were unsuited to serve as such tools.

Fichte disavowed having any plan for directly "improving and instructing mankind." His philosophy was of practical benefit to men only indirectly, in a pedagogic sense, by demonstrating the reality of existence and natural rights and the kind of moral philosophy and politics that follow from this.[122] Continuing the old tension threading right through the Enlightenment between philosophy and theology, the present controversy signified a clash between freedom to philosophize and court control and supervision. A crisis of the relationship of the professorate to princely authority, it ran deep because Fichte, Schelling, the Schlegels, Hegel, and Kant—and marginally even Reinhold—were working to subordinate theology, law, morality,

[117] "Jacobi to Fichte," in Jacobi, *Main Philosophical Writings*, 520.
[118] Jaeschke, "Messias der spekulativen Vernunft," 148–9; Josephson-Storm, *Myth of Disenchantment*, 73.
[119] Solé, "Intervención de F. H. Jacobi," 455. [120] Reinhold, "Letter to Fichte," 134.
[121] Reinhold "Letter to Fichte," 134–5, 141, 143; Boehm, *Kant's Critique of Spinoza*, 224–5.
[122] Fichte, "Selected Correspondence," 430, 438.

and the clergy to what they considered a higher set of principles beside full freedom of expression for the professoriate. More than a conflict between courts and universities, the controversy reflected a deeper collision between university faculties and rival conceptions of the professoriate's social role—traditional social control via theologians versus the call of the *Aufklärer* to collective political action to change society.[123]

Rebuffed by Goethe, Jacobi, and Reinhold, Fichte had scant hope of Schiller and none of rallying Kant, who now lost any wish to see Fichte become his generally acknowledged successor. Earlier, prefacing the *Critique of Pure Reason*'s second edition, in 1787, after the clashes over Lessing's alleged "Spinozism," Kant had pointedly re-opened the issue of whether Enlightenment reason is man's supreme implement, the overriding tool of human endeavor. Worried lest the mid-1780s *Pantheismusstreit* provoke an unpleasant theological reaction and Counter-Enlightenment backlash, he had proclaimed his critical philosophy uniquely indispensable for defending rational religion and morality, and repelling Spinozist "enthusiasm" and metaphysics.[124] Fichteanism being an invalid derivation from Kantianism, its relation to Spinozism was automatically suspect; but the principal danger for Kant in 1799 was that some of the professoriate, notably at Göttingen, were exploiting the Fichte furor to contest Kant's denial of "atheism in the critical philosophy." [125] Kant had recently ceased lecturing, but, awkwardly for Fichte, the "atheism" furor burst just as his personal rift with Kant became publicly known. By 1799 it was impossible even to mention Fichte to Kant without making the old man angry. Breaking with Weimar, Fichte found himself simultaneously breaking with Königsberg too. Kant's final intervention in the philosophical wars of the revolutionary decade occurred on 7 August 1799: Fichte's *Wissenschaftslehre*, he announced, is in no way true "Kritizismus." Recalling the Italian proverb "God protect us from our friends, from our enemies we can easily take care of ourselves," he pronounced Fichte's a "totally indefensible system" [*ein gänzlich unhaltbares System*], sheer muddle, a public declaration many considered "necessary," that caused quite a sensation.[126]

Another powerful interlocutor, the young Breslau-born theologian Schleiermacher, responded more supportively. In 1799 he published an anonymous booklet, *On Religion, Speeches to its Cultural Despisers*, expounding a theology ruling out all prospect of philosophical or theological definitions of God with unmistakable affinities to Kant's and Fichte's conclusions, except that Schleiermacher's prose exuded a religious passion, a "feeling" for God relentlessly aimed against Enlightenment skeptics, deists, and atheists.[127] Later among the foremost early nineteenth-century Prussian educational and religious reformers, Schleiermacher was destined to exert a

[123] Bauer and Gerber, "Politisierung," 136–7.
[124] Boehm, *Kant's Critique of Spinoza*, 192–3, 210.
[125] Kant, *Briefwechsel* iii. 273; Kuehn, *Kant*, 390.
[126] Kant, "Erklärung," 7 Aug. 1799, in Kant, *Briefwechsel* iii. 267–9; Kuehn, *Kant*, 413.
[127] Seysen, "Rezeption des Atheismusstreits," 175, 178–9.

major influence not just as a theologian and Bible critic but key higher education reformer. In 1799, however, it was his theory of religion that seized attention, becoming immediately highly controversial.[128] One's sense of one's own dependence on God can take many diverse forms, but for most it is feeling communicated through Jesus and the church; Christian sensibility, not creeds of churches and theological dogma—or philosophy—is the core of religious truth. Many, not least Hegel, found this radical subjectivism disturbing and excessively close to the ardent Romanticism latterly embraced by the Schlegels. Some labeled this controversial young clergyman a hypocrite preaching Christianity in church on Sunday mornings while, in his writings, insidiously seconding Fichte, Spinoza (whose philosophy he greatly admired), and pantheism.[129]

In the Germany of 1799 other noted champions of freedom of expression, freedom to philosophize, and freedom to criticize princely courts also offered support, including Friedrich Schlegel, who assured Fichte, in May 1799, that "your cause seems to be of universal importance. I believe it is the cause of philosophy itself, the cause of the age and the nation."[130] But that was precisely the problem. Many Jena students hailed from Prussia and Saxony and both regimes utterly condemned even the discreet pro-revolutionary outlook rooted in naturalism Fichte offered. Goethe and the Weimar court felt their predicament keenly. Jena performed a special role in German life and culture: renowned in all disciplines, it was the academic stronghold supplementing the literary headquarters of the entire German-speaking world, the base of Goethe, Schiller, Herder, and Wieland. Jena's professors and celebrated library stood at the forefront of the universities' efforts to recast philosophy, history, ethnic studies, aesthetics, Bible criticism, and ancient and oriental literatures into a new, more coherent secularizing whole. All the universities awaited Goethe's solution to a crisis caused by Fichte's prickly tactlessness plunging the Weimar court into deep embarrassment. Fichte's adversaries felt they were defending the entire academic sphere and youth from atheism, Spinozism, and political subversion. Declaring the "concept of God as a separate substance an impossible and contradictory concept," Fichte held there is no God who is "master of fate and dispenser of all happiness," and that "what they call God is an idol to me."[131] Christianity is "sublime" but not a system of doctrine revealing eternal truths, rather an appeal to the "moral sense of mankind."[132] Only lack of grasp of the individual's relation to the world, a stunted comprehension, leads to dogmatically insisting that God is a separate, independent being, the creator and organizer of the world, though it fulfills a legitimate need in many to imagine God in

[128] Seysen, "Rezeption des Atheismusstreits", 187–8

[129] Cousin, *Souvenirs*, 105; Crouter, *Friedrich Schleiermacher*, 252–4; Seysen, "Rezeption des Atheismusstreits," 189–90.

[130] Fichte, *Early Philosophical Writings*, 41–2.

[131] Fichte, *Appeal*, 109, 111–12; Cousin, *Souvenirs*, 146–7.

[132] Fichte, *Appeal*, 115, 117..

this way.[133] Is this not unadulterated "Spinozism," demanded critics, pointing to Fichte's "God" lacking all normative, coercive, and educational force, and, as such, surely a revolutionary menace to society?[134]

Adversaries were hardly likely to be assuaged by Fichte's urging religious authority's elimination and democratic government exclusively in learned publications, deploying only enlightened criteria deserving toleration "even under a monarchical government." He denied being any kind of active subversive or revolutionary; the princes, he argued, should grant us "civil security provided we live as peaceful, respectable citizens."[135] Every critic is acceptable provided "he performs no external action to actually overthrow existing constituted governments or put in their place one he prefers." Refuting his conclusions should be left to scholars. In March 1799, Weimar decided Fichte must receive a resounding public rebuke and be required to resign. To escape the unenviable Scylla and Charybdis of either incurring accusations of tolerating "atheism" in the university, or despotically violating academic freedom—equally unpalatable prospects—Goethe wanted punishment with lasting impact, but adroitly managed to minimize any redolence of reactionary court attitudes and repression. Fichte, accordingly, was condemned not for "Atheism" but fulfilling university duties in a careless, irresponsible manner.[136]

Fichte's "resignation," effectively his dismissal, on 18 April 1799 duly blighted his public standing for years, temporarily displacing him from the central position in academic life he occupied. Some Jena students vehemently protested, demanding his "dismissal" be rescinded, submitting two petitions to Duke Karl August reminding him that students flocked from all over Germany to hear Fichte lecture. Both petitions were signed by sizeable numbers, and both firmly rebuffed. The court additionally intervened to prevent Fichte finding any "place of refuge" near Jena or Weimar. His adversaries' goal, Fichte's wife, Johanna, surmised to Reinhold, was to force them to "flee to France" so as to claim he was "never a real German."[137] Protesting he was no "atheist," Fichte felt outrageously betrayed by the court, declaring his dismissal essentially a political ploy, part of the general drive against democrats and free-thinkers,[138] with the "atheism" charge a mere pretext. Weimar was violating academic freedom and freedom of thought and demeaning his status as a leading philosopher, by abjectly joining the wider effort of rulers to capture, distort, and dominate man's quest to shape his own inner life, promoting tyranny in support of social cliques, collusion that is the true "atheism."[139]

133 Wittekind, "Retorsion des Atheismus," 74, 77.

134 Almeida Carvalho, "Introducion histórica," 72–4.

135 Estes and Bowman, *Fichte and the Atheism Dispute*, 196, 200–1.

136 Landau, "Der rechtsgeschichtliche Kontext," 15.

137 Fichte, "Appellation," 350; Fichte, "Selected Correspondence," 440; Estes and Bowman, *Fichte and the Atheism Dispute*, 220, 227–8.

138 La Vopa, *Fichte*, 404, 423–4; Morujão, "Controversias teológicas," 311.

139 Wittekind, "Retorsion des Atheismus," 76.

20.4. A NEW VISION OF THE UNIVERSITY

Stripped of his Jena professorate, Fichte searched for "some place of refuge where I can for a while enjoy a bit of leisure in complete anonymity, safe from the literary and political news which fills me with an unconquerable and deadly disgust, and where I shall be protected from the anathemas of the priests and the stones of the faithful."[140] He fled to Berlin, withdrawing from the fray, and from 1800 began that slow, painful retreat from "democracy," atheism, and "Jacobinism," with which he was still firmly associated in 1800, toward the Francophobe, nationalist Romanticism that became his hallmark from 1806 onwards—a transition paralleling a wider shift, with profound consequences for the entire nineteenth century, of large segments of German philosophy and university life, encompassing Schiller, Schelling, Schlegel, and in key respects Hegel, away from Radical Enlightenment and engagement with democratic programs of renewal into an overarching, lofty German idealism stalwartly refusing to challenge publicly state, church, or university authorities.[141]

Overshadowed by growing French military and political preponderance, the overall political condition of Germany soon came to be fundamentally transformed. Under the Treaty of Lunéville (February 1801), the Holy Roman Emperor acknowledged France's possession of the left bank of the Rhine and likewise a need to compensate secular princes deprived of lands in consequence. The Imperial Reichstag's subsequent deliberations, continually prodded by Napoleon, led to a massive redrawing of the map by abolishing Germany's ecclesiastical states altogether along with many other ancient but small entities, a fundamental reordering announced in a declaration of February 1803 and proclaimed formally by the Emperor in April. The changes entailed massive transfers of population, power, status, and cultural influence, the largest territorial reshuffling of Germany since the Protestant Reformation affecting every level of life from the political and religious to the philosophical. Implementation on the ground was swift, much of it during 1802, well before the final proclamations. Germany's benefiting enlarged states—Bavaria, Württemberg, Hesse, Baden, and the Grand Duchy of Berg—were now all allies of Napoleon, with the last being administered by French officials under the nominal rule of his brother-in-law, Joachim Murat.

Stripped of political functions, revenues, and property, the ecclesiastical hierarchy stood decisively weakened. Several more Catholic universities were secularized at this point with professoriate and students becoming mixed Catholic–Protestant bodies, as at Würzburg (founded 1582),[142] or else, like Bamberg, Dillingen, and Fulda, along with thousands of monasteries and nunneries, simply dissolved. A catastrophic setback for Rome politically, and partial triumph for the secular Enlightenment and Lutheranism, the upheaval simultaneously entailed ejection of ecclesiastical nobility

[140] Fichte, "Selected Correspondence," 430–2, 440; Sauter, *Visions of Enlightenment*, 131–5.
[141] Hösle, *Short History*, 102–3; Calvié, "Début du siècle nouveau," 523–7, 534–5.
[142] Cousin, *Souvenirs*, 175; Schweigard, "Studentische Netzwerke," 337.

from their former bishoprics, abbeys, and ecclesiastical lands and revenues, clearing the way for a non-aristocratic higher clergy, more dedicated and learned as well as morally of higher caliber. In this respect, the 1801–3 redrawing of Germany's map was a reverse for aristocracy and victory for the "Religious Enlightenment." Equally, traditionally Protestant states like Baden and Hesse-Cassel now acquired sizeable Catholic populations which intensified pressure to de-confessionalize administration, law, and higher education. In several cases, rulers of enlarged principalities, suddenly finding themselves saddled with more universities than were needed, simply abolished academies in annexed areas as superfluous to needs, particularly where of a different confession to the annexing court. Duisburg University closed in 1804; Altdorf (founded in 1578), a Lutheran establishment near Nuremberg, was shut by the Bavarian ruler in 1809; in 1811, the same year he suppressed Franeker University in the Netherlands, Napoleon, planning a larger, more modern institution at Düsseldorf (which never materialized), closed the Grand Duchy of Berg's recently acquired Calvinist academy of Herborn (founded in 1584).

Closure and transfers, infused with philosophical wrangling and the *Atheismusstreit*, exerted a considerable impact on relations between states and universities, and the ideological struggle within universities. "Atheism" tinted the Jena uproar, but Fichte was not alone in believing the concerted opposition to his person and philosophy was basically political, part of a wider drive by princely courts to tighten censorship and control the professoriate, and to an extent he was right. But adversaries were equally justified in associating his philosophical naturalism with underground radical tendencies seeking to move beyond individual enlightenment and emancipation to mass social and political emancipation, collective action stemming from reading and universities directed against privilege, aristocracy, religious authority, and the princely courts. Despite his disavowals, Fichte's was ultimately a "philosophy of action," albeit indirect, mobilizing professors and students behind a vision of *Aufklärung* inherently adverse to princely and church authority.[143] The princes, declared Fichte, "are ashamed and afraid before the proponents of Enlightenment but, on the other hand, do not want to alienate the obscurantists."[144] He left Jena in April 1799; but even after his departure, the *Atheismusstreit* continued testing the university and ducal governments of Saxe-Weimar and Gotha. The flood of pamphlets showed little sign of abating. Religion, aristocracy, and princes had won on the surface, but deeper down the outcome seemed less clear politically and philosophically, especially as Fichte's efforts to modify his system after 1800, in part to counter Jacobi's charges, produced no new revised edition with any significant reformulation.[145]

Fichte left behind a formidable circle of sympathizers but this quickly dispersed. Friedrich Schlegel moved to France, in December 1801, after his novel *Lucinde* (1799)

[143] Bauer and Gerber, "Politisierung," 133, 136.
[144] Fichte, "Selected Correspondence," 427.
[145] Barth, "Pantheismusstreit, Atheismusstreit," 107.

scandalized the public through its uninhibited celebration of erotic love and his liaison with Mendelssohn's daughter, Dorothea Veit (1764–1839). Schlegel and Dorothea lived in Paris during 1802-4, marrying just as Napoleon consolidated his domestic despotism and grip on Germany, events that prompted the Schlegels to fundamentally change their views and repudiate revolution, republicanism, and "philosophy" along with Napoleon. While later Romanticism in literature and the arts, with its stress on exploring the self and freeing the personal emotions, and expressing individual identity, often detached itself from the Enlightenment, pre-1800 Romanticism at Jena and Weimar, as reflected in Schiller, Hölderlin, Schelling, and the Schlegels, far from detaching, had remained fused with late Enlightenment concerns and projects, an intensifying agent coupling emancipation of the individual with responsibility to society, politics, and building a new social order. Initially part of this tendency, after 1800 the Schlegels rebelled against early Romanticism's secular and revolutionary character. Equally, Friedrich took to denouncing Spinozism and pantheism as the inevitable outcome of philosophizing on the basis of reason, following Jacobi, whom he now hugely admired.[146] Attracted to ancient Hindu castes and tradition, Schlegel learned Sanskrit and searched instead for venerable archetypes exalting belief, hierarchy, and nobility, a creed to replace his earlier zeal for republicanism and secularism and help build a deeply conservative Romanticist religiosity. Conversion from "philosophy" to "religion" led on to his and Dorothea's conversion to Catholicism in 1808, alliance with Gentz, and finally public support for Metternich's reactionary policies.[147]

Schelling's notion of an entirely free ego reshaping reality radically, through imagination and power of thought, also began to strike Fichte, Hegel, and Hölderlin as too detached, and almost mystical, a sign Schelling too was abandoning the crusade to elevate man by teaching him how to be spiritually, morally, and politically free in the real world. Hegel, having sided with Fichte earlier, arrived in Jena in January 1801, effectively as Fichte's replacement as Jena's leading philosophical star, albeit with no intention of repeating his predecessor's mistakes. But more influential then were Von Humboldt and Schleiermacher, who, if louder than Kant and Fichte in embracing religion and proclaiming the university the servant of the state, nevertheless agreed with the radicals that universities should serve society as much as the state and not only function without denominational allegiance but enjoy full research autonomy and freedom of thought. Von Humboldt, who was well read in French and British as well as German Enlightenment literature, also concurred with the *Idéologues* that modern universities must make philosophy and philology the senior faculties, placing these at the forefront, ahead of theology and law, if they were to be adequate guides to the student body, a fitting inspiration to the public, and supervise the expansion of

[146] Schlegel, *Wesen der menschlichen Freiheit*, 9, 18, 22, 84 n. 6; Cousin, *Souvenirs*, 52.

[147] Cousin, *Souvenirs*, 48–9; Figueira, "Politics of Exoticism," 429, 432; Calvié, "Début du siècle nouveau," 531.

new sciences and disciplines.[148] Both Von Humboldt and Schleiermacher proved remarkably successful in securing the collaboration of enlightened princes while beneath the surface infusing a veiled but ambitious agenda of fundamental reform, exploiting the Napoleonic era's rushed transformation of university institutions, the opportunities the vast but overly sudden changes offered for discreet infiltration of the same advanced ideas the princes aimed to emasculate.

Between 1800 and 1812, with Napoleon in the ascendant, scope for a militant Counter-Enlightenment in the German universities, dishearteningly for prophets of faith and reaction, dwindled steadily. Uncompromising rationalization was everywhere the order of the day; in states allied to Napoleon, key universities, such as Leipzig, now had rectors directing them who were of pro-French and crypto-republican inclination.[149] Consolidating universities to create larger, more efficient units better able to accommodate the new sciences shaped higher education policy both in those areas directly incorporated into the Napoleonic empire and the Napoleonic daughter kingdoms, the Netherlands and "Westphalia," and in the unoccupied states. Of five long-established universities in King Jérôme's newly-carved "Kingdom of Westphalia" (1807–13) the three largest, Göttingen, Halle, and Marburg, after months of trepidation for the last, had their continued existence confirmed. Marburg looked dangerously vulnerable, having waned in recent years and boasting only twenty-nine professors, as against Göttingen's forty. Halle, on reopening in 1808, outside Prussia's reduced borders, and now temporarily incorporated into Westphalia, boasted forty-three. But when "King Jérôme" visited Marburg on 6 December 1807, the exceptional effort put into illuminating the town, arranging band music, and student singing had its effect. After lengthy consideration, Napoleonic "Westphalia" suppressed just two of its former five universities, Rinteln, now down to just twelve professors, and Helmstedt (founded in 1576) with twenty, both closing in 1809, with their books, facilities, and teachers transferred elsewhere, Rinteln's university library to Göttingen.[150]

Halle, key center of early Enlightenment "theological Wolffianism," lynchpin of the Prussian state's reconciling of theology and philosophy, and headquarters of Neolog reforming theology, among Germany's greatest academic centers, was closed by Napoleon in 1807. At the time, that seemed a much more crushing blow to Germany's higher education world than it subsequently proved. After reopening in "Westphalia," it was briefly closed for the second time following Napoleon's defeat in 1813, before permanently reopening under the Prussian crown in 1817.[151] Despite its temporary closures of 1807 and 1813, Halle handsomely profited in the end from another notable academic casualty—Wittenberg University, founded in 1502 and renowned

[148] Cousin, *Souvenirs*, 225; Lemberg, "Universität Marburg," 237; Crouter, *Friedrich Schleiermacher*, 141–2, 148, 162.
[149] Mühlpfordt, *Halle-Leipziger Aufklärung*, 314–16.
[150] Frijhoff, "Patterns," 86–7; Lemberg, "Universität Marburg," 224.
[151] Gall, *Wilhelm von Humboldt*, 161, 172; Sorkin, *Religious Enlightenment*, 123, 132–3, 163.

during the Lutheran Reformation, suppressed by Napoleon in 1813. Wittenberg's permanent closure was confirmed after the Prussian restoration, in 1817, with the library and facilities transferred to newly reopened Halle.[152] Meanwhile, Halle's temporary exclusion from Prussian territory lent added urgency to Prussia's state reform of higher education, enabling Von Humboldt to impart his subtle Radical Enlightenment stamp on the forming of the projected new University of Berlin, an opportunity that might otherwise have been more restricted.

The decision to create a new central Prussian state university in Berlin was taken by the Prussian royal cabinet in principle, after military defeat and Napoleon's severing off much of its territory, in September 1807.[153] Elaborating the plans was entrusted to Von Humboldt, working at a distance, with the court, from Konigsberg; consulting with Schleiermacher, Fichte, and others, the project was already well advanced by 1809. To replace the *ancien régime* conception, Von Humboldt, in line with his earlier thinking, envisaged a revolutionary late Enlightenment mega-university rooted in the new scholarship and science functioning as the prime agent of a new national outlook and moral character based not on religion, tradition, or ethnicity, but on forming individual character and the quest for extensive social and cultural amelioration. Research would be promoted above all else, with state backing for every field of knowledge. If Napoleon had shattered Prussia's military power, Germany must recognize Prussia's undiminished capacity for "true Enlightenment" [*ware Aufklärung*]. It was vital that the Prussian king should now step forward and secure Prussia's position in the front rank of culture and scholarship [*Wissenschaft*] linking Prussia inseparably to *Aufklärung*.[154]

Building on recent achievements of Jena, Halle, and Göttingen, Berlin University opened in 1810 with 262 students, two-thirds studying traditional vocational subjects, medicine, and law, but soon initiated an entirely fresh chapter in modern university history by eradicating all theological tutelage and consolidating academic freedom and freedom of research and expression as the guiding principles of modern nation forming.[155] The intellectual and moral formation students received from the Humboldtian university was conceived as essentially deriving from *Wissenschaft*, academic study, scholarship, and science gathered around the humanities, a process deemed an unending cumulative quest combining specialization and close study with cultivating a broader, richer general outlook and culture for the individual and the collectivity of the nation.[156] Instead of inculcating summaries of what was known, professors must now promote research and innovate and, by advancing knowledge and understanding of the whole, raise the moral and intellectual level of both

[152] Frijhoff, "Patterns," 84, 94. [153] Von Humboldt, "Antrag auf Errichtung," 143.

[154] Von Humboldt, *Sphere and Duties*, 65–70; Von Humboldt, "Antrag auf Errichtung," 143–4; Von Humboldt, "Über die innere und äussere," 152–3.

[155] Espagne, "Frères Humboldt," 132; Louden, *The World We Want*, 48–50.

[156] Nipperdey, *Germany*, 46–8.

individuals and society.[157] What was created was a neo-humanism grounded less in mathematics and the exact sciences—and less still religion—than in language studies, history, and the arts.

With Königsberg too distant and Frankfurt an der Oder too antiquated, Berlin became the hub of Prussia's post-1807 embrace of academic late Enlightenment. Although Von Humboldt aimed to retain both Königsberg and, "at least for now," Frankfurt an der Oder, he wanted both relegated to subsidiary status. Founded in 1506 and once Brandenburg's principal university, Frankfurt an der Oder was already sadly reduced, possessing barely 200 students when Von Humboldt's brother, Alexander, studied there in the late 1780s. Meanwhile, Breslau (formerly the Leopoldina, today Wrocław, one of the premier universities of Poland), maintained by Frederick the Great as a specifically Catholic university for Silesia, Von Humboldt did recommend for closure.[158] In 1810 the Prussian court, however, opted to close Frankfurt an der Oder instead (it was re-founded only in 1991), transferring the latter's science apparatus, books, and most professors and other resources to Breslau, which now became Prussia's second university, but stripped of its Catholic character and all theological bias.[159]

To guarantee autonomy and financial viability, Von Humboldt wanted the crown to assign Berlin, Prussia's new central university, permanently attached landed and other endowments; but his superiors never permitted the self-sufficiency and autonomy for which he had hoped.[160] This proved the main weakness of the Humboldtian university as a late Enlightenment model when compared with the foremost late Enlightenment university project in Britain, initiated at a much later stage but with notable success, in 1827, with the laying of the foundation stone of University College London, the brainchild of dissenter philanthropists guided by the British philosophic radicals Bentham, James Mill, and Francis Place. From the outset UCL was conceived as a Berlin-style mega-university equipped for all the sciences, expressly shorn of all religious connection, displaying innovative, reforming attitudes to teaching history, philosophy, law, modern languages, and the fine arts, but also solid independence of endowment.[161]

Berlin's success, and soon fame, powerfully impacted on even the most renowned older universities, which, by 1818, had suffered notable setbacks in prestige and student numbers. Göttingen stagnated at around 1,200 students from the late 1790s down to 1821, Jena fell back to 634, and Halle, boasting over 1,000 students in the 1780s, had notably lost ground by 1818, being reduced to only 550.[162] With

157 Espagne, "Frères Humboldt," 136, 146; Gall, *Wilhelm von Humboldt*, 147; Gare, "Democracy and Education," 18–19.

158 Von Humboldt, "Antrag auf Errichtung," 146–7; Wulf, *Invention*, 18.

159 Gall, *Wilhelm von Humboldt*, 160–1.

160 Von Humboldt, "Antrag auf Errichtung," 148–9; Espagne, "Frères Humboldt," 140; Gall, *Wilhelm von Humboldt*, 214–15.

161 Burston, *James Mill*, 73–5.

162 Kant, *Briefwechsel* iii. 274; [Jullien], *Revue encyclopédique* ii (1819), 168; [Jullien], *Revue encyclopédique* x (1821), 444; Cousin, *Souvenirs*, 70, Whaley, *Germany* ii. 522.

Napoleon's downfall and the new European settlement ordained by the Vienna Congress in 1814–15, Prussia was greatly enlarged, absorbing substantial territories in the west. This heralded yet another and now final round of closures and reorganization. Erfurt, where student numbers had reached minimal levels, provisionally closed in 1804 after over four hundred years (founded in 1392), and was permanently suppressed fifteen months later, in September 1816, following transfer to Prussia.[163] The longstanding but lapsed or antiquated universities of Duisburg, founded in 1555, Paderborn, founded as a Jesuit college in 1614, and Münster, also once a Jesuit college but re-established as a modernized Catholic university in 1780, all permanently closed in 1818, in conjunction with the Prussian crown's opening what became Berlin's successful western counterpart, the Humboldtian University of Bonn, founded in October 1818. Housed in the former prince-elector's palace, the new entity replaced the prince-archbishop's academy, founded in 1777. Within a year, Bonn already attracted impressive student numbers, and soon boasted thirty-seven professors, a medical school, botanical garden, observatory, cabinets of minerology, zoology, and technology, physics and anatomy laboratories, an art museum, a philological seminar, a library topping 25,000 volumes, many brought from Duisburg and other closed institutions, and a university press equipped with Greek, Hebrew, Syriac, and Arabic beside Western type.[164]

Fichte, having been living in Berlin for some years and having restored his reputation, after 1806, by stirring up national resentment to French occupation, in a remarkable turn-around was appointed professor of philosophy at Berlin, in 1810, and then, by his colleagues, elected university rector the following year. Accepted by the Prussian crown, his appointment to the Berlin rectorate reflected the rise of university autonomy, and bewildering complexity of university expansion during the opening years of the new century in terms of range of disciplines and research, the rush to find leading scholars and renowned scientists and gain cultural prestige. Complications associated with unreliable personal views of prominent scholars recruited could now be overlooked by the princely court provided there had been some adjustment to more conservative attitudes recently. When afterwards seeking to emulate Berlin's success, transferring the old Bavarian royal university founded originally at Ingolstadt in 1472 and transferred to Landshut in 1800 finally to Munich, in 1826, the new Bavarian king, Ludwig I, likewise caused a stir with several of his appointments. Expanding Munich University with impressive new buildings and facilities, the king appointed professors "of distinguished merit and celebrity" irrespective of their remoter past. Especially striking was the appointment of Joseph von Görres (1776–1848), once a notorious adherent of democratic republican doctrines, leading spokesman of the Coblenz republican club during the 1792–3 Rhenish Republic, and again in 1799–1800; during 1814–15, Görres had been a senior educational official on the Middle Rhine and founder of the *Rheinische Merkur*, a

[163] Märker, *Geschichte der Universität Erfurt*, 75–6.
[164] [Jullien], *Revue encyclopédique* ii (1819), 375.

paper with a crypto-republican character supporting constitutional movements suppressed by the Prussian crown in 1816. But more recently, the Bavarian court was satisfied, Görres, like Schlegel, had switched to Romantic right-wing politics and ardent Catholicism. On his appointment to Munich's principal chair of history, in 1827, the Prussian representative at court protested, citing the Baden government's readiness to "surrender the person of M. Görres into the hands of the Prussian authorities, if found within the Baden territory;" but all that was soon forgotten. Görres shone among Munich University's academic stars until his death in 1848.[165]

Reorganizing Germany's and much of Europe's universities was largely complete by the 1820s, but the ideological rift opened up within the academic sphere was far from resolved. The major new foundations at Berlin, Bonn, and Munich were widely praised; but there was also deep concern that such a massive agent of change was now ensconced at the very heart of political life and administration. Conservative anxieties seemed amply vindicated with the eruption of the 1820 revolutions in Spain, Portugal, Naples, and Piedmont, in all of which students and professors were more conspicuously prominent than ever. It was too late wholly to prevent the ill effects, acknowledged the British envoy in Berlin, "however powerful an example is afforded by the late transactions at Turin of the danger of such a body of young men being assembled in such a spot. The spirit, which has testified itself of late years amongst the German students, certainly is not less alarming than that, which existed amongst those of Italy; and here the building of the University is in the same street with the King's Palace, and in its immediate vicinity."[166]

If the "revolutionary spirit" that "animates these seats of learning in Germany," admonished Sir George Rose (1771–1849), a diplomat with long experience of European and American affairs and Britain's envoy to Prussia, in April 1819, "is not radically corrected, it would alone suffice to subvert the governments, such as they now exist, in a certain number of years; from them proceed in succession all those who fill every civil, and religious employment in the state, and who dedicate themselves to scientific and literary pursuits." Through compromising with Napoleonic reform, and enlighteners like Von Humboldt, Germany's princes had failed fully to address the consequences of the universities being a steadily growing seedbed of irreligious philosophy: "the opinions of the French philosophers met with early favour in Germany, and have long been disseminated more or less undisguisedly in its universities." Persons of rank had often failed to grasp "that so hideous a moral would become a very great political evil." Whatever their indignation at Napoleon's aggression, Germany's youth had "also learnt to view with extreme discontent those forms of government" prevailing in their country and favored by Britain. Many university students and scholars had fought in the wars of 1813–15 against Napoleon

[165] Taylor to Canning, Munich, 20 May 1826, in Freitag and Wende (eds.), *British Envoys* i. 293–5, 540–1; Blanning, *Romantic Revolution*, 136; Höffe, *Kant's Cosmopolitan Theory*, 155–6.

[166] Rose to Castlereagh, Berlin, 11 Apr. 1821, in Freitag and Wende (eds.), *British Envoys* i. 162; Broers, *Europe*, 131.

and become intensely politically conscious. The only way to halt what was at once a moral, political, and philosophical contagion sapping the foundations of monarchy, aristocracy, and religion, admonished Rose, was to introduce a better-concerted, fiercer repression. The states had either to secure general regulations applying to all the German Confederation's universities, endorsed by the German Diet— which seemed implausible—or agree "each state should recall its subjects to study at home; and then watch most carefully over the discipline, and course of studies pursued, and the spirit in which they are carried on in the upper seats of learning." The princes needed to end the old practice whereby professors received their incomes through student fees; for this encouraged them to court popularity, as Fichte had, by parading innovative views. Stalwart conservative values require professors to be firmly dependent on government: their salaries should be paid by the state "and they should be under its control in every way."[167]

Late Radical Enlightenment edged forward chiefly via the universities, the Gymnasium—a particular focus of Prussian government attention[168]—and reading clubs and forbidden societies. Germany's universities were directly contributing to the major crisis of political and religious values in Europe, the British envoy in Berlin reminded his superiors in London in 1819, threatening throne and altar through their students being "less circumscribed" than "any other class of citizen;" this helped philosophically-inclined academic fraternity to acquire "an exaggerated, and most mischievous idea of their own consequence, and weight" that disastrously "facilitated the propagation of pernicious principles among them."[169] In his *On the History of Religion and Philosophy in Germany* (1835), Heine explained that the conflict over liberty and "rights" which now so passionately stirs feelings in Germany had come to focus primarily on the universities and the "question of academic freedom" because, the authorities found, "political agitation (read: love of freedom) is to be found mostly at universities;" sovereigns were being "advised, from all sides, to suppress these institutes or at least change them into conventional teaching institutions."[170]

In the 1820s and 1830s persisted a near universal perception that Europe's universities had become the prime seedbed of republicanism, love of freedom, opposition to royalist legitimacy, and general fomenting of late Enlightenment ideas. "And what would science, research, or education matter to the princes," asked Heine sourly, "if the holy security of their thrones were in danger?" Had they not displayed cynical enlistment of religion and philistine attitudes frequently enough in the past with their purporting their sovereignty "is entrusted to them by God and where, heaven

[167] Rose to Castlereagh, Berlin, 13 Apr. 1819, in Freitag and Wende (eds.), *British Envoys to Germany*, i. 89–91.

[168] Barkin, "Social Control," 49.

[169] Rose to Castlereagh, Berlin, 24 July 1819, in Freitag and Wende (eds.), *British Envoys to Germany*, i. 106.

[170] Heine, *On the History of Religion*, 34.

commands, all earthly considerations must give way"?[171] The 1848 revolutions in Austria began in Vienna among crowds attending Metternich's funeral. Conspicuous among the printed flyers agitators distributed was an ode by a Jewish poet, Ludwig August Frankl (1810–94), a graduate of Vienna and Padua universities and warm advocate for the rights and dignity of all the Habsburg empire's peoples, entitled "The University": it extolled the students as freedom's prime fighters—and man's principal hope for a better future.[172]

171 Heine, *On the History of Religion*, 34–5.

172 Goldfarb, *Emancipation*, 201.

21

Radicalism and Repression in the Anglo-American World (1775–1815)

21.1. THE RADICAL TENDENCY

Untypical in certain respects, late eighteenth- and early nineteenth-century Britain, from the 1770s down to the 1820s, was nevertheless also, in key respects, a characteristically *ancien regime* society, especially as regards the political and social dominance of the aristocracy and gentry, continuing disabilities on Catholics, Jews, and Dissenters, and privileged status of the public church. Chiefly exceptional was the unexampled scale of her imperial success and unrivalled effectiveness of her "mixed government" constitution together with the unparalleled popular loyalty to king, country, and constitution. Conservative though he was, Scotland's greatest philosopher, David Hume, a warm advocate of the union of Scotland and England, abhorred the prevailing chauvinism and mood of self-congratulation, self-glorification, and aggressive loyalism suffusing late eighteenth-century England, and, during his last years, feared British prosperity was jeopardized by the "continual increase of our debts, in every idle war, into which, it seems, the mob of London are to rush every minister."[1] While exaggerating the precariousness of its prosperity and aggressiveness of its overseas expansion, Hume was not alone in asking whether the growing national consensus reflected a real, stable superiority over the rest or was dangerous illusion more than reality.

In any case where most gloried in their "confessional state," constructed on an "aristocratic, Christian and monarchical rationale," there were more than a few critical voices.[2] While the Glorious Revolution of 1688–91 "was a great work," agreed the Welsh radical theologian, Richard Price (1723–91), a fervent supporter of "Revolution-principles" but one construing these rather differently from most contemporaries, "it was by no means a perfect work, [. . .] all was not then gained which was necessary to put the Kingdom in the secure and complete possession of the blessings of liberty."[3] A small but growing and not insignificant fringe considered the

[1] Stewart, *Opinion and Reform*, 307–8. [2] Clark, "Eighteenth-Century Social History," 788.
[3] Price, *Discourse*, 35; Hammersley, *English Republican Tradition*, 158.

country's constitution and general organization far less satisfactory than it was then *de rigueur* in markets, taverns, and polite society to insist. Among the kingdom's major dissenting voices, amidst an overwhelming, increasingly intolerant national consensus, were Dissenters like Price and Priestley who objected not just to the narrow suffrage and corruption of the parliamentary system but also that the "toleration then [i.e. in 1688] obtained was imperfect" and that all kinds of penalties, exclusions, and disabilities continued to apply, irrationally and unjustly, to Dissenters, Catholics, Jews as well as Unitarians, not least exclusion from taking degrees at Oxford and Cambridge.[4]

"The toleration in England," complained Priestley, "notwithstanding our boasted liberty, is far from being complete."[5] Anglicanism remained the sole publicly established church linked to state and crown which meant there was some way to go before everyone became a truly autonomous conscience, free of what a renegade Cambridge don, John Jebb (1736–86), among the foremost of the objecting new English radicals of the late 1770s, called the "contagion of corrupted doctrine" maintained "by the craft and cunning of a designing and despotic priesthood."[6] If repression of radical opinions before 1775 was only occasional and sporadic, society's much-vented general scorn for and disapproval of public "atheists," backed by occasional legal interventions, sufficed to create the first stirrings of an intimidating atmosphere. The materialist deist Peter Annet (1693–1769), a Liverpool schoolmaster prosecuted for blasphemy in 1763 at the age of 69, was sentenced to be pilloried twice with a month in Newgate prison followed by a year of forced labor at Bridewell.[7]

Materialist freethinkers, suggested Annet, would always remain a sect wholly segregated by their ideas from most of society.[8] By the 1780s, the atmosphere had grown still more intimidating and by the early 1790s dramatically so. If radical ideas were to create a basis for effectively challenging the forms of society and culture in Britain then it was plain the first and perhaps most formidable adversary was not Parliament, crown, Anglican church, or even the aristocracy, but the combination of repressive law with chauvinistic loyalism and popular scorn compelling all disagreeing into a semi-concealed underground of inconspicuous intellectual networks. In England, complained Paine in April 1791, "where corruption has so completely subdued and strongly fettered human reason, the attempt of one or more obscure individuals to again erect the standard of forlorn reason, and take the field against her seemingly irresistible vanquisher, may appear desperate presumption, bordering upon insanity."[9]

Those comprehensively opposed to the British status quo, namely Britain's Radical Enlightenment critics, may have been a minuscule intellectual fringe with only

[4] Priestley, *Essay*, 186, 202, 211; Webb, "Emergence," 37; Webb, "Price," 161.
[5] Priestley, *Essay*, 128; Porter, *Enlightenment*, 412. [6] Jebb, *The Works* iii. 161.
[7] Harrison, "*Religion*," 87; Hudson, *Enlightenment and Modernity*, 98.
[8] Harrison, "*Religion*," 87–8; Hudson, *Enlightenment and Modernity*, 99–100.
[9] Paine, *Collection of Unknown Writings*, 74.

marginal support among the population, but were also acute, eloquent, and incisive observers, exuding oppositional passion, who, by the 1790s, had come to be associated with the spreading revolutionary wave evident on all sides, including Ireland, Italy, and the Low Countries, and hence were perceived as an immediate danger to the kingdom's security and integrity. Earlier, during the quieter era between the 1740s and the early 1770s, the old appetite for subversion and clandestine networks had noticeably receded. Early eighteenth-century British radical thought was strident in some respects, especially in declaiming against unrestrained royal prerogative, "priestcraft," ecclesiastical privilege, "superstition," intolerance, and unreasoning Bible authority. But limited religious toleration had not provoked major opposition after 1689 and objections to the government's zeal for newspaper and theater censorship was less than insistent. Scorn hard to rebut had occasionally been poured on what Price termed "the disgrace" of "the Test laws" and general readiness to "deprive of eligibility to civil and military offices, all who cannot conform to the established worship."[10] But the political thought of Sidney, Bolingbroke, Shaftesbury, and even Toland and Tindal, had remained, on the whole, too restrained, too "classical republican" and Hobbesian, too amenable to gentry dominance and too little concerned with electoral reform, furthering equality, eradicating royal power, widening personal autonomy, and attacking privilege and the aristocracy, to provide a viable platform for the needs of late eighteenth-century radicalism. The mid-eighteenth-century legacy of Toland, Shaftesbury, Tindal, Collins, and Gordon was an incipient radicalism too submerged, unsteady, and hesitantly presented in its republican concerns to afford the kind of comprehensive rationale for challenging Constitution and legal and social system needed to format the wide-ranging disaffection that first began to emerge powerfully during and after the American crisis.

While many specific grievances voiced after 1775 were not unknown during the century's middle decades, public controversies prior to the American Revolution suggest little real movement toward rallying behind a broad, coherent package of reforming principles simultaneously addressing all four main areas of disaffection—the Constitution, law, disabilities affecting Dissenters, and imperial sway (in America and Ireland in the first place, but also India and the Caribbean). During the middle decades, these remained separate, disparate areas of complaint, marginal to the overall picture. Few disputed that colonies, and not least Ireland, were England's rightful absolute domain, while the law and lawyers met mostly only deep respect. Excessive intervals between elections, seven-year parliamentary terms under the Septennial Act (1716) that replaced the 1694 Triennial Act, which had earlier maintained a three-year ceiling on the length of parliaments, flagrant corruption of the electoral process, and in most constituencies exceedingly narrow franchises within spectacularly uneven and antiquated constituency boundaries, were blatant enough defects for those who cared to look; but as yet few made an issue of it. Britain's

[10] Price, *Discourse*, 36.

Constitution was not without its imperfections, observed Hume, but precisely through being a delicate balance of divergently useful but imperfect principles, it functioned uncommonly well. Crown ministers *were* indeed corrupting Parliament and in a way infringing "liberty;" but Hume could not agree that such corrupt practices should therefore be swept away any more than he thought parliamentary elections should be more frequent or differently organized, or the Anglican church weakened. Retaining a vigorous "monarchical" element in the "mixed government" Constitution, he averred, positively required infrequent elections to the House of Commons.[11]

The majority perspective firmly attached to loyalism and moderation, bolstering the moderate Enlightenment which registered at the highest philosophical level in Hume's claims to the unchallengeable superiority of incoherence, imperfection, and inconsistency. Lower down, only a few worried that radical critics identified glaring inconsistencies in both the boasted "liberties" themselves, and the philosophical arguments buttressing the incomparable superiority of the constitution, and conservative championing of the aristocratic status quo. Until the late 1760s the strategy worked quite smoothly, evolving into a prevalent anti-intellectual and anti-philosophical culture centered on the curiously pervasive notion, both popular and among the ruling elite—almost a national creed and certainly a common psychological defense mechanism—that men of sense and character scrupulously avoid intellectual debate and especially "philosophy." But as the Enlightenment process itself proceeded, entrenched anti-intellectualism, a form of Counter-Enlightenment, for some almost part of the Constitution and unimpeachable, denying any need to find answers to the fraught questions the American Revolution would soon raise in an acute form, while remaining central to both elite and popular culture, increasingly came under siege.

Despite lingering traces of the radical legacy of Toland, Shaftesbury, Collins, Tindal, and Gordon, sustained, wide-ranging criticism of society and the political system in Britain subsided to remarkably low levels in the decades prior to the American Revolution. But then, after three or four decades of quiescence, the issue of parliamentary corruption in England suddenly surged up once more in the late 1760s with the eruption of the "Wilkes and Liberty" disturbances. An incipient clamor against parliamentary nepotism and public pressure for widening the franchise to allow more of the adult male population to vote was skillfully orchestrated by the rabble-rousing John Wilkes (1725–97), son of a distiller, whose spectacular clashes with Parliament helped spur the rise of a politically-orientated reform movement which, however, for the moment remained rather narrowly framed and decidedly chauvinistic in attitude. Wilkes had undeniable historical importance, being much the most celebrated domestic victim of the country's overweening aristocratic, royal, and parliamentary establishment during the 1760s. In 1769, Parliament made a

[11] Hume, *Essays*, 36; Israel, *Democratic Enlightenment*, 219; Pocock, *Barbarism* ii. 186, 220; Pocock, *Virtue, Commerce*, 135.

vigorous attempt to expel him from their midst, contrary to the wishes of his Middlesex constituents. With this, England's chief trouble-maker truly came to symbolize the cause of the unprivileged, ordinary citizen, being the first parliamentary figure to formally propose universal male suffrage in the British Parliament. But there was nothing universal or philosophical about his politics; to many, he seemed just a cynical, self-seeking politician who deep down remained largely indifferent to the issues of popular sovereignty, democracy, and constitutional liberties.[12]

Experience proved, moreover, that a genuine, effective radical program is inconceivable without first mobilizing what radicals and public alike termed "philosophy." What was needed but exceedingly hard to find in the 1760s and early 1770s was a sweepingly bold new theoretical framework. "Preparation for that revolution in favor of human happiness,"[13] as Price called the radical endeavor, necessarily required the "spread of the principles of humanity," which meant, as Price, Jebb, Priestley, Godwin, and Bentham in particular stressed, powerfully advancing the cult of reason in social, moral, and political affairs, the role of intellectual questioning and critical research, and uncompromising hostility to "mysteries." But far too many broad assumptions, dogmas, traditions, and beliefs underpinned the status quo for this not to invite, eventually, a new radicalism with a real prospect of establishing subversive communicating cells around the country. Unitarianism, chief breeding-ground of the new radicalism in Britain and America, suddenly began to gain ground dramatically, even while, for the moment, the general status of "philosophy" in Britain remained strikingly low compared to France, Germany, and Italy. In 1774, the first openly Unitarian chapel was established in London, an initiative led by Theophilus Lindsey (1723–1808), a former Cambridge fellow, Anglican defector, and soon ally of Priestley and Jebb, creating a focus for merging religious and political radicalism with which Franklin too associated.[14] While Priestley and the Unitarian radicals were not in all respects natural allies of atheists like Turner, Godwin, and Bentham, both teams were as one in seeing "reasoning" alone as mankind's "complete test of truth" in weighing the profoundest issues. Their invoking "reason" alone pitted them all as a bloc against the conservativism, moderate Enlightenment skepticism and cult of "honest gentlemen" of Hume, Smith, Ferguson, Gibbon, and, from 1787, Burke.[15]

21.2. UNITARIAN RADICAL ENLIGHTENMENT

Joseph Priestley (1733–1804), born to a Yorkshire dissenting family, and educated in "all the gloom and darkness of Calvinism," converted first to Arminianism whilst still

12 Goodwin, *Friends*, 44–5; Cash, *John Wilkes*, 235, 380, 382.
13 Price, *Political Writings*, 162.
14 Gascoigne, *Cambridge*, 197.
15 Turner, *Answer from a Philosophical Unbeliever*, Preface, p. xxvi; Himmelfarb, *Roads*, 94.

in his teens.[16] By the mid-1750s he had abandoned Arminianism for Arianism and flatly rejected "the Absurdity of the Trinitarian System." During his pastorate at the Mill Hill Chapel in Leeds (1767–73), he made a further transition from Arianism to an Unitarianism rejecting all theological "mysteries," maintaining that "Christ did not die to make satisfaction for the sins of men."[17] At the same time, he steeped himself in scientific study, embarking on a lifelong involvement in experimental chemistry including famous experiments with carbon dioxide and air. Priestley's politics, science, and philosophy were all inseparably tied to his Socinianism, a theological tendency certainly but distinctive in its unyielding insistence on the centrality of "reason," scientific observation, and philosophy, and denial of all supposedly divinely delivered ontological and social hierarchy. For Priestley, basing everything on "reason," being a strict "rationalist" did not mean advocating abstract reasoning but rather accepting only scientifically and historically verifiable facts—what he called the "language of the naked facts"[18]—observed data needing to be tied together via cogent argument. His endeavors at Mill Hill led to his materialism, determinism, and Socinianism becoming for him "equally parts of one system, being equally founded on accurate observations of nature, philosophical necessity (mechanical determinism) and fair deductions from the Scriptures."[19] Priestley, complained one of his fiercest critics, Thomas Reid (1710–96), "denies all mysteries. He thinks, and rejoices in thinking so, that plants have some degree of sensation. As to the lower animals, they differ from us in degree only, and not in kind."[20] Priestleyan radicalism was underpinned by this triad of positions, and while it has been questioned whether his materialistic monism did in fact weld the democratic political, religious, social, and intellectual planks of his radical program coherently together, the argument that Priestley was not a democrat remains manifestly a weak objection.[21]

It is "of the utmost importance," contended Priestley, in a sermon at Leeds in November 1771, that mankind's attention should be directed to the practice of virtue, as the one thing "absolutely necessary to their acceptance with God and their final happiness, and that the doctrine of the eternal obligation of the laws of virtue and religion should be frequently and forcibly, inculcated upon them."[22] This reductive theology, justifying and underpinning his sweeping reformism and universalism, involved rejecting all notion that God's plan envisages redemption as something reserved for a specific group defined by belief, that salvation is bestowed in exchange for faith. It was theology postulating the brotherhood of all men, and the oneness of religion, with respect to the future but also the present and past. Traditional church teaching, especially the dogma of Christ's divinity, he deemed a universal disaster: "for so long as Christians in general are chargeable with this fundamental error of

[16] Willey, *Eighteenth-Century Background*, 172; Hiebert, "Integration," 30.
[17] Priestley, *History of the Corruption* i. 154, 171; Webb, "Emergence," 36.
[18] Priestley, *History of the Corruption* i. 171–2.
[19] Priestley, *Disquisitions*, 220; Hiebert, "Integration," 38; Hampshire-Monk, "British Radicalism," 671.
[20] Reid, *Works* i. 52.
[21] Sakkas, "Joseph Priestley on Metaphysics."
[22] OHM MS Joseph Priestley MS i/iii, p. 64.

worshipping more Gods than one, Jews and Mahometans will always hold their religion in abhorrence" and there can be no "general spread of the Gospel."[23] Had Christ been all along recognized "a mere man approved of God, by signs and wonders which God did by him," Christians would never "have arrogated for him divine honours and consequently the worship that has been paid to the Virgin Mary, and other Popish saints, would not have followed: and the influence of these leading opinions, upon the whole mass of corruptions that came in like a deluge afterward, is easily traced."[24] No sooner had Priestley's enquiries hardened into his new persuasion, that there exists only one substance and that soul and matter are one, than the outcry against him, as he put it, "as an unbeliever, and a favourer of atheism, was exceedingly general and loud; and was echoed from quarters where more candour and better discernment might have been expected."[25]

Impressed, like Jebb, by d'Holbach's arguments, in his *Système de la nature*, against the soul's immortality, Priestley judged it "absolutely necessary to abandon the notion of a soul" if Christianity is to remain compatible with rigorous philosophy and science: "and, happily," he held, "the principles of [Christianity] are as repugnant to the notion [of the soul], as those of any modern philosophy."[26] Convinced that Unitarianism, materialism, and the "doctrine of philosophical necessity, are equally parts of one system,"[27] a system constituting a revolution in religion, science, and philosophy, he rightly believed this also entailed a revolution in politics. "For mechanism", he reasoned, "is the undoubted consequence of materialism," and entails necessity, and both mechanism and materialism are "eminently subservient," as he put it, "to the doctrine of the proper, or mere humanity of Christ."[28] How exactly Priestley reconciled materialism and necessitarianism with belief in divine Providence guiding the world, the special status of Scripture, and "Christ, being a man like ourselves" is far from altogether clear. But he always subsequently adhered to this synthesis. Deeply persuaded by the "argument from design" and averse to the "atheistick scheme [which] makes the very lowest of qualities, powers and perfections, namely passive, senseless matter, the first principle, from whence all things, beauty, regularity, intelligence, virtue, happiness arose," he unquestioningly accepted its logicality despite Hume's critique of the idea. [29] "Neither the hypothesis of chance blind and irregular, nor undesigning necessity," he averred in a Leeds sermon, "can account for the appearances of the universe." "The more we see of the wonderful structure of the world and of the laws of nature, the more clearly do we comprehend their admirable uses, to make all the percipient creation happy, a sentiment which cannot but fill the heart with unbounded love, gratitude, and joy."[30]

[23] OHM MS Joseph Priestley MS i/iii, i, p. 151. [24] Price, *A Free Discussion*, 52.
[25] Priestley, *Disquisitions*, Preface, p. xiv.
[26] Priestley, *Disquisitions*, 88; Willey, *Eighteenth-Century Background*, 169.
[27] Price, *A Free Discussion*, 241. [28] Price, *A Free Discussion*, 240–1.
[29] OHM MS Joseph Priestley MS i/iii, fos. 3, 12v.
[30] Quoted in Hiebert, "Integration," 46.

From 1775 onwards, Priestley half expected to remain, "like Mr Hobbes," for generations "under the imputation of absolute atheism."[31] To defend himself and his disciples against the charge that his "materiality of man, leads to atheism," Priestley tried to prove God's existence philosophically, essentially using the argument from design. Since the "maker of the table, or of the watch, must be different from the table or the watch," it is manifest, held Priestley, that the "maker of myself, of the world, and of the universe (meaning by it all the worlds that we suppose to exist) must be a being different from myself, the world or the universe."[32] This he considered a sufficient rebuttal of Spinoza, "who, making the universe itself to be God, did in fact, deny that there was any God."[33] But precisely here, retorted the Liverpool physician, medical researcher, and atheist, Matthew Turner (d. 1788), Priestley went astray. Reason is more cogently upheld by embracing "a principle of intelligence and design" in nature denying "that principle to be extraneous from itself." "The method which Dr Priestley has taken to prove the existence of a God," he objected, "is by arguing from effect to cause," since he "explodes that other pretended proof *a priori* which has so much raised the fame of Dr Clarke among other theologians." Priestley's strategy landed him in the same camp, therefore, as Turner himself, championing reason and scientific findings as the only basis of truth, a doctrine creating an unbridgeable rift between Priestleyan Unitarianism and the "theologians."[34] Curiously, while labeling Spinoza a devotee of "atheism," Hobbes, contended Priestley, "notwithstanding his heterodoxy in politics," was "no atheist, but a sincere Christian and a conscientious good man."[35]

Spiritual emancipation entailed the destruction of false notions of faith, "and consequently" the demolition, ultimately, of "the antichristian tyrannies that have supported them," by which Priestley meant the unholy trinity of monarchy, aristocracy, and (false) theology.[36] Since early in the eighteenth century, all Christian orthodoxies had, in the universities, loosely allied with dualistic systems in modern philosophy like those of Descartes, Locke, Leibniz, Wolff, and Kant, systems providing a rationale for explaining nature comprehensively in terms of "reason" while exempting Revelation, miracles, Providence, and all *supernaturalia* together with theological mysteries like the Eucharist from like rigorous tests of experience and rational examination on the ground that these pertained to a transcendental higher metaphysical sphere. Only philosophical Socinianism could logically combine with materialism, necessitarianism, and one-substance doctrine. Linking Socinianism with a determinist moral philosophy in Britain had begun with the vegetarian physician David Hartley (1705–57) in the 1740s, an Anglican rejecting Trinitarian Orthodoxy who, according to Priestley, "produced the greatest, and in my opinion the most

[31] Priestley, *Disquisitions*, Preface, p. xvi; Schofield, *Enlightened Joseph Priestley*, 56, 59–61.
[32] Priestley, *Disquisitions*, 148; Price, *A Free Discussion*, 365–6.
[33] Price, *A Free Discussion*, 253–4; Priestley, *Disquisitions*, 149.
[34] Turner, *Answer from a Philosophical Unbeliever*, 2.
[35] Turner, *Answer from a Philosophical Unbeliever*, Preface, p. xxviii.
[36] Priestley, *Disquisitions*, p. xxv.

favourable effect on my general turn of thinking through life,"[37] and exerted a crucial influence too on Jebb, Bentham, Coleridge, and James Mill.

A close friend of Jebb's father, in his *Observations on Man* (1749), a new edition of which was brought out by Priestley in 1775, Hartley expounded an innovative philosophy, almost a physics of the mind, designed to reconcile necessitarianism and materialism with Christian idealism. Not unlike Condillac, Hartley conceived the mind as a dynamic interaction of sensory experience and association of ideas, a purely material process producing ideas from vibrations in the brain transmitted via the nervous system. Since all men's minds function similarly, Hartley arrived at the notion of universal salvation in place of selective salvation. His removing the hard-and-fast distinction between body and mind, reconfiguring mind as something both receiving stimuli from, and working on, its social and physical context, helped lead Priestley to his doctrine of "necessity." Dismantling metaphysical dualism, Hartley constructed a compromise retaining practical Free Will within a necessitarian overall framework postulating a divinely determined development designed to promote the collective and individual well-being of men.[38] Here was a philosophy that seemingly opened the door to a British philosophical Radical Enlightenment of universal salvation through "reason" absorbing spiritual salvation into pure physical salvation in the here and now, erasing all *supernaturalia*, hierarchy, and salvation other than through works and practical piety.

Alongside Hartley and Jebb, Priestley flatly denied their common materialism and necessitarianism was Spinozistic or conflicted, as most interlocutors contended, with Christianity, morality, or justice. Priestley's materialism, unlike Turner's, Godwin's, and Bentham's, implied "everything is the divine power; but still, strictly speaking, everything is not the deity himself." "There is nothing in nature but God's agency," held Priestley, but rationally "making the Deity to *be*, as well as to *do* everything" removed his stance from "any thing like the opinion of Spinoza; because I suppose a source of infinite power, and superior intelligence, from which all inferior beings are derived."[39] The sole author of the corruption, superstition, and tyranny, admonished Priestley as Unitarian minister in Birmingham, was the "same great being who is also now, in the course of his providence, employing these means to purge his floor."[40] But why "so long a season of darkness" had to precede "the perfect day" and how exactly to conceive His "the best of purposes" remained troublingly unclear, Priestleyan Unitarian's great vulnerability. That God had permitted the long corruption of the church, the "gross darkness of that night which has for many centuries obscured our holy religion," as Priestley put it, in 1782,[41] and permitted the general sway of superstition and tyranny over men "for the best of purposes," was something Priestley's and Jebb's divine necessitarianism rendered certain yet

[37] Priestley, *Autobiography*, 76.

[38] Bower, *Hartley and James Mill*, 27–9; Page, *John Jebb*, 78–80.

[39] Page, *John Jebb*, 253, 337.

[40] Priestley, *History of the Corruption* i, Dedication, p. vi; Himmelfarb, *Roads*, 103–4.

[41] Priestley, *History of the Corruption* i, Dedication, p. v.

wholly inexplicable, a mystery as impervious to "reasoning" as any the ecclesiastics of the reviled main churches preached. Why had Christ not preached against superstition and why was it only now that the divine Majesty desired "superstition" to lapse?

Rational Dissent, especially the materialist Unitarianism of Priestley and Jebb, spearheaded the British Radical Enlightenment between the 1760s and 1815, eclipsing the more purely philosophical, one-substance tradition reaffirmed by Diderot, d'Holbach, and Condorcet. But Unitarian radicalism suffered from seemingly insuperable intellectual inconsistencies, contradiction rooted in its attempt to combine one-substance doctrine and science with a theology of divine Providence, Revelation, and salvation that eventually, during the early nineteenth century, undermined its viability.[42] Where the prolonged political repression that arose in the 1790s and persisted in Britain down to the end of the Napoleonic Wars failed to prevent most suppressed British reform societies, networks, and organizations from reviving in one form or another after 1815, the original intellectual spearhead, Rational Dissent, failed to survive as an active movement into the next century. The Priestleyan Unitarians proved uniquely well-placed to serve as a bridge between Radical Enlightenment and Christianity but only for a limited period, less than half a century.

Son of a senior Anglican clergyman in Ireland, John Jebb (1736–86), after a year studying at Trinity College Dublin, enrolled as a student at Peterhouse, Cambridge, in 1753, at a time when Latitudinarian Anglican theology proclaiming Locke and Newton the great pillars of mankind's rational and enlightened world-view remained unchallengeably hegemonic in the English universities. Jebb's combined religious and political radicalism, like Priestley's, emerged from convoluted personal spiritual striving. Combining Cambridge, and a career in the church, he became a fellow of Peterhouse in 1761 and ordained Anglican priest in 1763. In the mid-1760s he focused on Arabic and the Koran besides theology and Newton's mathematics, very much a general Enlightenment figure whose intellectual culture was Newtonian, Latitudinarian, and "moderate."[43] A declared Socinian from 1768—roughly the same time as Priestley—for him too Christ became exclusively human, the last great prophet whose Crucifixion never signified supernatural redemptive power. Original Sin Jebb (like Socinianism generally) dismissed as a superstitious myth. Meanwhile, his identifying with the cause of "Wilkes and Liberty" around this time tied his religious radicalism to a budding political radicalism, making him a largely isolated firebrand within the University.[44] Even before Priestley, Jebb perused the *Système de la nature*, taking detailed notes and agreeing with much he found there. Matter he now viewed as an active, not passive substance. Since his materialist conception of the mind left no room for traditional notions of the soul, or freedom of the will, by 1771–2 Jebb, concurring with d'Holbach, had discovered mankind's

[42] Donnelly, "Joseph Towers," 32–5; Johnston, *Hidden Wordsworth*, 176–7.
[43] Donnelly, "Joseph Towers," 20, 32–4.
[44] Price, *Discourse*, 17; Price, *Observations*, 44.

need for a single, universal moral code distinct from, and antagonistic to, anything offered by the churches.[45]

Renewing British radicalism from its philosophical core, through reconnection with Continental Radical Enlightenment, originates then in the early 1770s when d'Holbach's principal works and the *Histoire philosophique* exerted their maximum impact in France and internationally. But unlike its Continental counterpart, late Enlightenment British radicalism strove to secure comprehensive reform not via "enlightened despots" (though Diderot too had abandoned this route by 1770), or violent revolution from below, but by tirelessly promoting comprehensive reform of the system through publicity and debate, generating a complex mix of extra-parliamentary pressure politics, press campaigns, and carefully-targeted initiatives in the church and higher education. Jebb's was an approach consonant with the Unitarian view that progress and Man's Enlightenment is nothing other than the working of divine Providence active everywhere and continually advancing, albeit mostly in unobtrusive, non-violent ways. Even "unbelievers" and freethinkers like Turner, whom the Priestleyan Unitarians, Jebb and Price, hoped to convert but did not decry as did conventional "Christians," they deemed a valuable tool. "The writings of the unbelievers," declared Price, in 1787, "have done service to the Christian religion by causing a stricter enquiry into its evidence and clearing it of the rubbish which has been thrown upon it and the false doctrines which have been mingled with it."[46] Much of what France's unbelievers had to say about Christianity and the church Priestley, Price, and Jebb designated "a great public benefit" rather than blasphemy.

An embattled don, Jebb initially fought locally, establishing a movement to reform Cambridge, which he believed was infused with "an abominable spirit of bigotry and fanaticism" and in need of "a through reform" to raise standards, encourage diligence, and, by enhancing the University's "public utility," help it "flourish." He also wanted "non-Christians," Jews and others, admitted to the University. His outspoken critique, *Remarks upon the Present Mode of Education in the University of Cambridge* (1772), recommended expanding the decision-making power of the University by reducing the colleges' traditional autonomy so as to reorganize the curriculum and examinations system. Annual examinations for all students, noblemen included, he pronounced indispensable if zeal for study and academic performance were to be raised as he hoped. The non-theological curriculum, dominated by Newtonian natural philosophy with its strong emphasis on mathematics, Jebb, like Price, thought needed altering to include subjects useful for moral and political instruction, classics and history especially. Excessive stress on Newtonian mathematics he considered as "reprehensible" as the highly defective examination system since both prevented students learning about society, politics, and moral conduct.[47] Students from

[45] Jebb, *The Works* ii. 167–8; Page, "Liberty," 224; Sonnenscher, *Sans-Culottes*, 381–2.

[46] Price, *Political Writings*, 163.

[47] Price, *Observations*, 58; Page, *John Jebb*, 132–4; Gascoigne, *Cambridge*, 203–4.

aristocratic families, he proposed, should be examined annually, and treated like the rest, a recommendation rebuffed by the University Senate on the ground that such an innovation would antagonize the aristocracy and erode college autonomy.[48]

Jebb's campaign ignited a miniature civil war within academe during 1773–5, pitting a minority supporting comprehensive reform against the conservative opposition headed by the University vice-chancellor, college heads and Senate. Both sides resorted to newspapers and mobilizing the public. Aversion to his Cambridge proposals grew alongside abhorrence for his Unitarian and political views, the battle soon reverberating through British elite corridors.[49] He ceased performing Anglican clerical duties late in 1773. Before long, it became clear that Jebb had lost his battle with the "bigots and time-servers of Cambridge." He decided he had no alternative but to resign as an Anglican priest and Cambridge don. In a very public fashion he irrevocably sacrificed respectability and his privileged life with his pamphlet *A Short State of the Reasons for a late resignation* issued in October 1775,[50] which left his reputation at Cambridge in tatters and all prospect of success for his higher education reforms at an end. Examination reform at Cambridge was not again a topic for high table discussion until the 1820s. "I have had some experience of academical men," he remarked years later, "and should be very willing to exchange a few of our most orthodox men, with long faces and empty skulls, for the learning, talents and integrity of infidels."[51]

21.3. THE AMERICAN REVOLUTION IN BRITISH THOUGHT

The American crisis polarized opinion in Britain even before the war itself began. For most, in Britain, the ensuing conflict heightened pressure to display patriotic sentiment, extol Constitution, crown, and empire, and denounce "rebellion" unreservedly, pressure kept up by the press and sermons of the Anglican clergy who now stressed more than ever the godliness and oneness of faith, loyalism, and royalism. This only strengthened Priestley's conviction that "religion requires no civil establishment," that religion supported by government "instead of being any advantage, is a great incumbrance to a state, and in general highly unfavourable to its liberties."[52] Although not a few felt some degree of sympathy for the American cause, and many supported petitions to Parliament and the crown urging a more conciliatory policy toward the colonies, few backed the rebels publicly in definite, forthright terms, defying the loyalist outcry to the extent of agreeing with the *Histoire philosophique* that in America (and Ireland), Britain had become a despicable "tyranny," and calling

[48] Jebb, *Account of the Proceedings*, p. iii.
[49] Gascoigne, "Anglican Latitudinarianism," 231–2; Page, "Great Politicianness," 746.
[50] Page, "Great Politicianness," 747; Page, *John Jebb*, 144–5.
[51] Jebb, *Account of the Proceedings*, p. iv.
[52] Priestley, *Letters*, 53; Hampshire-Monk, "British Radicalism," 669–70.

on king and Parliament to suspend efforts to suppress the rebellion by force.[53] Very few agreed with Price and Jebb that American independence, as the latter put it in a speech in London, in August 1782, "is equally necessary to the establishment of American and English freedom."[54] Rather, for openly criticizing ministry, Parliament, and king, and justifying the Americans, radicals subjected themselves, recounted Price, "to much abuse and some danger."[55]

Nevertheless, once the fighting began, the radical claim that, contrary to Montesquieu, Britain's was not genuinely a mixed constitution, nor admirable, but a defective "juntocracy," government by royal ministers and their cronies without any worthwhile philosophic principles, diffused widely. If Paine's *Common Sense* (1776) stood unmatched for vehement repudiation of the Constitution, crown, class-system, and empire, not a few others presented comparably wide-ranging subversive oppositional perspectives.[56] Amid the flurry of radical booklets and petitions appearing in 1775–6, among the foremost was Price's *Observations on the Nature of Civil Liberty* (1776) where the American upheaval is proclaimed "a revolution by which Britons themselves will be the greatest gainers, if wise enough to improve properly the check that has been given to the despotism of their ministers, and to catch the flame of virtuous liberty which has saved their American brethren."[57] Britons must push for "free government" and render Parliament more representative, less corrupt, and more accountable. While still way out of line with majority opinion, with most Britons stalwartly rallying behind crown and elites, sympathizers with the American cause accounted for an increasingly significant segment of opinion. Admittedly, much of this protest kept to older ideological perspectives, not all Radical Enlightenment in character. Many protesters still thought in terms of the incomparable virtues of supposed ancient British traditions, precedents, laws, and constitutional practices.[58] A prominent example was Jebb's friend, Major John Cartwright (1740–1824), a Nottinghamshire landowner who, on a practical level, accomplished more than anyone in the late 1770s to connect American developments to the need for political reform at home, but who remained always chiefly preoccupied with precedent, "lost rights," and the constitutional past, heavily stressing the guiding role of the common law and lacking Price's and Priestley's cosmopolitanism. An outstanding, tireless combatant for parliamentary reform but in no way a radical enlightener, Cartwright expressed reservations about universal male suffrage and took no interest in general principles or "philosophy."[59] Only the fringe committed to democracy, universal and equal rights, and equality rooted in universal principles, writers and orators eschewing talk of past constitutions and precedent, dismissing "constitutions formed by chance, and

[53] *Histoire philosophique* (1780), ix. 257–75; Goodwin, *Friends*, 56–7; Page, *John Jebb*, 172.

[54] Jebb, *The Works* iii. 314.

[55] Price, *Observations*, 1.

[56] Priestley, *Letters*, 146; Pocock, *Virtue, Commerce*, 276; Foner, *Tom Paine*, 10, 12.

[57] Price, *Observations*, 2; Dickinson, "Friends," 18; Lieberman, "Mixed Constitution," 339.

[58] Priestley, *Letters*, 40; Paine, *Rights of Man*, 196–7.

[59] Hampshire-Monk, "On not Inventing," 141, 145; Lieberman, "Mixed Constitution," 341; Duthille, *Discours radical*, 2–4.

continually patched up" and supposed "superior to the plans of reason," as Wollstonecraft expressed their view, were "radicals" in the philosophical sense central to the late Enlightenment.[60]

Few then ventured to tie opposition to royal policy in America to a truly wide-ranging general critique of the British Constitution and institutions expressed in universal terms—a reluctance which, however, only intensified the exasperation of those who did. Conspicuous among these exceptional spirits were a group among the London Club of Honest Whigs, including Price, Priestley, Jebb, and James Burgh, with which, until he returned to America in 1775, Franklin too was associated.[61] These men felt impelled not just to demand more equal representation and annual parliaments, but for the first time to invoke natural rights, universal principles, and the philosophical basis of human freedom; and several, like Paine and Price, even rejected the doctrine of parliamentary supremacy in their quest for deeper, wider principles of social and political organization.[62] Forming a "completely new government on the principles of equal liberty and the rights of men," as Priestley put it, "without nobles" as "Dr Price expressively and happily said," the American Revolution exerted a consolidating, deepening, and unifying effect on the reforming aims and arguments of the most outspoken sections of Britain's opposition to crown, ministry, and Parliament, finally decisively shifting the emphasis away from particular historic rights to universal and equal rights, along lines outlined in French and now American radical thought.

Extra-parliamentary agitation in the late 1770s led to calls to form county associations and pressure Parliament for political reform. The "Westminster committee" or "association" set up in the Kings Arms Tavern in 1780 by a crowded meeting of local freeholders savoring speeches by Charles James Fox, Jebb, and others seeking to elect Fox to the Commons, to secure parliamentary reform, produced a report vividly illustrating the shift away from older forms, classical republicanism, Whiggism, and the Commonwealth tradition, to a broad Radical Enlightenment stance. What emerged was an organized movement committed to securing annual general elections, equally bounded constituencies, the secret ballot, salaries for MPs, and removal of property qualifications for candidates for election. The right of those who are taxed to be represented had hitherto been obscured, urged the report, in which Jebb had a hand, by the privileged status traditionally but wrongfully accorded to property. "Every man has an interest in his life, his liberty, his kindred, and his country," and without representation these interests, "as substantial, as land or money," possess no defense against the sway of rank and property.[63] Simply petitioning Parliament, concurred Jebb, in his *Address to the Freeholders of Middlesex*, would not bring

[60] O'Neill, *Burke–Wollstonecraft Debate*, 241; Dickinson, *Friends*, 56–8; Thomas, *Philosophic Radicals*, 18.

[61] Wood, *Americanization*, 86, 170; Dickinson, "Friends," 6; Foner, *Tom Paine*, 7.

[62] Paine, *Rights of Man*, 197, 220–1; Dickinson, "Friends," 22; Page, "Liberty," 205, 226.

[63] Paine, *Rights of Man*, 184–8; Dickinson, "Friends," 21; Hampshire-Monk, "British Radicalism," 666–7.

about reform: stronger, more sweeping methods were needed. It was Jebb who first formulated the idea, based on "general will" doctrine, that extra-parliamentary gatherings and special conventions have the right to override Parliament or any legislature should it persist in refusing to enact democratic reforms the people demand, and first suggested that withholding taxes might be a practicable method to step up the pressure.[64]

To radical enlighteners American Independence was something "equally necessary," as Jebb expressed it, in 1782, "to the establishment of American and English freedom."[65] Legally, Parliament was not bound to heed any representations from below, and was most unlikely to while crown and Lords remained sufficiently independent within the structure of government to defy any sign of the Commons weakening under outside pressure. Jebb's plan was for the associations to convene a national convention of delegates, "approved friends of liberty" chosen in proportion to population, to debate and formulate a public act comprehensively setting out all the reforms demanded of Parliament, first and foremost "equal, annual and universal representation" in the House of Commons.[66] Although Price and Priestley were less radical than Jebb or Paine, in terms of activism, they too unequivocally demanded moves towards universal male suffrage and the principle of democracy. There was no advocacy of violence or a resort to arms; but the American crisis decisively turned representative democracy into a theoretical possibility in British political life. Yet, as a program of practical politics, the goals remained unattainable, even inconceivable, within the prevailing class, cultural, and political context. This meant the status quo could only be seriously challenged by a revolution of philosophical principles enshrining ideals aimed at securing the "happiness" and interests of the individual, and the common welfare, on an egalitarian basis. To Jebb in his last years, the world situation, with scant progress being made, still looked distinctly gloomy. The English, Irish, and, still more, the empire's other subjects, he complained in September 1785, remain "helpless prey, to the depredations of ministers of state."[67] Where "in the extensive province of Quebec," ministers had established "an arbitrary government (which still prevails),"[68] in Ireland, the outlook was direr still, so that it had become the duty of those, like himself, assisting the "friends of liberty in Ireland," to encourage the Irish to resist.[69] At home, he sought to reform Parliament, but also limit parliamentary sovereignty by introducing educated public opinion more directly into the process of consultation and decision-making.[70]

Supporting political causes abroad and at home, linked by universal principles, also characterized the efforts of Jebb's remarkable wife, Ann Jebb (1735–1812), perhaps

[64] Gascoigne, "Anglican Latitudinarianism," 232.
[65] Jebb, *The Works* iii. 314; Page, "Liberty," 218–19.
[66] Page, "Liberty," 233; Page, *John Jebb*, 182–3.
[67] Jebb, *The Works* iii. 396.
[68] Jebb, *The Works*, Preface, pp. x–xi and iii. 387; Page, *John Jebb*, 172–3.
[69] Jebb, *The Works* iii. 386–7, 394; Page, "Great Politicianess," 750, 757.
[70] Hampshire-Monk, "British Radicalism," 667.

the first woman actively to propagate a comprehensive radical outlook by publishing articles (usually anonymously). Childless daughter of a Church of England vicar, she had emerged in her own right during the Cambridge fray as a resolute writer of letters to newspapers urging higher education reform. In her case too, Unitarianism, exalting reason and toleration and rejecting "mysteries," shaped a cosmopolitan, libertarian political activism based on universal principle which she strove to apply, collaborating with her husband and propagandizing on behalf of a wide range of causes—American Independence, the "Liberties of the Irish Nation," reform in India, universal suffrage, prison reform, and annual parliaments; from 1789, she emerged too as a staunch backer of the French Revolution.[71]

Radical Enlightenment scorned veneration of "mixed government" and the existing British Constitution and also abjured Montesquieu's endorsement of Britain's separation of crown, Parliament, and judiciary as quasi-independent powers, disapproving of full separation because this negated the claim that popular sovereignty is the overriding principle and a universal benefit for all peoples. Radical ideas drawing heavily on Rational Dissent thereby helped drive what was now a growing polarization, with a newly energized extra-parliamentary opposition gaining ground and splitting the intelligentsia but most of Britain's population rallying unapologetically behind the elites. Presbyterians and most other Dissenters were firmly directed by their clergy and creed to show loyalty to crown and Constitution, not sympathy for rebellion. The Methodist leader, John Wesley (1725–97), though no less anti-Calvinist than Price or Priestley, and like them dedicated to social and law reform and abolition of slavery, never challenged Anglican theology or its doctrine of peaceful acquiescence in authority and powerfully attacked radical ideas. In his sermons he especially denouncing the concept of popular sovereignty, here anticipating Burke's post-1787 uncompromising insistence on tradition, laws, and charters. Nothing could shake Wesley's conviction that there was more liberty "under a limited monarchy" than under democracy. He called upon the populace of England and Wales, who, after all, had "no more voice in the Parliament than the Americans" that "they must needs be subject" to crown and ministry from duty and "for conscience sake."[72] Methodists joined the Anglicans in accusing the likes of Jebb, Price, Priestley, and Paine of threatening to "unhinge all government, and overturn it from the foundation."[73]

Certainly, a good many Dissenters of whatever stripe sympathized with "no taxation without representation," especially since Dissenters were disproportionately numerous in precisely the fastest growing industrial areas of the Midlands and the North—Manchester, Birmingham, Sheffield, Liverpool, and Leeds—the cities most

[71] Page, "Great Politicianess," 750–7; Page, *John Jebb*, 194, 204, 225, 251–2; Duthille, *Discours radical*, 162.

[72] Semmel, *Methodist Revolution*, 65; Hampshire-Monk, "British Radicalism," 670–1; Shaw, *Miracles*, 178–9.

[73] Semmel, *Methodist Revolution*, 65; Dickinson, "Friends," 3.

chronically underrepresented in Parliament. This injustice, some also perceived, added to the existing system's bias hampering the interests of Britain's industrial–commercial sector in favor of the Anglican landed gentry.[74] Dissenters of many kinds regarded America as a bastion of religious liberty, deserving sympathy, even support against a crown, army, and Parliament enforcing not just political acquiescence—to which few objected—but also religious discrimination. Northern Ireland Presbyterians showed a particular inclination toward the American rebels. Some Presbyterians were angry too over George III's Canadian policy, especially the Quebec Act placing Catholics and Protestants in Canada on virtually equal footing. But these sympathizers with the American Revolution and its assemblies were not sympathizing on the basis of a radical program. If there was a tendency for such support to become radical in some cases, equally, as with Burke's stance, it could powerfully stiffen aversion to radical notions.

Burke endorsed Hume's doctrine regarding the limited scope of reason, likewise insisting on morality's rootedness in habit, feeling, and custom. What many contemporaries took to be his pro-American stance, and his support for resistance to oppression in Ireland, actually bore practically no resemblance to the egalitarian and democratic principles of radical writers like Jebb, Price, Paine, Godwin, Priestley, Wollstonecraft, or, later, Bentham. Though at this time openly hostile to the American Revolution in a way Burke did not appear to be, Bentham remained always a believer in the power of sound philosophy to transform the world fundamentally for the better.[75] Burke's ostensibly pro-American phase ended with his abrupt shift to an avowedly anti-democratic and anti-reformist conservative stance, from 1787, when he publicly approved Prussia's suppression of the democratic movement in the Netherlands. Henceforth, armed intervention to fight democrats was consistently recommended by a previously always illiberal but now openly reactionary Burke.[76] His seeming change of principles briefly baffled Mirabeau, Fox, Cloots, and Paine: for they mistakenly construed his post-1787 stance as a volte-face, as a startling lack of consistency. "That an avowed friend of the American revolution," complained Priestley in 1791, "should be an enemy to that of the French, which arose from the same general principles, and in a great measure sprung from it, is to me unaccountable."[77] Wollstonecraft was more accurate but no less cutting: "on what principle Mr Burke could defend American independence, I cannot conceive," she commented in 1790, "for the whole tenor of his plausible arguments settles slavery on an everlasting foundation."[78] Burke indeed never supported the American Revolution as a set of principles. Burke urged men to proceed sensibly, Paine reluctantly concluded, "without troubling ourselves about the principles of philosophy and politics," holding that

[74] Gibbs, *Joseph Priestley*, 192; Thomas, *Philosophic Radicals*, 130; Fitzpatrick, "Enlightenment," 122.
[75] Priestley, *Letters*, Preface, pp. v–vi, 23; Rosen, "Jeremy Bentham's Radicalism," 218.
[76] Israel, *Expanding Blaze*, 236–42. [77] Priestley, *Letters*, Preface, p. iv.
[78] Wollstonecraft, *Vindication of the Rights of Men*, 13; Gibbons, *Edmund Burke*, 167, 257 n. 5.

to proceed by way of logical conclusions is "ridiculous," ensuring an outcome in theory and practice that is then itself ridiculous.[79]

Jebb, Priestley, and William Godwin (1756–1836), a 20-year-old when the American Revolution commenced, took pride in their English heritage. But from the mid-1770s onward they also faced a growing emotional challenge with respect to national feeling and patriotism. Their supporting the American Revolution and universalist Enlightenment ideals, their commitment to what Priestley called the "rights of men," exposed them to the charge of disloyalty driven by a xenophobic mood surging up vigorously from 1789.[80] Price and Priestley, denouncing ignorance, "error and delusion," responded by trying to re-educate public opinion as to the true meaning of "patriotism."[81] While it is good to love our country as a "community of which we are members, as that body of companions and friends and kindred who are associated with us under the same constitution of government, protected by the same laws, and bound together by the same civil polity," it is sheer prejudice to suppose "love of it which is our duty" entails "any conviction of the superior value of it to other countries, or any particular preference of its laws and constitution of government." Patriotism, declared Price, in his *Discourse on the Love of Our Country*, delivered at a Dissenter meeting in London, in November 1789, is "certainly a noble passion; but, like all other passions, it requires regulation and direction."[82] True love of country arises from universal principles common to all men and understanding of Man's place in the world. "The chief blessings of human nature," he maintained, "are the three following: TRUTH, VIRTUE, and LIBERTY. These are therefore, the blessings in the possession of which the interest of our country lies and to the attainment of which our love of it ought to direct our endeavours."[83] What he and Priestley labeled "true patriotism" needed to be carefully distinguished from reprehensible chauvinism, which should be condemned. The next evening, Price attended a dinner with "the Revolutionists," as Godwin called the newly created "Revolution Society," meeting at the "London Tavern," where, amid the toasts and speeches of 4–5 November 1789, old-fashioned narrow patriotic radicalism exalting the traditional Whig pantheon from King Alfred through Hampden, Sidney, and Russell to Locke continued to rub shoulders with Paine's and Price's cosmopolitan, universalist, pro-American, and pro-French Radical Enlightenment.[84]

Impervious to the "rancorous invectives of Mr. Burke,"[85] Price redefined "patriotism" and loyalty to one's nation in terms relating it to the general predicament oppressing humanity: "our first concern, as lovers of our country, must be to enlighten it. Why are the nations of the world so patient under despotism? Why do they crouch to tyrants, and submit to be treated as if they were a herd of cattle? Is it not because they are kept in

[79] Paine, *Rights of Man*, 195. [80] Mori, *William Pitt*, 13; Philp, *Godwin's Political Justice*, 42, 77.
[81] Price, *Discourse*, 3. [82] Price, *Discourse*, 2; Priestley, *Letters*, 45; Paine, *Rights of Man*, 157.
[83] Price, *Discourse*, 11; St Clair, *The Godwins*, 44; Locke, *Fantasy of Reason*, 42.
[84] Duthille, *Discours radical*, 253, 263–4. [85] Morgan, *Memoirs*, 82.

darkness, and want knowledge? Enlighten them and you will elevate them."[86] "Much would have been lost "had Britain conquered" in America. The United States had won their freedom and were now "a place of refuge for opprest men in every region of the world." In this way the American War, "did great good by disseminating just sentiments of the rights of mankind, and the nature of legitimate government; by exciting a spirit of resistance to tyranny which has emancipated one European country [i.e. the Netherlands], and is likely to emancipate others; and by occasioning the establishment in America of forms of government more equitable and more liberal than any that the world has yet known."[87]

In his 1789 discourse Price—by this time a figure famous in France and the Netherlands as well as America and Britain—delivered a scathing indictment of "that spirit of rivalship and ambition which has been common among nations," barely veiling his view that British national feeling had unfortunately degenerated into "love of domination; a desire of conquest, and a thirst for grandeur and glory, by extending territory and enslaving surrounding countries"—though he left it unclear whether Wales and Scotland as well as Ireland, India, Canada, the Caribbean, and the Americas were included in his indictment. Once love of country becomes a "blind and narrow principle," it produces a well of prejudice against other peoples and useful device in the hands of corrupt government for "forming men into combinations and factions against their common rights and liberties." Paine made the same point still more abrasively when condemning militant loyalism as a tool of monarchical government for manipulating the British people against Swiss, Dutch, and French efforts to forge government "established on the representative system."[88] Ordinary patriotism, Price, Priestley, and Paine deemed incompatible with "universal benevolence" and a general plague inducing men to "attack one another's territories, to encroach on one another's rights, and to endeavour to build their own advancement on the degradation of all within the reach of their power."[89] "From a small spark kindled in America," agreed Paine, late in 1791, stressing the benefits for all men, "a flame has arisen, not to be extinguished."[90]

An early sign of what was to come, confirming the depth of the ideological rift pervading intellectual and cultural life in Britain after the American war, was the uproarious trial for sedition of William Davies Shipley, dean of St Asaph, in North Wales, in 1783. Already discernible here in embryo was an emerging tripartite moral, social and political struggle between moderate mainstream Enlightenment, Radical Enlightenment, and Counter-Enlightenment loyalism soon to rage in full fury. Shipley offended by republishing a pamphlet by his future brother-in-law, William Jones, the orientalist, entitled the *Principles of Government* (1782), a tract for the

[86] Price, *Observations*, 12; Porter, *Enlightenment*, 46.
[87] Price, *Observations*, 2. [88] Paine, *Rights of Man*, 162, 194, 268.
[89] Paine, *Rights of Man*, 6; Priestley, *Letters*, 45; Grenby, *Anti-Jacobin Novel*, 117.
[90] Paine, *Rights of Man*, 210.

Society for Constitutional Information of which he was a member, calling for political reform, frequent elections, and a more democratic franchise.[91] Jones's opinion, and that of the Society, citing Locke, that the Revolution principles of 1688 had not been sufficiently adopted in Britain, was by no means shared by most of the Welsh gentry presiding over their still largely rural countrymen whom they intended to keep as deferential as in the past. Shipley had wanted to bring the pamphlet out in Welsh but, retreating before the outraged reaction of local gentry, began with a reprint locally in English. Brought to trial for sedition by loyalist gentry, before the Wrexham magistrates, in April 1783,[92] he was defended by the Society for Constitutional Information and survived the first round intact. But his case was then transferred, resuming over a year later at Shrewsbury Assizes, in August 1784, amid a now huge national furor mixing angry denunciation with supportive reformist letters propagating the Society's views. Acquitted again, Shipley returned to Wrexham in triumph.

As in France, Holland, and America, republican and democratic tendencies notably gained ground in Britain through the 1780s and beginning of the 1790s. Unitarianism experienced a noticeable surge at this time, becoming rife at Cambridge following Jebb's departure and especially in the wake of another prominent don abandoning Anglicanism and the Trinity for Unitarianism, William Frend (1757–1841), a fellow of Jesus College expelled from the university in 1787, the year Wordsworth arrived there.[93] Coleridge too was originally radicalized during his student years in Cambridge (1791–4), chiefly by witnessing the university's persecution of his hero, Frend, a don stripped of his fellowship, in May 1793, for publishing an anti-war tract, *Peace and Union* (1793), deploring Britain's war against revolutionary France. The new revolutionary awareness surging in Britain in the 1780s, rightly averred Paine and the radical fraternity, was the fruit not of economic change, social forces, or religion, and certainly not of ordinary notions, but of "the enlightened state of mankind."[94] In Godwin's radical formation, French ideas supplemented by Priestley proved decisive.[95] "It is now twelve years," noted William Godwin in 1793, indicating 1781, since he personally first discovered "that monarchy was a species of government unavoidably corrupt." Before 1780, he had been a stalwart Tory and Dissenting minister; only since 1781 had his thinking been revolutionized, largely owing to the "great additional instruction" he had gained "from reading the most considerable French writers upon the nature of man in the following order, *Système de la nature* [d'Holbach], Rousseau, Helvétius," having been introduced to d'Holbach's *Système de la nature* and subsequently Helvétius' *De l'Esprit* through meeting a certain Frederick Norman, at Stowmarket, who possessed a collection of such books and liked discussing their contents.[96]

[91] Page, "Dean of St Asaph," 24–5; Porter, *Enlightenment*, 240, 403.
[92] Page, "Dean of St Asaph," 30.
[93] Johnston, *Hidden Wordsworth*, 176–7, 184.
[94] Paine, *Rights of Man*, 146.
[95] Locke, *Fantasy of Reason*, 19–20; Philp, *Godwin's Political Justice*, 78.
[96] Godwin, *Enquiry*, Preface, p. viii.

Like Bentham and Jebb, Godwin derived his universalism, concept of the "general good," and of "reason" as the motor driving man's destiny, together with his anti-monarchism, denunciation of aristocracy, and rejection of organized religion, from reading French radical *philosophes*.[97] French democratic republicans taught him the need to avoid the drawbacks and reject the "propriety of instituting different political governments suited to the characters, the habits, and prejudices of different nations," to dismiss, that is, the relativist ideology that, drawing on Montesquieu and Hume, "by many political reasoners has been vehemently maintained." By the late 1780s, Montesquieu's and Hume's political reasoning utterly lacked force in Godwin's mind.[98] Truth, he had learnt, is in reality "single and uniform" so that there must "in the nature of things be one best form of government, which all intellects, sufficiently roused from the slumber of savage ignorance, will be irresistibly incited to approve. If an equal participation of the benefits of nature be good in itself, it must be good for you and me and all mankind."[99]

French materialists changed his conception of society, as they had, equally, those of Jebb, Priestley, and Paine, beside destroying his former trust in religious orthodoxy, the Trinity, and eternal damnation, an impact supplemented by Priestley, with whom he corresponded and by whom he was brought to Unitarianism.[100] But, like some others, before long Godwin also outgrew Unitarianism. By 1788 he had relinquished organized religion altogether. If not yet an aggressively irreligious non-providential deist, like Paine or Thomas Holcroft (1745–1809)—the outspoken son of a London shoemaker turned writer, and translator from French of various Enlightenment texts including Frederick the Great's *Posthumous Works*—Godwin figured among the more prominent English "revolutionists" of the day, wholly rejecting organized religion along with the political and social system[101] On this basis, shortly before Louis XVI's flight to Varennes, in May 1791, he began drafting his famous *Enquiry concerning Political Justice*. While composing his *Enquiry*, he later recalled, a time when his uncompromising friend Holcroft, whom he had first met in 1786, was constantly prodding him on, the "reflections into which I was led by the doctrine of necessity, made me an atheist, to which doctrine I had hitherto been a resolute adversary."[102]

"An enlightened and virtuous country," agreed Price, "must be a free country."[103] The recent progress of mankind in moral and political principles, and "those revolutions in which every friend to mankind is now exulting," was encouragement "to us all in our endeavours to enlighten the world." To his mind, revolution had begun with

[97] Philp, *Godwin's Political Justice*, 78–80; St Clair, *The Godwins*, 14–15; Locke, *Fantasy of Reason*, 19, 40; Porter, *Enlightenment*, 455.

[98] Godwin, *Enquiry*, Preface, 157–9, 179.

[99] Godwin, *Enquiry*, 181; Evans, *Debating the Revolution*, 69–71.

[100] Locke, *Fantasy of Reason*, 19–20; Philp, *Godwin's Political Justice*, 78.

[101] Locke, *Fantasy of Reason*, 30; Philp, *Godwin's Political Justice*, 34, 161; St Clair, *The Godwins*, 38–9, 57.

[102] Locke, *Fantasy of Reason*, 30–1; Philp, *Godwin's Political Justice*, 34.

[103] Price, *Discourse*, 19.

Milton, Locke, Sidney, and Hoadly in England and Montesquieu, Fénelon, and Turgot in France. Paine, who produced a more consistent, democratic, and secular radicalism than any other late eighteenth-century English radical writer, was also the English author most consistently drawn to France and the French. Educated, he admonished Burke, in August 1788, "as all under English government are, to look on France as a contentious nation striving at universal monarchy and oppression," without assistance, he would never have realized this was just one more piece of deliberate imposture and obscurantism foisted by state, church, and society in eighteenth-century England that needed sweeping aside.[104] From the late 1780s, as his involvement with the French Revolution developed, he established contact with a widening circle of convinced republicans and, by 1791, was collaborating with Condorcet and the latter's circle meeting at the Paris Hotel de la Monnaie, propagating a full-blown republicanism in their new political journal.[105]

Price, Priestley, and especially Paine and Godwin, admittedly, strikingly unlike Helvétius and d'Holbach, and still more than Bentham later, sought to minimize government's role in regulating, administering, and reshaping society; this was perhaps the most striking difference between French and British Radical Enlightenment.[106] What essentially united all these thinkers was precisely Priestley's thesis that men could now, as he asserted in late in 1790, expect to see government organized in accord with and based on the 'general good' though achieving this far-reaching goal would be arduous and would require a concerted campaign of action in the sense of promoting and diffusing a particular form of Enlightenment. A common front based on fundamental principles was formed and clearly took shape well before 1789, reaching back in effect to the mid- and later 1770s.[107]

Although it is often claimed that the advent of the French Revolution changed the content of British philosophic radicalism fundamentally,[108] in fact, this type of British radicalism, the Radical Enlightenment tendency, seems to have been largely formed already prior to 1789, even if this key strand of republican thought, a mix of ingredients with Paineite egalitarianism as its backbone, has long been relatively ignored by a dominant historiographical tradition dismissing anti-monarchism and anti-imperialist democratic thinking tinged with atheism, or at least hostility to the main churches, as the creed of a narrow, unrepresentative, eccentric sect.[109] Meanwhile, if the agitation in France of 1787–9 aroused Price and some other British radicals—though not yet Paine—to fresh levels of ardor and exaltation, so it did initially many British "moderates," not least in Scotland.[110] If the mix constituting

[104] Paine to Burke, 7 Aug. 1788, in Nelson, *Thomas Paine*, 179–80.

[105] Nelson, *Thomas Paine*, 179–81; Baker, *Condorcet*, 304; Keane, *Tom Paine*, 285, 357.

[106] Priestley, *Letters*, 55, 142, 152; Foner, *Tom Paine*, 90; Hampshire-Monk, "British Radicalism," 669–70; Clark, *Thomas Paine*, 175.

[107] Priestley, *Letters*, 145.

[108] Grenby, *Anti-Jacobin Novel*, 143; Philp, "Disconcerting Ideas," 181.

[109] Taylor, "Down with the Crown," 53.

[110] Ahnert, *Moral Culture*, 122–5; Clark, *Thomas Paine*, 219, 221.

British radicalism in the 1780s and 1790s included traditionalist Commonwealthmen, enthusiasts for the ancient English constitution, unruly undergraduates, Unitarians, Paineites, Benthamites, and more, the authentic Radical Enlightenment core displayed a steely intellectual consistency that contrasted sharply with much of the agitation that passed as "radical." Intellectually coherent radicalism came basically in two varieties—Unitarian and materialist philosophical in the style of Helvétius and d'Holbach, strands displaying a high degree of ideological convergence. British radicalism, where it showed much capacity to be comprehensive and combine political reformism with general philosophy and social and moral theory, displayed much the same tendency toward materialism, necessitarianism, determinism, and moral utilitarianism as Radical Enlightenment in France, Italy, or Germany. In the English anti-Jacobin novels of the 1790s and opening years of the nineteenth century the "modern philosophy" is certainly dismissed as bizarre and eccentric; but the essential point, and the reason it became a literary *idée fixe*, was that it was very widely deemed pernicious, socially seditious, and exceedingly dangerous.[111]

21.4. EXPELLING BRITAIN'S RADICALS (1792–1802)

If Radical Enlightenment gained ground in Britain in the 1780s, the force of popular disapproval and opprobrium grew faster. Meanwhile, reacting to the violence and seeming anarchy of the French Revolution, especially from 1792, many moderates among the academic establishment and in established churches grew more rigid in their conservatism and rejection of representative democracy, not least in Scotland.[112] Godwin completed his great work, *An Enquiry concerning Political Justice* (1793), he observes in his preface, in a Britain swept by an unparalleled reactionary fervor everywhere mobilizing popular sentiment against revolutionary republican ideas. "The people of England have assiduously been excited," he records, "to declare their loyalty, and to mark every man as obnoxious who is not ready to sign the shibboleth of the Constitution. Money is raised by voluntary subscription to defray the expense of prosecuting men who shall dare to promulgate heretical opinions, and then: to oppress them at once with the enmity of government and of individuals." Those few, who like Paine, Godwin, Holcroft, Priestley, Cooper, Bentham, Ann Jebb, and Mary Wollstonecraft held fast to Radical Enlightenment principles in Britain through the early 1790s found themselves isolated and generally detested. During the 1780s, Prime Minister William Pitt had inclined to tolerant, liberal, and moderately reformist policies; from 1790, by contrast, abandoning his earlier inclination to widen civil liberties in Britain and Ireland, Pitt veered to a policy of domestic repression.[113]

[111] Grenby, *Anti-Jacobin Novel*, 107. [112] Ahnert, *Moral Culture*, 135–6.
[113] Mori, *William Pitt*, 17; Philp, *Godwin's Political Justice*, 6, 103–5.

Reinforcing popular chauvinism, loyalism, and anti-Jacobinism arose a number of militant conservative organizations such as the "Association for the Preservation of Liberty and Property against Republicans and Levellers" which at its height, in 1792–3, was the largest political organization in Britain.[114] In consequence, the abhorred creeds of republicanism, egalitarianism, unrestricted toleration, and universal and equal rights served, for decades, not just as targets of popular scorn but principles no one could for long openly champion without fleeing abroad. Something of a recognizable widespread trait already by the 1770s, in the 1790s religious and political anti-intellectualism became not so much an ingrained national characteristic as an indication that popular thinking and the general mood counted for more in Britain than on the Continent for defining general attitudes. "The ordinary person is by nature fearful," observed the German radical, Diez, in 1781, "and owing to this drive cries out against *Aufklärung* like the night owl against the onset of daylight." Everything unfamiliar alarms him. An illicit desire to innovate has always been leveled as a charge against almost all *Aufklärern der Vernunft* [enlighteners of reason]. "Socrates, Christ, Arius, Luther, Hobbes, and Spinoza all had to face this accusation."[115] The loyalist outcry against radicals in Britain in the 1790s was simply a more prolonged and widespread instance of the popular outcry against the Enlightenment in Bavaria in the mid-1780s, and Belgium in 1787–91. The common people reacted in much the same way to radical ideas everywhere in Europe and the Americas.

Still, Britain was unusual in the exceptional strength of popular support for the existing Constitution and rejection of the democratic tendency. Writing to President Washington from London, in August 1790, Gouverneur Morris (1752–1816), a leading New York "aristocrat" opposing the democratic tendency in the United States (albeit persuaded that many Englishmen pushed the interests of monarchy and aristocracy too far, and too blatantly), an unbending foe of Paine and radical ideas, noted that compared to Flanders, Italy, and parts of Germany, let alone France, where the democratic threat was formidable, England was remarkably "free from the contagion." Indeed, the "English seem in some respects to have changed sentiments and manners with the French. They are as far gone in Loyalty as their neighbours in republicanism. Happy America where alone (I verily believe) both freedom and virtue have their real and substantial existence."[116] What *did* change in 1789 was that radical thought in Britain confronted an unparalleled contrary surge of reactionary Counter-Enlightenment sentiment that dragged moderate Enlightenment opinion in its wake, forthrightly to the right into a rigid, ossifying anti-democratic moderatism.

London during the early 1790s, though by no means the only hub, became the prime engine-room of British philosophic radicalism, the focal point where Paine,

[114] Mori, *William Pitt*, 8, 17; Philp, *Godwin's Social Justice*, 6, 77; Cone, *English Jacobins*, 8, 17; Evans, *Debating the Revolution*, 47, 49, 162.

[115] Diez, *Apologie*, 68–9.

[116] Morris, *Diary* i. 574.

Godwin, Holcroft, and their following concentrated their activity and energies. It was the chief publishing center, the place where most of the repeated editions of Price's *Observations* were produced and whence the huge trans-Atlantic impact of Paine's *Rights of Man* (1791–2) emanated, the first 50,000 copies selling out in a few months despite its original publisher, Joseph Johnson, panicking early on in the printing process. During the early 1790s, radicals, inspired by Paine and Godwin especially, adopted a comprehensive view of how the world had become tyrannical and what humankind's emancipation involves, using naturalist "philosophy" to frame their unprecedentedly sweeping programs of political action. John Thelwall (1764–1834), widely-read and soon among the most notorious "English Jacobins," figured among Godwin's chief converts. Not a Godwinian in all respect—he adopted a more activist, provocative stance than his "philosophical father" and they quarreled bitterly in the mid-1790s—Thelwall was greatly impressed with the *Enquiry concerning Political Justice* and permanently embraced its principles, including its utilitarian moral theory stemming from Helvétius. For his fierce critique of empire, above all Britain's, Thelwall eventually turned to the French sources himself, commencing with the *Histoire philosophique* and Marmontel's *Les Incas*. He wrote two plays justifying the Tupac Amaru rebellion against Spain, and espousing emancipation of the slaves, partly reworkings of Marmontel.[117]

Enlightenment, man's progress, had begun, Price was convinced, in England with Milton, Locke, Sidney, and Hoadly, and in France with Montesquieu, Fénelon, and Turgot: "they sowed a seed which has since taken root, and is now growing up to a glorious harvest." It was mankind's recent progress in moral and political principles and "those revolutions in which every friend to mankind is now exulting," that imparted the true encouragement "to us all in our endeavours to enlighten the world." [118] Among key vehicles of formulation and dissemination in London were literary circles like that which crystallized around Joseph Johnson (1738–1809), the Unitarian bookseller who had come to London from Liverpool, in 1760, and whose bookshop, at St Paul's Churchyard, became a regular radical meeting place and literary club. On returning from Ireland, in 1787, it was among this circle that Mary Wollstonecraft found editorial work, in connection with Johnson's periodical, the *Analytical Review*, securing her niche alongside such prominent figures as Price, Priestley, Paine, Holcroft, Blake, and Godwin. There she laid the foundations of her feminism based on the democratic principles she first encountered in the circles around Price, Paine, and Godwin.[119] It was at a reception for Paine hosted by Johnson, in November 1791, that Godwin met Wollstonecraft, whom later, in March 1797, he was to marry.[120]

[117] Johnston, "Usual and Unusual Suspects," 25–6; Green, "John Thelwall's Radical Vision," 74.

[118] Price, *Discourse*, 14; Price, *Observations*, 49, 54–5; Dickinson, "Friends," 24.

[119] O'Neill, *Burke–Wollstonecraft Debate*, 109–12; Keane, *Tom Paine*, 304–5; Sher, *Enlightenment*, 380–1.

[120] St Clair, *The Godwins*, 64; Philp, *Godwin's Social Justice*, 176; Evans, *Debating the Revolution*, 150.

Swaying British opinion in favor of the French *Declaration of Rights* Price, Paine, and the others found to be an increasingly uphill task. Most governments, many Englishmen agreed, are "usurpations on the rights of men, little better than contrivances for enabling the few to oppress the many."[121] Few Englishmen would have quarreled with Price's claim, in 1789, that "in Russia, the common people are only a stock on the lands of grandees, or appendages to their estates, which like the fixtures in a house, are bought and sold with the estates."[122] Yet relatively few could be persuaded that mankind's general plight was any business of the English, or that such a principle required Britain to support, rather than fight, the democratic revolutions surging, since 1782, in Geneva, France, and Holland. Least of all could people be persuaded that the British Constitution left anything to be desired or that the English crown and empire shared in any oppressive traits readily attributed to foreign crowns and sway.

Price demanded full representation, equality, freedom of expression, and individual liberty for Britain: "an enlightened and virtuous country must be a free country."[123] There had long been tension between such an Enlightenment stance and the landed interest in Britain and, in cities like Liverpool and Bristol, also between Enlightenment and commerce, between radical ideas and the rising middle class.[124] But only after 1789, and especially 1791, the year that dominant opinion among the students and professors at Cambridge turned decisively against the Revolution,[125] did the reaction of landed gentry and commercial middle class against radical thought grow hardened, systematic, and vociferous, and American Federalist backing for this anti-democratic stance explicit. Condemned in England, Price additionally received the "harsh censures" of the US ambassador in London, America's great champion of "aristocratic republicanism," John Adams.[126]

Persons defiant and brazen enough to display busts of Price or Paine in their homes could be found, but after 1791–2 were more likely to appear in the growing stream of anti-Jacobin novels than in reality. Initiated by conservative political activists in the years 1791–5, between the years 1791 and 1805, a mere decade a half, astonishingly around fifty "anti-Jacobin" anti-philosophical novels were published in Britain and these played an appreciable part in mobilizing and escalating popular reaction against universal rights, "modern philosophy," and radical thought.[127] Loyalist reaction, not least in the novels, fixed attention on Paineite irreligious republicanism rather than Priestleyan Unitarianism as the principal foe, because the heightened conservative propaganda campaign of the period needed a more clear-cut, definitely irreligious, and readily demonized enemy. Irreligious Paineites were more loathed, and more hounded by Parliament, the courts, the papers, the "anti-Jacobin novel," and the

[121] Price, *Discourse*, 12. [122] Price, *Discourse*, 25. [123] Price, *Discourse*, 19.
[124] Fitzpatrick, "Enlightenment," 122–5, 130–1, 135.
[125] Roe, *Wordsworth and Coleridge*, 17–18. [126] Morgan, *Memoirs of the Life*, 79–80.
[127] Grenby, *Anti-Jacobin Novel*, 1–2, 6, 8; Hampshire-Monk, "British Radicalism," 683.

theater world than the likes of Price and Priestley, even though the latter too were heaped with vituperation.[128]

Priestley was increasingly harassed in Birmingham. The ugly reality of official repression, and government recruiting of networks of spies to report on suspect persons, groups, taverns, and crowded meetings of whatever sort, grew ubiquitous. Regularly denounced "with fury," as one contemporary put it, "both in sermons and pamphlets," Priestley found himself charged with "attacking the basis of moral obligation, and with forming designs to overturn by violence the constitution of his country;" to believe the pronouncements from the pulpit, he was "not only a blasphemer of his God, but a traitor to his king." One of Europe's most eminent thinkers and scientists, he could no longer "walk the streets without danger of personal insult."[129] Popular rage against radical ideas culminated in the Birmingham riots of July 1791, after a few brave souls, convened by Priestley, dared to celebrate, as they had on 14 July 1790, the French Revolution's accomplishments with speeches and a dinner. Despite riot warnings having gone out and troops sent to the area, the Home Office, Prime Minister, and everyone else were taken aback by the violence against the "friends of the Revolution" and Bastille Day celebrations, the intensity of bigotry displayed. Three days of furious "Church and King" rioting targeted first reformers and French Revolution supporters but then evolved into a fierce pogrom against Dissenters, marked, somewhat like the 1780 London Gordon riots against the Catholic community, by flagrant intimidation, extensive smashing of windows, and breaking down doors.[130] Several Dissenter homes were wrecked entirely. The yelling of "Church and King for ever; Down with the Presbyterians; and Damn Dr Priestley" climaxed in an attack on Priestley's own home that might well have been fatal had friends not fetched him away minutes earlier. His home, laboratory, and library were all completely wrecked. If the flames "gratified the bigotry of High Churchmen," commented one Priestleyite, they "consumed the most valuable apparatus for philosophical experiments that any private individual was ever possessed of, many manuscripts intended for publication, and a library of valuable books, the produce of many years selection."[131]

Tension surged up also in London, Manchester, Bristol, and Coventry. When Johnson panicked, in 1791, the printing of the first edition of Paine's *Rights of Man*, overseen by Holcroft and Godwin among others, had to be transferred midway to another still bolder publisher, in Fleet Street. By late 1793, around 200,000 copies are estimated to have been sold or distributed, an astounding figure given the typical novel sold under 1,500 copies at the time. Denouncing aristocracy, declaring England's laws "irrational and tyrannical," demanding the House of Lords be abolished, Paine celebrated the overthrow of French, and looked forward to the "extinction of German

[128] Worrall, *Theatric Revolution*, 107–8; Mori, *William Pitt*, 92–5; Himmelfarb, *Roads*, 112–13.

[129] [Heywood], *High Church Politics*, 36.

[130] Evans, *Debating the Revolution*, 19, 42, 46; Bloom, *Restless Revolutionaries*, 99.

[131] Evans, *Debating the Revolution*, 43; Gibbs, *Joseph Priestley*, 200–1.

despotism" while proclaiming his radical views in social theory, ethics, and politics relevant to Britain too. After the French Revolution, "it is natural to expect that other revolutions will follow," revolutions having "become subjects of universal conversation, and may be considered as the Order of the Day;" "revolutions are to be looked for" while "all attempts to oppose their progress will in the end be fruitless."[132] Declaring war on Britain's aristocratic–monarchical system, Paine ranged it with Europe's other monarchical tyrannies: "I do not believe," he confidently predicted, "that monarchy and aristocracy will continue seven years longer in any of the enlightened countries in Europe."[133]

Doubtless the radicals had a following throughout Britain, but its dimensions and potential were greatly exaggerated by fearful reporting and accounts. In the north of England, alarmed Home Office reports suggested, doctrines "alleged to have been propagated by Mr Paine [. . .] are known to many of the lowest people," supposedly including "many of our soldiers."[134] As a consequence, the repression steadily intensified. Paine's *Rights of Man*, the pre-eminent banner of Anglo-American radicalism, was pronounced a "seditious libel" by Parliament in February 1792. With his book prohibited and a royal proclamation issued three weeks later against seditious writings in general coming into force, Paine was formally charged with treason in May 1792. As he went about London during the summer of 1792, he found himself constantly tailed by government agents. Two months before his scheduled trial, he hurriedly slipped away, with two companions of the London Corresponding Society, via Dover to France. Hounded into exile, he was tried in absentia, at Guildhall, before a specially chosen jury. Yet, for some, he remained throughout a prophet; his writing had indeed created a small but raucous following.[135] Found guilty as charged by the government-packed jury, the gloss was rubbed off for the government by a diminutive but defiant crowd yelling support for Paine, his lawyer, and press freedom outside. As the trial ended, his lawyer was acclaimed outside Guildhall by the protesters shouting "Paine for ever!"[136]

Gestures of support for Paine worried the authorities and antagonized most opinion. What especially heartened conventional thinking were the indications that popular support for Paine, rowdy though it was sporadically, was dwarfed by the vast chorus of reaction against. After July 1792, intimidation and persecution continued but now mostly in more orderly fashion. Reactionary pressure was intensified by a two-way interaction—unceasing popular fury in concert with government strategy and sweeping parliamentary measures. The "Church and King" party expanded their campaign after Paine's flight to France, over the winter of 1792–3; in January 1793, Parliament passed its Aliens Act aimed at uncovering and halting subversive activities of foreign intruders and agents, an enactment paralleled a few years later by the

[132] Locke, *Fantasy of Reason*, 47; Himmelfarb, *Roads*, 152, 158, 160–1, 269; Foner, *Tom Paine*, 212–32.
[133] Paine, *Rights of Man*, 156. [134] Mori, *William Pitt*, 94; White, *London*, 547–8.
[135] Paine, *Rights of Man*, 155; Foner, *Tom Paine*, 219; Nelson, *Thomas Paine*, 202.
[136] Keane, *Tom Paine*, 345–8; Nelson, *Thomas Paine*, 232–4.

American Congress's "Aliens Acts" equally directed against philosophic radicals, like Volney and Gallatin, in particular. An atmosphere of deep suspicion and hostility toward foreign influences long prevailed.

Those few who, like Godwin, Holcroft, Priestley, Cooper, and Wollstonecraft, remained steadfast for Radical Enlightenment ideas through the early 1790s in Britain found themselves increasingly isolated and detested.[137] In many places, booksellers and publishers, Johnson among them, were prosecuted, searches organized for those pasting up or distributing handbills and "pamphlets of a seditious tendency," and landlords and the general public enlisted by country gentry and magistrates to assist with identifying trouble-makers and breaking up radical meetings.[138] "Paine burnings," that is burnings of Paine in effigy, were organized across England, one on the Cornhill, in Cambridge, a town where suspect tradesmen had their businesses wrecked and were encouraged or forced to leave. A loyalist declaration by 110 Cambridge area tavern-keepers vowed to report all reprobate undergraduates revealing "treasonable or seditious tendencies" in their pubs to the authorities.[139] In Manchester, one of England's most stressed cities, innkeepers formed a like loyalist union sworn to prevent radical political clubs hiring their premises. Over the winter of 1792–3, more local "Church and King" popular chauvinist "associations" were organized to further intimidate all who were contemplating sedition. In December 1795, Parliament passed its two "Gagging Acts" to protect "His Majesty's government" against sedition, the second of which, the "Seditious Meetings Act," effectively classed as treasonable all attempts to stir up popular discontent, all gatherings promoting disturbance, and all gatherings involving more than fifty people found to be discussing parliamentary reform or formulating petitions of grievance of any kind.[140]

The Radical Enlightenment's combining rejection of religious authority with democratizing republicanism was reflected by the repression as if by a mirror. In Britain, the international "Jacobin" threat was invariably identified as menacing religion and morals in the first place, and only secondarily the social fabric and Constitution, because this order of priorities was more conducive to arousing ordinary opinion and popular ire.[141] In addition, the "Anti-Jacobin" drive tended to harp on about foreign intellectual intrusion, fastening attention on *philosophes* being seen as a sure way to arouse xenophobic anger. "New Philosophy," the prime source of contagion, was deemed a mix of Voltaire, Rousseau, Price, Paine, and Godwin, not infrequently with allusions to Adam Weishaupt and the Illuminati thrown in. In this way, "Church and King" strategists succeeded in fixing all classes' attention on the dire consequences of the "New Philosophy," and on *philosophes* as the supposed

[137] Cone, *English Jacobins*, 142–3, 202–3; Philp, *Godwin's Political Justice*, 66–7.

[138] Locke, *Fantasy of Reason*, 80–6; Philp, "Disconcerting Ideas," 164, 166; Grenby, *Anti-Jacobin Novel*, 188.

[139] Holmes, *Coleridge*, 44, 47; Cone, *English Jacobins*, 143.

[140] Cone, *English Jacobins*, 218–19; Bloom, *Restless Revolutionaries*, 112–13; Johnston, "Usual and Unusual Suspects," 29–30.

[141] Grenby, *Anti-Jacobin Novel*, 66, 68–70; Israel, *Expanding Blaze*, 348–51.

supreme menace to society, religion, and morals, with plentiful allusion also to the perils of female forwardness arising from the ideas of Wollstonecraft and disciples of hers like the notorious Mary Hays (1759–1843).[142] But inciting xenophobic outrage came at the price of making considerably more of the British and American public aware than had been the case earlier that the "New Philosophy" or the "modern philosophy" *was* in fact the prime motor of democratic revolutionary fervor, the root of the "General Revolution" sweeping the globe and threatening the social system.

On the surface at least, repression worked: democratic republicanism was driven underground. The local pro-Revolution societies, led by the London Revolution Society formed in 1788 with Price, Priestley, and Hollis among its members—an organization supposedly established to celebrate the Glorious Revolution of 1688, but enthusiastically celebrating also the fall of the Bastille—all either ceased to exist during 1791–2, or were forced underground.[143] A more elusive nut to crack were societies that made no allusion to revolution, proposing gradual means and focusing just on parliamentary reform, headed by the "London Corresponding Society of the Unrepresented Part of the People of Great Britain" (LCS), founded by Thomas Hardy (1752–1832), at the Bell Tavern, off the Strand, in January 1792. A poor Piccadilly shoemaker greatly influenced by reading Price's *Observations*, calling for a nationwide network of English "corresponding societies" to press for parliamentary reform, before long Hardy was replaced as leader by the "radical tailor of Charing Cross," Bentham's future ally, Francis Place (1771–1854). At its height the LCS had a membership of around 3,500, paying a penny a week, a considerable proportion of whom were cobblers, weavers, watchmakers, and other artisans; they often met at a tavern on London's Islington edge.

Conspicuous at the LCS's famous 1794 Chalk Farm gathering, attended by some 2,000 Londoners on the Hampstead Road, in April 1794, was Thelwall, who, the next month, was among those arrested, and imprisoned in the Tower, in the biggest round-up of radicals in London of the entire 1790s. This occurred two days after the fourteenth and last of the LCS's grand banquets celebrating the Revolution where the toasts were "To The Rights of Man," a "Free Constitution," "Equal Laws and Liberty," and to the "Armies contending for Liberty." Most of 1794 Thelwall spent behind bars. The government's clumsy effort, at the Old Bailey in London, to convict those arrested of "treason" led to one of the most closely-followed and sensational group trials of the age.[144] Godwin, Wordsworth, and Coleridge were among an audience of onlookers often deeply agitated by the trials. Despite the 1794 treason trials' eventual collapse, due to insufficient evidence of "treason or subversion," targeting the LCS's leaders following passage of the government's Two Acts, proved effective: the membership dwindled rapidly. Hence, despite the acquittals, from the government's point of view, the 1794 treason trials were a success, especially in

[142] Grenby, *Anti-Jacobin Novel*, 1, 206–7.
[143] Cone, *English Jacobins*, 112–13; Philp, *Godwin's Political Justice*,, 163.
[144] Johnston, "Usual and Unusual Suspects," 28; Green, "John Thelwall's Radical Vision," 77, 79–80.

convincing most of the nation that there really did exist a "Jacobin" conspiracy to subvert the crown, Constitution, and liberties of England. The LCS's final attempt to stage an impressive mass meeting, organized outside St Pancras Church in London, was forcibly dispersed by the magistrates, and its leadership again arrested.

Abandoning his efforts in London, Thelwall ceased publishing his periodical the *Tribune* in April 1796; his subsequent efforts to disseminate radical ideas through lectures in Yarmouth, Derby, Norwich, and other provincial towns fizzled out, during 1797, in the face of intimidation and organized violence.[145] Place gave up, resigning his chairmanship also in 1797. It was around the time of their withdrawal from active politics, in the summer of 1797, a time of rumors of a possible French landing on the Somerset coast, that Thelwall, Wordsworth, and Coleridge, together with several other "violent democrats," were spotted gathering in the Globe Inn, at Nether Stowey, in Somerset. Aware Thelwall was in the vicinity, residing at nearby Alfoxton House, Home Office spies were sent to listen in on their conversations at the village tavern. References to a certain "Spy Nozey" briefly caused consternation until James Walsh, the principal Home Office agent sent to Somerset, an official trailing Thelwall since 1793, realized his literary suspects were discussing the philosopher "Spinoza," in whom Coleridge and Wordsworth both took a passionate interest, and that the scare was a ludicrous mix-up on the part of ignorant locals. Some, though, remained unconvinced and kept the relevant stretch of Somerset on high alert.[146]

Finally, in 1799, Parliament's Combination Acts declared the LCS "seditious" and ordered its complete suppression along with all other reform societies.[147] Overall, the campaign of repression, viewed as a joint parliamentary, judicial, ecclesiastical, and popular effort, had an immense impact on the country: for decades, republicanism, egalitarianism, comprehensive toleration, and democratic ideas were packaged together as objects of virulent common loathing, principles no one could openly champion without provoking a furious reaction. Systematic intimidation daunted some and forced others out of sight. Between 1797 and 1800, Wordsworth, Burns, and Coleridge, though never consistent, thoroughgoing radicals of the kind Shelley became later, all abandoned their pre-1797 support for the principles of the French Revolution and sympathy for Godwin.[148] British Radical Enlightenment survived through the 1790s only in small, inconspicuous underground groups furtively discussing Paine, Godwin, and "philosophy," now mostly obliged to avoid pubs, coffee-houses, student clubs, and bookshops. But while anti-monarchism and anti-imperialism remained attributes of a narrow, unrepresentative sect,[149] radicalism nevertheless proved ineradicable as a cultural

[145] Roe, *Wordsworth and Coleridge*, 234–5, 237.

[146] Roe, *Wordsworth and Coleridge*, 258–60; Johnston, *Hidden Wordsworth*, 526–8; Roberts, *Shelley*, 83 n.

[147] Cone, *English Jacobins*, 119–21, 210, 222–3; Bloom, *Restless Revolutionaries*, 90–3, 155; Morris, *British Monarchy*, 120–1.

[148] Grenby, *Anti-Jacobin Novel*, 171; Roe, *Wordsworth and Coleridge*, 200, 226; Johnston, *Hidden Wordsworth*, 527, 530–5.

[149] Taylor, "Down with the Crown," 53.

presence behind the scenes in London and in places as diverse as Birmingham, Manchester, Liverpool, Edinburgh, Glasgow, Belfast, and Cambridge.[150]

21.5. TOM PAINE AND THE RISE OF THE AMERICAN RADICAL INTELLIGENTSIA

The indictments, trials, and persecution of radicals in Britain culminated over a period of years, starting in 1792, in their effective expulsion from the country, initially mainly to France but, before long, principally to America. Denounced as a "traitor" to his own country and "wicked, malicious, seditious and ill-disposed person," Paine was specifically charged with propagating "seditious libel." If a few British and Irish political refugees, including some of the membership of the American democratic societies of the early 1790s, were barely literate artisans, most were journalists, teachers, tutors, lecturers, editors, and writers and it was these highly literate Paineites who polarized British culture and, after fleeing, enriched America's, especially Philadelphia's, Boston's, and New York's burgeoning intellectual life.[151]

A group identity drew these radicals in some sense together, but it was not one defined by social class, religious background, or profession.[152] The adhesive was basically ideological and intellectual; the membership, despite deriving from very diverse backgrounds, formed a steady, solid audience for the works of Price, Paine, Godwin, and Priestley and, from 1789, for feverish discussion of the Revolution. Egalitarian, international, uncompromisingly democratic, radicalism drew support from all over Britain and Ireland even if mainly from small highly articulate coteries including disillusioned Unitarians, estranged Oxford and Cambridge undergraduates like Coleridge early in his career, and the occasional autodidact artisan trained for manual work, like Holcroft and Francis Place. The latter, a well-known atheist and fervent bibliophile, and friend of James Mill, was also, unusually, a resolute labor organizer. A former journeyman-tailor who became a leather-breeches maker, Place was converted to radicalism by reading Paine; later he became Godwin's disciple, before eventually becoming Bentham's heroically loyal editorial assistant ceaselessly battling with the latter's notoriously convoluted, prolix style.[153]

Persecution was the vehicle that transferred British radicalism to the United States, just as, not infrequently, it helped propagate radical defiance also within Britain. By

[150] Fitzpatrick, "Enlightenment," 130–1; Porter, *Enlightenment*, 403–48; Israel, *Revolution of the Mind*, 31, 59.

[151] May, *Enlightenment*, 218–19; Durey, "Thomas Paine's Apostles," 193; Sheps, "American Revolution," 308.

[152] Thomas, *Philosophic Radicals*, 163; Philp, *Godwin's Political Justice*, 126–7, 228–9; Hampshire-Monk, "British Radicalism," 681.

[153] Thomas, *Philosophic Radicals*, 10, 38–9; Philp, *Godwin's Political Justice*, 125–7, 194; McKown, *Behold the Antichrist*, 118.

1792–3, driving out radicals was very much the order of the day.[154] In December 1792, a "Church and King" mob broke up the Unitarian democrat group in Manchester, in the process wrecking the print-shop of Matthew Falkner and William Young Birch, publishers of the *Manchester Herald*, a democratic paper which, over the winter of 1792–3, had openly opposed government preparations for war with revolutionary France. Abandoning their paper, the editors and several associates, from March 1793, headed for America. The Manchester group's leader was one of Burke's prime targets, Thomas Cooper (1759–1839), Oxford graduate, ardent democrat, and advocate of the *Rights of Man*, an acerbic personage devoted to chemistry and all the sciences. Cooper had scandalized opinion by traveling to Paris in November 1792 as the Manchester Constitution Society's envoy charged with announcing their solidarity with revolutionary France, and opposition to aristocracy and monarchy. Whilst there he conferred with Condorcet, then working on the world's first democratic constitution. Deeming the Anglican clergy as repressive as the priesthood in France, Spain, and Italy, Cooper concurred with Jefferson that those who "solemnly pretend to be the depositaries of the sacred truths of God himself" were the world's "great deceivers."[155] "So offensive" was Cooper to the "present spirit of the British government, that he can no longer in safety reside in this country," Jefferson learned, in August 1793, from a disciple of Paine's and Priestley's, Joseph Barnes, for whom Jefferson was "our great patron of republicanism, and of virtue." Cooper "therefore goes to seek asylum in the United States."[156]

Settling in Pennsylvania, Cooper worked as a journalist and soon became a leading scourge of the "aristocratic republicans," the Federalists. He also utilized his early months in North America to compile a survey of life and conditions designed to encourage other political fugitives to emigrate from Britain. Though then appalled (he abandoned his abolitionist views later) by southern slavery, and urging avoidance of the "unpleasant" climate, swamps, and mosquitoes of New Jersey, he was otherwise much taken with the United States. In Boston, New York, Philadelphia, and Baltimore, life was "much the same as in the large towns of Great Britain, such as Birmingham, Bristol, Liverpool, and Manchester." "Civil society," Cooper passionately believed, like the French materialists and Benthamites (against Rousseau), "is intended to promote the mutual happiness of the members of it, while they live together here on earth." He quickly proved as obnoxious to majority opinion in America as he had in England, leading to "persecution" lasting many years. Among his retaliatory writings was *The Scripture Doctrine of Materialism* (Philadelphia, 1823) where, admitting to being guided on the topic of the Church Fathers by Priestley, he denied the soul exists distinct from the body, asserting that "Christ and his Apostles were materialists" and claiming it matters hugely to the "welfare of

[154] Roe, *Wordsworth and Coleridge*, 18–19.
[155] Cooper, *Scripture Doctrine*, 328–9; Durey, "Thomas Paine's Apostles," 190, 193, 196.
[156] Jefferson, *Papers* xxvi. 715; Wood, *Empire of Liberty*, 724; Morris, *British Monarchy*, 86, 88.

society" that people should not believe in any *supernaturalia* or trust priests or pastors.[157]

Hounded from Birmingham, Priestley himself crossed the Atlantic with his ailing wife, seeking asylum, in June 1794. Arriving in Manhattan, he was greeted by a "Democratic Society of New York" delegation reading an address from James Nicholson (1763–1804), the society's president. "The governments of the old world present to us one huge mass of intrigue, corruption and despotism," proclaimed his speech of welcome; "most of them are now basely combined, to prevent the establishment of liberty in France, and to effect the total destruction of the Rights of Man."[158] Refusing offers of college presidencies and chairs, and assailed by the pro-Federalist press as a foe of religion and law and order, Priestley settled, hoping for tranquility and to establish his own college, in the village of Northumberland, Pennsylvania (ill-advisedly in Jefferson's opinion due to its remoteness). This unfortunate choice of location for basing a rejuvenated community of British radical refugees—which, however, never materialized— prevented the renowned exile from England from having as much impact as Jefferson, Cooper, and many others hoped.[159]

In Scotland and Ireland, meanwhile, government-sponsored hounding of radicals in the early 1790s proved still more unrelenting than in England.[160] Among prominent Scots driven out in the early and mid-1790s were James Tytler (1745–1804), editor of the *Encyclopedia Britannica*'s early editions, outlawed by the Scottish High Court for sedition in January 1793, who resettled in Massachusetts, becoming editor of the *Salem Register*, and James Callender (1758–1803), an Edinburgh clerk whose democratic egalitarianism was tinged with Scottish national sentiment. Callender absconded, in January 1793, before trial for publishing his subversive *Political progress of Britain* (1792); he too settled in Philadelphia, where, by 1794, he already figured among America's more trenchant commentators.[161] No less seditious with respect to the British government, and contemptuous of Washington's presidency, was the Irish journalist and bookseller Matthew Carey, whose bookshop on Market Street, in Philadelphia, became a focus of Irish political activism and cultural identity comparable to the city's circle of angry Scots refugee intellectuals.[162]

Among Irish radical journalists settling in America, none stood out more, though, than Denis Driscol (1762–1810), an Irish Catholic who converted to Anglicanism in 1789. At first, in the early 1790s, after receiving a vicarage, he had preached militant Loyalism both from the pulpit and in his first newspaper, *The Cork Gazette*, established in 1790. Quarrels and ejection from his curacy, the following year, prompted his discarding Loyalism and plunging into republican and soon also anti-Christian

[157] Cooper, *Scripture Doctrine*, 301, 303, 306, 316.

[158] Priestley, *Autobiography*, 133; Foner, *Democratic-Republican Societies*, 182, 423.

[159] Jefferson, *Papers* xxvi. 716; Gibbs, *Joseph Priestley*, 226–35; Malone, *Public Life*, 4, 12–13, 80–1.

[160] Munck, "Troubled Reception," 171; Durey, "Thomas Paine's Apostles," 194–5.

[161] Weisberger, *America Afire*, 206–7, 212, 237; Wood, *Empire of Liberty*, 258–61.

[162] Sher, *Enlightenment*, 544–5.

sentiments, thrusting aside a curate friend who "admonished and remonstrated in vain" against his adhering to "these infernal theories."[163] Denouncing church tithes, and calling for land redistribution to sustain the downtrodden Irish Catholic peasantry, Driscol demanded universal male suffrage, annual parliaments, and abolition of property qualifications for parliamentary candidates.[164] Hauled before the Cork Assizes, for sedition, in 1794, he was sentenced to two years imprisonment; but from gaol kept his paper going aided by his assistant, John Swiney, later among the many arrested in Ireland, for sedition, in 1798—he eventually also fled to America.

In the mid-1790s, Driscol's group resoundingly combined anti-Christianity with democratic republicanism and social reform, viewing themselves as heirs in Ireland to both the American and French revolutions: all the Cork radical enlighteners were Paineites, much to Paine's gratification.[165] In 1797, when his paper was eventually forced to close and he faced the prospect of a second trial and further imprisonment, Driscol finally abandoned the Irish political scene, emigrating in 1799 to New York, where he joined forces with Elihu Palmer to lead America's most outspoken deist coterie.[166] In New York too he set up America's first explicitly deist newspaper which first appeared on 8 November 1800, in the midst of the momentous presidential election of that year. He called it *The Temple of Reason*.[167]

[163] Quoted in Durey, "Irish Deism," 57–8.
[164] Durey, "Irish Deism," 57–8.
[165] Dickson, "Paine and Ireland," 136–7.
[166] Durey, "Irish Deism," 60, 63–5.
[167] Fischer, "Religion Governed," 17; Durey, "Irish Deism," 68.

22

The American Connection

22.1. NEW YORK RADICALISM

Democratic republican thinking, values, and tendencies notably gained ground in the United States from the Revolution's beginnings, in 1774–6, until the early 1790s, in the press, intellectual life, and among the public, a crucial development in world history. In this respect, America was swiftly followed by Switzerland, France, and the Netherlands, and still more divisively and tentatively, Ireland, Britain, Italy, Belgium, and Germany. Well before 1789, democratic republicanism and "universal and equal rights" had become a French and a global force. "From a small spark kindled in America," commented Paine late in 1791, stressing the benefits for England, Europe, and the world, "a flame has arisen, not to be extinguished."[1]

What mattered more than American independence and liberty, to Paine, more than the American Revolution itself—as was true too for Price, Priestley, Jebb, Godwin, and the principal British radicals, for Condorcet, Destutt, Volney, and their French equivalents, and Filangieri, Gorani, Mazzei, their Italian counterparts—was the inspiration imparted to Europe, and the rest of the world. From America "liberty, science and virtue," predicted Price optimistically, would spread overseas "till they become universal, and the time arrives when kings and priests shall have no more power to oppress, and that ignominious slavery which has hitherto debased the world is exterminated."[2] Diderot's and d'Holbach's ghosts, along with Condorcet, Volney, Mirabeau, Brissot, and Destutt, would have disagreed only with Price's last point: "I therefore, think I see the hand of Providence in the late war [in America] working for the general good."[3]

But after 1783 the American Revolution's legacy remained as divided as ever, a war of rival ideologies, Federalists with their "aristocratic republicanism" and veneration for the British model versus Jeffersonians and Paineites, propounding the democratic republic and "universal and equal rights" as a model for all. The Federalists held power and controlled the government through the 1790s, but Jefferson, always anxious to prevent his personal differences with Adams from becoming an

[1] Paine, *Rights of Man*, 210. [2] Locke, *Fantasy*, 40; Price, *Observations*, 3.
[3] Price, *Observations*, 3; Porter, *Enlightenment*, 425.

open split, or let the gulf between him and Washington become too obvious, and the wider ideological rift too aggravated,[4] remained confident Federalist thinking could not permanently dominate mainstream American political culture or public sentiment. "It is but too true," Jefferson confided to Paine, in the midst of the French Revolution, from Philadelphia, in June 1792, "that we have a sect preaching up and pouting after an English constitution of king, lords, and commons, with heads itching for crowns, coronets, and mitres. But our people, my good friend, are firm and unanimous in their principles of republicanism and there is no better proof of it than that they love what you write and read it with delight." American papers, he assured Paine, were full of extracts from the *Rights of Man*, the press serving to "separate the wheat from the chaff, and to prove that tho' the latter appears on the surface, it is on the surface only. The bulk below is sound and pure."[5] Although his and Adams's names were "thrown on the public stage as public antagonists," and though it was common knowledge that he and Adams "differ in our ideas of the best form of government," still Jefferson always strove to ensure they "differed as friends do." avoiding public rupture and antipathy.[6]

Paine and the "Rights of Man" remained central to the new American republic's political culture through much of the fifteen years he spent in Britain and France, after leaving US shores in 1787. Until 1796, there was no great reaction, as yet, among the American public against the French Revolution, and little so far against "universal rights," equality, Paine, and his heroic status. During the dramatic 1793–5 surge at Philadelphia, New York, Boston, and other cities of the so-called "Democratic Societies," and of student "Jacobin" enthusiasm at Princeton and other colleges, Paine and the "Rights of Man" were incessantly and fervently toasted at 4 July gatherings celebrating American Independence Day, along with endless toasts and eulogies cheering the fraternal union of the nascent American and French republics, constant commemoration of the continuing potency of the radicalism of '76 and American awareness of its renewal in the French upheaval's democratic tendency.[7]

But the picture changed drastically from the mid-1790s, especially 1796, thrusting Paine suddenly to the margins of American political culture. This happened mainly due to the increasing success of Washington, Hamilton, Adams, and the Federalists in steering mainstream opinion away from its former republican trajectory in which Jefferson had such confidence. Suddenly, enthusiasm for the French Revolution and republican France collapsed, and sentiment swung strongly behind Britain. Suddenly enthusiasm for Paineite values withered, helped by publication of Paine's irreligious *Age of Reason* (1794–5), which massively offended the clergy everywhere, American and European, and Paine's startling recklessness in publishing his opinion of George

[4] Wood, *Empire of Liberty*, 146–7, 500–1.

[5] Jefferson to Paine, Philadelphia, 19 June 1792, in Jefferson, *Writings*, 992; Newman, "Paine, Jefferson," 75.

[6] Jefferson to Adams, Philadelphia, 17 July 1791, in Jefferson, *Writings*, 981; Kloppenberg, *Toward Democracy*, 382–5, 766 n. 43.

[7] Israel, *Expanding Blaze*, 386–7; Bow, "'Jacobins' at Princeton," 94, 99–100.

Washington and his entourage as "apostates from the principles of the Revolution" in his open *Letter to General Washington* (1796). This ill-judged vehement outburst, denouncing Washington as the "patron of fraud" who cheated his own soldiers, accused the president of colluding in Paine's incarceration in Paris, Robespierre having imprisoned him for the "interests of America as well as France," styling the "silence of the American Government" during his incarceration in Paris as "connivance and consent."[8] Paine also ill-advisedly depicted Washington as an incompetent general deficient in courage.[9] The effect was sudden and palpable. At 4 July toasts all over America, Americans stopped raising their glasses to the former hero.[10] Paine's standing in America in the late 1790s plummeted so rapidly he feared to return to the United States following release from his Parisian prison despite being marginalized by the *Directoire*. From 1796, he felt distinctly apprehensive about a possible repeat, in America, of his 1792 British experiences: "the government of England honoured me with a thousand martyrdoms, by burning me in effigy in every town in that country, and their hirelings in America [i.e. Adams, Hamilton, Morris, and the Federalists] may do the same."[11]

Accordingly, Paine waited until Adams had been voted out and Jefferson became president, in 1801, and the menacing 1798 "Alien and Sedition Acts" were rescinded, before returning. But even after disembarking at Baltimore, on 30 October 1802, and settling again in America, he found himself besieged on every side by a sea of open hostility. His standing among the wider public had sunk to the point that most public comment on his person, writings, and opinions was vehemently antagonistic. Former allies and friends, including Benjamin Rush, publicly rebuked and repudiated him owing to his publicly-aired irreligion, especially his rejecting Christianity in *The Age of Reason*.[12] Once widely viewed as the very voice of the Revolution, he was now the vile "Jacobin" maligner of George Washington, the "living opprobrium of humanity," "infamous scavenger of all the filth which could be raked from the dirty paths which have been hitherto trodden by all the revilers of Christianity."[13] Washington's revered standing, he discovered too late, had transmogrified into a quasi-sacred dogma strictly out of bounds to critics. By openly assailing America's first president as an "apostate" from "true principles," Paine intensified the reaction against his own democratic principles, leaving himself almost totally isolated, forced back on the support of a tiny radical coterie, often consisting of British and Irish fugitives from royal justice across the Atlantic. Having provided a United States naval vessel to bring him back across the Atlantic without risk of British interception, some of the vituperation piled on Paine spilled onto Jefferson too. "Our pious President,"

[8] Paine, *Collection of Unknown Writings*, 11, 226 n. 302; Durey, "Thomas Paine's Apostles," 662; Newman, "Paine, Jefferson," 76–7; Israel, *Expanding Blaze*, 90, 179, 330.

[9] Paine, *Letter to George Washington*, 695, 718–20.

[10] Newman, "Paine, Jefferson," 78.

[11] Paine, *Complete Writings* ii. 912.

[12] Newman, "Paine, Jefferson," 87–9; Jacoby, *Freethinkers*, 60; Nelson, *Thomas Paine*, 312.

[13] Keane, *Tom Paine*, 456; Nelson, *Thomas Paine*, 306–7.

sarcastically reported the *Baltimore Republican; or The Anti-Democrat*, "thought it expedient to dispatch a frigate for the accommodation of this loathsome reptile."[14]

Paine had much the worst of the ensuing fierce exchanges in the churches and press. Though defended by the Philadelphia *Aurora* and the few other republican papers, the Federalist press, together with the preachers' sermons, succeeded in permanently wrecking Paine and his principles. He protested to Sam Adams at the mounting persecution he and his friends were being subjected to: "even error has a claim to indulgence, if not respect, when it is believed to be the truth."[15] No one had promoted freedom of the press in three great societies, the United States, Britain, and France, more insistently; but Paine had failed to grasp, during his absence, that opinion had come to be shaped chiefly by a growing need to appeal to the largely uneducated majority, as well as commercial pressures and the rivalry of lead editors, who were sometimes keener on pandering to common prejudices and assumptions than propagating fact, authentic debate, or revolutionary principles. Above all, the public had grown deaf to any plea that the Revolution had fallen short of its promises. Not only had the "Rights of Man" not been upheld, nor adult white male suffrage made universal, nor slavery abolished, but strenuous efforts were afoot, it appeared to hard-core democratic republicans, to curtail freedom of expression and democracy, expand executive power, and tie religious authority more closely to the regime.

During his last years, Paine tried to rebuild his American standing with a series of open letters "To the Citizens of the United States" aimed at regenerating "sparks from the altar of Seventy-Six." The American Revolution had shown how to refashion humanity by introducing a new kind of political system "in which the rights of all men would be preserved;" the United States was the inspiration of all. But Americans had not sufficiently adhered to their own Revolution's basic principles. Pennsylvania's former democratic constitution, which, between 1776 and 1790, had greatly appealed to radicals also in other states,[16] had, by 1790, to the applause of Federalists, been fundamentally refashioned by the state legislature's now conservative majority, following the two-chamber, one-man executive pattern prevailing in the other states, with an upper house dominated by Pennsylvania's informal aristocracy of privilege and money. On their governor, the state's legislators conferred full veto powers with a "great quantity of patronage," making him an echo of the British monarch, following the corrupt system Paine charged the other states with having "copied from England," so as to empower state governors to block whatever laws the state legislatures passed that they disliked.[17]

Except within his own narrow and hardening radical circle, Paine met with scant success. Besides being denounced as an out-and-out rebel against religion—his greatest heresy—his public attacks on Washington and Adams ill accorded with Jefferson's

[14] Keene, *Tom Paine*, 456; Belissa, "Légende grise," 138.
[15] Keane, *Tom Paine*, 475–8; Nelson, *Thomas Paine*, 312–13; Belissa, "Légende grise," 140–1.
[16] Richards, *Shays's Rebellion*, 68–9.
[17] Nash, *Unknown American Revolution*, 423–4; Newman, "Paine, Jefferson," 79.

post-1800 policy of softening the fierce ideological strife of the 1790s.[18] Although they concurred on matters of broad principle, and Paine visited Jefferson several times at the White House (to the irritation of Federalist critics), Paine nevertheless grew more and more isolated from mainstream political reality; at the same time, his private political fantasies assumed an unrealistically grandiose air. Should Napoleon succeed in invading England—as seemed possible, even likely, during 1803–5—Paine intimated to Jefferson, in September 1803, he planned to "make another passage across the Atlantic" to "assist in forming a Constitution for England."[19] England's monarchical–aristocratic–ecclesiastical system, he and some of his American and exiled British allies had convinced themselves, had now reached "a tottering condition and if Bonaparte succeeds, that government will break up." Among other, to his mind beneficial consequences of such a turn, the British Empire would disintegrate, finally emancipating Ireland and delivering Canada to the United States.[20]

During the late 1790s, studious moderate enlighteners introduced a totally fresh and astounding dogma onto the American scene, namely that the American and French Revolutions had nothing whatever in common, and had never shared any basic principles. This fitted with what had all along been Adams's own private view, but flatly contradicted what most people thought before 1796. This astounding new political dogma was reinforced by a key work entitled *The Origins and Principles of the American Revolution Compared with the Origin and Principles of the French Revolution* (Philadelphia, 1800) by the Silesian diplomat and writer, Friedrich von Gentz (1764–1832), translated and promoted in America by the future sixth president, Adams's son, John Quincy Adams (1767–1848). Von Gentz, "one of the most influential counter-revolutionary writers" of the era, having published his adulatory German rendering of Burke's *Reflections on the Revolution of France* (1791) in 1793, later, after 1814, became editor-in-chief of the Austrian crown's most reactionary decrees. An enthusiastic disciple of Locke and originally a constitutional monarchist supporter of moderate revolution, a follower of Mounier rather than Burke, he later came to regard dynastic legitimacy, social hierarchy, and aristocracy as so sacrosanct, so indispensable to every society, as to turn full against all dimensions of the French Revolution, becoming a pillar of German political reaction and anti-republicanism championing the rights of Louis XVIII against Napoleon. By 1814 Metternich's closest advisor, he long remained one of the Atlantic world's foremost reactionary ideologues, one who viewed the fight against the "new principles" of the French Revolution and the need to restore monarchy, aristocracy, and faith along with the guiding dominance of the big powers and British rule in Ireland, as a universal holy fight, a "fight to the death;" in 1819 and 1824 he had a major hand in further tightening the Habsburg press laws.[21]

[18] Ferling, *Adams vs. Jefferson*, 205.

[19] Aldridge, *Man of Reason*, 282.

[20] Paine to Jefferson, 23 Sept. 1803, in Paine, *Complete Writings* ii. 1448.

[21] Koch, "Power and Impotence," 588.

A great many people in America and Europe, Gentz acknowledged, believed the basic principles of the American and French revolutions were the same. This he considered hugely dangerous for everyone. Having been an ardent enthusiast for the French Revolution of 1789–91 in its moderate, monarchical phase, only changing his mind after intensive reflection and debate with other leading German enlighteners including Von Humboldt,[22] in his 1800 text he pronounced revolt on the basis of contract broken when the contract is between ruler and people, as in 1688 and 1776, perfectly allowable, as the incomparable Locke had shown, but popular sovereignty, democracy, and Paine's *Rights of Man* were not just absolutely unLockean but "criminal" and abominable.[23] Because "some of the most important personages, who made a figure in the French Revolution, scarce ten years before had been active on the theatre of that in America," and because French revolutionary leaders tried "to imitate the course, the plans, the measures, the forms and, in part the language of those, who had conducted that of America," and make that revolution "at once, the model and the justification of their own," it became "easy for those who felt an evident interest in seeing the French Revolution superficially compared" and placed on the same ground as that of America, "to draw the great majority of the public into this fundamentally false point of view."[24] Where the American Revolution was entirely justified in Lockean terms and constitutional law, the French was entirely unjustified. "The American Revolution was from beginning to end, on the part of the Americans, merely a defensive revolution; the French, from beginning to end, in the highest sense of the word, an offensive revolution."[25]

For Gentz, Adams, and John Quincy, the difference between the American and French revolutions was the difference between right and wrong, between Locke and anti-Locke, between the justified and the criminal.[26] Given this gulf in "essential principles" between the revolutions, it was supposedly near catastrophic that many American states had misguidedly prefaced their revised constitutions, and the Federal government had adopted as an addendum, general "declarations of rights." Yet the American Revolution, sensibly, was never intended as a model for others, whereas the French, disastrously, had become a universal model so that its principles now needed to be systematically discredited and eradicated everywhere, not just from constitutions and government but from intellectual life, the universities, and the press.[27] Paine, furthermore, had succeeded in persuading the misinformed mass of Americans as well as some Europeans that the two revolutions' principles were the same, and that the American Revolution, therefore, was a democratic model for the world; fortunately for good government, religion, and social hierarchy, "his *Common Sense* is a pamphlet just as contemptible, almost throughout, as remote from sound human

[22] Von Humboldt, *Briefe*, 464; Kuehn, *Kant*, 342.
[23] Berlin, *Roots*, 18; Cahen, "Correspondence," 97–8, 115; Jarrett, *Congress of Vienna*, 204.
[24] Von Gentz, *Origin and Principles*, 5–6.
[25] Von Gentz, *Origin and Principles*, 41.
[26] Von Gentz, *Origin and Principles*, 3–4, 28; Jarrett, *Congress of Vienna*, 263.
[27] Von Gentz, *Origin and Principles*, 55–6; Gall, *Wilhelm von Humboldt*, 270, 275, 318.

sense, as all the others by which, in later times, he has made himself a name."[28] "A "not unimportant proof of the accuracy" of his argument, showed Gentz, "lies in the unquestionable aversion of most great statesmen in America to the French Revolution, and to all what, since 1789, has been called revolutionary principles." Were not Adams, Washington, Hamilton, and Morris wholeheartedly averse to French revolutionary principles? To illustrate the depth of the fundamental ideological rift dividing the trans-Atlantic world, Gentz highlighted the disagreement between Brissot and Adams, in America, shortly before the French Revolution began, precisely over whether American principles were or were not applicable in Europe.[29]

Shortly to become a Federalist senator for Massachusetts (1803–8), John Quincy Adams warmly lauded Gentz for entirely rescuing the American Revolution finally "from the disgraceful imputation of having proceeded from the same principles as that of France."[30] Given the extent of the shift of mood against him, and antipathy of the preachers, Paine's feelings of apprehension and isolation, following his return, could only intensify. His position was made worse by the acerbic pugnaciousness of his own renewed assaults on the "aristocratic," pro-British tendency in America, and his sallies against church authority, Sabbath observance, and Christian "mysteries" published in the *Temple of Reason* and, a few years later, in *The Prospect; or, View of the Moral World*, a New York deist journal founded in 1803, edited by the blind American radical, Elihu Palmer (1764–1806). A former Connecticut minister and rebel against Calvinist orthodoxy, Palmer had first become a Unitarian minister and then, from 1791, a radical freethinker. Swimming flat against the American mainstream, he considered Paine "one of the first and best of writers and probably the most useful man that ever existed upon the face of the earth."[31] During its brief existence he edited *The Prospect* aided by his wife, Mary Powell, a lady whom he had converted to deism, who helped him in his blindness and who owned the boarding-house where they lived.[32] Their paper appeared irregularly for two years before folding in 1805.

In the America of 1805, uncompromising radical enlighteners like Paine, Driscol, Cooper, and Palmer were almost bound to acquire a persecution complex. Before embracing "deism," whilst serving as a Unitarian minister, in 1791, Palmer had badly blundered by announcing a scheduled sermon beforehand, in a Philadelphia paper, to be delivered by himself, denying Christ's divinity. On the appointed day, an "immense mob assembled at an early hour before the Universalist church" barring his entry;[33] the experience led him to abandon not just his sermon but Unitarianism and preaching altogether. Not long afterwards, blinded by the 1793 Philadelphia yellow fever epidemic, he had to abandon also his second career, as a lawyer; from

[28] Von Gentz, *Origin and Principles*, 41. [29] Von Gentz, *Origin and Principles*, 58.
[30] Knudsen, *Justus Möser*, 184–6.
[31] Israel, *Democratic Enlightenment*, 455; Wilentz, *Rise of American Democracy*, 352.
[32] Fischer, "Religion Governed," 17–18; Foner, *Tom Paine*, 258–9; Keane, *Tom Paine*, 463–4, 467–8.
[33] Fischer, "Religion Governed," 17.

1793, he worked as a full-time radical editor, orator, and organizer. As to Paine, Barlow, Freneau, Fellows, and the like, so to the militant blind Palmer of the mid-1790s it was outrageous that the American republic's governing faction—prior to the move to the new capital, Washington, then still in Philadelphia—should reveal themselves, as public opinion swung their way, vocal allies of the British aristocracy and Old World despots openly combating the "Rights of Man" and the French Revolution. "Whence this political apostasy," demanded Palmer, "this dereliction of good principles in our own country?"—meaning retreat from the universal, democratic, republican outlook radicals attached to the altar of '76 to the narrow, aristocratic, but also now populist, preacher-supported American exceptionalism characterizing the Federalist outlook.[34]

22.2. NEW YORK AND PHILADELPHIA RADICALISM REVIVED (1792–1806)

Armed with Locke and the preaching of the so-called "Second Great Awakening," Federalist conservatism gained formidable traction in the late 1790s. If both sides, Federalists and Jeffersonians, claimed to represent the true spirit of the American Revolution, the public increasingly endorsed the former's perspectives. Moreover, after the French Revolution ended, in 1799–1800, and especially from 1804 after Napoleon crowned himself French emperor and democratic and republican principles were suppressed in France, the United States stood alone as the world's only republic even nominally based (however imperfectly and precariously) on republican liberty, press freedom, and freedom of expression. Helped by the huge "Second Great Awakening" evangelical upsurge now in progress, Palmer feared that "Church and State may unite to form an insurmountable barrier against the extension of thought, the moral progress of nations and the felicity of nature." Were the principles of '76 to succumb on both sides of the Atlantic? The resumed fight for liberty and truth would be long, unrelenting, and arduous, and devolve for now on just a small band of valiant champions.

Yet, because the Revolution's basic principles had been so widely diffused in books and pamphlets, because the "guarantee for moral and political emancipation is already deposited in the archives of every school and college, and in the mind of every cultivated and enlightened man of all countries," a general reversal of American opinion against the democratic principles Paine, Palmer, Priestley, and Cooper stood for seemed unlikely to triumph in the long run across the board. The battle would be immensely arduous, but "it will henceforth be a vain and fruitless attempt to reduce the earth to that state of slavery of which the history of former ages has furnished such an awful picture."[35]

[34] Palmer, *An Enquiry*, 11; Belissa, "Légende grise," 144–5.
[35] Palmer, *An Enquiry*, 7; Palmer, *Principles*, 9.

Courage and enlightenment would defeat ignorance and prejudice in the end, and it was in most people's interest that they should. For the truth was, contended Palmer, that "those who oppose philosophy and bestow upon it harsh and malignant epithets, are interested in keeping up a privileged system of plunder and robbery, which makes nine-tenths of the human race absolute slaves to support the other tenth in indolence, extravagance, pride, and luxury."[36] Fortunately, the "cry of vengeance and merciless punishment against the benevolent philosophers of all countries of the present day, has not deterred them from the faithful discharge of their duty, and the most unremitting attention to the best interest of individual and national happiness."[37] Palmer's stalwart ally, Colonel John Fellows (1759–1844), fulsomely agreed that "religion, which means nothing but belief in idle, fantastic stories, owes its origin to ignorance and fears of mankind in remote and barbarous ages," but, being "found admirably adapted to the support of despotism," was "sedulously cultivated and rigidly enforced among nations, the enlightened part of which have long since ceased to be the dupes of its extravagant vagaries." "In short, it has been made a cheating, money-making business, and kings and priests, both equally useless, have divided the spoil. Kings could not exist without priests. Their trades exactly fit each other."[38]

The two main radical groups, based respectively in New York and Philadelphia, were a classic Radical Enlightenment movement and nowhere more so than in their tight linkage of rejection of religious authority with democratic republicanism. Paine, Palmer, Fellows, Cooper, Driscol, the poet Freneau, and their fraternities knowingly faced overwhelming odds—almost the entire American public—yet exerted a lasting effect, especially in New York and Philadelphia, precariously surviving but notably reinforced at this juncture by the arrival of more and more angry radicals expelled from Britain and Ireland. Palmer exhorted his following to prepare for the long haul, eloquently blending pessimism for the present with confidence in the ultimate irreversibility of the radical secular and democratic Enlightenment. It was a confidence regularly reiterated during these years also by Jefferson, Paine, Barlow, and others, and became a veritable article of faith among the Anglo-American radicals.[39] From 1796, with New York as his base, Palmer organized his "Deistical Society" of New York, setting up branches also in Philadelphia, Baltimore, and elsewhere. This organization, which Driscol joined on arriving, sympathizers called the Theophilanthropists and foes the "Columbian Illuminati."[40] "Science and truth, virtue and happiness" the Society proclaimed the sole "great objects to which the activity and energy of the human faculties ought to be directed."

"Mr Palmer, as a public speaker was equaled," according to Fellows, "by few, his delivery was graceful, his voice strong and sonorous."[41] A New York book-dealer

[36] Palmer, *Principles*, 160–1; Walters, *American Deists*, 263–4; Jacoby, *Freethinkers*, 55.
[37] Palmer, *Principles*, 161; Walters, *American Deists*, 276–7; Gilmartin, *Print Politics*, 3–4.
[38] Fellows, "Memoir," in Palmer, *Posthumous Pieces*, 9–10.
[39] Israel, *Expanding Blaze*, 418–22. [40] Kaye, *Thomas Paine*, 109; Durey, "Irish Deism," 65.
[41] Fellows, "Memoir," in Palmer, *Posthumous Pieces*, 9.

trading with neighboring cities, Fellows, who was also Barlow's publisher, seconded Palmer at every turn, aiding his activities and preserving his manuscripts from destruction after his death. The latter included his unfinished book *The Political World*, a work published later, in London in 1824, on Fellows's initiative, by the redoubtable English radical Richard Carlile (1790–1843). A Yale graduate and Revolutionary War veteran who had fought at Bunker Hill, Fellows remained prominent for many years among the small, resolute band around Palmer and Paine. He was also Paine's general agent in America and a "personal friend," publisher of several editions of *The Age of Reason*, and a skillful organizer. He later became manager of the New York City waterworks.[42] Philip Freneau (1762–1832), of Huguenot descent, also a veteran of the revolutionary war, a well-known radical poet and journalist with pantheist leanings, regularly assisted Palmer too, not least with finding large rooms in New York for delivering his freethinking talks.[43]

New York radicalism aspired to generate a continued enlightening and reform effort to serve as an exemplar for every people and every country.[44] If most Americans professed views differing fundamentally from the "Jacobin" principles of Paine, Palmer, and their circle, a few listened—and read. If most Americans learnt to revile modern "philosophers" and "philosophy" as foreign sedition and collusion with the French Revolution's "criminal" principles, Palmer countered with his 1797 oration on the "Moral and Political Improvement" of humanity and the *Principles of Nature Or, A Development of the Moral Causes of Happiness and Misery Among the Human Species* (New York, 1801). He also tried to build his following by renewing his old alliance with the Unitarians. However, this scheme foundered on another major public relations setback: in July 1801, an allied journalist advertised his forthcoming lecture, on morality, to be given in the very same Philadelphia Universalist church where he had been routed a decade earlier. To symbolically underline their public rupture with him, the Unitarian congregation elders posted themselves before the church entrance to prevent his entering.[45] But despite all setbacks, until dying of pleurisy while on another Philadelphia speaking engagement, in April 1806, Palmer remained undaunted and indefatigable in his efforts. After his death, the New York "Deistical Society" struggled on "for some years," reports Fellows, "but at length was discontinued for want of zeal in its members."[46] Radical Enlightenment was simply ceasing to inspire.

Palmer and his New York and Philadelphia bands of diehards insisted that modern "philosophy" alone could promote democratic, secular, egalitarian ideas as an international model, applicable to the whole world, in an integrated, argued fashion and present the American Revolution in its true light. "The philosophers, the patriots, the

[42] Cotlar, *Tom Paine's America*, 27.
[43] May, *Enlightenment in America*, 237, 326; Stewart, *Nature's God*, 193.
[44] Sheps, "American Revolution," 291; Jacoby, *Freethinkers*, 55. [45] Durey, "Irish Deism," 70.
[46] Fellows, "Memoir," in Palmer, *Posthumous Pieces*, 8; Israel *Expanding Blaze*, 391; Clark, *Thomas Paine*, 382.

philanthropists of all countries," he admonished his New York audience in 1797, "are combining the wishes of their hearts and the efforts of their minds to meliorate the condition of the human race; and, so they behold, in the progressive movement of intellectual power, the certain ruin, the inevitable destruction of those pernicious systems of error and superstition, of civil and religious despotism which have so long desolated the world and degraded the character of man."[47] That "religion brought her potent aid, To kings, their subjects to degrade," as Freneau pithily versified their group doctrine, was axiomatic for the New York circle.[48] Palmer, Fellows, and Freneau, like Paine and Barlow, could not have been clearer about the true nature of their "philosophy," that "mild and peaceful philosophy, whose object is the discovery of truth, and whose first wish is to emancipate the world from the double despotism of church and state," being at once anti-religious and politically revolutionary, while in character simultaneously American and French.

What kept the system of "slavery" in place the world around for millennia and now needed overcoming was conserved, guarded, institutionalized ignorance tied to "superstition," an edifice demolished only via an undeviating, more incisive, concerted international Enlightenment. The "grand object of all civil and religious tyrants," held Palmer, "the privileged impostors of the world, has been to suppress all the elevated operations of the mind, to kill the energy of thought, and through this channel to subjugate the whole earth for their special emolument." This was why "men are kept in a total ignorance of their rights by those whom they are taught to revere as beings of a higher order," and "it is not to be expected that they will be capable of that activity by which alone their privileges are to be regained. Slavery and fear have rendered them torpid and senseless, without acquiring knowledge sufficient to exercise a holy indignation against their oppressors."[49] Unlike the early socialists, who believed casting off the system of economic oppression imposed by capitalists is the path to liberate humankind, for the New York group, as for radical enlighteners generally, no path to human liberation from oppression exists other than that of defeating ignorance and superstition with anti-theological, one-substance philosophy. The "General Revolution" had already "destroyed innumerable errors," repulsed theological arrogance, and triumphantly advanced science and technology; "those moral and political systems, which have softened the savage and ferocious heart of man, and raised the ignorant slave from the dust, into the elevated character of an enlightened citizen" comprised the only truly universal liberating force available.[50]

In contrast to the socialists, radical enlighteners aimed not at overthrowing the economic system but changing how the masses think; for them, the trans-Atlantic revolutionary impulse proclaiming the oneness of the American Revolution with the French—not Jacobin tyranny, but the true French Revolution principles of Condorcet, Brissot, Volney, and Destutt—was the essence of their creed and movement. The

[47] Palmer, *An Enquiry*, 4. [48] Quoted in Stewart, *Nature's God*, 379.
[49] Palmer, *An Enquiry*, 4–5.
[50] Palmer, *Principles*, 159; Keane, *Tom Paine*, 497–500; Walters, *Revolutionary Deists*, 204.

Federalists' antipathy to the French Revolution they interpreted as self-interestedly tied to their aristocratic republicanism, adulation of Britain, and anti-democratic stance in American politics and social thought. It was no "uncharitable gesture," contended Palmer, in his published 1797 New York oration, "to suppose that those who indulge such violent resentments against the French nation, on account of the EXCESSES of the Revolution, are influenced by other sentiments than those that are purely humane and benevolent; and that some secret attachment to the British system of government has united itself with their political opinions." Those who "feel the strongest attachment to the French Revolution," he explained, "are the most decidedly opposed to those measures of our own government resembling the British scheme of policy; while, on the other hand, those who advocate those measures are not observed to speak with much affection relative to the true interests of France."[51] Where Washington, and his successor, John Adams (president: 1797–1801), were content for Americans to garner their Old World news from the British papers, approving the latter's ferocious bias against revolutionary France, the radicals searched in vain for an effective antidote. Briefly, Freneau, colluding with Jefferson, had used his paper, the *National Gazette* (1791–3), to provide a countervailing flow of reports, a pro-French slant chiefly extracted from the influential Dutch democratic Patriot paper, the *Gazette de Leyde*;[52] but that venture collapsed prematurely amid the ravages of the Philadelphia yellow fever epidemic.

The deteriorating Franco-American relationship aggravated by "this war-whoop of the pulpit," as Paine called the convergence of the preachers with Federalist doctrine, drove a deep psychological and ideological wedge between the two Atlantic republics—and between American mainstream society and the radicals. Churchmen embracing the Federalist appeal, eager to denounce the French Revolution and its "philosophist" American admirers, and ready to stretch the facts a little, began trumpeting the supposedly "Christian" sentiments of Washington and Adams.[53] In this way, the pulpit helped construct an entire new construing of the Revolution which the Federalist press then seconded with alacrity. America's civil privileges, admonished the Philadelphia *Gazette of the United States*, the semi-official paper of the Federalist regime, edited by John Fenno, on 14 August 1798, were now severely menaced by the "deathly embraces" of the "French fraternity" and "philosophical fanatics" attempting to raise a "cry of religious hatred and persecution," and subvert the "religious principles of the intrepid founders of our independence."[54]

Yet the radicals were not the only onlookers contemplating the emerging alliance of Federalists and Evangelical preachers in the late 1790s, and deeming it suspicious, if not downright fraudulent, a device for manipulating an ignorant public for crudely

[51] Palmer, *An Enquiry*, 13.

[52] Peterson, *Thomas Jefferson*, 444–6; Walters, *Revolutionary Deists*, 220–1; Cotlar, *Tom Paine's America*, 30, 180, 219 n. 32; Wilentz, *Rise of American Democracy*, 49–50.

[53] May, *Enlightenment in America*, 265–6; Sharp, "France and the United States," 213–14.

[54] Rosenfeld, *American Aurora*, 216; Brookhiser, *Alexander Hamilton*, 107; Bow, "'Jacobins' at Princeton," 116–22.

political ends. The manipulative rhetoric of the late 1790s also worried some genuine believers in a profound bond uniting Christianity with the Revolution's core values. In July 1797, David Tappan (1752–1803), an ardent adherent of Scots moral philosophy, and longstanding bulwark of Calvinist orthodoxy, holder of the Hollis Chair of Divinity at Harvard, a theologian loathing both radicals and Unitarians, nevertheless had serious doubts about the new ideology. Certainly, the "philosophic" tendency direly threatened the United States; but though a threat, he assured his brother, modern philosophy was at the same time being unwittingly aided by the Federalist leaders "who declaim against French principles, and yet resemble them in practice; who speak highly of religion and the clergy in charges to juries, in orations, toasts, or newspaper-paragraphs, and yet practically neglect or trample them underfoot."[55] When it came to church attendance the ruling elite showed little ardor. The devout must not be misled by bogus piety. Unlike Europe's conservatives the Federalists did precious little to bolster the sway of religious authority.

The Sedition Act (July 1798), which Adams did not initiate, but signed, and Hamilton, despite initial reservations, afterwards rebuked Adams for not enforcing vigorously enough, empowered the Federal government to counter foreign revolutionary influence by restricting entry of foreign radicals and deporting suspect "aliens."[56] What Jefferson, Madison, and democratic republican newspaper editors called a scandalous assault on liberty, designed to entrench religious bigotry, aristocracy, and presidential "informal monarchy," Hamilton judged urgently necessary to curb "immoderate criticism" of the government and "approbation of France."[57] If the Second Great Awakening fused with antipathy to the French Revolution opened the door to the "Alien and Sedition Acts," added support for a vigorous crackdown stemmed from growing prejudice against recent immigrants.

Adams's secretary of state charged with implementing "the Acts," Timothy Pickering (1745–1829), was a paranoid xenophobe considering Irish immigrants especially undesirable. A Massachusetts church deacon's son and a leading American detractor of revolutionary France (and democracy), Pickering ranked among Jefferson's foremost ideological foes.[58] The eventually four Alien and Sedition Acts of 1798 together exerted a considerable impact, marking a sea-change in early United States history, deepening the ideological rift in the nation, by imposing checks on immigrants and severe restrictions on collaboration with foreigners and the right to criticize government. The "Alien Act" empowered the president to register, place under surveillance, and also deport non-naturalized foreign nationals deemed "dangerous to the peace and safety of the United States." The greatest infringement of the

[55] May, *Enlightenment in America*, 264, 393 n. 26; Israel, *Expanding Blaze*, 108–9, 348–50.

[56] Ferling, *Jefferson and Hamilton*, 299–300; Federici, *Political Philosophy*, 88, 177; Furstenberg, *When the United States Spoke*, 371–3.

[57] Foner, *Story*, 43; Jacoby, *Freethinkers*, 45, 239; Wood, *Empire of Liberty*, 258–60; Federici, *Political Philosophy*, 176–7.

[58] Peterson, *Thomas Jefferson*, 621, 793; Burstein and Isenberg, *Madison and Jefferson*, 336, 616; Rana, *Two Faces*, 369 n. 37; Slack, *Liberty's First Crisis*, 82–3, 191.

Constitution and freedom of expression thus far, according to Jefferson and Madison, every single Supreme Court justice nevertheless endorsed the Four Acts' constitutionality. "The Acts" revealed just how bitterly divided public opinion and the state legislatures had become, how embedded in ideological strife was the America of 1798.

The Sedition Act was especially repressive. During 1798—9, no less than twenty-five New York, Philadelphia, Boston, and other journalists were arrested under this measure, with eleven duly charged and ten convicted.[59] Some were native-born, others recent or not so recent immigrants. First indicted under the Act was Dublin-born Matthew Lyon (1749–1822), who, in January 1798, became the first person to start a brawl in Congress after spitting on a Federalist Congressman who insulted him. Elected to Congress for Vermont, in 1797, despising "aristocrats," and a supporter of the pro-French Democratic societies, this "singular animal" from the "bog of Hibernia," as he was styled by William Cobbett (1763–1835), the fiery political writer and (at that time) firm Tory and anti-democrat, based in Philadelphia, was virtually the sole avowed Jeffersonian Congressman in New England.[60] Sentenced for mocking his opponents' "aristocratic" proclivities and Washington's fondness for "pomp, idle parade, and selfish avarice" in the *Vermont Journal*, "spitting Lyon" received four months in gaol and a hefty $1,000 fine. The only book he wished to take to prison, he retorted defiantly, was Volney's (atheistic) *The Ruins*. Returning to Vermont after his release, "spitting Lyon" found himself besieged in Trenton and New Brunswick by hostile mobs: "the hisses and hooting of the crowd," reported the Federalist press, "were loud and universal."[61] Anthony Haswell (1756–1816), the Vermont publisher who mounted a lottery to raise money to pay Lyon's fine—the same who had earlier published Ethan Allen's deist tract *Reason, the Only Oracle of Man* (1785)—was likewise tried under the Act for maligning the government in his papers and in a lottery advert; in May 1800, pronounced guilty of "seditious libel," he received two months' imprisonment and a $200 fine.

Likewise indicted for "libeling" the president "in a manner tending to excite sedition" was Franklin's grandson, Benjamin Franklin Bache (1769–98). Imprisoned in June 1798, he died soon after, in Philadelphia, aged only 29, from a fresh yellow fever outbreak, prematurely ending what Adams termed his "detestable career."[62] Another target, the Scotsman Callender, fled to Virginia, but was indicted there for styling Adams in a book endorsed by Vice-President Jefferson, his *The Prospect Before Us* (1799), a "repulsive pedant, a gross hypocrite and an unprincipled oppressor." Callender received nine months' imprisonment and a $200 fine.[63] Cooper, designated a "fugitive Englishman" and "journeyman of discontent and sedition"[64] in

[59] Sharp, *American Politics*, 218; Grant, *John Adams*, 405–8; Sheehan, *James Madison*, 28.

[60] Elkins and McKitrick, *Age of Federalism*, 709–11; Slack, *Liberty's First Crisis*, 15–16, 156–62.

[61] McCullough, *John Adams*, 494, 536; Rosenfeld, *American Aurora*, 198, 526–7, 532–3; Meacham, *Thomas Jefferson*, 317; Cotlar, *Tom Paine's America*, 241 n. 89.

[62] Rosenfeld, *American Aurora*, 169–70, 175, 207; Slack, *Liberty's First Crisis*, 121–3.

[63] McCullough, *John Adams*, 536–7; Buel, *Joel Barlow*, 232; Ferling, *Adams vs. Jefferson*, 136–7, 140.

[64] Malone, *Public Life*, 109, 112, 116; Volokh, "Thomas Cooper," 375–6; Slack, *Liberty's First Crisis*, 190–1.

the Federalist Press, was indicted for a piece approved by his mentor Priestley, published in November 1799, accusing Adams of incompetence and meddling with the judiciary—comparatively mild criticism pronounced "scandalous and malicious libel" by the judge who convicted him for "defaming" the president, fining him $400 with six months' imprisonment.[65]

Among internationally renowned foreign revolutionary freedom-fighters menaced by the Alien Act—none were formally prosecuted—were Volney, Priestley, the Genevan radical Gallatin, and Polish hero Kościuszko, whose hasty flight to evade deportation his friend Jefferson helped arrange.[66] After three years of *voyage philosophique* through the United States, Volney had latterly resided in Philadelphia, colluding with Jefferson and quarreling with conservatives (as well as Priestley, who publicly rebuked him for his "atheism"), uninhibitedly plunging into what he then called the "quarrel of English against French principles," pitting democratic republicanism against the champions of "aristocracy," finance, and empowered clergy. Americans exhibited neither greater good faith in politics, nor greater probity, nor thrift in financial affairs, nor, least of all, he concluded, less bias than Europeans. Nor did Volney find education more prized in the United States than Europe. Rather, in his view, America had unquestionably regressed since 1783.[67] Denounced as an agent plotting a French takeover of the (still Spanish-held) Louisiana territory—which some in the French government were indeed angling for—Volney too hurriedly departed.[68] Before leaving, he took charge of the manuscript of Jefferson's translation of most of his *Les Ruines* (1791), the book so dear to Lyon. An unsatisfactory first English version had appeared in 1796, rendered by the Welsh anti-slavery activist Morgan John Rhys (1760–1804), a radical Baptist minister, settled in Philadelphia, after being brought out earlier, in 1792, by the London Corresponding Society. A massive success in Britain, the book "made more Deists and Atheists," recorded the radical publisher, Richard Carlile, among British radicalism's supporters, "than all the other anti-Christian writings that have been circulated in this country."[69] Jefferson, who considered Helvétius "one of the best of men," and one of whose favorite writers was Condorcet,[70] re-translated Volney's sections on politics, oppression, and economic inequality, but not the last part, "The Origin and Filiation of Religious Ideas," where Volney contends men created God, rather than the reverse, to answer baffling cosmological questions. Back in France, in July 1798, Volney asked Barlow to complete the translation.[71] In 1802, the Jefferson–Barlow English version duly appeared at Paris, but without either Jefferson's or Barlow's name on the title-page

[65] Wood, *Empire of Liberty*, 257, 261; Verhoeven, *Americomania*, 300–1.

[66] Wood, *Empire*, 260; Nash and Gao Hodges, *Friends*, 161–2, 170; Slack, *Liberty's First Crisis*, 191.

[67] Volney, *Oeuvres* ii. 27; Chinard, *Volney et l'Amérique*, 83, 92, 100; Gaulmier, *Grand Témoin*, 271–2; Furstenberg, *When the United States Spoke*, 355–9.

[68] Volney, *Oeuvres* ii. 22–3; Buel, *Joel Barlow*, 259; Serna, "In Search," 260–1.

[69] William, "Morgan John Rhys and Volney's *Ruins*," 58–9.

[70] Scherr, "Thomas Jefferson," 88.

[71] Serna, "In Search," 262; Jacoby, *Freethinkers*, 115; Cotlar, *Tom Paine's America*, 241 n. 89.

since, with the "Second Awakening" mounting by the day, neither could afford to be publicly linked to Volney's undisguised atheism.[72]

Of "all the books that ever were published," asserted Palmer, Volney's *Ruins* was "pre-eminently entitled to the appellation 'Holy Writ' and should be read in the churches." If Volney, Jefferson, Barlow, Paine, Cooper, Fellows, Palmer, and "that rascal Freneau," as Washington had called him, all concurred on the "fatal effects of the Christian religion, relative to science, to morality and human happiness," very few others did.[73] Palmer believed that the "sound philosophy of the Enlightenment," when "Mirabeau, Rousseau, Voltaire, Hume and Bolingbroke, together with twenty other philosophers of France and England, combined their strength in the philanthropic cause of human improvement, and swept away the rubbish of human superstition," would eventually "emancipate the world from religious bondage," and contribute hugely to "ameliorating the moral condition of society." If the *philosophes* of the pre-1789 era had been beaten back "by the thundering voice of the church and the resentful malice of monarchical tyranny," this had merely emboldened those of "more modern times." The "present age is pre-eminently distinguished by a numerous and respectable band of philanthropic philosophers, whose labors are calculated to destroy error and elevate truth upon the ruins of every thing injurious to the peace and dignity of human society." If Paine's texts offered "truth with much simplicity [. . . and] irresistible force,"[74] Palmer's other key writers "entitled to the universal gratitude and applause of the human race" included Condorcet, Godwin, Barlow, and Volney, whom, incidentally, he cited far more frequently than Toland, Collins, or d'Holbach.[75]

Months before Jefferson took office as president in March 1801, it seemed increasingly likely, despite the knife-edge closeness of the November 1800 presidential election, among the most acrimonious in US history, that the Federalists, damaged by the unseemly split between Hamilton and Adams and a growing press campaign against the "Alien and Sedition Acts," were losing support and might be toppled. By 1800, the democratic republican press generally rapidly revived from its late 1790s slump.[76] Palmer, providing type and funds, contributed, working with two new allies both notably antagonistic to Federalists and preachers—James Cheetham (1772–1820), a former Manchester hatter, who arrived in New York in 1798 and acquired a printing business, and the newly arrived Driscol, who likewise established his paper in New York (moving to Philadelphia in 1802), a venture backed by Palmer and Cheetham and regularly featuring excerpts from Voltaire, Volney, and Condorcet. Cheetham, as editor of one of the most influential New York republican papers, *The American Citizen*, took to denouncing not just Federalists but, from 1801, also

[72] Buel, *Joel Barlow*, 259–60.

[73] Palmer, *Principles*, 135; Jacoby, *Freethinkers*, 115; Peterson, *Thomas Jefferson*, 604; Walters, *American Deists*, 182.

[74] Palmer, *Principles*, 158.

[75] Fischer, "Religion Governed," 17.

[76] Israel, *Expanding Blaze*, 358–9, 657.

Jefferson's presidency for timidity and leaving its pre-1801 republican promises unfulfilled. For some years, until the two quarreled bitterly, Cheetham also collaborated closely with Paine, repeatedly publishing large extracts from his writings. Cheetham signally helped beef up the New York radical circle and establish a tenuous ideological bridge connecting American radical circles with Britain and Ireland.[77]

On returning to the United States in 1802, Paine lived at first on the farm received in 1784 from the New York state legislature as remuneration for his revolutionary efforts, at New Rochelle, a seaside settlement thirty miles north-east of New York. Early in 1806, he moved into the city itself and it was there, despite suffering a stroke in late July 1806, that he embarked on his final phase of lively political meetings and immersion in radical debate (1806–8), surrounded by his few remaining allies, notably Fellows, Cheetham (initially), the Irish revolutionary Thomas Emmet (1764–1827), now a successful New York attorney, another New York attorney, Walter Morton, and De Witt Clinton (1769–1828), a radical democrat and future mayor of New York and New York State governor (1817–22). During his last three years (1806–9), Paine exhorted New Yorkers to become more active locally, nationally, and internationally, assuring especially the city's numerous Irish and British political refugees that Britain's political system was entirely "wrong, and never would be set right without a revolution, which was as certain as fate, and at no great distance in time."[78]

With Palmer's death, however, the New York movement, after flourishing for a decade, gradually but inexorably dwindled, not least owing to Paine's ferocious feud with Cheetham, which flared in 1807–9 into a great scandal tearing New York radicalism apart. Both men were permanently damaged by it. Cheetham considered Paine domineering, egocentric, unwilling to listen to others, and hypocritical in claiming to be a "deist" when his deism was just a screen for atheism. Paine publicly denounced Cheetham, in 1807, as an "impostor" and anti-French agitator "who cannot live without quarreling, nor write without abuse," "a disgrace to the republicans whose principle is to live in peace and friendship with all nations."[79] To Cheetham's charge that he drew ideas from Locke without proper attribution, he retorted that "I never read Locke nor had the work in my hand."[80] Cheetham, or "Cheat'em" as Paine began calling him, also became Paine's first (distinctly vicious) biographer.[81] But for his malicious attacks on their idol in the biography which appeared just months after Paine's passing, in late 1809, Cheetham was frozen out of the now shrinking New York radical fraternity. Madame de Bonneville, Paine's housekeeper and nurse, also successfully sued Cheetham in court for falsely claiming Paine had "seduced and abandoned her."[82] What the falling away of New York

[77] Macleod, "Thomas Paine," 221; Buel, *Joel Barlow*, 278.
[78] Keane, *Tom Paine*, 517–18; Belissa, "Légende grise," 146, 155.
[79] Paine, *Complete Writings* ii. 1017; Clark, *Thomas Paine*, 344–5, 372–3.
[80] Paine, *Collection of Unknown Writings*, 6; Nelson, *Thomas Paine*, 320.
[81] Kaye, *Thomas Paine*, 144; Keane, *Tom Paine*, 527, 532.
[82] Kaye, *Thomas Paine*, 123.

Radical Enlightenment in the new century's second decade reveals of the wider set of contradictions underlying the ultimate failure of the trans-Atlantic Radical Enlightenment is that, for all its universalism, and stress on promoting the welfare of society as a whole, Radical Enlightenment as an ideology could only appeal to highly-educated alienated fringes whose own lifestyle had been up-ended by the huge political and social upheavals of the era.

Despite assurances the "Alien and Sedition Acts" would lapse forthwith and its victims be compensated, Jefferson's inauguration as president proved a more hesitant, conciliatory, and less resounding start to the new century than the radical fraternity had hoped. Once tentatively in power, following his victory in the election of 1800, Jeffersonians found themselves hemmed in by their own supporters, by the narrowness, religious commitments, and special interests of their often (as in Jefferson's own case) predominantly Southern popular support, and hence adopting something of the split personality of Jefferson himself, especially with respect to black slavery. The Federalists collapsed at the polls; yet, on basic issues of values, there was no real reversing of the late 1790s shift of attitudes. Where, during the years 1790–6, reaction to the French Revolution in the United States and Britain had markedly diverged, with British opinion overwhelmingly negative and American sentiment toward French developments predominantly positive, the years 1796–1805 displayed a striking convergence, with a fiercely negative view of "philosophy," irreligion, democratic republicanism, and the French Revolution powerfully prevailing on both sides of the Atlantic.[83]

Accordingly, Jefferson's supporters almost immediately split into rival camps, divided between "moderates" and a much smaller bloc of radicals, with only the latter venerating Paine and the republican democratizers of 1776; extensive reform was either sporadic or firmly blocked. Bitter wrangling set in over education, Indian policy, religious tests for office-holding, the blasphemy laws, and Sunday observance restrictions. Those aiming to end black slavery and integrate the blacks found themselves pitted against those opposing abolition or who hesitated, those sympathetic to the Haitian revolution against those hostile to it (including Jefferson). Paine, Barlow, Price, Palmer, Cooper, Callender, Duane, Coram, Fellows, Cheetham, and Priestley, all prominent publicists propagating Radical Enlightenment in and from America in the years around 1800, fought on doggedly, providing the essential frame for a genuinely democratic and secularist republicanism in the new century. Their political thought fed on the tradition of popular sovereignty and the "common good" originating in the Continental radicalism of Raynal, Diderot, Helvétius, Beccaria, Dragonetti, Condorcet, Volney, and Sieyès. Especially, alien to older English republican and Lockean tradition but vital to Paine, Barlow, Coram, Cooper, and Palmer, was the belief that political tyranny is general in the world and locks together with social oppression and that both remained a looming threat in America, as well

[83] De Bolla, *Architecture of Concepts*, 276–7; Sharp, "France and the United States," 203, 206, 209, 212, 214.

as everywhere else: "too much reason had Raynal to say," exclaimed Coram, that "everywhere you meet with masters, and always with oppression. How often, says this venerable philosopher [in fact Diderot], have we heard the poor man expostulating with heaven, and asking what he had done that he should deserve to be born in an indigent and dependent station."[84]

Their conviction that enlightening the people was the path to success remained, for these few, as alluring, and elusive, as ever. In January 1806, Barlow, recently back from France, continued urging his plan, first proposed in 1802, for an American national institute modeled on the Institut de France, a cherished scheme he laid before America's Enlightenment-advocating new president. America's representative republican system was a unique and invaluable innovation in human political development, contrasting fundamentally with Napoleon's blinkered dictatorship. Representative democracy flourishes, argued Barlow, only on the basis of enlightenment, by expanding secular education and diffusing awareness, knowledge, and science. Welding science conducted in well-appointed laboratories and general research in the social sciences to the American Revolution, in a national institute, was hence essential to conserving and propagating the Revolution's core values at home and abroad. Promoting useful social and political studies would enable Americans to participate more fully in trans-Atlantic debate with European radical republicans and democrats. Europeans "give us credit for what we have done" but also point out "what we have omitted to do." Interacting with such an institute, they would "perhaps aid us with their lights, in bringing towards perfection a system, which may be destined to ameliorate the condition of the human race." Congress, "as well as our opulent citizens," would surely gladly join "in making a liberal endowment" for a national institute on the French model.[85]

Ever zealous for educational reform during his later years, Jefferson was enthusiastic. "No American had spoken more eloquently or more fully," observes one scholar, "for the radical impulse of the Enlightenment than Jefferson."[86] "I have often wished," he assured Barlow in February 1806, "we could have a Philosophical Society or academy so organized" that while the central body should be at the "seat of government, its members dispersed over the states, should constitute filiated academies in each state" so that "all the members wheresoever dispersed might be brought into action, and a useful emulation might arise between the societies."[87] Barlow's and Jefferson's joint endeavor produced a bill for a "National Academy and University at the city of Washington," combining features of a university, research institute, adult education center, national museum (incorporating Charles Wilson's Peale's renowned collection), and national academy. Based on Barlow's proposals, but drafted at the White House, it was a resounding late Enlightenment American appeal,

[84] Coram, *Political Inquiries*, 60–1; Durey, "Thomas Paine's Apostles," 665–8.
[85] May, *Enlightenment in America*, 311–12; Buel, *Joel Barlow*, 281–3.
[86] Wood, *Empire of Liberty*, 737.
[87] Jefferson to Barlow, 24 Feb. 1806, in Jefferson, *Writings*, 1160.

presented to Congress in March. To Jefferson's and Barlow's unmitigated dismay, it advanced only at a "snail-paced gait" before the nation's wise legislators shelved it.[88]

After Paine's death in 1809, and funeral at New Rochelle (where local Quakers refused to allow his burial in their churchyard), followed a period when radical groups and their journals "almost vanished from sight," a receding presenting a sad contrast with the dogged confidence Palmer, Fellows, and Paine had avowed around 1800, their belief that the public was on the verge of conversion to their views.[89] The radical ferment faded fast.[90] Ex-president Adams, who thought he had "done more harm than good," believed the "sooner Paine is forgotten, perhaps, the better." But the pressures and grievances of the era made it unlikely that he would be forgotten or that a total recession in radical activism would long continue.[91] While the mainstream Jeffersonian bloc rapidly mellowed, becoming more passive, conciliatory, and conservative, from 1801, the radical wing, or "violent democrats" as some called them, encompassing Fellows and the New York circle, William Duane, editor of the Philadelphia *Aurora*, and the Philadelphia doctor and activist Michael Leib (1760–1822), a radical Congressman in 1799–1806 and senator from 1809 to 1814, continued presenting themselves as unapologetic heirs of Paineism, of the pre-1800 Jefferson and the republican democratizers of 1776.[92] Like the earlier mid-1790s Democratic Societies, it was these "violent democrats" who, after 1810, continued the fight against Federalists, big money, and the arcane grip of the lawyers over the judicial process, especially by expanding Pennsylvania's lower legislative house's influence and lessening that of the governor and state senate.

Paine's reputation in the English-speaking world reached a nadir around the time of his death; but he remained in eclipse only briefly.[93] From the 1819 "Peterloo massacre" onwards, both his British and American standing noticeably revived while his Spanish American renown climbed steadily following publication of translations of his work into Spanish, at Philadelphia in 1811. Long after abandoning his early Toryism and crusade against revolutionary principles, but before becoming a famed democratic leader in England, Cobbett decided, before returning to England in 1819, to make amends for his own earlier attacks on Paine by writing a new biography of the man he now venerated, in part using materials supplied by Bonneville's daughter.[94] It was part of a growing trend. On 29 January 1825, forty freethinkers, led by Paine's and Palmer's old comrade and publisher, John Fellows—among the few who stuck by Paine and helped him financially in his last years—gathered in the artisan unions' regular meeting-place, Harmony Hall, New

[88] May, *Enlightenment in America*, 312; Peterson, *Thomas Jefferson*, 859–60.

[89] May, *Enlightenment in America*, 326; Newman, "Paine, Jefferson," 71–2.

[90] Kaye, *Thomas Paine*, 123; Nelson, *Thomas Paine*, 326–7.

[91] Clark, *Thomas Paine*, 390–1.

[92] Rush, *Letters* ii. 664, 996; Wood, *Empire of Liberty*, 426–7; Wilentz, *Rise of American Democracy*, 122–3.

[93] Foner, *Tom Paine*, 263–4; Munck, "Troubled Reception," 178–9; Macleod, "Thomas Paine and Jeffersonian America," 222.

[94] Kaye, *Thomas Paine*, 124–5; Ingrams, *Life and Adventures*, 156–8.

York, to deliver eulogies and drink rousing toasts to mark Paine's birthday and revive the cult of the reviled refugee author who had electrified all America with *Common Sense* half a century before.[95]

Observed annually from 1825, during the 1830s celebrating Paine's birthday grew into an elaborate secular ritual drawing hundreds of hard-core devotees of '76 to political banquets celebrating Paine and his principles at Boston, Albany, and Cincinnati besides Philadelphia and New York.[96] In mid-nineteenth-century Cincinnati, exalting Paine as a great American reformer and Enlightenment writer became a particular focus for numerous recent German immigrant radicals, or "Forty-Eighters." Thus, especially those who considered themselves victims of monarchical and aristocratic oppression prized his legacy; the great limitation was that few others did.

[95] Kaye, *Thomas Paine*, 127; Keane, *Tom Paine*, 519, 522.

[96] Foner, *Tom Paine*, 264; Kaye, *Thomas Paine*, 139–45; Honeck, *We are the Revolutionists*, 89.

23

The Spanish Revolution (1808–1823)

23.1. JOSEPHISM VERSUS RADICAL THOUGHT

The American Revolution's political impact, principles, publications, and propaganda were just one of several broad strands of Enlightenment which fundamentally transformed the Spanish-speaking world during the last quarter of the eighteenth century. By breaking the mold of tradition and Spain's existing structures of authority and governance, Enlightenment set the scene for one of the profoundest upheavals and most transformative dramas of the early nineteenth century.

In the late eighteenth century and early nineteenth, Spain remained a great power with a vast colonial empire that could in no way be isolated from the fall-out from the founding of the United States, or the French Revolution. If "for Spain, the issues raised by the American Revolution were, first and foremost, matters of foreign and colonial policy,"[1] and crown and church strove to keep it so, fencing Spain off from the intellectual ferment of the age while recovering lost imperial territories and prestige, the Spanish crown's goal in participating in the Atlantic War that secured American independence proved difficult. Carlos III (reigned: 1759–88), forced to cede the Floridas (modern Florida, Alabama, and Mississippi) to Britain in 1763, and resolved to recover the lost strategic hub of the Spanish Caribbean, Havana, entered the American war in 1779, without endorsing America's cause or (unlike France) directly allying with the new republic, primarily to regain lost territories and curb Britain's burgeoning empire—but he thereby courted a range of formidable challenges.

Madrid deliberately kept Spanish contact with the infant republic and acknowledgment of its Independence to a minimum, and subsidies to the rebels a secret (especially from Spain's subjects in the Indies). Embarrassed by its complicity in supporting colonial rebellion, initially Spain seemingly profited, recovering first West "Florida" (Alabama–Mississippi), with Mobile, in 1779, and, then, in 1782–3, after besieging Pensacola, Florida proper. Minorca was retaken by a joint Franco-Spanish force. But plans to eject the British from Honduras, and invade Jamaica (captured by the English from Spain in 1656), came to naught while, more generally, no land forces

[1] McFarlane, "American Revolution," 29, 32, 36.

could check Britain's naval might, or what the Salamanca professor and reformer, Pedro Estala (1757–1815), called the "colossal edifice of her maritime despotism" keeping the world's other empires under her dominion. Meanwhile, if Spain's rigid mercantilist trade system, strict regulation of shipping excluding foreign intrusion, imposition of religious authority over education and general culture, and the Inquisition's stranglehold on thought and conscience lent an aura of imperviousness and unmatched solidity to Spain's imperial system, much of this dominated only on the surface. Spain had its own deeply-rooted clandestine religious traditions and hidden secrets, rendering its vast, imposing, and impervious façade less impervious to the challenge of external influences and ideas than most assumed.

Crypto-Judaism especially evinced a continued vitality into the eighteenth century, conserving buried lines of clandestine thought and interaction amounting to an irrepressible underground psychology of revolt against ecclesiastical sway to which literally thousands of Inquisition trials in Spain and the New World, peaking only in the 1720s, attest. Even though this earlier sustained drive to suppress crypto-Judaism slackened markedly after 1740, a lingering aftermath of deeply-rooted clandestine deep hatred of established structures of authority, including the stifling Aristotelian scholasticism supposedly still orthodox in the universities, heightened by the very ferocity of the centuries-old repression, powerfully lingered. Superficially, the American Revolution appeared to have much less impact than elsewhere because newspaper and periodical reporting of issues and events was suppressed in the Spanish world far more vigorously than in other places; but this proved a deceptive criterion.[2]

Meanwhile, under Carlos III, Spain's moderate Enlightenment gained impressive momentum on a number of levels, but supposedly always strictly as the preserve of the crown, noted the education reformer and Condorcet disciple, Manuel José Narganes de Posada (1772–1823?), in 1807. Crown and church planned to adopt selected strands of Enlightenment while maintaining stability and keeping their repressive grip on the public sphere and general culture intact. But in part, inevitably, the effect was the opposite. For Bourbon royal policy proved that "our hopes," as Narganes put it—the expectations, that is, of Spain's budding underground of radical enlighteners, often fugitives like himself forced to flee abroad to escape the Inquisition—must remain unrealized under a monarchy keen to reform and import foreign influences where this enhanced imperial and economic power without compromising religion, but incapable of implementing real change at a deeper level.[3] In any case, the crown pulled back from its earlier pro-Enlightenment stance in the early 1790s, on realizing that clandestine and, from the autumn of 1792 crypto-republican, revolutionary cells were fast taking root in Spain's universities under the influence of the French Revolution. This occurred most noticeably at Salamanca, where many leading early nineteenth-century Spanish revolutionaries received their early intellectual formation, the first seeds of their subversive outlook originating in the 1770s and

[2] McFarlane, "American Revolution," 39–40.

[3] Narganes, *Tres Cartas*, 89–90, 102.

1780s when clandestine versions of d'Holbach's *Système de la nature* and Filangieri began circulating there among the more defiant professors and students.[4] An early sign of royal retreat was the abolition, in 1794, at Valencia, Grenada, and other universities, of the chairs in "Natural Right" philosophy introduced two decades before to teach Grotius and Pufendorf, because, more recently, these had increasingly been introducing students to Montesquieu, Rousseau, Filangieri, and other unsettling political thought.[5]

The crown's underlying predicament was insoluble because by the 1780s the Enlightenment in Spanish lands had ceased to be a royal and ecclesiastical preserve, having sunk deep roots, causing "conversions" in basic beliefs among not a few youths whose families intended them for the church, including some who did then embark on ecclesiastical careers, including a secretary general of the Inquisition no less, Juan Antonio Llorente (1756–1823). Llorente later identified 1784 as the year when he realized, after debate with an erudite personage in Calahorra, that the whole edifice of theology in which he had been raised consisted purely of *préjugés* and underwent a complete reversal in thinking. Yet for decades he continued publicly adhering to faith, ultramontane views, scholasticism, and Aristotelianism in a stringent manner.[6] His Radical Enlightenment revolt remained entirely secret and in no way hindered his ecclesiastical career. Secretary-general of the Inquisition in the years 1789–91 and entrusted with the Inquisition archives, it took three years for the inner clash between his views and outward functions to prompt him, in 1791, to resign, after which he devoted himself, still keeping his radical views secret, to assisting refugee French priests fleeing France. An ally of the reforming minister Jovellanos in the mid-1790s, by 1800 he had become a target for conservatives through refusing to be party to the mounting repression and, by 1801-7, languished in public "disgrace."[7]

The crown's post-1790 repudiation of the Enlightenment encouraged the unmistakably intensifying Inquisition censorship. Having banned Filangieri's great work, the *Science of Legislation* in 1790,[8] by the early and mid-1790s the Inquisition's revival was deeply alienating many of Spain's more resolute enlighteners. In a few cases, those outraged began rebelling at the edges by imbibing Condorcet and other radical Enlightenment writings translated into Spanish and circulated during the 1790s at Salamanca and elsewhere in manuscript. Among them was a young man soon among the foremost Spanish revolutionaries and translators of the era, José Marchena y Ruiz de Cueto (1768–1821), a student, then colleague of Ramón de Salas y Cortes (1753–1837), a Salamanca professor figuring among the Inquisition's boldest critics.[9] Forced to flee, Marchena settled in Bayonne where he emerged as one of Spain's first

[4] Álvarez de Morales, *La Ilustración*, 243–8; Mantecón, *España en tiempos*, 248; Fuentes, *José Marchena*, 38.
[5] Álvarez de Morales, *La Ilustración*, 246–7, 259–60.
[6] [Jullien], *Revue encyclopédique* XVIII (Apr. 1823), 28.
[7] [Jullien], *Revue encyclopédique* XVIII (Apr. 1823), 32–4.
[8] Trampus, "Entre Antonio Genovesi y Gaetano Filangieri," 80.
[9] Álvarez de Morales, *La Ilustración*, 244–95.

prominent republicans and a *philosophique* foe of all theocracy and *idées théocratiques* sworn to rescue what he considered true civic morality from organized religion;[10] no longer needing to disguise his atheistic personal philosophy in 1790s France, he proclaimed God and Nature identical, following d'Holbach.[11] His group of Spanish exiles in France colluded with Brissot and, from August 1792, clandestinely injected Brissotin revolutionary propaganda into Spain, especially via the clandestine *Gaceta de la Libertad y de la Igualdad.* Imprisoned during the Terror but released after Thermidor, Marchena's post-1795 Spanish political propaganda predictably projected Marat, Robespierre, and the Montagne as "monsters," and Brissot's faction as "mártires de la libertad" [martyrs of liberty].[12]

The French Revolution only intensified the Spanish crown's American Revolution dilemma. It was impossible to exclude revolutionary influences or prevent convergence of Enlightenment thought with revolutionary values. After a short war against France during 1793–5, Carlos IV (reigned: 1788–1808), guided by his corrupt, grasping chief minister, Godoy, abandoned his fellow monarchs and collaborated openly with revolutionary France. In 1796, Spain joined France in arms again chiefly to tackle British imperial power and its adjunct Portugal, a land revolutionaries too considered a "tranquil slavery" dominated by London. Hoping to wrest that kingdom from British domination, recover Gibraltar and other territory, and generally strengthen Spain's position overseas, Godoy landed the country in a strategic trap, leaving Spain's ports blockaded by the British navy, and Spain cut off from the Caribbean and Spanish America, causing a severe recession.[13] Britain reoccupied Minorca. Crushing defeat at Trafalgar (1805) did not persuade Godoy to end Spain's disastrous pact with France, which persisted with Spain's domestic condition steadily deteriorating as her shipping and trade became increasingly depleted, partly through weakness and partly still in expectation of partitioning Portugal.

But precisely Spain's abject post-1796 dependency on France unleashed further zeal for unofficial Enlightenment, a sense of urgency in linking enlightened ideas to political reform. In his *Cartas de un Español a un Anglomano* of 1805, the astute Estala, echoing Diderot and Raynal, reminded his countrymen of Spain's colossal decades-long humiliation at British hands and the immensity of the *imperio tiránico* Britain exercised over the seas and continents. Had not India been "desolated and reduced to the most miserable state"? The same oppressive sway covered much of the rest of the world.[14] Adding to his difficulties, Godoy found himself on bad terms with the heir to the throne, the future Fernando VII, and with much aristocratic and ecclesiastical as well as enlightened opinion. Then Napoleon, taking his humiliated ally for granted, proposing Portugal's partition, and likewise

[10] Marchena, *Essai de théologie*, Preface, p. A2, 12; Fuentes, *José Marchena*, 171–2.
[11] Brissot, *Mémoires* ii. 265–6; Fuentes, *José Marchena*, 106–10, 172.
[12] Sánchez-Blanco, *El Absolutismo*, 410–12; Fuentes, *José Marchena*, 93–4, 125–7.
[13] Estala, *Cartas* (1805), 54; Rodriguez, *Independence*, 32.
[14] Estala, *Cartas* (1805), 38–51, 102, 105.

considering that strategically important land a virtual British colony, under the Treaty of Fontainebleau (October 1807) secured passage for a French army to be sent into and across Spain to invade Portugal. When the French seized Lisbon, in November 1807, just failing to prevent the Portuguese court's flight, on British vessels, to Brazil, their commander, Junot, proclaiming France Portugal's savior, promised to end the *ancien régime* and feudalism, construct roads and canals, establish schools, and help the poor.

Spain's crisis, meanwhile, further intensified, opening rifts Napoleon was quick to exploit. With Portugal overrun by 50,000 Spanish and French troops, in Madrid King Carlos arrested his son and heir, Fernando, for plotting against him. In February 1808, exploiting Spain's increasingly divided, supine state, the French also occupied Barcelona and part of the Basque country. As general disarray spread, France's emperor—disastrously, he later realized—became tempted to exploit the turmoil to the full and try to establish mastery over a deeply fractured land of vast strategic, economic, and political significance for the Mediterranean and the Americas. Napoleon hoped to remodel the Spanish and Portuguese empires so as to heighten French hegemony in Europe and gain more leverage in South America and the Caribbean.

The Spanish Revolution (1808–23) began with the so-called "motín de Aranjuez (17–19 March 1808) when army officers supported by mobs orchestrated by court conspirators backing Fernando against Godoy seized the latter and forced Carlos IV to abdicate in his son's favor. Refusing to recognize him as king, Napoleon instead, under guise of favoring Fernando's cause (actually Napoleon scorned him utterly), persuaded him to accompany his special envoy, Murat, to confer with him at Bayonne, where he would be joined by his father. At Bayonne, Carlos cancelled his first abdication and, on 14 April, the emperor tricked Fernando into abdicating in favor of his father; but both quickly discovered that with Bonaparte as "mediator," they had placed the monarchy's future in his hands. Carlos was obliged to abdicate for the second time, and with Fernando secreted away under house arrest at the Loire chateau of Valençay (where he stayed until 1814), Napoleon proclaimed as king of Spain his elder brother, Joseph, now hastily summoned from Naples.

Besides controlling Spain in the interests of France, Napoleon was undoubtedly eager to bring Enlightenment, modernity, and non-Catholic perspectives to the country, and especially, he assured Roederer, abolish aristocratic feudal privilege and the Inquisition.[15] A constitution was promised to provide Spain with new representative and administrative mechanisms and other freedoms, a major turning-point in Spanish history and for Spanish America even if these freedoms mostly stayed on paper only. Before any changes could be introduced, however, a powerful uprising ensued among Madrid's illiterate popular classes, who stormed the capital's center, on 2 May (the *Dos de Mayo*, unforgettably dramatized by Goya). Anti-French rioters yelling that Fernando VII was Spain's true king filled the streets,

[15] Roederer, *Mémoires*, 220–1.

sacked the homes of prominent "traitors" complicit in enthroning Joseph, and installed Fernando's portrait in the city hall. Sporadic revolt spread to other provinces, commencing in Asturias, especially regions where provincial administrations had tamely accepted the Bourbons' dethronement.[16] On 9 May, the first of the regional juntas that sprang up to defy King Joseph, the *Junta General* of the principality of Asturias, declared war on Napoleon, and sent emissaries to Britain for support, establishing a pattern soon emulated elsewhere. But Napoleon's coup precipitated a broad reaction that amounted to considerably less than a solidly national response to foreign invasion, with many regions notably slow to follow Asturias's example. National sentiment was by no means strongly-developed, and among Spain's elites and clergy, prior to the late summer of 1808, there was no widespread rejection of the Bayonne *renuncias*, as the abdications in favor of Napoleon and "King Joseph" were known. In fact, the Madrid popular insurrection was decidedly out of step with initial reaction in large parts of Spain, where allegiance to "King Joseph" was avowed in churches, during high mass, before the sacraments, over many weeks, with the consequence that Joseph was publicly acknowledged by church and officialdom in most big cities except Cádiz and Alicante.[17]

Joseph reached Bayonne in June 1808 to meet the assembly of Spanish notables, ninety-one nobles and high officials out of the 150 Napoleon had summoned to proclaim his and their intention to regenerate Spain and Spanish America with sweeping reforms. These ninety-one participants, a mix of conservatives and reformers including several Spanish American representatives, convened as a constitutional convention, itself an astounding innovation, alive with talk, often enthusiastic, of secularizing church property, reducing Spain's monasteries and convents, and abolishing the Inquisition, which had just banned Diderot's *Oeuvres complètes*, in 1807.[18] Napoleon, though, deeming it necessary, on a temporary basis, to placate conservative opinion in Spain, shelved all measures concerning Inquisition, church property, and monasteries and guaranteed the Catholic faith would remain the sole permitted faith. Precisely this was what drew most of Spain's episcopate during the spring and early summer of 1808 to acknowledge "King Joseph" as Spain's monarch. Most of the enlightened professional and intellectual elite did too and with greater zeal, this element becoming known as the *Afrancesados*, those supporting reform under French auspices.[19]

While the deputies attending at Bayonne—some elected, most co-opted—never exceeded ninety-five in number, the assembly included many known enlighteners and other leading figures including the dukes of Frias, del Infantado, and Osuna, lending a veneer of *ancien régime* social as well as religious legitimacy to the *renuncias* and Spain's first constitution. The deputies were later praised by Bentham's Anglo-Irish

[16] Grab, *Napoleon and the Transformation*, 129.
[17] Fernández Sarasola, "Alternativas constitucionales," 32–3, 116.
[18] Tietz, "Diderot und das Spanien," 144.
[19] Rodríguez-López Brea, *Don Luis de Borbón*, 150; Larriba, "Estudio," 74; Roberts, *Napoleon*, 483–4.

ally and commissary sent to Spain to report back to Bentham on the 1820 Revolution, Edward Blaquiere (1779–1832), as men "long distinguished for the liberality of their sentiments, literary acquirements, and superior talents in all the branches of political knowledge."[20] On 7 July, Joseph was consecrated "king of Spain" by the archbishop of Burgos no less, and formally recognized by the royal councils. Spain's first national constitution, the *Estatuto de Bayona*, requiring legislative approval for royal decrees and taxation but otherwise leaving the monarch's power absolute, was signed by Joseph on 8 July. Resembling the autocratic, highly undemocratic French Constitution of the Year VIII (1799), it also introduced comprehensive legal, educational, and social reform following the Code Napoléon and also regular triennial meetings of the Cortes with, for the first time, regular Spanish American representation.[21]

The French reacted to the May insurrection with a vigorous crackdown including mass executions. This in turn provoked further resistance which, outside Madrid, built up through the summer into a wider rising, in some regions precipitating fierce battles between Bonaparte's troops and pro-Bourbon royalists. But much of the existing royal administration, not just in French-occupied Madrid but far beyond, *did* publicly accept and celebrate the Bayonne *renuncias* and Joseph's enthronement, along with most canons of Toledo cathedral and most of Spain's clergy generally—though the Spanish church afterwards sought to veil this subsequently embarrassing fact. Rather than a national uprising against French occupation what followed much more resembled a full-scale civil war.[22]

Most Spaniards remained loyal to church, traditionalism and Counter-Enlightenment; but a not inconsiderable slice of society by this time thought very differently. As a former minister of Carlos IV put it, in April 1808, everyone in Spain sympathizing with the French Revolution, especially many *gente de letras* [intelligentsia] and everyone with secret Jewish, masonic, or Protestant sympathies, stirred excitedly, avidly supporting the Bourbon dynasty's extinction and acknowledgment of "King Joseph."[23] The remark exactly captured the inner logic of Spain's Enlightenment: it was more than just a post-1750 transformation in thinking but, for many, release from a centuries-old iron oppression of mind and soul. Catholic Counter-Enlightenment reaction against new, reformist ideas in the Spain of 1808, in other words, was undeniably massive, but not so overwhelming it could extinguish the rising fervor of what had previously been hidden in clandestine wells of fervent opposition—bitter resentment of the vast cultural and religious apparatus of control, discipline, and repression.

Carlos III had introduced enlightened reforms attuned to the moderate Enlightenment fashion pervading Europe's courts from the 1760s to the 1780s but had included no structural reforms challenging aristocratic or ecclesiastical ascendancy

[20] Blaquiere, *Historical Review*, 133; Alonso, "A Great People," 104, 197.
[21] Fernández Sarasola, "Alternativas constitucionales," 44, 48–9.
[22] Rodríguez-López Brea, *Don Luis de Borbón*, 153, 185–6.
[23] Caro Baroja, *Judios* iii. 173.

over society, culture, and education, or that diluted mercantilism or royal absolutism.[24] Though no radical, Joseph for the first time provided Spain with a potentially anti-feudal, anti-clerical, and anti-Inquisition framework, creating scope for great Enlightenment projects the Bourbon monarchy declined to attempt. Meanwhile, in June 1808, the French occupied only a swathe of central Spain running from Madrid and Toledo to the Basque country and soon proved to have been overconfident of their military superiority. Dispatching military columns in all directions, marching simultaneously on Seville, Valencia, Zaragoza and Gerona, French commanders were astounded that all these columns were repulsed. Especially humiliating was the crushing of the Seville column. In July 1808, 20,000 French troops, trapped at Bailén, in the sherry-producing province of Jaén, weakened by defection of their Swiss contingents, having lost 2,500 killed in three bloodily repulsed attempts to break out (16–19 July 1808), surrendered, registering the first major French land defeat since the capitulation of Napoleon's army of Egypt, in 1801—Napoleon's gravest (European) non-naval setback between 1800 and 1812.

Following this reverse, the French lost much of their grip in central Castile, while the clergy, having initially acquiesced, from late July 1808, encouraged by the growing scale of the rebellion, came out *en masse* against Joseph in many parts and began actively inciting the people to rebel.[25] In August, the British threw their weight into the scales, landing an army in Portugal. The joint British–Portuguese army won a resounding victory at Vimeiro (21 August 1808). Joseph ordered a general evacuation to the line of the Ebro. By early autumn, the *antibonapartista* insurrection encompassed most of Spain. To consolidate royal government in the regions freed, a *Junta Central* was set up at Aranjuez, in September 1808, under the reforming conde de Floridablanca, a pillar of the royal Enlightenment dominant between 1760 and 1789, though dying soon afterwards, and replaced by Jovellanos. This *Junta Central* exercised some authority, first from Madrid then Seville, especially in southern and eastern Spain, and sporadically in the New World (assuming the functions of the old Council of the Indies),[26] but never acquired an effective grip over the rebellion as a whole, being unable to establish anything like ideological unity.

Distinctly shaken, Bonaparte decided, in early autumn, to go himself with an army to crush the rebellion. Despite tenacious resistance, most famously the heroic defense of Zaragoza, his forces swept across northern Spain. By now most of the population and clergy sided with the Patriots, so little was to be lost by introducing more bracing, more overtly anti-Catholic, reform measures than were stipulated at Bayonne. Madrid capitulated on 4 December 1808, entrenching the French again in the heart of Spain. That very day, Napoleon in person (not King Joseph), proclaimed the Inquisition's abolition.[27] The British, crushed at Corunna, had to evacuate. From

[24] Sánchez-Blanco, *El Absolutismo*, 313.
[25] Barrio Gonzalo, "Eclesiásticos afrancesados," 232, 241.
[26] Jovellanos, *A Sus Compatriotas*, 66; Breña, *Primer liberalismo español*, 96–9.
[27] Blaquiere, *Historical Review*, 118–19; Caro Baroja, *Judios* iii. 178; Broers, *Europe*, 160.

the French-occupied zone, twenty-two bishops and many other clergy fled, either to unoccupied parts of Spain or Portugal or elsewhere abroad, the bishops of Barcelona, Tarragona, Lérida, and Tortosa fleeing to Mallorca, though some other ecclesiastics, including some who had endorsed the revolt after Bailén, now again preaching humility and submission, resumed collaboration.[28] In March 1809 commenced the second French invasion of Portugal. Again Napoleon tried to exclude British shipping entirely from the Iberian Peninsula and convince the Americans that a reciprocal paralysis of French and British trade could only work to their advantage.[29] Regaining control of the Madrid press, especially the prestigious *Gaceta de Madrid*, Joseph turned it again into a propaganda tool of the *Afrancesados*; but equally, beyond French control, in Patriot Spain, the press, paradoxically, always heavily censured in the past, likewise found itself far freer than before.[30] To the disgust of churchmen high and low, Spain now had two (largely) free presses promoting reform and criticizing religious authority, values, culture, and education.

Napoleon spent only two months in the Peninsula, before leaving with some of his troops and riskily dispersing the rest. Soon enough, the tide turned yet again, first in Portugal, then Spain. By May 1809 the French were ousted from Portugal and, by July, also from Spain's north-western region, Galicia. Crucially, in April 1809, the Patriot *Junta* issued a "royal" decree convening a Spanish national Cortes in which colonies too would be represented. A steering committee, under Gaspar Melchor de Jovellanos (1744–1811), the renowned Asturian enlightener in semi-disgrace since 1789–90, but deemed the very embodiment of Spanish respectable court Enlightenment during Carlos III's reign and who, having been offered the post of interior minister under Joseph, pointedly refused, began to prepare and direct this foundational constitutional process. The Patriots' supreme national *Junta*, based from December 1808 until January 1810 in the Seville Alcázar, tried to balance conservatives and moderates, repel the radical fringe, and assume effective direction of the war and raise taxes, while consolidating the close "alliance" with Britain. But the French pushed back hard; the Supreme *Junta*'s forces were beaten in key battles, notably at Ocaña, a huge defeat for the anti-Napoleonists, in November 1809, and Alba de Tormes. In January 1810, the *Junta* had to abandon Seville for Cádiz.

Fundamental for late Enlightenment history, and Spain's political future, the popular rising had triggered a three-way, not a two-way, ideological and intellectual struggle, pitting moderate Enlightenment "Josephism" against outright conservatism while simultaneously, opposing both, fomenting a reformist, modernizing anti-Napoleonism acquiring a revolutionary republican tinge. A triangular conflict resulted not unlike that in Napoleonic Italy cutting right across the Patriot anti-French coalition.[31] Resistance to the French comprised three always distinct and

[28] Barrio Gonzalo, "Eclesiásticos afrancesados," 232–3, 239–40.
[29] Estala, *El Imparcial*, 168–9. [30] Larriba, "Estudio," 20.
[31] Durán López, "Construcción," 68–9; Broers, *Napoleonic Mediterranean*, 89–90, 106, 128–31.

incompatible factions vying to steer the national uprising—*absolutistas* wanting Spain's existing Constitution based on monarchy, aristocracy, and ecclesiastical authority restored intact; moderates headed by Jovellanos striving for social hierarchy with limited reform based on English notions of constitutional monarchy and aristocratic dominance of society and refraining from using counter-Enlightenment rhetoric;[32] and, finally, the foes of clergy and aristocracy, demanding a comprehensively new constitution on French lines.[33] The *absolutistas*, especially ecclesiastical foes of the French occupation, developed a vehement counter-Enlightenment creed insisting those Spaniards supporting the French had been led to infidelity and betrayal of the legitimate ruling dynasty by "philosophy."[34] Spain's triangular stasis exactly mirrored the Western world's general ideological, cultural, and religious fragmenting into Counter-Enlightenment, moderate Enlightenment, and Radical Enlightenment. Published on 26 October 1808, the *Junta Central*'s first public manifesto was deftly composed, at Jovellanos's prompting, by the prominent poet Manuel José Quintana (1772–1857) soon to be the *Junta*'s secretary-general, and central figure, "one of the most honest and accomplished Spaniards I ever knew," according to the journalist and religious reformer, José Maria Blanco White (1775–1841). A Cortes would be convened and, hinted Quintana and his colleagues, major reforms embarked on; but no indication was offered as to what changes were proposed.[35]

Enlightenment moderation was stalwartly championed by Jovellanos in such texts as his *Advice on the Convocation of the Cortes by Estates* (May 1809). Long opposed to the *philosophique* spirit, *la philosophie nouvelle* of the democratic tendency, Jovellanos extolled historical precedent and tradition, concurring with the *absolutistas* and Catholic apologists that nobility and clergy must retain their special status and privileged position. Moderates also wished to avoid the term "constitution," which too obviously smacked of American and French models inapplicable to the conservative social texture they sought to conserve.[36] What troubled Jovellanos was that moderation and cautious reform, extolling the unphilosophical, British "aristocratic" approach, was being drowned out by "seditious" writings now circulating in profusion, which he and his allies considered bound to corrupt opinion and discredit "legitimate government," benefiting only idle *políticos* of the cafés and sitting-rooms, as he styled the radicals.[37] Where Quintana rejected separate representation for the privileged orders, Jovellanos insisted separate orders were essential. Jovellanos "was a man of talent and of the highest honour," commented Blanco White, "but timid and

[32] Suanzes-Carpegna, "Image of the British System," 205, 208.

[33] Fernández Sarasola, "Alternativas constitucionales," 51.

[34] Aymes, "Mise en cause," 117–21.

[35] Hocquellet, *Résistance et Révolution*, 288; Breña, *Primer liberalismo español*, 93, 207.

[36] Sánchez-Blanco, *El Absolutismo*, 271; Fernández Sarasola, "Alternativas constitucionales," 55–6; Hocquellet, *Résistance et Révolution*, 287.

[37] Jovellanos, *A Sus Compatriotas*, Preface, p. xvii; Cuenca Toribio, *Guerra de la Independencia*, 152, 157; Fernández-Sebastián and Capellán, "Democracy in Spain," 57.

full of prejudices of the most injurious kind considering the circumstances in which he had to act. I believe he was duped by the worst of his colleagues."[38]

The war against Joseph unfolded without any unified command. At its base stood town and provincial *juntas* led by nobles, landowners, ecclesiastics, and officials taking the Patriot side. These *juntas* justified their actions in the name of the people, and modern historians sometimes label them "revolutionaries in spite of themselves."[39] But leaders and rank-and-file were mostly profoundly conservative in aims and values, while including some real republicans and revolutionaries, like Quintana, for whom sovereignty lay with the people. The latter rejected notions that thrones could be transferred by treaties, proclaiming the Bayonne *renuncias* illegitimate, but aspired to reorganize and modernize their country on republican and egalitarian lines, going further than Joseph especially as regards representative government and freedom of expression. The three-way ideological struggle impressed discerning observers not with the vigor of national feeling (which historians once grossly exaggerated) or religious allegiance, which counted for more, but rather the tragedy that deep factional splits prevented "the most enlightened men of Europe from uniting for the common good," and the calamity such a check represented to Enlightenment values, damaging, without their realizing it, a populace suffering the horrors of a ferocious civil war (a struggle graphically illustrated by Goya), exacerbated by religious passion and obscurantism.

A national assembly of some kind had to be convoked to legitimize and organize the war; but equally, the rebellion's dominant conservative elements did not wish this Cortes to be the instrument of sweeping reform demanded by a revolutionary fringe.[40] The clash was aired in pamphlets and increasingly, lamented Jovellanos, big city cafés, besides periodicals like the *Semanario Patriótico* (1808–12), chief paper of the *Junta*, founded in Madrid in September 1808, afterwards transferred to Seville and edited from May 1809, under Quintana's supervision, by Blanco White and the history professor and abolitionist, Isidro de Antillón (1778–1814).[41] Rescuing two decaying sets of the *Encyclopédie* of Diderot and d'Alembert from the Seville Inquisition dungeons, Blanco White assembled philosophical materials for their effort to re-educate the Spanish public so they could form meaningful up-to-date judgments about politics and the public arena. Spanish newspaper readers during 1808–9 not only first encountered, but were furiously plunged into contemporary political theory and constitutional debate. The crucial first question, as during the commencement of the French Estates-General, in May 1789, was whether the noble and ecclesiastical estates should, or should not, retain separate status in Spain's national assembly. Were the traditional forms and institutions conservative officials and nobles defended Spain's legitimate constitution? Jovellanos and the conservatives insisted they were;

38 Blanco White, *The Life* i. 147.
39 Carr, *Spain*, 90, 94–5; Hocquellet, "L'Invention," 172; Morange, "Opinion publique," 193.
40 Blanco White, *The Life* i. 149.
41 Fernández Sebastián, "Voice of the People," 226–7.

more forthright enlighteners denied this, discreetly at first but with mounting acerbity before long.[42]

Embracing the opposing Josephist faction, meanwhile, were many of Spain's foremost "enlightened" reformers, including Llorente, Estala, Narganes, Marchena, Fernández de Moratín, and Francisco Cabarrús (1752–1810), founder during Carlos III's reign of the Banco de San Carlos, first precursor of the modern Bank of Spain, and planner of several canals around Madrid, who became Joseph's finance minister. Fernández de Moratín, Juan Meléndez Valdés, Sebastian Miñano, and the law reformer and critic Juan Sempere y Guarinos, were all also well-known for Enlightenment zeal and for insisting on ignorance as the chief source of human intolerance, oppression, and bad government.[43] Leandro Fernández de Moratín (1760–1828), Spain's leading dramatist, became Joseph's librarian and literary advisor. Estala had had links with Juan Picornell (1759–1825), chief instigator of the republican conspiracies of San Blas in Madrid (1795) and La Guaira (1797) in Venezuela, but who had latterly come to reject republicanism, opting for enlightened despotism even in matters of theater reform. He continued to loath England's aristocracy, though, as "oligarchs" who every day "increase their opulence and tyranny," and Parliament as a clever device for persuading ordinary folk they are free, pay taxes freely, and live in a land where everything is intended for "their liberty," while in fact living under the *despotismo oligárquico* holding most English, Scots, and Irish under the "iron yoke of that infamous oligarchy."[44] For Narganes, Joseph's reign was an opportunity "to enlighten Spain," and end its misfortunes and misery through education; his guiding maxim, typical of French *Idéologie*, was that "desórdenes sociales nacen casi todos de la ignorancia de los hombres" [social disorders almost all derive from men's ignorance].[45]

Given the circumstances, Spain's Enlightenment zealots could not, or could no longer be, republicans, but differentiated vehemently between tyranny and enlightened reforming monarchy. Among the Spanish Revolution's chief publicists, culminating in his *Memorias para la historia de la Revolución de España* (published at Paris, in 1814–15), Llorente proceeded to dismantle every aspect of the Inquisition.[46] Entrusting him with the abolished Inquisition's archives, Joseph commissioned him to write the history of that formidable arm of repression. Among the many Josephist officials whose portraits Goya painted, in 1810, Llorente was also charged with implementing plans for reorganizing Spain into French-style equal administrative prefectures each to be divided into sub-prefectures.[47]

To reorganize Spain's local institutions and higher, middle, and lower education, Joseph, in February 1809, set up one of the chief reforming agencies of his reign, the

[42] Blanco White, *The Life* i. 146–7, 154; Breña, *Primer liberalismo español*, 93–5.

[43] Sánchez-Blanco, *Absolutismo*, 155–6, 369–71; Larriba, "Estudio," 21.

[44] Estala, *Cartas* (1805), 28–30.

[45] Narganes, *Tres Cartas*, 77, 90–1, 101.

[46] Grab, *Napoleon and the Transformation*, 134.

[47] [Jullien], *Revue encyclopédique* XVIII (Apr. 1823), 36; Esdaile, "Enlightened Absolutism," 67.

Ministerio del Interior, under Josef Martínez de Hervás, marqués de Almenara, an administrator in Paris during 1795–1806 handling financial transactions between the Spanish and French regimes, who had formed ties with the Bonaparte family.[48] Almenara set about reorganizing everything from commercial regulation, the justice system, police, and hospitals to historical and artistic monuments, the new *bibliotecas publicas* [public libraries] and the education system, aided by 490 officials, among them the republican atheist, Marchena. Another reforming body created by Joseph was his directorate of *Bienes Naciones* [national properties], placed under the finance ministry, with an administrative staff of 219, entrusted with dissolving monasteries and appropriating ecclesiastical properties "for the nation," initially headed by Llorente. Under the August 1809 royal dissolution of the religious orders, many of Spain's monasteries and friaries, possibly as many as two-thirds, were suppressed over the next four years, with the confiscated books used to set up "public libraries" in the main towns. Also established in Madrid, to disseminate Joseph's decrees, regulations, and propaganda was an *Imprenta Real* [Royal Press].[49]

In 1810, Almenara set up the "Junta de Instrucción publica y educación" to oversee education reform. Formalized in January 1811, this body, with Narganes, Estala, and Marchena all members of the governing committee, drew up a comprehensive "Plan general de educación" including choosing the textbooks destined for Spain's schools.[50] The planners, especially Narganes and Marchena, viewed as an urgent priority the reduction of the number of youths permitted to study theology in Spain's seminaries and universities, imposing caps calculated in relation to the actual need for parish priests in each diocese.[51] The scope of their undertaking was breathtaking. In Spain, it mattered far more to bring some education to the great majority, Narganes believed, than raise the higher education level, a point he thought France's *Idéologues* had insufficiently grasped: "the happiness of a nation does not depend on the enlightenment of a small number of individuals but on the level of civilization and sane reason of the most numerous classes."[52] A deadly civil war was in progress, fought with guns but still more with books and newspapers, a clash of world-views commencing the vast modern political conflict later to engulf early twentieth-century Spain—ideological strife unavoidable once Joseph began using gazettes and pamphlets to concert a vigorous propaganda campaign directed by the literary and intellectual elite whose support he aimed to ensure by showing he genuinely sought reform and amelioration.[53]

Reforming primary education in Spain was a gigantic challenge. A royal census of 1797 revealed that 304,613 boys between 6 and 13, that is between 20 and 30 per cent

[48] Roederer, *Mémoires*, 227 n.

[49] López Tabor, *Famosos traidores*, 53–6, 59; Cuenca Toribio, *Guerra de la Independencia*, 282–96; Muñoz Feliu, "Bibliotecas y Revolución," 462–3.

[50] Narganes, *Tres Cartas*, 114; Ruiz Berrio, "Introducción," 22–3; Fuentes, *José Marchena*, 245–7.

[51] Narganes, *Tres Cartas*, 110.

[52] Narganes, *Tres Cartas*, 77, 90; Ruiz Berrio, "Introducción," 57–8.

[53] Hocquellet, *Résistance et Révolution*, 263–76.

of the total, were attending 8,704 primary schools mostly staffed by priests and monks. Another 2,303 primary schools existed, supposedly teaching over 10 per cent of the female population of primary school age, around 88,000 girls; but girls, contemporary reports indicate, learnt only to recite prayers and acquire household skills, often without even being taught to read. With the onset of civil war between 1808 and 1814, school attendance dropped and female illiteracy rose possibly as high as 97 per cent. Male illiteracy, meanwhile, languished at around 80 per cent. Narganes judged Spanish primary education so mind-arrestingly backward and morally pernicious that in 1807 he had refused to accept that Spain actually possessed *educación primaria* [primary education] at all.[54] The key problem was not lack of resources, or cost, for massive resources had long been committed to Catholic education; the problem was strictly that of enlightenment: it was "sad" but certain that no nation had for centuries spent more liberally on public education than Spain and yet, no people was more "backward than us in useful kinds of knowledge."[55] The challenge was how to educate more children under a "sistema filosófico de instrucción primaria" [*philosophique* system of primary education] eradicating churchmen's grip over people's minds. In reforming primary education he especially favored the system of Johann Heinrich Pestalozzi.[56]

Joseph's regime made progress in reforming elementary, secondary, and higher education, but only in parts of the country. Reformers considered the state of secondary and higher education just as dire as that of the elementary schools. In all Spain, revealed the 1797 census, there existed only around 149 mainly ecclesiastical secondary schools, or *colegios*, teaching 7,250 students, most preparing for twenty-two universities, with 560 professors, teaching a mere 12,538 students in total. By European standards numbers of professors and students per university were so low as to make them irreparably unsuited for precisely what was needed—introducing new disciplines and sciences.[57] "The soup of the monasteries," remarked Narganes cuttingly, "is food you can count on to draw to universities many youths who, without this recourse, would have to devote themselves to more useful occupations and careers."[58] Philosophy teaching required fundamental restructuring, but still more requisite were the many new fields of study absent in Spain but now taught in France and elsewhere. There existed also one subject, Arabic, absent everywhere but necessary in Josephist Spain to "disinter the buried treasure in our libraries" and further a deeper grasp of the Spanish language.[59] Introducing new "sciences" is difficult everywhere, but especially in Spain, where availability of "books is very limited."[60] Unhelpful too was the traditional structure of secondary education, assigning central importance to learning Latin, the path to theology and metaphysics, and hence

[54] Narganes, *Tres Cartas*, 81.
[55] Narganes, *Tres Cartas*, 77–80.
[56] Narganes, *Tres Cartas*, 101; Ruiz Berrio, "Introducción," 20.
[57] Narganes, *Tres Cartas*, 105–6; Astigarraga, "España y la *Scienza*," 107.
[58] Narganes, *Tres Cartas*, 83.
[59] Narganes, *Tres Cartas*, 109.
[60] Narganes, *Tres Cartas*, 114.

priesthood, a structural obstacle Narganes considered even more harmful from a moral and social than scientific and educational standpoint—the "root that must be cut."[61] To provide a model, the formerly monastic Colegio de San Antón in Madrid, secularized by Joseph's officials in September 1809, was transformed, with Narganes as director, into a Napoleonic-style *lycée* guided by the educational principles of Condorcet, Destutt, and Pestalozzi.[62]

Enlightened reformers thus figured on both sides and were not always entirely clear as to which side they were on. Those publicly opting for Joseph not infrequently felt troubled by the depth of opposition, some on the Patriot side sympathized with Joseph's aims and following, and felt torn, sometimes yielding to popular sentiment, and opting for the Patriot side rather half-heartedly. A classic instance was Blanco White. A graduate of Seville University, son of an Irish Catholic merchant settled in Spain, and ordained as a Catholic priest, he had become estranged from the church through being assigned to hear nuns' confessions, deciding convent life was indeed deeply demoralizing. Especially he felt alienated by the church's unabashed use of religion to exert political sway over the uneducated. His friends mostly backed the Patriots, he recorded years later: "they believed that when the blind prejudices of the country had done their work in expelling the French from the Peninsula, the Liberal party would have it in their power to subdue the priesthood, whom they now allowed to enjoy a complete ascendancy as a temporary tool. To me such views appeared extremely absurd." Blanco White agonized, knowing "many of the most enlightened and honest Spaniards" supported Joseph.[63]

No atheist, indeed deeply religious in an unorthodox way, Blanco White was as convinced as Llorente, Cabarrús, Narganes, Gallardo, Marchena, or Estala that "if the people could be [. . .] delivered from a dynasty which was past all hope of improvement," the future benefits would be "great whatever the political humiliation of receiving a king from Napoleon's hands." Radical enlighteners loathed the arbitrary manner in which the coup had been engineered, but were promised a constitution with "an express acknowledgment of the right of the nation to be governed with her own consent, and not by the absolute will of the King." The Inquisition, chief apparatus of the degradation of Spain, would never return: the religious orders, that other wellspring of ignorance, vice, and mental slavery, would be drastically curbed. Spain, once "delivered from the mass of moral evil which prevented the natural development of its powers for good, would regenerate itself in less than half a century." Blanco White could see no point in a simple patriotism blinding men to the "faults of their country, as well as their own." Yet he broke with Joseph and the "French party" on hearing his own province had taken up arms against Bonaparte, feeling obliged to follow the masses. He crossed a land riven by civil war to reach Seville, the "most bigoted town in Spain—at that moment under the absolute control

[61] Narganes, *Tres Cartas*, 81–3; Álvarez de Morales, *La Ilustración*, 245.
[62] Ruiz Berrio, "Introducción," 20. [63] Blanco White, *The Life* i. 140.

of the most ignorant and superstitious populace, guided by that part of the clergy which was to me an object of equal horror and contempt."[64]

23.2. THE CÁDIZ CORTES AND 1812 CONSTITUTION

At Cádiz, the Patriot supreme Junta dissolved itself, leaving a five-man regency council to direct the war effort and convene the Cortes. By early 1810, the French had overrun all southern Spain except for besieged Cádiz and some remote areas where *guerillas* were active. After a long siege (April–July 1810), they also captured the border fortress town of Ciudad Rodrigo and launched their third invasion of Portugal. With British help, again the Portuguese repulsed them. The year 1811 in the Peninsula proved one of general deadlock. Spain had fragmented politically, spiritually, and ideologically. For the moment, Inquisition, monasteries, and the clergy generally, along with the nobility, retained their old sway and privileges in areas unoccupied by the French. Civil war permeated every dimension of national life; and soon those parts of Spanish America closest to the Peninsula and most easily communicated with from Spanish ports—Venezuela, Cuba, and New Granada.

The Cádiz Cortes held its opening session on 24 September 1810 in a large building today called the Real Teatro de las Cortes, proceeding without any communication with Patriot Spain's nominal monarch, "King" Fernando, who remained Napoleon's prisoner. The eventually 260 deputies included around sixty from the Americas, representing New Spain (Mexico), Peru, New Granada, Venezuela, Chile, Puerto Rico, and Santo Domingo beside the Philippines, mostly chosen by Creole elite city governments.[65] In the ensuing deliberations, Jovellanos and the moderate wing joined the conservatives in demanding restoration of the *antiguo regimen* with special status and privileges for nobility and clergy, and disallowing the term "constitution." But with Spain mostly under occupation, the conservative–moderate alliance found itself precariously positioned: representation was highly unrepresentative and, in such straitened circumstances, Jovellanos's strategy proved unworkable. A fringe of radicals, republicans, and democratic enlighteners, journalists, professionals, and café-frequenting literary men mostly, stiffened by Creoles averse to Spain's existing relationship with the colonies, threatened to gain the upper hand.

The Cortes, argued zealous reformers, required a coherent, meaningful reform program that could be presented as a plausible alternative to the *josefinos*' enlightened agenda. It was at the height of French fortunes, in 1810–11, with their offensive into Andalusia seemingly about to end the civil war, that leading figures, later pronounced traitors to their country, were most attracted to Joseph's banner. "Fear lest adherents of Joseph Buonaparte" win me over to their party, recorded Blanco White later, "was

[64] Blanco White, *The Life* i. 141–2. [65] Breña, *Primer liberalismo español*, 132–3.

the predominant feeling of both my father and mother."[66] With him supporting French revolutionary ideals, rejecting Bonapartism, and bitterly critical of the Seville Junta, his own mother, a deeply pious woman, was terrified lest her conscience compel her to denounce her own son to the Seville Inquisition. To escape his agonizing dilemma he boarded ship and permanently emigrated to England, where he edited a Spanish paper, *El Español*, sponsored by the British government and distributed in Spain and Spanish America, where his articles expounded a vigorously anti-*josefino* reform ideology. Hostile to conventional Christianity, he eventually gravitated to Unitarianism. First supporting autonomy for the colonies, he later also urged conceding independence to those demanding it, a stance which blighted his standing in Spain, causing former friends to abandon him and accuse him of "treason."

Patriots accused the *Bonapartistas* of disloyalty to crown and church; *Afrancesados* charged Patriots with lack of realism and obscurantism. Joseph's adherents, noted Blaquiere, while acknowledging the "patriotism of their competitors in the cause of reform, merely contend that much more might have been effected for the interests and happiness of Spain, without those sacrifices of blood and treasure occasioned by the war. Equally anxious for the regeneration of their common country, the leaders of this party had long advocated the absolute necessity of a change, though [before 1808] they entertained no idea of altering the existing dynasty."[67] Spain could neither reassert its prestige in the world nor ameliorate society without first achieving a thoroughgoing administrative, economic, educational renewal. The Bourbons were incapable of launching such a project, the "great work of reform could never be brought about, without a government possessing sufficient energy to inspire respect, with power to awe those formidable enemies" certain to "oppose every measure in favor of improvement and humanity."[68] Pro-French, exalting Bonaparte, the Madrid paper *El Imparcial*, edited by Estala between March and August 1809, emerged among Joseph's chief propaganda tools. Estala aimed to provide international news objectively and raise awareness of the country's plight at home and overseas. For the monarchical past he displayed only contempt: Spain's Habsburg and Bourbon kings he labeled "tyrants" who impoverished and depopulated the country.[69] Under Philip II "began the epoch of our ignorance that established as a system, reached its zenith in the seventeenth century, the golden age of Gothicism and the Inquisition."[70] Are the Bonapartes more foreign to Spain than the Habsburgs and Bourbons? Joseph he lauded for establishing public education and introducing true legality and constitutionality. The provinces, "free of the yoke of anarchy and English oppression," i.e. Joseph's Spain, more effectively sought justice, order, constitutional government, and improvement, he maintained, than the Patriot regions.[71] Fernando's despotic disposition and hounding of all dissidents after Napoleon's downfall would prove the accuracy of his judgment.

[66] Blanco White, *The Life* i. 157. [67] Blaquiere, *Historical Review*, 113, 131–2.
[68] Blaquiere, *Historical Review*, 116. [69] Estala, *El Imparcial*, 109–10, 124–5, 148–9.
[70] Estala, *El Imparcial*, 149. [71] Larriba, "Estudio," 52–3.

All three ideological blocs opposing Joseph, reactionaries, mixed government moderates, and constitutionalist radicals, diverged further than did *josefismo* from the trajectory of the Spanish Enlightenment of Carlos III.[72] Conservatives and clergy could easily outdo Joseph in seeking the support of the illiterate and ill-informed. Their problem was that their traditionalism seemed ridiculously threadbare and unappealing to literate elements even mildly committed to Enlightenment values. Their stance was often characterized less by authentic fidelity to the past than militant antipathy to *filosofismo, philosophes* and heretics, ideological antipathy to enlightened values and the principles of the American and French Revolutions. Facing two highly articulate ideological foes in the *josefinos* and the Patriot constitutionalists, Spanish conservatism in 1810–12 had little beside ecclesiastical admonitions to offer those little enticed by the mystique of monarchy and aristocracy. On the level of public debate at least, constitutionalist radicals, commanding as they did the free press, easily seized the initiative for their claims that only an ambitious Enlightenment reformism could counter *josefismo*.

Among the Cádiz Cortes' first decrees, on 18 October 1810, was its declaring liberty of the press.[73] "No sooner had liberty of the press been proclaimed," observed one contemporary, "than several eloquent [Spanish] writers, who had travelled and marked the progress of knowledge throughout the rest of Europe, almost exclusively devoted their talents to enlightening the people, and showing the advantages of civil freedom."[74] Political newspapers, as in France after the fall of the Bastille, became the decisive factor in deepening public awareness and advancing the revolutionary tendency whether Josephist or Patriot. The constitutionalist, in part republican, faction in the Cortes, buoyed by papers like *El Semanario Patriótico*, the *El Observador*, *El Voto de la Nación Española*, and also *El Espectador Sevillano*, established at Seville by a poet allied to Quintana but less radical, Alberto Lista, soon gained the upper hand. Conservative opinion lost the battle at Cádiz even more swiftly than the nobility lost at Versailles, in 1789, due to the press. The constitutionalist faction headed by Quintana centered around an intellectual circle formed by gatherings like the Seville Academia de Letras Humanas (founded in 1793), which he frequented with his close ally, Agustín Argüelles (1776–1844), a former bishop's secretary estranged from the church, and a leading promoter of press freedom and Beccaria's egalitarian legal theories in the Spanish-speaking world. Another leading opponent of the slave trade,[75] it was Argüelles who composed the preface to the 1812 Cádiz Constitution and authored the Cádiz Cortes decree of 22 April 1811 abolishing judicial torture. Other key figures were Álvaro Flóres Estrada (1766–1853), a progressive royal official and journalist, the jurist and Greek scholar Antonio Ranz Romanillos (1759–1830), the poet, journalist, and classicist Francisco Sánchez

[72] Durán López, "Construcción," 77–8.
[73] Hocquellet, "L'Invention," 172; Fernández Sebastián, "Voice of the People," 230.
[74] Blaquiere, *Historical Review*, 24.
[75] Agüero and Lorente, "Penal Enlightenment in Spain," 252–6.

Barbero (1764–1819), the constitutionalist journalist Manuel López Cepero (1778–1858), the Aragonese leader Lorenzo Calvo de Rozas (1780–1850), and Bartolomé José Gallardo (1776–1852), among the foremost intellectual figures of the 1808–12 revolution. A peasant's son trained in philosophy at Salamanca and bibliophile avid for French books and "philosophy," Gallardo was the author of the *Diccionario Crítico-Burlesco* (1811), among the more anti-clerical Spanish texts of the age.[76]

The Quintana faction succeeded in preventing the nobility and clergy forming separate estates in the Cortes. "With what right!" exclaimed an outraged Jovellanos, writing to a relative in 1811, are the nobility and clergy "defrauded" of their special representation in the Cortes? [77] Equality of all Spanish citizens under the law and fiscal regime was proclaimed. With formal privilege ended, the medieval military orders were abolished and, under a decree of August 1811, seigneurial jurisdiction annulled. Use of noble titles, arms, and liveries in municipal and other public affairs was forbidden.[78] A broad category of lands, including of the military orders and many monasteries, was disentailed and earmarked for sale. Far from resuming the agenda of the Spanish absolutist enlightened despotism of Carlos III, the 1810–12 Cádiz Cortes rendered itself sovereign in fact if not name, circumscribing Spain's putative sovereign, Fernando, with an array of restrictions. Those orchestrating these far-reaching changes, complained Jovellanos, were leading Spain toward a ruinous reign of "democracy."

But conservativism succumbed in the Cádiz legislature in a manner that could not occur on the ground. For it was the assembly, cafés, and newspapers that were captured by the journalists, teachers, professionals, and intellectuals swayed by French philosophy, not Spain. At Cádiz, they were too formidable for the few nobles and clergy taking refuge there to check, but they possessed nothing like that preponderance in the towns and countryside. Journalists and literary men dominated the Cádiz-based "Spanish revolution," as they had the French until June 1793: the adage "La libertad de la prensa es la principal base de la ilustración pública" [Liberty of the press is the principal foundation of public enlightenment] became the Spanish Revolution's presiding maxim and, as in Paris in 1789, the demand that public opinion prevail easily mingled with claiming "philosophy" "both preceded and made the Revolution."[79] But for the Spanish Revolution, even more than the French, this meant that the *ilustrados* [the enlightened] could not simply equate the view of the common people, whom they considered hopelessly unaware of their dire predicament and what was needed, with the "general will." The "popular cry of 1808,"

[76] Rodríguez López Brea, *Don Luis de Borbón*, 211, 218; Fernández Sarasola, "Portée des droits," 92, 96, 102; Hocquellet, *Résistance et Révolution*, 276–80.

[77] Broers, *Europe*, 209; Suárez, *Cortes de Cádiz*, 122; Suanzes-Carpegna, "Image of the British System," 208.

[78] Esdaile, "Enlightened Absolutism," 67–8; Fernández-Sebastián and Capellán, "Democracy in Spain," 57–8.

[79] Hocquellet, "L'Invention," 177; Morange, "Opinion publique," 195.

averred Blanco White, "even if it expressed the sentiments of the majority, no more merited the name of public opinion than the unanimous acclamations of a crowd at an Auto-da-Fé." Ignorance and fanaticism cannot be the "general will."[80] For many onlookers, the constitutionalist intelligentsia's rapid emergence only confirmed that what transpired was just the latest phase of the same age-old insidious underground heresy undermining religious faith, recast as *filosofismo*, impiety now rife everywhere, threatening all true Spanish values, tradition, education, and probity.[81] Drafting the new Spanish constitution was the work of Enlightenment zealots who then imposed it, more so even than in France in 1789 and 1791, contrary to the will of most people. If the reformers were right to insist conservatives represented only vested interests plus religion and Counter-Enlightenment, conservatives could justifiably counter that the reformers were, overall, even more unrepresentative of Spanish opinion.

The Spanish Revolution thus advanced simultaneously on two opposed fronts—*josefismo* in the French-occupied zone and constitutionalist reform in Cádiz Spain, both comprising uneasy coalitions of moderate and radical Enlightenment. From late 1808, Quintana regularly utilized the term "revolución española" [Spanish Revolution] to describe his constitutionalist, anti-clerical, and in part republican Patriot reformism, extolling the term "constitution," expressly comparing it to the French Revolution.[82] Acknowledged by all the Spanish American colonies except Venezuela and Buenos Aires, the Cádiz assembly planned a wholly new constitution for the empire. One deputy, invoking the famous Tennis Court Oath of 1789, exhorted the assembly to swear not to disperse until they had wholly perfected the new constitution. Ironically, the jurist entrusted with drafting its articles by the commission overseeing the process was none other than Ranz Romanillos, a principal participant in compiling Napoleon's 1808 Bayonne Constitution, and also its translator into Spanish and the third person to sign it. Having initially sworn allegiance to Joseph and served the *josefino* administration in Madrid in March 1809, he defected, joining the *antibonapartista* faction in Seville. An expert on the Napoleonic code and constitutional terminology allied with Quintana and the now dominant republican group in the Cortes, he now emerged as principal drafter of the new constitution.[83] By late August 1811, when the constitutional commission finalized its proposed draft, printed copies were circulated, and the main debate in the Cortes began, the *realistas* defending royal prerogative and noble privilege had lost a great deal of ground.[84]

The ideological warfare within the Cortes raged as bitterly as ever. "Moderate" displeasure that Spain's laws were not being restored, that the commission was imposing an entirely new construct based on French revolutionary principles, boiled over into a bitter quarrel over whether sovereignty derives from God and is divinely

[80] Blanco White, *Letters*; Morange, "Opinion publique," 193.
[81] Breña, "Introducción," 14 n.; Durán López, "Construcción," 81, 85–7.
[82] Breña, "Introducción," 14 n.; Breña, *Primer liberalismo español*, 207.
[83] Suárez, *Cortes de Cádiz*, 90–1; Hocquellet, *Résistance et Révolution*, 295, 297, 306.
[84] Suárez, *Cortes de Cádiz*, 103–5, 109; Fernández Sarasola, "Portée des droits," 96–7.

vested in kings, or resides in the people, as the American and French revolutions proclaimed, and as Article Three of the draft stated. Many wanted the new constitution to profess to be clarifying and modifying Spain's traditional laws rather than introducing *philosophique* principles. However, most agreed that sovereignty resides in the people, and that only a limited executive power rests with the king. Not only reactionaries, but some republican leaders, like Argüelles, who knew Bentham's texts, objected to the idea of natural basic rights. Argüelles also headed the Cortes opposition to full equality of rights for Spanish Americans.

Finalized in March 1812 in 141 articles, as against 146 in the Bayonne Constitution, the Cádiz Constitution made many concessions to the "moderate" standpoint and derived its content mainly from the French constitutional monarchist Constitution of 1791,[85] though unlike the French constitutions of 1791, 1793, and 1795, which all served as models, it featured no *Declaration of the Rights of Man*, such as Álvaro Flórez Estrada had urged in a draft composed in 1809. Such a general affirmation had been hotly debated by the assembly but it was finally agreed to avoid any general principle of equality. Nevertheless, the Cádiz Constitution was radical in crucial respects: numerous individual articles aimed at securing individual rights in a manner implying general equality in law and equality in taxation. It emulated the 1791–2 French republican tendency in closely restricting the executive power and marginalizing the judiciary, acknowledging supremacy of the legislature as the voice of national sovereignty. The king approved laws and headed the executive, armed forces, and diplomatic service, but possessed no separate right to initiate legislation, impose taxes, require subsidies, or introduce financial exactions of any sort, or even arrest or detain, and none to introduce exclusive privileges, or obstruct or suspend the legislature. Cortes deputies would not, as in the past, represent districts or towns but the nation in general, each notionally representing 70,000 citizens. The secular clergy lost their separate status and were limited in size. Under Cortes decrees of 25 January 1811 and 16 June 1812, special taxes were imposed on the church's property and tithes. In February 1813, all monasteries and convents with less than twelve inmates were dissolved and restrictions placed on the remainder as regards recruiting novices and collecting contributions from parishioners.[86]

There was no suggestion, for the moment, that the empire adopt a federal organization on the American model. Rather, the sweeping legal and administrative reforms envisaged a highly centralized system for the empire as a whole. A fundamental change was that American-born Spaniards, the *Criollos*, whose legal status had always been both different and inferior, now received full equality as citizens. The Constitution defined the "Spanish nation as the collectivity of the Spaniards of both hemispheres" and was highly innovative too in granting citizenship in principle to Spanish America's half-castes and indigenous peoples, while creating a two-tier hierarchy excluding those of African descent from automatic citizenship. Slavery was preserved in the manner of

[85] Scandellari, "Recepción," 129.
[86] Suárez, *Cortes de Cádiz*, 116–20, 127; Fernández Sarasola, "Portée des droits," 92–3, 99–100.

the American Constitution but Free Blacks could obtain citizenship through naturalization. In theory, Indians and mestizos all became Spanish citizens on the same basis as peninsular Spaniards. But the Cortes deliberately avoided allocating one American representative for every 70,000 inhabitants on an equivalent basis to metropolitan Spain, as this would mean conceding a majority of the Cortes seats to Spanish America—something it refused to countenance.[87] Spanish American votes hence counted for appreciably less than peninsular Spanish votes. On publication of the Constitution, a further Cortes decree "directed that a marble slab bearing the words 'Plaza de la Constitución' in gilt letters be conspicuously affixed in the principal square or market place of every town in the monarchy."[88]

Napoleon having abolished the Inquisition in Josephist Spain, in 1808, the Cádiz assembly abolished the Inquisition in *antibonapartista* Spain, in December 1812—but only following a bitter fight, with many deputies arguing that a secular body like the Cortes cannot abolish a holy institution that most Spaniards deeply venerated, authorized by papal bulls.[89] In theory, the Inquisition was no more. But few accepted that the church no longer had the power to prevent writers expressing doctrines of which the clergy disapproved. Freedom of expression and the press were proclaimed in theory but remained severely curtailed by the proviso that nothing contrary to Catholic belief could be said or published, special new diocesan councils being instituted to take over the Inquisition's task of enforcing religious censorship, suppressing forbidden books, and countering irreligious ideas.

23.3. REACTION (1814–1820)

Joseph held the upper hand until the spring of 1812 when Napoleon withdrew part of the French army from Spain to join his *Grande Armée* invading Russia. The turning-point occurred on 22 July 1812 when a combined British and Portuguese force heavily defeated the French near Salamanca. The two-and-a-half-year siege of Cádiz was then abandoned and the strategic position of Napoleon's troops in Spain deteriorated so fast Joseph already had to evacuate Madrid on 11 August. A final French counter-offensive followed, outflanking Wellington near Burgos, and forcing him into an epic withdrawal back to Portugal. But the tide quickly turned again. The *Afrancesados* began to flee; Joseph returned to France in March 1813, though Josephist final defeat occurred only with the Battle of Vitoria (21 June 1813), after which Bonaparte, with his power and European-state system disintegrating, offered to replace Fernando on the Spanish throne with greater powers than the Cádiz Constitution accorded in exchange for his allying with France against Britain and Portugal and promising to

[87] Fernández Sarasola, "Portée des droits," 100; Breña, *Primer liberalismo español*, 141, 146–7.
[88] Blaquiere, *Historical Review*, 54.
[89] Rodríguez-López Brea, *Don Luis de Borbón*, 211, 215–16.

keep those who had served Joseph in positions of trust and restore their property. Fernando cheerfully signed the offered treaty of Valençay (December 1813), returning to Spain in March 1814, but he did so without ratifying the treaty, the Cortes of Cádiz having stipulated they would acknowledge no arrangement entered into with Napoleon.

But with Bonaparte's power broken, the 1812 Constitution, among the foremost achievements of the Western Enlightenment, was, as a direct consequence, itself soon overthrown. Fernando, at first proceeding cautiously, solemnly swore to uphold the Constitution, freedom of the press, and other changes introduced by Cádiz as well as Joseph, albeit already designating the people "my vassals." But on finding most of the people had little sympathy for or understanding of the Cádiz Constitution, and urged on by the episcopate, within weeks he grew bolder. Cádiz constitutionalists saw themselves "represented in pamphlets and periodical publications as subversive of religion and the social order." Spain's restoration soon became, next to Piedmont, the most uncompromisingly repressive anywhere in Europe.[90] To the stupefaction of the Cádiz reformers, who had expected nothing of the sort, Fernando flagrantly reneged on all his promises. Crowds were incited to smash the Revolution's monuments, plaques, markers, and nameplates designating the central squares of Spanish towns "Plaza de la Constitución."[91]

For all their talk of the power of public opinion and the press, those who engineered the Cádiz Constitution, the revolution's backbone, were just a tiny fringe of editors, journalists, university jurists, and the like passionately committed to Enlightenment principles. In predominantly illiterate Spain, it was not difficult to persuade most people to accept that their country was menaced by a pernicious underground "conspiracy" of heretics—masons, Protestants, and Jews—the same old clandestine subversion that had so relentlessly gnawed at Spanish orthodoxy and loyalty for six centuries.[92] Emboldened by the weakness of popular support for the *constitucionales*, and gathering momentum of political reaction in France, Germany, and Britain, on 4 May 1814 Fernando dissolved the Cortes and abolished the Constitution, restoring church and nobility to their old privileges and rights.[93]

Follow-up measures included cancelling press freedom and the education reforms, releasing the church, by decree of 24 June 1814, from all contributions imposed by the Cortes, and reinstating the Jesuit order in Spain and its empire as a bulwark of Counter-Revolution. Exalting the resumed alliance of throne and altar, Fernando ordered restitution of all the seized properties of Spain's monasteries and convents without compensation to the buyers, according to a later report in the Paris *Revue encyclopédique*, though he also balanced his munificence, in this and other respects,

[90] Broers, *Napoleonic Mediterranean*, 257.
[91] Blaquiere, *Historical Review*, 25; Rodríguez-López Brea, *Don Luis de Borbón*, 255–6.
[92] Durán López, "Construcción," 84–5, 93; La Parra, *Fernando VII*, 295–7.
[93] Grab, *Napoleon and the Transformation*, 143; Cuenca Toribio, *Guerra de la Independencia*, 379–87.

by exacting hefty ecclesiastical donations specifically to the crown.[94] Glorying in his triumph, on 21 July 1814, Fernando proclaimed the end of private freedom of conscience and restoration of Spain's Inquisition tribunals with all powers intact; ten days later, he reinstated the Inquisition tribunals of Lima, Mexico City, and Cartagena de Indias.[95] Llorente, having fled to France in March 1814, where he afterwards published the first full-scale history of the Inquisition, the *Histoire critique de l'Inquisition espagnole* (Paris, 1817), was sentenced to perpetual banishment with confiscation of his belongings, including his noted Madrid library of over 8,000 books.[96] Nor did Ferdinand hesitate to use royal troops to round up the *constitucionales* who had so loyally supported him throughout against Napoleon. Some Patriot *liberales* fled in time but thousands, Quintana and Argüelles among them, were seized and imprisoned.

There followed six years of unremitting repression. The press was purged, decimated to a degree unparalleled in Europe. The sole newspapers in Madrid between 1814 and the resumption of the Revolution in 1820 were an official government gazette and ecclesiastical newssheets.[97] The Inquisition at once began compiling up-to-date lists of forbidden books, prominent among which was the Cádiz Constitution itself; Joseph's "public libraries" in main towns were dissolved and the books returned to the monasteries.[98] Anxious to erase every Cádiz innovation symbolically as well as actually, Spain's ultra-royalists collected all the reforming tracts and periodicals they could find published during the war, and, staging spectacular religious processions, ceremonially burnt heaps of prohibited published matter in public squares under ecclesiastical blessing. Mounds of condemned text were set alight "amidst the acclamations of the priesthood and their friends, after which high mass, and Te-Deum were sung with as much fervor as if it had been a real Auto da Fé!"[99]

Dedicated to full-blooded Counter-Enlightenment, Fernando had every intention of crushing the Cádiz *constitucionales* as thoroughly as the *josefinos*.[100] Commissions of investigation were set up resulting in numerous fresh arrests. Down to December 1815, some 450 prominent personages of rank were sentenced by three royal commissions, sixty imprisoned for four, six, eight, or ten years, forty-three banished abroad, twenty-six stripped of public offices, and 165 disgraced, fined, and ordered to pay costs. Arguëlles received eight years' imprisonment at Ceuta, Quintana, "one of the most celebrated living poets of Spain," six years at Pamplona; a Mexican delegate, Gutierrez de Terán, was banished for six years. A royal decree of 15 December 1815 confirmed the sentences of "nearly seventy individuals, composing what might be considered the soul of the liberal party in Spain."[101] Yet, through proscribing both

94 [Jullien], *Revue encyclopédique* XVIII (Apr. 1823), 164; La Parra, *Fernando VII*, 297–301.
95 Bethencourt, *The Inquisition*, 421–2.
96 [Jullien], *Revue encyclopédique* XVIII (Apr. 1823), 38.
97 [Jullien], *Revue encyclopédique* VII (Aug. 1820), 389.
98 Caro Baroja, *Judios* iii. 183; Muñoz Feliu, "Bibliotecas y Revolución," 471.
99 Blaquiere, *Historical Review*, 102, 160.
100 Blaquiere, *Historical Review*, 46.
101 Blaquiere, *Historical Review*, 107.

josefinos and anti-Josephist *constitucionales*, expelling on a scale unmatched by any other Restoration era monarch,[102] Fernando also greatly expanded the burgeoning pool of revolutionary *émigrés* circulating in Europe, powerfully reviving the Spanish liberation movement in exile. If droves of defeated democratic republicans, "moderates," and Napoleonists, ejected from posts, homes, and pensions in Italy, Germany, Austria, Poland, Britain, and Ireland beside France were exiled abroad,[103] the total ejected from Spain, estimated at around 12,000 families, was much the largest mass of ex-patriots from any European land.[104] Spanish political fugitives, many remaining committed activists, congregated in their thousands in semi-permanent refugee communities in France, Switzerland, Belgium, and England.

Superficially, Fernando triumphed, with church, nobility, and common people solidly behind him. But if Joseph's regime had been unstable, Fernando's restored absolutism of 1814 proved still more precarious internally and externally. Spanish exiles abroad openly called for Fernando's deposition and reinstatement of Carlos IV (residing in Rome) in his place, with even Marchena, now back in France, adopting this destabilizing tactic rather than urging republican revolution—a call Europe's legitimists could hardly dismiss outright.[105] To suppressed division at home and subversion beyond was added deep humiliation overseas. Between 1819 and 1823, United States secretary of state John Quincy Adams conducted negotiations with Spain that were among the most bullying and encroaching of the era. Beside losing the Floridas under the 1819 Adams–Onís treaty, the crown, pushed into one retreat after another, accepted a highly unfavorable redefinition of the Texas border and, for the first time, recognized United States sovereignty over the whole North American interior north of Texas stretching to the Pacific.[106] The American president's ground of justification for these acts "so little consonant to the moderate professions and frequent appeals of the infant Republic, to the laws of the nations," commented the Benthamite, Blaquiere, sarcastically, "was not derived from any disputes existing" between Spain and the United States but merely "Ferdinand's impotence to preserve his possessions, and cause his authority to be respected! It was certainly reserved for the publicists of North America to add this new clause to the ponderous folios of Grotius, Pufendorf, and that phalanx of sages who have written so much, and so vainly for the rulers and statesmen of the present day."[107]

Spanish post-1814 Counter-Enlightenment flourished against a backcloth of mounting unrest and disgruntlement which Fernando's obscurantism could only aggravate. A revolutionary variant of Freemasonry flourished and conspiracies formed, including one headed by a young Asturian general, Don Rafael del Riego y Nuñez (1784–1823). On 1 January 1820, led by conspiring officers under Riego, the

[102] [Jullien], *Revue encyclopédique* III (Aug. 1819), 493–4; Flores Estrada, *Representación*, 20–1, 38–9, 41.
[103] Aprile, *Siècle des Exiles*, 83–4; Isabella, *Risorgimento*, 22–30.
[104] [Jullien], *Revue encyclopédique* III (1819), 494.
[105] Suárez, *Crisis política*, 64–5; La Parra, *Fernando VII*, 350.
[106] Gould, *Among the Powers*, 178–80.
[107] Blaquiere, *Historical Review*, 190.

14,000 troops awaiting embarkation at Cádiz that Fernando planned sending to Spanish America for his projected reconquest of Buenos Aires and the River Plate, mutinied, demanding restoration of the Cádiz Constitution. The first time a royal army precipitated a revolutionary outcome against its own monarch in any European country, the mutiny itself initially failed. In Andalusia, peasantry and townspeople alike scarcely reacted, displaying near total indifference, while elsewhere most of the army stayed loyal. For weeks, until late February, Riego thought his rising had flopped, while the Spanish court stayed confident the insurrection was virtually crushed. But on 21 February rebellion erupted also at Corunna followed by other Galician towns, then Murcia, and, on 5 March, Zaragoza. Within days, popular revolutionary movements spread also elsewhere and soon to Madrid, causing Fernando's power suddenly to disintegrate.[108] Strikingly, revolutionary fervor for the first time, in several places, included attacks on Inquisition tribunals, prisons, and archives.

As usual, there was no direct correspondence between social pressures and revolutionary scripts: the decisive social factor, as before, was the drawing of the angry and aggrieved behind competing, highly vocal ideological blocs dedicated respectively to overthrowing the entire status quo, veneration of monarchy and the church with some reform, and militant defense of the status quo, or Counter-Enlightenment.[109] Deep splits within insurrectionary ranks obliged the leadership to show considerable caution. In particular, few dared speak of deposing, or punishing, the monarch. Trapped in insurgent hands, on 9 March 1820 Fernando proclaimed the Constitution's reinstatement, and the same day, the Inquisition's third abolition, with a show of royal hypocrisy that greatly reassured majority sentiment.[110] The people, all evidence confirmed, knew nothing of republicanism and cared nothing for the Inquisition's opponents; they revered king and church. Royal concessions were published on 10 March amidst an aura of supposed royal good intentions which the new regime deliberately encouraged and that conserved Fernando in general high esteem. To reassure the public, despite being under virtual house arrest, his every move during the remainder of the Revolution that could conceivably be presented, amidst changes flowing thick and fast, as manifesting royal approval, integrity, and pious intentions was made the most of.

23.4. THE FAILED REVOLUTION OF 1820–1823

Coinciding with no particular spike of economic distress or social deprivation, the 1820 insurrection introduced a distinctively Spanish style of revolution later ubiquitous in

[108] La Parra, *Fernando VII*, 375–8; Muñoz Sempere, *Inquisición Española como tema literario*, 69–70.
[109] Mantecón, *España en tiempos*, 118, 127, 266–7; La Parra, *Fernando VII*, 377.
[110] Suárez, *La Crisis política*, 66–7; Busaall, "Constitution," 112.

Spanish America, triggered by an initial coup, or *pronunciamiento* by army officers.[111] With the king's power broken, the political context changed dramatically and freedom of expression was again suddenly a reality. A fresh revolutionary "constitutional" government formed in Madrid, on 10 March. The Cádiz Constitution was publicly reaffirmed and sworn to amidst public fiestas spreading during the next days to many provincial cities, Cartagena on 11 March, Murcia on the 12th. All prisoners held for political subversion—Quintana at Pamplona, Argüelles on Majorca, and those in Inquisition gaols—were freed; those exiled abroad on political grounds were amnestied and recalled.[112] Numerous political fugitives who fled, in 1814, excitedly returned. Exhilaration at their sudden reversal of fortunes found expression in an unprecedented outpouring of newspapers, controversial leaflets, and radical texts trumpeting their return.

Where, during 1814–20, Spain boasted virtually no newspapers of any standing, hardly had the Revolution resumed than major papers reappeared, offering criticism, political analysis, debate, and international news. Especially notable were the revived *Gazeta de Madrid*, *El Constitucional*, handling constitutional debates, and *El Censor*, commencing on 5 August 1820, supported by the Cortes president, the conde de Toreno, one of those just released from prison, which, for a time, in Llorente's opinion, was Spain's leading pro-Revolution journal. Strikingly, all its editors, Lista, Amarita, Miñano, and Gómez Hermosillo, had been *josefistas* until 1814, championing Napoleon's 1808 Bayonne Constitution, not the Cádiz Constitution to which they now rallied. José Mamerto Gómez Hermosilla (1771–1837), a professor of Greek, had been secretary to Joseph's Madrid *superintendente* of police. Exiled to France in 1814, he returned, like the others, in 1820, joining forces with the Cádiz constitutional bloc; in 1823, he was to publish a three-volume scathing attack on *robespierriste* "Jacobinism," *El Jacobinismo*.[113] Stressing the need to heal old wounds, Llorente arranged leaflets, demanding a "union general" erasing all past division between the rival sets of 1808–14 reformers, calling on Cádiz adherents and *josefistas* alike to link arms.[114]

Cádiz supporters and *Afrancesados* did indeed join forces to an extent, though significant tensions remained. From exile, radicals and moderates, Patriots and *josefinos* alike, ejected in 1814, streamed back while those suppressed internally resumed writing and speaking at meetings.[115] Mexican and other Spanish American deputies at Cádiz, in 1810–13, also returned to aid the empire's much heralded revival on the consensual basis of 1812. Those just released from Spanish prisons included several eminent South American revolutionaries, among them Antonio Nariño (1764–1824) of New Granada (Colombia), an admirer of Franklin and the American and French revolutions who, in 1794, had disseminated his own Spanish translation

[111] Butrón Prida, "Liberté, Nation," 177, 183, 189.
[112] La Parra, *Fernando VII*, 378; Más Galvan, "Clero Murciano," 334.
[113] [Jullien], *Revue encyclopédique* VII (Aug. 1820), 389 and VIII (Oct. 1820), 191–3.
[114] López Tabor, *Famosos traidores*, 185–7.
[115] Fuentes, *José Marchena*, 281–3; Dérozier, *Manuel José Quintana*, 693, 700.

of the 1789 French "Declaration of the Rights of Man and the Citizen" in Peru and New Granada.[116] Briefly, hope soared that the South American insurrections could finally be resolved by an equitable and peaceful new compromise relationship with Madrid. A six-month ceasefire between crown and Spanish American revolutionaries was proclaimed and new constitutional arrangements proposed for the entire empire based on the "Cádiz" principles of 1812.[117]

Elections were held soon after the Cádiz Constitution's reintroduction, reportedly resulting in the selection of "men distinguished for talent and virtue, who have been besides proved by persecution and suffering."[118] Madrid especially plunged into "a state of the greatest excitement and exultation" as the political clubs of Fontana de Oro, Lorencini, and La Cruz de Malta opened their doors and crowds of avowed anti-Catholics, Carbonari, and Freemasons streamed into the open. For weeks the Madrid populace "enjoyed a continual festival" after work: "the Prado, Puerta del Sol, and the numerous streets which branch off from it in every direction," reported Blaquiere (whose trip to report on the revived revolution was funded by Bentham), "are immediately filled with people of all ranks, ages and sexes: the usual round of serenades and other musical parties, enliven the scene at night, while some popular play or patriotic chief attracts crowded audiences to the theaters. Many hundreds, and these of a respectable class, attend at the societies of the Cruz de Malta and Fontana de Oro, where some of the most eloquent men in Spain emulate each other in impressing the value of rational liberty, and the importance of constitutional government on the minds of their countrymen."[119] The smashed marble plaques designating Spain's former *plazas de la Constitución* were, during these weeks, "restored and consecrated amidst the rejoicings of the people. Such was the veneration in which these symbols of liberty were held by the Patriots, that many contrived to preserve fragments, which have been restored to light since March last, and are now sought for as valuable relics."[120]

Not just a sensational event for the Spanish-speaking world, the 1820–3 Spanish Revolution proved a rousing beacon for all Western humanity, instilling fresh hope into the literary and intellectual unrestricted Enlightenment everywhere. The revolutionary fervor electrifying Spain, Naples, Piedmont, and Lisbon in the summer of 1820 generated excitement right across Europe. The Holy Alliance and pro-Restoration powers, shocked by this fresh assault on crowns and religious authority so soon after the Vienna Congress, were deeply shaken by the ubiquitous upsurge of revolutionary exhilaration. Resurgence of Spanish constitutionalism occurred at a point when the Greek Revolution was yet to break out, but when France, Tory-dominated Britain, and Prussia were all fast wearying of reaction. England's ardently radical poet, Shelley, considering visiting Spain the following winter, and penned a stirring "Ode to Liberty" in 1820, styling revived revolutionary Spain "the lightning of

[116] Martínez Garnica, "Experiencia del Nuevo Reino de Granada," 379–80.
[117] Jarrett, *Congress of Vienna*, 309–10.
[118] Blaquiere, *Historical Review*, 17.
[119] Blaquiere, *Historical Review*, 6.
[120] Blaquiere, *Historical Review*, 54.

the nations," a blaze of light in a dark conservative sky.[121] Reactionaries everywhere took fright. "In a military nation as this," noted Britain's envoy at Berlin, "the precedent of a revolution effected by a revolting army imposing laws upon its sovereign is felt to be one of peculiar danger; but the most immediate, and national apprehension existing here is that of an explosion in France sympathetic with the convulsion in Spain, but infinitely more dangerous, and involving a war of aggression, and the defection of the Rhenish Provinces."[122]

With the advent of the Spanish revolution of 1820, motivated neither by *nacionalismo* nor by any new doctrine called "liberalism," as generations of later historians supposed, but chiefly by the promise of restoring an enlightened civil society, the entire trans-Atlantic world sat up. There is no "liberal *ilustrado*" [enlightened liberal] in Europe," proclaimed the educator and political activist José Joaquín de Mora (1783–1864), among the Revolution's leading radical ideologues, and Bentham's chief Spanish correspondent, in 1820, in a leaflet introducing the latter's (post-1810 radical) ideas in Spanish, "who did not see this event" as "*predecesor y anuncio*" of the "regeneration of the civilized nations."[123] Radicals everywhere rejoiced and all the more when Naples and the Greeks rose too. Lafayette, in Paris, felt intoxicated.[124] Still vainly hoping the United States would support and help fund the international "General Revolution," he became entranced by the prospect of a general wave of republican revolution emanating from Spain, Spanish America, Italy, and Greece, rolling back the world tide of reaction and royalism.[125] The revolutionary vanguard—intellectuals, artists, professors, and journalists—who had led in 1808–12 were again, from March 1820, the backbone of the 1820–3 Trienio. Like other early nineteenth-century revolutions, the 1820–3 Spanish upheaval proceeded in the name of the people but was a popular movement only in a limited sense. In content and direction, it was engineered by editors and literary men striving to create a *público ilustrado* [enlightened public] to fight both religious authority and royalism, acting despite and in part contrary to the traditionally-minded, so-called *vulgo irracional.*

Spain's epic struggle was viewed by radicals and reactionaries alike as essentially a battle between Enlightenment and Counter-Enlightenment against the backcloth of political reform. In places, civil war erupted as Fernando's ultra-royalist adherents reorganized and took up arms. Retreating to anti-constitutionalist strongholds, the not yet fully extinguished Inquisition, in 1821, uttered defiance against "philosophy" from remote strongholds, renewing its "ban" on Montesquieu.[126] For moderates, dominant for the moment, it was a struggle over how to reconcile religion and politics.

[121] Foot, *Red Shelley*, 209; Holmes, *Shelley*, 581, 583; Philp and Posada, "Liberalism and Democracy," 179.
[122] Rose to Castlereagh, Berlin, 26 Mar. 1820, in Freitag and Wende (eds.), *British Envoys* i. 141.
[123] *Consejos que dirige á las Cortes y al pueblo español Jeremías Bentham: traducidos del inglés por José Joaquín de Mora*, Prologue, 3; Alonso, "A Great People," 203.
[124] Neely, *Lafayette and the Liberal Ideal*, 136–8.
[125] Neely, *Politics and Conspiracy*, 205–8.
[126] [Jullien], *Revue encyclopédique* x (Apr. 1821), 170; Mantecón, *España en tiempos*, 240.

Moderates now enjoyed the support of the primate of the Spanish church since 1799, the cardinal-archbishop of Toledo, Don Luis de Borbón (1777–1823), the so-called "cardinal of the liberals." Another leading champion of "moderation" was Spain's eminent journalist exile in England, Blanco White, who had undergone an ideological conversion since emigrating: repudiating the radicalism with which he formerly aligned, he charged the framers of the 1812 Constitution with being doctrinaire, naive admirers of French ideas and Paine. Resuming contact with his old ally, Quintana, now again prominent in the Revolution, from England, Blanco White tried to dissuade him from restoring the 1812 Cádiz Constitution with its democratic features unaltered: Spain's revolutionaries, veterans of Cádiz and Josephism alike, he urged, must change course and adopt British "mixed monarchy" as their model. For otherwise, it would not be long, he predicted, before the *constitucionales* of 1820–3 would again be overwhelmed by popular ignorance "superstition," and a clergy supporting reaction.[127] And indeed, the revived Revolution began auspiciously but was soon again trapped in the old rift between radicals and moderates, with the latter seeking to conciliate crown and church, and alter the unicameral Cádiz Constitution by introducing a second, aristocratic upper chamber, ending its unity.[128] The renewed split between pro-Revolution "moderates" and militant anti-church radicals was bound to be exploited by the Holy Alliance, Europe's reactionary great power alliance staunchly backed, to Lafayette's infinite scorn,[129] by a deeply reactionary British government.

Poetry and art were avidly recruited to aid the revolution. In 1809–14, Joseph's ministers had planned a "Museo Josefino" as an enlightenment tool, on the site of the future Prado in Madrid, modeled on the Paris Musée Napoleon. The civil war had prevented the project materializing but an emasculated version survived after 1814 at court: Fernando inaugurated the Prado as an unseen royal repository in November 1819. However, it was the new revolution that converted the project into a major public undertaking: in 1820, the Prado opened to the public for the first time, one day per week initially, the restored legislature ordering the transfer to the new public collection of all significant Spanish pictures from the royal palaces in and around Madrid, beginning with those in the Buen Retiro and at Aranjuez. By January 1821, reported Llorente, in Paris, the Prado exhibited 332 paintings, including forty-four Velazquezes, forty-three Murillos, and twenty-eight Riberas.[130] But 1820–3 was above all a revolution of publications. With the Cortes' Freedom of the Press edict in place, and the Inquisition dismantled in much (though not all) of Spain, publishers, printers, and booksellers, exhilarated with sudden freedom to import into the Spanish-speaking world, set to work with alacrity. Just as happened in France between 1789 and 1793, in Spain and Portugal, during 1820, a press revolution completely transformed the public sphere, diffusing democratic republicanism as a powerfully

[127] Blanco White, *Life* i. 375; Murphy, *Blanco White*, 111; Breña, *Primer liberalismo español*, 410–11.
[128] Murphy, *Blanco White*, 111–12; Busaall, "Constitution," 122–3.
[129] Lafayette, *Mémoires* vi. 161.
[130] [Jullien], *Revue encyclopédique* IX (Jan. 1821), 192–3.

active Enlightenment concept.[131] Few texts propagating late Enlightenment radical political consciousness had enjoyed much circulation in Spanish prior to 1812.[132] Although some irreligious texts had seeped secretively and inconspicuously into Spain from the 1770s onwards, broad systematic linkage of revolutionary republicanism with rejection of religious authority surged up for the first time only during the Trienio, chiefly due to the revolutionary vanguard returning from exile avid to expose their native land to a cleansing torrent of Rousseau, Paine, Price, Priestley, Helvétius, d'Holbach, Filangieri, Condorcet, Volney, Constant, Say, and Bentham.

Unimpeded, they everywhere plied publications on political, social, moral, and religious issues of a kind strictly forbidden before 1808 and fiercely suppressed between 1814 and 1820. Much of the flow came from abroad but this was soon seconded, especially at Madrid, by presses within Spain, much as happened more briefly after 1793 in Haiti and during 1820 in revolutionary Naples and Piedmont.[133] Among jurists, professors, and lawyers, high-level constitutional theory became the rage, stimulated most notably by publication of the Spanish version of Benjamin Constant's recently published *Cours de politique constitutionelle* (1818–20), appearing in three volumes, at Madrid, in 1820, introducing the Constant of reform, constitutionalism, freedom of the press and abolition of slavery; for the next three years there was incessant invoking of Constant, along with Filangieri and Bentham as well as Montesquieu.[134] Llorente stressed the international significance of this sudden Spanish preoccupation with recent political science in Marc-Antoine Jullien's Paris *Revue Encyclopédique*.[135] Among its first actions, the reinstated Cortes ordered courses in political science introduced in the Spanish universities as a tool to modernize and enlighten Spain's political consciousness, not least by teaching Constant's three volumes under the title *Curso de politica constitucional*.[136]

Constant, Filangieri, and also Bentham, despite the latter's vigorous support for Spanish American independence grating on many Spanish leaders, were the three giants of political science who, in the Spain of 1820–3, imparted the firmest theoretical push in a radical direction.[137] The *Tratado de legislacion civil y penal* of Bentham appeared in 1822, rendered by the Aragonese jurist, Salamanca professor, and academic subversive, Marchena's old mentor, Ramón de Salas, who, together with José Joaquín de Mora, emerged as one of Bentham's two prime promoters in Spain.[138] Filangieri's chief work, banned by the Inquisition in 1790, had appeared in Josephist Madrid in 1813, in a Spanish rendering by D. Jaime Rubio in ten volumes, under the

[131] Popkin, "Colonial Media Revolution," 3–7; Israel, *Revolutionary Ideas*, 30–52; Ramos, "Democracy without the People," 77; Fernández-Sebastián and Capellán, "Democracy in Spain," 55–8.

[132] Usoz, "Political Economy and the Creation," 118.

[133] [Jullien], *Revue encyclopédique* VIII (Oct. 1820), 187, 193; [Jullien], *Revue encyclopédique* XVIII (Apr. 1823), 454–5.

[134] Suárez, *La Crisis política*, 67; Busaall, "Constitution," 113–15.

[135] Bethencourt, *The Inquisition*, 10–15.

[136] Pantoja Moran, *Supremo poder conservador*, 535.

[137] Scandellari, "Recepción," 129; Alonso, "A Great People," 199, 201.

[138] Fernández Sarasola, "Ramón de Salas y la Nueva Ciencia Jurídica," 640–1.

title *Ciencia de la Legislación*, but been suppressed the following year, under the Inquisition's renewed general ban on all republican and anti-clerical ideas, with many copies seized.[139] In the 1820s, though, Filangieri again powerfully rivaled Constant and Bentham as one of the three foremost radical constitutional pillars in both Spain and Spanish America. In 1821–2, a second Spanish edition of Filangieri appeared in six volumes at Madrid; three more editions then appeared in rapid succession—the third, again in ten volumes, at Bordeaux, shortly after the ending of Spain's short-lived press freedom in 1823 when the ban on Filangieri was re-imposed.[140] Condorcet's *Esquisse*, meanwhile, having circulated in manuscript inside Spain, in Spanish, translated by "D.J. de la C.Y.C.," since 1799, was first published in Spanish at Paris also in 1823.[141]

Much of the influx of political theory into the Spanish-speaking world in 1820–3, though, entailed simply catching up with the past, disseminating material largely familiar elsewhere. Montesquieu's *L'Esprit de Lois*, forbidden in Spain and Italy since the papal *Index Librorum Prohibitorum* in 1751, appeared in a five-volume Spanish translation at Madrid in 1820, followed by a three-volume edition.[142] Beccaria's 1764 classic, first rendered into Spanish as the *Tratado de los delitos y de las penas* in 1774, reappeared in its original version in 1820 and then, in 1821, in Juan Rivera's more assertive and "instrumental" new translation with one of Spain's major presses, Fermin Villalpando. The latter firm, though active in Madrid from 1794 to 1830, exclusively published Beccaria, Bentham, and Jean-Baptiste Say during the Trienio. Beccaria's *Tratado* reappeared in its new version in 1822, and, for the Spanish American market, at Philadelphia in 1823.

Spain's three principal political thought translators during the 1820–3 Revolution—Mora, Marchena, and Salas y Cortes—had all tangled with the Inquisition in the 1790s and subsequently for colluding in disseminating prohibited books and concepts. Denounced to the Inquisition in January 1792, Salas y Cortes had been stripped of his chair at Salamanca and, on 25 September 1796, sentenced to a year's detention in a monastery. Joining Joseph and the *Afrancesados* in 1808, he was prefect first of Guadalajara and later Toledo. On *josefismo*'s collapse, he returned to France but reappeared in 1820, becoming an elected member of the revolutionary Cortes. To him, freedom of the press was "la más importante de todas la libertades" [the most important of the freedoms]. Among other projects, he prepared a textbook entitled *Lecciones de Derecho público constitucional para las escuelas de España* (Madrid, 1821), designed to inculcate political thought awareness in secondary schools.

139 Varela Orol, "Poder e censura," 93, 116, 121.

140 Torrres Campos, *Bibliografía española contemporánea* i. 56–7; Trampus, "Entre Antonio Genovesi y Gaetano Filangieri," 84; Trampus, "Enlightenment in Global History," 121–2; Astigarraga, "España y la *Scienza*," 103–7.

141 Astigarraga and Menudo, "Condorcet en Espagne," 439, 445–6.

142 Torrres Campos, *Bibliografía española contemporánea* i. 56; Carlos Pérez Vaquero, "Introducción" to Montesquieu, *Del Espíritu de las Leyes* (Valladolid, 2008), 5–6.

While also promoting Bentham's influence on all sides, Salas chiefly admired Constant and Destutt de Tracy. Destutt's commentary on Montesquieu, criticizing *L'Esprit* for favoring "mixed government" and the British system, appeared in Spanish at Madrid in 1821, in an edition together with a Spanish *L'Esprit des Lois*, as *Comentario sobre el Espiritu de las Leyes* "translated by D. Ramón Salas."[143]

A still more subversive aspect of the influx from abroad, though, was the irreligious and atheistic stream which in its more vehement forms entered after 1820 still only in clandestine formats.[144] Here, Radical Enlightenment's old need for evasion and subterfuge persisted owing to the violent emotion such material provoked and the still resilient local grip of the bishops and clergy. This radical influx flowed mostly from Bordeaux, Paris, London, and Geneva rather than from within Spain, but again also partly from Spanish presses, although now with the names of translators and distributing booksellers (*libreros*) carefully obscured. A strikingly new phenomenon, clashing with Spain's past, this torrent had a traumatic effect. In reaction to the clergy's sanctioning the 1814–20 repression, there was now clearly a mounting appetite, once press freedom resumed, for irreligious books in Spanish with a militantly anti-clerical edge, a veritable flood of such material becoming widely available almost immediately. Notorious works vigorously banned by crown, bishops, and Inquisition for decades until 1820, or only seeping in rarely during the 1808–14 turmoil, poured in from early 1820, a much noted irruption that only intensified the triangular ideological war between moderate Enlightenment, radical Enlightenment, and Counter-Enlightenment, ideological warfare in Spain seething more and more under the surface during Fernando's unbending repression. During the 1820–3 Trienio, for the first time, but not the last, there surfaced a virulent strain of Spanish popular as well as intellectual anti-clericalism.

Given the depth of the split between moderates and radicals, the sudden flood of clandestine philosophical literature disseminating subversive attitudes toward religion and the church, as well as royalty and nobility, became a particularly divisive issue. If, initially, a boost for the revolution, the fact that leading "liberal" churchmen espoused the restored Constitution soon proved a double-edged sword. Don Luis de Borbón, cardinal-archbishop of Toledo and a member of the revolutionary *Junta* in Madrid, initially played an invaluable supporting role, issuing a printed circular to his clergy, dated 15 March 1820, ordering them to instruct their flocks to support the restored 1812 Constitution, and obey the revolutionary *Junta* and restored Cortes. A true Christian, clergy must impress on the faithful, can embrace toleration and enlightened principles as embodied in the Cádiz Constitution; the same message was read out in the seminaries. On 24 March, Borbón directed all curates of his archbishopric to stage public ceremonies of allegiance, swearing on the Gospel, to abide by the

[143] *Boletín de la Librería* 23 (1895/6), no. 10, p. 155.

[144] Muñoz Sempere, *Inquisición Española como tema literario*, 66, 68; Astigarraga and Menudo, "Condorcet en Espagne," 445–6.

restored Constitution.[145] *Absolutista* clergy refusing were punished. The problem was that even the most enlightened prelates could only go so far. Spain's clergy were now sharply divided into *absolutistas* and *liberales* but, by definition, the latter remained strictly moderate Enlightenment and could not countenance radical opinion.[146] Some bishops nominally embraced "freedom of the press." Toleration and "freedom of the press," as enacted by the revolutionary *Junta* on 11 March 1820, the cardinal-archbishop assured his clergy, were allowable, but only insofar as publications remained free of the "sarcasmos y de las injurías" [sarcasms and insults] of libertines and the irreligious.[147] Catholic freedom of conscience must not be confused with *libertinaje* (libertinage) and irreligion. On 29 April, the cardinal-archbishop issued an edict proposing to formulate rules for an enlightened modified censorship of texts judged "contrary to religion."[148] But such efforts to steer between Scylla and Charybdis provoked shrill opposition from right and left.[149] If freedom of expression and the press advanced further in 1820–3 than in 1808–13, this very fact deepened the rifts plaguing the 1820–3 revolution as such freedom increasingly lacked support among both clergy and public.

The influx of *philosophique* literature pillorying Christian doctrine exacerbated the difficulties trammeling the 1820–3 revolution especially following re-adoption of the Cádiz Constitution's special provisions for suppressing material detrimental to church and religion. The *Junta Suprema de Censura*, established by Cádiz in 1813 to exercise a reduced censorship in place of the Inquisition, was revived by the Cortes in June 1820, and again authorized to balance freedom of press against the need to prevent *philosophique* militant or demeaning criticism of church, clergy, and doctrine.[150] But then what exactly *was* banned, and what permitted? In 1813, the Cortes had accepted that "escritos prohibidos, o que sean contrarios a la religion" [prohibited books or those contrary to religion] were prohibited throughout the empire, with the Cádiz leadership charged with compiling detailed lists of forbidden publications; but no such lists ever appeared. Complaints that prohibited books "contrary to religion" were widely circulating obliged the Cortes, in April 1821, as in 1813, to ask the governing council to provide comprehensive lists for the guidance of church and state.[151] But still no guidance arrived and, instead, the bishops simply reaffirmed that all books "prohibidos por el Santo Oficio, subsisten prohibidos" [prohibited by the Holy Office remain prohibited], a stance scarcely acceptable to Spain's more ardent revolutionaries.[152] *Absolutista* bishops, with the Inquisition abolished from 9 March 1820, simply reissued pastoral circulars announcing that though the Holy Office itself

[145] Rodríguez López-Brea, *Don Luis de Borbón*, 287; Más Galvan, "Clero Murciano," 335.
[146] Más Galvan, "Clero Murciano," 335–6.
[147] Rodríguez López-Brea, *Don Luis de Borbón*, 286; Isabella, "Citizens or Faithful?" 564, 569.
[148] Varela Orol, "Poder e censura," 67.
[149] Rodríguez López-Brea, *Don Luis de Borbón*, 302–4.
[150] Establier Pérez, "Novela anticlerical y traducción," 67–92.
[151] Varela Orol, "Poder e censura," 46.
[152] Varela Orol, "Poder e censura," 44.

was suspended, its functions were not, suppression of condemned writings being an essential power now devolving on the episcopate. This provoked considerable protest: 1820 has rightly been called the "founding year of the revolutionary or modern anticlerical ideology" in Spain.[153]

Hardly surprisingly, the most active disseminators of texts of modern French "philosophy" undermining religion tended to be the most outspoken radical enlighteners, most obviously Salas and Marchena. After holding various posts in the Josephist administration between 1810 and 1813, the latter had resumed his life in exile successively in Perpignan, Nîmes, and Montpellier, busying himself with translating into Spanish key works that were published in southern France undoubtedly with the object of being smuggled across the Pyrenees, including his translations of Rousseau's *Émile* (Bordeaux, 1817) and Montesquieu's *Lettres persanes* (1818). After 1820, his renderings of Rousseau and Montesquieu reappeared inside Spain, as *Emilio traducido por J. Marchena* (2 vols., Madrid, 1821), *Julio o la nueva Héloise* (1821), and *Cartas persanas escritas en francés por Montesquieu puesto en castellano por D. J. Marchena, nueva edición* (2 vols., Cádiz, 1821). Rousseau's *Contrat social* had already appeared in Spanish, rendered by Marchena, much earlier.[154]

Returning from exile for the second time, Marchena settled in Seville in October 1820, at once hurling himself into political debate as one of Andalusia's leading anticlerical voices urging strict subordination of clergy to the enlightened state. On 6 November 1820, he delivered a speech before Seville's *sociedad patriótica* supporting the Cortes' law of 1 October reforming Spain's regular clergy and abolishing some monasteries in which he roundly denounced intrusive religious authority and questioned the character of organized religion. While some of the *sociedad* backed him, he and the society were fiercely denounced from the pulpit, stirring the city's less informed to a furious hostility which split the *sociedad* into Marchena supporters and declared adherents of *moderantismo*, significantly damaging Seville's constitutionalist constituency and obliging Marchena to depart, in December, only three months after arriving; he transferred to Madrid where he died soon afterwards, in January 1821.[155]

Texts harshly assailing theology, religious authority, and the church still appeared in the old clandestine fashion. In Spain during 1820–3, this principally meant works of d'Holbach, including *Le Bon-Sens*, appearing as *La Religion natural del Buen Cura Meslier* (also called *El Buen Sentido*),[156] with a second version, *El Buen-Sentido fundado en la Naturaleza* "translated and dedicated," states its dedication, "to the enlightenment of his fellow citizens by Citizen S.L.M.M.J. at 'Lisboa' at the 'Liberty Press' 1821"—a furtive publication reappearing in additional editions, in 1821

[153] Muñoz Sempere, *Inquisición Española como tema literario*, 68.

[154] *Boletín de la Librería* 22 (1894/5), no. 7, p. 109; [Jullien], *Revue encyclopédique* XVIII (Apr. 1823), 577; Torrres Campos, *Bibliografía española contemporánea* i. 72.

[155] Fuentes, *José Marchena*, 284, 287–8, 292–3, 298; Rodríguez López-Brea, *Don Luis de Borbón*, 315.

[156] Alberto Gil Novales, "Notas en torno a Lecturas de Larra," in *Revisión de Larra (Protesta o Revolución?")*, in *Annales Littéraires de l'Université de Besançon* 14 (1983), 35–42, here p. 36.

supposedly at "Londres" [Madrid?] and Bordeaux.[157] The *Système de la nature* (1770), long circulating clandestinely in Spain under the title *Sistema de la Naturaleza*, reappeared in editions published at Paris (1822) and Gerona (1823);[158] a complete Spanish versión of *La Morale universelle* (Amsterdam, 1776) came out in 1820 at Madrid, as *La Moral universal* translated by "Don Manuel Díaz Moreno," followed by two further editions in 1821. More widely diffused was an abbreviated version, *Elementos de la Moral Universal, o Catecismo de la Naturaleza* by "Barón de Olbach" (Madrid, 1820), which figured in a small incident after repression resumed in 1823, involving a former royal official at Veracruz, D. Florencio de Imaz, a native of the Basque region, recently expelled from Mexico by the revolutionaries there. On re-entering Spain he was found to be carrying forbidden books, including a copy of the *Elementos.* "The eagerness with which the *constitucionales* buy [forbidden works]," commented the Madrid official handling the case, "proves that irreligion abounds in their ideas."[159] Later editions, entitled *Principios de Moral Universal* "traducido por" D.M.L.G., were purportedly published in Valladolid.

Other d'Holbach works disseminated in Spain during the Trienio were the *Contagion sacrée* ("Londres" [Amsterdam], 1767), appearing as *El Contagion Sagrado, ó Historio natural de la Supersitición* (2 vols., Paris, Rodrique, 1822), and *Lettres à Eugénie* (1768) first published as *Cartas a Eugenia* at Paris, in 1810, "por M. Fréret," then again, at Madrid, in 1823.[160] The *Historia Crítica de Jesus Christo* translated by "P.F. de T. ex-jesuita," supposedly appeared at "Londres" in two volumes in 1822.[161] D'Holbach's *Essai sur les préjugés* (1769) appeared as the *Ensayo sobre las prejuicios, escrito en francés por el Baron de Holbach* translated "with additions by" *José Joaquín de Mora* (Madrid, 1823).[162] Volney's *Ruines* entered under the title *Meditaciones sobre la Ruinas* published in "London" in 1818, and Bordeaux in 1822.[163] Diderot's fierce denunciation of female cloister life, *La Religieuse*, available much earlier in English, German, and Italian, first appeared (at Paris) in Spanish, only in 1821, as "*La religiosa* "written in French by M. Diderot," translated by Don M.V.M.—initials sometimes said to be those of Marchena though there is no certainty as to who M.V.M. was.[164]

Before long, Blanco White's pessimism looked increasingly justified. Since 1821, *legitimista* risings against revolutionary Enlightenment had spread beyond the ultra-royalist areas of Navarre and Aragon to other areas. The Holy Alliance refused to tolerate the renewed Spanish Revolution: three of the world's foremost reactionary figureheads, Czar Alexander, Metternich, and Wellington, came in person, meeting at

157 Gil Novales, "Notas en torno a Lecturas," 40 n. 12; Naville, *Paul Thiry d'Holbach*, 134–9.
158 *Boletín de la Librería* 34 (1906/7), no. 7, p. 100.
159 Gil Novales, "Notas en torno a Lecturas," 36; Cushing, *Baron d'Holbach*, 103.
160 Cushing, *Baron d'Holbach*, 93–4. 161 Cushing, *Baron d'Holbach*, 95–6.
162 *Boletín de la Librería* (Publicacion mensual), 34 (1906/7), 91.
163 Establier Pérez, "Novela anticlerical y traducción," 74–5.
164 Jullien, *Revue encyclopedique* x (Apr. 1821), 200; Establier Pérez, "Novela anticlerical y traducción," 73; Tietz, "Diderot und das Spanien," 149.

Verona in October 1822, to concert the Four Powers' authorizing Louis XVIII, when ready, to send in the French royal army to crush the insurgency. In Madrid, in the legislature, much time was expended on interminable debates covering all legislative areas, with only excruciatingly slow progress being achieved. The Dirección General de Estudios, headed by Quintana, set up to revolutionize education, proved, much as in 1808–14, largely ineffective in its secularizing drive, owing to the deep rift between the two enlightenments, though it did eventually issue instructions for dissolving monasteries and converting them into schools, in April 1822, which registered some success.[165]

As the clouds gathered, from December 1822, French and other republican volunteers began arriving in Spain vowing to help defend the Revolution. Finally, in April 1823, in the name of legitimacy, monarchy, and religion 100, 000 French royalist troops poured over the Pyrenees with the Holy Alliance's blessing and made rapid progress. Lafayette, Fabvier, and other committed radicals hoped their republican propaganda would persuade some officers and men of the invading army to mutiny, emulating Riego's example in 1820, but nothing of the sort occurred.[166] While in France this royal enterprise, loudly trumpeted by Chateaubriand, now French minister of foreign affairs, but publicly vehemently condemned by Lafayette and Destutt, proved highly unpopular, within Spain, despite the revolution enjoying some support, in dramatic contrast to 1808, the common people, directed by their clergy, largely backed rather than opposed the French invasion.[167]

With Spain's army split and the church summoning the people to abominate the "godless" *constitucionales* as foes of faith and church, and help the invaders, constitutionalist efforts to engineer a repeat of the 1808 anti-French fury, this time against absolutism and for the revolution, dismally failed.[168] Conservatives demanded faith, monarchy, and repression of Enlightenment values, even on occasion invoking Rousseau's *Contrat social* to prove maintaining public religion requires organized, institutionalized intolerance and suppression of dissenters.[169] "Philosophy and its proud reason," insisted the bishops, "has done nothing but destroy: it proscribed virtue and canonized crimes; it reigned briefly: and who could count the laments this impious reign caused?[170] As the revolution collapsed under the weight of reaction and royalist invasion, foreign republicans who had enthusiastically come to support it scattered, many moving on to Greece.[171] During the regime's final weeks, the revolutionary government, beaten back to Seville, gathered its remaining publicists and such revolutionary papers as Narganes' *Gaceta española* there, to mount their final ideological stand, lambasting Louis XVIII, the Holy Alliance, and the unenlightened

165 Dérozier, *Manuel José Quintana*, 718–25.

166 Neely, *Politics and Conspiracy*, 233–4, 236–7.

167 Renauld, *Antoine Destutt de Tracy*, 192–3; Caron, "Mouvements insurrectionels," 57.

168 Mansel, *Paris between Empires*, 182; Butrón Prida, "From Hope to Defensiveness," 592, 595–6.

169 *Representación que el Illmo. Dean y Cabildo de la S.ta Iglesia metropolitana de Burgos hace á S.A.S. La regencia del reyno, pidiendo,* [primero], *Que se restablezca El santo Tribunal de la Inquisición* (Burgos, 1823), 7.

170 Ibid.

171 Neely, *Politics and Conspiracy*, 240.

sway of the ignorant and uninformed.[172] As the revolutionary regime collapsed, *legitimista* fury seethed throughout Andalusia. Among the victims at Seville where *absolutistas* rampaged through the streets yelling "Viva el rey!" and "Viva la religion!" was Gallardo, who in his *Diccionario Critico Burlesco* of 1811 had denounced "fanaticism" and corrupt clergy as the bane of Spain, and called "philosophy" the key to a better future. The mob destroyed his books and literary manuscripts, thousands of pages of his life's work, including his draft history of the Spanish theater.[173]

Freed by the French, Fernando exacted his revenge on *constitucionales* in a more orderly fashion. The Cádiz Constitution was voided for the second time, the Inquisition re-established, and General Riego publicly executed in Madrid on 7 November 1823. Many books published in Spain during 1820–3 were immediately banned in 1823–4 by the restored Inquisition.[174] Unremitting persecution of *constitucionales* and adversaries of church authority of every stripe took hold, going well beyond what Chateaubriand and the Holy Alliance had intended. Indeed, the impetus behind the 1823 uncompromising repression in Spain was almost entirely Spanish rather than French. Chateaubriand and his colleagues were increasingly dismayed by how little leverage royalist France actually gained through the invasion.[175] Repression followed much the same lines as in 1814 but with added refinements such as a special police surveillance system now established to spy on Spanish exiles at home and abroad. Over 6,000 opponents are known to have left Spain and gone into exile in 1823, over two-thirds to France and more than 700 to England.[176] A report by Fernando's police compiled in 1826 listed 143,749 individuals considered supporters of the suppressed Constitution and regime remaining under surveillance within Spain, with disproportionately large numbers in Valencia and Catalonia.[177]

For a time restored absolutist Spain seemed calm. Yet the consequences of Fernando's and the Inquisition's renewed triumph proved deeply ominous for Spain's future.[178] Aware how closely their status and property hinged on absolute monarchy, the clergy remained more involved in politics after the Trienio than before, more adamantly opposing constitutionalism, press freedom, and Enlightenment than prior to 1820, while those resenting absolutism and repression increasingly wrapped their opposition in overt antagonism to the clergy. The Inquisition was finally abolished in Spain a decade later, in 1834, but its shadow remained not just through the 1820s and 1830s but for decades after.[179] The sight of priests and friars stirring popular political emotion against constitutionalists silently nurtured a broad-based anti-clericalism, even in rural areas, hardly perceptible before 1820, heightening thirst for vehemently anti-Christian texts by d'Holbach and Diderot.

172 López Tabor, *Famosos traidores*, 247; Aprile, *La Révolution inachevée*, 231–2.

173 La Parra, *Fernando VII*, 457; Aymes, "Mise cause," 118.

174 Prado Moura, *Hogueras*, 201.

175 La Parra, *Fernando VII*, 490–2; Neely, *Lafayette and the Liberal Ideal*, 231.

176 Fuentes, "Geografía," 309, 311, 325.

177 Fuentes, "Geografía", 325–31.

178 Breña, *Primer liberalismo español*, 450–1.

179 Prado Moura, *Hogueras*, 234.

When renewed constitutional crisis attended by widespread unrest seized Spain in 1834–5, something dramatic occurred previously seen only incipiently—anti-clerical fury in the streets culminating in repeated attacks, especially in Madrid, Zaragoza-and Barcelona, on monasteries and priests, now with numerous monasteries being burned down.[180] In the 1820s were planted in Spanish soil the seeds of a deeply-rooted, long-term bitter, ideological civil war now with the clergy as the prime target.[181]

[180] Moliner Prada, "Anticlericalismo popular," 517, 520–2, 524–6, 528.
[181] Moliner Prada, "Anticlericalismo popular," 501–2.

24

Black Emancipation, Universal Emancipation, and the Haitian Revolution (1775–1825)

24.1. ENLIGHTENMENT, RADICAL ENLIGHTENMENT, AND BLACK EMANCIPATION

The radical critique of slavery diverged from other abolitionist movements of the late eighteenth and early nineteenth century, first tentatively, and after 1780 more insistently, in affirming the potential equality of black men in intelligence, capacities, moral standards, and rights, that is in their equal right, as Condorcet put it, to live under the laws "emanating from the general will of the citizenry."[1]

However fundamental the issue of abolition and however disturbing for many was the American Revolution's failure to abolish slavery, and initially also the failure in this respect of the Venezuelan and other Spanish American republican revolutions from 1808 down to the mid-1820s, there thus remains another wider, even more basic framework for the debate about black emancipation than issues of slavery and abolition—the Enlightenment controversy over race, universal rights, and the essential unity of mankind. Embracing social hierarchy, moderate mainstream Enlightenment did not feel particularly, or at least not strongly, impelled to put an end to slavery since it did not feel constrained to admit, much less proclaim, black equality and moral and intellectual equivalence. By contrast, Radical Enlightenment entailed wholly different social and political implications deriving from its divergent philosophical premises. If New World slaves often appeared "lazy and stupid," commented Condorcet in 1781, it was slavery alone that had made them so. *Philosophes* not only "sought to save millions of men from ignominy and death," he maintained, but "restore to a whole section of the world the sacred rights given to them by nature."[2]

Approaching early nineteenth-century black bondage straightforwardly from the perspective of Quaker or other religious agendas, or widely prevalent notions of moderate mainstream enlighteners, one gets no further than the slavery question. It was taken for granted by most of European and American opinion, by nearly all other

[1] Condorcet, *Political Writings*, 154; Condorcet, *Reflexions sur l'esclavage*, 42.
[2] Condorcet, *Reflexions sur l'esclavage*, 5, 19.

than the democratic revolutionary camp, that the world's black inhabitants either side of the Atlantic were inherently different, inferior, subordinate, and less intelligent and morally inherently more corrupt than white society. The clash between moderate and Radical Enlightenment hence has to be central to any study of the origins of modern black equality in general as well as the complex, unfolding ideological–political history of the Haitian Revolution. For it was almost exclusively late Radical Enlightenment, following Diderot, Raynal, d'Holbach, Condorcet, and their faction, that presented and fought for a comprehensive program of black emancipation that besides ending slavery encompassed education, training in skills, the arts, and sciences, and generally enabling the black population to rise to the moral and intellectual equality they were capable of and that, as the white's man's brothers and equals, was their due.

Condorcet here went further than anyone before him. His views on black emancipation evolved during the early stages of the American Revolution, certainly no later than 1777;[3] he wrote his most far-reaching denunciation of slavery and oppression of the blacks in 1781 (reprinted in 1788), basing his conclusions on a strikingly more comprehensive critique of contemporary values, moral standards, and social practice, and condemnation of colonial society, than did religious abolitionists at the time. To him, slavery pertained to a comprehensively corrupt social and moral system which, along with its other oppressive practices, deliberately incited strife and instigated local wars in Africa to promote European mercantile interests. "Politically regulated society can have no other goal than maintenance of the rights of those who make up society. Hence every law contrary to the right of a citizen or outsider is unjust, a veritable crime, authorizing violent resistance."[4] According to the *philosophique* culture forged by Diderot, d'Holbach, Helvétius, and the *Histoire philosophique*, afterwards consolidated by Condorcet, the *Idéologues*, and Bolívar, universal human rights override every other consideration, every other value system.

Revolutionary *philosophie moderne*, then, was key, and why those relatively few *philosophes* advocating abolition of slavery were mostly the same as those vociferously demanding women's emancipation.[5] All the great projects of amelioration, contended Condorcet, were put forward by *philosophes*, and not by others. *Philosophes* alone rejected black inferiority; *philosophes* alone denounced massacring Albigensians and Protestants; *philosophes*, not others, sought to diminish numbers of monks and remove Jesuits; only *philosophes* strove to abolish *corvées* and outdated penal laws.[6] Diderot's German disciple Wekhrlin similarly underlined the difference between *philosophie moderne* and other viewpoints regarding black emancipation: certainly one must rejoice that the Quakers' eyes had been opened to the truth that slavery cannot be "reconciled with the principles of equality, gentleness and humanity they profess;" in 1788, he joined Condorcet and Brissot in lauding the Quakers for

[3] Badinter and Badinter, *Condorcet*, 172, 175.
[4] Condorcet, *Réflexions sur l'esclavage*, 15.
[5] Davidson, "Feminism and Abolitionism," 104–5.
[6] Condorcet, *Réflexions sur l'esclavage*, 50–1.

initiating a process philosophical radicals now aspired to extend throughout the world. But equally, in the vast struggle to emancipate black peoples, he reminded readers, it was not Christianity but "philosophy" that played the primary role and afforded the real impetus.[7] For all the churches—except the Quakers and a few other Dissenters—kept to a reprehensible and obnoxious policy of acquiescence regarding slavery, the slave trade, and worldwide oppression of blacks: "Christianity" had accepted and endorsed slavery for millennia and, mostly, still did. Churches, Protestant and Catholic alike, instead of furthering emancipation, mostly impeded the process, preaching acceptance and submission on the pernicious basis that it is Christian souls, not bodies, that are equal.[8] Anglican churchmen, whether in Jamaica or the United States, were among the most obstructive. Even Methodists, though generally keener than Anglicans and Catholics to instruct slaves in Scripture, and the second dissenting church after the Quakers to publicly promote abolition, did so only very late in the (American) Revolution. Prodded by Francis Asbury (1745–1816), a recent English immigrant figuring among the principal founders of Methodism in America and the Second Great Awakening, they categorically pronounced slavery "contrary to the laws of God"—but only from their 1780 Baltimore conference onwards.[9]

Unlike the Christian Dissenting movement for black emancipation,[10] radical strategy pivoted on the idea that "natural morality" and universal natural right is the heritage of all men, that the "right of men" is inviolable and universal, rooted in the inherent equality of all, so that even voluntary slavery is unjustifiable.[11] The idea that black men are "our equals" in a moral, social, intellectual, and political sense was hence a principle adopted during the 1770s and 1780s only by "Radical Enlightenment" writers like Diderot, Helvétius, Pechméja, Condorcet, Deleyre, Wekhrlin, Raynal, Volney, and Brissot. It is a notable feature of late Enlightenment history that the sturdy resistance of groups of runaway black slaves, or *marrons*, in Dutch Surinam and escalating military campaigns, in the early 1770s, to suppress them, rendered issues of black slavery, resistance, and liberation a lively topic in French colonial policy-making and Parisian salon conversation already prior to the outbreak of the American Revolution in 1775. French focus on the topic was stimulated in particular by the 1770 and 1774 editions of Raynal's *Histoire Philosophique* which here, as in so many respects, proved a foundational late Enlightenment event.[12]

But it was not until the late 1780s, shortly before the French Revolution, that the clash between moderate and radical positions over black equality became a clear, conscious, and explicit rift. "You want to know why there are no black authors," exclaimed Brissot, in 1786, "or even any enlightened black men? What made you

[7] Condorcet, *Political Writings*, 151–2. [8] Wekhrlin, *Graue Ungeheuer* i (1784), 250–2, 255.

[9] Hirschfeld, *George Washington*, 203; Fergus, *Revolutionary Emancipation*, 48–51.

[10] Condorcet, *Réflexions sur l'esclavage*, 5, 50; Badinter and Badinter, *Condorcet*, 172–3.

[11] Condorcet, *Réflexions sur l'esclavage*, 15; Popkin, *You are all free*, 333, 341.

[12] Brissot, *Examen critique* (1786), 96–8; Condorcet, *Réflexions sur l'esclavage*, 50; Israel, *Democratic Enlightenment*, 416, 473; De Kom, *Wij slaven van Suriname*, 76–81.

what you are?" Education, circumstances; have either the one or the other favored the blacks? Made wretched by African despotism, enslaved in the Americas, "in Europe, they are condemned by public opinion, everywhere proscribed like the Jews; in a word, everywhere in an abject state."[13] By wise government and education a superstitious black, Jew, Turk, or Indian can be turned into a "républicain éclairé" [enlightened republican] with no more or less difficulty than a credulous and prejudiced white ignoramus, of which the supply is infinite.[14] In aptitude, whether for education, the arts, or business, contended Brissot, Condorcet, and other radicals, blacks are no different from whites. Here was the authentic radical stance. By the 1780s Enlightenment democratic republicans were increasingly confident in pronouncing the ignorance, indolence, religiosity, monarchism, and other generally alleged black "deficiencies" to be socially and institutionally induced. Their "vices," arose like those of their oppressors, the white planters, from society's basic structural flaws, the corrupting effects of monarchy, aristocracy, slavery, and religion.[15]

Radical Enlightenment and moderate Enlightenment were never more openly in collision than within the French Revolution, in 1789–92, and nowhere was the rift deeper than over black emancipation. During the early Revolution, Raynal's constitutional monarchist revolutionary friend, Pierre-Victor Malouet (1740–1814), owning plantations and slaves on Saint-Domingue and Louis XVI's former intendant for the navy at Toulon, long one of Raynal's principal sources of information about the Caribbean, succeeded in pulling Raynal himself over toward the moderate anti-republican (pro-slavery) viewpoint opposing the more radical anti-slavery views of Diderot, d'Holbach, Naigeon, Pechméja, and the rest.[16] One of the great clashes of revolutionary debate was between Radical Enlightenment offering anti-slavery arguments originally developed by Diderot, Deleyre, and Pechméja,[17] and now chiefly championed by Condorcet and Brissot, and pro-slavery "moderation" presented by "moderates" especially Malouet in part using the new post-1789 "converted" Raynal some scholars aptly designate "Raynal-Malouet." "Why should France be more free than Saint-Domingue?" exclaimed Brissot. "Is it the thermometer that should regulate the rights of men?"[18] The quarrel erupted in full fury with a pamphlet Malouet published at Neufchâtel in 1789 flatly rejecting the race equality preached by Condorcet and the *Amis des Noirs* in which he unfurled his sensational dread-stirring racist warning to the world: "la liberté des noirs, c'est leur domination! C'est le massacre ou esclavage des blancs, c'est l'incendie de nos champs, de nos cités!" [liberty of the blacks! That means their domination and the massacre or enslaving of the whites, the burning of our fields and cities].[19]

[13] Brissot, *Examen critique* (1786), 96–7.
[14] Brissot, *Examen critique* (1786), 103–4.
[15] Condorcet, *Réflexions sur l'esclavage*, 46–7.
[16] Salverda, "Involvement of Pierre-Victor Malouet," 236–7.
[17] On the role of Jean de Pechméja (1741–85), see Israel, *Democratic Enlightenment*, 423, 441, 926.
[18] Brissot, *Patriote français* xcv (11 Nov. 1789), 4.
[19] Salverda, "Involvement of Pierre-Victor Malouet," 237–8.

Malouet's intervention, seconded by other pro-slavery publicists, provoked a heated public controversy persisting in full force until the defeat of the moderate royalists in Paris in August 1792. The famous anti-republican letter Raynal wrote to the French revolutionary Assemblée Nationale retracting the more radical ideas expressed in the *Histoire philosophique*, dated 31 May 1791, alleged by radicals to have been co-written with Malouet (by then long a powerful countervailing influence on Raynal personally), was undoubtedly massaged by Malouet and other moderates.[20] As Brissot pointed out in an article in his *Le Patriote français* dated 4 June 1791, whether or not Malouet co-edited Raynal's 1791 *Addresse*, the latter unquestionably amounted to just a rehash of the pro-slavery views of Malouet, Maury, Mounier, and Lally-Tolendal.[21] The moderate (pro-slavery) Enlightenment stance presented in Raynal's 1791 *Addresse* was already being referred to in the polemics of 1791 as "Raynal-Malouet" to contrast it with Raynal's contrary pre-1791 anti-slavery stance dubbed "Raynal-Diderot et Pechméja."[22]

Brissot and Condorcet aimed not just to promote abolition, but more comprehensively emancipate the blacks through education, training, and helping to provide appropriate work.[23] *La philosophie moderne*, assisted by the *Histoire philosophique*'s major trans-Atlantic impact, was not just the chief source of guidance for the general democratic republican tendency of the revolutionary era, but spur for the activism demanding general black emancipation. If slavery needed eradicating compulsorily without compensating slave-owners, black emancipation was conceived by radicals as a comprehensive political and educational break with the past rather than just a purely legal transition, with public resources being assigned to assist, educate, and support the legally emancipated blacks.[24] Abolition, Condorcet, Mirabeau, Lafayette, and the Abbé Grégoire unanimously concurred, at a strategic meeting at the duc de La Rochefoucauld's home in Paris, shortly before the Bastille's fall, in June 1789, must occur in carefully prepared and publicized stages. This had been Condorcet's view all along; for he well knew the risks of violent revenge and disorder should the process get out of hand; only gradually, by stages, would the French Caribbean's free blacks and mulattoes and, eventually, all blacks under the French flag "be assimilated with the whites as regards political and civil rights;" this was the program actually implemented by the Brissotins three years later.[25]

The organization the revolutionary republican democrats, Brissot especially, established in Paris, following the English example, to work towards ending slavery, the *Société des Amis des Noirs*, had been inaugurated on 19 February 1788. By early

[20] Israel, *Revolutionary Ideas*, 157–9, 210, 212; Salverda, "Involvement of Pierre-Victor Malouet," 236, 238; Lüsebrink, *L'Adresse à l'Assemblée*, 16, 37.

[21] For the text of Brissot's article see Lüsebrink, *L'Adresse à l'Assemblée*, 104–16.

[22] Lüsebrink, *L'Adresse à l'Assemblée*, 7–8, 13–14, 21–3, 30–1.

[23] Brissot, *New Travels*, 237; De Luna, "Dean Street Style," 170, 173; Gilbert, *Black Patriots*, 245–7.

[24] Condorcet, *Réflexions sur l'esclavage*, 22–3; Badinter and Badinter, *Condorcet*, 174.

[25] Brissot, *Patriote français* xxiv (24 Aug. 1789), 4; Condorcet, *Réflexions sur l'esclavage*, 23–5; Badinter and Badinter, *Condorcet*, 292–3; Gainot, "Republican Imagination," 285–6.

1789 it boasted 141 members including Brissot, Condorcet, Mirabeau, Lafayette, Carra, Grégoire, Pétion, Clavière, and Cerisier; and soon also Olympe de Gouges[26]—though there is no sign that Paine ever joined, even during the early and mid-1790s, or lent active support to the black emancipation generally or the Haitian Revolution.[27] The *Amis des Noirs* saw themselves as working hand in hand with England's abolitionists and also Benjamin Franklin and other American enlighteners taking up the black cause in a similar spirit at the time. The last public document Franklin signed, in February 1790, two months before his death, was the Pennsylvania Abolition Society's renewed petition to Congress for the prompt outright abolition of slavery in America. A fitting conclusion to an extraordinary career, it achieved little beyond being read out in the Senate, by John Adams with "rather a sneer." Backed by a few senators like the Pennsylvania Scots democrat William Maclay (1737–1804), it provoked angry reactions from most Southern Congressmen, and personal attacks on Franklin, confirming America's deep divisions over Franklin as well as slavery.[28]

Prior to 1775, only a tiny portion, under 5 per cent of the Thirteen Colonies' black population, comprised free blacks. During the revolutionary turmoil, several paths opened whereby blacks could win their freedom, whether enlisting in militia regiments raised by Northern and Middle state governments to fight the crown, or by joining the British to fight the Americans, pushing the originally low threshold to over 8 per cent of the black total.[29] A parallel increase occurred also in the French plantation colonies during France's participation in the struggle on the American side (1778–83), with substantial numbers gaining their freedom by enlisting in militia units or on royal warships and privateers.[30] Nevertheless, growth of the French Caribbean slave population markedly accelerated during the two decades from the end of the 1760s down to 1790, even more than in the Thirteen Colonies, from approximately 379,000 to 650,000 with nearly two-thirds of this latter total, over 400,000, on Saint-Domingue. By 1790, there were nearly 180,000 black slaves on Martinique and Guadeloupe, and another 10,000 in Cayenne and several small islands, so that by the early 1790s the grand total in the French Caribbean was not far off the rising North American total now approaching 700,000.[31] The acceleration in Saint-Domingue was driven by the area under plantation cultivation there burgeoning at an exceptionally rapid rate. Given the high mortality rate, the slave trade was the essential motor of the black population's expansion in all France's plantation economies, imports from Africa increasing so that, by 1790, only about half the slaves of future Haiti were locally-born "Creoles," the rest having arrived in recent years on slave ships from Africa.

[26] Tulard, *Histoire*, 520; Blanc, "Une humaniste," 15.
[27] Clark, *Thomas Paine*, 93–7, 260; Israel, *Expanding Blaze*, 144–5, 406–7.
[28] Meleney, *Public Life*, 186–7; Israel, *Expanding Blaze*, 144, 147–50.
[29] Walsh, "African American Colonial Population," 194; Steckel, "African American Population," 436, 454.
[30] Régent, *France et ses esclaves*, 186.
[31] Burnard and Garrigus, *Plantation Machine*, 250–1; Cormack, *Patriots, Royalists*, 27–8; Steckel, "African American Population," 439; Spieler, "Abolition and Re-enslavement," 133.

Black slavery, to radical minds, was the glaring contradiction of the American Revolution, the great blemish marring the infant United States. Together with free blacks, the nearly half a million black slaves in the Thirteen United States at the gaining of Independence, in 1775, already far outstripped the total for Native Americans, who, in 1775, amounted at most to 150,000 in the entire republic. Blacks totaled practically 20 per cent of the United States population, then estimated by contemporaries at around three million. The black proportion remained at just under the 20 per cent level, attaining 700,000 during the 1790s as total US population passed four million.[32] Proportions of black to white were, of course, very different in the French Caribbean. By 1789 the French Caribbean far outstripped the British, Spanish, and Dutch colonies as the Western world's chief producer of sugar, coffee, indigo, and other Caribbean cash crops, rendering ratios of black to white in the French territories exceptionally high. Between 1770 and 1790, tropical cash crop exports from Saint-Domingue, Martinique, and Guadeloupe rose to a value of 217 million *livres*, nine million pounds sterling, approaching twice the level of total British Caribbean exports (five million).[33]

On Saint-Domingue in 1789 only 6 per cent of the population, around 35,000 people, was classified as "white," a category comprising three main groups: planters, "petits blancs," mostly skilled artisans and sailors, and officials (and ecclesiastics). The corresponding figure on Martinique was 11 per cent, some 10,600 persons, on Guadeloupe 14 per cent (13,700 persons), and in Cayenne (French Guyana) around 8 per cent (around 2,000).[34] Although the racial divide was always the main factor separating the population blocs in the Caribbean, one must not underestimate the rift between landowners and *petits blancs*, a sharp distinction fueling much of the faction-fighting surrounding the colonial assemblies. Only whites owning at least twenty-five blacks were admitted to the island assemblies, thereby excluding *petits blancs* along with the free blacks; for a time, this continued after 1789, thereby violating the Revolution's core principles in every respect.[35] The 1789 *Declaration of the Rights of Man* being wholly incompatible with all *ancien régime* societies based on social, racial, and religious hierarchy, hence of itself imparted a vigorous impulse to revolutionary *esprit* as a reforming force in the New World too. From August 1789 ensued a fiercely contested, widely publicized trans-Atlantic debate not least within France's National Assembly, with the anti-emancipationist and anti-egalitarian side backed by colonial and slaving interests based in Nantes and Bordeaux.

Radical Enlightenment, though integral to the American and French revolutions alike, produced major progress toward comprehensive black emancipation in the sense Brissot, Condorcet, and their circle understood it, especially in the latter case.

[32] Raphael, *People's History*, 388; Wood, *Empire of Liberty*, 509.

[33] Blackburn, *Overthrow*, 163; Burnard and Garrigus, *Plantation Machine*, 34–6, 167.

[34] Bourdin and Chappey, *Révoltes et revolutions*, 240; Belleau, "Love in the Time," 218; Cormack, *Patriots, Royalists*, 28.

[35] *Il est encore des Aristocrates* (BL R-328/11), 6–7; Cormack, *Patriots, Royalists*, 27.

Colonies were crucial to France's overseas trade, they acknowledged, and needed protecting from chaos and economic ruin. They designed no abrupt, precipitate abolition, they replied to charges the *Amis des Noirs* were seeking to disrupt France's colonies, commerce, and shipping. Slaves were supposedly not yet sufficiently "mature" to embrace freedom and equality in an orderly, constructive manner. But while slaves must first be conditioned and prepared, urged the *Société*, the revolutionary project of ending slavery had to be embarked on at once, striven for, justified, and planned to win over public opinion and create the necessary conditions.[36] The *Amis des Noirs*' ensuing press campaign impacted mainly through the pages of democratic republican papers, Brissot's *Patriote français*, Mirabeau's *Courrier*, the *Chronique de Paris*, Prudhomme's *Révolutions*, and so forth.[37]

During 1788–92, revolutionary black emancipation propaganda continued to be powerfully countered by the slaving interest and Caribbean planters.[38] Detailed proposals for emancipation issued by Condorcet, as the *Société*'s president, in December 1789, fed alarmist accusations, spread by Caribbean planters, claiming the *Société*'s destructive idealism would plunge the colonies into fearful mayhem, pillage, and strife. Unfamiliar with the actual Caribbean, already before 1789 Brissot, Condorcet, and their organization had been accused of being carried away by the "devouring zeal of their *philosophie théorique*;" of embracing disastrously impractical policies in defiance of Locke and Montesquieu.[39] Clashes over this in the revolutionary press and legislature were fierce, and the democratic republicans initially made little headway, in part because most National Assembly deputies (some 15 per cent of whom themselves owned properties in the colonies) were monarchists, committed *modérés* little persuaded by the *Société*'s egalitarian aims. Needing some philosophical counterweight to radical claims that slavery affronted morality and equal rights, the Caribbean landed oligarchy's spokesmen resorted especially to Montesquieu's relativism of climate and conditions. In the Caribbean, where whites could not easily work the fields, slavery was pronounced "natural," indispensable and hence justifiable. Montesquieu's argument in Book Seven of Part III of the *L'Esprit des Lois* that "there are countries where the heat debilitates the body, and so weakens resolve that men are not brought to arduous labor except through fear of punishment: there black slavery seems less shocking to our reason [. . .]" helped drive the slave-owners' ideological *machine de guerre*.[40]

Among principal promoters of Montesquieu as a pillar of racial as well as social *modérantisme* was a deputy for Martinique, Médéric-Louis Moreau de Saint-Méry (1750–1819), a prominent colonist and lawyer, like Malouet familiar with Saint-Domingue

[36] Brissot, *Patriote français* xxiv, 24 Aug. 1789, p. 4; Condorcet, *Political Writings*, 153; Thomas, *Slave Trade*, 520.

[37] Brissot, *Mémoires* ii. 276; Oldfield, *Transatlantic Abolitionism*, 54–5.

[38] Raimond, *Réflexions*, 4–5; Popkin, "Colonial Media Revolution," 4–5.

[39] Bertrand de Molleville, *Mémoires* ii. 244; Condorcet, *Réflexions sur l'esclavage*, 123–4.

[40] Montesquieu, *De L'Esprit* iii, book vii in *Oeuvres complètes*, 620; Israel, *Democratic Enlightenment*, 423–4; Pečar and Tricoire, *Falsche Freunde*, 119–20; Villaverde, "L'Abbé Raynal," 244, 261.

and the wider French Caribbean. He belonged to the Saint-Domingue *Cercle des Philadelphes*, the colony's principal academic scientific body, among the foremost Enlightenment gatherings anywhere in the Americas before 1789, a society founded in 1784 that boasted around sixty members at its height but that had to suspend its meetings amidst Saint-Domingue's turmoil, during 1791. An accomplished ethnographer knowing the Haitian Creole language and foremost early modern recorder of Voodoo practices,[41] at the same time Moreau de Saint-Méry was a propagandist for the alleged virtues of the white plantocracy and author of the best account of Saint-Domingue on the eve of the Revolution, his two-volume *Description topographique* describing the colony's ethnography, economy, and geography, written between 1785 and 1788 but unpublished until 1797.[42] Like Malouet a passionate enlightener, fervent for debate, propagating science, sociability, and newspapers, and promoting the theater, Moreau de Saint-Méry was adamantly "moderate Enlightenment," lauding Montesquieu and the principle of aristocracy. A slave-owning ideologue expressly rejecting universal and equal rights in favor of a race theory placing the white race at the top of the racial hierarchy, and justifying black slavery, he fled France after the rout of the moderates in 1792, seeking refuge in Philadelphia, where he published his book and stayed until 1798 running a bookstore renowned as a meeting-place for French *émigrés* in America.[43]

The Caribbean Revolution's first stage was thus an escalating war of moderate versus radical Enlightenment ideologies. In Paris during 1788–90, the press and the arts were the prime tools of *philosophe-révolutionnaires* promoting black emancipation. The pro-planter, colonial lobby hit back with their own successes in the arts, press, and theater. Having lambasted race prejudice, injustice, and slavery since 1785, reaffirming it in her *Réflexions sur les hommes nègres* (1788), Olympe de Gouges, feminist, democrat, and first French dramatist to present slavery, as well as divorce and illegitimacy, as contested themes on the stage, saw her abolitionist play *L'Esclavage des nègres* (or *Zamore et Mirza*) forced off the stage after three performances by agitation whipped up by the Paris Club Massiac, chief focus of pro-Revolution monarchist sentiment, and planter money and influence, in which Saint-Méry figured prominently. Olympe summoned France's "philosophes bons et sensibles" to fight harder for the Revolution's core egalitarian ideals.[44]

During early 1790, black emancipation, vigorously opposed by *modérantisme*, liberal monarchism, and the colonial interest, developed into one of the foremost, most passionately promoted causes of the Revolution. Besides petitioning the National Assembly for suppression of the slave trade, the *Amis des Noirs*' demanded the French Caribbean's free blacks and mulattoes receive political rights equal to those of

[41] Belleau, "Love in the Time," 223, 225–8.

[42] Belleau, "Love in the Time," 215; Burnard and Garrigus, *Plantation Machine*, 10, 53–4.

[43] Ghachem, "Montesquieu," 12–14; Popkin, *You are All Free*, 53–4.

[44] *Chronique de Paris* i/xlviii (10 Oct. 1789), 234 and ii/xv (15 Jan. 1790), 57; De Gouges, *Oeuvres*, 83–7; Verdier, "From Reform," 190; Belleau, "Love in the Time," 215; Blanc, "Une humaniste," 15–16.

whites, including political representation with their own deputies in the National Assembly.[45] A small group of mulattoes in Paris, around thirty initially, led by Julien Raimond (1744–1801), an educated and articulate mulatto of one-quarter African ancestry and three-quarters white, a wealthy indigo planter who himself owned some 200 slaves, allied to Brissot and Condorcet and encouraged by the Assembly's republican faction to organize politically, began pressing for recognition of black rights on the basis of the *droits de l'humanité* generally.[46] His Paris group were afterwards suspected of actively encouraging black insurgency against the white slave-owners of Saint-Domingue. In countering anti-abolitionist propaganda, the *Amis des Noirs* portrayed themselves as just a small opinion-forming faction inspired by high motives, in no way desiring to subvert France's prosperity.

Both sides' rhetoric grew more strident. If nobility were contemptible, Caribbean white planters were a thousand times worse, ruthlessly oppressing their slaves, discriminating against "free blacks," and deceiving the public; they treated slaves and free blacks alike as animals. The Club Massiac was pilloried as a "vile pillar" of "horrible aristocratie." That Saint-Domingue's whites were incomparably indolent, ignorant, and cruel as well as sexually-obsessed was supposedly the invariable impression of European visitors to the island.[47] Despite free blacks being as numerous on Saint-Domingue as whites,[48] nowhere were they admitted to positions of responsibility or dignity despite, complained the *Amis des Noirs*, mostly being harder working, braver, and more useful to the *patrie* than the scandalously indolent whites. Saint-Domingue's whites—at over 27,000, totaling 5,7 per cent of the population—may have been a shrinking proportion of the colony's population, but by 1789, due to steady immigration from France, nevertheless amounted to twice the total of whites on Jamaica and about half that for the entire British West Indies.[49]

In May 1791, finally yielding to the concerted efforts of the *Société*, and the mulatto circle around Julien Raimond, the French National Assembly voted that the colonies' free blacks should now receive voting rights where they met the property qualifications; but this the colonial assemblies flatly refused to countenance.[50] By the summer of 1791, the tensions in Saint-Domingue were proving hard to contain. In the north, a formidable slave insurrection, initiated with Voodoo ceremonies, broke out in August 1791, while in November 1791 fighting between *petits blancs* and free blacks engulfed Port-au-Prince, leading to a conflagration on 21 November that burned down most of the town, with each side blaming the catastrophe on the other. White colonists and

[45] Brissot, *Patriote français* cxv (1 Dec. 1789), 4 and cxvii (3 Dec.1789), 2.

[46] Granié, *De l'Assemblée*, 120; Régent, *La France*, 215; Burnard and Garrigus, *Plantation Machine*, 189–90, 262.

[47] Belleau, "Love in the Time," 216–18; Blanc, "Une humaniste," 16–17.

[48] Burnard and Garrigus, *Plantation Machine*, 97.

[49] *Il est encore des Aristocrates* (BL R-328/11), 5; Brissot, *Patriote français* xcv (11 Nov. 1789), 4; Brissot, *Mémoires* ii. 276; Bourdin and Chappey, *Révoltes et révolutions*, 242–3.

[50] Raimond, *Réflexions*, 6–7; Griggs and Prator, *Henry Christophe*, 10; Garrigus, "Opportunist," 11; Hunt, *Inventing*, 163.

their American supporters attributed the mounting chaos, and incipient black insurgency, to the activities of the Brissotin republicans; the Brissotins blamed it on the blinkered, reactionary attitude of the planters and *petits blancs*.[51]

Revolutionary *modérantisme* and the British model were then fatally handicapped by Louis XVI's defection and flight to Varennes. By late 1791, the French Caribbean's mulattoes and free blacks had become a major factor of instability and potential support for the Brissotin cause. The free blacks, asserted Destutt de Tracy in a major speech on 23 September 1791, if released "by us from oppression, will be our natural allies; it is neither just nor *politique* to abandon them."[52] Villette likewise recommended a strategy of allying with free blacks in Brissot's *Patriote français*.[53] By early 1792, the dangerous escalation of tensions throughout the French colonies, had caused a dramatic expansion of the local white militias and progressive tightening of security measures. To restrict local awareness of the disturbingly novel terms in which Caribbean affairs were being debated in France, Saint-Domingue's colonial assembly had, since the start of the Revolution, drastically curtailed local press reportage and discussion of everything relating to slavery and black rights, including free black protest and slave resistance in Saint-Domingue itself; in addition, in April 1792, the colonial assembly permanently closed its visitors' gallery.[54] The Revolution reached a crucial turning-point, and the planters' position weakened further with the Paris Assembly's edict of 4 April 1792, charging the colonists with violating basic human rights. Partly due to the Brissot circle's publicity campaign and partly to the black insurrection gaining momentum in northern Saint-Domingue since August 1791,[55] the measure, introduced by Brissot, ended the extensive autonomy enjoyed by the white colonists since 1789, and stepped up the drive against monarchism and aristocracy.

This edict elevated the Caribbean Revolution to an entire new level by dissolving the old colonial assemblies and reconstituting the island assemblies on the basis of equality of all the free population, white and black. Aimed at reasserting France's grip over its colonies by ending *ancien régime* racial hierarchy and winning over the free blacks to support the Revolution while shelving the slavery question temporarily,[56] it outraged the colonial assemblies of Martinique, Guadeloupe, Cayenne, and Saint-Domingue when news of it reached them during May and June. With this high-risk strategy, the Brissotins and their mulatto allies became the prime agents of the Caribbean Revolution, as was confirmed, following the downfall of monarchy and the Feuillants, in August 1792, by the closure of the principal colonial lobby in Paris, the Club Massiac and seizure of its papers.

[51] *Chronique du mois* (Jan. 1792), 88–108; Jordaan, *Slavernij en vrijheid*, 190, 222–3.

[52] Destutt de Tracy, *Premiers écrits*, 72.

[53] Raimond, *Réflexions*, 14; Burnard and Garrigus, *Plantation Machine*, 265–6.

[54] Popkin, *You are all free*, 78; Popkin, "Colonial Media Revolution," 7–8.

[55] Bourdin and Chappey, *Révoltes et révolutions*, 243; Garrigus, "Opportunist," 7; Klooster, *Revolution*, 98–9.

[56] Popkin, *You are all free*, 45–6; Popkin, "Colonial Media Revolution," 17.

To implement the changes, the revolutionary legislature dispatched 6,000 troops (bringing 30,000 rifles) to restore revolutionary authority in Saint-Domingue. With the troops arrived a Brissotin civil commission, headed by Léger-Felicité Sonthonax (1763–1813) and Étienne Polvérel (d. 1796). Sonthonax, a "disciple of Brissot" whose portrait hangs today—almost the sole white man so honored—in the national historical gallery at Port-au-Prince, had earlier predicted, in the *Révolutions de Paris* in September 1790, that Europe's monarchs and aristocrats would not long resist the "cries of philosophy and principles of universal liberty" spreading among the nations. A republican ideologue and champion of universal education openly hostile to the church (and all churchmen), aged only 29,[57] Sonthonax presided over the powerful commission sent to transform France's profile in the Caribbean (where he had never yet set foot). He set about implementing the April law, reconstituting the colony's assembly so as equitably to represent both free blacks and poor whites, soon becoming disgusted with the hypocrisy and reactionary views of the colony's whites, who took to opposing him at every turn.[58]

Dissolving the colonial assembly on Saint-Domingue, in October 1792, Sonthonax and his colleagues replaced it with an interim commission of twelve, comprising six whites and six blacks, including Charles Guillaume Castaing, among Cap-Français' principal propertied men of color and soon Sonthonax's most trusted black advisor, an eager supporter of the Revolution, educated in France. White royalist officers were purged. To help prepare black representatives for political life, the commissioners established a local mixed-race political club at Cap-Français affiliated to the (pre-1793 Brissotin) Jacobins. A state of acute tension was reached on 2 December 1792 when Sonthonax summoned several hundred mulatto and free black National Guard to face down a white militia unit encamped on the Champ-de-Mars, outside the town, refusing officers of mixed race, a confrontation between blacks and "foes of equality and the law of 4 April," as the *Patriote français* expressed it, leading to a violent clash. According to a letter from his brother in Saint-Domingue to Raimond in Paris, the affray resulted in the death of thirty whites and six free blacks, and only narrowly avoided becoming a pitched battle.[59] Castaing later returned to France where, in 1794, after being saved from the guillotine during the Terror, he married Françoise de Beauharnais, stepsister and cousin of Josephine; Napoleon (apparently prejudiced against blacks) reportedly viewed him with loathing.

Although the Brissotin commissioners failed to end the slave revolt in the northern hills, for a time this probably helped stabilize their grip on the colony as many disgruntled whites were now too apprehensive of black insurgency to risk directly opposing the revolutionary regime. For a time, the *commissaires* kept most of France's most valuable colony under revolutionary control, in contrast to Martinique where

[57] Brissot, *Mémoires* ii. 300–1; Régent, *France*, 242–3; Loft, *Passion, Politics*, 213; Popkin, *You are all free*, 87.

[58] Brissot, *Mémoires* ii. 293–4; Raimond, *Réflexions*, 35–6; Nesbitt, *Universal Emancipation*, 145–6.

[59] Girey-Duré, *Patriote français* 1278 (10 Feb. 1793), 164–5.

open royalist planter revolt against the Republic commenced in late September 1792; this was overwhelmed after a struggle in January 1793 by republican officials and troops backed by many *petits blancs*, but re-erupted with redoubled force in April 1793, again backed by some *petits blancs*. Aided by newly arrived French *émigrés*, Martinique's white colonists had largely defeated the Republic and its decrees, under the banner of *royalisme* and counter-revolution, proclaiming their alliance with the British (who captured Tobago from France in February 1793) many months before 7,000 British troops arrived on a powerful armada that completed the Revolution's defeat on Martinique and Guadeloupe between February and April 1794.[60] Fort Royal, Martinique's main naval and military base, recently renamed Républiqueville, now reverted to being called Fort Royal. On Saint-Domingue, beside rebel royalist white planters, newly arrived *émigrés*, and royalist free blacks, Sonthonax faced stubborn resistance from the *petits blancs*, especially white sailors and artisans servicing Saint-Domingue's ports and shipping. Subject to harsh discipline and largely illiterate, this deeply aggrieved element proved peculiarly receptive to the notion of racial superiority promoted by royalists and populist anti-*philosophique* decriers of the Revolution.

Facing burgeoning internal opposition, while fending off the land and sea forces of Britain and Spain, now at war with France, was no easy task. To complicate matters further, the commissioners became the butt of ferocious criticism directed at them by the Montagne in France. The Montagne, contrary to the views of those who associate Robespierre and his allies with the black emancipation movement, initially evinced considerably less concern for ending slavery, and more sympathy for the white planters, than the Brissotins.[61] Despite its efforts to improve the lot of Saint-Domingue's free blacks, friction between Sonthonax's regime and sections of the black populace intensified, many free blacks and *gens de couleur* refusing to share Castaing's pro-Sonthonax sympathies, preferred to remain a privileged group ranked above the slaves, who mostly found the newly proclaimed revolutionary principles deeply baffling. Illiterate, both slaves and poor free blacks, Sonthonax reported to Paris, had difficulty in grasping the abstract principles of republican liberty and equality, mostly preferring to think it was "their king" who wanted to free them and his royal will that was being thwarted by evil councilors and slave-owners. In insurgent districts, Catholic as well as Voodoo priests remained influential and many black rebels also abhorred the white democrats' overt irreligion. That many blacks preferred royalism and Catholic devotion to republican ideas, slaves especially, only confirmed to Sonthonax's mind that without *la philosophie* humans are hopelessly adrift and blind to their own true interests.[62] Sonthonax showed considerable

[60] Cormack, *Patriots, Royalists*, 123–4, 132, 173, 182–5.

[61] Bourdin and Chappey, *Révoltes et révolutions*, 249; Geggus, *Haitian Revolutionary Studies*, 161; Popkin, *You are all free*, 13–14; Israel, *Revolutionary Ideas*, 406–13; Cormack, *Patriots, Royalists*, 189.

[62] Blackburn, *Overthrow*, 197–9, 228–9; Régent, *France et ses esclaves*, 243–5; Girard, *Toussaint Louverture*, 122–3, 126.

sympathy for Saint-Domingue's black inhabitants in principle, but none for the northern insurgency which he considered madness rooted in religion.

But enough free blacks supported the revolutionary regime to thoroughly antagonize the white populace of Port-au-Prince, which grew so intransigent that, in April 1793, they had to be blockaded with the aid of local free blacks and then bombarded into submission. As the town fell, hundreds of royalist counter-revolutionary whites fled into the interior; others were caught and imprisoned. Jacmel was similarly reduced with black help. Soon the situation in the colonial capital, Cap-Français, too became extremely fraught. Again, the chief agents of counter-revolutionary unrest were neither free blacks nor slaves but obstreperous *petits blancs* championing white supremacy and the old colonial assembly. Sonthonax's Cap-Français adversaries, frequently white refugees from the interior insurgency, or sailors and merchants whose livelihoods were disrupted by the maritime war with Britain, became increasingly rancorous. A fraught situation became a full-scale crisis on 20 June, when the Cap-Français sailors mutinied and set siege to the Brissotin commission's headquarters, the governor's house.

Units of free black militia rallied to the commission's defense. Amid the fighting, and on their own initiative, initially merely as a local emergency measure, the commissioners issued the momentous edict of 21 June 1793, offering local slaves their freedom if they would fight for the Revolution. In consequence, the fighting and killing spread. Fires started; houses were pillaged. Finally, like Port-au-Prince earlier, the entire town was engulfed in flames and reduced to ashes. Besides several thousand blacks, over a thousand whites were butchered, often with their throats slit, in the dreadful slaughter. Whites who escaped did so mostly by reaching vessels in the harbor, often bringing (usually) female slaves with them. The survivors fled by sea to Philadelphia, New York, Charleston, and other North American ports, bringing lurid accounts of what had transpired and electrifying the American South with the frightening specter of a spreading Caribbean Revolution. "The situation of the Saint-Domingue fugitives," commented Jefferson amid the gloom, "(aristocrats as they are) calls aloud for pity and charity." "I become daily more and more convinced, that all the West India Islands will remain in the hands of the people of colour, and a total expulsion of the whites [will] sooner or later take place."[63]

24.2. TOUSSAINT LOUVERTURE'S BLACK REVOLUTION

The 21 June emancipation decree was a true historical landmark. Over the next four months, the emancipation process extended to the entire colony, the northern province receiving its own local decree, citing the *Declaration of Rights of Man*, on

[63] Quoted in Meacham, *Thomas Jefferson*, 255.

29 August.[64] By October 1793, all Saint-Domingue's slaves were officially free, though this still failed to rally the black insurgency in the interior to the Revolution's side. Toussaint Louverture (1743–1803), a highly talented former slave who had learnt to read and write and emerged during the summer of 1793 as the principal insurgent leader in the hills, construed "liberty" to mean independence from French control rather than allying with Sonthonax. Initially, he preferred playing off the Spaniards of the larger eastern (but less populated and cultivated) part of the island against the French.[65] In exchange for fighting for religion and monarchy against the Revolution, the Spanish authorities in Santo Domingo provided munitions and permitted rebel black commanders to operate on their own.

Saint-Domingue's revolutionaries had simultaneously to fight white *contre-révolutionnaires*, insurgent ex-slaves in the hills, invading Spanish troops arriving from Cuba, Puerto Rico, and Venezuela, and the British while fending off the Montagne in France. Britain continued recruiting hundreds of French *émigrés* for intervention in France *and* for its drive to strip France of its colonies.[66] In the same month Britain occupied Martinique, February 1794, Malouet, proclaiming the indispensable necessity of slavery in the West Indies,[67] negotiated the so-called "Whitehall Accord" proclaiming the French Caribbean royalists' backing for Britain's projected occupation of the French Caribbean generally. In Martinique, where around 82,000 slaves toiled alongside some 4,000 free blacks (4,3 per cent of the population), the British were warmly welcomed by the white planters but, for several weeks, stubbornly resisted by the governor and bands of French revolutionaries supported by blacks.[68] Guadeloupe's whites were equally deeply divided. In Saint-Domingue, the main allied incursion commenced in May 1794 with Spanish troops occupying the hill country astride the border, while in the south the British and *émigrés* seized Port-au-Prince and some coastal areas.

It was at this crucial point, from May 1794, with Sonthonax's authority crumbling, that the republicans were saved by none other than Toussaint, who now had second thoughts about the wisdom of opposing the Revolution allied to Spain and Britain, imperial powers plainly intent on restoring slavery along with monarchy and religion. As more Spanish troops arrived, Toussaint performed a sudden volte-face: publicly disavowing the "enemies of the Republic and the human race," he realigned his 4,000 men behind the beleaguered Sonthonax.[69] At this juncture, Toussaint had apparently not yet studied the French National Convention's emancipation decree proclaimed by the Montagnard-dominated National Convention in Paris intended to thwart the Caribbean Anglo-Spanish offensive by rallying black support against it. This initiative

64 Popkin, *You are all free*, 210–11; 234–5, 248–9; Garrigus, "Opportunist," 11; Hunt, *Inventing*, 165.

65 Raimond, *Réflexions*, 10; Popkin, *You are all free*, 250–1; Girard, *Toussaint Louverture*, 96, 133–4.

66 Raimond, *Réflexions*, 8, 10; Geggus, *Haitian Revolutionary Studies*, 18.

67 Raimond, *Réflexions*, 8, 15–16; Salverda, "Involvement of Pierre-Victor Malouet," 213–26.

68 Bourdin and Chappey, *Révoltes et révolutions*, 247; Cormack, *Patriots, Royalists*, 182–4.

69 Toussaint Louverture, *Lettres*, 155–8; Girard, *Haiti*, 43; Geggus, *Haitian Revolutionary Studies*, 130–5.

was pushed through by Danton, who, with another of his rousing speeches, helped secure the world's first general slave emancipation edict, dated 4 February 1794.[70] But, as Toussaint himself reports in a surviving letter, he *had* examined the decrees by June 1794 when he proclaimed the February edict happy news "for all the friends of humanity," and expressed keen interest in the progress of French arms in Europe.[71] His subsequent use of universalist Brissotin revolutionary language in letters to French commanders, a style originating in the *Histoire philosophique*, may not of itself be proof, but the evidence suggests that in the summer of 1794 Toussaint did become a revolutionary sincerely embracing Brissotin universalist rhetoric drawn from *la philosophie moderne*.[72] He readily adopted also the symbolic changes accompanying the Revolution's progress in Saint-Domingue, including the changed names of key locations, Port-au-Prince under Toussaint's regime keeping its Brissotin title "Port Républicain."[73]

The February 1794 decree, however significant in principle, exerted little immediate effect in the Caribbean since Saint-Domingue's slaves were already free while Britain barred implementation on Martinique, Sainte-Lucie, and Guadeloupe. Formal abolition ensued only in Cayenne where there were relatively few slaves, 10,400 comprising 78 per cent of the population. Abolition there was trumpeted amid fanfares on 14 June 1794, a few weeks before Robespierre's downfall. Under the emancipation decree's terms, the newly created black "citizens" had to register with their nearest municipality to obtain certificates of citizenship and to contract with their former owners, opting whether to work for wages or on a sharecropping basis. Freed slaves, under the Cayenne colonial assembly's regulations, were supposed not to move from their previous domiciles to seek new homes or employment without their former owners' permission. In effect, they were not entirely freed and did not always much benefit.[74]

Meanwhile, rumors circulated in the Caribbean (and the United States) that the Montagne, now masters in Paris, repudiated Sonthonax and his commission's actions and authority. Having crushed Brissot's faction, the victors canceled the commissioners' powers. As the Montagnard group dictatorship consolidated, the white anti-emancipationist camp recovered some lost ground.[75] Despite neo-Marxist historiography claiming the contrary, Robespierre and his allies hardly matched Brissotin radicality regarding racial egalitarianism or black (or women's, or Jewish) emancipation. A populist Counter-Enlightenment, *robespierrisme* was chiefly concerned with suppressing dissent, restricting freedom of expression, curtailing basic freedoms. Lavishly employing political untruths, Robespierre and his following preferred blaming the chaotic turmoil in Saint-Domingue and Martinique on the Brissotins rather

[70] Doyle, *Oxford History*, 412; Lawday, *Danton*, 240; Popkin, *You are all free*, 356.
[71] Toussaint Louverture, *Lettres*, 165, 172; Régent, *France et ses esclaves*, 249–50.
[72] Baggio and Augustin, "Introduction," 98–9; Girard, *Toussaint Louverture*, 96.
[73] Toussaint Louverture, *Memoir*, 60–1; Nesbitt, *Universal Emancipation*, 147–8.
[74] Bourdin and Chappey, *Révoltes et révolutions*, 243; Régent, *France et ses esclaves*, 252.
[75] Popkin, *You are all free*, 338, 344.

than on anti-revolutionary white colonists. Amar, the official drawing up the official indictment against Brissot, was particularly active in backing the white colonist lobby against the emancipationists; but in his Convention speech on 18 November 1793, Robespierre in person joined in, flagrantly perverting the truth by accusing the Brissot faction of colluding with Britain and deliberately arming Saint-Domingue's slaves to ruin France's colonies to help salvage monarchy, aristocracy, and Counter-Revolution.[76]

Raimond, the mulatto leader in Paris, still supported Brissot and Sonthonax well after it became unsafe to do so. After clashes with Montagnard and pro-colonist opponents at meetings of the Convention's colonial committee, he was arrested on 27 September 1793. Two representatives (one white) sent to petition the Convention to endorse Sonthonax's emancipation decrees were also imprisoned. Arriving with them, the black representative, Jean-Baptiste Belley (*c.*1746–1805), wounded while commanding the "free blacks" in the defense of Government House during the Cap-Français fighting of 20–21 June 1793, likewise received a frosty reception. A freed former slave born in Senegal, in September 1793 Belley was the first black to occupy a seat as a deputy in France's legislature. The impressive portrait of him alongside a bust of Raynal, painted later, in 1797, by the revolutionary artist Anne-Louis Girodet (1767–1824), the most celebrated of all pictures linking the French Revolution to black emancipation, made France's first black deputy look formidable and yet "beautiful." In 1793–4, Belley continued battling for black rights in Paris against stiff opposition.[77]

Initially amicable relations between white colonists and the Montagne based on common detestation of Brissotins failed to last beyond early 1794, however, due to the *émigré* alliance with Britain and the vast scale of Britain's offensive against France's Caribbean colonies. With Martinique's whites openly collaborating and those of Saint-Domingue also allied with Britain and Spain, colonist collusion with monarchy and aristocracy had simply grown too overt and treasonable for the Montagne to tolerate further. Most French Caribbean colonies were now either occupied or in open rebellion, leaving the Montagnard-dominated Convention little alternative but ignore Amar and the white colonists and, even if somewhat half-heartedly, push universal and equal rights and general emancipation of the slaves. *Robespierriste* hostility to Caribbean Brissotins nevertheless continued unremittingly. In June 1794, orders arrived from Paris for Sonthonax's arrest. Cornered by pro-Robespierre forces, at Jacmel, the commissioners who had freed Saint-Domingue's slaves were brought back to France and imprisoned. The executors of slavery's abolition were saved from the guillotine only by a fortunate delay: a week after Robespierre was toppled, the two Brissotin *commissaires* were freed.

The Caribbean revolutionary arena, meanwhile, had expanded well beyond Saint-Domingue and Cayenne as the French recovered some lost ground. A small fleet and

[76] McPhee, *Robespierre*, 173. [77] Crow, *Emulation*, 160–1.

1,200 troops arrived under a leader of the La Rochelle Jacobin Club, Victor Hugues (1770–1826), appointed civil commissioner for Guadeloupe with responsibility to emancipate the slaves there. Despite facing a superior British force, Hugues, helped by rebel slaves and "free blacks," recovered part of Guadeloupe and launched a successful mini-revolutionary onslaught from this enclave. Freeing all the island's 83,000 slaves, comprising 85 per cent of the population, by October 1794, he had beaten the fever-ridden 3,000-strong British garrison and royalist plantation-owners. Surrendering their supplies, thirty-eight cannon, some "free blacks," and 800 counter-revolutionary *émigrés*, the British were allowed to sail away. Using a guillotine specially brought from France, Hugues had several French noble *émigrés* executed. After seemingly extirpating slavery and royalism from Guadeloupe, he organized a privateer fleet financed by both the Republic and private investors, manned partly by black sailors, that over the next four years seized substantial numbers of British, Spanish, and American vessels. Hugues also fomented a prolonged black uprising against the British on Sainte-Lucie, St Vincent, and Grenada.[78]

The Caribbean revolutionary arena then widened dramatically further, from late 1794, following the French invasion and overthrow of the Orangist regime in the Dutch Republic which intensified the already bitter splits between democrats and Orangists on Curaçao and the five other Dutch Caribbean islands as well as Surinam and western Guyana, then both in Dutch possession. Neither Orangists nor Dutch republican Patriots in the Caribbean favored emancipating the slaves, but the Dutch "Patriots," being allied to France, could not prevent revolutionary propaganda being diffused on the Dutch islands, or Guadeloupe privateers manned by partly black crews frequenting Curaçao's strategically-placed harbor. In the poor Otrobanda section of Willemstad, the island's capital, blacks and mulattoes, including seamen from French vessels anchored nearby, held gatherings and took to singing provocative songs. Fights broke out between revolutionary sailors, often black or mulatto, and pro-British Orangist members of the Curaçao military garrison. Before long, a major mixed slave and free black revolt erupted both on Curaçao and, in May 1795, equally inspired by the French and Haitian revolutions and talk of founding a "republic," the neighboring Venezuelan region of Coro, where the insurgency took on a racially still more mixed character.[79] Among the biggest Caribbean black risings of the revolutionary era, the 1795 Curaçao and Coro risings, contemporary reports and correspondence confirm, were definitely triggered by reports of black emancipation in Saint-Domingue, Guadeloupe, Sainte-Lucie, and Cayenne.[80] In March 1795, mixed slave and free black revolts, flaunting standards inscribed "Liberté, Égalité ou la Mort" dispatched from Guadeloupe, erupted likewise on the formerly French islands of

[78] Bourdin and Chappey, *Révoltes et révolutions*, 243, 248; Cormack, *Patriots, Royalists*, 197–204, 224–5.

[79] Jordaan, "Patriots, privateers," 154–5; Jordaan, *Slavernij en vrijheid*, 18, 181; Soriano, *Tides of Revolution*, 117–19.

[80] Thomas, *Slave Trade*, 566; Klooster, "Rising Expectations," 66–7; Oostindie, *Ethnicity*, 58.

Grenada and St Vincent. Led by the legendary mulatto landowner Julien Fédon (d. 1796?), these too were inspired by the Haitian revolution and French republican propaganda, and initially successful on both islands. Fédon was long remembered as a local Caribbean folk hero.[81]

The Coro slave and "free black" revolt began on 10 May 1795 on a plantation in the sierra above Coro and spread rapidly to neighboring plantations. If relatively few blacks could read French revolutionary literature, Castaing, Toussaint, Raimond, and Belley were not the only ones who could. In the islands and on the neighboring mainland existed a small fringe of literate blacks, an incipient proto-intelligentsia in the making, susceptible to radical ideas, who helped foment the clandestine milieu from which the black revolutionary leaders emerged. In 1795, a *pardo* musician named Juan Bautista Olivares greatly alarmed the Caracas authorities on being found to have read and explained to mulatto and *pardo* friends Spanish translations of French Revolution documents expounding liberty and equality. In prison, Olivares proved "subversive and arrogant" enough to urge other "people of his own class to shake off the yoke of obedience and vassalage."[82] On the Coro peninsula, besides blacks, local Indians joined in the rising. Plantation houses were pillaged. On 12 May the main rebel force, led by José Leonardo Chirinos, a local *zambo* (son of a slave and an Indian woman) able to read and write, a free black married to a slave woman, advanced on the town but was defeated by the armed militia assembled by the local white populace. In the subsequent pursuit, many rebels were caught and brutally executed. Subsequent enquiries showed that whilst accompanying a Spanish merchant on Caribbean business trips, Chirinos had collected information about the French, Haitian, Curaçao, and Guadeloupe revolutions.[83]

Under the Franco-Spanish peace of Basel (1795), Spanish Santo Domingo was ceded to France. A region with a relatively large "white" population estimated at 50,000, some 60,000 *gens de couleur*, and only around 15,000 slaves—a tiny proportion compared to the French part of the island before 1793[84]—in theory, this further extended black emancipation and the strategic threat to Britain's Caribbean hegemony. But it was not until January 1801 that Toussaint's men entered Spanish Santo Domingo in force. Meanwhile, counter-revolutionary efforts in Haiti and Santo Domingo persisted through 1796–8, hampering efforts to restore order in war-torn Saint-Domingue and its decimated agriculture with continuing disturbances and conspiracies backed by both British and Spaniards (toward whom Toussaint remained particularly antagonistic). Struggling to curb the disorder instigated by "enemies of liberty and equality," Toussaint, ensconced in his mountainous strongholds, continued issuing proclamations in the name of the French Republic.[85] "It is absolutely necessary," he assured the new French governor, Étienne Laveaux, that

[81] Blackburn, *Overthrow*, 230–2; Spillemaker, "Guerres révolutionnaires," 120–1, 123, 127.
[82] Klooster, "Rising Expectations," 59–60; Soriano, *Tides of Revolution*, 72–4.
[83] Aizpurua, "Revolution," 99; Thibauld, "*Salus Populi*," 342; Soriano, *Tides of Revolution*, 141–2.
[84] Régent, *France et ses esclaves*, 258.
[85] Toussaint Louverture, *Lettres*, 337–8, 340–1, 346.

"citizens of these quarters conform to the laws of the Republic and keep themselves in proper order, and have a good citizen to command them, wise and very firm in good principles."[86] Having become a devotee of Raynal and the *Histoire philosophique*, Toussaint took to recommending that bible of global revolution to others and emphasizing Haitian blacks' right to be "French citizens," their desire to be "free and French." Suggesting Toussaint was indeed the "black Spartacus prophesied by Raynal" who would "avenge the outrages upon his race," Laveaux acknowledged his loyalty, in May 1796, appointing him Lieutenant-Governor.[87]

De facto control of Saint-Domingue only slowly slipped from the grip of the Paris *Directoire*. The turning-point occurred in 1797 when Toussaint suddenly broke with Sonthonax, who had returned to head the administration of Saint-Domingue in the spring of 1796. The exact nature of their rupture and brief power struggle has never been fully explained, though doubtless it was chiefly a question of who was now controlling the country. Since returning Sonthonax had worked to regain his grip on the Haitian Revolution and of the island itself.[88] Elbowing Sonthonax aside and assuming effective control of the island's governance and administration in effect meant repudiating the *Directoire*'s authority, which Toussaint now did but without saying so. Shortly after the French elections of March 1797 in which royalists briefly won control of the French lower legislature and seemed strong enough to begin dismantling the Revolution, with the area under direct French control in Saint-Domingue steadily contracting, Sonthonax was again seized by white colonists and, with Toussaint's agreement, dispatched to France. Colluding in deporting Sonthonax, the French Republic's last remaining *commissaire* on Haiti, Julien Raimond (though he too was afterwards sent back), briefly joined forces with Toussaint.[89]

During the 1797–8 transition period whilst Saint-Domingue hovered between remaining under France and full independence, the black revolutionists, ignoring calls to eliminate the island's remaining whites, consistently abjured outright independence.[90] Raimond's collaboration helped keep up the appearance that Toussaint governed Saint-Domingue for France under French revolutionary auspices. Indeed, at this stage Toussaint claimed to be more loyal to France than Sonthonax, and neither to be seeking full independence nor in any way seeking to turn on the whites. No one should suppose Sonthonax was more upright and republican than he, or "more of a friend to the liberty of the blacks." If Sonthonax seemed to speak in favor of liberty, he was actually a "monster" betraying the "republicans," a thoroughgoing scoundrel as

[86] Toussaint Louverture to Laveaux, 22 Feb. 1796, in Toussaint Louverture, *Lettres*, 305; Girard, *Toussaint Louverture*, 165.

[87] Griggs and Prator, *Henry Christophe*, 16–17; Toussaint Louverture, *Lettres*, 95; Oldfield, *Transatlantic Abolitionism*, 122; Conrad, "Enlightenment," 1014; Girard, *Toussaint Louverture*, 171.

[88] Girard, *Toussaint Louverture*, 166–7, 170.

[89] Toussaint Louverture to Laveaux, 12 Sept. 1797, in Toussaint Louverture, *Lettres*, 369–70; Blackburn, *Overthrow*, 238.

[90] Toussaint Louverture, *Lettres*, 374; Buck-Morss, "Hegel and Haiti," 834.

perfidious as Robespierre: "Robespierre too spoke of *la liberté* but what would have happened to the Republic without 9 Thermidor?"[91]

The Franco-Dutch Caribbean revolution of the mid-1790s precipitating black emancipation provoked the utmost alarm and consternation in London and Madrid. The revolution cast its shadow throughout the region just as the British and Spanish colonies promised to become much more lucrative, with the collapse of Saint-Domingue's sugar and coffee production creating boom conditions in Cuba, where many French planters from Saint-Domingue had sought refuge, and in Jamaica.[92] So alarming did resurgent Franco-Dutch democratic-revolutionary arms, privateering, and rhetoric in the Caribbean appear to Prime Minister Pitt that despite the disappointing results of the 1793–4 offensive, a renewed and expanded British counter-offensive was prepared and launched during 1795–6, under Sir Ralph Abercromby (1734–1801), commanding the largest expedition ever sent across the Atlantic until then, nearly 100 ships and 30,000 troops. This huge armada joined the substantial British forces already in the Caribbean, together representing a truly massive commitment of resources aimed at reversing the Revolution and black emancipation, and extending British sway.

With overwhelming naval and military superiority and supporting resources, this unprecedented counter-offensive secured several important gains. Grenada and Saint Vincent were recovered in June 1796; the western Guyana colonies of Demerara, Berbice, and Essequibo were seized from the Dutch; and in 1797 undefended Trinidad and Tobago were overrun. Finally, in 1800, Curaçao was taken. But, against this, there was also the humiliation of the final failure of Britain's five-year occupation of parts of coastal Haiti (1793–8) and the heavy repulse of an attack force of 7,000 troops, brought up in sixty vessels, after a two-week siege, during April and May 1797, of San Juan, capital of Puerto Rico.[93] France's National Convention dispatched much smaller expeditions to Guadeloupe and Saint-Domingue but, with black help, these sufficed to hold the line.[94] Yellow fever and malaria exacted an appalling toll on both the British seamen and troops and the many French *émigrés* and German mercenaries in British pay. Altogether over 50,000 British troops and sailors died or disappeared, through enemy action, disease, and desertion, combating the Caribbean General Revolution between 1793 and 1798 when the British withdrew the last of their troops from Saint-Domingue. Around half of these stupendous losses, some 25,000 dead, were incurred in the southern Caribbean on Guadeloupe, Grenada, Martinique, and Sainte-Lucie, where the British were stubbornly resisted by a mix of blacks and *petit blanc* republicans; about one-third of the total, some 14,000 troops, expired on Saint-Domingue.[95]

[91] Toussaint Louverture to Laveaux, 1 June 1798, in Toussaint Louverture, *Lettres*, 372–4.
[92] Thomas, *Slave Trade*, 530–1.
[93] Jiménez de Wagenheim, *Puerto Rico*, 101–3; Spillemaker, "Guerres révolutionnaires," 127.
[94] Geggus, "Cost of Pitt's Caribbean Campaigns," 699; Israel, *Revolutionary Ideas*, 416.
[95] Geggus, "Cost of Pitt's Caribbean Campaigns," 702–4; Cormack, *Patriots, Royalists*, 218.

Those disseminating "universal and equal rights" ideology widely around the Caribbean were not as a rule Haitian but more often white French republicans, together with rebel blacks from the smaller French colonies operating on sea and land from bases in Guadeloupe and the lesser Antilles, and Afro-Curaçaoans. Their main ally on Saint-Domingue, during the conflict of 1794–1800, was not Toussaint, who increasingly detached himself from the French from 1797, but the revolutionary mulatto leader André Rigaud (1761–1811), a literate goldsmith born of a white father and black mother who, from 1794, dominated Saint-Domingue's south, pursuing a more actively pro-French, republican agenda than Toussaint.[96] The essential impulse or agent of revolutionary subversion in the Caribbean thus remained France itself together with the republican clandestine Radical Enlightenment filtering through literate black minds, including Toussaint's and Rigaud's, channeled into subversion via Saint-Domingue, Guadeloupe, and Curaçao.

Although black representatives remained in the French National Assembly, from 1794 to 1799, real power on Saint-Domingue, by May 1798,[97] devolved onto local black leaders, Toussaint controlling the center and north, and Rigaud the south. For all his explicit republicanism, Rigaud nurtured a more racially hierarchical conception of Haitian society than Toussaint, whose army was principally composed of former slaves. Rigaud kept up more active ties with Guadeloupe and Curaçao but it was Toussaint who, in August 1800, finally won the struggle for Saint-Domingue. Anxious to consolidate the ex-colony's virtual independence, as he extended his reach over Haiti, Toussaint took to reassuring France's enemies, as he continued to do later, that Haiti's freed slaves did not aim (as Rigaud had) to export revolution to their colonies. He discontinued, in other words, his 1794–5 championing of the emancipating principles of the Revolution. Toussaint's post-1795 policy of isolationism and disengaging from conflict with Spain and Britain helped weaken the French Caribbean offensive and slowed the impetus of black emancipation outside Haiti. Still, consolidating liberty and freedom for Haiti's blacks, claimed Toussaint, as late as June 1798, meant remaining residually loyal to the French Republic.[98]

In France, concern lest the Revolution's republican achievements dissolve under the *Directoire*'s vacillations culminated in the coup of Brumaire (1799). Differently from previous *coups d'état*, Brumaire was inspired neither by the legislature, nor the *Directoire*, but a substantial, high-level group of disaffected political, legal, and constitutional reformers, orchestrated by Sieyès, including some of the foremost Radical Enlightenment theorists and journalists in the legislature and Paris Institute—Volney, Cabanis, Daunou, Marie-Joseph Chénier, Garat, and Say. If the Republic persisted on its current indecisive trajectory, believed the Brumairians, it would face inevitable eventual collapse.[99] They tried to realize their political–philosophical vision by securing the new human order of liberty, equal rights,

[96] Klooster, *Revolutions*, 105, 107.
[97] Fick, "Revolutionary S. Domingue," 25.
[98] Toussaint Louverture to Laveaux, 5 June 1798, in Toussaint Louverture, *Lettres*, 377; Girard, *Haiti*, 57.
[99] Welch, *Liberty*, 37–8; Bredin, *Sieyès*, 463–4.

freedom of expression, secularism, and representative constitutionalism, through authoritarian, extra-legal means.[100] Another leading voice for black emancipation, Lafayette, also supported the coup.[101]

Without actually declaring war on France, the United States, under Adams's presidency, increasingly sought, like Britain and Spain, to counter French revolutionary and democratic principles in the Atlantic world, and began moving closer to Britain. Converting Toussaint into a tool of American influence against revolutionary France became a particular aim of President Adams's fiercely Anglophile secretary of state, Timothy Pickering (1745–1829), an avowed foe of equality and the French Revolution. To establish normative commercial relations with the US and coax Toussaint to secede formally from France, placing Haiti under United States protection, Pickering sent an able consul-general (and yellow fever expert), Edward Stevens (1755–1834), who arrived in April 1799. For a time, collaboration was close and American support helped Toussaint capture Jacmel and defeat Rigaud. But Toussaint refused to terminate formal allegiance to France and insisted on remaining very much his own master. In January 1801, he sent a substantial force of black troops in into the former Spanish eastern two-thirds of Santo Domingo (ceded to France in 1795) which Napoleon planned to return to Spain with its former laws intact, to cement his Spanish alliance. Suspicious of the United States, Britain, Spain, and Napoleon, Toussaint, still conducting himself as a French republican general acting in the name of revolutionary France, now abolished slavery and erected French revolutionary flags on the Spanish part of the island.[102]

Maintaining the plantation system, trying to revive sugar exports and persuade freed slaves who had abandoned devastated interior and coastal areas to return to the land and resume agricultural work, remained high on Toussaint's list of priorities.[103] The spectacle of former slaves working their own seized land (albeit not yet always fully free), struggling to sustain Haiti's economy and population in defiance of foreign incursion, did not fail to have its effect. After succeeding Adams as president, in 1801, Jefferson suggested Saint-Domingue might become a safety-valve for America's own racial tensions, lessening the risk of the horrifying inter-racial violence in America he so dreaded. He conceived the idea of resettling, siphoning off, a portion of America's blacks in some remote quarter of North America, or else Africa, or else possibly the Caribbean. "The most promising portion of [the West Indies]," he assured Monroe, in November 1801, "is the island of St. Domingo, where the blacks are established into a sovereignty *de facto*, and have organized themselves under regular laws and

[100] Gaulmier, *Grand Témoin*, 234–6; Forsyth, *Reason*, 8–9; Harris, *Antoine d'Estutt de Tracy*, 28; Jainchill, *Reimagining Politics*, 198–200.

[101] Lafayette, *Mémoires* v. 245–6; Wood, "Benjamin Constant," 8.

[102] Brown, *Toussaint's Clause*, 123–4, 185; Cuevas Pérez and Dias Bido, *Presencia francesa*, 116–17; Fick, "Revolutionary S. Domingue," 36.

[103] Toussaint Louverture to Laveaux, 17 June and 22 Aug. 1795, in Toussaint Louverture, *Lettres*, 208–9, 236; Toussaint Louverture, *Memoir*, 52–3; Bourdin and Chappey, *Révoltes et révolutions*, 250; Fick, "Revolutionary S. Domingue," 33.

government." The prospect both attracted and troubled him: in Jefferson's thinking racial fear had come to eclipse his republicanism and commitment to equality.[104]

Writing to Toussaint in early 1801, Napoleon made no mention of any plan to reassert direct French control over Saint-Domingue; he merely urged Toussaint to continue his efforts to restore order and revive the island's agriculture. Having beaten Rigaud and occupying Spanish Santo Domingo in defiance of Napoleon,[105] Toussaint, at the zenith of his career, convened a constitutional convention in Haiti, choosing the deputies himself. He proclaimed Haiti's first constitution on 8 July 1801, abolishing slavery on the island forever, and declaring himself governor of all Hispaniola, both the French and Spanish parts, for life. But while initiating self-rule and the authoritarian traditions that characterized Haiti's development from then on, Toussaint's constitution still nominally acknowledged French sovereignty.[106] At first, Napoleon gave no indication of his displeasure. He did not share the principled stance of the *Amis des Noirs*, Volney, Say, or Destutt, but his recorded statements about Caribbean slavery during 1798–1800 betray no hint of any intention to reintroduce slavery—rather the contrary, though conceivably this was just well-masked guile.[107] While some of the international democratic republican revolutionary fraternity, like the Polish emancipator Kościuszko, angrily condemned Napoleon's ambition and quest for power from the outset,[108] many of the original Brumairian conspirators, including Volney and Constant, despite troubling doubts, still hoped that, through Napoleon, the core republican achievement and human rights could be salvaged and upheld.

For the time being, Napoleon had reason to continue under the guise of a republican general committed to revolutionary values, and he well knew that without endorsing permanent abolition of slavery there was scant likelihood of reconciliation with Saint-Domingue's black population. If it was in response to the First Consul's consolidation of personal power in France that Toussaint consolidated and extended his own during 1800–1, the news that Toussaint had extended his grip over Spanish Santo Domingo sufficiently annoyed Napoleon for him to cancel his initial confirmation of Toussaint's title as Lieutenant-Governor, provoking a rift between them. Plainly, Toussaint would obstruct all plans for reviving French power and empire in the New World, including the formerly flourishing French sugar trade and huge profits Bordeaux and Nantes had derived from it.

Napoleon's ambition first obtruded into the Caribbean during negotiations over the Peace of Amiens with Britain, in late 1801. At this point, he commenced preparations to restore French Caribbean power while (secretly) planning to reintroduce slavery in the French colonies to provide a social and economic base for renewed empire. Jefferson's narrow victory in the fall 1800 American presidential election

[104] Jefferson to Monroe, 24 Nov. 1801, in Jefferson, *Writings*, 1098.

[105] Brown, *Toussaint's Clause*, 174–5.

[106] Davis, *Problem of Slavery*, 30, 150; Bourdin and Chappey, *Révoltes et révolutions*, 249.

[107] Gueniffey, *Bonaparte*, 596–8, 657; Roberts, *Napoleon the Great*, 300–1; Cormack, *Patriots, Royalists*, 257.

[108] Nash and Gao Hodges, *Friends of Liberty*, 171–2.

removed the threat of war between the United States and France, and Pickering's agent from Cap-François. With Franco-American relations improving, the United States, Napoleon believed, would not oppose his reasserting French control over Haiti or France's and the Dutch Republic's numerous other lost colonies. Ignoring Volney, who tried to dissuade him from trying to re-subjugate the former Saint-Domingue, pointing out that the blacks would fight tenaciously for their freedom and that any European army sent out would suffer disastrous depletion from yellow fever, Napoleon pushed ahead despite knowing that sending an army to the Caribbean would antagonize Britain probably to the point of preferring to resume the war rather than acquiesce in France retrieving its lost New World possessions, power, and resources.[109]

Jefferson too could hardly countenance the kind of grandiose French American empire Napoleon had in mind. When, in May 1801, news reached America of the secret treaty of San Ildefonso (1 October 1800) whereby, in exchange for dynastic concessions in Tuscany, Spain's royal house transferred the entire (since 1763) nominally Spanish, North American Louisiana territory to France, there suddenly loomed the very real possibility of a colossal French empire arising in the Americas based on military force and practically adjoining the United States. The troops being sent to Saint-Domingue, Jefferson understood, "were to proceed to Louisiana after finishing their work," as he expressed it, in April 1802, "in that island." Where "Spain might have retained it quietly for years," French acquisition of the Louisiana territory, with control of New Orleans and the Mississippi estuary, the United States could not accept.[110] Such an attempted shift in the power and territorial balance in North America must blight Franco-American relations. "From that moment," concluded Jefferson, "we must marry ourselves to the British fleet and nation,"[111] a distasteful prospect in his eyes.[112]

Where Jefferson and his administration showed scant inclination, despite the libertarian and republican values they proclaimed, to encourage Haitian independence or champion universal black emancipation, or the international movement to suppress slavery, Bonaparte, still more cynically (but as yet only secretly),[113] repudiated the freedom and self-determination of Haiti's blacks altogether. Late in 1801, the First Consul dispatched two powerful fleets to the Caribbean—the smaller to Guadeloupe, Tobago, and Sainte-Lucie (all of which were recovered, though the latter two only fleetingly, being retaken by Britain in June 1803), and the larger, prepared in Brest, to Saint-Domingue, commanded by Charles Victor Emmanuel Leclerc (1772–1802), husband of Napoleon's favorite sister, Pauline, who had figured among Humbert's officers during the 1798 Irish expedition and closely supported

[109] Gaulmier, *Grand Témoin*, 256–7; Furstenberg, *When the United States Spoke French*, 387–90, 392.
[110] Quoted in Brown, *Toussaint's Clause*, 211.
[111] Jefferson, *Writings*, 1105; Matthewson, "Jefferson and Haiti," 245–6.
[112] Brown, *Toussaint's Clause*, 211; Burstein and Isenberg, *Madison and Jefferson*, 375–7, 379–80.
[113] Gueniffey, *Bonaparte*, 658; Roberts *Napoleon the Great*, 300–2; Cormack, *Patriots, Royalists*, 260–3.

Napoleon during the coup of Brumaire. Comprising fifty-four vessels, Leclerc's armada arrived off Cap-Français in February 1802, and landed the largest French force thus far ever sent to the Caribbean, 22,000 troops, subsequently reinforced, bringing total troop strength dispatched by Napoleon to Haiti considerably higher still, though perhaps not to the staggering 40,000 claimed by some historians.[114]

With this massive investment of French power, cash, and resources, as momentous as the British investment of 1796–7, the First Consul's objective was to carve a New World empire pivoting on Haiti and New Orleans and encompassing the entire Mississippi Valley. Saint-Domingue's main ports were swiftly occupied, as was the Spanish capital of Santo Domingo from where Leclerc's men ejected Toussaint's garrison that same month.[115] Overcoming initial resistance from black troops, the French also landed at Cap-Français. But one of Toussaint's commanders, Henry Christophe, supposedly (but probably not) without Toussaint's agreement, torched a good portion of the island's capital.[116] According to his later memoir, submitted to Napoleon whilst in captivity in France, Toussaint, absent from Cap-Français when Leclerc arrived, had never wanted to resist the French. The mayhem that ensued he blamed on Leclerc's lack of judgment and bludgeoning conduct.[117]

Leclerc freely posted up copies of Napoleon's decree proclaiming all citizens of Saint-Domingue, "whatever may be your origin and your color, are all Frenchmen; you are all free, and equal before God and the Republic," adding that the "Republic that has given us liberty [. . .] will never suffer it to be ravished from us."[118] This studied hypocrisy was part of Napoleon's three-stage devious plan for a revived French Saint-Domingue: first proclaim republican principles and promise the blacks their freedom while occupying the island's key strategic points; second, arrest and deport potential opponents; third, proceed to reintroduce slavery.[119] In any case, fighting soon resumed, with Toussaint re-supplied with weapons and powder by American merchants using outlying ports where Leclerc's blockade proved ineffective. Where British vessels were ordered to keep away, Jefferson made no effort to prevent Americans supplying the black insurgents through secondary ports. Leclerc found the United States administration much less co-operative in every way than Napoleon had expected: not only did Jefferson decline to co-operate with French agents, suppliers, and commissaries, or ease his financial difficulties, or help blockade Toussaint, but the Americans were plainly supplying the black insurgents.[120] By late March, sequestration of American cargoes and heavy-handed treatment of captured

[114] Geggus, *Haitian Revolutionary Studies*, 25; Matthewson, "Jefferson and Haiti," 209; Roberts, *Napoleon the Great*, 300.

[115] Cuevas Perez and Diaz Bido, *Presencia francesa*, 117.

[116] Toussaint Louverture, *Memoir*, 65, 157; Brown, *Toussaint's Clause*, 204–5; Girard, *Toussaint Louverture*, 236.

[117] Toussaint Louverture, *Memoir*, 58–9.

[118] Griggs and Prator, *Henry Christophe*, 21; Brown, *Toussaint's Clause*, 200–3.

[119] Roberts, *Napoleon the Great*, 300–1.

[120] Matthewson, "Jefferson and Haiti," 229–30; Brown, *Toussaint's Clause*, 216–17.

American skippers and crews resulting from the French attempting to enforce their prohibition on neutral ships entering Saint-Domingue's ports—a ban the United States refused to acknowledge—had provoked a serious quarrel between France and its fellow republic.

24.3. HAITIAN INDEPENDENCE

After three months' fighting, Leclerc defeated Toussaint and exacted his surrender, under terms agreed in May 1802. In the last days of the struggle, several of his own commanders, notably Henry Christophe (1767–1820), destined to play a central role in the Haitian Revolution's final stages, abandoned their chief and negotiated their own withdrawal separately. Under the terms of Christophe's surrender, Leclerc confirmed the basis of the new code for French Saint-Domingue would be "liberty and equality" and that "the negroes will be free."[121] At no stage was anything said about reintroduction of slavery. But already, in March 1802, when, under the Anglo-French Peace of Amiens, Britain returned Martinique (where slavery had been maintained intact), the French, contrary to expectation, made no move to abolish slavery there. When news arrived of new laws promulgated in Paris, in May, proclaiming re-establishment of slavery and the slave-trade in Guadeloupe and Cayenne (albeit for the moment avoiding use of the term "slavery"), general outrage convulsed the entire network of the French Caribbean's black communities, including Saint-Domingue. In Cayenne, slavery was presently reinstated by none other than the ruthless Hugues, now a loyal servant of Napoleon The man who had earlier introduced the "Terror" to the French Caribbean, and nominally abolished slavery in 1794, had also denied freedom of movement to the blacks, retaining what amounted to forced labor in place—tyrannical conduct earning him the epithets "Robespierre of the Caribbean" and "Robespierre's most perfect student."[122]

The cynical character of Napoleon's promises was suddenly plain for all to see. France had now abandoned its role, maintained since 1792, as herald of black emancipation in the trans-Atlantic world.[123] Black insurgency, having only just subsided in Haiti, immediately flared again, everyone now realizing Napoleon's real objective was permanent colonial rule with slavery reintroduced to work the sugar and coffee plantations producing for export to Europe.[124] Before this happened, though, in May 1802, Leclerc's officers, colluding with Henry Christophe and another leading black commander, General Jean-Jacques Dessalines (1758–1806), captured

[121] Griggs and Prator, *Henry Christophe*, 26–7; Régent, *France*, 265–6; Brown, *Toussaint's Clause*, 225.

[122] Spieler, "Abolition and Re-Enslavement," 146–7; Cormack, *Patriots, Royalists*, 200–1, 219–25.

[123] Geggus, "Louisiana Purchase," 120; Régent, *France*, 268, 273; Roberts, *Napoleon the Great*, 300–1.

[124] Brown, *Toussaint's Clause*, 219–20; Oldfield, *Transatlantic Abolitionism*, 165–6; Curran, *Anatomy*, 208–9.

the betrayed Toussaint by deception and deported him to France, where, imprisoned in the Jura, he died in April 1803 without being formally tried or sentenced.[125]

Restoring slavery on Guadeloupe immediately wrecked Leclerc's ideological and moral standing, rupturing his alliance with Christophe and Dessalines. Reversal of the black equality program stretched so far that abolitionist writings began to be suppressed in France and, in a decree of 13 Messidor of the Year X (2 July 1802), Napoleon even forbade free entry of free blacks and half-castes into France, permitted since 1791.[126] But Napoleon's monumental betrayal of the Rights of Man and Caribbean blacks in the end profited him nothing. From May 1802, resistance stiffened until, in October 1802 Christophe and all the black commanders who had collaborated openly broke with Napoleon and the French.[127] In the resumed fighting, the French slaughtered great numbers of black rebels, conducting themselves with a brutality in no way alleviated by their own mounting losses from yellow fever, which exacted an appalling toll of their army. Meanwhile, also in October, formal title to Louisiana was transferred from Spain to France, intensifying the incipient confrontation with the United States, especially when in November the Spanish acting governor of New Orleans, on Napoleon's orders, imposed a ban on American Mississippi river traffic freely passing to New Orleans, causing outrage among the settlers of Tennessee, Kentucky, and Ohio. By November 1802, when Leclerc himself died from the fever, all Haiti was in revolt against France and Napoleon's army there so depleted it was a mere feeble remnant of that of nine months before.[128]

Britain's blockade of Haiti resumed with the Anglo-French conflict, in May 1803, helping accelerate French Caribbean defeat. French recovery of Saint-Domingue, the London papers concurred with their government, would be even more menacing to Britain than a "black empire."[129] But it was especially the appalling losses from yellow fever that blighted Napoleon's New World imperial ambitions by depleting his army to the point that it could no longer hold the black insurgents at bay. Leclerc's brutal successor, General Rochambeau, was decisively defeated by his black opponents, under Dessalines, at the battle of Vertières (18 November 1803), near Cap-Français. By then, the army sent from France two years before had lost roughly two-thirds of its men. Horrified, Napoleon pronounced himself utterly sick of the Americas. "There was considerable dislike in Paris against the expedition to Domingo," Paine assured Jefferson, a year later, "and the events that have since taken place were then often predicted. The opinion that generally prevailed at that time was that the commerce of the Island was better than the conquest of it—that the conquest could not be accomplished without destroying the Negroes, and in that case the Island would be of no value."[130] Yellow fever spelt military defeat which, with resumption of war with

[125] Cuevas Pérez and Dias Bidó, *Presencia francesa*, 220, 227–9, 255.
[126] Popkin, *You are all free*, 380; Pitts, "Constant's Thought," 126.
[127] Griggs and Prator, *Henry Christophe*, 31; Girard, *Toussaint Louverture*, 235–6, 240, 258.
[128] Kukla, *A Wilderness*, 224–5; Régent, *France*, 268–9; Curran, *Anatomy*, 209–10.
[129] Régent, *France et ses esclaves*, 269.
[130] Paine to Jefferson, 1 January 1805, in Paine, *Writings*, ii. 1454.

Britain, ended all prospect of Haiti becoming Napoleon's lever for his New World ambitions.[131] His Haitian venture, admitted Napoleon toward the end of his life, "was the greatest error that in all my government I ever committed," quite an admission given the disastrous consequences of his invading Spain and Russia.[132]

Saint-Domingue's ex-slaves secured their hard-won freedom. After the November 1803 defeat, part of the decimated French army surrendered to the British, part returned to France, and a third remnant withdrew into occupied Spanish Santo Domingo so that, despite Haiti's independence, France retained a lingering foothold on the island overall. Independence was officially proclaimed by Dessalines on 1 January 1804, when the island's name was formally changed to Haiti, a landmark event in world history. Dessalines wrote to President Jefferson affirming Haiti's friendship for the United States and desire for commercial ties. But Jefferson rebuffed him; he and his supporters in Congress, while profiting from the Haitian struggle to secure the Louisiana Purchase, thereby vastly expanding the United States' territory, were unwilling to recognize Haiti's independence—mainly to avoid arousing adamantly hostile Southern opinion. Instead of acclaiming black liberty, Jefferson chose to treat Haitian independence as a threat; he sought to isolate and boycott the island to prevent Haiti's blacks becoming a force at sea.[133] Independent Haiti earned no gratitude in the event from Congress or Jefferson.[134] Haiti renounced subjection to France "forever" but Dessalines, the victor of Vertières, laced his proclamation with calls for true Haitians to manifest "eternal hatred" for the French "barbarians who had bloodied" their land for two centuries, almost openly inciting massacre of the remaining whites.[135]

If Jefferson, like Lafayette, Constant, Kościuszko, Destutt, Paine, and Toussaint, condemned Napoleon as they did Robespierre, as a monstrous foe of human rights and republican liberty, from 1804 Jefferson nevertheless colluded with Napoleonic France in seeking to stifle Haiti's revolution, which he feared might yet ignite black insurrection further afield, including the southern United States.[136] By February 1806, partly to mollify Napoleon, and Southern opinion, but chiefly to isolate Haiti, Jefferson's bloc in Congress formalized a permanent embargo on American navigation and trade with the world's first black republic.[137] The ban was strictly applied, with even the name "Haiti" being boycotted, the United States referring to the island still as "Saint-Domingue." This opened the door for Britain to act as chief patron and protector of Haitian independence down to the early 1820s, helping Haiti guard its shores against the French navy and the military remnant garrisoning Santo Domingo.

[131] Popkin, *You are all free*, 379; Furstenberg, *When the United States Spoke French*, 387, 390.

[132] Geggus, "Louisiana Purchase," 121; Roberts, *Napoleon the Great*, 303.

[133] White, *Encountering Revolution*, 164; Brown, *Toussaint's Clause*, 237–8.

[134] Wood, *Empire*, 368–9; Matthewson, "Jefferson and Haiti," 211.

[135] Souker, *Discours et proclamations*, 20, 22; Gainot, "Republican Imagination," 276–7; Ghachem, "Antislavery Script," 160.

[136] Egerton, "Race and Slavery," 75–6; Brown, *Toussaint's Clause*, 148.

[137] Brown, *Toussaint's Clause*, 268, 272, 276.

Jefferson's apprehensions seemed more than vindicated when Dessalines, in revenge for horrific massacres perpetrated by Leclerc and Rochambeau, personally directed massacres, between February and April 1804, in which the remaining 3,000 to 5,000 whites still living in Haiti were slaughtered.[138] Gruesome accounts of what transpired were widely publicized in South America, Europe, and the United States, the slaughter transmitting deep shock-waves throughout the Southern states. On learning that Napoleon, disavowing all republican pretense, was planning his own elevation to the rank of emperor, Dessalines adroitly forestalled him, having himself crowned "Jacques I, Emperor of Haiti" on 8 October 1804, seven weeks before Napoleon's coronation in Paris, on 2 December.

Dessalines, backed by Christophe and Pétion, proclaimed his imperial "constitution" on 20 May 1805: this abjured slavery forever, declaring all citizens equal, and made the crown of Haiti "elective" not hereditary, but provided no specific freedoms, conspicuously failing to declare individual liberty, freedom of expression, or press freedom.[139] Haiti's second constitution did adopt Haiti's new red and blue national flag, repudiated the term "negro," and sought to end friction between mulattoes and pure blacks, and between the African-born and Creoles, by declaring all members of Haitian society officially "blacks" (including even the handful of surviving whites, among whom figured what remained of 400 Polish soldiers who arrived with Leclerc but, as foreigners speaking no French, had been spared the butchery inflicted on the rest). Recognizing the Poles as fighters for the liberty of their oppressed nation, Dessalines bizarrely adopted them as his own personal elite bodyguard.[140] Despotic and notoriously brutal even by the chilling standards of Haiti's civil wars, the new emperor, whose autocratic style starkly contradicted the revolutionary principles of both the French and Haitian revolutions, was assassinated in an ambush, on 17 October 1806, at the age of 48.[141]

Dessalines' demise precipitated a struggle for power that soon gripped the entire country, pitting against each other the two foremost remaining leaders, Alexandre Pétion (1770–1818), supreme at Port-au-Prince and among the southern region's mulattoes, and Christophe dominating Cap-Français and the north. These two embodied the clash of basic principles and symbols dividing the new Haiti during the Revolution's remaining decade and a half. Son of a wealthy French white and mulatto freed woman, only one-quarter of African ancestry (a quadroon), Pétion had trained in France at the military academy in Paris, spending ten years in revolutionary France before returning to Haiti. Essentially a product of the French Revolution, more than the Haitian, and close ally of Rigaud during the 1799–1800 civil war, he had been exiled by Toussaint on Rigaud's defeat but had returned in the wake of Leclerc's

[138] Souker, *Discours et proclamations*, 22; White, Encounter*ing Revolution*, 177–9.

[139] Griggs and Prator, *Henry Christophe*, 35–6; Régent, *France*, 269–70; Popkin, "Colonial Media Revolution," 25.

[140] Zamoyski, *Holy Madness*, 131–2.

[141] Prévost, *Relation des glorieux événemens*, 212.

troops in 1802.[142] From this point on, Pétion and the Haitian republic of the south, endorsed by Grégoire and the heirs of the *Amis des Noirs* in Paris, represented French revolutionary principles in action as far as these survived anywhere, proclaiming republicanism, equality, and (rather implausibly) limited executive power. Christophe, who had served in the American Revolution as the slave of a French officer, from the outset exhibited a comprehensively more autocratic approach.

Ostensibly working together, Pétion and Christophe initially sought to maintain Haiti's unity as a single state; but this quickly broke down. Disagreeing as to how many representatives each part of the republic should have—although Christophe's domain was larger in area, North and South had roughly equal populations—Pétion convened a constituent assembly in Port-au-Prince with a manipulated majority of forty-one delegates for the South and thirty-three for the North. His revised constitution for the Republic, promulgated on 27 December 1806, confirmed Haiti's republican character and, on paper, assigned the lion's share of power to its "senate," leaving virtually none to the presidency.[143] Whilst their original accord pertained, Pétion preferred this arrangement since it envisaged Christophe as president. Christophe, however, rejected the draft and opted for war, leading his troops into the southern region. He defeated Pétion's supporters in a pitched battle, on 1 January 1807, but was repulsed from Port-au-Prince. The civil conflict subsequently lapsed into a mostly inactive stalemate. On 9 March 1807, the senate of the republic elected Pétion president for four years, a period during which he devoted his energies to clawing back the powers he had conspired to deprive Christophe of. The stalemate persisted largely unchanged until 1812 when Christophe again set siege to Port-au-Prince bombarding it for two months, but again unsuccessfully. For thirteen years after that, Haiti remained divided into two wholly separate rival states.[144]

24.4. "KING HENRY CHRISTOPHE" AND THE THWARTING OF BLACK MONARCHY

A pure black former slave without formal education but highly intelligent, Christophe had been one of Toussaint's top commanders, and a key administrative official helping oversee the efforts to revive agriculture and commerce. When Pétion became president of the southern part of Haiti, Christophe initially retained the title of "president" in the North; but his heart was not in republicanism. Facing opposition and conspiracies by plotters allied to Pétion, with France implacable and commercial relations with the United States non-existent,[145] Christophe sought an enduring alliance with Britain despite the fact that Britain, like the United States, was unwilling

[142] Souker, *Discours et proclamations*, 35–6, 40, Régent, *France*, 257–8, 265.
[143] Griggs and Prator, *Henry Christophe*, 40–1.
[144] Popkin, *You are all free*, 394.
[145] Brown, *Toussaint's Clause*, 292.

to formally recognize Haitian independence. Christophe too aspired to be an enlightened leader planning improvements but within a framework of aristocracy, revived ecclesiastical authority, and veneration for the British model to which he became strongly attached, leading him increasingly to admire the principle of monarchy.[146]

Constantly challenged in his ascendancy, Christophe's regime was never secure and strengthening his position remained throughout a prime concern. The great fortress crowning one of the highest points in his territory, initiated in 1805 while Dessalines was still "emperor," he expanded, crammed with cannon, and made his own, renaming it the "Citadelle Henry Christophe." Commanding northern Haiti's coastal strip, it was described in 1814 as "ce Palladium de la liberté, ce majestueux boulevart de l'indépendance;"[147] and was still under construction when Christophe's rule ended. Known today as the Citadelle Laferrière it remains among the most astounding historic fortresses of the Americas. Christophe's British alliance was built on acceptance, if not formal acknowledgment, of his personal sway in northern Haiti in exchange for preferential access to Haiti's ports and commerce and general deference to British interests, especially guaranteeing that the independent part of Haiti under his rule would make "no conquests out of their own island" and not trouble slavery in the British, Spanish, or any other West Indies. He kept to the bargain throughout his ascendancy. At one point, discovering a plot against British rule and slavery in Jamaica, among Jamaican exiles in Haiti, he demonstratively crushed it to secure additional British trust. As time passed, his London connections increased. Among his closest advisors during the last years of his dominance, and closest white associate, was his personal physician, Duncan Stewart, a remarkable Scotsman about whom little is known.

Britain prior to 1832 doggedly promoted monarchy in the world and firmly disapproved of republics. When, in March 1811, the senate in the South re-elected Pétion for a second term, Christophe announced that the North was now becoming a "kingdom" and proclaimed himself "King Henry I." The state coronation, on 2 June 1811, a spectacle attended by several British and American guests, was conducted by the new archbishop of Haiti, who placed Haiti's new magnificently bejeweled crown on the head of the former cook. The coronation was followed by eight days of public "rejoicing." Hierarchy was now the order of the day and even slavery was no longer entirely condemned. When Napoleon quashed the Spanish Bourbon monarchy, putting Joseph on the throne, in Madrid in 1808, Christophe sent arms, men, and money to Santo Domingo's *antibuonapartista* insurgents fighting for the Bourbons under Juan Sánchez Ramirez (1762–1811) against the French military remnant there under General Louis Ferrand. Aided by British naval vessels blockading Santo Domingo port from the sea, and by Christophe's men, Sánchez Ramirez, son of a wealthy landowner, defeated the French at the battle of Palo Hincado in November 1808, and set siege to Santo Domingo itself. Capitulating, in July 1809, the surviving

[146] Gainot, "Republican Imagination," 288–9.

[147] Prévost, *Relation des glorieux événemens*, 17.

French were evacuated soon after, replaced temporarily by a British garrison charged with overseeing Santo Domingo's restoration to Fernando VII's reactionary Spain.[148] Leclerc and Ferrand having restored slavery in the Spanish colony, Sánchez Ramirez, with Christophe's acquiescence, then kept slavery in place.

The monarchical ideology and symbols of Henry's realm, its coffers swollen by proceeds of his lucrative export trade to Britain, differed markedly from those of the "republic of Haiti" in the south. Northern Haiti's chief city, the former Cap-Français, was renamed "Cap-Henry" and its street names were deliberately de-republicanized so that its former "Rue de la Liberté," "de l'Egalité," and "quai des Républicains" were changed to exalt the person and entourage of the ruler.[149] Christophe commenced the largest of his nine palaces, in 1810, employing thousands of laborers for its construction, at a location just three miles from towering "Citadelle Henry Christophe." Completed in 1813, it was renowned for its splendor, the sumptuous feasts and events held there, and gardens in classical style, graced by fifteen marble statues imported from Italy. "Ce superbe palais royal, la gloire d'Hayti," as it was described in 1814, having caused the demise of many of those forced to work on it, was named "Sans-Souci" after Frederick the Great's palace at Potsdam, even though most features recalled rather the style of Louis XIV.[150]

A man of no formal education, Christophe carefully studied the trappings of monarchy. Correct terminology, etiquette, and procedure mattered greatly to him. To assist, he established an advisory group including a "history" reading circle headed by his advisor, Pompée Valentin Vasty (1735–1820), author of several works lauding monarchy and condemning republicanism, at which his trusted advisors read to him. Despite his fondness for Louis XIV and Versailles, his court etiquette he modeled principally on England's. Under the monarch, a Haitian black nobility was established, with princes of the royal family forming the next level down, and under them eight dukes and twenty-two counts, followed by thirty-seven barons and fourteen chevaliers.[151] Principal courtiers bore the magnificent gold and lapis lazuli crosses of his royal "Order of St Henry."[152] Among the counts was Julien Prevost, comte de Limonade, his secretary of state for foreign affairs and chief propagandist, author of the *Relation des glorieux événemens qui ont porté Leurs Majestés royales sur le trône d'Hayti* (1814). This text exalted "le grand Toussaint Louverture" as the founder of Haitian liberty but criticized him for being too trusting of the French and disastrously failing to secure full independence. Feeling insecure among his Haitian troops, Christophe recruited a special bodyguard of African soldiers known as the Dahomets, specially shipped over for the purpose with British assistance.[153]

148 Prévost, *Relation des glorieux événemens*, 15–16.
149 Griggs and Prator, *Henry Christophe*; Popkin, *You are all free*, 393.
150 Prévost, *Relation des glorieux événemens*, 19–20.
151 Griggs and Prator, *Henry Christophe*, 43.
152 Griggs and Prator, *Henry Christophe*, 210.
153 Griggs and Prator, *Henry Christophe*, 56.

King Christophe stood in unceasing rivalry with Pétion, "president for life" in the south. Henry's propaganda trumpeted the alleged longing of all true, patriotic Haitians to be reunited in one state under "King Henry" and the contemptible lack of patriotism of those obstructing this goal. Pétion he and Prevost denounced as weak, incompetent, and given to intrigue with Haiti's greatest enemy—the French. Rigaud and Pétion (who had sided with the former against Toussaint) were both really traitors, blocking reunion and perfidiously colluding with Paris.[154] Where King Henry, following the example of Toussaint and Dessalines, maintained the plantation system, Petion broke with this pattern, dividing the large plantations into small plots which were assigned to former soldiers and servants, with the result that southern Haiti's agriculture became a system of petty subsistence farming, unconnected with foreign trade and soon plunged in poverty. Christophe kept the sugar and coffee plantations of the north intact, as large blocs, leasing them out to his nobles and retainers though they remained legally part of the "national domain." His "rural code" required one-fourth of all cash crops to be paid to the crown and another fourth to the laborers, in wages, leaving half the proceeds to the ennobled estate-holders, a system that sustained trade with Britain while keeping his coffers and those of his nobility and senior ecclesiastics filled. Laborers had Sundays free but otherwise worked under stringent conditions. In the south, the peasants were freer but dreadfully poor while the state coffers were usually empty, a point much stressed in Henry's ceaseless anti-Pétion propaganda.[155]

Foreign onlookers often scorned Christophe's monarchical delusions and extolled Pétion as Toussaint's true heir, the Haitian Revolution's authentic embodiment, the veritable symbol of black representative government and republicanism—and none more so than South America's *Libertador*, Simon Bolívar. In an address to Bolivia's constituent assembly, in May 1826, Bolívar extolled Pétion as the model of a republican president and of how a new state can steer between the extremes of tyranny on the one hand and anarchy on the other, the twin perils menacing every society with ruin. Denouncing Dessalines, Christophe, and the Mexican tyrant, Iturbide, as *ambiciosos* raising empires of oppression on the people's hopes, Bolívar admonished the new republican president-to-be, in Bolivia, to closely emulate Pétion in Haiti, in respecting both constitution and people and venerating the basic principles on which true liberty is built, above all "equality," the fundamental principle of "civil liberty," precluding aristocracy and privilege and excluding religion from the public sphere. A true republican president should also be a strong executive in his proper sphere, including as military commander, and ensure his vice-president and successor was as reliable and respectful as Pétion's choice, Boyer.[156]

[154] Prévost, *Relation des glorieux événemens*, pp. xii–xiii; Prévost, *À ses concitoyens*, 2–3; Souker, *Discours et proclamations*, 35–6.

[155] Griggs and Prator, *Henry Christophe*, 46; Girard, *Haiti*, 67–8; Geggus, *Haitian Revolutionary Studies*, 28–9.

[156] Bolívar, *Obras Completas* iii. 763–8; Bolívar, *Writings*, 57.

Needless to say, Bolívar's republican image of Pétion was somewhat idealized. In reality, despite conflicting official ideologies, the two leaders' rivalry produced an unmistakable parallelism. By 1818, Pétion ruled virtually without referring to the legislature at all, reducing the difference between Christophe and himself to little more than a difference of name and trappings. Despite his flamboyant adornments, Henry Christophe proved a genuine "moderate enlightener." Among his proudest boasts—and it was no empty one—was that he brought schools, hospitals, and a university to northern Haiti. A network of schools in "Cap Henry" and other towns emerged during 1816–17 providing instruction in French and English "according to the English system." By the last years of his rule a close-knit group of British teachers and medical staff were directing a substantial complex of educational and medical institutions.[157] But at exactly the same time, in 1816, Pétion founded the *lycée* at Port-au-Prince, the Lycée Alexandre Pétion, that marked the commencement of the system of *lycées* on the French model that became the republic's standard secondary school format. The kingdom's hospitals, affirmed Stewart, in December 1819, were being admirably administered (under his own care): "I can safely say there is not a hospital in England where the sick are better supplied with all conveniences and necessaries than in the hospitals of Haiti."[158]

The concluding years of Henry's reign produced new challenges, casting Haiti's independence and the whole issue of black emancipation into a fresh light. The Bourbon monarchies of France and Spain, restored by the Vienna Congress, in 1814–15, and backed by Britain and the Holy Alliance, proclaimed a new world order undeviatingly based on the *ancien régime* principles of monarchy, aristocracy, religious authority—and slavery. "King Henry" and his neighbor Pétion both felt threatened by the revived legitimism fueling Louis XVIII's plans for recovering lost French colonies no less than Fernando VII"s for restoring the *ancien régime* in Spanish America, including Santo Domingo. In these years, Henry's principal advisor in England was the abolitionist, Thomas Clarkson (1760–1846), son of an Anglican vicar who, though a devout Anglican, had allied with Quakers and Methodists in the common fight against slavery. Reminding Clarkson it was not just Haiti but the status of the "African race" that was at stake, Henry repeatedly demanded to know why the British government still declined to recognize Haiti's independence and his "crown." Britain, explained Clarkson, could not risk damaging its alliance with Louis XVIII.[159] British recognition of Haiti's independence hence long remained as remote as that of the United States.[160] Clarkson also alerted Henry to the need to keep Haitian vessels under strict orders not to interfere with Spanish slaving vessels, shipping enslaved Africans to Spanish Caribbean ports under Fernando VII's colors; for under its agreement with Britain and the Holy Alliance to end the slave trade (but not slavery),

[157] Prévost, *Relation des glorieux événemens*, 5; Griggs and Prator, *Henry Christophe*, 62–3, 66.
[158] Stewart to Clarkson, Cap Henry, 4 Dec. 1819, in Griggs and Prator, *Henry Christophe*, 183.
[159] Griggs and Prator, *Henry Christophe*, 124–35, 183–4. [160] Brown, *Toussaint's Clause*, 293.

Spain remained entitled to ship slaves from Africa to its American possessions until May 1820. Henry acquiesced.[161]

Neither France, Spain, nor Britain wished Haiti to gain possession of Santo Domingo. But one of Clarkson's more ambitious schemes for Haiti was his suggestion that Henry should enlist the help of American abolitionists for transferring free blacks from the United States to Haiti. Should those, like Jefferson (and many others), interested in encouraging free black emigration from the United States to an enlarged Haiti be willing, on that account, to see Santo Domingo annexed, the United States might then agree to purchase Santo Domingo from Fernando VII and cede it to Haiti. "Spain would probably sell it to America," proposed Clarkson, "though she would not sell it to Your Majesty."[162] Clarkson also represented Haiti's predicament to Czar Alexander, on "King Henry's" behalf, urging the Holy Alliance to discourage the new French minister for the colonies (who was none other than Malouet) from pressing for resumption of French sovereignty over France's once most valuable colony. Alexander agreed to defend Haiti's cause in the Holy Alliance's "council of sovereigns," while Henry displayed his own enlightened credentials by writing to the Czar, in March 1819, aided by his advisory team: "too long has the African race been unjustly calumniated. Too long has it been represented as deprived of intellectual faculties, as scarcely susceptible of civilization, or government by regular and established laws; these false assertions spring from the avarice and injustice of men who have had the impiety to degrade the finest work of the Creator, as if mankind had not one common origin. These persons attribute to difference of color that which is only the result of [lack of] civilization and knowledge."[163]

Doubtless, Henry's "rhetoric of philanthropy and good intentions," as one of his British teachers later expressed it, was "to some extent a mask,"[164] but it was nevertheless a ringing tribute to the force of the Enlightenment in the early nineteenth-century Caribbean since he judged it fitting to assume this guise, making it a centerpiece of his royal policy and propaganda. Hemmed in by the Holy Alliance and his dependence on Britain, Henry avoided interfering to support the black cause in the Caribbean, United States, and South America and carefully avoided offending Louis XVIII and Fernando VII. In these respects he adopted the opposite stance to Pétion and Boyer, in the south. The Spanish revolution of 1820, and simultaneous revolutions in Italy and Greece, shook the Holy Alliance to its foundations but also presented fresh challenges to Haiti and the cause of black emancipation. That there was a moral bond linking Haiti to all the revolutions was acknowledged on both sides of the Atlantic, and the Holy Alliance sought to crush the revolutions, restore Fernando VII's tyranny, and strengthen Louis XVIII's role as the pillar of legitimacy,

[161] King Henry to Clarkson, Cap Henry, 20 Mar. 1819, in Griggs and Prator, *Henry Christophe*, 128.
[162] Clarkson to King Henry, London, 20 Feb. 1819, in Griggs and Prator, *Henry Christophe*, 124–5.
[163] King Henry to Czar Alexander, 20 Mar. 1819, in Griggs and Prator, *Henry Christophe*, 134–5.
[164] William Wilson to Clarkson, Cape Haytien, 5 Dec. 1820, in Griggs and Prator, *Henry Christophe*, 216.

reaction, and slavery in Latin America and the Caribbean. In one of his last letters to King Henry, in July 1820, Clarkson repeated his earnest admonition that France would very likely send an expeditionary force to try to retake Haiti if the civil conflict between the two Haitis resumed, or anything occurred "which should have the appearance of [Haitian] meddling with European concerns or with the present state of the slave colonies belonging to the different maritime powers of Europe." Should Haiti try to interfere with Caribbean slavery, Louis XVIII would probably be able "to engage every power in Europe to make common cause with France in the entire subjugation of Hayti."[165]

Henry Christophe, brutal and ruthless whatever his pretensions to enlightened values, was widely resented as a tyrant. In his last years, records one of the English teachers hired in Haiti, he also "became very licentious and prostituted the wives of most of his nobility."[166] Whether the revival of republican enthusiasm the 1820 revolutions generated in Europe and South America impacted also on Haiti, or whether "the revolution" (as one of the British teachers called it) that erupted in northern Haiti in the autumn of 1820 ensued purely from internal repression and discontent, the "kingdom of Haiti" too was gripped by agitation. In August 1820, Christophe suffered fits which left him paralyzed on one side and inactive. His nobles "and chiefs, no longer awed by his presence and activity," another British teacher explained, "began to express their abhorrence of the restraint in which they were held. The dissatisfaction quickly spread through all ranks, and the soldiers at Saint-Marc, a frontier town, openly revolted."[167]

Christophe ordered the garrison of Cap Henry to march against the mutineers, but on approaching the insurgent lines, on 6 October, they announced, drums beating and their lines drawn up, that "they would no longer bear a king, but be entirely free." The duke of Marmelade ripped off his Cross of the Order of St Henry and other decorations and declared himself no longer a duke; a count and other nobles followed suit. "At the Cape, the insurgents were joined by the mass of the inhabitants, the students from the College, and many criminals who were liberated." When finally, as his last resort, Henry sent his palace bodyguard to assail the rebels, the "republicans exhorted them to join in the cause of freedom; immediate desertion followed. Shouting "Vive la liberté! Vive l'indépendance! A bas le tyran! A bas Christophe!" the rebels advanced on the palace. On hearing this, realizing all was lost, King Henry Christophe retired to his rooms and shot himself through the heart.[168] The superb palace at Sans-Souci, the center of all the magnificence of Haiti, was pillaged the same night."[169] On 18 and 19 October the dismantling of the monarchy continued, with the king's two

[165] Clarkson to King Henry, 10 July 1820, in Griggs and Prator, *Henry Christophe*, 201.

[166] Griggs and Prator, *Henry Christophe*, 223.

[167] George Clarke to Clarkson, Cap Henry, 4 Nov. 1820, in Griggs and Prator, *Henry Christophe*, 210; Souker, *Discours et proclamations*, 55.

[168] Souker, *Discours et proclamations*, 39; Griggs and Prator, *Henry Christophe*, 217.

[169] Clarke to Clarkson, 10 July 1820, in Griggs and Prator, *Henry Christophe*, 211.

sons and some nobles who remained loyal, along with Vasty, being bayoneted to death in the prison yard or massacred nearby.

Pétion had died earlier in March 1818 and been succeeded by Jean-Pierre Boyer (1776–1850), who was also proclaimed "president for life" in southern Haiti. On 21 October 1820, Boyer, "by common consent of the people and the chiefs of the army," was declared "president" of both north and south Haiti. The goal of reunion Christophe had so loudly demanded without success was effortlessly accomplished by his death. All the "treasure private and public belonging to the late king" was transferred by President Boyer to Port-au-Prince. The orders and decorations of nobility were abolished. Cap Henry was renamed Cap Haitien, and Citadelle Henry Christophe became Citadelle Laferrière (since 1982 a UNESCO World Heritage Site). Henry's British-style education project was shelved: "the president, Boyer, seems indifferent to all establishment for the moral and intellectual improvement of his people," lamented Stewart to Clarkson in December 1820; "he has dismissed all the professors and schoolmasters who were employed by King Henry, and is unwilling to pay up the arrears of salaries due to them."[170] Finally, the plantation system Christophe had maintained was broken up during the 1820s, and the estates split into small plots.[171]

Boyer reunited the two Haitis and then, even if only provisionally, the entire island. Bolívar's South American triumphs had stirred revolutionary agitation in neighboring Santo Domingo. In November 1821, dissatisfied with the reformers in Madrid, a pro-independence group headed by a University of Santo Domingo professor, José Núñez de Cáceres (1772–1846), rose in revolt, seizing control of the "Spanish part of Haiti," as his "Declaration of Independence" termed what is today the Dominican Republic. Dated 1 December 1821, his declaration proclaimed Dominicans a "free people" no longer subject to a repressive, ungrateful Spain, deploring the country's 328 years of *pupilage* as servile submission and looking forward to the *Independencia* of all the Americas. It undertook to constitute a properly proportional representative government without the distortions of representation marring the Cádiz Constitution,[172] and raise education levels "because without that all efforts at social improvement are ineffective." It exalted the achievements of the University of "Santo Tomas de Aquino," the oldest higher education institution anywhere in the New World (founded in 1538), which for three centuries had awarded degrees in every field to the youth of Caracas, Puerto Rico, Cuba, and the "Spanish part of Hayti," placing Santo Domingo among the "focos principales de la ilustración Americana" [principal foci of the New World Enlightenment].[173]

Enlightenment then remained, in 1820–1, very much the badge of the Caribbean revolution. Invoking political theory, to show men leave the state of nature to form civil society for the sake of the benefits that accrue, giving them the perennial right to

[170] Stewart to Clarkson, 8 Dec. 1820, in Griggs and Prator, *Henry Christophe*, 222.
[171] Girard, *Toussaint Louverture*, 256.
[172] [Nuñez de Cáceres], *Declaratoria de Independencia* (1821), 5.
[173] [Nuñez de Cáceres], *Declaratoria de Independencia* (1821), 4.

resist tyranny and repressive institutions like the Inquisition;[174] the Santo Domingo declaration was a stirring text that, however, made no mention of slavery or any obligation to abolish it. Very soon, Spanish Haiti's revolution of 1820–2 proved to be two completely incompatible revolutions. On the one hand stood the "Independence" revolution of white elite landowners not necessarily seeking full independence for Santo Domingo, and evincing little of the "national sentiment" generations of historians later attributed to it, but rather "independence" from both Haiti and Spain, preferably as part of a loose confederation with Bolívar's Union of Gran Colombia. On the other hand stood the Santo Domingo revolution of the slaves, free blacks, and mixed bloods seeking the abolition of slavery and union with the two Haitis. Boyer, opposing the plans of the Santo Domingo landowners, gained the allegiance of several border towns and elements among Santo Domingo's non-white population eager for union with Haiti.

Although Boyer announced that he was entering Spanish Haiti "not as an invader" but to restore order, as the Haitian troops entered turmoil spread across the country. Núñez de Cáceres and his colleagues, after an abortive independence of only three months, yielded, submitting to the new union of three Haitis.[175] Under an edict of February 1822, slavery was abolished throughout the annexed territory. Núñez de Cáceres submitted but in private continued plotting for an autonomous Santo Domingo with its future tied to Spanish America rather than Haiti. His plotting caused President Boyer to send him into exile, in August 1822. Little did Núñez de Cáceres know that the university of which he was so proud and considered a focal point of the Spanish New World Enlightenment was experiencing the final year of its existence. Deemed a hotbed of white elitist opposition to black equality and the union of the three Haitis, during 1823 Boyer stopped the professors' salaries, letting courses lapse and the university fall into ruin. Ending slavery in Santo Domingo at once raised fears of revolution in nearby Puerto Rico, where slave conspiracies were uncovered at Bayamón (1821), near the north coast, and Naguabo (1823), at the island's eastern end, causing local authorities there and in Cuba to blame the seditious movements among their slaves on Haiti's example and what Haiti represented.[176] President Boyer had succeeded in absorbing "Spanish Haiti" into a newly expanded black Haitian Republic and in projecting the new threefold Haiti's image as a bastion of emancipation and enlightenment to the wider world.

The union of all the Haitis was to last twenty-three years. Boyer's ending of "King Henry's sway and of slavery in Santo Domingo while the escalating struggle in Spanish America was continuing and Europe convulsed by the 1820 revolutions, had the effect of suddenly renewing enthusiasm for the Haitian revolution among the radical fraternity in Europe and raising the Haitians' achievement in general esteem. No feature of French radical thought in the 1820s was more characteristic than

[174] [Nuñez de Cáceres], *Declaratoria de Independencia* (1821), 4–5.
[175] Souker, *Discours et proclamations*, 45; Girard, *Haiti*, 72.
[176] Jiménez de Wagenheim, *Puerto Rico*, 123–4.

repudiating Napoleon's efforts to reintroduce black slavery and extolling the political and cultural achievements of Haiti's blacks since their defeat of Napoleon's army there in 1802–3.

Among the most resolute voices condemning all notion that royalist France was entitled to recover Saint-Domingue was that of the Swiss economist, Sismondi, who, from 1814, forcefully presented economic arguments as to why it was against France's interest to invest again in slave-based plantation economics.[177] Attacking the race theories of both counter-enlighteners and liberal "moderates," and stressing the principle of equality and ability of the blacks to match Europe's best achievements in legislation, literature, and moral philosophy, became characteristic too. Through its efforts in literature and poetry, and writings on legislation and education, claimed the editor of the Paris *Revue Encyclopédique*, Marc Antoine Jullien, an ally of Sismondi, in January 1821, the "nation haïtienne" was "proving more and more that the black race is also part of the great human family, is endowed by Providence with the same moral and intellectual faculties that distinguish our race, and needs only to be cultivated and developed by the double influence of a good education and an enlightened and well-meaning administration, to figure honorably among the nations."[178] A year later, in January 1822, President Boyer wrote to Adamantios Korais and four other Greek leaders in exile in Paris, responding to Greek requests for Haitian support in their struggle for independence from the Ottoman empire. He was unable to send men, money, or supplies, he explained, but glad to lend moral support; defying the Vienna Congress powers, Haiti became the first state in the Western world to accord formal acknowledgment to Greek national aspirations.[179]

Summing up the Haitian revolution's significance for black emancipation and world history, Constant penned a remarkable passage in his *Mélanges de littérature et de politique* published in Paris in 1829. "The blacks of Haiti," he wrote, "have become very reasonable legislators, disciplined enough warriors, and statesmen as able and as polished as our diplomats." He ended with a prophetic passage warning contemporaries against absorbing into politics race theories purporting to justify inequality, "this new pretext" for imposing inequality and oppression that has no genuine basis in moral and political theory. Faced by severe obstacles, including the "dreadful servitude to which our infamous calculation subjected them," the Haitians' have "placed themselves at the level of the most perfect races, in terms not only of the necessary arts, but of social institutions whose intricacy we find so perplexing and management so difficult. Their constitution is better than most constitutions of Europe."[180]

[177] Oldfield, *Transatlantic Abolitionism*, 208–10.
[178] *Revue encyclopédique* IX (Jan. 1821), introductory editorial by Marc-Antoine Jullien, 15.
[179] Zamoyski, *Holy Madness*, 238. [180] Pitts, "Constant's Thought," 131–3, 137.

Part IV

The Enlightenment that Failed

25

Reaction and Radicalism

Germany and the Low Countries (1814–1830)

25.1. RESTORATION THWARTED

Adversaries socially, politically, and religiously, in terms of intellectual ferment and interaction of ideas, there can be little doubt that Leo Strauss was right to maintain that the moderate Enlightenment, or at least its many compromises, was the Radical Enlightenment's best friend. It was this especially that made the 1814–15 Restoration so widely and often a bitterly disheartening and disappointing experience not just for hard-core legitimists, reactionaries, and militant religionists but for a very large number of disappointed worldly noble *émigrés*, dispossessed ecclesiastics, and outcast princelings. If the Enlightenment registered an immense impact on the world's population in the half century down to 1800, it is no less true that it continued to do so during the first third or so of the nineteenth century in ways that remained no less divisive than they had earlier.

In the eyes of hardcore conservatives the post-1815 Restoration proved a decided failure. The mood of euphoria in reactionary circles in the immediate aftermath of Napoleon's downfall did not last long despite broad agreement among the victorious monarchies that a general restoration of monarchy, aristocracy, and ecclesiastical authority would now be imposed by the Allies on Europe and Europe's empires. Britain, the newly restored French monarchy, and Russia's Czar all supported the concerted reaction in all spheres that the Vienna Congress (October 1814–March 1815) sought to preside over in the German world, the Low Countries, Italy, and Scandinavia, but many smaller states refused to co-operate beyond a limited extent and it soon became obvious that what hardcore conservatives considered the insidious danger of democratic republican revolutionary radicalism had in no way been eradicated.

At the congress of great powers convened at Vienna (1814–15), Britain, Russia, Prussia, Austria, and Bourbon France together reached agreement on far-reaching measures to stabilize Europe's, and the colonial world's, "legitimist" new political order, a system of international relations and general principles of government further consolidated by the "Holy Alliance" (September 1815) of Russia, Austria, and Prussia. The conservative powers strove to restructure the post-1815 world on lines diametrically opposite to those envisaged by democratizing republicans, and sharply diverging also from Napoleon's reformism and state system. Yet, to stabilize and consolidate the uncompromisingly conservative world order based on royalism, aristocracy, and ecclesiastical authority they aspired to re-establish and agreed jointly to guarantee, Britain, Russia, and the other powers had perforce to collude to a great extent with the outcome of numerous revolutionary changes They also joined in supporting a new kind of interdenominational Protestant–Catholic–Orthodox social reactionary religious "orthodoxy" that was assuredly emphatic in exalting throne, altar, and divinely sanctioned government but also theologically bewilderingly undogmatic, not to say unprincipled, cosmopolitan, and flexible.

The Vienna Congress colluded especially in broadly endorsing the dynastic and territorial, and tacitly accepting the social, transformation of the central European state system. Far from there being any attempt to restore the pre-1789 "Holy Roman Empire," Austria, which for centuries had been entrenched as the presiding power among the German states, largely abandoned its ancient procedural primacy and bases in the west, the Austrian Netherlands (Belgium) and Rhenish enclaves, permitting Prussia to be compensated for its losses in its pre-1806 part of Poland by acquiring a massive bloc of north-western Germany, thereby ensuring precisely what Napoleon had striven to prevent, Prussia's German primacy, in exchange for Austria's own imperious new dominance in Italy. It was a dramatic outcome planned by Czar Alexander in consultation with Britain since 1804–5.[1] Hardly any of the dozens of pre-1789 German small states abolished by Napoleon were restored; rather, Bavaria, Württemberg, the Grand Duchy of Hesse (Grossherzogtum Hesse), and other middle-sized states Napoleon had created remained in the enlarged and profoundly reorganized condition in which the Napoleonic reforms had left them.

If one major Napoleonic entity, the so-called "Kingdom of Westphalia," with its capital at Cassel and population of two millions, a Napoleonic "model state," was dismantled altogether, it was the exception that proved the rule. When this "Kingdom of Westphalia," built from a disparate array of territories severed from states that had opposed Napoleon during the war of 1805–7 —an amalgamation of the former electorate of Hesse-Cassel, duchy of Brunswick, part of Hanover, and vestiges of several ecclesiastical states with nearly all Prussian territory west of the Elbe—was dissolved in 1813, Prussia and the Grand Duchy of Hesse each swelled with part of the collapsed state. The rest went to the restored principalities of Hanover which, in 1814, was converted into the 'Kingdom of Hanover' and the duchy of Brunswick. But the old Holy Roman Empire had been a confederacy of over three hundred states. There were thirty-nine states in the German Confederation created by the Congress of Vienna in 1814–15, among which only the four southern German states and five others—Austria, Prussia, Saxony, Hanover, and Brunswick—carried any political and

[1] Delfiner, "Alexander I," 147–8.

cultural weight.[2] At Berlin, the reforms of the Napoleonic era and need for concerted reform to achieve military success had brought to the fore several key figures who by no means thought as Metternich did, and it was far from obvious in 1815 that unqualified reaction and opposition to basic reform would dominate Prussian policy and attitudes. Indeed, Prussia was directly complicit in conserving and consolidating many of the most drastic Enlightenment changes the Napoleonic system had introduced, even if reform was also heavily constrained by respect for nobility.[3]

Hardcore repressive and reactionary monarchies subscribing to Counter-Enlightenment values were simply too few, it turned out, and too hampered by the rest, to engineer a genuine Counter-Enlightenment. These included Metternich's Austria, Prussia post-1817 (once Von Humboldt and the committed reformers were ousted from positions of influence), a few smaller German states, the Papacy, Fernando VII's Spain, and Russia once Czar Alexander abandoned his originally "enlightened" perspective to adopt a purely reactionary stance in 1819–20, plus, but here more in theory than practice, the restored French Bourbon monarchy. The effectiveness and solidarity of this narrowly-conceived monarchical new world order, based on social reaction and state-backed religion, was to a considerable degree offset, however, by two sizeable subsidiary categories of post-1815 principality—the "enlightened despotism" model to which Czar Alexander initially adhered until 1819 and the "mixed government" model based on moderate Enlightenment principles, entrenching a large measure of press and religious freedom, classically exemplified in 1815 by Britain and, in practice if not proclaimed values, by the newly restored French monarchy. To this category belonged also several other substantial and influential European states, notably Bernadotte's Sweden–Norway and the new "kingdom of the United Netherlands." These states forged a new Western reality that strongly appealed to the innumerable moderates traumatized by the French Revolution but rejecting reaction, the many demanding social hierarchy and aristocratic primacy but monarchy on the basis of moderation, modernization, press freedom, and reform.

Consequently, despite what is sometimes claimed, the overall picture failed to break with the Enlightenment pattern of social reformism, secularization, renewal of values through reason, and enlightened despotism to remotely the extent conservative theorists and Romantic writers in the mold of De Lamennais, Chateaubriand, Bonald, De Maistre, Da Costa, and the like demanded European society could and should revert to. It was a failure leaving authors of the religious Right exasperated and deeply frustrated. To De Maistre, the Congress of Vienna was a wholly inadequate response to the threat posed by the revolutionary ideologies of the age. Rather than sporadic repression and empty talk of legitimacy, a real Restoration would be based on religious authority and acceptance of the papacy as the true arbiter of men's affairs.[4] The authentic, pure "Restoration" of Chateaubriand was violated above all by the Vienna Congress's failure to remove a resilient and progressive group of

[2] Ramm, *Germany*, 139. [3] Clark, *Iron Kingdom*, 338–40.
[4] Ravera, "Joseph de Maistre and Italy," 190–1.

post-Napoleonic enlightened despotisms in northern Europe, selectively conserving absolutist forms of monarchical rule but openly combining these with non-royalist attitudes, further secularization, and upholding moderate Enlightenment principles.[5] Czar Alexander I (ruled: 1801–25) himself, held Chateaubriand, set a disastrous example when in Paris, in 1814, instead of spending his time with royalists and ecclesiastics, he chiefly conferred with *philosophes*, savants, and Paris Institut *Idéologues*![6] Russia's empire under Czar Alexander and its Polish annex had initially adhered to this "third way" before wholeheartedly embracing the "Holy Alliance," leading on to the brutal repressiveness of the Czar's last five years, and further repression after the Decembrist Conspiracy shook the Russian throne in December 1825. Many of the officers in St Petersburg who led or joined the Decembrist revolt aimed to transform Russia on the basis of the "British model"—limited monarchy, aristocratic domination, abolition of serfdom, and a restricted suffrage excluding the majority from the political sphere.

The kind of relentlessly reactionary policy pursued by Metternich and prevailing in much of Italy for some years, cemented by the close co-operation between the Austrian court and the Papacy during the period immediately following the Congress—symbolized by a visit to Rome made by the Emperor and Metternich in 1819—was far from successfully fully entrenched in most German capitals. Even where pure reaction was the order of the day, many restored courts after 1814–15 hardly exuded vitality, effectiveness, and vigor, or even a sustained resolve to purge enlighteners from office, influence, and professorships. Enlightened reform in Prussia during 1806–17 had introduced many far-reaching changes, including a new university system which subsequently led the Western world in the academic sphere and much of science and mathematics for the rest of the nineteenth century, widely-ventilated proposals for Jewish emancipation, and the promise of a full-blown Constitution that was admittedly later cancelled, but also many other reforms pushed through in the face of formidable opposition.

During the campaigns of 1812–13, Russia's summons to Europe, ardently backed by Freiherr vom Stein, a leading Prussian reformer, to rise for "freedom" against Napoleon actually exuded the deepest ambiguity and paradox.[7] Detestation of French hegemony and of Napoleon's despotism held together the marriage of convenience between reaction and anti-French enlightened reformers, brokered by Vom Stein and Von Humboldt, whilst the outcome of the war remained in doubt. But after the decisive battle of Leipzig (16–19 October 1813), this grand anti-Napoleonic alliance of Prussian ideological factions began to unravel, while never fully unraveling.[8] A thoroughgoing late Enlightenment reformer, Vom Stein's plans for modernization and freeing, and equalizing, the individual in Prussian society could not be combined or reconciled with the exigencies of restoring princely authority and noble privilege;

[5] Chateaubriand, *Memoires* ii. 295–8.
[6] Chateaubriand, *Memoires* ii. 297; Delfiner, "Alexander I," 133–4.
[7] Straub, *Wiener Kongress*, 54–7.
[8] Schroeder, *Transformation*, 451.

but this reality was long papered over. The Czar placed Vom Stein at the head of a council of officials that provisionally administered Germany's "liberated" territories and, although it quickly emerged that the former close collaboration between reformers and Prussian royal officialdom was breaking down because the aspirations of reformers and reactionaries were profoundly incompatible at every level,[9] it took years before an outright rift was acknowledged and acted on.

Admittedly, Western anti-Enlightenment fed, as it still feeds today, not only on what was inherited from the past but also on new forces. Thus, the so far distinctly few genuinely nationalist publicists like Ernst Moritz Arndt (1769–1860) could be relied on to condemn and revile Enlightenment, certainly, but also—though its importance was not yet as great as it later became—to act as a disruptive force in the world of hereditary princes and legitimacy. A powerful voice and brilliant versifier, fiercely anti-French, anti-Semitic, and anti-Polish, with a gift for stirring the hearts of those lower down the social scale, Arndt directly clashed with the priorities of the allied powers gathered at the Vienna Congress. Both nationalists and enlightened reformers often intensely disliked the new German state-system. Vom Stein too, like Arndt and the Prussian loyalists, had expected large territorial acquisitions by Prussia and drastic reduction of the now formidable system of middle-sized German states Napoleon had created with the deliberate intention of preventing the emergence of a powerful north German entity, and which the Allies were endorsing, as well as reversion of Alsace-Lorraine from France to Germany. Neither the Czar, nor Britain, nor Austria's chancellor, Metternich, the three chief brokers at the Vienna Congress, wished to see a major new power emerge in Germany and all agreed on maintaining the system of middle-sized German states as a buffer between France and the three main Holy Alliance powers, Russia, Austria, and Prussia. Hardly any participants in the Vienna Congress had much time for the liberation of peoples ideology animating Vom Stein as well as figures like Arndt.[10] Vom Stein, at loggerheads with both Czar and Prussian king, as well as Metternich and the British government, soon retired to his estates in disillusioned frustration.

Greatly enlarged by the Congress of Vienna toward the west as well as eastwards, with its population now almost reaching eleven million, the sprawling post-1814 Prussian monarchy was content to reverse many Enlightenment innovations, but proved distinctly unwilling to reverse some of the largest, most sweeping changes. This applied especially in the new Prussian Lower Rhine provinces amalgamated from several states now suppressed and where huge changes now ensued. Among the most fiercely reforming puppet states Napoleon forged in Germany had been the Grand Duchy of Berg (Grossherzogtum Berg), with its capital at Düsseldorf, a territory formed by amalgamating the pre-1800 duchies of Cleves, Mark, and Berg with lands of the ejected never-to-return prince-bishop of Münster. A principality originally placed under Napoleon's brother-in-law, Joachim Murat, on Murat's

[9] Arndt, *Erinnerungen*, 322–3.
[10] Arndt, *Erinnerungen*, 328–9; Straub, *Wiener Kongress*, 112–14.

transfer to Naples (following Joseph Bonaparte's transfer to the Spanish throne, in 1808), the territory fell under direct French administration, headed by Roederer, in the name of Prince Napoleon Louis Bonaparte (1804–31), infant son of King Louis, Napoleon's brother in Holland. While there was an oppressive aspect to the Napoleonic state system in Germany, as in Holland and Italy—taxes rose and great numbers of men were drafted into Napoleon's armies—a powerful reformist dimension brought about many fundamental changes, some supported in society, that were hard to reverse and after 1815 remained widely effective. The once entrenched privileged status of the local nobility and clergy remained greatly curtailed in the Rhineland under the post-1815 Prussian crown, while the respective Catholic, Lutheran, and Calvinist church authorities, each previously dominant in different sections of the north-western German states, failed to recover their former influence in government, education, and law. This predominantly Catholic area saw practically all its monasteries remain dissolved and former church schools and charitable institutions remain secularized, with its convents often converted into barracks or stables. The guilds, abolished in 1810, stayed abolished. The entire legal system had been transformed, brought under the Code Napoleon, which, among other consequences, liquidated what remained of feudal obligations affecting the Lower Rhine and Münsterland peasantry. Little of this was reversed after 1814.

In Berlin, despite arousing suspicion in conservative minds, Von Humboldt clung to his influential position and continued effort to get Prussia to adopt a constitution, as well as strove to shield the universities from court interference. The enlightener who risked irritating kings by making Fichte head of the philosophy faculty (1810–14) of the new University of Berlin, and even university rector, might veil his broad disagreements with the new reactionary mood, but was not one to abandon the Enlightenment project. If he gave "no indication whatever of a democratic tendency," he remained resolute and was not finally dismissed from government service until the intensified reactionary sweep of 1819–20 when, criticizing Prussia's following Metternich's course, he opposed the further crackdown following the Carlsbad decrees.[11] It was only in December 1819, with Von Humboldt's departure, that all talk of moderate press freedom and a Prussian constitution finally ceased at court in Berlin.[12]

Laws, institutions, and even outright repression, experience quickly proved, can only achieve so much. Even the purest reaction need not be at all effective in countering enlightened thinking and fierce anti-clericalism, as Fernando's Spain revealed for all to see. Much of the failure of the general Restoration of 1814–15 was simply due to the weakness and mediocrity of most conservative principalities, their sheer inability to counter Enlightenment ideas. The restored Papal state in Italy once again ruled over a large central Italian territory, but much to Metternich's

[11] Von Humboldt, *Briefe*, 398, 488; Gall, *Wilhelm von Humboldt*, 335–6; Reed, *Light in Germany*, 152; Levinger, *Enlightened Nationalism*, 204.

[12] Rose to Castlereagh, Berlin, 4 Jan., 1 Feb., and 26 Mar. 1820 in Freitag and Wende (eds.,) *British Envoys* i. 128, 131–2, 141; Gall, *Wilhelm von Humboldt*, 205–6.

dismay seemed incapable of organizing an even remotely competent administration, pursue clear lines of policy, or even maintain surveillance over the droves of radical-minded suspects, despite its obvious zeal for following Vienna's advice. "You can prop up a corpse," gloomily reported an Austrian commander from central Italy, to Vienna, in February 1832, "but to make it walk is impossible."[13]

The Vienna Congress, Holy Alliance, and general Restoration failed to achieve the goals conservative courtiers, aristocrats, diplomats, and clergy had counted on. Even in the Austrian Habsburg Empire, lingering Josephist tendencies and reluctance to surrender state powers and property gained since the 1780s, or return supervision of schools to parish clergy, hampered the reactionary drive in numerous ways. Austria's marriage laws and regulations relating to Jews and other religious minorities remained areas of unresolved continuing discrepancy, difficulty, and dispute. Officially, the Jesuits were re-admitted to the lands of the Austrian Empire in 1820, but in practice, despite papal pressure and protests, Jesuit establishments remained few and hemmed in by bureaucratic restrictions and supervision. Metternich was eventually able to force through improved terms and wider scope for Austria's Jesuits, in 1836, but a papal report on the state of Catholicism in Austria, of 1838, was remarkably pessimistic regarding religious Restoration in the empire, judging that the edifice of Josephism was far from fully dismantled in the manner both Papacy and Austrian court believed was needed; in most respects, efforts to expand the clergy, reimpose its sway, and reverse the 1780s educational reforms, had not succeeded.[14]

No one doubted that the three pre-eminent threats to Counter-Enlightenment, Restoration, legitimacy, and restored religious authority were the universities, the press, and networks of radicals and ex-revolutionaries expelled from the reactionary monarchies scattered across Europe living in exile. Sizeable untrammeled networks of political and intellectual dissident fugitives were mostly to be found congregating in Switzerland, Belgium, the smaller German states, and Paris but their shadow was felt everywhere. Large monarchies had plenty of clout with which to intimidate small courts but overall it proved impossible sufficiently to disperse the radical groups or effectively expunge Radical Enlightenment ideas and trends. "Measures have been taken," remarked the British envoy in Berlin, in 1819, welcoming the Carlsbad Decrees, jointly formulated by Prussia and Austria, to repress the "licentiousness of the press in certain newspapers in some of the small states in the center and north of Germany, whose undisguised tendency was highly revolutionary."[15] The July 1819 agreement following the Carlsbad conference, in August, required all newspaper, periodical, and pamphlet publications of less than twenty pages to submit to censorship before publication, and placed princely monitors at every university to remove politically undesirable professors and students.[16] But diplomatic observers remained

[13] Reinerman, *Austria and the Papacy* ii. 134–5.
[14] Reinerman, *Austria and the Papacy* ii. 270–1, 279–80, 294–6, 298.
[15] Rose to Castlereagh, Berlin, 20 July 1819, in Freitag and Wende (eds.), *British Envoys* i. 105.
[16] Cousin, *Souvenirs*, 153; Ramm, *Germany*, 148–9; Nipperdey, *Germany*, 247–9.

pessimistic about the efficacy of such efforts, not least due to political obstruction by some lesser states. "I very much fear," added the same envoy in November 1819, "that few of the German governments will meet the evil of the abuses of the Press as rigorously as Prussia has done, and that she will be left thus prominent with much inconvenience."[17]

Political and literary refugees were deemed particularly dangerous to stability, traditional thinking, and reactionary government, nurturing as they did political resentment and sharing their teachings with disaffected individuals staying at home, dissidents not exiled but barely tolerated, like the historian Jules Michelet (1798–1874), a passionate sympathizer with the ideals of 1789, and future author of the classic *Histoire de la Révolution française* (7 vols., 1847–53), a critic seething with hatred for the restored Bourbon monarchy. Evincing scant regard for Louis XVIII and none for his successor, Charles X (reigned: 1814–30), Michelet, a printer's son turned scholar and Vico disciple who became a Paris University professor, burned throughout the 1820s with a deep republican ardor for the great Revolution's democratic principles coupled with an irrepressible zeal to combat priests and church oppression.

Enlightenment was now in one sense in retreat, on the level of officialdom, but in another, deeper down, still gaining ground. Radical exiles, underground fugitives, and veteran critics inspired a largely veiled but growing home constituency of younger men bearing explosive grudges. The very nature of the generalized repression, forcing thought and activity underground, served to further concentration and segregation of radical thinking in intellectual, journalistic, and academic as distinct from professional, mercantile, or workers' circles. Censorship, the Restoration's broad impact, and the ideological reaction to it, in poetry, novels, painting, history, political thought, and social science, may have siphoned revolutionary impulses into allusion, sentiment, nostalgia, and visionary longing but could not quash the stream as such. Enlightenment radicals, as distinct from Napoleonists and moderates misleadingly designated "liberals" in France, Italy, and Spain, were doubtless a minority among the sizeable numbers forced into European exile from France, Germany, Poland, Italy, and Spain, as well as from Britain and Ireland to America and Australia, but Radical Enlightenment ranks remained considerable and, in literary and artistic as well as press and academic circles, indubitably expanding.

Between 1815 and 1830, the Romantic cult of revolution and conspiratorial opposition, refining and reworking memories of the revolutionary experience in journals, literature, drama, and poetry as well as philosophy, so profoundly permeated European intellectual life that this resumed "revolution of the mind" registered appreciable advances not just despite but, to a large extent, because of the repression.[18] Literature and art intensified awareness of the revolutionary experience and its meaning. The challenge of reaction and Counter-Enlightenment weighed so unremittingly on everyone outside agriculture, trade, and industry, that it generated its

[17] Rose to Castlereagh, Berlin, 3 Nov. 1819, in Freitag and Wende (eds.), *British Envoys* i. 120.
[18] Van der Veen, *Groot Nederland*, 8.

own counter-reaction in general culture. As Hegel suggested, a dialectical mechanism operated. If Romanticism nurtured reactionary views, as the Schlegels vividly demonstrated, it also inspired manifold radical, dissident paths. Moreover, Romanticism, as the Schlegels also showed, was often peculiarly conducive to abrupt volte-faces and reversals of direction. If there were impressive literary "apostates" changing course by defecting from the radical tendency, and breaking with their former associates, like Coleridge, Southey, and Wordsworth, all fiercely rebuked by Shelley for writings that "tainted the literature of the age, with the hopelessness of the minds from which it flows,"[19] Romanticism was no less potent in attracting converts and boosting revolutionary ardor infused with radical thought.

For crowns, ecclesiastics, aristocrats, and Counter-Enlightenment publicists everything suddenly deteriorated further with the revolutions of 1820 in Spain, Portugal, Greece, Naples, and Piedmont which proved, for all to see, that powerful revolutionary tendencies remained close at hand, able to mobilize the broad social grievances and discontent of the moment while invariably orchestrated by intellectuals, especially journalists, professors, students, literary men, and artists. The general scenario deteriorated further in conservative eyes, and still more inspiringly for Europe's radical intelligentsia, with Bolívar's stunning success in extinguishing Spanish monarchical rule in most of Spanish America and substituting in its place an entire network of independent republics. The transformation of Spanish America in the years 1820–5 looked like the resurgence of the European republican revolutionary wave that had cost the monarchies so much blood, effort, and treasure to overcome.[20] Both the 1820 and the 1830 revolutions have often been misleadingly presented by historians as if they were spontaneous initiatives of peoples, or classes, social forces seeking national liberation and constitutional changes. In reality, the socio-economic movements, powerful as they were, in themselves proved blind and anarchic, offering no political or moral direction: the direction, the scripts, derived almost exclusively from the targeted, underground coteries. Nationalist and Marxist historiography afterwards claimed the revolutions were actions of peoples or at least broad social segments moved by economic trends. Indeed, they were driven by profound social forces but became revolutionary movements only insofar as they followed the directives of political exiles, clandestine organizations, conspiratorial groups, and revolutionary reading societies acting on their own agendas always very differently from majority impulses. The leadership, rhetoric, priorities, and general orientation of the revolutionary movements in Europe mostly had little to do with slow shifts of broad "*mentalités*," conventional thinking, class, popular culture, social impulse, or economic factors. The revolutionary impulse sprang rather directly from fringe groups of highly articulate revolutionary veterans and intellectuals, a socially thoroughly unrepresentative mix of renegade nobles, defecting clergy, students, cashiered Napoleonist officers, artists, literary men and women, journalists, and academics.

[19] Foot, *Red Shelley*, 196. [20] Van der Veen, *Groot Nederland*, 85.

Claiming social and economic pressures "caused" the revolutions, always difficult to substantiate, has often led to misleading historiographical oversimplification. But this does not mean social factors were not basic to the story, only that divergent social and economic pressures drove blindly and indiscriminately in all directions. Bad harvests had a considerable impact. Industry changed the urban face of Britain, Belgium, and, more patchily, parts of France, Germany, and the north-eastern United States. Population growth accelerated everywhere, from 1815, noticeably expanding pauperism and destitution. Powerful social forces drew momentum also from other factors. Louis XVIII's refusal to re-employ most officers of Napoleon's army, many of whom had risen from relatively low social strata to high positions and, from 1814, found themselves adrift but unwilling to revert to inferior status, provided innumerable recruits for the exiled, underground "grande armée" of Liberty and the Romantic cult of Revolution.[21] Increases in university enrollment in Germany after 1815 went unmatched by any sufficient matching growth of employment opportunities in Germany's court bureaucracies, creating a trap that inevitably expanded the pools of highly qualified unemployed and frustrated graduates.[22]

Social factors generating distress and discontent, without the direction and guidance afforded by coherent, philosophically grounded ideology and a highly motivated fringe of professional revolutionaries, fomented only inchoate protest, contradictory impulses, and aimless insurgency, as easily harnessed by nationalism, Counter-Enlightenment bigotry, or authoritarian populism manipulating the credulous in the manner of the Montagne, as republican egalitarianism. The violent anti-Semitic movement that rocked Germany in 1819 with the pogroms called the "Hep-Hep riots" was as much an expression of social frustration as anything inspiring democratic agitation. These riots commenced in August 1819 in mixed Protestant–Catholic Würzburg, and rapidly spread to Bamberg, Bayreuth, Karlsruhe, Mannheim, Frankfurt, Koblenz, and Cologne, wrecking and pillaging Jewish quarters and communities as far as Hamburg and Lübeck. Not peoples, nor classes, and least of all broad cultural processes—a notion almost totally irrelevant—but rather the intelligentsia's disaffection with princely rule, bureaucracy, and religious sway focused the universal revolutionary credo of universal and equal human rights and free expression. Radical Enlightenment battled monarchy, aristocracy, and religious authority, but equally had to fight majority bafflement and bigotry. Alienated students and writers in these years renewed an Enlightenment radicalism of a growing sophistication and intellectual complexity that differed dramatically from the yearnings, dissatisfaction, and alienation of most peasants, workers, traders, housewives, and merchants. This striking and growing social differentiation and divergence had wide-ranging consequences and in many ways was society's tragedy, being a principal contributory factor in the collapse of the 1820, 1830, and 1848 revolutions and ultimately demise of the Radical Enlightenment itself.

[21] Bruyère-Ostells, *Grande Armée*, 26–9.
[22] Sperber, *Rhineland Radicals*, 70–1; Wende, *Radikalismus*, 22–3.

The main threat to restored hegemony of royalty, aristocracy, and ecclesiastical primacy derived, Europe's regimes were acutely aware, not from the common people, class, or particular interests, but clandestine underground intellectual opposition circles giving "countenance to persons of dangerous principles." Reminding his superiors that the "revolutionary spirit" in Germany was far from dead, in October 1817, the British envoy at Berlin emphasized that the principal threat, the source of "revolutionary effervescence," were the universities, professors, and students, with Jena "the most turbulent."[23] Italy was made ripe for the 1830 revolution by secretive, underground lodges of Carbonari, the underground milieu from which most notable personalities of the Risorgimento originally emerged. In Russian Poland, clandestine student groups throve not only in Vilnius (Vilna), where the underground student society of the Philomaths flourished between 1817 until broken up in 1823, but especially in Warsaw, Cracow, and Lemberg (Lwów).[24] Germany was no different. The Prussian court recalled all Prussian students from Jena to Prussia's own universities in April 1818, "under penalty of being excluded forever from all employments in their native country should they not obey this mandate instantly."[25] Yet Prussia, complained Britain's envoy, prior to Carlsbad, was still not repressing radical principles in universities vigorously enough.

The menace of "machinations of the revolutionists" was aggravated perhaps by economic hardship, by "slowness with which Germany recovers from the wounds inflicted in so many years of war, and defeat," and royal refusal to grant the promised constitution, but the general discontent directly threatened governments due to the "hold which the revolutionists have gained on the education of youth."[26] Reading societies and universities, not sectors of society, were the levers potentially unseating princes and churches. The Revolution was alive but hidden, simultaneously exciting and disappointing leading radical writers. Joint resolutions of the German Confederation in December 1835, again acknowledged that radical subversion in Germany was principally driven by a fringe of *Akademiker*, student organizations, and independent writers, two of the most notorious of whom, reportedly, were the journalist Ludwig Börne and poet Heinrich Heine.[27]

25.2. "ENLIGHTENED DESPOTISM" REVIVED: THE UNITED NETHERLANDS (1814–1830)

Important too for prolonging the late Enlightenment as a dominant cultural format in early nineteenth-century Europe were the new medium-sized monarchical–aristocratic

[23] Rose to Castlereagh, Berlin 29 Oct. and 11 Nov. 1817, in Freitag and Wende (eds.), *British Envoys* i. 76–8.
[24] Kienewicz, "Revolutionary Nobleman," 276.
[25] Rose to Castlereagh, Berlin, 10 and 13 Apr. 1819, in Freitag and Wende (eds.), *British Envoys* i. 89–90.
[26] Rose to Castlereagh, Berlin, 29 Dec. 2017, in Freitag and Wende (eds.), *British Envoys*, i. 82–3.
[27] Wende, *Radikalismus*, 21, 28.

entities—especially the new united kingdom of Sweden–Norway under King Bernadotte, the much expanded new kingdom of Bavaria, and the new Dutch kingdom, *Groot Nederland*, uniting the Netherlands, Luxembourg, and Belgium. Together these constituted a major obstruction to political reaction and especially the broader international effort to curb freedom of expression, reverse secularization, equality of cults, and Napoleonic legal and educational changes. In the Low Countries, as in Germany and Scandinavia, it was not "liberalism," "nationalism," or Restoration, but late Enlightenment that was central.

From 1804, Napoleon increasingly repudiated republics and republicanism and aborted the Batavian Republic in the years 1804–6 as he did those of Italy, exasperated by what he regarded as inadequate levels of Dutch and Italian contributions of troops and resources for his wars against allied coalitions. A transitional regime was installed in The Hague over the winter of 1804–5 headed by Rutger Jan Schimmelpenninck (1761–1825), a leading Patriot in the 1780s and 1790s, now Napoleon's anchor-man, and the Batavian Republic's last *Raadpensionaris* or state-pensionary. Schimmelpenninck did not wholly abandon his republican convictions, a blend of French democratic revolutionary theory and Dutch democratic traditions of the 1780s, but tried to placate Napoleon and hasten administrative unification and rationalization while preserving something of Dutch autonomy and the symbolism of 1795.

Transition from the Batavian Republic to the autocratic monarchy of the emperor's younger brother, Louis Napoleon (1778–1846), or Lodewijk Napoleon, as he now preferred to be called, who became "king" in June 1806 at the age of 27, represented a disgraceful regression from republican values in radical eyes. Politically, it nevertheless marked a vigorous acceleration of enlightened reform on many levels, a shift especially obvious in the administrative, fiscal, and legal spheres, and in the subordination and equalization of religious cults, a prominent feature of the new regimes throughout the Napoleonic state-system. Louis Napoleon sought to balance Catholic and Protestant ministers in his new royal state-council and allow Catholic communities equal scope with Protestants in building new churches. Though intended by his brother to be a reliable tool of his European strategy and French military requirements, as a newcomer in Holland but with a mind of his own, Louis Napoleon centralized the internal administration of the country with a raft of decrees issued in the early part of 1807, relying on his own trusted ministers, and did so with the clear intention of winning over local assent to his policies—in which he succeeded in good part, establishing a tradition of progressive, liberal monarchy which also reconciled in some measure, like the restored Orangist monarchy that followed, a good segment of the country's lingering "republican" sentiment.[28]

For centuries, Dutch cities and provinces had been administered by exclusive boards and committees of oligarchs. These were now replaced by ten autocratic department heads or prefects, called *landdrosten*, in whose hands police, military,

[28] Joor, *Adelaar en het Lam*, 73–5; Atteridge, *Napoleon's Brothers*, 164–6; Koekkoek, "Ware en vrije republiek," 256.

and civil powers combined, answerable to the king alone. These ten new departments corresponded to the old Dutch provinces except that Holland was now divided into two (North and South Holland, called respectively Amstelland and Maasland). However, now the departments were made strictly equal in status and format. Municipal government was thoroughly reformed too, becoming less autonomous and more standardized, each town of over five thousand inhabitants coming under a single burgomaster appointed by the monarch.[29] As in "Westphalia" and the rest of Napoleon's state system, the Code Napoleon replaced the former legal system (from May 1809) and, in August 1809, a royal decree regulated and equalized all the churches, fixing church ministers' salaries, and enforcing reversion of many church buildings to the Catholic community. A separate decree integrated Jewish life into Dutch society, stipulating full equality of Judaism as a state-regulated cult and removing lingering legal distinctions between Jews and non-Jews, one of the many key enlightened changes of the Napoleonic era the post-1814 Dutch monarchy retained.

Napoleon personally may have been more concerned with exacting resources and men, for his wars, than implementing far-reaching reform, but those he relied on to run his state-system, whether French, Dutch, German, or Italian, often had stronger Enlightenment commitments.[30] Stendhal was among the many middle-ranking French officials running the Napoleonic empire who, whether in France, Germany, or Italy, resented the relentless demands for men and money while wrapping this exasperation in an undogmatic neo-Jacobin republicanism that viewed the Revolution as primary and Napoleon as in some sense an accessory, if for the moment an indispensable, weapon in the revolutionary struggle against *ancien régime* princes, aristocrats, and churchmen.[31] Bonaparte's empire was exploitative, his armies pillaged; but his state system afforded a new organizational, legal, and constitutional framework enabling many gifted enlighteners and reformers of different nations to dismantle old laws, procedures, and institutions, and bring in improvements in theory and practice that could not otherwise have been introduced. Napoleon's system enabled the Western Enlightenment to attain its fullest, culminating late phase—and to powerfully survive beyond 1815. Given the wholesale abandonment of enlightened reform by Germany's, Italy's, and the Low Countries' secular and ecclesiastical princes in the years 1789–95, it was a process carried though in the teeth of increasing resistance from the reactionary Allied coalition and surging Counter-Enlightenment thinking and ideology, that could only have been achieved and consolidated via Napoleon's massive, unrelenting use of force.[32]

A key progressive reformer operating successfully within the Napoleonic state system was Izaak Jan Alexander Gogel (1765–1821), a revolutionary veteran and leader of the 1798 radical coup in Holland, recruited to serve Louis Napoleon and

[29] Joor, *Adelaar en het Lam*, 82–6. [30] Schroeder, *Transformation*, 380–2, 400.
[31] Imbert, *Métamorphoses*, 28.
[32] Knudsen, *Justus Möser*, 164; Israel, *Revolutionary Ideas*, 329–35.

afterwards Napoleon himself, who succeeded in introducing the first Dutch General Tax Law replacing the chaotic pre-1806 system of essentially regressive taxation. He had originally proposed his sweeping reform to remove provincial variations and municipal fiscal autonomy, equalizing the tax burden throughout the republic, in 1799; but though provisionally approved in March 1801, it was blocked by the Dutch democrats' defeat, in 1802, and reversion to a more federalized system. Gogel succeeded in bringing in his key reform in January 1806. It was characterized by the prime fiscal principle of Condorcet and Brissotin democratic republicans during the Revolution—the specifically Radical Enlightenment goal of switching to "progressive" direct taxation, placing the main fiscal burden on the middling and wealthier strata of society while shifting it away from excises on basic foodstuffs and components of everyday consumption to alleviate pressure on the growing numbers of impoverished.[33]

Son of a German officer in the old Republic's army who established himself as a merchant in Amsterdam in the early 1790s, Gogel first became prominent, in 1794, helping concert collaboration of the Dutch republican underground revolutionary movement with General Daendels and the invading French. Reviling Orangists, Orangism, aristocracy, and the *ancien régime*, no one more vividly illustrated conscious Radical Enlightenment piggybacking on the Napoleonic and post-Napoleonic state system. Frustrated by the Batavian Republic's vacillating moderation, from 1796 he edited one of Europe's foremost radical journals of the 1790s, the Amsterdam *De Democraten*, a paper mercilessly disparaging the old oligarchies.[34] Following the democratic republican coup of 1798, he had served as the Republic's minister of foreign affairs for a time, before the retreat from republican values, and re-federalization of 1802–5, drove him from office. He figured among the chief conspirators responding to Napoleon's efforts to subvert the Batavian Republic because he wanted more meaningful changes. Unlike other Dutch Patriots, he remained consistently committed to universal suffrage and equality (while also despising populism and mob unruliness) while collaborating both with the transformation of the Batavian Republic into the monarchy of Louis Napoleon, in 1806, and the dissolving of the monarchy into the French empire, in 1810. He proceeded throughout seeking to advance rationalization, democratization of society, and administrative improvement while mitigating the impact of Napoleon's increasingly vociferous exactions.

A true Enlightenment enthusiast, hardly had he become king of the Netherlands than Louis Napoleon began consulting advisors as to how to centralize, reform, and strengthen science and learning in his kingdom. He wanted to establish a counterpart to the *Institut de France* and, in January 1807, set up a commission to study this question which reported the following April. His commission, strikingly, selected as its model not Napoleon's revised format of 1803 but, rather, Condorcet's and

[33] Joor, *Adelaar en het Lam*, 382–9; Lok and Van der Burg, "The Dutch Case," 103.
[34] Schama, *Patriots*, 248.

Lakanal's earlier revolutionary concept of 1795, proposing more classes for the projected new royal academy, the first dedicated to the exact and mathematical sciences, the second political and social sciences with related disciplines like historical studies, and the third literature and language. On 4 May 1808, Louis Napoleon decreed the establishment of his Amsterdam Koninklijk Instituut van Wetenschappen (Royal Institute of Sciences) with a projected ninety-six members, covering all science and learning, including the arts. Its purpose was to co-ordinate and supervise the furthering of knowledge, including collecting from, and sending out, learned reports abroad.

The First Class, with thirty-six members, as in France, was devoted to the exact sciences (divided into six divisions); the Second Class, with twenty, dedicated to historical studies and Dutch language and literature, which became a recognized, state-promoted academic discipline for the first time (a policy afterwards continued by King William). The Third and Fourth Classes, each again with twenty members, were assigned to classical studies and philosophy, and lastly (as in France) the fine arts.[35] At the new royal academy's first general meeting, the physicist, Jan Hendrik van Swinden (1746–1823), a personality well-known in Paris and among the founders of the metric system, made clear to the assembled *érudits*, in his inaugural speech, that the new central body had different priorities from the older Dutch local learned societies: rather than local social and sociability functions, the new framework would be national, and mainly concerned to advance scholarship on an international level, filling gaps in knowledge by keeping vigilant watch on developments internationally, and especially promoting new discoveries, a goal supported not least by Holland's then internationally best-known scientist, Martinus van Marum (1750–1837), director of the Teylers Museum in Haarlem.[36] In the end, van Swinden and his colleagues failed to retain the 1795 "Second Class" devoted to social science and political theory with history, or to dissolve the local societies, which retained much of their vigor. Nevertheless, the new academy reinvigorated and changed the face of Dutch science and scholarship profoundly.[37]

The Prince of Orange's assumption of the title of "King of the Netherlands," on 16 March 1815, had the full approval of the European powers but was hardly a lesson in legitimacy and restoration of the old regime. Rather, from a Counter-Enlightenment perspective the change reflected a disconcerting continuity with the enlightened policies pursued in the Netherlands before 1814. In August 1815, William also secured from the victorious powers provisional authority over the former Austrian Netherlands (Belgium). Although the new monarchy failed to win general support in Belgium, it did successfully foment a sense of legitimacy and acceptance in the northern Netherlands by cultivating what was largely a false myth of national liberation from foreign occupation under its lead. Far from being a restoration, the

[35] Van der Burg, *Nederland onder Franse invloed*, 212–13.
[36] Van der Burg, *Nederland onder Franse invloed*, 213–15.
[37] Kloek and Mijnhardt, *1800: Blueprints*, 424–5.

new Dutch monarchy represented a total discontinuity in the course of modern Dutch history, above all by retaining most of the enlightened changes the Napoleonic regime had introduced. Although the period from the Batavian Revolution to the prince's return, in 1813, came to be both officially and popularly disparaged as the "French period," and taught in schools as an unfortunate lapse, a time of false foreign values despotically imposed, with Orange's collusion in British annexation of South Africa and other Dutch colonies conveniently overlooked, in reality, after 1815 the substantive changes of the revolutionary era were broadly retained and their Enlightenment character reaffirmed.[38] "King William I" remained steadfastly deaf to the incessant calls from Vienna and Berlin to curb freedom of expression and freedom to hold meetings, along lines adopted in Germany.[39]

For advancing democratic freedoms and equal human rights what chiefly mattered among Low Countries continuities after 1815 were the innovations affecting press freedom, minorities, and education, and demolishing ecclesiastical sway and privilege. After 1815, despite the resentment and opposition of most, followed huge further changes in schooling, especially in the southern Netherlands. But these were a continuation of the process of breaking down the church's grip over education and the press proceeding right through the revolutionary and Napoleonic era, the entire quarter-century 1790–1815, from which arose a new kind of enlightened intellectual elite. From the late 1780s onwards a vanguard of intellectuals, especially those formed subsequently by the *écoles centrales* and then Napoleon's *lycées*, doggedly continued, as they did equally also after 1815, to propagate robustly anti-popular Enlightenment views. Louis de Potter (1786–1859), a leader of the radical coterie during the Belgian revolution of 1830, for example, issuing from a minor noble lineage at Bruges that had supported Joseph II and fled during the *Vandernootiste* ascendancy of 1789–91, as a young man ardently infused with *jozefisme*, then later an ardent democratic republican venerating the French Revolution more than home-grown *Vonckisme*, flourished under the Napoleonic system, but never much admired Napoleon, who in his eyes betrayed the Revolution and republicanism. He spent most of the period 1811–21 in Florence and Rome where, thanks to official intercession, he gained access to the Vatican archives, enabling him to carry out research for a series of publications on ecclesiastical history which afterwards established him among Restoration Europe's foremost anti-clerical writers. In post-1814 Belgium, he became widely associated with the rising call for full religious toleration, including for Jews, and for further eradicating church influence from education.

If de Potter's fierce criticism of ecclesiastical privilege and authority did little to win him applause in Belgian society as such, ironically, for a decade or so it put him solidly in the good books of the court.[40] The king encouraged anti-Catholic publications of the kind de Potter produced, though that changed in the mid-1820s as de Potter

[38] Lok, "Establishment," 209–11; Lok and Van der Burg, "The Dutch Case," 108–9.
[39] Op de Beeck, *Verlies van België*, 77; Van der Veen, *Groot Nederland*, 7.
[40] Op de Beeck, *Verlies van België*, 14–16.

increasingly linked his uncompromising anti-clericalism with public displays of democratic republican sympathies. Among other public demonstrations, he helped organize the commemorative march in Brussels to honor the great revolutionary artist, Jacques-Louis David (1848–1825), who had twice been imprisoned by the Thermidorians and by Napoleon, and was buried in Brussels (Charles X having refused his burial in France), in December 1825.[41] King William's tolerant attitude decidedly helped render Brussels one of the prime centers of both French and German anti-monarchical, anti-Catholic, and anti-aristocratic exiles and agitation, as became conspicuous from the early 1820s when several major new opposition periodicals established themselves there. Especially notable, from 1821, was *Le Courier des Pays-Bas*, published by a group of opposition-minded young men later to emerge at the head of the 1830 Belgian revolution—Lucien Jottrand (1804–77), Alexandre Gendebien (1789–1869), Sylvain van der Weyer, and the future statesman Jean-Baptiste Nothomb (1805–81).

Among de Potter's most notable post-1815 initiatives was his establishing a small, subversive intellectual network, the so-called *Société de Douze* that gathered twice-weekly at the home of Philippe Lesbroussart (1781–1855), a former professor of the Brussels *École centrale* and then of the Université impériale de Bruxelles, to discuss politics and Belgium's future. The *Société de Douze* was successor to an earlier renowned elite society, the *Société de littérature de Bruxelles* founded in the Year VII (1800) as a kind of emanation of the revolutionary *École centrale de Bruxelles* dedicated to spreading appreciation of Voltaire and the *philosophes* and regularly debating philosophy, literature, and politics. Members of the *Société de Douze* included Adolphe Quetelet (1796–1874), mathematics professor and astronomer, a product of the Napoleonic Ghent *lycée*, who, in 1828, became principal founder of the Brussels Observatory, and was among the founders of European statistical social science, demography, and crime studies, the philosopher Louis Gruyer (1778–1866), and the learned jurist Jean-François Tielemans (1799–1888), later one of de Potter's closest collaborators. The Radical Enlightenment strand among the future leadership of the Belgian Revolution were all products of the *écoles centrales*, the Napoleonic secular education system—journalists, professors, and lawyers, often sons of Napoleonic officials, deeply committed to Enlightenment principles and unbendingly hostile to theology and the churches.

As dynast and monarch, alternating his royal residence between The Hague and Brussels, William stoutly resisted the democratic values the Dutch Republic proclaimed in 1795 and strove, motivated by dynastic and personal considerations, to foment a spirit of hierarchy and aristocracy. But it is not the case that the advent of monarchy marked a significant departure from the attitudes and system prevailing in the Low Countries between 1806 and 1813. Indeed, there were enough enlightened and progressive features of his rule for him to be able to win the willing support of key

[41] [Jullien], *Revue encyclopédique* 34 (1827), 54.

hardcore republican editors and intellectuals.[42] If some scholars view him more as an heir to Joseph II of Austria, or Frederick the Great, than Louis Napoleon, there is little doubt his administrative and economic reformism, education policies, secularizing church policy, museum policies, anti-Catholic attitude, and tolerationism made him a firm antagonist rather than protagonist of Restoration and Counter-Enlightenment values. In church policy, much to the fury of the restored Belgian bishops, he enforced much the same *tolérantisme* and "equality of cults" throughout the Low Countries as Joseph II, Louis Napoleon, and Napoleon; to his mind all the churches could equally contribute to the safeguarding of the people's moral uprightness.[43] In part a typical product of the Napoleonic system (between 1802 and 1806, as "prince of Fulda," he had been ally and pawn of Napoleon in Germany), he represented a continuation of the centralizing methods, style, and also personnel, of the Napoleonic kingdom of 1806 to 1813; indeed, many of the innovations he introduced, despite adornment with monarchical window-dressing, actually derived from the Batavian Republic.[44]

After 1814, there were many key continuities in personnel as, for example, with Cornelis Felix van Maanen (1769–1849), a former revolutionary and since 1806 Louis Napoleon's justice minister, whom, in 1815, William I confirmed as his justice minister. Until the mid-1820s, he presided over a relatively generous freedom of the press which proved vital to the French and German republican and Napoleonist fugitives exiled in Brussels during the 1820s. Adapting the Code Napoleon, including public registration of births, marriages, and deaths, to the Dutch context, it was van Maanen too who, in 1808, first created a centralized Dutch police force with broad responsibilities including overseeing the Dutch coastline, harbors, and fisheries.[45] Also Gogel, who at the time of the coup, in 1813, refused to break his oath of loyalty, and transferred to Paris to serve Napoleon there,[46] and by his own wish held no official position under King William, continued to stand in high regard, for some years remaining a royal advisor in the background.

There was no break either in school policy, which continued on the lines of Louis Napoleon's 1806 ordinance and even under the same Haarlem-based royal official, Adriaen Van den Ende (1768–1846) who drafted the 1806 measures and who, remarkably, continued supervising school policy until 1833. Having conceived and introduced the system compelling local government authorities to establish permanent "school funds" under state, not local, supervision and state-inspection of all schools, state-funded and private, as well compulsory division of all schools into levels according to age, it was also he who introduced blackboards and regulation of school punishment codes. When the Netherlands was formally annexed to France in 1810, a commission of French state school inspectors, among whom was Georges Cuvier,

[42] Koekkoek, "Ware en vrije republiek," 255–7.
[43] Santegoets, "Verenigd Koninkrijk," 233–4.
[44] Lok, "Establishment," 213–15; Van Sas, "Republiek voorbij," 98; Van der Burg, *Nederland*, 256–7.
[45] Joor, *Adelaar en het Lam*, 420–1, 458–60; Van der Veen, *Groot Nederland*, 53–5.
[46] Joor, *Adelaar en het Lam*, 473, 499; Van Sas, "Republiek voorbij," 89.

compiled a report on the Dutch school system, filed in 1811, pronouncing the Dutch primary school system indisputably superior to anything seen in France.[47] Under Louis Napoleon, Van den Ende and his staff established the tradition whereby the Netherlands regularly spent more on education per hundred thousand population than France or Britain, but it was William I who confirmed and continued this policy through the 1820s and 1830s.[48]

Louis Napoleon's and Van den Ende's education policy, especially their efforts to separate education from religion and secularize teaching, was not popular. The 1808 decree forbidding practicing preachers and priests, Protestant or Catholic, becoming regular teachers in state-supported primary schools met with widespread opposition, as did the concept of "algemene christendom" [general Christendom] figuring prominently in the new school regulations of Louis Napoleon's reign. Catholics viewed the concept as mere camouflage for indoctrinating children in attitudes and morality that in reality were essentially "Protestant," as did rabbis and Jewish parents. There was much opposition too to Van den Ende's standardized required lists of books for use in schools.[49] William I's school policies only extended the opposition earlier leveled at Van den Ende's reforms, especially in Belgium, where the Catholic clergy remained furious that they were just as far from recovering their pre-1794 hold over education and the schools, after 1815, as before. In Belgium, there was much resistance too to William's "algemene christendom" and his rigid language policy, favoring use of the Dutch language in schools even in areas where French was the main spoken tongue.[50]

Colonial affairs were another area of Enlightenment continuity. Under the terms of the Vienna settlement, Britain, in August 1816, returned to the Dutch those parts of south-east Asia occupied by the British during the latter part of the Napoleonic Wars, since 1811, other than the three most valuable Dutch colonies after Indonesia—South Africa, Ceylon, and western Guyana—which were permanently absorbed into the British empire. Returning Indonesia renewed the Dutch Enlightenment presence in south-east Asia. Earlier, under the British governor, Thomas Stamford Raffles (governor of the Dutch East Indies 1811–16, and later, in 1819, founder of Singapore), cataloging the historical monuments of Java had commenced and the Batavian Society of Sciences had been revived. On 23 April 1813, Raffles returned to contribute a famous discourse on the state and progress of the Koninklijk Bataviaasch Genootschap van Kunsten en Wetenschappen (Royal Batavian Society of Arts and Sciences), "Discours sur l'état et les progrès de la Société batavienne," to commemorate the thirty-fifth anniversary of the Society's founding in 1778; and in 1817 he published his *History of Java*.

In the East Indies, King William's prime concern was to promote Dutch commercial interests and exploit the territory, people, and resources for the benefit of the Dutch homeland. Nevertheless, Enlightenment concerns lent a particular character to

[47] Van der Burg, *Nederland*, 163.
[48] Van der Burg, *Nederland*, 152–5, 161, 192, 194, 196; Santegoets, "Verenigd Koninkrijk," 231.
[49] Van der Burg, *Nederland*, 155–6.
[50] Van der Burg, *Nederland*, 260.

the restored regime. Beside combating slavery, the new monarch dispatched a stream of scientists, artists, and topographical draughtsmen to collect reliable information of every kind. He issued instructions for certain kinds of statistics to be gathered, promoted study of the flora, fauna, history, archeology, and art of Java and the other islands, and took measures to secularize the government and administration of the islands as well as secularize study of Indonesia's religions. An Amsterdam-trained professor of natural history of German origin, prominent in the Netherlands in many fields, patronized before 1810 by Louis Napoleon, Caspar Georg Reinwardt (1753–1854), became royal "director" of agriculture, science, and the arts on Java, under the new royal governor-general. At Batavia, with Dutch rule restored, he spent over five years (1816–22) presiding over the progress of the sciences. Many of the antiquities Raffles had had gathered from various parts, including a number of massive statues of Hindu goddesses, one with an elephant head, were shipped back at this time and displayed in Amsterdam, along with a wide range of other East India curiosities.[51] Exploratory expeditions were organized into the interior of Java, to Bali, the Moluccas, and other less well-known parts of the archipelago to collect natural history items for both local and Dutch natural history collections—the objects sent back including an exceptionally large stuffed crocodile.[52] In May 1817, Reinwardt established the royal Javan botanical gardens adjoining Buitenzorg Palace, forty miles south of Jakarta (at modern Bogor), where Raffles had resided, and there collected plants and seeds from all over Indonesia, for their commercial potential but also as part of his scientific program. An all-round naturalist possessing also pharmaceutical and general medical expertise, Reinwardt also initiated programs of vaccination among the local population against various sicknesses, and sought to transfer the best medical advances achieved in Holland into Java.

The foremost western Enlightenment body in Asia after the Calcutta society, the *Bataviaasch Genootschap*, was especially proud of bringing all the sciences together to advance the Enlightenment in East Asia, while making the East Indies known in Europe. The *Société littéraire et scientifique* of Batavia (Jakarta), as it was first called, had brought out its first volume of proceedings in 1781. Its mission it had long viewed as one of propagating the arts and sciences in the East Indies, "contributing to the development of the intellectual and industrial faculties of both the native and foreign inhabitants of Batavia and all its dependencies."[53] By 1818 it had published nineteen volumes, including seven volumes of proceedings and discussions, representing one of the most monumental compilations of knowledge about Asia available to European contemporaries.[54] By 1826 the body, now known as the *Bataviaasch Genootschap van Kunsten en Wetenschappen*, had produced eleven volumes of proceedings and had ninety-five ordinary members resident at Batavia besides associates, staff, and eighty-

[51] [Jullien], *Revue encyclopédique* iv (1819), 176; Van Goor, *Nederlandse koloniën*, 201–2.
[52] [Jullien], *Revue encyclopédique* iv (1819), 175–6; Van Goor, *Nederlandse koloniën*, 194, 208.
[53] [Jullien], *Revue encyclopédique* xl (1828), 132–3.
[54] [Jullien], *Revue encyclopédique* v (1820), 18, 184.

six extraordinary members residing elsewhere in the East Indies, making a total membership of 201. Originally gathering in Batavia's main fortress, the society now convened in a building with a library, botanical garden, cabinet of natural history, and museum of antiquities and conducted regular correspondence with the learned societies of Calcutta and London besides those of Amsterdam, Rotterdam, Haarlem, and Utrecht, and with missionaries in Peking and Tranquebar. Beside a president and vice-president, it had eight directors, a secretary, librarian, and eight administrative staff.[55]

A particular burst of publications and *Verhandelingen* [Proceedings] appeared in 1825–8. With texts such as the "Description of the Island of Borneo," they sought to make known previously unknown regions, and promote ethnology, as with an account of the customs and manners of Sumatra. The 1826 Proceedings included an abridged Japanese grammar and catalogue of the most important Japanese books, the first contribution to Japanology of Philip Franz von Siebold (1796–1866), graduate of Würzburg and admirer of the Von Humboldts (especially Alexander), later to become the greatest of all late Enlightenment naturalists working in eastern Asia.[56] A survey of the plants of Java "and neighboring islands," compiled under the society's auspices, appeared in two volumes, in Brussels, in 1828. As well as promoting understanding of Indonesian art and history, the society strove to further research on medical and demographic aspects of neighboring parts of Asia, one result of which was an account of the 1817 cholera epidemic in Bengal by M. J. Renier Vos.

A marked change set in in the Netherlands, however, much as in Bavaria and several other Late Enlightenment "enlightened despotisms," from the late 1820s. Especially from 1827, William I exhibited increasingly authoritarian and repressive tendencies.[57] Newspapers began to be harassed and shut down, editors fined and gaoled. On 15 February 1830, Professor Tielemans was arrested in Brussels and imprisoned. He was tried together with de Potter and the journalist Adolphe Bartels (1802–62) for inciting revolt against the government; sentenced to seven years' exile, he settled in Paris, where he formed a committee to lend support to Belgian political refugees. De Potter was sentenced, in December 1828, to eighteen months' imprisonment and a 1,000 florins fine.

25.3. BAVARIA AND WÜRTTEMBERG AS LATE ENLIGHTENMENT STATES

As a late Enlightenment despotism the pre-1827 Dutch–Belgian model was paralleled by Bernadotte's Sweden–Norway and several middle-sized German states, most

55 [Jullien], *Revue encyclopédique* xl (1828), 133.
56 [Jullien], *Revue encyclopédique* xl (1828), 404, 442.
57 De Valk, "Weg naar de vrijheden," 567.

impressively Bavaria. The death in 1799 of the reactionary Elector, Charles Theodore, the last Bavarian ruler seeking religious uniformity, was greeted with relief by many and followed by far-ranging changes.[58] The new prince, Maximilian IV Joseph, who ruled Bavaria as "Elector" from 1799 to 1806 and "king" from 1806 to 1825, having resided much of his life in France and married two Protestant women in succession, fundamentally transformed the Bavarian court's character. Dismissing the papal nuncio, Father Lippert, Director of the College of Book Censorship, and other notoriously reactionary ministers from government service, in their place the new ruler chose as his chief advisor a well-known enlightener, Count Maximilian Joseph von Montgelas (1759–1838), supplemented by other ministers known to scorn the old order. Symbolically, the year 1799 marked the Enlightenment's most decisive leap forward in Bavaria.

Religious toleration was no easy step to take in deeply pious and reactionary Bavaria. Introduced in stages, it took several years before Lutherans and Calvinists were effectively on an equal legal footing with Catholics. Religious press censorship and the old confessional narrowness slowly drew to a close, though Mennonites and Herrnhuters secured merely the right of private worship and Jews long remained burdened with many pre-1799 disabilities and restrictions curtailing their rights and activities. Lutherans received their first large church in Munich in 1806. Bavaria's edict on religion of 24 March 1809 reaffirmed full equality of Lutheran and Calvinist rights in principle; nevertheless, the new regime still encountered stubborn lingering resistance in many districts, including to ending the sway of the Benedictine and other religious orders over the elementary schools and Bavaria's nineteen gymnasia.[59]

Montgelas, having studied at Ingolstadt and Strasbourg and when young, from 1779, for some years belonged to the Illuminati,[60] was regarded with particular suspicion and dread in German reactionary court circles and by many churchmen. Fusing monarchism and aristocratism with definite radical tendencies, a lifelong champion of secularization and foe of religious authority, from 1799 he emerged among the most wide-ranging of all late Enlightenment reformers. In March 1802, street begging by friars and monks, and collections for monasteries, were forbidden. In 1803 began a state-directed campaign of removal of crosses, chapels, small churches, and images from streets and country roads, though popular hostility to image-clearing from public places long remained especially intense. On government orders, building materials retrieved from dismantled churches were mostly employed for constructing and repairing schools, which greatly proliferated in number as well as becoming secular in character during the opening years of the century. Most monasteries were suppressed, church lands were extensively secularized, and monastic orders' art and book collections were appropriated by the state.

Secularization overshadowed all else; but there were also other major changes. Between 1803 and 1810, noble privilege was curtailed, serfdom's vestiges were

[58] Pinkard, *Hegel*, 249–51.
[59] Higby, *Religious Policy*, 101–3, 112–13, 127, 142–4.
[60] Schüttler, *Mitglieder*, 106.

abolished, and the bureaucracy elevated into a professional, salaried *Stand*. In February 1800, Maximilian invited proposals for a comprehensive revision of Bavaria's criminal code and trial procedures on the basis of the "proper principles of reason and civil life." Pressed to align with the Code Napoleon, a general reform of the Bavarian law codes and penal code, including abolition of judicial torture, followed. This too encountered opposition from the clergy and much of the populace. From a radical perspective the Code Napoleon was highly defective in its provisions on divorce, and approach to pregnancy and birth outside of wedlock, as it largely reversed the 1792–3 Brissotin principle of gender equality. But in Germany its provisions seemed far too innovative and contrary to church tradition to be easily accepted. Rehberg did not doubt that in its legal re-conceptualization of marriage and sexual relations, the Code Napoleon (1804) stood even more contrary to German sensibilities and tradition than French administrative practices or abolishing privilege and feudal vestiges.[61]

In the new Grand Duchy of Baden (Grossherzogtum Baden), a modified version of the Code Napoleon was adopted by Grand Duke Carl Friedrich in 1809, but again only over extensive protest. In post-Napoleonic late Enlightenment Bavaria, under the revised state criminal code of 1813, the principle that individual rights remove personal morality from the sphere of the law, that individual autonomy requires de-criminalization of all consensual sexual acts except where minors are involved, was fully adopted, so that extra-marital intercourse, extra-marital pregnancy, and homosexuality were now all de-criminalized.[62] But while nearly all German magistrates by this time urged milder penalties for "sexual crimes," conservative jurists still insisted fornication, extra-marital sex, and same-sex relations must continue to be defined, in statute and the courts, as criminal offenses. Not only in society and among the clergy, but also legal and bureaucratic circles, Montgelas's revisionism provoked widespread indignation and recrimination.

Montgelas impatiently confronted the recalcitrance of Catholic "Old Bavarians," as they called themselves, and their resentment of Bavaria's new Protestant subjects, who were widely deemed unwelcome intruders and foreigners—among whom, at this point, was Hegel, who regarded this typical attitude with great contempt, wholeheartedly agreeing with Montgelas's refusal to accept the traditional Bavarian notion that teachers must be subordinate to the church.[63] To fund state-run schools and gymnasia like that at Nuremberg, of which Montgelas made Hegel headmaster from 1808 to 1816, the government did not hesitate to seize private endowments from many church-run schools. A decree of June 1804 not only admitted Jewish boys to all the lower and higher schools of the Bavarian realm with full exemption from religious instruction, but, where no Jewish schools existed, obliged parents to send them to Christian schools while requiring Bavaria's *Generalschuldirektorium* [ministry of

[61] Hull, *Sexuality, State*, 372–92.
[62] Hull, *Sexuality, State*, 342–9.
[63] Pinkard, *Hegel*, 250–1, 291.

education] to ensure Jewish children's freedom of conscience was not interfered with by teachers in any way.[64]

Following the Franco-Bavarian peace of 1801, Montgelas steered Bavaria, tentatively at first, away from alliance with Austria and the Allies, though Maximilian Joseph long remained in two minds about whether to participate in Napoleon's demolition of the old German Empire and throw in his lot with France. Relations with Napoleon, pivotal to Bavaria's early nineteenth-century transformation, were tightened, in January 1806, by the marriage of Maximilian's eldest daughter, Princess Augusta Amalia (1788–1851), to Josephine's son and Napoleon's adopted heir, Eugène Beauharnais, in exchange for Napoleon's tempting offer, highly distasteful to Vienna and Berlin, to elevate Bavaria to the status of "kingdom."[65] Within months of this marriage, Napoleon arranged two more dynastic marriages designed to promote southern Germany's transformation into a buffer between France and the great powers, Prussia, Russia, and Austria, dominating Europe's eastern half. In April 1806, Karl Ludwig, heir to the Grand Duchy of Baden, married Stéphanie de Beauharnais, Josephine's cousin; in August 1807, the marriage, scheduled since 1803, between Napoleon's younger brother, Jérôme Bonaparte (1784–1860), who had now divorced his American wife (to whom he had professed himself deeply devoted), and Princess Catharina Frederica (1783–1835), daughter of Duke Frederick of Württemberg, finally took place. In exchange for becoming a military ally of France against the Allies, the duke was likewise elevated, becoming "King of Württemberg," and received several additional territories.[66] These alliance-building dynastic marriages mattered greatly to the political status and further development of the south German states as "enlightened despotisms" both before and after 1815.

Eugène Beauharnais's Bavarian marriage of January 1806 confirmed the status of the newly enlarged entity "Königreich Bayern," as a kingdom. "Bavaria" found itself substantially enlarged but also transformed through the addition of a whole collection of very diverse territories—twelve former Imperial Free Abbeys, the former partly Protestant Imperial Free City of Augsburg, the entirely Lutheran Imperial Free City of Memmingen with its population of 11,000, and the less than wholly Catholic former prince-bishoprics of Bamberg and Würzburg. Another predominantly Lutheran former Imperial Free City, Regensburg, was added in 1810. Bavaria's king, having married his eldest daughter to Eugène who had recently been proclaimed "viceroy" of the new "Kingdom of Italy" with its capital in Milan, with which, in March 1805, Napoleon replaced the amalgamation of Italian republics he had established in northern Italy in 1796–9, became a firm French ally fully integrated into Napoleon's new European state-system, a key component of Napoleon's Confederation of the Rhine and check on Prussia and Austria.

64 Higby, *Religious Policy*, 148; Holborn, *History of Modern Germany*, 391–2.

65 Chateaubriand, *Mémoires* ii. 130; Whaley, *Germany*, 617–18; Roberts, *Napoleon the Great*, 299, 394–5.

66 Roberts, *Napoleon the Great*, 369, 393, 395; Atteridge, *Napoleon's Brothers*, 147.

Following Napoleon's downfall, in 1814, Maximilian stuck to his enlightened policies, in opposition to Metternich and the Prussian court, and Eugène, expelled from France, remained a welcome refugee at court in Munich until his death in 1824. Despite the reactionary wave sweeping Europe from 1814 and onset of the Restoration, Montgelas clung to power for several years being only finally dismissed by "King Maximilian," accused by other courtiers of "having monopolized to himself exclusively all the power and patronage of the state," in 1817.[67] Although Montgelas's departure was followed by some softening of Bavaria's earlier anti-clerical stance and a concordat with the Papacy, his removal was no great concession to the clergy or a sign the king was ending his Enlightenment commitment, or educational or legal reforms. "The Concordat has excited considerable sensation here," reported the British envoy, from Munich, in January 1818:"it is indeed rather remarkable that a government which since the secularization of the clergy in 1803 has accorded less influence and fewer privileges to the Church than any other in Europe, should have ratified a treaty so favourable to the supremacy of His Holiness."[68] But to the church, the Bavarian concordat was by no means a satisfactory outcome. It yielded substantial compromises, restoring church control over Catholic marriages, greater opportunity to censor irreligious publications, and some compensation for seized land and revenues, but kept the bishops, as Napoleon had, in an entirely subordinate role in most areas of law and administration. Although only a fraction of the original stock of monasteries in the kingdom, around twenty, still survived, the religious orders received back only a small fraction of the properties seized.[69] It was still the king who nominated the bishops and drew episcopal boundaries to fit his kingdom's revised borders. Efforts to restore religious street processions and local mass pilgrimages to encourage popular zeal were still discouraged until 1830. Renewed disputes over jurisdiction, marriage law, and Protestant and Jewish rights soon flared up once more, re-aggravating the church–state friction only superficially resolved in 1821.

Montgelas's secretive style of rule, and reluctance to concede the principle of representative government, did end. Even if rather half-heartedly, in May 1818, the king issued the first Bavarian constitution installing a genuine form of parliamentary consultation, albeit based on a highly restricted suffrage. The constitution, received "with the greatest apathy and indifference," according to the British envoy, tightly confined the new legislature's sphere of competence, did nothing to secure "responsibility" of ministers, and "nothing for the liberty of the press." Still, ignoring papal protests, the constitution guaranteed freedom of worship on an equal basis to Catholics, Lutherans, and Calvinists (Protestants by this time comprising almost one-third of Bavaria's population), and was undoubtedly couched in "too liberal

[67] Hervey to Castlereagh, Munich, 26 Apr. 1817 in Freitag and Wende (eds.), *British Envoys* i. 260.
[68] Hervey to Castlereagh, Munich, 17 Jan. 1818, in Freitag and Wende (eds.), *British Envoys* i. 262.
[69] Higby, *Religious Policy*, 310–14, 320–9, 331; Nipperdey, *Germany*, 59.

and tolerating a spirit to give much pleasure to the Holy See."[70] Bavaria, moreover, refused to adopt the 1819 Carlsbad decrees with any vigor, remaining decidedly suspicious of the "exclusive and predominating influence of the courts of Berlin and Vienna over all the affairs of Germany." After being suppressed the previous year by Württemberg, Bavaria, since 1804, had been the home of the *Allgemeine Zeitung* published by the famous Tübingen publishers, Cotta, after 1815, now published at Augsburg and the most independent and widely-read newspaper in the entire German Confederation (circulation over 10,000).[71] Repeated protests from Berlin and Vienna that Bavaria was failing to curb press freedom sufficiently failed to produce "any alteration in the line of conduct the Cabinet of Munich seems determined to adhere to."[72]

Frustratingly for Vienna, Berlin, and also London, during the decade after 1815 Bavaria stubbornly resisted the prevailing Counter-Enlightenment tendency, and much the same held for neighboring Württemberg. The new "king of Württemberg," Wilhelm I (reigned: 1816–64), well-read and connected to various foreign courts, including that of Russia, showed little taste for Metternich's attitudes, which earned him the hostility of all the conservative courts. He utterly scorned "government so unenlightened and uncompromising as that of Spain," which seemed to him a clear case of "misrule arising out of the wealth and influence of the clergy."[73] Wilhelm, however, found still greater cause of alarm in the disposition he traced in France to put itself by degrees under the same monastic sort of government which had caused for some time the misfortunes of Spain. Having spent several years in Paris, he had held advanced views on many topics, and though never keen on broad suffrages and representation, became a classic late Enlightenment despot. His sister being married to "King Jérôme Bonaparte of Westphalia," the latter, on losing his Westphalian kingdom, received from the Württemberg court the title of "Prince of Montfort." Having close connections with Jérôme's court at Cassel before 1813, Wilhelm was known to have a high regard for several of the foremost enlighteners in Germany, including August Heinrich Freiherr von Trott (1783–1840), a former close advisor of Jérôme.

In 1824, the Prussian crown prohibited its subjects from studying at Tübingen as well as Basel, due to insufficient rigor on the part of the Württemberg and Swiss authorities in suppressing radical ideas.[74] King Wilhelm defied what was expected in

[70] Hervey to Castlereagh, Munich, 30 May 1818 and 5 Feb. 1819, in Freitag and Wende (eds.), *British Envoys* i. 263, 266; Nipperdey, *Germany*, 230.

[71] Straub, *Wiener Kongress*, 140–1; Koch, "Power and Impotence," 588; Moran, *Toward the Century*, 92–7.

[72] Hervey to Castlereagh, Munich, 3 and 17 Nov. 1819 and 3 Jan. 1820, in Freitag and Wende (eds.), *British Envoys* i. 271–2; Jarrett, *Congress of Vienna*, 216–18.

[73] Seymour to Canning, Stuttgart, 31 Jan. and 8 Feb. 1827, in Freitag and Wende (eds.), *British Envoys* i. 369–73.

[74] Wynn to Canning, Stuttgart, 6 and 18 June 1824, in Freitag and Wende (eds.), *British Envoys* i. 357–8; Ramm, *Germany*, 150.

Berlin and Vienna in various respects but especially his reluctance to impose stringent restrictions on university teaching and freedom of expression at home, whereby he aroused the ire of the Five Powers (Austria, Prussia, Russia, Britain, and France) imposing the new European order. He showed intransigence not just by issuing an ordinance for the liberty of the press, in 1817, but in and after 1819 openly expressing opposition to the Carlsbad decrees.[75] This gained him considerable popularity among radically-inclined university students. A famous scandal arose, in March 1824, when thirty-five students were arrested at Halle, followed by more arrests at other universities, after it was discovered, or at least rumored, that among those engaging in "dissemination of revolutionary principles" were agitators of the pan-German student movement aiming at German reunification who had "their eye on the present King of Württemberg" to be their eventual figurehead.[76]

Of course, post-1815 "enlightened" Württemberg, like Bavaria, Baden, and the Netherlands, always scrupulously maintained a wide separation between court Enlightenment, their "moderation," and republican, anti-aristocratic democratic radicalism. This was well illustrated by the List affair. A professor of state administration at Tübingen, Friedrich List (1789–1846) ranked among the leading economists of pre-1848 Germany. Convinced Germany's political and economic fragmentation was a principal cause of the country's growing numbers of poor, he became a passionate advocate of a national customs union, in 1819 becoming a founder of the *Deutscher Handels- und Gewerbeverein* [German Trade and Industry Union]. Later, with his book, *Das Nationale System der politischen Ökonomie* (1841), he emerged as chief advocate of a single border tariff around the entire German Confederation. But beside concern for the poor, he was "long celebrated," as the British representative in Stuttgart noted, "for the democratic nature of his political tenets." His scathing comments about the inadequacies of the Württemberg administration and the king's ministers led to his incurring the wrath of the court. Stripped of his professorship in 1819, he was nevertheless elected, in 1820, to the state legislature, where he continued criticizing the "principles of the king's government, and censured, abused and vilified unsparingly" everyone in the king's service. Arrested in 1822 and tried for sedition, he was sentenced to imprisonment but escaped. "He has taken refuge at Strasbourg," it was afterwards reported, "the asylum and rendezvous, with Basel, of the very numerous disciples of revolution whom Germany has of late years ejected from its bosom."[77] Afterwards, List worked as a journalist in Philadelphia for some years, before returning to Germany in 1832.

When it came to the validity of monarchy and aristocracy, then, conservatism prevailed. Due to List and other activists, King Wilhelm remained deeply worried about the proposed two-chamber constitution finally adopted in 1819 after two years of vigorous debate in his kingdom. The 1819 Württemberg constitution featured an

[75] Taylor to Castlereagh, Stuttgart, 21 Nov. 1819, in Freitag and Wende (eds.), *British Envoys* i. 328.
[76] Clanwilliam to Canning, Berlin, 8 Oct. 1824, in Freitag and Wende (eds.), *British Envoys* i. 202.
[77] Hamilton to Londonderry, 27 Apr. 1822, in Freitag and Wend (eds.), *British Envoys* i. 335–6.

upper chamber largely reserved for royalty and nobility, but with nobility and bishops also occupying a slice of the lower chamber. Württemberg's reformers, at loggerheads with the old nobility and Protestant clergy, had pressed for greater freedoms and less aristocratic presence. Hegel published an article at Heidelberg in 1817, reissued as a pamphlet in 1818, setting out his own view of the uproar over the Württemberg constitution, claiming it reflected a conflict between pre- and post-revolutionary forms of society and life, that the 'modern project' inevitably competed with the *ancien régime*, being "that which is rational and required of us because of the failures and insufficiencies of the older project."[78] Older conceptions of society, entailed commitments to hierarchy and status dividing individuals into groups based on ties of dependence of a kind irreconcilable with equality before the law, universal justice, and confessional freedom, causing friction that could ultimately be resolved only by adopting the modernizing view.

Württemberg's nobles and clergy defending the historic "rights" of elites, privilege, and veneration of old family names, Hegel portrayed as blind to how the march of history had transformed society's circumstances, interposing a fresh set of conditions in which the forms of dependence and status characteristic of the past lost their relevance. Conservatives were defending a position incompatible with the realities of modernity. But he also rejected the stance of the radicals. Rather, Hegel's position during the 1817–19 Württemberg constitution debate reflected his new conviction, renewing Kant's stress on the need to balance support for French revolutionary principles against the need to uphold order, law, and political stability as represented by the sovereign, that the French Revolution marked an inherently irreversible change reflecting an underlying logic in the reality of human development which is best managed by the sovereign state minimizing the damage and disruption (as Prussia was supposedly doing) from the inevitable resulting clashes of competing interests and principles.[79] There was much adverse reaction to Hegel's recommendations during the constitutional debate, including from several former friends, rebuking him for siding ultimately with the king against the people. Hegel's conception of representation, of how the interests of the different groups in society should be represented in the modern state, there was no concealing, placed the main responsibility in the hand of the state authorities even if his new intellectual and technocratic elite, replacing the nobility and clergy of the past, were trained to higher levels of awareness in the universities.[80]

Like Kant, the mature post-revolutionary Hegel aspired to secure the principles of the French Revolution without revolutionary upheaval disrupting lives and property, advocating universal principles of emancipation within a format as smoothly adapted to constitutional monarchy as possible.[81] If Kant softened the radical implications of

[78] Pinkard, *Hegel*, 405. [79] Cousin, *Souvenirs*, 196; Pinkard, *Hegel*, 403–7.
[80] Pinkard, *Hegel*, 411; Kouvelakis, *Philosophy and Revolution*, 40–1.
[81] Kouvelakis, *Philosophy and Revolution*, 42–3.

his core premises with temporizing compromises,[82] Hegel did so equally, at times degenerating, complained Nietzsche later, into open admiration of what exists, of the status quo, of success. Victor Cousin (1792–1867), soon to become the intellectual doyen of French post-1815 French academic moderate Enlightenment, an admirer of Kant and Hegel and fierce critic of Spinoza, was delighted to find, conversing with Hegel when visiting Heidelberg in 1817, that Germany's greatest living philosopher had apparently altogether given up his earlier republicanism and become as much a man of "moderation," the middle ground, and constitutional monarchy, as Cousin himself.[83]

Until 1830, both Bavaria and Württemberg remained models of late Enlightenment despotism. Maximilian's death, in October 1825, and the accession of his successor, King Ludwig I of Bavaria (reigned: 1825–48), given the latter's "disposition to mysticism" and love of miracles, did arouse apprehension among the progressive-minded that "increased power of the Catholic clergy" would follow. However, "nothing has yet been done," it was reported from Munich, in March 1826, "to confirm this apprehension,"[84] nor did anything so occur until 1830. At the ceremonial inauguration of Munich University, in 1826, an entity soon figuring among the foremost late Enlightenment higher education initiatives in Europe, Ludwig professed antipathy to all bigotry and obscurantism, explicitly guaranteeing freedom of expression and academic freedom.[85] After 1832, Bavaria, Hesse, and the others steadily shed their enlightened trappings of the 1820s. In February 1848, during the agitation preceding the outbreak of "this, useless, outrageous Revolution," as Schelling styled the new revolutionary upsurge, one of the Bavarian government's first preventive measures was to close Munich University and order all students not domiciled in the city to leave within forty-eight hours.[86]

Another key Bavarian initiative of the 1820s brought to fruition by King Ludwig was the construction of a vast new library, the Bayerische Hofbibliothek, on what afterwards became the Ludwigstrasse, the magnificent new, broad avenue dominating central Munich, to house the—for the epoch, since Montgelas's interventions—vastly expanded state book collections. Like Munich University's dramatic rise among Germany's principal higher education institutions, the Bavarian state library's triumphant apotheosis was closely linked to Montgelas's dissolution of fifteen of the eighteen monasteries formerly skirting Munich, commencing with suppression of the Carmelites, in December 1801, when their buildings were reassigned to the Munich Latin School.[87] Montgelas's 1803 *Sekularisation* decrees and their aftermath had created a unique opportunity for appropriating church properties and books. Over a million books, it is estimated, were removed from Bavarian ecclesiastical

[82] Schröder, "Radical Enlightenment," 46.
[83] Cousin, *Souvenirs*, 196; Moreau, "Réception du spinozisme," 245.
[84] Taylor to Canning, Munich, 17 Mar. 1826, in Freitag and Wende (eds.), *British Envoys* i. 293.
[85] Pinson, *Modern Germany*, 54.
[86] Schelling, *Das Tagebuch*, 34.
[87] Higby, *Religious Policy*, 183–4.

establishments of all categories between 1803 and 1813, the state library thereby becoming "one of the principal beneficiaries of the secularization of monastery books."[88] A celebrated late Enlightenment initiative, the Munich State Library burgeoned to become Europe's largest public library outside Paris. By 1819 it boasted 400,000 volumes, dwarfing even Göttingen where the famous library reportedly then possessed 280,000 books, 110,000 academic dissertations, and 5,000 manuscripts, and Dresden's royal library with 250,000 books, 100,000 dissertations, and 4,000 manuscripts, besides the renowned ducal library at Wolfenbüttel where Lessing had been director, with 190,000 books, 40,000 dissertations, and 4,000 manuscripts, and the Prussian royal library at Berlin, in 1819 comprising 160,000 volumes.

Munich thus became an emphatic vindication of the effectiveness of enlightened despotism as an agent of late Enlightenment. Munich and the above four other major libraries now vastly eclipsed even the best-furnished other German university libraries, which, located mostly away from capital cities, found themselves at a growing disadvantage. Marburg reportedly held only 55,000 books in 1819, Heidelberg 30,000, and Halle a mere 20,000.[89] Now in a class of its own, Munich remained for some time, until the British Museum reading-room and library facilities were built in the 1850s, Europe's second largest public library after the Paris Bibliothèque Nationale, now, of course, renamed the "Bibliothèque du Roi."

The Hofbibliothek's international prominence as one of Europe's greatest libraries reflected a late Bavarian Enlightenment that retained momentum until the end of the 1820s. Sharing the conservative Romantics' enthusiasm for the Middle Ages, Ludwig disagreed with Montgelas's and his father's Francophile and anti-clerical policies. He initiated a program of establishing new monasteries, raising the total in Bavaria from twenty in 1825 to thirty-four by 1832. But there arose no real Counter-Enlightenment movement at the Bavarian court until after the 1830 revolutions when a decidedly stronger reaction against constitutional freedoms and anti-clericalism set in. This became still more marked following the democratic republican ferment of the 1832 "Hambacher Festival" which finally jolted Bavaria into wholeheartedly joining Prussia in imposing vigorous repressive measures and tightening state censorship.[90] Among principal organizers of the epoch-making 1832 Hambacher Fest was a former leader of the Erlangen University student society, Johann Georg August Wirth (1798–1848), editor of the *Deutsche Tribune*, the main organ of the German press association or *Presse- und Vaterlandsverein*, a publication appearing in Munich from July 1831, and then Homburg, but suppressed by the Bavarian authorities in March 1832. It was this paper which, in April, played the chief role in clandestinely inviting radical societies and organizations all over Germany, and German exiles abroad, to attend the Hambach freedom festival, at which Wirth and other speakers publicly denounced Germany's princes as "traitors" to the people, designating press freedom the people's shield against arrogant, rapacious rulers, the eventual path to victory over tyranny.

88 Garrett, "Klostersturm," 64–5.

89 [Jullien], *Revue encyclopédique* iii (1819), 365.

90 Nipperdey, *Germany*, 326–9, 368–9; Pinson, *Modern Germany*, 52–4; Higby, *Religious Policy*, 331–3.

The three-day jamboree at Hambach Castle, in the Bavarian kingdom's outlying Palatinate region, proclaimed democratic values, human rights, and a future united Germany. Adopting as its symbol a tricolor of black, red, and gold, it introduced into subversive German political culture the colors later adopted by the Weimar Republic (the present-day German flag).

The organizers' basic goal, the peroration Wirth delivered at Hambach illustrates, was not German nationhood, unification, and certainly not "liberalism" (though Wirth later did drift toward both "moderation" and a nationalistic stance after around 1840). In 1832, what the leadership demanded was the overthrow of autocracy, censorship, and religious authority on the basis of "Freiheit, Aufklärung, Rationalität und Volkshoheit" [Freedom, Enlightenment, Rationality, and Sovereignty of the People].[91] Wirth called for the downfall of Germany's kings and princes not as a nationalist, but to establish democracy and republicanism together with fraternity of peoples, summoning Germans to contribute active fraternal support also to Polish, Italian, Hungarian, and Spanish liberty.[92] Stressing the Revolution's international character, he summoned the German people to rise against the Holy Alliance and their ally, Louis-Philippe's France, and fight for "Spain, Italy, Hungary, and Poland" as well as Germany. The 1830 July Revolution, insisted Wirth, had been disgracefully subverted by "liberal," anti-democratic financial interests, especially bankers, using the new French monarch Louis-Philippe to pamper and extend their wealth and property at the expense of democracy and the people's happiness.

France in 1830 had settled for a "liberal" monarchical compromise utterly bogus and false in the eyes of sincere *Republikaner.* No significant help for the German or international Revolution could henceforth be expected from France. Europe's revolutionaries should now look exclusively to themselves. Only the German people themselves could topple the repressive despotism Austria, Prussia, and Bavaria had imposed, but must do so as part of a Europe-wide revolutionary movement.[93] Wirth ended his peroration, urging the crowds to give three rousing cheers for the peaceful, brotherly "conföderirte republikanische Europa" [confederated republican Europe] of the future! In part a folk festival, with much singing and jollification over large beer-mugs, there was doubtless less commitment to radical principles among the crowds than the intellectual leadership liked to suppose.[94] The Bavarian court nevertheless sent in half the Bavarian army, 8,500 troops, to occupy Hambach. A month after the Fest, the Carlsbad Decrees were further tightened; now even one-page flyers, caricatures, and categories of longer text hitherto exempted were subjected to prior censorship.[95]

[91] Görisch and Mayer, *Untersuchungsberichte,* 42, 276–7, 280–1, 358; Wende, *Radikalismus,* 41–4.

[92] *Rede von Johann Georg August Wirth,* 1–3; Levinger, *Enlightened Nationalism,* 121–2.

[93] *Rede von Johann Georg August Wirth,* 4.

[94] Wegert, *German Radicals,* 153–6; Sperber, *Rhineland Radicals,* 112, 152, 175, 217–18.

[95] Sperber, *Rhineland Radicals,* 112; Koch, "Power and Impotence," 588; Sandkühler, "Positive Philosophie," p. xxxi.

Everyone connected with the Hambacher Fest was pursued afterwards by the Bavarian as much as Austrian and Prussian authorities: Börne hurried back to Paris where he died in February 1837. Wirth was caught in hiding and tried at Landau. By "republic," he declared, in a defiant eight-hour speech before his judges, he meant "the empire of reason, justice, humanity, freedom and happiness."[96] Condemned to lengthy imprisonment, he escaped in 1836, first to France, then Switzerland, spending the rest of his life in exile, apart from a brief return on the outbreak of the 1848 Revolution. Hambach marked a turning point not only for Bavaria but also several other German principalities, becoming the pretext, for example, for reversing the semi- freedom of expression conceded in 1831 in Grand-Ducal Hesse.[97] Protest and agitation against the post-Hambach repression continued for years on the part of German exiles in Switzerland, France, and Belgium, and clandestinely by students and professors at Heidelberg, Giessen, Göttingen, and Marburg. In 1834, the young dramatist Büchner created a considerable stir in Hesse with his *Hessischer Landbote* [The Hessian Courier], a defiant clandestine revolutionary pamphlet powerfully denouncing Germany's princes and aristocrats, including the Grand Duke, while simultaneously echoing Ruge's, Börne's, and Heine's incisive literary critique of the deep-seated deference to authority and acquiescence underpinning the "moderation" of German middle-class "liberalism," the people's feeble response to the growing repressiveness of the German states.[98]

No one asserted more passionately than Arnold Ruge (1802–80) that the German people had been duped by their governments in 1813–15 and would continue to be duped by ruling elites until philosophy showed them the way forward; among the Young Hegelians he became the figure most interested in organizing them as a political group.[99] Like Hegel and Bauer, he regarded history as a progressive movement, impelled by the "General Will," for realization of "freedom" within and also by the state, while also criticizing Hegel for his conciliatory, ambivalent stance.[100] No one was more virulently critical of the conventional notions of both the general public, and what he considered, notably in his *Self-Critique* of 1843, the undemocratic, impotent, unphilosophical wishy-washy "liberalism" of the day.[101] When would Germans abandon the unthinking deference and conventional piety that accomplishes nothing, he demanded, the stifling parochialism blocking all effort toward a better and freer society? The Germans, he maintained, "need the dissolution of liberalism into democratism" and only philosophy could show men how to make this indispensable transition.[102]

[96] Wegert, *German Radicals*, 147–8; Wende, *Radikalismus*, 23–5.
[97] Görisch and Mayer, *Untersuchungsberichte*, 11; Ohles, *Germany's Rude Awakening*, 37–41, 44.
[98] Görisch and Mayer, *Untersuchungsberichte*, 331, 335–45; 357; Ohles, *Germany's Rude Awakening*, 129; Nipperdey, *Germany*, 330.
[99] Ruge, "Self-Critique," 246–7.
[100] Berlin, *Against the Current*, 273–5.
[101] Nipperdey, *Germany*, 344.
[102] Ruge, "Self-Critique," 264–7; Israel, *Expanding Blaze*, 470.

Kant, Fichte, and Hegel had created a philosophical tendency, "were on the right path,"[103] as the young Feuerbach expressed it later, but failed to go far enough in rendering philosophy man's chief guide to both truth and reshaping reality in our world. On the surface, the defeat of the 1830 revolutions was an outright victory (outside Belgium, Baden, and Switzerland at least) for reactionaries, churchmen, and supporters of aristocracy. Veteran *Freiheitsfreunde* [Friends of Liberty], like Wirth, Ruge, Börne, and Heine, now furtively hiding in exile or plunged in dejection, or both, were left striving to preserve their old revolutionary morale and zeal, on a purely intellectual plane. If memories of 1830 and the Hambacher Fest in south-west Germany helped keep alive a vigorous commitment to basic rights, democracy, and Revolution in student networks and reading societies,[104] more generally the experience of 1830 dejected radicals and had a powerfully disorienting effect on "moderates," who across Europe felt ever more torn between the need for constitutional, religious, and educational reform and fear of social unrest and radicalism.[105] Disappointment, combined with frustration at the ambivalence, metaphysical fusion of revolutionary principles with individual passivity, and upholding state sovereignty and stability offered by Kant and Hegel, incited in the 1830s a final wave of defiant philosophical revolt against the religious and the social-political status quo, that of the so-called "Young Hegelians." What emerged was a relentless two-pronged assault, on religious authority, on the one hand, and, on the other, on metaphysical systems like those of Kant and Hegel professedly hindering the advance of democratic activism. It was amidst this splintered, disheartening post-1830 milieu that what might be termed the last chapter of the Radical Enlightenment was written.

[103] Feuerbach, *Pierre Bayle*, 340; Reed, *Light in Germany*, 56–7.
[104] Görisch and Meyer, *Untersuchungsberichte*, 42–3, 276–84.
[105] Sheehan, "The German States," 262–3.

26

British Philosophical Radicalism (1814–1830)

26.1. A NEW BEGINNING: BENTHAM AND THE GENTLER PATH

In Britain, repression, prosecutions for "atheism" under the blasphemy laws, and the crackdown on Paine's and like publications, continued, from 1792, for a remarkably prolonged span, for four decades until 1832. Aversion to radical thought as a threat to the established social and political order remained general and intense. Beside prohibiting seditious works, and imprisoning a few rebellious authors, publishers, and orators, the government in London tried to curtail political consciousness among the poor by repeatedly raising the duty on newspapers to minimize sales among the least instructed and informed. By 1819, the minimum cost of papers had risen to seven pence per issue, putting them out of reach for most and largely restricting sales to the middle classes and above. Unremitting pressure was kept up to discourage publication of new editions of subversive texts, or halt, as one observer expressed it, the "laudable exertions of Mr. Thomas Paine to bring disaffection and infidelity within the comprehension of the common people."[1]

However, not infrequently, the effect on certain minds was counter-productive. Oxford and Cambridge were not yet independent research universities but rather ecclesiastically-controlled preparatory schools, which was not a little off-putting to some. Converted, like not a few, by reading Paine and Godwin, the young Shelley, on arriving at Oxford from Eton (where he had been much bullied by other boys) in October 1810, already detested monarchy and was a committed republican; only a year later, in 1811, he was expelled from Oxford for clandestinely publishing an atheistic piece.[2] During the 1820s and early 1830s, blasphemy trials followed by fines and imprisonment remained still quite common in England; as late as 1841, a publisher of Shelley's "Queen Mab" was prosecuted. During the early and mid-1830s, the young Charles Darwin (1809–82), studying at Cambridge in the years 1828–31, inspired by Lamarck and Alexander von Humboldt, and meditating on the

[1] Johnston, *Hidden Wordsworth*, 767; Chadwick, *Secularization*, 106; Hamburger, *John Stuart Mill*, 72.
[2] Guinn, *Shelley's Political Thought*, 23–6; Roberts, *Shelley*, 242; Capaldi, *John Stuart Mill*, 103.

persecution of Galileo, felt no small trepidation at the thought of being exposed to retribution as an "atheist."[3]

In the United States public disapproval and blasphemy trials could no more than Britain's trials, imprisonments, and fines halt the continuous flow of radical literature from certain subversive presses, as is well illustrated by the uninterrupted stream of Paine editions and the reception of Elihu Palmer's principal work, his *Principles*, which first appeared in 1801, followed by a revised edition in 1802. A third American edition appeared in the year of Palmer's death, 1806, without naming any place of publication, merely announcing on its title-page that its aim was to present "philosophy" calculated to overthrow the "theology which has destroyed the harmony of nature, and demoralized the intelligent world." Illegally republished in London by subversive radicals in 1819 and 1823,[4] George E. Evans published further American editions of Palmer in 1830 and 1840; a final edition appeared in London in 1841. Even so, this uninterrupted clandestine flow does not mean intimidation did not exert a huge inhibiting effect—quite the contrary. In post-1815 London, noted that fascinating general propagator of radical thought, Richard Carlile (1790–1843), booksellers were mostly "afraid to sell" and readers to "purchase, to defy the authorities under such conditions."[5]

Cobbett, having returned to England and, by 1809, become disillusioned with the parliamentary system, concluded that neither of the ruling parties genuinely worked for the "national benefit;" from that year, he became a regular, leading, and caustic critic of the government. Consequently, the Tory ministry targeted him and his influential paper, the *Political Register*, too; the caricaturist Gillray took to depicting him as a "Jacobin." Tried for inciting mutiny and subversive criticism of the government in July 1810, he was sentenced to two years' imprisonment at Newgate and a £1,000 fine, which, unsurprisingly, made him more cautious but also privately still more scathing than before about the country's existing aristocratic status quo.[6] Subsequently returning to the fray in a more subdued fashion kept Cobbett out of trouble until early 1817, but then the government, unnerved by a series of mass meetings in London, in part stirred by the radical press, calling for parliamentary reform, passed the so-called "Gagging Act" declaring public meetings illegal except where authorized beforehand by a magistrate. Once again menaced by the threat of imprisonment, Cobbett returned, via Liverpool, to America, where he stayed until 1819.[7]

Yet most reformers and critics of the existing system, now including Cobbett, aimed to make the legislatures and the electoral system more representative without entertaining much thought of abolishing aristocracy and mixed government as such,

[3] Hamburger, *John Stuart Mill*, 69–70. [4] Fischer, "Religion Governed," 18.

[5] Nelson, *Thomas Paine*, 227; Nash, *Secularism*, 11–12; Hudson, *Enlightenment and Modernity*, 73, 145.

[6] Foot, *Red Shelley*, 34–5; Ingrams, *Life and Adventures*, 102–3, 117.

[7] Ingrams, *Life and Adventures*, 134–5, 141.

or curbing religious authority;[8] only a small, restricted core were authentic radical enlighteners in the sense of seeking to eliminate "aristocracy," install democracy, and institute secularism by transforming the people's thinking. Cobbett never developed plans to overhaul society as distinct from Parliament or assail Britain's aristocracy as the dominant social and political force. Also, where the Paines, Palmers, Fellows, Places, and Carliles were all anti-Christian "deist" or atheist, Cobbett remained a churchgoer and never took much interest in "philosophy," pronouncing one of Bentham's works he tried to read "puzzling and tedious beyond moral endurance."[9] While persisting in their efforts to spread the message, full-blown "radical enlighteners" at the same time remained wary lest the revolution in ideas and attitudes they sought to precipitate should meander violently off course in the wrong hands, plunging everyone, as the French Revolution had disastrously done during 1793–4, into the catastrophe of populist tyranny. To radical minds, it is worse than useless to oust kings, priests, and aristocrats by "such an utter overthrow as should leave us prey to anarchy, and give us illiterate demagogues for masters."[10]

"Cobbett's running away," as one or two radical critics referred to his absence during 1817–19, occurred at a crucial moment of rising agitation and unrest. After the end of the Napoleonic wars, diverse radical groups and journals started to regain lost momentum in London and, before long, also in Philadelphia, Boston, and New York. In Britain, more than America, revulsion against the unending, costly, and destructive wars, and the post-1815 economic depression, powerfully contributed to the post-1815 revival of radical thought. Hope, toasts, and banquets imparted a timeless, indestructible core to Paine's radical message, rendering his impact uniquely trans-Atlantic, while stimulating revived awareness of the American Revolution's abiding significance for the world, the continuing expectation of its "expanding blaze." This was the stirring message Cobbett brought back with him on returning, yet again, to England in 1819.[11] Paine and Palmer had embraced the doctrine of Brissot and Condorcet that the peoples of the world would ultimately support the radical cause; and that when, eventually, men did reject kings and priests, a world of democratic republics would arise where the general interest would oblige states to refrain from fighting each other in the way that monarchies normally did, and instead work for the good of the whole, of the majority, forging a new era of "perpetual peace."[12] British radicalism's revived trans-Atlantic dimension was reflected, in the years down to 1832, by a burst of admiration for the United States and their institutions, the reverse of the coin of the then fashionable English aristocratic and middle-class cultural disdain for America. Shelley, a self-proclaimed "democrat, philanthropist, and atheist," was among those who most clearly reflected this intellectual and emotional reaction: to him, the French

[8] Dickinson, *Liberty*, 229; Thomas, *Philosophic Radicals*, 2–3.
[9] Ingrams, *Life and Adventures*, 196. [10] Holmes, *Shelley*, 349.
[11] Ingrams, *Life and Adventures*, 157, 163–4.
[12] Whatmore, "French and North American," 224–6, 229–30.

Revolution was the "master theme of the epoch in which we live,"[13] America the model, and Tom Paine England's greatest hero.

The post-1815 depression and upsurge of discontent in England passed the subversive initiative in the pamphleteering and press war against the Tory government to several younger men, most notably Carlile who regarded Cobbett as still something of a reactionary. On returning to Liverpool, in November 1819, Cobbett was gratified to receive a warm welcome from the crowds. He brought with him the remains of Tom Paine, which, to the annoyance of some American radicals, he had had dug up, intending to organize a rousing re-burial in England. He planned a huge public event with massive publicity, a mass gathering, banquet, and toasts, and the erection of a bronze monument at Thetford (Paine's birthplace), to more effectively trumpet Paine as a national hero and object of a national cult. To his regret, Cobbett was forced to abandon his plans because Paine's bones got lost in transit, and partly also because, on reaching England, he found that, despite Peterloo and rising criticism of the government, the British public still remained, after all, predominantly either indifferent or hostile to Paine due to his irreligion.[14]

Nothing could clearer, in Britain as in America, that Enlightenment radicalism as such could not stir events, movements, or crowds; ordinary men were not interested in the writers of books or radical philosophy. But the London government and *The Times*, the leading London conservative paper, were by no means mistaken in assuming that, in Britain too, radical pamphleteers and journalists with their slogans and catchphrases could powerfully energize and steer angry crowds when these were already seriously aroused for other reasons. A few months before Cobbett's return, Carlile was among the speakers scheduled to address the crowded Chartist reform meeting at St Peter's Fields, Manchester, on 16 August 1819, when the banner-waving masses, estimated at over 60,000, brandishing signs reading "Parliaments annual, suffrage universal," were assailed by the yeomen cavalry charging into the crowds with sabres drawn, killing around fifteen and wounding hundreds.[15] Carlile escaped; later that month, hidden by friends, he launched a new paper, *The Republican*, a hard-hitting subversive journal accusing crown and magistracy of murdering the innocent Manchester protesters. Following news of Shelley's early death, in 1822, Carlile, his wife, and journal were also to become the foremost publicists striving to keep Shelley's name alive and disseminate his poetical and prose works.[16]

Shelley had penned several pieces of political theory prior to his drowning off the Tuscan coast in 1822, most notably *A Philosophical View of Reform*, written in 1819–20 but unpublished before the twentieth century, a text he composed at the same time

[13] Jager, "After Atheism," 622; Roberts, *Shelley*, 30.

[14] Seaman, "Thomas Paine," 168; Kaye, *Thomas Paine*, 125; Ingrams, *Life and Adventures*, 159, 163–4.

[15] Holmes, *Shelley*, 529–31; Bloom, *Restless Revolutionaries*, 134.

[16] Nash, *Secularism*, 11; Guinn, *Shelley's Political Thought*, 98, 101–2.

that he was working on his translation of Spinoza's *Tractatus Theologico-Politicus*.[17] *A Philosophical View* presented a gradual, open-ended cumulative perspective on the trans-Atlantic world's renewed revolutionary process, which he held to be political and social but driven by philosophical and literary subversion, by his international brotherhood of revolutionary writers, artists, and critics nourished on one-substance philosophy and democratic ideas, or, as he put it, the "new race that has arisen throughout Europe, nursed in the abhorrence of the opinions which are its chains."[18] "The just and successful Revolt of America" had initiated the revolutionary process leading to universal suffrage and had established the world's principal trans-Atlantic model. America "has no king," he explained, "that is no officer to whom wealth and from whom corruption flow. It has no hereditary oligarchy, that is it acknowledges no order of men privileged to cheat and insult the rest of the members of the State," and no "rotten boroughs," or "false representation, whose consequences are captivity, confiscation, infamy and ruin."[19]

Another conspicuous irritant to the establishment was the blistering attack on Britain's role as chief patron of reaction and royal "legitimacy" in the world mounted in the respectable press by the redoubtable Leslie Grove Jones (1779–1839), a former major in the Grenadier Guards, and Wellington's commandant at Brussels prior to Waterloo. Grove Jones stopped short of preaching outright rebellion but assaulted the revised world order decreed from Vienna and London from a specifically British radical perspective. Having witnessed the Restoration first hand in France, a visit to the United States, in 1817, completed his disillusionment with his former conventional views. He began waging ideological war on British Loyalism, taking particular satisfaction in elegantly infuriating the gentry establishment with abrasive letters to the London papers. The United States taught one to "contrast the free, happy, and flourishing condition of that country with the subjugated and degraded position of France" and all Europe under restored monarchy and compare the "principles of freedom and justice" triumphant in America with what he had learned to see as the despicable principles and practices of the Allies. He was appalled that the Anglican "pulpit has resounded with the obnoxious doctrines of passive obedience and non-resistance, of the infallibility of ministers and divinity of kings." He continually contrasted the baseness of "monarchical legitimacy" with the principles proclaimed by "Sidney and Locke, by Beccaria and Vattel, by Franklin and Condorcet, by Price and by Bentham."[20]

"Ameliorating and remodeling the constitutions of the old states of Europe" was unavoidable and essential, insisted Grove Jones, due to the "rapid strides which the human intellect is making, and which all the powers on earth cannot arrest." Even so, "it should not be recommended" to those reformers struggling to achieve the

[17] Guinn, *Shelley's Political Thought*, 46, 51–4; Roberts, *Shelley*, 83–4.
[18] Shelley, *Poetical Works* iv. 41; Roberts, *Shelley*, 44–5.
[19] Shelley, *A Philosophical View*; Guinn, *Shelley's Political Thought*, 53–4, 60, 64, 66.
[20] Grove Jones, *An Examination*, pp. ii– iv.

necessary transformation that they "imitate entirely the Americans." In particular, he contended, reflecting a feature that especially typified British philosophical radicalism at its height in the 1820s, Europeans should now eschew armed struggle and seek less violent means than had been tried in 1775 and 1789. Given the great strength of the royal courts and bitter legacy of recent wars, in post-1815 circumstances neither taking up arms nor furious pushes toward democratic republicanism could "promote the general happiness of the European states." Another vast struggle, renewing the French revolutionary conflict, would be just another useless, bloody resort to methods already tried, exhausted, and discarded. "What is only to be obtained by torrents of blood, should not be sought after, if otherwise attainable."[21] Europe must settle for less initially, and by gradual stages edge towards the American democratic model.

The key was to infiltrate more minds. Among the foremost English radicals of the era, Richard Carlile, a cobbler's son, originally from Devon, who left school at the age of 12, first discovered radical thought while working in London for a tinsmith in 1816–17, on being placed on short-time and growing familiar with the economic misery affecting much of the English working population. The mass distress of 1816 "opened my eyes" to the significance for readers from poor backgrounds of Paine's *The Rights of Man*, a work where, beside abolition of primogeniture and breaking up aristocratic estates, Paine calls for a shift of taxes from the poor and middle strata onto the wealthy and the aristocracy, and more generous public support for the poorest and most wretched.[22] More comprehensively and genuinely radical than Cobbett, within a few years Carlile emerged among the most resourceful and energetic republican, freethinking, Paineite publicists in Britain. Pondering the problem of the difficulty of communicating the truths of "philosophy" to the poor and barely educated inspired his plan to make fundamental radical texts available to the poorest readers by splitting them into small leaflets and running these off, without resorting to shops, selling them inconspicuously in the streets.

Astonishingly, Carlile's *The Republican* kept up its assault on monarchy and restricted suffrages from its clandestine place of production for nearly seven years, until December 1826. During the late 1820s, Carlile also formed a touring lecture and debating team with the freethinking ex-minister Robert Taylor, which, among other episodes, provoked, in May 1829, one of the most scandalous uproars in Cambridge's history. Having booked rooms in the town center, they posted up notices on the University Library doors, announcing meetings challenging the Cambridge theologians to answer their claim that Jesus Christ, alleged "of Nazareth, never existed; and that the Christian religion had no such origin as has been pretended; neither is it in any way beneficial to mankind." The University vice-chancellor organized Carlile's and Taylor's swift expulsion from the town but not before the event left a deep impression on, among others, the young Charles Darwin, a student figuring among

[21] Grove Jones, *An Examination*, 46–7.
[22] Paine, *Rights of Man*, 240–53, 256–9, 269; Seaman, "Thomas Paine," 150–1, 156–7.

the fifty or so "young collegiants" in Cambridge whom Carlile discovered to be "somewhat bold in avowing infidelity among each other."[23]

For decades, the radical tendency survived in Britain, tightly besieged, marginalized, and loudly howled down by the public, underground but uneradicated and remarkably tenacious. "You and your friends," averred Fellows, complimenting Carlile on the *Republican*'s surviving seven years under such conditions, and on his lively London discussion forum founded, in 1830, on the South Bank, known as the Blackfriars Rotunda, "have made a glorious stand in England, which surprises even us in America, who agree with you in sentiment. For although we are more at liberty to express our thoughts, there are few who have the boldness to do it with that freedom which you and your supporters have done."[24] No small compliment from Fellows, and no small paradox—one summed up still more incisively by Cooper: "in no other country is the wise toleration established by law, so complete as in this [the USA]. But in no other country whatever, is a spirit of persecution for mere opinions, more prevalent than in the United States of America. It is a country most tolerant in theory, and most bigoted in practice."[25] And Cooper, a doughty fighter eventually forced to resign from the presidency of South Carolina College (now the University of South Carolina) by local clergy, for irreligion, in 1833, was in a position to know.

But Carlile paid a steep price for his tenacity. A principal target of the Tory assault on press subversion during the post-Peterloo era, in November 1819 he was brought to trial on ten counts of blasphemous and seditious libel, less for his publicizing the Peterloo "murders," though that was a factor, than his 1819 edition of Paine's *Age of Reason* and re-edition of Palmer's *Principles of Nature.* His trial became a *cause célèbre*, observed, among others, by Shelley, who composed a 6,000 word defense of freedom of the press in protest: "in prosecuting Carlile, they have used the superstition of the Jury as their instrument for crushing a political enemy, or rather they strike in his person at all their political enemies." Carlile was indeed being singled out for severe punishment, declared the presiding judge, for "attacking the purity of that which we believe to be true, and of attempting to undermine that faith upon which all our hopes of happiness here and hereafter are founded." Sentenced to three years in Dorchester prison for publishing illegal blasphemous material, two for publishing Paine and one for Palmer, and a swingeing £1,500 fine, his prison sentence was doubled to six years after he presented evidence of his inability to pay the fine.[26]

For helping to publish *The Republican*, Shelley's "Queen Mab," suppressed by the government in 1821 as blasphemous and seditious, and other prohibited items whilst he languished in prison, and aiding his activities, several associates were likewise

[23] Quoted in Desmond and Moore, *Darwin*, 71.

[24] Fellows, "Memoir," in Palmer, *Posthumous Pieces*, 9–10.

[25] Cooper, *Scripture Doctrine*, 323.

[26] BL printed 1177/2 "Speech of the Hon. Mr. Justice Bayley"; Foot, *Red Shelley*, 31, 214–15; Clark, *Thomas Paine*, 404–6.

arrested, fined, or imprisoned, among them his wife, Jane, given two years behind bars in 1821.[27] In 1823, the Court of the King's Bench ordered the seizure of the entire contents of Carlile's Fleet Street offices and bookshop, out of which "such works as are not considered libelous" were then auctioned off to cover various smaller remaining unpaid fines. Seizure of his stock of 70,000 volumes destroyed Carlile's whole capital investment but enabled London's foremost radical martyr finally to walk free, in 1825. His harsh fate was a topic intensively discussed at the time in the circles of Bentham and his close ally (since 1808), James Mill (1773–1836).[28] Brought to trial yet again in January 1831, Carlile was sentenced to a further two and a half years of imprisonment for libel and sedition.

The democratic republican principles of the American and French revolutions, viewed as a trans-Atlantic force, were thus heavily repressed in Britain as well as continental Europe in and after 1814–15, but by no means decisively crushed. Rather, there is an important sense in which the Allied Powers' success in defeating Napoleon and dismantling the physical and territorial vestiges of the French Revolution actually helped revive those values on an inspirational, philosophical, and emotional level. Shelley, Heine, Stendhal, Sismondi, Michelet, Lamartine, and many another early nineteenth-century literary and intellectual voice powerfully reflected this remarkable literary and intellectual rebound. In Britain it was manifested above all in the movement of the philosophical radicals. If British repression of Radical Enlightenment proved unremitting in the years following Waterloo, it was precisely then that the new movement of "philosophical radicals" inspired by Bentham's increasing shift to the Left gained momentum. If Bentham's moral thought was in part radical already long before 1815, he embraced representative democracy only from around 1810 and his readership prior to the last years of the Napoleonic era was extremely limited: he only became a formidable intellectual and public force in Britain and in the trans-Atlantic world after 1814.[29]

From 1814–15, Bentham's general scheme for political reform in Britain, in its mature post-Waterloo phase, his and James Mill's plea for "democratic ascendancy," became one of the principal vehicles of radical thought and activism of the age. If, for James Mill, an admirer particularly of Millar among his Scots predecessors, all monarchs were "tyrants,"[30] Bentham's 350-page *Plan of Parliamentary Reform* (1817) not only proposed universal manhood suffrage, secret voting, equal electoral districts (one of the principles of the French Revolution), and annual parliaments, but unlike most other parliamentary reform proposals of the age (but in keeping with his early 1790s stance) demanded votes for women as well, a theme John Stuart Mill

[27] Foot, *Red Shelley*, 215–17; Nelson, *Thomas Paine*, 268; Holmes, *Shelley*, 542, 556–7.

[28] Hamburger, *John Stuart Mill*, 66, 72; Gilmartin, *Print Politics*, 49–50; Reeves, *John Stuart Mill*, 54, 272.

[29] Philp, *Godwin's Political Justice*, 72; Peonidis, "Jeremy Bentham's 'Unusually Liberal' Representative Democracy," 446–7.

[30] Bower, *Hartley and James Mill*, 202; Pitts, *Turn to Empire*, 127, 129.

would later take up more forcefully.[31] Contrary to the general opinion, Bentham now despised and considered indefensible the entire system of British common law as well as the Constitution. Typically for the radical mind-set, the late Bentham could never refrain from pouring abuse on lawyers.

The gestation of Bentham's post-1815 radical philosophy, though, had needed decades. Disgusted with the legal profession, he had early on abandoned thoughts of a legal career, devoting himself instead to studying philosophy and enlightenment.[32] He set out, as he put it, "to rear the fabric of felicity by the hands of reason and of law" by re-directing and regulating human behavior on the basis of a philosophical analysis aimed at maximizing for the greatest number of individuals in any given society that happiness which consists in the largest possible surplus of worldly pleasure over worldly pain. According to his own testimony, he was often "heard to say that he stands indebted for no small part for the ardour of his desire to render his labours useful to mankind on the largest scale" to reading Helvétius' *De l'Esprit*. In a letter to d'Alembert of 1778, he himself styled his budding system for the reform of jurisprudence as "founded on the ideas of M. Helvétius,"[33] and so indeed it was. From Helvétius, whose early death he keenly lamented, and Beccaria, he also derived his vision of the philosophical legislator with philosophically-based legal codes bursting from his pockets, who mobilizes the public to demand changes in the law so as to put the law to work to advance the happiness of the greatest number on a utilitarian basis.[34] It was Helvétius supplemented by Beccaria who also provided the ethical system, the framework of seeking bodily pleasures and fleeing from pain, that formed the basis of Bentham's moral thought and utilitarianism. Like Helvétius, d'Holbach, and Condorcet, he always viewed philosophy as a vast practical agenda resting on theoretical foundations designed to transform humanity and the world comprehensively.

However, Bentham mounted his campaign to change society without explaining to the public the philosophical foundations on which his crusade was based, believing, realistically enough, that trying to convert opinion to his ideas would be a waste of time, even counter-productive. Unoriginal though it was in basic principles, his vision of general amelioration was both radical and original in its increasingly detailed and ingenious application of the criterion of reason to analyzing men, laws, and reform proposals and in its comprehensive scope, stretching to prison and higher education reform. However, only in the years after Napoleon's downfall did Bentham and his philosophic radicals publicly adopt the key Radical Enlightenment principle that the pursuit of the "general happiness" is best pursued by democratic means aided by education, and that this will work not because men seek the common good directly

[31] Thomas, *Philosophic Radicals*, 28; Schofield, "Jeremy Bentham," 388–9, 401; Burston, *James Mill*, 203–5; Kloppenberg, *Toward Democracy*, 681–6.

[32] Schofield, "Jeremy Bentham," 393; Malik, *Question of Moral Compass*, 209.

[33] Bentham to d'Alembert, spring of 1778 in Bentham, *Correspondence* ii. 117–18.

[34] Burns, "Jeremy Bentham," 415–18; Rosen, "Jeremy Bentham's Radicalism," 226; Rosen, "Utilitarianism," 557; Devigne, *Reforming Liberalism*, 64.

(they seek only their own interest), but because the system of representation will, "in resolving clashes of interest, steer the whole in that direction, precisely as a result of each pursuing his or her own interest."[35] He and James Mill, who derived from an impoverished Scots background, were indefatigable in claiming education, not education in any traditional sense but education understood as applying the principle of "reason," is the principal tool for social and moral amelioration.[36]

Their thought certainly formed an all-round radical Enlightenment package in its atheism, anti-monarchism, anti-aristocratism, and, even if more vaguely, their argument that Bentham's "greatest happiness" principle at bottom means uniting men to maximize "social satisfaction" and protect one another from rapacious exploitation by individuals and vested interests, including monarchy and aristocracy.[37] Even so, after 1815 as before, there lingered a certain evasiveness and ambiguity about Bentham's critique of aristocratic dominance of society, as was true also of his ally James Mill, whose behavior and general attitude was often even more ambiguous, not to say deferential, regarding the aristocracy than Bentham's. Both men enjoyed staying in aristocratic houses; both wanted to radicalize society but without provoking social conflict, doing so with the approval and help of the more progressive Whig element among the aristocracy, and this precluded all harsh, sweeping rejectionism. In Mill—in contrast to Bentham, a longstanding opponent of colonial empires[38]—this tendency also involved refraining from comprehensive Radical Enlightenment with respect to anti-colonialism and anti-imperialism, as is plainly evident from his acceptance of the basic validity of the British Raj, and generally disdainful attitude to non-European peoples and cultures, in his principal work, his *History of British India*, on which he labored for over a decade (1806–17).[39]

A note of caution was understandable. On some points, discretion remained advisable even in post-1832 England: it would be to risk their public legal reform program and general strategy to denounce either monarchy, empire, or established church too openly, or put their names to their joint view of the generally accepted "argument from design" as a blatant affront to strict empiricism and "falling into the disease of extra-experimental persuasion."[40] No friend of what he scornfully dismissed as "Church-of-Englandism," Bentham despised the church but from the 1770s onwards always discreetly, adhering to his privately forthright but publicly muted, undeviatingly anti-religious stance. Revelation, miracles, organized religion, ecclesiastical authority, the formal disabilities retained by Oxford, Cambridge, and other British institutions to exclude Catholics, Dissenters, and Jews, to his mind were just additional tools of a contemptible but gigantic engine of manipulative control, an

[35] Burston, *James Mill*, 204.
[36] Bower, *Hartley and James Mill*, 205–8; Chadwick, *Secularization*, 30; Burston, *James Mill*, 216–18.
[37] Bower, *Hartley and James Mill*, 200–2; Weinstein, *Utilitarianism*, 166–7.
[38] Pitts, *Turn to Empire*, 103–15.
[39] Pitts, *Turn to Empire*, 124–8; Stuurman, *Invention of Humanity*, 404–9.
[40] Bentham and Grote, *Influence of Natural Religion*, 125.

appalling barrier to individual liberty and general happiness, forming a vast juggernaut—familiarly referred to by him as "the Jug."[41]

Hence, Bentham and his allies tended to avoid criticizing the Church of England directly, and to ignore Christianity in general, preferring to assail "natural theology," along with Platonism, in a more generalized way, so as to more indirectly sap theism and rationalized, Newtonian notions of Christianity.[42] For those who stayed and fought the radical fight within Britain, for the Carliles, Places, and the like, but also Bentham and Mill, Radical Enlightenment was in part a public appeal but nevertheless, still more, a continuing clandestine and submerged underground. As Thelwall had discovered, there was no other way to operate effectively in the Anglo-American public sphere down to the 1830s. No one had a greater impact on the early nineteenth-century English-speaking world, no one in this period was more quintessentially a Radical Enlightenment political theorist and philosopher than Bentham. Yet he was no outspoken, bold, and resolute spirit but rather renowned for vacillation, indecision, and timidity, judging it necessary throughout to keep much of his thought and general program hidden from the public gaze.

Thus, even when Bentham did attack belief in the supernatural and Christianity publicly, in his later years, he still did so in a partly concealed manner, pseudonymously. The clearest statement of his views on religion appearing in his lifetime, *The Influence of Natural Religion on the Temporal Happiness of Mankind* (1822), was an elegantly fashioned text, arranged from the usual jumble of his papers by his atheist ally George Grote (1794–1871), and published not only without either Bentham's or Grote's name on the title-page but under a misleading pseudonym (Philip Beauchamp) by Carlile's helpers during the time Carlile himself languished in prison.[43] The tract sets out to "ascertain whether the belief of posthumous pains and pleasures," to be administered "by an omnipotent Being, is useful to mankind—that is, productive of happiness or misery in the present life." "Adherence to the injunctions of religion," argued Bentham, "is something entirely different from an habitual performance of beneficial actions. For the latter are everywhere uniform and identical whilst the mandates of religion are infinitely various. And further, in mentioning the system of religion to which any individual belongs, we do not at all state whether his conduct is beneficent or pernicious—therefore an adherence to the system is perfectly consistent either with friendship or enmity to mankind."[44] If Christian or any other religious piety "inculcated performance or abstinence" merely according to whether such actions are positive or negative with regard to our present life, "religion would be precisely coincident with our present laws;" but of course it diverges from them massively. One can only conclude that the "influence possessed by natural religion

[41] Hamburger, *John Stuart Mill*, 61–3.
[42] McKown, *Behold the Antichrist*, 53–4; Burston, *James Mill*, 217; Reeves, *John Stuart Mill*, 12–13.
[43] Hamburger, *John Stuart Mill*, 63.
[44] Bentham and Grote, *Influence of Natural Religion*, 31, 65.

over human conduct is, with reference to the present life, injurious to an extent incalculably greater than it is beneficial."[45]

Among the most damaging of the "human antipathies" fomented by religion that "which the believer in a God bears to the unbeliever is the fullest, the most unqualified, and the most universal."[46] The antipathy of believers to unbelievers, pagans, members of other faiths, and atheists is so powerful, contended Bentham, that it ranks among the most immoral of all human emotions and most destructive of what he termed the "science of morality." He also believed that the churches, and in Britain especially the Anglican church, tended to obstruct the rational reform of education and the law, having a vested interest in keeping the people in a wretched condition, in "continued prostration of the understanding and the will."[47] These were sentiments fully shared by James Mill and his brilliant son, John Stuart, who avoided attending religious services from infancy onwards, throughout his life.[48] Another particularly noxious consequence of theological fervor, for Bentham, "is its coincidence and league with the sinister interests of the earth," or vested interests, the natural alliance in other words of priests with aristocracy and monarchy. Despite all this, some would argue that Bentham was "institutionally less than thoroughly secular;"[49] but surely this is just a weak quibble. If his metaphysics was Epicurean and Hobbist, Bentham's basic principle in ethics, that "moral conduct springs from the mutual wants and interests of mankind," and is uniform across the globe, and by its nature inherently conflicts with religious authority at every level, followed directly from Spinoza, Diderot, Helvétius, d'Holbach, and Condorcet.

Bentham purposely veiled his ideas wherever he calculated that exhibiting them might harm his standing and legal reform proposals, keeping back what was unmentionable, too much in conflict with conventional ideas, or too provocative according to what most deemed respectable, proper, and Christian. Regarding sexuality, he thought and privately wrote a good deal, sharing a degree of permissiveness and libertarianism entirely in line with the attitudes of Beverland and the Utrecht and Leiden "Spinozistic" fraternities of the 1670s, beside Helvétius, Diderot, and d'Holbach later, but equally entirely at odds with the restrained, inhibited manner in which practically everyone not party to Radical Enlightenment views, including even the rakes, thought about and discussed sexual issues in early nineteenth-century Britain. None of Bentham's freethinking libertinism and material dealing with sexual matters, including the sixty pages he wrote arguing for the decriminalization of homosexuality, saw the light of day for the next hundred and fifty years. Much then *had* to remain shrouded in obscurity. It was simply not helpful to furthering Bentham's cause or promoting the effectiveness of his strategy that the English public and intellectual

[45] Bentham and Grote, *Influence of Natural Religion*, 93; During, "Is Absolute Secularity Conceivable?," 160–2.

[46] Bentham and Grote, *Influence of Natural Religion*, 105, 154.

[47] During, "Is Absolute Secularity Conceivable?," 161.

[48] Hamburger, *John Stuart Mill*, 45.

[49] During, "Is Absolute Secularity Conceivable?," 162.

world should have any inkling of his views on sex or his blasphemous and irreligious general philosophy.[50] The full picture finally emerged only in the twentieth century.[51]

26.2. BENTHAMITE RADICALISM AS A POST-1815 BRITISH AND INTERNATIONAL IDEOLOGY

Consequently, while a private radical from early on, and in touch with Priestley, Price, and other radicals in the 1780s, publicly Bentham was in no sense a committed radical during the 1770s, 1780s, and the 1790s, or during the Napoleonic Wars that followed. An Oxford graduate and son of a Church of England Tory lawyer, he felt he ought to go along, on the surface at least, in Humean fashion, with the prevailing common English antipathy to the American Revolution and rejection of the French, except, in the latter case, briefly from the end of 1788 to 1792. Actually, Bentham privately harbored democratic and egalitarian leanings well before 1789. His utilitarian principles pushed him in this direction: his envisaging each individual's happiness as counting on an equal basis with the happiness of every other pressured him toward applying this principle, in the shape of universal or near universal suffrage and participation in the political sphere. In particular, he had long pondered universal manhood suffrage, the secret ballot, and unlimited freedom of the press, in preference to the existing system.[52]

Fleetingly, during 1789–91, he ventured to argue for these goals not just in personal manuscripts composed at that time but in communication with Mirabeau and Brissot, whose public ideology impressed him; at that time, he took to formulating more comprehensive political and legal reform than he had previously.[53] But repression, prejudice, and popular rejection of democratic principles in Britain were simply too overwhelming and intimidating for a declared, publicly proclaimed radicalism to be a practicable, sensible option for someone intent on introducing concrete reforms to the law, penal code, education, and institutions. Besides, by 1792 Bentham felt disillusioned with the Revolution and, consequently, pulled back, wholly suspending any willingness to express democratic sentiments publicly.[54] Appalled, like all the European pro-Revolution Enlightenment, by the excesses and anti-intellectual despotism of the Terror and the Montagne, he reached the height of his own public counter-revolutionary phase in the mid-1790s, the point at which he famously

[50] Burns, "Jeremy Bentham," 4–5; Marshall, *John Locke*, 718; Taylor, *Secular Age*, 610.

[51] Burns, "Jeremy Bentham," 4; Reeves, *John Stuart Mill*, 282; Quinn, "Jeremy Bentham," 614–15.

[52] Dickinson, *Liberty*, 246; James, "Bentham's Democratic Theory," 9, 12, 16; Rudan, "Securing the Future," 492–4; Duthille, *Discours radical*, 19.

[53] Thomas, *Philosophic Radicals*, 19; Schofield, "Jeremy Bentham," 382–3; Hampshire-Monk, "On not Inventing," 141–2; Rosen, "Jeremy Bentham's Radicalism," 219.

[54] James, "Bentham's Democratic Theory," 5.

dismissed "natural rights" as "rhetorical nonsense, nonsense upon stilts."[55] He even published a pamphlet in defense of "rotten boroughs," *Rottenness no Corruption*. But even there, paradoxically, he remained a veiled radical in rejecting the entire Western "natural law" tradition as a fallacy and a fiction. The soul of discretion, over many years, his constant tactic was to cultivate links with progressive aristocrats, men like Lord Henry Petty, third marquess of Lansdowne, who actually controlled "rotten boroughs," in the hope that they could procure him entry into Parliament.

Only during the last twenty to twenty-five years or so of his long life, long after the "stilts" remark, did Bentham emerge unequivocally into the limelight as a committed political radical. By 1809, privately converted to the cause of thoroughgoing political reform and the cause of democracy, the intolerant insularity and fierce chauvinism of the British national mood was beginning to appall him inwardly. However, his conversion to far-reaching, systematic political reform was still scrupulously kept from the public for the time being; both he and James Mill still confided most of their reformist plans strictly to their own circle. Only after Waterloo, and the re-emergence of a vigorous reform movement in England, did Bentham and Mill feel the situation had sufficiently altered for them to finally come out into the open, and publicize their schemes for "Parliamentary Reform"—not just in Britain, but also France, and everywhere else. Bentham, therefore, can be classified as a full-blown declared philosophical radical enlightener, committed to the primacy of the "general interest" in politics by democratic means guided by intellectual pressure, only from 1816–17. By the early 1820s, his "political radicalism was as unmistakable as his counter-revolutionism had been thirty years earlier."[56]

Even so, Bentham remained singularly self-absorbed. Eccentric, excessively sensitive, lacking experience of both politics and business, profoundly insecure in every practical situation, Bentham was not much of an orator, public spokesman, or political leader. He was heavily dependent on his regular team of attendants, Mill, Francis Place, and others, for even the simplest organizational matters. He was also peculiarly single-minded. With the basic outlines of his philosophic system fixed, in the 1770s, he lost his earlier openness to French and other thought and subsequently mostly "failed," as one observer expressed it, "in deriving light from other minds." Putting the fruit of his reflections, reading, and research into a mass of recondite manuscripts, he wrote indefatigably but tediously and obscurely, in a way that left most of it a vast unknown territory to others during his own era, often even to his most intimate associates.[57] None of his three closest allies in his fully radical phase, James Mill, Francis Place, and Sir Samuel Romilly (1757–1818), a descendant of a Huguenot family who had likewise known Mirabeau in the 1780s, another Beccaria disciple who was also a noted abolitionist in Parliament, were really disciples in the sense that they possessed a detailed knowledge of his texts and the overall range of his

[55] Burns, "Jeremy Bentham," 11.
[56] Burns, "Jeremy Bentham," 12; During, "Is Absolute Secularity Conceivable?," 160–1.
[57] Thomas, *Philosophic Radicals*, 25.

thought. They tended to concern themselves with different aspects of his ruminations, Romilly with legal reform, Mill chiefly educational and ethical reform. Least of all had Bentham much skill as a writer. His publications, which he prepared for the press with the utmost difficulty, usually struck readers as tedious to an uncommon degree. Yet he had a gift for inspiring those around him with his vision for mankind's general amelioration and, from 1815, exerted a growing impact on the world, thanks especially to the French versions of his work prepared by the Genevan exile Étienne Dumont (1759–1829)—the same Dumont driven from Geneva following the victory of the aristocrats there, in 1782, who had assisted Mirabeau as a speech-writer in 1789–90, a highly competent editor and translator. Having found Mirabeau too radical for his taste, Dumont also judged Bentham's hostility to religion and the British constitution excessive; but he stuck to his task and his French renderings helped make Bentham a formidable force for change, to a degree rivalled by practically no other early nineteenth-century thinker.

Between 1816 and the Great Reform Bill of 1832, the philosophic radicals, with Bentham as their head, were not just a central feature of the British political and cultural scene. Suddenly, their influence became a formidable force internationally, in Canada and Latin America as well as Italy, Greece, and throughout Europe. In the wake of the Spanish revolution, radical spirits immediately revived in England as elsewhere. Believing Spain "already free," Shelley rejoiced from self-imposed exile in Pisa as the unrest spread to Italy, Portugal, and Greece: "the world waits only the news of a revolution of Germany to see the tyrants who have pinnacled themselves on its supineness precipitated into the ruin from which they shall never arise."[58] A leading Benthamite radical in Italy during the 1820s was Melchiorre Gioia (1767–1829), a veteran democrat and republican from Piacenza who had renounced the priesthood in his youth and plunged into Helvétius, Diderot, and Rousseau. Imprisoned by the Austrians in Milan, prior to Napoleon's triumphal entry, in 1796, for publishing tracts calling for Italy to be "free, republican and provided with democratic institutions," he resumed his democratic campaign in 1797, with his *Dissertazione* on what kind of state would best suit Italy in the future, and his paper *Il Monitore italiano*. Gioia was convinced that the defeat of the Neapolitan revolution of 1799 and the other setbacks Italy had suffered were due to the "moral, political and religious prejudices that debase the Italian mind" and that (Radical) Enlightenment was the only effective and relevant cure. In the 1820s he infused his democratic republicanism with Benthamite utilitarianism.[59]

The Spanish revolution of 1820–3 presented the British government as well as the Holy Alliance with a thorny challenge. The Cádiz Constitution's prestige stood high not just in the Spanish-speaking world but also in Portugal and among the Italian radicals; in Britain and France, conservatives not only suspected Spain's

[58] Shelley, *Poetical Works* iv. 40–1; Guinn, *Shelley's Political Thought*, 72–3, 76–8.

[59] Gioia, *Dissertazione*, 253, 262–3; De Francesco, "How Not to Finish," 170–1; Romani, *Sensibilities*, 46–7, Israel *Revolutionary Ideas*, 644–6, 650, 654, 719.

revolutionaries of fomenting the revolution in Portugal, but also suspected Bentham and the philosophical radicals of encouraging them to do so.[60] The Greek revolution too showed its strongest Enlightenment credentials and most marked republican leanings during these years when the first Greek National Assembly, gathered at Epidauros, approved the first provisional constitution for Greece, in January 1822.[61] The best way to blunt the democratic tendency and rescue aristocracy, altar, and throne was to boost support for the many Spanish, Portuguese, and Greek Anglophile "moderates" rejecting "universal and equal rights," democratic republicanism, and radical ideas. Having emphatically abandoned his earlier radical views, Blanco White, Spain's most eminent "moderate" exile, and his ally, the Sevillean poet, Félix José Reinoso (1772–1841), accused the Cádiz Constitution framers and their adherents in 1820 of being doctrinaire, naive admirers of French radical ideas and disciples of the everywhere condemned Thomas Paine. Reinoso, a former *josefino* who had fled to France in 1814 and returned in 1820, now a fervent "moderate" and disciple of Burke gaining prominence in Seville, had taken to eulogizing England as a political model as ardently as Blanco White. But Blanco White, though likewise now devoted to Burke, had also for some years been the chief a propagator of Bentham's reputation in a land where Bentham was hardly known at all before 1815.[62] This created an ideologically highly tense, paradoxical situation. During the 1820–3 Spanish revolution, Blanco White tried to dissuade Quintana and his colleagues from restoring the 1812 Constitution with its democratic features unaltered. They should adopt "mixed monarchy" on the British pattern, as the correct path for Spain and all the European monarchies.

The dilemma, Burke versus Bentham, despite the latter's vigorous support for the Latin American revolutions, soon also extended to the entire Portuguese-speaking world. Having seized Portugal, commencing with a mutiny in the army barracks at Oporto in August 1820, the 1820 revolutionary wave spread to Rio de Janeiro, in February 1821. The Portuguese revolution of 1820 similarly presented the Allied powers and the West's philosophers with a testing exercise replete with political, religious, and intellectual conflicts. At Oporto, a junta was formed that convoked the long-moribund Portuguese national Cortes with its three estates of Clergy, Nobility, and People, and declared an urgent need for the Portuguese people to forge a modern national constitution. In the meantime, provisionally, the Cádiz Constitution was adopted in Portugal, in November 1820, intensifying the clash between democratic and aristocratic tendencies. At the same time, there was growing pressure for resumption of programs of enlightened economic regeneration on the model of the Pombal regime, aimed at revitalizing Portugal's ailing commerce and society on a Catholic basis. The "disastrous" 1808 and 1810 treaties with Britain were being

[60] Butrón Prida, "Hope to Defensiveness," 578, 582.
[61] Kitromilides, *Enlightenment and Revolution*, 316.
[62] Suanzes-Carpegna, "Image of the British System," 199, 208–10.

fiercely condemned for turning the country into an economic colony of Britain and ruining the country's crafts and industries. Having burned its last victim to death in 1761 and, in 1768, lost control over book censorship in Portugal, the Inquisition was abolished altogether by the new Portuguese Cortes in 1821; however, under the new constitution, as in Spain and Naples, most "liberals" (moderates) willingly helped ensure that the Catholic Church retained its monopoly over the outward, public practice of religion.

The finalized Portuguese constitution of 1822 was heavily based on the 1812 Cádiz model. But, as with the Spanish empire, upheaval in the metropolis entailed a mass of complications across the Atlantic. Ever since arriving in 1808, the Portuguese royal court, based at Rio, had exhibited a besieged, feverishly Counter-Enlightenment mentality, prohibiting printing presses, banning the importing of foreign books, and preventing the establishment of universities in Brazil, so as to exclude as far as possible foreign influence and Enlightenment ideas.[63] Throwing in its lot with religion and Counter-Enlightenment, the Portuguese court relied on Britain and the Holy Alliance, with their overarching power, to ensure the integrity and stability of Portugal's fragile absolute monarchy and empire. But suddenly, early in 1821, the king of Portugal and Brazil, Dom João VI (reigned: 1816–25), and his councilors, believing union of Portugal and Brazil and the stability of royal rule in Brazil and Portugal equally at risk, sought to quell the widespread agitation as quickly as they could by a conciliatory strategy, making hasty concessions.

On both sides of the Portuguese Atlantic, a flood of political pamphlets and new newspapers seized the attention of the educated elite. At the same time, as part of its deliberations over the Cádiz Constitution and search for a way out of the moderate–radical clash, the Portuguese Cortes ordered the political and legal works of Bentham to be rendered into Portuguese. In this way, the two Iberian revolutions became a battleground for opposing and irreconcilable British political ideologies. For advocating bicameralism and a Spanish upper house modelled on the London House of Lords, and division of powers, Blanco White found himself fiercely assailed by Bentham as this "Spanish Burkeite" and "admirer of Monarchical and Aristocratical vetos," in his 1820 tract addressed to the Spanish Cortes: "Spaniards! Think for yourselves," admonished Bentham. "Think whether, between an assembly of the ruling few thus constituted on the one part, and the interest of the subject many on the other part, there exists not a point-blank opposition, and that opposition an unchangeable one?" He claimed that an upper house, representing a noble class with immense estates and the clergy, whether in Spain or Portugal, Britain or Italy, possessing the power "in pursuit of its own particular and thence sinister interest, to frustrate all measures proposed by the representatives of the whole for the good of the whole," was an abomination to be avoided at all costs. For some time, Bentham had been highly critical of division of powers as any kind of aid to constitutional

[63] Wilcken, *Empire Adrift*, 79, 83.

liberty or bar to corruption and malpractice, condemning it as the "false principle of division of power."[64]

Were the foes of Spain's Burkeites and "moderates," the republican faction opposing the nobility and clergy, misguided, demanded Bentham, to be inspired "by Yankee-land, whose neck has, for these forty years been free from all such vermin, and who bids the habitable globe observe and declare, whether, in any and what respect, she is the worse for it?" Roundly disparaging Burke, Bentham urged the Portuguese to cease all vacillation and keep the Cádiz constitution: "adopt it as a mass. Take example," he wrote, unconsciously echoing Shelley's "Ode to Naples" (before the crushing of the Neapolitan revolution by an army sent by the Holy Alliance, early in 1821), "by your friends in Naples."[65] Regarding liberty of the press, the United States, once again, was far preferable not just to Fernando's absolutist monarchy and what was seen in Italy, but also to the British situation, for in America—since rescinding the Alien and Sedition Acts in 1800—government wholly lacked the abominable power to persecute contrary opinions in the way British ministers were doing with their campaign to suppress Paine.[66] Britain's constitution, or the "great Boa Constrictor with a coronet on his head," as he picturesquely styled it in addressing Spain's legislators, was solidly weighted in the interest of nobility and crown, rendering it hopelessly obsolete and defective: "this is legitimacy and social order under the matchless constitution, the envy and admiration of the world." His representations were hotly debated in both the Portuguese and Spanish Cortes, he was delighted to learn, besides the Madrid Club Cruz de Malta and the universities of Salamanca and Coimbra.[67]

Given its power to weaken religious authority, curb the prejudices of mankind, enhance individual liberty and happiness not least through sexual emancipation, and its capacity to generate legal and political reform, Bentham contended that the Enlightenment, or what he termed the "increase of light and wisdom throughout Europe" through the achievements of philosophers, was undoubtedly among the most important developments in the world ever.[68] Indefatigable in promoting the late Enlightenment, he believed the dwindling power of religious authority, intolerance, and obscurantism was the direct and natural result of diffusion of knowledge. Nothing is more costly to humans than the damage they suffer from "unenlightened" minds and beliefs. Yet his own philosophical movement was fated to falter and lose momentum, spiraling down into failure almost immediately after his death in 1832.

Philosophical radicalism in Britain aborted in the 1830s due to its abandonment of its democratic and universalist aims and, at the same time, and directly connected with this, losing its anchor in democratic universalism. It succumbed, as John Stuart

[64] James, "Bentham's Democratic Theory," 6–7; Rosen, "Thinking about Liberty," 13–14; Alonso, "A Great People," 201.

[65] Bentham, *Three Tracts*, 4–6, 47; Guinn, *Shelley's Political Thought*, 77.

[66] De Champs, *Enlightenment and Utility*, 179.

[67] Bentham, *Three Tracts*, 3–4, 9–10.

[68] Grayling, *Towards the Light*, 138; Porter, *Enlightenment*, 481–2.

Mill emphasized more than anyone, to intellectual retreat, parochialism, and distancing from the Enlightenment as a whole. John Stuart Mill (1806–73) had been brought up by his father lacking any religious allegiance, to take for granted the basic incoherence of theological views of the world. He ascribed his full conversion to the ideas of his father, and Bentham, when he was 15, in 1821, to reading Bentham's moral philosophy. The bookish youth was especially attracted by the doctrine that it is through "everyone drawing in the direction of his own happiness, [that] the happiness of the whole will be attained."[69]

After Bentham's death, however, the mature John Stuart became increasingly convinced that Bentham's utilitarianism betrayed serious weaknesses as a system of moral thought, indeed seemed incapable of inspiring a true moral consciousness. Explaining human motivation as Bentham had, entirely in a one-dimensional fashion, in terms of desire for pleasure and aversion to pain, had blinded him, he concluded, to the role of moral dimensions such as love of beauty, love of order, and feelings of honor in motivating men's higher actions. His system required extensive modification, in particular by redefining Bentham's "happiness" based on the pleasure principle by something more like "worthwhile-living."[70]

After 1832, the ground beneath the philosophic radicals rapidly crumbled as the parliamentary group at their head, in London, having joined forces with middle-class reformers aiming at a wider but still limited suffrage, proved unable to connect with the still disappointed and frustrated elements found among the post-1832 British majority which still lacked the right to vote. The resulting loss of appeal and impetus was reflected in the disappointing political career of one of Bentham's and James Mill's closest allies, George Grote (1794–1871), a rich banker and influential scholar of ancient Greek philosophy, especially Plato; later Grote also became a major historian (of ancient Greece).[71] From 1825, the group of radical reformers, led by James Mill, and including the later prominent John Arthur Roebuck (1802–79), met regularly in Grote's house, to thrash out the central ideas underpinning their "philosophic" radical movement. In the 1830s Grote became leader of the small group of radical MPs in the British Parliament, and the most learned and philosophically oriented. However, if "universally beloved for his extreme goodness," he was also "narrow," lamented John Stuart, "narrower than most other utilitarians of reading and education: more a disciple of my father than of anyone else;" in uprightness he resembled David Ricardo, "though a far inferior man to him in powers of intellect."[72] But by 1840, Grote was also a defeated parliamentary leader who had dismally failed to build the philosophic radicals into a purposeful political engine of reform.

In part, his failure was due to ingrained timidity. Like Bentham, Grote tended to avoid all public avowal of hostility to religion, the Anglican church and the dominant

[69] Capaldi, *John Stuart Mill*, 39–41.

[70] Devigne, *Reforming Liberalism*, 56, 100; Hamburger, *John Stuart Mill*, 43; Malik, *Quest for a Moral Compass*, 214–15; Kloppenberg, *Toward Democracy*, 621–2; Weinstein, *Utilitarianism*, 44–5, 78–9, 129.

[71] Devigne, *Reforming Liberalism*, 24–6.

[72] Thomas, *Philosophic Radicals*, 411; Capaldi, *John Stuart Mill*, 43; Reeves, *John Stuart Mill*, 309.

landed interest. Under pre-1832 conditions, this had been a strength, helping secure the radicals their niche. But in post-1832 circumstances it became distinctly more of a weakness preventing them from climbing further. Very different from Grote was the impulsive young Cornish baronet, the wealthy and eccentric Sir William Molesworth (1810–55), who likewise passionately adhered to the doctrines of Bentham and James Mill and like them was a private atheist but, unlike them, made no secret of his hostility to organized religion and the landed interest.[73] Yet he too failed to build a wider movement whether in Parliament or outside. In 1834–5 he founded the *London Review* together with the Mills to serve as the main organ of the philosophical radicals in disseminating their opinions to the public; after a few months it merged with the *Westminster Review* to become the *London and Westminster Review*, an outstanding journal of high quality and clear radical tendency.[74] For some years it was chiefly edited by John Stuart Mill. But once the 1830 European revolutions were defeated and Parliament's (very limited) 1832 Reform Act was secured, the British mood swung strongly against further reform, turning the 1830s into a decade of reviving Toryism and renewed vehement anti-intellectualism and anti-Europeanism so that the Mills' and Molesworth's enlightened tone found scant favor with the public.

Composing his *Autobiography* in the early 1850s, John Stuart Mill's verdict on the philosophic radicals, and Grote in particular, was unremittingly harsh. The 1830s in England had begun as a decade of promise, then turned into a "relapse into Toryism" and conservatism that was a general disaster for all. A more energetic and broad-minded figure might have created "a real Radical Party, for which the materials then existed; he could have put heart into the many younger men who would have been ready to join him—could have made them available to the extent of their talents in bringing advanced ideas before the public—could have used the House of Commons as a rostra or teacher's chair for instructing and impelling the public mind." But Grote and his team failed to do any of this and consequently lost the priceless opportunity. Grote possessed neither the intellectual breadth nor the political energy the situation required. For want of such a figure the "instructed Radicals sank into a mere *côté gauche* of the Whig party," the general level of which was unenviably mediocre. By the 1840s, all evidence showed, the British Enlightenment was well and truly sunk and beaten.

Among the main reasons for Molesworth's failure and that of John Stuart Mill's journal was a clash over philosophy, policy, and strategy which illustrates the essential dilemma at the heart of the philosophic radicals' post-1840 political marginalization. A direct consequence of John Stuart's particular stress on Enlightenment was his idea, akin to that of Auguste Comte, that "the instructed" must achieve a basic unanimity of view on key issues without which "the many" would not defer to their judgment and leadership; he recognized the kinship of Bentham's and his approach, viewed as a creed, to the idea of a society based on a single coherent moral, social, and philosophical outlook prized by Bonald and De Lamennais, however different these were

[73] Thomas, *Philosophic Radicals*, 190–1; Capaldi, *John Stuart Mill*, 124–5.
[74] Malik, *Quest for a Moral Compass*, 209.

theologically. In terms of the need for the basic principles of society to be coherent, meaningful, and disseminated downwards through society, the ultras were right.[75] The inspiration had to penetrate from the top down; for the Rousseauist and Montagnard idea of mandating representatives to bind them from below, he had nothing but scorn. The great risk in democracy, as he saw it, was precisely that representation could degenerate into Montagnard strict mandating and that the opinion of the mass would then paralyze, or drown out, all critical and independent thinking and research in the individual, a worry he shared with De Tocqueville.[76] Other philosophic radicals firmly disagreed, however, among them John Arthur Roebuck (1802–79), an Englishman born in India but raised in Canada, a disciple of Bentham and James Mill imbued with their doctrines who retained a lifelong involvement in Canadian and other colonial affairs; he returned to England in 1824 and became MP for Bath in 1832.

Where John Stuart Mill believed "in the advantages to be derived from an aristocracy of intellect," Roebuck had "no faith in any such Aristocracy."[77] A doctrinaire Benthamite and follower of James Mill in some respects, Roebuck also admired Rousseau and was emphatic in his commitment to popular sovereignty. Relatively poor and distant from the English upper social strata, he was more inclined to stress his democratic credentials than almost any other philosophic radical and became fiercely critical of the tone of the *London and Westminster Review* under John Stuart's management. This was more than just a difference of emphasis. For Roebuck was as convinced as Mill and the rest that their monopoly of the most advanced social and political thought of the age gave them an unbeatable edge, among the mass of the electorate, over their aristocratic and clerical enemies. Roebuck tried to rouse public opinion behind the radical cause with more energy than others but was just as defeated as they were by the growing conservatism of the great bulk of the electorate.

In 1837, the year that marked the start of Queen Victoria's reign, the Tories won a great electoral victory in Britain, crushing the hopes of Mill and the "instructed radicals" seemingly permanently. It began to appear as if the limited reform movement of the early 1830s, combining far-reaching political and social reform with cautious procedural gradualism, had run its course. Benthamism had failed as a public reform movement after all. It was at this point that John Stuart Mill began to feel seriously alienated from the "philosophic radicals" in Parliament in whom his father and he himself, thus far, had vested their hopes; soon he grew deeply critical of the vying circles that had formed around Grote and Roebuck. Retreating into permanent subsequent isolation, splendid and lofty but powerless, he no longer wished to be identified with them, claiming that "my radicalism is of a school, the most remote from theirs, at all points, that exists."[78]

[75] Hamburger, *John Stuart Mill*, 120; Fedi, *Comte*, 149–52.
[76] Jaume, *Tocqueville*, 224; Burrow, *Crisis of Reason*, 153–5; Kloppenberg, *Toward Democracy*, 632.
[77] Thomas, *Philosophic Radicals*, 196; Malik, *Quest for a Moral Compass*, 214–15.
[78] Capaldi, *John Stuart Mill*, 127–8; Reeves, *John Stuart Mill*, 134–6.

27

Failed Restoration in France (1814–1830)

27.1. LOUIS XVIII AND THE "HUNDRED DAYS"

When Napoleon's emperorship collapsed the first time, between January and March 1814, the returning French Bourbon dynasty did not yet possess the full support of all the Allies. After a quarter of a century of exile abroad, the restored dynasty were also unsure how much support, if any, they could count on in and around Paris, and more generally in France. More certain was that they needed to negotiate their re-entry and acceptance, especially with Napoleon's imperial senate which, with Napoleon gone, indicated its readiness to restore the monarchy and Bourbon dynasty but only under certain carefully specified conditions.

Hardcore reactionaries among the Allies had their hands tied to an extent, as did Louis XVIII's entourage, by the—at that time—relatively enlightened attitude of Czar Alexander, who issued a public declaration, dated 31 March 1814, that the Allies would "recognize and guarantee the Constitution that France shall adopt," pointedly inviting the Napoleonic senate to form a "provisional government."[1] Among the war-weary French people, there was scant willingness to prolong a vast European war carried on without interruption since 1804.[2] War-weariness offered a promising backcloth for the Restoration to an extent, but in claiming the throne in early 1814 Louis XVIII confronted, he recognized, an unprecedented and unpredictable situation. Most *émigré* Restoration plans, nurtured during many years of resentment and longing for revenge in exile, assumed a comprehensive royal Counter-Enlightenment and vengeance that would turn the clock back uncompromisingly in the institutional sphere, socially and religiously; but such schemes were not favored by all the Allies, nor did they suit the exigencies of a fraught domestic French scene that compelled the aspiring monarch to make immediate initial compromises. Metternich, moreover, troubled by the threat of Russian domination of Germany and Scandinavia, felt intensely worried about Russian designs, fearing, like Louis, lest the Czar, having absorbed Finland and most of Poland, rather than restore the Bourbons, might opt to break with Austria, ignore Prussia, and make the Swedish king, Bernadotte,

[1] De Staël, *Considerations*, 552, 558–60; Morgan, *Memoirs*, 84–5; Jennings, *Revolution*, 167–8.
[2] Leggiere, *Fall of Napoleon*, 536–7, 540, 552–3.

France's new monarch while weakening France territorially to strengthen Russia's hand further.[3]

Restoring monarchy, aristocracy, and church in France was, each in its own way, an immense undertaking posing a myriad of problems. The old landed aristocracy demanded restoration in status, titles, and wealth, at the apex of the social hierarchy, with the lower orders again made subordinate to them. France's ultra-royalists and the *émigré* Catholic press had since 1789 been demanding, along with a divinely sanctioned, publicly consecrated king ruling without constitutional constraint, full restoration of the church in all its eminence, appurtenances, and privilege; monarchy and religion had shown their ability to inspire the illiterate and traditional-minded with the great Vendéean revolt of 1793–4 and together propagated a reactionary ideology which had sustained the royal princes and their entourages whilst in exile in Germany. But could one turn back the clock in the manner returning nobles and ecclesiastics, and many country folk, expected, given that aristocratic and ecclesiastical lands had long since be sold off to new owners, absorbed by a new upper stratum of prosperous landowners, farmers, and city landowners, the church's regular orders had been ousted for over twenty years, and the entire administrative apparatus and legal and educational framework had been fundamentally transformed?

Beside the difficulties, averred Chateaubriand later, Louis XVIII made several crucial mistakes at the outset, seriously prejudicing the counter-enlighteners' prospects for a wide-ranging, truly comprehensive French Restoration. Understandably, Louis wanted an authentically royal army; but he should never have cashiered such a large proportion of the officers and men of Napoleon's army: by suddenly creating a vast pool of discontented men deprived of their salaries, pensions, and honors, and publicly dishonored, but free to talk and conspire among themselves, he denied himself the chance to genuinely win hearts and minds to loyalism, creating at a stroke a sea of internal sullenness and opposition. A second blunder hindering true reversion to *ancien régime* values, contended Chateaubriand, was Louis's openness, on approaching Paris in April 1814, to treat with Napoleon's senate at all. Headed by Talleyrand, they were urged to abjure Bonaparte, acknowledge the Restoration, and recognize the legitimate Bourbon line under specific conditions, first by the Czar and then in Louis's ill-advised, as he saw it, public statement, prior to any constitutional commission being set up, guaranteeing representative government, equality before the law (irrespective of titles), freedom of the press, freedom of expression, freedom of religious practice, and taxation only with consent—wide concessions formally incorporated and reaffirmed in the royal charter [*charte constitutionnelle*] of June 1814.[4] With such a disastrous start how could there be any authentic Counter-Enlightenment or true Restoration?

Yet there had been no easy way to avoid these initial concessions. Apprehensive of French power, the Allies wanted Napoleon's army largely disbanded. The Czar

[3] Leggiere, *Fall of Napoleon*, 494–5.
[4] Chateaubriand, *Mémoires* ii. 290–1, 298; Aprile, *1815 La Révolution inachevée*, 22–3.

favored constitutions at the time, and for Louis to secure his throne in an undisputed, smooth fashion, acquiescence in the *charte* looked advisable, even unavoidable, despite royalists like Chateaubriand feeling disgust at their about-to-be-restored monarch principally negotiating not with churchmen and royalists but with Talleyrand and Napoleonists.[5] According to the draft constitution settled by the various parties in April 1814, the French nation called Louis to the throne. Personally, Louis VIII abjured this principle, always deeming himself king by dynastic right and divine decree, not the people's wish; but his hurried public declaration expressing readiness to grant a "constitution" and representative government, along lines indicated by the imperial senate, issued just before he re-entered Paris as king—a seemingly necessary precaution at the time—had bound his hands. Effectively, in 1814–15, Louis acquiesced in substantial curbs on his power and a two-chamber restricted suffrage legislature.[6] Restoration, consequently, proved a relatively weak affair in France, more a story of reluctant continuity with forms and tendencies operative in France since Brumaire than a serious break with the past, and, humiliatingly, one even less authoritarian in many respects than Napoleon's regime.[7]

Unlike Fernando VII's Spain where, during 1814, royal absolutism was rigorously imposed and the Inquisition restored with undiminished powers, facilitating suppression of dissident political and religious publications, in France—to the disgust of hardline Counter-Enlightenment authors like Chateaubriand, the Provençal émigré Louis de Bonald (1754–1840), and the Savoyard Joseph de Maistre (1753–1821)—not only was popular sovereignty formally acknowledged, and royal ministers made responsible to the legislature, but royal support for reversion of ecclesiastical authority and property, though wholehearted in intention, in the event proved relatively flimsy in operation. The fundamental goals of the Restoration were to rebuild the ascendancy of monarchy and aristocracy everywhere in Europe and the trans-Atlantic world, and, tightly linked with this goal politically, restore religious authority to its former spiritual, cultural, and educational hegemony. None could doubt that church, aristocracy, and monarchy stood shoulder to shoulder as closely interdependent, intertwined allies. Yet so marginal were true legitimists in the reinstalling of the French monarchy during 1814–15 they were bound to feel estranged and indignant and consider the entire procedure devoid of real legitimacy. Despite their efforts and devoted resolve over many years, ultra-royalists felt bitter, disillusioned, and sidelined—so much so that Chateaubriand, or so he later claimed, considered re-emigrating to Switzerland.[8]

It was the officer corps and Napoleon's administrators who suffered the heaviest immediate loss of status and income. If great numbers of ordinary soldiers were sent home empty-handed, at least they had farms and skills to return to; but thousands of officers found themselves either with nothing, or struck off the active service lists on

[5] Chateaubriand, *Mémoires* ii. 295–7; Craiutu, *Virtue for Courageous Minds*, 189–90.
[6] Furet, *Revolutionary France*, 270; Price, *Perilous Crown*, 52–4.
[7] Pilbeam, "Impossible Restoration," 183–4.
[8] Chateaubriand, *Mémoires* ii. 299–300.

half-pay. The few retained in reformed royal regiments mostly found themselves placed beneath returning *émigré* royalists who had been living outside France for decades.[9] A great many imperial *fonctionnaires* likewise lost their positions—including the future novelist, Stendhal (Henri Beyle, 1783–1842), who, in 1814, had been on the verge of promotion to imperial prefect. From the Napoleonic administration and judiciary hundreds of officials were dismissed by the restored crown. Losing their careers, those deprived, along with French administrators expelled from the Low Countries, Westphalia, and other areas Napoleon had annexed to France, often sank into acute hardship, festering alongside the mass of cashiered army officers. Resentment widespread among military and ex-administrative personnel was rife too among those formerly staffing the revolutionary and Napoleonic navy. Imperial captains either stayed with reduced rank, placed under returning *émigrés*, or else, pensioned off, were replaced by aging aristocrats groomed for naval command before 1789. Both navy and naval shipbuilding were suddenly drastically reduced. At Toulon, Bourbon restoration plunged the great naval arsenal into severe recession, rendering thousands redundant. If, in 1815, during the Hundred Days [*Cent-Jours*], other economically-stricken locations such as Montauban often showed scant support for Napoleon, or the monarchy,[10] and popular hostility to Napoleon's unexpected reappearance characterized Marseille, Aix, and the countryside west of Toulon, which remained solidly royalist, France's main naval bases evinced only wild enthusiasm, all Toulon being promptly bedecked with (banned) tricolor flags.[11]

If royal weakness bred frustration and resentment among disappointed returning *émigrés* and clergy failing to receive the compensation and rewards expected, this in no way lessened the disgruntlement of purged republicans and Bonapartists. Under the terms of the Restoration, agreed in April 1814 with the expiring imperial senate, the king solemnly swore full amnesty for the past, complained the prominent opposition journalist Marc-Antoine Jullien (1775–1848); he had agreed to treat all Frenchmen alike. But once on the throne, the Bourbons "have exclusively called to their side, admitted to their councils, employed, and favored all the returned *émigrés*, former nobles and known foes of the Revolution, while rejecting, removing or abusing everyone in France who had faithfully served and defended their country." Having modified the draft constitution presented by Talleyrand and the "senate" after Napoleon's abdication, Louis seemed to imagine, contrary to the facts, that he had conceded the "constitution of 1814 as a royal charter and not as a right inherent in the sovereignty of the nation."[12]

Many groups in French society remained deeply hostile to the new order despite Louis XVIII's caution and moderation in most respects; yet, paradoxically and ironically, returning *émigrés* were among the most disgruntled. Louis could return neither the aristocracy nor the church to the levels of prestige, landownership, and

[9] Bruyère-Ostells, *Grande Armée*, 24–5. [10] Darrow, *Revolution*, 48.
[11] Crook, *Toulon*, 225.
[12] Palmer, *From Jacobin to Liberal*, 121–2; Aprile, *Révolution inachevée*, 19–21.

authority they enjoyed before 1789. In the eyes of the ultras, returning *émigrés*, and ardent counter-enlighteners, Louis was also excessively lenient with declared republican and Napoleonist elements remaining in the country. In their eyes, far too many unrepentant republicans and former revolutionaries were permitted to stay. Everyone involved in the trial and execution of Louis XVI was deemed a "regicide" and, along with a relatively small selection of other prescribed persons, banished permanently from France. But even some of these were then offered exemptions, including France's most celebrated living artist, Jacques-Louis David (1748–1825). Reluctant to lose him, Louis offered individual amnesty, which David refused, preferring self-imposed exile along with numerous other ex-revolutionaries residing in Brussels, where the United Netherlands' new monarch openly refused to bow in the slightest to Catholic reaction. Consensus-seeking, Louis XVIII also allowed Henri Grégoire to remain and revoked Benjamin Constant's expulsion order, permitting him to return after only a year of English exile.[13] Amnestied too were Maximin Isnard (1755–1825), among the few Brissotin leaders to survive the Terror, Barras, and, after three years' exile, Cambacérès. Some of these were reconciled: the once militantly anti-clerical Isnard henceforth publicly displayed his remorse each year by praying on the spot where Louis XVI had been guillotined.

Nevertheless, the remaining core of revolutionaries and Napoleonists expelled was substantial: Carnot, Barère, Vadier, Debry, Lakanal, Buonarotti, Thuriot, Drouet, Robert, the younger Lepeletier, and General Edouard Milhaud (1766–1833), among Napoleon's best cavalry generals (earlier a zealous republican), all set off into permanent or long-term exile. Billaud-Varenne contrived to escape from Cayenne to New York. Even the quintessentially "moderate" Abbé Jean Siffrein Maury (1746–1817), a constitutional royalist leader in the National Assembly during 1790–1 and foe of all republicans, democrats, Brissotins, and Montagnards, was expelled for having accepted the archbishopric of Paris from Napoleon, in 1810, in open defiance of king and pope. Poor Maury, having striven harder and more skillfully, and spoken out more forcefully, than anyone for religion, "moderation," and conservative values for over a quarter of a century of revolution, on arriving in the restored Papal States following expulsion from France, found himself imprisoned in Rome by the pope.

Those tainted with the 1793 regicide were often stringently dealt with, some permanently expelled. Yet Louis XVIII ended up tolerating, to an extent his Spanish, Prussian, and Austrian counterparts could not countenance, great numbers of former revolutionaries and professed republicans as well as Napoleonists, which automatically meant tolerating, through his reign, a vast undercurrent of anti-monarchical dissent within France and international subversive networking.[14] This flourishing conspiratorial undercurrent was then further conspicuously reinforced by the many exiled foreign revolutionaries fleeing from harsher repression elsewhere and seeking permanent refuge in France. This veritable host of veteran republicans, Josephists,

[13] Holmes, *Benjamin Constant*, 18–19; Neely, *Lafayette and the Liberal Ideal*, 116.
[14] Pilbeam "Impossible Restoration," 186.

and anti-ecclesiastical fugitives included Llorente, Marchena, the educationalist Manuel Narganes, the stalwart republican, anti-Napoleonist, and radical Luigi Angeloni (1759–1842), still planning to convert Italy into an American-style federal republic,[15] and Francesco Saverio Salfi (1759–1832), a leading Neapolitan republican and admirer of Filangieri exiled to Milan after the collapse of the Neapolitan republic of 1799, who spent the remainder of his life in Paris from 1815 to 1832 while still demanding a pan-Italian republic.[16] Returning to France in 1814, neither Marchena, who, after 1808, had been a prominent Napoleonist as editor of Joseph Bonaparte's official Madrid *Gaceta*,[17] nor Narganes ceased their old clandestine political activism and subversion; rather they and their associates kept in contact with underground opposition circles in Spain pouring scorn on the absolutist, Fernando, while continuing to translate and propagate Enlightenment texts in Spanish.[18]

Critics and opponents of the restored monarchy, within France and without, abounded on all sides. Llorente, whose *Histoire critique de l'Inquisition d'Espagne* appeared in French in 1817 (and Spanish in 1822), becoming the standard late Enlightenment condemnation of the Inquisition, was forbidden to teach in France but otherwise left alone by the royal authorities until December 1822 when he was banished for his open, public support of the renewed Spanish revolution of 1820–3.[19] With royal absolutist and Inquisition power in Spain again temporarily crushed during 1820–3, the *Afrancesados* domiciled in France celebrated and rushed to participate, many returning to Spain when the revived Spanish revolution issued an amnesty for all *Afrancesado* exiles in France, in September 1820; of these, a considerable portion, Goya among them, then fled back again, seeking renewed refuge in France when Fernando, with Louis's assistance, suppressed the revived Spanish revolution in the summer of 1823.[20]

Most on the center and Left were as disdainful of the paltry constitutional arrangements Louis conceded as the royalist ultras. Center and Left, usually unhelpfully bundled together by historians as "liberals," a highly misleading usage given how disparate was the mix, actually consisted of several very different elements—radicals (democratic republicans), "moderate" anti-democratic big property constitutional monarchists, and Napoleonists, all needing to be carefully differentiated. Napoleon might have suppressed the Republic, ended French press freedom, reintroduced black slavery in the French Caribbean, and suspended the Rights of Man more broadly, but the returning aristocracy and priesthood of 1814, followed by the Hundred Days, showed that at least he had kept the old aristocracy out and confined the priesthood to a highly restricted subordinate position. "Democratic France," later remarked one of the greatest ideological foes of the democratic republican tendency,

15 Körner, *America in Italy*, 85–7; Isabella, *Risorgimento*, 136–7, 231–2.
16 De Francesco, "How not to Finish a Revolution," 168; Isabella, *Risorgimento*, 134, 243.
17 Ruiz Berrio, "Introdución," 16, 19–22.
18 Fuentes, *José Marchena*, 222–58, 262–70; López Tabor, *Famosos traidores*, 19, 175.
19 [Jullien], *Revue encyclopédique* xviii (Apr. 1823), 41–4.
20 López Tabor, *Famosos traidores*, 262, 364–5.

the "liberal" historian-statesman, François Pierre Guillaume Guizot (1787–1874), remained unquestionably powerful beneath the surface despite the efforts of the restored Bourbon monarchy, and "owes much to the Emperor Napoleon. He bequeathed her two things of immense value: internally, a civil order solidly constituted; externally, a national independence strongly established by *la gloire*."[21] Both tendencies could be exploited in what Guizot considered an unfortunate, even disastrous, democratic direction as well as more constructively in moderate Enlightenment vein presided over by limited monarchy. A Protestant from Nîmes and firm Anglophile "moderate," but also a keen educationalist and acute political writer with a professorship in history at the Sorbonne from 1812, Guizot remained a lifelong foe of the failed reactionary tendency in post-1814 Bourbon France but equally hostile to popular sovereignty and democratic republicanism.[22]

Many dismissed *fonctionnaires* and military officers were left to find new, if lower positions, hurriedly swearing allegiance to the restored dynasty even when, as with Stendhal, they personally detested all monarchy, the Bourbons especially, and what he considered the abhorrent, philistine culture of Catholic Counter-Enlightenment. Frequently swearing allegiance in the most cynical fashion, they remained at heart unswerving republicans or Bonapartists.[23] Equally, reaction entrapped many an ambitious youth from a plebeian or peasant background, like the main protagonist in Stendhal's great novel *Scarlet and Black* (1830), in deep inner, veiled estrangement from authority and society, under the exigencies of a renewed aristocratic–ecclesiastical social system detested by them as repressive, hollow, and hypocritical. One point where Louis XVIII's biases converged with Napoleon's—went further in fact—and to which neither ultras nor constitutional monarchists were likely to object, was his campaign against radical ideas, his suppressing the Auteuil circle and purging "the Institute" of ideological undesirables. In March 1815, on royal orders, Garat, Roederer, Sieyès, Monge, and several others were dismissed from that body, leaving the Institut drastically clipped.[24] But a comprehensive, systematic, ideological clear-out was inconceivable.

Finally, there was also a large segment of society, in the France of 1814–15, bound to feel uneasy on account of possessing lands and rents acquired during the Revolution, knowing concerted efforts were under way to procure their return to *émigrés* and ecclesiastics.[25] Knowing the Restoration's fragility, Bonaparte escaped from his island prison off the Tuscan coast, after ten months' captivity, on 26 February 1815. After landing, he forthrightly ventured northwards. For a few days, it remained unclear whether he would receive mass support. Discontent with the Restoration was rife, but not such that it seemed likely Napoleon would, with ease, swiftly overthrow an

[21] Guizot, *De la démocratie*, 26; Holmes, *Benjamin Constant*, 17.
[22] Guizot, *De la démocratie*, 25–9; Jaume, *Tocqueville*, 256; Aprile, *Révolution inachevée*, 61–2.
[23] Stendhal, *Private Diaries*, 525–6; Blanning, *Romantic Revolution*, 127.
[24] Imbert, *Destutt de Tracy critique*, 75.
[25] Nagy, "Hommes d'action," 46–7; Bruyère-Ostells, *Grande Armée*, 24–8.

internationally supported, newly restored king, and at once regain the emperorship of France. Until early March, veteran observers like Sismondi, then in Paris, and Stendhal, in Milan, and most French, British, and Italian newspapers, viewed the flight from Elba more as a romantic escapade without much prospect of success than a realistic bid for power.[26] What followed stunned all Europe. Once defections from the crown started, they snowballed with astounding speed, revealing just how flimsy Louis XVIII's domestic support was. Garrison commanders, local functionaries, the common soldiers defected in droves. Louis, finding himself abandoned on all sides, had little alternative but flee, departing Paris on 19 March 1815, removing himself and his family in all haste via Lille and Ghent; by 20 March 1815, the Emperor was installed back in his old capital with all France at his feet. During the next few heady weeks, Paris stayed in a state of rare intoxication. At the Opera, Théâtre-Française, and other theatres, bands day after day accompanied exulting crowds in singing the Marseillaise and other revolutionary songs. The Restoration's innumerable opponents, not just veteran revolutionaries and Bonapartists but also youthful converts to radical thought and republicanism like the 17-year-old future philosopher, Auguste Comte (1798–1857), suddenly converted, like many a fellow student of the École Polytechnique, into zealous supporters of a potentate he formerly (and subsequently) detested. Later among Bonaparte's severest critics, the young Comte typified innumerable enthusiasts convinced Bonaparte had "changed entirely during his philosophic stay on the island of Elba," and abandoned his despotic dreams of conquest "that caused us so much harm during the first part of his reign," that the constitution he offered with its guarantees of full freedom of the press was genuine, and that henceforth he had "no other ambition than to be head of a free people and perfect civilization in France."[27]

Across France, especially in large towns (except Marseille), sprang up within two or three weeks hundreds of associations of Bonaparte supporters, active adherents called *féderés* drawn mostly from middle-class, professional, student, or administrative backgrounds with a smaller element, perhaps a fifth, consisting of artisans.[28] Virtually no churchmen joined them, but many recently appointed royal *fonctionnaires* did. If the Napoleon of 1815 found the Catholic clergy ranged solidly against him, Protestants and Jews mostly supported him; where there were substantial Protestant rural populations, as in the Cévennes and Gard departments in the south, Protestants mobilized *en masse* into "federations" to fight Bourbon loyalists and the threat of re-theologization of French life and law.[29] During the *Cent-Jours*, Napoleon's reappearance was viewed as an almost miraculous revival of the Revolution, an alluring, epoch-making reaffirmation of the past quarter-century's enlightened promises and benefits.

[26] Imbert, *Metamorphoses*, 83–4.

[27] Comte, *Correspondance générale* i. 9–10, 373; Comte, *Vie de Auguste Comte*, 50–1; Fedi, *Comte*, 19–20.

[28] Alexander, *Bonapartism*, 97–9.

[29] Alexander, *Bonapartism*, 97.

One veteran revolutionary who had later supported Napoleon, Jullien, at this point published two tracts welcoming the "Revolution's seventh" and hopefully last phase, confident it would consolidate all the most substantial gains for society since 1789.[30] *Féderés* abounded almost everywhere, including country towns and villages, at least among the more affluent and better educated. Certainly, as Marxist scholars object, workers and nearly all peasants and small shopkeepers, the great mass of the less literate, except in a few places stayed inactive and indifferent, supporting neither Bourbons nor Napoleon. In Brittany and the Vendée, rural and small-town armed insurrection surged yet again, eager to fight for religion, clergy, and crown. Nevertheless, the great wave of support for Napoleon in 1815 was no less real for being actually less a movement of adulation of Bonaparte the man, or a strain of enlightened despotism he represented, than for retrieving the gains, real and imagined, of the Revolution and Empire conflated into a single set of ideals and slogans, a vision enthusiastically papering over the deep rifts between the early Revolution, the democratic republican Revolution, Montagnard Counter-Enlightenment, and the Empire.

This helps explain the most astounding feature of the *Cent-Jours*—that such hardened veteran adversaries of Bonaparte as Constant, Sismondi, and Pierre-Louis Ginguené, former editor of *La Feuille villageoise* and a co-editor of the *Décade philosophique*, all rallied publicly to him.[31] While the enthusiasm probably did rekindle something of Napoleon's pre-1799 zeal for the Revolution and constitutions, "Napoleon's sudden return," observed Jullien perceptively, "was not the *cause* but *occasion* of the revolution that has occurred."[32] The consequent unifying program of revolutionary renewal was intellectually extremely vague and relied chiefly on emotion, patriotism, and the tricolor; but it also produced concrete reform proposals that elicited real appreciation. If there was scant pressure among the 1815 Bonapartiste *fédérés* for representative democracy or legislative supremacy, there was considerable hostility to the aristocratic interest and to archaic prejudice, superstition, and illiterate obscurantism along with support for a social egalitarianism based on merit and elimination of privilege. The 1815 Bonapartist insurrection featured a noticeable strand of militant anti-clericalism, openly deriding the priesthood and pious rural peasantry, which occasionally turned violent, as at Rennes in early April 1815 when a student mob attacked a local Catholic seminary.[33]

Napoleon can hardly have been in doubt as to what he needed to offer former republican critics and potential backers to gain their support. Among prominent figures invited to assist with formulating his constitutional declaration to the nation were Benjamin Constant and Lazare Carnot (1753–1823), one of the "regicides" of 1793, principal organizer of the French revolutionary army of 1794–6, and a leading

[30] Palmer, *From Jacobin to Liberal*, 119–20.
[31] Imbert, *Destutt de Tracy critique*, 75; Holmes, *Benjamin Constant*, 17–18; Craiutu, *Virtue for Courageous Minds*, 188–9.
[32] Quoted in Palmer, *From Jacobin to Liberal*, 119–20.
[33] Alexander, *Bonapartism*, 107; Jordan, *Napoleon and the Revolution*, 216–17.

member of the *Directoire*. The former, a longstanding political foe willing to forgive in exchange for real constitutional concessions, played the chief role in drafting Napoleon's *Acte Additionnel* (22 April 1815), or the "Benjamine" as some styled it, a constitutional accord, presented as adjusting the arrangements of 1804, providing for a two-chamber legislature, the upper house to be a chamber of peers.[34] On the other hand, Destutt de Tracy, still resenting Napoleon's rebuffing the *Idéologues*, along with others of pre-1814 republican stamp, refused to join the 1815 Bonapartist bandwagon.[35]

After Waterloo, and Napoleon's second abdication, ensued a noticeable change in attitude on the part of both Allies and the restored Bourbon regime. Treated relatively leniently in 1814, when France was reoccupied, after the Hundred Days "revolution" the mood was distinctly harsher. This time substantial allied military forces remained stationed in the country for many months, helping to foment an atmosphere of repression, active revenge, retribution, and punishment.[36] Purging the military and administration resumed with greater vigor than previously. Some 5,000 persons were tried for treason or sedition, and possibly as many as 50,000 officials dismissed from their posts.[37] During 1815, over 20,000 Napoleonist officers were discharged, disgraced, suspended from active service, or removed from the half-pay lists, many now emigrating abroad, an entire batch of cashiered generals settling in Philadelphia as well as other parts of the United States. The Paris École Polytechnique, founded in 1794 by Gaspar Monge and Lazare Carnot (now exiled from France), and reorganized and expanded by Napoleon, was suspended by royal order; a detachment of troops closed it down, the students being sent home at royal expense— among them Comte, who returned to Montpellier.

Fierce retribution fell on those the king had personally forgiven earlier but who had now betrayed him by participating in the Hundred Days. Marshal Michel Ney (1769–1815), risen from the ranks to become a general by 1796, prominent in many of Napoleon's greatest battles, was tried by the upper house of the legislature, the chamber of peers, with both Destutt and Volney refusing to participate, and then shot, in December 1815.[38] Official repression by the Bourbon court was supplemented with some sometimes erratically targeted informal retaliation usually expressing antipathy to republican anti-Catholicism rather than Bonaparte. On 2 August 1815, early in the second Restoration, Marshal Guillaume Brune (1763–1815), a captain in the National Guard in 1789, and friend of Danton active in suppressing the Girondin risings of 1793, who after 1798 commanded French armies in Italy and the Low Countries, and aided Bonaparte at Brumaire, despite having repudiated Bonaparte and backed Louis during 1814–15, was set upon and killed by a mob in Avignon who

[34] Jennings, *Revolution*, 158. [35] Renauld, *Antoine Destutt de Tracy*, 178–9.

[36] Furet, *Revolutionary France*, 280; Aprile, *Révolution inachevée*, 28–9; Jordan, *Napoleon and the Revolution*, 223.

[37] Bruyère-Ostells, *Grande Armée*, 24–5; Jennings, *Revolution*, 89.

[38] Gusdorf, *Conscience révolutionnaire*, 329; Aprile, *Révolution inachevée*, 30.

threw his corpse into the Rhone. Catholic thirst for revenge was greatly aroused in certain regions. In parts of Provence, notably Nîmes, popular anger and frenzy led to the slaughter of dozens of Protestants and Jews and briefly even the closure of Protestant churches.

27.2. ENLIGHTENMENT BARRIERS TO A GENUINE RESTORATION

But at no stage was there a purge of the intellectual and academic reformers of the revolutionary and Napoleonic era, who often, like Constant and Daunou (though now stripped of his post as state archivist), continued to hold prestigious teaching positions, and were now more antagonistic to reaction and faith than ever, while the brief 1815 cleansing of the military and officialdom did nothing more generally to placate either old Jacobins or thwarted Napoleonists, or those half won over in 1814.[39] There was no way royalty could prevent France abounding with those Stendhal called "my republicans" and demi-republicans devoted to personal liberty, secularism, and freedom of expression. It would be hard, perhaps impossible, to prevent permanent estrangement of those like Stendhal who knew all too well the Revolution's failings and the curbs Napoleon's autocracy had imposed, and provisionally accepted that Bourbon Restoration might afford the best chance of reconciling the disparate royalist, republican, and Bonapartist factions, but only as long as the crown tacitly tolerated the most essential freedoms.

One hardcore "Old Jacobin" remaining an inveterate foe of Bonaparte, the ex-mayor of Arles, Pierre-Antoine Antonelle (1747–1817) in 1814–15 definitely considered Bourbon Restoration the sole plausible available means to recover civil "liberty" from Bonaparte's arbitrary authoritarianism. Constant, permitted to resume his career in France, soon again, like Daunou, a leading professor of the Collège de France, a convinced libertarian seated among the Paris legislature's stalwarts of the Left alongside Lafayette and Daunou, once more emerged as a leading representative of the republican values of the Brissotin faction.[40] Flexible radicals, libertarian "republicans" at heart, like Volney and Destutt, remained unforgiving toward Napoleon since the latter's break with the *Idéologues*, but would prove equally antagonistic toward a constitutional monarchy showing any sign of moving against constitutionalism. The overriding point of any constitution, for radicals and "moderates" alike, was to advance human well-being. From the perspective of moderates like Guizot and Victor Cousin, or the inwardly radical stance of Volney and Destutt, stability,

[39] Gusdorf, *Conscience révolutionnaire*, 512; Holmes, *Benjamin Constant*, 19; Price, *Perilous Crown*, 83–7.

[40] [Jullien], *Revue encyclopédique* ix (Jan. 1821), 192; Fontana, *Benjamin Constant*, 98–105; Wood, "Benjamin Constant," 14–15.

restraint, freeing France from fanaticism remained the essential task of the precarious but thoroughly despised restored monarchy.[41]

There were other reasons too why Louis quickly reverted to the path of studied "moderation." Not a few aristocratic and ecclesiastical royalists, preferring Louis XVIII to Napoleon, had no wish to see him become an absolutist, a new "Louis XIV" profiting from the new more efficient centralized administration created by Bonaparte.[42] Napoleon's permanent exile was hence far from being an unambiguous victory for royalism. If Louis was to restore order and secure his fragile regime, wide-ranging comprehensive tolerationism and compromise were indispensable. The *Cent-Jours* vividly illustrated the social and economic factors fermenting behind the scenes, the widening of the ideological and intellectual divide profoundly troubling post-1815 France and Europe. The episode helps one see how divisive it had become that early nineteenth-century France and Europe inherited so much from the great Revolution that powerfully subsisted inextricably consolidated into the post-1815 European reality by Napoleon. This insuperable contradiction was especially evident in the fragility and vacillation of Louis XVIII's policies between 1815 and 1824 (when his successor embarked on a more determined royal reaction), and the refusal to embrace Counter-Enlightenment also in other countries under regimes supposedly ideologically committed to reaction but pragmatically committed, like Bavaria or Bernadotte's Sweden, to prolonging a Napoleonic-type moderate Enlightenment program of rationalization, amelioration, and reform.

The political, religious, and intellectual strategy of the Vienna Congress powers was to permanently entrench monarchy, aristocracy, and religion everywhere in Europe and the colonial empires by thoroughly crushing republicanism and Napoleonism but not necessarily the Enlightenment more broadly, especially in countries such as France, Germany, the Netherlands, and Scandinavia where espousing Counter-Enlightenment as an ally and inspiration was bound to be counter-productive in important respects. Aside from Spain and Russia, in fact, there were not many contexts where outright Counter-Enlightenment was feasible. As Vom Stein discovered at Berlin, moderate enlightened thinking could survive at court only by becoming the servant of reaction, which in post-1815 circumstances meant diluting the moderate Enlightenment tendency, politically and morally. But this left ample scope for eroding, eating away at the fragile Restoration behind the scenes, with most surviving impetus for renewed reform and improvement rooted in the suppressed underground Radical Enlightenment.

Above all, the 1815–48 era was always and invariably a war of three competing ideologies, reaction, moderation and radical reform. Superficially, reaction had triumphed. The Catholic Right swept the board in the French elections of August 1815, voting in a new National Assembly, the so-called *Chambre introuvable*, implacably royalist and aristocratic, that effectively dominated France for the first year of Louis

[41] Imbert, *Metamorphoses*, 42–3, 45.

[42] Imbert, *Destutt de Tracy critique*, 24.

XVIII's resumed reign. At this point, Romantic royalists, like Chateaubriand, were foremost among political visionaries envisaging Louis XVIII as ushering in a new age of liberty.[43] They believed France was theirs for the remaking in their image. But the mood did not last. The post-1815 era remained, if not an enlightened age (any more than the eighteenth century had been), then certainly an age of a passionately resurgent democratizing radicalism, on the one hand, and, on the other, a retreating, more aristocratic, calculated, enlightened "moderation" like Guizot's wanting extensive freedoms on the basis of constitutional monarchy and churches. Some key Counter-Enlightenment objectives were relatively easily secured in the circumstances, but these were of largely symbolic character. The difficulty was how to engineer a profounder, more authentic shift in attitudes and institutions. Louis lost no time in erasing the title "Code Napoleon" from the French *Code civil*, which, lightly revised, with divorce eradicated in accordance with a longstanding promise, received its new royal title in July 1816; but broadly the French legal system remained the Code Napoleon.[44] Spending on restoring churches, church art, and ecclesiastical education was massively stepped up in 1815–23 France, but much of this proved just flimsy window-dressing yielding unprecedented quantities of huge but mostly mediocre, uninspiring, and, in the eyes of many, depressing pious paintings supposedly representing holy scenes.

Restored monarchy was particularly eager to remove offending names of streets, foundations, institutions, museums, and educational establishments, everywhere discarding the attribute "national" and replacing it with royal, noble, or ecclesiastical designations. However, this often meant endorsing entities established by the crown only shortly before or during 1789–91, affording seemingly *ancien régime* titles but, as with the Louvre museum, actually sanctioning and renewing what were in fact revolutionary entities with a pronounced Enlightenment character. It was Louis XVI, for instance, who decreed the establishment of the Paris *Institution royale des jeunes aveugles* [Royal Institute for Blind Children], with its newly developed techniques, in 1786. In 1791, the National Assembly changed its name to *Institution nationale des jeunes aveugles*. Internationally renowned in the Napoleonic era, it inspired the creation of like public schools using the Paris methods to educate blind children, at Vienna (1805), Berlin (1806), Prague (1807), Amsterdam (1808), Dresden (1809), Zurich (1810), and Copenhagen (1811).[45] In 1814–15, the Paris foundation's name reverted to *Institution royale*, but this could not hide its essentially enlightened, experimental, innovative, and internationally renowned character.

Pragmatism thus became the adopted strategy of nearly all factions apart from the Counter-Enlightenment Right. Having little alternative, Louis XVIII realized, he had to retain the new legal system, departmental system introduced in 1789–90, and post-1789 forms of municipal government. After the Hundred Days, with a few exceptions,

[43] Chateaubriand, *Mémoires* ii. 259; Febvre, *Michelet*, 123–4; Serna, *Antonelle*, 421–8; Holmes, *Benjamin Constant*, 2–3, 237–8.

[44] Van der Burg, *Nederland*, 259.

[45] [Jullien], *Revue encyclopédique* ii (1819), 374.

the crown still made little sustained effort to recover aristocratic, ecclesiastical, or even royal properties sold off since 1789. But a full-blown Restoration capable of defeating revolutionary attitudes, radical and moderate, and rebuilding social hierarchy and religious authority in France required considerably more than just changing names and titles. Despite the fervent hopes of legitimists, ultra-royalists, and many churchmen, liberty of conscience, freedom to criticize, and Napoleon's virtual equality of cults all survived intact. They survived, moreover, with an undeniably considerably expanded measure of press freedom compared with anything the Montagne or Napoleon permitted, at any rate until the intensified reactionary drive of Charles X's reign (1824–30). There were still no public religious ceremonies in Louis XVIII's France consecrating monarchical power, and, crucially, no obligatory payment of tithes.

Regular clergy, monks, and friars represented the *ancien régime* throughout France as stalwartly as any element but were now again conspicuous less by their resumed limited presence than the colossal dimensions of their irreplaceable, permanent loss of monastic buildings, land, and property, and, in some areas, continuing near-total absence.[46] Compared to the 366,000 ecclesiastics, regulars and seculars, with eighteen archbishops and 128 bishops, and well over 2,000 monasteries and friaries, in France in 1788,[47] or even the 30,906 monks and friars and 1,940 monasteries in less populated Spain in 1835,[48] the revived French total in the 1820s looked astoundingly paltry. Catholics had fervently longed for their Bourbon Restoration, protested Claude-Hippolyte Clausel de Montals (1769–1857), later bishop of Chartres, in a pamphlet published in 1818, but now faced a deeply disillusioning, dismal prospect with France's army of churchmen besieged and afflicted on every side. Never had the church faced greater dangers or more formidable threats. Although many insipidly concurred with Napoleon that the church usefully lent form and discipline to society and shepherded the masses, among the more educated and higher strata, true men of faith and devotion had become rare. The post-1815 French clergy were acutely aware of the steep decline of French religion, a phenomenon especially striking in large cities and in schools and colleges. The most usual explanation for the all too obvious waning of *ancien régime* style fervor and piety was paucity of clergy and political weakness: "what is destroying religion and accelerating its rapid fall is the rarity and small number of ministers."[49]

Structurally, the French church's two gravest difficulties around 1820, both deeply menacing for its future, were lack of resources and that the Revolution and Napoleon had shattered the ties between church and higher education. Despite Bonaparte's Concordat, hardly any young men educated in his *lycées* and universities entered the priesthood, and little was done to reverse the ruin of the seminaries and *ancien régime*

[46] Flores Estrada, *Representación*, 82–3; Petiteau, "La Restauration," 31–2; Duprat, "Sacre de Charles X," 69–7.

[47] *Courier du Bas-Rhin* no. 8, pp. 61–2 (26 Jan. 1788).

[48] Molinar Prada, "Anticlericalismo popular," 505.

[49] Clausel de Montals, *Coup d'œil*, 14.

colleges, causing a universal chronic clergy shortage difficult to make good after 1815. Most priests surviving the 1793–4 de-Christianization campaign, while remaining priests, went into exile abroad. Now, three decades later, where still alive, they had nearly all been trained in seminaries prior to 1789 and were distinctly aging. Some had returned under the 1801 Concordat between Napoleon and the pope, with others holding out in exile until 1814, creating a subtle tension within the clergy between older and newer returned exiles. But much the greatest difficulty after 1815 was simply the French church's chronic lack of funds, its own economic resources. "When in 1790," observed the ecclesiastical journal *L'Ami de la religion et du Roi*, in 1815, "*la philosophie triomphante* set out to abolish religion, it found no surer expedient to reach its goal than to strip the clergy of their property."[50]

France faced a general acute paucity of priests, with even many of the bishops' seats scandalously remaining vacant for years.[51] Without having its pre-1789 lands and property returned, or new lands and property assigned, how could the church play the part expected of it under the Restoration? "Doubtless one cannot return to it entirely what the church used to possess [thirty] years ago, but what prevents restitution, after deduction of the royal treasury's payments to the clergy, that portion of its former property that was absorbed into the public domain?" Aside from paying preaching clergy's salaries, complained churchmen, the Napoleonic regime deliberately starved the church of resources. Behind a façade of compromise, Napoleon had done all he could "to weaken priestly authority." By the autumn of 1816, some French bishoprics still had between a third and half of all their curacies vacant.[52] Miserably deprived of funds for parishes, schools, and monasteries, the Restoration church lacked the resources to repair crumbling edifices so that everywhere in the countryside abounded abandoned churches. If the Restoration was to succeed, ways had to be found to salvage the Catholic clergy from the "humiliation of being salaried like a troop of workingmen."[53]Above all, the church lacked the means to generate, through the press, a sufficiently powerful counter-current to the torrent of irreligious literature the post-1815 monarchy did not actually encourage but, unlike the Spanish, Prussian, and Austrian regimes, proved too weak to curb.

Loss of resources, numbers, status, and power to condemn and censor drastically reduced the church's capabilities and independence, rendering it subservient to the state; and these setbacks were almost as much the doing of Napoleon, and now the Restoration, as of the Revolution. "In truth," commented one onlooker, Napoleon "wanted a phantom religion, a religion enslaved to him, like everything else."[54] Secularization and Radical Enlightenment had established deep roots especially among the professional and intellectual elite, which meant that beside its other handicaps and vulnerabilities, the French church in France, after 1815, found itself

[50] *L'Ami de la religion* iii (1815), 116. [51] Clausel de Montals, *Coup d'œil*, 12, 16.
[52] *L'Ami de la religion* ix. 291, 293, 295.
[53] F.L.M., "Dotation du clerge," in *L'Ami de la Religion* iii (1815), no. 60, pp. 113–14, 117–18.
[54] *L'Ami de la religion* iii (1815), 28.

constantly charged with being the hypocritical, subservient tool of political tyranny, even of infidel rulers. In 1821, early in the Greek revolt, the French press emanated harsh criticism of the faction calling itself "the friend of religion" for purveying a view of the world stemming not from true Christian allegiance but interest and bias, creating a "great perversion of political morality" built on strange prejudices, and for condemning outright all rebellion, including the Greek insurrection, and hence "embracing the cause of the Turks."[55]

A few surface changes were possible. From 1814, the change of tone in public secondary schools, in their "exterior conduct," was palpable, but the transition was so obviously purely outward that the pupils themselves frequently mocked the new minimalist perfunctory gestures of piety and acquiescence.[56] Napoleon's *lycées*, now renamed *collèges royales*, were essentially secular institutions where, until 1815, religious education, where taught at all, had been a minor formality so that genuinely devout parents, aware of the rampant indifferentism and secularism prevailing, were reluctant to send their sons to them. After 1815, public secondary schools remained the main recruiting ground for the universities, and although theology and religion again officially enjoyed prestige and high status, it remained hard to secure highly educated novices and train them as priests. Napoleon had gone but not the legacy of his *lycées* and universities in which, though now superficially royal colleges, faith still counted for nothing, complained Clausel de Montals, and "les talents seuls y sont comptés" [talent alone is esteemed]; a culture of ability and merit had wholly expunged religious devotion as society's guiding spirit.[57] An entire generation of schoolmasters and lecturers had been nurtured and trained on an irreligious "philosophy," changing French education fundamentally in ways that could not easily be reversed, even if such militant secularism was now stringently frowned on by the royal authorities. The result—highly deplorable in his opinion—observed Jullien, in October 1828, was that most teachers while no longer "directed" by *l'esprit philosophique* were not infused by anything sincere whatever; instead, the usual approach involved half-heartedly imparting traditional religious notions, rendering French education under the restored Bourbon throne unpersuasive, uninspiring, and contemptibly pedantic, unable to give students any sense of the general direction of things.[58]

27.3. POLITICAL IDEOLOGY AND THE REVOLUTIONARY TRADITION

Louis XVIII strove to overcome the debilitating consequences for the church of the 1801 Concordat under his 11 June 1817 new Concordat, under which no less than

[55] [Jullien], *Revue encyclopédique* x (1821), 147–8.
[56] *L'Ami de la religion* iii (1815) 3. [57] Clausel de Montals, *Coup d'œil*, 20–2.
[58] [Jullien], *Revue encyclopédique* xl (Oct. 1828), 8–9, 26.

forty-two additional bishoprics, suppressed by the Revolution, in 1791, and in abeyance since 1801, were reinstated. Episcopates were deemed pivotal to rebuilding religious authority and bolstering Counter-Enlightenment ideology of throne and altar entwined together as the highest principles. But despite instituting a new tax for the purpose (that was hardly popular in the country), most of Louis XVIII's additional bishoprics still remained vacant in 1818.[59] Although in 1805 Napoleon had terminated use of the Brissotin regime's revolutionary calendar introduced in 1793, after 1814 further adjustments to names and holidays were deemed necessary to lend France's revised calendar a sturdier religious gloss. The official year was now peppered with additional commemorations, saints' days, and memorial days marked by expiatory processions commemorating the martyrdoms of Louis XVI, Marie-Antoinette, and also Louis XVII, who had expired on 8 June 1795 aged 10, from tuberculosis contracted in confinement at the Temple prison in Paris.[60] An especially imposing funerary event, commemorating the anniversary of Louis XVI's execution in 1793, occurred on 21 January 1815, with the bells of churches throughout France pealing for a whole hour of public repentance. At Arras in October 1816, the anniversary of Marie-Antoinette's guillotining was marked in all the churches with local civic, judicial, and military authorities turning out in their finery accompanied by detachments of troops, headed by the bishop, whose sermon celebrated the growing success of the seminaries of Arras and St Omer in producing fresh "theologians."[61]

The receding, increasingly rural character of the church's support in society imparted a curiously sectional and provincial, almost marginal, stamp to the resurgent French Counter-Enlightenment. Undeniably, areas amenable to Counter-Enlightenment, and most associated with France's counter-revolutionary heroes, tended to be remote and out of step with the rest. In the Vendée, the 1793–4 religious conflict left deep scars locally and bitter memories. The bishop of Dol-de-Bretagne, chief diocese of that unreconciled rural region, together with the commander of the Vendée insurgents, General François de Charette (1763–96), a nobleman who also fought defending the Tuileries palace on 8 June 1795 and ranked among the best-remembered counter-revolutionary leaders executed in the Revolution, were now lionized before the public. They were presented as surpassing spiritual heroes central to the burgeoning new Catholic political–theological cult of anti-republican martyrdom. By 1827, commemorations and masses for Charette's soul adorned innumerable French churches, including all ninety-seven parishes of the former bishopric of Dol.[62] But precisely by intensifying the clash of Counter-Enlightenment and Enlightenment in France such a cult, redolent with idealizing the nobility,

[59] Clausel de Montals, *Coup d'œil*, 12.
[60] Furet, *Revolutionary France*, 274.
[61] *L'Ami de la religion* x. 7–8.
[62] Archives de la Vendée, mandements et actes épiscopaux des évêques de Luçon 4, no. 278/31 (18 Oct. 1823); Tulard, *Histoire et dictionnaire*, 639.

rendered Louis XVIII's monarchy only more, not less, divided and fraught. Despite special symbolic significance locally, due to lack of funds even the revived bishopric of Dol, its seat now transferred to Luçon, suffered a prolonged delay before a new prelate could be installed. Among the bishop's first *mandements*, dated October 1823, was his ordering a Te Deum to be held in his cathedral whereby the local populace could express joy and thanksgiving for the crushing of the Spanish revolution of 1820–3.[63]

Reactionary politics and theology in Restoration France linked arms. But quite apart from insufficiency of numbers and resources, there seemed no way to overcome the problem of the clergy's educational and social marginality stemming from reduced educational opportunities and social status. Napoleon's policies had simply created two sharply separated French ideological and intellectual spheres destined to eternal conflict with each other. Priests generally came not from the educational mainstream but either small private ecclesiastical colleges and seminaries, or from outside France; by 1820, practically all younger priests derived from marginal contexts with virtually none emanating from the country's state-supported main educational institutions. In this respect especially, *la philosophie* remained not just still entrenched, but seemingly winning its battle against organized piety and faith.[64] Only remote rural areas featured populations still manifesting the kind of unquestioning Catholic devotion widely encountered before 1789, which accentuated the declining social status and cultural apartness of the priesthood still more; one encountered persons unaffected by the "contagion of impiety" supporting their priests with fervor and energy, it seemed to many, only among the uneducated and unaware, among "les simples."

Still more complained bitterly of the crown's and church's inability to halt the torrent of irreligious books flowing from French presses. After 1815, there seemed to be no more hindrance to the flow than before. Without a more resolute effort at all levels of society, especially women and the rich, to raise standards of piety and faith, the church seemed doomed to a dismal, contracting role and increasing cultural marginality. In 1817, angry protests drew attention to announcements of the publication that year, in Paris, of sets of the complete works of both Voltaire *and* Rousseau, the former with the notes on Voltaire the impious Condorcet had added with all his "arrogance and bitterness." At the time of his pantheonization, in 1791, readers were reminded, Voltaire had been hailed as the Revolution's "premier auteur": "it was he," trumpeted the revolutionary press "who overthrew the chief and most formidable pillar of despotism, namely religious and priestly power." Everyone should join the fight for the "faith of Christians" to suppress the writings of the "two greatest enemies of Christianity."[65] Louis XVIII's minister of police was among those who joined the chorus complaining to the legislature about the slackness of book censorship and

[63] Archives de la Vendée, mandements et actes épiscopaux des évêques de Luçon 4, no. 278/31 (18 Oct. 1823).

[64] Clausel de Montals, *Coup d'œil*, 23, 27.

[65] *L'Ami de la religion* x. 369–76; Silvy, *Fidèles Catholiques aux Évêques*, 44.

newspaper surveillance. Members of the legislature and others disagreed over whether freedom to publish such material was or was not avoidable under Louis's 1814 *charte.* Either way, held the fervent Jansenist, Louis Silvy (1760–1847), France's clergy were not doing enough to combat *la philosophie moderne.* Monarchy and piety can only survive if religious authority holds a dominant position in society and culture. If society allows "this divine religion to continue to be insulted, derided and made abject by books like those of Voltaire and Rousseau" none can doubt that kingdom and church will undergo before long "another shock just as severe as the Revolution of 1789." A realm where minds are infected by the "errors of *la nouvelle philosophie*" is "lost," assuredly on the path to ruin. It was impossible for "this holy religion" to recover its old ascendancy over hearts [*sa puissance et son ascendant sur les coeurs*], if publishing *philosophique* works persisted. Revolution, averred Silvy, was in part retribution by divine providence for not suppressing impious books.[66] The bishops must redouble their efforts to persuade the king that his most vital interest lay in championing religion more vigorously.[67]

At every level, the Restoration left the returning stream of *émigré* aristocrats, priests, and office-holders, avid for reaction after decades of often harsh and discomforting exile abroad, frustrated and dissatisfied. Despite the surface calm, following the Hundred Days, resentment and frustration continually reinforced the ideological divide and widened it in unexpected ways. Compromises made by the French monarchy, no less than the Bavarian, Dutch–Belgian, and Swedish–Norwegian, and, until 1819–20, the Czar, greatly diluted the impact of "Holy Alliance" legitimism, censorship, and religious reaction, and in France and Belgium left republicans, democrats, and Napoleonists openly contemptuous of the new order feeling more exasperated than defeated. Many in France, scorning the monarchy and its puny church and nobility, silently fumed, vowing vengeance in the style of the hero of Stendhal's *Scarlet and Black*, on seeing young ecclesiastics of noble birth acquiring annual incomes three times larger than those of Napoleon's finest major-generals.[68] Contempt and alienation pervaded the intelligentsia, the schools, teaching profession, even sections of the clergy.

The thinness of the reactionary façade, and its educational failures, could only encourage a powerful radical response beneath the surface that was Europe-wide. The Vienna Congress's inconsistently repressive and intolerant international conservative order provoked a growing repugnance not only among radicals and "moderates" but even among many forthright champions of orthodoxy and Counter-Enlightenment. Especially French and Belgian Catholic militants and right-wing Romantics like Chateaubriand, De Maistre, De Lamennais, Bonald, and the young Victor Hugo, grew disgusted with the—from their standpoint—highly defective Restoration and deplorable tide of *philosophique* literature pouring from the presses. If pragmatism, restraint, and moderation reigned supreme, such moderation seemed ill-advised,

[66] Silvy, *Fidèles Catholiques aux Évêques*, 20–3.

[67] Silvy, *Fidèles Catholiques aux Évêques*, 10–14.

[68] Stendhal, *Scarlet and Black*, 44.

bogus, virtual sacrilege, to ultra-royalist critics.[69] Descended from an ancient Provençal noble family, Louis de Bonald (1754–1840) had fled to Heidelberg in 1791, publishing his first book, stressing the indissoluble linkage of authentic political power with religion, in 1796; between 1815 and 1822 he served as a deputy of the French national legislature and a royal education councilor. Hailed by De Lamennais as the "most profound philosopher in Europe to have appeared since Malebranche," he was the leading advocate in post-1814 France of vigorous censorship and new blasphemy and sacrilege laws to systematically punish impious speech and action. Christianity, he taught, is not just a religion but, with monarchy, the defender of the social and moral order. France reverting to republicanism would mean the end of "monarchical Europe, and a republican Europe would mean the end of civilization, religion, politics, society, the end of everything."[70] The Restoration he judged a disaster that had failed to reverse the Revolution.[71]

There was no shortage of published denunciations of *philosophisme* in the years following the Restoration, profiling the allegedly dire consequences of irreligious thought. Though alarmist and lurid in their rhetoric, declarations like that in the *Annales politiques, morales et littéraire* of 5 May 1816 were not inaccurate in their basic analysis. What threatened the conjunction of throne and altar in France was the "philosophical charlatanism" of the *idéologie* of Volney, Destutt, and Daunou, here deemed the very philosophical backbone of the Revolution, the "arguments making both egoism and anarchy sacred and that lead us to materialism and atheism," though, fundamentally, this was just the intellectual legacy of the "school of Diderot and d'Holbach."[72] The ecclesiastical journal *L'Ami de la religion et du Roi* drew some comfort, in August 1816, from the fact that among society's elites the vogue for reading eighteenth-century irreligious *philosophes*, apart from Voltaire and Rousseau (whose continued popularity seemed impregnable), was receding, a tendency perceptible since the late 1790s.[73] "Today one does not read d'Argens, nor La Mettrie, nor Helvétius, nor Diderot, nor d'Holbach. They are tedious, one agrees, and in their books one searches in vain for the grounds of the ephemeral reputation they received from those with an interest in praising them the better to accredit their doctrine."[74]

However, while Diderot, Helvétius, and d'Holbach, no longer in vogue, were ceasing to be read, their core ideas were being constantly reworked, and remained firmly entrenched in the minds and writings of innumerable pernicious heirs, young and old, the Destutts, Volney, Daunou, Jullien, Cabanis, and Say prominent among them. Hegel might dismiss *idéologie* in his 1821 Berlin lecture course as of scant importance philosophically,[75] but new editions of the *Idéologues*' works

[69] Berlin, *Crooked Timber*, 137; Aprile, *Révolution inachevée*, 15; Claudes, "Joseph de Maistre," 92, 95–9.

[70] Bonald, *Réflexions*, 105.

[71] De Lamennais, *Oeuvres complètes* i. 220; Aprile, *Révolution inachevée*, 15.

[72] Kennedy, "Ideology," 362.

[73] *L'Ami de la religion* v (1815), 2–11 and vi. 3.

[74] *L'Ami de la religion* vi, no. 210 (14 Aug. 1816), 3–4.

[75] Hegel, *Lectures* iii. 166.

stood incontrovertibly in vogue in France. Indeed, Destutt's writings, including his uncompromisingly radical and republican *Commentaire* on Montesquieu, banned under Napoleon and published for the first time in the new United Netherlands without the author's name, at Liège in 1817, finally appeared under his own name at Paris in 1819, and again at Paris in 1822 and 1828;[76] Destutt's works indisputably circulated more freely in France under the Restoration than they had under Napoleon, no small irony given that one of Destutt's principal maxims was: "esperer liberté et monarchie, c'est espérer deux choses dont l'une exclut l'autre" [to expect liberty and monarchy is to expect two things one of which excludes the other].[77]

With hindsight it might seem that any thoroughgoing transformation of society and culture along the lines Europe's reactionaries demanded was unrealistic, that ultra-royalist Catholic Counter-Enlightenment expectations of eliminating freedom of thought and "universal and equal rights" were simply an emotional, blind refusal to accept the world as it now existed.[78] The "philosophical" content of an immensity of enlightened printed books, journals, and pamphlets, admonished Jefferson, could never be wholly reversed or eradicated from the collective European and American mind. But to many at the time the ultras' program looked far from unrealistic; there seemed no great obstacle preventing obliteration of the emblems, purging the persons, and suppressing the ideas and books of the Enlightenment and Revolution. Had not Spain's restored monarchy, within weeks, succeeded, in 1814 and again in 1823, in overturning the Cádiz constitution (which the king had likewise sworn to uphold), restoring church and Inquisition to unchallenged supremacy along with their confiscated property, and revived the nobility? If Fernando VII too was less than wholly successful in purging administration and army of conspiring radicals and crypto-radicals, his regime's profound instability was not at first generally evident. In Prussia, liberalization of education, the press, and even the army advanced considerably between 1807 and 1814, and a constitution was promised; but after Von Humboldt's dismissal, in 1819, all was emphatically reversed, backed by a much tougher and more illiberal press policy than existed in France and a reactionary officer corps controlling the army. The same was true of Austria, Austrian Italy, Piedmont, Naples, and the Papal States. Pressure to end formal religious toleration and freedom of thought, and reverse the Enlightenment generally, along with a more systematic purging of suspect individuals and erasure of symbols, had to be stepped up if the traumatic twenty-five-year revolutionary reality was to be effectively ended. [79] To Legitimists, ultra-royalists, and Catholic reactionaries, Counter-Enlightenment could eradicate every monument to the Revolution's legacy whether in the form of ideas, buildings, institutions, plaques, statues, busts, pictures, insignia, or books, along with the

76 Jolly, "Introduction," 29–31; Carrithers, "An Appreciation," 33 n. 13.
77 Destutt de Tracy, *Commentaire*, 157–8; Jolly, "Introduction," 24–5.
78 McMahon, *Enemies*, 155–6.
79 Jennings, *Revolution*, 318.

obstructive, militantly anti-Catholic new regime in the Low Countries, and urgently needed to do so.[80]

On recovering his throne for the second time, Louis XVIII renewed his pledge to rule together with his legislature under a restricted suffrage, allowing a limited press freedom. Those dissatisfied with the new order provisionally went along with a working alliance of "republicans" and moderate *royalistes constitutionnels* supporting the Restoration as long as Louis respected the new constitution replete with personal liberty and freedom of expression.[81] This held the ultras in check. But Louis's cautious pragmatism with its concessions and compromises often struck not just republicans and Napoleonists but also ardent conservatives as an "unnatural and feeble government," self-contradictory, uninspiring, a hypercritical scenario all too apt to breed more dissatisfied, resentful republicans than more of the religiously devout, especially among the brighter pupils of secondary schools and colleges. Obvious instances were the young Auguste Comte, who, on leaving his Montpellier *lycée*, had scarcely enrolled, in August 1814, at the Paris École Polytechnique, a college loathed by royalists as a hotbed of Jacobinism, *bonapartisme*, and irreligion, than he embraced an intensely idealistic revolutionary republicanism;[82] and the future historian, Jules Michelet (1798–1874), a printer's son, by 1814–15 already a fiery republican youth, unwilling to show the slightest outward deference to the new order; a Paris University professor from the early 1820s, Michelet aimed to revive the democratic principles of the great Revolution while combating Restoration and clergy intellectually together with the false "Jacobinism" of Robespierre. For decades, Michelet devoted his energies to discrediting and undermining Louis XVIII's Restoration as well as urging readers, as he reminded Lamartine in November 1847, that the European public must on no account suppose "Robespierre was, among the people, the truly national man" [*l'homme vraiment national*].[83]

By 1815, moreover, some of the era's foremost literary figures had already imbibed, from *Idéologue* sources, the key ideas and influences that shaped their outlook and literary creativity. The irreligion and generally radical views of Stendhal (1783–1842) were already formed before 1814, principally by Helvétius, whom he first read in 1803, and, from 1805, Destutt, with whose help he sought to train his mind in exercising the materialists' truth-detecting procedural triad—"observation, analysis, judgment," the recipe that enables mankind to purge minds of unsound and false presumptions. Often in emotional turmoil, Stendhal resolved early on to be a close observer of the human heart, and especially stabilize himself and his ideas by adhering to Destutt's maxim "nosce te ipsum" [know thyself], as his chosen path to a secure

[80] Holmes, *Benjamin Constant*, 17.

[81] Serna, *Antonelle*, 427–8, 432; Holmes, *Benjamin Constant*, 16–17.

[82] Gouhier, *Vie de Auguste Comte*, 36–7, 41, 49.

[83] Michelet to Lamartine, 1 Nov. 1847, in Michelet, *Correspondance générale* v. 448–9; Finch, *French Literature*, 63.

personal happiness.[84] For the rest of his life, Stendhal felt guided by the "astonishing change in all my ideas" Destutt's *idéologie* occasioned.[85]

Furthermore, if boycotted by fashionable society, pre-1789 *philosophes* were still wildly in demand among students and the opposition-minded, and frequently reprinted, circulating almost as if officially permitted despite furious condemnation by Chateaubriand, De Maistre, Bonald, De Lamennais, and other chief prophets of reaction. Such texts were rightly considered the principal root of the Revolution.[86] *Philosophisme*, the greatest challenge to the Restoration, was defined by the Loyalist paper *L'Ami de la religion et du Roi* as a phenomenon first arising in the seventeenth century with the systems of "Socinus, Hobbes, Spinoza, Bayle and some others now less well known," thinkers with few followers unable to dent the robust solidity of religious authority in society,[87] but which, evolving during the early eighteenth century in England, the land of Herbert, Blount, Shaftesbury, Toland, Collins, Tindal, and Woolston, into deism and irreligion, grew into a powerful, broad-based tendency. Initially lagging behind England, France soon caught up thanks to Voltaire. However, it was principally Diderot, affirmed this journal, in 1815, who transformed the process into a serious menace to the existing order. A journal founded in 1814 that ceased publication during the Hundred Days but resumed on Louis XVIII's return, *L'Ami de la religion et du Roi* also attributed to Diderot the most subversive pages of *De l'Esprit* (1756; actually by Helvétius), the *Système de la Nature* (1770; actually by d'Holbach), and the *Histoire philosophique des Deux Indes* (1770). Above all, the *Encyclopédie* in Diderot's hands became *une affaire de parti*, a formidably potent publication, widely disseminated and exalted by his following, and widely deemed to have contributed "more than any other to accrediting *la philosophie*."[88]

Diderot, followed by "Helvétius with his crude metaphysics," the *Bélisaire* (1767; by Marmontel), and other irreligious writers of that coterie produced large-scale works supplemented by a stream of brochures by Naigeon, Condorcet, Damilaville, and others, which fatally disseminated *le philosophisme*, the quintessence of the revolutionary creed. After 1770, *philosophisme* dominated the French literary–intellectual scene, lamentably saturating Paris, and "penetrated the provinces," conquering the upper strata of society while also infiltrating the mass of the common people. *Philosophisme* addressed society in terms disastrously exaggerating the common people's "rights" and ruinously indoctrinating them with false notions of sovereignty, independence, and liberty. "To the people, they depicted authority as despotism, religion as a superstition. Pamphlets full of exaltation and bitterness excited their minds."[89] Their arguments inverted "all notions of duty, and threw all [existing] principles of government into doubt," overturning religious authority comprehensively. Among the worst and most violently crypto-republican of these radical texts,

[84] Stendhal, *Private Diaries*, 390–1.
[85] Stendhal, *Private Diaries*, 47, 68, 88, 91, 98, 157, 199, 201; Kennedy, "Ideology," 360–1.
[86] McMahon, *Enemies*, 158–9, 165.
[87] *L'Ami de la religion* v (1815), 2–3.
[88] *L'Ami de la religion* v (1815), 6.
[89] *L'Ami de la religion* v (1815), 10.

Le Système de la nature [of d'Holbach] not only preached atheism, and shamelessly reviled priests, but with inconceivable impudence insulted kings, calling monarchs *usurpateurs*, and *oppresseurs*, and inviting peoples to regain their rights. "Tant de soins, d'efforts et de livres produisirent leur effet. La Révolution eût lieu" [So many preparations, efforts and books produced their effect. The Revolution took place].[90]

Félicité de Lamennais (1782–1854), like Bonald, emerged as one of the greatest French Catholic publicists of the early nineteenth century, commencing in 1817 with his *Essai sur l'indifférence en matière de religion* portraying "religious indifference" as a historical, philosophical, and psychological phenomenon. His thoroughness betrayed an intellectual outlook not just eloquent and steeped in Enlightenment literature, citing Hobbes, Voltaire, Rousseau, Montesquieu, Diderot, Condorcet, Raynal, Gibbon, Shaftesbury, Chubb, Blount, and Bolingbroke repeatedly, but itself a product of the Enlightenment. As cultural phenomena, the "indifférence monstrueuse" and "tolérance universelle" he and Bonald relentlessly assailed stemmed not from within irreligious "philosophy" itself, he argued, but underlying psychological and cultural impulses rendering the appearance, or pretense, of intellectual superiority, rather than reasoning as such, the most prized of qualities. "La honte de paraître crédule" [the shame of appearing to be credulous] is the "vraie cause de l'incrédulité" [true cause of incredulity].[91] Judged as reasoning, the atheistic thought of Diderot and Condorcet, and deism of Voltaire and Rousseau, possessed scant originality, being derived, De Lamennais went to considerable lengths to show, from the early English deists. Unoriginal, they were also philosophically incoherent, Rousseau's eloquent writing being no more than an "assemblage d'incohérence, d'absurdités et de contradictions."[92]

Ancient Greek philosophy had first introduced atheism and religious indifference into the world, notes De Lamennais, but Epicurus and the Epicurean sect had wisely understood they needed to keep their thoughts strictly to themselves and not challenge the public cult, since public order, morality, and respect for institutions depend on religion. Making good use of Gibbon, De Lamennais contended that the Roman Empire's decline and fall followed from moral decay which in turned resulted from philosophy undermining religion.[93] Gibbon scoffed at religion privately while perfectly grasping that religion is indispensable to society, regularly attending church and revering the Anglican church outwardly.[94] Enlightenment philosophy proclaims the dignity, equality, and imprescriptible rights of man and then pretends three-quarters of all humanity are the victims of religious imposture. Philosophy, by pronouncing religion and its doctrines to be imposture while acknowledging its *necessité indispensable* to morality, society, and politics, as Voltaire, Rousseau, and

[90] *L'Ami de la religion* v (1815), 11.
[91] Bonald, *Réflexions*, 103; De Lamennais, *Oeuvres complètes* i. 56, 211.
[92] Bonald, *Réflexions*, 100; De Lamennais, *Oeuvres complètes* i. 51, 65, 83–4.
[93] De Lamennais, *Oeuvres complètes* i. 23–6, 28.
[94] De Lamennais, *Oeuvres complètes* i. 51–4.

Gibbon all do, admits to being totally in contradiction with itself, pure "ignorance" and imposture.[95]

Auguste Comte, beginning to formulate his Positivist system in the years around 1820, and having its main lines in place by 1825, concurred with De Lamennais, Bonald, and De Maistre that the Revolution, followed by Napoleon, hurled France into profound moral turmoil and that the recipes of pre-1789 *philosophes* are insufficient to construct a lasting social stability enabling the state to afford the security and other advantages that it should. Like De Lamennais and Constant, he accused Rousseau of forging a false kind of popular sovereignty that foments only anarchy. But he firmly denied religion and royalism can fill the chasm; that to his mind was just sliding back to a sullied past, an earlier stage of human development. The answer to mankind's predicament, he urged, at that time viewing himself very much as the heir of Condorcet (later, from the mid-1840s, Comte's thought assumed a more mystical, quasi-religious character), is to redouble the emphasis on science and the laws of nature as man's sole source of verifiable, trustworthy, genuine truth and only legitimate and lasting ground for moral and political truth. All truth constitutes one single system of rules and science, so that morality and politics too possess a single, unquestionably scientific basis, one that lies exclusively in a rational democratic republicanism and a new kind of moral and intellectual "communion" taught by experts but imbibed by, and gradually becoming the creed of, the whole people, completing the Revolution of 1789–99 by means of a final, further stage of enlightenment.[96]

Philosophisme from Diderot via d'Holbach and Helvétius down to 1789 and Condorcet, and then first to *Idéologie* and eventually Comte's Positivism, hence continued still to be obsessively projected alike by the Counter-Enlightenment Right, and renewed Radical Enlightenment as the principal engine of demolition of *ancien régime* values. In 1815, Enlighteners moderate and radical, whatever their disillusionment, could at least celebrate Napoleon's military triumphs, transient though these proved, for giving Europe and the world sufficient time and space to digest the great reformist impulses, and consolidate the revolutionary gains which thereby became too firmly entrenched to be reversed by Counter-Enlightenment. The Code Napoleon and administrative and educational innovations of the French empire, and all the principles of the Enlightenment lived on as an institutionalized reality in post-1815 Europe that could neither be denied nor countered. The Napoleonic legacy formed an insuperable barrier to the French Counter-Enlightenment, to all sliding back. The challenge was to build further on this solid foundation, renewing and extending the Western Enlightenment.

An encouraging illustration, contended Jullien, writing in the *Revue encyclopédique* in 1819, was the contrast between the situation of the Jews of France with that in Germany, where their deteriorating position was the work of oppressive princes

[95] De Lamennais, *Oeuvres complètes* i, 28, 51–3, 439; Jaume, *Tocqueville*, 75.

[96] Gouhier, *Vie de Auguste Comte*, 102–3; Fedi, *Comte*, 20–2, 29, 36–7; Jaume, *Tocqueville*, 97.

and of Counter-Enlightenment thinking. Jullien reiterated the typical Radical Enlightenment perspective on the Jewish problem in Europe: for some time "the friends of humanity" [*les amis de l'humanité*] had pondered the Jewish question and clearly established that Christian oppression over the centuries is the chief cause of the "l'abrutissement de leurs facultés intellectuelles" [the debasement of their intellectual faculties], of the degradation of Jews' moral and aesthetic sensibility. However, since Jewish emancipation in France one had seen them detach themselves more and more from religious traditions, and habits and practices "incompatible with the duties of the citizen." Following emancipation, French Jews had "served under the colors with distinction," successfully applied themselves to science and the arts, become honest businessmen, honorable functionaries: "in short, they have become citizens but without ceasing to be *Israélites*.[97]

Only Enlightenment "philosophy," held De Lamennais, prevents religion from peacefully reigning over European society. The answer was to show greater respect for the simplicity of ordinary folk. De Lamennais eulogized the Spanish common people for heroically rising against the tyrant Napoleon, in 1808, in the name of religion, whereas the philosophical radicals spouting about liberty foment only religious indifference leading to tyranny and servitude.[98] Disorder and crime plague society, but, he claimed, are a direct consequence of philosophy's assault on faith. There will always be the poor and hence always a need to console them, which can never be philosophy's task.[99] But stressing poverty and society's defects to assail "philosophy" proved a risky strategy: during the 1830s, De Lamennais increasingly became a divisive force within the church, by urging churchmen to associate themselves more closely and energetically with helping the poor.

With its dependence on faith and tradition, and weakness among the highly literate of middle-class and professional background, Restoration Counter-Enlightenment found it difficult to supply a teachable doctrine adapted to persuading youth and to recapturing the schools, colleges, and universities. Romanticism could do some of the work by countering Enlightenment stress on "reason" with a new emphasis on emotion, feeling, and symbolism suffused with melancholia and nostalgia. By in setting the individual starkly apart from both authority and the crowd, Romanticism remained essentially a cultural filter and intensifier, rather than a specific ideological program in its own right. Reinvigorating both Left and Right rather than the middle ground, its effect was to sharpen in some respects but not substantially change the basic triangular split in the Western Enlightenment separating radical reform from "moderation" and setting both against Counter-Enlightenment. Romanticism merely reconfigured this basic divide in predominantly literary and artistic terms. If early nineteenth-century Romanticism in political thought, literature, and painting was

97 [Jullien], *Revue encyclopédique* iii (1819), 494–7.
98 De Lamennais, *Oeuvres complètes* i. 41, 44.
99 De Lamennais, *Oeuvres complètes* i. 385, 399, 403.

both conservative and Leftist, both equally feeding on disillusionment, melancholy, and nostalgia, the pain of foreign exile and reverses of the Revolution and Napoleonic era firmly steered much Romanticist longing into resurgent revolutionary ardor and ambition. Backward-looking though it often appeared, Romanticism, Stendhal recognized, with its striving to break conventional bounds, was a decidedly "modern" phenomenon, a highly charged response to the challenges and dilemmas of an age of far-reaching cultural and social alienation.[100]

"France is tranquil," observed Shelley with satisfaction, in 1821, "in the enjoyment of a partial exemption from the abuses which its unnatural and feeble government are vainly attempting to revive."[101] The numerous Frenchmen who had gone into exile, voluntary or involuntary, in 1814–15 had evolved into a new species of *émigré*, reinforcing the post-1815 tendency for political exiles to become an international fraternity infused with ideologies uncompromisingly anti-Legitimist, anti-aristocratic, and anti-clerical. And unlike the clandestine intellectual networks of the eighteenth century, these exiles had a fully developed Radical Enlightenment democratic republican ideology at hand, the principal organs of which the Bourbon monarchy was in no position to challenge let alone suppress outright. There was many a Michelet, many ardent French republicans in the France of 1820, as there were also abroad.

27.4. A LATE ENLIGHTENMENT *MACHINE DE GUERRE*: THE *REVUE ENCYCLOPÉDIQUE*

Among post-1815 radical journals published in France, the most noteworthy mouthpiece of Radical Enlightenment views and aspirations was that edited by Marc-Antoine Jullien, the *Revue encyclopédique* (1819–31). Established in 1819 with the strong encouragement of Volney shortly before his death, with an eye to filling a gap in the existing press in France by providing a comprehensive guide to the progress of human knowledge in all its *rapports* with the social order, it sought to make the perfecting of society via this interplay "easily accessible" to all levels of intelligence and "all types of readers." Bentham, who had ties with the project via Jean-Baptiste Say, called it "that monthly journal which is the journal of the rest of the civilized world."[102]

Unconnected with "nationalism," nothing to do with "liberalism," the journal existed, explained Jullien, to serve the "general interests of humanity," among which, plainly, he counted his and his colleagues' scarcely veiled support for the revolutions in Spain, Portugal, Spanish America, Naples, and Greece.[103] Their plan

[100] Finch, *French Literature*, 63. [101] Shelley, *Poetical Works* iv. 41.

[102] [Jullien], *Revue encyclopédique* vii (July 1820), 35–6; Schoorl, *Jean-Baptiste Say*, 93; De Champs, *Enlightenment and Utility*, 169.

[103] [Jullien], *Revue encyclopédique* xvii (Jan. 1823), 21.

was to rally all the savants, publicists, *philosophes*, *encyclopédistes*, and *littérateurs*, French and foreign, to resume the task of advancing the Enlightenment in its most essential aims and purposes, to relate the "march and continuing progress of human knowledge" to improving the social order, to "consider the sciences and their results from a *philosophique* perspective," that is the progress of "l'esprit humain" in relation to "l'avancement social" [social advancement] and the general interest.[104] The editors' purpose was to rally and interconnect all the scientists and men of learning in the world to provide a regular mechanism of communication linking all dimensions of the Enlightenment together.[105]

France's geographical position, outgoing intellectual culture, and "spirit of sociability" made her in some sense European civilization's foyer, creating a particular need for a general French-language Enlightenment review reporting the progress of *la philosophie*, the sciences and arts everywhere.[106] The editors planned to offer reviews of all the "most instructive and most useful" publications in every field of knowledge. While aspiring to be objective, impartial, and scientific, they were, at the same time, unwilling to allow royalist and Catholic publications to persuade the public that the Revolution was something detrimental, undesirable, or bad in essence; rather, they strove to curb the profound harm caused, they believed, by misguided writers admonishing readers that the Revolution propagated *fausses doctrines*. Whatever its mistakes, the Revolution was "pure in principles," a wholly "necessary" consequence with profound causes, endorsed by all "honest and enlightened men of the nation." If the current rules of discussion, in France, forbade discussion of whether or not the nobility should exist, and even impeded their campaign against slavery, they decried attacking the *Declaration of the Rights of Man* as intolerable and pernicious.[107] A conscious strand of the Radical Enlightenment, the *Revue encyclopédique* was above all devoted to "propagation de l'esprit philosophique" internationally. "It is by the influence, and the continuous action of *l'esprit philosophique*" that little by little "abuses disappear, laws become more perfect, and all the movements of the social body become better regulated."[108]

A key feature of the project was the journal's gathering reports on the progress of higher education and the sciences, and the global general progress of "enlightenment," from all quarters of the world, not least the United States, a regular link maintained through the philosophical societies of Philadelphia, Boston, Charleston, and New York. An early report from the Russian city of Odessa, dated 1 November 1818, observed that Greeks formed a majority of the city's population, a community ardent for the "bien general de la Grèce" and well-being of Greeks everywhere: Odessa's Greek schools had made excellent progress, and both ancient and modern

[104] [Jullien], *Revue encyclopédique* v (1820), 11, 14–15; Palmer, *From Jacobin to Liberal*, 177–9.
[105] [Jullien], *Revue encyclopédique* ix (1821), 7.
[106] [Jullien], *Revue encyclopédique* i (1819), 5–24.
[107] [Jullien], *Revue encyclopédique* x (1821), 95–9; Schoorl, *Jean-Baptiste Say*, 131–2.
[108] [Jullien], *Revue encyclopédique* xl (1828), 8–9; Whatmore, "Democrats and Republicans," 45.

Greek dramas, rendered into modern Greek, were being staged in Odessa with success.[109] The revue's chief Spanish reporter was Llorente, who supplied well-informed accounts of Spain's domestic situation and the reinstated Inquisition, the latest works prohibited, and the Inquisitors' efforts to prevent Estrada's London periodical *El Español constitucional* eulogizing British institutions, from entering Spain. Estrada's salutary "Address" to Fernando VII "caused so much disquiet in Madrid that all the agents of the police and of the Inquisition" were set to work tracking down copies. Yet, no matter how unenlightened, Fernando could not stifle Spain's Enlightenment altogether. If France, in 1819, counted over sixty societies and academies devoted to the sciences and arts, Restoration Spain lamentably boasted a mere seventeen such bodies.[110]

Until the 1830 revolutions the *Revue encyclopédique* served as prime standard-bearer of progress in the world of *l'esprit philosophique.* By this key term, Jullien, hardened veteran of the great Revolution, meant mankind's slow and arduous progress toward democratic, republican modernity in all its aspects, including political economy, a dimension thus far sadly neglected in France.[111] The goal of Jullien and his principal collaborators—Say, the Abbé Grégoire, Llorente, Salfi for Italy, and the "honnête et judicieux" Sismondi, as Michelet called him, expert in history as well as economics—was nothing if not sweeping and ambitious—representative democracy, condemning *robespierriste* direct democracy, free expression, free press, secularization, ending slavery, generating social equality, and promoting the "general interest" above all particular vested interests whether aristocratic, ecclesiastical, landowning, or commercial. The team advanced their agenda by disseminating radical ideas (including Bentham's) to promote radical politics internationally and advance universal secular education together with a dash of economic redistribution along the lines recommended by Say and Sismondi; in other words, it represented the mature and final version of the ideology of Diderot, d'Holbach, Raynal, Condorcet, the Brissotins, and the *Idéologues.*

Theirs was a late Enlightenment philosophical radicalism ceaselessly decrying populism and Robespierre's "dictatorship," a democratic radicalism repudiating the Montagne, Napoleon, the British "model," and the "Holy Alliance," strictly on the basis of representative democratic republicanism. From its founding in 1819, through the early 1820s, the *Revue encyclopédique* also discreetly promoted the tremendous new revolutionary developments occurring in Spain, Italy, Greece, and Latin America, keeping the public informed, giving meaningful guidance and direction, and providing a key pro-Revolution discussion forum, an intellectual meeting-point serving all Europe while enabling the international radical leadership to concert the new revolutions' foreign publicity. Radicals also needed a concrete, convincing

[109] [Jullien], *Revue encyclopédique* i (1819), 175–6.

[110] Llorente's articles in the *Revue encyclopédique* i (1819), 281–2, 355–6, 405–48.

[111] Palmer, *From Jacobin to Liberal*, 180; Febvre, *Michelet*, 115; Trampus, *Naissance du langage*, 149; Schoorl, *Jean-Baptiste Say*, 122, 131.

model, and for some years there was a lively discussion as to whether the United States, the world's sole existing representative republic moving toward universal male suffrage, actually provided that model. The *Revue encyclopédique* indeed stood out among European journals for promoting a generalized political and cultural democratic republican *Américanisme.*[112] At this juncture, most leading radical voices supporting the 1820s revolutions, including Bentham, Angeloni, Rocafuerte, Fenimore Cooper, Lafayette, and Jullien himself, continued to exalt and eulogize the United States, Jullien perceiving America as the one major society that was genuinely democratizing, the "only modern society," as he expressed it in the *Revue encyclopédique,* "established from the outset on a rational basis, with no need to compromise with vicious precedents." By 1825, every state of the Union except Rhode Island, Virginia, and Louisiana had adopted the principle of universal white male suffrage.[113] But was the United States genuinely fitted to be designated the world's supreme model for philosophical radicals, the sole major stable, free republic "where liberty enlivens all institutions"?[114]

Confirmation of the United States' unparalleled role, held Jullien, was its implementing—startlingly alone among major world powers at the time—the Enlightenment's (and Napoleon's) scheme for Jewish emancipation and integration. In the Old World, *ancien régime* anti-Jewish restrictions and disabilities earlier dismantled by the Revolution and Napoleon had now brought about a partial resegregation, excluding the Jews from mainstream society and public careers—except in France and the Low Countries. The barriers had been reinstated in 1814–15 with both official and widespread popular support, as well as church backing, most obviously in Germany and central Europe. Of course, prejudice and Old World bigotry persisted in the United States too; not all barriers to Jewish integration had yet disappeared there either. In Maryland, Jews remained still legally debarred "as Jews" from holding public office.[115] But in America, claimed Jullien, vestiges of Counter-Enlightenment prejudice and obscurantism directed against the Jews lacked broad legal, institutional, and educational endorsement and were already a target of organized protest. In America, such bias was just a ridiculous remnant about to disappear, not a basic ingredient of an entire anti-philosophical system of religious and reactionary thought, culture, and practice as in Europe. However crass, American anti-Semitism was not basic to an entire social and political hierarchical value-system sanctioned by churches, Papacy, and a towering "Holy Alliance" of oppression eradicable only by massive revolutionary force.

By consolidating its own Revolution and removing nearly all social, legal, and cultural barriers which in Europe continued to block progress towards liberty, the United States alone could now supposedly march "directly to a certain level of perfection without having to pass through the dreadful ordeal of [further]

[112] Rémond, *Les États-Unis* i. 421–7; Isabella, *Risorgimento*, 48–9, 98.
[113] Wood, *Radicalism*, 294. [114] [Jullien], *Revue encyclopédique* x (Apr. 1821), 381.
[115] Israel, *Expanding Blaze*, 488–9.

revolutions."[116] America required no new upheaval and frenzy of change to propel it toward democracy and secularism, whereas post-1815 Europe did. Universal male suffrage in America was surely a tremendous landmark in humanity's advance. "Even should the cloud of barbarism and despotism again obscure the science and liberties of Europe," Jefferson admonished Adams, in 1821, the United States "remains to preserve and restore light and liberty to them. In short the flames kindled on the 4th of July 1776, have spread over too much of the globe to be extinguished by the feeble engines of despotism. On the contrary they will consume those engines, and all who work them."[117]

But was this perspective correct? Was the United States genuinely a beacon lighting the path for the radical fraternity? The "America" venerated by Europe's and Latin America's radical republicans in the 1820s was not exactly the actual America familiar to its citizens, but an European ideological and literary abstraction, a remote ideal nurtured by a radical vanguard presenting a potent ideology for the 1820s. Various skeptics harbored doubts. Sismondi published an incisive critique in the *Revue encyclopédique*, in January 1827, that attracted attention in Switzerland and America, as well as France. Once a conservative foe of the Revolution, since 1814, appalled, like Bentham, by "la Restauration" and the Holy Alliance,[118] Sismondi had turned radical, repudiating his old allegiance to "mixed government" and the empirical, experience-based approach of political thinkers extolling Locke, Hume, Smith, Burke, and Ferguson. Now firmly against those defending the old aristocratic order, he had taken to championing the democratic republicanism of Condorcet, Jefferson, and the Brissotins.[119]

Discarding moderate and embracing radical Enlightenment, Sismondi, we have seen, shifted leftwards politically and in political economy. In his *Nouveaux Principes d'économie politique* (1819), while criticizing Adam Smith and David Ricardo for excessively relying on the notion of a natural equilibrium in economic development, he articulated his new theory of economic cycles, consumption, excess production, and market oscillations. Social and political intervention, held Sismondi, is always requisite to shield the poor and vulnerable from market downturns and their unavoidably harsh effects. Though never a socialist and later sternly rebuked by Marx, his was among the major voices of the democratic enlightened of the 1820s repudiating classical economics along with American and French veneration of the "British model."[120] American-style federal republicanism was undeniably proving a growing inspiration for the world, as recent developments in Spanish America proved; but there were as many worrying as promising signs. With twenty-four states in the

116 [Jullien], *Revue encyclopédique* v (Jan. 1820), 7, 15–16; Palmer, *From Jacobin to Liberal*, 181; Isabella, *Risorgimento*, 43–4.

117 Jefferson to Adams, 12 Sept. 1821, *Adams–Jefferson Letters* ii. 575.

118 Stelling-Michaud, "Sismondi," 157, 160; De Luca, "Benjamin Constant," 111; Tillet, "Place ambigue de Jean-Louis de Lolme," 204–5.

119 Stelling-Michaud, "Sismondi," 154–5; De Luca, "Benjamin Constant," 110–12.

120 Schoorl, *Jean-Baptiste Say*, 161–2.

United States and another twenty-four in the newly proclaimed "United States of Mexico," plus seven more loosely confederated "republics" in Central America, American federalism had latterly become the dominant constitutional model for the entire New World. Conceivably, Brazil, Peru, and other emerging new nations would eventually all follow suit, becoming federal republics. But when one delved deeper, the progress represented by these new "republics" looked fragile and defective.

History's chief lesson, held Sismondi in the mid-1820s, is that whatever ideals they announce, governments serve the interests of dominant elites and encourage, or fail to restrain, instead of combating, the ubiquitous oppression of society's *classes inférieures*. Lower classes toil to provide the wealth and services the world's elites appropriate and enjoy, yet, paradoxically and unjustly, exactly these segments are the least protected, favored, and assisted by governments. Here was the prime source of injustice in the world, the pattern of global history, as his own researches on the Middle Ages showed, and the chief dilemma of philosophy, a conundrum the truly enlightened, like the *Revue encyclopédique*'s editors, could not escape grappling with. Only by advancing the "happiness" of the poor and weak, by lending support and protection, can the security of the rich and stability of society be ensured. The trend hitherto, especially in Britain, had been to oppress the poor inexorably, strip the destitute of all respect, and brutalize them by keeping them as unaware and ignorant as possible.[121]

Was the United States different? The Sismondi of the late 1820s saw little reason to think so. Rather, the rapidly growing lowest class of society in America, held in abject slavery, found itself even more wretched and miserable than the oppressed of Britain or France, more downtrodden than the slaves of ancient Greece and Rome, or serfs of contemporary Russia and Poland. In the United States, the slaves' misery was intensified by the whites' abiding dread and suspicion of the black race, so that, even after successive generations, aspiring black freemen could not attain equality with the oppressor. There were a million and a half slaves in the United States in 1827, according to the latest statistics, he recorded (accurately),[122] and another 235,557 free blacks,[123] hence, nearly two million out of a total of nine million inhabitants. Since 1775, blacks consistently comprised more than 20 per cent of American society (in fact between 18 and 19 per cent). While the total American population since 1775 had roughly trebled, now surpassing Britain's, the proportion that was black, and direly oppressed, remained unchanged. "It is necessary to say it: it was for American republicans who have long possessed their liberty and Enlightenment, to set an example of humanity; but they had done the opposite." In America, racial prejudice was more offensive, degrading, and cruel even than in the newly founded Ibero-American republics. Sismondi's conclusions provoked a storm of protest; he failed to

[121] Sismondi, "L'Amérique," 34; Palmer, *From Jacobin to Liberal*, 192–3.
[122] Steckel, "African American Population," 435.
[123] Steckel, "African American Population," 435; Palmer, *From Jacobin to Liberal*, 193.

note, retorted critics, abolitionism's strength and the emancipation trends of New England and the rest of the North.[124]

The reactionary mood in France, having intensified in 1816 with the election of a predominantly ultra-royalist and ultra-Catholic legislature,[125] surged again following the sensational assassination on 13 February 1820, by a workingman, Louis Pierre Louvel (1783–1820), of Charles Ferdinand d'Artois, duc de Berry (1778–1820), nephew of Louis XVIII, the childless youngest son of the heir to the throne, Charles, and only direct heir. The assassination of the man who, at the start of the crisis of the Hundred Days, in March 1815, then aged 47 and an experienced officer, had been named commander-in-chief by a royal court desperate to halt the royal army's disintegration, provoked a furious outburst of reactionary sentiment.[126] His assassin, a participant in the *Cent-Jours*, had long exulted in Louis XVI's execution in 1793, and considered all Bourbons traitors to their country. Stabbing his victim in the chest, outside the Paris Opera, was intended to finally extirpate the Bourbon royal line; but Berry's wife, Marie-Caroline de Bourbon-Sicile, was pregnant at the time and subsequently gave birth to a boy, Henri, duc de Bordeaux, who, after Charles X's overthrow in the 1830 July Revolution, was recognized by ultras as the true, legitimate heir to the French throne.

Charles X (reigned: 1824–30), Louis XVIII's successor, was more active than his brother in seeking financial compensation for nobles deprived of their lands in the Revolution, and more forcefully promoted the ecclesiastical interest. It was clear from the moment of his accession that he would follow a more resolutely reactionary course. Where Louis had forgone the ancient ritual of the consecration of kings at their coronation in Reims, Charles made a point of reviving it. One of nineteenth-century France's greatest writers, Victor Hugo (1802–85), during the early and mid-1820s a royalist and admirer of Chateaubriand, yet to begin his slow, lifelong political odyssey from extreme Right to Left, was among those invited to the new king's consecration. To celebrate, he composed an *Ode au sacre* denigrating the Revolution and Napoleonic reforms as a catalogue of betrayal, arrogance, and denial of divine mystery and invoking Louis XVI as a glorious royal martyr doubly sanctified "at altar and scaffold." Yet, just two years later, by 1827, disillusioned, he was already revising his view of Bonaparte; before long, he shifted further, becoming an ardent republican.[127]

Bishops and clergy rallied enthusiastically behind the new king, more than ever exalting the ties between monarchy and religion while exhorting the public to pay more toward the cost of re-adorning churches and construction and consecration of more memorials and shrines promoting the cult of martyrs, saints, and suffering

[124] Sismondi, "L'Amérique," 34–6; [Jullien], *Revue encyclopédique* xxxiv (Apr. 1827), 54; Körner, *America in Italy*, 199, 201.

[125] Holmes, *Benjamin Constant*, 19.

[126] Pilbeam, "Impossible Restoration," 188–9; Price, *Perilous Crown*, 106–8.

[127] Duprat, "Sacre de Charles X," 70–1; Mansel, *Paris between Empires*, 184; Blanning, *Romantic Revolution*, 163–5.

loyalists and clergy persecuted under the Revolution. Charles encouraged their striving for a general culture of "Restoration," artistic and intellectual, as well as political and social. But France's last Bourbon king failed to restore the religious orders, or reverse the changes in education to the extent he wanted; nor did he and his advisors succeed in transforming the major public museums and institutes or generate an authentic new "Restoration" architectural style.[128] But until the spring of 1829, when he appointed the fervently religious Jules de Polignac (1780–1847) chief minister, Charles was not so obdurate as to try to rule directly against the wishes of the majority of France's legislature.[129]

With Polignac at the helm he did make that fatal shift, although, paradoxically, Polignac was no admirer of the *ancien régime,* or foe of the division of powers, or of the British system, but was particularly keen to accord privileged predominance to the aristocracy and was intensely religious.[130] Within months, the Bourbon monarchy was overthrown by a new revolution. Beneath the surface, the late Enlightenment story, after 1815, in France, thus remained in one important respect one of basic continuity: through three abruptly different periods together forming France's "Age of the late Enlightenment"—the revolutionary decade (1789–99), the Napoleonic era (1799–1815), and the so-called "Restoration" (1815–30). Through all three the same underlying tripartite ideological conflict continued pitting moderate Enlightenment versus Radical Enlightenment and both against Counter-Enlightenment, all vying to dominate the social, political, and cultural scene.

[128] Pérouse de Montclos, *Paris*, 507.
[129] Pilbeam, "Impossible Restoration," 190.
[130] Price, *Perilous Crown*, 123–4.

28

Bolívar and Spinoza

28.1. ENLIGHTENMENT APPLIED TO REVOLUTIONARY POLITICS

At the time of the American Revolution, and in its wake, it was widely believed in radical circles that a broad Spanish American Revolution would soon follow and that further, revolutionary republicanism would eventually ignite a chain reaction throughout the European New World empires: these would surely all "shake off their foreign dependence," as Barlow expressed it, "and burst the ties which now bind them to European governments."[1] Writing in *Le Politique Hollandois*, in 1783, Cerisier judged this a welcome outcome for humanity and the world that would contribute significantly to building the better world order and consequent world peace he and other radical publicists predicted would one day materialize.[2]

Others seriously doubted whether "Spaniards" were a people fitted, by experience and character like Genevans and Americans, for "les grandes révolutions." The English and their American brethren, argued one pro-American pamphlet published in Holland, were decidedly better suited for such enterprises, New World Spaniards being passive types, proverbially inclined to indolence.[3] Among those propagating this view was the German naturalist, explorer, geographer and ethnographer, Alexander von Humboldt (1769–1859), who, during and after the five years he toured Spanish America (1799–1804), came to be generally considered the Western world's unrivalled expert on the region. "There was no great love for Spain," he concurred, but passivity and general conformity struck him as far more characteristic of New World Creoles than any hints of rebellion, though he himself was inspired by the American and French revolutions and eager for Spain to be ousted. In meetings with the young Simon Bolívar (1783–1830), in Europe, in 1804–5, Von Humboldt continued to insist on the New World Spaniards', "the Creoles'," ineradicable indolence. Bolívar in fact shared this view in large part but also believed there was scope for

[1] Barlow, *Two Letters to the Citizens*, 68, 80.
[2] Cerisier, *Le Politique Hollandois* v (Mar. 1783), 52–3.
[3] *Réplique au Second Discours* (Kn. 19248), 28, 33.

precipitating revolution by means of vigorous intervention, political and intellectual, from outside.[4]

While Spanish American Creole society appeared sunk in indolence, provincialism, and the past, spending its time playing cards, drinking, and consorting with prostitutes, countered the *Histoire philosophique*, behind the scenes sophisticated young elite Creoles could be found, especially after finishing their education in Europe, with minds fashioned by enlightened teaching, reading, and discussion. The decisive years of Bolívar's own intellectual formation, 1804–6, were spent in Paris, where he became an avid reader of the main Enlightenment authors;[5] early on, he was captivated by Diderot and the *Histoire philosophique*, the "most radical, most global and most systematic" denunciation of colonialism then available.[6] By 1804, South American Creoles of this stamp, often tutors, editors, and *littérateurs* but also jurists and army officers, were frequently Enlightenment zealots ardently scheming basic change.[7]

Bolívar's becoming an Enlightenment enthusiast was part of a wave commencing a quarter of a century earlier: subversive "new philosophy" entering from abroad first acquired dangerous momentum in Spain during the mid-1770s, noted several observers, including the Cistercian Father, Antonio José Rodríguez, author of *El Philoteo* (Madrid, 1776),[8] as it happened just when the American Revolution was beginning. The pamphlet *España Triunfante en el actual siglo filosófico* [Spain Triumphant in the Present Philosophic Century], published at Madrid, in 1786, a satire on the now widely condemned underground new "philosophic religion" seeking to usurp the place of the Catholic religion, portrayed it as a seditious force seeping into Spain and now widespread, a philosophy forging not just new dogmas and a new morality but its own culture and rites. This "new philosophy" was a creed that "in imitation of the Christian religion would soon acquire its own Apostles, martyrs, and confessors."[9] While most Spaniards fiercely resisted, dismayingly, in Spain too, "la filosofía," the all-ravaging army of "philosophy" eroding faith, morality, and society, foe of all men honest and good, was unmistakably gaining ground.

Among key leaders of this new political-ideological Enlightenment creed was the Venezuelan officer, Francisco de Miranda (1750–1816), later to be Spanish America's first great *Libertador*. On garrison duty at Melilla, in 1775, Miranda, shared with a fellow Creole officer, a Peruvian named Manuel Villalta, a large cache of forbidden books and manuscripts. Arrested, in Seville in November 1778, for possessing prohibited texts (and obscene pictures), Villalta was reported to have joined many conversations with Miranda and others at Melilla and Cádiz, in which irreligious books and ideas were the chief themes. By 1779, now in Madrid, Miranda possessed

4 Bolívar, *Discurso*, 19; Madariaga, *Bolívar* i. 136–7; Zapata, *Libros que leyó*, 50–1, 60; Arana, *Bolívar, American Liberator*, 64; Wulf, *Invention of Nature*, 136–8.

5 O'Leary, *Memorias* i. 58–63; Madariaga, *Bolívar* i. 140.

6 Stuurman, "Diderot en Raynal. Verlichtingsvisies," 112; Lovera de Sola, *Simón Bolívar*, 288–91.

7 *Histoire philosophique* (1780) iv. 405–6.

8 Herrero, *Orígenes*, 105–7; Sánchez-Blanco, *Absolutismo*, 225.

9 [D.J.C.], *España Triunfante*, 38–9.

around 230 predominantly Enlightenment books, some in multiple volumes, including the *Histoire philosophique*, d'Holbach's *Système de la nature*, Helvétius' *De l'Esprit*, Diderot's *Lettre sur les Aveugles*, Beccaria and *L'An 2440* of Mercier with its electrifying prophecy of a massive black slave revolt foreshadowing liberation of all the slaves of the Indies.[10]

A royal commissioner touring the Caribbean and Mexico between 1780 and 1783, Don Francisco de Saavedra de Sangronis (1746–1819), among the best-informed observers of the empire's general condition at the time, a leading reformer of the Spanish administration in Cuba who also helped plan Spain's re-conquest of the Floridas during the American War, concluded that Spain must either lose its empire in a "short time" or else consolidate on a wholly fresh basis. If the latter, Spanish America's administrative, economic, and cultural institutions and administration must be comprehensively reformed on the basis of Enlightenment thinking acceptable to the Spanish court in Madrid, to deflect the American Revolution's appeal.[11] Should Spain continue as before "with tyranny and oppression" without transforming the attitudes and conduct of peninsular Spaniards in positions of responsibility, Spain's empire could not long avoid the predicted "fatal catastrophe."[12] Intellectual upheaval caused on the one hand by the American Revolution and, the other, by the unremitting influx of French books of which one finds "allí immensa copia" that "va haciendo una especie de revolución en su modo de pensar" [an immense quantity that effects a kind of revolution in their way of thinking] represented a fundamental threat to crown, church and empire.[13] New-World-born Spaniards, the Creoles, "are today in a very different situation from a few years ago, having enlightened themselves a lot in a short time." Today, "thousands of copies of the works of Voltaire, Rousseau, Robertson, the Abbé Raynal, and other modern philosophers which those natives [i.e. Creoles] read with a special enthusiasm" were circulating in "our America."[14] By the 1790s, Filangieri's influence too pervaded Ibero-American elite circles.[15] Later Spanish American commentators fully confirmed the identification of the 1770s as the decisive decade when white Spanish Americans underwent "this revolution" in Enlightenment ideas that seeded the great revolutionary movement commencing in 1808.[16] Miranda and Bolívar classically exemplified this Ibero-American "revolution of the mind" ushering in revolution.[17]

The viceroy of New Granada (today Colombia), reporting to Madrid in July 1781, at the height of a major insurgency that shook Spain's grip on the northern Andes in the early 1780s, was another who assured royal ministers that the American

[10] Rodríguez de Alonso, *Siècle*, 40–2.
[11] Saavedra, *Memorias*, 134, 149, 202; Weber, *Bárbaros*, 159; Morales Padrón, "México," 356–7.
[12] Morales Padrón, "México," 357.
[13] Saavedra, *Memorias*, 134; Ruiz Martínez, *Librería*, 25–6; McFarlane, "American Revolution," 41–2.
[14] Ruiz Martínez, *Librería*, 25–6; Weber, *Bárbaros*, 35.
[15] Morelli, "Quito frente a la crisis," 431–3; Israel, *Democratic Enlightenment*, 397, 399, 517–18.
[16] Rocafuerte, *Ensayo Político*, 31; Walter, "Revolution, Independence," 109.
[17] Bolívar, *El Libertador*, 9–12; Israel, *Democratic Enlightenment*, 503.

Revolution held considerable allure for discontented Creoles. New Granada's sudden unprecedented internal social turmoil had worsened, he explained, "because the form of *independencia* won by the English colonies of the North is now on the lips of everyone [participating] in the [South American] rebellion."[18] Most people, being illiterate, knew practically nothing about it, but Spanish America's social elites understood all too well the significance of American independence. This applied not least to Bolívar, who, on returning from Europe, spent most of the first half of 1807 in the United States, mainly in Charleston where he landed (ill with fever), and then Philadelphia. Much impressed by Philadelphia, Bolívar in later life remained nearly as captivated by the renown of Washington as of Napoleon.

The young Bolívar plunged into Enlightenment thought and literature, even before his first visit to Europe, owing to his tutor in Caracas, Simon Rodríguez (1769–1854), among the Venezuelan capital's best-known schoolmasters, an unruly but ardent Enlightenment zealot always insisting on the need to expand literacy among the common populace. Intoxicated with Rousseau, steeped in education theory, and by 1794 a renowned education reformer, Rodríguez was a man of illegitimate birth brimming with social resentment. He soon paid a hefty price for loathing monarchy. Suspected of involvement in the 1797 Picornell conspiracy against the crown, Bolívar's teacher and guardian was forced to flee, abandoning job and home in Venezuela forever.[19] Permanently banished from the Indies, he later migrated to France. Comrades in Paris in 1804–6, in May 1805 Bolívar and Rodríguez journeyed to Italy together. Bolívar remained in touch with his old mentor in later years, and always recognized him as his intellectual "maestro," even while feeling some annoyance at Rodríguez's relentless efforts to convert him into his intellectual disciple.[20]

Bolívar was just 14 when, in July 1797, the Caracas authorities uncovered the first Venezuelan conspiracy, inspired by reports of the American, French, and Haitian revolutions, to seize the colony. The conspirators, including mulatto militiamen, *pardos*, *zambos*, poor whites, some regular soldiers, and also white officials and traders, were led by the ardently republican and egalitarian Juan Bautista Picornell (1759–1825), a veteran Spanish agitator imprisoned in Venezuela for sedition, and a hacienda-owner, Manuel Gual.[21] The plot's two headquarters, government investigation discovered, were Picornell's prison cell and the barber-shop of a 38-year-old *pardo* of La Guaira named Narciso del Valle, where mulatto, black, and *pardo* artisans and soldiers congregated, turning it into a veritable school of subversive republican and egalitarian ideas and recruiting-center for insurrection. Having studied at Salamanca, Picornell is known to have been drawn, like Miranda, Rodríguez, and Bolívar,

[18] Archivo General de Indias (Seville) section: Santa Fe 578/1 Viceroy Florez to Gálvez, 11 July 1781.

[19] Madariaga, *Bolívar*, i. 98; Arana, *Bolívar, American Liberator*, 33–7; Soriano, *Tides of Revolution*, 15–16, 45.

[20] Bolívar, *Obras Completas* i. 22–3; Rojas, *Ideas educativas*, 25, 37, 43; Lovera de Sola, *Simon Bolívar*, 183, 185–6, 195, 213, 218.

[21] Jordaan, "Patriots, privateers," 101–3; Fulgencio López, *Juan Bautista Picornell*, 75, 80–1, 85, 88, 135.

to subversion against Spain by philosophical literature, especially the *encyclopédistes*.[22] When the conspiracy was betrayed and the first arrests made, government enquiries uncovered evidence the conspirators had held subversive seminars in which radical texts—Raynal, Rousseau, and Paine's *Rights of Man* (in French)—were read and discussed, attended by some French-speaking prisoners from Saint-Domingue kept at La Guaira. Many persons were implicated in these subversive gatherings, including Rodríguez now fled to Baltimore.[23]

Bolívar first visited Paris between January and March 1802 when Napoleon, still supposedly "republican," was at the height of his prestige, a circumstance that left a vivid impression on the 18-year-old. After briefly returning to Venezuela with his young Spanish bride, who died of fever a few months later, leaving him distraught and vowing to remain a widower for the rest of his life, he returned to Europe in 1803, again spending time in Spain, before revisiting Paris in May 1804, six months before Napoleon crowned himself emperor in Notre-Dame cathedral but when he was already being proclaimed "emperor of the French." That the man he had deeply admired as the very "symbol of liberty and glory" and republican steadfastness should reveal himself to be a hypocrite and tyrant long filled him with disgust.[24]

The question of Bolívar's philosophical views, intellectual formation, and the impressions he gathered in France, matter not just for understanding Bolívar, but for correctly grasping the course of the Spanish American Revolution. To understand, it is essential to get away from notions of nationalism and liberalism. For the crisis precipitated in Spain's culture and Spanish America by the Enlightenment ran very deep. The post-1770 transformation in Creole elite education and print culture, causing Enlightenment ideas to flood into the Spanish New World, one must bear in mind, had little to do with social movements or economic forces in a Marxist sense and nothing to do with "nationalism" or "liberalism," however much historians and others sought to use these labels to appropriate and distort interpretation of the upheaval later. While the ideologies driving the great upheaval laying the ground for Spanish America's emancipation, constitution-making, and ending slavery and the Inquisition, were Enlightenment concepts, these ideas, powered by centuries-old grievances and longstanding resentments, as Saavedra de Sangronis stressed, came in two very different and conflicting formats.

On the one hand stood the royal, official "moderate" approach calling for urgent reforms, integration, transformation by prudent and responsible officials, and profound change of attitude leading to the dependencies being treated like provinces of Spain rather than "colonies." A key facet of this "moderate strategy was the careful, structured reforming of Spanish America's colleges, replacing their conservatism, scholasticism, and ecclesiasticism with up-to-date erudition, science, and legal

[22] Fulgencio López, *Juan Bautista Picornell*, 73, 75, 91–2; Thibauld, "*Salus Populi*," 342–3; 160–1, 169–80.

[23] Fulgencio López, *Juan Bautista Picornell*, 35, 80, 89; Soriano, *Tides of Revolution*, 157–60.

[24] Bolívar, *Obras Completas* i. 25; O'Leary, *Memorias* i. 58–63; Madariaga, *Bolívar* i. 142.

thought, so as to tackle one of the foremost problems confronting crown and church—that sons of leading Creole families, like Miranda and Bolívar, often drifting to France to finish their education, were imbibing their Enlightenment ideas abroad.[25] Without such large-scale reform, the more subversive approach, rejecting the Spanish crown and its claims, was bound to gain ground. Those, including Miranda and Bolívar, to whom it seemed that Spain desired only to extract everything it could from its colonies, keeping them permanently in subjection—the rebellious fringe, schooled in radical ideas since the 1770s—had to be kept firmly in check. This committed would-be reformers of royal and ecclesiastical absolutism seeking the empire's further centralization, militarization, and commercialization, while rejecting the popular sovereignty underpinning Miranda's, Rodríguez's, and Bolívar's creed, to unending intellectual war with Spanish America's alienated radical fringe.

The three years spent in France and Italy during his early twenties were the crucible of Bolívar's intellectual and political awakening. During this period of ardent discussion (not least with Rodríguez and Von Humboldt), he imbibed Western Enlightenment in all its aspects, including revolutionary politics.[26] At this time too began his estrangement from organized religion. Although numerous churchmen later claimed the great Bolívar was a good Catholic, according to his aide-de-camp from 1818, General Daniel O'Leary (1801–54), whose testimony is the best we have, the mature Bolívar was "a complete atheist," albeit one believing outward forms of religion were necessary for government and who regularly attended mass for the sake of appearances. There was one churchman among his ideological heroes, the sixteenth-century Dominican friar, Fray Bartolomé de Las Casas (1484–1566), whom he eulogized in a manifesto he issued from Jamaica in September 1815. But Las Casas he admired not for his religion but as a "great philosopher and philanthropist," who tirelessly defended the New World Indians against the colonial forced labor system, the *encomienda*, and spent years endeavoring to beneficially reorganize Indian life in his southern Mexican bishopric of Chiapas. Having fought for recognition of the equal human status of the American Indians at the 1550 Valladolid disputation, in Spain, Las Casas's fame lived on in Mexico and the Caribbean; eulogizing him, was, for Bolívar, a way of tying the principles of racial equality and universal justice to Spanish America's past while simultaneously reviving the "black legend of Spanish cruelty."[27]

Spain in Bolívar's view had subjected all Spanish America to insufferable oppression for centuries, keeping its population in total "ignorance" by means of "superstition," and "weakness" by means of tyranny.[28] There was no way the young Bolívar could avoid Rodríguez's intoxication with Rousseau, but Rousseau by no means

[25] Bolívar, *Carta de Jamaica*, 86–9; Morales Padrón, "México," 357.

[26] Lynch, *Simón Bolívar*, 20, 24–6, 37; Arana, *Bolívar, American Liberator*, 62–7.

[27] Bolívar, *Carta de Jamaica*, 78–9, 84–5; Bolívar, *Obras Completas* i. 152–3, 159; Zapata, *Libros que leyó*, 153.

[28] Bolívar, *Obras Completas* i. 176.

figures prominently in Bolívar's thought world or personal lists of books, while his mature thought was decidedly unRousseauist. Rousseau, for one thing, believed republican liberty could be achieved only in small states while Bolívar dreamed of creating a vast republic. Rousseau exalted the simplicity, morality, and traditional attitudes of rural folk whereas Bolívar considered ordinary beliefs, the commonplace attitudes and culture of the Spanish American population, altogether fatal to his republican program; the latter was feasible to his mind only insofar as he could "enlighten" and educate the people, by which he chiefly meant oust superstition, tradition, and deference from their minds. Rousseau could never have agreed that "reason" is the exclusive key and an unremitting course of "enlightenment" to change everything, especially how ordinary people think, the only way forward. Where Rousseau's individual is intrinsically good but corrupted by society, Bolívar's individual is hopelessly weak and unreliable until elevated by the *fuerza colectiva* [collective force] and rules of society. Bolívar's "general will," meanwhile, his *fuerza colectiva*, stood much closer to Diderot's and d'Holbach's than Rousseau's. Bolívar rejected particularist notions affixing his "greatest happiness" principle to universal human rights, universal secular morality, and equality. Finally, Bolívar by no means shared Rousseau's passive, neutralist attitude toward political action; on the contrary, there was no more fervent advocate of undaunted political activism—at any rate by the enlightened.[29]

Bolívar never invokes Rousseau and, though he immensely enjoyed reading Voltaire,[30] was decidedly no Voltairean either. If the seeds of his intellectual outlook originated in Rodriguez's pedagogy, his years in France, 1804–6, widened and consolidated his broad Radical Enlightenment vision, as did visiting Britain between July and September 1810 when he explored London on foot and met Bentham, holding a discussion with him in his garden. The man who knew Bolívar best in later life (from around 1818), his aide-de-camp, the Irish Catholic officer O'Leary, who, between 1835 and 1840, wrote the most detailed contemporary narrative of his life, records that "metaphysics was Bolívar's favourite study but that it is to be regretted that the skeptical philosophy should have established such profound roots in his mind. Helvétius, d'Holbach, and Hume among others were the authors whom Rodriguez advised him to study. Bolívar admired the austere independence of Hobbes despite the marked monarchical tendencies in his writings: but what captivated him most were the speculative opinions of Spinoza and in these, perhaps, we should seek the origin of some of his own political ideas."[31] The few scholars aware of the significance of this statement assume Bolívar's familiarity with Spinoza's philosophy began with Rodríguez's mentoring, as seems likely though O'Leary does not say so. The latter

[29] Bolívar, *Discurso*, 19–21; Madariaga, *Bolívar* i, 165; Acosta, "Bolívar" de Marx," 86; Rojas, *Ideas educativas*, 43, 45; Zapata, *Libros que leyó*, 63–4.

[30] Madariaga, *Bolívar* i. 16.

[31] O'Leary, *Memorias* i. 63; here I am particularly indebted to the insights and scholarship of Jorge Dávila in his *Bolívar y Spinoza Reflejos Doctinarios* (Merida, Venezuela, 2013) and what follows is to an extent a dialogue with his admirably pertinent thesis.

does emphasize, though, that Bolivar's (purely inner) rejection of the Christian faith and skepticism about religion began with the fervently irreligious Rodríguez.[32] More important, meanwhile, is O'Leary's emphasis on Spinoza being Bolívar's principal philosophical inspiration; for this urgently prompts the question how far this fundamental fact about Bolívar—and hence for understanding modern Latin America—is indeed connected with the evolving of Bolívar's guiding social, moral, and political ideas.[33]

Bolívar was decidedly no Christian in his private sphere of reading and thought.[34] Ever since Salvador de Madariaga's book on *Bolívar* (1951), a few have grasped that Bolívar's basic political concepts stand closer to Spinoza than Rousseau, Montesquieu, Hume, or Voltaire. Especially Bolívar's view of the "general will" as a collective "conatus"—the collective essence of society conceived as a power primed to conserve itself as well as possible—savors of Spinozism. Of course, it is exceedingly difficult for modern scholarship, as for South American nationalist historiography, to accept that Bolívar's basic ideas, far from being Rousseauist, and even less Montesquieuan, are basically "Spinozist" in the eighteenth-century sense of the term, and one can expect sturdy resistance to the suggestion; but it is not a judgment easily set aside.[35] For Bolívar, nothing can be achieved unless the majority are "enlightened" by an oppositional intellectual and moral elite rejecting the assumptions and institutions on which society is currently based, a vanguard dedicated to eradicating generally-accepted notions rooted in religious authority, aristocracy, and monarchy.

While there is no clear evidence it was Rodríguez who injected this Spinozist dimension into Bolívar's mind, or who prompted him to spend "hours in smoke-choked cafés," arguing about Spinoza (Madariaga assumed it was under Rodríguez's "direction" that Bolívar first "devoured" Spinoza),[36] it does seem *spinozisme* as a broad tendency became the guiding thread in Bolívar's intellectual outlook, though it is not unlikely, despite O'Leary's testimony, that it was rather the influence of Diderot, d'Holbach, Raynal, Volney, and later Sismondi that put it there. While in Paris until 1806, Bolívar immensely enjoyed the theater and ballet, dallying around the Palais Royale and Comédie Française, and frequenting the bookshops. Moreover, in Paris, he got to know several other young South Americans of radical republican stamp and vehement Enlightenment enthusiasm who encouraged him in his then already powerfully anti-authoritarian impulses, notably the similarly-aged Vicente Rocafuerte of Guayaquil (1783–1847), later second president of Ecuador (1834–9). A radical likewise converted to republicanism in France, Rocafuerte, like Bentham, remained friendly with Bolívar for many years before eventually emerging among his harshest critics.[37]

[32] O'Leary, *Memorias* i. 1; Dávila, *Bolívar y Spinoza*, 21, 23–4.
[33] O'Leary, *Memorias* i. 63–4; Dávila, *Bolívar y Spinoza*, 21, 24; Van Reijen, *Argentijnse gezicht*, 137.
[34] Madariaga, *Bolívar* i. 161, 163, 165.
[35] Bolívar, *Discurso*, 21, 26–7, 29.
[36] Arana, *Bolívar, American Liberator*, 36, 53, 59–60.
[37] Wulf, *Invention of Nature*, 143–4.

From 1808, Spanish American Creole unease with the old order suddenly gained vast leverage from the chaos arising from Bonaparte's invasion of Spain. Although most of the populace lamented their legitimate monarch's misfortunes, and Spanish America's viceroys, regional judicial high courts (*audiencias*), district governors, and city councils (*ayuntamientos*) all loyally adhered to the deposed Bourbon monarch, disavowing Joseph in Madrid, the collapse of effective imperial control inevitably created a chronically destabilized scenario. Power at local level suddenly devolved onto local town governments, which often convened emergency open meetings of local notables and prolonged conferring among the elites, which, in turn, fomented local power struggles in almost every regional center.[38] Rumor, conspiracy, and sedition everywhere intensified long-established underground subversive tendencies, aggravated further in Venezuela and New Granada by unrest spilling over from the French and Haitian revolutions.[39] The ubiquity of the sedition (as well of Counter-Enlightenment royalism) clearly shows the rupture was only *triggered*, not caused, by Napoleon's invasion. Chronic instability in turn produced insurrection, uprisings following the lines of the earlier conspiracies of the 1780s and 1790s, commencing in Upper Peru (Bolivia) and northern Chile.[40]

Insurrection erupted in Buenos Aires, Santiago de Chile, Charcas, and also Quito, where active plotting began in late 1808 following the dethronement of Fernando. In Quito province, which had been attached to New Granada since 1739 but now detached itself, emergency gatherings of the local noble elite established a *Junta* to represent royal sovereignty in their region.[41] Officially, the *Junta* swore allegiance to Fernando and undertook to defend religion and fight Napoleon; but its actions served local Creole ambition and interests.[42] The Quito *audiencia*'s presiding royal official was deposed on 10 August 1809. Royalist troops regained control after three months—but not for long: renewed disturbances enabling a second *Junta* to seize Quito in September 1810. On 15 February 1812 a "congress" of delegates proclaimed the Quito *audiencia*'s area of jurisdiction a separate union of "provinces forming the state of Quito" [modern Ecuador]. Among the revolt's leading figures was Bolívar's comrade, the *guayaquileño* (from Guayaquil) Rocafuerte, who from 1808 until 1814 stayed in Spain as a Cortes deputy representing Quito province, an ally of the Cádiz *liberales*.

During the Spanish American Revolution's early stages, the leadership mostly adopted a continental perspective, proclaiming "la revolución de América" in general, rather than one identifying with the particular countries corresponding to the old imperial viceroyalties and captaincies-general. There was practically no budding "national" identity in any of the future Spanish American republics. Napoleon's

[38] McFarlane, "American Revolution," 44–5; Breña, *Primer liberalismo español*, 87–8.
[39] Thibaud, "Salus Populi," 341; Jordaan, *Slavernij*, 181.
[40] Irisarri, *Semanario Republicano* iii (21 Aug. 1813), 20–1; Minchom, *People of Quito*, 242–3.
[41] Rodríguez, "Cultura política clerical," 294; Morelli, "Quito frente a la crisis," 420–1.
[42] Minchom, *People of Quito*, 242–3; Andrien, "Soberanía y revolución", 327–9, 333.

invasion simply unleashed pre-existing tensions affecting all classes, especially local particularism and the two warring Enlightenment ideologies, which together fragmented all Spanish America, like Spain, into implacably warring factions. Even Lima, chief bulwark of royalism, religion, and Counter-Enlightenment during the risings of 1808–14, where the press was more effectively muzzled than elsewhere, featured a clandestine paper, the *Diario Secreto de Lima*, which in 1811 briefly propagated not "national" or "liberal" but specifically Enlightenment views and political subversion. Nothing could be more erroneous than to suppose the Spanish American Enlightenment "did not reach the point of applying the idea of freedom and equality to relations between peoples, and did not produce a concept of colonial liberation or war of independence."[43] Quite the reverse: it was the unstoppable incursion of Raynal, Diderot, Filangieri, Paine, Volney, Bentham, and Sismondi (a favorite of Bolívar's), with the example of America's and Europe's revolutions, that provided the rationales and principles rendering the war of liberation possible, affording the inspiration, rhetoric, and constitutional arrangements enabling the great *Libertadores*, Miranda and Bolívar especially, to accomplish what they did.

28.2. PHILOSOPHY OF A MILITARY GENIUS

In May 1809, the Seville *Junta Suprema* removed Venezuela's former captain-general for vacillation, replacing him with Vicente Emparán (1747–1820), governor of Cumaná province, among the Spanish New World's more distinguished administrators and a keen reformer friendly with Von Humboldt.[44] Emparán, despite winning the applause of the *caraqueño* elite by opening Venezuela's commerce to the outside world against the Seville *Junta*'s explicit orders, could not control the situation. The Venezuelan landed elite, noticed deeply alarmed royal authorities, were steeped in subversive local "conspiracy." By mid-April 1810, news of the French breakthrough in Andalusia, fall of Seville, and blockade of Cádiz brought friction between Fernando's adherents and reform-minded Venezuelans, some among the latter, including Emperán, being rightly suspected of *josefismo*. "Secret" meetings, penetrated by the regional high court (*audiencia*), led to several high-status individuals being arrested.[45] But on 19 April 1810 a mixed group of Creole and peninsular elite figures toppled Emperán and the *audiencia*, establishing a *Junta Suprema* supposedly embodying the sovereignty of all the "inhabitants of the United Provinces of Venezuela." The coup deeply divided local opinion, being denounced by radicals, on one side, and conservatives headed by the archbishop, *audiencia*, and the ousted *absolutista* officials, on the other. It immediately alienated supporters of the Cádiz

[43] Lynch, *Simón Bolívar*, 36.
[44] Walter, "Revolution, Independence," 109–10; Osterhammel, *Transformation*, 476.
[45] Leal Curiel, "Juntismo Caraqueño," 404–7; Quintero, "Movimiento," 392–5.

regime along with particularists disliking direction from Caracas even more than Madrid, who were strongly entrenched in Coro and Maracaibo.[46] Reaffirming their loyalty to the crown—with which Bolívar, who had watched Fernando VII in Madrid, and despised him utterly, strongly disagreed—the *Junta* in fact represented the local landed elite's initial bid for power.

With Venezuela verging on de facto independence but also fast descending into anarchy, the Caracas *Junta Suprema* tried to reorganize the country's administration and fiscal and commercial regime, abolishing some royal taxes, including Indian tribute, ending the slave trade, and also formally opening the country's commerce with United States and Britain, terminating Spain's longstanding, mercantilist trade monopoly. Bolívar, preferring more forthright language and methods, expressed astonishment that the new leadership, with their hesitant, tentative style, got anywhere at all. Delegations were prepared to be sent to the United States and Britain to seek backing, supplies, and arms. Although initially regarded with suspicion as being too radical, anti-Spanish, and hot-headed, the insurrectionary leaders accepted Bolívar's offer to help pay for as well as lead the commission sent to England.

Arriving on a British warship, Bolívar and his team docked at Portsmouth in July 1810. No sooner had negotiations with the British government commenced, at Apsley House, on the edge of Hyde Park, than the feuding between Bolívar and the moderates deepened. Defying instructions forbidding formal renunciation of allegiance to Fernando, Bolívar, for whom Fernando's incarceration by Napoleon in France was fitting retribution for the *Conquistadores*' seizing Montezuma and the Inca emperor Atahualpa, three centuries before,[47] proceeded to do exactly what he was ordered not to do—but with inconclusive results, since his diplomatic papers clearly stated the opposite of what Bolívar claimed were the Venezuelan people's wishes. As Fernando's ally, the British government were unwilling to undermine him.[48] Bolívar's delegation also had orders not to join forces with General Miranda, the exiled icon of revolution, Radical Enlightenment, and irreligiosity, now living in London, repudiated totally by Spain's crown and church. Again Bolívar disobeyed, visiting Miranda in Grafton Street, a hotbed of conspiracy where the revolutionary general kept his now no less than 6,000 books. As the sole internationally famous Ibero-American revolutionary, and veteran of both the American and French revolutions, Bolívar urged him to return to orchestrate Venezuela's revolution. Bolívar and Miranda spent months in each other's company, often in Hyde Park, Richmond, or Kew Gardens, locked in discussion over how to revolutionize the world. Reluctant initially, Miranda was won round. On separate ships both men returned to Venezuela, in December 1810.[49]

The Cádiz assembly's quarrel with the Caracas *Junta* revolved around sovereignty, jurisdiction, and commerce. To reaffirm Spain's sovereignty and imperial trade

[46] Leal Curiel, "Juntismo Caraqueño," 399–400; Thibaud, "Salus Populi," 360–2.
[47] O'Leary, *Memorias* i. 75; Bolívar, *Carta de Jamaica*, 89–91.
[48] Arana, *Bolívar, American Liberator*, 89–91.
[49] O'Leary, *Memorias* i. 77; Lynch, *Simón Bolívar*, 49–54; Arana, *Bolívar, American Liberator*, 92–5.

restrictions, Cádiz, backed by three Venezuelan provinces—Coro, Maracaibo, and Guyana—sent naval forces from Cuba and Puerto Rico to police Venezuela's coast. Nor could the Caracas *Junta* prevent some Venezuelan regions and towns holding elections to choose deputies for the Cádiz Cortes scheduled for March 1811. "Electors" were chosen at parish level by propertied free males over 25; these "electors" then selected the deputies. Though, on one level, feuding between insurgents and loyalists over independence, Venezuela's internal power struggle was actually a complex four-cornered contest: royalists against the rebel elite's *Junta Suprema*, with both battling particularists, local foes of the landed elite, and all factions meeting resistance from local *castas*, *pardos*, and *zambos*. Where particularist regional opposition was strong, as at Coro, one found large *pardo*, slave, and Indian ethnic concentrations wholly lacking any sense of solidarity with the Creole elite.[50] As the chaos of what Bolívar called the "revolutionary hurricane" worsened, foreign observers grew increasingly gloomy about the prospects and none more so than Blanco White, the anglophile editing the foremost independent trans-Atlantic Spanish-language periodical of the day, *El Español* (1810–14), in London. Influential in Chile, Mexico, Quito, and Buenos Aires as well as the Caribbean and Spain, Blanco White's paper, like publications rejecting royal absolutism, agreed with opposition enlighteners like Castelli, Roscio, and Irisarri demanding "liberty," equality with peninsular Spaniards, and more toleration, but rejected their resort to arms and, at first, the talk of independence.

During 1810–11, most of Spanish America plunged into chaotic turmoil, and Blanco White, like many others, did not believe the Revolution could succeed. Neither Spain nor Spanish America seemed to him, in 1810, sufficiently educated or "prepared to profit by a revolution."[51] Revolution would make sense if "led by well-meaning and impartial men, and were it not the interest of many to oppose all their efforts;" but in existing circumstances, slaughter and civil war would be the only result.[52] Writing to Lafayette, in November 1813, Jefferson hoped for Spanish America's "emancipation" and did not doubt South America's ability to break away one day, but for now he too considered its populace, plunged in the "most profound ignorance, brutalized by superstition, and in complete subjection to their clergy," incapable, despite possessing intelligent and able leaders, of breaking out of their stifling religious and social despotism. To him too, these revolutions looked premature, a view that eventually, by stages, Bolívar would come to share also. For men trapped in pre-Enlightenment structures of thought there was, to their minds, simply no way forward to a better society and life for all.[53] Democratic republicanism must

[50] Laviña, "Participación de pardos," 168–9.
[51] Irisarri, *Semanario Republicano* ii (14 Aug. 1813), 10–12.
[52] Blanco White, *Life* iii. 328; Breña, *Primer liberalismo español*, 400–4.
[53] Jefferson to Lafayette, Monticello, 3 Nov. 1813, in Lafayette, *Mémoires* v. 291–2; Breña, "Ideas," 142–4.

fail, radical observers agreed, where the people are not taught what it is and how to sustain it.

Briefly, the insurrections succeeded at Santiago (Chile) and Buenos Aires though even there they were resisted by upcountry regions of what is today Chile's south, by north-west Argentina and neighboring Montevideo. As yet, no single declaration of independence actually materialized. Strife or outright civil war gripped virtually the entire continent while confusion of principles and goals blurred the conflicting lines of allegiance within each viceroyalty and captaincy-general, and between regionalist and centralizing factions. As the vast drama unfolded, regional authority disintegrated, exacerbating tensions generated by caste, class, ecclesiastical status, and slavery. Amidst the spectacular collapse of order, and hope (and fears) of British or American intervention, many thirsted for more compelling and coherent direction. Given the absence of clear goals and revolutionary focus, a significant development in distant Philadelphia was the translation project of Manuel García de Sena (1780–1816), a Venezuelan based there since 1803, rendering into Spanish key extracts of Paine together with the American *Declaration of Independence*, the United States Constitution, and the state constitutions of Massachusetts, Connecticut, New Jersey, Pennsylvania, and Virginia. Like many Spanish American intellectuals, García de Sena shared Paine's conviction that the American Revolution represented a giant step forward in man's understanding of government and politics and that it was the American Revolution's essential principles the French Revolution had carried further.[54] The quest for a broader and more coherent Spanish American revolutionary consciousness depended, he believed, on teaching the American Revolution and its constitutional outcome, an idea reinforced by a separate Spanish rendering of Paine's *Common Sense* appearing in 1811, in London, by the Peruvian Manuel José de Arrunátegui. García de Sena and Arrunátegui wanted the entire New World, North and South America, to converge in terms of republican attitudes and practice.[55]

Until 1821, the "Tom Paine" propagated by the revolutionary leadership remained fragmentary, however, consisting only of *Common Sense* plus short extracts from his other writings. *The Rights of Man* failed to appear until an abbreviated version was bought out in translation, at Philadelphia, by Matthew Carey in 1821. But what *was* made available helped shape Spanish America's incipient radical tendency. Five thousand copies of the Philadelphia Paine compilation, demanding independence from Spain and repudiation of aristocracy, presenting the turmoil gripping Spanish America as part of the wider global struggle of "liberty" against "oppression," reached Venezuela, with some seeping through to New Granada and New Spain (Mexico) besides Cuba and Puerto Rico.[56] *La Independencia de Costa Firme justificado por Thomas Paine treinta años ha* [The Independence of the Mainland justified by Thomas Paine Thirty Years Ago] (Philadelphia, 1811) was followed by García de

[54] García de Sena, *Independencia*, 33.
[55] Bastin, Echeverri, and Campo, "Translation," 59–61; Billias, *American Constitutionalism*, 115, 123.
[56] Aldridge, *Early American Literature*, 233.

Sena's rendering of John McCulloch, *A Concise History of the United States until 1807* (Philadelphia, 1812). Both attracted attention in leading reformist Spanish American papers like the *Gazeta de Caracas* (January 1812),[57] further entrenching Paine's thought and before long rendering him the pre-eminent publicist evoking American solidarity with the Spanish American Revolutions and Europe's "General Revolution." Paine's arguments for republicanism as a model preferable to the 1812 Cádiz Constitution's constitutional monarchism began to penetrate.[58] Among those debating Paine's ideas in the *Gazeta* was a leading Caracas journalist, Juan Germán Roscio (1763–1821).

There is little sign, though, that Bolívar took much interest in Paine, though he knew his works. Bolívar Enlightenment was always of a more sweeping, universalist kind, more philosophical in character than Paine's, more concerned with the moral and anti-religious roots of civic virtues, and with "General Will" theory, and also more insistent on avoiding the North American federal revolutionary model (which he deemed unsuited to South American conditions).[59] Nevertheless, Bolívar fully concurred with attacks on the "moderate" stance launched across South America by the radical, democratic republican trend in revolutionary thought.

During 1813, the ephemeral Chilean republican paper *Semanario Republicano de Chile*, for example, edited by the Guatemalan Antonio José Irisarri (1786–1868), a key figure in the Chilean revolution of 1810 and commander of the Santiago National Guard, chided "moderates" of the Spanish reform party, like Blanco White, for urging merely modest changes, supporting "mixed government," and endorsing Spain's imperial claims over Spanish America.[60] Reviling all royalists, Irisarri mocked Spanish Americans who lamented Napoleon's seizure of Spain as a "great calamity" when they should celebrate a priceless opportunity for securing independence. How contemptible that many "weep over the misfortune of Fernando!"[61] On completing his education in Europe, Irisarri had joined Miranda, Roscio, Rocafuerte, and Bolívar in maintaining republics promote happiness of peoples more, and better, than kings, and in ridiculing the clergy's claims that royalty is instituted by God.[62] "Lack of enlightenment of the popular masses," exploited by base ambition, had "always been the reef on which republics perish,"[63] which nothing better illustrated than the French Revolution. "Thus I believe the firmest support of republics is Enlightenment and virtue; and dread with pain in my soul the truth that a people lacking these qualities cannot be republican" but will always revert to tyranny, growing more wretched than before. Only Enlightenment produces a sustainable, meaningful outcome, capable of

[57] Aldridge, *Early American Literature*, 221, 224–6.

[58] Bastin, Echeverri, and Campo, "Translation," 60–1; Brewer-Carías, *Constituciones de Venezuela* i. 126–7.

[59] Bolívar, *Discurso*, 22–3; Lynch, *Simón Bolívar*, 32; Dávila, *Bolívar y Spinoza*, 28, 37.

[60] Irisarri, *Semanario Republicano* ii (14 Aug. 1813), 9–14; Walter, "Revolution, Independence," 120.

[61] Irisarri, *Semanario Republicano* i (7 Aug. 1813), 2–4.

[62] Irisarri, *Semanario Republicano* vii (18 Sept. 1813), 49–50.

[63] Irisarri, *Semanario Republicano* viii (25 Sept. 1813), 53.

benefiting the whole, ameliorating society, and securing peace. Unlike Bolívar, though, Irisarri believed, like Roscio, that this was most likely under a constitution like that of the United States.[64] He regularly cited Paine's views, the American example, and the urgent need for South American "Washingtones."[65]

Miranda's return improved prospects for radical measures to demolish royal government and ecclesiastical primacy, but only briefly. Avowed republican foe of monarchy, aristocracy, gender inequality, slavery, and religious authority, steeped in Raynal and *philosophique* literature since the 1770s, Miranda's trans-Atlantic revolutionary record spanned unmatched over three decades.[66] With meetings, demonstrations, and through the press, his following briefly gained ground. When, in March 1811, thirty delegates representing seven of Venezuela's ten provinces convened as a national Congress, in Caracas Cathedral, the "moderate" majority, representing top landowning families and preferring more autonomy to full independence, failed to block the radicals who had mobilized considerable pressure in the streets, cafés, and Caracas press. As a result, Venezuela's first *Declaration of Independence* was proclaimed on 14 July 1811. The ceremony also saw the unfurling, once again, of the yellow, blue, and red tricolor, the first flag of Venezuela, that Miranda had devised in emulation of the French, Dutch, Rhenish, and Italian revolutionary tricolor banners of the 1790s, and introduced when first declaring Venezuelan independence from Spain, at Jacmel, in Haiti, on 12 March 1806. A Bill of Rights and a decree conceding freedom of the press followed. Bolívar and a few other landowners freed their slaves (something none of the Virginia Founding Fathers had done).

Venezuela's Act of Independence (5 July 1811) followed after rowdy scenes in Caracas, and a vigorous radical push with Miranda and Bolívar well to the fore. The Act, and the new republic's constitution, finalized in December 1811, were drawn up by commissions headed by Roscio, editor of the *Gazeta de Caracas*, who, like Miranda and Francisco Javier Yanes (1776–1846), another Venezuelan founder invoking Paine's *Common Sense*, figured prominently in the anti-monarchical democratic republican revolutionary vanguard to which Bolívar too belonged. *Soberanía popular* should always preside in politics: "all should take part in what affects everyone; it is for everyone to approve what concerns everyone."[67] All Spanish America languished under the triple yoke of oppression: monarchy, feudal privilege, and popular ignorance linked to ecclesiastical authority, held Roscio who defined monarchy as a means of enslaving men with the help of theologians. The Bible does not contradict sovereignty of the people. Eulogizing Paine as chief propagandist of the North *and* South American Revolution, his later pamphlet, *El Triumpho de la Libertad sobre el despotismo* (Philadelphia, 1817), full-frontally assailed the

[64] Irisarri, *Semanario Republicano* viii (25 Sept. 1813), 63–4, 70.
[65] Irisarri, *Semanario Republicano* xii (28 Oct. 1813), 89.
[66] Breña, "Ideas, acontecimientos," 141; Gleijeses, "Limits of Sympathy," 481.
[67] Roscio, *Triumfo de la Libertad*, 11, 25, 28, 71–2; Ruiz Barrionuevo, "Juan German Roscio," 182–3, 189.

church's teaching that monarchs derive their authority and power from God.[68] The basic principles of Roscio's and Miranda's Venezuela constitution of 1811— repudiation of monarchy, aristocracy, slavery, and religious authority, universal and equal rights, full freedom of expression and the press, and division of powers—Bolívar afterwards maintained, were partly correct, but also had serious faults even if, in his view, it was especially the way the 1811 constitution applied its principles that was unrealistic, too complicated and unsuited to local conditions, causing the 1811 coup's subsequent failure.[69]

Venezuela's first constitution abolished hereditary privilege and titles, instituting elections for the legislature and equality before the law (for non-slaves), and suppressed the slave trade (but not yet slavery itself).[70] Discarding the designation "Spanish America," the Venezuelan constitution located the country geographically in the "continente Colombiano" [Columbian continent], declaring: "We, the People of the States of Venezuela, on the basis of our sovereignty, proclaim the seven provinces here represented to be Venezuela's 'United States.'"[71] The judiciary was pronounced a separate branch and placed under a Supreme Court, again in the American manner. The 1811 constitution, though, avoided an American-style presidency, the one North American feature Bolívar did rate highly, adopting instead a three-man executive, or triumvirate (resembling the 1799 French constitution), one of whom was Roscio. Elected for four-year terms, the 1811 Caracas executive, to Miranda's annoyance, was deliberately kept weak to ensure legislative primacy.[72] The only feature of the United States' political system that Bolívar deemed worthy of emulation in Spanish America, apart from a separate judiciary, was what he termed the "American President's right to choose his own successor," as he described Washington's succession by Adams, and Jefferson's by Madison.[73]

Bolívar and Miranda were dismayed too by the new constitution's emulating the 1791 French constitution in electing members of its new legislature indirectly, via "electors," formally distinguishing between "active" and "passive" citizenship, and restricting voting rights to adult males over 25 who met substantial property qualifications (raising the 20 per cent of the population that was white into a broad new racial elite). The constitution, some believed, excessively deferred to how most people thought in its first article proclaiming the Catholic faith the "one and exclusive religion of the inhabitants of Venezuela" and charging Congress with excluding all other "public or private" religions.[74] Eclectically forged by professors, journalists, and professional revolutionaries like Roscio and Yanes, Venezuela's first constitution, like

[68] Ruiz Barrionuevo, "Juan Germán Roscio," 182–3; Israel, *Expanding Blaze*, 443.

[69] Bolívar, *Discurso*, 21–3, 26.

[70] Billias, *American Constitutionalism*, 125–7.

[71] Brewer-Carías, *Constituciones de Venezuela* i. 560.

[72] Bailyn, *Atlantic History*, 106; Brewer-Carías, *Constituciones de Venezuela* i. 113, 563.

[73] Bolívar, *El Libertador*, pp. xxxviii–xxxix; Bushnell, *Simón Bolívar*, 4, 96–7; Fitz, *Our Sister Republics*, 227–8.

[74] Brewer-Carías, *Constituciones de Venezuela* i. 117, 555–6; Arana, *Bolívar, American Liberator*, 102–3.

Mexico's several years later, was fiercely criticized by some, above all for adopting American-style federalism. Venezuela emulated the American model especially in adopting a "federal constitution," declaring each of its states "sovereign," along with separation of powers and a two-chamber national legislature respectively called the "House of Representatives" and the "Senate." However, Venezuela's upper house, instead of stipulating an equal, fixed number of senators per state, as in the United States, followed Cádiz in providing one senator for every seventy thousand inhabitants. Bolívar remained a lifelong opponent of Spanish American emulation of North American federalism, which he claimed needed a society of "saints" and the force of miracles to function effectively.[75]

Before long, the revolutionary wave also engulfed New Granada (Colombia), including Quito and Panama, territory estimated by Bolívar, relying on Von Humboldt, to have two and a half million inhabitants.[76] In November 1809, the Bogotá city council had issued a manifesto highly critical of royal policies, denouncing discrimination against Creoles. Drafted by a leading critic of the royal administration, Camilo Torres Tenorio (1766–1816), it demanded equal representation for "American Spaniards" in the Cádiz Cortes. True fraternal union between European and American Spaniards could follow only from justice and equality. Had the British crown pondered carefully "perhaps today it would not be regretting the secession of its [American] colonies. Pride and a superiority complex meant losing rich colonies unable to comprehend why, being vassals of the same sovereign, they could not (while other provinces could) send representatives to the nation's legislative body, a parliament enacting laws and imposing taxes they had not approved."[77] Calling for "progreso de la luces" [progress of Enlightenment], and "ideas of humanity for all classes of society," Tenorio demanded abolition of slavery and the slave trade, ending "Indian tribute," and regularization of Indian land tenure rights.[78] Months of behind-the-scenes pressure, backed by popular demonstrations, enabled Bogotá's Creole notables, critics, and activists to force the viceroy to concede a *Junta Suprema*, comprising twenty-seven Creole and peninsular notables, which, in July 1810, provisionally assumed the viceroyalty's government.[79] Proclaiming an equitable "union" of peninsular and Creole Spaniards, this *Junta* promptly repudiated the Cádiz regency council and expelled both viceroy and *audiencia* from the country, albeit still voicing nominal allegiance to Fernando. However, the Bogotá *Junta Suprema* soon found itself defied by regional elements. In the north-eastern provinces of Santa Marta and Río Hacha and the south, a tenacious royalism resisted. At coastal Cartagena, opponents demanded a loose federal confederacy not dominated by Bogotá. New Granada thus split, like Venezuela, into three or rather probably four principal blocs—centralist republicans

[75] Bolívar, *Discurso*, 22; Brading, *Classical Republicanism*, 11; Dávila, *Bolívar y Spinoza*, 52–4, 59, 63.
[76] Bolívar, *Carta de Jamaica*, 83.
[77] Martínez Guarnica, "Experiencia," 372; Vanegas, "Actualización," 379.
[78] Rodríguez, *Independence*, 70–1; Martínez Guarnica, "Experiencia," 372–3; Vanegas, "Actualización," 378.
[79] Martínez Guarnica, "Experiencia," 375; Vanegas, "Actualización," 387.

seeking an independent, unified New Granada, Cádiz regency council loyalists wanting to keep loose ties with Spain, regional particularists and ultra-royalist Catholics directed by reactionary clergy.

Here, too, García de Sena's Spanish renderings of Paine and North American state constitutions helped give voice to republican sentiment. Throughout the Spanish American Revolution's early stages (1808–13), despite the indispensable military functions of generals like Miranda and Bolívar, it continued to be opposition-minded jurists, journalists, professors, and intellectuals, prominent members of the Enlightenment societies and reading clubs since the 1770s, who headed the New Granadian, as well as Venezuelan, Argentinian, Chilean, Bolivian, and Ecuadorian revolutions. Among presiding figures in New Granada were the veteran enlightener Antonio Nariño (1764–1824), the botanist and editor Miguel de Pombo (1779–1816), José Felix Restrepo (1760–1832), botanist and professor of history at the Popoyán royal college, and the naturalist and journalist, Francisco José de Caldas (1768–1816). Reviling absolutism, scholasticism, and clergy, Caldas, a founder of the science of mapping and analyzing plant distribution according to different geographical conditions, had like the others collaborated with the great Von Humboldt in several local scientific expeditions. In 1810, he became co-editor, alongside Pombo, of New Granada's first newspaper printing republican revolutionary rhetoric, the thrice-weekly *Diario Político de Santa Fé*.[80] The New Granada revolutionary intelligentsia's doyen, Nariño, had led a subversive *círculo literario* in Bogotá ever since 1789; an admirer of Franklin and zealot for the American and French revolutions, he had clandestinely disseminated his own translation of the 1789 French "Declaration of the Rights of Man and the Citizen" in New Granada and also Peru.[81] His library of 1,800 volumes, including Bayle's *Dictionnaire* and Raynal, had been seized by the crown in August 1794 when he first came under suspicion of plotting rebellion.

The first issue of the *Diario Político* deplored the confusion and uncertainty gripping New Granada, and stressed the need for a genuinely enlightened newspaper enabling "our Francklines and Washingtones to spread light."[82] A *discurso* on press freedom the paper published in October 1810 tightly linked political servitude under monarchy to religious *fanatismo* and general ignorance, and political liberty inextricably to press freedom and "Enlightenment," the true salvation of man.[83] As most of the populace preferred "superstition and fanaticism" to "reason and philosophy," Pombo, Nariño, Restrepo, and Caldas conceived their task to be a gargantuan uphill challenge. Representatives from those provinces willing to participate convened as New Granada's "Congreso General" in December 1810, but proved unable to restore unity. Each New Granadian "state" abandoning royalism during 1810–11 adopted its

[80] Von Humboldt, *Wiederentdeckung*, 292, 362; Elías Ortiz and Martínez Delgado, *El Periodismo*, xxiii–xxxiii.

[81] Von Humboldt, *Wiederentdeckung*, 477–8; Martínez Garnica, "Experiencia," 379–80; Ruiz Martínez, *Librería de Nariño*, 209, 394.

[82] Elías Ortiz and Martínez Delgado, *El Periodismo*, 29–30.

[83] Elías Ortiz and Martínez Delgado, *El Periodismo*, 123–6.

own "Declaration of the Rights of Man and the Citizen," eclectically selecting divergent wording and precedents—often from the 1793 and 1795 French constitutions. Although most clergy, and all New Granada's bishops, condemned the revolutionary leadership, there was no alternative, once again, given obstinately ingrained attitudes, but to recognize Catholicism as the exclusive religion. (Knowing its indispensability, García de Sena had systematically deleted Paine's sallies against churches, clergy, and religious authority from all his editions at the outset.)

Here, too, federalism and the American model dominated early constitutional debates.[84] New Granada's Congress, convening in Bogotá in February 1811, "fascinated by the brilliance and prosperity of the United States of North America," tried to judiciously balance the American and the French models, but leaned more to the former. With Pombo, Nariño, and others extolling the United States, New Granada's "states" modeled their constitutions each on a different American state constitution, so that "in one province reigned, with small alterations," complained Restrepo, "the fundamental laws of Pennsylvania," here those of Massachusetts, and there those of Maryland. However, experience soon proved these "constitutions, while wisely devised for North America, were inadequate to maintain order among New Granada's inhabitants," saturated as they were in "superstition" and the "habit of slavish submission."[85] Here again Bolívar rejected the early efforts at constitution-founding as fundamentally defective in conception. In 1811–14, *Republicanos federalistas* promoted a vision of the "United Provinces of New Granada" as a new United States, he complained, "preserving a wide autonomy for the individual "states," borrowing the "fundamental base of the constitution from the most exaggerated federal system that has ever existed." Nariño and the historian José Manuel Restrepo (1781–1863) soon likewise regretted this approach, judging the American state constitutions "too liberal for peoples educated under the harshest despotism."[86]

New Granada's revolution too quickly fragmented, descending into civil war with a mix of ultra-royalists and Cádiz Patriots controlling the south, Panama, and parts of the north-east, centralist republicans holding Bogotá, and *republicanos federalistas* defending what remained of the "United States of Colombia." But it outlasted Venezuela's first republic, which survived only a year and twenty days from July 1811 to July 1812, with royalists nominally loyal to Cádiz, often mobilizing *pardos* and slaves against the rich, steadily gaining ground, as many appalled Venezuelans began to glimpse how closely the Independence movement and leadership was tied not just to European revolutionary tradition, but irreligion and rejection of religious authority, causing many poor people and most blacks and *pardo* half-castes, who had little grasp of the complexities of republicanism, to opt for church and king against the Republic, a struggle increasingly characterized by cruelty and slaughter. Before long, two more Venezuelan "States"—Barcelona and Cumaná—defected to the Cádiz

[84] Rodríguez, *Independence*, 150–7.
[85] Bolívar, *Carta de Jamaica*, 105, 109; Restrepo, *Historia de la Revolución* v. 27–8.
[86] Restrepo, *Historia* v. 27.

Patriots and royalists (for the moment allied), turning Venezuela's civil war into a conflict of five provinces against five. Miranda was proclaimed generalissimo of the fledgling republic with unrivalled powers but, lacking sufficient support, was unable to hold the line. By this stage he had ceased collaborating, and begun quarreling, with Bolívar.[87] In desperation, Miranda ordered the arrest of all peninsular Spaniards and promised black slaves willing to fight for independence their freedom. But the archbishop of Caracas proved better able to secure the lower orders' loyalty. Blanco White's *El Español* accused Venezuela's elite of using radical Jacobin principles to cloak their own material self-interest, to oppress Venezuela's non-whites.[88] Independent Venezuela's collapse accelerated with the arrival of royalist troops from Puerto Rico that deployed at loyalist Coro and overran much of western Venezuela. This setback was followed by a massive earthquake, on 26 March 1812, that devastated Caracas and La Guaira, burying thousands in the rubble and demolished Miranda's barracks. Wrecking republican bases while leaving Coro, Maracaibo, and other royalist strongholds intact, the disaster, despite leaving piles of corpses under collapsed churches and monasteries, was sufficiently one-sided to assist the clergy assuring parishioners that divine providence manifestly favored the royalist side.[89]

On 25 July 1812, increasingly unwilling to take the offensive, fearful of the consequences of a deepening civil war, and depressed by desertions from his force, Miranda offered to capitulate to the Cádiz Cortes.[90] An enraged Bolívar, denouncing his "treason," led a group of dogged republicans who seized Miranda in La Guaira just before his planned departure by sea.[91] When the republican leaders were then almost trapped by royalist forces, Miranda was left chained in a cell, at the royalists' mercy. Bolívar contrived to escape to nearby Curaçao—then under British control—with a few followers; there he remained for two months, raising funds and making useful connections among local Sephardic Jews, including an Amsterdam lawyer, Mordechai Ricardo, a cousin of the economist David Ricardo, and uncle, ironically, of the Counter-Enlightenment poet and convert to Christianity, Isaac da Costa, back in Holland, who ardently opposed the Spanish American Revolution and supported Fernando.[92] Also on Curaçao, Bolívar composed his so-called Cartagena Manifesto, admonishing New Granadians to avoid the ruinous divisions, lack of discipline, and executive weakness that had doomed the first Venezuelan republic, a text published as he landed in New Granada, in December 1812.[93]

On the Venezuelan republic's collapse, Miranda, Roscio, and other captured revolutionary leaders were sent for trial to Spain, where, as Joseph's regime crumbled, the Cádiz regency council representing the British-backed Spanish crown regained

[87] O'Leary, *Memorias* i. 98–9; Brewer-Carías, *Constituciones de Venezuela* i. 119–20.
[88] Murphy, *Blanco White*, 78–9, 83.
[89] Rodríguez, *Independence*, 117; Klooster, *Revolutions*, 138.
[90] Rodríguez, *Independence*, 117–18; Adelman, *Sovereignty*, 214.
[91] Brice, "Bolívar de Marx", 39, 43; see also Marx, "Bolívar," 10.
[92] Van der Veen, *Groot Nederland*, 41.
[93] Bolívar, *Obras Completas* i. 41–8; Van der Veen, *Groot Nederland*, 41–2, 66.

ground through 1812–14. As the Cádiz-style constitutional revolution gained momentum in Spain and Venezuela alike, royalist-held areas of northern South America held elections at parish level on the basis of universal suffrage, including Indian and mixed populations (but excluding the black minority), proceeding with questionable fairness and usually controlled by local Creole elites. But, for the first time, less affluent whites, mixed bloods, and some Indians found themselves thrown pell-mell into political participation, concerning which most lacked even the sketchiest notion.[94] However, the royalist position was far weaker than it seemed at first due to a growing split between Cádiz constitutionalists and ultra-royalists ignoring Cádiz, and trying to capitalize on the deepening republican defeat. In 1813, a round of confiscations of estates of rebel leaders, including Bolívar, further added to disorder, now more chaotic, brutal, and gruesome than ever.

In New Granada Bolívar joined with the *federalistas*, soon confirming his growing reputation as an able and indefatigable military commander. Pushing the royalists from a large swathe of Cartagena's hinterland, he captured the border town of Cúcuta on 28 February 1813, demanding that federalist New Granada now invade Venezuela since no South American republic could be free whilst others languished in chains. This met with a mixed response, but eventually General Bolívar, as he now was, received the half-hearted permission of Nariño and the Bogotá regime to seize Venezuela's western border areas (but not advance on Caracas). Crossing back with only 500 men, a largely New Granadian force, Bolívar urged them to be "loyal republicans" and fight for all Hispanic America, plunging into a ruinously rash venture by challenging the royalist regime. But royalist Venezuela had become a textbook instance of how to rapidly lose local support through atrocities and excessive brutality. Royalist ruthlessness, and the ideological rift opened by the ultra-royalists against the Cádiz constitutionalists, enabled Bolívar to make startling advances. Recruiting "republicans" by the hundred, and ignoring all orders, he advanced on Caracas, crushing the main royalist force near Valencia. The Venezuelan capital capitulated on 6 August 1813. Acclaimed on all sides, he entered Caracas in triumph, the *cabildo*, or city government, conferring on him the title of "El Libertador."

As the bitter fighting and breakdown of order continued, enlightened professors and professionals found themselves sidelined, as military commanders increasingly stepped into their shoes. By late 1813 and early 1814, Bolívar was virtual dictator of Venezuela apart from the stubbornly royalist Coro locality. Refusing to re-install the decentralized federal republic of 1811, he insisted Venezuela's Congress establish a much more unified and centralized republic, practically under his own sole command.[95] Veneration for the American model, so pronounced earlier, receded markedly during these years except in New Spain (Mexico). With time, Bolívar's incessant calls for a powerful executive and centralization of power seemed to many, including close subordinates, to reflect zeal for a power structure especially suiting his own

[94] Elliott, *Empires*, 386–7. [95] Bushnell, *Simon Bolívar*, 15.

increasingly Napoleonic aspirations. Yet Bolívar proved entirely unique, whatever his ambition, in his ability over many years to combine military genius with a profound, lasting preoccupation with "philosophy" and enlightened values focused on constitution-building, propagating republicanism, and combating popular ignorance.

Meanwhile, with Napoleon's defeat, Fernando had ample cause for satisfaction. Joseph, toppled, fled via France to the United States, where he spent the next seventeen years in Philadelphia, living in splendor on the proceeds of Spanish crown jewels brought with him from Madrid. Restored to the throne, Fernando entered Madrid in triumph. On 4 May 1814, supported by church, nobility, and common people, Fernando abolished the Cádiz Constitution,[96] suppressing all constitutional rights and liberties while issuing a peremptory admonition to his rebellious New World subjects to return to their pre-1808 obedience.[97] From mid-1814, throughout Spanish America, opposition to the Revolution, popular royalism fired chiefly by ecclesiastics and religious zeal, steadily gained ground. In New Granada, Ecuador, and Peru, and now again in Venezuela, many blacks and ethnic half-castes flocked anew to the royalist banner. The "fanatismo religioso" of priests and monks aroused the *vulgo ignorante* in part, protested José Manuel Restrepo, by accusing revolutionaries of violating Catholic shrines, images, and crucifixes.[98] Under growing pressure, New Granada's "states" with American-style constitutions dismantled or suspended their more libertarian clauses. By May 1814 Nariño, despite promising (like Bolívar) freedom to hacienda and mine slaves joining his army, faced unavoidable defeat.[99] In October 1814 royalist troops, sent south from Peru, also crushed the Patriots in Chile, leaving Argentina for the moment, in Jullien's words, South America's "last asylum of independence and liberty."[100]

Assured of Holy Alliance and British backing, Fernando in February 1815 followed up his successes in Spain by dispatching a formidable armada across the Atlantic hoping to restore royal power and authority, not least to secure urgently needed New World silver and other resources to stave off bankruptcy in Spain. Forty-seven vessels carrying 10,800 troops, this force extended Fernando's royalist counter-revolution first to Venezuela, then South America more generally. Europe's great powers supported the project, a fact that outraged Bolívar, who claimed their backing was unlikely to continue for long, being contrary to their basic interests.[101] Fernando's aristocratic and ecclesiastical supporters on both sides of the Atlantic were eager to regain their own lost revenues, posts, and New World emoluments while promising few or no benefits for supporters lower down. Bentham, increasingly hostile to empire in general, and following Spanish and Spanish American developments closely at this point, believed most European as well as American Spaniards would benefit

[96] Carr, *Spain 1808–1939*, 120–1; Rodriguez, *Independence*, 105, 171.
[97] Restrepo, *Historia* v. 62–3; Suárez, *Cortes de Cádiz*, 197–8; Durán López, "Construcción," 93.
[98] Restrepo, *Historia* v. 26, 110–11, 137, 139.
[99] Restrepo, *Historia* v. 52, 78; Hamnett, "Popular Insurrection," 309–12.
[100] [Jullien], *Revue encyclopédique* xviii ((1823), 482–3.
[101] Bolívar, *Carta de Jamaica*, 87, 89.

materially should Spain be stripped of its American colonies as only the upper strata profited from the colonial governorships, colonial trade, and the bishoprics; the rest just paid taxes, or performed military or naval service, to support the vast and unwieldy imperial structure.[102]

The king and his advisors knew Bolívar's Creole troops in Venezuela had been weakened through repeated bloody encounters with local royalist forces consisting largely of non-whites. Evacuating Venezuela, Bolívar fell back on Cartagena in September 1814, even before the royal army sent out under Don Pablo Morillo y Morillo (1775–1837), conde de Cartagena, a veteran commander wounded at Trafalgar, hardened in the Peninsular War fighting against Joseph from 1808, arrived. Morillo's forces had an easy job completing the pacification of Venezuela. Next, Morillo, capable but brutal, invaded New Granada where Bolívar, commanding the opposing forces, had recently retaken Bogotá for the local republicans. During the spring of 1815, helped by the Anglo-American War (1812–15), which impeded the flow of weapons and munitions to the insurgents from the United States, the royalists won several further victories. Again, the less educated heeded the church's exhortations more than those of the republican leadership. Weakened too by the continuing rift between federalists and centralizers, Bolívar withdrew temporarily to Jamaica, leaving the great coastal fortress city of Cartagena, northern South America's most prosperous commercial metropolis, defended by 4,000 Patriots, to rescue what remained of his now severely depleted army, hoping to return refurbished.

Besieged by 6,000 Spanish troops and 3,000 Venezuelan royalists, to the great dismay of all republicans, in December 1815, after an 106-day epic siege that left the city in ruins, Cartagena capitulated.[103] Bogotá was retaken by Morillo, in May 1816. During 1814–17, the Revolution comprehensively collapsed in Spain, Venezuela, New Granada, and most of Spanish America. From 1814, the insurgents faced severe reverses also in Chile. To all appearances, Counter-Enlightenment was triumphing and republicanism everywhere, except in Argentina, collapsing. All monuments erected throughout the empire commemorating the Cádiz constitution and citizen rights were demolished and Spanish America's civic main squares, lately renamed in honor of constitutions, reverted to strictly royal and religious titles. Jefferson, Lafayette, and Bentham all lamented: but commentators sympathizing with the Revolution were mostly less dismayed by royalist brutality and the reactionary views of the clergy than by the common people's lukewarm attitude toward the republican cause and the leaders battling in its name.[104] In his *Carta de Jamaica*, Bolívar emphasized Spanish America's backwardness in cultural, social, and political terms, blaming centuries of deep passivity, under oppression, for forging a sphere of servitude where tyranny usurps all the rights and powers of the citizen, stripping men of all sense of what elevates mankind to a life of liberty. It is harder, Montesquieu had

[102] Carr, *Spain 1808–1939*, 122–3; Schofield, *Utility and Democracy*, 208–9, 287; Isabella, *Risorgimento*, 45.
[103] [Jullien], *Revue encyclopédique* iii (July 1819), 345–51; Fitz, *Our Sister Republics*, 162–3.
[104] Schofield, *Utility and Democracy*, 208–10.

rightly averred, to "salvage a people from servitude, than to conquer a free one."[105] Spanish Americans had shown they do not sufficiently possess the *conato* (impulse), the collective will, to secure *instituciones liberales*, he contended, expressing the point in Spinozistic terms, the *conatus* arising from "the instinct that all men have to aspire to their greatest possible happiness" based on justice, liberty, and equality and initially attained when civil societies are founded; due to age-old Spanish oppression, they had fought for it too hesitantly and weakly. It is not hard to imagine a suddenly unchained people hurling itself into the sphere of liberty, but, like Icarus, with its wings undone, immediately falling straight into the abyss.[106]

Where France, Spain, and Holland had rushed to aid the fledgling United States in their struggle with Britain, no power in 1814–15, noted Bolívar, backed the Spanish American Revolution militarily.[107] Between 1815 and 1819, possessing no real foothold anywhere in northern or central South America, and with Bolívar in Jamaica, the Revolution survived only on the shoulders of those insurgents escaping with, or after him, on islands of the Caribbean. The republican leaders still resisting, preaching liberty, toleration, and equal rights in New Granada, were one by one captured by Morillo and shot, Pombo at Bogotá, in July 1816, Caldas in October. Yet the repression's very brutality, which for six months continued unremittingly, during which Morillo himself reckoned he executed some 7,000 prisoners with thousands more imprisoned, or exiled, helped keep the embers of rebellion alive. From a royalist and ecclesiastical counter-revolutionary standpoint, the draconian financial exactions Morillo collected in "pacified" areas also proved counterproductive.[108] Another factor that during the years 1815–19 slowly and painfully helped turn around history's verdict on Bolívar's great undertaking, from crushing defeat to astounding triumph, was the end of the Napoleonic Wars in Europe and the Anglo-American war: the sudden release on the New World precisely during those years of numerous demobilized, unemployed soldiers and sailors willing to volunteer for revolution in distant parts, and immense quantities of no longer needed muskets and munitions, lent much added impetus. The vast post-1815 flow of arms, munitions and volunteers passed mainly from Britain and Holland via New York, Philadelphia, New Orleans, St Thomas, Jamaica, and Curaçao.[109]

Aware that Alexander von Humboldt possessed a more comprehensive knowledge of Spanish America than any other living man, Bolívar studied the latter's four-volume "essay" on the political state of New Spain (1808–11), among the greatest late Enlightenment works, and, inspired by reading Von Humboldt, penned his morale-lifting "Letter from Jamaica" [*Carta de Jamaica*], a piece blending pessimism about Spanish American society with his fervent prediction that Spain would never rebuild

[105] Bolívar, *Carta de Jamaica*, 81, 95–9, 109, 160; Oostindie, *Ethnicity*, 60.
[106] Bolívar, *Carta de Jamaica*, 108–11; Dávila, *Bolívar y Spinoza*, 24, 78.
[107] Bolívar, *Obras Completas* i. 176.
[108] Hamnett, "Popular Insurrection," 314, 316, 318–19; Adelman, *Sovereignty*, 275.
[109] Blaufarb, "Révolution armée," 176–7, 183–5, 189–90, 193.

its Spanish American empire and could not sustain its effort at reconquest for long, lacking the resources, nor be assisted by other European powers for long, a re-subjugated Latin America not being in Europe's interest.[110] All Spanish America, including Mexico, would eventually break away; but whether it would also be free depended on bridging the differences between the different racial groups, on finding the way to a true republican solution for its political and social difficulties. Chile, he predicted, would achieve republican peace and stability more readily than Argentina and the rest.[111] Peru, like Venezuela and New Granada, would suffer the turmoil and disruption of a white elite resisting a democratic outcome empowering the non-white strata, blacks, Indians, and mestizos, resenting the tyranny of centuries and avenging the murder of Moctezuma and Tupac Amaru. [112] What then is true "democracy"? For Bolívar, democracy was less a question of constitutional procedures or electoral systems than securing basic rights and freedoms for all the people on an equal basis. Certainly, democracy must be based on representation, and hence elections. Like d'Holbach, he scorned "absolute democracy," direct democracy of the sort Rousseau favored, as being of no use whatever: "un pueblo ignorante es un instrumento ciego de su propria destrucción" [an ignorant people is the blind instrument of its own destruction]; it was a fair enough summary of Spinoza's principle that society's true object is the "common good" but that we, humankind, are generally deflected, "misled by power and cult" [*sed potentia et cultu decipimur*]. Bolívar's true "democracy" was the effective securing of men's rights and freedoms, the "General Will" overcoming distraction through good direction, attaining the essence of what the people need and, where their ideas can be improved, in an idealized sense want. [113]

Dismissing Rousseau's belief in man as basically good but corrupted by society, Bolívar thought the clergy right to claim an individual, left to himself, is a wretched, miserable creature, but wrong in inferring from this their false doctrine of Original Sin. To redeem men from their degradation and misery what is required is not theology, which only deepens their degradation, but the well-constructed republic securing men's rights and freedoms, something unattainable without first elevating men to a higher educational and moral level. Bolívar was above all an Enlightenment revolutionary who saw elevating all classes of society together in awareness and civic virtues as the key: "el hombre puede elevarse sobre si proprio a poder de ejemplos y por la educación" [man can elevate himself above what he is by force of example and by education].[114] Hence, "a democratic system" introduced too fast can only bring Spanish America to ruin since experience showed the great majority were simply too ignorant and under the thumb of ecclesiastics for a genuinely representative framework to be viable. "We are a region plagued by vices acquired from Spain, throughout

[110] Bolívar, *Carta de Jamaica*, 79–81; Wulf, *Invention of Nature*, 178–9.

[111] Bolívar, *Carta de Jamaica*, 119–21. [112] Bolívar, *Obras Completas* i. 153, 163.

[113] Bolívar, *Discurso*, 21; Rojas, *Ideas educativas*, 44–5; Dávila, *Bolívar y Spinoza*, 65.

[114] Bolívar, *Carta de Jamaica*, 108–9; Dávila, *Bolívar y Spinoza*, 29, 37, 64.

history a mistress of cruelty, ambition, meanness, and greed." Saving South America's fledgling republics required a firm executive vested in one leader dispensing justice and wisdom, ruling benevolently for life, able to command, stabilize, and consolidate while fostering an enlightened elite able to elevate society to the requisite level.[115] This was his answer to a predicament he saw as the fundamental difficulty confronting Latin America, a politics functioning by creating a democratic base through deploying arguments and concepts to undermine "superstition" and dogmatic false ideology, slowly dissolving the socially destructive force of ignorance, a version of Spinoza's activist democratic republicanism, since the 1980s reviving among the democratic Left intelligentsia in Argentina and Brazil.[116]

From Jamaica, Bolívar transferred to Haiti, where he and the ten shiploads of insurgents he led were warmly welcomed. On Haiti, which he got to know well, and where he stayed for two separate periods in quick succession, he established his base first, like Miranda in 1806, at Jacmel. Conferring with the world's then sole black republican president, Alexandre Pétion, in southern Haiti's "national palace," which he found appropriately adorned with portraits of Raynal, Grégoire, and Wilberforce, he promised, in exchange for a safe haven and aid, to abolish slavery in all areas he liberated. With Pétion supplying guns, munitions, and troops, as well as a printing-press for Bolívar's Spanish-language propaganda, Bolívar publicly vowed to abolish slavery everywhere he could in Spanish America, a declaration that further enhanced his stature among radicals—even if, at the time, he had no other recourse and his declaration was partly from calculation, to attract black support.[117] Transferring from Jacmel, with a growing stream of volunteers and refugees arriving, Bolívar and his men regrouped at Aux Cayes, a port facing New Granada, on Haiti's south-western coast.[118] In February 1816, Bolívar wrote asking Pétion whether he wished him, in his manifestos published in South America, to proclaim the black leader "l'auteur de notre liberté" [the author of our liberty].[119] Worrying about the reaction in Europe, Pétion asked him not to, to avoid Haiti antagonizing Fernando, and hence Louis XVIII and the Holy Alliance.[120]

The year 1816 marked the low-point. Yet the Spanish American Revolution clearly remained alive not just on Haiti and Jamaica but among the refugee networks from the mainland found throughout the Caribbean, and at New Orleans, Philadelphia, and New York, and also at sea and among fugitives lying low in the cities, mountains, and valleys of the viceroyalties. Bolívar's first expedition to the mainland from Haiti,

[115] Arana, *Bolívar, American Liberator*, 176–7.

[116] Tatián, *Spinoza. Filosofía terrena*, 12–13, 44, 68, 156; Van Reijen, *Argentijnse gezicht*, 16–17, 22.

[117] Klooster, *Revolutions*,140; Oostindie, *Ethnicity*, 58; Blanchard, *Slavery and Abolition*, 9–10, 196; Lombardi, *Decline and Abolition*, 41.

[118] Souker, *Discours et proclamations*, 38; Zamoyski, *Holy Madness*, 205.

[119] Bolívar, *Obras Completas* i. 189.

[120] Klooster, *Revolutions*, 140; Blanchard, *Slavery and Abolition*, 9–10, 196; Lombardi, *Decline and Abolition*, 41; Geggus, "Slave Rebellion," 39.

in April 1816, was repulsed, and before long he found himself again encamped "in the asylum of all the republicans in this part of the world," as he styled Haiti. Another revolutionary group based in southern Haiti at that juncture was that of General Martín Javier Mina y Larrea (1789–1817), a Navarrese patriot who had led a guerilla band against Napoleon in Navarre in 1808–10 and was now stirring revolution in Spanish America without wanting to advance national causes, or anyone's independence, purely to combat Fernando's tyranny; from Haiti he landed in New Spain in November 1816 with several hundred men. Captured by royalists a year later, he was shipped to Spain, where he was executed by firing squad. Bolívar's second foray into Venezuela from Haiti, between May and August 1816, was an unmitigated failure too. He returned for the third time to Haiti to rebuild his fortunes, and now also to create a rudimentary armed fleet.

Bolívar's third incursion from Haiti, however, launched in December 1816, gained the foothold that led on eventually to the triumphs of 1819 and liberation of Spanish America. Returned to Venezuela, he now used his small fleet not just for transportation of men and supplies but, as his support and resources expanded, to blockade the Venezuelan coast. His admiral, from 1816 until he died in 1821, was a young Curaçao merchant of part Jewish descent, one of the arms importers from Europe, Luis Brion (1782–1821), among Bolívar's most steadfast allies. Imbued with the republicanism of the Batavian Republic, Brion would have liked to turn Curaçao into the main base for supplies and munitions fueling the South American Revolution as it had once fueled that in North America; but the Dutch governor was under orders from The Hague to distance himself from the insurgents and proceed as an ally of monarchical Spain[121]—though later, after Brion's death, from July 1822, King William did defy the Holy Alliance by recognizing the new Spanish American republics and permitting ships flying Spanish American republican flags to enter Dutch Caribbean ports, hoping to be compensated for antagonizing his fellow monarchs by Curaçao becoming the chief staple-place for the Spanish America trade.[122]

For many months, Bolívar and his minuscule army, numbering a few hundreds, much troubled by insubordination and infighting, remained largely cut off in a remote, inland eastern region of Venezuela. Through 1817 and 1818, to all appearances he represented no real threat to Spain's resurgent Spanish American ascendancy. Brion sank his entire personal fortune in Bolívar's stalled enterprise—to his own eventual ruin and despair. For a time, Bolívar achieved little more than disseminate republican propaganda and calls for the abolition of black slavery, for which his friend, Von Humboldt, along with Lafayette and other leading late Enlightenment voices, warmly praised him.[123]

[121] Van der Veen, *Groot Nederland*, 63–7.

[122] Van der Veen, *Groot Nederland*; Blaufarb, "Révolution armée," 181.

[123] Wulf, *Invention of Nature*, 182–3; Neely, *Lafayette and the Liberal Ideal*, 206–7.

28.3. TRIUMPH AND FAILURE IN SPANISH AMERICA

The gloom of 1813–17 lifted only when a mixed Argentine–Chilean insurgent force, the so-called "Army of the Andes," under General José de San Martín (1778–1850), in a spectacular march across the Andes of a kind never before attempted and widely deemed impossible, surprised the royalist forces in Chile at the decisive battle of Chacabuco (12 February 1817), captured Santiago and then Valparaiso, in a few weeks virtually ejecting Spain from Chile. This infused Bolívar and his aides, and republican activists throughout the Caribbean, with renewed inspiration, but also a powerful new challenge. Anxious not to be stranded behind, they became obsessed with the lure of similarly advancing dramatically, mounting a vast pincers movement of liberation sweeping southwards to meet San Martín's northwards thrust, freeing all South America from Spain. Uneasy lest San Martín reach Lima first and, securing the central Andean viceroyalty, acquire the major honors as Spanish America's *Libertador* and the decisive role in reshaping the vast new entity, Bolívar became more than ever fixated on the idea of forging an immense Spanish American republic of emancipation, freedom, and well-being, ideologically united, independent, and free. But Bolívar and his force, hard pressed by Morillo, remained frustratingly pinned to the defensive for many months, hemmed into an inhospitable waste far to the south-east of Caracas. It was at this time that Bolívar first met O'Leary, the man who got to know him best and reported his life and thought in greatest detail. A volunteer with an Anglo-Irish contingent raised by agents promoting South American liberation in Britain, sent to eastern Venezuela in five ships sailing in May 1818, O'Leary's volunteer band had to penetrate a great distance inland through tropical forest, ascending the Orinoco, to join Bolívar's still minuscule army.

Bolívar's great breakthrough as military commander came the following year. It was preceded by a significant new political development. On 15 February 1819, at the small, remote south-eastern inland town of Angostura (today Ciudad Bolívar), on the Orinoco, the *Libertador*, accompanied by a body of notables drawn from across the country, inaugurated Venezuela's Second National Congress. For the first time, he proposed his own draft constitution. He had for some time been busy formulating what he considered the optimal constitution for Venezuela in present fraught circumstances and lost no time in expounding his long-pondered constitutional principles to the gathered assembly. A people for centuries kept in abject ignorance by Spain faced a political predicament that was essentially new, requiring carefully-crafted innovation in political theory and constitution-making. Bolívar accepted the first Venezuelan constitution's basic principles with respect to rejecting monarchy and aristocracy, universal and equal rights, freedom of expression and the press, and equality between the races. Black slavery must end. All men are equal whatever their color. Contrary to Hobbes, basic human rights carry over into the republic, he declared, and are the essence of popular sovereignty.[124]

[124] Bolívar, *Discurso*, 22, 25; Zapata, *Libros que leyó*, 65–6.

A strong one-man executive would be an essential feature of the new constitution.[125] Not only British "mixed government" but also the United States federal model, all *federalismo*, he rejected out of hand because Venezuela represented a very different kind of society, requiring a centralized non-federal system. Not yet ready for true representative government, Spanish America remained subject to deep divisions, particularly ethnic divisions: "we are more a mixture of Africa and America than we are children of Europe." Rifts difficult to resolve could be overcome only by means of an effective system providing strong centralized government and unity. "Unity," he insisted, above all was indispensable.[126] The hardest and most vital task, in a case such as Venezuela, involved in constructing a viable democracy that works for the good of all, is to educate the ignorant majority lacking any notion of what a true democratic republic is, or even, due to centuries of oppression, any inkling of justice or fair government, any concept of the requisite civic virtues. For this purpose, he recommended creating a hereditary senate that would not be a "nobility" in a traditional sense but comprise those leading the fight for the republic, an aristocracy of mind and action, of *libertadores*, a highly-educated vanguard teaching the rest the new values and thinking, in place of the old.[127]

Resigning all his powers under the Old Congress, and suggesting that no one man should hold supreme power for too long,[128] the next morning, at the age of 35, and at the height of his military and intellectual powers, the assembly elected him "president of Venezuela." His Angostura speeches made no mention of any plans for carrying the Revolution forward into New Granada, without waiting to recapture Caracas from the royalists first, or the strongholds on the Venezuelan coast. In a strategic move that nonplussed his own officers and men, and the skeleton government in Angostura, he led his army in a lightning march as difficult and astounding as that of San Martín, over the Andes, crossing Venezuela far to the south of Caracas, along the river system, under exceedingly testing conditions, then crossing the Arauca River into New Granada, at Tame, on the Andes' eastern side well to the north-east of Bogotá. Crossing the Andean eastern cordillera by a passage Morillo's officers thought too difficult to attempt, he incurred heavy losses in men, animals, and equipment, but also the opportunity, once across, to recover with no Spanish forces anywhere near to oppose him. Descending the slopes, he advanced on New Granada's capital. The ensuing battle of Boyacá was Bolívar's greatest triumph and the turning-point in the struggle in northern South America. Fought on 7 August 1819, it was a huge victory for the republicans, Bogotá falling into their hands just hours afterwards. Their triumph yielded control of all the strategic routes north, south, east, and west. "In just one day," commented Morillo, "Bolívar has undone all we have accomplished in five years of this campaign, and with a single battle reconquered all the territory the

[125] Bolívar, *Discurso*, 23, 31; Rojas, *Ideas educativas*, 45.
[126] Bolívar, *Discurso*, 17, 20–7; Bolívar, *Obras Completas* ii. 531; Dávila, *Bolívar y Spinoza*, 56.
[127] Bolívar, *Discurso*, 28–9; Brading, *Classical Republicanism*, 11; Dávila, *Bolívar y Spinoza*, 28.
[128] Bolívar, *Discurso*, 17.

king's soldiers have won in the course of so many past conflagrations."[129] Bolívar proceeded at once to organize a provisional republican government for New Granada, without concealing his plans to join New Granada to Venezuela to form a stronger, more stable entity through their union.

The *Libertador* was soon trudging back toward Venezuela, recruiting more troops in the towns and regions of Tunja and Pamplona while retracing his steps to Angostura, where he arrived on 11 December 1819. At the gathering of Venezuela's Congress three days later, he officially proposed the union of Venezuela with New Granada and Quito, to form a vast new entity to be called the "Republic of Gran Colombia." Congress duly complied, naming Bolívar "president" of the whole and Roscio vice-president on the Venezuelan side, with Nariño afterwards becoming vice-president on the New Granada side. But the union at once posed a host of problems, organizational difficulties and issues of principle. The centralist independence bloc in Bogotá resumed their feuding with New Granada federalists while Quito recalcitrantly reverted to royalist control. The local Patriot regime at Quito, deeply divided since 1809–12, aspired less to full independence than autonomy from both Bogotá and Lima, with power monopolized by the local Creole elite, ideas for Ecuador's republican future that hardly converged with Bolívar's.[130]

Rocafuerte, Quito's republican theorist, agreed that the Enlightenment is the exclusive ground of all democratic republican revolution, and that Filangieri figured among the most useful republican theorists they were jointly promoting in Spanish America. Rocafuerte professed to derive his political ideas from Filangieri in the first place, and secondly Montesquieu and Mably. Few other Spanish American revolutionaries indeed were as adamantly republican, but this included his views on executive power, which diverged from his Venezuelan comrade in crucial respects.[131] After participating from 1816 to 1820 in the revolutionary movement in Quito, and then Lima, later he reworked his political ideas, from 1820, at Philadelphia. His *Necessary Ideas for every Independent American People that Wants to Be Free* (1821) summed up Rocafuerte's reflections on twelve years of revolutionary struggle, like his *Ensayo Politico* (New York, 1823), envisaging the Revolution as the offspring of the American and French revolutions together. Only republicanism is valid; all monarchy he rejected outright as "superstition."[132] Where courts and kings—even in constitutional monarchies—cost exorbitant sums, the United States' president, following the "immortal example of the great Washington," contents himself with a modest annual salary.[133] The function of "religion" is to bolster the "morality of society" via toleration and "not by maintaining opulent archbishops" like those of Toledo, Lima, and Santiago de Chile expending revenues of thousands of

[129] Quoted in Arana, *Bolívar, American Liberator*, 235.
[130] Andrien, "Soberanía y revolución," 331–4.
[131] Rocafuerte, *Ensayo Político*, 8; Bolívar, *Carta de Jamaica*, 117–19; Trampus, *Naissance du langage*, 127–8; Trampus, "Enlightenment in Global History," 121.
[132] Rocafuerte, *Ideas necesarias*, 9–10; Fernández Sebastián, "Voice of the People," 231–2.
[133] Rocafuerte, *Ideas necesarias*, 4, 6.

pesos annually.[134] For him too the guiding democratic republican principle was that "all men are born equal" and share basic rights, that without press freedom there can be no defense of those rights or communication of basic truth to the people. For him too there is no other legitimate basis for representative government than equality of rights. Legitimate government therefore can only be based on popular sovereignty and every government failing to protect men's rights may legitimately be overthrown. Thus far he and Bolívar were as one.

The French Revolution began well and should have converted the rest of the world to the same principles as the American. But it had unfortunately been wrecked by the "hipocritas Robespierres," "ambiciosos San-Just," execrable Couthones, and other Montagnard "monsters of humanity" perpetrating the most "atrocious crimes."[135] "All the disorders occurring in France during the course of its Revolution," held Rocafuerte, "have had their origin not in the principle of equality of rights, but in violation of this principle."[136] Given France's failure, the American Revolution, believed Rocafuerte, was of unique relevance to Spanish America, causing him to supplement his texts with Spanish renderings of the American *Declaration of Independence*, the 1778 American Articles of Confederation, the American Constitution, and extracts from Paine's *Common Sense*. America's *Declaration of Independence*, he declared humanity's "verdadero decálogo político" [true political Decalogue] which, after many years, would eventually accomplish for the entire world what Moses' Decalogue had taken forty centuries to do in the moral sphere.[137] For him, unlike Bolívar, Thomas Paine "contributed more than anyone else to wresting the despotic scepter from the hands of royalism;"[138] The prime model for Hispanic Americans must be the institutional framework forged by "Franklin, Hancock, Hamilton, and that series of great men, whose wisdom the world admires and will admire forever."[139]

Praising Washington, Adams, and John Quincy Adams, as well as Franklin and Jefferson, Rocafuerte sought to spread "among us the spirit of liberty and tolerance that stems from the wise sentiments of the heroes and great men of North America."[140] Rejecting property qualifications for the right to vote, Rocafuerte declared universal and equal rights and representative democracy the only valid basis for representation.[141] For him, no less than Roscio, Nariño, and Irisarri, and like Bolívar, the overriding challenge confronting the Revolution was not Spain's obduracy but the struggle against ignorance, the fight "between darkness and light." Without Enlightenment "philosophy" Spanish Americans could not attain the exalted moral and political standards of the "Washingtones, Franklines y Jeffersones," and would justly be scorned by future generations for not cultivating "in our soil the delicate plant of liberty." America's

[134] Rocafuerte, *Ensayo Político*, 31. [135] Rocafuerte, *Ideas necesarias*, 3–4.
[136] Rocafuerte, *Ideas necesarias*, 78.
[137] Rocafuerte, *Ideas necesarias*, 2–3; Isabella, *Risorgimento*, 47.
[138] Rocafuerte, *Ideas necesarias*, 8, 11–12, 45–6, 61–2; Rocafuerte, *Ensayo Político*, 22, 3773; Aldridge, *Early American Literature*, 232.
[139] Rocafuerte, *Ideas necesarias*, 7–8; Aguilar Rivera, *Ausentes del universo*, 76–9.
[140] Rocafuerte, *Ideas necesarias*, 17. [141] Rocafuerte, *Ideas necesarias*, 66, 71–2, 74, 77–8.

political system, which he admired without any of Bolívar's reservations, should ultimately, he thought, be that of all the Americas. The New World needed to share in a pan-American constitutionalism rooted in the principles of Washington, Adams, Jefferson, and Madison.[142] In the early 1790s, Barlow had already urged his countrymen to consider whether they were content for the eventually independent other New World republics "to be our rivals, and consequently our enemies after the example of the states of Europe" or whether a way could "be prepared and they be persuaded to adopt our principles, to form with us a great union of political interests, and make of the whole but one confederated empire."[143] Rocafuerte's New World would contrast with royalist Europe and the Holy Alliance, becoming the world's chief promoter of human well-being and happiness, "la verdadera patria de la filosofía, de la tolerancia religiosa y de la libertad política" [true homeland of philosophy, religious toleration, and political liberty]. This elective and representative future common model, Rocafuerte dubbed the *sistema Colombiano*.

Soon after Bolívar proclaimed his union of Venezuela, New Granada, and Quito, republican prospects suddenly vastly improved with the advent of the new Spanish Revolution, commencing among the very troops, gathered in Cádiz, intended to reinforce royalism and religion in Spanish America. As the upheaval in Spain took hold, instead of reinforcements, Morillo received, in March 1820, astounding new instructions: he was to cease military operations against the Spanish American rebellion and, instead, negotiate, according full equality to Venezuelans and New Granadians as Spanish citizens, and guaranteeing all freedoms encased in the Cádiz Constitution. Morillo's ordering a ceasefire and publishing the news of restoration of the Cádiz Constitution, in June 1820, was bound to rapidly further erode Spain's strategic position and bolster that of the republicans. It also meant the end of court aristocracy in Spanish South America, and the end of the Inquisition, the final suppression of its tribunals at Lima, Cartagena, and Mexico City. The struggle between royalism and republicanism continuing without pause since 1808 lapsed into an uneasy unofficial truce, formalized by treaty in November.[144] A month later, Morillo embarked for Spain, never to return.

Negotiations with the constitutional government in Madrid followed, during 1821. From that moment Spain's position in the New World swiftly disintegrated while Bolívar strove to consolidate his huge republic of Gran Colombia (comprising modern Colombia, Venezuela, Panama, and Ecuador). More and more, he demanded a relentlessly centralized, enduring, authoritarian structure, and began exhibiting the Napoleonist tendencies that appalled Rocafuerte and became his undoing, though certainly they had their benevolent side. While only a few blacks, escaped slaves, or freemen ever joined his campaigns in Colombia, Venezuela, Ecuador, and Peru, and

[142] Rocafuerte, *Ensayo Político*, 6–7, 36; Rodríguez, "Cultura política clerical," 305; Krauze, *Redeemers*, 26–7.
[143] Barlow, *Two Letters to the Citizens*, 80.
[144] Breña, *Primer liberalismo español*, 44–5; Rodríguez, "Cultura política clerical," 304–5.

despite the hostility of most landowners, and the antipathy to his policies among Southern Congressmen in the United States, he kept his promise to Pétion and the Haitians, constantly insisting on universal and equal rights and, where possible, freeing the slaves.[145]

Bolívar's negotiators in Spain were authorized to swap Panama or Quito for full recognition but on no account to concede any constitutional arrangement or ties linking Spain to the main body of Gran Colombia. Full independence was his *sine qua non*. Elections to choose deputies for the Cortes in Spain proceeded in royalist and some other areas including Ecuador and parts of Venezuela; but already by April 1821 the armistice with Spain broke down. The Patriots captured Coro in early June. On 24 June 1821, Bolívar won the battle of Carabobo, the encounter that finally broke the royal presence in Venezuela, leading to the fall of Caracas, and the end of the war in northern South America. A month later a victorious San Martín, leading a motley army of half-castes, blacks, and foreigners, gained the upper hand also in central Peru, occupying Lima, though few Peruvian whites joined the independence movement as yet and many strongpoints in the viceroyalty, including Spain's great coastal stronghold at Callao, remained in royalist hands for several more years.

As part of his scheme to eclipse San Martin as chief Liberator of Spanish America, Bolívar aspired to join at least Quito and Guayaquil to his Gran Colombia. San Martín was no intellectual or constitutional theorist in the manner of Bolívar or Rocafuerte. Nor was he a sworn republican in principle like Bolívar, Rocafuerte, Roscio, or Nariño but flexible in his principles. His military triumphs were spectacular, though, and as the now renowned Liberator of Argentina, Chile, and Peru, it appeared he would soon also free Upper Peru (Bolivia) and Ecuador. A race commenced at this point to prize Quito from royalist hands with both republican armies facing stubborn resistance. By the spring of 1822, Bolívar and his able subordinate, Sucre, had the upper hand in Ecuador but had also thoroughly alienated San Martín, who was outraged on learning Bolívar planned to absorb Ecuador too into Gran Colombia. Quito fell to Sucre in May 1822; Bolívar made his triumphal entry into the city on 16 June, to the acclaim of the cheering masses.[146] By the time Bolívar and San Martín finally met, near Guayaquil in Ecuador, the latter was much the weaker party politically. Learning while at sea, sailing northward from Peru, that Quito province had now been formally annexed to Gran Colombia, a distraught San Martín at first refused to land. Three long private meetings finally took place between Bolívar and the liberator of Chile and Peru. The two great commanders profoundly disagreed on Ecuador's future, how to liberate Upper Peru (Bolivia), and over which political system was right for the future Peruvian state.

Courteous and diplomatic in their talks, Bolívar thoroughly scorned San Martín's views. By this time, San Martín found himself quite baffled by the political quagmire facing him in Peru, finding it impossible to reconcile the vying factions at Lima,

[145] Lombardi, *Decline and Abolition*, 42; Blanchard, *Slavery and Abolition*, 195–6.

[146] Arana, *Bolívar, American Liberator*, 286–7.

convene a congress, or formulate a constitution. He had delayed convening a Peruvian Congress, and presenting a constitution, it turned out, because, unlike Bolívar, Rocafuerte, and Roscio, he preferred a monarchical system in line with British and Holy Alliance wishes, and hoped to find a suitably qualified prince from Britain, Germany, or even Spain willing to accept the new Peruvian crown. Refusing to send any significant force into Peru to assist while San Martín remained at the helm, no sooner had the Argentine, his authority collapsing, given up his schemes for a Peruvian monarchy, and departed in despair, than Bolívar entered the scene, calling for Spain to be permanently ousted from all South America and Peru turned into a republic allied to Gran Colombia. But with the anti-Spanish factions fiercely divided—indeed on the verge of civil war—and royalists still strongly entrenched at many points, Bolívar's scheme faced innumerable difficulties.[147] Sucre was sent ahead to assume command of the "Peruvian" army (actually more Chilean, Argentine, and Colombian than Peruvian), but he too was unable to subdue the chaotic situation. In June 1823, a 9,000-strong royalist army recaptured Lima, forcing Sucre and Peru's makeshift Congress to withdrew to Callao. Not until August would the Colombian Congress in Bogotá authorize their president, Bolívar, to lead their army from Ecuador into Peru. He recaptured Lima only to lose it again, together with Callao, in February 1824. Greatly helped though he was by the revolution in Spain and the split on the royalist side resulting from the French invasion of Spain and brief Spanish civil war of 1823, Bolívar only slowly gained the upper hand in Peru.

Fernando's crushing the constitutionalists in Spain with Louis XVIII's help, fortunately for Bolívar, only deepened the split among the Peruvian royalists. Declaring himself sole true "defender of throne and altar" in all Peru, the Basque commander of Upper Peru (Bolivia), Pedro Antonio Olañeta (1770–1825), first repudiated the "liberal" viceroy, De la Serna, and then in January 1824 initiated full-scale civil war among the royalists, pitting Upper Peru's "throne and altar" bloc against constitutionalist Lower Peru. After De La Serna inadvisably sent most of the royal army to fight in Bolivia, Bolívar staged yet another epic march over the Andes, once more stretching his men to the limit, culminating in his triumph at the battle of Junen (6 August 1824), the capture of Cuzco, and then finally the securing of Lima. The remaining task of defeating royalism in southern Peru the *Libertador* left to Sucre, whose victory over the royalists at Ayacucho (9 December 1824), between Cuzco and Lima, effectively ended the struggle in Lower Peru. The final stage of the epic South American struggle was the fight for Upper Peru, which ended in April 1825. All that remained in Spanish hands, after that, was the fortress of Callao, which finally surrendered to Bolívar's men on 22 January 1826.

Sucre summoned a constituent assembly to gather on 8 July 1825 in Chuquisaca (formerly Charcas, today Sucre), where he proclaimed the independence of Upper Peru, naming the new republic Bolivia after the *Libertador*, and offered its presidency

[147] Lynch, *Simon Bolívar*, 188–92; Breña, *Primer liberalismo español*, 448.

to Bolívar, who was then traversing southern Peru and who readily accepted, aiming to use his second presidency to reconcile the warring factions "with impartiality."[148] Peru too offered him their "presidency for life" but that office he refused. From Cuzco he proceeded slowly southwards, bringing with him his mobile library of works of his favorite enlighteners, Helvétius, Montesquieu, Filangieri, Sismondi, and Bentham. Bolívar then embarked on a celebratory tour of the new republic lasting many months, visiting in turn La Paz, Potosí, and Chuquisaca while, as "president," devising a revised version of his model South American constitution to fit Bolivia. Again, he combined guaranteeing freedoms and emancipation of the slaves with a strong presidency for life, which he hoped would be the model adopted in Peru and Ecuador too.[149]

A powerful executive Bolívar deemed necessary not as a permanent republican fixture but provisionally, being convinced, much like Diderot and Raynal, that Spanish America was culturally and intellectually chronically backward compared to Europe.[150] His network of republics, which he proposed calling the "Federation of the Andes," he wanted to stretch from Panama to Potosí with each republic possessing its own constitution and legislature but with the whole federation linked together by a common president and army, and common basic laws and principles capable of transcending local divisions. This wider union would be a loose confederacy, with federalism as such strictly avoided within each of the constituent republics. Addressing Bolivia's constituent assembly, Bolívar urged in addition that the future constitution should exclude religious authority and ceremonies from any public role, or association with the state, since religion should remain a purely private affair. The state should simply guarantee freedom of religion and freedom of thought without associating itself with any creed.

Enlightenment political theory down to Bentham was the essential backcloth. Among recent political theorists, Bolívar had long admired the utilitarian philosophy and political thought of Bentham, as well as Helvétius and d'Holbach, and sought to apply the French and the British philosophic radicals' wholly secularist principles while at the same time seeking to avoid, as far as possible, antagonizing the prelates. His private view, he assured close confidants, was that their "credulity and ignorance makes the [Catholic] Christians into idolators," but this was a strictly personal matter which should not obtrude into the public realm.[151] Helvétius and Bentham had both shown how the monarchical–ecclesiastical–noble framework of the past must be replaced by a republican morality of equality enthroning the good of the entire community as society's chief political goal. In August 1825, praising Bolívar's achievements and recalling their meeting in his London garden, in 1810, Bentham himself

[148] Bolívar, *Obras Completas* ii. 246–7.
[149] Bolívar, *Obras Completas* i. 214 and iii. 763–9; Isabella, *Risorgimento*, 47.
[150] Stuurman, "Diderot en Raynal. Verlichtingsvisies," 114–15.
[151] Bolívar, *Obras Completas* iii. 769; Dávila, *Bolívar y Spinoza*, 113–15.

wrote encouragingly, enclosing additional copies of several of his books, including his *Constitutional Code*.[152]

From 1819 to 1830, presiding over the huge, short-lived Gran Colombia, Bolívar nurtured his grandiose republican vision, seeking to forge a highly centralized authoritarian structure. It was not his intention to be either the ally or guardian but rather the tamer of Spanish America's proud landowning elites. Bolívar was not a man of family or class, indeed never showed any interest whatever in his estates, or amassing personal wealth, or family schemes.[153] As Spanish American society matured and became readier for the full responsibilities of republicanism, the world without, informed by Von Humboldt, would increasingly come to appreciate a continent that would one day emerge from its age-old fragility and become strong, vigorous, and uplifting. His prophetic stance, ambition, and Napoleonist tendencies unquestionably had their benevolent side. He fulfilled his promise to appoint some black officers to the Gran Colombian army, but antipathy to this feature, and the dread of *pardocracia* it aroused, only further added to the growing opposition within the white elite that he already faced.[154]

Bolívar, while debating constitutional arrangements for Bolivia and Peru, also planned a grand conference of all the Spanish American republics to gather at Panama, to agree on the principles and inaugurate his confederacy of the Andes. This Congress of Panama needed in his view to be a purely Spanish American convention committed to republicanism and equality of races that should gather and confer without Brazil, then officially still an empire, and without the United States, which maintained racial subordination and slavery. He wanted it to convene too without Haiti, which was not ethnically "mixed," in his particular sense, but rather defined itself as purely a black republic, which he felt would not be a helpful influence.[155] Opponents in Bogotá arranged for the United States and Brazil to be invited nevertheless, albeit neither wished to attend. Nor did Argentina or Chile, while Bolivia's delegation failed to arrive in time. The grand event Bolívar planned as the culmination of Spanish America's liberation, and his republican crusade, intended to fill the Franciscan friary where the congress was planned with groundbreaking debate and republican theory lasting for months, broke up in complete failure, after only three weeks (22 June–15 July 1826), in July 1826, a terrible disappointment to the *Libertador*.

Still more disillusioning was the deteriorating situation in Gran Colombia and Bolívar's loss of leverage in Peru, where the local white elite increasingly rejected him and his egalitarian policies. In Peru, his constitutional arrangements collapsed within months. He left the central Andes forever on 3 September 1826, returning, via

[152] Lynch, *Simon Bolívar*, 244–5.

[153] Bolívar, *Obras Completas* i. 23; Brading, *Classical Republicanism*, 13–15; Dávila, *Bolívar y Spinoza*, 101, 108.

[154] Lombardi, *Decline and Abolition*, 42; Blanchard, *Slavery and Abolition*, 195–6; Oostindie, *Ethnicity*, 63–4.

[155] Oostindie, *Ethnicity*, 62–3.

Guayaquil, to Bogotá in November 1826. His return, though, also proved discouraging as it rapidly emerged that the Colombian elite felt little sympathy for his constitutional principles, vision of Gran Colombia, or aspirations for a grand South American federation. The problem was that Colombia remained as deeply divided between warring factions as ever. In July 1824, the Colombian Congress had removed his exceptional powers in their own domain, leaving Bolívar, who planned to unite as much of Hispanic America as possible under his personal leadership, in a peculiarly ambiguous position. Part of the Congress wanted Colombia to become a single republic under its former federal constitution of 1815 with a notably weak executive, while Bolívar's burgeoning world renown, and the triumphant end of the conflict with Spain, kept his standing at a level that made it hard for his foes in Bogotá to displace him from the public arena as they aspired to do. By way of compromise, the Congress renewed his presidency with more limited powers.

If he was to save the union with Venezuela, where Bogotá's ascendancy was resented, Bolívar had to act quickly. Staging a magnificent triumphal entry into Caracas on 12 January 1827, he stayed for some months trying to iron out innumerable problems. But while preoccupied with Venezuela his standing in Colombia, Ecuador, and Peru eroded further. To reassert his authority, he sailed to Cartagena, gathered an army, and advanced on Bogotá, which he entered on 10 September 1827, peremptorily demanding that Congress provisionally confer on him absolute power to resolve the Republic's formidable difficulties. They complied but also voted for a Grand National Convention to revise Colombia's constitution, to convene in February 1828, at Ocaña. With his foes spreading rumors that he was planning to crown himself "king" of Colombia, Bolívar deliberately refrained from attending the congress, preferring to stay at a location ninety miles away, from where he communicated with O'Leary, and made it clear to the Convention, that he considered the republic to be in an unacceptably disorderly and chaotic state, that Colombia must remain a republic but become one with a stronger executive.[156] But his staying away left the fight between supporters and opponents unresolved, reducing the entire event to stalemate. While his supporters wanted the union conserved with a strong centralizing executive, his rapidly proliferating opponents, the Colombian federalists, demanded decentralization and reversion to a weak executive.

When, eventually, the constitutional convention broke up in deadlock, in June, its rulings were formally rejected by the Bogotá city government, which gathered the signatures of all the city's notables and petitioned Bolívar to return to the capital and accept absolute power in the Republic. He readily accepted, re-entering Bogotá to the general acclaim of the populace.[157] This caused the opposition to resort to conspiracy, culminating in some kind of attempted coup on 25 September 1828 which was forcefully suppressed. Aware that the students and professors of Bogotá's newly reformed university were spearheading the "republican" opposition against him,

[156] Bolívar, *El Libertador*, 88–94; Van der Veen, *Groot Nederland*, 84.
[157] Lynch, *Simon Bolívar*, 232–9.

Bolívar at this point decided to revise the University curriculum especially as regards teaching political thought. Gran Colombia by 1828 was engulfed in ideological warfare, one strand of which, suddenly, was a quarrel over the appropriateness of Bentham's ideas. Recent experience and his difficulties with students and professors caused Bolívar to revise his judgment about Bentham, with whom he had still been on good terms in early 1827. On 10 March 1828 he issued orders forbidding the teaching in "any of the universities of Colombia of Bentham's treaties on legislation."[158]

During the last two years of his life, 1828–30, Bolívar shifted to—and proclaimed theoretically—an expanded, more authoritarian, and seemingly Napoleonist vision of presidential power which considerably damaged his image both locally and internationally. Many former admirers, Bentham, Rocafuerte, and most noteworthy Italian republicans living in exile outside Italy, apart from Angeloni, now came to regard him as an unwelcome Caesarian figure, a power-hungry hypocrite, betraying the republican ideal he had once so passionately avowed.[159] Meanwhile, he also became increasingly sick with the tuberculosis that was soon to kill him, causing loss of much of his formerly renowned energy and powers of concentration.

Yet despite his now tarnished reputation and final failure, there are grounds for arguing that Bolívar acted as he did in his final phase not in despicable emulation of monarchy, as many charged, but to defend authentic republican ideals against the curse of faction and grasping local elites.[160] Here again, one discerns perhaps the pervasive significance for him of a Spinozist conception of a collective "conatus," an equalizing "common good" seeking the best possible political frame for sustaining individual rights and freedoms as determined not by votes but by situation, stage of development, and reason. Finally, he had to accept his failure, dying in a mood of profound pessimism, blaming three vast unconquerable foes—ignorance, ecclesiastical authority, and the power of local elites—for undermining and destroying his vision and the authentic "General Will" of the people, to the permanent loss of all Spanish America.[161] In the last weeks of his life he felt a particular bitterness at what he saw as the ingratitude of the Venezuelan Congress, which effectively debarred him from returning to his own country during his dying days. He expired at a country retreat near Cartagena.

The gloomy assessments of Jefferson, Adams, Madison, Monroe, Blanco White, and finally Bolívar himself, in his "Message" to the Ocaña Convention, proved all too accurate. Dogged resolve and Bolívar's incomparable military skills, together with the triumphs of the joint Argentine–Chilean forces in Peru, eventually did free Spanish America from Spain but failed to establish viable and stable republican institutions. Ecclesiastical power was curbed, the Inquisition eradicated, and an even greater scourge of humanity, black slavery, curtailed, though it was not finally abolished in

[158] Bolívar, *El Libertador*, 214–15; Rojas, *Ideas educativas*, 120–2.
[159] Rojas, *Ideas educativas*, 122–3; Isabella, *Risorgimento*, 59.
[160] Lynch, *Simon Bolívar*, 239.
[161] Dávila, *Bolívar y Spinoza*, 69, 73, 93, 113.

Bolivia until 1831, Colombia (and Panama) in 1851,[162] Venezuela in 1854, and Peru in 1855. Mexico, Colombia, Venezuela, and the other new republics acquired splendid constitutions on paper but exhibited precious little genuine republican liberty or freedom of expression in practice. Gran Colombia, observed President John Quincy Adams in May 1823, had a constitution "almost identical with our own."[163] Yet, it was a kind of mirage, altogether unable, like the other republics, to effectively consolidate its declared liberties.

During the mid-nineteenth century, as the Enlightenment increasingly faded, Bolívar's reputation receded and, in some quarters, disparagement of his life and legacy escalated. Karl Marx denounced many rulers and public figures, but few great men were so pilloried by him as Bolívar, about whom he wrote an article for a New York encyclopedia published in 1858, projecting him as the "most dastardly, most miserable and meanest of blackguards," a figure of no positive significance for humanity.[164] The most talented and determined of all the South American revolutionaries though he was, Bolívar left no lasting democratic or equal rights constitutional political legacy of any substance. Among the saddest shades surrounding the legacies of once venerated great men are the perverse distortions subsequent regimes introduce to manipulate the public veneration surrounding them. "Bolivarianism" remains a considerable force today in Spanish America, but there is little agreement as to what exactly it signifies.

[162] Oostindie, *Ethnicity*, 60–2.

[163] Quoted in Johnson, "United States–British Rivalry," 346.

[164] Krauze, *Redeemers*, 464.

29

Marx and the Left's Turn from Radical Enlightenment to Socialism (1838–1848)

Engels, Plekhanov, and other founders of Marxology, and the Marxist view of the history of Marxism, identified Spinoza as a key precursor of Marx, a philosopher persuaded the world must be interpreted purely in this-worldly terms, that all reality is governed by a single set of rules, that there are no supernatural realities or forces, no miracles or revelation, and thus no theology. In 1982, the great French Marxist thinker, Louis Althusser, traced the history of Western materialism as a line running from Epicurus and Lucretius via Machiavelli, Spinoza, Hobbes, and Rousseau to Marx, progressively demolishing metaphysics as traditionally understood and hence all teleology and divine intervention.[1]

According to this perspective, Spinoza foreshadowed Marxism by reforming philosophy itself on a basis of "materialism," a secular modernity anchored in a wholly immanent world-view. Since all reality is and can be no other than this-worldly and nothing exists outside or beyond it, all understanding, values, morality, and grounded significance is identifiable and defined by the same single, universal, and coherent set of natural laws. There is and can be no meaningful or justifiable religious authority or religious education. Yet Karl Marx (1818–83) himself, in 1844, in his *Holy Family* and again early in 1846, in the *German Ideology*, disdainfully dismissed Spinoza not as any kind of precursor but merely another of the seventeenth-century's "metaphysicians" rendered irrelevant by eighteenth-century French materialism.[2]

If there is reason to be cautious concerning how Marx positioned himself in the mid-1840s, arguably Plekhanov too was being somewhat misleading, oversimplifying considerably, in presenting Spinoza as Marxism's direct precursor. Certainly, this claim was powerfully reiterated, among other occasions in a lecture by A. M. Deborin marking the 250th anniversary of Spinoza's death, at the Communist Academy in Moscow, in February 1927, subsequently published in German at Vienna in the

[1] Morfino, *Temps de la multitude*, 167.

[2] Giancotti Boscherini, "Matérialisme chez Spinoza," 187–8; Terpstra, "Spinoza en de anti-naturalistische filosofie," 1–2; Tatián, *Spinoza. Filosofía terrena*, 143.

collection, *Spinozas Stellung in der Vorgeschichte des Dialektischen Materialismus* [Spinoza's Place in the Pre-history of Dialectical Materialism]: "in all Plekhanov's works," claimed Deborin, "there evidently runs like a red thread the foundational thought that Marxism, as a world-view, is nothing other than a kind of Spinozism" [*Art Spinozismus*].[3] Correctly identifying and characterizing the relationship of Marx to Spinoza, and Marxism to Spinozism, requires more than just a few words, or an easy formula, and, as we shall see, matters considerably for grasping key developments in early nineteenth-century intellectual, ideological, and general history.

At the point the young Marx attended university, in Berlin, the Western Enlightenment was decidedly faltering. Prussia's post-1815 monarchy undoubtedly prolonged and to a degree promoted late court Enlightenment, partly via educational reform and conserving features of the Napoleonic system, and partly through vigorous steps to weaken the Catholic church in large parts of north-west Germany annexed to Prussia in 1814–15 by the Congress Powers. The post-1806 reforming faction in the Prussian government—Hardenberg, Stein, and Wilhelm Von Humboldt—viewed their grand project of state revival as one of rationalizing the Prussian state and its laws, furthering education and elevating the population and, especially in Von Humboldt's case, furthering the "ennoblement of mankind" generally.[4] By 1850, Prussia had a literacy rate of approximately 85 per cent of the population, as against 61 per cent for France and 52 per cent for England.[5] If not the first modern state to proclaim education and adequate literacy a generalized enlightened goal—that was revolutionary France—Prussia was certainly the first to render the project of educating its entire population a social and cultural reality, in this respect going well beyond contemporary France or Britain, and by so doing potentially opening up to all classes many of the then still novel social, economic, and political complexities of modernity.

Prussia pushed literacy, education, and potential access to the Enlightenment further, to a wider spectrum of society, than was seen anywhere else in the early nineteenth century apart from the Netherlands. The first large state successfully to impose compulsory elementary education, by 1848 Prussia had no less than 29,000 teachers trained in forty-two pedagogical institutes, boasting a schools system far in advance, as Engels observed, of the restricted, class-based school system at the time still operative in Britain. Numbers of university students per thousand of population in Prussia, as in Germany generally, likewise rose higher than elsewhere.[6] Still more important for propagating reforming ideas and in some quarters revolutionary fervor and comprehensive opposition to government and officialdom, down to the revolutionary upheavals of 1848 and after, these teachers were both more highly trained and

[3] Thalheimer ansd Deborin, *Spinoza's Stellung*, 41; Moreau, "Reception du spinozisme," 248.
[4] Levinger, *Enlightened Nationalism*, 45–6.
[5] Barkin, "Social Control and the Volksschule," 50.
[6] Barkin, "Social Control and the Volksschule," 32, 41–2.

tended to be more independent, critical, and dissident in outlook than teachers in Britain, France, or America.[7]

Prussia's court-directed official late Enlightenment had as its primary goal achieving a better organized and more efficient, harmonious, and unified society and body politic.[8] Yet, paradoxically, it was precisely the continuing Enlightenment impetus behind Prussia's expanding education, universities, libraries, and press during the early nineteenth century that accounts for the unprecedented intensity and focus of Prussia's campaign of repression during this period with its focus on the educational sector. By creating a new dialectical tension in German society simultaneously fomenting spread of radical ideas, and efforts to counter their propagation, it spurred the further growth of the Radical Enlightenment tendency. A key social as well as intellectual stimulus prodding the aggressive, uncompromising oppositional attitude of the new generation of young philosophers emerging in the wake of Hegel, the "Young Hegelians," was their newly widened access to academic careers as doctoral candidates and lecturers at the new Prussian universities and elsewhere, followed by finding themselves officially blocked from proceeding on academic and other respected career paths due to their being drawn to freethinking and atheistic philosophical tendencies. Official exclusion from academic careers, the fate of every one of the Young Hegelians,[9] guaranteed lifelong social marginalization and resentment which in turn further stiffened their long-term oppositional stance toward state and church. This did not necessarily produce rejection of all religious authority linked to democratizing republicanism, but where it did, as with the young Karl Marx until 1844—that is, in Marx before "Marxism"—the result was—albeit in his particular case notably temporary, and short-lived (1837–44)—vigorous adherence to Radical Enlightenment as a tradition of thought and criticism.

Born at Trier, on the extreme western edge of Germany, on 5 May 1818, Marx descended from a long line of rabbis on both sides. In 1824, his father, Herschel Mordechai Marx (1777–1838), son of a local rabbi but an Enlightenment zealot and admirer of Voltaire and Lessing, who had earlier converted to Lutheranism, arranged for his 6-year-old son likewise to be baptized into the Lutheran church. Thoroughly schooled in the state system, from the age of 17 onwards the young Marx studied successively at the universities of Bonn and Berlin, where "I broke off all the connections I had hitherto contracted, made rare and reluctant visits, and tried to steep myself in learning and art;" before long, he also abandoned his original vocational orientation, the law, to devote himself wholeheartedly to his new intellectual passion, "philosophy."[10] Hardly surprisingly, the young Marx's unstinting embrace of "philosophy" rapidly developed into simultaneous revolt against, and profound psychological alienation from, both Jews and Judaism *and* Christians and Christianity.

[7] Nipperdey, *Germany*, 230–6; Barkin, "Social Control and the Volksschule," 42.

[8] Levinger, *Enlightened Nationalism*, 48–9. [9] Sperber, *Karl Marx*, 64, 69–70, 73–5.

[10] Marx to Heinrich Marx, 10 Nov. 1837, in Marx, *Early Texts*, 2, 7–8; Berlin, *Karl Marx*, 69.

After first embracing "Idealism," joining the following of Kant and Fichte, Marx turned to the writings of Hegel. Joining the Young Hegelian stream, *Neuhegelianismus*, at Berlin, Marx's principal mentor (and soon close friend), the figure under whom he chiefly worked during his key early intellectually formative phase (1839–41), was an exceptionally divisive and controversial young professor, Bruno Bauer (1809–82). Earlier associated with theology and the "Right Hegelians" aiming to reconcile Hegel with "Christian" values and religion, Bauer had changed course in 1838, the same year Feuerbach published his *Pierre Bayle*, the book immediately preceding his materialist critique of Hegelianism (1839). Performing a dramatic volte-face, Bauer now opted for the radical tendency in religion and politics.[11] With his *Kritische Darstellung des Alten Testaments* (1838), a work explaining all the biblical "miracles" in naturalistic terms wholly banishing the supernatural, Bauer joined Feuerbach in publicly denying Christianity, thereby abandoning all prospect of remaining socially respectable—already three years before Feuerbach published his most notorious work *Das Wesen des Christentums* (1841). Bauer broke with Hegel, Christianity, established academe (and before long the Prussian state), making full use of his famously incisive, polemical writing style. Briefly, he assumed a position of leadership among the "Young Hegelians," becoming chief initiator of their common further radicalization.

Derided in respectable circles as the "Messiah of Atheism" in texts such as his banned article *Das entdeckte Christentum* (1843), Bauer condemned Christianity outright as a denial of human freedom and reason while rejecting deism as a "foggy morning" and eulogizing the "atheistic Enlightenment" defined as the unification of Spinozism with Voltaireanism.[12] As a public foe of Christianity and churchmen Bauer was surpassed, in the public eye, by Feuerbach and by David Friedrich Strauss (1808–74), whose *Das Leben Jesu* (1835–8) firmly separated, in a way much criticized by Bauer, the historical Jesus from what Strauss considered the largely mythical "Jesus" fabricated by early Christians to fit their highly contrived conception of his theological significance.[13] But in radical circles Bauer surpassed Feuerbach and Strauss in bringing out the social and political implications of rejection of religious authority and presenting "atheistic Enlightenment" as a historical and living intellectual tradition.

Like Bauer and other aspiring young philosophers at the time, for several years Marx greatly venerated Hegel, a philosopher who claimed to be fulfilling and transcending Spinoza's philosophy but who did not publicly detach nature, politics, and the course of history from "Christian" values and theology in the way, according to the Young Hegelians, he did, or virtually did, in private conversation—as Spinoza had, and Bauer, Feuerbach, Strauss, Stirner, and others, including Moses Hess, now did. Nor, since the great turn in German thought around 1800, did Hegel any longer preach systematic opposition to the monarchical state. However, like Bauer and the

[11] Bensussan, "Feuerbach et le 'secret'," 115. [12] Bauer, *Christianity Exposed*, 1–6.
[13] Rotenstreich, "For and Against Emancipation," 11.

other Young Hegelians, Marx believed Hegel was more subversive of religion and conventional attitudes in reality than appeared on the surface, a contention grounded by invoking the "esoteric" Hegel who allegedly often contradicted the exoteric Hegel.[14] All the same, theology and Christian values were, if only in the haziest fashion, kept on board by Hegel and he had continued to affirm the ultimate superiority of monarchy, aristocracy, and Christianity over democratic republicanism and irreligion. This entirely failed to satisfy the young Marx.

In Marx's intellectual development, importantly, anti-Scripturalism and rejection of all theology clearly preceded his short-lived emphatic democratism, and both his anti-theology and democratism clearly preceded, and for a time presided over, his developing outlook as a whole, unaccompanied prior to 1844 by the slightest hint of socialism or interest in class-struggle. The concept of the "proletariat" so central in Marx's mature theory of society is mentioned for the first time—and then used, very differently from later, to mean dissolution of classes into a union of thought and action—only in 1843.[15] Critique of organized religion, miracles, and especially religious authority, steeped in Bauer's post-1838 and Feuerbach's vehement anti-theologism and anti-Hegelianism, remained the main thrust in Marx's thought for some years before becoming linked to a particular notion of "democracy" which he shared with Bauer and Feuerbach but less so with the others. This sequence of stages is of crucial importance because this pre-1844 linkage, fundamental and passionate in Marx until he reached his own great intellectual turning-point, in the mid-1840s, was a political tendency rarely evinced so emphatically by other Young Hegelians.

In short, for five to six years Marx adhered in a more conspicuous and uncompromising fashion than most to a classic Radical Enlightenment trajectory prior to sharply swerving away toward economic theory, socialism, and communism. Socialism he converted to only in 1844, "the year in which German socialism was born," as it has been put,[16] partly owing to his friendship and soon close collaboration with Friedrich Engels (1820–95), whom he encountered for the first time in November 1842, and partly also to Moses Hess and socialist circles he encountered in Paris. Earlier, Marx passed through successive intellectual stages, but his entire development from 1838 to 1844 was that of a late Enlightenment radical with what later emerged as "Marxism" being then so remote on the horizon as to be totally invisible. Only from 1844, when he first began studying economic theory,[17] did he defect from and abandon classic Radical Enlightenment, defined as democratic republicanism joined to rejecting religious authority, forming a (mostly non-violent) revolutionary thrust principally geared to changing how men think.

Marx's doctoral dissertation, written under Bauer's supervision, deals with post-Aristotelian Hellenistic philosophy and its relation to Aristotelianism, especially Bauer's favorite Greek thinker, Epicurus, viewed by them both as an epoch-making

[14] David McLellan, "Introduction" to Marx, *Early Texts*, p. xiii.
[15] Haubtmann, *Proudhon*, 41. [16] Stedman Jones, *Karl Marx*, 208.
[17] Tiran, "Jean-Baptiste Say," 586.

figure in mankind's early intellectual self-emancipation. During 1838–41, Marx the doctoral student filled whole notebooks with jottings from readings around Epicurus and Epicureanism, and came to think of Epicurus as "der grösste Griechische Aufklärer" [greatest Greek enlightener].[18] By 1838, the *annus mirabilis* of both Bauer and Feuerbach, the project unfolding in Marx's mind centered on the total severance of philosophy and everything meaningful from theology and the outright repudiation of religion. By 1839, prodded by Bauer, it seemed bizarre to the young Marx that anyone should think there exists a meaningful analogy between Socrates and Christ. "If there is an analogy between Socrates and Christ, this could only be in this sense that Socrates is philosophy embodied while Christ is religion personified."[19] "As long as a single drop of blood pulses in her world-conquering and totally free heart," affirms Marx in his thesis, concurring with Bauer and Feuerbach, "philosophy will continually hurl the cry of Epicurus at her opponents: the profane man is not the one destroying the gods of the multitude but the one who foists the multitude's doctrines onto the gods."[20]

Marx's doctoral thesis, presented and examined at the University of Jena in April 1841, was a project motivated by intense youthful philosophical zeal but also the practical goal of eventually securing, with Bauer's assistance, a Prussian university teaching post. In particular, Marx hoped to relocate to Bonn, from where Bauer, who had now been obliged to leave Berlin and take up a professorial post there, continued directing his studies by letter.[21] While preparing for the oral encounter forming part of the doctoral examination, Marx had heeded Bauer's advice that on these occasions, the discussion turns "principally and regularly around Aristotle, Spinoza and Leibniz" so that tactically immersing himself in those thinkers would strengthen his hand.[22] This is presumably why, only shortly after entering the world of Young Hegelianism, Marx read and extensively annotated Spinoza's *Theological-Political Treatise* and his letters, compiling a montage of sections filling a whole notebook with extracts and quotes lending a particular emphasis that seems to have played a significant formative role in his subsequent intellectual development.

At the same time, he took to studying the atheist and materialist d'Holbach. The order of Marx's notes on Spinoza and d'Holbach, and conspicuous lack of interest in Spinoza's *Ethics*, confirm that he became a radical atheist and foe of metaphysics first, in 1838–41, and only afterwards became a radical democrat due to working out the results of the earlier phase, with both early shifts occurring some years before he began studying economic theory or made any move toward becoming a Marxist.[23]

[18] Tortarolo, "Epicurus and Diderot," 385.

[19] Quoted in Rubel, "Marx à la recontre de Spinoza," 10.

[20] Marx, *Early Texts*, 13; Lecompte, *Marx et le baron d'Holbach*, 149, 151–2; Hull, "Marx's Anomalous Reading," 19, 28; Sperber, *Karl Marx*, 65–8.

[21] Rubel, "Marx à la recontre de Spinoza," 8; David McLellan, "Introduction" to Marx, *Early Texts*, p. xiii.

[22] Rubel, "Marx à la recontre de Spinoza," 8.

[23] Igoin, "De l'ellipse," 216; Lecompte, *Marx et le baron d'Holbach*, 158–60.

Prior to linking materialism, naturalism, and rejection of Christianity to democracy in the highly significant way he did in 1841–3, Marx's study of Spinoza and d'Holbach, and gathering of extracts from their texts, set the scene for his democratic republican phase. One strand of this, his notes clearly show, was a focus on Spinoza's idea, revived by Mendelssohn in his *Jerusalem*, that the Mosaic state, unlike the Christian state, required only obedience to laws governing outward conduct for the common good, not dogmata or beliefs. This lent the Mosaic state in the thought world of the pre-Marxist Marx a valuable, special status.

Encountering Spinoza partly in deference to Bauer, and assuredly never with the passionate zeal for the *Ethics* exhibited soon afterwards by his English female near-contemporary George Eliot (1819–80), Marx filled a whole notebook with extracts. Filling thirty-eight pages, amounting to 160 extracts in all, drawn from the 1802 Jena Latin edition of the *Tractatus Theologico-Politicus* edited by H. E. G. Paulus, Marx selected and notably reordered especially quotes pertaining to miracles, and the nature of biblical prophecy and politics, assembling these with another sixty extracts taken from the 1841–2 Berlin edition of Spinoza's letters.[24] His careful selection and reordering illustrates a powerful predisposition to view the course of history as the only divine providence there is and history itself, like Spinoza, Hegel, Bauer, Heine, and Hess, as the only meaningful definition of God's will. Since "God or nature" fixed the laws of nature and the course of history, either there are no sins and no evil, or else, as Marx expressed it, annotating Spinoza's letter of January 1665 to Willem Blyenburgh, "vel nulla dari peccata, nullumve malum, vel Deum ea peccata atque illud malum efficere" [or God Himself is author of sin and evil].[25]

Several scholars have noted the strikingly conspicuous reluctance of nearly all scholars of modern thought, Marxist and non-Marxist alike, to consider the intimate link between Spinoza and Marx during the early stages of the latter's intellectual development, particularly during 1841–3. Here is a topic philosophers evidently prefer to ignore. Isaiah Berlin, in his 1939 biography of Marx, subsequently revised several times, makes no mention of Spinoza. Even in France and Italy, where a rigorous "Spinozist Marxism" later arose, impelled especially by Louis Althusser (1918–90) and Antonio Negri—the former a powerful critic of the orthodox Marxism of his day whose lingering influence has been especially marked in Latin America from the late 1960s onwards and, in whose eyes, Spinoza engineered the crucial philosophical "revolution" in the history of philosophy on which Marx subsequently built—little effort was made, as one scholar expressed it, "to relate Spinoza and Marx to one another in a direct, explicit and sustained manner."[26] But given that Marx was a vehement radical democrat and atheist undeniably almost totally uninterested in

[24] Reproduced in *Cahiers Spinoza* 1, ed. A. Igoin, A. Lecrivain, Alexandre Matheron, Pierre-François Moreau, and M. Schneider (Paris, 1977), 31–157; see also Rubel, "Marx à la recontre de Spinoza," 13–14.

[25] Marx, "Trois Cahiers," 98–9; see Spinoza, *Letters*, 132.

[26] Tosel, *Spinoza, ou l'autre (in)finitude*, 131; Casarino, "Marx before Spinoza," 180, 219; Terpstra, Spinoza en de anti-naturalistische filosofie," 5–6.

economic history, the proletariat, and class warfare for approximately six years before his conversion to socialism, this avoidance and non-focus is not just bizarre but distinctly misleading. Obviously, Marx's prior commitment to Radical Enlightenment must be examined and related to his subsequent conversion to socialism, while the entrenched aversion of Marxology, and the scholarly world more generally, to addressing Marx's early engagement with Spinoza and the radical tendency needs to be recognized as itself a significant quirk of modern intellectual history.

Marx's choice of extracts from the *Tractatus Theologico-Politicus*, it is worth noting, dramatically changes the order and simplifies the logic of Spinoza's argument, rearranging Spinoza into what at the time represented, for Marx, a kind of secular personal "Bible." Focusing on chapters VI (on Miracles), XIV (on faith), and XV on the relationship of reason and theology, he worked his way from demolishing Revelation and all theology to drawing the consequences for social criticism, politics, and law. His very first quote is taken from Spinoza's paragraph 233: "et ex nulla re clarius existentiam Dei probari posse existimat [vulgus], quam ex eo, quod natura, ut putant, suuum ordinem non servet" [the multitude supposes the existence of God is proven by nothing more clearly than what they perceive as nature failing to follow its normal course].[27] Already for Marx then, as for Bauer and Feuerbach, God and religion in every traditional sense, including Hegel's conception of the "Christian" monarchy, was devoid of all validity. Divine governance of the world, for Marx as Spinoza, signified "fixum illum et immutabililem naturae ordinem, sive rerum naturalium concatenationem" [that fixed and immutable order of nature, or interconnection of natural things].[28]

Marx's early thought, shaped by Bauer and Feuerbach, was in a sense a variant of Spinozist materialism, naturalism, anti-providentialism, and anti-Scripturalism which, before long, became dramatically infused with zeal for democratic transformation. During this formative early period, until 1844, Spinoza helped organize and define not only Marx's general outlook and moral thought but also his political stance, his self-awareness as an active, committed democratic republican revolutionary.[29] Moving in logical steps, savoring the universal determinism he found in Spinoza's Latin, Marx cheerfully set about hacking down "monarchy" and the system of princes, and aristocracy.[30] Strikingly, his early conception of democracy was one of conserving collective "natural right," with the consequence that the more any given state conserves that "right" the more it conforms to democracy and nature, is stable and resolves friction and inner contradictions; correspondingly, the less it conserves that right and is hierarchical the more it is oppressive and despotic. Whether he "owed" this to his own insight while merely finding confirmation in Spinoza, or was indebted for his early combined philosophical–political democratic stance more specifically

[27] Spinoza, *Theological-Political Treatise*, 81; Spinoza, *Opera* iii. 81.
[28] Marx, "Trois Cahiers," 86–7. [29] Dobbs-Weinstein, *Spinoza's Critique of Religion*, 68.
[30] Tosel, "Pour une étude systématique," 129–30; Rubel, "Marx à la recontre de Spinoza," 12.

and directly to Spinoza (even if guided by Bauer, Feuerbach, Hegel and Hess), remains unclear, and perhaps hardly matters.

Marx's stance, in any case, was essentially Spinozistic and directly linked to his rejecting Hegel's claims to have transcended and completed Spinoza's philosophy by joining divine providence to the course of history conceived as the course of nature. He shared Feuerbach's view that Hegel represented the final guise of "theology" and very likely Feuerbach's conclusion that full separation of philosophy from theology, and its purification, incomplete and insufficient in Hegel, had already been equally incomplete and impure in Spinoza, whose failure to complete the "revolution" in thought that he had embarked on marked the starting-point not just of modern materialism but, equally, of the impurity and deviations from reality of German Idealism.[31] In short, between 1839 and 1844 Marx held to a broader, more genuine allegiance to Spinozist democratic radicalism, combining political radicalism with full rejection of religious authority, than any of his philosophical predecessors or associates—Hegel, Fichte, Schelling, Hess, or Bauer—and adhered to this striking stance at a time when there existed, as yet, no hint of his subsequent plunge into economics, the ideology of class-warfare and the world of communism.

Wielding Spinoza in one hand and his critique of Hegelianism in the other, by 1841 the young Marx was already making a name for himself in German radical circles. At this time viewed as the public ally of Bauer, an academic rebel and leading younger member of an angry and burgeoning young Prussian fraternity, he seemed almost terrifying to some, herald of a militantly anti-theological new species of philosophical "Montagne."[32] Among those impressed was Moses Hess (1812–75), who, in September 1841, wrote about him to his friend Berthold (Moses Baruch) Auerbach (1812–82), a German Jewish author estranged from Judaism less due to his university studies at Tübingen, Munich, and Heidelberg than to reading Spinoza, and whose novelistic biography, *Spinoza* (1837), and German edition of Spinoza's texts, did more at this time to familiarize the public and intelligentsia with the figure of Spinoza, and popularize his image, than any other single effort. Auerbach devoted far more passion, time, and energy to reviving Spinozism than Marx, Heine, or Hess, but was less willing to see Spinoza as a total foe of religion and outright revolutionary. He was at one, though, with Heine and Marx in refusing Hegel's notion of Christianity as a higher stage of spirituality superseding Judaism, and at this stage shared also Heine's aversion to the vehement *Antijudaismus* articulated by Hess and Bauer (and before long also Marx). At the same time, Auerbach rebuked Heine for seeking to found a new philosophical quasi-religion in place of Judaism.[33] For Auerbach, Spinoza led the way from the ghetto into a partly secular, multi-faith modernity where the Jew could integrate while adhering to his own religious traditions and identity.

"Dr. Marx, as my new idol is called," reported Hess to Auerbach, in September 1841, at a time when he too was immersing himself in the "new German philosophy"

[31] Bensussan, "Feuerbach et le 'secret'," 120–1. [32] Ruge, *Briefwechsel* i. 239.
[33] Rose, *German Question, Jewish Question*, 226; Schwartz, *First Modern Jew*, 56–7.

of the Young Hegelians, "is still a very young man (at the most around twenty-four years old)." But it was he "who will give medieval religion and politics the last push, as he combines a cutting wit with the deepest philosophical seriousness; imagine Rousseau, Voltaire, Holbach, Lessing, Heine and Hegel united in one person—I mean 'united' and not blended—then you have Dr. Marx."[34] Precisely these characteristics, however, obviated whatever prospect of a university career the fiery young philosophical convert had set out with. Completing his studies, Marx discovered, to his disgust, that even being a long-converted "Lutheran," unsympathetic to his Jewish origins, in post-1815 Restoration Germany left all paths to a university career closed to him, due chiefly to his undisguised radicalism. Needing an alternative career, he entered the tumultuous world of opposition journalism while privately continuing his studies, and remaining as unremittingly subversive as ever, but as yet entirely in the Radical Enlightenment sense without the slightest hint of faith in the primacy of the economic or involvement in class-warfare.

During 1841, transferring to Bonn, briefly, to be near Bauer and relying still on his guidance, Marx collaborated with him on the latter's projected journal, the *Atheistic Archives* that never appeared, and his book, the *Last Trump over Hegel, the Antichrist*, written provocatively as if by a devout Pietist, alerting co-religionists to the atheistic menace concealed behind Hegel's apparently innocent verbiage. Marx failed to get his sections ready in time, however, and Bauer, losing patience, went ahead and published without his input, one of several episodes at this juncture causing some cooling of their originally amiable collaboration. Bauer, in any case, was dismissed from his university post by the Prussian authorities in March 1842, for religious and political subversion, a development that definitively ended Marx's hopes of life in academe.[35] Hurling his energy into journalism, he showed his mettle early on, later in 1842 becoming chief editor of a new paper in Cologne (until banned by the Prussian government in early 1843), the *Rheinische Zeitung*. Here, he collaborated with several allies, notably Hess, who had founded the paper and who attended the weekly editorial meetings and first acquainted Marx with another editor, Engels. A fervent socialist averse to Proudhon and some other strands of French socialism, Hess soon also found himself increasingly out of step with Marx and other (predominantly Young Hegelian) contributors at that stage still detached from and to a degree averse to socialism (as well as Hess's mystical idealism). Having been turned down for editorship of the paper in favor of Marx, who at that time was considered less openly radical, as well as uncontaminated by socialist tendencies, by the autumn of 1842 Hess, vigorously parading his communist ideology, grew increasingly alienated from his own creation.[36]

[34] Hess, *Briefwechsel*, 79–80. Hess to B. Auerbach, Cologne, 2 Sept. 1841; Berlin, *Karl Marx*, 67; Marcuse, "Heine and Marx," 112.

[35] Berlin, *Karl Marx*, 69, 72; Lecompte, *Marx et le baron d'Holbach*, 161; Sperber, *Karl Marx*, 73–5.

[36] Na'aman, *Emanzipation und Messianismus*, 115–16; Kouvelakis, *Philosophy and Revolution*, 130; Evans, "Marx and the *Rheinische Zeitung*," 2–3.

During his brief editorship of the *Rheinische Zeitung*, Dr Marx was unmistakably an avowed "atheist," foe of monarchy, and revolutionary activist, and already a kind of philosophical guru exerting a considerable impact on those he met. A leading figure in radical circles, he was not, though, at this stage, even a neophyte in the spheres of socialism and economic theory, towards which for the time being he remained both distant and mildly hostile rather than neutral.[37] Like Hess, Börne, and his future associate, Heine, Marx passionately rejected and deeply abhorred every strand, legal, doctrinal, and institutional, of Restoration "Christian" Germany's princes, courts, aristocracy, police forces, and ecclesiastical authorities, and, becoming averse also to Hegel, was beginning to assume his lifelong favorable view of the French, the Enlightenment, and accomplishments of the French Revolution. But while emphatically a radical democrat and revolutionary who already believed Germany ripe for Revolution in 1842–3, he still viewed "philosophy," changing men's ideas, radical thought, not social and economic forces, as the agent of revolutionary change. In short, until 1844, by which time he had reached the age of 26, Marx was a classic adherent of the "Radical Enlightenment" and not in any respect a socialist.

Eager to promote anti-Catholic sentiment in the heavily Catholic environment of Cologne and the Rhineland, one main path along which the Prussian crown sought to utilize the late Enlightenment, the authorities initially proved relatively lenient regarding Hess's and Marx's violently anti-clerical paper.[38] Marx's strategy (with which Hess disagreed) was to exploit this elbow-room by masking somewhat the paper's political and social radicalism while concentrating on assailing churchmen and religious authority. Marx's first article for the *Rheinische Zeitung*, published in July 1842, was a scathing assault on a reactionary rival paper, the *Kölnische Zeitung*, for its attacks on Young Hegelians and the anti-Christian tendency of the "new philosophical school," which it denounced as treason against philosophical reason itself. "Of course, from the beginning you only recognize as scholarly research what is merely your way of looking at things, it is easy for you to prophesy; but how," retorted Marx, "is your affirmation more valid than that of the Indian Brahmin who proves the Vedas' sanctity by reserving to himself alone the right to read them!" What sense did it make to call the secularized post-1815 Prussian monarchy of 1840 a Christian or "religious state"? His obscurantist adversaries had forgotten the existing Prussian civil code was fashioned by philosophy, not religion, just as the Code Napoleon was fashioned "not from the Old Testament but the ideas of Voltaire, Rousseau, Condorcet, Mirabeau, Montesquieu and the French Revolution. Ignorance is a demon; it is to be feared it will yet play many a tragedy."[39]

Marx's pre-1844 radicalism, then, combined rejection of Christianity and Judaism with a fierce general critique of organized religion along lines expounded by Bauer, Feuerbach, Hess, and other Young Hegelians with an initially less fervent rejection of monarchy, a stance he shared with Bauer, Feuerbach, and Arnold Ruge (1802–80)

[37] Hess, *Briefwechsel*, 80; Silberner, "Moses Hess als Begründer," 24; Lundgren, *Moses Hess*, 28–30.
[38] Silberner, "Moses Hess als Begründer," 19–20. [39] Marx, *Early Texts*, 39, 42.

among leading Young Hegelians at that time but not with the rest. "The monarchical principle in general," he agreed with Ruge, writing from Cologne in March 1843, "is the despised, despicable, dehumanized man; and Montesquieu was quite wrong to allege that it is honor. He gets out of the difficulty by distinguishing between monarchy, despotism, and tyranny. But these are names for one and the same concept, and at most denote differences in customs, though the principle remains the same." Catholic and Protestant obscurantism and the ignorance of the masses, held Marx at this time, constituted the great barrier to the coming revolution. But 1842, as it happened, proved a crucial year in central Europe for the revolutionary underground's evolution following publication, at Leipzig, of Lorens Stein's widely-read *Der Sozialismus und Kommunismus*, presenting these as a wholly new and disturbing social movement. The German public and Prussian authorities for the first time took serious note of socialism and communism and began sounding the alarm bells internationally.[40]

Marx at this juncture embraced the idea that democracy is the primal and also the most natural, comprehensive, and ubiquitously relevant form of state however much generally submerged by oppression monarchical, aristocratic, and ecclesiastical. It was the democratic republic, he insisted, that is the original and most "natural" form, as Spinoza and Paine argued before him, and the form, as Spinoza explains in one of the *Tractatus Theologico-Politicus* passages Marx had extracted and annotated in 1841, that "accords the maximum of individual liberty to all men."[41] "All other constructions of the state are a certain, definite, and particular form of the state. In democracy alone the formal principle is at the same time the material principle." Here Marx deliberately opposed Hegel, who assigns this role to modern monarchy shorn of feudalism, especially Prussia's monarchy. Only democracy, in Marx's pre-1844 view, united the universal and the particular in politics, resolving all contradictions; monarchy, despite Hegel's claims, was a truncated variant buttressed by false theological dogmata.[42]

At this stage in his development, Marx also borrowed from Spinoza directly or indirectly and shared with Bauer and Feuerbach a deep preoccupation with the idea that organized religion is in its essence an imposed political ideology designed to promote submission and obedience that functions by deluding believers into beliefs which it is contrary to their own interest to adopt.[43] Both Spinoza and the pre-Marxist Marx maintain in classic Radical Enlightenment fashion that organized "priestcraft" is indispensable to despotism and inherently the enemy of the majority despite, paradoxically, being adhered to fervently by the majority. It was more to Spinoza's system, then, than Hegel's that the pre-Marxist Marx owed his political

[40] Na'aman, *Emanzipation und Messianismus*, 115.
[41] Marx, "Trois Cahiers," 60–1; Urbinati, *Representative Democracy*, 174, 279 n. 42.
[42] Marx, *Early Texts*, 64–7; Tosel, "Pour une étude systématique," 130; Hull, "Marx's Anomalous Reading," 21–2.
[43] Hull, "Marx's Anomalous Reading," 22.

framework—his insistence that morality and religion are wholly separate, that the laws of nature govern everything so that "natural right" governs not only the behavior of individuals but the formation of the state, and the idea that the more that state conserves the "natural right" of the masses, the more it is "democratic," serving its primal function and beneficial. In fact, none of the other Young Hegelians so boldly reworked and reaffirmed Spinoza's principle that "democracy is the truth of democracy; monarchy is not the truth of democracy," as Marx himself expressed it, meaning monarchy is ultimately just democracy perverted and betrayed, democracy inconsistent with itself.[44] "It goes without saying," noted Marx, in 1843, reaffirming this profoundly unHobbesian, Spinozist insight foreign also to Kant and Hegel, "that all forms of state have democracy for their truth and that they are untrue insofar as they are not democracy."[45]

The young Karl Marx looked forward keenly to the democratic revolution, the resumption of the Great French Revolution which he, like Hess, was convinced was gradually reviving. All monarchs and monarchists he deemed fundamentally opposed to Germany's new "idealists who want only the consequences of the French Revolution and, therefore, in the final count, always a republic and an organization of free human beings instead of the system of dead objects." But he was convinced too that the coming upheaval would be wholly useless if not based on a new general consciousness, a fundamentally new way of thinking arising from oppressed humanity's having long and carefully taken stock of its situation and become enlightened. Authentic political revolution occurs only when man's self-confidence, when human freedom, is "aroused again in the hearts of these people. Only this feeling that vanished from the world with the Greeks, disappearing under Christianity into the blue mist of the heavens, can again transform society into a community of human beings united for their highest aims, into a democratic state."[46]

Rather ironically, given his subsequent embrace of the proletariat from December 1843, during the years 1838–43, while intensely preoccupied with Hegel, Bauer, Epicurus, Spinoza, and d'Holbach, Marx evidently harbored an almost contemptuous view of the masses and distinctly shared Spinoza's, Toland's, d'Holbach's, Shelley's and John Stuart Mill's dread of the active ignorance of the unschooled multitude. From Holland, in March 1843, he assured Ruge, whom he had met the previous year and with whom he agreed on plans for a future working relationship, that in the Netherlands the standing of the "Prussian despotism" (which had forced Ruge to leave Prussia and move to Dresden) had sunk rather low. Free men outside Germany invoking the "impending revolution" to which he eagerly looked forward, even the dull Dutch, considered the despotic Prussian monarchy altogether abysmal; happily,

[44] Igoin, "De l'ellipse," 216; Dobbs-Weinstein, *Spinoza's Critique of Religion*, 67; Tosel, *Spinoza, ou l'autre (in)finitude*, 133–4.

[45] Igoin, "De l'ellipse," 225–6; Dobbs-Weinstein, *Spinoza's Critique of Religion*, 67; Kouvelakis, *Philosophy and Revolution*, 304.

[46] Marx to Ruge, undated, Cologne, May 1843, Marx Engels Internet Archive, Letters Archive, *Deutsch-Französischer Jahrbücher*, 1843.

such international "shame is actually the victory of the French Revolution over the German patriotism that defeated it in 1813," though unfortunately "in Germany, even shame is not yet felt; on the contrary, these miserable people are still patriots."[47]

The pre-Marxist Dr. Marx judged the democratic republic the fittest mechanism for resolving social contradictions, raising men to their highest level of fulfillment, and ensuring the state eschews policies and laws serving vested minority interests, like those of kings, aristocracy, and clergy exploiting the majority. Pursuit of the "general will" based on the democratic republic protecting the people from the influence of particular interests remained a pronounced feature of Marx's Radical Enlightenment phase and was not a trait he was likely to have derived from Hegel, Bauer, Hess, or Feuerbach, or even Rousseau. Hence, restoring proper emphasis to what one scholar termed "the occluded relation between Spinoza and Marx" helps here by revealing that Marx's notes, rearranging the order of ideas he extracted from Spinoza's *Theological-Political Treatise*, look uncannily like the source of his early political orientation and "source of [Marx's] radical critique of Hegel and the left Hegelians."[48] Admittedly, Marx's estrangement from Hegel was not straightforward and rooted in various impulses, including the influence of Hess; but Hess too, during the years 1841–3 when collaborating with Marx, oriented himself chiefly by Spinoza rather than any other thinker—though, ironically, Hess was less strongly drawn than "Marx before Marxism" to Spinoza's democratic theory.

A text composed in the weeks from March to August 1843, Marx's *Zur Kritik der Hegelschen Rechtsphilosophie*, the same as that in which he first discusses the "proletariat," marks a key transition in the evolution of his early thought. Borrowing from Feuerbach and Hess, Marx here rebukes Hegel for compromising with "Christian values, monarchy and aristocracy," and joins Hess in declaring that Christianity and Bauer's version of radicalism both revolutionize men on an excessively individual basis, producing a secularized version of Christian salvation in terms of individual re-education rather than collective social transformation. Bauer's radical Enlightenment, he thought, lacked the democratic republican dimension. While he refers to "the proletariat," stressing the need for collective as opposed to individual salvation, for the moment Marx still remained firmly within the Radical Enlightenment rather than socialist fold: it is still collective "enlightenment," the march of progress guided by *Philosophismus*, and not faith in the primacy of the economic, that is the principal source of our awareness and knowledge of reality, and chief mechanism of revolutionary change. Realities of class were not yet a significant factor: "today when theology itself has foundered," asserts his *Einleitung* (published in February 1844), the most unfree thing in German history, our status quo, will be shattered by philosophy." "Just as philosophy finds its material weapons in the proletariat, so the

[47] Marx to Ruge, undated, Mar. 1843, Marx Engels Internet Archive, Letters Archive, *Deutsch-Französischer Jahrbücher*, 1843.

[48] Dobbs-Weinstein, *Spinoza's Critique of Religion*, 68; Igoin, "De l'ellipse de la théorie," 215–16; Matheron, "*Traité Theologico-Politique* vu," 160, 212.

proletariat finds its spiritual weapons in philosophy; and once the lightning of thought has struck deeply into this naïve soil of the people, the emancipation of the Germans into men will be accomplished."[49] He went on to explain that the "emancipation of Germany is the emancipation of man. The head of this emancipation is philosophy, its heart is the proletariat. Philosophy cannot realize itself without transcending the proletariat, the proletariat cannot transcend itself without realizing philosophy. When all interior conditions are fulfilled, the day of German resurrection will be heralded by the crowing of the Gallic cock."[50]

Marx's thought in 1843 and early 1844 remained essentially democratic, undogmatic, and republican. In *Zur Kritik*, Marx identifies not just absolute monarchy but likewise constitutional monarchy and the British "mixed government" model as the primal foe of both intelligentsia and common people, "a hybrid," he assured Ruge, in March 1843, "which from beginning to end contradicts and abolishes itself." For the Marx of 1841–3 "democracy is the solution to the riddle of every constitution. In it we find the constitution founded on its true ground—real human beings and the real people."[51] Convinced democracy means more than a form of state, Marx defines it, rather, as the essence of politics, the ultimate triumph of the general will: "monarchy is necessarily democracy in contradiction to itself whereas the monarchical moment is no moment, is no contradiction within democracy. Monarchy cannot, while democracy can, be understood in terms of itself, and while "democracy is content and form; monarchy should be only form, but adulterates the content."[52] Here once again he unfolds a characteristically Spinozist stance, following his 1841 Spinoza extracts, projecting the idea that the collective good is the highest law and that God or Nature rules over men most crucially through political sovereigns, rather than religious authority. Nor did Marx ignore another key Spinozist topos—the claim that morality and religion are entirely separate and that the only religious doctrines possessing true moral validity are justice and charity, which must both become detached and embodied in state policies and laws.

Where, for Hess, love of truth, justice, and charity remained the core of Spinoza's living message to men, and his personal guideline for decades, in Marx this feature remained less prominent throughout his early 1840s phase, but by no means entirely absent.[53] "The specifically Christian law-giver cannot recognize morality as a sphere sacred in itself and independent," averred Marx in an article "by a Rhinelander" in February 1842, banned in Germany, eventually published by Ruge at Zurich in 1843, "for he appropriates its inner universal essence for religion. Independent morality violates the universal bases of religion, and the particular concepts of religion are contrary to morality. Morality knows only its own universal and rational religion, and religion only its particular positive morality." Hence the new wave of press censorship

[49] Marx, *Critique of Hegel's "Philosophy of Right,"* 138, 142. [50] Marx, *Early Texts*, 128–9.
[51] Kouvelakis, *Philosophy and Revolution*, 273–85; Rose, *Jewish Philosophical Politics*, 155.
[52] Marx, *Critique of Hegel's "Philosophy of Right,"* 29.
[53] Matheron, "*Traité Theologico-Politique* vu," 182–3.

proclaimed in Germany in the name of Christian piety and authority "must reject the intellectual heroes of morality—Kant, Fichte, Spinoza, for example—as irreligious and violating discipline, morals and exterior responsibility. For these moralists start from a contradiction in principle between morality and religion, for morality is based on the autonomy of the human mind whereas religion is based on its heteronomy [i.e. subjection to others]."[54]

It was not long before even the massaged visage of Marx's radical paper became unacceptable to the Prussian government. By late 1842, losing patience, several German courts together began harassing all publications emanating from Left, democratic republican, and Young Hegelian circles, with much of German society enthusiastically supporting the crackdown. "It is impossible for me to write under Prussian censorship," exclaimed Marx, writing to Ruge from Cologne, "or live in Prussian air." The famous *Leipziger Allgemeine Zeitung* was closed by the Saxon government in December 1842; Marx's and Hess's *Rheinische Zeitung* ceased publication, under official pressure, in March 1843. Suppression of the radical press, stepped up without any real sign of protest from the reading public, meant the end not only of Marx's career in democratic republican journalism, in Germany, but a decisive setback to hopes, not least Marx's own expectations, of mobilizing the reading public behind the republican democratic cause.[55] Left Hegelian journalism no more offered a serious career prospect within Germany than the academic path. During the months of his chief editorship of the *Rheinische Zeitung*, Marx adhered consistently to the Radical Enlightenment general stance he embraced between 1838 and 1844, and it was this creed that forced his exile from Germany, in November 1843.

At the point Marx ceased publishing the *Rheinische Zeitung*, he had just been asked by the "president of the Israelites here" to support the local Jewish communities' petition to the regional provincial assembly "on behalf of the Jews." Somewhat half-heartedly, Marx agreed, "although I find the Israelite faith repugnant; yet Bauer's opinions [his viewing Christianity as a higher form of consciousness than Judaism, and Jewish rights as an irrelevant "particularist" reform] seem to me too abstract." Marx supported Jewish emancipation at this time perhaps only because he considered rising Jewish resentment useful to the Revolution (which Bauer did not) and because he believed it necessary to punch as many holes in the Christian state as possible and "smuggle in the rational as far as we can. At least it must be attempted—and the embitterment [of the Jews] grows with every petition that is rejected."[56] Despite contemptuously rejecting Judaism as a system of belief, and identifying Jews above all with the money system, Marx played his own small part in the fight for Jewish emancipation, expressing support for equal Jewish rights and at Paris, in 1844, in the

[54] Marx, "Remarks on the Latest Prussian Instruction on the Censorship." in Marx, *Early Texts*, 29–30; Rubel, "Marx à la recontre de Spinoza," 15.

[55] Stedman Jones, *Karl Marx*, 208.

[56] Marx to Ruge, Cologne, 13 Mar. 1843. Marx Engels Internet Archive, Letters Archive, *Deutsch-Französischer Jahrbücher*, 1843; Marx, *Early Texts*, 60; Evans, "Marx and the *Rheinische Zeitung*," 9.

Deutsch-französischer Jahrbücher, rebuking Bauer for an anti-Semitism fiercer and more systematic than even his own.[57]

In Marx's *Rheinische Zeitung* articles readers found as much emphasis as in Bauer on the role of ideas in shaping the course of history and the human condition, and the need to change minds, hearts, and human consciousness in order to lift humanity from our existing world of misery, slavery, and oppression to a better one. Estranged from Bauer personally from 1842, Marx was also now beginning to learn something about the world of socialism and communism from Hess. But during 1842–3, apart from a new stress on society rather than liberation of the individual, he was not yet shifting toward socialism or communism as such but rather toward a closer alliance with Ruge and Germany's and Switzerland's democratic radicals.[58] Bauer, too, still a leader of the radical opposition and the revolutionary movement in Germany, continued to exhibit (apart from his vehement anti-Semitism) the distinctive features of the Radical Enlightenment stance. Only later did he more broadly repudiate democratic values. For the pre-1848 Bauer, ameliorating society still meant above all changing the people's consciousness through spreading radical ideas. Increasingly abandoned by his former radical following, Bauer subsequently during the 1850s developed very differently, reverting back to a right-wing, anti-religious stance steeped in a supposedly secularizing anti-Semitism that began assuming a markedly racist character.[59]

Philosophisme the pre-1848 Bauer still considered the principal revolutionary agent, and his estranged former disciple Marx, for the moment, took a similar view. In classic Radical Enlightenment fashion, linking their systematic attack on religious authority and theology to democratic republicanism, Bauer identified Robespierre (like all radical enlighteners) as the supreme, contemporary outright enemy of the Enlightenment, highlighting not just the Terror and Robespierre's crimes but, equally, the *robespierriste* reaction against *philosophisme*, atheism, and cosmopolitanism. By December 1792, contended Bauer, Robespierre had fully set his face against the "correct" revolution that he should have promoted, betraying the great Revolution in particular by failing to enthrone "*Philosophismus* in the place of [mere] political revolution."[60] Marx meanwhile rebuked Bauer less for his *Antijudaismus*, to which he had no great objection,[61] than for staying too abstract and intellectual, too narrow in approach, focusing excessively on "political emancipation" and the individual when he should seek, in a fuller, more comprehensive way, collective "human emancipation" under the state. Hess had earlier criticized Bauer for precisely these tendencies. In *Die letzten Philosophen*, a critique of Bauer published in 1843, Hess classified Bauer and Stirner as essentially secularized "Christian philosophers," who were too abstract,

[57] Avineri, "Marx and Jewish Emancipation," 445–50; Levin, *Jewish Socialist Movements*, 104.
[58] Evans, "Marx and the *Rheinische Zeitung*," 2–3, 24–5; Sperber, *Karl Marx*, 134, 140.
[59] Rotenstreich, "For and Against Emancipation," 32–4.
[60] Bauer, *Geschichte der Politik, Cultur und Aufklärung* i. 233–7.
[61] Wistrich, "Socialism and Judeophobia," 118–19.

too concerned with reducing human individuals to intellectual atoms with no real social binding, turning them into secularized Christian "souls" without realizing it; both were insufficiently rooted in social reality. Preoccupied with emancipating and secularizing the human individual, most Young Hegelians seemed unconcerned with transforming the community, with society.

Marx during the last year or so of his career as a radical enlightener thus aligned with, indeed appears to have extensively borrowed from without acknowledging it, certain of the views of Hess and his circle, the group calling itself "True Socialism," especially when accusing Bauer of confusing general "human emancipation" with mere "political emancipation."[62] This social stress during 1843 was something new in Marx's work; he was beginning to emphasize the significance of the social whole. If for Marx prior to 1844, "philosophy" remained the primary agent for changing men's consciousness and ideas, the tool of actual legal, institutional, and social change remained the state, the instrument with which, as with Spinoza and Hegel earlier, the improved general legal, moral, and political freedom must be realized. It is the state that educates its members, declared Marx, in July 1842, "by converting the aim of the individual into general aims, crude instinct into moral inclination, natural independence into spiritual freedom, through the individual finding his good in the life of the whole and the whole in the frame of mind of the individual."[63] Even in 1843, then, there was little sign of Marx's pending defection from Radical Enlightenment to faith in the primacy of the economic and the creed of class-war, to an unalterable, inexorable, "scientific" materialist dialectic permitting no scope for doubt or disagreement.

Zur Kritik marks rather the culmination of Marx's "Spinozist" phase. But already here Marx contends that great revolutions require more than just *Philosophismus*, even if this is still what chiefly counts; they require also a "passive element, a material basis." While a radical enlightener could accept that "theory will be realized in a people only insofar as it is the realization of their needs," and endorse Marx's idea that "it is not enough that thought strive to actualize itself, actuality must itself strive toward thought," we do perhaps glimpse at least the first seeds of his later vision of human history as an inexorable material process, a dialectic of shifts in property and economic relations, and control of resources, interpreted in terms of class-struggle such as no radical enlightener could endorse. "The emancipation of Germany is the emancipation of man. The head of this emancipation is philosophy, its heart is the proletariat. Philosophy cannot be actualized without the abolition [*Aufhebung*] of the proletariat, the proletariat cannot be abolished without the actualization of philosophy."[64] Here, Marx was nearing rupture with the Radical Enlightenment, on the threshold of the break.

[62] Hull, "Marx's Anomalous Reading," 25; Rotenstreich, "For and Against Emancipation," 23–4.
[63] Evans, "Marx and the *Rheinische Zeitung*," 6.
[64] Marx, *Critique of Hegel's "Philosophy of Right,"* 142.

Marx moved to Paris from Cologne in October 1843, encountering a great city in ferment, not least among its astoundingly large community of German exiles, which had grown slowly under the Bourbon Restoration but rapidly since 1830, rising from around 7,000 in 1831 to no less than 59,000 by 1846, by when one in twenty of the French capital's inhabitants was a German ex-patriot.[65] Marx's "Marxism" first took root in this new milieu. No doubt his sudden discovery of proletarian misery and potential for revolution owed much to actually seeing a large impoverished pool of labor for the first time; but it was also due to meeting the French socialist intelligentsia, especially Proudhon, and exiled foreign intellectuals of every stripe. It was at the Café de la Regence, at the Place du Palais Royale, once frequented by Diderot, that he resumed contact with Engels, on 28 August 1844. They found themselves wholly agreeing regarding classical economics' faults and the inherent antagonism between capitalism and the working class. Starting from an atheism, materialism, and naturalism proximate to those of Bauer, Heine, and Hess, Marx, spurred by Engels, now suddenly plunged into reading economic theory and, before long, began identifying economic exploitation driven by class interest as the driving force of history and true cause of universal but avoidable misery and false consciousness—oppression cast off only by a revolution of social forces in which appropriation and confiscation assume vast proportions, a revolution rooted in and shaped by economic development and class-conflict.[66] The point of revolution now was to capture and transform the economic system. "Philosophy," from being the principal agent, now found itself relegated to superstructure and essentially irrelevant to the revolutionary process itself, even if still significant for learning the true nature of the human condition. With class war, proletarian capture of the economic system, now the chief engine of universal liberation; the Enlightenment's earlier overridingly decisive role was excised from the picture.

Furthermore, Marx's shift to economics and the concept of class-warfare, abandoning his earlier Spinozistic conception of "democracy" and stress on freedom of expression, went hand in hand with a growing dogmatism and fierce intolerance of those, like Bauer, and soon also Ruge, Heine, and Hess, dissenting from his newfound framework and analysis. Coinciding with his ideological turn, Marx broke with all those former friends and allies who refused to join his unabashed leap into a new and very different ideological world to that he had inhabited hitherto. Neither Hess nor Heine much influenced this fundamental shift in Marx's outlook, which derived chiefly from debate with French socialist leaders and Engels, except that the break between Marx and Ruge at this point did significantly parallel the simultaneous rupture, in 1844–5, between Hess and Auerbach, with the latter claiming it is not the masses, but more enlightened, better-educated elements in society who are the vehicle of history able to elevate society to superior status rooted in higher values. During 1844–5, Hess accused his famously gentle and withdrawn former comrade of

[65] Mansel, *Paris between Empires*, 389–90.
[66] Mansel, *Paris between Empires*, 390–1; Stedman Jones, *Karl Marx*, 161, 173–9.

living in a fairy-tale world of Spinozism and sympathy for the poor: by rejecting communism and socialism, Auerbach was opposing the *Erlösung der Menschheit* [redemption of mankind].[67]

Marx and Hess briefly converged at a superficial level, both embracing communism. By 1844, both deemed the Enlightenment to have failed and believed communism offered a path to transformation of the human condition that would render mankind happier by abolishing class-war, money, and private property. For Marx and Hess communism was no longer just a theory but a doctrine sanctioned by factual reality that all radicals were duty bound to endorse and support. Nevertheless, a wide gap opened between them. For Hess, human suffering and alienation are universal facts deriving from innate inadequacy, rather than the outcome of prevailing economic conditions, with the result that Hess nowhere attempts any truly searching economic analysis; to him, class warfare was not a meaningful doctrine and creating a better society remains essentially an ethical project. For Marx, who soon tired of Hess's moralistic approach and idealism, alienation was an affair of the proletariat increasingly strictly defined as an economic category.

Marx, Hess, and also Heine were all alive to the misery of the working poor and injustice of their plight. The Revolt of the Silesian Weavers, about which Heine wrote one of his most moving, socially engaged poems, "Die schlesischen Weber," occurred in 1844, the same year as his meeting Marx.[68] Shared rejection of the existing order, shared radicality of temperament, afforded some scope for a common revolutionary outlook, as did Heine's detestation of censorship and aristocracy and contempt for autocratic government as something rooted in ignorance, fear, and theological repression of the individual. But authentic emancipation with constructive results, for Heine, occurs by individual and collective revolt against oppression rooted in insight, understanding, and awareness, not revolt against a rigorously exploitative economic system by social forces.[69] In Paris, from 1844, the increasingly acrid and acerbic Dr. Marx, dropping all allegiance to the Enlightenment, became a different kind of thinker than previously, one that Heine, Hess, Brauer, and Ruge were soon to discover was not particularly amiable. Marx's private comments depict Heine as eloquent and discerning, but also a corrupt, timid, charmingly unreliable liar. While Marx poked jibes at Heine behind his back, Heine felt a growing antipathy to the "clenched fists," as he caricatured the Communists, with the unappealing "idea of absolute equality [. . .] that broods in their barbarous heads."[70]

Heine had earlier expressed his premonition of the pent-up force of proletarian frustration in his *Lutetia*, a collection of newspaper reports from the period 1840–3 for the *Augsburger Allgemeine Zeitung*, profiling the resentment that had "Communism" as its "secret name." He questioned its antagonism to the existing "bourgeois" order, and felt uneasy about Marx's prediction of future class war. "How will it end?

[67] Rose, *German Question, Jewish Question*, 234–5. [68] Marcuse, "Heine and Marx," 118.
[69] Sammons, *Heinrich Heine*, 262–3; Marcuse, "Heine and Marx," 116.
[70] Quoted in Marcuse, "Heine and Marx," 120–1; Berlin, *Karl Marx*, 97–8.

No one knows but gods and goddesses acquainted with the future."[71] Where Marx and Engels were to proclaim in their *Communist Manifesto*, in 1848, that "Communists everywhere support every revolutionary movement against the existing social and political order of things," Heine, much like his hero Spinoza, and Shelley and Bentham, believed mass participation in disorder, led by the ill-informed, must be the wrong way, that most revolts and revolutionary movements turn out to be disasters yielding only anarchic Montagnard devastation, vandalism, and bloodshed to no purpose.[72]

Steeped in Spinoza only a few years before, from 1844 Marx, most strikingly in his *The Holy Family*, his most extended attack on Bauer and the Young Hegelians, offered with it no small dose of veiled self-criticism.[73] Composed between September and November 1844, Spinoza he now classified, along with Descartes, Malebranche, and Leibniz, among the "metaphysicians" misleading and deluding mankind. Flat contrary to his stance earlier, and to later Marxology which again adopted a more positive view of Spinoza's thought, Marx abruptly repudiates him.[74] Spinoza's conflation of matter and thought, might be a form of materialism but he had refused to elevate thought over matter or matter over thought. For Spinoza, matter and thought remained two parallel and in status equal aspects of one and the same thing. In Hegel, by contrast, the "ultimate identity" of matter and thought is an idealism subordinating matter to thought via the dialectic of negation of the negation. Because one dimension is subordinated to the other while the two still converge into one, but now as the result of a dialectical process of negation producing negation, what in Spinoza is a relatively static state of nature, in Hegel more obviously forms a historical process. Young Hegelians, and henceforth Marx, retained this distinctive feature while reversing Hegel's order: thought now becomes the passive adjunct subordinate to matter. Hegel and Marx equally diverged, but in opposite directions, from the unifying equality of status Spinoza and Heine lent mind and matter, idea and object, thought and being.[75]

By 1845 Marx's rupture with Radical Enlightenment, what has been termed the "disjunction between Marx's initial, democratic and republican political goals and his further communist ones,"[76] was complete. Ruge reacted with increasing exasperation to Hess's secular communistic theology and Marx's burgeoning economic determinism. Seeing that socialism and communism represented a very different revolutionary tradition from that which he and his colleagues espoused, he henceforth viewed socialism as a form of "mystification," a disastrously wrong turn, bound to generate irresolvable disunity and strife between rival oppositional movements—as indeed

[71] Kouvelakis, *Philosophy and Revolution*, 83.
[72] Marx and Engels, *Communist Manifesto*, 65; Marcuse, "Heine and Marx," 124.
[73] Sperber, *Karl Marx*, 161–3.
[74] Lecompte, *Marx et le baron d'Holbach*, 172; Moreau, "Réception du spinozisme," 248.
[75] Tosel, *Spinoza, ou l'autre (in)finitude*, 129; Albiac, "Sujets déterminés," 105.
[76] Sperber, *Karl Marx*, 134.

it did.[77] To reduce man's significance to his economic role and circumstance struck Ruge as a betrayal of basic humanity as well as philosophy and the democratic republican tradition. Accordingly, he summoned the enlightened to fight communism with all possible vigor and rescue the "true" individual from the communists' "mystical, reactionary claws."[78] The meaningful "whole," he insisted, is not economic society but the democratic republic. As theorists and authors promoting what amounted to a kind of "religious sect," Ruge pronounced the *Kommunisten* worse than intellectually confused: they were perfidious intriguers and deceivers, promising an utterly false, impossible, and mystical new *evangelium* of economic happiness to the poor, a highly damaging doctrinal deviancy liable to ruin the fight for democracy, freedom, and enlightenment.[79] Here history would prove Ruge prescient.

What Marx retained from Hegel and the Young Hegelians, placing his mature thought on a quite different plane from Spinoza's anti-theological immanentism, then, was the concept of an irreversible, iron law of history inexorably pushing in a particular direction, an irreversible process whereby material forces occasion unremitting class-struggle in turn determining the vagaries and shifts of thought structures. If Europe's first wave of socialist theorists, Owen, Fourier, and Saint-Simon, derived their notions of community of goods, and other communitarian notions superseding the egoism underlying the moral theories of the democratic radicals, from distillations of Christianity, traditions of Christian Millenarianism and Radical Reformation, during the 1840s socialists equally still seemed to be forging a secularized "new religion."[80] Deluded and sidetracked, according to democratic radicals,[81] the socialists seemed set on fabricating a new obscurantist theology, that of "the proletariat," with quasi-priestly dogma and bitter internal disputation to go with it: Fourier, Proudhon, Blanc, Blanqui, Weitling, Marx, and the "artisan communists" were all at each others' throats; and along with their new theology arrived fresh forms of intolerance and dogmatism, with dissenters being formally excommunicated at solemn meetings. This new variety of inquisitorial procedure gained high visibility with the condemnation and expulsion from the communist movement of Wilhelm Weitling (1808–71), among Germany's leading early communists. In early adulthood a garment worker in Leipzig, Dresden, and Vienna, Weitling had acquired socialist leanings through reading and his activism from Paris street battles of the late 1830s. His first book, *Die Menschheit, wie sie ist und wie sie sein sollte* [Humanity as it is and should be], of 1838, combined pleas for ending outrageous wealth inequality with calls to revolutionary action and renewal of the (radical, democratic) *Aufklärung*. He urged jettisoning all former notions about politics and society in favor of a brotherhood of all men, and permanently erasing national and

[77] Ruge, *Polemische Briefe*, 390, 398, 412; Wende, *Radikalismus im Vormärz*, 127–8; Vaccaro, *Socialismo e umanesimo*, 274, 278–80.
[78] Ruge, *Polemische Briefe*, 374, 377.
[79] Ruge, *Polemische Briefe*, 412; Israel, "Poststructuralist and Postcolonial Criticism," 31–8.
[80] Claeys, "Early Socialism," 896, 900, 903.
[81] Albiac, "Sujets déterminés," 100–1.

religious divisions. Capital should be reorganized into public funds vested in national banks, operated solely for the benefit of families and society.

Partly inspired by Hess, Weitling ardently admired Babeuf and Buonarotti, and was actually the first in Europe or America to fuse a clear communist vision with summoning mass revolutionary action.[82] Tried and imprisoned in Zurich for sedition and blasphemy in 1845 (depicting Jesus as a communist and as Mary's illegitimate son), and deported from Switzerland, Weitling transferred to Paris, where he gained prominence in the socialist movement there.[83] But at a meeting of the Brussels *Kommunistischen Korrespondenzkommitee*, in March 1846, with Marx presiding, he found himself arraigned as part of a campaign to eradicate two condemned heresies from the communist movement—non-Marxist "artisan communism" and incorrect "philosophische Kommunismus."[84] Such dogmatism, doctrinal manipulation, and power-seeking, placing Marx and Engels at the head of the budding communist movement in Germany and neighboring lands, thoroughly shocked Hess. By 1845, Marx had broken with Bauer, Ruge, Weitling, and Hess, as well as Heine. Scornful of Hess, unforgiving toward Weitling, who, in late 1847, transferred to New York, where he gained a renewed reputation among the German immigrants pouring into the United States at that point and where he at once began organizing workers' associations (as well as introducing improvements to sewing machines), Marx developed a quite irrational hatred of Ruge.[85] Even after Weitling settled permanently in New York, the battle between him and Marx dragged interminably on.

Hess broke with Marx and his budding Marxist movement during 1846. In the *Communist Manifesto* written in December 1847 and January 1848, during the early stages of the 1848 revolutions, Marx and Engels publicly denounced Hess's communism, dismissing his group's idealistic "true socialism" and "philosophy of action" as philosophical nonsense derived from misunderstood French sources, a tool of reactionary interests, and "robe of speculative cobwebs, embroidered with flowers of rhetoric."[86] By then Hess was retreating from his earlier activism, Marx having wholly eclipsed him, Weitling, and all the rest as a communist theoretician and leader. "Communism is already acknowledged by all European Powers," announced Marx and Engels, in the *Communist Manifesto* in 1848, "to be itself a Power;"[87] yes indeed, and they might have added, but did not, that theirs was a displacing power wresting democratic republicanism's former oppositional leadership role from its hands. Communism became a "power" under the direction of Marx. Even so, it would be hard to claim Marx ever matched Hess's passion for human dignity, truth, freedom, and justice, or the insights of the radical enlighteners from whom Marx so abruptly broke away. Among his characteristic innovations as a social theorist, noted Marx, in

[82] Haubtmann, *Proudhon*, 444–5. [83] Haubtmann, *Proudhon*, 632, 637.

[84] Hess, *Briefwechsel*, 150–1. Weitling to Hess, Brussels, 31 Mar. 1846; Sperber, *Karl Marx*, 178–81; Stedman Jones, *Karl Marx*, 212–16.

[85] Weiss, *Moses Hess*, 72–6; Stedman Jones, *Karl Marx*, 334, 343.

[86] Marx and Engels, *Communist Manifesto*, 59; Heller, *Moses Hess*, 18, 21; Berlin, *Karl Marx*, 136–7.

[87] Marx and Engels, *Communist Manifesto*, 33.

a letter of 1852, was the idea that class-struggle "necessarily leads to the dictatorship of the proletariat" and that this "dictatorship" is the tool that will bring about the justice and happiness promised by his "classless society."[88] In its conflictual agenda, authoritarianism, and displacement of the intellectual process of enlightening, it was a concept remote indeed from the Radical Enlightenment.

These developments permanently blighted toleration and free criticism in Marxist circles, quashing Marx's own earlier teaching on liberty of expression. In lending socialism an ultimately ethical motivation, Hess undoubtedly remained closer to Spinoza, at least in that respect. Where Marx distanced himself from the radical camp, forging a dogmatic, unalterable Marxist ideological and economic logic,[89] Hess's socialism, not unconnected with his break with Marx, remained a moral idealism.[90] By pushing determinism and materialism to the point that individual understanding of the world, individual agency, and moral responsibility are all curtailed, Marx did indeed create a new international movement, and an irreversible divergence from radical thought. If Spinoza and Marx were agreed in affirming that religious authority does not exist, Marx had always largely ignored, despite its sporadic presence in his extracts from Spinoza, Spinoza's view that true "religion" and piety nevertheless do exist.[91] This was not a lesson Hess ever forgot. The essential difference between "religion" based on "charity and justice" and "superstition," held Spinoza in a letter to Oldenburg annotated by Marx, and implying that no revealed religion is a "religion" in his sense, is that "haec ignorantiam, illa autem sapientiam pro fundamento habeat"—that the latter has ignorance, the former wisdom for its basis.[92]

Attempts to reform Marxist theory in France in the 1960s and 1970s, later influential in Latin America too, featured a sustained call, associated in particular with Louis Althusser,[93] to use Spinoza's philosophy as the necessary correcting tool to fight the dogmatic straitjacket and moral negativism of Marxist doctrine, stripping away Marx's own theological fixity and post-Hegelian metaphysics while reinforcing the plea for freedom to philosophize, and freedom in the social sciences generally. Hegel, Marx, Hess, and Spinoza were all searching for a higher state, the optimal condition of man, and the underlying logic of things that transforms the picture. Spinoza (followed here by Hess) championed "compatibilism," arguing that our being determined by the force of nature does not mean lack of freedom to align with necessary truths, to choose between "religion" and "impiety," wisdom and ignorance, the common good and purely selfish options.[94] In re-routing materialism by integrating it with a modified Hegelian dialectic and class-warfare, argued Althusser, Marx avoided both mechanistic notions of causality and an organicist model, instead

[88] Marx to Weydemeyer, London, 5 Mar. 1852 in Marx and Engels, *Selected Works* ii. 452.

[89] Lundgren, *Moses Hess*, 2. [90] Vaccaro, *Socialismo e umanesimo*, 281.

[91] Matheron, "*Traité Théologio-Politique* vu," 175, 183. [92] Marx, "Trois Cahiers," 124–5.

[93] Terpstra, "Spinoza en de anti-naturalistische filosofie," 14–15.

[94] Smith, *Spinoza's Book of Life*, 78–9; Albiac, "Sujets déterminés," 105, 107; Bove, "Bêtes ou automates," 157.

attaining an immanent conception of substance close to Spinoza's. According to Althusser, both Marx's insistence that history is made by the masses and the doctrine of class-warfare can be linked to Spinoza's influence on Marx.[95] Yet it seems a tenuous argument.

Contrary to Marx, Spinoza was highly averse to assigning directive power over the course of history to the masses. Though living nearly two centuries before Marx, there is arguably less mystification and metaphysics in Spinoza's account of how amelioration, progress toward the democratic republic, can occur than in either Hess's utopianism or Marx's dogmatic inevitable triumph of the proletariat. In the end Althusser too failed satisfactorily to fuse Spinozism with Marxism. Althusser's personal tragic dead-end, and feeling of ultimate failure, to an extent reflected perhaps the general problem all Marxism encounters when trying to join forces with Spinozism, the barrier posed by the basic incompatibility of Spinoza's naturalism and conception of the whole as an infinite individual capable of infinite change but without in any way changing overall, with Marx's and Althusser's idea that philosophy is ultimately "class-struggle" translated into theory.

[95] Morfino, *Temps de la multitude*, 240–1.

30

Conclusion

The "Radical Enlightenment Thesis" and its Critics

This present volume spanning the entire relevant era from before the rise of the Radical Enlightenment in the 1650s and 1660s, down to the revolutions of 1830 and 1848, completes what is far from a "simple" argument. Profiling the Radical Enlightenment as philosophical rejection of religious authority tied to democratizing republicanism helps show what precisely it was that differentiates the novel elements of the late seventeenth-century nascent Radical Enlightenment from earlier, pre-1650 clandestine philosophical–theological revolt against the prevailing religious, social, and political order—that is, from Radical Renaissance rooted in rediscovery of Lucretius, on the one hand, and, on the other, key currents of Radical Reformation rooted especially in Socinianism.

Certainly, notions that the churches were tyrannical and corrupt, their teachings fabricated and false, that medieval social hierarchy, morality, and monarchy were all ungrounded in "true religion" and fundamentally unjust, while exalting universal toleration and the rudiments of physics and astronomy, all had deep roots reaching back way before the 1660s. But Radical Renaissance and Radical Reformation, we have seen, both differed from Radical Enlightenment in crucial respects: beside the political passivity and underground evasiveness of the first, and theological wrapping of the latter, they differed also through evolving as they did before the early Scientific Revolution, the Galilean breakthrough based on observation, experiment, and mathematical reasoning which introduced mathematically precise, verifiable laws of nature as a decisive criterion, equations that could ultimately be conceived together as an overarching edifice of unalterable laws governing the entirety of physical reality. For without that crucial shift to mathematically-based science, philosophically conceptualizing all physical reality as a coherent, unified, and comprehensive system of natural laws (which first entered the scene with Descartes) remained impossible.

The Italian philosopher and historian of science Paolo Casini correctly claimed "moderates" like Voltaire, Montesquieu, and Hume stood closer to the undogmatic "esprit systématique" some consider the true spirit of the Enlightenment than the more ambitious systematic "esprit de système" associated with Spinoza, d'Holbach,

Condorcet, or Volney. But Casini also claimed the former were more "modern" than the latter because they supposedly stood closer to the true scientific spirit of the age. This seems questionable since the latter consists of far more than just an experimental approach.[1] Radical Enlightenment's conviction that mathematic science provides the exclusive criterion of all that is true, that this criterion rigorously applied leads ineluctably to denial of miracles, divine providence, and religious authority, along with embracing principles of equality and democracy, from the 1660s generated an activist, non-Lucretian, profoundly anti-sceptical Enlightenment that was something fundamentally new and modern. To turn the existing mix into an active force capable of seriously challenging the status quo required a particular combination of circumstances first encountered, we have argued, in the late seventeenth-century Dutch Republic, a context encouraging the fusing of appreciation of recent science and preoccupation with reforming philosophy with an activist reforming republican democratic movement urgently seeking solutions to pressing political challenges direly threatening what for many were the precious new freedoms and unprecedented toleration afforded by the Dutch Golden Age.

Throughout the Enlightenment era a close connection persisted between comprehensive rejection of religious authority and adopting democratizing social and political programs. "Democratizing" here is defined as promoting the equal right of every citizen to an equal personal autonomy, freedom of speech, thought, and to criticize, the equal right, that is, to enjoy the freedoms and benefits of the state, closely tied to rejection at every level of the hereditary principle and abolishing differentiated group "rights." Anti-aristocratic republicanism of this type was from the outset fused with viewing true government as government in accord with a strictly secular "common good" or "general will" governing the goals and duties of government, a form of ideology first widely promoted by Diderot and d'Holbach, a "general will" conceived in universalist, non-Rousseauist terms. However, this all-important democratizing tendency, rejecting monarchy, aristocracy, the hereditary principle, and all notion of differentiated "rights" for different groups, only included explicit demands for broader representation via elections tending toward universal suffrage from the late eighteenth century onwards.

For the early pre-1720 period, one or two figures who do not fully meet the criteria for inclusion in the Radical Enlightenment category—outright rejection of religious authority tied to secularizing and democratizing republicanism—nevertheless figured in the story because they significantly contributed to building the complex but coherent edifice of radical thought. Anthonie van Dale (1644–1715), and Henri de Boulainvilliers (1659–1722), in particular, received attention in the first volume because each initiated more effectively than anyone else a tendency that became an indispensable building block in the long-term development of the tradition. Van Dale did not reject religious authority as such, nor advocate a democratizing republicanism.

[1] Paganini, *Filosofie clandestine*, 158.

He figures only because he demonstrated more systematically than anyone else down to 1700 that all ancient oracles of the Greeks and Romans were fraudulent, and that supernatural forces never played any part at all in ancient religion, while also using his exceptional expertise with the relevant ancient texts to argue all demonic power, divination, and sorcery without exception is likewise non-existent, all ancient belief groundless and mythical.[2] Boulainvilliers figured because he was a key transmitter, via forbidden manuscripts, of crypto-Spinozism as an underground, irreligious philosophy in early eighteenth-century France; no attempt is made to conceal his also being an apologist for aristocracy.[3]

The linkage of two, at first glance seemingly separate, lines of critique, opposing both the prevailing social–political system and prevailing forms of religious authority, derives from what at one point I termed the "necessary connection between one-substance metaphysics and Radical Enlightenment political and social reformism," a phrase that has given rise to considerable misunderstanding.[4] By this I meant not, as a number of critics misunderstood, that one-substance monism, atheistic materialism, always or inevitably leads to egalitarian attitudes and ideas of equality—the examples of Hobbes, La Mettrie, and Goethe sufficiently prove this was not at all the case, something that has been obvious all along—but rather that such a metaphysics is "necessary," meaning indispensable, for conceptually demolishing every claim, every conceivable justification, for a providentially-intended and governed history of morality, social hierarchy, caste and gender relations, all bases for divinely-sanctioned kingship.[5] This coupling of elements proved decisive throughout although, as we have seen, this conjunction did not prevent some radicals, like Cabanis and (the pre-1800) Fichte, re-introducing woman's subordination to man within marriage by substituting for divine intention and divine law allegedly "natural" reasons for subordinating women.

Many materialist atheists like La Mettrie or Goethe embraced forms of one-substance "Spinozism" in metaphysics while rejecting radical political theory and "general will," and refusing to identify the democratic republic as the best form of government—or "ignorance" and "superstition" as the chief pillars of tyranny.[6] Hence, they were not part of the Radical Enlightenment. The "necessity" claimed in the phrase above, and similar passages, refers to awareness of the unavoidable need to counter religious authority's wide domain in order to sustain and justify sweepingly reformist political and social views. Churchmen active during the French Revolution

[2] Van Dale, *Verhandeling*, 3–4, 150–1, 200–19, 234, 278; Israel, *Radical Enlightenment*, 363–6.

[3] Pečar and Tricoire, *Falsche Freunde*, 22.

[4] Rosenblatt, "Rousseau, the 'Traditionalist'," 634; Ferrone, *The Enlightenment*, 165; Stalnaker, "Jonathan Israel in Dialogue," 640; Stuurman, "Pathways," 227–35; Lord, "Spinoza on Natural Inequality," 127–9; for the correct definition, see Israel, *Democratic Enlightenment*, 2; Devellennes, "Radical Atheism," 161, 173.

[5] Israel, *Democratic Enlightenment*, 2; Simon, "Hume et les 'lumières radicales'," 382, 391; Stalnaker, "Jonathan Israel in Dialogue," 640; Lord, "Spinoza on Natural Inequality," 127–8.

[6] Israel, *Enlightenment Contested*, 43, 796–7, 811–12; this mistake is made by several commentators and repeated in Piet Steenbakker's review of the Ducheyne volume.

rightly claimed to be not just aristocracy's and royalty's best, most effective ideological asset, but everywhere in practice their chief resource for stirring militant popular counter-revolutionary sentiment among ordinary folk. "Alone through their [i.e. the priesthood's] heroic resistance," averred the conservative *Gazette de Paris*, in January 1791, "can you [the aristocracy] be rescued from the Revolution."[7] This was perfectly true. Religious authority, commentators pointed out, not least Camille Desmoulins and Johann Ludwig Ewald, was undoubtedly the most robust and reliable support that kings and aristocracy as well as prelates possessed against universal and equal rights and against democratic subversion. Religion alone, rightly declared Da Costa, could defeat the "barbaric actions" of the Spanish constitutionalists of 1820: it is God who "entrusts scepters to kings" and it is enlightened constitutionalism that perverts God's will expressed as the order of things as they are.[8]

Thus, the Radical Enlightenment thesis by no means maintains that substance monism is per se more democratic than deism as many have totally misread it as claiming; what it contends is that monism eliminates divine providence whereas revealed religion, and authentic deism, do not, with the result that both the latter remained more obviously conducive to creeds and philosophies claiming divine providence regulates the universe according to a benevolent divine plan, envisaging the universe as functioning along providentially directed lines. Accordingly, Radical Enlightenment is more strictly and comprehensively at odds and irreconcilable with religious authority for all of society, including the uneducated, than Voltairean deism, Humean skepticism, or other creeds. Conversely, conceptions of nature specifying a divinely-given moral order conform far better than monist systems to upholding doctrines of a benignly intended hierarchy of social orders including, along Rousseauist lines, the idea that woman's adjunct status to men is ordained as well as "natural." Equally, deism remained always more conducive to "fixity of species" premises, just as Voltaire emphasized, than evolutionary theories, while evolutionary theories better fit with monism.[9] The point the thesis makes about divine governance of the world, therefore, is that monism is at every point better and more completely equipped, if not always more certain, than revealed religion, and all forms of theism and genuine deism, to counter claims of divine sanction for hierarchy, tradition, unequal gender relations, and the existing moral, social, and political order. What the historical and textual record of the French and American, as well as the lesser revolutions of the era, confirms therefore is not that "there is a necessary link between atheism and radical politics"—a (widespread) misreading—but rather, as one scholar expressed it, "that there exist particularly strong resonances between the two positions."[10]

Radical Enlightenment, then, was (and is) a set of attitudes. Just because a writer or thinker is associated with or claimed to be influenced by a radical thinker by no

[7] Israel, *Revolutionary Ideas*, 180–2. [8] Da Costa, *Bezwaren*, 54–6, 69, 71.
[9] Cohen, *Science, libertinage*, 251–66, 357–68.
[10] Lord, "Spinoza on Natural Inequality," 127, 136–7; Devellennes, "Radical Atheism," 173.

means necessarily signifies their actually belonging to the Radical Enlightenment stream in any meaningful sense. The Marquis de Sade, an atheist steeped in clandestine philosophical literature and venerating d'Holbach, is cited by several renowned critics of the whole undifferentiated Enlightenment, such as Horkheimer, Adorno, and Charles Taylor, as a professed champion of Enlightenment values who supposedly illustrates its profound moral shortcomings, the alleged limitations of "Enlightenment humanism," whereas in reality, as Schröder pointed out, his case proves nothing of the kind. Rather, de Sade's boundless hedonism and immoralism rendered him the very "antipode of Enlightenment morality" even without his heaping violently misogynist abuse on Charlotte Corday (1768–93), the female martyr to Brissotin values who stabbed the counter-enlightener, Marat, to death in his bath.[11]

My arguing for the primacy of ideas in Enlightenment history has given rise to another widely repeated, inaccurate notion: that the Radical Enlightenment thesis is "not much interested in the social and institutional contexts through which the Enlightenment was articulated."[12] This is totally wrong. Actually, what is really meant with this charge is that very little shaping significance is assigned to popular sentiment and cultural trends, like freemasonry or the public's adulation of Rousseau, in determining the forming of Enlightenment ideas and strategies. Lilti, Margaret Jacob, and other "negative critique" stalwarts regularly complain that the "Radical Enlightenment thesis" presented in my work is *histoire idéaliste*, presumably because ideas receive a prominent role. But it is not idealist history in any meaningful sense since ideas are not presented as causing the onset or outcome of major events, determining the general direction of the historical process, and still less as determining attitudes and policies of particular groups in society, but only as shaping ideologies, reforming initiatives, legislative agendas, and the like.[13] Contrary to the "negative critique's" claims, the thesis is not intellectual history generalized but intellectual history at all levels in constant combination and fusion with social, political, religious, and economic history.

Clashes between Enlightenment ideologues were far from being mere intellectual disagreements. Conflicting strategies of publicity and political activism profoundly reflected social grievances and changes, and growing socio-economic tensions. To adequately understand such controversies, one must view them as cultural and social events focusing not just on key texts and ideas, but also on the surrounding publicity, reviews, journals, court cases, police interventions, debates in legislatures, ecclesiastical councils, universities, etc. and consider the economic context. General social factors always have primacy, then, in determining the direction and character of events and developments. Viewed as a vast upheaval that shook France to the foundations, the French Revolution was assuredly a story of mass protest, rioting, and disruption, primarily shaped by social unrest and resentment. So, equally, was the

11 Schröder, "De Sade—an Heir?," 260–1, 267; Domenech, *L'Éthique des Lumières*, 49, 214–15, 217.
12 Chisick, "Of Radical and Moderate Enlightenment," 62.
13 Balázs, "Jean-Jacques Rousseau," 182.

Jacobin victory over the Brissotins, the outcome having nothing to do with which side had the intellectually more compelling ideas. Only as regards proclaiming universal and equal rights, emancipation of (often highly unpopular) minorities, proposing equal rights for women, upholding freedom of the press, theater, and expression, total dismantling of ecclesiastical authority (against the sentiments of most), and constitutional and educational reform, that is in its ideological and legislative programs, was the Revolution only minimally shaped by ordinary men and women, popular action, *mentalités*, or broad cultural trends, and principally by Radical Enlightenment concepts generating political agendas. Exclusively here are social and the cultural context altogether secondary and ideas primary.

This is neither inconsistency nor idealism, nor ideologically charged as some reviewers complain, but straightforward analysis based on empirical examination of evidence of many kinds. Undoubtedly, Hunt, Jacob, and Lilti are right, for example, to insist "Rousseau had an infinitely greater impact on his contemporaries than either Diderot or Raynal."[14] In the eyes of most of society he was the "handbook of the citizen." These critics' basic error lies in supposing that what applies to most applies also to the republican vanguards, the circles leading the democratic factions of the American, French, Italian, Liège, Mainz, Genevan, Dutch, Jeffersonian, and Bolivarist revolutions for whom Rousseau, far from being an overwhelming inspiration, was deliberately, systematically, and not infrequently even disdainfully set aside. Typical of the attitude, Bolívar had no regard for Rousseau whatsoever precisely because so many around him were addicted to his writing. Prior to the French Revolution, the radical enlighteners who became the backbone of the post-1789 democratic revolutionary vanguard were likewise either longstanding detractors and non-admirers of Rousseau like Condorcet, Volney, Paine,[15] and Jefferson or else, like Brissot, Buzot, or Cloots, former ardent Rousseau admirers who backtracked in the late 1780s, and took to emphatically and publicly repudiating their previous enthusiasm for Rousseau.[16]

Rousseau, we must remember, was an ex-radical, once belonging to Diderot's circle, who retained some radical characteristics but, after breaking with the Diderot and d'Holbach circles, in 1757, switched to opposing them, promoting a divergent conception of virtue, truth, natural rights, and *volonté générale*, presenting notions less amenable to universal and equal rights, cosmopolitanism, gender equality, and anti-colonialism and much more readily allied to particularism, anti-intellectualism, dictatorship, gender prejudice, race prejudice, and propping up religious authority, in other words Counter-Enlightenment. So it is hardly surprising that Rousseau became an altogether marginal, rejected influence in Jeffersonian and Bolivarist as well as d'Holbachian and Condorcet's circles.[17] It is true that many vigorous critics of the

[14] Mondot and Revauger (eds.) "Margaret Jacob and Jonathan Israel Debate," in *Lumières* xiii, p. 169.

[15] Clark, *Thomas Paine*, 227–8.

[16] Burns, "Jacques-Pierre Brissot," 516, 526; Bevilacquer, "Conceiving the Republic," 554, 557–60.

[17] As Maria José Villaverde, Graeme Garrard, in his *Rousseau's Counter-Enlightenment* (2003), and others rightly point out.

Radical Enlightenment thesis claim that its account of Rousseau is wrong and that Rousseau is an obvious "problem" for the thesis where supposedly he does not fit; but the reader should note that this frequently repeated claim is largely rhetorical without evidence or cogent reasoning being offered as to why; the few attempts to show that Rousseau is wrongly interpreted here have themselves been shown to be clearly mistaken about this in fundamental ways.[18]

Radical Enlightenment was cosmopolitan to its fingertips, and profoundly universalist. Ending monarchy, establishing the Rights of Man on an equal basis (1789), and a general revaluation of all values could only be engineered by the most reform-oriented wing of the Enlightenment. Not just democratization but also the French Revolution's plans for universal compulsory education, proclaimed, above all, by Condorcet, Lakanal, and Daunou in the years 1792–4, and calls for universal peace and the idea of the brotherhood of all peoples, were inherent in such cosmopolitanism, all these ideals being saturated in Radical Enlightenment concepts, language, and philosophical categories, not Rousseauist ones, and still less *robespierrisme*. The same was true of secularization, if not of the term itself which was invented only later, then certainly the reality—conscious elimination of everything miraculous, religious, and ecclesiastical, everything proclaimed in churches including Robespierre's "Supreme Being," from political authority, officially supported education, and basic legislative principles.

Robespierre's public attacks on the atheist and materialist *philosophes* hence quite accurately identified the principal Left-leaning ideological opposition to his oppressive authoritarian populist ideology—as the adversaries of Rousseau. The key Mainz revolutionary journals during 1792–3, striving to spread appreciation of *repräsentative Demokratie* in Germany proclaiming the benevolent universalism of the future, the *Universal-Republik* and the *Universal-Konstitution*, consistently aligned German revolutionary democratic thought with that of France, Holland, Italy, and also Britain and America, publishing not only the speeches of Forster, Dorsch, and Wedekind but equally those of Condorcet, Paine, Price, Cloots, and Gorani.[19] Conversely, Robespierre's populism, anti-intellectualism, and fervent Rousseauism were anathema to all radical enlighteners—as defined here—no less than to moderates and outright counter-revolutionaries. Condorcet loathed Robespierre just as Robespierre detested him. Thorild styled Robespierre an "all-consuming crocodile;"[20] directly contrary to de Sade, the German radical republican poet, Hölderlin, passionate for the Revolution, rejoiced when Charlotte Corday stabbed the "abominable tyrant" Marat to death. Paine utterly reviled "the faction of Robespierre" who incarcerated him in the Paris Luxembourg prison for eleven months.[21] When describing the remote origins of Britain's and other countries' aristocracy as rooted in "robbery," calling

[18] See the debate about Rousseau in JHI 77 (2016), 627–35 and 649–77.
[19] Forster and Wedekind, *Der Patriot*, vol. 1/A, pp. 1–3, 5–20.
[20] Muschik, "Ideen der Französischen Revolution," 173–4.
[21] Beck, "Hölderlin als Republikaner," 41; Macor, "Friedrich Hölderlin and the Clandestine Society," 105.

the progenitors of modern aristocracy "thieves," Paine tellingly styled Europe's early medieval nobility the "Robespierre and the Jacobins of that day."[22] Equally, Paine justly lamented that "it was the real republicans [i.e. Condorcet, Brissot, Cloots, etc.] who suffered most during the time of Robespierre."[23]

Robespierre's and more generally Montagnard exaltation of the "ordinary" abundantly exemplifies d'Holbach's and Condorcet's (and Spinoza's) axiom that despotism, dictatorship, cultural vandalism, and violent oppression chiefly feed on popular ignorance, illiteracy, credulity, and gullibility, on what the ordinary man for the moment (unfortunately but hopefully avoidably, in the future) wrongly believes and thinks.[24] Ignorance is what rallies the masses behind oppressive populism and dictatorship like that inspired by Marat and Robespierre, as ignorance likewise fosters subservience to priests and priestcraft. To radical enlighteners it seemed their Enlightenment's overriding task was to cure mankind of its ignorance, credulity, and fanaticism. Pervading the Radical Enlightenment's whole history lingered a deep dread not of the *multitudo*, as Spinoza called it, itself, but of the ignorance of the multitude, fear greatly amplified by Marat, Robespierre, and the Terror. Montagnard branding of Paine, Brissot, and Condorcet "enemies of the Revolution" together with the notion that ordinary folk are morally pure, the prime criterion of legitimacy in politics without need of "enlightenment" or changing their ideas, Rousseau's "simple souls," opened an unbridgeable rift between Montagnard exalting of ordinariness and the common man, and both categories of enlighteners, moderate and radical.

Over the last decade, the Radical Enlightenment controversy has escalated on all sides in an unexpected and unintended but at times spectacular fashion. Yet, given that political and social systems based on universal and equal rights are, since World War II, the essence of Western and Eastern modernity, and in these volumes Radical Enlightenment is identified as the enduring prime source of the universal and equal cosmopolitan values infusing our "modernity," it was perhaps inevitable, given the high stakes, that the exchanges over the Radical Enlightenment thesis should at times have become distinctly heated.[25] As always in scholarly controversies, conflicting allegiances and issues of principle play a part in the background to the debate. A mix of influences contribute to the rhetorical edge of the "negative critique," among them Postmodernist hostility to "grand narratives" and the Enlightenment "grand narrative" in particular, antipathy to finding intellectual history placed center stage, dislike at seeing the American and French revolutions closely bracketed together and declared to be sharing common basic principles, opposition to seeing organized religion cast in an essentially negative, unenlightened light, in some cases socialist doctrines, and, finally, here and there aversion to seeing England de-centered from its traditional place of primacy in early Enlightenment studies.

[22] Paine, *Complete Writings* ii. 582.
[23] Paine, *Complete Writings* ii. 600.
[24] Israel, *Revolutionary Ideas*, 698.
[25] Wolin, "Introduction to the Symposium," 616–17; see also Villaverde in "L'Abbé Raynal," 231–7.

There is considerable antagonism, noted Frank Mertens in 2001, to finding Locke displaced by Spinoza as the "father of liberal democracy" and to any notion that Spinoza, not Locke, put forward the "first fully developed theory of liberal democracy."[26] There is also considerable and equally unjustified antagonism to the "notion that the fault lines of the Enlightenment led to virulent ideological fractures during the Revolution," indeed shaped the ideological course of the Revolution, for accepting this as a guiding and "compelling idea" necessarily undermines a great part of the recent historiography of the French Revolution, much of which has shown undeviating persistence and ideological ingenuity in insisting on the Revolution being something essentially new and seeking to detach the Revolution from, or rather ignoring, as much as possible, its pre-1789 French anti-monarchist and republican as well as American, Dutch, Swiss, and Paineite radical origins and total immersion in Enlightenment ideas.

The cumulative effect of preferring Postmodernism, cultural history, *mentalité* approaches, Anglocentrism, socialism, religious allegiance, and French Revolution ideology with a strong Marxist and anti-intellectual bias, has been to add an enormously imposing mass to the "negative critique" consensus. Imbruglia cites Casini, Chappey, Missé, Ferrone, Armenteros, Wright, Baker, Jacob, Lilti, Verbeek, Moyn, Jones, Stuurman, Chisick, Bell, Van Kley, Hunt, Edelstein, McMahon, and De Dijn as leading stalwarts comprehensively opposed to the thesis, heading the burgeoning demolition team noisily hacking away at my version of the Radical Enlightenment story.[27] But to these, many more distinguished names must be added, voices no less loudly dismissing the Radical Enlightenment thesis as reductive, reified, oversimplified, teleological, based on "shaky evidence" and unacceptable "cherry-picking," notably Goldenbaum, Sluiter, Thomson, Munck, Jürgens, Melamed, Bove, De Boer, Stalnaker, Peña, Rosenblatt, Beth Lord, Pečar, Tricoire, Jeremy Popkin, and Francesco Benigno, whose view that the thesis is "teleological" is wholly incomprehensible in the context of my argument but whose refrain that it is based on a "Manichaean logic" chimes well with the view of many others. The most systematic, sustained attempted rebuttals, however, remain Lilti's and La Vopa's, both published in 2009.[28]

Those rejecting the thesis are undoubtedly the larger phalanx and this certainly suffices to convince many readers that they *must* be right. Still, during the quarter century it has taken to complete this undertaking, numerous scholars of various nationalities, while not necessarily agreeing in every respect and often suggesting improvements or refinements, have intervened to support the basic schematization and classification. Several among this block, the "positive critique," using or supplementing the thesis in seminars and public debates as well as publications, have indeed contributed to developing and strengthening key aspects. Prominent among them

[26] Mertens, "Radical Political Theory," 86.
[27] Imbruglia, "Illuminismo e Rivoluzione," 56; Goldenbaum, "Some Doubts," 72 n. 19.
[28] Benigno, "Lumi e lanterne," 963, 982–3; Pečar and Tricoire, *Falsche Freunde*, Vorwort.

since the thesis began evolving in 1993, are Giuseppe Ricuperati, Frederik Stjernfelt, Wim Klever, Matthew Stewart, Günter Mühlpfordt, Winfried Schröder, Antony McKenna, Frank Grunert, Wayne Hudson, Gianni Paganini, Michiel Wielema, Sonja Lavaert, Maria José Villaverde, Charles Devellennes, Charles T. Wolfe, Paul Cliteur, Marta García-Alonso, Richard Wolin, Ian Leask, Andrew Weeks, Julie Henry, Landon Frim, Roberto Aramayo, Antonio Hermosa, Laurent Jaffro, and Diego Lucci. Leask and Jaffro, considering my original formulation too timid, notably reinforced the claim that Toland was far more decisively indebted to Spinoza for the radical dimensions of his thought than most scholars had been willing to countenance: and indeed the latest research shows Toland's "Spinozism" to be more, not less, extensive than I originally maintained and altogether more crucial than anything drawn from Locke. Although many "negative critique" supporters have intervened to applaud as "incisive" and "devastating" Chisick's, Edelstein's, and others' rebuttal of my arguments about d'Holbach, this turns out to be actually one of the weakest parts of the "negative critique" and Devellennes is prominent among those who helped show just how utterly wrong Chisick's and Jacob's view about d'Holbach is. Agreeing that the radical critique of religion and tradition does broadly align with promoting a secular morality in people's lives, and hence egalitarianism in society, and republicanism in politics,[29] Schröder judged the thesis insufficiently broad in another key respect—failure to draw attention to the Radical Enlightenment's sweeping, blanket rejection of *all* previous philosophy.[30]

There are also a few voices who remain, as it were, half and half in both the positive and negative camps, having significantly contributed to the thesis's evolution but also vigorously criticizing key aspects, notably Wiep van Bunge and Siep Stuurman. With Richard Popkin, my chief interlocutor during the earliest formative phase (1993–5) when I first began assembling my Radical Enlightenment thesis, the case is different. We profoundly disagreed about Spinoza and especially Bayle whom he insisted on viewing as a thoroughgoing "sceptic," not a clandestine atheist and unflinching moral rationalist, and foe of all theology, as McKenna and Mori have shown him to be; but Richard Popkin's generous encouragement and unflagging willingness to go over the ground again and again played a major part, at the most formative time, in helping conceptualize and formulate the strands of the overall concept.

Meanwhile, scholars (and we should add philosophers) "rarely consider," as one commentator accepting the basic usefulness of dividing the Enlightenment into Moderate and Radical Enlightenment put it, the "subsequent development of the Enlightenment's legacy in the nineteenth century."[31] De Tocqueville and John Stuart Mill exemplify nineteenth-century recognition of the underlying trend in the Western world toward democracy, urges Nathan Wolloch, suggesting the "aim of the Radical

[29] Schröder, "De Sade—an Heir?," 260.

[30] Schröder, "Radical Enlightenment from a Philosophical Perspective," 44–51.

[31] Wolloch, "Alexis de Tocqueville, John Stuart Mill," 359; on this see also Jürgens, "Contesting Enlightenment Contested," 57–8.

Enlightenment to further democracy was eventually achieved, thanks to the peaceful, slow and deliberate means proffered by the Moderate Enlightenment, more than by political revolutions." One might conclude, he adds, that "while the Enlightenment was a varied historical phenomenon, it had a predominant core ideological outlook, which was most typically manifested by the Moderate rather than the Radical Enlightenment."[32] But here we see, once again, how urgent is the need to reaffirm and further clarify the "Radical Enlightenment" thesis as it has stood since 2001: for it never sought to suggest revolutionary transformation of society by democratizing and secularizing must arise from sudden, violent overturning, especially not where demagoguery and popular prejudices figure prominently. On the contrary, Spinoza, Bayle, and d'Holbach were all notably reluctant to sanction violent revolution. Spinoza took a negative, highly jaundiced view of the English Revolution of the 1640s, not because it was a revolution, executed Charles I, or tried to do away with monarchy, but because it was dominated by prevailing popular and religious notions culminating in Cromwell's tyranny; to him, it was all wasted effort because it amounted to a mere *mutatio tyranni*; d'Holbach's view was identical.[33]

Radical Enlightenment, hence, was quintessentially revolutionary but never necessarily tied to violent revolution. After 1815, the great poet "red Shelley" typified a new intensified radical plea, in part reacting to the Terror in France, mirrored too by Grove Jones, for more peaceful, gradual, morally preferable methods to achieve radical democratic goals than those tried by the failed efforts of the early 1790s; but in doing so merely renewed an approach that, from the *cercle spinoziste* onwards, had always been deeply characteristic. However euphoric for some, the cult of democratic revolution between 1775 and 1848, advocating violent mass action as the method to attain democracy, and remove religious authority from law, education, and the public sphere, never had anything intrinsically to do, as Imbruglia too observed, with the Radical Enlightenment as such. To suppose love of peace and "moderation," gentle methods and a peaceable disposition, means Moderate as against Radical Enlightenment would be extremely misleading: it is not a question of methods or approach, or aversion to bloodshed, but basic conceptual ground-plan and ultimate goals.

Were the 1830s and 1840s really an end-point? The developing split between socialism and Radical Enlightenment, and socialism's displacing Radical Enlightenment as the main opposition to the status quo in the Western world, did entail a fundamental change in the way the prevailing social, political, and religious status quo was challenged intellectually and politically. But there is perhaps a still more basic reason for seeing the Radical Enlightenment's effective end in the revolutions of 1830 and 1848: after vast effort and extravagantly raised hopes, the revolutions' failure to transform Europe politically resulted during the middle years of the century in a great wave of revulsion against the whole business of revolutionary transformation of politics and society, against fighting for democratic and egalitarian ideals, and

[32] Wolloch, "Alexis de Tocqueville, John Stuart Mill," 359.
[33] D'Holbach, *Système social*, 260; Goggi, "Spinoza et la Révolution anglaise," 391–3, 397–403.

universal and equal rights. Disheartening, abject failure after decades of revolutionary effort engendered deep disillusionment in the non-socialist part of the generation of thinkers, writers, and artists shaped by the revolutionary upheaval and that grew up in its wake.

If 1848–9 was the "revolution of the intellectuals," its colossal failure caused what one historian has aptly called the "disillusionment of the intellectuals,"[34] molding a mid- and late nineteenth-century era of pessimism and abiding isolation of many of the West's leading minds from society and the masses. It was a reaction of deep dismay, even disgust, with existing society and trying to change it on the basis of high-sounding ideals, that, for some, made Schopenhauer the guiding hero of the age, the towering pessimist philosopher who ranks among Spinoza's fiercest critics, the thinker who charged Spinoza with presenting a hopeless, deceptively optimistic path to "happiness" and freedom through fighting ignorance and seeking to reconstitute society on the basis of "reason."[35] For many, disillusionment engendered retreat from youthful radicalism into deep religious mysticism (as with Dostoevsky), or, following Schopenhauer and Nietzsche, lofty and acerbic philosophical disdain. The Enlightenment's failure also encouraged new forms of racism, imperial sway, and right-wing ideology, or alternatively, as with Michelet and Alexander Herzen, putting pre-1848 republican fervor on the back-burner and immersing oneself in new, bizarrely remote fixations, in Michelet's case "a kind of idiosyncratic nature-mysticism."[36] Most frequently, though, profound dismay led simply to withdrawal into an exaggerated cult of the arts as with Wagner, Flaubert, and another disillusioned participant in the 1848 risings, abandoning politics almost immediately afterwards, Baudelaire. With democratic radicalism lapsing, the Italian *Risorgimento* found itself suspended between the conservatism of Piedmontese constitutional monarchy and the prospect of class-war. The age of Cavour, Napoleon III, Bismarck, Queen Victoria, budding socialism, South America's post-Bolívar republican breakdown, and the American Civil War, was an age of retreat from Enlightenment ideals in Europe and the Americas alike,[37] away from activism and ardor for democratic renewal.

This mid- and late nineteenth-century global phenomenon of profound fatigue with radical ideas is also what explains this volume's title. No doubt this last volume of the series contains imperfections that are well worth pointing out, focusing on, and correcting. It is precisely the value of close text and evidence-based scholarly debate and criticism that it brings defects to light and helps iron them out, thereby improving the quality of the finished product. It also provides an opportunity for all concerned to re-examine prevailing assumptions and conclusions from opposing viewpoints.

The intensity and scale of the controversy reflects its importance and how much is at stake. No one better captured the ultimate implications of this scholarly battle than

[34] Burrow, *Crisis of Reason*, 24, 27–9, 54–5.
[35] Moreau, "Réception de spinozisme," 246–7.
[36] Burrow, *Crisis of Reason*, 26.
[37] For the American angle to this, see Israel, *Expanding Blaze*, 568–614.

Richard Wolin, who contrasts twentieth-century, especially Postmodernism's, rejection of the "teleological optimism" of such (pre-1848 inspired) giants as Hegel, Comte, and Marx with the post-Postmodernist (i.e. Radical Enlightenment) argument that unless we do maintain our intellectual anchorage in universal and equal rights, democratic republicanism, and individual liberty, the twin secularizing and democratizing processes in motion since the late seventeenth century, "we risk succumbing to the moral disorientation and political catastrophe that left such deep and permanent scars on the twentieth century."[38]

Despite the sheer mass of the "negative critique" it is not easy to find solid arguments on their side that stand up to careful examination and it has to be admitted that some of their claims are spectacularly weak. One commentator, heartily agreeing "there is very little evidence" to support the claim Spinozist thinkers had a "truly conclusive notion of democracy that would have extended civic rights not just to a propertied elite but to all adults," and eager to back Jacob's claim that d'Holbach was no radical enlightener but firmly committed to absolute monarchy, substantiates her broadly damning dismissal of the overall thesis by reminding readers that the Abbé Raynal came out in publicly-declared opposition to the French Revolution. This proves it "very hard to maintain [. . .] that the transition to a more modern and democratic political culture in France was linked to the spread of atheism and materialism, or anything that can be plausibly described as a 'radical Enlightenment'."[39] If anyone is impressed with this they should note that this prominent backer of the "negative critique" totally ignores the fact that, in 1790–2, a dozen indignant commentators, Brissot and Condorcet among them, wrote in to the Paris papers protesting that the now elderly and decrepit Raynal's disavowal of the Revolution (probably manipulated by Malouet) totally contradicted—as indeed it did—the entire logic of the *Histoire philosophique*, which, they rightly insisted, remained a principal source of inspiration for the Revolution. The radical press uniformly condemned Raynal's letter of disavowal as an "infame tromperie." Even Raynal himself admitted his disavowal roundly contradicted the democratic arguments he and Diderot had put forward in the *Histoire philosophique*.[40] In other words, this "negative critique" intervention is so severely muddled it ends up actually bolstering instead of denting the Radical Enlightenment thesis by providing a splendidly typical example of the utter flimsiness of the mighty background chorus's principal refrains.

Remarkably little effort has been made, one has to accept, to carefully cross-examine the main empirical sub-theses on which the Radical Enlightenment argument as a whole rests. It might seem strange that the "negative critique" relies so much on its chorus line appeal, leaving nearly all the thesis's main structural

[38] Wolin, "Introduction to the Symposium," 617; Wolin, "In Praise of *philosophie*," 100–4.

[39] De Dijn, "Politics of Enlightenment," 800.

[40] Brissot, *Patriote français* xxix (29 Aug. 1789), 4–5, and 667 (6 June 1791), 626–7; [Condorcet], *Bibliothèque de l'Homme Public* III (1792), part iii, pp. 161–70; Israel, *Revolutionary Ideas*, 157–9, 706; also Imbruglia, "Illuminismo e rivoluzione," 69.

components on which the so-called "grand narrative" rests unexamined. Hardly any of the main steps in the argument have been closely criticized in terms of text and evidence at all, let alone "*a fondo* [thoroughly]" as one Italian commentator rather ridiculously claimed, not even such key components as the propositions that the *cercle spinoziste* introduced a profoundly new form of republicanism and conception of human freedom, that the chief issue in eighteenth-century republicanism is the growing split between aristocratic and democratic republicanism, that the *Encyclopédie* was a hidden *machine de guerre* deeply subversive politically as well as religiously and philosophically, or that Voltaire spent his last decade fighting a *guerre civile* with the more radical *philosophes* and clearly envisaged a deep rift between his following and those atheists and materialists who were "not royalists." But then this striking across-the-board failure to examine closely or seriously is perhaps not so strange when we consider that the evidence obviously largely supports these basic contentions. Given all these features, one is vividly reminded of Bayle's stricture that on fundamental issues not only is the view of the majority all too likely to be comprehensively wrong but even *consensus omnium*, the agreed view of all, must be treated with great reserve and suspicion by the searcher after truth.[41] The concurrence of many while solid evidence and cogent argument is conspicuously lacking from what they say, does sway some readers temporarily, but, at a deeper level such a curious situation actually weakens the larger phalanx, in this case the "negative critique," because its apparently massive consensus only further encourages its stupendous and glaring failure practically everywhere to look more closely and to engage seriously.

Consequently, a key problem in this controversy is the essentially rhetorical character of most of the main objections. La Vopa considers the Radical Enlightenment thesis guilty of supposing whenever a "thinker was a Spinozist, he must have subscribed to the entire array of radical positions, even though some were left immanent and unstated."[42] Lilti, Ferrone, La Vopa, and others agree that in my view Radical Enlightenment "originated" in Spinoza's philosophy and that I try to make all radicals conform to a Spinozist format. But as I have repeatedly explained *I do not* argue that the Radical Enlightenment originated in Spinoza's, or indeed in any, philosophy but in the political crisis in the Dutch Republic during the third quarter of the seventeenth century. Every statement (including Wikipedia's) that the Radical Enlightenment thesis is "Spinoza-based" or that its ideas "originated" in Spinoza's philosophy is factual nonsense. From the moment *Radical Enlightenment* (2001) appeared, the argument has been for an abundance of disparate sources shaping impulses that are ultimately social—defiance of and protest against the existing order. Fundamental in shaping the Radical Enlightenment were neo-Epicureanism, philosophical Socinianism, Lodewijk Meyer's "radical Cartesianism," Bayle's pseudo-skepticism, Meslier's attack on religion and aristocracy, Shaftesbury's "deism," Priestley's materialism, and Bentham's post-1815 utilitarianism, just to

[41] Israel, *Enlightenment Contested*, 71–82.

[42] La Vopa, "A New Intellectual History?," 727.

mention eight component influences. If Radical Enlightenment did indeed first arise among the *cercle spinoziste*, that is the circle around Spinoza, not only were the Radical Enlightenment's sources disparate but the starting-point, the *cercle spinzoiste* as such, demonstrably did not arise with the ideas of Spinoza himself. The characteristic coupling of rejection of religious authority with democratic republicanism first powerfully and clearly arose, as argued at length in *Radical Enlightenment*, in the writings of Van den Enden, the Brothers Koerbagh, Meyer, and the Brothers De La Court.

The "all roads lead to Spinoza" line of attack, attributing to my approach the idea that an entire segment of the Enlightenment and the revolutionary tendency it inspired "originates with the enigmatic Dutch philosopher," certainly helps make the thesis look "simplistic."[43] It powerfully adds to the mighty chorus. It has proved helpful in rallying support for the "negative critique" by further appealing to Post-modernists, traditionalists, the devout, the Marxist, and all who dislike non-theological "grand narratives" as well as old-style intellectual history (which this is not), but this misrepresentation too in the end only weakens the "negative critique" still further. For this misplaced insistence not only reflects failure to engage seriously but amounts to outright distortion. Such claims do not even connect with let alone do anything to rebut the central argument, which is that anyone comprehensively repudiating religious authority while seeking and combining this with democratizing republicanism belongs to the Radical Enlightenment, even if such voices never mention Spinoza at all, here classically including Meslier and Condorcet. Meslier's writing owed nothing to Spinoza, and he only recognized the significant affinities between his own thought and Spinozism after composing most of his immense secret *Testament*. Meslier was in no way indebted to Spinozism and never remotely a Spinozist; yet his thought has rightly been described as "the perfect poster-figure for Israel's thesis" because he grounded his radical politics rejecting all monarchy and aristocracy in a materialism linked to atheism.[44]

In any case, a scrupulous "unity and coherence" of the sort found in Meslier, Spinoza, d'Holbach, Condorcet, or the late Bentham, though not infinitely rare, was far beyond most writers' capabilities moderate or radical. Radical Enlightenment comprised a large number of authors, publicists, dramatists, poets, and mentors of divergent backgrounds and tendencies and, inevitably, more lesser and undistinguished than great minds. The only criterion being "imposed" for inclusion within the category is comprehensive rejection of religious authority combined with a democratizing republicanism.[45] There are no grounds whatever for calling this an "iron logic" that distorts and distorted reasoning based on "cherry-picking"—a much-loved recurring item of the chorus refrain, delightfully easy to repeat when

[43] Ferrone, *The Enlightenment*, 162; Jacob, "Heavenly City," 50; Chisick, "Of Radical and Moderate Enlightenment," 61.
[44] Devellennes, "Radical Atheism," 161–2.
[45] On this point, see Israel, *Democratic Enlightenment*, 698–9, 748–51, 754–5, 757–8.

unsubstantiated. If enlighteners clearly combined eradication of religious authority with a democratizing crypto-republican tendency or declared republicanism, like Toland, Diderot, Helvétius, d'Holbach, Condorcet, Volney, Destutt, Lessing, Herder, Fichte, and the post-1814 Bentham, they are included; if they opt for one substance in their metaphysics like La Mettrie or Goethe but do not reject the existing political and social status quo then they are excluded. This is a purely empirical test. Even if a mistake occurs in a particular case, there is nothing rigid or reified in the procedure.

Rather than the thesis imposing an "iron logic" as the chorus insists, it was precisely the difficulty of affording sufficient coherence, imparting a robust logic to this highly complex, wide-ranging, and difficult strategy and set of social impulses, that gained Spinoza his uniquely prominent position in the unfolding Radical Enlightenment story from beginning to end, in a way neither Toland, nor Diderot, d'Holbach, Condorcet, Bentham, or anyone else ever came near rivaling. This was because, as Bayle contends, Spinoza was the first thinker to turn "atheism" in the sense of rejection of divine revelation, providence, and miracles, "atheism" excluding the ecclesiastical voice from the political process, into a fully worked-out, coherent philosophical system, a system tied to systematic anti-Scripturalism and equipped with a formidable democratic republican political theory. Neither Hobbes not Locke offered anything remotely like this. Spinoza was also the first major thinker to present religious authority allied to untreated, unreformed popular thinking, ordinary people's gut assumptions, as foundational to political "tyranny." During the late seventeenth and eighteenth centuries, 'Spinoza' was universally recognized as the most formidable advocate of the "atheist" tendency and most successful in establishing a creed threatening to overturn the existing moral and social order. Leibniz, Lessing, and Kant were all agreed about this.

From 1673, when the Swiss commander Stouppe became the first to identify "Spinozism" as an underground "sect" chiseling away at all accepted values, a clandestine tradition rejecting the prevailing social, moral, religious, and political order, it became commonplace to cite Spinoza as chief inspirer of this new creed challenging the hegemony of Christianity; this is simply historical fact readily investigated even if, until recently, a reality rarely acknowledged by historians. A Europe-wide reality, it has been demonstrated in great detail for France in Alan Kors's latter volumes on "atheism," *Naturalism and Unbelief in France, 1650–1729* (2016).[46] The most striking (and challenging) conclusion emerging from two of Kors's latter volumes (diverging slightly from his argument of 1990) is assuredly the unparalleled centrality he recognizes was accorded, throughout the meandering French debate surrounding "atheism," to "Spinoza." Spinoza loomed always above and beyond, more prominently and formatively, than Bruno, Machiavelli, Hobbes, Toland, or any other early modern thinker, and this remained true throughout the period under review until the age of Bolívar, Heine, Bauer, and Marx.

[46] Kors, *Naturalism and Unbelief*, 69–101; and my review of Kors's two volumes in the JMH for 2018.

Lilti in particular has been widely applauded for attacking the Radical Enlightenment thesis's supposedly rigid categories, rejecting all notion of "opposing definite currents that are defined once and for all," for his effective dissolving all such classification presenting two vying enlightenments with his relentless stress on ambiguity and "meaning instability."[47] His tireless appeals to "signification slippage" are indeed very likely the "negative critique's" most powerful card, but, contrary to Antonio Negri and others claiming it has overturned the thesis completely, when carefully examined, it is an 'ambiguity' thesis which, far from being "devastating," in fact amounts to hardly anything. Clinging to Roche, Derrida, and Foucault, he admonishes that the entire Radical Enlightenment thesis dangerously rests on representing the vast eighteenth-century discussion surrounding "spinozisme" as meaningful in flagrant disregard of Postmodernist warnings to beware of "sliding of significations" and "instability of textual meanings." But if we investigate carefully, his fiercely protesting against the false appearances of coherence warned against by Postmodernist deconstruction enthusiasts can in the end scarcely be claimed to comprise much of a plus for the "negative critique."[48] Certainly, a great many applaud Lilti for "incisively" lambasting the supposedly artificial "teleology of philosophical radicalism, linking Spinoza and the French Revolution," but it is impossible to find any real substance behind his resounding rhetoric– or that of La Vopa.

Rhetorically, Lilti sounds impressive; the problem is the facts. Does anyone, can anyone, when it comes to the evidence, back Roche and Lilti in a serious discussion when dozens of texts prove the term *spinozisme* was constantly used in eighteenth-century polemics surrounding Montesquieu, Diderot, Voltaire, and d'Holbach, and that "spinozisme" played a pivotal intellectual role in eighteenth-century Europe in a way that no other category did? If the term did not have an absolutely fixed meaning (who would expect that?) one would need to be very foolish indeed to try to argue, using multiple texts, that it did not have a consistent and formidably concrete core. Such a stance would be completely nonsensical. *Spinozisme* could exhibit marginally different meanings in different contexts; the intellectual historian must, as always, be on his guard, and sensitive to such shades of difference; but there were basic, strict limits to how the term was used. Nothing in the world can make the category *spinozisme* as employed from 1673 down to the 1840s compatible with miracles, Revelation, religious authority, deism, mysticism, skepticism, Aristotelian substances, Platonic ideals, Cartesian dualism, Lockean dualism based on *supra rationem*, fixity of species, and more; it invariably and undeviatingly signified conflating body and soul, God and Nature, and the laws of physics and rules of mathematics into one unified body of doctrine leaving no reserved area for divine providence, Scriptural authority, *supra rationem*, or skepticism. It always meant a hylozoic vision of the world compatible

[47] Stalnaker, "Jonathan Israel in Dialogue," 645, 647; Lilti, "How Do We Write the Intellectual History?," cue 50.

[48] Lilti, "How Do We Write the Intellectual History?," cue 19.

with evolutionary theories such as Toland and later Diderot and d'Holbach developed and one strictly incompatible with revelation, mysteries, magic, sorcery, divine governance of the world, and fixity of species. There was no *spinozisme* that was not also Tolandian, d'Holbachian, and Diderotian. To suppose that when Boulainvilliers, Voltaire, and Diderot invoke *spinozisme* they had nothing concrete in mind, and that neither did the great German figures of the eighteenth century, Leibniz, Wolff, Lessing, Goethe, Herder, Mendelssohn, Kant, Fichte, and Schelling, who all spent a great part of their energy disputing and writing about Spinoza, is sheer delusion. Lilti's and Roche's argument that Spinoza was interpreted in the eighteenth century in a bewildering variety of ways so that eighteenth-century "Spinozism" did not represent any sort of meaningful tradition, that "spinozisme" was not a "theoretical corpus" but instead just a slogan, "un scandale, la figure extrême de l'hétérodoxie,"[49] is nothing but a Postmodernist scholarly fiction, an ultimately ridiculous position which only further confirms the utter emptiness and groundlessness of the "negative critique" overall.

Lilti does also attempt a little more, trying to undercut the *cercle spinoziste* subthesis by arguing that even if one concedes that something remarkable and unusual occurred in the Holland of the 1660s and 1670s, the argument is invalid since the Dutch context was too different from the rest of Europe to be relevant while the thinkers involved, apart from Spinoza, were soon forgotten and played little part in eighteenth-century European thought generally. But the dramatic contrast the Dutch republican political model presented with Louis XIV's absolutist monarchical Europe was precisely what made the Dutch Republic and with it the unique scenario concocted by the *cercle spinoziste* appealing to key foreign radicals like Toland, Shaftesbury, Radicati, Leti, Tindal, Mandeville, Saint-Glain, Tyssot, and Boulainvilliers. Lilti compounds his error here by suggesting the *cercle spinoziste* apart from Spinoza had no wider European impact. But the De La Courts and Bekker were not forgotten; Lodewijk Meyer remained uninterruptedly a continuous topic of debate from Leibniz through Baumgarten to Semler in eighteenth-century Germany.[50] To top his cake, Lilti, like La Vopa, then also throws in a final additional error: following Popkin, he wrongly construes Bayle as a fideist and skeptic.[51]

Much undoubtedly is at stake. The very fact it has become so "virulent" a contest with accusations abounding of "bias," "unscholarly use of sources," "idealism," "essentialism," "reductionism," and "rigidity," notes Vincenzo Ferrone, shows the issues remain unresolved and that it will take time before final conclusions can be drawn.[52] To an extent this is true. But it is arguable that the debate in the form it has taken since 2009 drags on, especially since the appearance of the Ducheyne,

[49] Lilti, "Comment écrit-on l'histoire intellectuelle," 188–9, 192.

[50] Bordoli, *Ragione e scrittura*, 38–9; Lavaert and Schröder, "Introduction," 8–9; Lavaert, "Lieutenants," 152; Krop, "Philosophia S. Scripturae Interpres," 92–3.

[51] Israel, "L'Histoire intellectuelle des Lumières," 243.

[52] Ferrone, *The Enlightenment*, 162; Israel, "'Radical Enlightenment': A Game-Changing Concept," 17.

García-Alonso, and Niekerk volumes, that is since 2017,[53] not because there are solid arguments on both sides but merely because of the power of one side's chorus line: the "negative critique," in massed ranks, insistently and rhetorically dismisses the Radical Enlightenment as "deeply flawed and problematic" chanting about "cherry-picking" without seriously examining the arguments let alone successfully substantiating their objections of which there is no trace, thinking nothing else is needed.

The "modernity" of the Radical Enlightenment, in confrontation with Moderate Enlightenment, Counter-Enlightenment, Rousseau, and Robespierre, matters still today profoundly. The "happiness of a society" [le Bonheur d'une société], held the pre-1789 Condorcet, like Brissot, Cérutti, Desmoulins, Volney, Destutt, Bonneville, Robert, and other leading pre-1789 democratic republicans, figures such as Price, Priestley, Paine, Barlow, and Jefferson, increases the more equal human rights are established and respected.[54] Equality being the basis of universal "rights of mankind," it follows, stressed Condorcet, in 1788, that women must eventually escape the oppression husbands and fathers heap on them, and in a truly enlightened democratic republic will one day equally share in universal rights; women's status and interests will be equivalent to men's, as should be their education. All free, independent humans need to learn the same things. Female participation in politics will eventually become a reality too.[55] Outlawed and hounded to death by Robespierre and the Montagne, this pre-eminent theorist of democratic constitutionalism, black emancipation, and universal secular education, likewise emerged during the French Revolution as a leading champion of women's emancipation.[56]

Abolition of slavery, black and Jewish emancipation, and a generalized equality of the races and sexes, along with curtailing religious authority, abolishing aristocracy, and universal compulsory education, according to radical enlighteners, follow ineluctably from the premises of 1776 whereas for moderate enlighteners like Adams, Morris, Burke, Mounier, Malouet, and Adam Smith such revolutionary conclusions are false. Not only were they *not* the veritable doctrine of the American Revolution, such notions, complained the moderates, wrecked the French Revolution, clashed with the then universally admired "aristocratic" British model, and everywhere needed resisting. Moderate enlighteners bowed to monarchy and aristocracy, championed restricted suffrages, and, even if sometimes reluctantly and half-heartedly, until the 1830s (and sometimes later) accepted the inevitability of slavery under certain climes along with female subjection to male dominance; above all, they embraced the necessity of church guidance for the majority.[57] Where for Adam Smith, following Locke's reasoning, property rights come first and trump personal

[53] For detailed recent comparison of the opposed critiques, see Steffen Ducheyne (ed.), *Reassessing the Radical Enlightenment* (2017) and Marta García-Alonso, *Les Lumières radicales et le politique* (2017).

[54] Condorcet, "De l'influence de la Révolution," 7; Condorcet, *Réflexions sur l'esclavage*, 71–2.

[55] Condorcet, *Lettres d'un Bourgeois*, 281–7; Condorcet, *Tableau historique*, 554.

[56] Israel, *Revolutionary Ideas*, 123–5, 396–8, 707–8; Green, *History of Women's Political Thought*, 204–6; Davis, "Radical Enlightenment and . . . Women's Equality," 300.

[57] Condorcet, *Réflexions sur l'esclavage*, 67, 71, 82–3, 133; Fergus, *Revolutionary Emancipation*, 605.

rights and ownership, precluding black emancipation and the common good—for pre- and post-1789 radicals basic human rights, despite their fears of West Indian slave insurrection, emphatically overrule all property rights so that slaves should be emancipated without compensation to slave-owners, and, for those radicals most fully consistent with their principles, like Condorcet, women immediately emancipated by changing the laws relating to marriage, inheritance, and divorce and educating them together with and like the male population.[58]

Respect for universal and equal human rights must logically end all oppression, not just formal slavery, argued radical enlighteners, but informal slavery and eventually also all forms of discrimination and exploitation together with the curse of war, enabling all peoples around the globe to support and fraternize with, rather than fight, each other.[59] For in democratic republics it can never be in the interest of the majority for governments, legislatures, and states to fight one another. If it is true that amidst the dangers and dilemmas of our contemporary world, Radical Enlightenment offers a superior alternative to either traditional religion or an enfeebling, ultimately absurd Postmodernism, endlessly trumpeting 'ambiguity and "signification slippage" allied to a failed multiculturalism of supposedly equally valid autonomous identities,[60] then Radical Enlightenment has never been more relevant than today. After 1789 and during the century that followed the "Enlightenment that failed" universal and equal rights were widely resisted, secularization opposed, women's rights blocked, black emancipation obstructed, Jewish emancipation reversed, and representative democracy drastically postponed and derailed. Freedom of speech, thought. and to criticize was, as it still is, massively infringed. From 1848, Radical Enlightenment's appeal inexorably receded. It has yet fully to revive, and despite the incipient resurgence of universal and equal human rights after 1945 now once again appears to be stalling if not in full retreat.

[58] Condorcet, *Réflexions sur l'esclavage*, 82–3; Pitts, *Turn to Empire*, 30–1, 51–2; Fergus, *Revolutionary Emancipation*, 34; Phillipson, *Adam Smith*, 223; Hill and Montag, *Other Adam Smith*, 184–5.

[59] Condorcet, "De l'influence de la Révolution," 26–7; it is yet one more basic category mistake, definitely wrong—but still a current thesis—that Enlightenment "universal rights" attached to particular states and were *not* the predecessor of post-1948 human rights as a universal measure for all mankind, a view championed by Moyn and endorsed by Stuurman that needs adding to the long list, that boundless catalogue of misunderstanding, error and misrepresentation which constitutes the "negative critique;" see Moyn, *The Last Utopia*, 24–7.

[60] Cliteur and Gordon, "Enlightenment in Contemporary Cultural Debate," 312, 330.

Bibliography

General Abbreviations

AHR	*American Historical Review*
AHRF	*Annales historiques de la Révolution française*
BJECS	*British Journal of Eighteenth-Century Studies*
BJHPh	*British Journal for the History of Philosophy*
BMGN	*Low Countries Historical Review*
CHEPh	*The Cambridge History of Eighteenth-Century Philosophy*, ed. Knud Haakonssen (2 vols., Cambridge, 2006)
CHEPTh	*The Cambridge History of Eighteenth-Century Political Thought*, ed. M. Goldie and R. Wokler (Cambridge, 2006)
Corpus	*Corpus: revue de philosophie* (Paris X–Nanterre)
CPB	*Correspondance de Pierre Bayle*, ed. A. McKenna et al. (15 vols; Oxford, 1999–2017)
EJHE	*European Journal of the History of Economic Thought*
EJPTh	*European Journal of Political Theory*
EPRF	*Etica e Politica. Rivisita di Filosofia* (online publication, Department of Philosophy, University of Trieste)
ESB	*Études sur le XVIIIe siècle. Université libre de Bruxelles*
FHS	*French Historical Studies*
GWN	*Geschiedenis van de Wijsbegeerte in Nederland*
HAHR	*Hispanic American Historical Review*
HEI	*History of European Ideas*
HPTh	*History of Political Thought*
IHR	*Intellectual History Review*
JAE	*Jaarboek De Achttiende Eeuw*
JES	*Journal for Eighteenth-Century Studies*
JHI	*Journal of the History of Ideas*
JHPh	*Journal of the History of Philosophy*
JMEH	*Journal of Modern European History*
JMH	*Journal of Modern History*
Kn.	W. P. C. Knuttel, *Catalogus van de Pamfletten-verzameling berustende in de Koninklijke Bibliotheek*
LIAS	series: *Sources and Documents to the Early Modern History of Ideas* (Amsterdam)
MIH	*Modern Intellectual History*
OHM	Oxford, Harris Manchester College, Manuscripts
PAPS	*Proceedings of the American Philosophical Society*
RDE	*Recherches sur Diderot et sur l'Encyclopédie*
RSI	*Rivista Storica Italiana*
SECC	*Studies in Eighteenth-Century Culture*
SHPhSc	*Studies in History and Philosophy of Science*

SVEC	*Studies on Voltaire and the Eighteenth Century* (Geneva and Oxford)
TJEAS	*Taiwan Journal of East Asian Studies*
TvG	*Tijdschrift voor Geschiedenis*

Abbreviations of Libraries, Collections of Manuscripts and Collections of Official Printed Edicts and Prohibitions

ARH	The Hague, Algemeen Rijksarchief
AUB	Amsterdam: Universiteitsbibliotheek
BL	London: British Library
BRL VH	Brussels, Royal Library of Belgium, section Manuscripts and rare printed items
GrUB	Greifswald, Universitätsbibliothek
GUB	Göttingen: Universitätsbibliothek
HHL	Harvard University, Houghton Library
HKB	The Hague: Koninklijke Bibliotheek (Royal Library)
PBN	Paris: Bibliothèque Nationale
PFL	Princeton, Firestone Rare Books Library
RLC	Royal Library, Copenhagen
YBL	Yale Beinecke Library
YSL	Yale Sterling Memorial Library

Primary

Adams, John, *Novanglus; or, A History of the Dispute with America* (Boston, 1774).

Adams, John, *Thoughts on Government applicable to the present State of the American Colonies* (Philadelphia, 1776).

Adams, John, *The Works of John Adams, Second President of the United States* (10 vols., Boston, 1850–6).

The Adams–Jefferson Letters: The Complete Correspondence between between Thomas Jefferson and Abigail and John Adams, ed. L. J. Cappon (2 vols., Chapel Hill, NC, 1959).

L'Ami de la religion et du Roi, Journal ecclésiastique, politique et littéraire (journal: Paris, 1814–59).

L'Anatomie de la Cabale, ou Les Affaires presentés dans leur vrai jour (n.p. [Brussels?], 1790). BRL VH

d'Argens, Jean-Baptiste de Boyer, marquis, *Lettres Chinoises, ou Correspondance philosophique, historique et critique* (5 vols., The Hague, 1739–40).

d'Argens, Jean-Baptiste de Boyer, marquis, *Lettres Juives ou Correspondance philosophique, historique et critique entre un Juif voiageur en differens états de l'Europe et ses correspondans en divers endroits* (1738; 2nd edn., 6 vols., The Hague, 1742). PFL

d'Argens, Jean-Baptiste de Boyer, marquis, *Mémoires secrets de la République des Lettres ou le théatre de la vérité* (7 vols., Amsterdam, 1744).

Audrein, Yves, *Apologie de la religion contre les prétendus philosophes* (Paris, 1797).

*Avis au public sur le Troisième Volume de l'*Encyclopédie (n.p., n.d.). BL

Bachaumont, *Mémoires secrets pour servir à l'histoire de la république des Lettres en France depuis MDCCLXII jusqu'à nos jours* (36 vols., "Londres," 1780–9).

Baczko, Bronislaw, *Une Éducation pour la démocratie. Textes et projets de l'époque révolutionnaire* (Paris, 1982).

Bahrdt, Car Friedrich, *Geschichte seines Lebens, seiner Meinungen und Schicksale* (4 vols., Frankfurt, 1790).

Bahrdt, Car Friedrich, *On Freedom of the Press and its Limits* (1787) in J. Ch. Laursen and J. van der Zande (eds.), *Early French and German Defenses of Freedom of the Press* (Leiden, 2003), 92–172.

Barlow, Joel, *A Letter to the National Convention of France on the Defects in the Constitution of 1791* (London, 1792).

Barlow, Joel, *Two Letters to the Citizens of the United States* (New Haven, 1806).

Barruel, Abbé Auguste, *Les Helviennes, ou Lettres Provinciales philosophiques* (1781–8; 5 vols., 7th edn., Paris, 1830).

Barruel, Étienne, *Observations sur l'instruction publique, particulièrement sur les écoles centrales* (Paris, An VIII, Germinal [spring 1800]).

Bauer, Bruno, *Christianity Exposed. A Recollection of the Eighteenth Century, and a Contribution to the Crisis of the Nineteenth Century* (1843), ed. Paul Trejo (Lewiston, NY, 2002).

Baumgarten, Siegmund Jacob, *Nachrichten einer Hallischen Bibliothek* (8 vols., 1748–51).

Bayle, Pierre, *Dictionnaire historique et critique* (1697; 4 vols., Amsterdam, Leiden, The Hague, and Utrecht, 1740).

Bayle, Pierre, *Correspondance*, ed. E. Labrousse and A. McKenna (15 vols., Oxford, 1999–2017).

Beccaria, Cesare, *On Crimes and Punishments* (1764), ed. R. Bellamy (Cambridge, 1995).

Beccaria, Cesare, "Pensieri sopra la barbarie e coltura delle nazioni e su lo stato selvaggio dell'uomo," in Venturi (ed.), *Riformatori Lombardi*, 106–12.

Bentham, Jeremy, *Correspondence*, in *The Collected Works of Jeremy Bentham*, ed. J. H. Burns et al. (12 vols. thus far, London and Oxford, 1968–).

Bentham, Jeremy, *A Fragment on Government*, ed. J. H. Burns and H. L. A. Hart (Cambridge, 1988).

Bentham, Jeremy, *The Influence of Natural Religion on the Temporal Happiness of Mankind*, ed. D. McKown (1822; New York, 2003).

Bentham, Jeremy, *The Principles of Morals and Legislation* (Amherst, NY, 1988).

Berlinische Montaschrift, ed. F. Gedike and J. E. Biester (Berlin, 1783–96).

Blanco White, Joseph, *The Life of the Rev. Joseph Blanco White, written by Himself* (3 vols., London, 1845).

Blaquiere, Edward, *An Historical Review of the Spanish Revolution* (London, 1822).

Bolingbroke, Henry St John, Viscount, *The Philosophical Works*, ed. R. Wellek (5 vols., New York and London, 1977).

Bolingbroke, Henry St John, Viscount, *Political Writings*, ed. David Armitage (Cambridge, 1997).

Bolívar, Simón, *Carta de Jamaica* (6 Sept. 1815), ed. Jorge Dávila in *Escrito en Jamaica* (Mérida, Venezuela, 2015), 73–129.

Bolívar, Simón, *Discurso de Bolívar en el Congreso de Angostura (15 de Febrero de 1819)* (Caracas, 1919).

Bolívar, Simón, *Obras Completas* (3 vols., Havana, Cuba, 1950).

Bolívar, Simón, *El Libertador: Writings of Simon Bolívar*, ed. D. Bushnell (Oxford, 2003).

Bonald, Louis de, *Réflexions sur la Révolution de 1830 et autres inédits*, ed. Jean Bastier (Paris, 1988).

Bonnet, Charles, *Mémoires autobiographiques*, ed. R. Savioz (Paris, 1948).

Boulainvilliers, Henri de, *Oeuvres philosophiques*, ed. Renée Simon (2 vols., The Hague, 1973–5).

Boulainvilliers, Henri de, *La Vie de Mahomed* ("Londres" [Amsterdam?], 1730).

Boulainvilliers, Henri de, *Essais sur la noblesse de France contenans une dissertation sur son origine et établissement*, ed. J. F. de Tabary ("Amsterdam" [Rouen], 1732).

Boulainvilliers, Henri de, *État de la France* (8 vols., "à Londres," 1752), YSL.

[Boulanger, Nicolas-Antoine], B.I.D.P.E.C., *Recherches sur l'origine du Despotisme oriental* ("Londres" [Amsterdam?], 1762]). PFL

Boulanger, Nicolas-Antoine, *L'Antiquité Dévoilée par ses usages* (3 vols., Amsterdam, 1777).

[Boulanger and d'Holbach], *Recherches sur l'origine du Despotisme oriental*, ouvrage posthume de Mr. B.I.D.P.E.C. ("Londres" [Amsterdam?], 1762]).

[Boulanger and d'Holbach], *Examen critique de la vie et des ouvrages de Saint Paul avec une dissertation sur Saint Pierre* ("Londres" [Amsterdam], 1770). BL

Brandolini, Aurelio Lippo, *Republics and Kingdoms compared*, ed. James Hankins (Cambridge, MA, 2009).

[Brissot de Warville, Jacques-Pierre], *Recherches philosophiques sur le droit de propriété considéré dans la nature* (n.p., 1780; repr. Paris, n.d).

[Brissot de Warville, Jacques-Pierre], *Bibliothèque philosophique du législateur* (10 vols., "Berlin," 1782).

[Brissot de Warville, Jacques-Pierre], *Lettres philosophiques sur Saint Paul, sur sa doctrine, politique, morale et religieuse, et sur plusieurs points de la religion chrétienne, considérés politiquement* (Neuchâtel, 1783).

[Brissot de Warville, Jacques-Pierre], *Le Philadelphien à Genève, ou Lettres d'un Américain sur la dernière Révolution de Genève* ("Dublin" [Amsterdam?], 1783).

[Brissot de Warville, Jacques-Pierre], *Correspondance universelle sur ce qui intéresse Le Bonheur de l'Homme et de la société* ("Londres" [Neuchâtel], 1783).

[Brissot de Warville, Jacques-Pierre], *Tableau de la situation actuelle des Anglois dans les Indes Orientales* (Paris, 1784).

[Brissot de Warville, Jacques-Pierre], *Lettre à l'Empereur sur l'atrocité des supplices qu'il a substitués comme adoucissement à la peine de mort* (Brussels, 1787).

[Brissot de Warville, Jacques-Pierre], *New Travels in the United States of America* (1788), ed. D. Echeverria (Cambridge, MA, 1964).

[Brissot de Warville, Jacques-Pierre], *Mémoire aux États-Généraux sur la necessité de rendre dès ce moment la presse libre* (Paris, June 1789).

[Brissot de Warville, Jacques-Pierre (ed.)], *Le Patriote français. Journal libre, impartial et national* (journal: Paris, 1789–93).

[Brissot de Warville, Jacques-Pierre], *Mémoires* (Paris, 1911).

Bruno, Giordano, *The Cabala of Pegasus*, ed. S. L. Sondergard and M. U. Sowell (New Haven, 2002).

Burke, Edmund, *A Vindication of Natural Society* (1756), in *The Works of the Right Honourable Edmund Burke* (6 vols., London, 1815) i. 1–80.

Burke, Edmund, *Pre-Revolutionary Writings*, ed. Ian Harris (Cambridge, 1993).

Burke, Edmund, *Reflections on the Revolution in France* (1790), ed. F. M. Turner (New Haven, 2003).

Cabanis, Pierre-Jean-Georges, *Opinion de Cabanis sur les réunions s'occupant d'objets politiques* (Paris, n.d. [1795?]). **BL.**

Cabanis, Pierre-Jean-Georges, *Oeuvres complètes* (5 vols., Paris, 1823–5).

Capasso, Giambattista, *Historiae Philosophiae Synopsis sive De Origine, et Progressu Philosophiae* (Naples, 1728).

Capellen, Joan Derk van der, *Aan het Volk van Nederland* (1781), ed. H. L. Zwitzer (Amsterdam, 1987).

Carra, Jean-Louis, *L'Orateur des États-Généraux, pour 1789* (2 vols., Paris, 1789).

Carrol, William, *Spinoza Reviv'd* (London, 1709).

Castillon, M. J. de, *Observations sur le livre intitulé* Systême de la Nature (Berlin, 1771).

Catalogue des livres de la Bibliothèque de feu M. le Baron d'Holbach (Paris, 1789). BL

Censure de la Faculté de Théologie de Paris contre un livre qui a pour titre Histoire philosophique et politique [. . .] par G. T. Raynal (Paris and Liège, 1782).

Cerisier, Antoine-Marie, *Ontwerp om de Republiek door eene heilzaame vereeniging der belangen [. . .] gelukkig [. . .] te maaken* (known as the *Leidse Ontwerp*) (Leiden, 1785). Kn. 21045

Cerisier, Antoine-Marie, *Observations impartiales d'un vrai Hollandois à ses compatriotes* (n.p., 1778). Kn. 19191

Cerisier, Antoine-Marie, *Le Politique hollandois* (journal: Leiden, 1780–5).

Cérutti, Joseph Antoine, *Mémoire pour le peuple françois* (Paris, 1788).

Cérutti, Joseph Antoine, *Vues générales sur la Constitution françoise* (Paris, 1789).

[Charrière, Isabelle de (Belle van Zuylen)], *Éclaircissemens relatifs à la publication Des* Confesssions *de Rousseau, Avec des réflexions sur la réputation, les apologies de MM. Céruti et d"Holback* (n.p., n.d., but Paris, 1789); also in Charrière, *Oeuvres complètes* x (Amsterdam, 1981). BL

Chastellux, François Jean, marquis de, *De la felicité publique, ou Considérations sur le sort des hommes dans les différentes époques de l'histoire* (Amsterdam, 1772).

Chastellux, François Jean, marquis de, *Discours sur les avantages ou les desavantages qui résultent pour l'Europe de la découverte de l'Amérique* in H. J. Lüsebrink and A. Mussard (eds.), *Avantages et desavantages de la découverte de l'Amérique. Chastellux, Raynal et le concours de l'Académie de Lyon* (Saint-Étienne, 1994).

Chateaubriand, François-René, vicomte de, *Mémoires d'outre-tombe*, ed. Pierre Clara (3 vols., Paris, 1973).

Chénier, Marie-Joseph de, *Dénonciation des Inquisiteurs de la pensée* (25 Aug. 1789) (Paris, 1789).

La Chronique de Paris (journal appearing from August 1789 to August 1793), ed. Louis-Pierre Manuel, Rabaut Saint-Etienne, Cloots (et al.).

Clarke, Samuel, *A Demonstration of the Being and Attributes of God* (1705), ed. E. Veilati (Cambridge, 1998).

Clavière, Etienne, and J. P. Brissot, *De la France et des États-Unis ou De l'importance de la Révolution de l'Amérique pour le bonheur de la France* ("Londres," 1787).

Cloots, Anarcharsis, *Voeux d'un Gallophile* (Amsterdam, 1786).

Cloots, Anarcharsis, *De Algemeene Republiek of Aanspraak aan de ombrengers der dwingelanden* (Dunkirk, 1792).

[Cloots, Anarcharsis], *La Certitude des preuves du mahométisme ou Réfutation de l'examen des Apologistes de la Religion Mahométane par Ali-Gier Ber, Alfaki* ("Londres" [Amsterdam?], 1780).

B.d.C.d.V.d.G [Cloots, Anarcharsis], *Lettre sur les juifs à un ecclesiastique de mes amis* (Berlin, 1783).

Comte, Auguste, *Correspondance générale et confessions* i (1814–40) (Paris and The Hague, 1973).

Condillac, Étienne Bonot de, *Essay on the Origin of Human Knowledge*, ed. H. Aarsleff (Cambridge, 2001).

Condorcet, Jean-Antoine-Nicolas de Caritat, marquis de, *Oeuvres complètes*, ed. L. S. Caritat et al. (21 vols., Brunswick and Paris, 1804).

Condorcet, Jean-Antoine-Nicolas de Caritat, marquis de, *Réflexions sur le commerce des bleds* ("Londres" [Paris?], 1776).

Condorcet, Jean-Antoine-Nicolas de Caritat, marquis de, *Vie de Voltaire*, vol. vi of *Oeuvres complètes*.

Condorcet, Jean-Antoine-Nicolas de Caritat, marquis de, *Réflexions sur l'esclavage des nègres* (Neuchâtel, 1781).

Condorcet, Jean-Antoine-Nicolas de Caritat, marquis de, "De l'influence de la Révolution de l'Amérique sur l'Europe" (1786), in *Oeuvres de Condorcet*, ed. A. Condorcet O'Connor and M. F. Arago (12 vols., Paris, 1847), vol. viii.

Condorcet, Jean-Antoine-Nicolas de Caritat, marquis de, "Sentiments d'un républicain sur les assemblées provinciales et les États Généraux" (1788), in *Oeuvres de Condorcet* vol. viii.

Condorcet, Jean-Antoine-Nicolas de Caritat, marquis de, *Lettres d'un Bourgeois de New Haven à un citoyen de Virginie* (1788), in Philip Mazzei, *Recherches historiques et politiques sur les États-Unis* (4 vols., Colle, 1788), i. 267–371.

Condorcet, Jean-Antoine-Nicolas de Caritat, marquis de, *Réflexions sur la Révolution de 1688, et celle du 10 août 1792* ("Dunkirk," 1792). BL

Condorcet, Jean-Antoine-Nicolas de Caritat, marquis de, *Tableau historique des progrès de l'esprit humain. Projets, Esquisse, Fragments et Notes (1772–1794)*, ed. J. P. Schandeler and P. Crepel (Paris, 2004).

Condorcet, Jean-Antoine-Nicolas de Caritat, marquis de, *Ce que les citoyens ont droit d'attendre de leurs représentans* (speech of 7 Aug. 1791) (Paris, 1791).

Condorcet, Jean-Antoine-Nicolas de Caritat, marquis de, Sur "La Politique naturelle" (d'Holbach), in *Bibliothèque de l'Homme publique* 6 (1790), 62–226.

Condorcet, Jean-Antoine-Nicolas de Caritat, marquis de, *Plan de constitution présenté à la Convention Nationale les 15 et 16 février 1793, l'An II de la République* (Paris, 1793).

[Condorcet, with Charles de Peyssonel et al.], *Bibliothèque de l'Homme Public* (journal: Paris, 1790–2).

Cooper, Thomas, *Philosophical Writings*, ed. Udo Thiel (3 vols., Bristol, 2001).

Cooper, Thomas, "The Scripture Doctrine of Materialism" (1823), in Cooper, *Philosophical Writings*, iii. 99–308.

Coppens, B., *Chronique des revolutions belgique et liégeoise* (Beauvechain, 1992).

Coram, Robert, *Political Inquiries: to which is added a Plan for the General Establishment of Schools throughout the United States* (Wilmington, DE, 1791).

Correspondance inédite de Condorcet et de Turgot (1770–1779), ed. Ch. Henry (Paris, 1883).

Courier du Bas-Rhin (journal: ed. Jean Manzon (Cleves (Prussia), 1768–98).

Cousin, Victor, *Souvenirs d'Allemagne. Notes d'un journal de voyage en l'année 1817*, ed. D. Bourel (Paris, 2011).

Damnatio et prohibitio operis in plures tomos distribuiti, cujus est titulus, Encyclopédie (Rome, 3 Sept. 1759).

Da Costa, Isaac, *Bezwaren Tegen den Geest der Eeuw* (Leiden, 1823).
Dale, Anthonie van, *De Oraculis veterum ethnicorum* (1683; 2nd edn., Amsterdam, 1700).
Dale, Anthonie van, *Verhandeling van de oude orakelen der heydenen* (1687; new edn., Amsterdam, 1718).
Dangerous Positions: or, Blasphemous, Profane, Immoral and Jesuitical Assertions, faithfully discovered (London, 1708).
Deleyre, Alexandre, *Tableau de l'Europe, pour servir de supplément à l'*Histoire philosophique [. . .] des Deux Indes ("Amsterdam" [Maastricht?], 1774).
Delisle de Sales, Jean-Baptiste, *De la philosophie de la Nature ou traité de morale pour l'espèce humaine* (1770; 6 vols. "à Londres" [Amsterdam], 1777).
Delisle de Sales, Jean-Baptiste, *De la Philosophie du bonheur* (2 vols., Paris, 1797).
Démeunier, Jean-Nicolas, *L'Esprit des usages et des coûtumes des différents peuples* (3 vols., "Londres" [Paris], 1776).
Démeunier, Jean-Nicolas, *L'Amérique indépendente, ou les différentes constitutions des treize provinces, qui se sont érigées en républiques sous le nom d'États-Unis de l'Amérique* (3 vols., Ghent, 1790).
Destutt de Tracy, Antoine, *Premiers écrits*, ed. Claude Joly (Paris, 2011).
Destutt de Tracy, Antoine, *Analyse raisonée de l'Origine de tous les cultes ou religion universelle* (1799; Paris, 1804).
Destutt de Tracy, Antoine, *Éléments d'idéologie*, ed. H. Goulier (1801; 2 vols., Paris, 1970).
Destutt de Tracy, Antoine, *Commentaire sur* l'Esprit des Lois *de Montesquieu*, ed. Claude Jolly (Paris, 2016).
Diderot, Denis, *Oeuvres*, ed. Laurent Versini (4 vols., Paris, 1994).
Diderot, Denis, *Oeuvres complètes*, ed. I. Assezat and M. Tourneux (20 vols., Paris, 1875–7).
Diderot, Denis, *Oeuvres complètes*, ed. R. Lewinter (15 vols., Paris, 1969–73).
Diderot, Denis, *Oeuvres philosophiques*, ed. P. Vernière (Paris, 1990).
Diderot, Denis, *Correspondence*, ed. G. Roth and J. Varloot (15 vols., Paris, 1955–70).
Diderot, Denis, *Pensées philosophiques*, in Diderot, *Oeuvres philosophiques* (Paris, 1990), 9–55.
Diderot, Denis, *Le Rêve d'Alembert*, in Verniere (ed.), Diderot, *Oeuvres philosophiques*, 249–385.
Diderot, Denis, *De l'Interprétation de la nature* (1753) in *Oeuvres complètes*, 165–245.
Diderot, Denis, *Le Neveu de Rameau*, ed. Jean-Pol Caput (Paris, 1972).
Diderot, Denis, *Pages inédites contre un tyran*, ed. Franco Venturi (n.p., 1937).
Diderot, Denis, *Political Writings* trans. and ed. J. H. Mason and Robert Wokler (Cambridge, 1992).
Diderot, Denis, *Commentaire sur Hemsterhuis*, ed. G. May, in F. Hemsterhuis, *Lettre sur l'homme*, 44–513 (New Haven, 1964).
Diderot, Denis, *Principes de politique des souverains* (1775), in *Oeuvres complètes*, ed. J. Assezat ii. 459–502.
Diderot, Denis, *Supplément au voyage de Bougainville*, ed. A. Adam (Paris, 1972).
Diderot, Denis, *Apologie de l'abbé Galiani* (1770), in M. Barrillon (ed.), Diderot, *Apologies* (Marseille, 1998), 63–133.
Diderot, Denis, *Fragments échappés du portefeuille d'un philosophe*, in *Oeuvres complètes*, ed. J. Assézat vi. 444–57.
Diderot, Denis, *Lettre apologétique de l'abbé Raynal à M. Grimm* (1781), in Barrillon (ed.), Diderot, *Apologies*, 135–58.
Diderot, Denis, *Essai sur le règnes de Claude et de Néron et sur les mœurs et les écrits de Sénèque* (2 vols., "Londres" [Amsterdam?], 1782).

Diderot, Denis, and Jean le Rond d'Alembert, *Encyclopédie ou Dictionnaire raisonné des sciences, des arts et des métiers* (17 vols., Paris, Geneva, and Neuchâtel, 1751–72).

Diez, Heinrich Friedrich, *Apologie der Duldung und Pressfreiheit* (n.p., 1781).

Diez, Heinrich Friedrich, *Benedikt von Spinoza nach Leben und Lehren* (Dessau, 1783).

Dragonetti, Giacinto, *A Treatise on Virtues and Rewards* (London, 1769).

Dohm, Christian Wilhelm von, *Geschichte der Engländer und Französen im östlichen Indien* (Leipzig, 1776).

Dohm, Christian Wilhelm von, *Denkwürdigkeiten meiner Zeit oder Beiträge zur Geschichte vom letzten Viertel des achtzehnten und vom Anfang des neunzehnten Jahrhunderts (1778 bis 1806)* (4 vols., Lemgo and Hanover, 1814).

Dohm, Christian Wilhelm von, *Exposé de la Révolution de Liège en 1789* (Liège, 1790).

Doria, Paolo Mattia, *Discorsi critici filosifici intorno alla filosofía degl' antichi, e degli moderni* (Venice, 1724).

Doria, Paolo Mattia, *Difesa della metafisica degli antichi filosifi contro il signor Giovanni Locke* (2 vols., Venice, 1732).

[Dubuisson, P. U.], *Lettres critiques et politiques sur les colonies* [. . .] adressés à G. T. Raynal (Geneva, 1785).

Dumont, Étienne, *Souvenirs de Mirabeau*, ed. J. Bénétruy (Paris, 1951).

Dupont de Nemours, Pierre Samuel, *De l'origine et des progrès d'une science nouvelle* (1768; repr. Catania, 1992).

Edelmann, Johann Christian, *Moses mit aufgedeckten Angesichte* (3 vols., "Freyburg" [i.e. Berleburg], 1740).

[D.J.C.], *España triunfante en el actual siglo filosófico* (Madrid, 1786).

Enden, Franciscus van den, *Free Political Propositions and Considerations of State*, trans. and ed. Wim Klever ("Vrijstad," 2007).

Esprit de Guillaume-Thomas Raynal, Recueil également nécessaire à ceux qui commandent et à ceux qui obéissent (2 vols., "Londres" [Paris?], 1782). PBN

Ewald, Johann Ludwig, *Über Revolutionen ihre Quelle und die Mittel dagegen* (1792; 2nd edn., Berlin, 1793).

Exposé des droits des Colonies Britanniques pour justifier le projet de leur indépendance (Amsterdam, 1776). Kn. 19118

[Feller, François Xavier de, SJ], "Flexier de Reval," *Catéchisme philosophique, ou recueil d'observations propres à défendre la religion chrétienne contre ses ennemis* (1772; Liège and Brussels, 1773).

[Feller, François Xavier de, SJ] *Journal historique et littéraire* (journal: Liège, Brussels, and Maastricht, 1773–94).

Ferguson, Adam, *An Essay on the History of Civil Society* (Edinburgh, 1767).

Ferguson, Adam, *Institutes of Moral Philosophy for the Use of Students in the College of Edinburgh* (Edinburgh, 1773; repr. New York, 1978).

Ferguson, Adam, *Remarks on a pamphlet lately published by Dr Price, intitled* Observations on the nature of civil liberty (London, 1776).

Ferguson, Adam, *Principles of Moral and Political Science* (2 vols., Edinburgh, 1792; repr. 1978).

Feuerbach, Ludwig, *Pierre Bayle. Ein Beitrag zur Geschichte der Philosophie und Menschheit* (Berlin, 1989).

Fichte, Johann Gottlieb, *Early Philosophical Writings*, ed. D. Beazeale (Ithaca, 1988).

Fichte, Johann Gottlieb, "Selected Correspondence," in Fichte, *Early Philosophical Writings*, 355–44.
Fichte, Johann Gottlieb, *Foundations of Natural Right* (1795), ed. F. Neuhouser (Cambridge, 2000).
Fichte, Johann Gottlieb, "On the Ground of our Belief in a Divine World-Governance," in Estes and Bowman (eds.), *J. G. Fichte*, 17–29.
Fichte, Johann Gottlieb, "Appeal to the Public" (1799), in Estes and Bowman (eds.), *J. G. Fichte*, 85–125.
Fichte, Johann Gottlieb, *Foundations of Transcendental Philosophy* [Wissenschaftslehre novo methodo] (1799), ed. D. Beazeale (Ithaca, 1992).
Fichte, Johann Gottlieb, *Schriften zur Revolution* (Cologne, 1967).
Fichte, Johann Gottlieb, *Fichte. Ausgewahlt und vorgestellt von Günter Schulte* (Munich, 1996).
Filangieri, Gaetano, *La Scienza della legislazione*, critical edn. ed. A. Trampus (7 vols., Venice, 2003–4).
Finestrad, Joaquin de, *El Vasallo instruido en el estado del Nuevo Reino de Granada y en sus respectivas obligaciones* (1789; Bogotá, 2000).
Forner, Juan Pablo, *Discursos filosóficos sobre el hombre* (Madrid, 1787).
Forner, Juan Pablo, *Preservativo contra el Atheismo* (Seville, 1795).
[Forsskål, Peter], *Tankar om Borgerliga Friheten* (Stockholm, 1759).
[Forsskål, Peter], *Thoughts on Civil Liberty*, ed. David Goldberg et al. (Stockholm, 2009).
Forster, Georg, *Werke, sämtliche Schriften, Tagebücher, Briefe*, ed. K. G. Popp et al. (18 vols., Berlin, 1968–82).
Fortgesetzte Sammlung von Alten und Neuen Theologischen Sachen, Büchern, Urkunden, Controversien Leipzig periodical. GUB
Franklin, Benjamin, *The Papers*, ed. L. W. Labaree et al. (43 vols. thus far; New Haven, 1959–).
Frederick the Great, king of Prussia, *Examen de l'*Essai sur les préjugés ("Londres" [Berlin], 1770).
Frederick the Great, king of Prussia, "A Critical Examination of the *System of Nature*," in the *Posthumous Works of Frederic II, king of Prussia* trans. Th. Holcroft, vol. 5 (London, 1789), 147–75.
Freitag, S., and P. Wende (eds.), *British Envoys to Germany, 1816–1866* (2 vols., Cambridge, 2000–2).
[Frend, William], *An Account of the Proceedings in the University of Cambridge, against William Frend* (Cambridge, 1793).
Fréron, Elie Catherine, *L'Année Littéraire, ou Suite des lettres sur quelques écrits de ce temps* (292 vols., Paris, 1755–90).
Galiani, Ferdinando, *Dialogues sur le commerce des blés* (1770; Paris, 1984).
Galiani, Ferdinando, *Correspondance avec Madame d'Epinay* [. . .] *Diderot* [. . .]. *D'Holbach* etc. (2 vols., Paris, 1881, repr. 2005).
Garat, Dominique-Joseph, *Mémoires historiques sur la vie de M. Suard, sur ses écrits, et sur le XVIIIe siècle* (2 vols., Paris, 1820).
Genlis, Stephanie Félicité, comtesse de, *Religion considered as the only Basis of Happiness and true Philosophy* (2 vols., Dublin, 1787).
Genovesi, Antonio, *Discorso sopra il vero fine delle lettere e delle scienze* (1753), in F. Venturi (ed.), *Illuminati Italiani*, vol. 5 (Milan, 1965), 84–131.
Genovesi, Antonio, *Elementa Metaphysicae mathematicum in morem adornata* (1743–5; 4th edn., 5 vols., Naples, 1760).

Genovesi, Antonio, *Lezioni di comercio o sia d'economia civile* (1765; 2 vols., Bassano, 1769).
Genovesi, Antonio, *Note sul Spirito delle Leggi del signore di Montesquieu* (4 vols., Naples, 1777).
Gentz, Friedrich von, *The Origin and Principles of the American Revolution compared with the Origin and Principles of the French Revolution* (Philadelphia, 1800).
Gibbon, Edward, *The Autobiographies*, ed. J. Murray (London, 1896).
Gibbon, Edward, *Memoirs of my Life and Writings* (Keele, 1994).
Ginguené, Pierre-Louis, *Lettres sur les* Confessions *de J. J. Rousseau* (Paris, 1791).
Godwin, William, *An Enquiry concerning Political Justice and Its Influence on General Virtue and happiness* (2 vols., London, 1793). BL
[Godwin, William], *History of the Internal Affairs of the United Provinces from the year 1780, to the Commencement of Hostilities in June 1787* (London, 1787).
Goeree, Willem, *De Kerklyke en Weereldlyke Historien* (1705; 2nd edn., Leiden, 1729).
Gorani, Count Giuseppe, *Il Vero Dispotismo* ("Londra" [i.e. Geneva], 1770).
Gorani, Count Giuseppe, *Recherches sur la science du gouvernement* (1786; trans. of 2nd edn., 2 vols., Paris, 1792).
Gorani, Count Giuseppe, *Mémoires secrets et critiques des cours, des gouvernemens, et les moeurs des principaux états de l'Italie* (3 vols., Paris, 1793).
Granié, Pierre, *Lettre à M... sur la philosophie dans ses rapports avec notre gouvernement* (Paris, 1802).
Griggs, E. L., and Clifford H. Prator (eds.), *Henry Christophe and Thomas Clarkson: A Correspondence* (New York, 1968).
Grolman, Ludwig Adolf Christian von, *Die neuesten Arbeiten des Spartacus und Philo in dem Illuminaten-orden jetzt zum erstenmal gedruckt* (n.p. [Frankfurt am Main], 1793).
Grolman, Ludwig Adolf Christian von, *Kritische Geschichte der Illuminaten-Grade* (n.p. [Frankfurt am Main], 1793).
Grund, Francis J., *Aristocracy in America* (1839), ed. Armin Mattes (Columbia, MO, 2018).
Gurdon, Brampton, *The Pretended Difficulties in Natural or Reveal'd religion No Excuse for Infidelity* (London, 1723).
Haller, Albrecht von, *Tagebuch seiner Beobachtungen über Schriftsteller und über sich selbst* (2 vols., Berne, 1787).
Hamilton, Alexander, James Madison, and John Jay, *The Federalist*, ed. T. Ball (Cambridge, 2003).
Hansen, Joseph (ed.), *Quellen zur Geschichte des Rheinlandes im Zeitalter der französischen Revolution* (4 vols., Bonn, 1931–3).
Hegel, G. W. F., *Lectures on the History of Philosophy* 1825–6, vol. iii, ed. R. F. Brown (Oxford, 1986).
Helvétius, Claude-Adrien, *Réflexions sur l'homme et autres textes*, ed. Jean-Pierre Jackson (Paris, 2006).
Helvétius, Claude-Adrien, *De L'Esprit* (Paris, 1758; repr. 1988).
Helvétius, Claude-Adrien, *Le Bonheur, Poéme, en six chants* ("Londres" [Amsterdam], 1772).
Helvétius, Claude-Adrien, *De l'homme: de ses facultés intellectuelles et de son éducation* (1773; repr. 2 vols., Paris, 1989).
Helvétius, Claude-Adrien, *Correspondance générale*, ed. A. Dainard et al. (3 vols., Toronto and Oxford, 1981–91).
Helvétius, Claude-Adrien, *Notes de la main d'Helvétius publiées d'après un manuscrit inédit*, ed. A. Keim (Paris, 1907).

Herder, Johann Gottfried, *Selected Early Works, 1764–1767*, ed. E. A. Menze and K. Menges (University Park, PA, 1992).

Herder, Johann Gottfried, *Gott. Einige Gespräche über Spinoza's System* (1787; 2nd edn., Gotha, 1800).

Herder, Johann Gottfried, *Ideen zur Philosophie der Geschichte der Menschheit* (4 vols., Riga, 1785).

Herder, Johann Gottfried, *Philosophical Writings*, ed. M. N. Forster (Cambridge, 2002).

Herder, Johann Gottfried, *Another Philosophy of History* (1774), ed. I. D. Evrigenis and D. Pellerin (Indianapolis, IN, 2004).

Hess, Moses, *Briefwechsel*, ed. E. Silberner (The Hague, 1959).

Histoire de l'Académie Royale des Sciences (annual journal: Paris, 1702–97).

Histoire philosophique et politique des établissemens et du commerce des Européens dans les deux Indes by Raynal, Diderot, Deleyre, etc. (6 vols., Amsterdam, 1770).

Histoire philosophique et politique des établissemens et du commerce des Européens dans les deux Indes (6 vols., Amsterdam, 1774).

Histoire philosophique et politique des établissemens et du commerce des Européens dans les deux Indes (10 vols., Geneva, 1780) [one third of which is the work of Diderot].

Holbach, baron d', Paul-Henri Thiry, *Le Christianisme dévoilé ou, Examen des principes et des effets de la religion chrétienne* (repr. Paris, 2006).

Holbach, baron d', Paul-Henri Thiry, *La Contagion sacrée ou, Histoire naturelle de la superstition* (1768; repr. Paris, 2006).

Holbach, baron d', Paul-Henri Thiry, *Lettres à Eugénie ou, Préservatif contre les préjugés* (1768; repr. Paris, 2007).

Holbach, baron d', Paul-Henri Thiry, *Essai sur les Préjugés ou, De l'Influence des opinions sur les mœurs et sur le bonheur des hommes* ("Londres" [Amsterdam], 1770).

Holbach, baron d', Paul-Henri Thiry, *Système de la nature, ou Des Loix du monde physique et du monde moral* (1770; 2 vols., "Londres" [Amsterdam], new edn. 1781, repr. Paris, 1990).

Holbach, baron d', Paul-Henri Thiry, *Histoire critique de Jésus-Christ, ou, Analyse raisonnée des Évangiles* (n.p. [Amsterdam] 1770) in d'Holbach, *Oeuvres philosophiques complètes*, vol. ii, ed. Jean-Pierre Jackson, 645–815.

Holbach, baron d', Paul-Henri Thiry, *La Politique naturelle, ou discours sur les vrais principes du gouvernement* (1773; repr. Paris, 1998).

Holbach, baron d', Paul-Henri Thiry, *Système social, ou principes naturels de la morale et de la politique* (1773; repr. Paris, 1994).

Holbach, baron d', Paul-Henri Thiry, *Le Bon-Sens du Curé Jean Meslier suivi de son Testament* ("Londres" [Amsterdam, 1772) repr. of the edn of "Bruxelles, 1829," Hildesheim, 1970).

Holbach, baron d', Paul-Henri Thiry, *La Morale universelle, ou, Les Devoirs de l'homme fondés sur sa nature* (3 vols., Amsterdam, 1776).

Holbach, baron d', Paul-Henri Thiry, *Éthocratie ou Le Gouvernement fondé sur la morale* (Amsterdam, 1776), in d'Holbach, *Oeuvres philosophiques complètes*, vol. iii, ed. Jean-Pierre Jackson (Paris, 2000), 590–707.

Holberg, L., *Memoirs of Lewis Holberg* (London, 1827).

Hölderlin, Friedrich, *Sämtliche Werke*, ed. F. Beissner et al. (8 vols., Stuttgart, 1946–85).

Humboldt, Wilhelm von, *Briefe*, ed. H. Gollwitzer (Munich, 1952).

Humboldt, Wilhelm von, "Antrag auf Errichtung der Universität Berlin," in W. von Humboldt, *Schriften zur Bildung*, ed. G. Lauer (Stuttgart, 2017), 143–51.

Humboldt, Wilhelm von, *The Sphere and Duties of Government*, trans J. Coulthard (1854; repr. Bristol, 1996).
Hume, David, *Treatise of Human Nature* (1739) (Buffalo, NY, 1992).
Hume, David, "Of Superstition and Enthusiasm" (1741), in R. Wolheim (ed.), *Hume on Religion*.
Hume, David, *Essays Moral, Political and Literary*, ed. E. F. Miller (1741; Indianapolis, IN, 1985).
Hume, David, *Dialogues concerning Natural Religion*, in R. Wolheim (ed.), *Hume on Religion*, 99–204.
Hume, David, *An Enquiry concerning Human Understanding* (1748), ed. E. Steinberg (2nd edn., Indianapolis, IN, 1993).
Hume, David, *An Enquiry concerning the Principles of Morals* (1751), ed. T. L. Beauchamp (Oxford, 1998).
Hume, David, *The Natural History of Religion* (1757), in J. C. A. Gaskin (ed.), David Hume, *Principal Writings on Religion* (Oxford, 1993), 134–93.
Hume, David, *The History of England from the Invasion of Julius Caesar to The Revolution of 1688* (6 vols., Indianapolis, IN, 1983).
Hume, David, *Letters*, ed. J. Y. T. Greig (2 vols., Oxford, 1969).
Hume, David, *Life and Correspondence of David Hume*, ed. J. H. Burton (2 vols., Edinburgh, 1846).
L'Impie démasqué, ou Remontrance aux écrivains incrédules ("Londres" [Paris?], 1773).
Index Librorum prohibitorum Pii Sexti jussu editus (Rome, 1786). BL
Indice último de los libros prohibidos y mandatos expurgar para todos los reynos y señorios del católico rey de las Españas (Madrid, 1790).
Irhoven van Dam, Wilhelmus van, *Courier van Europa* (journal: Amsterdam, 1783–5).
Jacobi, Friedrich Heinrich, *The Main Philosophical Writings*, trans. G. di Giovanni (Montreal, 1994).
Jacobi, Friedrich Heinrich, *Schriften zum Spinozastreit*, ed. K. Hammacher and I. Piske (2 vols., Hamburg, 1998).
Jamin, Nicolas, *Pensées théologiques relatives aux erreurs du temps* (1768; new edn., Riom, 1798).
Jebb, John, *The Works Theological, Medical, Political and Miscellaneous* (3 vols., London, 1787).
Jefferson, Thomas, *The Political Writings*, ed. M. D. Peterson (Monticello, VA, 1993).
Jefferson, Thomas, *Writings*, ed. M. D. Peterson (New York, 1984).
Jelles, Jarig, *Belydenisse des algemeenen en Christelycken Geloofs* (Amsterdam, 1684).
Journal des décrets de l'Assemblée Nationale, ed. François-Jérôme Riffard de Saint Martin (5 vols., Paris, 1789–91).
[Jullien, Marc Antoine], *Revue encyclopédique ou analyse raisonnée des productions les plus remarquables dans la littérature, les sciences et les arts* (journal: Paris, 1819–35).
Justification de la résistance des Colonies Américains aux oppressions du Gouvernement Britannique ("Londres," 1776). Kn. 19120
Kames, Lord, Henry Home, *Essays on the Principles of Morality and Natural Religion* (1751).
Kames, Lord, Henry Home, *Six Sketches on the History of Man* (Philadelphia, 1776).
Kames, Lord, Henry Home, *Elements of Criticism*, ed. P. Jones (6th edn., 2 vols., Indianapolis, IN, 2005).

Kant, Immanuel, *Gesammelte Schriften* edition of the Königlich Preussischen Akademie der Wissenschaften (35 vols., Berlin, 1902–97).

Kant, Immanuel, *Critique of Practical Reason*, trans. L. White Beck (3rd edn., London, 1993).

Kant, Immanuel, *Was ist Aufklärung? Ausgewählte kleine Schriften*, ed. H. D. Brandt (Hamburg, 1999).

Kant, Immanuel, *Religion within the Boundaries of Mere Reason*, ed. A. Wood and G. di Giovanni (Cambridge, 1998).

Kant, Immanuel, "What does it mean to orient oneself in thinking?," in Kant, *Religion within the Boundaries*, 3–14.

Kant, Immanuel, "On the Use of Teleological Principles in Philosophy" (1788), in Robert Bernasconi (ed.), *Race* (Oxford, 2001), 37–56.

Kant, Immanuel, *Lectures on Metaphysics*, ed. K. Ameriks (1997; repr. Cambridge, 2001).

Kant, Immanuel, *Toward Perpetual Peace: A Philosophical Sketch*, in P. Kleingeld (ed.), Immanuel Kant, *Toward Perpetual Peace and Other Writings on Politics, Peace, and History* (New Haven, 2006) 67–109.

Kant, Immanuel, *Groundwork of the Metaphysics of Morals*, ed. M. Gregor (Cambridge, 1997).

Kant, Immanuel, *Critique of Judgment*, trans. J. H. Bernard (New York, 1951).

Kant, Immanuel, *Briefwechsel von Imm. Kant*, ed. H. E. Fischer (3 vols., Munich, 1912–13).

Die Korrespondenz des Illuminatenordens vol. i *(1776–1781)*, ed. R. Markner, M. Neugebauer-Wölk, and H. Schuttler (Tübingen, 2005).

Koerbagh, Adriaen, *A Light Shining in Dark Places to Illuminate the Main Questions of Theology and Religion* (1668), ed. Michiel Wielema (Leiden, 2011).

Kuyper, Frans, *Bewys dat noch de schepping van de natuur noch de mirakelen, die de H. Schrift verhaalt tegen de natuurlijke reeden strijdig zijn* (Amsterdam, 1685).

La Beaumelle, Laurent Angliviel de, *Mes pensées ou Le qu'en dira-t-on*, ed. C. Lauriol (Geneva, 1997).

La Beaumelle, Laurent Angliviel de, *La Spectatrice danoise; ou, L'aspasie moderne; ouvrage hebdomdaire* (Copenhagen, 1749–50).

[La Beaumelle, Laurent A. de] L.B.L.D.A, *L'Asiatique tolérant* ("Paris" [Amsterdam], 1748). AUB

La Beaumelle, Laurent Angliviel de, *Suite de la Defense de* L'Esprit des Loix (1751; repr. Geneva, 1753). IAS

La Beaumelle, Laurent Angliviel de, *Pièces pour et contre* L'Esprit des Loix (Geneva, 1752).

La Court, Johan de, *Consideratien en exempelen van Staat, omtrent de fundamenten van allerley regeeringe* (Amsterdam, 1660).

[La Court, Pieter de], *Interest van Holland, ofte gronden van Hollands-Welvaren* (Amsterdam, 1662).

[La Court, Pieter de], *Aanwijsing der heilsame politike gronden en maximen van de Republike van Holland en West-Vriesland* (Leiden, 1669). BL

[La Court, Pieter de], V.D.H. *Le Vrai Interet de la Hollande* translated by I.N.D.P. [Jean Nicolas de Parival] (Amsterdam?, n.d.).

[La Court, Pieter de], *The True Interest and Political Maxims of the Republic of Holland and West-Friesland written by John de Witt and other Great men in Holland* (London, 1702).

Lakanal, Joseph, *Rapport fait au nom du Comité d'Instruction Publique* (23 Ventose, An III (Paris, 1795).

Lakanal, Joseph, *Aperçu des Dépenses des divers objets d'instruction publique présenté au comité d'instruction publique* (Paris, Year III).

Lalande, Jérôme, *Voyage en Italie contenant l'histoire et les anecdotes les plus singulières de l'Italie* (2nd edn., Paris, 1786).

Lamourette, Adrien, *Pensées sur la philosophie de l'incrédulité* (Paris, 1786).

Lardizábal y Uribe, Manuel de, *Discurso sobre la penas contrahido a las leyes criminales de España para facilitar su reforma* (Madrid, 1782).

Lau, Theodor Ludwig, *Meditationes philosophicae de Deo, Mundo, Homine* (1717) (Stuttgart, 1992).

Le Clerc, Jean, *Mr. Le Clerc's Extract and Judgment on the Rights of the Christian Church, translated from his Bibliotheque choisie* (London?, 1711?).

Leenhof, Frederik van, *De Prediker van de wijzen en magtigen konink Salomon* (Zwolle, 1700). AUB

Leenhof, Frederik van, *Het leven van de wijzen en magtigen konink Salomon* (Zwolle, 1700). AUB

Leibniz, Gottfried Wilhelm, *Philosophical Essays*, ed. R. Ariew and Dan Garber (Indianapolis, IN, 1989).

Leibniz, Gottfried Wilhelm, *Theodicy*, ed. A. Farrer (La Salle, IL, 1985).

Leland, John, *A View of the principal Deistical Writers* (3 vols., London, 1755–7; repr. New York, 1978).

Lessing, Gotthold Ephraim, *Gesammelte Werke*, ed. P. Rilla (10 vols., Berlin, 1954–8).

Lessing, Gotthold Ephraim, "Des Andreas Wissowatius Einwurfe wider die Dreieinigkeit," in *Gesammelte Werke*, vii. 489–535.

Lessing, Gotthold Ephraim, *Philosophical and Theological Writings*, trans. and ed. H. B. Nisbet (Cambridge, 2005).

Lessing, Gotthold Ephraim, *Ernst und Falk*, in Nisbet (ed.), *Philosophical and Theological Writings*, 184–216.

Lessing, Gotthold Ephraim, *Briefe*, ed. H. Kiesel, in G. E. Lessing, *Werke und Brief*, ed. W. Barner (3 vols., Frankfurt, 1987).

Lessing, Gotthold Ephraim, *Anti-Goetze*, in H. G. Göpfert (ed.), G. E. Lessing, *Werke in drei Banden* (Munich, 1982), iii. 477–546.

Lettre à Monsieur Raynal (Marseille, 17 Mar. 1789).

Lettre sur l'invasion des Provinces Unies à M. Le Comte Mirabeau, et sa réponse (Brussels, 1787).

Lettres de Genève (1741–193) à Jean Henri Samuel Formey, ed. A. Bandelier and F. S. Eigeldinger (Paris, 2010).

Lichtenberg, Georg Christoph, *Werke* (Hamburg, 1967).

Lichtenberg, Georg Christoph, *Schriften und Briefe*, ed. W. Promies (6 vols., Munich, 1968).

[Lilburne, John?], *A Declaration to the free-born People of England: Concerning the Government of the Commonwealth* (London, 1654).

Llano Zapata, José Eusebio, *Memorias histórico-físicas, crítico-apologéticas de la América meridional* (Lima, 2005).

Locke, John, *Epistola de Tolerantia*, ed. R. Klibansky (Oxford, 1968).

Locke, John, *Political Writings*, ed. David Wootton (London, 1993).

Locke, John, *The Second Treatise of Government* (*c.*1681), in Locke, *Political Writings*, 261–387.

Locke, John, *An Essay concerning Human Understanding*, ed. P. H. Nidditch (Oxford, 1975).

Locke, John, *The Reasonableness of Christianity* (1695), ed. G. W. Ewing (repr. Washington, DC, 1989).

Locke, John, *Some Thoughts concerning Education*, ed. J. W. and J. S. Yolton (Oxford, 1989; repr. 2003).

Luxdorphs samling af trykke-frihedens skrifter (collection of printed pamphlets dating from 1770–3, in RLC).

Luzac, Elie, *Hollands rijkdom behelzende den oorsprong van den koophandel, en van de magt van desen staat* (3 vols., Leiden, 1780).

Mably, Gabriel Bonnot de, *Collection complète des Oeuvres de l'Abbé de Mably* (15 vols., Paris, "l'an III de la République" [1794/95]).

Mably, Gabriel Bonnot de, *Observations sur le gouvernement et les lois des États-Unis d'Amérique* (1783) in *Collection complète* viii. 337–85.

[Maistre, Joseph de], *Considérations sur la France* (n.p., 1797).

Malesherbes, Chrétien Guillaume de Lamoignon de, *Mémoires sur la librairie et sur la liberté de la presse* (Chapel Hill, NC, 1979).

Maleville, Guillaume, *La Religion naturelle et la révelée établie sur les principes de la vraie philosophie* (6 vols., Paris, 1756–8).

Mallet du Pan, Jacques, *Considérations sur la nature de la Révolution de France* ("Londres," 1793).

Mandeville, Bernard, *The Fable of the Bees*, ed. F. B. Kaye (2 vols., Indianapolis, IN, 1988).

Mandeville, Bernard, *Free Thoughts on Religion, The Church and National Happiness* (London, 1720).

[Mandeville, Bernard], *The Virgin Unmask'd* (London, 1709). BL

Marchena, José, *Essai de théologie* (Paris, 1797).

Maréchal, Pierre-Sylvain de, *Catéchisme du Curé Meslier* (n.p. [Paris], 1790).

Maréchal, Pierre-Sylvain de, *Dictionnaire des athées anciens et modernes* (Brussels, 1833).

Maréchal, Pierre-Sylvain de (with Jacques Grasset de Saint-Sauveur), *Costumes civils actuels de tous les peuples connus* (1784; 2nd edn., 4 vols., Paris, 1788).

Marx, Karl, "Trois Cahiers d'étude de l'année 1841," in *Cahiers Spinoza* i (Paris, 1977), 29–157.

Marx, Karl, *Early Texts*, ed. David McLellan (Oxford, 1971).

Marx, Karl, *Critique of Hegel's "Philosophy of Right"* (1843), ed. J. O'Malley (Cambridge, 1970).

Marx, Karl, *Capital: A Critical Analysis of Capitalist Production*, vol. i (Moscow, 1961).

Marx, Karl, and Friedrich Engels, *The Holy Family, or, Critique of Critical Critique* (1844) (Moscow, 1956).

Meiners, Christoph, *Briefe über die Schweiz* (4 vols., Berlin, 1784–90).

Meiners, Christoph, *Ueber die Natur der Völker im südlichen Asien auf den ostindischen und Südsee-Inseln*, in *Göttingisches Historisches Magazin* vii (1790), 258–306.

Meiners, Christoph, *Historische vergleichung der Sitten, und Verfassungen der Gesetze, und Gewerbe, des Handels und der religion, der Wissenschaften, und Lehranstalten des Mittelalters mit denen unsers Jahrhunderts* (3 vols., Hanover, 1793).

Mémoires authentiques et intéressans ou histoire des comtes Struensee et Brandt (Copenhagen, 1789).

Mémoires véridiques de la Révolution de Liège commencée le 18 Aout 1789 (Liège, 1789). BRL

Mercier, Louis Sebastien, *De J. J. Rousseau considéré comme l'un des premiers auteurs de la Révolution* (2 vols., Paris, 1791).

[Mercier, Louis Sebastien], *Memoirs of the Year Two Thousand Five Hundred*, trans. W. Hooper (London, 1772).

Meyer, Johann, *Die Närrische Welt in ihrer Narrheit, Oder endeckte Quellen der Atheisterey und Freydenckerey* (Breslau, 1752). GUB

Meyer, Lodewijk, *Philosophy as the Interpreter of Holy Scripture* (1666), ed. L. C. Rice and F. Pastijn (Milwaukee, 2005).

Mill, John Stuart, *The Collected Works*, vols. xii and xiii: *The Earlier Letters of John Stuart Mill 1812–1848*, ed. F. E. Mineka (2 vols., Toronto, 1963).

Millar, John, *Observations concerning the Distinction of Ranks in Society* (London, 1771).

[Mirabeau, Honoré Gabriel Riqueti, comte de], *Des Lettres de cachet et des prisons d'état* (1778) (2 vols., "Hambourg," 1782).

[Mirabeau, Honoré Gabriel Riqueti, comte de], *Essai sur le despotisme* (1775; 3rd edn., n.p., 1792).

[Mirabeau, Honoré Gabriel Riqueti, comte de], *Considérations sur l'ordre de Cincinnatus* ("Londres" [Amsterdam?], 1784).

[Mirabeau, Honoré Gabriel Riqueti, comte de], *Avis aux Hessois et autres peuples de l'Allemagne, vendus par leurs princes à l'Angleterre* (1777; 3rd edn., Paris, 1792).

[Mirabeau, Honoré Gabriel Riqueti, comte de], *Aux Bataves sur le stathouderat* (n.p. [Amsterdam?], 1788).

[Mirabeau, Honoré Gabriel Riqueti, comte de], *De la monarchie prussienne sous Frédéric le Grand* (6 vols., "Londres," 1788).

Miranda, Francisco de, *Diario de viaje a Estados Unidos* (1783–4) (Santiago, Chile, 1998).

Miranda, Francisco de, *Archivo del General Miranda. Viajes, Diarios (1750–1785)*, vol. i (Caracas, 1929).

Moniglia, Tommaso Vincenzo, *Dissertazione contro i materalisti e altri increduli* (2 vols., Padua, 1750).

Montesquieu, Charles de Secondat, Baron de, *Oeuvres complètes*, ed. D. Oster (Paris, 1964).

Montesquieu, Charles de Secondat, Baron de, *Défense de l'Esprit des Lois*, in *Oeuvres complètes*, 808–22.

Morellet, Abbé André, *Lettres*, ed. D. Medlin et al. (3 vols. Oxford, 1991–6).

Morellet, Abbé André, *Mémoires sur le dix-huitième siècle et sur la Révolution française* (2 vols., Paris, 1822).

[Morelly], *Code de la Nature, ou le véritable Esprit de ses Loix* ([Amsterdam?], 1755).

Morgan, Thomas, *The Moral Philosopher* (1737; repr. New York, 1977).

Morgan, William, *Memoirs of the Life of the Rev. Richard Price*, in *Enlightenment and Dissent* 22 (2003), 1–95.

Mounier, Jean-Joseph, *Considérations sur les gouvernemens et principalement sur celui qui convient à la France* (Versailles, 1789).

Mounier, Jean-Joseph, *De l'Influence attribuée aux philosophes aux franc-maçons et aux Illuminés sur la Révolution de la France* (Tübingen, 1801).

Muñoz, Juan Bautista, *Historia del Nuevo Mundo*, vol. i (Madrid, 1793).

Münter, Balthasar, *Theologiae naturalis polemicae specimen exhibens historiam et refutationem systematis illius quod a Benedicto de Spinoza nomen habet* (n.p., 1758). GUB

Münter, Balthasar, *Bekehrungsgeschichte des vormaligen Grafen und Königlichen Dänischen Geheimen Cabinetsministers Johann Friedrich Struensee* (Copenhagen, 1772).

Naigeon, Jacques-André, "Lettre sur la mort de M. le Baron d'Holbach," in Naville, *Paul Thiry d'Holbach*, 452–5.
Naigeon, Jacques-André, *Adresse à l'Assemblée Nationale sur la liberté des opinions* (Paris, 1790).
Naigeon, Jacques-André, *Philosophie ancienne et moderne* (3 vols., Paris, 1791).
Naigeon, Jacques-André, *Mémoires historiques et philosophiques sur la vie et les ouvrages de Denis Diderot* (repr. Geneva, 1970).
Naigeon, Jacques-André, and d'Holbach (eds.), *Le Militaire philosophe, ou Difficultés sur la religion proposées au Père Malebranche*, ed. Jean-Pierre Jackson (Paris, 2008).
[Naigeon?], *Discours préliminaire* (1770), printed as appendix to Vercruysse, *Bicentaire*, 39–56.
Narganes de Posada, José Manuel Narganes, *Tres Cartas sobre los vicios de la instrucción pública en España* (Madrid, 1809).
Necker, Jacques, *De l'importance des opinions religieuses* ("Londres" [Paris], 1788).
Die Neue Mainzer Zeitung oder der Volksfreund (journal: Mainz, 1792–3).
Nieuhoff, Bernard, *Over Spinozisme* (Harderwijk, 1799).
Notice des écrits les plus célébres, tant imprimés que manuscripts, qui favorisent l'incrédulité, ou dont la lecture est dangéreuse aux esprits foibles (*c.*1744), in *La Lecture Clandestine* (1993), ii. 178–92.
Nouvelles Observations sur la seconde lettre de Mr de Pinto à l'occasion des troubles de l'Amérique septentrionale ("Londres," 1776). Kn. 19125
Nuix, Juan, *Reflexiones imparciales sobre la humanidad de los españoles en las Indias, contra los pretendidos filósofos y políticos* (Madrid, 1782).
Nuñez de Cáceres, José, *Declaratoria de Independencia del Pueblo Dominicano* (Santo Domingo, 1821).
Observations sur plusieurs assertions extraites littéralement de l'Histoire philosophique des [. . .] deux Indes (Amsterdam, 1776).
Ochs, Peter, *Reden*, ed. Christian Bectin (Basel, 1998).
Oldisworth, William, *A Dialogue between Timothy and Philadeus* (3 vols., London, 1709–11).
O'Leary, Daniel Florence, *Memorias del General Daniel Florencio O'Leary* (3 vols., Caracas, 1952).
Ontwerp om de Republiek door eene heilzaame vereeniging der belangen van regent en burger van binnen gelukkig en van buiten gedugt te maaken (Leiden, 1785), ed. Wybo Fijnje et al. Kn. 21045, HKB
[Paalzow, Christian Ludwig], "Vorbericht des Uebersetzers," in [d'Holbach], *System der Natur, oder von der Gesetzen der physischen und moralischen Welt* (Frankfurt, 1783), pp. i–x.
Paape, Gerrit, *De Aristocraat en de Burger* (Rotterdam, 1785). Kn. 21046
Paape, Gerrit, *De Hollandsche wijsgeer in Braband* (4 vols., Antwerp and Dordrecht, 1788–90).
Paape, Gerrit, *De Hollandsche wijsgeer in Vrankrijk* (Dordrecht, 1790).
Paape, Gerrit, *De Zaak der verdrukte Hollandsche Patriotten voor de vierschaar der Menschlijkheid gebragt* (Dunkirk, 1790).
Paape, Gerrit, *Mijn vrolijke wijsgeerte in mijne ballingschap* (Dordrecht, 1792).
Paape, Gerrit, *Mijn Tegenwoordig Vaderland of wijsgeerige geschiedenis van Vrankrijk* (3 vols., Dordrecht, 1792).
Paape, Gerrit, *De onverbloemde geschiedenis van het Bataafsch Patriottismus* (Delft, 1798).

[Paape, Gerrit], *Het Leven van zijne Doorluchtigste Hoogheid Willem de Vijfden* [. . .] *bijgenaamd de Bederver van zijn Vaderland* (Dunkirk, 1791).
Pagano, Franceso Mario, *Saggi Politici de' principi, progessi e decadenza delle società* (2 vols., Naples, 1791–2).
Paine, Thomas, *The Complete Writings of Thomas Paine*, ed. Philip S. Foner (2 vols., New York, 1945).
Paine, Thomas, *A Collection of Unknown Writings*, ed. Hazel Burgess (New York, 2010).
Paine, Thomas, *Common Sense*, ed. I. Kramnick (Harmondsworth, 1976).
Paine, Thomas, *The American Crisis* nos. 1 to 3 (Philadelphia, 1777).
Paine, Thomas, *Rights of Man* (1790), ed. E. Foner (New York, 1985).
Paine, Thomas, *The Age of Reason* (1794–5), ed. K. Walters (Peterborough, Ontario, 2011).
Paine, Thomas, *Letter to George Washington* (Paris, July 1796) in Paine, *Complete Writings* i. 691–723.
Paine, Thomas, *Political Writings*, ed. Bruce Kuklick (Cambridge, 1989).
Palacio y Viana, Josef de, *Defensa de los puntos mas interesantes a la religion acometidos por los incrédulos* (Madrid, 1788).
Palmer, Eliahu, *An Inquiry relative to the Moral and Political Improvement of the Human Species* (New York, 1797).
Palmer, Eliahu, *Principles of Nature or, A development of the Moral Causes of Happiness and Misery Among the Human Species* (New York, 1801).
Palmieri, Giuseppe, *Riflessioni sulla pubblica felicità relativamente al regno di Napoli* (Naples, 1787).
Parival, Jean-Nicolas, *Abregé de l'histoire de ce siècle de fer contenant les misères et calamitez des derniers temps* (Leiden, 1653).
Paulian, Aime-Henri, *Le Véritable Système de la nature* (2 vols., Avignon, 1788).
Paulus, Pieter, *Vrage: in welken zin kunnen de menschen gezegd worden gelyk te zyn?* (1793; 4th edn., Haarlem, 1794). HKB
Pétion, Jérôme, *Avis aux François sur le salut de la Patrie* (Paris, 1788).
[Petit, Émilien], *Observations sur plusieurs assertions, extraites littéralement de l'*Histoire Philosophique des [. . .] deux Indes (Amsterdam, 1776).
Pilati, Carlantonio, *Ragionamenti intorno alla legge naturale e civile* (1764; Venice, 1766).
Pilati, Carlantonio, *Di una Riforma d'Italia* (1767; 2nd edn., "Villafranca" [Venice], 1770). BL
Pilati, Carlantonio, *Lettere di un viaggiatore filosofo*, ed. G. Pagliero (Bergamo, 1990).
Pinto, Isaac de, *Précis des arguments contre les matérialistes* (The Hague, 1740). BL
Pinto, Isaac de, *Letters on the American Troubles* (London, 1776). BL
Pinto, Isaac de, *Réponse de Mr. I. de Pinto aux observations d'un homme impartial, sur sa lettre à Mr S.B., docteur en médicine à Kingston dans la Jamaïque* (The Hague, 1776). BL
Pinto, Isaac de, *Second Lettre de Mr de Pinto à l'occasion des troubles des colonies, contenant des reflexions politiques* (The Hague, 1776). Kn. 19124, HKB
[Pinto, Isaac de], *Lettre de Mr**** [I. de Pinto] *à Mr S.B* [. . .] *au sujet des troubles qui agitent actuellement toute l'Amérique Septentrionale* (The Hague, 1776). Kn. 19122, HKB
Plans d'enseignement suivis par les professeurs à l'école centrale du departement de Doubs (Besançon, Year IX (1801). BL
Platner, Ernst, *Philosophische Aphorismen* (2 vols., Leipzig, 1776–82).
Polignac, Melchior, Cardinal de, *L'Anti-Lucrèce* (1749; new edn., 2 vols., Paris, 1767).
Pontoppidan, Eric, *Abhandlung von der Neuigkeit der Welt* (2 vols., Copenhagen, 1758). GUB

Pontoppidan, Eric, *Kraft der Wahrheit den atheistischen und naturalistischen Unglauben zu besiegen* (Copenhagen, 1763). GUB

Portalis, J. E. M., *De l'usage et de l'abus de l'esprit philosophique durant le XVIIIe siècle* (1798; new edn., Paris, 2007).

Posada, E., and P. M.Ibañez (eds.), *Relaciones de mando. Memorias presentados por los gobernantes del Nuevo Reino de Granada* (Bogotá, 1910).

Prévost, Julien, *Relation des glorieux événemens qui ont porté Leurs Majestés Royales sur le trône d'Hayti* (Cap Henry [Cap Haïtien], Haiti, 1811).

Price, Richard, *Observations on the Importance of the American Revolution and the Means of Making it a Benefit to the World* (London, 1785).

Price, Richard, *A Discourse on the Love of our Country* (2nd edn., London, 1789).

Price, Richard, *Political Writings*, ed. D. O. Thomas (Cambridge, 1991).

Priestley, Joseph, *An Essay on the first Principles of Government and on the nature of Political, Civil and Religious Liberty* (Dublin, 1768).

Priestley, Joseph, *An Examination of Dr. Reid's* Inquiry into the Human Mind on the Principles of Common sense (London, 1774).

Priestley, Joseph, *Disquisitions relating to Matter and Spirit* (1777) (New York, Garland repr., 1976).

Priestley, Joseph, *The Doctrine of Philosophical Necessity Illustrated* (1777) (New York, Garland repr., 1976).

Priestley, Joseph, *An History of the Corruptions of Christianity* (2 vols., Birmingham, 1782).

Priestley, Joseph, *Letters to the Right Honourable Edmund Burke* (Birmingham, 1791).

Proby, W. C., *Modern Philosophy and Barbarism* (London, n.d. [1794?]).

Procès-Verbal de l'Inauguration solemnelle de l'École Centrale d'Instruction publique de Bourges (n.p., Year III). BL R 372/1

[Prudhomme, Louis-Marie, and A. Tournon], *Révolutions de Paris* (journal: Paris, 1789–90).

Quesnay, François, *Examen de l'examen du livre intitulé Principes sur la liberté du commerce des grains* (1768) (Catanea, 1988).

Radicati di Passerano, Alberto, *A Philosophical Dissertation upon Death* (London, 1732). BL

Radicati di Passerano, Alberto, *Twelve Discourses concerning Religion and Government, inscribed to all Lovers of Truth and Liberty* (2nd edn., London, 1734).

Radicati di Passerano, Alberto, *Recueil de pièces curieuses sur les matières les plus intéressantes* (Rotterdam, 1736). BL

Radicati di Passerano, Alberto, *Discorsi morali, istorici e politici*, ed. D. Canestri (Turin, 2007).

Radicati di Passerano, Alberto, *A Succinct History of Priesthood, Ancient and Modern* (London, 1737).

Raimond [Raymond], Julien, *Réflexions sur les véritables causes des troubles et des désastres de nos colonies, notamment sur ceux de Saint-Domingue* (Paris, 1793).

Raynal, Guillaume Thomas François, *A Philosophical and Political History of the British Settlements and Trade in North America* (2 vols., Edinburgh, 1776).

Raynal, Guillaume Thomas François, *Révolution de l'Amérique* ("Londres," 1781).

Raynal, Guillaume Thomas François, *The Revolution of America* (London, 1781).

Raynal, Guillaume Thomas François, *Adresse de Guillaume-Thomas Raynal remue par lui-même à M. le president le 31 Mai 1791, et lue à l'Assemblée le même jour* (Paris, 1791).

[G.T.] *Raynal Demasqué, ou Lettres sur la vie et les ouvrages de cet écrivain* (Paris, 1791).

Reflexions d'un Belge Patriote, ou Comparaison respective de la Révolution de France avec celle du Brabant ("Londres," 1790). BRL V/63

Rehberg, August Wilhelm, *Sammtliche Schriften* (4 vols., Hanover, 1828–9).
Rehberg, August Wilhelm, *Untersuchungen über die französische Revolution* (2 vols., Hanover, 1793).
Reimarus, Hermann Samuel. *Apologie oder Schützschrift für die vernünftigen Verehrer Gottes*, ed. G. Alexander (2 vols., Frankfurt, 1972).
Reimarus, Hermann Samuel, *Die vornehmsten Wahrheiten der natürlichen Religion* (2 vols., Göttingen, 1985).
Reinhold, Karl Leonhard, *Letters on the Kantian Philosophy*, ed. Karl Ameriks (Cambridge, 2005).
Reinhold, Karl Leonhard, "Letter to Fichte," in Estes and Bowman, *J. G. Fichte*, 127–43.
Relation exacte De ce qui s'est passé à Bruxelles, dans les journées du 16 et 17 mars 1790 (Brussels, 1790). BRL VH
*Réponse à la Censure de la Faculté de Théologie de Paris contre l'*Histoire philosophique [. . .] *des* Deux Indes ("Londres" [Paris?], 1782). PBN
Restrepo, José Manuel, *Historia de la Revolución de la República de Colombia* (5 vols., Paris, 1827).
Reynaud, Abbé Marc-Antoine, *Le Delire de la nouvelle philosophie ou errata du livre intitulé* La Philosophie de la nature (Paris, 1775).
Riem, Andreas, "On Enlightenment," in J. Schmidt (ed.), *What is Enlightenment*? (Berkeley, 1996).
Rivarol, Antoine de, *De la philosophie moderne* (Hamburg, 1797; 2nd edn,. n.p., 1799).
Robert, François, *L'Ami de la Liberté applaudissant aux généreux efforts de la Belgique* (Paris, 10 Nov. 1790). BRL VH
Robertson, Geoffrey (ed.), *The Levellers: The Putney Debates* (London, 2018).
Robertson, William, *The History of America* (4th edn., London, 1783).
Robespierre, Maximilien, *La Défenseur de la Constitution* (journal: Paris, 1792–3).
Robespierre, Maximilien, *Oeuvres completes*, ed. E. Hamel (10 vols., Paris, 1910–67).
Robespierre, Maximilien, *Lettres de Maximilien Robespierre membre de la Convention Nationale de France à ses commettans* (Paris, 1792–3).
Robespierre, Maximilien, "Exposition de mes principes" afterwards inserted in *Le Defenseur de la Constitution* no. 1, pp. 7–61.
Robespierre, Maximilien, "Discours sur la religion, La République, l'esclavage," Discours of 18 Floreal Year II (7 May 1794).
Robespierre, Maximilien, "Sur les rapports des idées religieuses et morales avec les principes républicaines" (Paris, 2006).
Rocafuerte, Vicente, *Ideas necesarias a todo pueblo americano independiente: Que quiera ser Libre* (Philadelphia, 1821).
Rocafuerte, Vicente, *Ensayo político: El Sistema Colombiano popular, electivo* (New York, 1823).
Roederer, Pierre Louis, *Mémoires sur la Révolution, le consulat et l'empire*, ed. O. Aubry (Paris, 1942).
Roederer, Pierre Louis, *The Spirit of the Revolution of 1789*, ed. M. Forsyth (Aldershot, 1989).
Roederer, Pierre Louis, *Des sociétés particulières telles que clubs, réunions, etc.* (Paris, 1799).
Roederer, Pierre Louis, *De la philosophie moderne, et de la part qu'elle a eue à la Révolution française* (Paris, 1799).
Roederer, Pierre Louis, *Discours prononcé par Roederer orateur du gouvernement sur le projet relatif à l'instruction publique* (24 Floreal An 10) (Paris).

Rousseau, Jean-Jacques, *Discours sur les sciences et les arts*, ed. J. Roger (1971; repr. Paris, 1992).
Rousseau, Jean-Jacques, *The Social Contract and Discourses*, ed. G. D. H. Cole, J. H. Brumfitt, J. C. Hall, and P. D. Jimack (repr. London, 1993).
Rousseau, Jean-Jacques, *A Discourse on the Origin of Inequality* in Cole et al. (eds.), Rousseau, *The Social Contract and Discourses*, 31–126.
Rousseau, Jean-Jacques, "Lettre à Voltaire," 18 Aug. 1756, in Rousseau, *Oeuvres complètes* (25 vols., Paris, 1826), xx. 307–33.
Rousseau, Jean-Jacques, *Lettre à M. d'Alembert sur son article "Genève"* (1758), ed. M. Launay (Paris, 1967).
Rousseau, Jean-Jacques, *Émile* (1762; trans B. Foxley, Everyman edn., repr, London, 1969).
Rousseau, Jean-Jacques, *Lettres écrites de la Montagne* (2 vols., Amsterdam, 1764).
Rousseau, Jean-Jacques, *Rousseau Judge of Jean-Jacques: Dialogues*, in R. D. Masters and Chr. Kelly (eds.), *The Collected Writings of Rousseau*, vol. i (Hanover, MA, 1990).
Rousseau, Jean-Jacques, *Considérations sur le gouvernment de Pologne*, in Rousseau, *Discours sur l'économie politique*, ed. Barbara de Negroni (Paris, 1990), 161–309.
Rousseau, Jean-Jacques, *Projet de constitution pour la Corse*, in Rousseau, *Discours sur l'economie politique*, ed. Barbara de Negroni (Paris, 1990), 101–60.
Rousseau, Jean-Jacques, *Les Rêveries du promeneur solitaire* (1782), ed. H. Roddier (Paris, 1960).
Rousseau, Pierre, *Journal Enyclopédique* (304 vols., Liège and Bouillon, 1756–93).
Ruge, Arnold, "A Self-Critique of Liberalism" (1843), in L. S. Stepelevich (ed.), *The Young Hegelians: An Anthology*, (Atlantic Highlands, NJ, 1983), 237–59.
Ruge, Arnold, *Polemische Briefe* (Mannheim, 1847).
Ruge, Arnold, *Briefwechsel und Tagebuchblätter aus den Jahren 1825–1880*, ed. P. Nerrlich (2 vols., Berlin, 1886).
Rush, Benjamin, *The Autobiography of Benjamin Rush*, ed. G. W. Corner (Princeton, 1948).
Saavedra y Sangronis, Don Francisco Arias de, *Memorias inéditas de un ministro ilustrado* (Seville, 1992).
Salfi, Franceso Severio, *L'Italie au dix-neuvième siècle* (Paris, 1821).
Say, Jean-Baptiste, *Traité d'Économie Politique, ou Simple Exposition de la manière dont se forment et se consomment les richesses* (new edn., 2 vols., Paris, 1814).
Say, Jean-Baptiste, *De l'Angleterre et des Anglais* (Paris, 1815).
Say, Jean-Baptiste, *Lettres à M. Malthus sur différens sujets d'économie politique* (Paris, 1820).
Schelling, F. W. J., *System of Transcendental Idealism* (1800) (Charlottesville, VA, 1978).
Schelling, F. W. J., *Philosophy and Religion* (1804), trans. K. Ottmann (Putnam, CT, 2010).
Schelling, F. W. J., *Das Tagebuch 1848*, ed. H. J. Sandkühler (Hamburg, 1990).
Schiller, Friedrich von, *Philosophische Briefe* (1786), ed. A. Holthusen ((Hamburg, 1937).
Schiller, Friedrich von, *Universalhistorische Schriften* (1789–92), in Otto Dann (ed.), *Friedrich Schiller Historische Schriften und Erzählungen* 1 (Frankfurt, 2000), 409–510.
Schiller, Friedrich von, *On the Aesthetic Education of Man* (1794), trans. R. Snell (Mineola, NY, 2004).
Schimmelpenninck, R. J. *Verhandeling over eene wel ingerigte volksregeering* (Leiden, 1785).
Shaftesbury, Anthony Ashley Cooper, third earl of, *Essai sur le mérite et la vertu*, trans. D. Diderot (2nd edn., Paris, 1998).
Shaftesbury, Anthony Ashley Cooper, third earl of, *Characteristics of Men, Manners, Opinions, Times*, ed. Lawrence E. Klein (Cambridge, 1999).

Shaftesbury, Anthony Ashley Cooper, third earl of, "Pathologia, sive explicatio affectuum humanorum secundum doctrinam Socraticorum" (1706), in HEI 39 (2013), 221–40.
Shelley, Percy Bysshe, *The Poetical Works*, ed. H. Buxton Forman (5 vols., London, 1892).
Shelley, Percy Bysshe, *A Philosophical Review of Reform*, ed. T. W. Rolleston (Oxford, 1920).
Sieyès, Abbe Emmanuel-Joseph, *Essai sur les privilèges* (1788; new edn., n.p. [Paris], 1789).
Sieyès, Abbe Emmanuel-Joseph, *Qu'est-ce que le Tiers Etat?* (1788; 3rd edn., Paris, 1789).
Silvy, Louis, *Les fidèles catholiques aux évêques et à tous les pasteurs de l'Église de France: au sujet des nouvelles éditions des oeuvres de Voltaire et de Rousseau* (Paris, 1817).
Sinnhold, Johann Niklaus *Historische Nachricht von der bekannten und errissenen sogenannte Wertheimische Bibel* (Erfurt, 1737).
Sismondi, J. C. L., *Recherches sur les constitutions des peuples libres*, ed. M. Minerbi (Geneva, 1965).
Sismondi, J. C. L., *Nouveaux principes d'économie politique* (2 vols., Paris, 1819).
Sismondi, J. C. L., "De l'Amérique," in *Revue Encyclopédique* 33 (Jan. 1827), 17–40.
Smith, Adam, *Essays on Philosophical Subjects*, ed. W. P. D. Wightman and J. C. Bryce (Oxford, 1980).
Smith, Adam, *The Theory of Moral Sentiments* (1759), ed. D. D. Raphael and A. L. Macfie (Oxford, 1976).
Smith, Adam, *An Inquiry into the Nature and Causes of the Wealth of Nations*, ed. J. E. Thorold Rogers (2 vols., 2nd edn., Oxford, 1880).
Smith, Adam, *A Catalogue of the Library of Adam Smith*, ed. J. Bonar (New York, 1966).
Smith, Samuel Stanhope, *An Essay on the Causes of the Variety of Complexion and Figure in the Human Species* (Philadelphia, 1788).
Sonnenfels, Joseph von, *Über die Afschaffung der Tortur* (Zurich, 1775).
Sonnenfels, Joseph von, *Politische Abhandlungen* (Vienna, 1777).
Spinoza, Benedict de, *Opera*, ed. Carl Gebhardt (4 vols., Heidelberg, 1925).
Spinoza, Benedict de, *The Letters*, trans S. Shirley (Indianapolis, IN, 1995).
Spinoza, Benedict de, *Korte Geschriften*, ed. F. Akkerman et al. (Amsterdam, 1982).
Spinoza, Benedict de, *Tractatus Theologico-Politicus*, ed. Jonathan Israel (Cambridge, 2007).
Spinoza, Benedict de, *Tractatus Politicus*, trans. Samuel Shirley (Indianapolis, IN, 2000).
Spinoza, Benedict de, *Collected Works*, ed. E. Curley, 1 vol. thus far (Princeton, 1985).
Staël, Anne-Louise-Germaine, Mme de, *Letters on the Works of J. J. Rousseau* (London, 1789).
Staël, Anne-Louise-Germaine, Mme de, *Considerations on the Principal Events of the French Revolution*, ed. A. Craiutu (Indianapolis, IN, 2008).
Stendhal (Marie-Henri Beyle), *The Private Diaries of Stendhal*, ed. R. Sage (New York, 1954).
Stendhal (Marie-Henri Beyle), *Scarlet and Black*, trans. M. Shaw (1953).
Suplemento al Indice expurgatorio del año de 1790 (Madrid, 1805).
Taillandier, M. A. H. (ed.), *Documents biographiques sur P. C. F. Daunou* (Paris, 1841).
Temple, Sir William, *Observations* (1672; Cambridge, 1932).
Temple, Sir William, *Five Miscellaneous Essays*, ed. S. H. Monk (Ann Arbor, 1963).
Der Teutsche Merkur, ed. Chr. Wieland (Weimar, 1773–89).
Thiebault, Dieudonné, *De l'enseignement dans les Écoles centrales* (Strasbourg, Year V).
Thorild, Thomas, *Samlade Skrifter*, ed. S. Arvidson (12 vols., Stockholm and Lund, 1933–97).
Thorild, Thomas, *Dissertationes* in GrUB Ab 938, ex biblioteca academica.
Thorild, Thomas, "Critik over Montesquieu," in Th. Thorild, *Samlade Skrifter*, ed. S. Arvidson ii. 279–85.

Thorild, Thomas, "Critik öfver Montesquieu under Juris Professoris Doctor Anders Hernberghs presiderende" (22 Mar. 1788) (Uppsala, 1788).

Thorild, Thomas, *Om den almindelige forstands frihed: Til kongen og folket* (Copenhagen, 1793).

[Thorild, Thomas], *The Sermon of Sermons on the Impiety of Priests and the Fall of Religion* (London, 1789). GrUB

Tindal, Matthew, *The Rights of the Christian Church asserted* (London, 1706).

Tindal, Matthew, *A Defence of the Rights of the Christian Church* (2nd edn., London, 1709).

Tindal, Matthew, *A New Catechism with Dr. Hicke's Thirty Nine Articles* (1709; 3rd edn., London, 1710). YBL

Tindal, Matthew, *Christianity as Old as the Creation* (London, 1731).

Toland, John, *Christianity not Mysterious* (1696) (repr. New York and London, 1978).

Toland, John, *Anglia Libera, or The Limitation and Succession of the Crown of England explain'd* (London, 1701).

Toland, John, *The Art of governing by Partys: particularly, in Religion, in Politics, in Parliament, on the Bench and in the Ministry* (London, 1701).

Toland, John, *Letters to Serena* (London, 1704), ed. Ian Leask (Portland, OR, 2013).

Toland, John, *Socinianism truly stated being an Example of fair Dealing in all theological Controverseys* (London, 1705).

Toland, John, *The Jacobitism, Perjury and Popery of High Church-Priests* (London, 1710).

Toland, John, *An Appeal to Honest People Against Wicked Priests* (London, 1710). YBL

Toland, John, *Reasons for Naturalizing the Jews in Great Britain and Ireland* (1714), ed. H. Mainusch, *Studia Delitzschiana* ix (Stuttgart, 1965).

Toland, John, *Pantheisticon* (1720) (repr. of 1751 edn., New York and London, 1976).

Toland, John, *The Primitive Constitution of the Church of England* (1726), ed. L. Jaffro (Paris, 2003).

Toland, John, *On the Manner, Place and Time of the Death of Giordano Bruno of Nolae*, trans. and ed. B. Begley, *Journal of Early Modern Studies* iii (2014), 103–15.

Tone, Theobald Wolfe, *An Address to the People of Ireland* (Belfast, 1796).

Triple Parallèle de la Révolution des Sept Provinces en 1579, [. . .] *de la Révolution des Treize États Unis en 1776* [. . .] *et de la Révolution des Onze États Unis en 1790, sous Joseph II* (Brussels, 1790). BRL

Toussaint Louverture, François-Dominique, *Lettres à la France. Idées pour la libération du Peuple Noir d'Haïti (1794–1798)*, ed. A. M. Baggio and R. Augustin (Bruyères-le-Châtel, 2011).

Toussaint Louverture, François-Dominique, *The Memoir of General Toussaint Louverture*, ed. Philippe Girard (Oxford, 2014).

Turgot, Anne-Robert-Jacques, Baron de l'Aulne, "Reflexions sur les *Pensées Philosophiques* de Diderot" (1746), in *Oeuvres*, ed. G. Schelle (5 vols., Paris, 1913) i. 87–97.

Turgot, Anne-Robert-Jacques, Baron de l'Aulne, *Reflections on the Formation and Distribution of Wealth*, trans. K. Jupp (London, 1999).

Turgot, Anne-Robert-Jacques, Baron de l'Aulne, *Recherches sur les causes des progrès et de la décadence des sciencees et des arts ou Réflexions sur l'histoire des progrès de l'esprit humain*, in Turgot, *Oeuvres*, i. 116–42.

Turgot, Anne-Robert-Jacques, Baron de l'Aulne, *Discours sur les avantages que l'établissement du christianisme a procurés au genre humain* (1750), in Turgot, *Oeuvres*, i. 194–214.

Turgot, Anne-Robert-Jacques, Baron de l'Aulne, *Tableau philosophique des progrès successifs de l'esprit humain* (1750), in Turgot, *Oeuvres* i. 214–35.

Turgot, Anne-Robert-Jacques, Baron de l'Aulne, *Plan de deux discours sur l'histoire universelle* (*c*.1751), in Turgot, *Oeuvres* i. 275–323.

Turgot, Anne-Robert-Jacques, Baron de l'Aulne, *Reflections on the Formation and Distribution of Wealth* (1766; London, 1793).

Turner, Matthew, *Answer to Dr Priestley's* Letters to a Philosophical Unbeliever (London, 1782).

Vallée, G. (ed.), *The Spinoza Conversations between Lessing and Jacobi* (Lanham, MD, 1988).

Valsecchi, Antonio, *Ritrati e vite letterarie e paralleli di G. J. Rousseau, del sig.* Di *Voltaire, di Obbes, e di Spinosa, e vita di Pietro Bayle* (Venice, 1816).

Vandeul, Mme De, *Mémoires pour servir à l'histoire de la vie et des ouvrages de Diderot* in Diderot, *Oeuvres complètes*, ed. J. Assezat i, pp. xxix–lxviii.

Van den Enden, Franciscus, *Free Political Propositions and Considerations of State* (1665), trans. and ed. Wim Klever ("Vrijstad," 2007).

Van der Hoop, H. J., *Réfutation des Considérations impartiales et du project d'adresse aux États* (Brussels, 1790).

[Van der Noot (also Vandernoot), Henrik], *Manifeste du Peuple Brabançon* (n.p., 24 Oct. 1789). BRL VH

Vergani, Paolo, *Traité de la peine de mort* (Paris, 1782).

The Villanous Principles of the Rights of the Christian Church Asserted, etc., Confuted by Scripture (London, 1708). BL

Volney, Constantin François, *Voyage en Syrie et en Egypte* (2 vols., Paris, 1787).

Volney, Constantin François, *Extrait d'un ouvrage imprimé à Rennes intitulé* La Sentinelle du Peuple (Paris, 1789). PBN

Volney, Constantin François, *Discours prononcé dans la Chambre du Tiers-État* (8 May 1789) (Paris, 1789).

Volney, Constantin François, *An Abridgement of the Law of Nature, or, Catechism of French Citizens* (London, 1796).

Volney, Constantin François, *Oeuvres* (2 vols., Paris, 1989).

Voltaire, François-Marie Arouet de, *Oeuvres complètes de Voltaire*. ed. M. Auguis et al. (97 vols., Paris, 1828–34.)

Voltaire, François-Marie Arouet de, *Correspondence and Related Documents*, ed. Th. Besterman (51 vols., Toronto, Geneva, and Oxford, 1968–77).

Voltaire, François-Marie Arouet de, [Abbé Bazin], *La philosophie de l'historie* (n.p. [Geneva?], 1765).

Voltaire, François-Marie Arouet de, *Dieu. Réponse de Mr de Voltaire au* Système de la Nature (Château de Ferney, 1770).

Voltaire, François-Marie Arouet de, *Questions sur l'Encyclopédie par des amateurs* (9 vols., n.p., 1770).

Voltaire, François-Marie Arouet de, *The Complete Works of Voltaire* (The Voltaire Foundation), vol. xv (Oxford, 1992).

Voltaire, François-Marie Arouet de, *Il faut prendre un parti ou le principe d'action. Diatribe* (1772) in *Oeuvres Complètes de Voltaire*, new edn. xxviii (melanges no. vii) (Paris, 1879), 517–54.

Voltaire, François-Marie Arouet de, *Essai historique et critique sur les dissensions des Églises de Pologne* ("Basle" [Geneva?], 1767).

Voltaire, François-Marie Arouet de, *Essai sur les mœurs et l'esprit des nations*, ed. R. Pomeau (2 vols., Paris, 1963).

Voltaire, François-Marie Arouet de, *Extrait des sentiments de Jean Meslier*, in Voltaire, *Oeuvres complètes* xliii. 254–327.

Voltaire, François-Marie Arouet de, *Traité sur la Tolérance*, ed. R. Pomeau (Paris, 1989).

Voltaire, François-Marie Arouet de, *Dictionnaire philosophique*, ed. Chr. Mervaud (2 vols., Oxford, 1994).

Voltaire, François-Marie Arouet de, *Homélies prononcés à Londres en 1765 dans une assemblée particulière* xliii. 331–417.

Voltaire, François-Marie Arouet de, *Le Philosophe ignorant* (1766), ed. J. L. Carr (London, 1965).

Voltaire, François-Marie Arouet de, *Lettres à son altesse M. le Prince de Brunsvick* (1767), in Voltaire, *Oeuvres complètes* xliv.

Voltaire, François-Marie Arouet de, *De la Paix perpetuelle par le docteur Goodheart* (1769), in Voltaire, *Oeuvres completes* xxviii. 403–28.

Voltaire, François-Marie Arouet de, *Histoire du parlement de Paris* (1769).

Voltaire, François-Marie Arouet de, *Lettres de Memmius à Ciceron* (1771), in Voltaire, *Oeuvres complètes* xxviii. 437–63.

Voltaire, François-Marie Arouet de, *Notes de M. de Morza sur les systèmes* (1772), in Voltaire, *Oeuvres complètes* xvi. 248–76.

Voltaire, François-Marie Arouet de, *Mémoires pour servir à la vie de M. de Voltaire écrits par lui-même*, vol. ii of Condorcet, *Vie de Voltaire* (London, 1791).

Voltaire, François-Marie Arouet de, *Corpus des notes marginales de Voltaire* (5 vols. thus far, Berlin and Oxford).

Voltaire, François-Marie Arouet de, *Political Writings*, ed. D. Williams (Cambridge, 1994).

[Voltaire], "Idées republicaines, par un citoyen de Genève" (1762), in *Oeuvres complètes de Voltaire*, ed. Ch. Lahure, xviii (Paris, 1860), 544–56.

[Voltaire], *Lettre d'un Quaker à Jean-George Le Franc de Pompignon* (n.p. [Geneva?], 1763].

[Voltaire], "Tout en Dieu. Commentaire sur Mallebranche," in Voltaire, *L'Évangile du jour contenant Paix perpetuelle* ("Londres" [Amsterdam, 1769)], 54–70.

[Voltaire], *Fragmens sur l'Inde* [. . .] *et sur plusieurs autres sujets* ("Londres," 1774).

[Voltaire], *Corpus des notes marginales de Voltaire*, ed. T. Voronova (5 vols. thus far, Berlin, 1979–94).

[Vonck, Jean-François], *Considérations impartiales sur la position actuelle du Brabant* (n.p., Jan. 1790).

Vreede, Pieter, *Waermond en Vryhart. Gesprek over de Vryheid der Nederlandren; en den aert der waere Vryheid* ("Holland," 1783). Kn. 20400, HKB

Vreede, Pieter, *Beoordeelend en ophelderend verslag van de Verhandeling over de Vryheid* (Arnhem, 1783). Kn. 2045, HKB

[Vreede, Pieter?], *Zakboek van Neerlands Volk, voor Patriotten, Antipatriotten, Aristokraten en Prinsgezinden* (Dordrecht, 1785). Kn. 21041, HKB

Wedekind, Georg Christian, et al. (eds.), *Der Patriot, eine Wochenschrift* (journal: Mainz, 1792–3).

Wekhrlin, Wilhelm Ludwig, *Chronologen* (periodical: 12 vols., Frankfurt and Nuremberg, 1779–84).

Wekhrlin, Wilhelm Ludwig, *Das Graue Ungeheuer* (periodical: 31 vols., Nuremberg, 1784–7).

Wekhrlin, Wilhelm Ludwig, *Hyperboreische Briefe* (periodical: 6 vols., Nuremberg, 1788–90).

Wekhrlin, Wilhelm Ludwig, *Paragrafen* (periodical: Nuremberg, 1790–2).

Wildman, Sir John, *A Call to all the Soldiers of the Army by the Free People of England* (London, 1647).

Wildman, Sir John, *A Letter to a Friend, advising in this Extraordinary Juncture, how to free the Nation from Slavery* (London, 1689).

Wirth, Johann Georg, *Die politische Reform Deutschlands* (Strasbourg, 1832).

Wiszowaty, Andrzej, *Religio rationalis seu de rationis judicio in controversiis etiam theologicis ac religiosis adhibendo* (Amsterdam, 1685).

Wiszowaty, Andrzej, *Spooren der Deugden en breidels der zonden* (Amsterdam, 1703).

Wollaston, William, *The Religion of Nature Delineated* (London, 1724).

Wollstonecraft, Mary, *A Vindication of the Rights of Woman* (1792), in M. Wollstonecraft, *Political Writings*, ed. J. Todd (London, 1993), 67–296.

Wollstonecraft, Mary, *The Collected Letters*, ed. J. Todd (London, 2003).

Wollstonecraft, Mary, *Letters Written during a Short Residence in Sweden, Norway and Denmark* (London, 1796).

Wotton, William, *A Letter to Eusebia occasioned [by] My Toland's Letters to Serena* (London, 1704).

Secondary

Acosta, Vladimir, "El 'Bolívar' de Marx," in Inés Quintero and V. Acosta (eds.), *El Bolívar de Marx* (Caracas, 2007).

Adelman, J., "The Rites of Statehood," HAHR xc (2010), 391–422.

Agüero, Ajeandro, and Marta Lorente, "Penal Enlightenment in Spain: From Beccaria's Reception to the First Criminal Code," in J. Astigarraga (ed.), *The Spanish Enlightenment Revisited* (Oxford, 2015), 235–63.

Ahnert, Thomas, *The Moral Culture of the Scottish Enlightenment, 1690–1805* (New Haven, 2014).

Alberola, A., and E. Larriba (eds.), *Las élites y la "Revolucion de Espana" (1808–1814)* (San Vicente de Raspeig, 2010).

Albertone, M. (ed.), *Il repubblicanesimo moderno* (Naples, 2006).

Albertone, M. "Democratic Republicanism: Historical Reflections on the Idea of Republic in the 18th Century," HEI 33 (2007), 108–30.

Albertone, M. "Thomas Jefferson and French Economic Thought," in Albertone and Francesco (eds.), *Rethinking*, 123–46.

Albertone, M., and A. De Francesco (eds.), *Rethinking the Atlantic World: Europe and America in the Age of Democratic Revolutions* (Basingstoke, 2009).

Alexander, R. S., *Bonapartism and Revolutionary Tradition in France: The Fédérés of 1815* (Cambridge, 1991).

Allen, R. C., "David Hartley's New Words for Action: 'Automatic' and 'Decomplex'," *Enlightenment and Dissent* xx (2001), 1–22.

Alonso, Gregorio, "'A Great People Struggling for their Liberties': Spain and the Mediterranean in the Eyes of the Benthamites," HEI 41 (2015), 194–204.

Altena, Peter, "Een 'Oude Hellenbroeksman' en de Radicale Verlichting," GWN 5 (1994), 139–67.

Altena, Peter, *Gerrit Paape (1752–1803). Levens en werken* (Nijmegen, 2012).

Ambri, Paola Berselli, *L'Opera di Montesquieu nel settecento italiano* (Florence, 1960).

Amidsen, Asser, *Til nytte og fornøjelse. Johann Friedrich Struensee (1737–1772)* (Copenhagen, 2002).

Ameriks, Karl, "Introduction" to Reinhold, *Letters*, pp. ix–xxxv.

Ameriks, Karl, *Interpreting Kant's* Critiques (Oxford, 2005).

Amoh, Y., "Ferguson's Views on the American and French Revolutions," in Heath and Merolle (eds.), *Adam Ferguson*, 73–86.

Amunátegui, Miguel Luis, *Los Precursores de la independencia de Chile* (3 vols., Santiago, 1909).

Anderson, M. S., "The Italian Reformers," in H. M. Scott (ed.), *Enlightened Absolutism* (Basingstoke, 1990), 55–74.

Andrès, B., *La conquête des lettres au Quebec* (1759–99) (Montreal, 2007).

Andries, L., Les Imprimeurs-libraires Parisiens et la liberté de la presse (1789–95)," *Dix-Huitième Siècle* xxi (1989), 247–61.

Ansart-Dourlen, M. *L'Action politique des personnalités et l'idéologie jacobine* (Paris, 1998).

Antognazza, Maria Rosa, *Leibniz on the Trinity and the Incarnation* (New Haven, 2007).

Antognazza, Maria Rosa, "Natural and Supernatural Mysteries: Leibniz's *Annotatiunculae subitaneae* on Toland's *Christianity not Mysterious*," in Schröder (ed.), *Gestalten*, 29–40.

Aprile, Sylvie, *1815–1870 La Révolution inachevée* (Paris, 2010).

Aramayo, Roberto, "Radical and Moderate Enlightenment: The Case of Diderot and Kant," in J. Rohbeck, D. Brauer, and C. Roldán (eds.), *Philosophy of Globalization* (Berlin, 2018), 315–26.

Arato, Franco, "Savans, philosophes, journalistes: l'Italie des dictionnaires encyclopédiques," *Dix-Huitième Siècle* xxxviii (2006), 69–82.

Armenteros, Carolina, "Joseph de Maistre, Heir of the Enlightenment," in J. D. Burson and U. Lehner (eds.), *Enlightenment and Catholicism in Europe* (Notre Dame, IN, 2014), 125–43.

Armenteros, Carolina, and R. A. Lebrun (eds.), *Joseph de Maistre and his European Readers* (Leiden, 2011).

Armitage, David, *The Ideological Origins of the British Empire* (Cambridge, 2000).

Armitage, David, *The Declaration of Independence: A Global History* (Cambridge, MA, 2007).

Armitage, David, "Globalizing Jeremy Bentham," *History of Political Thought* xxxii (2011), 63–82.

Armitage, D. and S. Subrahmanyam (eds.), *The Age of Revolutions in Global Context* (Basingstoke, 2010).

Artigas-Menant, G., *Du secret des clandestins à la propagande voltaireienne* (Paris, 2001).

Astigarraga, Jesús, "I Traduttori spagnoli di Filangieri e il risveglio del dibattito constituzionale (1780–1839)," in A. Trampus (ed.), *Diritti e costituzione* (Bologna, 2005), 231–90.

Astigarraga, Jesús, Political Economy and Legislation: The Great Success of Filangieri's *Scienza della legislazione* in Spain (1780–1839)," *Nuevo Mundo Mundos Nuevos, Coloquios* 2006 (online publication posted 18 Mar. 2006).

Astigarraga, Jesús, "España y la Scienza della Legislazione de Gaetano Filangieri," in Verdo et al., *Entre Nápoles y América*, 101–19.

Astigarraga, Jesús (ed.), *The Spanish Enlightenment Revisited* (Oxford, 2015).

Astigarraga, Jesús, and José Manuel Menudo, "Condorcet en Espagne: à propos d'une traduction manuscrite de l'Esquisse," *Dix-Huitième Siècle* 50 (2018), 431–48.

Aston, Nigel, *Religion and Revolution in France, 1780–1804* (Washington, DC, 2000).

Atteridge, A. H., *Napoleon's Brothers* (1909; new edn., Stroud, 2007).

Avineri, Shlomo, "Marx and Jewish Emancipation," *JHI* 25:3 (1964), 445–50.
Avineri, Shlomo, *Moses Hess: Prophet of Communism and Zionism* (New York, 1985).
Aymes, Jean-René, "La Mise en cause des élites et, en particulier, des 'philosophes' et des 'savants' pendant la Guerre de l'Indépendance," in Alberola and Larriba, *Las élites*, 107–25.
Baczko, Bronislaw, *Une éducation pour la démocratie: textes et projets* (Paris, 1982).
Baczko, Bronislaw, *Ending the Terror: The French Revolution after Robespierre* (Cambridge, 1994).
Baczko, Bronislaw, "The Terror before the Terror? Conditions of Possibility, Logic of Realization," in K. M. Baker (ed.), *The Terror*, Vol. 4 of *The French Revolution and the Creation of Modern Political Culture* (Oxford, 1994), 19–38.
Baczko, Bronislaw, "Comment est fait un tyrant [. . .] Thermidor et la légende noire de Robespierre," in Jean Ehrard (ed.), *Images de Robespierre* (Naples, 1996), 29–54.
Baczko, Bronislaw, *Politiques de la Révolution française* (Paris, 2008).
Bailyn, Bernard, *The Ideological Origins of the American Revolution* (Cambridge, MA, 1992).
Baker, E., "Lucretius in the European Enlightenment," in S. Gillespie and P. Hardie (eds.), *The Cambridge Companion to Lucretius* (Cambridge, 2007), 274–88.
Baker, K. M., *Condorcet: From Natural Philosophy to Social Mathematics* (Chicago, 1975).
Baker, K. M., "Representation," in Baker (ed.), *Political Culture* i. 469–92.
Baker, K. M., "Revolution," in Colin Lucas (ed.), *The Political Culture of the French Revolution* (Oxford, 1988), 41–62.
Baker, K. M., *Inventing the French Revolution* (Cambridge, 1990).
Baker, K. M. (ed.), *The Political Culture of the Old Regime*, Vol. 1 of *The French Revolution and the Creation of Modern Political Culture* (4 vols., Oxford, 1987).
Baker, K. M., and P. H. Reill (eds.), *What's Left of Enlightenment?* (Stanford, 2001).
Baker, K. M., and Dan Edelstein (eds.), *Scripting Revolution: A Historical Approach to the Comparative Study of Revolutions* (Stanford, 2015).
Ballazs, Peter, "Le Matérialisme athée d'un 'Jacobin' hongrois," *La Lettre Clandestine* xvii (2009), 326–47.
Balazs, Peter, "Jean-Jacques Rousseau est-il un auteur radical?," in García-Alonso, *Lumières radicales*, 171–94.
Balcou, Jean, *Fréron contre les philosophes* (Geneva, 1975).
Baldi, Marialuisa, *David Hume nel settecento italiano* (Florence, 1983).
Ballstadt, Kurt, *Diderot: Natural Philosopher* (Oxford, 2008).
Bancarel, G., "Élements de la stratégie éditoriale de Raynal," in Bancarel and Goggi (eds.), *Raynal*, 121–41.
Bancarel, G., and G. Goggi (eds.), *Raynal de la polémique à l'histoire* (Oxford, 2000).
Barbour, R. "Moral and Political Philosophy: Readings of Lucretius from Virgil to Voltaire," in S. Gillespie and P. Hardie (eds.,) *The Cambridge Companion to Lucretius* (Cambridge, 2007), 149–66.
Baridon, M., "Les Concepts de nature humaine et de perfectibilité dans l'historiographie des Lumières de Fontenelle à Condorcet," in *L'histoire au dix-huitième siècle. Centre Aixois d'Études et de Recherches sur le XVIIIème siècle* (Aix-en-Provence, 1980), 353–74.
Barkin, Kenneth, "Social Control in the Volksschule in Vormärz Prussia," *Central European History* xvi (1983), 31–52.
Barnard, F. M., *Herder on Nationality, Humanity and History* (Montreal, 2003).
Barnouw, Dagmar, "*Eräugnis*: Georg Forster on the Difficulties of Diversity," in Wilson and Holub (eds.), *Impure Reason*, 322–43.

Barrio Gonzalo, Maximiliano, "Los eclesiásticos afrancesados durante la Guerra de Independencia," in Alberola and Larriba, *Las élites*, 227–56.

Barth, Ulrich, "Pantheismusstreit, Atheismusstreit und Fichte's Konsequenzen," in K. M. Kodalle and M. Ohst (eds.), *Fichtes Entlassung. Der Atheismusstreit vor 200 Jahren* (*Kritisches Jahrbuch der Philosophie* 4 (1999), 101–23.

Bartlett, R. C., *The Idea of Enlightenment, a Post-Mortem Study* (Toronto, 2001).

Barton, H. Arnold, *Northern Arcadia: Foreign Travelers in Scandinavia 1765–1815* (Carbondale, IL, 1998).

Baumstark, M., "The End of Empire and the Death of Religion: A Reconsideration of Hume's Later Political Thought," in R. Savage (ed.), *Philosophy and Religion in Enlightenment Britain* (Oxford, 2012), 231–57.

Beales, Derek, *Joseph II: Against the World 1780–1790* (Cambridge, 2009).

Beck, Adolf, "Hölderlin als Republikaner," *Hölderlin-Jahrbuch* xv (1967/8), 28–52.

Bedjaï, Marc, "Libertins et politiques: le comte de Guiche," *Revue de la Bibliothèque Nationale* 44 (1992), 29–33.

Beermann, M., *Zeitung zwischen Profit und Politik. Der* Courier du Bas-Rhin *(1767–1810)* (Leipzig, 1996).

Beiser, F. C., *The Sovereignty of Reason* (Princeton, 1996).

Beiser, F. C., *Schiller as Philosopher: A Re-Examination* (Oxford, 2005).

Beiser, F. C., *Enlightenment, Revolution and Romanticism. The Genesis of Modern German Political Thought (1790–1800)* (Cambridge, MA, 1992).

Belaval, Yvon, *Études sur Diderot* (Paris, 2003).

Belissa, Marc, "La Légende grise des dernières années de Thomas Paine en Amérique, 1802–9," AHRF 360 (2010), 133–72.

Belissa, Marc, "Les Leçons de républicanisme de Thomas Paine (1802–1807)," AHRF 363 (2011), 59–84.

Belissa, Marc, and Yannick Bosc, *Robespierre: la fabrication d'un mythe* (Paris, 2013).

Belissa, Marc, and Julien Louvrier, "Robespierre dans les publications françaises et Anglophones depuis l'an 2000," AHRF 371 (2013).

Bell, David, *The Cult of the Nation in France: Inventing Nationalism, 1680–1800* (Cambridge, MA, 2001).

Bell, David, "A Very Different French Revolution," *New York Review of Books*, 10 July 2014.

Belleau, Jean-Philippe E., "'Love in the Time of Hierarchy': Ethnographic Voices in Eighteenth-Century Haiti," in L. Woff and M. Cipolloni (eds.), *The Anthropology of the Enlightenment* (Stanford, CA, 2007), 209–36.

Bénétruy, J., *L'Atelier de Mirabeau* (Geneva, 1962).

Benigno, Francesco, "Lumi e lanterne: una rivoluzione di philosophes?," RSI 129 (2015), 961–88.

Benítez, Miguel, *La Face cachée des Lumières* (Paris, 1996).

Benítez, Miguel, *Le Foyer clandestin des Lumières: nouvelles recherches sur les manuscrits clandestins* (2 vols., Paris, 2013).

Benot, Yves, *Diderot: de l'athéisme à l'anticolonialisme* (Paris, 1970).

Benot, Yves, *La Guyane sous la Révolution, ou l'impassse de la Révolution pacifique* (Kourou, 1997).

Benot, Yves, "Diderot, Raynal et le mot 'colonie'," in France and Strugnell (eds.), *Diderot*, 140–52.

Benot, Yves, "Y a-t-il une morale matérialiste?," in Fink and Stenger (eds.), *Être matérialiste*, 81–91.

Berlin, Isaiah, *Karl Marx*, ed. Henry Hardy (5th edn., 2013).

Bernasconi, R., "Kant as an Unfamiliar Source of Racism," in Ward and Lott (eds.), *Philosophers*, 145–66.

Berry, C. J., *Social Theory of the Scottish Enlightenment* (Edinburgh, 1997).

Berry, C. J., "Lusty Women and Loose Imagination," HPTh xxiv (2003), 415–33.

Berti, Francesco, "Modello britannico, modello americano e antidispotismo," in A. Trampus (ed.), *Diritti e constituzione. L'opera di Gaetano Filangieri e la sua fortuna europea* (Bologna, 2005), 19–60.

Berti, Silvia, "Repubblicanesimo e Illuminismo radicale nella storiografia di Franco Venturi," in M. Albertone (ed.), *Il Repubblicanesimo moderno. L'idea di repubblica nella riflessione storica di Franco Venturi* (Naples, 2006), 155–86.

Betz, John R., *After Enlightenment: The Post-Secular Vision of J. G. Hamann* (Malden, MA, 2009).

Bevilacqua, Alexander, "Conceiving the Republic of Mankind in the Political Thought of Anarchasis Cloots," HEI 38 (2012), 550–69.

Biagioni, Mario, *The Radical Reformation and the Making of Modern Europe* (Leiden, 2017).

Bianchi, Lorenzo, "Modération non sans tentations radicales: le cas de Montesquieu," in García-Alonso (ed.), *Lumières radicales*, 341–54.

Biard, Michel, *La Liberté ou la mort: mourir en député 1792–1795* (Paris, 2015).

Bietenholz, P. G., *Daniel Zwicker (1612–1678): Peace, Tolerance and God the One and Only* (Florence, 1997).

Blamires, Cyprian, "Beccaria et l'Angleterre", in Porret (ed.), *Beccaria*, 69–81.

Blamires, Cyprian, *The French Revolution and the Creation of Benthamism* (Basingstoke, 2008).

Blanc, Olivier, "Une humaniste au XVIIIe siècle: Olympe de Gouges," in E. Morin-Rotureau (ed.), *1789–1799: combat de femmes. La Révolution exclut les citoyennes* (Paris, 2003), 15–34.

Blank, Andreas, "D'Holbach on Self-Esteem, Justice, and Cosmopolitanism," in *Eighteenth-Century Studies*, 49 (2016), 439–53.

Blanning, T. C. W., *The Culture of Power and the Power of Culture: Old Regime Europe* (Oxford, 2002).

Blanning, T. C. W., The *Pursuit of Glory: The Five Revolutions that Made Modern Europe, 1648–1815* (New York, 2007).

Blanning, T. C. W., *The Romantic Revolution* (London, 2010).

Blaufarb, Rafe, "'La Révolution armée, la révolution victorieuse": comprendre la conquête de l'indépendance de l'Amérique latine," AHRF 393 (2018), 175–93.

Bloch, O., "L'Héritage libertin dans le matérialisme des Lumières," *Dix-Huitième Siècle* xxiv (1992), 73–82.

Blom, Hans W., "Grotius and Socinianism", in M. Mulsow and Jan Rohls (eds.), *Socinianism and Arminianism: Antitrinitarians, Calvinists and Cultural Exchange in Seventeenth-Century Europe* (Leiden, 2005).

Blom, Hans W., "Styles of Heterodoxy and Intellectual Achievement: Grotius and Arminianism," in Mortimer and Robertson (eds.), *Intellectual Consequences of Religious Heterodoxy*, 47–73.

Blom, Philip, *Enlightening the World: Encyclopédie. The Triumph of Reason in an Unreasonable Age* (London, 2004).

Blom, Philip, *A Wicked Company: The Forgotten Radicalism of the European Enlightenment* (New York, 2010).

Bloom, Clive, *Restless Revolutionaries: A History of Britain's Fight for a Republic* (Stroud, 2010).

Boehm, Omri, *Kant's Critique of Spinoza* (Oxford, 2014).

Boes, Maria, "Women and the Penal System in Frankfurt am Main, 1562–1696," *Criminal Justice History* xiii (1992), 61–73.

Boes, Maria, "'Dishonourable' Youth, Guilds and the Changed World View of Sex, Illegitimacy and Women in Late-Sixteenth-Century Germany", *Continuity and Change* xviii (2003), 345–72.

Böhm, G., *Ludwig Wekhrlin (1739–1792). Ein Publizistenleben des achtzehnten Jahrhunderts* (Munich, 1893).

Bohnen, Klaus, "Lessing und Dänemark," in W. Barner and M. Reh (eds.), *Nation und Gelehrtenrepublik. Lessing im europäischen Zusammenhang*, Sonderband, Lessing Yearbook (Munich, 1984), 305–14.

Bohnert, Christiane, "Enlightenment and Despotism: Two Worlds in Lessing's *Nathan the Wise*," in Wilson and Holub (eds.), *Impure Reason*, 344–63.

Bohorquez-Morán, Carmen, *Francisco de Miranda* (Paris, 1998).

Bongie, L. L., *David Hume: Prophet of the Counter-Revolution* (1965; 2nd edn., Indianapolis, IN, 2000).

Bonnerot, Olivier-Henri, "Louis-Sebastien Mercier: lecteur et éditeur de Jean-Jacques Rousseau," in Thiery (ed.), *Rousseau, l'*Émile *et la Révolution*, 415–23.

Bordoli, Roberto, *Ragione e scrittura tra Descartes e Spinoza* (Milan, 1997).

Bordoli, Roberto, *L'Illuminismo di Dio: alle origini della mentalità liberale* (Florence, 2004).

Bordoli, Roberto, "The Monopoly of Social Influence: The Jus circa sacra around Spinoza," in Lavaert and Schröder (eds.), *The Dutch Legacy*, 121–49.

Borghero, Carlo, "Sparta tra storia e utopia. Il significativo e la funzione del mito di Sparta nel pensiero di Jean-Jacques Rousseau," in G. Solinas (ed.), *Saggi sull' Illuminismo* (Cagliari, 1973), 254–318.

Borghero, Carlo, *Interpretazioni, categorie, finzioni. Narrare la storia della filosofia* (Florence, 2017).

Borrelli, Gian Franco, "Hobbes e la teoria moderna della democrazia," *Trimestre* xxiv (1991), 243–63.

Bosc, Yannick, "Le Conflit des libertés: Thomas Paine et le débat sur la déclaration et la constitution de l'an III," AHRF 327 (Jan.–Mar. 2002), 99–105.

Bosc, Yannick, "Le Conflit des conceptions de la république et de la liberté: Thomas Paine contre Boissy d'Anglas," in M. Belissa, Y. Bosc, and F. Gauthier (eds.), *Républicanisme et droit naturel* (Paris, 2009), 101–15.

Bosc, Yannick, "Liberté et propriété: sur l'économie politique et le républicanisme de Condorcet," AHRF 366 (2011), 53–82.

Bosc, Yannick, "Robespierre libéral," AHRF 371 (2013), 95–11.

Bosc, Yannick, *La Terreur des Droits de l'Homme: la républicanisme de Thomas Paine et le moment thermidorien* (Paris, 2016).

Bosc, Yannick, and Florence Gauthier, "Introduction à la réédition" of Albert Mathiez, *La Réaction thermidorienne* (Paris, 2010), 2–52.

Botting, Eileen Hunt, "Wollstonecraft in Europe, 1792–1904," HEI 39 (2013), 503–27.

Botting, Eileen Hunt, "The Early Rousseau's Egalitarian Feminism," HEI 43 (2017), 732–44.

Boulad-Ayoub, J., "Voltaire et Frederic II, critiques du *Système de la nature*," in Boulad-Ayoub (ed.), *Paul Henri Thiry, Baron d'Holbach*, 39–66.

Boulad-Ayoub, J (ed.), *Paul Henri Thiry, Baron d'Holbach: epistemologie et politique au XVIIIe siècle. Corpus. Revue de philosophie* xxii/xxiii (Paris, 1992).

Bourdin, Jean-Claude, *Diderot: le matérialisme* (Paris, 1998).

Bourel, D., *Moses Mendelssohn: la naisssance du judaïsme moderne* (Paris, 2004).

Bourke, Richard, *Empire and Revolution: The Political Life of Edmund Burke* (Princeton, 2015).

Bourke, Richard, "Rethinking Democracy." MIH 13 (2016), 247–59.

Bouwie, Andrew, *Schelling and Modern European Philosophy* (London, 1993).

Bove, Laurent, *La Stratégie du conatus: affirmation et résistance chez Spinoza* (Paris, 1996).

Bow, Charles Bradford, "'Jacobins" at Princeton in Student Riots, Religious Revivalism and the Decline of Enlightenment, 1800–1817," MIH 14 (2017), 35–65.

Boyle, Nicholas, *Goethe. The Poet and the Age* I: *The Poetry of Desire (1749–1790)* (Oxford, 1991).

Brading, David, *Classical Republicanism and Creole Patriotism. Simon Bolívar (1783–1830) and the Spanish American Revolution* (Cambridge Centre for Latin American Studies, 1983).

Bradley, J. E., and D. van Kley (eds.), *Religion and Politics in Enlightenment Europe* (Notre Dame, IN, 2001).

Braida, L., "Censure et circulation du livre en Italie en XVIIIe siècle," JMEH iii (2005), 81–99.

Braun, Th. E. D., "Diderot, the Ghost of Bayle," *Diderot Studies* xxvii (1998), 45–55.

Breazeale, Daniel, "Fichte and Schelling: The Jena Period," in K. M. Higgins and R. C. Solomon (eds.), *The Age of German Idealism* (London, 1993), 138–80.

Breña, Roberto, *El primer liberalismo español y los procesos de emancipación de América, 1808–1824* (Mexico City, 2006).

Brewer, Holly, "Slavery, Sovereignty and 'Inheritable Blood': John Locke and the Origins of American Slavery," AHR 122 (2017), 1038–78.

Broadie, Alexander, *The Scottish Enlightenment* (Edinburgh, 2001).

Broadie, Alexander (ed.), *The Scottish Enlightenment* (Cambridge, 2003).

Broers, Michael, *Europe under Napoleon* (London, 2015).

Broers, Michael, *The Napoleonic Mediterranean: Enlightenment, Revolution and Empire* (London, 2017).

Broers, Michael, P. Hicks, and A. Guimerá (eds.), *The Napoleonic Empire and the New European Political Culture* (Basingstoke, 2012).

Brommich, David, *The Intellectual Life of Edmund Burke* (Cambridge, MA, 2014).

Brooke, Christopher, "How the Stoics became Atheists," *The Historical Journal* xlix (2006), 387–402.

Brooke, Christopher, "Locke *en particulier* [. . .]: Revisiting the Relationship between Locke and Rousseau," in C. Miqueu and M. Chamie (eds.), *Locke's Political Liberty: Readings and Misreadings*, SVEC 4 (Oxford, 2009), 69–82.

Brown, Alison, *The Return of Lucretius to Renaissance Florence* (Cambridge, MA, 2010).

Brown, Eric, "Politics and Society," in J. Warren (ed.), *The Cambridge Companion to Epicureanism* (Cambridge, 2009), 179–96.

Brown, G. S., *Toussaint's Clause: The Founding Fathers and the Haïtian Revolution* (Jackson, MI, 2005).

Brown, Michael, *The Irish Enlightenment* (Cambridge, MA, 2016).
Brown, Robert, "Social Sciences," in CHEPh ii. 1069–1105.
Brown, Stuart, "Locke as Secret 'Spinozist': The Perspective of William Carroll," in Van Bunge and Klever (eds.), *Disguised and Overt Spinozism*, 213–34.
Brown, Stuart, "Theological Politics" and the Reception of Spinoza in the Early English Enlightenment," *Studia Spinozana* 9 (1993), 181–200.
Bruyère-Ostells, Walter, *La Grande Armée de la liberté* (Paris, 2009).
Buchan, James, *Adam Smith and the Pursuit of Perfect Liberty* (London, 2006).
Buck-Morss, S., *Hegel and Haïti* (Pittsburgh, 2009).
Buckley, M. J., *At the Origins of Modern Atheism* (New Haven, 1987).
Buel, Richard, *Joel Barlow* (Baltimore, 2011).
Buijs, Peter, *De Eeuw van het geluk* (Hilversum, 2007).
Buisman, Jan Wim, *Verlichting in Nederland, 1650–1850. Vrede tussen rede en religie?* (Nijmegen, 2013).
Bunge, Wiep (Louis) van, *Johannes Bredenburg (1643–1691). Een Rotterdamse Collegiant in de ban van Spinoza* (Rotterdam, 1990).
Bunge, Wiep (Louis) van, "Rationaliteit en Verlichting," *De Achttiende Eeuw* 32 (2000), 145–64.
Bunge, Wiep (Louis) van, *From Stevin to Spinoza: An Essay on Philosophy in the Seventeenth-Century Dutch Republic* (Leiden, 2001).
Bunge, Wiep (Louis) van, "The Modernity of Radical Enlightenment," *De Achttiende Eeuw* 41 (2009), 137–43.
Bunge, Wiep van, and W. Klever (eds.), *Disguised and Overt Spinozism around 1700* (Leiden, 1996).
Bunge, Wiep van, Henri Krop, et al. (eds.), *The Dictionary of Seventeenth and Eighteenth-Century Dutch Philosophers* (2 vols., Bristol, 2003).
Burgess, G., and M. Festenstein (eds.), *English Radicalism 1550–1850* (Cambridge, 2007).
Burnard, Trevor, and John Garrigus, *Atlantic Capitalism in French Saint-Domingue and British Jamaica* (Philadelphia, 2016).
Burns, James, "Jacques-Pierre Brissot: From Scepticism to Conviction," HEI 38 (2012), 505–26.
Burns, J. H., "Jeremy Bentham: From Radical Enlightenment to Philosophic Radicalism," *The Bentham Newsletter* 8 (1984), 4–14.
Burrow, J. W., *The Crisis of Reason: European Thought, 1848–1914* (New Haven, 2000).
Burstin, Haim "Entre théorie et pratique de la Terreur: un essai de balisage," in Michel Biard (ed.), *Les politiques de la Terreur, 1793–1794* (Rennes, 2008), 39–52.
Burston, W. H., *James Mill on Philosophy and Education* (London, 1973).
Buruma, Ian, *Taming the Gods: Religion and Democracy on Three Continents* (Princeton, 2010).
Busaall, J., "Constitution et 'gouvernement des modernes' dans l'Espagne du 'Trienio liberal'," in Jean-Phillippe Luis (ed.), *La Guerre d'Indépendence espagnol et le libéralisme au XIX siècle* (Madrid, 2011), 111–24.
Busnelli, Manlio, *Diderot et l'Italie* (1925; repr. Geneva, 1970).
Butrón Prida, Gonzalo, "From Hope to Defensiveness: The Foreign Policy of a Beleaguered Liberal Spain, 1820–1823," *English Historical Review* 133 (2018), 567–96.
Butterwick, R., S. Davies, and G. Sánchez Espinosa (eds.), *Peripheries of the Enlightenment* (Oxford, 2008).

Buys, Ruben, "Without Thy Self, Thou Hast No Means [. . .]: Pieter Balling, the Radical Enlightenment and the Legacy of Dirck Volckertsz Coornhert," *Church History and Religious Culture* 93 (2013), 363–83.

Cahen, Raphael, "The Correspondence of Friedrich von Gentz," in Armenteros and Lebrun (eds.,) *Joseph de Maistre*, 95–121.

Calvié, Lucien, "Le Début du siècle nouveau: le débat intellectuel et politique en Allemagne autour de 1800," *Archives de Philosophie* 81 (2018), 523–36.

Cañizares-Esguerra, Jorge, *How to Write the History of the New World: Histories, Epistemologies and Identities in the Eighteenth-Century Atlantic World* ((Stanford, 2001).

Cañizares-Esguerra, Jorge, *Nature, Empire and Nation: Explorations of the History of Science in the Iberian World* (Stanford, 2006).

Canovan, M., "Paternalistic Liberalism: Joseph Priestley on Rank and Inequality," *Enlightenment and Dissent* ii (1983), 23–37.

Canziani, Guido (ed.), *Filosofia e religione nella letteratura clandestina. Secoli XVII e XVIII* (Milan, 1994).

Capaldi, Nicholas, *John Stuart Mill: A Biography* (Cambridge, 2004).

Capra, Carlo, "Alle origini del moderatismo e del Giacobinismo in Lombardia: Pietro Verri e Pietro Custodi," *Studi historici* xxx (1989), 873–90.

Capra, Carlo, *I progressi della ragione. Vita di Pietro Verri* (Bologna, 2002).

Capra, Carlo, "Habsburg Italy in the Age of Reform," *Journal of Modern Italian Studies* x (2005), 218–33.

Carbonero y Sol, Leon, *Indice de los libros prohibido por el Santo Oficio de la Inquisición Española* (Madrid, 1873).

Cardenas Acosta, Pablo, *El movimiento comunal de 1781 en el Nuevo Reino de Granada* (1960; 2nd edn., 2 vols, Bogotá, 1980).

Carey, D., and L. Festa (eds.), *Postcolonial Enlightenment: Eighteenth-Century Colonialism and Postcolonial Theory* (Oxford, 2009).

Carey, Daniel, "Two Strategies on Toleration: Locke, Shaftesbury and Diversity," in C. Miqueu and M. Chamie (eds.), *Locke's Political Liberty: Readings and Misreadings*, SVEC 4 (Oxford, 2009), 51–67.

Carey, Daniel, and Sven Trakelhun, "Universalism Diversity and the Potcolonial Enlightenment," in D. Carey and L. Festa (eds.), *The Postcolonial Enlightenment: Eighteenth-Century Colonialism and Postcolonial Theory* (Oxford, 2009), 240–80.

Carhart, M., *The Science of Culture in Enlightenment Germany* (Cambridge, MA, 2007).

Carhart, M., and Robertson, John, "The Enlightenments of J. G. A. Pocock," *Storia della Storiografia* xxxix (2001), 123–51.

Carlsson, Ulla, and D. Goldberg (eds.), *The Legacy of Peter Forsskål: 250 Years of Freedom of Expression* (Gothenburg, Sweden, 2017).

Carpanetto, Dino, "Voltaire, la lumière et la théorie de la connaissance," in Kölving and Mervaud (eds.), *Voltaire et ses combats* i. 39–45.

Carpanetto, Dino, and Giuseppe Ricuperati, *Italy in the Age of Reason, 1685–1789* (London, 1987).

Carrion Caravedo, U., "La Soberanía en Baquijano y Carrillo," in A. Castro (ed.), *Filosofia y Sociedad en el Peru* (Lima, 2003) 63–74.

Carrithers, D. W., "An Appreciation of the *Spirit of the Laws*," in Carrithers et al. (eds.), *Montesquieu's Science of Politics*, 1–40.

Carrithers, D. W., "Democratic and Aristocratic Republics," in Carrithers et al. (eds.), *Montesquieu's Science of Politics*, 109–58.

Carrithers, D. W., M. A. Mosher, and P. A. Rahe (eds.), *Montesquieu's Science of Politics: Essays on* The Spirit of the Laws (Oxford, 2001).

Casalini, B., "*L'Esprit* di Montesquieu negli Stati Uniti durante la seconda metà del XVIII secolo," in D. Felice (ed.), *Montesquieu e i suoi interpreti* (2 vols., Pisa, 2005) i. 325–55.

Casarino, Cesare, "Marx before Spinoza: Notes toward an Investigation," in D. Vardoulakis (ed.), *Spinoza Now* (Minneapolis, 2011), 179–234.

Casini, Paolo, "Spinoza, il materialismo, e i radicali liberi," *Rivista di filosofia* 97 (2006), 387–408.

Cassirer, Ernst, *The Philosophy of the Enlightenment* (1932; Princeton, 1979).

Celenza, Christopher, *The Lost Italian Renaissance* (Baltimore, 2004).

Censer, J. R., *Prelude to Power: The Parisian Radical Press, 1789–1791* (Baltimore, 1976).

Chakrabarty, Dipesh, *Provincializing Europe* (2000; Princeton, new edn., 2008).

Champion, Justin, *The Pillars of Priestcraft Shaken: The Church of England and its Enemies 1660–1730* (Cambridge, 1992).

Champion, Justin, "John Toland: The Politics of Pantheism," *Revue de Synthèse* 4 (1995), 259–80.

Champion, Justin, "'The Men of Matter': Spirits, Matter and the Politics of Priestcraft, 1701–1709," in G. Paganini, M. Benítez, and J. Dybikowski (eds.), *Scepticisme, Lumières, clandestinité et libre pensée* (Paris 2002), 115–50.

Champion, Justin, *Republican Learning: John Toland and the Crisis of Christian Culture, 1696–1722* (Manchester, 2003).

Chappuis, Pierre, "Joseph Gorani et la Suisse," *Schweizerische Zeitschrift für Geschichte* ii (1952), 363–85.

Charbonnel, P., "Remarques sur la futurologie politique du groupe Holbach-Diderot, 1773–1776," SVEC 151 (1976), 449–66.

Charbonnel, P., "Le Réquisitoire de Seguier," in Boulad-Ayoub (ed.), *Paul Henri Thiry, Baron d'Holbach*, 15–37.

Chartier, Roger, *Les Origines culturelles de la Révolution française* (Paris, 1990).

Cherni, A., *Diderot: l'ordre et le devenir* (Geneva, 2002).

Chiaramonte, José Carlos, *La Ilustración en el Río de la Plata. Cultura eclesiástica y cultura laica durante el Virreinato* (Buenos Aires, 2007).

Chisick, H., "Interpreting the Enlightenment," *The European Legacy* xiii (2008), 35–57.

Chisick, H., "Of Radical and Moderate Enlightenment," in Ducheyne, *Reassessing*, 48–60.

Chopelin-Blanc, C., *De l'apologétique à l'Église constitutionelle: Adrien Lamourette (1742–1794)* (Paris, 2009).

Chopelin-Blanc, C., "Adrien Lamourette (1742–1794): The Unconventional Revolutionary and Reformer," in J. D. Burson and U. Lehner (eds.), *Enlightenment and Catholicism in Europe* (Notre Dame, IN, 2014), 107–23.

Chouillet, Anne-Marie (ed.), *Les Ennemis de Diderot* (Paris, 1993).

Chouillet, Jacques, "La Politique de Diderot entre la société démocratique et l'état hierarchisé," in A. Mango (ed.), *Diderot. Il Politico, il filosofo, lo scrittore* (Milan, 1986), 23–37.

Chukwudi Eze, E., *Race and the Enlightenment* (Oxford, 1997).

Ciappara, Frans, *Enlightenment and Reform in Malta 1740–1798* (Malta, 2006).

Citton, Yves, *L'Envers de la Liberté: l'invention d'un imaginaire spinoziste dans la France des Lumières* (Paris, 2006).

Citton, Yves, "L'Invention du Spinozisme dans la France du XVIIIe siècle," in Secrétan, Dagron, and Bove (eds.), *Qu'est-ce que les Lumières "radicales"?*, 309–24.

Citton, Yves, "À quoi servent les Lumières radicales?," *Lumières* xiii (2009), 135–56.

Claeys, Gregory, "Early Socialism as Intellectual History," HEI 40 (2014), 893–904.

Clark, Christopher, *Iron Kingdom: The Rise and Downfall of Prussia 1600–1947* (London, 2007).

Clark, H. C., *Compass of Society: Commerce and Absolutism in Old Regime France* (Lanham, MD, 2007).

Clark, J. C. D., *Thomas Paine. Britain, America, and France in the Age of Enlightenment* (Oxford, 2018).

Clarke, Joseph, *Commemorating the Dead in Revolutionary France* (Cambridge, 2007).

Clemens, Gabriele, "The Swiss Case in the Napoleonic Empire," in Broers et al. (eds.), *Napoleonic Empire*, 132–42.

Cliteur, Paul, and G. Gordon, "The Enlightenment in Contemporary Cultural Debate," in B. Labuschagne and R. Sonnenschmidt (eds.), *Religion, Politics and Law: Philosophical Reflections on the Sources of Normative Order* (Leiden, 2009), 311–31.

Cochrane, Eric, *Tradition and Enlightenment in the Tuscan Academies 1690–1800* (Rome, 1961).

Coffrey, John, "The Toleration Controversy during the English Revolution," in Christopher Durston and J. Maltby (eds.), *Religion in Revolutionary England* (Manchester, 2006), 42–68.

Cohen, Claudine, *Science, libertinage et clandestinité à l'aube des Lumières* (Paris, 2011).

Cohen, Joshua, *Roussseau: A Free Commuity of Equals* (Oxford, 2010).

Colie, Rosalie, *Light and Enlightenment* (Cambridge, 1957).

Colley, Linda, *Britons: Forging the Nation 1707–1837* (New Haven, 1992).

Comte-Sponville, A., "La Mettrie: un 'Spinoza moderne'?," in Olivier Bloch (ed.), *Spinoza, au XVIIIe siècle* (Paris, 1990), 133–50.

Cone, Carl B., *The English Jacobins: Reformers in Late 18th Century England* (New York, 1968).

Conrad, Sebastian, "Enlightenment in Global History," AHR 117 (2012), 999–1027.

Cook, Alexander, "Volney and the Science of Morality," *Humanities Research* 16 (2010), 7–28.

Cook, Alexander, "The Great Society of the Human Species: Volney and the Global Politics of Revolutionary France," IHR 23 (2013), 309–28.

Cook, Alexander, "Between the Old World and the New: C. F. Volney and the Politics of Travel Writing, 1782–1803," AHRF 385 (2016), 87–108.

Cormack, William, *Patriots, Royalists and Terrorists in the West Indies: The French Revolution in Martinique and Guadeloupe* (Toronto, 2019).

Corno, Philippe, "La Loi révolutionnairé du divorce et ses représentations théatrales," *Dix-Huitième Siècle* xli (2009), 61–77.

Cotlar, Seth, *Tom Paine's America: The Rise and Fall of Transatlantic Radicalism in the Early Republic* (Charlottesville, VA, 2011).

Cottebrune, Anne, *Mythe et realité du "Jacobinisme allemand"* (Lille 2001).

Courtney, C. P., "Les Metamorphoses d'un best-seller: *l'Histoire de Deux Indes* de 1770 à 1820," in Bancarel and Goggi (eds.), *Raynal*, 109–20.

Crampe-Crasnabet, M., "Les Articles ÂME dans l'*Encyclopédie*," RDE xxv (1998), 91–9.

Cremona, V. R. de Longis, et al., *Catalogo dell edizioni italiani, 1789–1799* (Naples, 1993).

Criautu, Aurelian, *Liberalism under Siege* (Lanham, MD, 2003).

Criautu, Aurelian, "Rousseau and Madame de Staël: A Surprising Dialogue," in Rosenblatt and Schweigert (eds.), *Thinking with Rousseau*, 235–51.

Criautu, Aurelian, *A Virtue for Courageous Minds: Moderation in French Political Thought, 1748–830* (Princeton, 2012).

Cristani, Giovanni, *D'Holbach e le rivoluzioni del globo* (Florence, 2003).
Cronk, Nicholas, "Voltaire (non) lecteur de Nieuwentijt," *Revue Voltaire* vii (2007), 169–81.
Crouter, R., *Friedrich Schleiermacher between Enlightenment and Romanticism* (Cambridge, 2005).
Crowe, B. D., "'Theismus des Gefühls.' Heydenreich, Fichte and the Transcendental Philosophy of Religion," JHI 70 (2009), 569–92.
Cuenca Toribio, José Manuel, *La Guerra de Independencia: un conflicto decisivo (1808–1814)* (Madrid, 2006).
Culoma, M., *La Religion civile de Rousseau à Robespierre* (Paris, 2010).
Cuneou, T., and R. van Woudenberg (eds.), *The Cambridge Companion to Thomas Reid* (Cambridge, 2004).
Curran, Andrew, "Buffon et l'histoire naturelle des Africains," *Dix-Huitième Siècle* 44 (2012), 183–99.
Curran, Andrew, *Diderot and the Art of Thinking Freely* (New York, 2019).
Curran, Mark, *Atheism, Religion and Enlightenment in Pre-Revolutionary Europe* (Woodbridge, 2012).
Dabhoiwala, F., "Lust and Liberty," *Past and Present* 207 (May 2010), 89–179.
Dagen, Jean, *L'Histoire de l'esprit humain dans la pensée française de Fontenelle à Condorcet* (Paris, 1977).
Dagron, Tristan, "Neo-spinozisme ou anti-spinozisme? Le Cas de Toland," in Secrétan, Dagron, and Bove (eds.) *Qu'est-ce que les "Lumières radicales"* (Paris, 2007), 325–41.
Dagron, Tristan, *Toland et Leibniz: l'invention du néo-spinozisme* (Paris, 2009).
Dahlberg, L., "The Habermasian Public Sphere: Taking Difference Seriously?," *Theory and Society* xxiv (2005), 111–36.
Dakin, D., *Turgot and the* Ancien Régime *in France* (New York, 1980).
Damrosh, Leo, *Jean-Jacques Rousseau: Restless Genius* (New York, 2005).
Darnton, Robert, *The Literary Underground of the Old Regime* (Cambridge, MA, 1982).
Darnton, Robert, *The Forbidden Best-Sellers of Pre-Revolutionary France* (London, 1996).
Darnton, Robert, "Two Paths through the Social History of Ideas," in H. Mason (ed.), *The Darnton Debate: Books and Revolution in the Eighteenth Century* (Voltaire Foundation, 1999), 251–94.
Darrow, Margaret, *Family, Class, and Inheritance in Southern France, 1775–1825* (Princeton, 1989).
Darwall, S., "Hume and the Invention of Utilitarianism," in Stewart and Wright (eds.), *Hume*, 58–82.
Darwall, S., "Norm and Normativity," in CHEPh ii. 987–1025.
Davidson, Denise, "Feminism and Abolitionism: Transatlantic Trajectories," in S. Desan, Lynn Hunt, and W. M. Nelson (eds.), *The French Revolution in Global Perspective* (Ithaca, 2013), 101–10.
Davidson, Ian, *Voltaire in Exile: The Last Years, 1753–78* (New York, 2004).
Davies, S., "L'Irlande et les Lumières," *Dix-Huitième Siècle* xxx (1998), 17–35.
Dávila, Jorge, *Bolívar y Spinoza. Reflejos doctrinarios* (Mérida, Venezuela, 2013).
Davis, D. B., "New Sidelights on Early Antislavery Radicalism," *William and Mary Quarterly* 3rd ser. xxviii (1971), 585–94.
Davis, D. B., *The Problem of Slavery in the Age of Revolution, 1770–1823* (New York, 1999).
Davis, J. A., "The Napoleonic Era in Southern Italy: An Ambiguous Legacy?," *Proceedings of the British Academy* lxxx (1993), 133–48.
Davis, Jennifer J., "The Radical Enlightenment and Movements for Women's Equality in Europe and America (1673–1825)," in Ducheyne (ed.), *Reassessing*, 292–308.

Davis, John, "The Spanish Constitution of 1812 and the Mediterranean Revolutions (1820–25)," *Bulletin for Spanish and Portuguese Historical Studies* 37 (2013), online article 7.
Davis, M. T. (ed.), *Radicalism and Revolution in Britain, 1775–1848* (Basingstoke, 2000).
Davis, Timothy, "The Historical Context of the General Glut Controversy," in Steven Kates (ed.), *Two Hundred Years of Say's Law* (Cheltenham, 2003), 133–50.
Davison, R., *Diderot et Galiani: étude d'une amitié philosophique* (Oxford, 1985).
De Bolla, Peter, *The Architecture of Concepts: The Historical Formation of Human Rights* (New York, 2013).
De Champs, Emmanuelle, *Enlightenment and Utility: Bentham in French, Bentham in France* (Cambridge, 2015).
De Dijn, Annelien, "The Politics of Enlightenment: From Peter Gay to Jonathan Israel," *The Historical Journal* 55 (2012), 785–805.
De Dijn, Annelien, "Montesquieu's Controversial Context: The Spirit of Laws as a Monarchist Tract," *History of Political Thought* xxxiv (2013), 66–88.
De Francesco, A., "How not to Finish a Revolution," in Imbruglia (ed.), *Naples*, 167–82.
De Kom, Anton, *Wij slaven van Surinme* (1934; new edn., Amsterdam, 2017).
Delaney, J., *Rousseau and the Ethics of Virtue* (London, 2006).
De Lange, M. H. "John Toland en Hermann Samuel Reimarus over de wonderen in het Oude Testament," *Nederlands Theologisch Tijdschrift* xlvi (1992), 1–9.
D'Elia, D. J., *Benjamin Rush: Philosopher of the American Revolution* (Philadelphia, 1974).
Delinière, Jean, "Polémique à propos d'un poème à la gloire de la liberté de l'Amérique," in R. Krebs and J. Moes (eds.), *La Révolution Américaine vue par les périodiques de langue allemande, 1773–1783* (Paris, 1992), 53–67.
Delpiano, Patrizia, *Il governo della lettura. Chiesa e libri nell'Italia del Settecento* (Bologna, 2007).
De Luca, Stefano, "Benjamin Constant and the Terror," in H. Rosenblatt (ed.), *The Cambridge Companion to Constant* (Cambridge, 2009), 92–114.
De Luna, F., "The Dean Street Style of Revolution: J. P. Brissot, jeune philosophe," FHS xvii (1991), 159–90.
Deneys, Henri, "Volney, Auteuil et la composition des *Ruines* (1791)," in Jean-Paul de Lagrave (ed.), *Madame Helvétius et la Société d'Auteuil* (Oxford, 1999), 103–22.
Deneys-Tunne, A., *Un autre Jean-Jacques Rousseau* (Paris, 2010).
Denis, Marcelle, *Comenius* (Paris, 1994).
Dent, Nicholas, *Rousseau* (Abingdon, 2005).
De Poortere, M., *Les Idées philosophiques et littéraires de Mme. de Staël et Mme. de Genlis* (New York, 2004).
Desan, Suzanne, "The Politics of Intimacy: Marriage and Citizenship in the French Revolution," in S. Knott and B. Taylor (eds.), *Women, Gender and Enlightenment* (Basingstoke, 2005), 630–48.
Desan, Suzanne, "Foreigners, Cosmopolitanism, and French Revolutionary Universalism," in S. Desan, Lynn Hunt, and W. M. Nelson (eds.), *The French Revolution in Global Perspective* (Ithaca, 2013), 86–100.
Deseure, Brecht, "Revolutionaire geschiedenispolitik in de Zuidelijke Nederlanden (1792–1799)," in BMGN 125 (2010), 25–47.
Deseure, Brecht, "Pre-Revolutionary Provinces in a Post-Napoleonic State: Piecing Together the United Kingdom of the Netherlands, 1813–1815," BMGN 133 (2018), 98–121.

Desprat, Jean-Paul, *Mirabeau: l'excès et le retrait* (Paris, 2008).
Dessertine, Dominique, "Le Divorce et l'amour pendant la Révolution," in E. Morin-Rotureau (ed.), *1789–1799: combat de femmes. La Révolution exclut les citoyennes* (Paris, 2003), 202–22.
Devellennes, Charles, "A Fourth Musketeer of Social Contract Theory: The Politics of the Baron d'Holbach," HPTh xxxiv (2013), 459–78.
Devellennes, Charles, "Utility contra Utilitarianism: Holbach's International Ethics," *Journal of International Political Theory* 10 (2014), 188–205.
Devellennes, Charles, "D'Holbach radical: contrat social et éthocratie dans la pensée politique du baron," in García-Alonso (ed.), *Lumières radicales* (2017), 321–40.
Devellennes, Charles, "Radical Atheism: Jean Meslier in Context," in Ducheyne (ed.), *Reassessing*, 160–77.
De Vet, Jan, "Verlichting en Christendom in Nederland," in W. Fritschy and J. Toebes (eds.), *Het Onststaan van het moderne Nederland (1780–1830)* (Nijmegen, 1996), 95–122.
De Vet, Jan, "Spinoza en Spinozisme en enkele 'Journaux de Hollande'", *Mededelingen vanwege het Spinozahuis* 83 (Delft, 2002).
Devigne, Robert, *Reforming Liberalism. J. S. Mill's Use of Ancient Religious, Liberal and Romantic Moralities* (New Haven, 2006).
De Vriese, M., *Beschaven! Letterkundige genootschappen in Nederland, 1750–1800* (Nijmegen, 2001).
Dhondt, L., "De conservatieve Brabantse ontwenteling van 1789 en het proces van revolutie en contrarevolutie in de Zuidelijke Nederlanden tussen 1780 en 1830," TvG 102 (1989), 422–50.
Dickinson, H. T., "'The Friends of America': British Sympathy with the American Revolution," in Davis (ed.), *Radicalism*, 1–29.
Dickson, P. G. M., "Joseph II's Reshaping of the Austrian Church," *The Historical Journal* xxvi (1993), 89–114.
Di Domenico, Maria Giovanna, *Natura, Uomo, Dio. Saggio sull' antropologia di d'Holbach* (Naples, 1994).
Di Giovanni, George, "Introduction" to Jacobi, *Main Philosophical Writings*, 3–167.
Dingli, Laurent, *Robespierre* (Paris, 2004).
Dioguardi, Gianfranco, *Attualità dell'Illuminismo milanese* (Palermo, 1998).
Diop, D., "L'Anonymat dans les articles politiques de l'*Encyclopédie*," *La Lettre Clandestine* viii (1999), 83–102.
Dirks, N. B., *Castes of Mind: Colonialism and the Making of Modern India* (Princeton, 2001).
Dixon, Simon, *Catherine the Great* (New York, 2009).
Dobbs-Weinstein, Idit, "The Paradox of a Perfect Democracy: From Spinoza's *Theological-Political Treatise* to Marx's *Critique of Ideology*," in H. Sharp and J. E. Smith (eds.), *Between Hegel and Spinoza: A Volume of Critical Essays* (London, 2012), 189–208.
Dobbs-Weinstein, Idit, *Spinoza's Critique of Religion and its Heirs, Marx, Benjamin, Adorno* (Cambridge, 2015).
Domenech, Jacques, *L'Éthique des Lumières* (Paris, 1989).
Domenech, Jacques, "Éthique et révolution," in R. Thierry (ed.), *Rousseau, l'*Émile *et la Révolution* (Paris, 1992), 37–42.
Domenech, Jacques, "D'Holbach et l'obsession de la morale," *Corpus: Revue de philosophie* 22 (1993), 103–15.

Donnert, Erich (ed.), *Europa in der frühen Neuzeit. Festschrift für Günter Mühlpfordt* vol. ii (Cologne, 1997).

Dorigny, Marcel, "The Abbé Grégoire and the *Société des Amis des Noirs*," in J. Popkin and R. Popkin (eds.), *The Abbé Grégoire and his World* (Dordrecht, 2000), 27–39.

Dorigny, Marcel (ed.), *Les Abolitions de l'esclavage de L. F. Sonthonax à V. Schoelcher* (New York, 2003).

Dorigny, Marcel, and Yves Benot, *La Société de les Amis des Noirs, 1788–99* (Paris, 1998).

Dorigny, Marcel, and Yves Benot (eds.), *1802: Rétablissement de l'esclavage dans les colonies françaises* (Paris, 2003).

Dowe, Dieter, H. G. Haupt, D. Langewiesche, and J. Sperber (eds.), *Europe in 1848: Revolution and Reform* (New York, 2000).

Doyle, William, *The Aristocracy and its Enemies in the Age of Revolution* (Oxford, 2009).

Droixhe, Daniel, "Raynal à Liège: censure, vulgarisation, revolutions", in H. J. Lüsebrink and M. Tietz (eds.), *Lectures de Raynal* (Oxford, 1991), 205–33.

Dubois, Laurent, *A Colony of Citizens: Revolution and Slave Emancipation in the French Caribbean (1787–1804)* (Williamsburg, VA, 2001).

Dubos, N. "Hobbes et les Lumières radicales," in *Lumières* 13 (Special issue: *Lumières radicales, Radicalisme des Lumières*, Bordeaux, 2009), 35–63.

Duchet, Michele, *Diderot et l'*Histoire des Deux Indes *ou l'Écriture fragmentaire* (Paris, 1978).

Ducheyne, Steffen, (ed.) *Reassessing the Radical Enlightenment* (Abingdon, 2017).

Duerloo, Luc, "De kleuren en symbolen van de Brabantse Onwenteling," in H. Bots and W. Mijnhardt (eds.), *De Droom van de Revolutie. Nieuwe benaderingen van het Patriottisme* (Amsterdam, 1988), 93–7.

Duflo, Colas, *Diderot philosophe* (Paris, 2003).

Duflo, Colas, "Diderot and the Publicizing of Censorship," in M. Laerke (ed.), *The Use of Censorship in the Enlightenment* (Leiden, 2009), 121–35.

Duflo, Colas, "Diderot et la fin de la clandestinité," *La Lettre Clandestine* 19 (2011), 25–39.

Dulac, Georges, "Les Modes d'intervention de Diderot en politique," in France and Strugnell (eds.), *Diderot*, 121–39.

Dulac, Georges, "Le Discours politique de Pétersbourg," RDE 1 (1986), 32–58.

Dunn, John, *Setting the People Free: The Story of Democracy* (London, 2005).

Dupré, Louis, *The Enlightenment and the Intellectual Foundations of Modern Culture* (New Haven, 2004).

Durey, Michael, "Thomas Paine's Apostles: Radical Emigrés and the Triumph of Jeffersonian Republicanism," *William and Mary Quarterly* xliv (1987), 661–88.

During, Simon, "Is Absolute Secularity Conceivable?," IHR 27 (2017), 151–69.

Duthille, Remy, *Le Discours radical en Grande-Bretagne, 1768–1789* (Oxford, 2017).

Duthille, Remy, "The Right of Resistance in Richard Price and Joseph Priestley," HEI 44 (2018), 419–32.

Edelstein, Dan, *The Terror of Natural Right* (Chicago, 2009).

Edelstein, Dan, "Enlightenment Rights Talk," JMH 86 (2014), 530–65.

Edelstein, Dan, *On the Spirit of Rights* (Chicago, 2019).

Edmond, Rod, "Island Transactions: Encounter and Disease in the South Pacific," in F. A. Nussbaum (ed.), *The Global Eighteenth Century* (Baltimore, 2003), 251–62.

Egerton, D. R., "Race and Slavery in the Era of Thomas Jefferson," in Frank Shuffelton (ed.), *The Cambridge Companion to Thomas Jefferson* (Cambridge, 2009), 73–82.

Ehrard, Jean, *L'Idée de nature en France dans la première moitié du XVIIIe siècle* (Geneva, 1981).

Ehrard, Jean, "Voltaire vu par Montesquieu," in Kölving and Mervaud (eds.), *Voltaire et ses combats* ii. 939–51.

Ehrard, Jean, *L'Esprit des mots: Montesquieu en lui-même et parmi les siens* (Geneva, 1998).

Eijnatten, Joris van, "Opklaring, opwekking en behoud. Religieus conservatisme in Nederland, 1780–1840," GWN 10 (1999), 9–24.

Eijnatten, Joris van, *Liberty and Concord in the United Provinces: Religious Toleration and the Public in the Eighteenth-Century Netherlands* (Leiden, 2003).

Eire, Carlos, *Reformations: The Early Modern World, 1450–1650* (New Haven, 2016).

Ellis, E., *Kant's Politics: Provisional Theory for an Uncertain World* (New Haven, 2005).

Emerson, R. L., *Essays on David Hume, Medical Men and the Scottish Enlightenment* (Farnham, 2009).

Enciso Recio, Luis Miguel, "La divulgación de los saberes," in Luigi da Rosa et al. (eds.), *Spagna e Mezzogiorno d'Italia nell'etá della transizione (1650–1760)* (2 vols., 1997), ii. 281–355.

Erdozain, Dominic, "A Heavenly Poise: Radical Religion and the Making of the Enlightenment," IHR 27 (2017), 71–96.

Erker, B., and W. Siebers, "Das Bahrdt-Pasquill," in U. Goldenbaum (ed.), *Appell an das Publikum. Die öffentliche Debatte in der deutschen Aufklärung, 1687–1796* (2 vols., Berlin, 2004) ii. 897–939.

Escobar Villegas, Juan Camilo, and A. León Maya Salazar, "Otras 'luces' sobre la temprana historia política de Colombia, 1780–1850: Gaetano Filangieri y 'La ruta de Napoles a las Indias Occidentales'," *Co-Herencia* iv (2006), 79–111.

Esdaile, Charles, "Enlightened Absolutism versus Theocracy in the Spanish Restoration, 1814–1850," in D. Laven and L. Riall (eds.), *Napoleon's Legacy: Problems of Government in Restoration Europe* (Oxford, 2000), 65–81.

Espagne, Michel, "Les Frères Humboldt et l'idée d'Université," in M. Espagne (ed.), *La Sociabilité européenne des frères Humboldt* (Paris, 2016), 131–50.

Espinosa Antón, Francisco Javier, "Los proyectos de paz y el cosmopolitismo en la Ilustración," *Araucaria* 16 (2014), 5–23.

Establier Pérez, Helena. "Novela anticlerical y traducción en el Trienio Liberal. Diderot, Lewis y Radcliffe en España," *Dicenda. Cuadernos de Filología Hispánica* 30 (2012), 67–92.

Estes, Yolanda, and C. Bowman (eds.), *J. G. Fichte and the Atheism Dispute (1798–1800)* (Farnham, 2010).

Evans, Chris, *Debating the Revolution: Britain in the 1790s* (New York, 2006).

Evans, Michael, "Marx and the *Rheinische Zeitung*," in *Manchester Papers in Politics* 5 (1995).

Everdell, W. R., *Christian Apologetics in France, 1730–1790* (Lewiston, NY, 1987).

Faccarello, G., "'Nil repente!' Galiani and Necker on Economic Reforms," EJHE 1 (1994), 519–50.

Fajn, Max, "The Attitude of the *Journal des Hommes Libres* towards the Babouvists," *International Review of Social History* xix (1974), 228–44.

Farr, J., "'So vile and miserable an estate': The Problem of Slavery in Locke's Political Thought," *Political Theory* xiv (1987), 263–89.

Farr, J., "Locke, Natural Law and New World Slavery," in Miqueu and Chamie (eds.), *Locke's Political Liberty* (Oxford, 2009), 165–88.

Farr, J., and D. L. Williams (eds.), *The General Will: The Evolution of a Concept* (Cambridge, 2015).

Fauré, Christine, "L'Exclusion des femmes du droit du vote pendant la Révolution française et ses conséquences durables," in E. Morin-Rotureau (ed.), *1789–1799: combat de femmes. La Révolution exclut les citoyennes* (Paris, 2003), 163–77.

Febvre, Lucien, *Michelet, Créateur de l'histoire de France* (Paris, 2014).

Federici, M. P., *The Political Philosophy of Alexander Hamilton* (Baltimore, 2012).

Fedi, Laurent, *Comte* (2000; 2nd edn., Paris, 2004).

Fehn, Ernst-Otto, "Moralische Unschuld oder politische Bewusstheit? Thesen zur Illuminatischen Ideologie und ihrer Rezeption," in Reinalter (ed.)., *Der Illuminatenorden*, 207–26.

Feiner, Shmuel, *The Jewish Enlightenment* (Philadelphia, 2002).

Feiner, Shmuel, "On the Threshold of the "New World": *Haskalah* and Secularization in the Eighteenth Century," *Jahrbuch des Simon-Dubnow-Instituts* vi (Leipzig, 2007), 33–45.

Felice, Domenico, *Per una scienza universale dei sistemi politico-sociali. Dispotismo, autonomía della giustizia e carattere delle nazioni nell'* Esprit des Lois *di Montesquieu* (Florence, 2005).

Fergus, Claudius, *Revolutionary Emancipation: Slavery and Abolitionism in the British West Indies* (Baton Rouge, 2013).

Ferguson, Moira, "Mary Wollstonecraft and the Problematic of Slavery," in M. J. Falco (ed.), *Feminist Interpretations of Mary Wollstonecraft* (University Park, PA, 1996), 125–49.

Fernández Sarasola, Ignacio. "Ramón de Salas y la Nueva Ciencia Jurídica," *Teoría y Realidad constitucional* 28 (2011), 633–48.

Fernández Sebastian, Javier, "From the 'Voice of the People' to the Freedom of the Press," in Astigarraga (ed.), *Spanish Enlightenment Revisited*, 213–33.

Fernández Sebastian, Javier, "Democracy in Spain", in Joanna Innes and Mark Philp (eds.), *Re-Imagining Democracy in the Mediterranean, 1780–1860* (Oxford, 2018), 53–74.

Ferret, Olivier, *La Fureur de nuire: échanges pamphlétaires entre philosophes et antiphilosophes (1750–1770)* (Oxford, 2013).

Ferrone, Vincenzo, *I Profeti dell'illuminismo* (1989; 2nd edn., Bari, 2000).

Ferrone, Vincenzo, *La società giusta ed equa. Repubblicanesimo e diritti dell'uomo in Gaetano Filangieri* (Rome, 2003).

Ferrone, Vincenzo, *Una scienza per l'uomo. Illuminismo e Rivoluzione scientifica nell' Europa del Settecento* (Turn, 2007).

Ferrone, Vincenzo, *Lezioni Illuministiche* (Bari, 2010).

Ferrone, Vincenzo, *The Enlightenment: History of an Idea* (Princeton, 2015).

Fink, B., and G. Stenger (eds.), *Être matérialiste à l'âge des Lumières* (Paris, 1999).

Finlay, Christopher J., *Hume's Social Philosophy* (London, 2007).

Firode, A., "Locke et les philosophes français," in François de Gandt (ed.), *Cirey dans la vie intellectuelle: la réception de Newton en France* (Oxford, 2001), 57–72.

Fischer, Kirsten, "'Religion governed by Terror': A Deist Critique of Fearful Christianity," *Revue française d'Études Américaines* 125 (2010), 13–22.

Fischer, Norbert, "Reduktion der Religion auf Moral?," in N. Fischer (ed.), *Kant und der Katholizismus* (Freiburg, 2005), 282–302.

Fisher, J. R., *Bourbon Peru, 1780–1824* (Liverpool, 2003).

Fitting, Peter, "Buried Treasures: Reconsidering Holberg's Niels Klim in the World Underground," *Utopian Studies* 7 (1996), 93–112.

Fitzpatrick, M., "Enlightenment in Late-Eighteenth-Century Liverpool," in Butterwick et al. (eds.), *Peripheries*, 119–44.

Fix, Andrew, *Prophecy and Reason, the Dutch Collegiants in the Early Enlightenment* (Princeton, 1991).
Fleming, Thomas, *The Great Divide: The Conflict between Washington and Jefferson that Defined America, Then and Now* (Boston, 2015).
Flores Galindo, Alberto, "República sin ciudadanos," *Fronteras. Revista del Centro de investigaciones de historia colonial* (Bogotá) i (1997), 13–33.
Floss, Pavel, "The Problem of Comenius' Sensualism," in M. Kyralova and J. Privratika (eds.), *Symposium Comenianum 1982. The Impact of J. A. Comenius on Educational Thinking and Practice* (Uhersky Brod, 1984), 102–7.
Fogelin, R. J., "Hume's Scepticism," in Norton (ed.), *Cambridge Companion to Hume*, 90–116.
Fogelin, R. J., *A Defense of Hume on Miracles* (Princeton, 2003).
Folkerts, Heinz, *Die Bedeutung französicher Denker des 18. Jahrhunderts für die Herausbildung eines Freiheitsbewusstseins in Spaniens südamerikanischen Kolonien* (Würzburg, 1969).
Foner, Eric, *Tom Paine and Revolutionary America* (1976; revised edn., 2005).
Foner, Eric, *The Story of American Freedom* (New York, 1999).
Fontana, B., *Benjamin Constant and the Post-Revolutionary Mind* (New Haven, 1991).
Forget, Evelyn, "Jean-Baptiste Say and Spontaneous Order," *History of Political Economy* 33 (2001), 193–218.
Foot, Paul, *Red Shelley* (1980; new edn., London, 1984).
Force, Pierre, "Helvétius as an Epicurean Political Theorist," in N. Leddy and A. S. Lifschitz (eds.), *Epicurus in the Enlightenment* (Oxford, 2009), 105–18.
Forst, Rainer, *Toleranz im Konflikt* (Frankfurt, 2003).
Förster, Eckart, *The Twenty-Five Years of Philosophy: A Systematic Reconstruction* (Cambridge, MA, 2012).
Förster, Eckart, "Goethe's Spinozism," in Förster and Melamed (eds.), *Spinoza and German Idealism*, 85–99.
Förster, E., and Y. Y. Melamed (eds.), *Spinoza and German Idealism* (Cambridge, 2012).
Forster, M. N., *Kant and Scepticism* (Princeton, 2008).
Forster, M. N., "Herder and Spinoza," in Förster and Melamed (eds.), *Spinoza and German Idealism*, 59–84.
Förster, Wolfgang (ed.), *Aufklärung in Berlin* (Berlin, 1989).
Fossati, W. J., "Maximum Influence from Minimum Abilities: La Mettrie and Radical Materialism," in B. Sweetman (ed.), *The Failure of Modernism* (Mishawaka, IN, 1999), 45–57.
Fraenckel, Carlos, "Reconsidering the Case of Elijah Delmedigo's Averroism and Its Impact on Spinoza," in Anna Akasoy and G. Giglioni (eds.), *Renaissance Averroism and its Aftermath: Arabic Philosophy in Early Modern Europe* (Dordrecht, 2013), 21–36.
France, P., and A. Strugnell (eds.), *Diderot: les dernières années, 1770–84* (Edinburgh, 1985).
Frandsen, Steen Bo, "Denmark 1848: The Victory of Democracy and the Shattering of the Conglomerate State," in Dowe et al. (eds.) *Europe in 1848*, 288–311.
Frängsmyr, Tore, *Wolffianismens genombrott i Uppsala* (Uppsala, 1972).
Franklin, Caroline, "Romantic Patriotism as Feminist Critique of Empire," in S. Knott and B. Taylor (eds.), *Women, Gender and Enlightenment* (Basingstoke, 2005), 551–64.
Frasca-Spada, M., and P. J. E. Kail, *Impressions of Hume* (Oxford, 2005).
Freedman, Jeffrey, *Books without Borders in Enlightenment Europe* (Philadelphia, 2012).
Freund, Gerhard, "Ein Trojaner. Lessings Reimarus-Fragmente als Anfrage an die zeitgenössische Theologie," in Steiger (ed.), *500 Jahre Theologie in Hamburg*, 133–52.

Frijhoff, Willem, "Patterns," in H. De Ridder-Symoens (ed.), *A History of the University in Europe*, vol. ii (Cambridge, 1996), 43–110.

Froidcourt, Georges de, *L'Abbé Raynal au pays de Liège* (Liège, 1946).

Fromm, H., *Bibliographie deutscher Übersetzungen aus dem Französischen 1700–1948* (6 vols., Baden, 1950–3).

Fruci, Gian Luca, "Democracy in Italy," in Joanna Innes and Mark Philp (eds.), *Re-Imagining Democracy in the Mediterranean, 1780–1860* (Oxford, 2018), 25–50.

Fubini, Riccardo, *Humanism and Secularization* (Durham, NC, 2003).

Fuentes, Juan Francisco, *José Marchena. Biografía política e intelectual* (Barcelona, 1989).

Fuentes, Juan Francisco, "Geografía del liberalismo español en la década ominosa," in Alberola and Larriba (eds.), *Las élites*, 309–31.

Furet, François, *Interpreting the French Revolution* (1978; Cambridge and Paris, 1978).

Furet, François, *Revolutionary France, 1770–1880* (1988; Oxford, 1995).

Furet, François, "Rousseau and the French Revolution," in C. Orwin and N. Tarcov (eds.), *The Legacy of Rousseau* (Chicago, 1997), 168–82.

Furet, F., and M. Ozouf, "Deux légitimations historiques de la société française au XVIIIe siècle: Mably et Boulainvilliers," in *L'Histoire au Dix-Huitième Siècle* (Aix-en-Provence, 1980), 233–49.

Gaddo, Irene, and E. Tortarolo, *Secularizzazione e modernità* (Rome, 2017).

Gainot, Bernard, "The Republican Imagination and Race: The Case of the Haïtian Revolution," in Albertone and De Francesco (eds.), *Rethinking*, 276–93.

Gall, Lothar, *Wilhelm von Humboldt. Ein Preusse von Welt* (Berlin, 2011).

Galliani, R., "Mably et Voltaire," *Dix-Huitième Siècle* iii (1971), 181–94.

Gallop, G., "Ideology and the English Jacobins," *Enlightenment and Dissent* v (1986), 3–20.

Garces, Marina, *Nueva Ilustración radical* (Barcelona, 2017).

García-Alonso, Marta, "Jonathan Israel et Carl Schmitt: révolution philosophique versus contre-révolution théologique," in García-Alonso (ed.), *Lumières radicales*, 355–85.

García-Alonso, Marta (ed.), *Les Lumières radicales et le politique: études critiques sur les travaux de Jonathan Israel* (Paris, 2017).

Gardner, Catharine, "Catharine Macaulay's Letters on Education," *Hypatia* 13 (1998), 118–32.

Gargett, G., "Jacob Vernet: Theologian and *Anti-philosophe*," BJECS xvi (1993), 35–52.

Garnai, Amy, *Revolutionary Imaginings in the 1790s: Charlotte Smith, Mary Robinson, Elizabeth Inchbald* (Basingstoke, 2009).

Garnot, B., "Les Peines corporelles en Bourgogne au XVIIIe siècle," in Porret (ed.), *Beccaria*, 215–22.

Garrard, Graeme, *Rousseau's Counter-Enlightenment* (Albany, NY, 2003).

Garraway, D., *The Libertine Colony: Creollization in the Early French Caribbean* (Durham, 2005).

Garre, Arran, "Democracy and Education: Defending the Humboldtian University and the Democratic Nation-State as Institutions of the Radical Enlightenment," *Concrescence: The Australian Journal of Process Thought* 6 (2005), 3–27.

Garrett, A., "Human Nature," in CHEPh i. 160–233.

Garrett, J., "Klostersturm and Secularisation in Central Europe: What happened to the Libraries?," *Theological Librarianship* 8 (2015), 61–9.

Garrigus, J. D., "Opportunist or Patriot? Julien Raimond (1744–1801) and the Haitian Revolution," *Slavery and Abolition* 28 (2007), 1–21.

Gascoigne, J., *Cambridge in the Age of Enlightenment* (Cambridge, 1989).
Gascoigne, J., "The German Enlightenment and the Pacific," in L. Woff and M. Cipolloni (eds.), *The Anthropology of the Enlightenment* (Stanford, 2007), 141–71.
Gaskin, J. C. A., *Hume's Philosophy of Religion* (1978; Basingstoke, 1988).
Gaskin, J. C. A., "Hume on Religion," in Norton (ed.), *Cambridge Companion to Hume*, 313–44.
Gatti, Hilary, *Ideas of Liberty in Early Modern Europe* (Princeton, 2015).
Gauchet, Marcel, *La Révolution des Droits de l'homme* (Paris, 1989).
Gauchet, Marcel, *La Révolution des pouvoirs* (Paris, 1995).
Gauchet, Marcel, *The Disenchantment of the World: A Political History of Religion* (new edn., Princeton, 1999).
Gauthier, David, *Rousseau: The Sentiment of Existence* (Cambridge, 2006).
Gauthier, Florence "Albert Mathiez, historien de la Révolution française," AHRF 353 (2008), 95–112.
Gauthier, Florence, *Triomphe et mort de la Révolution des Droits de L'Homme et du Citoyen* (Paris, 2014).
Gauthier, Florence, "Political Economy in the Eighteenth Century: Popular or Despotic?," *Economic Thought* iv (2015), 47–66.
Gawlick, Günter, "Epikur bei den Deisten," in Paganini and Tortarolo (eds.), *Der Garten*, 323–39.
Gawoll, Hans-Jürgen, "Karl Heinrich Heydenreich: Spinozismus als Metaphysik und Vernunftglaube," in Schürmann, Waszek, and Weinreich (eds.) *Spinoza im Deutschland*, 407–28.
Gay, Peter, *The Enlightenment: An Interpretation: The Rise of Modern Paganism* (1966; New York, 1977).
Gay, Peter, *The Enlightenment: An Interpretation. The Science of Freedom* (1969; New York, 1977).
Gayot, G., "War die französische Freimaurerei des 18. Jahrhunderts eine Schule der Gleichheit?," in H. E. Bödecker and E. François, *Aufklärung und Politik* (Leipzig, 1996), 235–48.
Geffarth, R. D., *Religion und arkane Hierarchie. Die Orden der Gold- und Rosenkreuzer* (Leiden, 2007).
Geggus, David, *Slavery, War and Revolution: The British Occupation of Saint Domingue, 1793–1798* (Oxford, 1982).
Geggus, David, "The Cost of Pitt's Caribbean Campaigns, 1793–1798," *The Historical Journal* 26 (1983), 699–706.
Geggus, David (ed.), *The Impact of the Haitian Revolution in the Atlantic World* (Columbia, SC, 2001).
Geggus, David, *Haitian Revolutionary Studies* (Bloomington, IN, 2002).
Geggus, David, "Slave Rebellion in the Age of Revolution," in W. Klooster and Gert Oostindie (eds.), *Curaçao in the Age of Revolutions, 1795–1800* (Leiden, 2011), 23–56.
Germana, N. A., "Herder's India," in L. Wolff and M. Cipolloni (eds.), *The Anthropology of the Enlightenment* (Stanford, 2007), 119–37.
Geuna, Marco, "Republicanism and Commercial Society in the Scottish Enlightenment," in Van Gelderen and Skinner (eds.), *Republicanism* ii. 177–95.
Ghachem, Malik, "The Antislavery Script: Haiti's Place in the Narrative of Atlantic Revolution," in Baker and Edelstein (eds.), *Scripting Revolution*, 148–65.

Ghibaudi, Silvia Rota, *La fortuna di Rousseau in Italia (1750–1815)* (Turin, 1961).
Gibbons, Luke, *Edmund Burke and Ireland* (Cambridge, 2003).
Gillespie, M. A., *The Theological Origins of Modernity* (Chicago, 2009).
Girard, Philippe, *Haïti: The Tumultuous History from Pearl of the Caribbean to Broken Nation* (New York, 2005).
Girard, Philippe, *Toussaint Louverture* (New York, 2016).
Glausser, W., "Three Aproaches to Locke and the Slave Trade," JHI li (1990), 199–216.
Glebe-Møller, Jens, *Struensees vej til skafottet: Fornuft og åbenbaring i Oplysningstiden* (Copenhagen, 2007).
Glebe-Møller, Jens, "Deismus in Dänemark," in Schröder (ed.), *Gestalten*, 101–11.
Godechot, J., *The Counter-Revolution: Doctrine et Action, 1789–1804* (1961; English edn., Princeton, 1961).
Godechot, J., *France and the Atlantic Revolution of the Eighteenth Century* (London, 1971).
Godineau, Dominique, *Citoyennes tricoteuses: les femmes du peuple à Paris pendant la Révolution française* (Aix-en-Provence, 1988).
Godman, P., *Die geheime Inquisition. Aus den verbotenen Archiven des Vatikans* (Munich, 2001).
Goetschel, Willi, *Spinoza's Modernity: Mendelssohn, Lessing, Heine* (Madison, WI, 2004).
Goggi, Gianluigi, "Les *Fragments politiques* de 1772," in G. Dulac and J. Varloot (eds.), *Editer Diderot*, SVEC 254 (Oxford, 1988), 427–62.
Goggi, Gianluigi, "Diderot et le concept de civilization," *Dix-Huitième Siècle* xxix (1997), 353–73.
Goggi, Gianluigi, *De l'*Encyclopédie *à l'éloquence républicaine* (Paris, 2013).
Goggi, Gianluigi, "Spinoza contre Rousseau: un commentaire de certains passages de Diderot et de d'Holbach," in Goggi, *De l'*Encyclopédie *à l'éloquence républicaine*, 155–83.
Goggi, Gianluigi, "Spinoza et la Révolution anglaise," in Goggi, *De l'*Encyclopédie *à l'éloquence républicaine*, 391–421.
Goldberg, David, "Who was Peter Forsskål?," in Carlsson and Goldberg (eds.), *Legacy of Peter Forsskål* (Göteborg, 2017), 13–25.
Goldenbaum, Ursula, "Beziehungen der jungen Berliner Zeitungsschreiber Mylius und Lessing zu französischen Aufklärern," in U. Goldenbaum and A. Kosenina (eds.), *Berliner Aufklärung* 1 (Hanover, 1999), 69–100.
Goldenbaum, Ursula, "Der 'Berolinismus': Die preussische Hauptstadt als ein Zentrum geistiger Kommunikation in Deutschland," in Förster (ed.), *Aufklärung in Berlin*, 339–62.
Goldenbaum, Ursula, "Kants Parteinahme für Mendelssohn im Spinoza-Streit 1786," in Rolf-Peter Horstmann et al. (eds.), *Kant und die Berliner Aufklärung. Akten des IX. Kant-Kongresses* (Berlin 2001), v. 176–85.
Goldenbaum, Ursula., "Some Doubts about Jonathan Israel's New Compartmentalization of Enlightenment," in Grunert (ed.), *Concepts of (Radical) Enlightenment* (2014), 52–80.
Goldie, Mark, "John Locke and the Reputation of the First Earl of Shaftesbury," in Müller (ed.), *Shaping Enlightenment Politics*, 71–85.
Goldie, Mark, and R. Wokler (eds.), *The Cambridge History of Eighteenth-Century Political Thought* (Cambridge, 2006).
González Sánchez, Carlos Alberto, "Libros europeos en las Indias del siglo XVIII," in Kohut and Rose (eds.), *Formación*, 337–65.
Goodell, E., *The Noble Philosopher: Condorcet and the Enlightenment* (Buffalo, NY, 1994).

Goodman, Albert, *The Friends of Liberty: The English Democratic Movement in the Age of the French Revolution* (London, 1979).
Goodman, D., *The Republic of Letters* (New York, 1994).
Gouhier, Henri, *Rousseau et Voltaire* (Paris, 1983).
Gordon, Daniel, "The Great Enlightenment Massacre," in H. Mason (ed.), *The Darnton Debate: Books and Revolution in the Eighteenth Century* (Voltaire Foundation, 1999), 129–56.
Gordon, Daniel, *Postmodernism and the Enlightenment: New Perspectives in Eighteenth-Century French Intellectual History* (New York, 2001).
Gorman, Th. K., *America and Belgium: A Study of the Influence of the United States on the Belgian Revolution of 1789–90* (London, 1925).
Gouhier, Henri, *La Vie d'Auguste Comte* (Paris, 1965).
Gouhier, Henri, *Rousseau et Voltaire: portraits dans deux miroirs* (Paris, 1983).
Gourevitch, V., "The Religious Thought," in Riley (ed.), *Cambridge Companion to Rousseau*, 193–246.
Grab, Alexander, *Napoleon and the Transformation of Europe* (Basingstoke, 2003).
Grab, Walter, *Norddeutsche Jakobiner. Demokratische Bestrebungen zur Zeit der französischen Revolution* (Frankfurt, 1967).
Graczyk, A., "Le Théâtre de la Révolution," *Dix-Huitième Siècle* xxi (1989), 395–410.
Grant, James, *John Adams. Party of One* (New York, 2005).
Grashoff, Udo, *Johann Friedrich Struensee. Arzt, Staatsmann, Geliebter der Königin* (Halle, 2008).
Green, Georgina, "John Thelwall's Radical Vision of Democracy," in Poole (ed.), *John Thelwall*, 71–81.
Green, Jonathan, "Immanuel Kant, Friedrich Gentz, and the Possibility of a Prudential Enlightenment," MIH 14 (2017), 35–65.
Green, Karen, "Catharine Macaulay's French Connections," *Eighteenth-Century Life* 41 (2017), 59–72.
Greentree, Shane, "'Writing against Sophie': May Hays's Female Biography as Enlightenment Feminist Critique of Jean-Jacques Rousseau's *Émile*," *Eighteenth-Century Life*, 41 (2017), 73–88.
Gregory, Brad S., *The Unintended Reformation* (Cambridge, MA, 2012).
Gregory, Tullio, "*Libertinisme érudit* in Seventeenth-Century France and Italy," BJHPh 6 (1998), 323–49.
Greminger, Ueli, *Sebastian Castellio. Eine Biografie aus den Wirren der Reformationszeit* (Zurich, 2015).
Grenby, M. O., *The Anti-Jacobin Novel: British Conservatism and the French Revolution* (Cambridge, 2001).
Groetsch, Ulrich, *Hermann Samuel Reimarus (1694–1768): Classicist, Hebraist, Enlightenment Radical in Disguise* (Leiden, 2015).
Grossmann, W., *Johann Christian Edelmann. From Orthodoxy to Enlightenment* (The Hague, 1976).
Gründer, Karlfried, and W. Schmidt-Biggemann (eds.), *Spinoza in der Frühzeit seiner religiösen Wirkung* (Heidelberg, 1984).
Grunert, Frank, *Concepts of (Radical) Enlightenment*, in IZEA *Kleine Schriften* no. 5 (Halle, 2014).
Guehenno, Jean, *Jean-Jacques Rousseau* (2 vols., London and New York, 1966).

Guerci, Luciano, "Les Catéchismes républicains en Italie (1796–1799)," *La Revolution française. Cahiers de l'Institut d'Histoire de la Révolution française* 1 (2009).

Guilhaumou, Jacques, *L'Avènement des porte-parole de la république (1789–1792)* (Paris, 1998).

Guilherme, Alexandre, *Fichte and Schelling: The Spinoza Connection* (Saarbrücken, 2009).

Guillaumont, Patrick, *La Pensée démo-économique de Jean-Baptiste Say et de Sismondi* (Paris, 1969).

Gusdorf, Georges, *La Conscience révolutionnaire. Les Idéologues* (Paris, 1978).

Guy, Marcel, "L'Enseignement de l'histoire dans les écoles centrales," AHRF 53 (1981), 89–122.

Guyer, Paul, *Kant's System of Nature and Freedom: Selected Essays* (Oxford, 2005).

Haakonssen, Knud, "The Structure of Hume's Political Theory," in Norton (ed.), *Cambridge Companion to Hume*, 182–221.

Haakonssen, Knud, "Natural Jurisprudence and the Theory of Justice," in Broadie (ed.), *Scottish Enlightenment*, 205–21.

Haakonssen, K. (ed.), *The Cambridge History of Eighteenth-Century Philosophy* (2 vols., Cambridge, 2006).

Haaser, Rolf, "Sonderfall oder Pradigma? Karl Friedrich Bahrdt und das Verhältnis von Spätaufklärung und Gegenaufklärung in der hessen-darmstädtischen Universitätsstadt Giessen," in Donnert, *Europa* ii. 247–85.

Habakkuk, J., *Marriage, Debt, and the Estates System: English Landownership, 1650–1950* (Oxford, 1994).

Haechler, Jean, *L'Encyclopédie: les combats et les hommes* (Paris, 1998).

Hallberg, P., "Translation on Trial: The 'Virginia Declaration of Rights' (1776) in Sweden," HEI 42 (2016), 1–21.

Hallberg, P., "Johann Gottfried Herder on European Ethnographic Representation," IHR 26 (2016), 497–517.

Hamburger, Joseph, *John Stuart Mill on Liberty and Control* (Princeton, 1999).

Hammersley, Rachel, "Jean-Paul Marat's *The Chains of Slavery* in Britain and France, 1774–1833," *The Historical Journal* xlviii (2005), 641–60.

Hammersley, Rachel, *The English Republican Tradition and Eighteenth-Century France* (Manchester, 2010).

Hammersley, Rachel, "Rethinking the Political Thought of James Harrington," HEI 39 (2013), 354–70.

Hampshire-Monk, I., "British Radicalism and the Anti-Jacobins," in Goldie and Wokler (eds.), *Cambridge History of Eighteenth-Century Political Thought*, 660–87.

Hampshire-Monk, I., "On Not Inventing the English Revolution," in Burgess and Festenstein (eds.), *English Radicalism*, 135–56.

Hampshire-Monk, I., "Edmund Burke's Changing Justification for Intervention," repr. in I. Hampshire-Monk (ed.), *Edmund Burke* (Farnham, 2009), 343–78.

Hampshire-Monk, I., "Edmund Burke and Empire," in D. Kelly, *Lineages of Empire* (Oxford, 2009), 117–36.

Hampson, Norman, *Saint-Just* (Oxford, 1991).

Hankins, James, "Introduction" to Brandolini, *Republics and Kingdoms*, pp. ix–xxvi.

Hanou, A. J., "Verlichte vrijheid," in E. O. G. Haitsma Mulier and W. R. E. Velema (eds.), *Vrijheid. Een geschiedenis van de vijftiende tot de twintigste eeuw* (Amsterdam, 1999), 187–211.

Hargraves, N., "Beyond the Savage Character," in L. Wolff and M. Cipolloni (eds.), *The Anthropology of the Enlightenment* (Stanford, 2007), 103–18.

Harris, E. E., "Spinoza's Treatment of Natural Law," in C. De Deugd (ed.). *Spinoza's Political and Theological Thought* (Amsterdam, 1984), 63–72.

Harris, James A., *Hume: An Intellectual Biography* (Cambridge, 2015).

Harris, James A., "The Epicurean in Hume," in Leddy and Lifschitz (eds.), *Epicurus*, 161–81.

Haskell, Y., "Religion and Enlightenment in the Neo-Latin Reception of Lucretius," in Gillespie and Hardie (eds.), *Cambridge Companion to Lucretius*, 185–201.

Harrison, Peter, "Adam Smith and the History of the Invisible Hand," JHI 72 (2011), 29–44.

Hassner, Pierre, "Rousseau and the Theory and Practice of International Relations," in C. Orwin and N. Tarcov (eds.), *The Legacy of Rousseau* (Chicago, 1997), 200–19.

Hauben, P. J., "White Legend against Black: Nationalism and Enlightenment in a Spanish Context," *The Americas* xxxiv (1977), 1–19.

Haug, Christine, "Die Bedeutung der radikal-demokratischen Korrespondenzgesellschaft 'Deutsche Union' für die Entstehung von Lesegesellschaften in Oberhessen im ausgehenden 18. Jahrhundert," in Donnert (ed.), *Europa*, 299–322.

Head, Brian W., *Politics and Philosophy in the Thought of Destutt de Tracy* (New York, 1987).

Heath, E., and V. Merolle (eds.), *Adam Ferguson: History, Progress and Human Nature* (London, 2008).

Heirwegh, Jean-Jacques, "La Fin de l'Ancien Régime et les révolutions," in H. Hasquin (ed.), *La Belgique autrichienne 1713–1794* (Brussels, 1987).

Helmers, Helmer, *The Royalist Republic: Literature, Politics and Religion in the Anglo-Dutch Public Sphere, 1639–1660* (Cambridge, 2015).

Hemming, T. D., E. Freeman, and D. Meaking (eds.), *The Secular City: Studies in the Enlightenment* (Exeter, 1994).

Henrich, Dieter, *Between Kant and Hegel: Lectures on German Idealism* (Cambridge, MA, 2003).

Henry, Julie, "L'Égalitarianisme et la rationalité sont-ils des visées radicales et spinozistes?," in García-Alonso, *Lumières radicales*, 27–50.

Herman, Ingo, *Knigge. Die Biografie* (Berlin, 2007).

Herr, Richard, *The Eighteenth-Century Revolution in Spain* (Princeton, 1958).

Herrero, Javier, *Los orígines del pensamiento reaccionario español* (Madrid, 1971).

Herrero Sánchez, Manuel, "Introducción" to M. Herrero Sánchez (ed.), *Repúblicas y republicanismo en la Europa moderna (siglos XVI–XVIII)* (Madrid, 2017), 17–89.

Herzog, Tamar, *A Short History of European Law* (Cambridge, MA, 2018).

Hess, Jonathan, *Germans, Jews and the Claims of Modernity* (New Haven, 2002).

Hesse, Carla, *The Other Enlightenment: How French Women became Modern* (Princeton, 2001).

Heyd, Michael, "The Limits of Toleration in the Early 18th Century: Shaftesbury's *Letter Concerning Enthusiasm* and the Reactions to it," in C. Berkvens-Stevelinck et al. (eds.), *The Emergence of Tolerance in the Dutch Republic* (Leiden, 1997).

Hiebert, E. N., "The Integration of Revealed Religion and Scientific Materialism in the Thought of Joseph Priestley," in L. Kieft and B. R. Willeford (eds.), *Joseph Priestley. Scientist, Theologian and Metaphysician* (Lewisburg, 1980), 27–61.

Higby, Chester P., *The Religious Policy of the Bavarian Government during the Napoleonic Period* (1918; repr. New York, 1967).

Hill, Mike, and W. Montag, *The Other Adam Smith* (Stanford, 2015).
Himmelfarb, G., "Two Enlightenments: A Contrast in Social Ethics," *Proceedings of the British Academy* cxvii (2001), 297–324.
Himmelfarb, G., *Roads to Modernity* (New York, 2004).
Hirschfeldt, Johan, "Freedom of Speech, Expression and Information in Sweden: A Legacy from 1766," in Carlsson and Goldberg (eds.), *Legacy of Peter Forsskål*, 53–70.
Hobohm, Hans-Christoph, "Le Progrès de l'*Encyclopédie*: la censure face au discours encyclopédique," in Mass and Knabe (eds.), *L'Encyclopédie*, 69–96.
Hoeckermann, A. "Thomas Thorild, der skandinavische Lessing," *Greifswalder Tageblatt. Sonntags-Blatt* viii (1883), 26–7.
Höffe, Otfried, *Kant's Cosmopolitan Theory of Law and Peace* (2001; English trans. Cambridge, 2003).
Höjer, T. T., *Bernadotte, Maréchale de France* (Paris, 1943).
Holborn, Hajo, *A History of Modern Germany, 1648–1840* (Princeton, 1964).
Holenstein, A. Th. Maissen, and M. Praak (eds.), *The Republican Alternative: The Netherlands and Switzerland Compared* (Amsterdam, 2008).
Hollewand, Karen, *The Banishment of Beverland: Sex, Sin, and Scholarship in the Seventeenth-Century Dutch Republic* (Leiden, 2019).
Holm, Edvard, *Nogle Hovedtræk af Trykkefrihedstidens Historie 1770–1773* (Copenhagen, 1885).
Holmes, Richard, *Shelley: The Pursuit* (London, 1974).
Holmes, Richard, *Coleridge: Early Visions* (London, 1989).
Holmes, Stephen, *Benjamin Constant and the Making of Modern Liberalism* (New Haven, 1984).
Hont, Istvan, *Jealousy of Trade* (Cambridge, MA, 2005).
Höög, Victoria (ed.), *What is Left of the Enlightenment? Insikt och Handling* 26 (Lund, 2018).
Hope Mason, John, *The Irresistible Diderot* (London, 1982).
Hope Mason, John, "Materialism and History: Diderot and the *Histoire des deux Indes*," *European Review of History* iii (1996), 151–60.
Hope Mason, John, "Portrait de l'auteur accompagné d'un fantôme: *l'Essai sur les règnes de Claude et de Néron*," in France and Strugnell (eds.), *Diderot*, 43–61.
Horkheimer, Max, and Adorno, Theodor W., *Dialectic of Enlightenment* (new edn., New York, 2000).
Hösle, Vittorio, *Morals and Politics* (Notre Dame, IN, 2004).
Hösle, Vittorio, *A Short History of German Philosophy* (Princeton, 2017).
Hsia, Adrian, "Euro-Sinica: The Past and Future," TJEAS 1 (2004), 17–58.
Hubatsch, Walther, *Frederick the Great: Absolutism and Administration* (London, 1973).
Hudson, Wayne, *The English Deists: Studies in Early Enlightenment* (London, 2009).
Hudson, Wayne, *Enlightenment and Modernity* (London, 2009).
Hudson, Wayne, "Atheism and Deism Demythologized," in Hudson, Lucci, and Wigelsworth (eds.), *Atheism and Deism Revalued*, 13–23.
Hudson, Wayne, D. Lucci, and J. R. Wigelsworth (eds.), *Atheism and Deism Revalued: Heterodox Religious Identities in Britain, 1650–1800* (Farnham, 2014).
Hudson, Wayne, D. Moggach, and M. Stamm, *Rethinking German Idealism* (Aurora, CO, 2016).
Hufton, O., *Women and the Limits of Citizenship in the French Revolution* (Toronto, 1992).

Hufton, O., *Europe: Privilege and Protest (1730–1789)* (1980; repr. Oxford, 2000).
Hull, Gordon, "Marx's Anomalous Reading of Spinoza," *Interpretation* 28 (2000), 18–31.
Hull, I. V., *Sexuality, State and Civil Society in Germany, 1700–1815* (Ithaca, 1996).
Hulliung, M., *The Autocritique of Enlightenment: Rousseau and the* Philosophes (Cambridge, MA, 1994).
Hüning, Dieter, "Die Grenzen der Toleranz und die Rechtsstellung der Atheisten," in L. Danneberg et al. (eds.), *Säkularisierung in den Wissenschaften seit der Frühen Neuzeit* ii (Berlin, 2002), 219–73.
Hunt, Lynn, *Politics, Culture and Class in the French Revolution* (Berkeley and Los Angeles, 1984).
Hunt, Lynn, *Inventing Human Rights: A History* (New York, 2007).
Hunt, Lynn, "Revolutionary Causes: Was Louis XVI Overthrown by Ideas?," *The New Republic*, 31 July 2014.
Hunter, Graeme, *Radical Protestantism in Spinoza's Thought* (Aldershot, 2005).
Hunter, Ian, "Kant's Religion and Prussian Religious Policy," MIH 2 (2005), 1–27.
Hunter, Ian, "Secularization: The Birth of a Modern Combat Concept,"' MIH 12 (2015), 1–32.
Hunter, Ian, "Secularisation: Process, Program, and Historiography," IHR 27 (2017), 7–29.
Hutchings, K., *Kant, Critique and Politics* (London, 1996).
Igoin, Albert, "De l'ellipse de la théorie politique de Spinoza chez le jeune Marx," *Cahiers Spinoza* 1 (1977), 213–28.
Ihde, A. J., "Priestley and Lavoisier," in E. N. Hiebert, A. J. Ihde, and R. E. Schofield (eds.), *Joseph Priestley: Scientist, Theologian and Metaphysician* (Lewisburg, NJ, 1980), 62–91.
Illing, Peter, "Montesquieu's Shadow: Debating Reform in the Austrian Netherlands," HEI 35 (2009), 330–6.
Imbert, Pierre-Henri, *Destutt de Tracy, critique de Montesquieu ou De la Liberté en matière de politique* (Paris, 1974).
Imbruglia Girolamo (ed.), *Naples in the Eighteenth Century* (Cambridge, 2000).
Imbruglia, Girolamo, "Due opposte letture napoletane dell *Esprit des lois*," in D. Felice (ed.), *Montesquieu e i suoi interpreti* (2 vols., Pisa, 2005), i. 191–210.
Imbruglia, Girolamo, "Indignation et droits de l'homme chez le dernier Diderot," in G. Goggi and D. Kahn (eds.), *L'Édition du dernier Diderot* (Paris, 2007), 125–76.
Imbruglia, Girolamo, "Enlightenment in Eighteenth-Century Naples," in Imbruglia (ed.), *Naples*, 70–94.
Imbruglia, Girolamo, "Utopia e repubblicanesimo: un'oppsizione illuministica," in Albertone (ed.), *Repubblicanesimo moderno*, 347–68.
Imbruglia, Girolamo, "Civilisation and Colonisation: Enlightenment Theories in the Debate between Diderot and Raynal," HEI 41 (2015), 858–82.
Imbruglia, Girolamo, "Illuminismo e rivoluzione: il problema della violenza," *Passato e Presente. Rivista di storia contemporanea* 100 (2017), 56–72.
Ingrams, Richard, *The Life and Adventures of William Cobbett* (London, 2005).
Iofrida, Manlio, "Matérialisme et hétérogénéité dans la philosophie de Toland," *Dix-Huitième Siècle* 24 (1992), 39–52.
Irmscher, Hans Dietrich, "Goethe und Herder—eine schwierige Freundschaft," in M. Kessler and V. Leppin (eds.), *Johann Gottfried Herder. Aspekte seines Lebenswerkes* (Berlin, 2005), 233–70.
Isabella, Maurizio, *Risorgimento in Exile: Italian Émigrés and the Liberal International in the Post-Napoleonic Era* (Oxford, 2009).

Isabella, Maurizio, "Citizens or Faithful? Religion and the Liberal Revolutions of the 1820s in Southern Europe," MIH 12 (2015), 555–78.

Israel, Jonathan I., *Dutch Primacy in World Trade, 1585–1740* (Oxford, 1989).

Israel, Jonathan I., *The Dutch Republic: Its Rise, Greatness and Fall, 1477–1806* (Oxford, 1995).

Israel, Jonathan I., *Conflicts of Empires* (London, 1997).

Israel, Jonathan I., *Radical Enlightenment: Philosophy and the Making of Modernity* (Oxford, 2001).

Israel, Jonathan I., "Religious Toleration and Radical Philosophy in the Later Dutch Golden Age (1668–1710)", in R. Hsia and H. Van Nierop (eds.), *Calvinism and Religious Toleration in the Dutch Golden Age* (Cambridge, 2002), 148–58.

Israel, Jonathan I., "The Early Dutch Enlightenment as a Factor in the wider European Enlightenment," in Wiep van Bunge (ed.), *The Early Enlightenment in the Dutch Republic* (Leiden, 2003), 215–30.

Israel, Jonathan I., "Meyer, Koerbagh and the Radical Enlightenment Critique of Socinianism," GWN 14 (2003), 197–208.

Israel, Jonathan I., "The Intellectual Origins of Modern Democratic Republicanism (1660–1720)," EJPTh iii (2004), 7–36.

Israel, Jonathan I., "Dr Bontekoe's Views on Spinoza and the Spread of Spinozism published in the Year 1680," in *Studia Spinozana* xvi (2008), 221–41.

Israel, Jonathan I., "French Royal Censorship and the Battle to Suppress the *Encyclopédie* of Diderot and d'Alembert, 1751–1759," in M. Laerke (ed.), *Use of Censorship* (Leiden, 2009), 61–74.

Israel, Jonathan I., "Equality and Inequality in the Late Enlightenment," *De Achttiende-Eeuw* xli (2009), 5–22.

Israel, Jonathan I., *A Revolution of the Mind: Radical Enlightenment and the Intellectual Origins of Modern Democracy* (Princeton, 2010).

Israel, Jonathan I., "The Philosophical Context of Hermann Samuel Reimarus' Radical Bible Criticism," in Martin Mulsow (ed.), *Between Philology and Radical Enlightenment: Hermann Samuel Reimarus (1694–1768)* (Leiden, 2011), 183–200.

Israel, Jonathan I., "L'Histoire intellectuelle des Lumières et de la Révolution: une incursion critique," *La Lettre Clandestine* 19 (2011), 173–225.

Israel, Jonathan, *Democratic Enlightenment: Philosophy, Revolution and Human Rights, 1750–1790* (Oxford, 2011).

Israel, Jonathan I., "Democracy and Equality in the Radical Enlightenment: Revolutionary Ideology before 1789," in Albertone and De Francesco (eds.), *Rethinking*, 46–60.

Israel, Jonathan I., "Spinoza and the Religious Radical Enlightenment," in Mortimer and Robertson (eds.), *Intellectual Consequences of Religious Heterodoxy*, 181–204.

Israel, Jonathan I., "Natural Virtue versus Book Learning: Rousseau and the Great Enlightenment Battle over Education," *European Journal of Developmental Psychology*, 2012 supplement, 6–17.

Israel, Jonathan I., "Diderot, D'Holbach et la question de la Chine," in A. Mothu (ed.), *La Lettre clandestine*, vol. xx: *L'Érudition et la littérature philosophique clandestine* (Paris, 2012), 185–99.

Israel, Jonathan I., *Revolutionary Ideas: An Intellectual History of the French Revolution from The Rights of Man to Robespierre* (Princeton, 2014).

Israel, Jonathan I., "Northern Varieties: Contrasting the Dano-Norwegian and Swedish-Finnish Enlightenments," in Ellen Krefting et al. (eds.), *Eighteenth-Century Periodicals as Agents of Change: Perspectives in Northern Enlightenment* (Leiden, 2015), 17–45.

Israel, Jonathan I., "Andrzej Wiszowaty (Wissowatius), Bayle, Leibniz, and the Critique of Polish Socinianism in Meyer's *Philosophia*," in M. Dowlaszewicz, J. Skubisz, and J. Urbaniak (eds.), *De Deught behoeft geen Loftrompet* (Feestbundel Stefan Kiedroń) (Wrocław, 2015), 83–9.

Israel, Jonathan I., "Leo Strauss and the Radical Enlightenment," in W. Schröder (ed.), *Reading Between the Lines: Leo Strauss and Early Modern Philosophy* (Berlin, 2015), 9–28.

Israel, Jonathan I., "Rousseau, Diderot, and the Radical Enlightenment": A Reply to Helena Rosenblatt and Joanna Stalnaker," JHI 77 (2016), 649–77.

Israel, Jonathan I., "Les 'Lumières radicales' comme théorie générale de la modernité démocratique séculière, et ses critiques," in García-Alonso (ed.), *Lumières radicales*, 387–436.

Israel, Jonathan I., "'Radical Enlightenment': A Game-Changing Concept," in Ducheyne (ed.), *Reassessing the Radical Enlightenment* (2017), 15–47.

Israel, Jonathan I., *The Expanding Blaze: How the American Revolution Ignited the World, 1775–1848* (Princeton, 2017).

Israel, Jonathan I., "Rousseau and d'Holbach: The Revolutionary Implications of *la philosophie anti- Thérésienne*," in Rosenblatt and Schweigert (eds.), *Thinking with Rousseau*, 149–74.

Israel, Jonathan I., "Toward the Nordic Model: Scandinavian Enlightenment Viewed as a Gradual Edging toward Universal and Equal Rights," in Thomas Bredsdorff and Søren Peter Hansen (eds.), *Det lange lys. 2000-tals spørgsmål, 1700-tals svar* (Copenhagen, 2017), 15–49.

Israel, Jonathan I., "Spinoza's Formulation of the Radical Enlightenment's Two Defining Doctrines: How Much did he owe to the Dutch Golden Age Political-Theological Context," in Charles Ramond and Jack Stetter (eds.), *Spinoza in 21st Century American and French Philosophy: Metaphysics, Philosophy of the Mind, Moral and Political Philosophy* (London, 2018), 335–48.

Israel, Jonathan I., "Jewish Emancipation in the Western World (1780–1860): What Kind of Enlightenment Made it Possible?," *Proceedings of the Israel Academy of Sciences and Humanities* IX (Jerusalem, 2018), no. 6, pp. 109–29.

Israel, Jonathan I., "Shaftesbury, an Early Voice of the Radical Enlightenment," in Müller (ed.), *Shaping Enlightenment Politics*, 89–97.

Israel, Jonathan I., "Poststructuralist and Postcolonialist Criticism of the 'Moderate Enlightenment' is Partly Justified," in Höög (ed.) *What is Left of the Enlightenment*, 17–43.

Jacob, M. C., *The Radical Enlightenment: Pantheists, Freemasons and Republicans* (revised edn., London, 2003).

Jacob, M. C., *Strangers Nowhere in the World: The Rise of Cosmopolitanism in Early Modern Europe* (Philadelphia, 2006).

Jacob, M.C., "The Radical Enlightenment: A Heavenly City with Many Mansions," in Ducheyne (ed.), *Reassessing*, 48–60.

Jacob, M.C., *The Secular Enlightenment* (Princeton, 2019).

Jacob, M.C., and Wijnand Mijnhardt (eds.), *The Dutch Republic in the Eighteenth Century* (Ithaca, 1992).

Jacoby, Susan, *Freethinkers: A History of American Secularism* (New York, 2004).

Jaeschke, Walter, "De Messias der spekulativen Vernunft," in K. M. Kodalle and M. Ohst (eds.), *Fichtes Entlassung. Der Atheismusstreit vor 200 Jahren* (*Kritisches Jahrbuch der Philosophie* 4 (1999) 143–57.

Jaffro, Laurent, "Toland and the Moral Teaching of the Gospel," in R. Savage (ed.), *Philosophy and Religion in Enlightenment Britain* (Oxford, 2012), 77–89.

Jaffro, Laurent, "L'Ecclésiologie de John Toland," in Toland, *Primitive Constitution*, 16–138.

Jaffro, Laurent, "Qu'est-ce qu'être déiste?," *La Lettre Clandestine* 21 (2013), 273–89.

Jaffro, Laurent, "La Normativité morale de l'Écriture chez Spinoza, Locke et Toland," in L. Simonutti (ed.), *Religious Obedience and Political Resistance in the Early Modern World* (Turnhout, 2015), 413–33.

James, Michael, "Bentham's Democratic Theory at the Time of the French Revolution," *The Bentham Newsletter* 10 (June 1986), 5–16.

James, Susan, "Spinoza the Stoic," in T. Sorell (ed.), *The Rise of Modern Philosophy* (Oxford, 1993), 289–316.

Jarrett, Mark, *The Congress of Vienna and its Legacy* (London, 2014).

Jarrick, Arne, *Back to Modern Reason* (1992; Liverpool, 1999).

Jarvis, Katie, *Politics in the Marketplace: Work, Gender, and Citizenship in Revolutionary France* (New York, 2019).

Jaume, Lucien, *Tocqueville: The Aristocratic Sources of Liberty* (Princeton, 2008).

Jaume, Lucien, "Robespierre chez Machiavel? Le Culte de l'Être suprême et le 'retour aux principes'," *Sguardo. Rivista de Filosofia* 13 (2013), 219–30.

Jaume, Lucien, *Le Religieux et le politique dans la Révolution française: l'idée de régénération* (Paris, 2015).

Jaynes J., and W. Woodward, "In the Shadow of the Enlightenment: Reimarus and his Theory of Drives," *Journal of the History of the Behavioural Sciences* x (1974), 144–59.

Jeandeau, René, *Sismondi précurseur de la législation sociale contemporaine* (Bordeaux, 1913).

Jen-Guo S. Chen, "Providence and Progress: The Religious Dimension in Adam Ferguson's Discussion of Civil Society," in Heath and Merolle (eds.), *Adam Ferguson*, 171–86.

Jennings, Jeremy, *Revolution and the Republic: A History of Political Thought in France since the Eighteenth Century* (Oxford, 2011).

Jennings, L. C., *French Anti-Slavery: The Movement for the Abolition of Slavery in France 1802–1848* (Cambridge, 2000).

Jespersen, K. J. V., "The Rise and Fall of the Danish Nobility, 1600–1800," in H. M. Scott (ed.), *The European Nobilities in the Seventeenth and Eighteenth Centuries* ii (1995; 2nd edn. London, 2007), 43–71.

Jimack, P., "Obéissance à la loi et révolution dans les dernières œuvres de Diderot," in France and Strugnell (eds.), *Diderot*, 153–68.

Jimack, P., "The French Enlightenment 1: Science, Materialism and Determinism," in S. Brown (ed.), *British Philosophy and the Age of Enlightenment* (London, 1996), 228–50.

Joary, Jean-Paul, *Diderot et la matière vivante* (Paris, 1992).

Johnson, H. C., *The Midi in Revolution: A Study of Regional Political Diversity, 1789–1793* (Princeton, 1986).

Johnston, K. R., "Usual and Unusual Suspects: John Thelwall, William Godwin and Pitt's Reign of Terror," in Poole (ed.), *John Thelwall*, 25–37.

Jolly, Claude, "Introduction" to Destutt de Tracy, *Commentaire*, 7–49.

Jolley, Nicholas, *Locke: His Philosophical Thought* (Oxford, 1999).

Jones, Peter M., *Agricultural Enlightenment: Knowledge, Technology and Nature, 1750–1840* (Oxford, 2016).

Joor, Johan, *De Adelaar en het Lam. Onrust, opruiing en onwilligheid in Nederland (1806–1813)* (Amsterdam, 2000).

Jordaan, Han, *Slavernij en vrijheid op Curaçao* (Zutphen, 2013).

Jordan, David R., *Napoleon and the Revolution* (Basingstoke, 2012).

Josephson-Storm, Jason, *The Myth of Disenchantment: Magic, Modernity, and the Birth of the Human Sciences* (Chicago, 2017).

Jourdan, A., "Le Culte de Rousseau sous la Révolution," in L'Aminot (ed.), *Politique et révolution*, 57–77.

Judge, Jane, "Provincial Manifestos: Belgians Declare Independence, 1789–1790," *De Achttiende Eeuw* 47 (2015), 127–45.

Jurdjevic, M., "Virtue, Commerce and the Enduring Florentine Republican Moment," JHI 62 (2001), 721–43.

Jürgens, Hanco, "Welke Verlichting? Tijdaanduidingen en plaatsbepalingen van een begrip," *De Achttiende Eeuw* xxxv (2003), 28–53.

Jürgens, Hanco, "Contesting *Enlightenment Contested:* Some Questions," *De Achttiende Eeuw* xxxix (2007), 52–71.

Kafker, F. A., and S. L. Kafker, *The Encyclopedists as Individuals* (Oxford, 2006).

Kaiser, Thomas, "Politics and Political Economy in the Thought of the Idéologues," *History of Political Economy* 12 (1980), 141–60.

Kaitaro, Timo, *Diderot's Holism* (Frankfurt, 1997).

Karpossy, Bela, "Neo-Roman Republicanism and Commercial Society: The Example of Eighteenth-Century Berne," in Van Gelderen and Skinner (eds.), *Republicanism* ii. 227–47.

Kates, Gary, The *Cercle Social*, the Girondins and the French Revolution (Princeton, 1985)

Kates, Gary, "From Liberalism to Radicalism: Tom Paine's Rights of Man," JHI 50 (1989), 569–87.

Kaye, H. J., *Thomas Paine and the Promise of America* (New York, 2005).

Keane, John, *Tom Paine: A Political Life* (1995; new edn., London, 1996).

Kempski, Jürgen von, "Hermann Samuel Reimarus als Ethnologe," in Hermann Samuel Reimarus, *Allgemeine Betrachtungen über die Triebe der Thiere* (Göttingen, 1982), i, 21–56.

Kempski, Jürgen von, "Spinoza, Reimarus, Bruno Bauer—drei Paradigmen radikaler Bibelkritik," in *Hermann Samuel Reimarus (1694–1768): ein "bekannter Unbekannter,"* 96–112.

Kenkel, Karen, "The Personal and the Philosophical in Fichte's Theory of Sexual Difference," in Wilson and Holub (eds.), *Impure Reason*, 278–97.

Kennedy, Emmet, "Ideology from Destutt de Tracy to Marx," JHI 40 (1979), 353–68.

Kennedy, Emmet, *A Cultural History of the French Revolution* (New Haven, 1989).

Kennedy, Emmet, *Secularism and its Opponents from Augustine to Solzhenitsyn* (New York, 2006).

Kerry, Paul, *Enlightenment Thought in the Writings of Goethe* (Rochester, NY, 2001).

Kersting, W., "Politics, Freedom and Order: Kant's Political Philosophy," in P. Guyer (ed.), *The Cambridge Companion to Kant* (Cambridge, 1992), 342–66.

Kidd, Colin, "Constitutions and Character in the Eighteenth-Century British World," in P. M. Kitromilides (ed.), *From Republican Polity to National Community* (Oxford, 2003), 40–61.

Kim, Minchul, "Volney and the French Revolution," JHI 79 (2018), 221–42.

Kirby, D. G. *Northern Europe in the Early Modern Period: The Baltic World, 1492–1772* (London, 1990).

Kitromilides, P. M., "The Enlightenment and the Greek Cultural Tradition," HEI xxxvi (2002), 39–46.

Kitromilides, P. M., *Enlightenment and Revolution: The Making of Modern Greece* (Cambridge, MA, 2013).

Klein, S. R. E., *Patriots republikanisme. Politieke cultuur in Nederland (1766–1787)* (Amsterdam, 1995).

Kloek, Joost, and Mijnhardt Wijnand, *1800: Blueprints for a National Community* (Assen, 2004).

Kloppenberg, James, *Toward Democracy: The Struggle for Self Rule in European and American Thought* (New York, 2016).

Knaap, G. J., "Slavery and the Dutch in Southeast Asia," in Oostindie (ed.), *Fifty Years Later*, 193–206.

Knibiehler, Yvonne, "Les Médecins des Lumières et la 'nature feminine'," in E. Morin-Rotureau (ed.), *1789–1799: combat de femmes. La Révolution exclut les citoyennes* (Paris, 2003), 127–42.

Knippenberg, J. M., "The Politics of Kant's Philosophy," in R. Beiner and W. J. Booth (eds.), *Kant and Political Philosophy* (New Haven, 1993), 155–72.

Knoll, R., *Johann Georg Hamann, 1730–1788. Quellen und Forschungen* (Bonn, 1988).

Kobuch, A., *Zensur und Aufklärung in Kursachsen* (Weimar, 1988).

Koekkoek, René, "'Eene ware en vrije Republiek,' Jan Konijnenburg, *De Republikein* en de uitvinding van de moderne republiek," *De Achttiende Eeuw* 42 (2010), 236–59.

Koerner, L., *Linnaeus: Nature and Nation* (Cambridge, MA, 1999).

Kohut, Karl, and S. V. Rose (eds.), *La formación de la cultura virreinal iii. El Siglo XVIII* (Madrid, 2006).

Kolakowski, Leszek, *Chrétiens sans Église: la conscience religieuse et le lien confessionnel au XVIIe siècle* (1965; new edn., Paris, 1987).

Kölving, U., and Ch. Mervaud (eds.), *Voltaire et ses combats* (2 vols., Oxford, 1997).

König, Hans-Joachim, "La rebelión de los Comuneros de Nueva Granada en 1780/1 y la formación de un orgullo proprio neogranadino," in Kohut and Rose (eds.), *Formación*, 255–72.

Kopitzsch, F., "Altona-ein Zentrum der Aufklärung am Rande des dänischen Gesamtstaats," in K. Bohnen and S. A. Jorgensen (eds.), *Der dänische Gesamtstaat* (Tübingen, 1992), 91–118.

Körner, Axel, *America in Italy: The United States in the Political Thought and Imagination of the Risorgimento, 1763–1865* (Princeton, 2017).

Kors, Alan, *Atheism in France, 1650–1729* (Princeton, 1990).

Kors, Alan, "Skepticism and the Problem of Atheism in Early-Modern France," in G. Paganini et al. (eds.), *Scepticisme, Clandestinité et Libre Pensée* (Paris, 2002), 47–65.

Kors, Alan, *Epicureans and Atheists in France, 1650–1729* (Cambridge, 2016).

Kors, Alan, *Naturalism and Unbelief in France, 1650–1729* (Cambridge, 2016).

Kors, Alan (ed.), *Encyclopedia of the Enlightenment* (4 vols., Oxford, 2003).

Kossmann, Ernst, *Political Thought in the Dutch Republic* (Amsterdam, 2000).

Kouvelakis, Stathis, *Philosophy and Revolution from Kant to Marx* (2003; London and New York, 2018).

Krause, Sharon, "History and the Human Soul in Montesquieu", HPTh xxiv (2003), 235–61.

Krause, Sharon, "Despotism in the *Spirit of the Laws*," in Carrithers, Mosher, and Rahe (eds.), *Montesquieu's Science*, 231–71.

Krause, Sharon, "Freedom, Sovereignty, and the General Will in Montesquieu," in Farr and Williams (eds.) *General Will*, 147–72.

Krebs, Roland, "Le 'Deutsches Museum' et l'Indépendance Américaine," in R. Krebs and J. Moes (eds.), *La Révolution américaine vue par les périodiques de langue allemande (1773–1783)* (Paris, 1992), 1–21.

Krebs, Roland, *Helvétius en Allemagne ou la tentation du matérialisme* (Paris, 2006).

Krop, Henri, "A Dutch *Spinozismusstreit*: The New View of Spinoza at the End of the Eighteenth Century," LIAS xxxii (2005), 185–211.

Krop, Henri, "The Secularism of Spinoza and his Circle," in Tomaszewska and Hämäläinen (eds.), *Sources of Secularism*, 73–99.

Krop, Henri, *Spinoza. Een paradoxale icoon van Nederland* (Amsterdam, 2014).

Kuchlbauer, Simon, *Johannes Amos Comenius' anti-sozinianistische Schriften. Entwurf eines intergriven Konzepts von Aufklärung* (Dresden, 2001).

Kuehn, Manfred, *Kant: A Biography* (Cambridge, 2001).

Kühler, W. J., *Het Socinianisme in Nederland* (1912; new edn., Leeuwarden, 1980).

Labbé, François, *La Gazette littéraire de Berlin (1764–1792)* (Paris, 2004).

Ladd, E. C., "Helvétius and d'Holbach: la moralization de la politique," JHI xxiii (1962), 221–38.

Laerke, Mogens, *Leibniz lecteur de Spinoza* (Paris, 2008).

Laerke, Mogens, "Introduction" to M. Laerke (ed.), *The Use of Censorship in the Enlightenment* (Leiden, 2009), 1–21.

Laerke, Mogens, "The Anthropological Analogy and the Constitution of Historical Perspectivism," in M. Laerke, Justin Smith, and Eric Schliesser (eds.), *Philosophy and its History: Aims and Methods of the Study of Early Modern Philosophy* (New York, 2013), 7–29.

Lafarga, Francisco, *Voltaire en España (1734–1835)* (Barcelona, 1982).

Lafrance, G. "Idée rousseauiste du droit et le discours jacobin," in R. Thiéry (ed.), *Rousseau, "Émile" et a la Révolution* (Paris, 1992), 27–36.

Lagier, Raphael, *Les Races humaines selon Kant* (Paris, 2004).

Lamb, Robert, "Labour, Contingency, Utility," in Poole (ed.), *John Thelwall*, 51–60.

L'Aminot, Tanguy (ed.), *Politique et révolution chez Jean-Jacques Rousseau*, SVEC 324 (Oxford, 1994).

Landau, Peter, "Der rechtsgeschichtliche Kontext des Atheismusstreits," in K. M. Kodalle and M. Ohst (eds.), *Fichtes Entlassung. Der Atheismusstreit vor 200 Jahren* (*Kritisches Jahrbuch der Philosophie* 4 (1999), 15–30.

Landon, William, "Bridging the Supposed Chasm: Tyranny, Republicanism and Lucretius' Influence on *The Prince* and the *Discourses*," in N. Gardini and M. McLaughlin (eds.), *Machiavelli's Prince: Traditions, Text and Translations* (Rome, 2017), 63–79.

Langford, Paul, *A Polite and Commercial People: England, 1727–1783* (Oxford, 1989).

La Parra López, Emilio, "The Monarchy at Bayonne and the Constitution of Cadiz," in Broers et al. (eds.), *Napoleonic Empire*, 260–9.

La Parra López, Emilio, *Fernando VII. Un rey deseado y detestado* (Barcelona, 2018).

Larrère, Catherine, "*L'Esprit des Lois*, tradition et modernité," in Larrère and Volpilhac-Auger (eds.), *1748, l'année*, 141–60.

Larrère, Catherine, "Diderot et l'atomisme," in J. Salem (ed.), *L'Atomisme aux XVIIe et XVIIIe siècles* (Paris, 1999), 151–65.

Larrère, Catherine, "D'Alembert and Diderot: les mathématiques contre la nature?," *Corpus* xxxviii (2001), 75–94.

Larrère, Catherine, "Montesquieu and Liberalism," in R. E. Kingston (ed.), *Montesquieu and his Legacy* (Albany, NY, 2009), 279–301.

Larrère, Catherine, "Women, Republicanism and the Growth of Commerce," in Van Gelderen and Skinner (eds.), *Republicanism* ii. 139–56.

Larrère, Catherine, "Montesquieu on Economics and Commerce," in Carithers et al. (eds.), *Montesquieu's Science*, 335–73.

Larrère, C., and C. Volpilhac-Auger (eds.), *1748, l'année de* l'Esprit des Lois (Paris, 1999).

Lascoumes, P., "Beccaria et la formulation d'un ordre public moderne," in Porret (ed.), *Beccaria*, 109–17.

Lauriol, Claude, *La Beaumelle: un Protestant cévenol entre Montesquieu et Voltaire* (Geneva, 1978).

Laursen, John Christian, "David Hume and the Danish Debate about Freedom of the Press in the 1770s," JHI lix (1998), 167–72.

Laursen, John Christian, "Spinoza in Denmark and the Fall of Struensee, 1770–1772," JHI 61 (2000), 189–202.

Laursen, John Christian, "Luxdorph's Press Freedom Writings Before the Fall of Struensee in Early 1770's Denmark–Norway," *The European Legacy* 7 (2002).

Laursen, John Christian, "Censorship in the Nordic Countries, *c.*1750–1890," JMEH iii (2005), 100–16.

Lavaert, Sonja, "Radical Enlightenment, Enlightened Subversion, and Spinoza," *Philosophica* 89 (2014), 49–102.

Lavaert, Sonja, "Lieutenants of the Commonwealth: A Political Reading of *De Jure Ecclesiasticorum*," in Lavaert and Schröder (eds.), *The Dutch Legacy*, 150–64.

Lavaert, Sonja, and W. Schröder, "Introduction" to Lavaert and Schroder (eds.), *The Dutch Legacy*, 1–15.

Lavaert, Sonja, and W. Schröder (eds.), *The Dutch Legacy: Radical Thinkers of the 17th Century and the Enlightenment* (Leiden, 2017).

La Vopa, A. J., "Conceiving a Public: Ideas and Society in Eighteenth-Century Europe," JMH lxiv (1992), 79–116.

La Vopa, Anthony, *Fichte: The Self and the Calling of Philosophy, 1762–1799* (Cambridge, 2001).

La Vopa, A. J., "A New Intellectual History? Jonathan Israel's Enlightenment," *Historical Journal* 52 (2009), 717–38.

La Vopa, A. J., *The Labor of the Mind: Intellect and Gender in Enlightenment Cultures* (Philadelphia, 2017).

Leask, Ian, "Introduction" to Toland, *Letters to Serena*, 9–3.

Leask, Ian, "Stoicism Unbound: Cicero's *Academica* in Toland's *Pantheisticon*, BJHPh 25 (2017), 223–43.

Leask, Ian, "The Undivulged Event in Toland's Christianity not Mysterious," in Hudson et al. (eds.), *Atheism and Deism Revalued*, 63–80.

Leask, Ian, "Speaking for Spinoza? Notes on John Toland's *Origines Judaicae*," in Ducheyne, *Reassessing*, 143–59.

Leca-Tsiomis, M., *Écrire l'*Encyclopédie: *Diderot: de l'usage des dictionnaires à la grammaire philosophique* (Oxford, 1999).

Lecompte, Denis, *Marx et le baron d'Holbach* (Paris, 1983).

Leddy, N., "Adam Smith's Critique of Enlightenment Epicureanism," in B. Leddy and A. S. Livschitz (eds.), *Epicurus in the Enlightenment* (Oxford, 2009), 183–205.

Leeuwenbergh, Bart, "Bayle and Mandeville: Republic or Monarchy," GWN 12 (2001), 89–96.
Leggiere, M. V., *The Fall of Napoleon: The Allied Invasion of France* (Cambridge, 2007).
Lehmann, William C., *Henry Home, Lord Kames and the Scottish Enlightenment* (The Hague, 1971).
Lehner, Ulrich, *The Catholic Enlightenment: The Forgotten History of a Global Movement* (Oxford, 2016).
Leigh, Ralph, "Le 'Contrat Social': Oeuvre Genevoise?," *Annales de la Société Jean-Jacques Rousseau* xxxix (1972/7), 93–111.
Lemberg, Margret, "Die Universität Marburg im Königreich Westphalen," in A. Hedwig, K, Malettke, and K. Murk (eds.), *Napoleon und das Königreich Westphalen. Herrschaftssystem und Modellstaatspolitik* (Marburg, 2008), 223–38.
Lerner, M. H., "Radical Elements and Attempted Revolutions in Late-18th-Century Republics," in Holenstein et al. (eds.), *Republican Alternative*, 301–20.
Leroux, Serge, "Un Dieu rémunérateur et vengeur comme fondement-garantie de la morale," in Kölving and Mervaud (eds.), *Voltaire et ses combats* i. 739–50.
Le Ru, Véronique, *D'Alembert philosophe* (Paris, 1994).
Le Ru, Véronique, "L'Aigle à deux têtes de l'*Encyclopédie*: accords et divergences de Diderot et de d'Alembert de 1751 à 1759," RDE xxvi (1999), 17–26.
Le Ru, Véronique, *Subversives Lumières: L'Encyclopédie comme machine de guerre* (Paris, 2007).
Leuwers, Hervé, *Robespierre* (Paris, 2014).
Levinger, Matthew, *Enlightened Nationalism: The Transformation of Prussian Political Culture, 1806–1848* (Oxford, 2000).
Levy, D. G., and H. B. Applewhite, "Women, Radicalization and the Fall of the French Monarchy," in Applewhite and Levy (eds.), *Women and Politics in the Age of Democratic Revolution* (Ann Arbor, 1990), 81–107.
Levy, Jacob, "Montesquieu's Constitutional Legacies," in R. E. Kingston (ed.), *Montesquieu and his Legacy* (Albany, NY, 2009), 115–37.
Lilti, Antoine, *Le Monde des salons: Sociabilité et mondalité à Paris auu XVIIIe siècle* (Paris, 2005).
Lilti, Antoine, "Sociabilité et mondanité," FHS xxviii (2005), 415–45.
Lilti, Antoine, "Comment écrit-on l'histoire intellectuelle des Lumières?," *Annales* lxiv (2009), 171–206.
Lilti, Antoine, "The Kingdom of Politesse: Salons and the Republic of Letters in Eighteenth-Century Paris," *Republics of Letters* 1 (Stanford, 2009).
Lilti, Antoine, "Et la civilization deviendra générale: l'Europe de Volney ou l'orientalisme à l'épreuve de la Révolution," *La Révolution française* 4 (2011).
Lilti, Antoine, *Figures publiques: l'invention de la celébrité, 1750–1850* (Paris, 2014).
Lilti, Antoine, "How Do we Write the Intellectual History of the Enlightenment? Spinozism, Radicalism and Philosophy," *Viewpoint Magazine*, 22 May 2017, pp. 1–16.
Lindroth, Sten, *A History of Uppsala University: 1477–1977* (Stockholm, 1976).
Lion, Henri, "L'Éthocratie de d'Holbach," *Annales révolutionnaires* xv (1923), 378–96.
Linton, M., *The Politics of Virtue in Enlightenment France* (Basingstoke, 2001).
Loayza Valda, J., "La Revolución en Charcas y la Universidad de San Francisco Xavier de Chuquisaca," in *Bicentenario del primer grito de libertad en Hispanoamérica, 25 de Mayo 1809* (Sucre, 2009), 121–30.

Locke, D., *A Fantasy of Reason: The Life and Thought of William Godwin* (London, 1980).
Loft, Leonore, "J.-P. Brissot and the Problem of Jewish Emancipation," SVEC 278 (1990), 465–75.
Loft, Leonore, *Passion, Politics and Philosophie: Rediscovering J. P. Brissot* (Westport, CT, 2002).
Lok, Matthijs, "Vijanden van de Verlichting. Antiverlichting en Verlichting in de Europese intellectuele geschiedenis," TvG 2014.
Lomonaco, Fabrizio, *Tolerance: Stages in Modernity from Holland to Italy* (Berne, 2005).
Lomonaco, Fabrizio, "Barbeyrac e Voltaire dalla virtù della tolleranza al ciritto di libertà religiosa," *Logos* (Università degli Studi di Napoli Federico II), ii/iii (2007/8), 73–93.
López Tabar, Juan, *Los famosos traidores. Los afrancesados durante la crisis del Antiguo Régimen (1808–1833)* (Madrid, 2001).
Lord, Beth, "Spinoza on Natural Inequality and the Fiction of Moral Equality," in Ducheyne, *Reassessing*, 127–42.
Louden, R. B., *The World We Want: How and Why the Ideals of the Enlightenment still Elude Us* (New York, 2007).
Lough, John, "Helvétius and d'Holbach," *The Modern Language Review* xxxiii (1938), 360–84.
Lough, John, *Essays on the* Encyclopédie *of Diderot and d'Alembert* (London, 1968).
Louth, Ch., "Coleridge und Friedrich Schlegel als Lessing-Leser," in K. Feilchenfeldt et al. (eds.), *Zwischen Aufklärung und Romantik* (Würzburg, 2006), 150–64.
Lucci, Diego, "Deism, Freethinking and Toleration," HEI 43 (2017), 345–58.
Lucci, Diego, "William Wollaston's Religion of Nature," in Hudson, Lucci, and Wigelsworth (eds.), *Atheism and Deism*, 119–38.
Lucci, Diego, "John Locke on Atheism, Catholicism, Antinomianism, and Deism," EPRF 20 (2018), 201–46.
Luciani, Paola, "Les Répercussions de la propagande philosophique des tragédies de Voltaire en Italie: Mahomet," in Kölving and Mervaud (eds.), *Voltaire et ses combats* ii. 1501–12.
Lundberg, David, and Henry F. May, "The Enlightened Reader in America," *American Quarterly* 28 (1976), 262–93.
Lundgren, Svante, *Moses Hess, Religion, Judaism and the Bible* (Åbo, 1992).
Lurbe, Pierre, "Matière, nature, movement chez d'Holbach et Toland," *Dix-Huitième Siècle* 24 (1992), 53–62.
Lüsebrink, Hans-Jürgen, "Zur Verhüllung und sukzessiven Aufdeckung der Autorschaft Diderots an der *Histoire des Deux Indes*," in T. Heydenreich (ed.), *Denis Diderot (1713–1784). Zeit, Werk, Wirkung. Zehn Beiträge* (Erlangen, 1984), 107–26.
Lüsebrink, Hans-Jürgen, "Aufgeklärter Humanismus. Philosophisches Engagement am Beispiel der Kontroverse über die 'Menschenrassen'," in R. Reichardt and G. Roche (eds.), *Weltbürger, Europäer, Deutscher, Franke. Georg Forster zum 200. Todestag* (Mainz, 1994), 188–95.
Lüsebrink, Hans-Jürgen, and R. Reichardt, *The Bastille: A History of a Symbol of Despotism and Freedom* (Durham, NC, 1997).
Lüsebrink, Hans-Jürgen, "Zensur, Exil und Autoidentität (Diderot, Raynal)," in W. Haefs and Y. G. Mix (eds.), *Zensur im Jahrhundert der Aufklärung* (Göttingen, 2007), 145–56.
Lüsebrink, Hans-Jürgen, *L'Adresse à l'Assemblée Nationale (31 Mai 1791) de Guillaume-Thomas Raynal. Positions, Polémiques, Répercussions* (Paris, 2018).

Lüsebrink, Hans-Jürgen, and M. Tietz (eds.), *Lectures de Raynal.* L'Histoire des deux Indes *en Europe et en Amérique au XVIIIe siècle* (Oxford, 1991), 205–33.

Lussu, Maria Luisa, *Bayle, Holbach e il dibattito sull' ateo virtuoso* (Genoa, 1997).

Luttrell, B., *Mirabeau* (Carbondale, IL, 1990).

Lutz, Donald, "Relative Influence of European Writers on Late Eighteenth-Century American Political Thought," *The American Political Science Review* 78 (1984), 189–97.

Lynch, A. J., "Montesquieu and the Ecclesiastical Critics of *l'Esprit des Lois*," JHI xxxviii (1977), 487–500.

Lynch, John, *Simón Bolívar: A Life* (New Haven, 2006).

McClure, George, *Doubting the Divine in Early Modern Europe* (Cambridge, 2018).

MacCulloch, Diarmaid, *The Reformation: A History* (New York and London, 2003).

McDaniel, Iain, *Adam Ferguson in the Scottish Enlightenment* (Cambridge, MA, 2013).

Macé, Laurence, "Les Lumières françaises au tribunal de l'Index et du Saint-Office," *Dix-Huitième Siècle* xxxiv (2002), 13–25.

McFarlane, Anthony, "Civil Disorders and Popular Protest in Late Colonial New Granada," HAHR lxiv (1984), 17–54.

McFarlane, Anthony, "The American Revolution and the Spanish Monarchy," in S. P. Newman (ed.), *Europe's American Revolution* (Basingstoke, 2006), 26–50.

McKenna, A., "Le Norme et la transgression: Pierre Bayle et le socinianisme," in Pierre Dubois (ed.), *Normes et transgression au XVIIIe siècle* (Paris, 2002), 117–36.

McKenna, A., "D'Épicure à Jamet en passant par Bayle," in Paganini and Tortarolo (eds.), *Der Garten*, 247–75.

McKenna, A., "Épicurisme et matérialisme au XVIIe siècle: quelques perspectives de recherche," in Secrétan, Dagron, and Bove (eds.), *Qu'est-ce que les Lumières "radicales"* (Paris, 2007), 75–85.

McKenna, A., "La Place de Pierre Bayle dans les Lumières radicales," in Garcia-Alonso (ed.), *Lumières radicales*, 51–81.

McKenna, A., "Recherches sur la philosophie clandestine à l'Age classique," in McKenna and Mothu (eds.), *La Philosophie clandestine*, 3–14.

McKenna, A., and Alain Mothu (eds.), *La Philosophie clandestine à l'Age Classique* (Paris, 1997).

McKown, Delos B., *Behold the Antichrist: Bentham on Religion* (Amherst, NY, 2004).

McMahon, D. M., *Enemies of the Enlightenment* (Oxford, 2001).

McMahon, D. M., and Samuel Moyn (eds.), *Rethinking Modern European Intellectual History* (Oxford, 2014).

McManners, J., *Church and Society in Eighteenth-Century France* (2 vols., Oxford, 1998).

McNaughton, David, "British Moralists of the Eighteenth-Century: Shaftesbury, Butler and Price," in Stuart Brown (ed.), *British Philosophy and the Age of Enlightenment*, Routledge History of Philosophy vol. v (London and New York, 1996).

McNutt, Jennifer Powell, *Calvin Meets Voltaire: The Clergy of Geneva in the Age of Enlightenment, 1685–1798* (Farnham, 2013).

Macor, Laura, "Friedrich Hölderlin and the Clandestine Society of the Bavarian Illuminati," *Philosophica* 88 (2013), 103–25.

McShea, R. J., *The Political Philosophy of Spinoza* (New York, 1968).

Madariaga, Salvador de, *Bolívar* (1951; new edn., 2 vols., Madrid, 1975).

Magrin, Gabriele, "Confutare Montesquieu. La critica di Condorcet," in D. Felice (ed.), *Montesquieu e i suoi interpreti* (2 vols., Pisa, 2005) i, 377–411.

Maiolani, D., "Mably e il repubblicanesimo dei lumi," *Il Pensiero Politico* xxxiv (2001), 73–94.

Maire, C., *De la cause de Dieu à la cause de la nation: le Jansénisme au XVIIIe siècle* (Paris, 1998).

Maissen, Thomas, *Die Geburt der Republic* (Göttingen, 2006).

Maissen, Thomas, "Die Erfinder der modernen Schweiz," in *NZZ Geschichte* 1 (Apr. 2015), 26–49.

Malcolm, Noel, "Hobbes, Ezra and the Bible," in N. Malcolm, *Aspects of Hobbes* (Oxford, 2002), 383–431.

Malik, Kenan, *The Quest for a Moral Compass: A Global History of Ethics* (London, 2014).

Mansel, Philip, *Paris between Empires: Monarchy and Revolution, 1814–1852* (London, 2001).

Mantecón, Tomás, *España en tiempos de Ilustración* (Madrid, 2013).

Marand-Fouquet, Catherine, *La Femme au temps de la Révolution* (Paris, 1989).

Marcuse, Ludwig, "Heine and Marx: A History and a Legend," *The Germanic Review* xxx (1955), 110–24.

Margerison, P., *L. Roederer: Political Thought and Practice during the French Revolution* (Philadelphia, 1983).

Märker, Almuth, *Geschichte der Universität Erfurt (1392–1816)* (Weimar, 1993).

Marshall, John, *John Locke, Toleration and Early Enlightenment* (Cambridge, 2006).

Martin, Jean-Clement, *Violence et Révolution: essai sur la naissance d'un mythe national* (Paris, 2006).

Martin, Jean-Clement, *Nouvelle histoire de la Révolution française* (Paris, 2012).

Martin, Jean-Clement, *Robespierre: la fabrication d'un monstre* (Paris, 2016).

Martin-Haag, É., *Voltaire: du Cartésianisme au Lumières* (Paris, 2002).

Martin-Haag, E., *Un aspect de la pensée politique de Diderot* (Paris, 1999).

Martínez Garnica, A., "La Experiencia del Nuevo Reino de Granada," in A. Ávila and P. Pérez Herrero (eds.), *La Experiencias de 1808 en Iberoamérica* (Madrid and Mexico City, 2008), 365–80.

Martus, Steffen, *Aufklärung. Das deutsche 18. Jahrhundert—ein Epochenbild* (Berlin, 2015).

Más Galvan, Cayetano, "El Clero Murciano durante el trienio liberal," in Alberola and Larriba (eds.), *Las élites*, 333–47.

Mason, Pamela, "The Genevan Republican Background to Rousseau's Social Contract," *History of Political Thought* xiv (1993), 547–72.

Mass, E., and P. E. Knabe (eds.), *L'Encyclopédie et Diderot* (Cologne, 1985).

Masseau, D., *Les Ennemis des philosophes: l'antiphilosophie au temps des Lumières* (Paris, 2000).

Mastellone, Salvo, "Italian Enlightenment and the Swedish Constitution during the Age of Liberty (1719–1772)," in N. Stjernquist (ed.), *The Swedish Riksdag in an International Perspective* (Stockholm, 1989), 112–17.

Mathan, Anne de, "Le Fédéralisme Girondin: histoire d'un mythe national," AHRF 393 (2018), 195–206.

Matheron, Alexandre, "Le Traité *Théologico-Politique* vu par le jeune Marx," *Cahiers Spinoza* 1 (1977), 159–212.

Matheron, Alexandre, *Individu et communauté chez Spinoza* (Paris, 1988).

Mathiez, Albert, *Autour de Robespierre* (Paris, 1957).

Maticorena Estrada, M. (ed.), *Colección documental de la Independencia del Peru* 1. *Los ideológos* vol. 3. *José Baquíjano y Carillo* (Lima, 1976).

Mattes, Armin, "Tocqueville and Grund on Democracy and Aristocracy in America," in Grund, *Aristocracy in America*, 28–52.

Matthey, Christine, "L'Ombre et les Lumières: une vision française de l'Espagne au XVIIIe siècle," *Dix-Huitième Siècle* xl (2008), 413–30.

Maxwell, Kenneth, "Pombal, the Paradox of the Enlightenment and Despotism," in H. M. Scott (ed.), *Enlightened Absolutism* (Basingstoke, 1990), 75–118.

Maxwell, Kenneth, "Pombal" in *Essays on Empire and Other Rogues* (London, 2003).

May, H. F., *The Enlightenment in America* (1976; new edn., New York, 1978).

Mazza, E., "Hume's 'Meek' Philosophy among the Milanese," in Frasca-Spada and Kail (eds.), *Impressions*, 213–43.

Mazzolini, Renato G., "Linnaeus and Michele Enrico Sagramoso: Knight of the Order of Malta," in Marco Beretta and Alessandro Tosi (eds.), *Linnaeus in Italy: The Spread of a Revolution in Science. Uppsala Studies in History of Science* 34 (Sagamore Beach, MA, 2007).

Méchoulan, Henry, R. H. Popkin, G. Ricuperati, and L. Simonutti (eds.), *La formazione storica della alterità. Studi di storia della tolleranza nell'età moderna offerti a Antonio Rotondò* (3 vols., Florence, 2001).

Meinsma, K. O. *Spinoza et son cercle* (1896; expanded French edn., Paris, 1983).

Meissner, Jochen, *Eine Elite im Umbruch. Der Stadtrat von Mexico zwischen kolonialer Ordnung und unabhängigem Staat* (Stuttgart, 1993).

Melamed, Y., "Salomon Maimon and the Rise of Spinozism in German Idealism," JHPh xlii (2004), 67–96.

Melamed, Y., "Omnis determinatio est negatio": Determination, Negation, and Self-Negation in Spinoza, Kant and Hegel," in Förster and Melamed (eds.), *Spinoza and German Idealism*, 175–96.

Melamed, Y., "Charitable Interpretations and the Political Domestication of Spinoza," in M. Laerke, J. Smith, and E. Schliesser (eds.), *Philosophy and its History* (Oxford, 2013), 258–77.

Mellor, Anne, "English Women Writers and the French Revolution," in S. E. Melzer and L. W. Rabine (eds.), *Rebel Daughters: Women and the French Revolution* (New York, 1992), 255–72.

Melzer, Arthur, M., *Philosophy between the Lines: The Lost History of Esoteric Writing* (Chicago, 2014).

Menant, S., "Les Relations de Voltaire avec la Russie," in Poussou et al. (eds.), *L'Influence*, 209–15.

Merrill, Thomas W., *Hume and the Politics of Enlightenment* (Cambridge, 2015).

Mertens, Frank, "Franciscus van den Enden: tijd voor een herziening van diens role in het ontstaan van het Spinozisme," in *Tijdschrift voor filosofie* 51 (1994), 77–37.

Mertens, Frank, "Radical Political Theory in the Netherlands of the Early Modern Period," GWN 12 (2001), 77–87.

Mertens, Frank, *Van den Enden en Spinoza* (Voorschoten, 2012).

Merz-Horn, S., *Georg Forster (1754–1794): Die Kasseler Jahre* (Kassel, 1984).

Mestre Sanchis, Antonio, *La Ilustración española* (Madrid, 1998).

Mestre Sanchis, Antonio, *Apología y crítica de España en el siglo XVIII* (Madrid, 2003).

Métraux, Alexandre, "Über Denis Diderots physiologisch interpretierten Spinoza," *Studia Spinozana* 10 (1994), 121–34.

Meynell, H. A., *Postmodernism and the New Enlightenment* (Washington, DC, 1999).
Michael, M., "Locke, Religious Toleration and the Limits of Social Contract Theory," *History of Philosophy Quarterly* xx (2003), 21–40.
Michman, Jozeph, *The History of Dutch Jewry during the Emancipation Period 1787–1815* (Amsterdam, 1995).
Middelfort, H. C. E., *Exorcism and Enlightenment* (New Haven, 2005).
Miert, Dirk van, "The Janus Face of Scaliger's Philological Heritage: The Biblical Annotations of Heinsius and Grotius," in Van Miert, Nellen, Steenbakkers, and Touber (eds.), *Scriptural Authority*, 91–108.
Miert, Dirk van, H. Nellen, P. Steenbakkers, and J. Touber (eds.), *Scriptural Authority and Biblical Criticism in ihe Dutch Golden Age* (Oxford, 2017).
Mignini, Filippo, "*Een Ligt schijnende in duystere plaatsen*: Adriaen Koerbagh tra averroismo e libertinismo," in G. Licata (ed.), *L'Averroismo in età moderna* (Macerata, 2013), 167–200.
Mihaila, I., "L'*hylozoïsme* de Diderot," in Fink and Stenger (eds.), *Être matérialiste* 185–97.
Mijnhardt, Wijnand, *Tot heil van't Menschdom. Culturele genootschappen in Nederland, 1750–1800* (Amsterdam, 1987).
Mijnhardt, Wijnand, "The Dutch Enlightenment," in Jacob and Mijnhardt (eds.), *Dutch Republic*, 197–223.
Mijnhardt, Wijnand, *Over de moderniteit van de Nederlandse Republiek* (Utrecht, 2001).
Mijnhardt, Wijnand, "The Construction of Silence: Religious and Political Radicalism in Dutch History," in W. van Bunge (ed.), *Early Enlightenment in the Dutch Republic, 1650–1750: Selected Papers of a Conference Held at the Herzog August Bibliothek Wolfenbuttel, 22–23 March 2001*, Brill's Studies in Intellectual History, (Leiden, 2003), 231–62.
Mijnhardt, Wijnand, "The Limits of Present-Day Historiography of Republicanism," *De Achttiende Eeuw* 37 (2005), 75–89.
Mijnhardt, Wijnand, "Urbanization, Culture and the Dutch Origins of the European Enlightenment," BMGN 125 (2010), 141–77.
Miller, James, *Rousseau: Dreamer of Democracy* (New Haven, 1984).
Miller, Nicholas, *John Millar and the Scottish Enlightenment* (Oxford, 2017).
Milton, J. R. (ed.), *Locke's Moral, Political and Legal Philosophy* (Aldershot, 1999).
Minart, Gerard, *Pierre Daunou, l'anti-Robespierre: de la Révolution à l'empire. L'Itinéraire d'un juste (1761–1840)* (Toulouse, 2001).
Minchom, Martin, *The People of Quito, 1690–1810: Change and Unrest in the Underclass* (Boulder, CO, 1994).
Minerbi, Marco, "Introduzione" to Sismondi, *Recherches*, 7–75.
Miquieu, Christophe, *Spinoza, Locke et l'idée de citoyenneté: une génération républicaine à l'aube des Lumières* (Paris, 2012).
Mokyr, Joel, *Industrialization in the Low Countries, 1795–1850* (New Haven, 1976).
Moliner Prada, Antonio, "El Anticlericalismo popular durante el Bienio 1834–5," *Hispania Sacra* 49 (1997), 498–541.
Mondot, Jean, "La Reception de Raynal en Allemagne: l'exemple de Wekhrlin," in Lüsebrink and Tietz (eds.), *Lectures de Raynal*, 189–204.
Mondot, Jean, "Wekhrlin et la Révolution d'Amérique," in Krebs and Moes (eds.), *Révolution Américaine*, 125–36.
Monod, A., *De Pascal à Chateaubriand: les défenseurs français du Christianisme de 1670 à 1802* (1916; New York, 1971).

Moore, James, "Montesquieu and the Scottish Enlightenment," in R. Kingston (ed.), *Montesquieu and his Legacy* (Albany, NY, 2009), 179–95.
Morales Padrón, F., "México y la independencia de Hispanoamerica en 1781 según un comisiado regio: Francisco de Saavedra," *Revista de Indias* xxix (1969), 335–58.
Moreau, Pierre-François, "Épicure et Spinoza: la physique," *Archives de philosophie* lvii (1994), 459–69.
Moreau, Pierre-François, "La Réception du spinozisme aux XIXe et XXe siècles," in Pierre-François Moreau and Charles Raymond (eds.), *Lectures de Spinoza* (Paris, 2006),.
Moreau, Pierre-François, "Spinoza est-il spinoziste?," in Secrétan, Dagron, and Bove (eds.), *Qu'est-ce que les Lumières "radicales"* (Paris, 2007), 287–98.
Moreau, Pierre-François (ed.), *Architectures de la raison* (Paris, 1996).
Moreau, Pierre-François, and Ann Thomson (eds.), *Matérialisme et passions* (Lyons, 2004).
Morfino, Vittorio, *Le Temps de la multitude* (Paris, 2010).
Mori, Gianluca, *Bayle philosophe* (Paris, 1999).
Mori, Gianluca, *L'Ateismo dei moderni. Filosofia e negazione di Dio da Spinoza a d'Holbach* (Rome, 2016).
Mornay, D., *Les Origines intellectuelles de la Révolution française (1715–1787)* (1933; 6th edn., Paris, 1967).
Morris, Marilyn, *The British Monarchy and the French Revolution* (New Haven, 1998).
Mortier, Roland, *Diderot en Allemagne (1750–1850)* (1954; repr. Geneva, 1986).
Mortier, Roland, "Diderot and Penal Law: Objections to Beccaria," in F. Jost (ed.), *Aesthetics and the Literature of Ideas* (Newark, NJ, 1990), 203–13.
Mortier, Roland, *Le Coeur et la raison: recueil d'études sur le dix-huitième siècle* (Oxford, 1990).
Mortier, Roland, "Les Héritiers de 'philosophes' devant l'expérience révolutionnaire," in Mortier, *Cœur*, 454–66.
Mortier, Roland, *Anarcharsis Cloots ou l'utopie foudroyée* (n.p., 1995).
Mortier, Roland, "Diversités culturelles: Aufklärung allemande—Lumières françaises," in Grunert and Vollhardt (eds.), *Aufklärung als praktische Philosophie* (Tübingen, 1998), 21–30.
Mortier, Roland, *Les Combats des Lumières* (Ferney-Voltaire, 2000).
Mortier, Roland, *Lumières du XVIIIe siècle* (Athens, 2003).
Mortimer, Sarah, "Human and Divine Justice in the Works of Grotius and the Socinians," in Mortimer and Robertson (eds.), *Intellectual Consequences*, 75–94.
Mortimer, Sarah, and John Robertson (eds.), *The Intellectual Consequences of Religious Heterodoxy 1600–1750* (Leiden, 2012).
Mossner, E. C., *The Life of David Hume* (1954; Oxford, 3rd revised edn., 2001).
Mothu, Alain, "L'Édition de 1751 des *Opinions des Anciens*," *La Lettre Clandestine* iii (1994), 45–53.
Mothu, Alain, "Les Vanités manuscrites des esprits forts," *La Lettre Clandestine* vi (1997), 65–9.
Mothu, Alain, "Un Curé 'Janseniste' lecteur et concepteur de manuscrits clandestins: Guillaume Maleville," *La Lettre Clandestine* vi (1997), 25–50.
Mothu, Alain, "Un Morceau des plus hardis et des plus philosophiques qui aient été faits dans ce pays-ci," *Corpus* xliv (2003), 35–56.
Mothu, Alain, "Athéisme et politique à la Renaissance: le cas du *Cymbalum Mundi* (1537)," EPRF 20 (2018).

Motta, Franco, "Le condanne inquisitoriali della 'Scienza della legislazione', in Trampus (ed.), *Diritti e Costituzione*, 291–335.

Moureau, F., "Du clandestin et de son bon usage au XVIIIe siècle," *La Lettre Clandestine* vi (1997), 271–83.

Moyar, Dean, "Thought and Metaphysics: Hegel's Critical Reception of Spinoza," in Förster and Melamed (eds.), *Spinoza and German Idealism*, 197–213.

Moyn, Samuel, *The Last Utopia: Human Rights in History* (Cambridge, MA, 2010).

Moyn, Samuel, "Mind the Enlightenment," *The Nation* (posted: 12 May 2010).

Muceni, Elena, "Mandeville et les 'Lumières radicales'," in García-Alonso (ed.), *Lumières radicales*, 85–102.

Mühlpfordt, G., "Barhdts Weg zum revolutionären Demokratismus," *Zeitschrift fur Geschichtswissenschaft* xxix (1981), 99–1017.

Mühlpfordt, G., "'Europarepublik im Duodezformat' Die internationale Geheimgesellschaft 'Union'," in H. Reinalter (ed.), *Freimaurer und Geheimbünde in 18. Jahrhundert in Mitteleuropa* (Frankfurt, 1983).

Mühlpfordt, G., *Halle-Leipziger Aufklärung. Kernstück der Mitteldeutschen Aufklärung* (Halle, 2011).

Mühlpfordt, G., *Demokratische Aufklärer* (2 vols., Halle, 2014).

Müller, Patrick, "An Equal Commonwealth: Lord Ashley and the Republican Project of the Late 1690s," in Müller (ed.), *Shaping Enlightenment Politics*, 115–33.

Müller, Patrick (ed.), *Shaping Enlightenment Politics: The Social and Political Impact of the First and Third Earls of Shaftesbury* (Berlin, 2018).

Müller, Thomas Christian, "Switzerland 1847/49: A Provisional Successful End of a Democratic Revolution," in Dowe et al., *Europe in 1848*, 210–41.

Müller, Winfried, *Universität und Orden. Die bayerische Landesuniversität Ingolstadt zwischen der Aufhebung des Jesuitenordens und der Säkularisation (1773–1803)* (Berlin, 1986).

Müller-Seidel, W., and W. Riedel (eds.), *Die Weimarer Klassik und ihre Geheimbünde* (Würzburg, 2003).

Mullett, Michael, *Radical Religious Movements in Early Modern Europe* (London, 1980).

Mulsow, M., *Moderne aus dem Untergrund. Radikale Frühaufklärung in Deutschland, 1680–1720* (Hamburg, 2002).

Mulsow, M., "The 'New Socinians': Intertextuality and Cultural Exchange in Late Socinianism," in M. Mulsow and J. Rohls (eds.), *Socinianism and Arminianism: Antitrinitarians, Calvinists and Cultural Exchange in Seventeenth-Century Europe*, Brill's Studies in Intellectual History (Leiden, 2005), 49–78.

Mulsow, M., *Freigeister im Gottsched-Kreis. Wolffianismus, studentische Aktivitäten und Religionskritik in Leipzig, 1740–1745* Göttingen, 2007).

Mulsow, M., "Adam Weishaupt als Philosoph," in Müller-Seidel and Riedel (eds.), *Weimarer Klassik*, 27–66.

Mulsow, M., *Prekäres Wissen. Eine andere Ideengeschichte der Frühen Neuzeit* (Berlin, 2012).

Mulsow, M., "Karl von Knoblauch und Georg Friedrich Werner als Materialisten," in M. Mulsow and G. Naschert (eds.), *Radikale Spätaufklärung in Deutschland, Einzelschicksale-Konstellationen-Netzwerke*, in *Aufklärung Interdiziplinäres Jahrbuch* vol. 24 (Hamburg, 2012), 91–112.

Mulsow, M., *Enlightenment Underground: Radical Germany, 1680–1720* (Charlottesville, VA, 2015).

Mulsow, M., *RadikaleFrühaufklärung in Deutschland, 1680–1720* (2 vols., Göttingen, 2018).

Mulsow, Martin, and Claudia Schmitz, "Eigennutz, Statuserhaltung und Naturzustand: Tradierungen des ethisch-politischen Epikurismus vom 15. bis 17. Jahrhundert," in Paganini and Tortarolo (eds.), *Der Garten*, 47–85.

Munck, Thomas, "The Danish Reformers," in Scott (ed.), *Enlightened Absolutism*, 245–63.

Mungello, D. E., "European Philosophical Responses to Non-European Culture," in D. Garber and M. Ayers (eds.), *Cambridge History of Seventeenth-Century Philosophy* (Cambridge, 2003), i. 87–100.

Muñoz Feliu, Miguel, "Bibliotecas y Revolución: La Política bibliotecaria de José I," *Bulletin Hispanique* 120 (2018), 461–71.

Muñoz Sempere, Daniel, *La Inquisición Española como tema literario. Política, historia y ficción en el crisis del Antiguo Régimen* (Woodbridge, 2008).

Muschik, A. "Die Ideen der Französischen Revolution in Schwedisch-Vorpommern," *Baltische Studien* 93 (2007).

Muthu, Sankar, *Enlightenment against Empire* (Princeton, 2003).

Na'aman, Shlomo, *Emanzipation und Messianismus. Leben und Werk des Moses Hess* (Frankfurt, 1982).

Naess, Harald, "Holberg and the Age of Enlightenment," in Harald Naess (ed.), *A History of Norwegian Literature* (Lincoln, NB, 1993), 54–75.

Nash, David, *Secularism, Art and Freedom* (Leicester, 1992).

Nash, G. B., *The Unknown American Revolution* (London, 2006).

Nash, G. B., "International Repercussions and Reconsiderations of the American Revolution," in Armitage and Subrahmanyam (eds.), *Age of Revolutions*, 1–19.

Nash, G. B., and Soderlund, J. R., *Freedom by Degrees: Emancipation in Pennsylvania and its Aftermath* (New York, 1991).

Nassar, D., "Spinoza in Schelling's Early Conception of Intellectual Intuition," in Förster and Melamed (eds.), *Spinoza and German Idealism*, 136–55.

Nauen, Franz Gabriel, *Revolution, Idealism and Human Freedom: Schelling, Hölderlin and Hegel and the Crisis of Early German Idealism* (The Hague, 1971).

Naves, R., *Voltaire et l'*Encyclopédie (Paris, 1938).

Naville, Pierre, *Paul Thiry d'Holbach et la philosophie scientifique au XVIIIe siècle* (5th edn., Paris, 1943).

Neely, Sylvia, *Lafayette and the Liberal Ideal, 1814–1824: Politics and Conspiracy in an Age of Reaction* (Carbondale, IL, 1991).

Negri, Antonio, *Spinoza for our Time: Politics and Postmodernity* (New York, 2013).

Negroni, B. de, "Le Rôle de la citation de Bayle à Voltaire," *La Lettre Clandestine* viii (1999), 35–54.

Neidleman, J., "The Sublime Science of Simple Souls: Rousseau's Philosophy of Truth," HEI 39 (2013), 815–34.

Neiman, Susan, *Evil in Modern Thought: An Alternative History of Philosophy* (Princeton, 2002).

Nennon, Monika, "Gender in Rousseau's *Julie ou La Nouvelle Héloïse* and its German Reception: Radical or Moderate?," in Niekerk (ed.), *Radical Enlightenment in Germany*, 238–63.

Nesbitt, Nick, *Universal Emancipation: The Haitian Revolution and the Radical Enlightenment* (Charlottesville, VA, 2008).

Newman, Simon P. (ed.), *Europe's American Revolution* (Basingstoke, 2006).

Newman, Simon P., "Paine, Jefferson and Revolutionary Radicalism in Early National America," in S. P. Newman and P. S. Onuf (eds.), *Paine and Jefferson in the Age of Revolutions* (Charlottesville, VA, 2013), 71–94.

Niblett, M., "Man, Morals and Matter: Epicurus and Materialist Thought in England from John Toland to Joseph Priestley," in N. Leddy and A. S. Lifschitz (eds.), *Epicurus in the Enlightenment* (Oxford, 2009), 137–59.

Nicolet, Claude, *L'Idée républicaine en France* (Paris, 1982).

Niekerk, Carl (ed.), *The Radical Enlightenment in Germany: A Cultural Perspective* (Leiden, 2018).

Niekerk, Carl, "Introduction: How Radical was the German Enlightenment," in Niekerk (ed.), *Radical Enlightenment in Germany*, 1–45.

Niezen, R., "The *Aufklärung*'s Human Discipline", IHR xix (2009), 177–96.

Nijenhuis, I. J. A., *Een joodse* philosophe, *Isaac de Pinto (1717–1787)* (Amsterdam, 1992).

Nilsen, H. F., "Republican Monarchy: The Neo-Roman Concept of Liberty and the Norwegian Constitution of 1814," MIH 16 (2019), 29–56.

Nilsson, Göran, "Sweden 1848—On the Road to the Middle Way," in Dowe et al., *Europe in 1848*, 325–37.

Nisbet, H. B., "Lucretius in Eighteenth-Century Germany," *The Modern Language Review* 81 (1986), 97–115.

Nooijen, A., "Balthasar Bekker's *Betoverde Weereld* and Freethinking in Germany," in Marie-Hélène Queval (ed.), *Orthodoxie et Héterodoxie. Libertinage et Religion en Europe au temps des Lumières* (Saint-Etienne, 2010), 63–74.

Nola, Robert, "The Young Hegelians, Feuerbach and Marx," in K. M. Higgins and R. C. Solomon (eds.), *The Age of German Idealism* (London, 1993), 290–329.

Noordenbos, O., "De eeuw der Verlichting," *De Gids* 134 (1971), 446–53.

Nordenstreng, K., "Freedom of Speech in Finland, 1766–2016," in Carlsson and Goldberg (eds.), *Legacy of Peter Forsskål*, 71–91.

Norton, D. F., "Hume, Human Nature, and the Foundations of Morality," in Norton (ed.), *Cambridge Companion to Hume*, 148–81.

Norton, D. F., and M. Kuehn, "The Foundations of Morality," in CHEPh ii. 941–86.

Norton, D. F. (ed.), *The Cambridge Companion to Hume* (Cambridge, 1993).

Nuovo, Victor, "Locke's Proof of the Divine Authority of Scripture," in R. Savage (ed.), *Philosophy and Religion in Enlightenment Britain* (Oxford, 2012), 56–76.

Nuovo, Victor, *John Locke: The Philosopher as Christian Virtuoso* (Oxford, 2017).

Nyman, Elmor, *Indragningsmakt och tryckfrihet 1785-1810* (Stockholm, 1963).

O'Brien, Patrick Karl, "The Impact of the Revolutionary and Napoleonic Wars, 1793–1815, on the Long-Run Growth of the British Economy," *Fernand Braudel Center Review* xii (1989), 335–95.

O'Dea, M., and Whelan, K. (eds.), *Nations and Nationalisms* (Oxford, 1995).

Oergel, Maike, *(Re-)Writing the Radical Enlightenment, Revolution and Cultural Transfer in 1790s Germany, Britain and France* (Berlin, 2012).

Offen, Karen, *The Woman Question in France, 1400–1870* (Cambridge, 2017).

Ogonowski, Zbigniew "Der Sozianismus und die Aufklärung," in P. Wrzecionko (ed.), *Reformation und Frühaufklärung in Polen* (Göttingen, 1977), 78–156.

O'Hagan, Timothy, *Rousseau* (London, 1999).

O'Hara, Kieron, *The Enlightenment: A Beginners' Guide* (London, 2010).
Ohles, Frederik, *Germany's Rude Awakening: Censorship in the Land of the Brothers Grimm* (Kent, OH, 1992).
Ohst, Martin, "Fichte's Entlassung," in K. M. Kodalle and M. Ohst (eds.,) *Fichtes Entlassung. Der Atheismusstreit vor 200 Jahren* (*Kritisches Jahrbuch der Philosophie* 4 (1999), 9–14.
Oittinen, Vesa, "Peter Forsskål, a Radical Reformer," in Charlotta Wolff, T. Kaitaro, and M. Ahokas (eds.), *The Enlightenment: Critique, Myth, Utopia* (Frankfurt, 2011), 133–49.
O'Keefe, C. B., *Contemporary Reactions to the Enlightenment (1728–1762)* (Paris, 1974).
Oltra, Joaquín, and M. A. Pérez Samper, *El Conde de Aranda y los Estados Unidos* (Barcelona, 1987).
O'Neill, D., *The Burke-Wollstonecraft Debate* (University Park, PA, 2007).
Onfray, Michel, *Les Ultras des Lumières* (Paris, 2007).
Oostindie, Gert, "The Enlightenment, Christianity and the Surinam Slave," *The Journal of Caribbean History* xxvi (1992), 147–70.
Oostindie, Gert, *Fifty Years Later: Antislavery, Capitalism and Modernity in the Dutch Orbit* (Pittsburgh, 1996).
Oostindie, Gert, *Ethnicity in the Caribbean* (1996; new edn., Amsterdam, 2005).
Oostindie, Gert, "Same Old Song? Perspectives on Slavery in Surinam and Curaçao," in Oostindie, (ed.), *Fifty Years Later*, 179–92.
Op de Beek, Johan, *Het Verlies van België. De strijd tussen de nederlandse koning en de Belgische revolutionairen in 1830* (Amsterdam, 2015).
Orain, Arnauld, "Le Journal oeconomique, le cercle de Gournay et le pouvoir monarchique," *Dix-Huitième Siècle* 45 (2013), 565–83.
Otto, R., *Studien zur Spinozarezeption in Deutschland im 18. Jahrhundert* (Frankfurt, 1994).
Oudin, Ch., *Le Spinozisme de Montesquieu: étude critique* (Paris, 1911).
Oustinoff, P. C., "Notes on Diderot's Fortunes in Russia," in O. E. Fellows and N. L. Torrey (eds.), *Diderot Studies* (Syracuse, 1949), 121–42.
Pabst, Adrian, "Political Economy of Virtue: Civil Economy, Happiness and Public Trust in the Thought of Antonio Genovesi," EJHE 25 (2018), 582–604.
Packham, Catherine, "The Physiology of Political Economy: Vitalism and Adam Smith's *Wealth of Nations*," JHI 63 (2002), 465–81.
Paganini, Gianni, "Hume et Bayle: conjonction locale et immaterialité de l'âme," in M. Magdalaine et al. (eds.), *De l'Humanisme aux Lumières, Bayle et le protestantisme* (Oxford, 1996), 701–13.
Paganini, Gianni, *Les Philosophies clandestines à l'âge classique* (Paris, 2005).
Paganini, Gianni, "L'apport des courants sceptiques à la naissance des lumières radicales," in Secrétan, Dagron, and Bove (eds.), *Qu'est-ce que les Lumières "radicales"?*, 87–104.
Paganini, Gianni, *Skepsis: le débat des modernes sur le scepticisme* (Paris, 2008).
Paganini, Gianni, "Charron et el scepticisme des modernes," *Corpus, revue de philosophie* 55 (2008), 231–49.
Paganini, Gianni, "Hobbes, Gassendi and the Tradition of Political Epicureanism," in Paganini and Tortarolo (eds.), *Der Garten*, 113–37.
Paganini, Gianni, *Introduzione alle filosofie clandestine* (2005; new edn., Bari, 2008).
Paganini, Gianni, "Scetticismo e certezza," in G. Paganini and E. Tortarolo (eds.), *Illuminismo. Un vademecum* (Turin, 2008).
Paganini, Gianni, "Early Modern Atheism and Renaissance Philosophy," IHR 26 (2016), 25–31.

Paganini, Gianni, "Le Moment machiavélien de Pierre Bayle," *Archives de Philosophie* 81 (2018), 709–28.

Paganini, Gianni, "Enlightenment before the Enlightenment," EPRF 20 (2018), 183–200.

Paganini, Gianni, and E. Tortarolo (eds.), *Der Garten und die Moderne. Epikureische Moral und Politik vom Humanismus bis zur Aufklärung* (Stuttgart, 2004).

Paganini, Gianni, M. Benítez, and J. Dybikowski (eds.), *Scepticisme, Clandestinité et Libre Pensée* (Paris, 2002).

Pagden, Anthony, "The Effacement of Difference," in G. Prakash (ed.), *After Colonialism: Imperial Histories and Postcolonial Displacements* (Princeton, 1995), 129–52.

Pagden, Anthony, *The Enlightenment and Why it Still Matters* (Oxford, 2013).

Page, Anthony, "'Liberty has an Asylum': John Jebb, British Radicalism and the American Revolution," *History* lxxxvii (2002), 204–26.

Page, Anthony, *John Jebb and the Enlightenment Origins of British Radicalism* (Westport, CT, 2003).

Palmer, Ada, *Reading Lucretius in the Renaissance* (Cambridge, MA, 2014).

Palmer, R. R., *From Jacobin to Liberal: Marc-Antoine Jullien, 1775–1848* (Princeton, 1993).

Pancaldi, G., *Volta: Science and Culture in the Age of Enlightenment* (Princeton, 2003).

Pantoja Moran, David, *El Supremo poder conservador. El diseño institucional en las primeras constituciones mexicanas* (Mexico City, 2005).

Pappas, J. N., "Voltaire et la guerre civile philosophique," *Revue d'histoire littéraire de la France* (1961), 525–49.

Pappas, J. N., *Voltaire and d'Alembert* (Bloomington, IN, 1962).

Pappas, J. N., "Diderot, d'Alembert et l'*Encyclopédie*," *Diderot Studies* iv (1963), 191–208.

Parikh, I., "The Need of the Third World for Humanism," in P. Kurtz and T. J. Madigan (eds.), *Challenges to the Enlightenment: In Defence of Reason and Science* (New York, 1994).

Parker, Grant, *Agony of Asar: A Thesis on Slavery by the Former Slave, Jacobus Elisa Johannes Capitein, 1717–1747* (Princeton, 2001).

Parker, Noel, "Souveraineté et providence chez Rousseau," in L'Aminot (ed.), *Politique et révolution*, 21–33.

Pascal, Jean-Noel, "Diderot dans le *Dictionnaire anti-philosophique* de Dom Mayeul-Chaudon," in Chouillet (ed.), *Ennemis*, 91–100.

Passannante, Gerard, *The Lucretian Renaissance: Philology and the Afterlife of Tradition* (Chicago, 2011).

Pasta, Renato, "Dei delitti e delle pene et sa fortune en Italie," in Porret (ed.), *Beccaria*, 119–48.

Pätzold, D., *Spinoza, Aufklärung, Idealismus. Die Substanz der Moderne* (1995; 2nd edn., Assen, 2002).

Paul, Jean-Marie, "Reimarus et le Curé Meslier: Évolution et Révolution," in J. Moes and J.-M. Valentin (eds.), *De Lessing à Heine: une siècle de relations littéraires et intellectuelles entre la France et l'Allemagne* (Paris, 1985), 73–91.

Peabody, S., "*There are no Slaves in France*" (New York, 1996).

Pearson, R., *Voltaire Almighty* (London, 2005).

Pečar, Andreas, and D. Tricoire, *Falsche Freunde. War die Aufklärung wirklich die Geburtsstunde der Moderne?* (Frankfurt, 2015).

Pecharroman, O., *Morals, Man and Nature in the Enlightenment: A Study of Baron d'Holbach's Work* (Washington, DC, 1977).

Pellerin, P., "Naigeon: une certaine image de Diderot sous la Révolution," RDE xxix (2000), 25–44.

Peña, Javier, "Lumières radicales et démocratie," in García-Alonso (ed.), *Lumières radicales*, 303–19.

Peonidis, F., "Jeremy Bentham's 'Unusually Liberal' Representative Democracy," HEI 37 (2011), 446–53.

Pepe, Luigi, "Les Milieux savants en Italie dans la deuxième moitié du 18e siècle," *Dix-Huitième Siècle* xl (2008), 211–28.

Peronnet, M., "Police et religion à la fin du XVIIIe siècle," AHRF 200 (1970), 375–97.

Perrot, Jean-Claude, *Une Histoire intellectuelle de l'économie politique* (Paris, 1992).

Peset, M., and J. L. Peset, *Gregorio Mayans y la reforma universitaria* (Valencia, 1975).

Phelan, J. L., *The People and the King: The Comunero Revolution in Colombia, 1781* (Madison, WI, 1978).

Phillipson, N., "Adam Smith as Civic Moralist," in I. Hont and M. Ignatieff (eds.), *Wealth and Virtue: The Shaping of Political Economy in the Scottish Enlightenment* (Cambridge, 1983), 179–202.

Phillipson, N., *Adam Smith: An Enlightened Life* (London, 2010).

Philp, Mark, *Godwin's Political Justice* (London, 1986).

Philp, Mark, "Disconcerting Ideas," in Burgess and Festenstein (eds.), *English Radicalism*, 157–89.

Philp, Mark, *Reforming Ideas in Britain: Politics and Language in the Shadow of the French Revolution* (Cambridge, 2014).

Philp, Mark, and E. Posada-Carbó, "Liberalism and Democracy," in Joanna Innes and Mark Philp (eds.), *Re-Imagining Democracy in the Mediterranean, 1780–1860* (Oxford, 2018), 179–204.

Pii, Eluggero, "Republicanism and Commercial Society in Eighteenth-Century Italy," in Van Gelderen and Skinner (eds.), *Republicanism* ii. 249–74.

Pilbeam, Pamela, "The 'Impossible Restoration': The Left and the Revolutionary and Napoleonic Legacies," in D. Laven and L. Riall (eds.), *Napoleon's Legacy: Problems of Government in Restoration Europe* (Oxford, 2000), 183–97.

Pinkard, T., *Hegel: A Biography* (Cambridge, 2000).

Pinkard, T., *German Philosophy, 1760–1860: The Legacy of Idealism* (Cambridge, 2002).

Piquet, Jean-Daniel, *L'Émancipation des Noirs dans la Révolution française (1789–1795)* (Paris, 2002).

Pitassi, Maria-Christina, "Bayle, the Bible and the Remonstrant Tradition at the Time of the *Commentaire philosophique*," in Van Miert, Nellen, Steenbakkers, and Touber (eds.), *Scriptural Authority*, 257–69.

Pitts, Jennifer, *A Turn to Empire: The Rise of Imperial Liberalism in Britain and France* (Princeton, 2005).

Pitts, Jennifer, "Constant's Thought on Slavery and Empire," in H. Rosenblatt (ed.), *The Cambridge Companion to Constant* (Cambridge, 2009), 115–45.

Platon, Mircea, "Robespierre's *Éloge de Gresset*: Sources of Robespierre's Anti-Philosophe Discourse," IHR 20 (2010), 479–502.

Pocock, J. G. A., *The Machiavellian Moment* (Princeton, 1975).

Pocock, J. G. A., "The Dutch Republican Tradition," in Jacob and Mijnhardt (eds.), *The Dutch Republic*, 197–223.

Pocock, J. G. A., *Virtue, Commerce and History* (Cambridge, 1985).

Pocock, J. G. A., "Spinoza and Harrington," BMGN 102 (1987), 435–49.

Pocock, J. G. A., *Barbarism and Religion* (6 vols., 1999–2010).

Poirier, Jean-Pierre, *Turgot: laissez-faire et progrès social* (Paris, 1999).

Polasky, J. L., *Revolution in Brussels, 1787–1793* (Brussels, 1985).

Polasky, J. L., "The Success of a Counter-Revolution in Revolutionary Europe: The Brabant Revolution of 1789," TvG 103 (1989), 413–21.

Polasky, J. L., "Women in Revolutionary Brussels," in Applewhite and Levy (eds.), *Women and Politics in the Age of Democratic Revolution* (Ann Arbor, 1990), 147–62.

Polasky, J. L., *Revolutions without Borders: The Call to Liberty in the Atlantic World* (New Haven, 2015).

Pomeau, René, *Politique de Voltaire* (Paris, 1963).

Pomeau, René, *La Religion de Voltaire* (Paris, 1969).

Poole, Steve (ed.), *John Thelwall: Radical Romantic and Acquitted Felon* (London, 2009).

Popkin, Jeremy, *News and Politics in the Age of Revolution* (Ithaca, 1989).

Popkin, Jeremy, "Dutch Patriots, French Journalists and Declarations of Rights: The *Leidse Ontwerp* of 1785," *The Historical Journal* xxxviii (1995), 553–65.

Popkin, Jeremy, "Robert Darnton's Alternative (to the) Enlightenment," in H. Mason (ed.), *The Darnton Debate: Books and Revolution in the Eighteenth Century* (Voltaire Foundation, 1999), 105–28.

Popkin, Jeremy, Review of Jonathan Israel, *Revolutionary Ideas*, in *H-France Review* vol. 15 (2015), no. 66, pp. 1–8.

Popkin, Jeremy, "A Colonial Media Revolution: The Press in Saint-Domingue, 1789–1793," in *The Americas* 75 (2018), 3–25.

Popkin, J. D., with Richard Popkin (eds.), *The Abbé Grégoire and his World* (Dordrecht, 2000).

Popkin R. H., "The Philosophical Basis of Eighteenth-Century Racism," in H. E. Pagliaro (ed.), *Racism in the Eighteenth Century* (Cleveland, 1973).

Popkin, R. H., and A. Vanderjagt (eds.), *Scepticism and Irreligion in the Seventeenth and Eighteenth Centuries* (Leiden, 1993).

Porret, Michel (ed.), *Beccaria et la culture juridique des Lumières* (Geneva, 1997).

Porret, Michel (ed.), *Sens des Lumières* (Geneva, 2007).

Porret, Michel, and C. Volpilhac-Auger (eds.), *Le Temps de Montesquieu. Actes du colloque international de Genêve (28–31 Oct. 1998)* (Geneva, 2002).

Porset, Charles, "Voltaire et Meslier: état de la question," in Olivier Bloch (ed.), *Le Matérialisme du XVIIIe siècle et la littérature clandestine* (Paris, 1982), 193–204.

Porset, Charles, "Position de la philosophie de Voltaire," in Kölving and Mervaud (eds.), *Voltaire* i. 727–38.

Porter, Roy, "The Scientific Revolution: A Spoke in the Wheel?," in R. Porter and M. Teich (eds.), *Revolution in History* (Cambridge, 1986), 290–316.

Porter, Roy, *Enlightenment: Britain and the Creation of the Modern World* (London, 2000).

Postigliola, A., *La città della ragione. Per una storia filosofica del settecento francese* (Rome, 1992).

Pott, Martin, "Einleitung" to Theodor Ludwig Lau, *Meditationes philosophicae*, 9–54.

Poussou, Jean-Pierre, et al. (eds.) *L'Influence française en Russie au XVIIIe siècle* (Paris, 2004).

Prado Moura, Ángel de, *Las Hogueras de la intolerancia. La Actividad represora del Tribunal Inquisitorial de Valladolid (1700–1834)* (Valladolid, 1996).

Price, Munro, *The Perilous Crown: France between Revolutions (1814–1848)* (London, 2007).

Prince, Michael, *Philosophical Dialogue in the British Enlightenment* (Cambridge, 1996).
Proust, Jacques, *Diderot et l'*Encyclopédie (1962; Paris, 1995).
Quinn, Malcolm, "Jeremy Bentham on Liberty of Taste," HEI (2017), 614–27.
Quintili, Paolo, *La Pensée critique de Diderot* (Paris, 2001).
Quintili, Paolo, "Note critiche sulo spinozismo e l'anticartesianismo di Diderot," in C. Borghero and A. Del Prete (eds.), *L'Uomo, Il Filosofo, Le Passioni* (Florence, 2016), 267–79.
Quintili, Paolo, "Diderot dans les Lumières Radicales," in García-Alonso (ed.), *Lumières radicales*, 263–80.
Rachum, I., *"Revolution": The Entrance of a New Word into Western Political Discourse* (Lanham, MD, 1999).
Racine, K., *Francisco de Miranda: A Transatlantic Life in the Age of Revolution* (Wilmington, DE, 2003).
Racine, K., "Love in the Time of Liberation," in J. Maher (ed.), *Francisco de Miranda, Exile and Enlightenment* (London, 2006), 88–115.
Racine, K., "British Cultural and Intellectual Influence in the Spanish American Independence Era," HAHR xc (2010), 423–54.
Rahe, Paul A., *Soft Despotism, Democracy's Drift: Montesquieu, Rousseau, Tocqueville and the Modern Prospect* (New Haven, 2009).
Rahe, Paul A., "Forms of Government," in Carrithers et al. (eds.), *Montesquieu's Science of Politics*, 69–108.
Rahe, Paul A., *Montesquieu and the Logic of Liberty* (New Haven, 2009).
Ramond, Charles, "Ne pas rire, mais comprendre": la recéption historique et le sens général du spinozisme," *Kairos. Revue de Philosophie* 11 (1998), 97–125.
Randolph, John, "The Space of Intellect and the Intellect of Space," in McMahon and Moyn (eds.), *Rethinking*, 212–31.
Ranieri, John J., *Disturbing Revelation: Leo Strauss, Eric Voegelin and the Bible* (Columbia, MI, 2009).
Rao, A. M., *Il Regno di Napoli nel Settecento* (Naples, 1983).
Rao, A. M., "The Feudal Question, Judicial Systems and the Enlightenment," in Imbruglia (ed.), *Naples*, 95–117.
Rauch, Leo, "Hegel, Spirit and Politics," in K. M. Higgins and R. C. Solomon (eds.), *The Age of German Idealism* (London, 1993), 254–89.
Ravitch, N., "The Abbé Fauchet: Romantic Religion during the French Revolution," *Journal of the American Academy of Religion* xlii (1974), 247–62.
Rebejkow, Jean-Christophe, "Les 'Notes sur la réfutation des Dialogues sur le commerce des blés' de Diderot," *Studi Francesi* xxxix (1995), 467–77.
Rees, John, *The Leveller Revolution: Radical Political Organisation in England, 1640–1650* (London, 2016).
Régent, Frédéric, *La France et ses esclaves* (Paris, 2007).
Reinalter, Helmut (ed.), *Der Illuminatenorden (1776–1785/87)* (Frankfurt, 1997).
Reinalter, Helmut, "Ignaz Edler von Born und die Illuminaten in Österreich," in Reinalter (ed.), *Der Illuminatenorden*, 351–91.
Reinerman, A. J., *Austria and the Papacy in the Age of Metternich* (2 vols., Washington, DC, 1989).
Renauld, Georges, *Antoine Destutt de Tracy: homme de la liberté, pionnier de l'enseignement secondaire laïque et républicain* (Paris, 2000).

Rétat, Pierre, "1789: Montesquieu aristocrate," *Dix-Huitième Siècle* xxi (1989), 73–82.
Rey, R., "Diderot à travers la correspondence entre Haller et Bonnet," in Chouillet (ed.), *Ennemis*, 113–26.
Rhoden, N. L., and I. K. Steele (eds.), *The Human Tradition in the American Revolution* (Wilmington, DE, 2000).
Rials, Stéphane, *La Déclaration des droits de l'homme et du citoyen* (Paris, 1988).
Ricuperati, G., "La cultura italiana nel secondo settecento europeo," in Santato (ed.), *Letteratura italiana*, 33–64.
Ricuperati, G., *Frontiere e limiti della ragione*, ed. D. Canestri (n.p., 2006).
Ricuperati, G., "Scrivere dell'Europa del dissenso: itinerari e percorsi della ragione," in Radicati, *Discorsi morali*, ed. Canestri, pp. i–xliv.
Riedel, Manfred, "Historizismus und Kritzismus. Kants Streit mit G. Forster und J. G. Herder," *Kantstudien* 72 (1981), 41–57.
Riedel, Wolfgang, "Aufklärung und Macht. Schiller, Abel und die Illuminaten," in Müller-Seidel and Riedel (eds.), *Weimarer Klassik*, 107–125.
Rigotti, Francesca, "Biology and Society in the Age of Enlightenment," JHI xlvii (1986), 215–33.
Rihs, Charles, *Voltaire: recherches sur les origines du matérialisme historique* (Paris and Geneva, 1962).
Rihs, Charles, *Les philosophes utopistes* (Paris, 1970).
Riley, P., "Rousseau's General Will," in R. Wokler (ed.), *Rousseau and Liberty* (Manchester, 1995), 1–28.
Riley, P., "Kant on the General Will," in J. Farr and D. L. Williams (eds.), *The General Will: The Evolution of a Concept* (Cambridge, 2015), 333–49.
Riley, Patrick (ed.), *The Cambridge Companion to Rousseau* (Cambridge, 2001).
Ripley, B. R., "Adams, Burke and Eighteenth-Century Conservatism," *Political Science Quarterly* 80 (1965), 216–35.
Riskin, J., *Science in the Age of Sensibility* (Chicago, 2002).
Roberts, Andrew, *Napoleon the Great* (New York, 2015).
Roberts, Hugh, *Shelley and the Chaos of History* (University Park, PA, 1997).
Roberts, Michael *The Age of Liberty: Sweden 1719–1772* (Cambridge, 1986).
Robertson, John, *The Case for the Enlightenment: Scotland and Naples, 1680–1760* (Cambridge, 2005).
Robertson, John, "Do we Need More than One Enlightenment?," *De Achttiende Eeuw* 43 (2011), 8–27.
Robertson, John, *The Enlightenment: A Very Short Introduction* (Oxford, 2015).
Robbins, Caroline, *The Eighteenth-Century Commonwealthman* (Cambridge, MA, 1961).
Robbins, Caroline, "The Lifelong Education of Thomas Paine (1737–1809)," PAPS 127 (1983), 135–42.
Robisco, Natalie-Barbara, *Jean-Jacques Rousseau et la Révolution française* (Paris, 1998).
Roche, Daniel, "La Diffusion des Lumières: un exemple: l'académie de Châlons-sur-Marne," *Annales* 19 (1964), 887–922.
Roche, Daniel, "Les Anglais à Paris," in D. Balani et al. (eds.), *Dall'Origine dei Lumi alla Rivoluzione* (Rome, 2008), 489–512.
Roche, Daniel, "Lumières concrètes: savoirs, pratiques, échanges," in Porret (ed.), *Sens des Lumières*, 91–7.

Rockmore, T., *Kant and Idealism* (New Haven, 2007).
Rodríguez, Jaime E., *The Independence of Spanish America* (Cambridge, 1998).
Rodríguez, Jaime E., "La cultura política-clerical en el Reino de Quito y Ecuador," in Peer Schmidt, S. Dorsch, and H. Herold-Schmidt (eds.), *Religiosidad y Clero en América Latina (1767–1850)* (Cologne, 2011), 285–306.
Rodríguez de Alonso, Josefina, *Le Siècle des Lumières conté par Francisco de Miranda* (Paris, 1974).
Roe, Nicholas, *Wordsworth and Coleridge: The Radical Years* (Oxford, 1988).
Roger, Jacques, "Diderot et Buffon en 1749," *Diderot Studies* iv (1963), 221–36.
Roger, Jacques, *The Life Sciences in Eighteenth-Century French Thought* (1963; Stanford, 1997).
Roger, Jacques, *Buffon: A Life in Natural History* (1989; Ithaca, 1997).
Rohls, Jan, "Herders 'Gott'," in M. Kessler and V. Leppin (eds.), *Johann Gottfried Herder: Aspekte seines Lebenswerkes* (Berlin, 2005), 271–91.
Rojas, Armando, *Ideas educativas de Simón Bolívar* (Caracas, 1976).
Romani, Roberto, "All Montesquieu's Sons: The Place of *esprit général, caractère national*, and *mœurs* in French Political Philosophy, 1748–1789," SVEC 362 (Oxford, 1998), 189–235.
Romani, Roberto, "The Republican Foundations of Sismondi's *Nouveaux Principes d'économie politique*," HEI 31 (2005). 17–33.
Romani, Roberto, *Sensibilities of the Risorgimento: Reason and Passions in Political Thought* (Leiden, 2018).
Rosa, Mario, "Sulla condanna dell' 'Esprit des Loix' e sulla fortuna di Montesequieu in Italia," *Rivista della chiesa in Italia* xiv (1960), 411–28.
Rosanvallon, Pierre, *Democracy Past and Future* (New York, 2006).
Rose, Paul Lawrence, *German Question/Jewish Question: Revolutionary Antisemitism from Kant to Wagner* (Princeton, 1990).
Rosen, Frederick, "Jeremy Bentham's Radicalism," in Burgess and Festenstein (eds.), *English Radicalism*, 217–40.
Rosen, Frederick, "Utilitarianism and the Reform of the Criminal Law," in Goldie and Wokler (eds.), *Cambridge History of Eighteenth-Century Political Thought*, 547–72.
Ronsenblatt, Helena, *Rousseau and Geneva* (Cambridge, 1997).
Ronsenblatt, Helena, "Rousseau, the 'Traditionalist'," *JHI* 77 (2016), 627–35.
Rosenblatt, H., and P. Schweigert (eds.), *Thinking with Rousseau: From Machiavelli to Schmitt* (Cambridge, 2017).
Rosendaal, Joost, *Bataven! Nedrlandse vluchtelingen in Frankrijk, 1787–1795* (Nijmegen, 2003).
Rosendaal, Joost, *De Nederlandse Revolutie. Vrijheid, Volk en vaderland, 1783–99* (Nijmegen, 2005).
Rosenthal, Michael, "Persuasive Passions: Rhetoric and the Interpretation of Spinoza's Theological-Political Treatise," in *Archiv für Geschichte der Philosophie* 85 (2003), 249–68.
Rossel, S. H. "Holberg and his Times," in L. Holberg, *Jeppe of the Hill and Other Comedies*, trans. G. S. Argetsinger and S. H. Rossel (Carbondale, IL, 2014).
Rossignol, Marie-Jeanne, "The American Revolution in France," in Newman (ed.), *Europe's American Revolution*, 51–71.
Rosso, C., "De Volney à Melchiorre Delfico: l'histoire, une discipline aussi inutile que dangéreuse," in Jean Roussel (ed.), *L'Heritage des Lumières: Volney et les Idéologues* (Angers, 1988), 345–56.

Röthlin, Niklaus, "La *Société économique de Berne* e le débat sur la législation criminelle," in Porret (ed.), *Beccaria*, 169–75.

Rothschild, E., *Economic Sentiments: Adam Smith, Condorcet, and the Enlightenment* (Cambridge, MA, 2001).

Rotta, Salvatore, "Voltaire in Italia," *Annali della Scuola Normale Superiore di Pisa*, Lettere, Storia e filosofia, series II, vol. xxxix (1970), 387–444.

Roudaut, M., "Ambiguités et limites de la tolérance radicale de l'*Aufklärung*," *Lumières* xiii (2009), 117–34.

Rousseaux, Xavier, "Doctrines criminelles, pratiques pénales et projets politiques: le cas des possessions habsbourgeoises (1750–1790," in Porret (ed.) *Beccaria*, 223–52.

Rowe, Michael, "A Tale of Two Cities: Aachen and Cologne in Napoleonic Europe," in Broers et al. (eds.), *Napoleonic Empire*, 123–31.

Rubel, Maximilien, "Marx à la rencontre de Spinoza," *Cahiers Spinoza* 1 (1977), 7–28.

Rudan, P., "Securing the Future: Jeremy Bentham's *A Fragment On Government* and the American Revolution," *History of Political Thought* xxxiv (2013), 479–506.

Ruiz Martínez, Eduardo, *La libraría de Nariño y los Derechos del Hombre* (Bogotá, 1990).

Rumore, Paola, *Materia Cogitans. L'*Aufklärung *di fronte al materialismo* (Hildesheim, 2013).

Russo, Elena, "The World of the Salons: Sociability and Worldliness in Eighteenth-Century Paris," *Reviews in History* (Institute of Historical Research, London), review no. 2041 (Jan. 2017) (ISSN 1749-8155).

Ryerson, Richard Alan, *John Adams's Republic: The One, the Few and the Many* (Baltimore, 2016).

Saada, A., *Inventer Diderot* (Paris, 2003).

Sa'adah, Anne, *The Shaping of Liberal Politics in Revolutionary France* (Princeton, 1990).

Sahmland, I., "Georg Forsters Wirken als Freimaurer und Rosenkreuzer," in Reichardt and Roche, *Weltbürger*, 167–95.

St Clair, William, *The Godwins and the Shelleys: A Biography of a Family* (Baltimore, 1989).

Sakkas, Evangelos, "Joseph Priestley on Metaphysics and Politics: Jonathan Israel's 'Radical Enlightenment' Reconsidered," HEI 45 (2019), 104–16 (published online 12 July 2018).

Sala-Molins, Louis, *Le Code Noir ou le Calvaire de Canaan* (Paris, 1987).

Salatowsky, Sascha, *Die Philosophie der Sozinianer. Transformationen zwischen Renaissance-Aristotelismus und Frühaufklärung* (Stuttgart, 2015).

Salatowsky, Sascha, "Socinian Headaches: Adriaen Koerbagh and the Antitrinitarians," in Lavaert and Schröder (eds.), *The Dutch Legacy*, 165–203.

Salaün, F., "Voltaire face aux courants matérialistes de son temps," in Kölving and Mervaud (eds.), *Voltaire et ses combats* i. 705–18.

Salaün, F., *L'Ordre des mœurs: essai sur la place du matérialisme dans la société française du XVIIIe siècle* (1734–1784) (Paris, 1996).

Salmon, J. H. M., "Liberty by Degrees: Raynal and Diderot on the British Constitution," HPTh xx (1999), 87–106.

Salverda, Reinier, "The Involvement of Pierre-Victor Malouet with Raynal's *Histoire des Deux Indes*," in A. Antonella and Gianlucca Goggi (eds.), *Autour de l'abbé Raynal: genèse et enjeux politique de* l'Histoire des Deux Indes (Lausanne, 2018), 213–26.

Sánchez-Blanco Parody, Francisco, *Europa y el pensamiento español del siglo XVIII* (Madrid, 1991).

Sandkühler, Hans Jorg, "Positive Philosophie und demokratische Revolution," in Schelling, *Das Tagebuch*, pp. xxiii–lxi.

Sandrier, A., *Le Style philosophique du baron d'Holbach* (Paris, 2004).
Santato, Guido (ed.), *Letteratura italiana e cultura europea tra Illuminismo e Romanticismo* (Geneva, 2003).
Santinello, Giovanni (ed.), *Models of the History of Philosophy* (1991; Dordrecht, 1993).
Santucci, Antonio (ed.), *L'età dei Lumi. Saggi sulla cultura settecentesca* (Bologna, 1998).
Sassen, F., *Geschiedenis van de wijsbegeerte in Nederland* (Amsterdam, 1959).
Saul, J. R., *Voltaire's Bastards: The Dictatorship of Reason in the West* (New York, 1993).
Sauter, H., "Paul Thiry von Holbach (1723–89)," *Pfälzer Lebensbilder* i (1964), 108–41.
Sauter, M. J., *Visions of the Enlightenment: The Edict on Religion of 1788 and the Politics of the Public Sphere in Eighteenth-Century Prussia* (Leiden, 2009).
Scandellari, S., "La Diffusión del pensamiento criminal de Gaetano Filangieri en España," *Nuevo Mundo, Mundos nuevos* Year 7, no. 7 web journal: http//nuevomundo.revues.org.
Scandellari, S., "La recepción del pensamiento criminal de Gaetano Filangieri en España," in Verdo et al., *Entre Nápoles y América*, 121–38.
Schaich, Michael, *Staat und Öffentlichkeit im Kurfürstentum Bayern der Spätaufklärung* (Munich, 2001).
Schaich, Michael, "A War of Words? Old and New Perspectives on the Enlightenment," *Bulletin of the German Historical Institute, London* xxiv (2002), 29–56.
Schandeler, Jean-Pierre, *Les Interprétations de Condorcet: symboles et concepts (1794–1894)* (Oxford, 2000).
Schechter, Ronald, *A Genealogy of Terror in Eighteenth-Century France* (Chicago, 2018).
Scherr, Arthur, "Thomas Jefferson versus the Historians: Christianity, Atheistic Morality, and the Afterlife," *Church History* 83 (2014), 60–109.
Schleich, Thomas, *Aufklärung und Revolution* (Stuttgart, 1981).
Schmidt, Alexander, "Self-Cultivation (*Bildung*) and Sociability between Mankind and the Nation: Fichte and Schleiermacher on Higher Education," in E. Frazer and Chr. Brooke (eds.), *Ideas of Education: Philosophy and Politics from Plato to Dewey* (London, 2013), 160–77.
Schmidt, James, "What Enlightenment was: How Moses Mendelssohn and Immanuel Kant Answered the Berlinische Monatsschrift," JHPh xxx (1992), 77–101.
Schmidt, James, *What is Enlightenment? Eighteenth-Century Answers and Twentieth-Century Questions* (Berkeley and Los Angeles, 1996).
Schmidt, Peer, "Against 'False Philosophy': Bourbon Reforms and Counter-Enlightenment in New Spain (1759–1788)," in R. Piper and P. Schmidt (eds.), *Latin America and the Atlantic World* (Cologne, 2005), 137–5.
Schmidt-Biggemann, W., "Edifying versus Rational Hermeneutics: Hermann Samuel Reimarus's Revision of Johann Adolf Hoffmann's 'Neue Erklärung des Buchs Hiob'," in Martin Mulsow (ed.), *Between Philology and Radical Enlightenment: Hermann Samuel Reimarus (1694–1768)* (Leiden, 2011), 41–74.
Schneewind, J. B., *The Invention of Autonomy. A History of Modern Moral Philosophy* (Cambridge, 1998).
Schneewind, J. B., "The Active Powers," in CHEPh i. 593–607.
Schneider, R. A., *Public Life in Toulouse, 1463–1789* (Ithaca, 1989).
Schnepf, Robert, "Enlightened Radicals- A Possible Difference between Spinoza and Van den Enden," in Grunert (ed.), *Concepts*, 95–111.
Schober, Angelika, "Diderot als Philosoph," in T. Heydenreich (ed.), *Denis Diderot (1713–1784). Zeit, Werk, Wirkung. Zehn Beiträge* (Erlangen, 1984), 35–42.

Schofield, Philip, "Jeremy Bentham, the French Revolution and Political Radicalism," HEI 30 (2004), 381–401.

Schofield, R. E., "Monism, Unitarianism and Phlogiston in Joseph Priestley's Natural Philosophy," *Enlightenment and Dissent* xix (2000), 78–90.

Schofield, R. E., *The Enlightened Joseph Priestley* (University Park, PA, 2004).

Schom, Alan, *Napoleon Bonaparte* (New York, 1998).

Schoorl, Evert, *Jean-Baptiste Say: Revolutionary, Entrepreneur, Economist* (London, 2013).

Schrikker, A., *British and Dutch Colonial Intervention in Sri Lanka, 1780–1815* (Leiden, 2007).

Schröder, Winfried, *Spinoza in der deutschen Frühaufklärung* (Würzburg, 1987).

Schröder, Winfried, *Ursprünge des Atheismus. Untersuchungen zur Metaphysik- und Religionskritik des 17. und 18. Jahrhunderts* (Stuttgart, 1998).

Schröder, Winfried, "Der Deismus in der Philosophie der Neuzeit," in Schröder (ed.), *Gestalten*, 7–27.

Schröder, Winfried, "Radical Enlightenment from a Philosophical Perspective," in Frank Grunert (ed.), *Concepts of (Radical) Enlightenment*, in series IZEA (Interdisziplinäre Zentrum für die Erforschung der Europäischen Aufklärung, Halle), Kleine Schriften, no. 5 (Halle, 2014), 44–51.

Schröder, Winfried, "De Sade—an Heir to the Radical Enlightenment?," in Ducheyne, *Reassessing*, 259–73.

Schröder, Winfried (ed.), *Gestalten des Deismus in Europa* (Wiesbaden, 2013).

Schroeder, Paul, *The Transformation of European Politics, 1763–1848* (Oxford, 1996).

Schulte, Christoph, *Die jüdische Aufklärung. Philosophie, Religion Geschichte* (Munich, 2002).

Schürman, E., N. Waszek, and F. Weinreich (eds.), *Spinoza im Deutschland des achtzehnten Jahrhunderts* (Stuttgart, 2002).

Schütt, R, *"Ein Mann von Feuer und Talenten": Leben und Werk von Carl Friedrich Cramer* (Göttingen, 2005).

Schutte, G. J., "Gereformeerden en de Nederlandse revolutie in de achttiende eeuw," TvG 102 (1989), 496–516.

Schweigert, Jörg, "Studentische Netzwerke im Zeichen der Französischen Revolution," *Aufklärung Interdisziplinäres Jahrbuch* 24 (2012), 317–44.

Scott, H. M., "Conclusion: The Continuity of Aristocratic Power," in Scott (ed.), *European Nobilities* ii. 377–99.

Scott, H. M. (ed.), *Enlightened Absolutism: Reform and Reformers in Later Eighteenth-Century Europe* (Basingstoke, 1990).

Scott, H. M. (ed.), *The European Nobilities in the Seventeenth and Eighteenth Centuries*, vol. ii (1995; 2nd edn., Basingstoke, 2007).

Scott, Jonathan, "Classical Republicanism in Seventeenth-Century England and the Netherlands," in Van Gelderen and Skinner (eds.), *Republicanism* i. 61–81.

Scrivener, M., "John Thelwall's Political Ambivalence," in Davis (ed.), *Radicalism*, 69–83.

Scrivener, M., "Thelwall's Two Plays against Empire," in Poole (ed.) *John Thelwall*, 117–24.

Scurr, Ruth, *Fatal Purity: Robespierre and the French Revolution* (London, 2006).

Seaman, J. W., "Thomas Paine: Ransom, Civil Peace and the Natural Right to Welfare," *Political Theory* 16 (1988), 120–42.

Sebastiani, Silvia, "'Race', Women and Progress in the Scottish Enlightenment," in S. Knott and B. Taylor (eds.), *Women, Gender and Enlightenment* (Basingstoke, 2005), 75–96.

Secrétan, Catherine, T. Dagron, and L. Bove (eds.), *Qu'est-ce que les Lumières "radicales"? Libertinage, athéisme et spinozisme dans le tournant philosophique de l'âge classique"* (Paris, 2007).
Seidler, M. J., "The Politics of Self-Preservation," in T. Hochstrasser and P. Schröder (eds.), *Early Modern Natural Law Theories: Context and Strategies in the Early Enlightenment* (Dordrecht, 2003), 227–55.
Seif, U., "Der missverstandene Montesquieu," *Zeitschrift für Neuere Rechtsgeschichte* xxii (2000), 149–66.
Seip, Anne-Lise, "The Revolution of 1848 on the Norwegian Scene," in Dowe et al. (eds.), *Europe in 1848*, 312–24.
Semmel, B., *The Methodist Revolution* (New York, 1973).
Senarclens, Vanessa de, *Montesquieu, historien de Rome* (Geneva, 2003).
Sens, A., "Dutch Antislavery Attitudes in a Decline-Ridden Society, 1750–1815," in Oostindie (ed.), *Fifty Years Later*, 89–104.
Serna, Pierre *Antonelle: aristocrate révolutionnaire 1747–1817* (Paris, 1997).
Sewell, William H., *A Rhetoric of Bourgeois Revolution: The Abbe Sieyès and* What is the Third Estate? (Durham, NC, 1994).
Seysen, Christian, "Die Rezeption des Atheismusstreits bei F. Schleiermacher," in K. M. Kodalle and M. Ohst (eds.), *Fichtes Entlassung. Der Atheismusstreit vor 200 Jahren*, Kritisches Jahrbuch der Philosophie 4 (1999), 175–90.
Sgard, Jean, "Diderot vu par les *Nouvelles ecclésiastiques*," RDE xxv (1998), 9–19.
Shackleton, Robert, *Montesquieu: A Critical Biography* (Oxford, 1961).
Shank, J. B., *The Newton Wars and the Beginning of the French Enlightenment* (Chicago, 2008).
Sharp, James R., "France and the United States at the End of the Eighteenth Century," in Albertone and De Francesco (eds.), *Rethinking*, 203–18.
Shek Brnardić, T., "The Enlightenment in Eastern Europe," *European Review of History* xiii (2006), 411–35.
Shell, Susan Meld, "Kant's True Economy of Human Nature," in Brian Jacobs and P. Kain (eds.), *Essays on Kant's Anthropology* (Cambridge, 2003), 194–229.
Sher, R. B., *The Enlightenment and the Book* (Chicago, 2006).
Shklar, J. N., "Jean d'Alembert and the Rehabilitation of History," JHI 42 (1981), 643–64.
Shovlin, John, *The Political Economy of Virtue* (Ithaca, 2006).
Silberner, Edmund, "Moses Hess als Begründer und Redakteur der *Rheinischen Zeitung*," *Archiv für Sozialgeschichte* 4 (1964), 5–44.
Silberner, Edmund, *Moses Hess: Geschichte seines Leben* (Leiden, 1966).
Silva, Renan, "Del mecenazgo al vacío. Los ilustrados de Nueva Granada como intelectuales modernos," in Kohut and Rose (eds.), *Formación*, 535–58.
Simon, Alexandre, "Hume et les 'Lumières radicales'," *Dialogue* 49 (2010), 381–94.
Skeaff, Christopher, *Becoming Political: Spinoza's Vital Republicanism and the Democratic Power of Judgment* (Chicago, 2018).
Skjönsberg, Max, "Adam Ferguson on Partisanship, Party Conflict and Popular Participation," MIH 16 (2019), 1–28.
Skornicki, Arnauld, "La Découverte de l'économie," *Dix-Huitième Siècle* 46 (2014), 253–67.
Skousen, Mark, "Say's Law, Growth Theory and Supply-Side Economics," in Steven Kates (ed.), *Two Hundred Years of Say's Law* (Cheltenham, 2003), 99–105.

Skrzypek, Marian, "Le Libertinisme polonais et la littérature clandestine," in McKenna and Mothu (eds.), *La Philosophie clandestine*, 509–20.

Skunke, Marie-Christine, "Jean-Jacques Rousseau in Swedish Eyes around 1760," in Butterwick and Davies (eds.), *Peripheries of Enlightenment*, 87–103.

Slavin, Morris, *The Left and the French Revolution* (Atlantic Highlands, NJ, 1995).

Smith, D. W., *Helvétius: A Study in Persecution* (Oxford, 1965).

Sonenscher, M., *Before the Deluge: Public Debt, Inequality, and the Intellectual Origins of the French Revolution* (Princeton, 2007).

Sonenscher, M., *Sans-Culottes* (Princeton, 2008).

Soriano, Cristina, *Tides of Revolution: Informatiom, Insurgencies and the Crisis of Colonial Rule in Venezuela* (Albuquerque, 2018).

Sorkin, David, *The Religious Enlightenment: Protestants, Jews and Catholics from London to Vienna* (Princeton, 2008).

Sörlin, S., "Science, Empire and Enlightenment," *European Review of History* xiii (2006), 455–72.

Sörlin, Sverker, and O. Fagersttedt, *Linné och han apostlar* (Stockholm, 2004).

Soto Arango, Diana, "La enseñaza ilustrada en las universidades de América colonial," in D. Soto Arango et al. (eds.), *La Ilustración en América colonial* (Madrid, 1995), 91–119.

Souker, Michel, *Discours et proclamations dans l'histoire d'Haïti (1804–1986)* (Delmas, Haiti, 2015).

Spalding, A. and P., "Der rätselhafte Tutor bei Hermann Samuel Reimarus: Begegnung zweier radikaler Aufklärer in Hamburg," *Zeitschrift für Hamburgische Geschichte* lxxxvii (2001), 49–64.

Spangler, M., "Science, philosophie et littérature: le polype de Diderot," RDE xxiii (1997), 89–107.

Spector, Céline, *Montesquieu et l'émergence de l'économie politique* (Paris, 2006).

Sperber, Jonathan, *Karl Marx: A Nineteenth-Century Life* (New York, 2013).

Spieler, Miranda, "Abolition and the Reenslavement in the Caribbean: The Revolution in French Guiana," in S. Desan, Lynn Hunt, and W. M. Nelson (eds.), *The French Revolution in Global Perspective* (Ithaca, 2013), 132–47.

Spillemaker, Frédéric, "Guerres révolutionnaires, conspirations et naissance de l'indépendance sud-américain," AHRF 395 (2019), 119–41.

Spitz, Jean-Fabien, "From Civism to Civility: d'Holbach's Critique of Republican Virtue," in Van Gelderen and Skinner (eds.), *Republicanism* ii. 107–22.

Spruit, Leen, "Introduzione" to L. Spruit (ed.), Jarig Jelles, *Professione della fede universale e Cristiana* (Macerata, 2004).

Spur, David, "Gibbon et la Révolution genevoise de 1792," in V. Cossy et al. (eds.), *Genève lieu d'Angleterre, 1725–1814* (Geneva, 2009), 269–79.

Squadrito, K., "Locke and the Dispossession of the American Indian," in Ward and Lott (eds.), *Philosophers on Race*, 101–24.

Stafford, James, "The Alternative to Perpetual Peace," MIH 13 (2016), 63–91.

Stalnaker, Joanna, *The Unfinished Enlightenment: Description in the Age of the Encyclopedia* (Ithaca, 2010).

Stalnaker, Joanna, "How does Enlightenment End?," in Höög (ed.), *What is Left of the Enlightenment*, 45–70.

Stammen, Theo, "Adolf Freiherr von Knigge und die Illuminatenbewegung," in Müller-Seidel and Riedel, *Weimarer Klassik*, 67–89.

Starobinski, J., *Le Remède dans le mal* (Paris, 1989).

Staum, Martin, *Cabanis: Enlightenment and Medical Philosophy in the French Revolution* (Princeton, 1980).

Staum, Martin, *Minerva's Message: Stabilizing the French Revolution* (Montreal, 1996).

Stedman Jones, G., *An End to Poverty?* (London, 2004).

Stedman Jones, G., *Karl Marx, Greatness and Illusion* (London, 2016).

Steenbakkers, Piet, Jetze Touber, and Jeroen van de Ven, "A Clandestine Notebook (1678–1679) on Spinoza, Beverland, Politics, the Bible and Sex," LIAS 38/2 (2011), 225–361.

Steiger, Johann Anself, "Ist es denn ein Wunder? Die aufgeklärte Wunderkritik," in J. A. Steiger (ed.), *500 Jahre Theologie in Hamburg* (Berlin, 2005), 112–30.

Steinbrügge, L., *The Moral Sex: Woman's Nature in the French Enlightenment* (1992; New York, 1995).

Stenger, G., "Le Matérialisme de Voltaire," in Fink and Stenger (eds.), *Être matérialiste*, 275–85.

Stephenson, R. "The Coherence of Goethe's Political Outlook," in C. P. Magill (ed.), *Tradition and Creation: Essays in Honour of Elizabeth Mary Wilkinson* (London, 1978), 77–88.

Stewart, J. B., *Opinion and Reform in Hume's Political Philosophy* (Princeton, 1992).

Stewart, M. A., "Religion and Rational Theology," in Broadie (ed.), *Scottish Enlightenment*, 31–59.

Stewart, M. A., "Hume's Historical View of Miracles," in Stewart and Wright (eds.), *Hume*, 171–200.

Stewart, M. A., "Arguments for the Existence of God: The British Debate," in CHEPh ii. 710–30.

Stewart, M. A., "Hume's Intellectual Development, 1711–52," in Frasca-Spada and Kail (eds.), *Impressions*, 11–58.

Stewart, M. A., and J. P. Wright (eds.), *Hume and Hume's Connexions* (Edinburgh, 1994).

Stewart, Matthew, *Nature's God: The Heretical Origins of the American Republic* (New York, 2014).

Stiening, G., "Zur Bedeutung von Lessings Spinoza-Rezeption," in Schürmann et al. (eds.), *Spinoza in Deutschland*, 193–220.

Stjernfelt, Frederik, "'Radical Enlightenment': Aspects of the History of a Term," in Ducheyne, *Reassessing*, 80–103.

Stoicea, Gabriela, "When History meets Literature: Jonathan Israel, Sophie von La Roche, and the Problem of Gender," in Niekerk (ed.), *Radical Enlightenment in Germany*, 211–37.

Straub, Eberhard, *Der Wiener Kongress. Das grosse Fest und die Neuordnung Europas* (Stuttgart, 2014).

Stroumsa, G. G., *A New Science: The Discovery of Religion in the Age of Reason* (Cambridge, MA, 2010).

Strugnell, A., *Diderot's Politics* (The Hague, 1973).

Strugnell, A., "La Voix du sage dans *l'Histoire des Deux Indes*," in France and Strugnell (eds.), *Diderot*, 30–42.

Strugnell, A., "Religion and the Secular City in Raynal's *Histoire des deux indes*," in Hemming, Freeman, and Makin (eds.), *Secular City*, 179–90.

Stuurman, Siep, "The Canon of the History of Political Thought: Its Critique and a Proposed Alternative," *History and Theory* xxxix (2000), 147–66.

Stuurman, Siep, "Pathways to the Enlightenment," *History Workshop Journal* liv (2002), 227–35.

Stuurman, Siep, *François Poulain de la Barre and the Invention of Modern Equality* (Cambridge, MA, 2004).

Stuurman, Siep, "The Voice of Thersites: Reflections on the Origins of the Idea of Equality," JHI (2004), 171–89.

Stuurman, Siep, *The Invention of Humanity: Equality and Cultural Difference in World History* (Cambridge, MA, 2017).

Suanzes-Carpegna, Joaquin Varela, "The Image of the British System of Government in Spain (1759–1814)," in Astigarraga (ed.), *Spanish Enlightenment Revisited*, 193–211.

Sutcliffe, Adam, *Judaism and Enlightenment* (Cambridge, 2003).

Swenson, James, *On Jean-Jacques Rousseau Considered as One of the First Authors of the Revolution* (Stanford, 2000).

Tackett, Timothy, *Becoming a Revolutionary* (Princeton, 1996).

Tackett, Timothy, *The Coming of the Terror in the French Revolution* (Cambridge, MA, 2015).

Tamamy, Saud M. S, *Averroes, Kant and the Origins of the Enlightenment. Reason and Revelation in Arab Thought* (New York, 2014).

Tamm, D., "Beccaria et le climat de réformes dans les pays du Nord," in Porret (ed.), *Beccaria*, 189–94.

Tapper, A., "The Beginnings of Priestley's Materialism," *Enlightenment and Dissent* 1 (1982), 73–82.

Tarantino, G., *Lo scrittoio di Anthony Collins* (Milan, 2007).

Taranto, Pascal, *Du déisme à l'athéisme: la libre-pensée d'Anthony Collins* (Paris, 2000).

Tarborrellii, Tara, "Il Gentleman e le passioni: Locke e Shaftesbury a confronto," in C. Borghero and A. Del Prete (eds.), *L'Uomo, Il Filosofo, Le Passioni* (Florence, 2016), 137–52.

Tarin, R., *Diderot et la Révolution Française* (Paris, 2001).

Taub, Liba, "Cosmology and Meteorology," in J. Warren (ed.), *The Cambridge Companion to Epicureanism* (Cambridge, 2009), 105–24.

Tavoillot, Pierre-Henri, *Le Crepuscule des lumières* (Paris, 1995).

Taylor, A., *"Down with the Crown": British Anti-Monarchism since 1790* (London, 1999).

Taylor, Barbara, "Rousseau and Wollstonecraft," in Rosenblatt and Schweigert (eds.), *Thinking with Rousseau*, 211–34.

Taylor, Charles, *A Secular Age* (Cambridge, MA, 2007).

Taylor, Rodney, *Perspectives on Spinoza in Works by Schiller, Büchner and C. F. Meyer* (New York, 1995).

Tazbir, Janusz, "Die Sozinianer in der zweiten Hälfte des 17. Jahrhunderts," in P. Wrzecionko (ed.), *Reformation und Frühaufklärung in Polen* (Göttingen, 1977), 9–77.

Thalheimer, A., and A. Deborin, *Spinozas Stellung in der Vorgeschichte des dialektischen Materialismus* (Vienna, 1928).

Thomas, William, *The Philosophic Radicals* (Oxford, 1979).

Thompson, J. M., *Robespierre* (1935; new edn., Oxford, 1988).

Thomson, Ann, "Les Lumières radicales sont-elles panthéistes?," in Secrétan, Dagron, and Bove (eds.), *Qu'est-ce que les "Lumières radicales"?*, 243–58.

Thomson, Ann, *Bodies of Thought: Science, Religion and the Soul in the Early Enlightenment* (Oxford, 2008).
Thomson, Ann, "La Mettrie et l'épicurisme," in Paganini and Tortarolo (eds.), *Der Garten*, 361–81.
Thomson, Ann, "Diderot, l'*Encyclopédie* et les Lumières radicales," RDE 49 (2014), 259–64.
Thomson, Ann, "French Eighteenth-Century Materialists and Natural Law," HEI 42 (2016), 243–55.
Tietz, M., "Diderot und das Spanien der Aufklärung," in S. Jüttner (ed.), *Présence de Diderot. Internationales Kolloquium zum 200. Todesjahr von Diderot an der Universität G. H. Duisburg* (Frankfurt, 1990), 276–97.
Tilgner, Hilmar, *Lesegesellschaften an Mosel und Mittelrhein im Zeitalter des aufgeklärten Absolutismus* (Stuttgart, 2001).
Tillet, E., *La Constitution anglaise, un modèle politique et institutionnel dans la France des Lumières* (Aix-en-Provence, 2001).
Tiran, André, "Karl Marx lecteur de Jean-Baptiste Say," in A. Tiran (ed.), *Jean-Baptiste Say: Influences, critiques postérité* (Paris, 2010), 581–611
Tomas y Valiente, Francisco, "El humanitarismo illustrado en España y el Discurso de J. P. Forner sobre la tortura," in L. Berlinguer and F. Colao (eds.), *Illuminismo e dottrine penali* (Milan, 1990), 373–402.
Tomaszewska, Anna, and H. Hämäläinen (eds.), *The Sources of Secularism: Enlightenment and Beyond* (2017).
Topazio, V. W., "Diderot's supposed Contribution to d'Holbach's Works," *Publications of the Modern Language Association* 69 (1954), 173–88.
Torres Campos, Manuel, *Bibliografía española contemporánea del derecho y de la política, 1800–1880* (2 vols., Madrid, 1883).
Torrey, N. L., "Voltaire's Reaction to Diderot," *Proceedings of the Modern Language Association of America* 50 (1935), 1107–47.
Tortarolo, Edoardo, *La ragione sulla Sprea* (Bologna, 1989).
Tortarolo, Edoardo, *L'Illuminismo* (Rome, 1999).
Tortarolo, Edoardo, *La ragione interpretata* (Rome, 2003).
Tortarolo, Edoardo, "Epicurus and Diderot," in Paganini and Tortarolo (eds.), *Der Garten*, 383–98.
Toscano, Alberto, *Fanaticism: On the Uses of an Idea* (London, 2010).
Tosel, André, *Spinoza, ou l'autre (in)finitude* (Paris, 2008).
Tosel, André, "Pour une étude systématique du rapport de Marx à Spinoza: remarques et hypothèses," in Tosel, Moreau, and Salem (eds.), *Spinoza au XIXe siecle*, 127–47.
Tosel, André, Pierre-François Moreau, and J. Salem (eds.), *Spinoza au XIX siècle* (Paris, 2007).
Trampus, Antonio (ed.), *Diritti e costituzione. L'opera di Gaetano Filangieri e la sua fortuna europea* (Bologna, 2005).
Trampus, Antonio, "Entre Antonio Genovesi y Gaetano Filangieri: el nacimiento del lenguaje constitucional moderno," in Verdo et al., *Entre Nápoles y America*, 65–119.
Trampus, Antonio, "Enlightenment in Global History: On Filangieri's Science of Legislation and the Transformation of Political Language in Classical Liberalism," in *Le Siècle des Lumières* vi (Moscow, 2018), 110–24.
Travers, R., "Imperial Revolutions and Global Repercussions," in Armitage and Subrahmanyam (eds.), *Age of Revolutions*, 144–66.

Tribe,, K., "Cameralism," in CHEPTh, 525–46.

Trohler, Daniel, "Switzerland and the Netherlands in the 18th Century: The Republican Discourse of Public Virtues," *De Achttiende Eeuw* 37 (2005), 90–104.

Trousson, R., *Jean-Jacques Rousseau* (Paris, 2003).

Trousson, R., *Denis Diderot ou le vrai Prométhée* (Paris, 2005).

Umbach, M., *Federalism and Enlightenment in Germany, 1740–1806* (London, 2000).

Urbinati, Natalia, "Condorcet's Democratic Theory of Representative Government," EJPTh 3 (2004), 53–75.

Urbinati, Natalia, *Representative Democracy* (Chicago, 2006).

Urbinati, Natalia, "Republicanism after the French Revolution: The Case of Sismonde de Sismondi," JHI 73 (2012), 95–109.

Usoz, Javier, "Political Economy and the Creation of the Public Sphere during the Spanish Enlightenment," in J. Astigarraga (ed.), *The Spanish Enlightenment Revisited* (Oxford, 2015), 105–27.

Uzgalis, W., "On Locke and Racism," in Ward and Lott (eds.), *Philosophers on Race*, 81–100.

Vaccaro, G. Battista, *Socialismo e umanesimo nel pensiero di Moses Hess (1837–1847)* (Naples, 1981).

Van Dam, Michiel, "Een spirituele revolutie? Geloof en zelfrepresentatie tijdens de Brabantse Omwenteling (1787–1790)," JAE (2017), 11–22.

Van der Burg, Martijn, *Nederland onder Franse Invloed* (Amsterdam, 2009).

Van der Veen, Sytze, *Groot Nederland en Groot Colombia (1815–1830). De Droom van Willem 1* (Hilversum, 2015).

Van de Velde, Paul, "The Orientalist, Artist and Writer, J. G. Haafner (1755–1809) Caught between Enlightenment and Romanticism," in *Dutch Crossing* xxxix (1989), 88–95.

Van Duzer, Ch. H., "Contribution of the *Idéologues* to French Revolutionary Thought," *The Johns Hopkins University Studies in Historical and Political Science*, liii, no. 4 (Baltimore, 1935), 143–76.

Van Gelderen, Martin van, and Quentin Skinner (eds.), *Republicanism: A Shared European Heritage* (2 vols., Cambridge, 2002).

Van Goor, J., *De Nederlandse Koloniën. Geschiedenis van de Nederlandse expansie 1600–1975* (Bilthoven, 1994).

Van Horn Melton, James, "From Enlightenment to Revolution: Hertzberg, Schlözer and the Problem of Despotism in the late Aufklärung," *Central European History* xii (1979), 103–23.

Van Horn Melton, James, *The Rise of the Public in Enlightenment Europe* (Cambridge, 2001).

Van Horn Melton, James, "The Nobility in the Bohemian and Austrian Lands, 1620–1780," in H. Scott (ed.), *European Nobilities*, 171–208.

Van Kempen, Michiel, *Een Geschiedenis van de Surinaamse literatuur* (5 vols., Paramaribo, 2002).

Van Kley, D. K., *The Religious Origins of the French Revolution* (New Haven, 1996).

Van Kley, D. K., "Christianity as Casualty and Chrysalis of Modernity," AHR cviii (2003), 1081–1104.

Van Kley, D. K., "Religion and the Age of 'Patriot Reform'," JMH lxxx (2008), 252–95.

Van Malssen, Tom, "Pantheism for the Unsuperstitious: Philosophical Rhetoric in the Work of John Toland," *International Journal of Philosophy and Theology* 74 (2013), 274–90.

Van Reijen, Miriam, *Het Argentijnse Gezicht van Spinoza* (Kampen, 2010).

Van Rossem, Stijn, "Politieke prenten. De Brabantse Omwenteling in vogevlucht," JAE (2017), 23–37.

Van Sas, N., "De Republek voorbij. Over de transitie van republikanisme naar liberalisme," in F. Grijzenhout, N. Van Sas, and W. Velema (eds.), *Het Bataafse experiment. Politiek en cultuur rond 1800* (Nijmegen, 2013), 65–100.

Vanysacker, D., "Verlicht ultramontaan: een *contradictio in terminis*?", *De Achttiende Eeuw* xxxii (2000), 97–115.

Vardi, Liana, *The Physiocrats and the World of the Enlightenment* (Cambridge, 2012).

Varela Orol, Concha, "Poder e censura: prohibitorum Libraria," in Concha Varela Orol and Martin González Fernández, *Heterodoxos e malditos. Lecturas prohibidas na Universidade de Santiago* (Santiago de Compostela, 2002), 31–121.

Vatar, Michael, "Introduction" to Schelling, *System*, pp. xi–xxxvi.

Vega, Judith, "Feminist Republicanism and the Political Perception of Gender," in Van Geldern and Skinner (eds.), *Republicanism* ii. 157–74.

Velema, W. R. E., *Enlightenment and Conservatism in the Dutch Republic: The Political Thought of Elie Luzac (1721–1796)* (Assen, 1993).

Velema, W. R. E., "Verlichting in Nederland: het voorbeeld van de politieke theorie," GWN v (1994), 45–53.

Velema, W. R. E., *Republicans: Essays on Eighteenth-Century Dutch Political Thought* (Leiden, 2007).

Velema, W. R. E., *Omstreden oudheid. De Nederlandse achttiende eeuw en de klassieke politiek* (Amsterdam, 2010).

Venturi, Franco, *Jeunesse de Diderot (1713–1753)* (Paris, 1939).

Venturi, Franco, *Le origini dell'Enciclopedia* (1946; 3rd edn., Turin, 1977).

Venturi, Franco, *L'antichità svelata e l'idea del progreso in N. A.Boulanger (1722–1759)* (Bari, 1947).

Venturi, Franco, "Postille inedite di Voltaire ad alcune opere di Nicolas-Antoine Boulanger e del barone d'Holbach," *Studi Francesi* v (1958), 231–40.

Venturi, Franco, *Settecento riformatore* (5 vols., Turin, 1969–90).

Venturi, Franco, "La Première Crise de l'ancien régime (1768–1776)," in Mortier and Hasquin (eds.), *Études sur le XVIIIe Siècle* vii (1980), 9–24.

Venturi, Franco, *Pagine repubblicane* (Turin, 2004).

Venturi, Franco, *Alberto Radicati di Passerano* (Turin, 2005).

Venturi, Franco (ed.), *Riformatori Lombardi, Piemontesi e Toscani*, vol. 3 of *Illuministi Italiani* (Milan, 1958).

Verbeek, Theo, "Spinoza on Natural Rights," IHR xvii (2007), 257–75.

Vercruysse, Jeroom, *Bicentaire du* Système de la nature, *textes holbachiens peu connus* (Paris, 1970).

Vercruysse, Jeroom, *Bibliographie descriptive des écrits du Baron d'Holbach* (Paris, 1971).

Vercruysse, Jeroom, "Les Pamphlets de la Révolution belge (1787–1791)," *Revue belge de philosophie et d'histoire* 91/2 (2013), 317–26.

Verdo, G., F. Morelli, and E. Richard (eds.), *Entre Nápoles y Amerca. Ilustración y cultura jurídica en el mundo hispánico (siglos XVIII y XIX)* (Lima, 2012).

Vermeulen, H. F., *Early History of Ethnography and Ethnology in the German Enlightenment (1710–1808)* (Leiden, 2008).

Vermij, Rienk, *De Geest uit de fles. De Verlichting en het verval van de confessionele samenleving* (Amsterdam, 2014).

Vernière, Paul, *Spinoza et la pensée française avant la Révolution* (1954; 2nd edn., 1982).

Verri, L., "Legge, potere, diritto," in D. Felice (ed.), *Montesquieu e i suoi interpreti* (2 vols., Pisa, 2005), 357–75.

Versini, L., "Diderot et la Russie," in Poussou et al. (eds.), 223–34.
Vierhaus, Rudolf, "Aufklärung und Freimaurerei in Deutschland," in H. Reinalter (ed.), *Freimaurer und Geheimbünde im 18. Jahrhundert in Mitteleuropa* (Frankfurt, 1983), 115–39.
Villani, Pasquale, *Mezzogiorno tra riforme e rivoluzione* (Rome and Bari, 1974).
Villari, R., "Antonio Genovesi e la ricerca delle forze motrici dello sviluppo sociale," in Balani et al. (eds.), *Dall'origine dei Lumi*, 605–20.
Villaverde Rico, Maria José, *Rousseau y el pensamiento de Las Luces* (Madrid, 1987).
Villaverde Rico, Maria José, "Rousseau, lecteur de Spinoza," SVEC 369 (1999), 107–39.
Villaverde Rico, Maria José, "Spinoza, Rousseau: dos concepciones de democracia," *Revista de Estudios Politicos* cxvi (2002), 85–106.
Villaverde Rico, Maria José, *La Ilusión republicana. Ideales y mitos* (Madrid, 2008).
Villaverde Rico, Maria José, "L'Abbé Raynal, philosophe radical," in García-Alonso (ed.), *Lumières radicales*, 229–61.
Vocelka, Karl, "Enlightenment in the Habsburg Monarchy," in O. P. Grell and R. Porter (eds.), *Toleration in Enlightenment Europe* (Cambridge, 2000), 196–211.
Vogel, Ursula, "'But in a Republic, men are needed': Guarding the Boundaries of Liberty," in Robert Wokler (ed.), *Rousseau and Liberty* (Manchester, 1995), 213–30.
Voitle, Robert, *The Third Earl of Shaftesbury, 1671–1713* (Baton Rouge and London, 1984).
Volpilhac-Auger, Catherine, "Une modération radicale? Montesquieu," in Secrétan, Dagro, and Bove (eds.), *Qu'est-ce que les "Lumières radicales"?* 389–97.
Vovelle, Michel, "Robespierre dans l'historiographie universitaire républicaine," in Jean Ehrard (ed.), *Images de Robespierre* (Naples, 1996), 163–96.
Vyverberg, Henry, *Human Nature, Cultural Diversity, and the French Enlightenment* (New York, 1989).
Waeber, Peter, *Sismondi: une biographie* (Geneva, 1991).
Wahnich, Sophie, *In Defence of the Terror: Liberty or Death in the French Revolution* (2012; new edn., London, 2015).
Waite, Gary, *David Joris and Dutch Anabaptism, 1524–1543* (Waterloo, Ontario, 1990).
Walker, Ch. F., *Smoldering Ashes: Cuzco and the Creation of Republican Peru, 1780–1840* (Durham, NC, 1999).
Walker, Ch. F. "Shaking the Unstable Empire," in A. Johns (ed.), *Dreadful Visitations: Confronting Natural Catastrophe in the Age of Enlightenment* (London, 1999), 113–44.
Wall, Ernestine van der, "Orthodoxy and Scepticism in the Early Dutch Enlightenment," in Popkin and Vanderjagt (eds.), *Scepticism and Irreligion*, 121–41.
Wall, Ernestine van der, "Geen natie van atheisten. Pieter Paulus (1753–1796) over godsdienst en mensenrechten," *Jaarboek der Nederlandse letterkunde* (1997), 45–62.
Walters, K. S., *The American Deists: Voices of Reason and Dissent in the Early Republic* (Lawrence, KS, 1992).
Walters, K. S., *Benjamin Franklin and his Gods* (Urbana and Chicago, 1999).
Walton, Charles, *Policing Public Opinion in the French Revolution* (New York, 2009).
Wangermann, Ernst, *From Joseph II to the Jacobin Trials* (1958; 2nd edn., Oxford, 1969).
Wangermann, Ernst, "Reform Catholicism and Political Radicalism in the Austrian Enlightenment," in R. Porter and M. Teich (eds.), *The Enlightenment in National Context* (Cambridge, 1981), 127–40.
Ward, J. K., and T. L. Lott (eds.), *Philosophers on Race: Critical Essays* (Oxford, 2002).

Ward, Lee, *The Politics of Liberty in England and Revolutionary America* (Cambridge, 2004; new edn., 2010).

Watt, J. R., "Suicide, Gender and Religion: The Case of Geneva," in J. R. Watt (ed.), *From Sin to Insanity: Suicide in Early Modern Europe* (Ithaca, 2004), 138–57.

Weber, Peter, "Mirabeau und die Berliner Aufklärer," in P. Weber, *Literarische und politische Öffentlichkeit. Studien zu Berliner Aufklärung* (Berlin, 2006), 169–82.

Weeks, Andrew, *Valentin Weigel: German Religious Dissenter, Speculative Theorist and Advocate of Tolerance* (Albany, NY, 2000).

Weeks, Andrew, "From Radical Reformation to Mystical Pre-Enlightenment," in Niekerk (ed.), *Radical Enlightenment in Germany*, 80–111.

Weil, Françoise, "L'Impression des tomes VIII à XVII de l'*Encyclopédie*," RDE 1 (1986), 85–93.

Wertheim-Gijse Weenink, A. H., *Democratische bewegingen in Gelderland, 1672–1795* (Amsterdam, 1973).

Wessell, L. P., *G. E. Lessing's Theology: A Reinterpretation* (The Hague, 1977).

Weststeijn, Arthur, *Commercial Republicanism in the Dutch Golden Age: The Political Thought of Johan and Pieter de La Court* (Leiden, 2012).

Whakey, L., *Radicals, Politics and Republicanism in the French Revolution* (Stroud, 2000).

Whaley, Joachim, *Germany and the Holy Roman Empire*, vol. 2 (1648–1806) (Oxford, 2012).

Whatmore, Richard, "Democrats and Republicans in Restoration France," EJPTh 3 (2004), 37–51.

Whatmore, Richard, "Rousseau and the *Représentants*: The Politics of the *Lettres Écrites de la Montagne*," MIH 3 (2006), 385–314.

Whatmore, Richard, "'Neither Masters nor Slaves': Small States and Empire in the Long Eighteenth Century," in D. Kelly (ed.), *Lineages of Empire* (Oxford, 2009), 53–81.

Whatmore, Richard, "The Role of Britain in the Political Thought of the Genevan Exiles of 1782," in V. Cossy et al. (eds.), *Genève lieu d'Angleterre, 1725–1814* (Geneva, 2009), 185–97.

Whatmore, Richard, *Against War and Empire: Geneva, Britain and France in the Eighteenth Century* (New Haven, 2012).

Whatmore, Richard, "Venturi and Republicanism in Eighteenth-Century Geneva," in Albertone (ed.), *Repubblicanesimo moderno*, 431–48.

Whatmore, Richard, *What is Intellectual History?* (Cambridge, 2016).

White, Jerry, *London in the Eighteenth Century: A Great and Monstrous Thing* (London, 2012)

Wickwar, W. H., *Baron d'Holbach: A Prelude to the French Revolution* (1935; repr. New York, 1968).

Wielema, Michiel, "Een onbekende aanhanger van Spinoza," GWN iv (1993), 21–40.

Wielema, Michiel, "Oneloof en atheïsme in vroegmodern Europa," TvG 114 (2001), 332–53.

Wielema, Michiel, *The March of the Libertines: Spinozists and the Dutch Reformed Church (1660–1750)* (Hilversum, 2004).

Wielema, Michiel, "Introduction" to Hendrik Wyermars, *Den Ingebeelde Chaos*, ed. M. Wielema (Hilversum, 2015).

Wigelsworth, J. R., *Deism in Enlightenment England* (Manchester, 2009).

Wigelsworth, J. R., "'God can require nothing from us, but what makes for our Happiness'; Matthew Tindal on Toleration," in Hudson, Lucci, and Wigelsworth (eds.), *Atheism and Deism*, 139–55.

Wigelsworth, J. R., "'God always acts suitable to his character, as a wise and good being': Thomas Chubb and Thomas Morgan on Miracles and Providence," in Hudson, Lucci, and Wigelsworth (eds.), *Atheism and Deism*, 157–72.

Wilentz, Sean, *The Rise of American Democracy* (New York, 2005).
Wilke, J., "Die Thematisierung der Französischen Revolution in der deutschen Presse," *Francia* xxii (1995), 61–98.
Willey, Basil, *The Eighteenth-Century Background* (1940; Harmondsworth, 1962).
Williams, Bernard, *Truth and Truthfulness* (Princeton, 2002).
Williams, D. L., *Condorcet and Modernity* (Cambridge, 2004).
Williams, D. L., *Rousseau's Platonic Enlightenment* (University Park, PA, 2007).
Williams, D. L., "Spinoza and the General Will," in Farr and Williams (eds.), *The General Will*, 115–46.
Wilson, Catherine, "The Enlightenment Philosopher as Social Critic," IHR (2008), 413–25.
Wilson, Catherine, *Epicureanism at the Origins of Modernity* (Oxford, 2008).
Wilson, Catherine, "Epicureanism in Early Modern Philosophy," in J. Warren (ed.), *The Cambridge Companion to Epicureanism* (Cambridge, 2009), 266–86.
Wilson, W. Daniel, *Geheimräte gegen Geheimbünde. Ein unbekanntes Kapitel der klassisch-romantischen Geschichte Weimars* (Stuttgart, 1991).
Wilson, W. Daniel, "Der politische Jacobinismus wie er leibt und lebt. Der Illuminatenorden und revolutionäre Ideologie," *Lessing Yearbook* xxv (1993), 133–84.
Wilson, W. Daniel, "Enlightenment's Alliance with Power: The Dialectic of Collusion and Opposition in the Literary Elite," in Wilson and Holub (eds.), *Impure Reason*, 364–84.
Wilson, W. Daniel, "Goethe and Schiller, Peasants and Students: Weimar and the French Revolution," in M. Oergel (ed.), *(Re)Writing the Radical Enlightenment: Revolution and Cultural Transfer in 1790s Germany, Britain and France* (Berlin, 2012), 61–71.
Wilson, W. Daniel, "Commercial Realities, Republican Principles," in Van Gelderen and Skinner (eds.), *Republicanism* ii. 293–310.
Wilson, W. D., and R. Holub (eds.), *Impure Reason: Dialectic of Enlightenment in Germany* (Detroit, 1993).
Winkle, Stefan, *Struensee und die Publizistik* (Hamburg, 1982).
Winkle, Stefan, *Die heimlichen Spinozisten in Altona und der Spinozastreit* (Hamburg, 1988).
Winkler, K. P., "Perception and Ideas, Judgment," in CHEPh i. 234–85.
Winter, M., "Georg Philipp Wucherer (1734–1805): Grosshändler und Verleger," *Archiv fur Geschichte des Buchwesens* xxxvii (1992), 1–98.
Withers, Ch. W. J., *Placing the Enlightenment* (Chicago, 2007).
Wittekind, Folkart, "Die 'Retorsion des Atheismus': Der Atheismusstreit im Kontext von Fichtes früher Religionstheorie," in K. M. Kodalle and M. Ohst (eds.), *Fichtes Entlassung. Der Atheismusstreit vor 200 Jahren* (*Kritisches Jahrbuch der Philosophie* 4 (1999), 61–79.
Wokler, Robert, "The Influence of Diderot on Rousseau," in SVEC 132 (1975).
Wokler, Robert, *Social Thought of J. J. Rousseau* (New York, 1987).
Wokler, Robert, *Rousseau* (Oxford, 1995; new edn., 1996).
Wokler, Robert, "The Enlightenment Project as Betrayed by Modernity," HEI xxiv (1998), 301–13.
Wolfe, Charles T., "Determinism/Spinozism in the Radical Enlightenment: The Cases of Anthony Collins and Denis Diderot," *International Review of Eighteenth-Century Studies* 1 (2007), 37–51.
Wolff, L., *Inventing Eastern Europe* (Stanford, 1994).
Wolff, L., *The Enlightenment and the Orthodox World* (Athens, 2001).
Wolheim, R., "Introduction" to R. Wolheim (ed.), *Hume on Religion* (1966; London, 1971), 7–30.

Wolin, Richard, "Introduction to the Symposium," JHI 77 (2016), 615–26.

Wolin, Richard, "In Praise of *Philosophie*: The Actuality of Radical Enlightenment," in Höög (ed.), *What is Left of the Enlightenment*, 97–113.

Wolloch, Isser, "The Ambiguities of Revolution in the Nineteenth Century," in I. Wolloch (ed.), *Revolution and the Meanings of Freedom in The Nineteenth Century* (Stanford, 1996).

Wolloch, Nathaniel, "Alexis de Tocqueville, John Stuart Mill and the Modern Debate of the Enlightenment," *The European Legacy. Toward New Paradigms* 23 (2018), 349–64.

Wolterstorff, N., *Thomas Reid and the Story of Epistemology* (Cambridge, 2001).

Wolterstorff, N., "God and Darkness in Reid," in J. Houston (ed.), *Thomas Reid* (Edinburgh, 2004), 77–101.

Wood, Allen, *Kant* (Oxford, 2005).

Wood, Allen, "Fichte on Freedom: The Spinozistic Background," in Förster and Melamed (eds.), *Spinoza and German Idealism*, 121–35.

Wood, Gordon, *Empire of Liberty: A History of the Early Republic 1789–1815* (New York, 2009).

Wood, P. B., "The Natural History of Man in the Scottish Enlightenment," *History of Science* 28 (1990), 89–123.

Woolf, Stuart, *A History of Italy 1700–1860* (London, 1979).

Wootton, David, "The Republican Tradition: From Commonwealth to Common Sense," in D. Wootton (ed.), *Republicanism, Liberty and Commercial Society 1649–1776* (Stanford, 1994), 1–41.

Wootton, David, "David Hume the Historian," in Norton (ed.), *Cambridge Companion to Hume*, 281–312.

Wootton, David, "Helvétius: From Radical Enlightenment to Revolution," *Political Theory* xxviii (2000), 307–36.

Worrall, D., *Theatric Revolution: Drama, Censorship and Romantic Subcultures 1773–1832* (Oxford, 2006).

Wrecionko, Paul, "Die Sozinianer und der Sozinianismus im Widerstreit der Beurteilingen," in P. Wrzecionko (ed.), *Reformation und Frühaufklärung in Polen* (Göttingen, 1977), 244–72.

Wright, J. K., *A Classical Republican in Eighteenth-Century France: The Political Thought of Mably* (Stanford, 1997).

Wright, J. K., "The Idea of a Republican Constitution in Old Regime France," in Van Gelderen and Skinner (eds.), *Republicanism* i. 289–306.

Wulf, Andrea, *The Invention of Nature: Alexander von Humboldt's New World* (New York, 2016).

Yasukata, Toshimasa, *Lessing's Philosophy of Religion and the German Enlightenment* (New York, 2002).

Yennah, R., "Rousseau et la révolution," in L'Aminot (ed.), *Politique et révolution*, 35–47.

Young, B. W., *Religion and Enlightenment in Eighteenth-Century England* (Oxford, 1998).

Young, David, "Despotism and the Road to Freedom: Cesare Beccaria and Eighteenth-Century Lombardy," SECC xiii (1984), 271–9.

Young, J. C., *Colonial Desire, Hybridity in Theory, Culture and Race* (London, 1995).

Young, Julian, *Friedrich Nietzsche: A Philosophical Biography* (Cambridge, 2010).

Zagorin, P., *How the Idea of Religious Toleration Came to the West* (Princeton, 2003).

Zambelli, P., *La Formazione filosofica di Antonio Genovesi* (Naples, 1972).

Zammito, J. H., *The Genesis of Kant's Critique of Judgment* (Chicago, 1992).

Zammito, J. H., *Kant, Herder and the Birth of Anthropology* (London, 2002).
Zapata, Ramón, *Libros que leyó el Libertador Simon Bolívar* (Bogotá, 1997).
Zaretsky, Robert, *Catherine and Diderot: The Empress, the Philosopher and the Fate of the Enlightenment* (Cambridge, MA, 2019).
Zaretsky, R., and J. T. Scott, *The Philosophers' Quarrel: Rousseau, Hume and the Limits of Human Understanding* (New Haven, 2009).
Zarka, Yves Charles, F. Lessay, and J. Rogers (eds.), *Les Fondements philosophiqes de la tolérance* (3 vols., Paris, 2002).
Zarone, Giuseppe, *Etica e politica nell' utilitarianismo di Cesare Beccaria* (Naples, 1971).
Zeuske, M., *Francisco de Miranda und die Entdeckung Europas* (Münster and Hamburg, 1995).
Zurbuchen, S., "Republicanism and Toleration," in Van Gelderen and Skinner (eds.), *Republicanism* ii. 47–71.

Index

For the benefit of digital users, indexed terms that span two pages (e.g., 52–53) may, on occasion, appear on only one of those pages.